YEARBOOK OF THE
UNITED NATIONS

Special Edition
UN Fiftieth Anniversary
1945-1995

Yearbook of the United Nations
Special Edition
UN Fiftieth Anniversary
1945-1995
Sales No. E.95.I.50

Prepared by the Department of Public Information, Yearbook Section, United Nations, New York. Although the *Special Edition* of the *Yearbook* is based on official sources, it is not an official record.

Chief Editor: Yobert K. Shamapande.

Senior Editor for Special Edition: Christine B. Koerner.

Senior Editor: Kathryn Gordon.

Editors/Writers: Peter Jackson, Melody C. Pfeiffer.

Staff Writers: Kikuko Maeyama, Kazumi Ogawa, Pio Schurti.

Contributors: Yuri Dudin, Harold Fruchtbaum, Amaryllis Jao, Greta Jones, Shari Kaplan, Dmitri Marchenkov, Lorraine Moneypenny.

Copy Editors: Alison M. Koppelman, Janet E. Root.

Indexer: Manjit Misra.

Editorial Assistants: Lawri M. Moore, Nidia H. Morisset, Leonard M. Simon, Elizabeth Tabert.

Typesetter: Sunita Chabra.

How to obtain volumes of the *Yearbook*

Yearbook Volumes 1-41 (1946-1987) are available in microfiche. Recent volumes may be obtained through bookstores worldwide, or in the United States, Canada and Mexico from Kluwer Law International, 101 Philip Drive, Norwell, Massachusetts 02061; in all other countries from Kluwer Law International, P.O. Box 85889, 2508 CN The Hague, Netherlands.

They are also available from United Nations Publications, Sales Section, Room DC2-853, United Nations, New York, N.Y. 10017, or from United Nations Publications, Palais des Nations, Office C-115, 1211 Geneva 10, Switzerland.

YEARBOOK
OF THE
UNITED
NATIONS

Special Edition
**UN Fiftieth Anniversary
1945-1995**

**Department of Public Information
United Nations, New York**

Martinus Nijhoff Publishers
THE HAGUE / BOSTON / LONDON

COPYRIGHT © 1995 UNITED NATIONS

Published by Martinus Nijhoff Publishers
P.O. Box 85889, 2508 CN The Hague, Netherlands

Kluwer Law International incorporates the
publishing programmes of Martinus Nijhoff Publishers

Sold and distributed in the U.S.A. and Canada
by Kluwer Law International,
101 Philip Drive, Norwell, MA 02061, U.S.A.

In all other countries, sold and distributed
by Kluwer Law International,
P.O. Box 85889, 2508 CN The Hague, Netherlands

Yearbook of the United Nations
Special Edition—UN Fiftieth Anniversary
ISBN: 0-7923-3112-5
ISSN: 0082-8521

UNITED NATIONS PUBLICATION
SALES NO. E.95.I.50

Printed in the United States of America

Foreword

HALF A CENTURY AGO, States from around the world launched an extraordinary experiment in cooperation. They created an institution to advance peace, human rights, international justice and economic and social development. This new Organization, the United Nations, not only would serve the particular interests of its Member States, but also would work on behalf of all humanity.

In the following five decades, the United Nations made progress in every area of its Charter. The unique concept of peace-keeping was created, in which troops are deployed not for the purpose of war, but to provide a foundation for peace. The sanctity of human rights was enshrined in international agreements achieved through the world Organization, and mechanisms were formed to protect these rights. International law gained wider acceptance and application in world affairs, and appropriate institutions of support were established or strengthened. Social and economic development were consolidated and advanced, as the international community coordinated its efforts to reduce disease, hunger and suffering in the world's poorest countries. Most important of all, the United Nations kept alive the ideal of multilateralism, even during the bleakest years of the postwar period.

Today, we stand at a second threshold in international cooperation.

Today Member States are working together more closely, on a greater range of issues, than ever before. But dangerous new threats to human well-being have come to the fore. Environmental degradation and disaster, crime and social disarray defy the powers of individual States. At a time when one system of order has disappeared and its successor has yet to be formed, ethnic, communal and other rivalries threaten many nations with conflict inside their borders.

Facing new opportunities and new dangers, the international community must renew its commitment to global cooperation. If we are to build upon the legacy that is ours, we must show vision and perseverance equal to that of those who founded the world Organization.

By understanding the accomplishments of the past, we can prepare for the future. Through a combination of narrative and key historical documents, this *Special Edition* of the *Yearbook* offers a picture of the extraordinary achievements of the United Nations over the past 50 years. I hope that it may foster knowledge of the United Nations history, pride in its achievements and courage to take up and to master the challenges to come.

Boutros BOUTROS-GHALI
Secretary-General
New York
June 1995

Contents

Origins of the United Nations

Part One: *International peace and security*

Part Two: *International law*

Part Three: *Emerging nations*

Part Four: *Economic and social development*

velopment Association, 277; International Finance Corporation, 277; International Monetary Fund, 277; International Civil Aviation Organization, 278; Universal Postal Union, 278; International Telecommunication Union, 279; World Meteorological Organization, 279; International Maritime Organization, 280; World Intellectual Property Organization, 280; International Fund for Agricultural Development, 281; United Nations Industrial Development Organization, 281; World Trade Organization, 282.

Part Five: *Human rights questions*

Into the twenty-first century

. . . And those who were there

Figures

About the *Special Edition* of the *Yearbook*

This *Special Edition* of the *YEARBOOK OF THE UNITED NATIONS* is a contribution to the important commemoration of the United Nations fiftieth anniversary. Divided into five substantive parts, the book captures the history of the United Nations—from the Atlantic Charter of 1941 to the Dumbarton Oaks Conversations of 1944, from the Yalta Agreement to the adoption of the Charter of the United Nations at San Francisco in 1945—and provides a context for the present and future challenges of the Organization.

It highlights the United Nations major achievements and developments over the past 50 years in the areas of international peace and security, development and strengthening of international law, disarmament, decolonization and the advancement of economic and social progress. It recounts the critical role of the United Nations in dealing with the early crises relating to the questions of Palestine, Korea, the Congo, the Suez Canal and others. It also reviews the increasingly complex recent United Nations peace-keeping operations and related activities worldwide.

It further highlights the Organization's humanitarian challenges, major development initiatives, the quest for the protection of human rights and a complex social agenda to expand opportunities, eradicate poverty and uplift human society. The final section—Into the Twenty-first Century—attempts to provide a future outlook of the United Nations based on the mandates resulting from many world conferences which have laid the foundations of a new international consensus for an expanded future development agenda.

Selection of material

Since its first publication in November 1947, the *Yearbook of the United Nations* has provided the most comprehensive and in-depth coverage of the activities of the United Nations, based on official documents. To date, 45 regular volumes have been published and have been the main source of the materials used in this *Special Edition*. The materials were selected on the basis of their significance in highlighting the various milestones, turning points and developments over the past 50 years. Excerpts are linked by narrative to put them into a proper context and illustrate the evolution of certain issues on the United Nations agenda. These materials are supplemented by new texts, written on the basis of official documents, to cover the periods when no *Yearbook* existed or to elaborate the current issues. Selected bibliographical materials used in the preparation of the various narrative texts are listed by respective chapter at the end of the book.

Quotations set in large type at the start of each chapter are taken from the Charter of the United Nations, unless indicated otherwise, to reflect the primary missions of the Organization.

Typefaces and styles used

In order to differentiate between the new narrative and excerpts taken from past editions, the new texts are printed in a sans serif typeface known as Univers. Excerpts are printed in the regular Baskerville type used in the *Yearbook*, with the sources cited in brackets at the end of the relevant texts as shown in the examples below.

Many variations are evident in styles and usage of English language in the excerpts. As the English language has evolved over the years, the *Yearbook* has changed along with it. In addition, the attentive reader will discern that some American English present in the earlier editions was eventually replaced by a consistently English usage found in latest editions of *The Concise Oxford Dictionary of Current English*. Other inconsistencies simply reflect evolutions in United Nations style and the format of the *Yearbook* itself.

Names of countries

Several changes have occurred in the names of countries. Many former colonial territories changed their names following independence: Belgian Congo became Congo (Leopoldville) and later Zaire, Southern Rhodesia became Zimbabwe. Other countries have changed names again thereafter: for example, Burma has become Myanmar, Dahomey became Benin and Upper Volta is now Burkina Faso. The reader should also recall that the seat of China in the United Nations was occupied by the representatives of Chiang Kai-shek until 25 October 1971.

Examples of the Typefaces Used

Newly written narrative for this edition:

In 1946, the United Nations Children's Fund (UNICEF) was established to provide a framework for advocacy on behalf of children and to increase decision-making and public awareness of their special needs. The protection of children's rights has remained a major concern of the United Nations and led to the adoption of the 1989 Convention on the Rights of the Child. The United Nations in 1990 held a World Summit for Children, which adopted the World Declaration on the Survival, Protection and Development of Children and a Plan of Action for its implementation.

Excerpts taken from past editions:

Women were to be protected from discrimination in the field of health care under article 12, ensuring access to such services as those relating to family planning, pregnancy, confinement and postnatal care, free where necessary, and nutrition, and from discrimination in other areas of economic and social life by article 13, ensuring equal rights to family benefits, bank loans, mortgages and other forms of financial credit, and participation in recreational activities, sports and cultural life. Article 14 applied the provisions of the Convention to rural women.

[YUN 1979, p. 890]

ABBREVIATIONS USED IN THE *SPECIAL EDITION*

ACC	Administrative Committee on Coordination
ANC	African National Congress of South Africa
ASEAN	Association of South-East Asian Nations
CCD	Conference of the Committee on Disarmament
CIS	Commonwealth of Independent States
CPC	Committee for Programme and Coordination
DHA	Department of Humanitarian Affairs
DPI	Department of Public Information
EC	European Community
ECA	Economic Commission for Africa
ECAFE	Economic Commission for Asia and the Far East
ECDC	economic cooperation among developing countries
ECE	Economic Commission for Europe
ECLAC	Economic Commission for Latin America and the Caribbean
ESCAP	Economic and Social Commission for Asia and the Pacific
ESCWA	Economic and Social Commission for Western Asia
FAO	Food and Agriculture Organization of the United Nations
GATT	General Agreement on Tariffs and Trade
GDP	gross domestic product
IAEA	International Atomic Energy Agency
ICAO	International Civil Aviation Organization
ICITO	Interim Commission for the International Trade Organization
ICJ	International Court of Justice
ICRC	International Committee of the Red Cross
IDA	International Development Association
IFAD	International Fund for Agricultural Development
IFC	International Finance Corporation
ILO	International Labour Organisation
IMF	International Monetary Fund
IMO	International Maritime Organization
IPF	indicative planning figure (UNDP)
IRO	International Refugee Organization
ITO	International Trade Organization
ITU	International Telecommunication Union
LDC	least developed country
NATO	North Atlantic Treaty Organization
NGO	non-governmental organization
NSGT	Non-Self-Governing Territory
OAS	Organization of American States
OAU	Organization of African Unity
ODA	official development assistance
OECD	Organisation for Economic Cooperation and Development
ONUC	United Nations Operation in the Congo
OPEC	Organization of Petroleum Exporting Countries

PAC	Pan Africanist Congress of Azania
PLO	Palestine Liberation Organization
SDR	special drawing right
TDB	Trade and Development Board (UNCTAD)
TNC	transnational corporation
UN	United Nations
UNAMIR	United Nations Assistance Mission for Rwanda
UNAVEM	United Nations Angola Verification Mission
UNCED	United Nations Conference on Environment and Development
UNCHS	United Nations Centre for Human Settlements (Habitat)
UNCTAD	United Nations Conference on Trade and Development
UNDOF	United Nations Disengagement Observer Force (Golan Heights)
UNDP	United Nations Development Programme
UNEP	United Nations Environment Programme
UNESCO	United Nations Educational, Scientific and Cultural Organization
UNFICYP	United Nations Peace-keeping Force in Cyprus
UNFPA	United Nations Population Fund (formerly United Nations Fund for Population Activities)
UNHCR	Office of the United Nations High Commissioner for Refugees
UNICEF	United Nations Children's Fund (formerly United Nations International Children's Emergency Fund)
UNIDO	United Nations Industrial Development Organization
UNIFIL	United Nations Interim Force in Lebanon
UNIKOM	United Nations Iraq-Kuwait Observation Mission
UNITAR	United Nations Institute for Training and Research
UNOMIG	United Nations Observer Mission in Georgia
UNOSOM	United Nations Operation in Somalia
UNPROFOR	United Nations Protection Force
UNRPR	United Nations Relief for Palestine Refugees
UNRRA	United Nations Relief and Rehabilitation Administration
UNRWA	United Nations Relief and Works Agency for Palestine Refugees in the Near East
UNSCOP	United Nations Special Committee on Palestine
UNTAC	United Nations Transitional Authority in Cambodia
UNTAG	United Nations Transition Assistance Group (Namibia)
UNU	United Nations University
UPU	Universal Postal Union
WFP	World Food Programme
WHO	World Health Organization
WIPO	World Intellectual Property Organization
WMO	World Meteorological Organization
WTO	World Trade Organization
YUN	*Yearbook of the United Nations*

Origins of the United Nations

" We the peoples of the United Nations...
do hereby establish an international organization
to be known as the United Nations."

An organization for the postwar world

Four months after the outbreak of war in Europe on 1 September 1939, the design of a postwar world with the means of maintaining international peace and security emerged as a subject for analysis and planning in a number of capitals. While the defeat of the Axis Powers held the highest priority, postwar foreign policy could not be neglected if the victory to come was to open the way to a stable and just world order.

A muted hint that at the highest level of government the idea of founding an international organization to replace the failed League of Nations was under consideration appeared in the last paragraph of the Atlantic Charter issued on 14 August 1941. In this joint declaration by the President of the United States and the Prime Minister of the United Kingdom, they declared their belief that "pending the establishment of a wider and permanent system of general security", the disarmament of nations threatening aggression "is essential". With the Declaration of Four Nations on General Security, issued in Moscow on 30 October 1943, "the necessity of establishing at the earliest practicable date a general international organization" was publicly recognized by the Allied Powers. The Dumbarton Oaks Conversations 10 months later shaped the design of the future United Nations. On 25 April 1945, as the Axis armed forces faced final defeat, the United Nations Conference on International Organization opened in San Francisco. Two months later, on 25 June, the representatives of 50 Governments unanimously approved the Charter of the United Nations. It came into force on 24 October 1945.

Origin and evolution

Declaration by United Nations

The term, "The United Nations," was suggested by Franklin Delano Roosevelt. It was first used in the Declaration by United Nations, and at the San Francisco Conference it was unanimously adopted as the name of the new international organization as a tribute to the late President of the United States.

On January 1, 1942, the representatives of 26 nations that were fighting against the Axis aggressors signed in Washington, D.C., a Declaration by United Nations. This is the first landmark in the evolution of the United Nations. The text of the Declaration is as follows:

The Governments signatory hereto,

Having subscribed to a common program of purposes and principles embodied in the Joint Declaration of the President of the United States of America and the Prime Minister of the United Kingdom of Great Britain and Northern Ireland dated August 14, 1941, known as the Atlantic Charter,

Being convinced that complete victory over their enemies is essential to defend life, liberty, independence and religious freedom, and to preserve human rights and justice in their own lands as well as in other lands, and that they are now engaged in a common struggle against savage and brutal forces seeking to subjugate the world,

DECLARE:

(1)   Each Government pledges itself to employ its full resources, military or economic, against those members of the Tripartite Pact and its adherents with which such government is at war.

(2)   Each Government pledges itself to co-operate with the Governments signatory hereto and not to make a separate armistice or peace with the enemies.

The foregoing declaration may be adhered to by other nations which are, or which may be, rendering material assistance and contributions in the struggle for victory over Hitlerism.

DONE at Washington, January First, 1942.

The original signatories of the Declaration[1] were:

---

[1]France and Denmark were generally regarded as having been identified with the United Nations from the beginning, as the French authorities abroad had carried on hostilities and the Danish Minister in Washington had signified the adherence of all free Danes to the Allied cause. As the Declaration was signed by governments, they could not at that time, however, formally adhere to it.

France, when the French National Committee was constituted as a government, adhered formally to the Declaration. Denmark, which was not liberated until after the opening of the San Francisco Conference was admitted as one of the United Nations by the Conference.

United States	Guatemala
United Kingdom	Haiti
U.S.S.R.	Honduras
China	India
Australia	Luxembourg
Belgium	Netherlands
Canada	New Zealand
Costa Rica	Nicaragua
Cuba	Norway
Czechoslovakia	Panama
Dominican Republic	Poland
El Salvador	South Africa
Greece	Yugoslavia

In addition to the original 26 signatories, 21 nations adhered to the Declaration. Below is a list of the adherents, together with the dates of communications of adherence:

Mexico	June 5, 1942
Philippine Commonwealth	June 10, 1942
Ethiopia	July 28, 1942
Iraq	January 16, 1943
Brazil	February 8, 1943
Bolivia	April 27, 1943
Iran	September 10, 1943
Colombia	December 22, 1943
Liberia	February 26, 1944
France	December 26, 1944
Ecuador	February 7, 1945
Peru	February 11, 1945
Chile	February 12, 1945
Paraguay	February 12, 1945
Venezuela	February 16, 1945
Uruguay	February 23, 1945
Turkey	February 24, 1945
Egypt	February 27, 1945
Saudi Arabia	March 1, 1945
Syria	March 1, 1945
Lebanon	March 1, 1945

Atlantic Charter

The signatories of the United Nations Declaration subscribed to the "common program of purposes and principles" embodied in the Atlantic Charter—the Joint Declaration made by the President of the United States and the Prime Minister of the United Kingdom on August 14, 1941. The Charter reads:

The President of the United States of America and the Prime Minister, Mr. Churchill, representing His Majesty's Government in the United Kingdom, being met together, deem it right to make known certain common principles in the national policies of their respective countries on which they base their hopes for a better future for the world.

First, their countries seek no aggrandizement, territorial or other;

Second, they desire to see no territorial changes that do not accord with the freely expressed wishes of the peoples concerned;

Third, they respect the right of all peoples to choose the form of government under which they will live; and they wish to see sovereign rights and self-government restored to those who have been forcibly deprived of them;

Fourth, they will endeavour, with due respect for their existing obligations, to further the enjoyment by all States, great or small, victor or vanquished, of access, on equal terms, to the trade and to the raw materials of the world which are needed for their economic prosperity;

Fifth, they desire to bring about the fullest collaboration between all nations in the economic field with the object of securing, for all, improved labour standards, economic adjustment and social security;

Sixth, after the final destruction of the Nazi tyranny, they hope to see established a peace which will afford to all nations the means of dwelling in safety within their own boundaries, and which will afford assurance that all the men in all the lands may live out their lives in freedom from fear and want;

Seventh, such a peace should enable all men to traverse the high seas and oceans without hindrance;

Eighth, they believe that all of the nations of the world, for realistic as well as spiritual reasons, must come to the abandonment of the use of force. Since no future peace can be maintained if land, sea or air armaments continue to be employed by nations which threaten, or may threaten, aggression outside of their frontiers, they believe, pending the establishment of a wider and permanent system of general security, that the disarmament of such nations is essential. They will likewise aid and encourage all other practicable measures which will lighten for peace-loving peoples the crushing burden of armaments.

FRANKLIN D. ROOSEVELT
WINSTON S. CHURCHILL

Dated August 14, 1941.

Moscow Declaration on General Security

On October 30, 1943, the Foreign Ministers of the United States, the United Kingdom and the U.S.S.R. and the Chinese Ambassador to Moscow issued the Declaration of Four Nations on General Security, which contemplated the establishment at the earliest practicable date of a general international organization, based upon the principle of the sovereign equality of all peace-loving States and open to membership by such States, large and small, for the maintenance of international peace and security.

The text of the Declaration is as follows:

The Governments of the United States of America, the United Kingdom, the Soviet Union and China:

United in their determination, in accordance with the Declaration by the United Nations of January 1, 1942, and subsequent declarations, to continue hostilities against those Axis powers with which they respectively are at war until such powers have laid down their arms on the basis of unconditional surrender;

Conscious of their responsibility to secure the liberation of themselves and the peoples allied with them from the menace of aggression;

Recognizing the necessity of ensuring a rapid and orderly transition from war to peace and of establishing and maintaining international peace and security with the least diversion of the world's human and economic resources for armaments;

JOINTLY DECLARE:

1. That their united action, pledged for the prosecution of the war against their respective enemies, will be continued for the organization and maintenance of peace and security.

2. That those of them at war with a common enemy will act together in all matters relating to the surrender and disarmament of that enemy.

3. That they will take all measures deemed by them to be necessary to provide against any violation of the terms imposed upon the enemy.

4. That they recognize the necessity of establishing at the earliest practicable date a general international organization, based on the principle of the sovereign equality of all peace-loving States and open to membership by all such States, large and small, for the maintenance of international peace and security.

5. That for the purpose of maintaining international peace and security pending the re-establishment of law and order and the inauguration of a system of general security, they will consult with one another and as occasion requires with other members of the United Nations with a view to joint action on behalf of the community of nations.

6. That after the termination of hostilities they will not employ their military forces within the territories of other States except for the purposes envisaged in this declaration and after joint consultation.

7. That they will confer and co-operate with one another and with other members of the United Nations to bring about a practicable general agreement with respect to the regulation of armaments in the postwar period.

> V. Molotov
> Anthony Eden
> Cordell Hull
> Foo Ping-sheung

Moscow, October 30, 1943

UN conferences on economic and social problems

Before the establishment of a general international organization, as contemplated in the Moscow Declaration, a number of United Nations conferences were held to discuss certain special problems. As a result of these conferences a number of specialized agencies were subsequently established.

The first of these conferences was the United Nations Conference on Food and Agriculture, held in Hot Springs, Virginia, from May 18 to June 3, 1943, which set up an Interim Commission on Food and Agriculture to draw up a Constitution of the Food and Agriculture Organiza-

tion of the United Nations. On October 16, 1945, FAO came into being when its Constitution was signed.

The Conference of Allied Ministers of Education, which first met in London in October 1942, drafted plans for a United Nations Educational and Cultural Organization. These plans served as a basis of discussion at the United Nations Conference for the Establishment of an Educational, Scientific and Cultural Organization, held in London from November 1 to 16, 1945, which drew up the Constitution of the United Nations Educational Scientific and Cultural Organization (UNESCO).

The Agreement creating the United Nations Relief and Rehabilitation Administration was signed in Washington on November 9, 1943, by representatives of 44 nations, and on the following day the first meeting of the UNRRA Council took place in Atlantic City, New Jersey. It may be noted that UNRRA was the first of the United Nations agencies formally to come into being.

The United Nations Monetary and Financial Conference was held at Bretton Woods, New Hampshire, from July 1 to 22, 1944. The Conference drafted the Articles of Agreement of the International Monetary Fund and the Articles of Agreement of the International Bank for Reconstruction and Development. The Articles of Agreement both of the Fund and of the Bank came into force on December 27, 1945, and the inaugural meeting of the Boards of Governors of these two institutions took place in Savannah, Georgia, U.S.A., from March 8 to 18, 1946.

The International Civil Aviation Conference was held in Chicago from November 1 to December 7, 1944. It drafted a Convention on International Civil Aviation and an Interim Agreement on International Civil Aviation. The Provisional (Interim) International Civil Aviation Organization came into being on August 15, 1945.

Dumbarton Oaks Conversations

The first concrete step toward the creation of a general international organization was taken in the late summer of 1944, when the Dumbarton Oaks Conversations took place. The first phase of the conversations was between the representatives of the U.S.S.R., the United Kingdom and the United States from August 21 to September 28, and the second phase between the representatives of China, the United Kingdom and the United States from September 29 to October 7. As a result of these conversations the four powers reached a number of agreements which were embodied in the Dumbarton Oaks Proposals. The text of the Proposals reads:

PROPOSALS FOR THE ESTABLISHMENT OF A GENERAL INTERNATIONAL ORGANIZATION

There should be established an international organization under the title of The United Nations, the Charter of which should contain provisions necessary to give effect to the proposals which follow.

CHAPTER I
PURPOSES

The purposes of the Organization should be:

1.   To maintain international peace and security; and to that end to take effective collective measures for the prevention and removal of threats to the peace and the suppression of acts of aggression or other breaches of the peace, and to bring about by peaceful means adjustment or settlement of international disputes which may lead to a breach of the peace;

2.   To develop friendly relations among nations and to take other appropriate measures to strengthen universal peace;

3.   To achieve international co-operation in the solution of international economic, social and other humanitarian problems; and

4.   To afford a centre for harmonizing the actions of nations in the achievement of these common ends.

CHAPTER II
PRINCIPLES

In pursuit of the purposes mentioned in Chapter I the Organization and its members should act in accordance with the following principles:

1.   The Organization is based on the principle of the sovereign equality of all peace-loving states.

2.   All members of the Organization undertake, in order to ensure to all of them the rights and benefits resulting from membership in the Organization, to fulfill the obligations assumed by them in accordance with the Charter.

3.   All members of the Organization shall settle their disputes by peaceful means in such a manner that international peace and security are not endangered.

4.   All members of the Organization shall refrain in their international relations from the threat or use of force in any manner inconsistent with the purposes of the Organization.

5.   All members of the Organization shall give every assistance to the Organization in any action undertaken by it in accordance with the provisions of the Charter.

6.   All members of the Organization shall refrain from giving assistance to any state against which preventive or enforcement action is being undertaken by the Organization.

The Organization should ensure that states not members of the Organization act in accordance with these principles so far as may be necessary for the maintenance of international peace and security.

CHAPTER III
MEMBERSHIP

1.   Membership of the Organization should be open to all peace-loving states.

CHAPTER IV
PRINCIPAL ORGANS

1.   The Organization should have as its principal organs:

a.   A General Assembly;
b.   A Security Council;
c.   An International Court of Justice; and
d.   A Secretariat.

2.   The Organization should have such subsidiary agencies as may be found necessary.

CHAPTER V
THE GENERAL ASSEMBLY

Section A—Composition

All members of the Organization should be members of the General Assembly and should have a number of representatives to be specified in the Charter.

Section B—Functions and Powers

1.   The General Assembly should have the right to consider the general principles of co-operation in the maintenance of international peace and security, including the principles governing disarmament and the regulation of armaments; to discuss any questions relating to the maintenance of international peace and security brought before it by any member or members of the Organization or by the Security Council; and to make recommendations with regard to any such principles or questions. Any such questions on which action is necessary should be referred to the Security Council by the General Assembly either before or after discussion. The General Assembly should not on its own initiative make recommendations on any matter relating to the maintenance of international peace and security which is being dealt with by the Security Council.

2.   The General Assembly should be empowered to admit new members to the Organization upon recommendation of the Security Council.

3.   The General Assembly should, upon recommendation of the Security Council, be empowered to suspend from the exercise of any rights or privileges of membership any member of the Organization against which preventive or enforcement action shall have been taken by the Security Council. The exercise of the rights and privileges thus suspended may be restored by decision of the Security Council. The General Assembly should be empowered, upon recommendation of the Security Council, to expel from the Organization any member of the Organization which persistently violates the principles contained in the Charter.

4.   The General Assembly should elect the non-permanent members of the Security Council and the members of the Economic and Social Council provided for in Chapter IX. It should be empowered to elect, upon recommendation of the Security Council, the Secretary-General of the Organization. It should perform such functions in relation to the election of the Judges of the International Court of Justice as may be conferred upon it by the Statute of the Court.

5.   The General Assembly should apportion the expenses among the members of the Organization and should be empowered to approve the budgets of the Organization.

6.   The General Assembly should initiate studies and make recommendations for the purpose of promoting international co-operation in political, economic and social fields and of adjusting situations likely to impair the general welfare.

7.   The General Assembly should make recommendations for the co-ordination of the policies of interna-

tional economic, social and other specialized agencies brought into relation with the Organization in accordance with agreements between such agencies and the Organization.

8. The General Assembly should receive and consider annual and special reports from the Security Council and reports from other bodies of the Organization.

Section C—Voting

1. Each member of the Organization should have one vote in the General Assembly.

2. Important decisions of the General Assembly, including recommendations with respect to the maintenance of international peace and security; election of members of the Security Council; election of members of the Economic and Social Council; admission of members, suspension of the exercise of the rights and privileges of members, and expulsion of members; and budgetary questions should be made by a two-thirds majority of those present and voting. On other questions including the determination of additional categories of question to be decided by a two-thirds majority, the decisions of the General Assembly should be made by a simple majority vote.

Section D—Procedure

1. The General Assembly should meet in regular annual session and in such special sessions as occasion may require.

2. The General Assembly should adopt its own rules of procedure and elect its President for each session.

3. The General Assembly should be empowered to set up such bodies and agencies as it may deem necessary for the performance of its functions.

CHAPTER VI
THE SECURITY COUNCIL

Section A—Composition

The Security Council should consist of one representative of each of eleven members of the Organization. Representatives of the United States of America, the United Kingdom of Great Britain and Northern Ireland, the Union of Soviet Socialist Republics, the Republic of China and, in due course, France, should have permanent seats. The General Assembly should elect six states to fill the non- permanent seats. These six states should be elected for a term of two years, three retiring each year. They should not be immediately eligible for re-election. In the first election of the non-permanent members three should be chosen by the General Assembly for one-year terms and three for two-year terms.

Section B—Principal Functions and Powers

1. In order to ensure prompt and effective action by the Organization, members of the Organization should by the Charter confer on the Security Council primary responsibility for the maintenance of international peace and security and should agree that in carrying out these duties under this responsibility it should act on their behalf.

2. In discharging these duties the Security Council should act in accordance with the purposes and principles of the Organization.

3. The specific powers conferred on the Security Council in order to carry out these duties are laid down in Chapter VIII.

4. All members of the Organization should obligate themselves to accept the decisions of the Security Coun-

cil and to carry them out in accordance with the provisions of the Charter.

5. In order to promote the establishment and maintenance of international peace and security with the least diversion of the world's human and economic resources for armaments, the Security Council, with the assistance of the Military Staff Committee referred to in Chapter VIII, Section B, paragraph 9, should have the responsibility for formulating plans for the establishment of a system of regulation of armaments for submission to the members of the Organization.

Section C—Voting

(Note: The question of voting procedure in the Security Council is still under consideration.)

Section D—Procedure

1. The Security Council should be so organized as to be able to function continuously and each state member of the Security Council should be permanently represented at the headquarters of the Organization. It may hold meetings at such other places as in its judgment may best facilitate its work. There should be periodic meetings at which each state member of the Security Council could if it so desired be represented by a member of the government or some other special representative.

2. The Security Council should be empowered to set up such bodies or agencies as it may deem necessary for the performance of its functions including regional sub-committees of the Military Staff Committee.

3. The Security Council should adopt its own rules of procedure, including the method of selecting its President.

4. Any member of the Organization should participate in the discussion of any question brought before the Security Council whenever the Security Council considers that the interests of that member of the Organization are specially affected.

5. Any member of the Organization not having a seat on the Security Council and any state not a member of the Organization, if it is a party to a dispute under consideration by the Security Council, should be invited to participate in the discussion relating to the dispute.

CHAPTER VII
AN INTERNATIONAL COURT OF JUSTICE

1. There should be an International Court of Justice which should constitute the principal judicial organ of the Organization.

2. The Court should be constituted and should function in accordance with a Statute which should be annexed to and be a part of the Charter of the Organization.

3. The Statute of the Court of International Justice should be either (a) the Statute of the Permanent Court of International Justice, continued in force with such modifications as may be desirable, or (b) a new Statute in the preparation of which the Statute of the Permanent Court of International Justice should be used as a basis.

4. All members of the Organization should *ipso facto* be parties to the Statute of the International Court of Justice.

5. Conditions under which States not Members of the Organization may become parties to the Statute of

the International Court of Justice should be determined in each case by the General Assembly upon recommendation of the Security Council.

CHAPTER VIII
ARRANGEMENTS FOR THE MAINTENANCE OF INTERNATIONAL PEACE AND SECURITY, INCLUDING PREVENTION AND SUPPRESSION OF AGGRESSION

Section A—Pacific Settlement of Disputes

1. The Security Council should be empowered to investigate any dispute, or any situation which may lead to international friction or give rise to a dispute, in order to determine whether its continuance is likely to endanger the maintenance of international peace and security.

2. Any state, whether member of the Organization or not, may bring any such dispute or situation to the attention of the General Assembly or of the Security Council.

3. The parties to any dispute the continuance of which is likely to endanger the maintenance of international peace and security should obligate themselves, first of all, to seek a solution by negotiation, mediation, conciliation, arbitration or judicial settlement, or other peaceful means of their own choice. The Security Council should call upon the parties to settle their dispute by such means.

4. If, nevertheless, parties to a dispute of the nature referred to in paragraph 3 above fail to settle it by the means indicated in that paragraph they should obligate themselves to refer it to the Security Council. The Security Council should in each case decide whether or not the continuance of the particular dispute is in fact likely to endanger the maintenance of international peace and security, and, accordingly, whether the Security Council should deal with the dispute, and, if so, whether it should take action under paragraph 5.

5. The Security Council should be empowered, at any stage of a dispute of the nature referred to in paragraph 3 above, to recommend appropriate procedures or methods of adjustment.

6. Justiciable disputes should normally be referred to the International Court of Justice. The Security Council should be empowered to refer to the Court, for advice, legal questions connected with other disputes.

7. The provisions of paragraph 1 to 6 of Section A should not apply to situations or disputes arising out of matters which by international law are solely within the domestic jurisdiction of the state concerned.

Section B—Determination of Threats to the Peace or Acts of Aggression and Action With Respect Thereto

1. Should the Security Council deem that a failure to settle a dispute in accordance with procedures indicated in paragraph 3 of Section A, or in accordance with its recommendations made under paragraph 5 of Section A, constitutes a threat to the maintenance of international peace and security, it should take any measures necessary for the maintenance of international peace and security in accordance with the purposes and principles of the Organization.

2. In general the Security Council should determine the existence of any threat to the peace, breach of the peace or act of aggression and should make recommendations or decide upon the measures to be taken to maintain or restore peace and security.

3. The Security Council should be empowered to determine what diplomatic, economic, or other measures not involving the use of armed force should be employed to give effect to its decisions, and to call upon members of the Organization to apply such measures. Such measures may include complete or partial interruption of rail, sea, air, postal, telegraphic, radio and other means of communication and the severance of diplomatic and economic relations.

4. Should the Security Council consider such measures to be inadequate, it should be empowered to take such action by air, naval or land forces as may be necessary to maintain or restore international peace and security. Such action may include demonstrations, blockade and other operations by air, sea or land forces of members of the Organization.

5. In order that all members of the Organization should contribute to the maintenance of international peace and security, they should undertake to make available to the Security Council, on its call and in accordance with a special agreement or agreements concluded among themselves, armed forces, facilities and assistance necessary for the purpose of maintaining international peace and security. Such agreement or agreements should govern the numbers and types of forces and the nature of the facilities and assistance to be provided. The special agreement or agreements should be negotiated as soon as possible and should in each case be subject to approval by the Security Council and to ratification by the signatory states in accordance with their constitutional processes.

6. In order to enable urgent military measures to be taken by the Organization there should be held immediately available by the members of the Organization national air force contingents for combined international enforcement action. The strength and degree of readiness of these contingents and plans for their combined action should be determined by the Security Council with the assistance of the Military Staff Committee within the limits laid down in the special agreement or agreements referred to in paragraph 5 above.

7. The action required to carry out the decisions of the Security Council for the maintenance of international peace and security should be taken by all the Members of the Organization in co-operation or by some of them as the Security Council may determine. This undertaking should be carried out by the members of the Organization by their own action and through action of the appropriate specialized organizations and agencies of which they are members.

8. Plans for the application of armed force should be made by the Security Council with the assistance of the Military Staff Committee referred to in paragraph 9 below.

9. There should be established a Military Staff Committee the functions of which should be to advise and assist the Security Council on all questions relating to the Security Council's military requirements for the maintenance of international peace and security, to the employment and command of forces placed at its disposal, to the regulation of armaments, and to possible disarmament. It should be responsible under the Security Council for the strategic direction of any armed forces placed at the disposal of the Security Council. The

Committee should be composed of the Chiefs of Staff of the permanent members of the Security Council or their representatives. Any member of the Organization not permanently represented on the Committee should be invited by the Committee to be associated with it when the efficient discharge of the Committee's responsibilities requires that such a state should participate in its work. Questions of command of forces should be worked out subsequently.

10. The members of the Organization should join in affording mutual assistance in carrying out the measures decided upon by the Security Council.

11. Any state, whether a member of the Organization or not, which finds itself confronted with special economic problems arising from the carrying out of measures which have been decided upon by the Security Council should have the right to consult the Security Council in regard to a solution of those problems.

Section C—Regional Arrangements

1. Nothing in the Charter should preclude the existence of regional arrangements or agencies for dealing with such matters relating to the maintenance of international peace and security as are appropriate for regional action, provided such arrangements or agencies and their activities are consistent with the purposes and principles of the Organization. The Security Council should encourage settlement of local disputes through such regional arrangements or by such regional agencies, either on the initiative of the states concerned or by reference from the Security Council.

2. The Security Council should, where appropriate, utilize such arrangements or agencies for enforcement action under its authority, but no enforcement action should be taken under regional arrangements or by regional agencies without the authorization of the Security Council.

3. The Security Council should at all times be kept fully informed of activities undertaken or in contemplation under regional arrangements or by regional agencies for the maintenance of international peace and security.

CHAPTER IX
ARRANGEMENTS FOR INTERNATIONAL ECONOMIC AND SOCIAL CO-OPERATION

Section A—Purpose and Relationships

1. With a view to the creation of conditions of stability and well-being which are necessary for peaceful and friendly relations among nations, the Organization should facilitate solutions of international economic, social and other humanitarian problems and promote respect for human rights and fundamental freedoms. Responsibility for the discharge of this function should be vested in the General Assembly and, under the authority of the General Assembly, in an Economic and Social Council.

2. The various specialized economic, social and other organizations and agencies would have responsibilities in their respective fields as defined in their statutes. Each such organization or agency should be brought into relationship with the Organization on terms to be determined by agreement between the Economic and Social Council and the appropriate authorities of the specialized organization or agency, subject to approval by the General Assembly.

Section B—Composition and Voting

The Economic and Social Council should consist of representatives of eighteen members of the Organization. The states to be represented for this purpose should be elected by the General Assembly for terms of three years. Each such state should have one representative, who should have one vote. Decisions of the Economic and Social Council should be taken by simple majority vote of those present and voting.

Section C—Functions and Powers of the Economic and Social Council

1. The Economic and Social Council should be empowered:

a. to carry out, within the scope of its functions, recommendations of the General Assembly;

b. to make recommendations, on its own initiative, with respect to international economic, social and other humanitarian matters;

c. to receive and consider reports from the economic, social and other organizations or agencies brought into relationship with the Organization, and to co-ordinate their activities through consultations with, and recommendations to, such organizations or agencies;

d. to examine the administrative budgets of such specialized organizations or agencies with a view to making recommendations to the organizations or agencies concerned;

e. to enable the Secretary-General to provide information to the Security Council;

f. to assist the Security Council upon its request; and

g. to perform such other functions within the general scope of its competence as may be assigned to it by the General Assembly.

Section D—Organization and Procedure

1. The Economic and Social Council should set up an economic commission, a social commission, and such other commissions as may be required. These commissions should consist of experts. There should be a permanent staff which should constitute a part of the Secretariat of the Organization.

2. The Economic and Social Council should make suitable arrangements for representatives of the specialized organizations or agencies to participate without vote in its deliberations and in those of the commissions established by it.

3. The Economic and Social Council should adopt its own rules of procedure and the method of selecting its President.

CHAPTER X
THE SECRETARIAT

1. There should be a Secretariat comprising a Secretary-General and such staff as may be required. The Secretary-General should be the chief administrative officer of the Organization. He should be elected by the General Assembly, on recommendation of the Security Council, for such term and under such conditions as are specified in the Charter.

2. The Secretary-General should act in that capacity in all meetings of the General Assembly, of the Security Council, and of the Economic and Social Council and should make an annual report to the General Assembly on the work of the Organization.

3.   The Secretary-General should have the right to bring to the attention of the Security Council any matter which in his opinion may threaten international peace and security.

CHAPTER XI
AMENDMENTS

Amendments should come into force for all members of the Organization when they have been adopted by a vote of two-thirds of the members of the General Assembly and ratified in accordance with their respective constitutional processes by the members of the Organization having permanent membership on the Security Council and by a majority of the other members of the Organization.

CHAPTER XII
TRANSITIONAL ARRANGEMENTS

1.   Pending the coming into force of the special agreement or agreements referred to in Chapter VIII, Section B, paragraph 5, and in accordance with the provisions of paragraph 5 of the Four-Nation Declaration, signed at Moscow, Oct. 30, 1943, the States parties to that Declaration should consult with one another and as occasion arises with other Members of the Organization with a view to such joint action on behalf of the Organization as may be necessary for the purpose of maintaining international peace and security.

2.   No provision of the Charter should preclude action taken or authorized in relation to enemy States as a result of the present war by the Governments having responsibility for such action.

Yalta Agreement

In February 1945, Prime Minister Churchill, President Roosevelt and Marshal Stalin met at Yalta in the Crimea. A report was issued after the conference which contained the following passage:

We are resolved upon the earliest possible establishment with our Allies of a general international organization to maintain peace and security. We believe that this is essential, both to prevent aggression and to remove the political, economic and social causes of war through the close and continuing collaboration of all peace-loving peoples.

The foundations were laid at Dumbarton Oaks. On the important question of voting procedure, however, agreement was not there reached. The present Conference has been able to resolve this difficulty.

We have agreed that a Conference of United Nations should be called to meet at San Francisco in the United States on the 25th April 1945, to prepare the charter of such an organization, along the lines proposed in the informal conversations of Dumbarton Oaks.

The Government of China and the Provisional Government of France will be immediately consulted and invited to sponsor invitations to the Conference jointly with the Governments of the United States, Great Britain and the Union of Soviet Socialist Republics. As soon as the consultation with China and France has been completed, the text of the proposals on voting procedure will be made public.

China and France were consulted. The Chinese Government agreed to join in sponsoring the invitations. The French Government agreed to participate in the conference but decided not to act as a sponsoring nation.

The countries qualifying for invitations were those nations which had declared war on Germany or Japan by March 1, 1945, and had signed the United Nations Declaration.

The invitations were issued on March 5 and contained the proposals for voting referred to in the Report of the Crimea Conference. The terms of invitation read as follows:

The Government of the United States of America, on behalf of itself and of the Governments of the United Kingdom of Great Britain and Northern Ireland, the Union of Soviet Socialist Republics and the Republic of China, invites the Government of (name of Government invited) to send representatives to a Conference of the United Nations, to be held on April 25, 1945, at San Francisco in the United States of America, to prepare a charter for a general international organization for the maintenance of international peace and security.

The above-named Governments suggest that the Conference consider, as affording a basis for such a charter, the proposals for the establishment of a general international organization which were made public last October as a result of the Dumbarton Oaks Conference, and which have now been supplemented by the following provisions for Section C of Chapter VI:

C.   Voting

1.   Each member of the Security Council should have one vote.

2.   Decisions of the Security Council on procedural matters should be made by an affirmative vote of seven members.

3.   Decisions of the Security Council on all other matters should be made by an affirmative vote of seven members, including the concurring votes of the permanent members; provided that, in decisions under Chapter VIII, Section A, and under the second sentence of paragraph 1 of Chapter VIII, Section C, a party to a dispute should abstain from voting.

Further information as to arrangements will be transmitted subsequently. In the event that the Government of (name of Government invited) desires in advance to present views or comments concerning the proposals, the Government of the United States of America will be pleased to transmit such views and comments to the other participating Governments.

Preliminary discussions on the Dumbarton Oaks Proposals

Inter-American Conference on Problems of War and Peace

The Dumbarton Oaks Proposals were being studied and discussed by the nations of the world, severally as well as individually. From February 21 to March 8, 1945, for instance, twenty Members of the Union of American Republics met in Mexico

City to consider the problems of war and peace. In a resolution the Inter-American Conference suggested that the following points be taken into consideration in the formulation of a definitive charter of the proposed international organization:

(a) The aspiration of universality as an ideal toward which the Organization should tend in the future;

(b) The desirability of amplifying and making more specific the enumeration of the principles and purposes of the Organization;

(c) The desirability of amplifying and making more specific the powers of the General Assembly in order that its action, as the fully representative organ of the international community may be rendered effective, harmonizing the powers of the Security Council with such amplification;

(d) The desirability of extending the jurisdiction and competence of the International Tribunal or Court of Justice;

(e) The desirability of creating an international agency specially charged with promoting intellectual and moral co-operation among nations:

(f) The desirability of solving controversies and questions of an inter-American character, preferably in accordance with inter-American methods and procedures, in harmony with those of the General International Organization;

(g) The desirability of giving an adequate representation to Latin America on the Security Council.

British Commonwealth Conference

From April 4 to 13, 1945, talks were held in London between representatives of the British Commonwealth as a preliminary to the San Francisco Conference. They were attended by the representatives of Australia, Canada, India, New Zealand, the Union of South Africa and the United Kingdom. The statement issued at the close of the meetings contained the following passage:

We have examined, generally and in detail, the tentative proposals resulting from the Dumbarton Oaks Conversations, and we have had a valuable exchange of views. We are agreed that the proposals provide the basis for a charter of such an organization, fully recognizing that in certain respects they call for clarification, improvement and expansion.

Committee of Jurists

The Dumbarton Oaks Proposals provided that there should be an International Court of Justice as the principal judicial organ of the organization, but the Proposals left open the question of whether the Court's Statute should be the Statute of the Permanent Court of International Justice with such modifications as were necessary, or a new Statute based on that of the Permanent Court.

The United States Government, acting on behalf of itself and the other governments sponsoring the San Francisco Conference, invited a Committee of Jurists to meet in Washington for the purpose of preparing a Draft Statute of the Court and submitting it to the San Francisco Conference. Jurists from 44 countries met from April 9 to 20, 1945.

The Committee felt that it was for the San Francisco Conference to decide whether the Court should be established as a new Court or as a continuance of the Permanent Court of International Justice established in 1920. The question affected particularly the operation of treaties containing references to the jurisdiction of the Permanent Court.

The Committee took the Statute of the Permanent Court as a basis and proceeded to revise it article by article. The revision consisted, on the one hand, of the effecting of certain adaptations of form, and on the other hand, of the introduction of certain new features considered desirable.

On the nomination of judges the Committee did not reach any agreement. It submitted two alternative texts—one retaining the system of nomination by national groups and the other introducing a system of nomination by governments. The Committee suggested that one-third of the judges should be elected every three years, instead of a complete election every nine years.

On the question of obligatory jurisdiction the Committee could not reach a unanimous agreement. Some jurists wanted to see the principle of obligatory jurisdiction affirmed in the new Statute, while others preferred to retain the optional clause. In the end two alternative texts embodying both views were presented.

A provision for amendment, based on a United States proposal, was adopted to fill what was felt to be a lacuna in the old Statute. The Committee called to the attention of the San Francisco Conference the importance of formulating rules for the execution of the Court's decisions, and the necessity of adjusting the situation as regards States which were parties to the Statute of the Permanent Court of International Justice but not Members of the United Nations.

Question of trusteeship

The question of trusteeship was placed tentatively on the agenda of the Dumbarton Oaks Conversations, but no provisions concerning it were included in the Dumbarton Oaks Proposals. It was understood that the question would be a subject of subsequent study and would be placed on the agenda of the United Nations Conference. At Yalta the matter was discussed and agreement was reached on the following policy:

(1) That the five Governments with permanent seats in the Security Council should consult each other prior to the United Nations Conference on providing machinery in the World Charter for dealing with territorial trusteeships which would apply only to (a) existing mandates of the League of Nations; (b) territory to be detached from the enemy as a result of this war; and

(c) any other territory that may voluntarily be placed under trusteeship.

(2) That no discussions of specific territories were to take place during the preliminary consultations on trusteeships or at the United Nations Conference itself. Only machinery and principles of trusteeship should be formulated at the Conference for inclusion in the Charter, and it was to be a matter for subsequent agreement as to which territories within the categories specified above would actually be placed under trusteeship.

Chinese proposals

In the second phase of the Dumbarton Oaks Conversations the Chinese Government had put forward certain proposals which were agreed to at that time between China, the United Kingdom and the United States. The Government of the U.S.S.R. agreed to join in sponsoring the proposals for presentation to the San Francisco Conference. The proposals, which were submitted to the San Francisco Conference on May 1, 1945, were:

(1) The Charter should provide specifically that adjustment or settlement of international disputes should be achieved with due regard for principles of justice and international law.

(2) The Assembly should be responsible for initiating studies and making recommendations with respect to the development and revision of the rules and principles of international law.

(3) The Economic and Social Council should specifically provide for the promotion of educational and other forms of cultural co-operation.

UN Conference on International Organization

Composition of the Conference

The Government of the United States, on behalf of itself and the other sponsoring Governments, on March 5, 1945, invited the Governments that had signed or adhered to the United Nations Declaration and had declared war against Germany or Japan to send representatives to the San Francisco Conference, officially known as the United Nations Conference on International Organization, beginning on April 25, 1945. The complete list of the sponsoring Governments and the invited Governments is as follows:

Australia	Dominican
Belgium	Republic
Bolivia	Ecuador
Brazil	Egypt
Canada	El Salvador
Chile	Ethiopia
China	France
Colombia	Greece
Costa Rica	Guatemala
Cuba	Haiti
Czechoslovakia	Honduras

India	Philippine
Iran	Commonwealth
Iraq	Saudi Arabia
Lebanon	Syria
Liberia	Turkey
Luxembourg	Union of South Africa
Mexico	Union of Soviet
Netherlands	Socialist Republics
New Zealand	United Kingdom
Nicaragua	United States of
Norway	America
Panama	Uruguay
Paraguay	Venezuela
Peru	Yugoslavia

The invitation to Poland, which was an original signatory of the United Nations Declaration, was withheld at that time pending the formation of a Polish Provisional Government of National Unity. On April 27, 1945, the San Francisco Conference adopted the following resolution on Poland:

The Governments of the United Nations express to the people of Poland their sympathy and their admiration. They hope that the constitution of a Polish Government recognized as such by the sponsoring nations will make it possible for Polish delegates to come and take part as soon as possible in the work of the Conference.

On April 30 the Conference approved the admission of Argentina, the Byelorussian S.S.R. and the Ukrainian S.S.R. On June 5 Denmark, which had just been liberated, was invited to attend the Conference. A total of 50 nations attended.

Organization and procedure of the Conference

The chairmen of the delegations of the sponsoring Governments presided in rotation at the plenary sessions of the Conference. They were: Edward R. Stettinius, Jr., of the United States; Anthony Eden, of the United Kingdom; Dr. T. V. Soong, of China; and V. M. Molotov, of the U.S.S.R. Lord Halifax later deputized for Mr. Eden, Dr. V. K. Wellington Koo for Dr. Soong, and Andrei A. Gromyko for Mr. Molotov. The chairmen of these delegations held private meetings from time to time with Mr. Stettinius presiding, and on May 3 the chairman of the French delegation was invited to attend those private meetings.

The Conference established four general committees: A Steering Committee, consisting of the chairmen of all delegations, with Mr. Stettinius presiding, was to consider major questions of policy and procedure. An Executive Committee, consisting of fourteen members—the chairmen of the delegations of the four sponsoring Governments and the chairmen of the delegations of Australia, Brazil, Canada, Chile, Czechoslovakia, France, Iran, Mexico, the Netherlands and Yugoslavia—with Mr. Stettinius presiding, was to make recommendations to the Steering Committee. A Co-ordination Committee, consisting of one representative of each of the fourteen members of the Executive Committee was to assist the Executive Committee and to supervise the final drafting of the Charter. A Credentials Committee, consisting of the chairmen of the delegations of Ecuador, Luxembourg, Nicaragua, Saudi Arabia, Syria and Yugoslavia, was to verify the credentials of the representatives.

The Conference was divided into four commissions and twelve technical committees. All delegations were represented on the commissions and the committees.

Each commission had a President and a Rapporteur, who were nominated by the Steering Committee and approved by the Conference. An Assistant Secretary-General of the Conference served as the secretary of each commission. Each commission was to develop general principles to guide its technical committees.

Each technical committee had a Chairman and a Rapporteur, who were nominated by the Steering Committee and approved by the Conference. Each committee was to formulate recommendations on various parts of the agenda assigned to it.

. . .

Commission & *Committee*	*Title*
Commission I	General Provisions
Committee I/1	Preamble, Purposes & Principles
Committee I/2	Membership, Amendment & Secretariat
Commission II	General Assembly
Committee II/1	Structure and Procedures
Committee II/2	Political & Security Functions
Committee II/3	Economic and Social Co-operation
Committee II/4	Trusteeship System
Commission III	Security Council
Committee III/1	Structure and Procedures
Committee III/2	Peaceful Settlement
Committee III/3	Enforcement Arrangements
Committee III/4	Regional Arrangements
Commission IV	Judicial Organization
Committee IV/1	International Court of Justice
Committee IV/2	Legal Problems

The Secretary-General of the Conference was Alger Hiss; the Deputy Secretary-General was John Ross. The Secretariat consisted of 1,058 persons, not including the United States Army and Navy personnel and volunteer workers. The expenses of the Conference, estimated at somewhat less than $2,000,000, were met by the United States as the host government.

Each delegation to the Conference had one vote. Any question of procedure was decided by a majority of the votes of the delegations present and voting;

all other questions were decided by two thirds of the votes of the delegations present and voting.

The official languages of the Conference were Chinese, English, French, Russian and Spanish. The working languages were English and French. Addresses in English or French were interpreted into the other language, and addresses in any other language into both English and French.

Agenda of the Conference

At a meeting of the chairmen of the delegations on April 27 it was agreed that the agenda of the Conference should be "the Dumbarton Oaks Proposals, as supplemented at the Crimea Conference, and by the Chinese Proposals agreed to by the sponsoring Governments, and the comments thereon submitted by the participating countries."

The four sponsoring Governments themselves submitted jointly to the Conference on May 5 a series of amendments to the Dumbarton Oaks Proposals.

. . .

It would be impossible . . . to include all the amendments and proposals submitted to the Conference and to go into the details of the work of the Commissions and Committees. In the following pages an attempt is made to point out some of the vital issues discussed at the Conference and some of the main contributions of the Conference to the drafting of the Charter of the United Nations.

Preamble, Purposes and Principles

The Dumbarton Oaks Proposals did not contain any Preamble. Chapter I of the Proposals was devoted to the Purposes, and Chapter II to the Principles, of the United Nations. The Charter in its final form contains a Preamble, and the Purposes and the Principles which constituted Chapters I and II of the Dumbarton Oaks Proposals became Articles 1 and 2 of Chapter I of the Charter.

The task of drafting the Preamble and Purposes and Principles was assigned to Committee I/1. Several delegations had proposed that the Charter should contain a Preamble, and several drafts were submitted. It was found difficult to draw a clear-cut distinction between the Preamble, the Purposes and the Principles of the United Nations. After some discussion the Committee finally made the distinction in these paragraphs:

(1)   The "Preamble" introduces the Charter and sets forth the declared common intentions which brought us together in this Conference and moved us to unite our will and efforts, and made us harmonize, regulate, and organize our international action to achieve our common ends.

(2)   The "Purposes" constitute the *raison d'être* of the Organization. They are the aggregation of the common

ends on which our minds met; hence, the cause and object of the Charter to which Member States collectively and severally subscribe.

(3) The chapter on "Principles" sets, in the same order of ideas, the methods and regulating norms according to which the Organization and its Members shall do their duty and endeavour to achieve the common ends. Their understandings should serve as actual standards of international conduct.

More briefly, the Preamble sets forth the intentions of the participating Governments, the Purposes constitute the *raison d'être* of the United Nations, and the Principles serve as the standards of international conduct.

Committee I/1 accepted as a working basis the Preamble submitted by the Union of South Africa.

. . .

On the proposal of the United States delegation, supported by the delegations of the U.S.S.R., the Ukrainian S.S.R., China, France and Latin American countries, the phrase "The High Contracting Parties" in the original draft proposed by South Africa was changed to "We the Peoples of the United Nations." However, it was recognized that the Charter, by its nature, must be an agreement between the Governments of the United Nations. Accordingly, at the end of the Preamble the clause was inserted that " . . . our respective Governments through their representatives assembled in the city of San Francisco . . . have agreed to the present Charter of the United Nations and do hereby establish an international organization to be known as the United Nations."

It was suggested in the Dumbarton Oaks Proposals that the name of the organization should be "The United Nations." Committee I/1 unanimously adopted the name as a tribute to President Franklin Delano Roosevelt, who was the first to suggest it. Commission I and the Conference accepted the name without dissent.

The Preamble has the same validity as the Purposes and Principles. The report of the Rapporteur of the Committee I/1 contains the following remarks:

The provisions of the Charter, being in this case indivisible as in any other legal instrument, are equally valid and operative. The rights, duties, privileges and obligations of the Organization and its Members match with one another and complement one another to make a whole. Each of them is construed to be understood and applied in function of the others.

It is for this reason, as well as to avoid undue repetition, that the Committee did not find it necessary to mention again in each paragraph relevant dispositions included in other paragraphs of the same chapter or other chapters. It was, nevertheless, unavoidable at times to make some repetition.

May the explanation given above dispel any doubts as to the validity and value of any division of the Char-

ter, whether we call it "Principles," "Purposes," or "Preamble."

It is thus clear that there are no grounds for supposing that the Preamble has less legal validity than the two succeeding chapters (Purposes and Principles). We found it appropriate to state the last remark, which could otherwise be taken for granted.

Chapter I of the Charter lists four Purposes, which constitute the *raison d'être* of the United Nations.

The Conference agreed that the first and foremost purpose of the United Nations was "to maintain international peace and security, and to that end: to take effective collective measures for the prevention and removal of threats to the peace, and for the suppression of acts of aggression or other breaches of the peace, and to bring about by peaceful means, and in conformity with the principles of justice and international law, adjustment or settlement of international disputes or situations which might lead to a breach of the peace." The Dumbarton Oaks Proposals did not contain the words "in conformity with the principles of justice and international law." On the proposal of China, the four sponsoring Governments agreed that "the Charter should provide specifically that adjustment or settlement of international disputes should be achieved with due regard for principles of justice and international law." The phrase "with due regard" was changed by Committee I/1 to read "in conformity with."

The second purpose of the United Nations is "to develop friendly relations among nations based on respect for the principle of equal rights and self-determination of peoples, and to take other appropriate measures to strengthen universal peace." The words "based on respect for the principle of equal rights and self-determination of peoples" were introduced at the San Francisco Conference; they were not in the Dumbarton Oaks Proposals.

The third purpose of the United Nations is "to achieve international co-operation in solving international problems of an economic, social, cultural, or humanitarian character, and in promoting and encouraging respect for human rights and for fundamental freedoms for all without distinction as to race, sex, language, or religion." The words "in promoting and encouraging respect for human rights and for fundamental freedoms for all without distinction as to race, sex, language, or religion" were introduced at the San Francisco Conference; they were not in the Dumbarton Oaks Proposals.

The fourth purpose of the United Nations is "to be a centre for harmonizing the actions of nations in the attainment of these common ends." The words "to afford" in the Dumbarton Oaks text, which at the time denoted an eye to the future, were changed to "to be."

Chapter I of the Charter lists seven Principles which should serve as the standards of international conduct. The Principles as finally agreed upon at the San Francisco Conference were substantially the same as those contained in the Dumbarton Oaks Proposals.

The first principle is that "the sovereign equality" of all the Members of the United Nations. The Moscow Declaration of October 30, 1943, and the Dumbarton Oaks Proposals used the expression "the sovereign equality of all peace-loving States." At San Francisco "all peace-loving States" was changed to read "all its [United Nations] Members." The term, "sovereign equality" according to the report of the Rapporteur of Committee I/1, means:

(1)   that States are juridically equal;
(2)   that each State enjoys the right inherent in full sovereignty;
(3)   that the personality of the State is respected as well as its territorial integrity and political independence; and
(4)   that the State should, under international order, comply faithfully with its international duties and obligations.

The second principle is that "all Members, in order to ensure to all of them the rights and benefits resulting from membership, shall fulfil in good faith the obligations assumed by them in accordance with the present Charter." The words "in good faith" were added by Commission I, upon the suggestion of the Colombian delegation.

The third principle is that "all Members should settle their international disputes by peaceful means in such a manner that international peace and security, and justice, are not endangered." This followed the wording of the Dumbarton Oaks Proposals, except the words "and justice", which were added upon the proposal of the Bolivian delegation.

The fourth principle is that "all Members shall refrain in their international relations from the threat or use of force against the territorial integrity or political independence of any State, or in any manner inconsistent with the Purposes of the United Nations." The words "against the territorial integrity or political independence of any State" were not in the Dumbarton Oaks Proposals; they were inserted upon the demand of several delegations which thought there should be a more specific guarantee in the Charter against any violation of territorial integrity and political independence. A New Zealand amendment that "all Members undertake collectively to resist any act of aggression against any Member" gained considerable support but failed to secure the necessary two-thirds majority.

The fifth principle is that "all Members shall give the United Nations every assistance in any action it takes in accordance with the present Charter, and shall refrain from giving assistance to any State against which the United Nations is taking preventive or enforcement action."

The sixth principle is that "the Organization shall ensure that the States which are not Members of the United Nations act in accordance with these Principles so far as may be necessary for the maintenance of international peace and security." The French delegation proposed the addition to the fifth principle of a clause to the effect that membership in the United Nations was incompatible with the status of permanent neutrality. It was understood, however, that the fifth and sixth principles, properly interpreted, would cover the French amendment.

The seventh principle is that "nothing contained in the present Charter shall authorize the United Nations to intervene in matters which are essentially within the domestic jurisdiction of any State or shall require the Members to submit such matters to settlement under the present Charter; but this principle shall not prejudice the application of enforcement measures under Chapter VII." In the Dumbarton Oaks Proposals a similar paragraph was to be found in Section A, Chapter VIII, dealing with pacific settlement of disputes. The Proposals used the expression "matters which by international law are solely within domestic jurisdiction of any State concerned." The sponsoring nations themselves proposed that the paragraph should be transferred to the chapter on the Principles of the United Nations, and they reworded the expression to read "matters which are essentially within the domestic jurisdiction of any State." The representatives of Uruguay, Belgium and Peru, however, expressed regret that the Charter did not establish the rule of international law as the criterion of what matters were essentially within domestic jurisdiction.

Membership

Chapter III (on Membership) of the Dumbarton Oaks Proposals contained only one Article, which stated that "membership of the Organization should be open to all peace-loving States."

In the Charter, membership is dealt with in Chapter II, which contains four Articles. The task of drafting the provisions for membership was assigned to Committee I/2.

The Committee made a distinction between original Members and future Members. The original Members are those States which, having participated in the United Nations Conference on International Organization or having previously signed the United Nations Declaration, signed and ratified the Charter. New Members are those peace-loving States which accept the obligations contained in the Charter and, in the opinion of the organization, are able and willing to carry out such obligations. According to the report of the Rapporteur of Committee I/2, it was understood that:

This distinction did not imply any discrimination against future Members but that the normal course of events required it. Before new Members can be admitted the Organization must exist, which in turn implies the existence of original Members. On the other hand the definition adopted would serve to calm the fears of certain nations participating in our deliberations which, properly speaking, are not States and which for this reason might be denied the right of membership in the Organization.

In the deliberations of Committee I/2, the delegations of Uruguay and some other nations took the position that all States should be Members of the United Nations and that their participation was obligatory. That is to say, it would not be left to the choice of any nation whether to become a Member of the United Nations or to withdraw from it. Other delegations believed that universality in this sense was an ideal toward which it was proper to aim but which it was not practicable to realize at once.

The Committee considered two other fundamental problems: (1) the relation existing between membership and the observance of the principles and obligations mentioned in the Charter; and (2) the extent to which it was desirable to establish the limits within which the organization would exercise its discretionary power with respect to the admission of new Members.

The unanimous opinion of the Committee was that adherence to the principles of the Charter and complete acceptance of the obligations arising therefrom were essential conditions to participation by States in the organization. Nevertheless, two principal tendencies were manifested in the discussions. On the one hand, there were some who declared themselves in favor of inserting in the Charter specific conditions which new Members should be required to fulfil, especially in matters concerning the character and policies of governments. On the other hand, others maintained that the Charter should not limit the organization in its decisions concerning requests for admission.

The term "all peace-loving States" was retained, while the qualifications for membership were elaborated. To declare oneself "peace-loving" does not suffice to acquire membership in the organization. It is also necessary to prove two things: that a nation is ready to accept the obligations of the Charter and that it is able and willing to carry out such obligations.

With respect to the admission of new Members, Committee I/2 recommended, and Commission I and the Conference approved the following interpretative commentary originally submitted on June 19, 1945, by the delegation of Mexico, and supported by the delegations of Australia, Belgium, the Byelorussian S.S.R., Chile, France, Guatemala, the Ukrainian S.S.R., the United States and Uruguay.

It is the understanding of the delegation of Mexico that paragraph 2 of Chapter III [Article 4, Chapter II, of the Charter] cannot be applied to the States whose regimes have been established with the help of military forces belonging to the countries which have waged war against the United Nations, as long as those regimes are in power.

The Charter provides that the admission of any State to membership in the United Nations will be effected by a decision of the General Assembly upon the recommendation of the Security Council. This was recommended by Committee II/1. It was stated in the report of the Rapporteur of that Committee that "the purpose of the Charter is primarily to provide security against a repetition of the present war and that, therefore, the Security Council should assume the initial responsibility of suggesting new participating States." However, it was understood that this provision did not "weaken the right of the General Assembly to accept or reject a recommendation for the admission of a new Member, or a recommendation to the effect that a given State should not be admitted to the United Nations."

The question of withdrawal aroused much discussion in the Committee. On the one hand, it was argued that it would be contrary to the conception of universality. On the other hand, it was asserted that a sovereign nation could not be compelled to remain in the organization against its will. In the end the Committee decided against the inclusion in the Charter of a withdrawal clause. Instead it adopted a declaration on withdrawal, the text of which, as revised by Commission I, was as follows:

The Committee adopts the view that the Charter should not make express provision either to permit or to prohibit withdrawal from the Organization. The Committee deems that the highest duty of the nations which will become Members is to continue their co-operation within the Organization for the preservation of international peace and security. If, however, a Member because of exceptional circumstances feels constrained to withdraw, and leave the burden of maintaining international peace and security on the other Members, it is not the purpose of the Organization to compel that Member to continue its co-operation in the Organization.

It is obvious, particularly, that withdrawal or some other form of dissolution of the Organization would become inevitable if, deceiving the hopes of humanity, the Organization was revealed to be unable to maintain peace or could do so only at the expense of law and justice.

Nor would a Member be bound to remain in the Organization if its rights and obligations as such were changed by Charter amendment in which it has not concurred and which it finds itself unable to accept, or if an amendment duly accepted by the necessary majority in the Assembly or in a general conference fails to secure the ratification necessary to bring such amendment into effect.

It is for these considerations that the Committee has decided to abstain from recommending insertion in the Charter of a formal clause specifically forbidding or permitting withdrawal.

The questions of suspension and expulsion gave rise to a lengthy exchange of views in Committee I/2. These questions were dealt with in the Dumbarton Oaks Proposals in Chapter V (on the General Assembly), but they were transferred to Chapter II (on Membership) in the Charter. In the discussions, some representatives maintained that expulsion would be contrary to the concept of universality, while the majority thought that the primary purposes of the United Nations were peace and security, not universality. In the end the Committee recommended and Commission I and the Conference adopted the following provisions:

A Member of the United Nations against which preventive or enforcement action has been taken by the Security Council may be suspended from the exercise of the rights and privileges of membership by the General Assembly upon the recommendation of the Security Council. The exercise of these rights and privileges may be restored by the Security Council.

A Member of the United Nations which has persistently violated the Principles contained in the present Charter may be expelled from the Organization by the General Assembly upon the recommendation of the Security Council.

Organs

Chapter IV (on Principal Organs) of the Dumbarton Oaks Proposals suggested that the United Nations should have four principal organs—a General Assembly, a Security Council, an International Court of Justice and a Secretariat—and should have such subsidiary organs as might be found necessary. This matter was assigned to Committee I/2.

Upon the recommendation of Committee II/3, the Economic and Social Council was made a principal organ, and upon the recommendation of Committee II/4, the Trusteeship Council was likewise made a principal organ.

Committee I/2 added a new Article: "The United Nations shall place no restrictions on the eligibility of men and women to participate in any capacity and under conditions of equality in principal and subsidiary organs."

These provisions constitute Chapter III (Organs) of the Charter.

General Assembly

Matters relating to the structure and procedure of the General Assembly were assigned to Committee II/1. The functions and powers of the General Assembly with respect to the maintenance of peace and security, the promotion of economic and social co-operation and the operation of international trusteeship were assigned respectively to Committee II/2, Committee II/3 and Committee II/4.

Chapter V of the Dumbarton Oaks Proposals as amended by the sponsoring Governments was used as the basis of discussion in Committee II/1 and Committee II/2. The work of Committee II/3 and Committee II/4 will be discussed later.

Structure and procedure

On the structure and procedure of the General Assembly the suggestions of the Dumbarton Oaks Conversations were generally accepted with minor changes and additions.

The Dumbarton Oaks text stated that all Members of the organization should be members of the General Assembly and should have a number of representatives. Committee II/1 recommended that each Member ''shall have not more than five representatives in the General Assembly.''

Some delegations proposed that the public and the press of the world should have free access to the sessions of the General Assembly, but other delegations thought that the question should be dealt with as a procedural matter by the General Assembly itself. The Committee recommended and Commission I and the Conference approved the following statement to be included as a part of the official record of the Conference:

The Conference is of the opinion that regulations to be adopted at the first session of the General Assembly shall provide that, save in exceptional cases, the sessions of the General Assembly shall be open to the public and the press of the world.

Functions and powers

On the functions and powers of the General Assembly, Committee II/2 made certain very significant recommendations which tended to strengthen the position of the General Assembly.

In the first place, the Committee recommended and the Conference approved what is now Article 10 of the Charter, which makes the General Assembly the overseeing and reviewing organ of the United Nations. The text of the Article, as finally adopted, was as follows:

The General Assembly may discuss any questions or any matters within the scope of the present Charter or relating to the powers and functions of any organs provided for in the present Charter, and, except as provided in Article 12 (matters under the consideration of the Security Council), may make recommendations to the Members of the United Nations or to the Security Council or to both on any such questions or matters.

In the second place, the relationship between the General Assembly and the Security Council was further clarified by Committee II/2. The Dumbarton Oaks Proposals had suggested that "the General Assembly shall receive and consider annual and special reports from the Security Council." While this was retained in the Charter, Committee II/2 added an interpretation that the General Assembly, when considering annual and special reports from the Security Council, might exercise the powers of discussion and recommendation. This interpretation was embodied in the report of the Rapporteur of Commission II and adopted by the Conference in these words:

> Commission II calls particular attention to the word "consider" as used in the Charter in connection with reports of the Security Council and other organs. It is the intention of Commission II that this word shall be interpreted to encompass the right to discuss, and that the power of the Assembly to discuss and make recommendations as defined in Articles 10, 11, 12 and 14 is not limited in any way with respect to its consideration of reports from the Security Council.

In the third place, Committee II/2 recommended a new Article, which is now Article 14 of the Charter. The Article, as finally adopted, read as follows:

> Subject to the provision of Article 12 [matters under the consideration of the Security Council], the General Assembly may recommend measures for the peaceful adjustment of any situation, regardless of origin, which it deems likely to impair the general welfare or friendly relations among nations, including situations resulting from a violation of the provisions of the present Charter setting forth the Purposes and Principles of the United Nations.

In the discussions of Committee II/2, the problem of the revision of treaties was brought up. Some representatives thought that any reference to the revision of treaties would tend to weaken the structure of international obligations and might be an invitation to the enemy States to seek a revision of peace treaties. In the end the Committee recommended the more general and inclusive phrase, "peaceful adjustment of any situation, regardless of origin." The Committee also made some minor changes in the Dumbarton Oaks text with respect to the elective, administrative and budgetary functions and powers of the General Assembly.

Security Council

Matters relating to the structure and procedure of the Security Council were assigned to Committee III/1. The functions and powers of the Security Council with respect to pacific settlement, enforcement arrangements and regional arrangements were assigned respectively to Committee III/2, Committee III/3 and Committee III/4. Chapters VI and VIII of the Dumbarton Oaks Proposals as supplemented by the Yalta agreement and amended by the sponsoring Governments served as the basis

of discussion of these four Committees of Commission III.

Structure and procedure

The Dumbarton Oaks Proposals had suggested that the United States, the United Kingdom, the U.S.S.R., the Republic of China, and, "in due course," France should have permanent seats in the Security Council. On the suggestion of the Canadian representative, Committee III/1 deleted the words "in due course."

The Dumbarton Oaks Proposals had suggested that the General Assembly should elect six States to fill the non-permanent seats. Pursuant to an amendment of the sponsoring Governments, Committee III/1 decided to add the following clause: "due regard being specially paid, in the first instance to the contribution of Members of the United Nations to the maintenance of international peace and security and to the other purposes of the Organization, and also to equitable geographical distribution."

Perhaps the most controversial issue in the San Francisco Conference was the voting procedure of the Security Council. The text of the procedure, known as the Yalta formula, which was finally adopted by the Conference as Article 27 of the Charter, read:

> 1. Each member of the Security Council shall have one vote.
> 2. Decisions of the Security Council on procedural matters shall be made by an affirmative vote of seven members.
> 3. Decisions of the Security Council on all other matters shall be made by an affirmative vote of seven members including the concurring votes of the permanent members; provided that, in decisions under Chapter VI, and under paragraph 3 of Article 52, a party to a dispute shall abstain from voting.

During the debate there was wide disagreement on the interpretation of the voting formula. Committee III/1 established a Sub-Committee for the purpose of clarifying the doubts that had arisen in the course of the discussion. On May 22 representatives other than those of the sponsoring Governments on that Sub-Committee addressed 23 questions on the exercise of the veto power to the representatives of the sponsoring Governments on the Sub-Committee.

On June 7 the delegations of the sponsoring Governments issued the following statement on the voting procedure of the Security Council:

> Specific questions covering the voting procedure in the Security Council have been submitted by a Sub-Committee of the Conference Committee on Structure and Procedures of the Security Council to the Delegations of the four Governments sponsoring the Conference—the United States of America, the United

Kingdom of Great Britain and Northern Ireland, the Union of Soviet Socialist Republics, and the Republic of China. In dealing with these questions, the four Delegations desire to make the following statement of their general attitude towards the whole question of unanimity of permanent members in the decisions of the Security Council.

I

1. The Yalta voting formula recognizes that the Security Council, in discharging its responsibilities for the maintenance of international peace and security, will have two broad groups of functions. Under Chapter VIII, the Council will have to make decisions which involve its taking direct measures in connection with settlement of disputes, adjustment of situations likely to lead to disputes, determination of threats to the peace, removal of threats to the peace, and suppression of breaches of the peace. It will also have to make decisions which do not involve the taking of such measures. The Yalta formula provides that the second of these two groups of decisions will be governed by a procedural vote—that is, the vote of any seven members. The first group of decisions will be governed by a qualified vote—that is, the vote of seven members, including the concurring votes of the five permanent members, subject to the proviso that in decisions under Section A and a part of Section C of Chapter VIII parties to a dispute shall abstain from voting.

2. For example, under the Yalta formula a procedural vote will govern the decisions made under the entire Section D of Chapter VI. This means that the Council will, by a vote of any seven of its members, adopt or alter its rules of procedure; determine the method of selecting its President; organize itself in such a way as to be able to function continuously; select the times and places of its regular and special meetings; establish such bodies or agencies as it may deem necessary for the performance of its functions; invite a Member of the organization not represented on the Council to participate in its discussions when that Member's interests are specially affected; and invite any State when it is a party to a dispute being considered by the Council to participate in the discussion relating to that dispute.

3. Further, no individual member of the Council can alone prevent consideration and discussion by the Council of a dispute or situation brought to its attention under paragraph 2, Section A, Chapter VIII. Nor can parties to such dispute be prevented by these means from being heard by the Council. Likewise, the requirement for unanimity of the permanent members cannot prevent any member of the Council from reminding the Members of the organization of their general obligations assumed under the Charter as regards peaceful settlement of international disputes.

4. Beyond this point, decisions and actions by the Security Council may well have major political consequences and may even initiate a chain of events which might, in the end, require the Council under its responsibilities to invoke measures of enforcement under Section B, Chapter VIII. This chain of events begins when the Council decides to make an investigation, or determines that the time has come to call upon States to settle their differences, or make recommendations to the parties. It is to such decisions and actions that unanimity of the permanent members applies, with the important proviso, referred to above, for abstention from voting by parties to a dispute.

5. To illustrate: in ordering an investigation, the Council has to consider whether the investigation—which may involve calling for reports, hearing witnesses, dispatching a commission of inquiry, or other means—might not further aggravate the situation. After investigation, the Council must determine whether the continuance of the situation or dispute would be likely to endanger international peace and security. If it so determines, the Council would be under obligation to take further steps. Similarly, the decision to make recommendations, even when all parties request it to do so, or to call upon parties to a dispute to fulfil their obligations under the Charter, might be the first step on a course of action from which the Security Council could withdraw only at the risk of failing to discharge its responsibilities.

6. In appraising the significance of the vote required to take such decisions or actions, it is useful to make comparison with the requirements of the League Covenant with reference to decisions of the League Council. Substantive decisions of the League of Nations Council could be taken only by the unanimous vote of all its Members, whether permanent or not, with the exception of parties to a dispute under Article XV of the League Covenant. Under Article XI, under which most of the disputes brought before the League were dealt with and decisions to make investigations taken, the unanimity rule was invariably interpreted to include even the votes of the parties to a dispute.

7. The Yalta voting formula substitutes for the rule of complete unanimity of the League Council a system of qualified majority voting in the Security Council. Under this system non-permanent members of the Security Council individually would have no "veto." As regards the permanent members, there is no question under the Yalta formula of investing them with a new right, namely, the right to veto, a right which the permanent members of the League Council always had. The formula proposed for the taking of action in the Security Council by a majority of seven would make the operation of the Council less subject to obstruction than was the case under the League of Nations rule of complete unanimity.

8. It should also be remembered that under the Yalta formula the five major Powers could not act by themselves, since even under the unanimity requirement any decisions of the Council would have to include the concurring votes of at least two of the non-permanent members. In other words, it would be possible for five non-permanent members as a group to exercise a "veto." It is not to be assumed, however, that the permanent members, any more than the non-permanent members, would use their "veto" power wilfully to obstruct the operation of the Council.

9. In view of the primary responsibilities of the permanent members, they could not be expected, in the present condition of the world, to assume the obligation to act in so serious a matter as the maintenance of international peace and security in consequence of a decision in which they had not concurred. Therefore, if a majority voting in the Security Council is to be made possible, the only practicable method is to provide, in respect of non-procedural decisions, for unanimity of

the permanent members plus the concurring votes of at least two of the non-permanent members.

10. For all these reasons, the four sponsoring Governments agreed on the Yalta formula and have presented it to this Conference as essential if an international organization is to be created through which all peace-loving nations can effectively discharge their common responsibilities for the maintenance of international peace and security.

II

In the light of the considerations set forth in Part I of this statement, it is clear what the answers to the questions submitted by the Sub-Committee should be, with the exception of Question 19 (with respect to the preliminary question as to whether a matter is procedural). The answer to that question is as follows:

1. In the opinion of the Delegations of the sponsoring Governments, the Draft Charter itself contains an indication of the application of the voting procedures to the various functions of the Council.

2. In this case, it will be unlikely that there will arise in the future any matters of great importance on which a decision will have to be made as to whether a procedural vote would apply. Should, however, such a matter arise, the decision regarding the preliminary question as to whether or not such a matter is procedural must be taken by a vote of seven members of the Security Council, including the concurring votes of the permanent members.

In the course of the debate that ensued, several delegations indicated that they would be more favourably inclined to accept the proposed voting procedure if a revision of that procedure were made possible at another conference. They hoped that such a revision would not be subject to the rule of unanimity of the permanent members of the Security Council.

The Australian representative proposed that decisions of the Security Council with respect to pacific settlement of disputes should be made by a majority of any seven members, i.e., should be considered as decisions on procedural matters. The Australian representative stated that he was reluctantly prepared to accept the veto power in connection with enforcement measures, but that in pacific settlement of disputes no one power should block any Council decisions. The Australian amendment, like several others, was not adopted.

Committee III/1, Commission III and eventually the Conference adopted the Yalta voting formula, which constitutes Article 27 of the Charter. The statement of the delegations of the sponsoring Governments on the voting procedure of the Security Council, however, was not formally accepted as the official interpretation of Article 27.

Committee III/1 agreed to the Dumbarton Oaks recommendations: (1) that Members of the United Nations should confer upon the Security Council primary responsibility for the maintenance of international peace and security and should agree that in carrying out these duties under this responsibility the Security Council should act on their behalf; (2) that in discharging these duties the Security Council should act in accordance with the Purposes and Principles of the United Nations; and (3) that Members should obligate themselves to accept the decisions of the Security Council and to carry them out in accordance with the provisions of the Charter.

Pacific settlement

Section A of Chapter VIII of the Dumbarton Oaks Proposals was the subject matter considered by Committee III/2, which made some changes in the order and wording of the paragraphs. The substance of this section constitutes Chapter VI of the Charter.

The Committee thought the first Article in this Chapter should set forth the basic obligations of Members to settle disputes by pacific means. The Dumbarton Oaks text had stated that parties to a dispute should seek a solution ''by negotiation, mediation, conciliation, arbitration or judicial settlement, or other peaceful means of their own choice.'' Committee III/2 added ''inquiry'' and, upon the recommendation of Committee III/4, ''resort to regional agencies or arrangements'' to the list of pacific means.

The Dumbarton Oaks text had suggested that any State, whether a Member of the organization or not, might bring any dispute, or any situation which might give rise to a dispute, to the attention of the General Assembly or of the Security Council. Committee III/2 revised this text so as to make it clear: (1) that any Member might bring any dispute or situation to the attention of the General Assembly or of the Security Council; and (2) that a State, not a Member of the organization, might bring only a dispute (not a situation) to the Assembly or the Council if it accepted in advance the obligations of pacific settlement as provided in the Charter. It was understood that the enemy States in the Second World War ''shall not have the right of recourse to the Security Council or the General Assembly until the Security Council gives them this right.''

Committee III/2 agreed to the Dumbarton Oaks recommendations, as amended by the sponsoring Governments: (1) that the Security Council might investigate any dispute, or any situation which might lead to international friction or give rise to a dispute, in order to determine whether the continuance of the dispute or situation was likely to endanger international peace and security; (2) that the Security Council might, at any stage of such dispute, recommend appropriate procedures or methods of adjustment; and (3) that the Security Council, if it deemed that the continuance of a dispute was in fact likely to endanger the maintenance of international peace and security, might recommend appropriate procedures or actual terms of settlement. With respect to the last clause, it was understood that such a recommendation "possessed no obligatory effect for the parties."

Enforcement arrangements

Section B of Chapter VIII of the Dumbarton Oaks Proposals was the basis of discussion in Committee III/3. The substance of this section, as amended and adopted by the Conference, constitutes Chapter VII of the Charter.

According to the Dumbarton Oaks Proposals, the Security Council "should determine the existence of any threat to the peace, breach of the peace or act of aggression and should make recommendations or decide upon the measures to be taken to maintain or restore peace and security." Several delegations proposed that the term "aggression" might be defined or explained, but the majority of the Committee thought that a preliminary definition of "aggression" went beyond the scope of the Charter and that the modern techniques of warfare rendered any definition of "aggression" impossible. The Committee decided to adhere to the Dumbarton Oaks text.

The Chinese delegation introduced a new paragraph to the effect that, before making recommendations or deciding upon enforcement measures, the Security Council might call upon the parties to a dispute to comply with such provisional measures as it might deem necessary and desirable, such provisional measures being without prejudice to the rights, claims and position of the parties concerned, the failure to comply with such provisional measures to be duly taken account of by the Council. The substance of this paragraph became Article 40 of the Charter.

In using the word "recommendations" in the two preceding paragraphs, Committee III/3 intended to indicate the action of the Security Council under the provisions of pacific settlement, and at the same time the Committee realized that the Security Council would in reality pursue simultaneously two distinct actions, one having for its object the settlement of the dispute, and the other the taking of enforcement or provisional measures. The Committee was unanimous in the belief that, in the case of flagrant aggression imperilling the existence of a Member, enforcement action should be taken without delay.

Committee III/3 agreed to the Dumbarton Oaks recommendations: (1) that the Security Council might call upon Members to employ measures not involving the use of armed forces, such as severance of economic and diplomatic relations, to give effect to its decisions; and (2) that, should these measures prove to be inadequate, the Council might take such action by land, sea or air forces as might be necessary to maintain international peace and security.

The Dumbarton Oaks Proposals contemplated that the forces put at the disposition of the Security Council should take the form of national contingents furnished by Members according to special agreements to be negotiated subsequently. On this matter the French delegation proposed a new draft, which became Article 43 of the Charter. The draft read:

In order that all Members of the Organization should contribute to the maintenance of international peace and security, they should undertake to make available to the Security Council, on its call and in accordance with a special agreement or agreements, armed forces, assistance and facilities, including rights of passage necessary for the purpose of maintaining international peace and security. Such agreement or agreements should govern the numbers and types of forces, their degree of readiness and general location, and the nature of the facilities and assistance to be provided. The special agreement or agreements should be negotiated as soon as possible on the initiative of the Security Council and concluded between the Security Council and Member States or between the Security Council and groups of Member States. All such agreements should be subject to ratification by the signatory States in accordance with their constitutional processes.

The Dumbarton Oaks Proposals had suggested that a Military Staff Committee should be established to advise and assist the Security Council on all questions relating to the Council's military requirements, to the employment and command of forces, to the regulation of armaments and possible disarmament; that the Military Staff Committee should consist of the Chiefs of Staff of the permanent members of the Security Council or their representatives; and that any Member not represented on the Committee should be invited by the Committee to be associated with it when the efficient discharge of the Committee's responsibilities required that such a State should participate in its work.

Upon the suggestion of the Canadian delegation, Committee III/3 added a new paragraph which became Article 44 of the Charter. It read:

When a decision to use force has been taken by the Security Council, it shall, before calling upon any Member not represented on it to provide armed forces in fulfilment of its obligations under the preceding paragraph, invite such Member, if it so requests, to send a representative to participate in the decisions of the Security Council concerning the employment of contingents of its armed forces.

Under this paragraph every Member not represented on the Security Council may participate, with the right of voting, in the deliberations of the Council when it is a question of the utilization of its armed forces. To repeat the expression of the Netherlands representative, the principle of "no military action without representation" was accepted by Committee III/3.

The Philippine delegation proposed and the Mexican delegation seconded an amendment that the Military Staff Committee should be composed of the Chiefs of Staff of all the Members of the United Nations. The amendment was not adopted, on the grounds that the Committee should be a small group so that it might be able to make decisions on military matters and that if the forces of a country not represented on the Committee were used there was no question but that the military staff of that country would be consulted.

Regional arrangements

Section C of Chapter VIII of the Dumbarton Oaks Proposals was referred to Committee III/4. The substance of this section constitutes Chapter VIII of the Charter.

The Dumbarton Oaks Proposals had suggested that "nothing in the Charter precludes the existence of regional arrangements or agencies for dealing with such matters relating to the maintenance of international peace and security as are appropriate for regional action, provided such arrangements or agencies and their activities are consistent with the Purposes and Principles of the United Nations." This was accepted by Committee III/4.

The Egyptian delegation introduced a definition of regional arrangements which read:

There shall be considered as regional arrangements organizations of a permanent nature grouping in a given geographical area several countries which, by reason of their proximity, community of interests, or cultural, linguistic, historical or spiritual affinities, make themselves jointly responsible for the peaceful settlement of any disputes which may arise between them and for the maintenance of peace and security in their region, as well as for the safeguarding of their interests and the development of their economic and cultural relations.

This amendment was not adopted, on the ground that it might not cover all the situations which might come under the term "regional arrangements."

Committee III/4 agreed to the Dumbarton Oaks recommendation that the Security Council should encourage pacific settlement of local disputes through regional arrangements or by regional agencies, either on the initiative of the States concerned or by reference from the Security Council. However, the Committee added a new paragraph to the effect that this provision did not impair the application of Articles 33 and 35 of the Charter.

Committee III/4 also agreed to the Dumbarton Oaks recommendation that the Security Council should, when appropriate, utilize regional arrangements or agencies for enforcement action under its authority, but no enforcement action should be taken under regional arrangements or by regional agencies without the authorization of the Security Council. The Committee approved an exception, suggested by the sponsoring Governments. It recommended that measures under regional arrangements directed against the renewal of aggressive policy by any enemy State of the Second World War might be taken without the authorization of the Security Council until such time as the United Nations might be charged with the responsibility for preventing further aggression by any such State.

Committee III/4 wrote a new paragraph which read as follows:

Nothing in the present Charter shall impair the inherent right of individual or collective self-defence if an armed attack occurs against a Member of the United Nations, until the Security Council has taken the measures necessary to maintain international peace and security. Measures taken by Members in the exercise of this right of self-defence shall be immediately reported to the Security Council and shall not in any way affect the authority and responsibility of the Security Council under the present Charter to take at any time such action as it deems necessary in order to maintain or restore international peace and security.

This paragraph, however, was not inserted in Chapter VIII of the Charter, which deals with regional arrangements, but became Article 51 of Chapter VII, which deals with enforcement measures.

International economic and social co-operation

Chapter IX of the Dumbarton Oaks Proposals constituted the agenda of Committee II/3. The substance of that chapter, as amended by Committee II/3, became Chapter IX, International Economic and Social Co-operation, and Chapter X, The Economic and Social Council, of the Charter.

Committee II/3 made certain significant contributions to the drafting of Chapters IX and X of the Charter.

In the first place, the Committee unanimously recommended that the Economic and Social Council be listed as one of the principal organs of the United Nations. This recommendation expressed the opinion of the Committee that international economic and social co-operation was of the utmost importance to the success of the United Nations as a whole.

In the second place, the Committee greatly enlarged and broadened the objectives which the United Nations should promote in the economic and social fields. It recommended that the United Nations should promote:

(a)   higher standards of living, full employment, and conditions of economic and social progress and development;

(b) solutions of international economic, social, health and related problems; and international cultural and educational co-operation;

(c) universal respect for, and observance of, human rights and fundamental freedoms for all without distinction as to race, sex, language or religion.

There were some misgivings as to whether this statement of objectives might not be taken to imply that the United Nations might interfere in the domestic affairs of Member States. The Committee agreed to include in its record a statement to the effect that nothing in the provisions relating to international economic and social co-operation "can be construed as giving authority to the Organization to intervene in the domestic affairs of Member States."

Committee II/3 accepted the Dumbarton Oaks recommendation that the Economic and Social Council should consist of eighteen members elected by the General Assembly for three-year terms. The Committee specified that one third of the members of the Council should retire every year. It rejected amendments designed to give permanent representation to the great Powers or to make membership dependent upon economic and social importance.

As to the functions and powers of the Economic and Social Council, Committee II/3 recommended that, under the authority of the General Assembly, the Council might initiate studies and make recommendations with respect to international economic, social, cultural, education, health and related fields; make recommendations for the purpose of promoting respect for, and observance of, human rights and fundamental freedoms; prepare draft conventions and call international conferences on matters falling within its competence; enter into agreements with specialized agencies and co-ordinate the activities of and receive reports from such agencies. The Committee suggested that the General Assembly, however, and not the Economic and Social Council, should examine the administrative budgets of the specialized agencies.

The Dumbarton Oaks Proposals had suggested that the various specialized economic, social and other agencies should be brought into relationship with the United Nations. Committee II/3 recommended that this provision should apply only to those inter-governmental agencies having wide international responsibilities, as defined in their basic instruments, in economic, social, cultural, educational, health and related fields. It was understood that the term "inter-governmental agencies" should be interpreted to mean agencies set up by agreement among governments. It was further understood that the United Nations should not deprive any specialized agency of its responsibilities in its own specialized field as defined in its basic instrument.

Committee II/3 further recommended that the Economic and Social Council might make suitable arrangements for consultation with non-governmental organizations which were concerned with matters within its competence.

In the course of the Committee's discussions, a number of statements and declarations relating to specific problems of international co-operation were made by national delegations. The French delegation issued a statement on cultural co-operation; the Brazilian and Chinese delegations a joint declaration regarding international health co-operation; the Greek delegation a declaration regarding the reconstruction of devastated areas; the Brazilian delegation a declaration on the status of women; the Panamanian delegation a declaration on the question of migration; the United States delegation a statement on the control of dangerous drugs. The Committee thought that its terms of reference did not permit it to pass resolutions on these matters; it decided to keep the texts of the statements and declarations on its record.

International trusteeship

The Dumbarton Oaks Proposals did not contain any provisions relating to the establishment of an international trusteeship system. At Yalta President Roosevelt, Prime Minister Churchill and Premier Stalin agreed that the San Francisco Conference should discuss only the machinery and principles of trusteeship and that specific territories to be placed under trusteeship should be a matter of subsequent negotiation and agreement.

Consequently Committee II/4 was assigned the task of drafting provisions "on the principles and mechanism of a system of international trusteeship for such dependent territories as may by subsequent agreement be placed thereunder."

On the basis of a number of proposals, the delegations of Australia, China, France, the U.S.S.R., the United Kingdom and the United States submitted a Working Paper to the Committee on May 15. The text of the Working Paper was as follows:

A. General Policy

1. States Members of the United Nations which have responsibilities for the administration of territories inhabited by peoples not yet able to stand by themselves under the strenuous conditions of the modern world accept the general principle that it is a sacred trust of civilization to promote to the utmost the well-being of the inhabitants of these territories within the world community, and to this end:

(i) to insure the economic and social advancement of the peoples concerned;

(ii) to develop self-government in forms appropriate to the varying circumstances of each territory; and

(iii) to further international peace and security.

2. States Members also agree that their policy in respect to such territories, no less than in respect to their metropolitan areas, must be based on the general prin-

ciple of good neighbourliness, due account being taken of the interests and well-being of other members of the world community, in social, economic and commercial matters.

B. Territorial Trusteeship System

1. The Organization should establish under its authority an international system of trusteeship for the administration and supervision of such territories as may be placed thereunder by subsequent individual agreements and set up suitable machinery for these purposes.

2. The basic objectives of the trusteeship system should be: (a) to further international peace and security; (b) to promote the political, economic, and social advancement of the trust territories and their inhabitants and their progressive development toward self-government in forms appropriate to the varying circumstances of each territory; and (c) to insure equal treatment in social, economic and commercial matters for all Members of the United Nations, without prejudice to the attainment of (a) and (b) above, and subject to the provisions of paragraph 5 below.

3. The trusteeship system should apply only to such territories in the following categories as may be placed thereunder by means of trusteeship arrangements: (a) territories now held under mandates; (b) territories which may be detached from enemy States as a result of this war; and (c) territories voluntarily placed under the system by States responsible for their administration. It would be a matter for subsequent agreement as to which territories would be brought under a trusteeship system and upon what terms. The trusteeship system should not apply to territories which have become Members of the United Nations.

4. The trusteeship arrangement for each territory to be placed under trusteeship should be agreed upon by the States directly concerned and should be approved as provided for in paragraphs 8 and 10 below.

5. Except as may be agreed upon in individual trusteeship arrangements placing each territory under the trusteeship system, nothing in this chapter should be construed in and of itself to alter in any manner the rights of any States or any peoples in any territory.

6. The trusteeship arrangements in each case should include the terms under which the territory will be administered and designate the State which should exercise the administration of the territory or designate the United Nations Organization itself to exercise the administration of the territory.

7. In addition, there may also be designated, in the trusteeship arrangement, a strategic area or areas which may include part or all of the territory to which the arrangement applies.

8. All functions of the Organization relating to such strategic areas, including the approval of the trusteeship arrangements and their alteration or amendment, should be exercised by the Security Council. The basic objective as provided for in paragraph B.2 above should be applicable to the people of each strategic area. The Security Council may avail itself of the assistance of the Trusteeship Council provided for in paragraph 11 below to perform those functions of the Organization under the trusteeship system relating to political, economic and social matters in the strategic areas, subject to the provisions of the trusteeship arrangements.

9. It shall be the duty of the State administering any trust territory to insure that the territory shall play its part in the maintenance of international peace and security. To this end the State shall be empowered to make use of volunteer forces, facilities and assistance from the territory in carrying out the obligations undertaken by the State for the Security Council in this regard and for local defense and the maintenance of law and order within the territory.

10. The functions of the Organization with regard to trusteeship arrangements for all areas not designated as strategic should be exercised by the General Assembly.

11. In order to assist the General Assembly to carry out those functions under the trusteeship system not reserved to the Security Council, there should be established a Trusteeship Council which would operate under its authority. The Trusteeship Council should consist of specially qualified representatives, designated (a) one each by the States administering trust territories, and (b) one each by an equal number of other States named for three-year periods by the General Assembly.

12. The General Assembly, and under its authority, the Trusteeship Council, in carrying out their functions, should be empowered to consider reports submitted by the administering State to accept petitions and examine them in consultation with the administering State, to make periodic visits to the respective territories at times agreed upon with the administering State, and to take other action in conformity with the trusteeship arrangements.

13. The administering authority in each trust territory within the competence of the General Assembly should make an annual report to the General Assembly upon the basis of a questionnaire formulated by the Trusteeship Council.

Committee II/4 adopted the Working Paper as a basis of discussion. As to the "general policy" in the Working Paper, the Committee found that it was desirable to change the description of Non-Self-Governing Territories as being "inhabited by peoples not yet able to stand by themselves under the strenuous conditions of the modern world" to that of territories "whose peoples have not yet attained a full measure of self-government." The Committee added a further obligation requiring the administering powers to transmit regularly to the Secretary-General statistical and other information relating to the economic, social and educational conditions of the territories they administered. The Committee changed the "general policy" into a "declaration," which eventually became Chapter XI of the Charter.

As to the "territorial trusteeship system" in the Working Paper, Committee II/4 made some significant changes. In the first place the Committee recommended that the promotion of the progressive development of the peoples of Trust Territories should be directed toward "independence" as well as "self-government." In the second place, the Committee suggested that the trusteeship system should encourage respect for human rights and fundamental freedoms for all without distinction as to race, sex, language or religion.

The Committee agreed to the provisions in the Working Paper that the trusteeship system should apply to such territories in the following categories as might be placed thereunder by means of Trusteeship Agreements (a) territories now held under mandate; (b) territories which might be detached from enemy States as a result of the Second World War; and (c) territories voluntarily placed under the system by States responsible for their administration.

The Working Paper had suggested a "conservatory clause" to the effect that, until individual Trusteeship Agreements were concluded, nothing in the provisions concerning the trusteeship system should be "construed in and of itself to alter in any manner the rights of any States or any peoples." The Committee added at the end of this paragraph the following words, "or the terms of existing international instruments." It inserted a new paragraph, however, to the effect that the conservatory clause should be not interpreted as giving grounds for delay or postponement of the negotiation and conclusion of Trusteeship Agreements.

With regard to the terms of Trusteeship Agreements, the Committee accepted with some minor changes the recommendations of the Working Paper. The terms of trusteeship should be agreed upon by the "States directly concerned" and should designate the Administering Authority. In any Trust Territory a strategic area or areas might be designated. All functions of the United Nations relating to Trust Territories, other than strategic areas, should be exercised by the General Assembly, and those relating to strategic areas by the Security Council.

In the course of the discussion the Egyptian delegation proposed: (1) that the General Assembly should have the power to terminate the status of trusteeship of a territory and declare the territory to be fit for full independence; and (2) that whenever an Administering Authority violated the terms of trusteeship, or ceased to be a Member of the United Nations or was suspended from membership in the United Nations, the organization should transfer the territory under trusteeship to another Administering Authority. These proposals, however, were not adopted.

Committee II/4 recommended the creation of a Trusteeship Council as a principal organ of the United Nations. The Council was to consist of: (a) those Members administering Trust Territories; (b) those permanent members of the Security Council which were not Administering Authorities; and (c) as many other Members elected for three-year terms by the General Assembly as might be necessary to ensure that the total number of members of the Trusteeship Council was equally divided between those which administered Trust Territories and those which did not.

The Committee agreed to the definition of the functions and powers of the Trusteeship Council as suggested in the Working Paper, and wrote several paragraphs on the voting and procedure of the Council.

The provisions on the International Trusteeship System constitute Chapter XII of the Charter, and those on the Trusteeship Council, Chapter XIII.

International Court of Justice

Chapter VII of the Dumbarton Oaks Proposals and the report of the Committee of Jurists constituted the agenda of Committee IV/1.

The basic question the Committee had to resolve was whether the Permanent Court of International Justice should be continued as an organ of the United Nations or whether a new Court should be established. After balancing the advantages to be gained and objections to be overcome in adopting either course, the Committee recommended the establishment of a new Court. This was thought to be in keeping with provisions to be proposed in the Charter, under which all Members of the United Nations are *ipso facto* parties to the Statute of the International Court of Justice and a State not a Member of the United Nations may become a party to the Statute on conditions to be determined by the General Assembly upon the recommendation of the Security Council.

Committee IV/1 recommended that each Member of the United Nations should undertake to comply with the decision of the Court in any case to which it was a party. The Committee added another paragraph to the effect that, should any party fail to comply with the decision of the Court, the other party could have recourse to the Security Council, which might make such recommendations or decide upon such measures as to give effect to the decision.

The Committee of Jurists had presented two alternative texts relating to the nomination of judges, one retaining the system of nomination by national groups, the other instituting a system of nomination by governments. The majority of Committee IV/1 thought that the system of nomination by national groups had worked very well in the past; the Committee therefore decided to recommend the retention of the system. As to the election of judges, two views were expressed: one favoured election by both the General Assembly and the Security Council, the other election by the General Assembly alone. In the end the Committee decided to recommend that both the Assembly and the Council should take part in the election of judges and that an absolute majority should be required in each body.

There was a general desire on the part of the Committee to establish compulsory jurisdiction for the Court. However, some of the delegates feared that insistence upon compulsory jurisdiction might impair the possibility of obtaining general accord to the Statute as well as to the Charter itself. It was in that spirit that the Committee recommended the adoption of the optional clause.

The Committee proposed that the procedure in amending the Statute should be the same as that in amending the Charter, but it added that the Court itself should have the power to propose amendments to the Statute.

Secretariat

The task of drafting provisions for the Secretariat was assigned to Committee I/2. Chapter X of the Dumbarton Oaks Proposals was the agenda of the Committee.

The Dumbarton Oaks text had suggested that there should be a Secretary-General, who was to be elected by the General Assembly upon the recommendation of the Security Council. The sponsoring Governments proposed an amendment providing that there should be four Deputy Secretaries-General elected in the same way. However, Committee I/2 did not adopt this amendment.

The Committee accepted the Dumbarton Oaks recommendations: (1) that the Secretary-General should be the chief administrative officer; (2) that the Secretary-General should act in that capacity in all meetings of the General Assembly and the Councils; (3) that he should make an annual report to the General Assembly on the work of the Organization. After considerable discussion the Committee also agreed to the Dumbarton Oaks suggestion that the Secretary-General might bring to the attention of the Security Council any matter which in his opinion might threaten international peace and security.

The Committee recommended that the Secretariat should be truly international in character; that the members of the staff should not receive instructions from any governments and the Members of the United Nations should not seek to influence the members of the staff. It further recommended that the paramount consideration in the employment of the staff should be the necessity of securing the highest standards of efficiency, competence and integrity, and that due regard should be paid to the importance of recruiting the staff on as wide a geographical basis as possible.

Legal problems

Committee IV/2 was assigned the task of drafting provisions regarding such legal matters as the judicial status of the United Nations, the privileges and immunities of the United Nations, registration of treaties, treaty obligations inconsistent with the Charter and interpretation of the Charter.

The Committee recommended that the United Nations should enjoy in the territory of each Member such legal capacity as might be necessary for the fulfilment of its purposes and that representatives of the Members of the United Nations and officials of the United Nations should enjoy such privileges and immunities as were necessary for the independent exercise of their functions.

It recommended that every treaty and every international agreement should be registered with the Secretariat and published by it and that no party to any such treaty or agreement which had not been registered might invoke that treaty or agreement before any organ of the United Nations.

It further recommended that in the event of a conflict between the obligations of the Members of the United Nations under the Charter and their obligations under any other international agreements, their obligations under the Charter should prevail.

As to the question, how and by what organ or organs the Charter should be interpreted, the Committee decided that it would be neither necessary nor desirable to make any explicit provision in the Charter. It made the following statement for the record:

If two Member States are at variance concerning the correct interpretation of the Charter, they are of course free to submit the dispute to the International Court of Justice as in the case of any other treaty. Similarly, it would always be open to the General Assembly or to the Security Council, in appropriate circumstances, to ask the International Court of Justice for an advisory opinion concerning the meaning of a provision of the Charter. Should the General Assembly or the Security Council prefer another course, an *ad hoc* committee of jurists might be set up to examine the question and report its views, or recourse might be had to a joint conference. In brief, the Members or the organs of the Organization might have recourse to various expedients in order to obtain an appropriate interpretation.

Amendments

Committee I/2 was charged with the responsibility for drafting provisions relating to amendments to the Charter.

Chapter XI of the Dumbarton Oaks Proposals contained only one Article on amendments. This was amended as follows:

Amendments to the present Charter shall come into force for all Members of the United Nations when they have been adopted by a vote of two thirds of the Members of the General Assembly and ratified in accordance with their respective constitutional processes by two thirds of the Members of the United Nations, including all of the permanent members of the Security Council.

The Dumbarton Oaks Proposals did not provide for the calling of a general conference to review the Charter. The sponsoring Governments proposed an amendment providing for such a conference to meet the wishes expressed by several delegations. After lengthy debate on the voting procedure and the time limit for calling a general conference, the Committee decided to recommend the following provisions:

A General Conference of the Members of the United Nations for the purpose of reviewing the present Charter may be held at a date and place to be fixed by a two-thirds vote of the members of the General Assembly and by a vote of any seven members of the Security Council. Each Member of the United Nations shall have one vote in the conference.

Any alteration of the present Charter recommended by a two-thirds vote of the conference shall take effect when ratified in accordance with their respective constitutional processes by two thirds of the Members of the United Nations including all the permanent members of the Security Council.

If such a conference has not been held before the tenth annual session of the General Assembly following the coming into force of the present Charter, the proposal to call such a conference shall be placed on the agenda of that session of the General Assembly, and the conference shall be held if so decided by a majority vote of the members of the General Assembly and by a vote of any seven members of the Security Council.

Signing of the Charter

At the final plenary session of the San Francisco Conference on June 25, 1945, the Charter of the United Nations was unanimously approved, the heads of the 50 delegations standing to mark their vote in favor.

President Harry S. Truman attended this final session in person and addressed the Conference on the conclusion of its historic task. He congratulated the delegates of all 50 nations upon having produced a solid structure on which could be built a better world.

On the following day the signing ceremony took place in the Veterans War Memorial Building at San Francisco. China, in recognition of its long-standing fight against aggression, was accorded the honor of being the first to sign. It was arranged that the signatures of the U.S.S.R., the United Kingdom and France should follow, and then, in alphabetical order, the remaining nations, with the United States, as host country, signing last. As each delegation came forward to sign, its chairman made an official speech to commemorate his country's participation in the work of the Conference.

Ratification of the Charter

Under Article 110, the Charter of the United Nations, together with the Statute of the International Court of Justice, was to come into force upon the deposit with the Government of the United States of ratifications by China, France, the U.S.S.R., the United Kingdom, the United States, and by a majority of the other signatory States.

On October 24, 1945, the Charter came into force when the five permanent members of the Security Council and 24 other signatory States had deposited their ratifications with the Government of the United States. On that date the United States Secretary of State signed a Protocol of Deposit of Ratifications, which read as follows:

WHEREAS, paragraph 3 of Article 110 of the Charter of the United Nations, signed at San Francisco on June 26, 1945, provides as follows:

"3. The present Charter shall come into force upon the deposit of ratifications by the Republic of China, France, the Union of Soviet Socialist Republics, the United Kingdom of Great Britain and Northern Ireland, and the United States of America, and by a majority of the other signatory states. A protocol of the ratifications deposited shall thereupon be drawn up by the Government of the United States of America, which shall communicate copies thereof to all the signatory States.";

WHEREAS, the Charter of the United Nations has been signed by the Plenipotentiaries of fifty-one states;

WHEREAS, instruments of ratification of the Charter of the United Nations have been deposited by

the Republic of China on September 28, 1945,
France on August 31, 1945,
the Union of Soviet Socialist Republics on
    October 24, 1945,
the United Kingdom of Great Britain and
    Northern Ireland on October 20, 1945, and
the United States of America on August 8, 1945;
    and by

Argentina on September 24, 1945,
Brazil on September 21, 1945,
the Byelorussian Soviet Socialist Republic on
    October 24, 1945,
Chile on October 11, 1945,
Cuba on October 15, 1945,
Czechoslovakia on October 19, 1945,
Denmark on October 9, 1945,
the Dominican Republic on September 4, 1945,
Egypt on October 22, 1945,
El Salvador on September 26, 1945,
Haiti on September 27, 1945,
Iran on October 16, 1945,
Lebanon on October 15, 1945,
Luxembourg on October 17, 1945,
New Zealand on September 19, 1945,
Nicaragua on September 6, 1945,
Paraguay on October 12, 1945,
the Philippine Commonwealth on October 11, 1945,
Poland on October 24, 1945,
Saudi Arabia on October 18, 1945,
Syria on October 19, 1945,
Turkey on September 28, 1945,
the Ukrainian Soviet Socialist Republic on
    October 24, 1945,
Yugoslavia on October 19, 1945;

AND WHEREAS, the requirements of paragraph 3 of Article 110 with respect to the coming into force of the Charter have been fulfilled by the deposit of the aforementioned instruments of ratification;

NOW THEREFORE, I, James F. Byrnes, Secretary of State of the United States of America, sign this Protocol in the English language, the original of which shall be deposited in the archives of the Government of the United States of America and copies thereof communicated to all the States signatory of the Charter of the United Nations.

DONE at Washington this twenty-fourth day of October, one thousand nine hundred forty-five.

James F. Byrnes

Secretary of State
of the United States of America

After the signature of this Protocol the following States deposited their instruments of ratification:

Country	Date of Deposit
Australia	November 1, 1945
Belgium	December 27, 1945
Bolivia	November 14, 1945
Canada	November 9, 1945
Colombia	November 5, 1945
Costa Rica	November 2, 1945
Ecuador	December 21, 1945
Ethiopia	November 13, 1945
Greece	October 25, 1945
Guatemala	November 21, 1945
Honduras	December 17, 1945
India	October 30, 1945
Iraq	December 21, 1945
Liberia	November 2, 1945
Mexico	November 7, 1945
Netherlands	December 10, 1945
Norway	November 27, 1945
Panama	November 13, 1945
Peru	October 31, 1945
Union of South Africa	November 7, 1945
Uruguay	December 18, 1945
Venezuela	November 15, 1945

[YUN 1946-47, pp. 1-34]

PART ONE

International peace and security

*"To maintain international peace and security, and
to that end: to take effective collective measures for
the prevention and removal of threats to the peace, and for the
suppression of acts of aggression or other breaches
of the peace, and to bring about by peaceful means, and in
conformity with the principles of justice and international law,
adjustment or settlement of international disputes or
situations which might lead to a breach of the peace "*

Chapter I

The evolving UN agenda: making and keeping peace

The first of the purposes of the United Nations outlined in its Charter was "To maintain international peace and security . . . ." Over the past 50 years, concrete measures have been taken by the United Nations Security Council, the principal organ vested with the primary responsibility for the maintenance of international peace and security, to achieve this purpose, as set out in Chapters VI and VII of the Charter. Chapter VI provided that international disputes "likely to endanger the maintenance of international peace and security" could be brought to the attention of the Security Council or the General Assembly. The Council was expressly mandated to call on the parties to settle their disputes by peaceful means, to recommend appropriate procedures or methods of adjustment and, in addition, to recommend actual terms of a settlement. The action of the Council in this context has been limited to making recommendations; essentially, the peaceful settlement of international disputes must be achieved by the parties themselves, acting on a voluntary basis to carry out the decisions of the Council in accordance with the Charter.

Within days of its very first meeting on 17 January 1946 at Westminster, London, the Security Council was called upon to act when Iran complained that the presence of Soviet troops on its soil had caused a situation which threatened peace. It would be but the first of a series of problems whose complexity required insight, delicate diplomacy and innovation in situations made even more difficult by powerful contending forces. History, ideology, economics, race and religion generated highly combustible mixtures of fear and mistrust.

Each of the critical situations brought before the United Nations contributed to the 50-year evolution

of peace-keeping, peacemaking and what came to be known as preventive diplomacy, a concept requiring constant expansion in perspective due to the changing nature of conflicts, from mainly inter-State wars to intra-State conflicts.

United Nations peace-keeping operations evolved as, essentially, holding actions to stop hostilities and control conflicts. They were born of necessity, largely improvised, a practical response to a problem requiring action. As the United Nations practice has evolved over the years, peace-keeping operations have come to be defined as operations involving military personnel, but without enforcement powers, undertaken by the United Nations to help maintain or restore international peace and security in areas of conflict. With an escalation of regional conflicts worldwide, peace-keeping operations have increased (see figure 1). These operations are voluntary and are based on consent and cooperation. While they involve the use of military personnel, they achieve their objectives not by force of arms.

Peace-keeping operations have been most commonly employed to supervise and help maintain cease-fires, to assist in troop withdrawals, and to provide a buffer between opposing forces. However, peace-keeping operations have also served as flexible instruments of policy adapted to a variety of uses, including helping to implement the final settlement of a conflict. These operations have never been purely military; they have always included civilian personnel to carry out essential political or administrative functions, sometimes on a very large scale.

The Congo crisis of the 1960s saw the introduction of United Nations peace-keeping operations in Africa. More recently, large-scale military and civilian contingents have been deployed to various African

FIGURE 1
United Nations peace-keeping operations as at April 1995

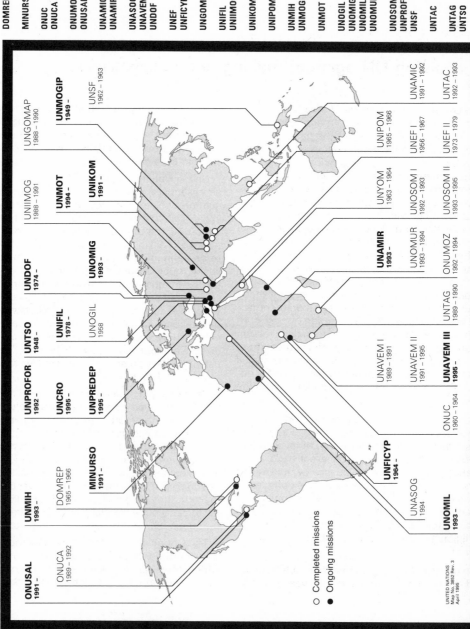

DOMREP	Mission of the Representative of the Secretary-General in the Dominican Republic
MINURSO	United Nations Mission for the Referendum in Western Sahara
ONUC	United Nations Operation in the Congo
ONUCA	United Nations Observer Group in Central America
ONUMOZ	United Nations Operation in Mozambique
ONUSAL	United Nations Observer Mission in El Salvador
UNAMIC	United Nations Advance Mission in Cambodia
UNAMIR	United Nations Assistance Mission for Rwanda
UNASOG	United Nations Aouzou Strip Observer Group
UNAVEM	United Nations Angola Verification Mission
UNDOF	United Nations Disengagement Observer Force
UNEF	United Nations Emergency Force
UNFICYP	United Nations Peace-keeping Force in Cyprus
UNGOMAP	United Nations Good Offices Mission in Afghanistan and Pakistan
UNIFIL	United Nations Interim Force in Lebanon
UNIIMOG	United Nations Iran-Iraq Military Observer Group
UNIKOM	United Nations Iraq-Kuwait Observation Mission
UNIPOM	United Nations India-Pakistan Observation Mission
UNMIH	United Nations Mission in Haiti
UNMOGIP	United Nations Military Observer Group in India and Pakistan
UNMOT	United Nations Mission of Observers in Tajikistan
UNOGIL	United Nations Observation Group in Lebanon
UNOMIG	United Nations Observer Mission in Georgia
UNOMIL	United Nations Observer Mission in Liberia
UNOMUR	United Nations Observer Mission Uganda-Rwanda
UNOSOM	United Nations Operation in Somalia
UNPROFOR	United Nations Protection Force
UNSF	United Nations Security Force in West New Guinea (West Irian)
UNTAC	United Nations Transitional Authority in Cambodia
UNTAG	United Nations Transition Assistance Group
UNTSO	United Nations Truce Supervision Organization
UNYOM	United Nations Yemen Observation Mission

○ Completed missions
● Ongoing missions

UNITED NATIONS
Map No. 3852 Rev. 3
April 1995

States, in particular Angola, Mozambique, Namibia, Somalia and South Africa, to promote peaceful transitions to democracy and independence as well as to foster political reconciliations and humanitarian relief efforts in areas affected by continuing civil conflicts.

Military operations to keep peace in Asia began with the United Nations Military Observer Group in India and Pakistan, followed by the Korean conflict and recently by a large-scale operation in Cambodia. The peace-keeping contingents in Central America, Cyprus, Europe and the Middle East have worked to transform the role of the United Nations in the conduct of international relations. While contributing significantly to the peaceful resolution of conflicts, these extraordinary demands have also taken a toll on United Nations resources and its capacity to respond to non-peace-keeping challenges.

As a standard, peace-keeping operations eventually end in a new phase of civilian operations which give greater emphasis to technical assistance for development of the countries concerned.

Africa

Angola

A protracted armed conflict between the Angolan nationalists and Portuguese forces lasted from 1961 until 1975 when Angola attained independence. As a newly independent country embarked on the process of nation-building, forces both within and outside it undermined that process. Fighting erupted between the three factions of the nationalist movement, each seeking to win absolute dominance. Outside powers, including South Africa, became increasingly involved, as they attempted to influence the future political shape of Angola. The country became a focus of cold-war confrontation. With the assistance of Cuban troops, the Movimento Popular de Libertação de Angola (MPLA), one of the three major political factions, took control of most of the country and gained wide recognition as the Government of Angola.

In December 1988, Angola, Cuba and South Africa signed an agreement on a timetable for the total withdrawal of Cuban troops. To verify their withdrawal, the Security Council established the United Nations Angola Verification Mission (UNAVEM) at the request of Angola and Cuba.

UNAVEM was charged with the task of verifying the phased and total withdrawal of Cuban troops from Angola in accordance with a timetable agreed between the two Governments. The withdrawal was completed by May 1991—more than one month before the scheduled date. Meanwhile, Angola requested the United Nations to verify the agreements for the

monitoring of a cease-fire and of the Angolan police, as foreseen in the Peace Accords signed by the Government and the União Nacional para a Independência Total de Angola (UNITA) during the same month. Under a new and later enlarged mandate entrusted by the Security Council, UNAVEM II observed the first-ever elections in Angola, held in September 1992. Soon thereafter, however, the situation deteriorated and hostilities resumed. The Security Council, in September 1993, imposed an oil and arms embargo against UNITA. In the meantime, the United Nations continued its efforts to facilitate the resumption of the peace negotiations which resulted eventually in the signing of the Lusaka Protocol in November 1994. UNAVEM II was to monitor and verify all major elements of the Protocol, including a cease-fire, and provide good offices to the parties. In December 1994, the Security Council extended the mandate of UNAVEM II until 8 February 1995.

Burundi

The United Nations became involved in Burundi, where widespread ethnic violence erupted following a plane crash in April 1994 which killed the Presidents of Burundi and Rwanda. It was estimated that between 25,000 and 100,000 people were killed and some 700,000 fled to neighbouring countries. Following reports of the rapid deterioration of the country's security situation, the Security Council dispatched, in August, a fact-finding mission. Despite the formation of a coalition Government in October, the situation remained unstable, leading some relief organizations to withdraw or suspend their operations. The Secretary-General recommended the maintenance in Zaire of a military presence for rapid intervention if the situation in Burundi so required, the deployment of guards to protect humanitarian organization teams, and strengthening the office of his Special Representative, which included helping organize a national debate early in 1995 on the problems of relations between the Hutu and Tutsi communities.

The Congo crisis

The Congo crisis of 1960 marked a new beginning for United Nations peace-keeping operations in Africa. Immediately after it attained independence from Belgium on 30 June 1960, the Congo (now Zaire) began to disintegrate as a result of a major civil disorder. Belgium sent its troops back into the country, with the stated aim to protect and evacuate Europeans. In the wake of that intervention, Moise Tshombe, the President of the mineral-rich Province of Katanga, which provided the country with more than half of its resources, proclaimed Katanga's independence.

Upon a request by the Congolese Government of President Joseph Kasa-Vubu and Prime Minister Patrice Lumumba, the Security Council on 14 July authorized Secretary-General Dag Hammarskjöld to provide the Congo with United Nations military assistance. In less than 48 hours, the first contingents began to arrive. At its peak, the United Nations Force in the Congo, which was made up of contingents from States other than the great Powers and placed under exclusive United Nations command, had a strength of 20,000 troops. The United Nations Operation in the Congo (ONUC) also included a civilian component of 2,000 experts who helped ensure the continuation of essential public services jeopardized by the large-scale departure of European personnel.

The original standing orders to the United Nations troops were to use force only in self-defence. As the internal conflict worsened, however, the Security Council authorized the use of force as a last resort to prevent civil war, and later it authorized the use of force to remove mercenaries.

The initial successes of the United Nations Force in bringing about the withdrawal of Belgian troops did not resolve the problem, as the secessionist regime of Katanga remained, assisted by European mercenaries and advisers. For 11 months, after the army Chief, Colonel Joseph Mobutu, seized power in Leopoldville, in the middle of a conflict between Prime Minister Lumumba and President Kasa-Vubu, there was no legal Government in the country and the United Nations troops had to carry out their mandate of keeping order in cooperation with whatever local authority existed. The murder of Patrice Lumumba in February 1961 worsened the crisis, and the Soviet Union declared its loss of confidence in the Secretary-General. Nevertheless, a majority of Member States, within a now deeply divided Organization, continued to support the Secretary-General and the conduct of ONUC.

With United Nations help, the constitutional crisis was resolved, the national Parliament reconvened in June 1961, and a national unity Government was created under Cyrille Adoula. However, the secessionists in Katanga remained intransigent, and an unsuccessful attempt by the United Nations to negotiate the peaceful reintegration of the Province was followed by clashes initiated by mercenary-led Katanga forces. While trying to restore peace to the Congo, Secretary-General Dag Hammarskjöld was tragically killed in a plane crash near Ndola, Zambia, on 18 September 1961. Shortly after appointing Ambassador U Thant of Burma as Acting Secretary-General, the Security Council authorized him to use the requisite force to complete removal of the mercenaries from the Congo. When the Katanga side did not react promptly to a "plan of national reconciliation" proposed by U Thant, United Nations troops, largely unopposed, acted and, on 14 January 1963, Tshombe ended his secession. With the reintegration of Katanga, the

United Nations Force began to phase out in February 1963 and the Force was completely withdrawn by 30 June 1964.

Political developments

When the General Assembly considered the situation in the Republic of the Congo (Leopoldville) during the second part of its fifteenth session in March-April 1961, the situation was complicated by the continuing constitutional crisis, marked by the existence of several rival authorities in the country.

The Chief of State, Joseph Kasa-Vubu, had replaced the "Council of Commissioners-General" on 9 February 1961 by a "provisional government" headed by Joseph Ileo. The latter, however, had not been approved by Parliament, which had been adjourned by the Chief of State on 11 October 1960. The "government" set up in Stanleyville in December 1960, headed by Antoine Gizenga, Vice-Premier in the first Government of the Congo (Leopoldville), continued to exercise authority in Orientale and Kivu provinces. The provincial government of Katanga in Elisabethville, headed by Moise Tshombe, and the authorities in Bakwanga, in the southern part of the Kasai province, continued to claim independence. In this situation, the United Nations Operation in the Congo (ONUC) was endeavouring to prevent the leaders holding the reins of power from using force to subdue their opponents. At the same time, ONUC intensified its efforts to induce the leaders to solve their differences through negotiation and conciliation.

Concerned at the grave situation, particularly after the death of Patrice Lumumba, the first Premier of the country, the Security Council adopted a resolution on 21 February 1961 urging the United Nations to take immediately all appropriate measures to prevent the occurrence of civil war, including the use of force if necessary in the last resort. It also urged measures for the immediate evacuation of all Belgian and other foreign military and paramilitary personnel and political advisers not under United Nations command and mercenaries, the convening of Parliament, the reorganization of Congolese armed units and an investigation into the circumstances of the death of Mr. Lumumba and his colleagues.

After considering the report of the United Nations Conciliation Commission for the Congo, which had visited the country in January-February 1961, and the reports of the Secretary-General on the implementation of the Security Council resolution, the General Assembly adopted three resolutions on 15 April 1961.

By the first resolution (1599(XV)), it: expressed its conviction that the central factor in the grave situation in the country was the continued presence of Belgian and other foreign military and paramilitary personnel, political advisers and mercenaries in total disregard of repeated resolutions of the United Nations; called upon the Belgian Government to comply fully and promptly with the will of the Security Council and the General Assembly; and decided that the above-mentioned foreign personnel should be completely withdrawn and evacuated.

By the second resolution (1600(XV)), it: called upon the Congolese authorities to desist from attempting a military solution to their problems; urged the immediate release of all members of Parliament and provincial assemblies and all other political leaders under detention; urged the convening of Parliament without delay, with safe conduct and security extended to its members by the United Nations, so that it might take the necessary decisions concerning the formation of a national Government and the future constitutional structure of the Republic; and appointed a commission of conciliation to assist the Congolese leaders to achieve reconciliation and end the political crisis.

By the third resolution (1601(XV)) it established a Commission of Investigation—consisting of four persons nominated by the Governments of Burma, Ethiopia, Mexico, and Togo—to investigate the circumstances of the death of Patrice Lumumba and his colleagues. (The members of the Commission were U Aung Khine (Burma), Teschome Hailemariam (Ethiopia), Salvador Martínez de Alva (Mexico) and Ayite d'Almeida (Togo)).

. . .

In a progress report on 17 May 1961, the Secretary-General recalled the measures taken by United Nations forces to avert the danger of emerging civil war, and the apprehension and evacuation of 37 mercenaries. He transmitted an agreement with President Kasa-Vubu under which the President accepted the Security Council resolution of 21 February and the United Nations undertook to provide assistance in its implementation, particularly with regard to the repatriation of foreign personnel and the re-organization of the National Army. The agreement, the Secretary-General reported, had been initialled by United Nations representatives on 17 April 1961 and approved by the Secretary-General on 26 April 1961. A representative of the Secretary-General began discussions with President Kasa-Vubu on measures to re-organize the National Army on a basis which would apply to the Republic as a whole.

The Secretary-General also reported on the progress of discussions by his representative, Ambassador Sahbani of Tunisia, with the Government of Belgium from 20 March 1961 on arrangements for the immediate withdrawal of Belgian personnel covered by the Security Council resolution.

The Belgian Government had accepted the resolution, but its views on implementation had been unsatisfactory. A slight change in the position became apparent with the change of government in April, but it remained far short of what was required by the Security Council resolution. The position, as stated in a letter of 6 May 1961 by the new Belgian Minister of Foreign Affairs, was regarded by the Secretary-General and the Advisory Committee on the Congo as not being in accord with the letter or spirit of the resolution. Negotiations were subsequently resumed, and on 12 July 1961 the Secretary-General met with the Belgian Foreign Minister, Paul-Henri Spaak, in Geneva. While some progress was made in regard to the withdrawal of Belgian military personnel originally placed at the disposal of the Congo and now active in Katanga, no agreement was reached in regard to mercenaries and "volunteers."

On 25 May 1961, the Secretary-General announced a re-organization of the administrative arrangements for the Congo operation. The Special Representative of the Secretary-General in the Congo, Ambassador Rajeshwar Dayal, of India, was relieved at his own request. He had gone to United Nations Headquarters for consultations on 10 March; Mekki Abbas had been Acting Special Representative in Leopoldville until Mr. Dayal's resignation. Sture C. Linner, formerly Chief of United Nations Civilian Operations in the Congo, was appointed Officer-in-Charge of the United Nations Operation in the Congo as of 25 May 1961.

Convening of Parliament and establishment of a national Government

Representatives of the Secretary-General held discussions with the various authorities in the Congo on the question of convening Parliament as urged by the Security Council and the General Assembly, and every effort was made by ONUC to facilitate a rapprochement between the Congolese leaders. While divisive tendencies had seemed to prevail at the Tananarive Conference in March 1961, a conference at Coquilhatville in April-May 1961 advocated a re-organization of the Congolese Government on a federal basis. Mr. Tshombe, who opposed this development at Coquilhatville, was detained by the Leopoldville authorities.

On 12 May 1961, President Kasa-Vubu announced that Parliament would be re-convened at Leopoldville in the near future and requested United Nations assistance and protection for this purpose. Four days later, Mr. Gizenga wrote to the Secretary-General that his "government" had decided to convene an extraordinary session of Parliament under ONUC protection at Kamina. This move was supported in letters to the President of the Security Council by the representatives of Albania, Czechoslovakia, Poland and the USSR.

Following strenuous efforts to bring about a rapprochement between the principal factions involved, representatives of the Secretary-General succeeded in arranging a meeting of delegations from Leopoldville and Stanleyville on 13 June 1961 at ONUC headquarters in Leopoldville. The two delegations reached an agreement on 19 June that Parliament would meet at the University of Lovanium, Leopoldville, and that all the members of Parliament and its administrative personnel should be housed during the session in Lovanium itself and should have no contacts with the outside world. They agreed to ask the United Nations to ensure that the army and police at Leopoldville and adjoining zones did not carry arms during the period of the parliamentary session. The United Nations was also requested: to take various other protective measures, including the provision of free passage of members of Parliament; to invite all other political factions to subscribe to the agreement; and to continue to accord its good offices to the parties concerned in seeking a real and satisfactory solution to the Congolese crisis. The Secretary-General accepted all the responsibilities devolving upon the United Nations under this agreement.

The agreement was subsequently subscribed to by the authorities in South Kasai, but not by the authorities in Elisabethville, though the representatives of the Leopoldville authorities and Mr. Tshombe had signed a protocol on 24 June 1961 for the convening of Parliament and on several other matters relating to the economic and administrative re-integration of Katanga into the Republic.

On 23 June 1961, Mr. Gizenga announced that eight Belgian soldiers who had been imprisoned in Stanleyville since January 1961 would be released.

On 5 July 1961, the President of the Republic issued an Ordinance convening Parliament. Under security and safe conduct arrangements devised by the United Nations in close co-operation with the authorities from Leopoldville and Stanleyville, members of Parliament assembled at Lovanium from 16 July. The Senate began to hold its sessions on 22 July and the House of Representatives on 23 July. On 1 August, the President of the Republic nominated Cyrille Adoula as *formateur* of Government.

On 2 August 1961, Mr. Adoula presented his Government to the two Houses of Parliament and described it as a Government of national unity and political reconciliation. He stated that his Government would: draw up a new constitution for the country; ensure the observance of fundamental freedoms and human rights and the maintenance of law and order; release all political prisoners and others imprisoned without valid cause; re-organize and re-unite the armed forces; and annul the secession of Katanga in the very near future. He expressed gratitude to the United Nations for its assistance and pledged that his Government would honour its obligations as a Member of the United Nations and execute the resolutions of the Security Council and the General Assembly so long as the sovereignty of the Congo was not affected. He added that his Government would strive for co-operation with the United Nations in the formulation as well as in the execution of projects and would use every means to implement rapidly the agreement of 17 April. He also expressed the desire to conclude promptly an agreement on the status of the United Nations in the Congo, elaborating the details of the application of the basic agreement of 27 July 1960 between the United Nations and the Congolese Government on the operation of the United Nations Force.

On the same day, both Houses of Parliament unanimously adopted a resolution to the effect that from the time the new Government obtained a vote of confidence in the Houses, no other Government might claim to act as the constitutional Government, and that the new Government of national unity would be the legal successor of the first Central Government of the Republic of the Congo. The two Houses then approved a new Government, led by Mr. Adoula; the vote was unanimous, except for one abstention in the House of Representatives.

. . .

In response to a letter of 10 August 1961 from Prime Minister Adoula, the Secretary-General, on 13 August, expressed satisfaction at the establishment of a constitutional Central Government, to which the Security Council and the General Assembly had attached the greatest importance. He confirmed that in response to the decisions of Parliament, the United Nations would deal with Mr. Adoula's Government as being the Central Government and would render all its aid and assistance exclusively to that Government.

On 10 September 1961, at the unanimous request of the Council of Ministers, Prime Minister Adoula extended an invitation to the Secretary-General to visit Leopoldville to discuss with them the framework within which the details of the aid and support by the United Nations could be worked out in relation to the future programme of the Government. He added that such a visit would provide the opportunity for the Government to express its high appreciation for the untiring efforts of the United Nations in the course of its action in the Congo. The Secretary-General immediately accepted the invitation and arrived in Leopoldville on 13 September 1961.

Problem of foreign military personnel and mercenaries in Katanga: developments from July to November 1961

Meanwhile, negotiations of United Nations representatives with the Belgian Government and with the Katanga authorities for the evacuation of foreign military and paramilitary personnel and political advisers and mercenaries, as called for by the Security Council, were encountering great difficulties.

The Katanga provincial authorities refused to take effective action to remove the foreign elements without whom the secessionist movement might have collapsed. For its part, the Belgian Government said that it was prepared to help in the removal of its professional officers and non-commissioned officers who had been serving in the Congo and were now in command of the *gendarmerie*, but it professed to be unable to do anything about the "volunteers" and mercenaries. The latter were not the traditional colonial administrative and military elements, but mostly non-Belgian adventurers and soldiers of fortune, including outlawed elements previously involved in extremist activities in Algeria and elsewhere; they fostered extremist attitudes in Katanga, too.

The ONUC effort was also obstructed by certain foreign financial interests, especially the *Union Minière du Haut-Katanga*, which provided economic and political sustenance for the secessionist movement, including the high wages of the mercenaries and the purchase of military equipment and warplanes.

In April 1961, 44 mercenaries who were members of the unit known as the *compagnie internationale* were apprehended by the United Nations and evacuated from the Congo. By mid-June, an estimated 60 more mercenaries had withdrawn from Katanga, and on 24 June the *compagnie* was formally dissolved by the provincial government.

In June 1961, a United Nations military mission reported that there were 510 foreign officers and non-commissioned officers active in the *gendarmerie* as against 142 Congolese cadres. Of the non-Congolese, 208 were the remaining Belgian professional military men; 302 were mercenaries.

Between June and August 1961, ONUC authorities evacuated several of Mr. Tshombe's foreign military and political advisers. A joint commission was established with the Katangese authorities to list such foreign personnel, both those in official posts and those acting unofficially, who were to be repatriated.

On 24 August 1961, the President of the Republic issued an Ordinance for the immediate expulsion of all non-Congolese officers and mercenaries serving in the Katanga forces who had not entered into a contractual engagement with the Central Government. On the same day, the Prime Minister, on behalf of his Government, requested United Nations assistance in the execution of the Ordinance. This request provided the United Nations with the legal authority to take action within the Congo to implement the evacuation provision of the Security Council resolution.

As the Katangese authorities countered with a campaign of inflammatory statements and rumours against the United Nations which created an atmosphere of tension, the United Nations was soon compelled to take security precautions in Elisabethville. On 28 August, it placed a surveillance on Radio Katanga, the *gendarmerie* headquarters and other key points and installations and proceeded to take measures for apprehending foreign military personnel and mercenaries.

Informed of the objectives of the United Nations action, Mr. Tshombe announced later in the day that the services of foreign personnel in the Katanga armed forces were terminated and that his Government approved of their evacuation. The Belgian Consul, in agreement with his colleagues in the consular corps in Elisabethville, offered to undertake the responsibility for ensuring the surrender and repatriation of all such foreign military personnel. Relying on this undertaking, the United Nations thereupon refrained from continuing to search for and apprehend such personnel and suspended the security measures.

These arrangements, however, were not scrupulously observed. Only the Belgian Army officers placed by the Belgian Government at the disposal of Katanga were dealt with under this procedure, and even in the case of these officers, delays or administrative exemptions were proposed. By 9 September 1961, 273 foreign officers and mercenaries had been evacuated, and 65 were awaiting repatriation, but at least 104 failed to report.

Profiting from the relaxation of evacuation measures, foreign officers and mercenaries soon began to re-infiltrate into the *gendarmerie*. Together with some elements in the local non-African population, they began to exercise an adverse influence on the Katanga authorities. The actions of the Katanga *Sûreté* led by non-Congolese officers, the inflammatory broadcasts of Radio Katanga and the spreading rumours caused panic among the Baluba population who began to throng into United Nations camps seeking protection. By 9 September 1961, the number of these refugees had reached 35,000 and created not only a very serious problem for the United Nations but a situation likely to lead to tribal and civil war. Meanwhile, the Katanga authorities inspired demonstrations against the United Nations, and reports were received of conspiracies directed against the United Nations Force.

In view of the deteriorating situation, the United Nations representative called on the consuls in Elisabethville on 9 September 1961 and asked them to ensure the immediate departure of their nationals among the non-Congolese officers and mercenaries, failing which the United Nations would have to resume action for implementing the Security Council resolution. On 11 September, the deputy United Nations representative in Elisabethville was arrested on orders given by a non-Congolese officer of the *Sûreté*. In view of the long series of wrongful acts committed by the non-Congolese officers of the *Sûreté* against the United Nations and of their actions against the Baluba population, ONUC representatives, acting under the Security Council resolution of 21 February 1961, requested the Katanga authorities to evacuate these officers within 48 hours. Instead of acceding to this request, the Katanga authorities reinforced their police force and began to maintain heavily armed patrols and guard posts at all public buildings and other installations. A meeting of United Nations representatives with Mr. Tshombe and members of his government on 12 September 1961, in an attempt to obtain a lessening of tension and assurance on the prompt evacuation of foreign officers and mercenaries, proved fruitless.

On 13 September, the United Nations Force took security precautions similar to those applied on 28 August in order to prevent threats to the maintenance of law and order while it resumed its task of apprehending and evacuating foreign military and paramilitary personnel. During this operation, fire was opened on the United Nations troops on several occasions, particularly from the building in which the Belgian "consulate" had its offices, and the ONUC troops returned the fire. United Nations units guarding the radio station and the post office were repeatedly attacked. Non-Congolese officers and mercenaries were observed leading the attacks. A number of European residents, otherwise regularly employed, participated in the attacks, and extensive sniping fire was directed against United Nations troops and positions by non-African residents.

Despite persistent efforts by United Nations representatives to obtain a cessation of hostilities, the attacks continued and spread to Jadotville, Kamina and other areas. A number of foreign officers who had gone into hiding after 28 August 1961 reappeared. A jet fighter, piloted by a non-Congolese, strafed and bombed United Nations troops and airports under United Nations control, making it impossible to provide re-inforcements to the hard-pressed United Nations Forces, which had no war planes. A company of the United Nations Force, sent to Jadotville at the urgent request of the consular corps to protect the non-Congolese population, was attacked by a large *gendarmerie* force under non-Congolese leadership and subjected to strafing and bombing by the jet fighter. On the

other hand, there were no clashes whatever between the United Nations troops and units of the Katanga *gendarmerie*, whose foreign officers had been duly withdrawn.

After repeated efforts to contact Mr. Tshombe to end the fighting, the United Nations representative in Elisabethville received a message from him, through the British Consul, at midnight on 16 September, proposing a meeting in Northern Rhodesia. Informed of this message, the Secretary-General, who was then in Leopoldville, replied to Mr. Tshombe reaffirming the desire of the United Nations to ensure a cessation of hostilities. He pointed out that the cease-fire would occur automatically on the United Nations side, as it was permitted to open fire only in self-defence. He asked that the Katanga authorities order an immediate and effective cease-fire and offered to meet personally with Mr. Tshombe at Ndola, Northern Rhodesia, to find peaceful methods of resolving the present conflict, thus opening the way to a solution of the Katanga problem within the framework of the Congo.

The Secretary-General and his party took off for Ndola from Leopoldville on 17 September, but the flight ended tragically in the crash of the aircraft and the death of the Secretary-General and his party consisting of seven United Nations staff members and two ONUC Swedish soldiers. Six Swedish crew members also lost their lives.

The Secretary-General's mission was immediately taken up by Sture Linner and his colleagues. On 19 September, Mahmoud Khiari, Chief of the ONUC Civilian Operations, flew to Ndola, where, on the next day, he and Mr. Tshombe signed a provisional agreement for an immediate cease-fire. They agreed that there should be no movement of troops to re-inforce garrisons or positions; also, the movement of arms and ammunition and other military devices was prohibited. A joint commission of four members was to be set up to fix the respective positions of the troops of both sides, to arrange the exchange of prisoners, to supervise the application of the agreement and to seek ways and means of placing the relations between the United Nations and the Katanga authorities on a basis of mutual understanding.

The United Nations representative made clear the following points: that the agreement was of a strictly military nature; that it applied solely to the United Nations Force in Katanga and the armed forces of Katanga, that it would not apply outside Katanga; that it had no political intention or aim; and that the conclusion of the agreement would in no way affect the resolutions of the Security Council and the General Assembly. The agreement became final on 24 September 1961 when approval of its terms by the United Nations Headquarters was communicated to Mr. Tshombe.

. . .

After further negotiations, the Katanga authorities and ONUC signed a protocol on 13 October 1961 for the implementation of the cease-fire agreement of 20 September. The protocol provided for: the release of prisoners on 16 October; the creation of three sub-commissions for the supervision of the application of the cease-fire agreement; a return to positions held on 12 September; and the return of the post office, radio station and several other positions held by the United Nations in Elisabethville in return for certain assurances by Katanga authorities. The United Nations agreed that it would consider that the cease-fire had been violated in the event that the Katangese *gendarmerie* countered an attack from the outside.

. . .

The text of the approval, transmitted to Mr. Tshombe on 23 October 1961, stated that the conditions set forth as the basis for the approval of the cease-fire agreement of 20 September 1961 were equally applicable to the protocol. It stated, too, that approval of the protocol involved no derogation of the unity, territorial integrity or independence of the Congo, of the sovereignty of the Republic of the Congo or of the authority of the Central Government. It also noted the agreement during the discussions that full compliance with the requirements of a paragraph in the Security Council resolution of 21 February 1961 (paragraph A-2) concerning the withdrawal of foreign military personnel and mercenaries was a condition essential to the effective application of the protocol.

. . .

Concurrently with the efforts for a cessation of hostilities, ONUC attempted to impress upon the Katanga authorities the imperative need, in the interests of the people of the province and the Congo as a whole, to undertake serious contacts with the Central Government with a view to achieving a peaceful solution of the issues dividing them. It offered assurances guaranteeing the safety of Mr. Tshombe and his representatives during any visit to Leopoldville for such discussions. Two emissaries of Mr. Tshombe went to the capital on 18 October 1961 with Mr. Khiari and presented a memorandum from Mr. Tshombe to the Prime Minister. They returned to Elisabethville on 23 October with a message from the Central Government that it was prepared to examine any proposals within the framework of the parliamentary institutions established by the *Loi fondamentale* and in accordance with the principle of legality. The Central Government announced its readiness to receive Mr. Tshombe and his colleagues in Leopoldville for such discussions.

Meanwhile, the Katanga authorities failed to respect a number of provisions of the protocol of 13 October 1961. The prisoners—190 ONUC prisoners and 240 Katangese prisoners—were exchanged, after some delays, on 25 October, and ONUC withdrew from several positions as agreed in the protocol. But the Officer-in-Charge of the United Nations Operation reported on 2 November that the Katanga authorities had failed to fulfil several of their obligations and had resumed a violent propaganda campaign against the United Nations. A large number of foreign personnel, chiefly mercenaries, remained in Katanga. It had become more difficult than before to identify and apprehend the mercenaries, as they had begun to serve in civilian garb and take cover in various forms of civilian employ. (ONUC reports indicated that 237 persons covered by the Security Council resolution, chiefly mercenaries, remained in Katanga in November 1961.) The United Nations was obligated to continue to care for some 35,000 refugees in Elisabethville, as they refused to return to their homes for fear of reprisals by the local police forces or members of Mr. Tshombe's Canokat *Jeunesse.*

In the latter part of October 1961, military engagements occurred on the border of Kasai and Katanga provinces between Central Government forces and the Katanga forces. Some probing attacks by both sides were reported. The Central Government forces were reported to have advanced some distance into Katanga and to have been forced by air and ground attacks to retreat. Prime Minister Adoula sent the Chief of Staff of the National Army to Kasai to halt the military operations in order to establish a favourable climate for talks with the Katanga authorities. Mr. Tshombe, however, protested the alleged genocide by the National Army.

Towards the end of the month, small Katangese aircraft attacked troops, civilians and communications inside the Kasai border. As these operations over Kasai were a civil war action and involved non-Congolese military personnel in violation of the Security Council resolution of 21 February 1961, and, moreover, constituted a military movement in contravention of the cease-fire agreement of 20 September, United Nations representatives in Elisabethville enjoined the Katanga authorities on 31 October to ground all military aircraft immediately. They indicated that unless this was done, the United Nations would be obliged to take counter-action and bring down aircraft engaged in offensive military operations in Kasai.

. . .

Report of Commission of Investigation on the deaths of Mr. Lumumba and his colleagues

On 11 November 1961, the report of the Commission of Investigation established by the General Assembly in April by resolution 1601(XV) of 15 April 1961 to investigate the circumstances of the deaths of Patrice Lumumba, Maurice Mpolo and Joseph Okito, was circulated to the Security Council and the General Assembly.

The Commission's efforts to arrange a visit to the Congo did not materialize, owing chiefly to the objections of the Leopoldville authorities.

After the establishment of a constitutional Central Government in the Congo, its Minister of Foreign Affairs informed the Commission on 19 September 1961 that the Congolese Government had the right and duty to investigate the affair and punish the perpetrators of the crime. The United Nations would be kept informed of the progress of the investigation.

The report of the Commission to the Security Council and General Assembly contained an account of the evidence it had gathered and certain conclusions it had reached. The Commission concluded: (1) that the weight of evidence was against the official version of the Katanga provincial government that Mr. Lumumba and his colleagues had been killed by certain tribesmen on 12 February 1961; (2) that the evidence indicating that the prisoners had been killed on 17 January 1961 in a villa near Elisabethville, probably by certain mercenaries in the presence of Katanga provincial officials, seemed to be substantially true; and (3) that President Kasa-Vubu and his aides and Mr. Tshombe and his aides, particularly the Katanga Interior Minister, Mr. Munongo, should not escape the responsibility.

Consideration by Security Council, 13-24 November

In a cable of 1 November 1961 to the President of the General Assembly, the Emperor of Ethiopia expressed concern at the deterioration of the situation in the Congo and suggested that the Security Council must take prompt and decisive action.

On 3 November 1961, the representatives of Ethiopia, Nigeria and the Sudan requested that the Security Council be convened to consider the situation caused by the lawless acts of mercenaries in the province of Katanga.

The Security Council met on 13 November 1961 and decided to consider the situation in the Congo, including the matter brought to its attention by these three powers. The Council considered the question at eight meetings through 24 November, with the participation of the representatives of Belgium, Congo (Leopoldville), Ethiopia, India and Sweden, who were invited, at their request.

. . .

Initiating the discussion in the Security Council on 13 November 1961, the representative of Ethiopia stated that a grave situation had been caused by the continued foreign intervention in Katanga and the military build-up in the province. Since it seemed that the Katanga authorities would not evict foreign military personnel and mercenaries as required by the Council's resolution of 21 February 1961, he suggested that the Council should adopt clear directives authorizing the Acting Secretary-General to evict them by force. He also called for measures by the Council to stop interference in Katanga through territories on the borders of the province. He said that the United Nations Command should help the efforts of the constitutional Central Government, which had been set up in August, to restore law and order in the country and remove the threat of foreign intervention against its territorial integrity.

The Foreign Minister of the Congo (Leopoldville) stated that all efforts by the Central Government towards a peaceful solution of the Katanga problem, within the framework of the *Loi fondamentale*, had failed because of the intransigence and duplicity of Mr. Tshombe, who had been supported by foreign mercenaries. Since the Congolese National Army alone did not have the necessary means to dispose of the Katangan secession, he argued that the United Nations had the duty to expel the mercenaries or deliver them to Congolese justice. (On 13 November 1961, the Congolese Government communicated to the United Nations the text of an Ordinance providing for the punishment of non-Congolese officers and mercenaries serving in the Katangese forces who had not entered into contract with the Central Government. It requested the United Nations henceforth to place all mercenaries at the disposal of the Central Government.) The Foreign Minister also requested United Nations assistance in the reorganization and strengthening of the National Army so that his Government could ensure the maintenance of law and order in the country and avoid dependence on other States. He said that such assistance by the United Nations would not involve intervention in Congolese domestic affairs, as it would be given at the request of the legal Government and as its purpose would be to prevent foreign intervention rather than involvement in any internal conflict.

The Foreign Minister of Belgium stated that his Government, since taking office in April 1961, had attempted to co-operate effectively with the United Nations in the implementation of its decisions even when it did not agree with the decisions. He claimed that it had complied with the United Nations decisions concerning the evacuation of political advisers and military and paramilitary personnel. It had refrained from providing any military assistance to the Katanga authorities, had taken measures to prevent recruitment of Belgian mercenaries for Katanga and had co-operated with the United Nations in the withdrawal of a large number of mercenaries. He claimed that his Government could not be held responsible for the

Belgian mercenaries who might be in Katanga in defiance of the law, without its knowledge and against its instructions. He complained that the United Nations had made unfounded accusations against Belgium, especially in connexion with the events of 28 August and 13 September, and asked for an impartial international investigation. He stated that his Government recognized the Central Government of the Congo as the legitimate Government in all the country and was opposed to the secession of Katanga. It had provided substantial technical assistance to the Congo, despite the absence of diplomatic relations, and only wished to continue such assistance without interfering in the country's political life.

. . .

On 14 November 1961, Ceylon, Liberia and the United Arab Republic submitted a draft resolution by which the Security Council would: reaffirm earlier resolutions; deprecate secessionist activities carried out in Katanga—with the aid of external resources and foreign mercenaries—and armed action against the United Nations forces; authorize the Secretary-General to take vigorous action, including the use of requisite measures of force, for the apprehension, detention or deportation of all foreign mercenaries and other "hostile elements" as laid down in the resolution of 21 February 1961; request the Secretary-General to take all necessary measures to prevent the entry of such elements or of war material; demand that all secessionist activities in Katanga should cease forthwith; and declare full and firm support for the Central Government of the Congo.

The sponsors argued that the United Nations should declare its support to the constitutional Central Government established in August and should give a clear mandate to the Acting Secretary-General to deal with the problem of foreign intervention in Katanga. They expressed confidence that he would use his mandate wisely and judiciously and stated that their proposal would not close channels for conciliation.

During the discussion, all Council members expressed opposition to secessionist activities in Katanga and to foreign interference in the Congo. Several representatives, however, voiced reservations about certain provisions of this draft resolution.

. . .

On 20 November, Ceylon, Liberia and the United Arab Republic submitted a revision of their draft resolution. By the new text, the Council would, among other things, declare that all secessionist activities were contrary to the *Loi fondamentale* and Council resolutions, while specifically demanding that such activities then taking place in Katanga should cease forthwith. They stated that though the Council had no official information

tion concerning secessionist activities outside Katanga, they were willing to declare opposition to such activities anywhere in the Congo.

On the same day, the United States submitted several amendments to the joint draft resolution; these were revised on 21 November and again on 24 November.

During the discussion which followed, the USSR representative indicated that he would not object to certain of the amendments but would oppose several others. Among the United States amendments which he was willing to support were the proposed revisions to the preamble, whereby the Council would: deplore all armed action in opposition to the authority of the Congolese Government, specifically action then being carried on in Katanga; note with deep regret the recent and past actions of violence against United Nations personnel; and recognize that the Congolese Government was exclusively responsible for the conduct of Congo's external affairs. He also did not object to a revision of the paragraph which would authorize the Secretary-General to take action to apprehend, detain or deport persons covered by the Security Council resolution of 21 February . . . .

The USSR representative opposed the other United States amendments. One of these would have the Council authorize the Secretary-General, in consultation with the Congolese Government, to remove weapons of war which had illegally entered Katanga "or any other region of the Congo," or to prevent their use against the United Nations or the Republic of the Congo or the civilian population. Another United States amendment would have the Council ask the Secretary-General to assist the Congolese Government to re-organize and re-train its armed forces. A third amendment would have the Council ask the Secretary-General to take steps he considered necessary, including negotiation and conciliation, to achieve the immediate political unity and territorial integrity of the Congo.

With regard to the first of these amendments, the USSR representative proposed deletion of the reference to other regions of the Congo on the grounds that it would distract attention from the central problem of colonial intervention in Katanga and that war material had not illegally entered regions other than Katanga. Opposing the provision of assistance to Congolese armed forces, he stated that it was an enormous task which did not fall within the functions of the United Nations at the present time. He added that the Acting Secretary-General had authority under the Council's resolution of 21 February 1961 to extend appropriate assistance and that a special decision on that matter in the present resolution would only distract attention from the main problem. Further, the third amendment seemed to imply negotiations with the secessionists in Katanga, which, in his delegation's view, were inappropriate and harmful. He added that political unity had been achieved in the Congo through the convening of Parliament and that territorial integrity would be attained only when the so-called independent state of Katanga was liquidated.

The United States representative and several other members argued that the amendments were essential to meet the needs of the situation and were consistent with the intent of the three-power draft resolution. They stated that recent events described in the report of 19 November 1961 by the Officer-in-Charge of the United Nations Operation had shown the threats to the maintenance of law and order arising from a lack of discipline in certain Congolese armed units, and they suggested that urgent action was required to rebuild the armed forces, in accordance with the earlier decisions of the Council, so that they might be able to perform their functions. They stressed the importance of making every effort to solve the Congolese problems by negotiation, conciliation and other peaceful means to the greatest extent possible.

The Foreign Minister of the Congo (Leopoldville) expressed the view that there was no contradiction between the draft resolution and the United States amendments and the Soviet sub-amendment. He asked for assistance to his Government in order to build an effective army and stated that little progress had been made in this respect since the agreement of April between the United Nations and the President of the Congo. He supported the amendment on removing or preventing the use of illegally imported arms. He said that though there existed no secession other than that in Katanga, his Government would not object to the declaration condemning all secession. As to the question of negotiations and conciliation towards a peaceful solution of the Katanga problem, he added that the repeated efforts of his Government had been frustrated by the attitude of Mr. Tshombe and the interference of foreign interests.

The United Kingdom representative said that he would support the draft resolution with the United States amendments but expressed misgivings about the provisions concerning the use of force. He also stated that United Nations officials should not interpret the provisions and act in such a way as to endanger the uneasy peace in Katanga, especially in view of the existence of a cease-fire agreement with the Katanga authorities. The representative of France stated that though his delegation deplored secessionist and mercenary activities in Katanga, it would abstain on the vote, as it felt that the United Nations should not become a party to any internal conflict and that use

of force could bring results contrary to those sought by the Council.

. . .

The Council then adopted the United States amendments to which the USSR did not object. The amendment to authorize the Secretary-General to remove or prevent use of weapons of war which had entered illegally into Katanga and other regions was rejected, having received only six votes. (The representative of the USSR voted against it after his sub-amendment to delete a reference to other regions was rejected. France, the United Arab Republic and the United Kingdom abstained, and Ceylon did not vote.) The other United States amendments failed of adoption because of the adverse vote of the USSR. The three-power draft resolution, as amended, was then adopted by 9 votes, with France and the United Kingdom abstaining.

The representative of the United States stated, in connexion with this resolution, that it could in no way be regarded as implying a diminution of the authority previously granted to the Secretary-General and expressed confidence that the Acting Secretary-General would continue to carry out all the resolutions to the full effect. The USSR representative expressed the hope that the Acting Secretary-General would scrupulously implement the provisions of the resolution without covering them in any special or political interpretation. The United Kingdom representative stated that he had abstained because of the rejection of some of the United States amendments. The Foreign Minister of the Congo (Leopoldville) thanked the Security Council for its decision and pledged full cooperation to the Acting Secretary-General.

The Acting Secretary-General told the Security Council that he intended to discharge the responsibilities entrusted to him, in connexion with the question of the activities of the mercenaries in Katanga, with determination and vigour and to employ as much as possible of the total resources available to the United Nations operation toward that end. He pointed out, however, that the recent events in the Congo showed that the Central Government was at that stage unable to assume an increased responsibility in the sphere of law and order. As the need for continuing United Nations assistance in that field was still critical in many parts of the Congo, it might be necessary from time to time to establish temporary priorities in the continuing efforts to achieve the various objectives of the United Nations. He noted that all of the United Nations responsibilities flowing from past resolutions continued with new emphasis, as they had been reaffirmed in the present resolution. They included the responsibility with regard to the training and re-organization of the Congolese armed forces under the terms of the previous Security Council resolutions. He appealed to United Nations Member States for more troops at the present critical stage and expressed the view that a gradual reduction in the size of the Force might be possible after the current phase of disorder and secessionist threat was over. He assured the Council that the United Nations would redouble its efforts to achieve peaceful reconciliation of the differences which endangered the unity of the country.

Finally, with regard to the murder of 13 Italian members of the United Nations Force on 11 November, which had been condemned by members of the Security Council, he stated that ONUC was taking all possible measures to see that all who were guilty of the crime would be severely punished. He pointed out, however, that this tragedy was but one of a long series of such experiences suffered with patience and fortitude by the United Nations personnel at the hands of undisciplined troops in the Congo.

Developments from
24 November to 21 December 1961

On 27 November 1961, the Acting Secretary-General and the Minister for Foreign Affairs of the Republic of the Congo signed an agreement on the legal status, facilities, privileges and immunities of the United Nations Organization in the Congo. It laid down the details of the application of the basic agreement signed on 27 July 1960 and was to be deemed to have taken effect from the date of the arrival of the first elements of the United Nations. The agreement made it clear that the responsibilities of the United Nations Force for the maintenance of public order, peace and security would be discharged in accordance with its interpretation of the mission assigned to it by the Security Council. It would not apply to domestic laws, regulations and procedures, which would remain fully within the responsibility of the Congolese authorities. The United Nations would not have recourse to the use of force except as a last resort and subject to the restrictions imposed by its mandate and the resolutions of the Security Council and the General Assembly. Both parties undertook to co-ordinate their actions in the maintenance of public order and to adopt the principle of mutual consultation.

Meanwhile, the Katanga authorities launched a propaganda campaign of increasing violence against the United Nations in violation of the provisions of the protocol of 13 October 1961. The campaign became highly inflammatory after the adoption of the Security Council resolution of 24 November. Mr. Tshombe and his colleagues alleged that the United Nations had decided to launch a war on Katanga and called on the Katangese to prepare to fight against the United Nations. The rousing of public feeling against the United

Nations and the incitement to violence against the United Nations personnel, despite the protests of the United Nations representatives, soon led to grave incidents.

. . .

It soon appeared, however, that the Katanga authorities were unable to control their forces, especially the "para-commandos." Incidents increased after the departure of Mr. Tshombe on 1 December for Brazzaville and Paris.

On 2 December 1961, United Nations troops at the Elisabethville airport disarmed some drunken Katangan gendarmes when they molested several Congolese women. Other gendarmes and police opened fire on the United Nations troops and were also disarmed and detained. United Nations representatives contacted the Katanga authorities in order to deliver the prisoners to them, but, in the meantime, the Katanga *gendarmerie* began to patrol the town and set up roadblocks to impede vital United Nations communications. United Nations personnel were molested at the roadblocks, and several were detained by the "para-commandos." The *gendarmerie* units were withdrawn on the night of 2-3 December at the demand of the United Nations, and the latter delivered the prisoners to the Katanga authorities. The next morning, however, the *gendarmerie* returned to the town and resumed manning the roadblocks. Several incidents occurred, and by the morning of 4 December, one member of the United Nations Force was killed, two were wounded and a number missing. Later that day a roadblock, manned by a strong force, was set up on the road from the airport to the city, thus cutting communications between the ONUC headquarters and the airport and severing the only exit available to ONUC troops in the city. Though the Katanga authorities undertook, at the demand of United Nations representatives, to remove the roadblock, it soon became apparent that they were only engaged in a delaying manoeuvre and that the *gendarmerie* was planning to encircle the airport and attack and destroy the United Nations Force. On 5 December, United Nations troops cleared the roadblock by force; one Indian officer of the United Nations Force was killed and four men wounded in the action, while the Katanga forces lost at least 38 gendarmes and "para-commandos" and two non-Congolese mercenaries.

After this defensive action by the United Nations to regain freedom of movement, the Katanga forces engaged in a series of aggressive actions, attacking or sniping at United Nations positions. A Katanga airplane dropped three bombs at the airfield. On the morning of 6 December, the Katanga Minister of Interior made an inflammatory broadcast accusing the United Nations of declaring war on Katanga and calling upon the people to fight against the United Nations Force. In order to prevent the arrival of further crowds of disorderly Katangese gendarmes in Elisabethville and to prevent further attacks by Katanga planes, the United Nations planes attacked the airports at Jadotville and Kolwezi and certain other points. United Nations troops cleared a number of roadblocks in Elisabethville. They also undertook to disarm the Katanga *gendarmerie* at Manono where they had been strengthened in violation of the cease-fire and caused tension.

The Katanga forces, aided by non-Congolese civilians and mercenaries, intensified sniping attacks against United Nations positions and hampered the freedom of movement of United Nations troops. They followed a consistent pattern of sniping and shelling from civilian homes and from the immediate vicinity of hospitals, schools and similar institutions. ONUC headquarters was under constant mortar attack. Violating the laws of war, the gendarmes attacked the Baluba refugee camp and inflicted a number of casualties.

. . .

The United Nations Force in Elisabethville was in a particularly unfavourable position when hostilities were launched against it by the Katangese gendarmes, because about one-half of its units were carrying out a periodic peaceful rotation. While re-inforcements were rushed to the scene, in part with the assistance of air transport provided by the United States, the ONUC troops refrained from major defensive action. They were, however, obliged to clear several roadblocks and positions from which the Katangese gendarmes fired on United Nations positions. In its anxiety to avoid endangering civilian lives and property, the United Nations Force was at serious disadvantage, as the Katanga forces consistently used the presence of civilians and civilian installations to shield their activities. The mercenary-led gendarmes also endeavoured, without success, to draw the ONUC troops into house-to-house fighting in town; this would have caused heavy civilian casualties.

On 10 December 1961, the Acting Secretary-General issued a statement saying that military action had been forced on the United Nations by a series of deliberate attacks against United Nations personnel and positions and by the impeding of the freedom of movement in Elisabethville. Only when negotiations had proved fruitless, because of repeated instances of bad faith by the Katanga political leaders and their failure to implement agreed measures, did the United Nations undertake military action with the greatest reluctance. Its purpose was to regain and assure freedom of movement, restore law and order, and defend United Nations personnel and positions. The Acting Secretary-General added that the military action would be pursued only up to such time as these objectives were achieved by military or other

means and satisfactory guarantees were obtained for the future. The United Nations would also need to be satisfied that it would be able to pursue the implementation of the Security Council and General Assembly resolutions without hindrance. He stated that he would welcome any initiative which would enable the achievement of the aims as peacefully and as speedily as possible.

The re-inforcement of the United Nations troops in Elisabethville was completed on 14 December and, as the Katangese attacks continued, ONUC undertook a more active role in securing freedom of movement. Between 15 and 17 December, ONUC forces captured several important positions around the perimeter of Elisabethville, including the main *gendarmerie* camp. ONUC struck from the air at certain installations of the *Union Minière du Haut-Katanga* which, despite repeated warnings, were used for sniping at United Nations troops. On 18 December, United Nations troops began to patrol the streets of Elisabethville to re-establish law and order.

During all the fighting, the United Nations gave all possible assistance to civilians and showed great restraint despite sniping from civilian houses. The Katangese forces, on the other hand, inflicted damage on civilian areas, often by missing their targets during attacks on United Nations positions. Many press dispatches, however, misrepresented the facts on the operation and exaggerated the loss of life and property suffered by the civilians.

In cables on 8 and 9 December 1961, the Foreign Minister of Belgium informed the Acting Secretary-General that the military operations in Katanga and the death of several Belgian civilians killed by United Nations troops had aroused profound emotion in Belgium. He urged that the United Nations troops should scrupulously respect the obligations of the Geneva Convention regarding the safeguarding of the lives and property of the civilian population. He denied allegations against the *Union Minière* and asked for the protection of its telecommunications installations, which were of great importance to the population. He questioned the legal basis of the action taken by the United Nations and expressed the view that the operations seemed to be out of proportion with the mandate given to the Secretary-General. In replies of 8 and 15 December, the Acting Secretary-General reviewed the course of events which led to the hostilities, explained the United Nations objectives and denied allegations against the United Nations troops. He stated that the *Union Minière* had assisted the Katanga authorities against the United Nations by supplying arms and equipment, providing working papers for mercenaries and in other ways. He offered to provide protection to the company if it ceased to carry out its hostile activities against the ONUC.

In cables on 15 December 1961, the President of the Republic of the Congo (Brazzaville) called for an immediate cease-fire in Katanga and requested that the Security Council convene immediately to reconsider the action taken by the United Nations. The representative of Congo (Brazzaville) stated, in a note to the Acting Secretary-General, that his Government considered that the continuation of military operations would exceed the limits set by the obligations of the United Nations Force and would imply a deliberate intention to intervene in the settlement of Congo's internal political problem. The Acting Secretary-General replied on 15 December that he would fully support the desirability of a cease-fire on the basis outlined in his statement of 10 December. On 16 December, the President of the Congo (Brazzaville) informed the Acting Secretary-General that his Government had regretfully decided to forbid aircraft engaged in transport on behalf of ONUC to land in or fly over its territory. The Acting Secretary-General replied on the same day that this action would constitute a grave hindrance to the fulfilment of United Nations purposes and would violate the obligations of the Republic under the Charter and the Security Council resolutions. (The Security Council did not accede to the request for a meeting to consider the messages from the Republic of the Congo (Brazzaville).)

The Acting Secretary-General informed the Advisory Committee on the Congo on 16 December 1961 that he had also received appeals for a cease-fire from the representatives of the United Kingdom, Belgium and Greece and from the President of Madagascar. He stated that he was always ready to consider reasonable proposals for a cease-fire provided that the United Nations objectives were safeguarded.

. . .

The Acting Secretary-General stated that the United Nations would do all in its power to facilitate such a meeting at a place acceptable to the Prime Minister and would give assurances in regard to the personal security of Mr. Tshombe. After agreement with Prime Minister Adoula, he designated representatives to assist in the negotiations and announced that, though there would be no cease-fire agreement, the United Nations troops in Katanga would hold their fire for the duration of the talks unless fired upon.

Fighting soon subsided in Elisabethville, except in the *Union Minière* area where the Katanga forces and non-Congolese civilians and mercenaries subjected the United Nations troops to heavy mortar fire causing many casualties. The United Nations Force occupied the *Union Minière* factory on 19 December 1961 and captured a large quantity of arms. They repulsed an attack by a *gendarmerie* platoon on the next day.

A meeting between Prime Minister Adoula and Mr. Tshombe was arranged on 19 December 1961, with the assistance of the United Nations and the United States, at Kitona, a former Belgian military base under ONUC control. It ended on 21 December when Mr. Tshombe, as president of the provincial government of Katanga, made a declaration accepting the application of the *Loi fondamentale* of the Congo; recognizing the indissoluble unity of the Republic and the authority of the Central Government over all parts of the Republic; recognizing President Kasa-Vubu as Head of State; agreeing to the participation of Katanga's representatives in the Governmental Commission to be convened at Leopoldville on 3 January 1962 to study the draft Constitution; pledging to take all necessary steps to enable Parliament members from Katanga to discharge their national mandate from 27 December 1961; agreeing to place the Katanga *gendarmerie* under the authority of the President of the Republic; and pledging to ensure respect for the resolutions of the General Assembly and the Security Council and to facilitate their implementation. Though the declaration contained no reservation on his part, Mr. Tshombe added in a letter to the United Nations representative, Ralph J. Bunche, that he had not been able to consult the competent authorities in Katanga so as to be authorized to speak on their behalf and that he proposed to do that on his return and inform the Central Government of the steps to be taken with a view to the application of the declaration.

Developments between 21 December 1961 and 30 January 1962

In accordance with the Kitona declaration, Mr. Tshombe announced his readiness to send Katanga parliamentarians to Leopoldville to participate in the session of the Parliament. He also dispatched three Katanga officials to Leopoldville to participate in discussions for the modification of the constitutional structure of the country. ONUC provided transport to the parliamentarians and officials and gave assurances guaranteeing their safety during their stay in Leopoldville and return to Elisabethville.

With respect to the other provisions of the Kitona declaration, Mr. Tshombe took the position that they should be discussed by the provincial assembly. He summoned the assembly to meet in Elisabethville on 3 January 1962 and asked the United Nations for assistance in transporting the deputies. President Kasa-Vubu, on the other hand, promulgated an Ordinance to convoke the provincial assembly to meet in extraordinary session at Kamina, but Mr. Tshombe replied to him through ONUC channels contending that convocation by the President was irregular and contrary to the *Loi fondamentale*. The provincial assembly met in

Elisabethville on 3 January and on the next day, when a quorum was obtained, decided to set up a commission to study the implications of the Kitona declaration.

On 5 January 1962, Mr. Tshombe approached ONUC with a request for the services of a neutral juridical expert to assist the provincial assembly and its commission. He confirmed this request in a letter of 15 January, making it clear that the expert would not be asked to express any opinion on matters of substance, but would only examine the form and presentation of the conclusions drawn from the assembly's discussions. The United Nations consulted Prime Minister Adoula, who stated that he had no objection to the provision of a legal expert for the limited purpose indicated. The Acting Secretary-General then assigned the Legal Counsel of the United Nations, Constantin Stavropoulos, to the task.

Meanwhile, tension in Elisabethville diminished after the conclusion of the Kitona talks, and military activities directly involving the Katangese *gendarmerie* and ONUC forces ceased almost completely. ONUC took immediate measures to help restore normal civilian life. Joint patrols were organized by ONUC and the Elisabethville police to maintain public order, particularly to halt looting of a large number of houses which had been deserted. ONUC assisted the Elisabethville police to bring about the evacuation of houses which had been illegally occupied by members of various tribes (especially Baluba) who had fled from their own communes in fear of attacks by the *gendarmerie* and by foreign elements. These measures helped greatly to restore law and order in Elisabethville.

The problem of mercenaries continued, however, as the hard core of this group remained at large, having succeeded in evading apprehension by ONUC forces. Recruitment of mercenaries in certain foreign countries did not cease after the Kitona declaration.

United Nations representatives continued to press the Katanga authorities in the strongest terms for the urgent and complete elimination of all remaining mercenaries from Katanga. Little progress was made in that respect, though Mr. Tshombe reiterated his Government's intention to liquidate the problem and provided information on the dismissal or expulsion of some mercenaries.

In order to reduce the influx of mercenaries and the illicit arms traffic into Katanga, the Acting Secretary-General addressed communications to the Permanent Representatives of the United Kingdom and of Portugal on 29 and 30 December 1961, respectively, soliciting their co-operation and proposing that United Nations observers be stationed at a few selected airports and roads through which transit from Rhodesia and Angola into Katanga takes place. Neither Government accepted the Secretary-General's proposal, though for different reasons.

. . .

In view of the continued presence of mercenaries in Katanga, United Nations representatives, acting on instructions from the Acting Secretary-General, warned the Katanga authorities on 24 and 25 January 1962 that unless urgent steps were taken to eliminate the mercenaries, not only in Elisabethville but also in other towns, ONUC would not hesitate to take all necessary measures to do so.

In a letter on 27 January 1962, Mr. Tshombe stated that his government was determined to expel the mercenaries who were still in Katanga within a month. It was also prepared to give the United Nations a list of all mercenaries who had been in Katanga. He proposed that a joint commission of civilian representatives of the United Nations and the Katanga government be set up to seek out any mercenaries who tried to escape the consequences of the measures taken. He stated that the proposed joint commission would have free access to all places in Katanga.

The Officer-in-Charge of the United Nations Operation in the Congo replied on 30 January agreeing to the idea of one or more joint commissions on the understanding that the United Nations representation in the commissions should not be limited to civilians and stating that the elimination of the mercenaries should be undertaken immediately and should not be subject to the time-limit of one month.

On 30 January, Mr. Tshombe delivered to the United Nations representative a list of foreign officers who had been serving in the Katanga *gendarmerie* up to 28 August 1961 when, according to him, the services of foreign officers were terminated.

Meanwhile, on 1 January 1962, mutinous soldiers of the Congolese National Army committed acts of brutality in Kongolo, north Katanga. They killed twenty-two Catholic missionaries, most of them Belgians, as well as many Congolese, and sacked the town. Soon after news of the disturbances was received, an ONUC officer flew to Kongolo to help evacuate non-Congolese priests and nuns from the area. The evacuation was completed successfully, and no casualties were reported after 1 January. The Central Government undertook an investigation into the events.

In reply to communications from the representative of Belgium about this incident, the Acting Secretary-General stated that the United Nations had been prevented from stationing troops in the Kongolo area owing to the determined opposition of the Katanga *gendarmerie*. The *gendarmerie*, then 1,800 strong, withdrew on 30 December 1961, leaving the town to the mercy of a small and disorderly detachment of the Congolese National Army. As neither ONUC nor the Central Government had been informed of this move, the United Nations was unable to ensure the protection of persons by direct ONUC action. The Acting Secretary-General pointed out, further, that the activities of the mercenaries and the attacks by the Katanga *gendarmerie* in Elisabethville had strained the available resources of the United Nations Force and had sharply circumscribed its ability to assist in the maintenance of law and order.

. . .

Developments from 30 January to 23 February 1962

On 2 February 1962, in response to continued pressure by United Nations representatives for measures to ensure the expulsion of the mercenaries, Mr. Tshombe stated that he would accept two joint commissions, composed of civilian and military representatives, to expedite the implementation of United Nations resolutions. He explained that he had not meant to make the operation conditional on any time-limit. The two commissions were formed on 7 and 8 February and left on their first visits, one to Jadotville and the other to Kipushi, on 9 February.

During joint meetings of the two commissions on 8 February and on subsequent dates, the United Nations representatives asked for lists and various particulars concerning the mercenaries and for lists of foreign personnel in the *Sûreté* and the Katanga police. They also asked for a list of areas where the Katanga forces were stationed and their strength. The Katangese members, on 12 and 16 February 1962, delivered a list of 89 "other volunteers" (in addition to those on the list transmitted on 30 January 1962) who were said to have left on 8 February. Apart from the locations of units where most of these mercenaries had served, they provided no further information.

In discussions with Mr. Tshombe, the United Nations representatives also emphasized the urgent need for the presence of United Nations troops at Jadotville, Kolwezi and other locations. Mr. Tshombe stated on 7 February 1962 that such an arrangement, under the circumstances, would call for psychological preparation of the population. He suggested that the resumption of the operations of the *Union Minière* plant at Lubumbashi and the return of the Katanga *gendarmerie* to Camp Massart would be helpful. The Officer-in-Charge of the United Nations Operation in the Congo agreed to these measures on condition that ONUC would maintain measures to ensure the necessary supervision of the activities of the Lubumbashi factory and that the return of the *gendarmerie* to Camp Massart would be synchronized with the entry of ONUC forces into Jadotville and Kolwezi.

The Commission of the Katanga provincial assembly continued discussions on the implementation of the Kitona declaration of 21 December.

. . . The commission had adopted a report on 7 January providing for compliance with the *Loi fondamentale* and the authority of the Central Government only after a number of stated conditions had been met. After discussion with the legal expert, who stated that his terms of reference did not permit assistance in the preparation of such a document, the commission decided to prepare a report adopting the Kitona declaration without reservations and adding observations relating to the implementation of its terms. A new report was then prepared with the assistance of the legal expert and approved on 13 February. . . . On 15 February the provincial assembly adopted the commission's draft resolution with further amendments.

Under this resolution, the Katanga assembly accepted the "draft declaration of Kitona" as a "potential basis of discussion with a view to the settlement of the Congolese conflict." It authorized the Katanga government to establish contact with the Central Government with a view to arriving at a solution by negotiation and peaceful means in the spirit of the "draft" declaration. It proceeded to recommend that in a spirit of conciliation, the Central Government must: forgo taking punitive measures against any civil or military officers who might have executed the orders of the Katanga government since 30 June 1960; avoid sending to Katanga civil or military officers who might be hostile to the Katanga authorities; refrain from sending to Katanga armed forces liable to spread disorder or panic among the population; refrain from showing any form of partiality in the internal dissensions of Katanga and from opposing the restoration of the Katanga government's authority over the whole of the province; take the necessary measures to balance the budget of the country; and prohibit all monetary, fiscal or administrative measures liable to prejudice the economic and financial situation of Katanga or the smooth running of public services. The assembly also recommended that the work of preparing the new constitution should be speedily concluded. Finally, it reserved the right to ratify the agreements which might be concluded between "the authorities in Leopoldville and those of Katanga."

On 16 February 1962, Prime Minister Adoula expressed disappointment at a statement made by Mr. Tshombe in the Katanga provincial assembly and at the resolution adopted, but sent an invitation to Mr. Tshombe for a meeting in Leopoldville to discuss the procedure for carrying out the Kitona declaration. On the same day, Mr. Tshombe suggested a personal meeting with Mr. Adoula to discuss a solution of the problems in the spirit of the Kitona declaration. On 19 February, Mr. Adoula sent three messages to Mr. Tshombe asking for information on appointments of officers in the Katanga _gendarmerie_, inviting Katanga _gendarmerie_ commanders to a meeting to discuss the re-organization of the National Army and suggesting a session of the provincial assembly, attended by all elected representatives under United Nations security arrangements, to help settle the internal problem of Katanga.

In response to requests by Mr. Tshombe, ONUC offered him and his party guarantees for their security during their visit to Leopoldville. The guarantees were to cover the whole period of the visit and were to include complete freedom to decide the time of the return to Elisabethville. Mr. Tshombe arrived in Leopoldville on 15 March 1962.

(YUN 1961, pp. 57-79)

The situation in the Congo (Leopoldville) during 1963 was marked by the completion of an important phase of the United Nations Operation in the Congo (ONUC), as most of the aims of the Operation had been in large measure fulfilled. However, as the Secretary-General stated in a report to the Security Council on 17 September 1963, it was considered necessary for the United Nations to exercise vigilance and to continue its military assistance over a transitional period to assist the Congolese Government in maintaining law and order.

On 4 February 1963, the Secretary-General reported to the Security Council regarding the extent to which the mandates given to ONUC by the Council's resolutions had been fulfilled and indicated the tasks still to be completed.

With respect to the maintenance of the territorial integrity and the political independence of the Congo, he stated that it might reasonably be concluded that the secession of Katanga which threatened those objectives was now at an end. Moreover, he felt, there was no direct threat to the independence of the Congo from external sources. That part of ONUC's mandate had thus been largely fulfilled.

Assistance by ONUC to the Congolese Government in the maintenance of law and order was continuing. Vast improvements had been achieved in this regard, and a substantial reduction of the United Nations Force was therefore being made.

Similarly, the mandate to prevent civil war in the Congo, given to ONUC in February 1961, could be considered to have been substantially fulfilled—especially after the formation in August 1961 of a Government of National Unity—with the termination of secessionist activities in Katanga. . . .

As far as the removal of foreign military, paramilitary and advisory personnel and mercenaries was concerned, the Secretary-General reported that ONUC's mandate was for all practical purposes completed.

In view of these accomplishments, the phase of active involvement of United Nations troops had been concluded, and a new phase of the Operation was beginning, which would give greater emphasis to civilian operations and technical assistance. Already, ONUC civilian operations, involving collaboration between the United Nations and the specialized agencies, had helped to provide essential public services.

(YUN 1963, p. 3)

Tragic end of a mission of peace— investigation into the circumstances leading to the death of Dag Hammarskjöld

Secretary-General Dag Hammarskjöld was on a mission of peace to meet with Moise Tshombe in an effort to restore order between United Nations troops and the secessionist Katanga forces when he, together with seven other United Nations staff members and the Swedish crew, was killed in an air crash on 18 September 1961 near Ndola in Zambia. In November 1961, Ambassador U Thant, then Permanent Representative of Burma to the United Nations, was appointed Acting Secretary-General for the remainder of Dag Hammarskjöld's five-year term of office.

Immediately upon receiving news of the air crash, which resulted in the deaths of Mr. Hammarskjöld and the 15 others accompanying him, the United Nations appointed two aeronautical experts from the International Civil Aviation Organization (ICAO) as observers at the technical investigation being carried out by the Rhodesian authorities under annex XIII to the Convention on International Civil Aviation. The United Nations observers, as well as representatives of Sweden, the State of registry of the aircraft, participated fully in the work of the Board of Investigation, which extended over a three-month period.

In the meanwhile, on 27 September 1961, Ghana, India, the United Arab Republic and Venezuela—later joined by Brazil, Cambodia, Cyprus, Morocco, Nigeria and Togo—requested that the following item be included in the agenda of the General Assembly's sixteenth session: "An international investigation into the conditions and circumstances resulting in the tragic death of Mr. Dag Hammarskjöld, and members of the party accompanying him."

An explanatory memorandum with the request noted that there was world-wide concern about the circumstances surrounding the accident. While observing that some national inquiries were being conducted or were envisaged, it proposed that the United Nations should itself make a thorough probe into the circumstances resulting in the tragic death of Mr. Hammarskjöld and a number of other international civil servants. World public opinion, the memorandum added, expected that a full and impartial international investigation be carried out to ascertain the exact circumstances of the tragic accident, the conditions which compelled the Secretary-General and his party to undertake the flight at night without adequate security or other precautionary measures, and other matters which might have a bearing on the accident.

On 13 October 1961, acting on the recommendation of its General Committee, the General Assembly decided to place the item on its agenda and to discuss it at a plenary meeting.

The Assembly considered the subject on 26 October 1961. Before the Assembly was a draft resolution submitted by the following 14 members: Ceylon, Congo (Leopoldville), Cyprus, Ghana, India, Libya, Morocco, Nepal, Nigeria, Senegal, Togo, Tunisia, United Arab Republic and Venezuela.

By this 14-power text, the Assembly, noting that the concern prevailing in the world about the tragedy and the circumstances surrounding it warranted an international investigation, noting also that inquiries had been or were being conducted by Governments or parties concerned, and considering it desirable and necessary, irrespective of such inquiries, that an investigation be carried out under the authority and auspices of the United Nations, would: (1) express its profound shock and sorrow at the death of Mr. Hammarskjöld and the persons who died with him in the service of the United Nations, namely: Heinrich A. Wieschhoff, Vladimir Fabry, William Ranallo, Miss Alice Lalande, Harold M. Julien, Serge L. Barrau, Francis Eivers, S. O. Hjelte, P. E. Persson, Per Hallonquist, Nils-Eric Aahréus, Lars Litton, Nils Göran Wilhelmsson, Harold Noork and Karl Erik Rosén; (2) offer its sincere condolences and deep sympathy to the families; (3) decide that an investigation of an international character should be held into the conditions and circumstances surrounding the tragedy and more particularly as to: *(a)* why the flight had to be undertaken at night without escort, *(b)* why its arrival at Ndola was unduly delayed, as reported, *(c)* whether the aircraft, after having established contact with the tower at Ndola, lost that contact, and the fact of its having crashed did not become known until several hours afterwards, and if so, why, and *(d)* whether the aircraft, after the damage it was reported to have suffered earlier from firing by aircraft hostile to the United Nations, was in a proper condition for use; (4) further decide to appoint an investigation commission of five eminent persons and request it to report its findings to the President of the General Assembly; (5) request all Governments and parties concerned and the appropriate specialized agencies to extend their full co-operation and assistance; and (6) decide to consider in the appropriate Assembly Committee the question of offering suitable remuneration to the families of the victims.

In support of the draft resolution, the representatives of India, Morocco and Venezuela urged that an investigation should be carried out under the auspices of an international body in order to satisfy public opinion and allay the world-wide concern aroused by the magnitude of the tragedy and its political and historical importance. The representatives of Cyprus, Ghana, Morocco, Togo and Tunisia considered that the United Nations owed it to Mr. Hammarskjöld and the others who perished with him to conduct a proper investigation which would also be a tribute to their memory. The representative of Cyprus held that an international investigation conducted under United Nations auspices would ensure an independent and impartial inquiry.

Many representatives, including those of Cyprus, Ghana, Honduras, Morocco, Sweden, Tunisia and Venezuela, considered it necessary to examine the rumours, fears and speculations to which the tragedy had given rise and to provide answers thereto. The representatives of Togo, Morocco and Venezuela thought the investigation should determine any responsibilities involved. The representatives of India and Venezuela stressed that the investigation should help to prevent the occurrence of such disasters in the future and to ensure maximum protection for those performing functions in the service of the United Nations.

Representatives of Cyprus, India, Tunisia and Venezuela considered that there should be no conflict between the United Nations investigation and other investigations and that the results of previous investigations could facilitate the task of the United Nations Commission.

The Swedish representative noted that his Government was represented on the Rhodesian commission of experts already established, the work of which would be of value when the new body began its work.

The United Kingdom representative welcomed the statements that the United Nations investigation would in no way conflict with the investigations conducted and contemplated by the Federation of Rhodesia and Nyasaland. The United Kingdom, he assured the Assembly, would co-operate in carrying out the resolution and in assisting the work of the United Nations Investigation Commission.

The representatives of Cyprus, Ghana, India and Venezuela pointed out that the United Nations investigation would cover a much wider field and would be more embracing in its character than the national or technical inquiries.

At the same meeting, on 26 October 1961, the General Assembly unanimously approved the 14-power draft resolution by 97 votes to 0, as resolution 1628(XVI).

. . .

On 8 December 1961, the General Assembly appointed the following as members of the United Nations Commission of Investigation: Justice Samuel Bankolé Jones of Sierra Leone, Raúl Quijano of Argentina, Justice Emil Sandström of Sweden, Rishikesh Shaha of Nepal and Nikol Srzentic of Yugoslavia.

The Commission held an organizational session at United Nations Headquarters in New York from 15 to 22 December 1961 and unanimously elected Rishikesh Shaha as Chairman and Raúl Quijano as Rapporteur. During its session in New York, the Commission considered the programme and organization of its work, decided on the relationship of its investigation to those going on in Rhodesia and heard a preliminary report from one of the United Nations observers about the Rhodesian investigation in which he had participated.

By a letter of 8 December 1961, the Permanent Representative of the United Kingdom informed the President of the General Assembly that a federal Commission of Inquiry would be established by the Federation of Rhodesia and Nyasaland which would conduct a public inquiry into the accident. On behalf of the Federation, he invited the United Nations to designate a member of this Commission. Similar requests, he said, had been made by the Federal Government to the Governments of Sweden and the United Kingdom and to ICAO.

The President of the General Assembly, in accordance with a suggestion by the United Kingdom, referred the invitation to the United Nations Commission of Investigation.

After careful consideration, it was concluded that the harmonization desired by the General Assembly between the different investigations could best be achieved by co-operation and exchange of information, but the investigations themselves should be kept separate. Consequently, it was decided that the United Nations would not appoint a member to the Federation's public Commission of Inquiry. At the same time, the United Nations Commission discussed with the appropriate authorities the best methods for effecting co-operation and exchange of information. It was also agreed that the United Nations Commission would begin its hearings in Rhodesia as early as possible in 1962 immediately after the Federation's Commission had completed its public hearings.

[YUN 1961, pp. 162-64]

Liberia

A civil war began in 1989 as rebel forces seeking to depose the Government made major territorial gains and advanced on the capital, Monrovia. A series of cease-fires failed to hold. By 1994, more than half of the country's population had become refugees as a result of the civil conflicts.

The United Nations Observer Mission in Liberia (UNOMIL), established in 1993, was the first United Nations peace-keeping mission undertaken in cooperation with a peace-keeping operation already set up by another organization. Initially intended to last for a seven-month period, UNOMIL was to work with the Military Observer Group (ECOMOG) created by the Economic Community of West African States in implementing the Cotonou Peace Agreement signed in July 1993 between the three warring factions. The agreement laid out a continuum of action, from a cease-fire through disarmament and demobilization to the holding of national elections. Due to renewed fighting, the peace process and the fulfilment of UNOMIL's role were hampered to the point that UNOMIL strength was temporarily reduced and all UNOMIL team sites were evacuated except for those in the Monrovia area. In October 1994, the Security Council extended UNOMIL's mandate until 13 January 1995, stipulating that any decision to return it to the authorized level would depend on a real improvement in the security situation.

Mozambique

After 14 years of devastating civil war, the Government of Mozambique and the Resistência Nacional Moçambicana (RENAMO) signed a General Peace Agreement in October 1992. The United Nations was requested to undertake a major role in monitoring implementation of the Agreement, and to perform specific functions in relation to the cease-fire, elections and humanitarian assistance. In December 1992, the Security Council established the United Nations Operation in Mozambique (ONUMOZ) whose mandate, in accordance with the Agreement, included four important elements: political, military, electoral and humanitarian. From the outset of ONUMOZ operations, various delays and difficulties of a political, administrative and logistical nature seriously impeded implementation of the Agreement. Due to determined United Nations efforts, many of the difficulties were overcome and, by the beginning of May 1993, ONUMOZ was fully deployed. By the beginning of 1994, political developments in the country allowed an increasing shift of focus from monitoring cease-fire arrangements to general verification of police activities and the respect of civil rights. With the beginning of the demobilization in March 1994, the implementation of the General Peace Agreement entered another critical phase, and in April the President announced that general elections would be held in October. Following the elections, ONUMOZ started the major withdrawal of its personnel. With the installation of Mozambique's new Parliament on 8 December and the inauguration of Joaquim Alberto Chissano as President the following day, ONUMOZ's mandate formally ended at midnight on 9 December.

Namibia

Namibia, formerly a German colony of South West Africa, was seized by South Africa in 1915 during the First World War. In 1920, the League of Nations gave South Africa a Mandate over the Territory. In 1946, the United Nations recommended the placement of the Territory under the newly created United Nations Trusteeship System. South Africa, however, refused to do so.

In 1966, by General Assembly resolution 2145(XXI), the United Nations revoked South Africa's Mandate over the Territory and assumed direct responsibility for it. Also in the same year, the South West Africa People's Organization (SWAPO) launched a guerrilla war to gain independence. In 1967, the United Nations Council for South West Africa (renamed Namibia in 1968) was established to administer the Territory until independence.

For more than two decades, the United Nations demanded South Africa's withdrawal and the transfer of power to the Namibian people. South Africa, however, continued its illegal occupation and rejected all United Nations proposals to move the Territory towards independence. In the meantime, a bitter armed conflict raged over Namibia with devastating consequences for the entire southern African region.

In 1978, the United Nations Security Council approved resolution 435 (1978) containing the settlement plan for Namibian independence. It called for a cease-fire in the Namibian conflict, the holding of free and fair elections under United Nations auspices and a peace-keeping operation in Namibia.

While South Africa had accepted in 1980 the settlement plan for Namibia, it did not agree to proceed towards a cease-fire; instead, it attached new conditions which were not acceptable to the United Nations. Negotiations stalled.

In December 1988, after many years of warfare, political conflicts and diplomatic efforts, Angola, Cuba and South Africa signed an agreement which opened the way to the implementation of the United Nations plan endorsed by resolution 435(1978) for the settlement of the Namibian problem. The mandate of the United Nations Transition Assistance Group (UNTAG) was to supervise implementation of the plan, scheduled to start on 1 April 1989 and create the conditions for the holding of free and fair elections for a Constituent Assembly leading to independence.

UNTAG was one of the most complex operations ever undertaken by the United Nations. It had to carry out a variety of tasks, including monitoring the dismantling of the South African military presence and the confinement of the forces of SWAPO to base; monitoring the conduct of the South West Africa Police; ensuring the repeal of discriminatory laws, amnesty, and release of prisoners and detainees; assisting in the return of refugees; and registration of voters and supervision and control of the electoral process.

Registration of voters began in July 1989, at registration centres set up all over the country, which had been divided into 23 electoral districts. Some 2,200 rural registration points were covered by 110 mobile registration teams. When the process concluded on 23 September, more than 700,000 Namibians had registered to vote.

At its height, during the elections from 7 to 11 November 1989, UNTAG had an overall strength of almost 8,000 personnel, consisting of about 2,000 civilians (including more than 1,000 international personnel, many of them seconded by their Governments specifically for the elections), 1,500 police and approximately 4,500 military forces.

The elections, intended to choose 72 delegates to the Constituent Assembly, saw a voter turnout of 97 per cent. UNTAG monitored the balloting and counting of votes. On 14 November, the Special Representative of the Secretary-General declared that the elections had been free and fair. SWAPO obtained 41 seats in the Assembly, followed by the Turnhalle Alliance with 21 seats, and 10 seats were shared by five smaller parties. The Assembly drafted a new Constitution, which was approved on 9 February 1990, leading to Namibia's independence on 21 March. The Secretary-General, at Windhoek, administered the oath of office to Sam Nujoma, the leader of SWAPO, who became Namibia's first President. On 23 April 1990, Namibia became the 160th Member of the United Nations.

Rwanda

For centuries Rwanda has experienced civil conflicts between the Hutu majority and Tutsi minority resulting in large-scale massacres. Renewed ethnic strife in the 1990s led to the August 1993 Arusha Peace Agreement between the Government and the rebels of the Tutsi-led Rwanda Patriotic Front (RPF), aimed at ending the continuing armed conflict.

In October 1993, the Security Council established the United Nations Assistance Mission for Rwanda (UNAMIR) to assist in implementing the Agreement. UNAMIR's mandate was to expire following national elections and the installation of a new Government, to take place no later than December 1995. Following a plane crash in April 1994 at Kigali, the capital of Rwanda, in which the Presidents of Burundi and Rwanda were killed, widespread violence of ethnic and political dimensions broke out throughout the country. Fighting between government forces and RPF intensified and the security situation deteriorated rapidly, with large-scale massacres taking place, making it impossible for UNAMIR to fufil its original mandate. In May, the Security Council expanded UNAMIR's mandate to enable it to contribute to the security and protection of refugees and civilians and to provide security and support for relief operations. At the same time, the Council imposed an arms embargo on the country. The protracted violence created an almost unprecedented humanitarian crisis. According to estimates, Rwanda's pre-war population of 7.9 million had fallen to 5 million by October, and internally displaced persons numbered from 800,000 to 2 million. There were more than 2 million refugees in Zaire, the United Republic of Tanzania, Burundi and Uganda. At the same time, it was estimated that some 360,000 refugees had returned to Rwanda spontaneously since the cease-fire on 18 July. The victims of the genocidal slaughter could number as many as 1 million.

In November, the Security Council decided to establish an international tribunal to prosecute persons responsible for genocide and other violations of international humanitarian law in Rwanda. The Council extended UNAMIR's mandate until June 1995, which included good offices to help achieve national reconciliation.

Somalia

For decades, Somalia was torn by civil and inter-clan strife. In 1991, following the flight of General Mohammad Siyad Barre, fighting intensified among the rival factions causing thousands of civilian casualties. The civil war, drought and banditry resulted in a devastating famine that threatened millions with starvation. By 1992, Somalia was a country without a Government. With United Nations consent, the United States moved troops to Somalia to safeguard the delivery of food to the starving. The United Nations took control of the Somalia operation in 1993.

The restoration of peace and protection of humanitarian relief were central tasks of the operation in Somalia. While great success was achieved in eliminating mass starvation, the political and security situation in the country remained volatile and even deteriorated progressively, especially in Mogadishu. The goal of national reconciliation was becoming ever more elusive and the protracted political impasse created a vacuum of civil authority

and governmental structure, which left the United Nations and the United Nations Operation in Somalia II (UNOSOM II) with no function to build on. In the face of continuing inter-clan fighting and banditry, the presence of UNOSOM II troops had limited impact on the peace process and on the security situation. Based on the conclusion of a seven-member Security Council mission, the Council in November 1994 extended the mandate of UNOSOM II for a final period until 31 March 1995. None of the Somali factions, the humanitarian agencies or non-governmental organizations requested a longer extension.

South Africa and apartheid

The racial policies of South Africa first came before the United Nations in 1946, when India complained about the enactment of legislation against South Africans of Indian origin. Beginning in 1952, the wider question of racial conflict arising from South Africa's policy of apartheid was included in the agenda of the General Assembly. The two items continued to be discussed separately until they were combined in 1962. The South African Government consistently maintained that the matter was essentially within its domestic jurisdiction and that under the Charter the United Nations was barred from considering it.

The Assembly, in 1952, established a three-man commission to study the racial situation in South Africa and called on all Member States to bring their policies into conformity with their obligations under the Charter to promote the observance of human rights and fundamental freedoms. South Africa refused to recognize the United Nations Good Offices Commission, which, nevertheless, submitted three reports in 1953, 1954 and 1955. It also refused to heed the Assembly's repeated appeals to revise its apartheid policies in the light of the Charter.

Treatment of people of Indian origin in the Union of South Africa

The question of the treatment of people of Indian origin in the Union of South Africa was first brought before the General Assembly by India in 1946, and was discussed at the first, second, third, fifth and sixth sessions. None of the resolutions adopted by the Assembly had been implemented before the opening of its seventh session.

On 12 January 1952, during its sixth session, the General Assembly adopted resolution 511(VI) recommending the establishment of a commission of three members to assist the parties, namely India, Pakistan and the Union of South Africa, in carrying through appropriate negotiations. If members of the commission were not nominated by the parties, the Secretary-General was requested, at his discretion, to assist them with a view to facilitating negotiations and, after consulting the Governments concerned, to appoint an individual for the purpose. The resolution stipulated that the question should be included in the agenda of the Assembly's seventh session.

Report of the Secretary-General

In a special report on 10 October 1952, the Secretary-General informed the General Assembly of developments since the adoption of resolution 511(VI) including the failure of the parties concerned to nominate members to the proposed commission. On 22 February 1952 the Union of South Africa informed the Secretary-General that it was not able to accept the terms of the resolution, as it constituted interference in a matter which was essentially within the Union's jurisdiction, but expressed readiness to participate in a round-table conference on the basis of the formula agreed to at Capetown in February 1950, a formula which allowed the widest freedom of discussion to all parties without any further conditions.

India, on 27 February 1952, indicated that, for reasons previously explained, it could not agree to the resumption of the negotiations on the basis proposed by the Union's Government. The reasons included refusal of the Union not to add to the disabilities of persons of Indian origin pending the proposed round-table conference. It added that, in view of the Union's reply, the nomination of the joint representative of India and Pakistan on the proposed commission could serve no useful purpose.

On 3 March 1952 Pakistan stated that, in view of the conflicting and irreconcilable points of view contained in the communications from the Union Government and India, it was clear that no useful purpose would be served by nominating the joint representative.

Subsequent consultations with representatives of the three Governments concerned and with those of other Governments forced the Secretary-General, the report stated, to the conclusion that there was at present no possible solution to the problem and that, consequently, the appointment of an individual under the terms of paragraph 3 of resolution 511(VI) was not yet opportune.

The special report concluded by stating that in late September 1952 the three Governments concerned informed the Secretary-General of their recent positions regarding resolution 511(VI), positions which were substantially the same as those taken in the course of the debate at the Assembly's sixth session.

Pursuant to resolution 511(VI), the question was placed on the provisional agenda of the Assembly's seventh session. At the 79th meeting of the General Committee, on 15 October, and at the 380th plenary meeting, on 16 October 1952, the representative of the Union of South Africa argued that the subject was not one which could be appropriately considered by the Assembly because it concerned a matter essentially within the domestic jurisdiction of the Union of South Africa.

The General Committee recommended its inclusion. The General Assembly, by 46 votes to one, with 6 abstentions, rejected a formal proposal of the representative of the Union Government to exclude the item from the agenda. It then referred the question to the *Ad Hoc* Political Committee which considered it at its 8th to 12th meetings from 3 to 11 November 1952.

Consideration by the Ad Hoc *Political Committee*

Opening the debate in the *Ad Hoc* Political Committee, the representative of the Union of South Africa stated that Article 2, paragraph 7, of the Charter debarred the Assembly from considering the matter since it fell wholly within the domestic jurisdiction of his Government. He could not, therefore, deal with the merits of the question. Certain facts, however, should be reiterated in order that the "complaint"—or, to be more correct, the "campaign"—against the Union of South Africa might be seen in its true colours. While the Charter, as drafted in San Francisco, remained unchanged, his Government would continue its stand and would not consider itself bound to give effect to Assembly resolutions on the matter.

What could the United Nations gain, he asked, by continuing year after year to adopt resolutions which, because they were unconstitutional, his Government could not accept?

The Union Government, he pointed out, had repeatedly indicated its willingness to enter into direct negotiations on the matter with India and Pakistan on the basis of the formula agreed upon between the three Governments in Capetown in 1950. Did India sincerely desire to achieve a solution on the matter, he asked, or was it merely endeavouring to keep the issue before the United Nations in order to further its own political interests? Not once since 1946 had India given any real proof that it wished to seek an amicable settlement. On the contrary, it had applied trade sanctions against South Africa and resorted to tactics which gave world opinion a distorted picture of the facts and encouraged intransigence among people of Indian origin in that country.

Despite the alleged hardships to which they were being subjected, the people of Indian origin continued to remain in the country even though the South African Government had offered to provide them with free passage to India and to pay them a special allowance.

By affording India an annual opportunity to pursue its vendetta against the Union of South

Africa, the United Nations was not acting in the interest of international peace and goodwill. He hoped that the Committee would state clearly that the Assembly did not intend to permit the United Nations to be used, unconstitutionally and improperly, as a propaganda forum for the promotion of a campaign of vilification against a Member State.

The representative of India reviewed her country's attempts since 1946 to solve the problem by direct negotiations. In accordance with resolution 265(III) it had been agreed in Capetown in 1950 to convene a round-table conference to explore all possible ways and means of settling the question. That conference had not taken place, she stated, because the Union Government had continued its policy of racial discrimination not only by its action under the Asiatic Land Tenure Amendment Act of 1949 but also by the adoption of a new racial segregation law known as the Group Areas Act. The Union Government had ignored the request of India and Pakistan to delay the enforcement of the latter Act so that the purpose of the proposed conference would not be defeated.

In resolutions 395(V) and 511(VI) the General Assembly affirmed that a policy of racial segregation (*apartheid*) was necessarily based on doctrines of racial discrimination and made various recommendations for the purpose of assisting the parties to carry through appropriate negotiations, meanwhile calling upon the Union Government to refrain from the implementation of enforcement of the Group Areas Act. The South African Government, the representative of India declared, had refused to enter into any negotiations with the Governments of India and Pakistan. It was pursuing a policy of denying elementary human rights and fundamental freedoms, systematically and deliberately, to the vast majority of its non-white nationals, and events in South Africa were moving rapidly towards inevitable catastrophe. Race tension was increasing dangerously. India believed it to be its duty to plead once more before the Assembly the cause of the non-white nationals of the Union of South Africa and, in particular, that of the people of Indian origin, who were victims of that Government's policy of racial segregation. In the face of the rapidly deteriorating situation resulting from the enforcement of laws which violated the fundamental principle of the Charter, the Indian representative called on the Assembly to make a new attempt to seek an amicable settlement of the problem. India hoped that the pressure of world opinion, exercised through the United Nations, would induce the Union Government to collaborate in the quest for a solution. It was the duty of the United Nations to defend human values and fundamental human rights without distinction of colour, race or religion.

Otherwise, its prestige and authority would be seriously impaired.

Accordingly, at the eighth meeting of the *Ad Hoc* Political Committee on 3 November, the representative of India introduced a draft resolution, sponsored jointly by Afghanistan, Burma, Egypt, India, Indonesia, Iran, Iraq, Lebanon, Liberia, Pakistan, the Philippines, Saudi Arabia, Syria, Thailand and Yemen. Under that draft resolution the General Assembly would:

> (1) note that the Government of the Union of South Africa had continued to enforce the Group Areas Act in contravention of resolutions 395(V) and 511(VI) and would establish a United Nations Good Offices Commission with a view to arranging and assisting in negotiations between the parties to solve the dispute in accordance with the principles and purposes of the Charter and the Universal Declaration of Human Rights; and (2) call upon the Union Government to suspend implementation of enforcement of the Group Areas Act pending the conclusion of such negotiations and would include the item in the agenda of the eighth session.

At the twelfth meeting on 11 November the sponsors added a clause stating that the members of the Good Offices Commission should be nominated by the President of the General Assembly.

The representative of Pakistan noted that the question of competence of the United Nations had once again been raised by the Union of South Africa in spite of the decisions taken on the question by the overwhelming majority at previous sessions of the General Assembly. He recalled that only two delegations had voted against resolution 511(VI). Consequently, he said, the question of competence should no longer be raised. The fact that fifteen Governments were jointly sponsoring a draft resolution should be regarded by the Union of South Africa as a sign of the times. That Government must ask itself why the resolutions on the question were adopted by an increasing number of votes each year. It was in pursuance of certain moral principles which actuated the larger part of humanity that the question had been again submitted to the United Nations.

It was not possible, he declared, to reconcile the Group Areas Act adopted in June 1950 with resolution 103(I) of the Assembly whereby the Member States had pledged themselves to take the most prompt and energetic steps in order to put an immediate end to racial discrimination in the world. Articles 2 and 3 of the Act established a distinction according to colour among the Union's inhabitants in order to determine their right to occupy or own property in a given region. That constituted racial discrimination designed to segregate various elements of the population.

The question was the action to be taken by the United Nations. The Assembly had already recommended direct negotiation between the parties, and it was proposed that that recommendation should be renewed. The Government of Pakistan would be happy to participate in such negotiations. Unfortunately this had hitherto been impossible because the Union Government had not agreed to even a temporary halt in the passage or enforcement of the Group Areas Act which would have been a necessary condition for successful negotiations. He reviewed the failure of the measures envisaged in resolution 511(VI) and declared that, despite the failure of these very moderate measures, the United Nations must not give up, but must adopt energetic measures to end religious persecution and racial discrimination in accordance with resolution 103(I).

Assertions by the Union of South Africa that any action by the United Nations would constitute interference should not cause the United Nations to drop the question, he said. The Assembly could not cast aside the Universal Declaration of Human Rights; it should reaffirm the principles on which the United Nations was founded. Moreover, it was impossible to say that the stand of any Government would never change. His Government did not give up hope that the Union Government would eventually accede to the United Nations appeal. It was for these reasons that Pakistan had associated itself with the other sponsors of the draft resolution.

Speaking in full support of the draft resolution, the representatives of Afghanistan, Burma, Cuba, Egypt, Ethiopia, Guatemala, Haiti, Indonesia, Iran, Iraq, Lebanon, Liberia, the Philippines, Poland, Saudi Arabia, Syria, the USSR, Uruguay and Yugoslavia emphasized that there could be no question of the competence of the General Assembly. The previous resolutions on the matter showed that the Assembly considered the question a matter of international concern. These representatives strongly objected to the South African Government's policy of racial discrimination and segregation as an offence to human dignity and a clear violation of the Charter and the Universal Declaration of Human Rights. Disregard by that Government of the Assembly's repeated recommendations was a direct challenge to principles which the Union Government had undertaken to respect, they said. They denied that there was any intention to interfere in the domestic affairs of the Union of South Africa or any feeling of hostility or ill-will towards the Union Government, and considered the draft resolution a moderate and conciliatory one designed to find a solution to the existing deadlock and offering a practical approach towards a peaceful settlement. All urged an early resumption of negotiations and expressed hope that the Union would realize the gravity of the deteriorating situation and would co-operate with the

United Nations in bringing about a solution of the problem. Several supporters considered that the Union Government's policy would inevitably lead to disturbances and was a potential threat to international peace and security.

The representative of Afghanistan asserted that the Union Government's policy of racial discrimination and segregation contained the seeds of destruction of South African society. Its economic structure had been built on the labour of the non-white population and the unity of the country depended on the harmonious co-operation of individuals and groups in ensuring the voluntary and continuous exchange of goods and services. Thus, apart from moral and humanitarian considerations, it was primarily in South Africa's own interest to put an end to its unfair racial policy.

The representative of Mexico stated that a truly democratic society was still an ideal towards which all peoples strove, but which was still far from realization anywhere. The Committee was merely seeking a reasonable and practical solution for a problem which threatened to weaken the cordial relations which existed with the Union of South Africa.

The representative of Poland declared that the essence of the South African Government's laws which violated fundamental rights and were permeated by a spirit of fascism, was the degradation of human beings, a weapon in a calculated campaign to maintain the non-whites in a position of economic subservience. His country's own experience made it protest all the more vigorously against racial discrimination. The attempt of the Union Government to perpetuate its policies was doomed to failure in a world where oppressed peoples were clamouring for liberation. South Africa could not stem that tide by terror, he said.

World opinion looked to the United Nations to remedy this state of affairs, said the representative of Haiti; by its dilatory action, the Organization ran a risk of undermining its own prestige.

In expressing support of the draft resolution and its desire for a peaceful settlement of the question in accordance with the Charter, the representative of the USSR said that his Government's position was dictated by one of the fundamental principles of its policy: equality of political, economic and cultural rights for all without distinction of race. He stated that the question of the treatment of people of Indian origin in the Union of South Africa could not be considered as being exclusively within the domestic jurisdiction of the Union of South Africa as it involved violation of bilateral agreements concluded in 1927 and 1932 between the Government of India and the Union of South Africa, thereby making the matter one of international concern. The South African Government, by its attitude and its policy, was violating Article

1, paragraphs 2 and 3, of the Charter. That South Africa was practising racial discrimination in violation of paragraph 2 of that Article, he stated, was not denied by the South African representative and was proved by the texts of paragraphs 2 (1) and 4 (2) of the Group Areas Act.

While stating that they would vote in favour of the draft resolution, the representatives of Brazil, China, Ecuador and the United States opposed some of its provisions, particularly the fourth paragraph of the operative part calling for the suspension of the Group Areas Act.

The representative of the United States favoured conciliation rather than recrimination. He pointed out that to translate ideas into realities in the field of human relations was a long and difficult task. Despite difficulties, the direction was clearly marked by the Charter. The test was not just how bad conditions were in a country, but whether efforts were being made there to improve those conditions. There appeared to be a serious difference, he thought, between the national policy of South Africa and the whole current of modern philosophy and scientific knowledge and the line of conduct endorsed in the Charter. His Government hoped that the discussion might create an atmosphere favourable to negotiations. The United Nations should not attempt to impose any solution. Progress could be hoped for only to the extent that the parties were willing to confer. Resolutions should not be such as to excite adverse nationalist reactions, but ought rather to follow the path of accommodation through negotiation. While the United States would support the draft resolution as a whole, it felt it contained certain doubtful provisions. It was inadvisable to censure a piece of national legislation and appear to set a condition preceding negotiations between the parties.

While supporting the draft resolution, the representatives of El Salvador, Israel and Mexico suggested that the resolution be framed so as to be more readily acceptable to the Union of South Africa. The representative of Israel said that the primary concern should be to bring the parties into direct negotiation so that they might find a ground for understanding rather than express feelings and convictions. No good offices commission could reach a settlement if the parties refused to engage in direct negotiations.

The representatives of Denmark, Norway and Sweden likewise supported the resolution but said that they would abstain on the fourth paragraph concerning the suspension of the Group Areas Act. This paragraph, they considered, was not worded in such a way as to facilitate renewal of negotiations in a friendly atmosphere. The representative of Denmark suggested a number of deletions.

Expressing doubts about the competence of the Assembly and opposition to some provisions of the draft resolution, particularly its references to the Group Areas Act, the representatives of Argentina, Australia, Belgium, Colombia, France, the Netherlands, New Zealand, Turkey and the United Kingdom indicated that, while anxious that the parties open direct negotiations, they would abstain from voting on the draft resolution.

The United Kingdom was anxious lest, while examining delicate questions involving the domestic policy of any State, the *Ad Hoc* Committee run the risk of increasing tension between the countries concerned instead of promoting friendly relations, its representative declared. The legal situation was far from clear. Parts of the resolutions adopted by the Assembly, he considered, constituted intervention in matters within South Africa's domestic jurisdiction. It was difficult to ascertain whether by reason of earlier agreements between the governments concerned the problem went beyond the national competence of the Union and the United Nations was justified in considering it.

The representative of France observed that, despite good intentions, the draft resolution was not likely to offer a solution but rather to delay it. His Government remained convinced that a solution acceptable to all could only be reached through direct negotiation among the parties to the dispute.

The representative of Australia considered the matter outside the competence of the United Nations. He declared that the fact that the question had been the subject of Assembly resolutions in no way implied that it was no longer the domestic jurisdiction of the State directly concerned. It was not sufficient to point to certain Articles of the Charter to justify the consideration of questions which, even if of international interest, were nevertheless a domestic concern. Article 2, paragraph 7, by reason of its position in the Charter, governed the application of all the other Articles.

A change of public opinion within a country was never, he remarked, a rapid process and could not be hastened as the result of the intervention of other countries. Aside from the merits or demerits of the law on which the Assembly was being asked to pass judgment, the Australian representative emphasized the explosive and undesirable consequences of exploiting racial issues in the United Nations. They could not be ignored but their solution required great wisdom and tolerance and could only be usefully discussed by those directly concerned. He believed that the parties should be urged to open direct negotiations.

At the conclusion of the debate, the South African representative expressed appreciation of the friendly sentiments which had been expressed towards his country by a number of delegations. His Government again urged that the provisions of Article 2, paragraph 7, of the Charter be respected.

Its attitude was based on that fundamental principle which governed relations between the Organization and its Members. His delegation would have to vote against the joint draft resolution.

He repeated his Government's willingness to discuss with India and Pakistan possible ways and means of settling the matter. It was prepared to reopen direct negotiations on the understanding that these would not involve any departure from or prejudice to the standpoint of the respective Governments in regard to the question of domestic jurisdiction. Such talks, while not related to any Assembly resolutions, would permit the parties to hold a full, free and unfettered discussion.

The representative of India concluded the discussion by saying that the sponsors did not feel that the provisions of the draft resolution could be amended. She said that the representative of South Africa had implied that India had refused to reopen negotiations with the Union. However, when the preliminary talks had been held at Capetown in 1950, it had appeared that the Union had meant to discuss only the repatriation of people of Indian origin and not the removal of the discriminatory measures to which they were subject. That was one of the main reasons why negotiations had been broken off. That this was his Government's only interest was demonstrated by the South African representative's silence when asked whether his Government would be prepared to repeal the Group Areas Act if the proposed negotiations resulted in an understanding.

Concerning the charges that the Indian Government had applied economic sanctions, she recalled that trade relations between India and South Africa had been broken off in 1946 by the United Kingdom. The charge of an Indian vendetta against the Union could not be taken seriously in view of the grave concern shown during the discussion by the vast majority of the Member States.

The *Ad Hoc* Political Committee at its 12th meeting on 11 November adopted the joint draft resolution, paragraph by paragraph, by votes ranging from 42 to 1, with 12 abstentions, to 30 to 12, with 16 abstentions, the latter a roll-call vote on the fourth operative paragraph, concerning suspension of the Group Areas Act.

The draft resolution as a whole was adopted by 41 votes to 1, with 16 abstentions.

Consideration by the General Assembly in plenary session

The report of the *Ad Hoc* Political Committee was considered by the General Assembly at its 401st plenary meeting on 5 December 1952. The draft resolution was adopted by a roll-call vote of 41 to 1, with 15 abstentions.

. . .

After the vote, the representative of India said that the continuous disregard by South Africa of previous resolutions of the General Assembly was not calculated to increase confidence in the United Nations. The Assembly was aware of the grave deterioration of the situation in South Africa. His delegation still hoped that the Union would respond to the overwhelming desire of the Assembly. His delegation sought negotiation, conciliation and a peaceful settlement and would persevere in the hope that the conscience of the world would find an echo in South Africa.

The representative of the Union of South Africa concluded the discussion by restating his position. Article 2, paragraph 7, of the Charter denied the Organization the right to intervene in a matter which was essentially within the domestic jurisdiction of his Government. The matter with which the resolution dealt was undeniably such a matter. His Government was not prepared to settle it under the Charter. India knew that all it had to do was to come and discuss the matter outside the Organization and divorced from any resolutions taken by the Organization. That was the standing offer of his Government.

The text of the resolution adopted (615(VII)) read:

"The General Assembly,

"Recalling its resolutions 44(I), 265(III), 395(V) and 511(VI) relating to the treatment of people of Indian origin in the Union of South Africa,

"Noting that the Government of the Union of South Africa has expressed its inability to accept General Assembly resolution 511(VI) in respect of the resumption of negotiations with the Governments of India and Pakistan,

"Noting further that the Government of the Union of South Africa has continued to enforce the Group Areas Act in contravention of the terms of General Assembly resolutions 511(VI) and 395(V),

"1. *Establishes* a United Nations Good Offices Commission consisting of three members to be nominated by the President of the General Assembly, with a view to arranging and assisting in negotiations between the Government of the Union of South Africa and the Governments of India and Pakistan in order that a satisfactory solution of the question in accordance with the Purposes and Principles of the Charter and the Universal Declaration of Human Rights may be achieved;

"2. *Requests* the Good Offices Commission to report to the General Assembly at its eighth session;

"3. *Requests* the Secretary-General to provide the members of the Commission with the necessary staff and facilities;

"4. *Calls upon* the Government of the Union of South Africa to suspend the implementation or enforcement of the provisions of the Group Areas Act, pending the conclusion of the negotiations referred to in paragraph 1 above;

"5. *Decides* to include the item in the provisional agenda of the eighth session of the General Assembly."

At the 411th plenary meeting on 22 December the President of the General Assembly announced the appointment of Cuba, Syria and Yugoslavia as members of the Good Offices Commission.

The question of race conflict in South Africa

On 12 September 1952 Afghanistan, Burma, Egypt, India, Indonesia, Iran, Iraq, Lebanon, Pakistan, the Philippines, Saudi Arabia, Syria and Yemen requested that the question of race conflict in South Africa resulting from the policies of *apartheid* of the Government of the Union of South Africa be placed on the agenda of the seventh session of the General Assembly.

An explanatory memorandum stated that this race conflict in the Union of South Africa was creating a dangerous and explosive situation, which constituted both a threat to international peace and a flagrant violation of the basic principles of human rights and fundamental freedoms enshrined in the Charter. The memorandum said that under the policy of *apartheid*, which implied a permanent white superiority over the 80 per cent of the population who were non-whites, the following measures were being taken: segregation of races under the notorious Group Areas Act, complete segregation in public services, suppression of democratic movements advocating racial equality under the Suppression of Communism Act, barring of non-whites from combat service, withholding of voting or other political rights from non-whites except in Cape Province, confinement of Africans to reserves and restriction of their movement, exclusion of non-whites from skilled work under the Mines Works Amendment Act and provision of vastly inferior educational and housing conditions for non-whites. The policy of *apartheid* not only challenged all that the United Nations stood for but was contrary to specific and repeated recommendations in Assembly resolutions 103(I), 217(III), 395(V) and 511(VI) urging the ending of racial discrimination. Unable to secure redress by constitutional methods, the non-whites of the Union had been compelled to launch a non-violent resistance movement against unjust and inhuman racial policies. It was therefore imperative, the memorandum concluded, that the General Assembly urgently consider the question so as to prevent further deterioration and effect a settlement in accordance with the Charter.

At the 79th meeting of the General Committee on 15 October, the representative of the Union of South Africa protested formally against the inclusion of the item in the agenda. After hearing statements from the representatives of India, Iraq and the United Kingdom the Committee recommended that the item be included.

On 17 October the General Assembly, at its 381st plenary meeting, considered the recommen-

dation of the General Committee. The representative of the Union of South Africa, supported by the representatives of Australia and the United Kingdom, challenged the competence of the Assembly to consider the item and asked that the Assembly decide upon that question before voting on the recommendation of the General Committee to include the item in the agenda. Under rule 80[1] of the rules of procedure, he introduced a draft resolution to the effect that the Assembly, having regard to Article 2, paragraph 7, of the Charter, should decide that it was not competent to consider the item.

The representatives of Chile and Iraq stated that all questions relating to human rights were within the Assembly's competence. Moreover, the representative of Chile argued, the question before the Assembly was the Committee's recommendation for inclusion of the item in the agenda, not the question of competence which could be dismissed only after the item was on the agenda. The President ruled that the proposal of the Union of South Africa was in order. After an appeal against the President's ruling, the latter was over-ruled by a roll-call vote of 41 to 10, with 8 abstentions.

. . .

The representative from South Africa then moved that the item should be excluded from the agenda on the ground that the United Nations was not competent to deal with or even discuss the matter. The General Assembly, by a vote of 45 to 6, with 8 abstentions, decided to accept the General Committee's recommendation to include the item in the agenda.

At its 382nd meeting on 17 October, the General Assembly referred the item to the *Ad Hoc* Political Committee which considered the question at its 13th to 21st meetings from 12 to 20 November 1952.

Consideration by the Ad Hoc Political Committee

The representative of the Union of South Africa outlined the factors which, in his Government's opinion, should preclude discussion of the item. Article 2, paragraph 7, absolutely prohibited any intervention by the United Nations in the domestic affairs of Member States, with the single exception of the application of enforcement measures by the Security Council under Chapter VII. The word "intervene" was not used, he argued, in the narrow restrictive sense of dictatorial interference but included such interference as the discussion of, and passing of resolutions by the Assembly on, the essentially domestic affairs of a Member State. Even the right of discussion conferred on the Assembly by Articles 10 and 11 could

---

[1]Rule 80 states that any motion calling for a decision on the competence of the General Assembly to adopt a proposal submitted to it shall be put to a vote before a vote is taken on the proposal in question.

not be invoked if the discussion constituted such intervention.

The Charter, he argued, left it to each Member individually to decide upon the methods of achieving such objectives mentioned in Article 55 as higher standards of living, full employment and respect for human rights. Action at an international level, on the other hand, was to be taken only by agreement between States. The pledge of international co-operation given in Article 56 to promote the purposes of Article 55 did not diminish the right of States to repel interference in their domestic affairs, or authorize the United Nations to take dictatorial action by way of discussion or resolutions.

Neither the Charter nor the Declaration of Human Rights, which set a standard for future achievement, nor any other international instrument contained a binding definition of human rights against which the actions of the South African Government could be tested.

It had been further alleged, he said, that conditions in South Africa constituted a threat to the peace. But such a threat could exist only when the territorial integrity or political independence of another State was threatened. It was both unrealistic and mischievous to allege the existence of such a threat in consequence of legitimate State action designed to deal with purely domestic matters which did not affect the legitimate interests and rights of other States. If the Committee could be led to believe that racial or other forms of segregation—which existed in a large number of countries—education, housing, conditions of recruitment for the armed services, the administration of justice and other matters referred to in the memorandum were not entirely within the domestic jurisdiction of a State, then the same must hold good for matters such as tariff, immigration and fiscal policies which certainly affected relations between States but which nevertheless continued to be the sole responsibility of the individual government concerned.

Article 2, paragraph 7, he said, served as a counter-balance to the absolute right of veto of the Great Powers and granted to the small nations protection of their inherent right freely to manage their domestic affairs. But for the compromises exemplified for the Great Powers by the right of veto and for the small Powers by Article 2, paragraph 7, there could have been no Charter.

Until such time as the Charter was amended by constitutional means, it must remain inviolate. It would be wise and statesmanlike to reflect carefully before taking any steps likely to result in the disintegration of the United Nations which could still become the greatest bulwark of world peace and security.

Accordingly, the South African representative introduced a motion, under rule 120 of the rules of procedure, whereby the Committee, having regard to Article 2, paragraph 7, would find that it had no competence to consider the item.

The representative of India stressed that the issue of competence could not be considered until the Committee had been enabled to weigh that issue against the background of the facts of *apartheid* policy as practised by the Union of South Africa. *Apartheid* policy, she declared, sought to force the 80 per cent of the population who were non-white into perpetual economic and social servitude by racial discrimination and segregation in violation of human rights and fundamental freedoms and of the principles of the Charter.

After reviewing the principal legislative acts adopted to implement that policy, the Indian representative declared that the non-white population, deprived of legal means to seek redress of its grievances, had begun a campaign of passive resistance. Selected volunteers, after advance notice to the police authorities, defied various laws and regulations deriving from the *apartheid* policy. Over 7,000 persons had sought arrest and been sentenced to imprisonment. Despite great provocation by the police and fanatical white elements, the peaceful character of the movement had been maintained.

The international implications of South African policies, she observed, were clear to all Member States which had pledged themselves to uphold basic principles of the Charter concerning the observance of human rights. The situation was imperilling the entire continent of Africa. Unless the United Nations acted rapidly, the world would be threatened with a new conflict.

India, she concluded, would welcome a study of the situation with a view to assisting the South African Government to resolve it on a humanitarian and rational basis of mutual toleration and understanding among all racial groups. It did not seek to condemn South Africa; it harboured no rancour; it sought only to end a situation as degrading to those who enforced the discrimination laws as to the victims. In addition to the South African motion (see above), the Committee had before it:

(1) *An eighteen-Power joint draft resolution* by Afghanistan, Bolivia, Burma, Egypt, Guatemala, Haiti, Honduras, India, Indonesia, Iran, Iraq, Lebanon, Liberia, Pakistan, Philippines, Syria, Saudi Arabia and Yemen, by which the General Assembly would:

(1) note the communication by thirteen Members on the question of race conflict in South Africa; (2) state that one of the purposes of the United Nations was to achieve international co-operation in promoting and encouraging respect for human rights and fundamental freedom for all; (3) recall its resolution 103(I) calling on all governments to take energetic

steps to end religious and so-called racial persecution; (4) refer to its resolutions 395(V) and 511(VI) holding that a policy of *apartheid* was based on doctrines of racial discrimination; and (5) state that international co-operation could not be furthered and that international peace might be disturbed by policies of racial discrimination and persecution. In its operative part the draft resolution would have the Assembly: (1) establish a commission to study the international aspects and implications of the racial situation in the Union of South Africa in the light of the Charter and the resolutions of the United Nations on racial persecution and discrimination, and to report its findings to the eighth session of the Assembly; (2) invite the Union of South Africa to co-operate with the commission; and (3) decide to retain the question on the agenda of the eighth session.

(2)   *A joint draft resolution by Denmark, Iceland, Norway and Sweden* which consisted of the first three paragraphs of the eighteen-Power joint draft resolution and four new paragraphs.

These four new paragraphs, which had originally been moved as an amendment to the eighteen-Power draft to replace the last two paragraphs of the preamble and all but the last paragraph of the operative part, would have the General Assembly, recognizing that the methods of Members for giving effect to their Charter pledges might vary with circumstances such as the social structure of the States concerned and the different stages of development of the various groups within the country:

(1)   declare that in a multi-racial society, respect for human rights and the peaceful development of a unified community were best assured when patterns of legislation and practice were directed towards ensuring equality before the law of all persons, and when economic, social, cultural and political participation of all racial groups was on a basis of equality; (2) affirm that governmental policies not directed towards those goals were inconsistent with pledges of Members under Article 56 of the Charter; and (3) call upon all Members to bring their policies into conformity with their Charter obligations to promote the observance of human rights and fundamental freedoms.

The representatives of Denmark, Norway and Sweden explained the position of the Scandinavian countries. While they could not subscribe to the rather extreme position taken by the South African representative on the Assembly's competence, they could not agree, also, to all the provisions of the eighteen-Power draft resolution. They felt that the United Nations, in matters of racial discrimination, could make recommendations but was not competent to prescribe specific measures to be imposed on a State. The establishment of a fact-finding commission, they considered, was a step on which the Assembly lacked jurisdiction. Moreover, such a commission was not likely to achieve any practical results. These representatives affirmed the competence of the Assembly to discuss the question, stating that the Charter imposed on Members the obligation not to bar discussion or adoption of recommendations by the United Nations on their policies in the field of human rights. They cited previous Assembly recommendations on racial policies of Member States as well as recommendations for the investigation of alleged forced labour, despite objections regarding competence.

As regards the merits of the question, the representative of Norway stated that he could not accept the South African representative's contention that the matters complained of did not constitute a violation of human rights and fundamental freedoms as laid down in the Charter. Mere reading of the Group Areas Act, he maintained, appeared to justify the claim that the Act legalized actions which all Member States had pledged to abandon.

(3)   The following amendments to the eighteen-Power joint draft resolution were also placed before the Committee:

(a)   *An amendment by Brazil* which would alter the terms of reference of the proposed commission by directing it to study the racial situation in the Union of South Africa "with due regard to the provisions of Article 2, paragraph 7", and to report its "conclusions" instead of its "findings" to the General Assembly. The representative of Brazil explained that the proposed amendment was to remove all misunderstanding concerning the powers of the proposed commission and the competence of the Assembly. The Committee he said, must respect the limitation imposed upon it by the Charter and must not encroach upon the domestic jurisdiction of States.

(b)   *An amendment by Ecuador* which would: (1) eliminate from the study of the proposed commission examination of "the international aspects and implications of" the racial situation in order, as its representative said, to make the proposal less controversial; (2) delete the last paragraph of the preamble which, he stated, prejudged the question to be studied by prescribing a strong criterion for that study; and (3) also delete the last operative paragraph providing for retention of the question on the agenda of the eighth session.

(c)   *An amendment by Israel* which would have the proposed commission report "its conclusions to the Secretary-General for transmission to the Members of the United Nations" instead of report "its findings to the eighth session of the General Assembly". The representative of Israel felt that to perpetuate items by placing them on the agenda year after year, without regard to intervening developments, might be harmful and was a practice which should be discouraged.

(d)   *An oral proposal by Mexico* which would supplement the first part of the Brazilian amendment by directing the commission to study the racial situation with due regard not only to the provisions of Article 2, paragraph 7, but also to the provisions of Article

1, paragraph 3, Article 13, paragraph 1 (b), Article 55 (c) and Article 56 of the Charter. The proposed commission would thus, the representative of Mexico said, be given balanced terms of reference; it would have an adequate legal basis on which to operate; it would be taking account of the Charter guarantee against intervention in domestic affairs, on the one hand, and of the Charter guarantees regarding human rights, on the other hand. The representative of Brazil accepted the amendment.

(e) *A USSR amendment* to the first operative paragraph which proposed that the commission to be set up should study the racial situation not only in the light of the Charter provisions enumerated but also in the light of Article 1, paragraph 2, which proclaimed that one of the purposes of the United Nations was to develop friendly relations among the nations based on respect for the principle of equal rights and self-determination of peoples.

The representative of India submitted, on behalf of the sponsors, and after consultation with the representatives of Brazil, Ecuador and Mexico, a revision of the eighteen-Power joint draft resolution which deleted from the original text the last paragraph of the preamble and amended the terms of reference of the commission proposed in the first operative paragraph, thus incorporating the Brazilian amendment and the first two parts of the Ecuadorean amendment. The representative of Ecuador withdrew the third part of his amendment. At the same time the representative of India suggested on behalf of the sponsors that, so far as the membership of the proposed commission was concerned, the President of the General Assembly should nominate as members three persons from a panel of experts on race relations selected by the sponsors of the draft and submitted to the President before the item was dealt with in plenary meeting.

The representatives of Australia, Belgium, France, New Zealand, and the United Kingdom supported, in general, the position of South Africa on the meaning of the Charter provision on domestic jurisdiction and the nature of international commitments on human rights. They were of the opinion that the policy of *apartheid* in South Africa was not a threat to the peace and that the suggested Assembly action was both improper and dangerous to the United Nations and unlikely to contribute to a solution of the problem. They held that United Nations interference, even to the extent of discussion, could only exacerbate racial antagonism in the Union of South Africa and might even be harmful to international relations, thus defeating the very purposes which the sponsors of the item had hoped to achieve.

Nothing, it was stated, was more obviously a matter of a country's domestic jurisdiction than the relationship which it had decided to maintain between persons of varying races living within its borders. If the General Assembly was considered in the present instance to be competent under Articles 55 and 56, it must in strict logic be regarded as having jurisdiction to deal not only with human rights but also with the economic, social and cultural activities referred to in Article 55. In other words, no aspect of the internal affairs of a State would be free from interference by the Organization.

Clearly, the purpose of any discussion or resolution was to modify a situation and that was precisely the meaning of the word "intervention". Article 2, paragraph 7, therefore applied to such discussion.

Even if it was argued that the situation in South Africa had become a matter of world interest, it could not be seriously claimed that thereby it became removed from the sphere of domestic jurisdiction to the international jurisdiction of the United Nations. Indignation at policies of racial or social discrimination pursued by certain governments, however well-founded, was not sufficient to make a question a threat to international peace. No flood of refugees had crossed from South Africa to a neighbouring State. On the contrary, statistics indicated that each year 100,000 Africans entered the Union of South Africa of their own free will. Except for New Zealand which abstained on all draft resolutions, these representatives supported the South African draft resolution but abstained on the others.

In reply, the representative of India said that one of the purposes of the United Nations, as stated in Article 1, paragraph 3, of the Charter, was to promote respect for human rights and fundamental freedoms for all. Under Article 10, the Assembly could discuss any question within the scope of the Charter and make recommendations on it to the Members. Moreover, Article 13 required the Assembly to initiate studies and make recommendations to assist in the realization of human rights for all. Under Article 14, the Assembly could recommend measures for the peaceful adjustment of a situation resulting from a violation of the provisions of the Charter. Respect for human rights having been included in the Charter, any infringement of those rights was a matter within the Assembly's competence. Article 55 of the Charter also required the United Nations to promote respect for human rights and fundamental freedoms for all. Its Members had pledged themselves under Article 56 to take action in co-operation with the Organization for the achievement of those purposes. Finally, Article 2, paragraph 2, stated that Members should fulfil in good faith the obligations assumed by them in accordance with the Charter. Thus the provisions of the Charter clearly established the competence of the Assembly to consider the question under discussion. Acceptance of the contention that the Assembly was not competent would open to challenge the validity of all the decisions by the General Assembly relating to the infringement of human rights.

The General Assembly was also empowered to consider the question under Article 11 of the Charter because the situation in South Africa resulting from the policy of *apartheid* was grave and clearly constituted a threat to international peace, the maintenance of which was one of the primary purposes of the United Nations. The concept of a threat to peace was not confined to the case of a threat to the territorial integrity and political independence of a State. Flagrant breaches of human rights by the government of a State could have serious repercussions outside that State and could affect international peace.

Turning to the argument that Article 2, paragraph 7, precluded the General Assembly from considering the item, the representative of India said that there were two essential prerequisites to its application. First, there must be intervention by the United Nations and, secondly, the matter in question must be essentially within the domestic jurisdiction of a State.

"Intervention" in this connexion had been authoritatively defined, he said, as a legal measure applied by the United Nations and accompanied by enforcement or threat of enforcement. In his opinion, Article 2, paragraph 7, did not preclude a consideration of situations arising from violations of human rights nor prevent the Assembly from making recommendations on such situations.

Concerning the word "essential" as used in Article 2, paragraph 7, he observed that international law maintained a clear distinction between matters within the domestic jurisdiction of a State and those which had passed into the international domain. A matter ordinarily within the domestic jurisdiction of a State could cease to be so and become the subject of an international obligation if, for example, it formed part of the terms of a treaty. The Charter was a multilateral treaty; the question of human rights and fundamental freedoms had therefore passed into the international domain. Thus the policy of *apartheid* had become a matter of international concern and could not be treated as being essentially within the domestic jurisdiction.

As neither of the two prerequisites existed necessary to the application of Article 2, paragraph 7, the Assembly was competent to act.

A large majority of the Committee, including the sponsors of the eighteen-Power resolution, joined with India in expressing, with varying degrees of emphasis and frequently with illustrations drawn from their national experience, their moral indignation at the policy of racial inequality in the Union of South Africa. Specifying their views on how it violated the Charter and created conditions which

were a threat to international peace, they affirmed the competence of the United Nations and the need for constructive action. Apart from the representatives of the eighteen Powers sponsoring the joint draft resolution, this majority included the representatives of Bolivia, Brazil, the Byelorussian SSR, Chile, Cuba, Czechoslovakia, Ecuador, El Salvador, Ethiopia, Israel, Mexico, Poland, Saudi Arabia, Syria, the Ukrainian SSR, the USSR, Uruguay and Yugoslavia. They opposed the South African resolution, supported the eighteen-Power draft resolution and abstained on the Scandinavian draft resolution, except for the Byelorussian SSR, Czechoslovakia, Mexico, Poland, the Ukrainian SSR and the USSR which opposed the latter.

Speaking as a sponsor of the eighteen-Power draft resolution, the representative of Pakistan said that by lowering the status of the original inhabitants of South Africa to the advantage of a minority representing the conquerors of that country, the Government of the Union of South Africa was practising a form of colonialism against which a struggle was being waged in the United Nations. The present dispute as regards the Assembly's competence was a part of that struggle. When asked to alter their inflexible policies, the European colonial Powers and their friends immediately raised the issue of United Nations competence. On the other hand, he said, the support of most North and South American countries was heartening. The representative of Pakistan warned the colonial Powers that attempts to enforce their position by raising legal technicalities, by brute force and by inhuman laws would finally result in an inevitable bloody clash. The strong moral right of the African peoples to rebel could not be denied. Fortunately, he concluded, the United Nations possessed the means and the wisdom to transform what would otherwise be a bloody revolution into a bloodless one.

While recognizing that the situations existing in many Member States were very far from the Charter ideal, several representatives, including those of Costa Rica, Cuba, Haiti, Liberia and Uruguay stated that their Governments were doing everything in their power to remedy the situation. Unfortunately the Union of South Africa, on the other hand, it was stated, was taking action that aggravated still further the discrimination existing in that country and refused to discuss the substance of the question. To show that it was possible to achieve co-operation between all the racial groups in a country, representatives cited the examples of Ecuador, Mexico, Indonesia and Haiti. It was said that the Union Government's uncompromising attitude had made such co-operation impossible for the time being.

Many supporters emphasized that they wished to have friendly relations with the Union of South Africa and that they had no intention of intervening in its internal affairs. The eighteen-Power draft resolution, said the representative of Mexico, was not intended to offend or condemn South Africa. Mexico was not voting against any nation but for a principle and against the violation of that principle. The proposed commission, said the representative of Indonesia, was a moderate and realistic approach which would help place the problem in its true perspective.

In expressing their strong support for the eighteen-Power draft resolution, the representatives of the USSR and other Eastern European States particularly stressed the connexion between racial discrimination and colonialism.

The representatives of Czechoslovakia and the USSR stated that the racial policies of the South African Government were designed to perpetuate the colonial domination of its ruling circles over oppressed and exploited peoples. The Union Government's policy, they maintained, represented a systematic and conscious violation of the Charter and its consequences were a threat to international peace and security.

The representative of the USSR added that the proposed commission might not only contribute to a solution of the South African problem, but to the elimination of racial persecution in other countries. He expressed the position of the Eastern European governments when he opposed all amendments attempting to weaken the original text and criticized strongly the Scandinavian draft resolution which, he declared, consisted of pious hopes designed to cover up South Africa's violation of the Charter. His Government vigorously rejected its reflection of the view that, while increasing restrictions were objectionable, existing restrictions might be countenanced.

During the debate, the representative of Liberia proposed that the Committee hear a native of South Africa, Professor Z. K. Matthews, an authorized representative of the African National Congress. The Chairman appealed to him not to press his request in order not to create a precedent by granting a hearing to a private individual in a political committee and because he could have a letter from Professor Matthews circulated as a Committee document. On 19 November, at the request of the delegation of Haiti, a letter from Professor Matthews, dated 17 November, was circulated in which he stated that he had been instructed by his college in South Africa, which had been subjected to warning pressure by the Union Government, not to accept an invitation to appear.

A number of representatives, including those of Canada, China, Peru and the United States, supported the Scandinavian compromise proposal. They expressed the conviction that the United Nations was competent to discuss racial policy of a Member State but questioned the correctness or the desirability, in terms of actually improving race relations

in South Africa, of doing more than appeal to all Member States to bring their policies into conformity with the Charter obligation of promoting the observance of human rights.

The representative of the United States maintained that the South African representative's interpretation of Article 2, paragraph 7, narrowed excessively the scope of the Assembly's powers to discuss the vital question of human rights. The representative of Canada added that it also impaired the Assembly's right to make recommendations for the peaceful adjustment of any situation deemed likely to impair friendly relations among nations. They, however, felt that the Assembly should proceed with great caution. The representative of the United States questioned the wisdom of the South African Government, however, in adopting a policy of racial segregation at a time when world trends were against it. He considered that a policy of increased restriction was incompatible with the generally accepted interpretation of the obligations of the Charter.

The representative of Peru felt that, until an effective legal instrument obliging nations to implement human rights had been ratified, the General Assembly, in exercise of what might be called its moral jurisdiction, could do no more than appeal to the goodwill of States to promote their observance. Any coercion would exacerbate South African nationalism and tend to stiffen the resistance of the South African Government.

A number of representatives, including those of Canada, Denmark, Iceland, the Netherlands, New Zealand, Norway, Sweden and Turkey, remarked that they would support a request for an advisory opinion from the International Court of Justice on the question of competence. The representative of Denmark declared that, in the absence of such an authoritative legal opinion and because of the divergence of views on competence, even if the matter was of great concern to many Member States, the General Assembly should proceed with the greatest caution.

In a final statement, the Indian representative said that the facts adduced by the sponsoring delegations of the eighteen-Power draft resolution had not been controverted. All the arguments against this draft had been on the purely legal ground of competence. Concerning doubts expressed about the establishment and effectiveness of a commission, he said that, even if the Union Government did not co-operate, the commission could still collect and examine legislation and other evidences regarding the problem. It was the duty of the United Nations to study the situation. As to the Scandinavian draft resolution, there seemed little object in reinstating declarations, however praiseworthy, which had already been made in the Charter and in many previous Assembly recommendations. The question before the Committee referred to the specific policy of *apartheid* in the Union of South Africa and called for a specific solution.

In his concluding remarks, the representative of South Africa described Article 2, paragraph 7, as a safeguard against the use of the United Nations as a means of prosecuting feuds and rivalries in the spotlight of a world organization. Such absolute insurance against intervention was necessary because widely divergent domestic problems could not be solved by a single universal approach. There was as yet no legally binding international instrument on human rights. The Charter called only for their promotion through international co-operation.

Certain representatives, he said, seemed to consider that the Charter might be interpreted to suit changing events. But the United Nations had no right to act as a supra-national organization and to usurp the sovereignty of individual Members. His Government recognized the dynamic nature of the United Nations, but it persisted in its adherence to certain constant principles, such as the San Francisco interpretation of the Charter.

The charge that the alleged happenings in South Africa threatened the peace was without foundation and a reprehensible attempt to persuade the United Nations to intervene in domestic affairs.

It was not true that conditions in South Africa were leading to a general conflagration on the African Continent. If, however, the South African Government were to allow the agitators and their foreign masters to go about their subversive work, the situation might indeed become serious.

On 20 November the *Ad Hoc* Political Committee proceeded to vote on the draft resolutions and the amendments.

The motion submitted by the Union of South Africa was rejected by a roll-call vote of 45 to 6, with 8 abstentions.

The USSR amendment to the eighteen-Power draft resolution was adopted by 29 votes to 5, with 23 abstentions. The amendment of Israel was rejected by 33 votes to 2, with 23 abstentions. The various paragraphs of the eighteen-Power draft resolution were adopted by votes ranging from 44 to 1, with 12 abstentions, to 32 to 7, with 18 abstentions. The joint draft resolution as a whole, as amended, was adopted by a roll-call vote of 35 to 2, with 22 abstentions.

The Committee then voted, paragraph by paragraph, on the joint draft resolution submitted by Denmark, Iceland, Norway and Sweden. All paragraphs were adopted except the last paragraph of the preamble recognizing that the methods for giving effect to their Charter pledges might vary with circumstances such as the social structure of the State concerned. That paragraph was rejected by a vote of 20 to 17, with 21 abstentions.

The draft resolution as a whole, as modified, was approved by a roll-call vote of 20 to 7, with 42 abstentions.

*Consideration by the
General Assembly in plenary session*

The report of the *Ad Hoc* Political Committee was considered by the General Assembly at its 401st plenary meeting on 5 December 1952. The representative of the Union of South Africa introduced a motion under rule 80 of the rules of procedure by which the Assembly would, in view of the Charter provisions on the question of domestic jurisdiction, declare itself unable to adopt either of the two draft resolutions recommended in the report. The motion was rejected by a roll-call vote of 43 to 6, with 9 abstentions.

. . .

The Assembly then voted on resolution A recommended by the *Ad Hoc* Political Committee (originally the eighteen-Power draft resolution). The first operative paragraph establishing a commission was voted on by roll-call and adopted by 35 votes to 17, with 7 abstentions.

. . .

The draft resolution as a whole was adopted by a roll-call vote of 35 to 1, with 23 abstentions.

. . .

Before the voting on resolution B (originally the joint draft resolution by Denmark, Iceland, Norway and Sweden), the representative of Mexico expressed opposition to including the first paragraph of the preamble, referring to the specific situation in South Africa, in a resolution which, he said, was a noble general declaration of principles on matters of racial discrimination. He requested a separate vote on that paragraph.

The paragraph was adopted by 25 votes to 10, with 18 abstentions.

The draft resolution as a whole was adopted by a roll-call vote of 24 to 1, with 34 abstentions.

. . .

The representatives of the United Kingdom, France, India, and the Union of South Africa explained their votes.

The representatives of France and the United Kingdom stated that, in the view of their delegations, the placing of the item on the agenda and all discussion on the substance of it was out of order, as the matter was essentially within the domestic jurisdiction of South Africa. They had accordingly abstained from voting on the two draft resolutions except on the first operative paragraph of Draft Resolution A, establishing a commission. They had voted against this paragraph, since they considered it a clear violation of Article 2, paragraph 7, of the Charter.

The representative of India declared that India had abstained on Resolution B because it did not have a direct bearing on the issue of race conflict in South Africa. The Assembly, she continued, could not shut its eyes to the fact that in South Africa there was an ever growing intensification of the policy of racial discrimination through all channels open to a government. Human rights and fundamental freedoms were being denied on the grounds of race and colour to an overwhelming majority by a small minority which retained all the resources of the State in its hands. All Member States must rally whenever the principles and purposes of the Charter were challenged. Africa and Asia would no longer accept the indignities imposed on them in the name of a white civilization. The demand was for a human civilization based on the universal standards of the Charter.

The representative of the Union of South Africa stated that, in adopting the two resolutions, the Assembly had not only denied to his Government its rights under the Charter but had clearly established a precedent in consequence of which it would in future seek to intervene by discussion and the adoption of resolutions on any matter of purely domestic concern. He had been instructed by his Government, he said, to state that it would continue to claim the protection inscribed in Article 2, paragraph 7, of the Charter and that it must therefore regard any resolution emanating from a discussion on, or the consideration of, the present item as *ultra vires* and, therefore, as null and void.

The resolutions adopted by the Assembly (616 A & B (VII)) read:

A

"*The General Assembly,*

"*Having taken note* of the communication dated 12 September 1952, addressed to the Secretary-General of the United Nations by the delegations of Afghanistan, Burma, Egypt, India, Indonesia, Iran, Iraq, Lebanon, Pakistan, the Philippines, Saudi Arabia, Syria and Yemen, regarding the question of race conflict in South Africa resulting from the policies of *apartheid* of the Government of the Union of South Africa,

"*Considering* that one of the purposes of the United Nations is to achieve international co-operation in promoting and encouraging respect for human rights and fundamental freedoms for all, without distinction as to race, sex, language or religion,

"*Recalling* that the General Assembly declared in its resolution 103(I) of 19 November 1946 that it is in the higher interests of humanity to put an end to religious and so-called racial persecution, and called upon all governments to conform both to the letter and the spirit of the Charter and to take the most prompt and energetic steps to that end,

"*Considering* that the General Assembly has held, in its resolutions 395(V) of 2 December 1950 and 511(VI) of 12 January 1952, that a policy of racial segregation

(*apartheid*) is necessarily based on doctrines of racial discrimination,

"1. *Establishes* a Commission, consisting of three members, to study the racial situation in the Union of South Africa in the light of the Purposes and Principles of the Charter, with due regard to the provision of Article 2, paragraph 7, as well as the provisions of Article 1, paragraphs 2 and 3, Article 13, paragraph 1 b, Article 55 c, and Article 56 of the Charter, and the resolutions of the United Nations on racial persecution and discrimination, and to report its conclusions to the General Assembly at its eighth session;

"2. *Invites* the Government of the Union of South Africa to extend its full co-operation to the Commission;

"3. *Requests* the Secretary-General to provide the Commission with the necessary staff and facilities;

"4. *Decides* to retain the question on the provisional agenda of the eighth session of the General Assembly."

B

"*The General Assembly,*

"*Having taken note* of the communication dated 12 September 1952, addressed to the Secretary-General of the United Nations by the delegations of Afghanistan, Burma, Egypt, India, Indonesia, Iran, Iraq, Lebanon, Pakistan, the Philippines, Saudi Arabia, Syria and Yemen, regarding the question of race conflict in South Africa resulting from the policies of *apartheid* of the Government of the Union of South Africa,

"*Considering* that one of the purposes of the United Nations is to achieve international co-operation in promoting and encouraging respect for human rights and fundamental freedoms for all, without distinction as to race, sex, language or religion,

"*Recalling* that the General Assembly declared in its resolution 103(I) of 19 November 1946 that it is in the higher interests of humanity to put an end to religious and so-called racial persecution, and called upon all governments to conform both to the letter and to the spirit of the Charter and to take the most prompt and energetic steps to that end,

"1. *Declares* that in a multi-racial society harmony and respect for human rights and freedoms and the peaceful development of a unified community are best assured when patterns of legislation and practice are directed towards ensuring equality before the law of all persons regardless of race, creed or colour, and when economic, social, cultural and political participation of all racial groups is on a basis of equality;

"2. *Affirms* that governmental policies of Member States which are not directed towards these goals, but which are designed to perpetuate or increase discrimination, are inconsistent with the pledges of the Members under Article 56 of the Charter;

"3. *Solemnly calls upon* all Member States to bring their policies into conformity with their obligation under the Charter to promote the observance of human rights and fundamental freedoms."

At its 411th plenary meeting on 21 December 1952, the General Assembly, on the proposal of the President, decided that the Commission, established under paragraph 1 of resolution 616 A (VII) should be composed of the following persons: Ralph Bunche, Hernán Santa Cruz and Jaime Torres Bodet.[2]

[YUN 1952, pp. 291-306]

Sharpeville massacre

On 21 March 1960, at Sharpeville, South African police fired on peaceful demonstrators protesting the requirement that all Africans carry "reference books", killing 69 people and wounding 180 others. As a result, the Security Council took up the question of apartheid for the first time on 30 March 1960 when it met to consider the incident at the request of 29 African and Asian Member States. Subsequently, the General Assembly proclaimed 21 March as the International Day for the Elimination of Racial Discrimination, to be observed annually.

Consideration by Security Council

On 25 March 1960, the representatives of 29 African and Asian Members of the United Nations requested an urgent meeting of the Security Council "to consider the situation arising out of the large-scale killings of unarmed and peaceful demonstrators against racial discrimination and segregation in the Union of South Africa." They considered that the situation had grave potentialities for international friction, which endangered the maintenance of international peace and security.

The 29 states requesting the meeting were: Afghanistan, Burma, Cambodia, Ceylon, Ethiopia, the Federation of Malaya, Ghana, Guinea, India, Indonesia, Iran, Iraq, Japan, Jordan, Laos, Lebanon, Liberia, Libya, Morocco, Nepal, Pakistan, the Philippines, Saudi Arabia, Sudan, Thailand, Tunisia, Turkey, the United Arab Republic and Yemen.

On 30 March, the Security Council decided, without objection, to place the matter on its agenda on the same day. It discussed the matter at six meetings between 30 March and 1 April 1960.

The representatives of Ethiopia, Ghana, Guinea, India, Jordan, Liberia, Pakistan and the Union of South Africa were invited to participate, without a vote, in its deliberations.

The Council's decision to place the item on its agenda was the subject of comment by several speakers.

The representatives of France and the United Kingdom, deploring the "tragic incidents" in South Africa, stated that the fact that they had not opposed the decision to place the item on the Council's agenda did not mean that they had abandoned their traditional stand that nothing in the United Nations Charter authorized the United Nations to intervene in matters falling essentially within the domestic jurisdiction of a Member state. The French representative added that France had always disapproved strongly of practices of racial discrimination and segregation.

The representative of Italy felt that there were some contradictions within the Charter itself between the need to give practical expression to the Charter provisions concerning human rights and fundamental freedoms and those which aimed at protecting states from interference in their internal affairs. Italy's stand was determined by the special political circumstances which appeared to justify some kind of exceptional procedure.

The USSR representative pointed out that the question of United Nations competence in the matter had been settled long ago and that the General Assembly had repeatedly called upon the Union Government to review its *apartheid* policy. These latest events were a new development and endangered the maintenance of peace in the African continent.

The United States representative, explaining why his Government favoured Council consideration of the recent events in South Africa, said, among other things, that in a situation such as that existing in South Africa, Article 2(7) of the Charter (which precludes United Nations intervention in matters essentially within the jurisdiction of any state) had to be read in the light of Articles 55 and 56 (dealing with the promotion of respect for human rights and fundamental freedoms, among other things).

The representative of the Union of South Africa protested against the refusal to hear the Union's views on the question of placing the item on the Council's agenda. Including the item in the agenda was, in his view, a violation of the basic principle enshrined in Article 2(7) of the United Nations Charter.

He rejected the argument that recent events in South Africa constituted a situation which might lead to international friction or give rise to a dispute likely to endanger international peace and security. For such an eventuality, there had to be at least two parties which, within the framework of the Charter, had to be sovereign independent states. South Africa, he said, had no intention of provoking such a dispute or creating such a situation.

Apart from legal objections, the South African representative wondered why, when so many disturbances and riots leading to serious losses of life had occurred throughout the world during the past 12 months, the Union of South Africa had been singled out. He also wondered whether all Members favouring inclusion of the item in the agenda

---

[2]On 30 March 1953 the General Assembly, on the proposal of the President, decided to appoint Henri Laugier of France and Dantès Bellegarde of Haiti to replace Ralph Bunche and Jaime Torres Bodet on the Commission, as the last two named were unable to serve on that body.

would, in their turn, willingly submit their efforts to maintain law and order in their own countries to consideration by the Council.

As to the reference made to the mass killing of unarmed and peaceful demonstrators against racially discriminatory and segregationist laws in South Africa, he said that the Union Government had already arranged for full judicial inquiries to be made. It was also considering the appointment of a commission to inquire into the contributory factors and deal with broader aspects of the problem.

The South African representative went on to explain that a splinter organization of extremists had organized a mass demonstration to protest against the carrying of reference books, a system which had been instituted when the pass system was abolished in 1952; these books were for identification and applied to men and women of all races. By intimidation, these extremists had managed to gather a group of approximately 20,000 persons in Sharpeville and about 6,000 in Langa. The police had been instructed to exercise normal control, but the demonstrators had threatened the police and then attacked them with various weapons. The police had been forced to fire in self-defence, he went on, in order to forestall greater bloodshed.

The Union Government, he stressed, considered that the annual discussion of South Africa's racial policies in the United Nations had inflamed the situation; if the present discussion served as an incitement to further demonstrations and riots, the blame would fall squarely on the Council.

In conclusion, he said that since the item had been placed on the agenda, he would have to report to his government for further instructions.

Spokesmen in the Council for those delegations which had brought the situation before the Council maintained that the Council was competent to discuss the matter. Among the points made in this connexion were the following: The tragic happenings in South Africa had international ramifications and created a threat to the maintenance of international peace and security. These events—which had caused world-wide concern, which had potentialities for international friction and disharmony and which were directly opposed to the spirit and letter of the United Nations Charter—could not be brought within the strait jacket of Article 2(7) of the Charter. They were directly attributable to the Union Government's *apartheid* policy which the United Nations General Assembly had repeatedly condemned. Moreover, Article 2(7) of the Charter could not be invoked to prevent United Nations organs from fulfilling their duties under Articles 55 and 56, which dealt with promoting respect for human rights and freedoms.

These points were among those made variously by the spokesmen for Ceylon, Ethiopia, Ghana, Guinea, India, Jordan, Liberia, Pakistan and Tunisia.

Also reviewed—by the representatives of Tunisia and India, among others—were the events which had come to the Council's attention. It was pointed out that a peaceful campaign had been launched on 21 March 1960 in a number of South African towns in protest against the requirement that all Africans carry passes at all times in order to move about in their own country. Africans had left their passes at home and convened peacefully before the offices of police commissioners to allow themselves to be arrested for failure to carry passes. In the township of Vereeniging, demonstrators moving towards the police office were halted by police using tear-gas bombs and opening fire in order to disperse the peaceful population. In Sharpeville, the police had brought in armoured vehicles which fired at the crowd while jet fighter planes had flown overhead to scatter and frighten the demonstrators. Accounts from eyewitnesses and official sources varied, but a conservative figure was 74 dead and 184 wounded for the one day of 21 March. The Union Government's allegations that the demonstrators had fired at the police was only self-exculpatory and designed to appease the mounting protest of world opinion.

The world had been stirred by these tragic incidents, not only because of the brutal intervention of the police against peaceful demonstrators, but also because of the dire consequences thus illustrated of the systematic and resolute policy of racial discrimination and of its dangers and risks to world peace.

At one point in the debate, Tunisia proposed that the President of the Council ask the South African representative, who had absented himself from the Council table, whether he wished to reply and thereby continue to take part in the discussion. The United Kingdom representative said it could be assumed that the South African representative would be receiving instructions and would therefore be in a position to say whether he would return to the Council table.

The Tunisian motion was not carried for lack of the required majority, the vote being 6 for and 0 against, with 5 abstentions.

In the course of the subsequent discussion, the United Kingdom representative said that his Government recognized the indisputable right and duty of any government to use the forces at its disposal to maintain law and order in its own territory. It was equally conscious of the strong feelings of concern which the events in South Africa on 21 March had produced in many parts of the world, including the United Kingdom, the policy of which in Africa was non-racial. But the problem of racial adjustment was not easy. The Council, he said, should be guided by the effect which its deliberations would have on the situation and on the people concerned. Attempts from the outside to impose changes in the internal policies of a government, particularly one of strong nationalist feeling, were likely to produce an effect contrary to that intended. He urged the Council not to do anything that would make the situation in South Africa worse.

The representative of China appealed to the Union Government to reverse its *apartheid* policy which was the main cause of the tragic events of 21 March. In the present case, his delegation, which had always urged the need for reconciliation and recognized that racial prejudice could not be abolished with a single stroke, was interested more in reconstruction than in condemnation.

The representative of France, stressing the principle of full equality of all men, said that a solution could not be imposed from outside. He hoped that the South African Government would take the road of a liberal evolution and that, at the same time, the African organizations in that country would exercise the greatest restraint and moderation so as to prevent the recurrence of the tragic events.

The Italian representative, pointing out that his country had always opposed racial discrimination, thought that the difficult problems of a multiracial society should not be belittled. The Council should be careful in proceeding further; for any action, not properly weighed, could frustrate hopes for favourable developments.

The USSR representative, ascribing the events in South Africa to policies of racial discrimination, declared that the Council was duty-bound to condemn the inhuman actions of the South African authorities and warn them of the possible consequences of these actions. The Council should take immediate steps to end the situation in South Africa and to ensure that the African peoples there be given all their rights in accordance with the Charter and the Universal Declaration of Human Rights.

The representative of Argentina pointed out that whereas the General Assembly had been able to disapprove and ask for reconsideration of South Africa's racial policies, the position of the Council was different. The Council was acting by virtue of Article 35, paragraph 1, of the United Nations Charter (which, among other things, permits any Member State to bring to the Council's attention any dispute or any situation which might lead to international friction). The Council should adopt decisions which made an effective contribution towards improving the situation in South Africa.

The representative of Poland, criticizing the Union Government's *apartheid* policies, considered it the Council's duty to help in establishing peace in South Africa through the creation of a rule of human rights.

On 31 March 1960, Ecuador proposed a draft resolution whereby the Council, recognizing that the situation complained of resulted from the Union Government's racial policies and its continued disregard of the General Assembly's resolutions calling for a revision of these policies, would, among other things: (1) recognize that the situation in South Africa had led to international friction, and, if continued, might endanger international peace and security; (2) deplore the fact that the recent disturbances in the Union should have led to the loss of life of so many Africans and extend its deepest sympathies to the families of the victims; (3) deplore the Union Government's policies and actions which had given rise to the present situation; (4) call upon the Union Government to initiate measures aimed at bringing about racial harmony based on equality in order to ensure that the present situation did not continue or recur and to abandon its policies of *apartheid* and racial discrimination; and (5) request the Secretary-General, in consultation with the Union Government, to take such measures as would adequately help in upholding the purposes and principles of the Charter and to report to the Security Council whenever necessary and appropriate.

In support of the draft resolution, the United States representative stated that, while his country realized that the problems of the multiracial society were difficult and took a long period to solve, it nevertheless felt that a new beginning could be made in South Africa.

The USSR representative said that he would vote for the draft resolution although he felt that the paragraph requesting certain measures of the Secretary-General tended to shift responsibility from the Council to the Secretary-General. The Council had recognized the existence of a situation that might endanger international peace and security, and the draft resolution should propose measures whereby the Council could rectify the situation.

The Tunisian representative considered that the draft resolution represented the strict minimum compatible with the Council's heavy responsibilities and with the gravity of the situation. The representative of Italy supported it because it reflected the political and moral principles which had guided the Council's debate and did not exceed the limits of the Charter.

Reiterating his earlier arguments about the Council's competence to consider the question, the representative of South Africa stated that his Government would view in a serious light any resolution by the Council in regard to the local disturbances.

On 1 April 1960, the Council adopted Ecuador's resolution by 9 votes to 0, with 2 abstentions (France and the United Kingdom).

Explaining his abstention, the United Kingdom representative said that the resolution went beyond the scope of the proper function of the Council and that it would have been more effective if the weighty discussion in the Council had been left to make its own impact. The representative of France, while strongly disapproving of the policy of racial discrimination, had doubts about the legitimacy and the timeliness of the action proposed in the resolution.

Various representatives of the Governments that had been invited to participate in the Council's debate indicated that they had wished for a stronger resolution. The Council had, however, recognized that the situation in South Africa had led to international friction which, if continued, might endanger international peace and security. They hoped that the Council would continue to have the problem before it and that the Union Government would make the resolution the starting point of a new chapter in race relations in South Africa.

Subsequent developments

On 19 April 1960, the Secretary-General submitted an interim report informing the Council that he had accepted a proposal of the Union Government for preliminary consultations with the Prime Minister and the Union's Minister of External Affairs in London. These consultations would be preliminary to a visit to the Union. In that regard, the Union Government had informed him that it would be better to defer his proposed visit to South Africa until the judicial commissions had completed their inquiry and submitted their reports. It was expected that the Secretary-General's visit would take place in the latter part of July or early August 1960. The consultations provided for in the Council's resolution would be undertaken on the basis of the authority of the Secretary-General under the Charter. It was agreed between the Union Government and the Secretary-General that consent of the Union Government to discuss the Council's resolution with him would not require prior recognition from the Union Government of the United Nations authority.

On 11 October 1960, the Secretary-General issued a second interim report in which he pointed out that, owing to circumstances concerning the United Nations Operation in the Republic of the Congo (Leopoldville), he had been unable to visit the Union of South Africa, as envisaged in his first interim report. However, a new invitation had been extended to him on 28 September 1960 to visit the Union early in January 1961. He hoped to arrange for the visit at that time and to explore with the Prime Minister the possibility of arrangements which would provide for appropriate safeguards of human rights, with adequate contact with the United Nations.

In a report to the Security Council dated 23 January 1961, the Secretary-General stated that he had visited the Union of South Africa between 6 and 12 January 1961 and had had consultations with the Prime Minister at six meetings on 6, 7, 10 and 11 January 1961. He had had unofficial contacts with members of various sections of the South African community in Cape Town, Umtata (Transkei), Johannesburg and Pretoria. With regard to the request made of him by the Security Council resolution, he stated that, during discussions between himself and the Union's Prime Minister, no mutually acceptable arrangement had been found so far. In his view, this lack of agreement was not conclusive, and he wished to give the matter further consideration. The exchange of views in general had served a most useful purpose. The Secretary-General did not consider the consultations as having come to an end, and he looked forward to their continuation at an appropriate time with a view to further efforts on his side to find an adequate solution to the problem. The Union's Prime Minister, he said, had indicated that further consideration would be given to questions raised in the course of their talks and had stated that "the Union Government, having found the talks with the Secretary-General useful and constructive, had decided to invite him at an appropriate time, or times, to visit the Union again in order that the present contact may be continued."

[YUN 1960, pp. 142-47]

International campaign against apartheid

As the political and human rights situation in South Africa further deteriorated, United Nations efforts to end apartheid intensified. From 1967 onward, the United Nations encouraged Governments and peoples to take a wide range of measures to isolate the South African regime and demonstrate solidarity with those who were oppressed. After the General Assembly in December 1973 declared that the regime had no right to represent the people of South Africa, whose authentic representatives were the liberation movements recognized by the Organization of African Unity, South Africa was excluded from participating in the Assembly, as well as from most United Nations specialized agencies. By 1975, it was effectively excluded from all United Nations organs and, in 1977, the Security Council imposed a mandatory arms embargo against it—the first such action under Chapter VII of the Charter against a Member State. In 1985, when South Africa proclaimed a state of emergency and escalated repression, the international community again reacted strongly, as the Council, for the first time, called on Governments to take significant economic measures against South Africa. South Africa became increasingly isolated as the international community sought to take concerted action against it. At the end of 1989, as South Africa moved more and more towards change, the General Assembly, at its sixteenth special session, adopted by consensus the Declaration on Apartheid and its Destructive Consequences in Southern Africa, (resolution S-16/1) which—for the first time—laid down internationally agreed steps towards a negotiating climate and principles for a united, non-racial and democratic South Africa, and prescribed a programme of action to achieve that goal.

That General Assembly Declaration read as follows:

Declaration on *Apartheid* and its Destructive Consequences in Southern Africa

We, the States Members of the United Nations,

Assembled at the sixteenth special session of the General Assembly, a special session on *apartheid* and its destructive consequences in southern Africa, guided by the fundamental and universal principles enshrined in the Charter of the United Nations and the Universal Declaration of Human Rights, in the context of our efforts to establish peace throughout the world by ending all conflicts through negotiations, and desirous of making serious efforts to bring an end to the unacceptable situation prevailing in southern Africa, which is a result of the policies and practices of *apartheid*, through negotiations based on the principle of justice and peace for all:

Reaffirming our conviction, which history confirms, that where colonial and racial domination or *apartheid* exist, there can be neither peace nor justice,

Reiterating, accordingly, that while the *apartheid* system in South Africa persists, the peoples of Africa as a whole cannot achieve the fundamental objectives of justice, human dignity and peace which are both crucial in themselves and fundamental to the stability and development of the continent,

Recognizing that, with regard to southern Africa, the entire world is vitally interested that the processes in which that region is involved, leading to the genuine national independence of Namibia and peace in Angola and Mozambique, should succeed in the shortest possible time, and equally recognizing that the world is deeply concerned that destabilization by South Africa of the countries of the region, whether through direct aggression, sponsorship of surrogates, economic subversion or other means, is unacceptable in all its forms and must not occur,

Also recognizing the reality that permanent peace and stability in southern Africa can only be achieved when the system of *apartheid* in South Africa has been eradicated and South Africa has been transformed into a united, democratic and non-racial country, and therefore reiterating that all the necessary measures should be adopted now to bring a speedy end to the *apartheid* system in the interest of all the people of southern Africa, the continent and the world at large,

Believing that, as a result of the legitimate struggle of the South African people for the elimination of *apartheid*, and of international pressure against that system, as well as global efforts to resolve regional conflicts, possibilities exist for further movement towards the resolution of the problems facing the people of South Africa,

Reaffirming the right of all peoples, including the people of South Africa, to determine their own destiny and to work out for themselves the institutions and the system of government under which they will, by general consent, live and work together to build a harmonious society, and remaining committed to doing everything possible and necessary to assist the people of South Africa, in such ways as they may, through their genuine representatives, determine to achieve this objective,

Making these commitments because we believe that all people are equal and have equal rights to human dignity and respect, regardless of colour, race, sex or creed, that all men and women have the right and duty to participate in their own government, as equal members of society, and that no individual or group of individuals has any right to govern others without their democratic consent, and reiterating that the *apartheid* system violates all these fundamental and universal principles,

Affirming that *apartheid*, characterized as a crime against the conscience and dignity of mankind, is responsible for the death of countless numbers of people in South Africa, has sought to dehumanize entire peoples and has imposed a brutal war on the region of southern Africa, which has resulted in untold loss of life, destruction of property and massive displacement of innocent men, women and children and which is a scourge and affront to humanity that must be fought and eradicated in its totality,

Therefore we support and continue to support all those in South Africa who pursue this noble objective. We believe this to be our duty, carried out in the interest of all humanity,

While extending this support to those who strive for a non-racial and democratic society in South Africa, a point on which no compromise is possible, we have repeatedly expressed our objective of a solution arrived at by peaceful means; we note that the people of South Africa, and their liberation movements who felt compelled to take up arms, have also upheld their preference for this position for many decades and continue to do so,

Welcoming the Declaration of the *Ad Hoc* Committee of the Organization of African Unity on Southern Africa on the question of South Africa, adopted at Harare on 21 August 1989, and subsequently endorsed by the Heads of State or Government of Non-Aligned Countries at their Ninth Conference, held at Belgrade from 4 to 7 September 1989, as a reaffirmation of readiness to resolve the problems of South Africa through negotiations. The Declaration is consistent with the positions contained in the Lusaka Manifesto of two decades ago, in particular regarding the preference of the African people for peaceful change, and takes into account the changes that have taken place in southern Africa since then. The Declaration constitutes a new challenge to the Pretoria régime to join in the noble efforts to end the *apartheid* system, an objective to which the United Nations has always been committed,

Noting with appreciation that the Commonwealth Heads of Government, at their meeting held at Kuala Lumpur from 18 to 24 October 1989, noted with satisfaction the strong preference for the path of negotiated and peaceful settlement inherent in the Declaration adopted at Harare on 21 August 1989, and considered what further steps they might take to advance the prospects for negotiations,

Also noting with appreciation that the Third Francophone Conference of Heads of State and Government, held at Dakar from 24 to 26 May 1989, likewise called for negotiations between Pretoria and representatives of the majority of the people with a view to the establishment of a democratic and egalitarian system in South Africa,

Consequently, we shall continue to do everything in our power to increase support for the legitimate struggle of the South African people, including maintaining international pressure against the system of *apartheid* until that system is ended and South Africa is transformed into a united, democratic and non-racial country, with justice and security for all its citizens,

In keeping with this solemn resolve, and responding directly to the wishes of the majority of the people of South Africa, we publicly pledge ourselves to the positions contained hereunder, convinced that their implementation will lead to a speedy end of the *apartheid* system and herald the dawn of a new era of peace for all the peoples of Africa, in a continent finally free from racism, white minority rule and colonial domination,

Declare as follows:

1. A conjuncture of circumstances exists, which, if there is a demonstrable readiness on the part of the South African régime to engage in negotiations genuinely and seriously, given the repeated expression of the majority of the people of South Africa of their longstanding preference to arrive at a political settlement, could create the possibility to end *apartheid* through negotiations.

2. We would therefore encourage the people of South Africa, as part of their legitimate struggle, to join together to negotiate an end to the *apartheid* system and agree on all the measures that are necessary to transform their country into a non-racial democracy. We support the position held by the majority of the people of South Africa that these objectives, and not the amendment or reform of the *apartheid* system, should be the goals of the negotiations.

3. We are at one with the people of South Africa that the outcome of such a process should be a new constitutional order determined by them and based on the Charter of the United Nations and the Universal Declaration of Human Rights. We therefore hold the following fundamental principles to be of importance:

(*a*) South Africa shall become a united, non-racial and democratic State;

(*b*) All its people shall enjoy common and equal citizenship and nationality, regardless of race, colour, sex or creed;

(*c*) All its people shall have the right to participate in the government and administration of the country on the basis of universal, equal suffrage, under a non-racial voters' roll, and by secret ballot, in a united and non-fragmented South Africa;

(*d*) All shall have the right to form and join any political party of their choice, provided that this is not in furtherance of racism;

(*e*) All shall enjoy universally recognized human rights, freedoms and civil liberties, protected under an entrenched bill of rights;

(*f*) South Africa shall have a legal system that will guarantee equality of all before the law;

(*g*) South Africa shall have an independent and non-racial judiciary;

(*h*) There shall be created an economic order that will promote and advance the well-being of all South Africans;

(*i*) A democratic South Africa shall respect the rights, sovereignty and territorial integrity of all countries and pursue a policy of peace, friendship and mutually beneficial co-operation with all peoples.

4. We believe that acceptance of these fundamental principles could constitute the basis for an internationally acceptable solution that will enable South Africa to take its rightful place as an equal partner among the world community of nations.

A. Climate for negotiations

5. We believe that it is essential that the necessary climate be created for negotiations. There is an urgent need to respond positively to this universally acclaimed demand and thus create this climate.

6. Accordingly, the present South African regime should, at the least:

(*a*) Release all political prisoners and detainees unconditionally and refrain from imposing any restrictions on them;

(*b*) Lift all bans and restrictions on all proscribed and restricted organizations and persons;

(*c*) Remove all troops from the townships;

(*d*) End the state of emergency and repeal all legislation, such as the Internal Security Act, designed to circumscribe political activity;

(*e*) Cease all political trials and political executions.

7. These measures would help create the necessary climate in which free political discussion can take place—an essential condition to ensure that the people themselves participate in the process of remaking their country.

B. Guidelines to the process of negotiations

8. We are of the view that the parties concerned should, in the context of the necessary climate, negotiate the future of their country and its people in good faith and in an atmosphere which, by mutual agreement between the liberation movements and the South African régime, would be free of violence. The process could commence along the following guidelines:

(*a*) Agreement on the mechanism for the drawing up of a new constitution, based on, among others, the principles enunciated above, and the basis for its adoption;

(*b*) Agreement on the role to be played by the international community in ensuring a successful transition to a democratic order;

(*c*) Agreed transitional arrangements and modalities for the process of the drawing up and adoption of a new constitution, and for the transition to a democratic order, including the holding of elections.

C. Programme of action

9. In pursuance of the objectives stated in this Declaration, we hereby decide:

(*a*) To remain seized of the issue of a political resolution of the South African question;

(*b*) To step up all-round support for the opponents of *apartheid* and to campaign internationally in pursuance of this objective;

(*c*) To use concerted and effective measures, including the full observance by all countries of the mandatory arms embargo, aimed at applying pressure to ensure a speedy end to *apartheid;*

(*d*) To ensure that the international community does not relax existing measures aimed at encouraging the South African régime to eradicate *apartheid* until there is clear evidence of profound and irreversible changes, bearing in mind the objectives of this Declaration;

(*e*) To render all possible assistance to the front-line and neighbouring States to enable them: to rebuild their economies, which have been adversely affected by South Africa's acts of aggression and destabilization; to withstand any further such acts; and to continue to support the peoples of Namibia and South Africa;

(*f*) To extend such assistance to the Governments of Angola and Mozambique as they may request in order to secure peace for their peoples, and to encourage and support peace initiatives undertaken by the Governments of Angola and Mozambique aimed at bringing about peace and normalization of life in their countries;

(*g*) The new South Africa shall, upon adoption of the new constitution, participate fully in relevant organs and specialized agencies of the United Nations.

10. We request the Secretary-General to transmit copies of the present Declaration to the South African Government and the representatives of the oppressed people of South Africa and also request the Secretary-General to prepare a report and submit it to the General Assembly by 1 July 1990 on the progress made in the implementation of the present Declaration.

Following legalization of previously banned political organizations and freeing of some of the political prisoners, negotiations between the Government and major parties took place, facilitated by the United Nations. From September 1992 onward, the United Nations Observer Mission in South Africa helped strengthen the structures set up under the National Peace Accord signed in 1991. A Multi-party Negotiating Council was convened in 1993 to prepare an interim constitution and organize elections for April 1994. On 10 May 1994, Nelson Mandela was inaugurated as the new President of the Republic of South Africa and the Government of National Unity was installed. Shortly afterwards, the Security Council terminated the mandatory arms embargo and all other measures against South Africa, and, in June, the General Assembly welcomed South Africa back to the community of nations.

Western Sahara

In 1990, after years of conflict between the Moroccan forces and the Frente para la Liberación de Saguía el-Hamra y de Río de Oro (Polisario Front), the two sides signed a cease-fire agreement. The United Nations planned to conduct a referendum to determine whether the Territory should become independent or remain under Morocco.

The referendum on self-determination of the people of Western Sahara, to be conducted by the United Nations in co-operation with the Organization of African Unity, was originally scheduled for January 1992.

However, owing to fundamental differences in the interpretation of the main provisions of the plan for the settlement of the conflict, particularly with respect to the criteria for the eligibility to vote, the United Nations Mission for the Referendum in Western Sahara (MINURSO), established in 1991, was unable to proceed in conformity with the original timetable. Nevertheless, MINURSO successfully monitored the cease-fire agreed by the two parties.

The Secretary-General's consultations with the parties during his visit to the area in November 1994 indicated that the political will existed to move the process forward. He hoped that by the end of March 1995, progress achieved in the identification and registration of voters would enable him to recommend 1 June 1995 as the date for the start of the transitional period, with the referendum to take place in October 1995.

Asia

Cambodia

Following a long history of internal political conflicts in Cambodia, negotiations towards peace culminated in the conclusion of the 1991 Paris settlement agreements which called for their implementation under United Nations auspices. The negotiations had drawn impetus from the General Assembly's urging and call for cooperation by the major parties to the Cambodia conflict.

The mandate of the United Nations Transitional Authority in Cambodia (UNTAC), set up by the Security Council in 1992 in accordance with the Paris Agreements, was one of the most complex and ambitious ever undertaken by a United Nations operation. It included aspects relating to human rights, the organization and conduct of general elections, military arrangements, civil administration, the maintenance of law and order, the repatriation and resettlement of refugees and displaced persons, and the rehabilitation of essential infrastructures during the transitional period. At the same time, it was planned as a traditional peace-keeping operation, based on the agreement and cooperation of the parties and relying on political authority and persuasion rather than on force.

As envisioned by the Paris Agreements, the elections that created the Constituent Assembly took place as scheduled in May 1993, leading to the formation of a new Government of Cambodia in September of that year. With the establishment of the government, the mandate of UNTAC was brought to a successful conclusion. Following its termination, the Council, upon the request of the Cambodian Government, decided to establish a 20-member United Nations Military Liaison Team until

May 1994 to assist with residual military matters relating to the Paris Agreements. In accordance with the principles of the Agreements, the Secretary-General's Special Representative, aided by three military advisers, continues to maintain close cooperation with the Government, as well as with the Special Representative for Human Rights in Cambodia and other United Nations bodies.

Cyprus

Cyprus became independent of British rule in August 1960, with a Constitution intended to balance the interests of the island's Greek Cypriot and Turkish Cypriot communities, which made up approximately 80 and 18 per cent of the population respectively. A treaty between Cyprus, Greece, Turkey and the United Kingdom guaranteed the basic provisions of the Constitution and the territorial integrity and sovereignty of Cyprus. The application of the provisions of the Constitution, however, encountered difficulties and led to a succession of constitutional crises. The accumulated tension between the two communities resulted in the outbreak of violence in December 1963.

After all attempts to restore peace failed, the Security Council in March 1964 unanimously recommended the establishment of the United Nations Peace-keeping Force in Cyprus (UNFICYP), with a mandate to use its best efforts to prevent a recurrence of fighting, as well as to contribute to the maintenance of law and order and a return to normal conditions. By September 1964, the Force had managed to restore calm to the island. Since then, the Council has periodically extended UNFICYP's mandate, usually for six months at a time.

The situation in Cyprus

The situation in Cyprus and the establishment and presence of the United Nations Force on the island were among the major events with which the United Nations was concerned in 1964.

A relative calm prevailed in Cyprus after the creation of the Republic in 1960. But political differences between the two main communities, concentrated mainly on some provisions of the Constitution and of the Treaties of Guarantee and of Alliance, remained unsettled. The situation gradually deteriorated and disturbances and communal fighting erupted in December 1963.

. . .

On 27 December 1963 the Security Council met to consider a complaint by Cyprus against Turkey for acts of aggression and intervention in the internal affairs of Cyprus. After hearing statements by the representatives of Cyprus, Turkey and Greece, the Council adjourned, to be reconvened when and if it was considered appropriate by the members.

On 15 January 1964, a conference was opened in London in which representatives of Cyprus, Greece, Turkey and the United Kingdom participated. The conference did not produce agreement. The Cyprus Government insisted on a unitary independent state, with protection for the Turkish Cypriot community, whereas the Turkish Cypriot leaders requested the geographical separation of the two main communities. In response to a United Kingdom suggestion that its force in Cyprus should be replaced by military contingents from member countries of the North Atlantic Treaty Organization (NATO) and other countries, the Cyprus Government insisted that any peace-keeping force should come under the direct control of the United Nations and that the whole issue should be brought before the Security Council.

On 13 January 1964, the Secretary-General, in a report to the Council, stated that the Cyprus Government had requested him, in December 1963, to appoint a personal representative to look into the situation in Cyprus. Later, the Governments of the United Kingdom, Greece and Turkey had associated themselves with that request. In his next report, on 17 January, the Secretary-General informed the Council of his decision to designate Lieutenant-General P. S. Gyani, of India, as his Personal Representative to observe, for a period up to the end of February 1964, the progress of the joint peace-keeping operation in Cyprus (which consisted of military units of the United Kingdom—stationed in Cyprus by virtue of the Treaty of Establishment between the United Kingdom, Greece, Turkey and Cyprus—and of national contingents of Greece and Turkey stationed in Cyprus under the Treaty of Alliance between Greece, Turkey and Cyprus). At the invitation of the Governments participating in the London conference, he had sent José Rolz-Bennett, his Deputy *Chef de Cabinet*, to London on 16 January for consultations, outside of the Conference, with the representatives of the parties concerned, in connexion with the request that a personal representative of the Secretary-General be sent to Cyprus.

Consideration by Security Council (17 February-4 March)

Discussions were held in the Security Council, between 18 February and 4 March 1964, and led to the adoption on 4 March of a resolution setting up a United Nations peace-keeping force in Cyprus—the United Nations Force in Cyprus (UNFICYP)—for a period of three months and providing for the appointment of a mediator to seek a peaceful solution and an agreed settlement of the Cyprus problem.

The Council debates followed a request made on 15 February, both by the United Kingdom and Cyprus, for an urgent meeting of the Council.

In a letter accompanying its request, the United Kingdom stressed the grave deterioration of the situation in Cyprus and asked the Council to take appropriate steps to ensure that the dangerous situation could be resolved with full regard to the rights and responsibilities of all parties concerned.

The United Kingdom stressed the constitutional aspects of the problem and referred, in particular, to the London agreement of 19 February 1959 establishing the basic structure for the Republic, including some principles in the Cyprus Constitution governing the relations between the Greek and Turkish Cypriot communities. It also referred to the Treaty of Guarantee of 16 August 1960 under which the Governments of the United Kingdom, Greece and Turkey had guaranteed the independence, territorial integrity and security of Cyprus and the basic provisions of the Constitution.

In its letter, the United Kingdom also declared that the peace-keeping force in Cyprus, consisting of the military units of the guarantor powers stationed in the island which, at the request of the Cyprus Government, were assisting in securing the observance of the cease-fire, would have to be augmented in order to restore conditions of internal security. Agreement on arrangements for the establishment of an international peace-keeping force had been reached among the guarantor powers and certain other Governments, including that of the United States. However, because of the inability of the Government of Cyprus to agree, it had not been possible to implement the agreement.

Cyprus, in its request of 15 February, asked urgently for a meeting of the Security Council to consider the increasing threat from war preparations and declarations of the Turkish Government which made the danger of the invasion of Cyprus obvious and imminent.

When the Council began its discussion of the problem on 18 February, the debate was concentrated mainly on possible measures to accommodate the dangers in the situation in Cyprus, on the creation of a United Nations Force in the island and on legal questions linked to the independence of Cyprus.

The United Kingdom representative again stressed the link between the basic articles of the Cyprus Constitution, the provisions of the Treaty of Guarantee and the establishment of an independent Cyprus in 1960. The principal purpose of these agreements, it was pointed out, was to safeguard the rights and interests of both the Greek and Turkish Cypriot communities. The right reserved to the guarantor powers under the Treaty of Guarantee was not an unlimited right of unilateral action but the right to take action to reestablish the state of affairs created by the Treaty.

Cyprus had thereby undertaken certain obligations and so long as it carried them out there would be no question of intervention. The British Government accepted the principle of an international force under the control of the Council.

The Minister for Foreign Affairs of Cyprus stated that Turkey was pursuing a policy of provocation towards Cyprus, based on a well prepared plan to advance further the idea of communal separation with the ultimate aim of partition. He asked whether the Governments of the United Kingdom, Greece and Turkey maintained that they had a right of military intervention under the Treaty of Guarantee, particularly in view of the United Nations Charter. He firmly rejected the interpretation that the Treaty had given Turkey the right to unilateral action. Both the Treaty of Guarantee and the Treaty of Alliance had been concluded in circumstances which had precluded a free choice for Cyprus, and the Constitution had been foisted on the Republic. He charged that efforts had been made at the London Conference to prevent Cyprus from bringing the question before the Council. He requested that an international peace-keeping force in Cyprus should be under control of the Council and that its terms of reference should also provide for assistance to the Government of Cyprus in the restoration of law and order and the protection of the integrity and independence of the Republic.

The representative of Turkey noted that the Greek Cypriot representative had requested the meeting of the Council in December 1963 on the unsubstantiated claim that there was a threat of an imminent attack from Turkey. The purpose of the Zurich and London agreements, he said, had been to ensure full harmony between the two main communities, to safeguard the interests of the guarantor powers and to bring peace to the area. The Treaties and the Constitution were in complete accord with a resolution (1287(XIII)) which the General Assembly had unanimously adopted on 5 December 1958 (whereby the Assembly expressed its confidence that continued efforts would be made by the parties involved in the Cyprus question to reach a peaceful, democratic and just solution in accordance with the United Nations Charter). The Greek Cypriot leaders wished to obtain, through the United Nations, abrogation of the Treaties. In that connexion, he recalled that in November 1963 the President of Cyprus, Archbishop Makarios, submitted to the Vice-President, Dr. Kuchuk, and to the three guarantor powers, a memorandum containing 13 proposals for amending the basic articles of the Constitution so as to take away from the Turkish community the rights which had been considered as essential for its protection. The proposals had been rejected by the Turkish Cypriot community and by Turkey.

Could the Council, he asked, suspend or amend an international treaty which had been duly negotiated, signed and ratified? Peace and stability, he declared, could best be maintained in Cyprus through the peaceful co-existence of the two main communities, each master of its own affairs.

Rauf Denktash, Chairman of the Turkish Communal Chamber in Cyprus, who had been invited by the President to speak, with the consent of the Council, stated that difficulties had arisen in Cyprus because the Greek Cypriots demanded union with Greece while the Turkish Cypriots had wanted union with Turkey or, at least, partition of the island. In his view, the Zurich and London agreements represented a compromise settlement in Cyprus between equals and not between a majority and a minority. He said that, from the beginning, Archbishop Makarios had intended to change the Constitution, abrogate the Treaties and use the independence of the Republic as a springboard for *enosis* with Greece. The Turkish community in Cyprus stood for the Constitution. Changes to the Constitution that might be necessary could be made only through discussion and not by massacres, such as had taken place in the previous two months in Cyprus.

The representative of Greece considered that the Treaty of Guarantee had not given to the signatory powers the right of unilateral intervention. If the need arose for an interpretation of the Treaties, only the International Court of Justice could give it authoritatively. His Government had accepted the principle of an international force on the condition that its terms of reference would safeguard the maintenance of the independence and territorial integrity of Cyprus.

In the opinion of the USSR representative, the problem before the Council was one of a threat of direct military aggression against the independence and territorial integrity of Cyprus in violation of Article 2, paragraph 4, of the United Nations Charter. The Council had the right to expect from the United Kingdom and Turkey a direct assurance that military force would not be used against Cyprus. As a result of the unequal Treaties, he added, the British bases and the military forces of three members of the North Atlantic Treaty Organization (NATO) had been placed in Cyprus, designed to destroy the independence of the Republic. The USSR spokesman urged all States concerned to exercise restraint and to consider realistically all possible consequences of an armed invasion of Cyprus. Only the people of Cyprus, he said, had the right to decide how to solve their domestic problems.

The United States representative observed that the Treaty of Guarantee formed an integral part of the arrangements which had created the Republic of Cyprus. He stressed that the Council could not abrogate, nullify or modify, either in fact or effect, the Treaty of Guarantee or any international treaty. At the moment, no country was threatening the independence of Cyprus. What was, however, possible, in accordance with the Treaty, was an action for the re-establishment of the state of affairs created by the Treaty. He requested the Council to bring about prompt agreement on an international peace-keeping force and contribute to the re-establishment of conditions in which a long-term political solution could be sought by a United Nations mediator with due regard to the interests of all parties concerned.

On 25 February, the Secretary-General informed the Council of his discussions with the parties principally involved in the problem to determine to what extent common ground might be found in their views. He said that the discussions had been undertaken within the context of the Charter and bearing in mind at all times the authority of the Council. The question of sending a peace-keeping force to Cyprus would not arise without the concurrence of the Council. The presence of his Personal Representative, General Gyani, in Cyprus had been useful in keeping him informed about the situation and had contributed to alleviating tensions in the island. He hoped that the Council would find a reasonable and practical way out of the apparent impasse, and said he would be continually available to the Council to assist towards reaching a solution.

The representative of France considered that an interpretation of the Zurich and London agreements was a matter for the International Court of Justice and not for the Council. The Council could not modify the agreements, and changes could only be negotiated among the parties concerned. He asked the Council to appeal to all interested parties to end bloodshed in Cyprus and, thereafter, to help in solving the problem of ensuring a peaceful future.

The representative of Morocco suggested that if the Turkish minority was clinging desperately to the Zurich and London agreements it was because they saw in those agreements the only guarantees on which they could rely to ensure their rights. He warned against any unilateral challenges to those guarantees. He expressed the hope that an amendment to the guarantees would, if undertaken in a spirit of respect for the rights of the communities, give the necessary guarantees to the Turkish minority in Cyprus.

The representative of the Ivory Coast maintained that the unilateral denunciation of a treaty was invariably a source of conflict and war. He stressed that a constitution was primarily a domestic affair, not the subject of bargaining with the outside world. He supported the idea of appointing a mediator, accepted by the parties, who would have the twofold mission of helping the Cypriot communities to negotiate a reform of the constitution and the parties to find suitable ways of re-adapting the treaties to the new conditions.

The representative of Norway considered that it was not for the Council to pass judgement either on the constitution of a United Nations Member State or on treaties which had been negotiated as an integral part of the whole process of granting independence to that State. He also felt that the international peace force should be established without financial obligation by the United Nations.

The representative of Czechoslovakia said there was nothing to indicate that the Government of Cyprus would not be willing to ensure to the Turkish community real and full equality in all respects. He expressed the view that the obligations of the United Nations Charter must prevail over all other interests, including the rights and obligations emanating from the unequal treaties imposed on Cyprus.

The representative of China believed that the constitutional arrangements in Cyprus were inseparably linked with a number of international instruments whose purpose was the maintenance of harmony between the two communities. The Council, as a political body, was not in a position to pass judgement on the merits of the constitutional arrangements, agreements and treaties.

The representative of Bolivia supported the request of Cyprus for revision of the Zurich and London agreements and noted that the Council could and should create conditions which would allow a re-examination or a renegotiation of the Treaties.

On 2 March 1964, Bolivia, Brazil, the Ivory Coast, Morocco and Norway submitted a joint draft resolution, by the operative part of which the Council would: (1) call upon all United Nations Member States, in conformity with their obligations under the Charter, to refrain from any action or threat of action likely to worsen the situation in the sovereign Republic of Cyprus or to endanger international peace; (2) ask the Government of Cyprus, which had the responsibility for the maintenance and restoration of law and order, to take all additional measures necessary to stop violence and bloodshed in Cyprus; (3) call upon the communities in Cyprus and their leaders to act with the utmost restraint; (4) recommend the creation, with the consent of the Government of Cyprus, of a United Nations peace-keeping force in Cyprus, whose composition and size would be established by the Secretary-General, in consultation with Cyprus, Greece, Turkey and the United Kingdom, and whose commander would be appointed by the Secretary-General and report to him. The Secretary-General would keep the Governments providing the force fully informed and would report periodically to the Council on its operations; (5) recommend that the function of the force should be, in the interest of preserving international peace and security, to use its best efforts to prevent a recurrence of fighting and, as necessary, to contribute to the maintenance and restoration of law and order and a return to normal conditions; (6) recommend that the stationing of the force should be for a period of three months, all costs being met in an agreed manner by the Governments providing the contingents and by the Government of Cyprus, while the Secretary-General might also accept voluntary contributions for that purpose; (7) recommend that the Secretary-General designate, in agreement with the Governments of Cyprus, Greece, Turkey and the United Kingdom, a mediator for the purpose of promoting a peaceful solution and an agreed settlement of the problem confronting Cyprus; and (8) request the Secretary-General to provide from funds of the United Nations for the remuneration and expenses of the mediator and his staff.

The representative of the USSR said that, although the joint draft resolution was not wholly satisfactory, its aim was to prevent aggression against Cyprus and safeguard the lawful rights of the Republic. The USSR would abstain in the vote on the fourth operative paragraph of the text (namely, that recommending the creation of a peace-keeping force), since it embodied procedures which would circumvent the Council. In supporting the draft as a whole, he said, the USSR was taking account of the fact that the Government of Cyprus considered it useful despite its defects.

The Secretary-General said that he intended, in accordance with established practice concerning previous United Nations peace-keeping forces, to keep the Council promptly and fully informed about the organization and operation of the force. The force, unlike those in Gaza and the Congo, would have a fixed and firm duration of three months, which could be extended beyond that date only by a new action of the Council.

On 4 March 1964, the joint draft resolution was voted upon as follows: Operative paragraph 4, on the creation of a peace-keeping force, (on which a separate vote was requested by the USSR) was adopted by 8 votes to 0, with 3 abstentions (Czechoslovakia, France, the USSR); the draft resolution as a whole was adopted unanimously.

Explaining his vote, the French representative said that, without entertaining the slightest doubt about the Secretary-General's wisdom and prudence, France considered that the Council was going very far in the direction of the delegation of powers to a single individual. He declared that this decision could in no case be considered as a precedent.

The representative of Czechoslovakia said he had serious doubts about giving the Secretary-General responsibilities which should, under the Charter, be part of the Security Council's functions.

On 13 March 1964, the representative of Turkey informed the Secretary-General that, on 12 March, his Government had sent a note to Archbishop Makarios in a last attempt to stop the massacre of the Turkish Cypriots, failing which Turkey had decided, under the Treaty of Guarantee, to take appropriate action. Also on 13 March, the Secretary-General appealed to the Turkish Government to refrain from any action which would worsen the already tragic situation in Cyprus.

On the same day, the representative of Cyprus requested an immediate emergency meeting of the Council, stating that there was a clear threat of imminent invasion of Cyprus by Turkish forces.

When the Council met on 13 March, the Secretary-General said that the United Nations Peace-keeping Force would be established without further delay and that elements of it would soon be deployed in Cyprus.

The representatives of Bolivia, Brazil, the Ivory Coast, Morocco and Norway submitted a joint draft resolution by the operative part of which the Council would: (1) reaffirm its call upon all United Nations Member States, in conformity with their obligations under the Charter, to refrain from any action or threat of action likely to worsen the situation in the sovereign Republic of Cyprus or to endanger international peace; and (2) request the Secretary-General to press on with his efforts to implement the Council's resolution of 4 March 1964 and request Member States to co-operate with the Secretary-General to that end.

On 13 March, the Council unanimously adopted the five-power draft resolution.

Subsequent reports by Secretary-General

In several reports during the period between 16 March and 15 June 1964, the Secretary-General informed the Council of the formation, functioning, operations and status of the Peace-keeping Force in Cyprus, as well as of developments in connexion with the United Nations Mediator's mandate. On 25 March, the Council was informed that Lieutenant-General Gyani, whom he had appointed Commander of the Force, would assume command on 27 March, at which time the Force would become operational under the Council's resolution of 4 March. On 26 March, the Secretary-General informed the Council that, with the agreement of the Governments of Cyprus, Greece, Turkey and the United Kingdom, he had designated Sakari S. Tuomioja as the United Na-

tions Mediator in Cyprus. On 11 May, he informed it that Galo Plaza was going to Cyprus as his Special Representative, directly responsible to him, to conclude negotiations of essential non-military matters and without impinging upon the efforts of the Mediator or upon the functions of the Commander of the Force.

. . .

On 15 June, the Secretary-General submitted to the Council the first comprehensive report on the United Nations operations in Cyprus for the period from 26 April to 8 June 1964.

The report analyzed the military as well as the political, economic, social and judicial aspects of the Cyprus situation. The United Nations Force in Cyprus (UNFICYP) had, in its few months' activities, made a valuable contribution to the cause of peace in Cyprus, the report noted. During the period under review there had been no military incidents which involved major clashes. The presence of the Force had undoubtedly prevented a recurrence of open fighting, but the tension in the island had not substantially lessened. Both the Greek and the Turkish Cypriots had taken advantage of the comparative lull to strengthen their military positions. Areas of tension remained mainly in Nicosia, the Kyrenia Pass and the Kokkina-Mansoura area in the north-west of the island. There was no major progress towards removing fortifications or disarming civilians. The decision of the Cyprus Government to introduce conscription and to organize and equip an army had increased the tension, since it might lead to a corresponding arms increase on the Turkish Cypriot side. It was also feared that, in the attempt by the Government to restore law and order by itself, violence and fighting might again break out.

The report also said that the recurrent threat of landing by Turkish military forces, the importation of smuggling of arms into Cyprus, the lack of any progress in achieving freedom of movement on the roads and the question of missing persons and of abductions remained very serious causes of tension. A certain amount of progress had been reported in the solution of some economic, social and judicial problems, but it was clear that economic considerations, even if difficulties started to be seriously felt in both main communities, were not likely to be an important factor affecting political considerations and decisions in the forthcoming period.

The Secretary-General reported that the presence of contingents of the Greek and Turkish national armies had caused a problem because of their one-sided attitudes. He said that the Greek contingent would readily place itself under the United Nations command if a similar arrangement could be made with the Turkish contingent. The report also stressed that further progress and a proof of the usefulness of UNFICYP could only be possible if the two communities and their leaders were willing to show more flexibility in their positions.

UNFICYP in June consisted of 6,238 military personnel from Austria, Canada, Denmark, Finland, Ireland, Sweden and the United Kingdom and 173 civilian police from Austria, Australia, Denmark, New Zealand and Sweden.

The Secretary-General said that informal consultations on the question of extending the operational period of UNFICYP with Council members, States providing contingents and voluntary monetary contributions, and the Government of Cyprus had indicated, generally, that an extension of the Force was favoured.

He announced the resignation of General Gyani and the appointment of General K. S. Thimayya, also of India, as the new Commander. He also pointed out that the method of financing the Force was most unsatisfactory because of the uncertainty of voluntary contributions.

The report added that the Mediator, Mr. Tuomioja, had been in consultation with the parties concerned in order to find a sufficient measure of common ground to develop the basis for a long-term political solution. In the prevailing circumstances, the Mediator's task was not likely to lead to positive results in a relatively short time.

Consideration by Security Council (18-20 June 1964)

The Council considered the Secretary-General's report at four meetings held between 18 and 20 June. It was generally agreed that the situation in Cyprus was still far from satisfactory. Members concurred in the view that the presence of the United Nations Force in the island had prevented a recurrence of open clashes and fighting and there was a consensus that the Force's mandate should be extended for another period of three months.

The representative of Turkey said that the situation in Cyprus, instead of showing improvement, had deteriorated, because of a complete disregard by the Greek Cypriot authorities of the resolution of 4 March 1964. They had further aggravated the situation by completely disregarding the Constitution, by instituting military conscription and by importing arms. He declared that UNFICYP had full authority to stop the importation of arms and to prevent both communities from arming themselves. He stressed that the decision of the Turkish contingent in Cyprus to move to a new garrison could not be used as a pretext by Archbishop Makarios for unilaterally denouncing the Treaty of Alliance. He condemned the policy of abductions and inhuman acts as exemplified in the Greek Cypriot attack at St. Hilarion Castle in May. He expressed his disappointment over cer-

tain conclusions in the report and maintained that UNFICYP was not in Cyprus to establish the authority of the Greek Cypriots over the whole island. In his view, the Government of Cyprus could not be recognized as lawful.

The representative of Cyprus appreciated the efforts made by the Secretary-General, the United Nations Mediator and UNFICYP, but he stressed that, despite the Council's resolutions of 4 and 13 March, the threat of invasion by Turkey continued. He maintained that his Government had every right to import arms and organize its defence as long as Turkey did not give assurance of non-intervention in Cyprus. His Government considered the Treaty of Alliance as terminated after its request to the Governments of Greece and Turkey to order their contingents back to camps in Nicosia had not been complied with by Turkey. Turkey had also rejected the proposal of the Secretary-General to place its contingent under the Commander of UNFICYP, while Greece had agreed to do so. He also condemned the practice of taking hostages, exercised by both communities in Cyprus. He reiterated that the non-participation of the Turkish Cypriots in the Government had been brought about by the Turkish Cypriots in December in pursuit of their objective to try to create a separate state. Finally, he assured the Council of his Government's full co-operation with UNFICYP but added that it was not prepared to accept curtailment of any of its sovereign rights.

The representative of Greece reiterated his Government's support of the United Nations efforts in Cyprus and its decision to put the Greek contingent in Cyprus under UNFICYP Command or to withdraw it, if similar arrangements could be made with Turkey. He stressed that Greece was not following a policy of expansionism with regard to Cyprus. Greece had been in favour of self-determination since 1955 and, in his view, that was the only peaceful way of determining the will of the majority in countries.

On 19 June, Bolivia, Brazil, the Ivory Coast, Morocco and Norway submitted a joint draft resolution by which the Council would: (1) reaffirm its resolutions of 4 and 13 March 1964; (2) call upon all Member States to comply with them; (3) take note of the Secretary-General's report; and (4) extend the stationing in Cyprus of the United Nations Force for an additional period of three months, ending 26 September.

The representative of the United Kingdom said that UNFICYP had accomplished one of its major objectives in preventing a recurrence of fighting. His Government was concerned with the evidence of an arms build-up in the island and with incidents involving abduction and the taking of hostages. Supporting renewal of the mandate of

UNFICYP, he said that it was likely that the withdrawal of the Force might lead to a resumption of the fighting.

The USSR representative emphasized that the threat of military aggression against Cyprus had not yet been averted and that foreign interference in its internal affairs still continued. He stressed that the Council's resolutions of 4 and 13 March had created the necessary conditions for a just solution of the Cyprus conflict. He was not opposed to the extension of the Force's mandate, provided that there would be no widening of the Force's function and that the financing would be on the same basis as stated in the 4 March resolution.

The United States representative considered the extension of the Force's mandate essential for preventing an early resumption of fighting, which could develop into more serious conflict. He hoped that the parties in Cyprus would avoid further acts such as the competitive inflow of arms, which might lead to an aggravation of the situation. He viewed as serious the practice of taking hostages and, particularly, the abduction of UNFICYP personnel. Finally, he appealed to all Member States to respond to the Secretary-General's request for financial contributions.

The French representative stressed the need to achieve, first, a relaxation of tension and to restore calm on the island. In that respect, progress had been limited. He hoped that UNFICYP would, within the framework of the resolution of 4 March, help to establish conditions under which the solution of the basic problems could be undertaken. He declared that the taking of hostages and importation of arms were in contradiction to the Council's resolutions.

On 20 June 1964, the five-power draft resolution was adopted unanimously.

Consideration by Security Council in August 1964

Tension in Cyprus, however, continued. The Secretary-General expressed his concern over the seriousness of the situation in exchanges of communications with the parties directly concerned and with some other Member States.

Early in August, the fighting between the two main communities was renewed in various parts of Cyprus, and there were air and naval actions by Turkey in the north-west areas of the island.

On 8 August, Turkey requested an urgent meeting of the Council to consider the serious situation created in Cyprus by the renewed and continuing attempts of the Greek Cypriots to subdue by force of arms the Turkish community in Cyprus. Cyprus also requested an immediate meeting of the Council as a matter of utmost urgency in view of the deliberate and unprovoked armed aerial attacks against the unarmed civilians of Cyprus carried out by aircraft of the Turkish Air Force.

When the Council met, on the evening of 8 August, the President informed the members that all efforts made by UNFICYP to bring about a cease-fire in the spots where fighting had occurred had not yet met with success.

The representative of Cyprus informed the Council that Turkish warships were heading for Cyprus for the purpose of invasion.

The representative of Turkey declared that the Greek Cypriots had made their military preparations during the last few weeks and, on 5 August, had unleashed offensives on several Turkish Cypriot localities in the island, particularly in the Kokkina-Mansoura area. Those developments had been brought to the attention of the Secretary-General, of UNFICYP and of the other guarantor powers. UNFICYP was unable to act and to exercise its mandate. Therefore Turkey had, under its rights by the Treaty of Guarantee, decided to stop the further attacks of the Greek Cypriots in the north-west areas by sending its military aircraft to attack exclusively Greek Cypriot military targets as a limited police action. He stressed that the air attacks were intended to halt Greek Cypriot aggression and that they would stop when it stopped. He viewed as a threat the statement made by the Interior Minister of Cyprus that an unrestrained assault against the entire Turkish population would be made unless the Turkish air attacks stopped by 9 August. The Council was requested to consider measures to put an end to the Greek Cypriot aggression against the Turkish Cypriot population, to stop any further importation of military equipment and personnel, to control all entry points into Cyprus and to consider a gradual and controlled disarmament of both sides.

The representative of Cyprus said that Turkey, despite its obligations under the United Nations Charter, had used force and bombed with napalm the unarmed Greek Cypriot population in some parts of Cyprus. He denied that Government forces had started an attack on the Turkish Cypriots in the north-west of the island and reviewed the events preceding the fighting in that area. The renewed attack by the Turkish Cypriots was merely provocation as a preliminary to intervention. He reminded the Council that the resolution of 4 March 1964 did not recognize any other government authority in Cyprus than the Government of Cyprus and did not give any status to the rebels as a fighting force that must be respected by the United Nations.

The representative of Greece noted that Turkey, which contended that the action of its air force was intended to protect a civilian minority attacked by the Cyprus Government forces, had not called for an urgent meeting of the Council to explain the facts and to ask that measures be taken by the Council. He stressed that the Council was confronted by an undeniable act of aggression by Turkey. If the attacks continued, Greece would assist Cyprus by all the military means available to it. He informed the Council of his Government's call for an immediate end to hostilities and for a peaceful solution of the question.

The USSR representative declared that the foreign armed intervention in the domestic affairs of Cyprus was very serious, having possible grave consequences for peace in the Eastern Mediterranean area. He warned the Council that it could not admit that one sovereign State could arrogate to itself the right to undertake so-called police measures against another sovereign State, as such a policy could only undermine and destroy the United Nations Charter. The Council should demand the immediate cessation of military acts against Cyprus and respect for the sovereignty of Cyprus in accordance with the Charter and previous decisions of the Council.

On 9 August, the Council's President, on the suggestion of the Ivory Coast, and with the agreement of all members of the Council, made an appeal to the Government of Turkey "to cease instantly the bombardment and use of military force of any kind against Cyprus" and to the Government of Cyprus "to direct the armed forces under its control to cease firing immediately."

The same day, the United States representative stressed that the responsibility of the Council was to stop hostilities which brought with them the danger of international war. He introduced a draft resolution, co-sponsored by the United Kingdom, which was approved on 9 April in a revised form by 9 votes with 2 abstentions (Czechoslovakia and the USSR). By this text, the Council: (1) reaffirmed the President's appeal; (2) called for an immediate cease-fire by all concerned; (3) called upon all concerned to co-operate fully with the United Nations Commander in the restoration of peace and security; and (4) called on all States to refrain from any action that might exacerbate the situation or contribute to the broadening of hostilities.

On 10 August, the Secretary-General issued a statement to the effect that the Governments of Cyprus and Turkey had responded positively and without conditions to the appeal of the President of the Council for a cease-fire.

The same day, Cyprus requested another immediate meeting of the Council to consider the extreme urgency of developments in Cyprus and to prevent any further aggravation of the situation.

When the Council met on 11 August, the representative of Cyprus informed it that Turkey had made another air attack on Cyprus on 10 Au-

gust, that overflights of Cyprus by Turkish aircraft continued and that supplies to the Turkish Cypriot strongholds in Kokkina had been sent from Turkey by sea, all in violation of the cease-fire and of the Council's resolution of 9 August.

The Turkish representative declared that the present cease-fire was meaningless, unless there was a withdrawal of the Greek Cypriots to the positions they had occupied before 5 August.

The Secretary-General informed the Council that firing had come to an end in Cyprus on the ground and in the air. He also mentioned cases of violation of the cease-fire.

After further discussion, the President summed up the agreed views of the members of the Council as follows: After hearing the report of the Secretary-General and the statements of the representatives of Cyprus, Greece and Turkey and of the members of the Council, the Council: (i) noted with satisfaction that the cease-fire was being observed throughout Cyprus; (ii) requested the parties to comply with the resolution of 9 August 1964 in its entirety; (iii) asked all Governments to stop all flights over the territory of Cyprus in violation of its sovereignty; (iv) requested the Commander of UNFICYP to supervise the cease-fire and to reinforce its units in the zones which were the sphere of the recent military operations so as to ensure the safety of the inhabitants; and (v) requested all concerned to co-operate with and to assist the Commander of the Force in achieving this purpose.

The Secretary-General communicated this consensus of views to the Governments of Cyprus and Turkey.

Developments during September 1964

Following the Council's meetings in August, the Government of Cyprus gradually imposed economic restrictions on the Turkish Cypriots in some parts of the island. The question of the rotation of part of the Turkish contingent in Cyprus reached an impasse with possible serious consequences.

The Secretary-General informed the Council on 21 and 29 August that additional financial support was required for the continuation of the Force's maintenance in Cyprus.

In Geneva, Switzerland, the Mediator continued efforts to promote an agreed political settlement of the Cyprus problem.

On 10 September, the Secretary-General submitted his second comprehensive report to the Council on the United Nations Operation in Cyprus covering the period from 8 June to 8 September. In this report, the Secretary-General indicated that the situation in the island had remained tense, although UNFICYP had done much to keep the peace and promote a return to normal conditions. The Cyprus Government and the Turkish Cypriot community had continued to build up their military strength and to fortify their positions. The tension prevailing in the island had culminated in August with the fighting in the Tylleria area and the subsequent intervention of the Turkish air force. Since then, the situation had been generally quiet. But the Secretary-General observed that this situation was an unstable one, and he drew attention to two developments in particular which might cause the tension to rise again; first, the deadlock over the rotation of part of the Turkish contingent in Cyprus, which was normally to take place at the end of August and, second, the economic restrictions imposed by the Cyprus Government on the Turkish Cypriot community.

The Secretary-General pointed out that the Security Council resolution of 4 March 1964 had defined the functions of UNFICYP only in general terms and that the lack of clarity in UNFICYP's mandate had been a serious handicap in its operations. However, despite this handicap, UNFICYP had functioned well. While it had not been able altogether to prevent a recurrence of fighting, as at St. Hilarion and in the Tylleria area, its presence was a major factor in bringing the fighting in those areas to an end and in preventing it from escalating. UNFICYP's efforts had also resulted in considerable improvement in the security situation and as regards a return to normalcy, although conditions in the island undoubtedly were still far from satisfactory. While admitting that strong reasons could be adduced against maintaining a United Nations force in Cyprus, the Secretary-General believed that—despite all the handicaps—to withdraw UNFICYP at this time could lead to utter disaster in the island. He indicated that all the four Governments which the Security Council resolution of 4 March required him to consult wished the Force to be extended. The Secretary-General considered, however, that, in the event that the Security Council was inclined to extend the Force for another three-month period, he had to call the Council's attention to two problems: the inadequacy of the financial support of the Force so far given by Member States, and the need for clarifying the mandate of the Force.

In his report, the Secretary-General also informed the Security Council that the Mediator on Cyprus, Ambassador Sakari Tuomioja, had died on 9 September as a result of the stroke which he had suffered on 16 August. In this connexion, he later informed the Council on 16 September that, in agreement with the four Governments concerned, he had designated his then Special Representative in Cyprus, Galo Plaza, as the new Mediator.

In an addendum to the report dated 15 September, the Secretary-General informed the Council that, in a message of the same date, President Makarios had advised him that the Cyprus Government had decided to remove any economic restrictions in the island. The President also indicated that his Government was ready: to order the removal of all the armed posts throughout Cyprus, provided that the Turkish Cypriot leadership would do the same; to afford protection and financial assistance to those Turkish Cypriots who wished to be resettled in their homes; to grant a general amnesty; and to accept any suggestion of the United Nations in respect of practical security measures designed to contribute to the pacification of the island, provided such measures would not affect the political solution of the problem.

The Security Council considered the Secretary-General's report at meetings held between 16 and 25 September 1964.

The representative of Cyprus said his Government was willing to accept the extension of the UNFICYP mandate for an additional three months on the basis of the Council's resolution of 4 March and with the understanding that the function of UNFICYP would respect the sovereign rights and authority of the Cyprus Government.

After citing the message of 15 September of the President of Cyprus to the Secretary-General, he reviewed again the fighting in the Kokkina-Mansoura area and the Turkish air attacks. It was necessary, he said, to clarify whether Turkey had acted in such a manner with the tolerance of some of its allies in NATO. He also reiterated his Government's decision to abrogate the Treaty of Alliance and, in consequence, its request that the Turkish contingent leave Cyprus.

The representative of Turkey welcomed the conclusion in the Secretary-General's report that there should be some clarification concerning actions the Force might take in the discharge of its mandate. He contradicted the statement of the Cyprus representative on the question of fighting in the Kokkina-Mansoura area and stressed that the Council had neither condemned nor condoned the Turkish action; no one had said that Turkey should stand aside. As for the Cyprus Government's proposals of 15 September, he reiterated that the solution of the Cyprus question could not be imposed by force on the Turkish minority. He also spoke of the continuing arms build-up in Cyprus and of the economic restrictions imposed on the Turkish Cypriot population.

Members of the Council supported the view that UNFICYP had played an essential part in preventing the outbreak of total civil war and in alleviating the suffering of the people of the island, and considered that extension of the Force's mandate was needed. It was understood that the solution of the Cyprus question had to be sought and found in Cyprus on a peaceful and reasonable basis by the two communities, through the newly appointed Mediator. Members of the Council also took account of the lifting of restrictions on essential supplies by the Government of Cyprus and of restraint by the parties concerned in the question of the rotation of the Turkish contingent.

Disagreement among Council members on some of the functions of UNFICYP remained, as did the question of the protection of Cyprus in case of foreign intervention and the methods of financing the United Nations operation.

On 25 September, Bolivia, Brazil, the Ivory Coast, Morocco and Norway jointly submitted a draft resolution whereby the Council would: (1) reaffirm its resolutions of 4 March, 13 March, 20 June and 9 August 1964 and the consensus expressed by the President at its meeting on 11 August 1964; (2) call upon all United Nations Member States to comply with the above-mentioned resolutions; (3) extend the period in which UNFICYP would be stationed in Cyprus for another three months, ending 26 December 1964, in conformity with the terms of the resolution of 4 March 1964; and (4) request the Secretary-General to keep the Council informed regarding the compliance of the parties concerned with the provisions of this resolution.

On the same day (25 September), the Security Council adopted the five-power text unanimously as resolution 194(1964).

At the same meeting of the Council, the Secretary-General expressed his intention of continuing to seek full respect for the freedom of movement of UNFICYP and to initiate any action necessary for the implementation of the Force's mandate. He informed the Council about an arrangement with the parties concerned for reopening the Nicosia-Kyrenia road under the exclusive control of UNFICYP and of his appointment of Ambassador C. Bernardes, of Brazil, as his Special Representative in Cyprus. He also appealed to all Member States to contribute towards meeting the costs of the peace-keeping operation, stating that, in his view, the existing method of voluntary contributions was unsatisfactory.

Secretary-General's report for period between 10 September and 12 December

There was a general improvement in the situation in Cyprus in the last few months of 1964. There were no major incidents during those months and the economic restrictions imposed by the Cyprus Government on the Turkish Cypriot community were considerably relaxed. In accordance with the agreement announced by the Secretary-General in the Security Council, the

scheduled rotation of the Turkish national contingent took place at the end of October and the Nicosia-Kyrenia road was reopened under the exclusive control of UNFICYP. This was followed by a general easing of restrictions on the freedom of movement of the population throughout the island.

This improvement, however, was a precarious one, as the position of the leaders of both communities remained basically unchanged and the tension continued to be high. In order further to promote a return to normal conditions, UNFICYP submitted to the Cyprus Government and the Turkish Cypriot leadership a series of suggestions to that end, but one side or the other was unable to accept most of them lest its case should be prejudiced with regard to the final settlement of the Cyprus problem.

The search for an agreed settlement of the problem continued with the new Mediator. But he noted that the amelioration of the day-to-day situation in Cyprus had not yet had the effect of eliminating the differences of view among the parties concerned as to a political solution of the problem.

This state of affairs was reflected in the third report of the Secretary-General on the United Nations Operation in Cyprus, which covered the period from 10 September to 12 December.

In his report, the Secretary-General stated that the general situation in Cyprus was improving and that the cease-fire was being observed, but that basic factors of the Cyprus question remained essentially unchanged. Acute political conflict and distrust between the leaders of the two communities and the passions stirred among the communities' members still were creating a state of potential civil war. Basically, the life and economy of the island remained disrupted and abnormal; there was no normal functioning of the Government administration in areas controlled by the Turkish Cypriots.

The report stressed that UNFICYP activities were still indispensable for the welfare of the people in Cyprus and for the maintenance of conditions in which the search for a long-term solution could be further pursued. The Secretary-General recommended the prolongation of UNFICYP's mandate for a further period of three months and urged all Member States and the specialized agencies to contribute to the financing of UNFICYP.

Consideration by Security Council on 18 December 1964

When the Council met on 18 December to consider the report, the representative of Cyprus said there had been no major incidents in the island during the last part of 1964. His Government had done its utmost to promote a return to normal conditions in Cyprus, even overlooking in certain cases its security requirements, but the leaders of the rebels had continued to demand a return to the Constitution of 1960, which they had destroyed by their actions against the State. The proposals made by the President of Cyprus on 15 September still stood, even if they had not so far met with the proper response from the Turkish Cypriot side. In no circumstances would there be acceptance by the people of Cyprus of a federal system or partition. He urged an effective new contribution by UNFICYP to a return to normalcy, provided that such measures did not affect the defence requirements of the island and did not prejudice the solution of the political problem. He reiterated his Government's view of the danger to Cyprus constituted by the continued illegal presence of the Turkish military contingent.

The Turkish representative said that the Council was now faced with a new approach by the Greek Cypriot leaders, who were trying to impose their own solution by gradual extension of their unlawful authority over the area where Turks had taken refuge. He stressed that the Turkish Cypriot community was still subjected to severe hardship, that it could not be left at the mercy of those who had attempted to annihilate it and that an agreed solution was the only lasting one for Cyprus.

The Greek representative noted that the peaceful solution of the Cyprus question was an urgent matter. He stressed that the peaceful intentions of the Government of Cyprus were reflected in President Makarios' message of 15 September to the Secretary-General. However, the Turkish Cypriot leaders had found it necessary to continue to prevent contact between Greeks and Turks in the island.

At the same meeting of the Council, Bolivia, Brazil, the Ivory Coast, Morocco and Norway submitted a joint draft resolution by which the Council would: (1) reaffirm its resolutions of 4 March, 13 March, 20 June, 9 August and 25 September 1964 and the consensus expressed by the President on 11 August 1964; (2) call upon all Member States to comply with the above-mentioned resolutions; (3) take note of the report by the Secretary-General; and (4) extend the stationing of the United Nations Peace-keeping Force in Cyprus, established under the Council resolution of 4 March, for an additional period of three months, ending 26 March 1965.

The five-power text was adopted unanimously by the Council as resolution 198(1964).

[YUN 1964, pp. 150-63]

Developments following the 1974 coup d'état

The situation changed dramatically following a *coup d'état* by the Cyprus National Guard in July 1974 against the Cyprus Government headed by President Makarios, and the subsequent landing of Turkish military forces. UNFICYP endeavoured to arrange local and general cease-fires, patrolled the battle zone, evacuated foreigners and did its best to ensure the safety of civilians. When a cease-fire came into effect in August 1974, the Turkish and Turkish Cypriot forces were in control of the northern part of the country. This necessitated a change in UNFICYP's operations. In particular, the Force has maintained since then a buffer zone between the two sides, extending approximately 180 kilometres across the island. UNFICYP also carries out humanitaran functions and supports relief efforts.

Strict adherence to the military status quo in the buffer zone has become a vital element in preventing a recurrence of the fighting. UNFICYP investigates and acts on all violations of the cease-fire and the military status quo.

The Secretary-General began his good offices functions in Cyprus in 1964. Since 1966, his Special Representatives have been actively involved in promoting an agreed overall settlement. After the events of 1974, the Security Council, in March 1975, requested the Secretary-General to undertake a new mission of good offices. Since then, the successive Secretaries-General and their Special Representatives have been trying to find a formula acceptable to both Cypriot communities.

In December 1994, the Secretary-General stated that the situation in Cyprus remained generally quiet, but subject to sudden tensions generated by events outside as well as within the country. However, the excessive level of armaments and forces in Cyprus and the rate at which they were being strengthened were a cause of concern. The Security Council extended the mandate of UNIFCYP until 30 June 1995, expressing concern that there had been no progress towards a final political solution and urging the leaders of both communities to promote tolerance and reconciliation.

Iran-Iraq

In September 1980, after a series of international disputes, war broke out between Iran and Iraq. The United Nations efforts to end the conflict began soon thereafter as Secretary-General Kurt Waldheim offered his good offices to work for a peaceful settlement. In accordance with the United Nations Charter, the Secretary-General brought to the attention of the Security Council the threat to the maintenance of international peace and security posed by that conflict. By resolution 479(1980) of 28 September 1980, the Security Council, *inter alia,* called upon Iran and Iraq to refrain immediately from any further use of force and to settle their dispute by peaceful means. That war lasted for almost eight years.

In August 1988, as a result of intensive negotiations between the Secretary-General and the two

Foreign Ministers, Iran and Iraq agreed to a cease-fire to end the war. During the conflict, the United Nations was able to play a role in the issue of the bombing of civilian population centres in both countries. Missions dispatched by the Secretary-General confirmed the use of chemical weapons and investigated the situation of prisoners of war. To verify, confirm and supervise the cease-fire and troop withdrawal to the internationally recognized boundaries, the United Nations Iran-Iraq Military Observer Group (UNIIMOG) was established. The operation was terminated in February 1991, with the completion of the withdrawal of the remaining forces.

Iraq-Kuwait crisis

In August 1990, Iraq invaded and occupied Kuwait. The Security Council condemned the invasion and demanded Iraq's immediate and unconditional withdrawal and, a few days later, instituted economic sanctions against Iraq.

In November, the Council allowed Iraq one final opportunity until 15 January 1991 to comply with its demand. The day after the deadline passed, the armed forces of those States cooperating with Kuwait began air attacks against Iraq, as authorized by the Council. Following a three-day ground offensive in February, Kuwait was liberated and returned to its legitimate Government. In April 1991, the Security Council set detailed conditions for a cease-fire and established machinery for ensuring those conditions. It established a demilitarized zone along the boundary between Iraq and Kuwait, to be monitored by a United Nations observer unit.

The United Nations Iraq-Kuwait Observation Mission (UNIKOM), which also monitors the Khawr Abd Allah waterway, has successfully contributed to the calm prevailing along the border. Following a series of incidents on the newly demarcated boundary involving Iraqi intrusions into the Kuwaiti side of the demilitarized zone and unauthorized retrieval of property from Kuwaiti territory, the Security Council in February 1993 expanded UNIKOM's mandate to include the capacity to take physical action to prevent or redress small-scale violations of the demilitarized zone or the boundary. In addition to these tasks, UNIKOM provided technical support to other United Nations missions working in the area, in particular to the Iraq-Kuwait Boundary Demarcation Commission until its dissolution in May 1993, and to the United Nations office dealing with the return of property from Iraq to Kuwait. Until February 1994, UNIKOM also assisted with the relocation of Iraqi citizens from the Kuwaiti side of the border to Iraq, following the demarcation of the international boundary.

Confrontation in Korea

Outbreak of hostilities

The question of Korea's unification and independence came before the United Nations for the first time in 1947, at the second regular session of the General Assembly. The efforts of the United Nations Temporary Commission on Korea, established that year to assist in the creation of a national Government through free elections, failed. Eleven months before the outbreak of armed conflict between North and South Korea, the Commission reported that the embittered propaganda and hostile activities between the two parts of Korea rendered the prospect of unification more and more remote.

On 25 June 1950, the United States and the Commission informed the Secretary-General that North Korean forces had invaded the territory of the Republic of Korea. The same day, the Security Council declared the attack to be a breach of the peace and called for an immediate cease-fire and withdrawal of North Korean forces to the 38th parallel. As the fighting continued, the Council two days later recommended that Member States furnish such assistance as necessary to repel the armed attack and restore international peace and security in the area. In the meantime, the United States announced that it had ordered its air and sea forces to give cover and support to the South Korean troops. Three days later, it informed the Council that it had ordered a naval blockade of the entire Korean coast and authorized the use of ground forces as a further response to the Council's 27 June resolution.

On 7 July, the Council recommended that all Member States providing military forces make them available to a unified command under the United States. A United States General, Douglas MacArthur, was designated Commanding General and troops from 16 nations, medical units from five others and all the military forces of the Republic of Korea were placed under the Unified Command and authorized to fly the United Nations flag.

The question of the independence of Korea had been considered by the General Assembly at its second, third and fourth sessions. At its second session the Assembly in resolution 112(II) had established a Temporary Commission to assist and hasten the participation of elected Korean representatives in the consideration of the question of Korean independence, and to observe that these representatives were in fact duly elected by the Korean people. The Byelorussian SSR, Czechoslovakia, Poland, the Ukrainian SSR, the USSR and Yugoslavia did not take part in the vote establishing the Commission, maintaining that the Assembly's refusal at that session to permit Korean representatives to take part in its discussions of the question at a time when questions affecting the independence of their country were being discussed contravened the provisions of the Charter and the right of self-determination of peoples.

The Temporary Commission was unable to secure access into North Korea and, after consulting the Interim Committee, as authorized by the General Assembly, it observed the elections in the areas of Korea south of the 38th parallel of latitude, which resulted in the establishment of the Government of the Republic of Korea. At its third session, in December 1948, the General Assembly in resolution 135(III) declared this Government a lawful government and the only such government in Korea. It recommended that Governments take this declaration into account in establishing their relations with the Government of the Republic of Korea. It also recommended the withdrawal of the occupying forces. It set up a United Nations Commission on Korea to lend its good offices to bring about the unification of Korea and the integration of all Korean security forces; the Commission was to facilitate the removal of barriers to economic, social and other friendly relations caused by the division of the country. In 1949, at its fourth session, the General Assembly in resolution 293(IV) decided to continue the Commission in being, with much the same terms of reference except that it was directed to observe and report any developments that might lead to military conflict in Korea.

Both in 1948 and 1949 the representatives of the Byelorussian SSR, Czechoslovakia, Poland, the Ukrainian SSR and the USSR had maintained that the General Assembly did not have the right to take any action with regard to Korea as that matter had been covered by the Moscow Agreement and should be dealt with by the Allied Governments concerned. The establishment of the Temporary Commission, they stated, was illegal since it was in violation of international agreements. They held that the unification of Korea and the establishment of a unified democratic State should be left to the Korean people themselves.

Complaint of aggression upon the Republic of Korea before the Security Council

On 25 June 1950, the United States informed the Secretary-General that North Korean forces had invaded the territory of the Republic of Korea at several points in the early morning of that day. Stating that this was a "breach of the peace and an act of aggression" the United States requested an immediate meeting of the Security Council to deal with the situation.

On the same day the United Nations Commission on Korea informed the Secretary-General that according to a statement of the Government of the Republic of Korea, attacks had been launched in strength by the North Korean forces all along the 38th parallel. The Pyongyang Radio announcement that the South Korean forces had launched an attack across the parallel during the night, the Commission stated, was declared to be entirely false by the President and Foreign Minister of the Republic of Korea in the course of a conference with the Commission's members. Stating that the situation was assuming the character of a full-scale war and might endanger international peace, the Commission suggested that the Secretary-General should consider the possibility of bringing the matter to the Security Council's attention.

Resolution of 25 June 1950

These communications were considered by the Council at its 473rd meeting on 25 June. On the proposal of the United States, the representative of the Government of the Republic of Korea was invited to sit at the Council table during the consideration of the question. The United States representative presented a draft resolution which would have the Council call upon the authorities in North Korea to cease hostilities and to withdraw their armed forces to the border along the 38th parallel. It would, also, request the United Nations Commission on Korea to observe the withdrawal of the North Korean forces to the 38th parallel and to keep the Security Council informed on the execution of the resolution. The Council, it was provided, would call upon all Members of the United Nations to render every assistance to the United Nations in the carrying out of the resolution and to refrain from assisting the North Korean authorities.

The representatives of the Republic of Korea, China, France, Cuba and Ecuador urged speedy action by the Council to deal with the situation, the representatives of the Republic of Korea, China and Cuba stating that the Council was faced with an act of aggression. The representative of France stated that the matter was of particular concern to the United Nations in view of the part which the Organization had played in establishing the Republic of Korea. Support for the United States draft resolution was expressed by the representatives of the United Kingdom, France and Ecuador; and the representative of Egypt, welcoming the Council's endeavour to bring about a cessation of hostilities, stated that he might be able to support the draft resolution if certain changes were made. The United Kingdom proposed an amendment to request the United Nations Commission on Korea to communicate its fully considered recommendation on the situation with the least possible delay. Following consultations between some of the representatives, various paragraphs of the United States draft resolution were amended and the revised draft resolution was adopted by the Council first in parts and then as a whole. The representative of Norway expressed his support of the amended resolution.

The first, second and third paragraphs and the first paragraph of the operative part were adopted by 9 votes, with 1 abstention (Yugoslavia) and one member absent (USSR);[3] the first clause of paragraph I (see below) of the operative part was adopted by 10 votes, with 1 member absent (USSR); the second clause of paragraph I of the operative part and paragraph II and III were adopted by 9 votes, with 1 abstention (Yugoslavia), and 1 member absent (USSR). The amended draft resolution as a whole was adopted by 9 votes, with 1 abstention (Yugoslavia), and 1 member absent (USSR). . . .

At its 474th meeting on 27 June, the Security Council had before it three cablegrams from the United Nations Commission on Korea. The Commission reported that, having considered the latest reports of its military observers resulting from direct observation along the 38th parallel during the period ending 48 hours before hostilities had begun, its present view was that the authorities in North Korea were carrying out a well-planned, concerted and full-scale invasion of South Korea; and that South Korean forces had been deployed on a wholly defensive basis on all sectors of the 38th parallel. The Commission also expressed unanimous gratification at the Security Council's resolution of 25 June. It stated, however, that it was convinced that the North Koreans would neither heed the Council's resolution nor accept the Commission's good offices, and suggested that the Council might consider calling on both parties to agree on a neutral mediator, or request Member Governments to undertake immediate mediation. It warned that in the light of military operations already in progress, the question of a cease-fire and a withdrawal of North Korean forces might prove ''academic''.

The representative of the United States submitted a draft resolution proposing that the Security Council note that the authorities of North Korea had not complied with the resolution of 25 June, and that urgent military measures were required to restore international peace and security. The draft resolution would also recommend that the Members of the United Nations furnish such assistance to the Republic of Korea as might be necessary to repel the armed attack and restore international peace and security in the area.

After submitting his draft resolution, the representative of the United States read the statement which the President of the United States had made on that day. This statement announced, *inter alia,* that, in conformity with the Council's call upon all Members of the United Nations to render every assistance to the United Nations in the execution of its resolution of 25 June he (the President of the United

States) had ordered United States air and sea forces to give cover and support to South Korean troops. The President of the United States also announced in this statement that he had ordered the Seventh Fleet to prevent any attack on Formosa and had called upon the Chinese Government on Formosa to cease all air and sea operations against the mainland. Orders had also been issued, he said, to accelerate military assistance to the Philippines and to the forces of France and the Associated States in Indo-China.

The representative of Yugoslavia, stating that, unfortunately, Korea and the Korean people were victims of ''spheres of influence'', maintained that the Council should not, after two days fighting, abandon hope that the parties would negotiate in their own interest and in that of international peace. The Council, he said, should help the Korean people by addressing to them an even more pressing appeal to cease hostilities and by suggesting to them a procedure of mediation with the good offices of the Security Council. He therefore proposed a draft resolution which would have the Council renew its call for the cessation of hostilities, initiate a procedure of mediation between the parties and, to this end, invite the Government of the People's Republic of Korea to send a representative immediately to the United Nations Headquarters, with full powers to participate in the procedure of mediation.

The representatives of the Republic of Korea, France, the United Kingdom, China, Cuba, Norway and Ecuador expressed support for the United States draft resolution. They held that the situation had become even more serious since the adoption of the Council's resolution of 25 June, since the North Korean authorities had ignored this resolution and had flouted the authority of the United Nations. The representative of China stated that he was obliged to oppose the Yugoslav draft resolution since he believed that any mediatory effort on the part of the Security Council at the present stage would be useless. The representatives of Egypt and India stated that, lacking instructions from their Governments, they would be unable to participate in the voting.

In the course of their statements, the representatives of France, the United Kingdom, China, Cuba, Norway and Ecuador welcomed the declaration of the President of the United States whereby United States air and sea forces had been ordered to give

---

[3]The USSR representative had withdrawn from the Council on 13 Jan. 1950, stating that he would not participate in the Council's work until ''the representative of the Kuomintang group had been removed'', and that the USSR would not recognize as legal any decision of the Council adopted with the participation of that representative and would not deem itself bound by such decisions. He returned to the Council on 1 Aug. 1950 when the presidency of the Council devolved upon him, according to the rule of monthly rotation.

the troops of the Government of the Republic of Korea cover and support.

The Council adopted the United States draft resolution by 7 votes to 1 (Yugoslavia) with 1 member absent (USSR) and 2 members (Egypt, India) not participating in the voting [resolution S/1511]. It rejected the Yugoslav draft resolution by 7 votes to 1 (Yugoslavia) with 1 member absent (USSR) and 2 members (Egypt, India) not participating in the voting.

. . .

Communications from Members
concerning the resolutions of 25 and 27 June

On 29 June the Secretary-General transmitted the Council resolution of 27 June to all Member States of the United Nations, and asked what assistance, if any, each would give to the Republic of Korea. A number of communications were received. . . .

In a communication dated 13 July 1950, the Permanent Representative of the USSR to the United Nations requested the Secretary-General to circulate as an official document of the Security Council the text of a statement made by the Deputy Foreign Minister of the USSR in Moscow on 4 July on the Korean question. In this statement, the Deputy Foreign Minister of the USSR declared, *inter alia*, that the events in Korea were the result of a provocative attack by the troops of the South Korean authorities on the frontier areas of the Korean People's Democratic Republic, and that the attack had been the outcome of a premeditated plan. He stated that the United States had resorted to open armed intervention in Korea and that the successive moves of the United States had disclosed its aggressive plans in Korea.

The United States, the statement continued, had confronted the United Nations with a *fait accompli*, in view of the fact that it had started its armed intervention in Korea before the convening of the Security Council on 27 June. Moreover, it was argued, the 27 June resolution of the Council was a gross violation of the Charter inasmuch as it had received six votes only, the seventh being that of "the Kuomintang representative" who unlawfully occupied China's seat in the Security Council and had been adopted in the absence of two permanent members of the Council, the USSR and China. Furthermore, the resolution had violated one of the most important principles of the United Nations, namely that of non-intervention in the domestic matters of States. This action showed, the statement of the Deputy Foreign Minister of the USSR continued, that the Council was not acting as a body which was charged with the main responsibility of the maintenance of peace, but as a tool utilized by the ruling circles of the United States for the unleashing of war. He maintained that the resolution of the Security Council

constituted a hostile act against peace. If the Council valued the cause of peace, he observed, it should have attempted to reconcile the fighting sides in Korea before it adopted such a "scandalous resolution".

The real aims of American armed intervention in Korea were to deprive Korea of its national independence, to prevent the formation of a united democratic Korean State and forcibly to establish in Korea an anti-popular regime which would allow the ruling circles of the United States to convert the country into their colony and use Korean territory as a military and strategic springboard in the Far East.

Referring also to the question of Formosa and to the situation in French Indochina, he submitted that President Truman's statement of 27 June showed that the United States had gone over from a policy of preparing aggression to direct acts of aggression simultaneously in a number of countries in Asia, and had thus disregarded its obligations to the United Nations. The Koreans, he went on, had the same right to arrange, at their own discretion, their internal national affairs as the North Americans had held and exercised when they united the Northern and Southern States in a single national State.

In conclusion, the statement said, the United Nations would fulfil its obligations to maintain peace only if the Security Council demanded "the unconditional cessation of American military intervention and the immediate withdrawal of American armed forces from Korea".

Creation and operation of the Unified Command

Resolution of 7 July 1950

At the Council's 476th meeting on 7 July, the United Kingdom representative, calling attention to the necessity for co-ordinating the assistance which the Council's resolution of 27 June had recommended should be furnished by Members to the Republic of Korea, presented a joint French-United Kingdom draft resolution providing: for the creation of a unified command under the United States. In addition to its sponsors, the representatives of China, Cuba and Norway spoke in favour of the joint draft resolution, which was adopted by the Council by 7 votes, with 3 abstentions (Egypt, India and Yugoslavia) and 1 member absent (USSR). The resolution read as follows:

The Security Council,
Having determined that the armed attack upon the Republic of Korea by forces from North Korea constitutes a breach of the peace,
Having recommended that Members of the United Nations furnish such assistance to the Republic of Korea as may be necessary to repel the armed attack and to restore international peace and security in the area,

1. *Welcomes* the prompt and vigorous support which governments and peoples of the United Nations have given to its resolutions of 25 and 27 June 1950 to assist the Republic of Korea in defending itself against armed attack and thus to restore international peace and security in the area;

2. *Notes* that Members of the United Nations have transmitted to the United Nations offers of assistance for the Republic of Korea;

3. *Recommends* that all Members providing military forces and other assistance pursuant to the aforesaid Security Council resolutions make such forces and other assistance available to a unified command under the United States;

4. *Requests* the United States to designate the commander of such forces;

5. *Authorizes* the unified command at its discretion to use the United Nations flag in the course of operations against North Korean forces concurrently with the flags of the various nations participating;

6. *Requests* the United States to provide the Security Council with reports as appropriate on the course of action taken under the unified command.

Following the Council meeting, the Secretary-General handed to the United States representative on the Security Council the United Nations flag which had been used in Palestine. In accordance with the resolution, the United States designated General MacArthur as Commander-in-Chief of the United Nations Forces in Korea. The flag was presented to General MacArthur in Tokyo on 14 July by General J. Lawton Collins, Chief of Staff of the United States Army.

First Report of the Unified Command

At the Council's 477th meeting on 25 July 1950 the United States representative communicated the text of an exchange of letters between the President of the Republic of Korea and the Supreme Commander of the United Nations Forces, regarding the assignment to the latter of the command authority over all military forces of the Republic of Korea during the period of the continuation of the state of hostilities. He also communicated the text of the United States Far East Command communiqué announcing the establishment of the United Nations Command and the text of the first report to the Council by the United States Government on the course of action taken under the Unified Command.

The President expressed appreciation of the report as giving a clear account of the initial stages of the aggression launched by the North Korean army and an impression of the speed and determination with which the available forces of the United States and other Member States were thrown into the breach to uphold the principles of the United Nations. The representatives of France, the United Kingdom, Cuba, China, India and Ecuador associated themselves with his statement.

Consideration by the Security Council of the Korean question during August and September

On 27 July 1950, the Permanent Representative of the USSR to the United Nations, who had been absent from the meetings of the Security Council since 13 January 1950, announced that, in accordance with the established procedure of the alphabetical rotation of the Security Council presidency each month, he was assuming the Council presidency in August. He set a meeting of the Council for 1 August.

(YUN 1950, pp. 220-30)

In August and September 1950, the Security Council held several meetings concerning the question of Korea. The Council debates were predominated by super-Power confrontations between the United States and USSR and their allies. While the United States supported the United Nations Unified Command in Korea with its General MacArthur as the Supreme Commander, the USSR did not recognize it. Serious differences also emerged between the West and East on the contentious issue of the recognition of the People's Republic of China as an interested party of the Korean question, and attempts to link the "Complaint of armed invasion of Taiwan (Formosa)" and "Complaints of aggression upon the Republic of Korea".

In view of this, the USSR refused to recognize the reports of the United Nations Command in Korea submitted by the United States.

With regard to item 3 of the provisional agenda, the United States representative objected to its implication that the USSR was the only nation interested in a peaceful settlement of the question; the wording of the item already on the Council's agenda permitted all Council members to express their views fully and to make proposals for terminating the breach of the peace.

The President, speaking as the representative of the USSR in support of item 3 of the provisional agenda, stated that the position of his Government and delegation was that it was the duty of the Security Council to adopt immediately measures for the peaceful solution of any international conflict which constituted a threat to peace and security. He maintained that the United States on the contrary aimed at seizing Korea and extending the scope of aggressive war and did not wish, therefore, even to discuss the cessation of aggression, putting an end to armed intervention and the termination of hostilities. He charged that the United States, under the title of the agenda item "Complaint of aggression upon the Republic of Korea", was attempting to cast the blame for events in Korea on the Government of the People's Republic of Korea; but, as shown in the statement of 4 July of the Deputy Foreign Minister of the USSR, there had been a provocative attack of South Korean forces on the frontier areas, with the participation of United States military advisers. This attack had taken place according to a plan previously prepared by and with the knowledge and agreement of highly placed United States officials.

The USSR representative referred to the definition of aggression approved in May 1933 by a League of Nations Committee, composed of representatives of seventeen States, and said that according to this definition the military operations of the United States against the Korean people were acts of direct armed aggression, which, he said, could not be justified by any strategic or other considerations. The war between the North and South Koreans was, he maintained, not a war between two States, but an internal conflict between two groups of the Korean people temporarily split into two camps under two separate authorities. The United Nations was debarred by the Charter from intervening in such an internal matter.

. . .

The representatives of the United Kingdom, Ecuador, France, Cuba, Norway and China in general expressed agreement with the views expressed by the representative of the United States.

. . .

At the 482nd meeting on 3 August, the Council decided by 8 votes to 1 (USSR), with 2 abstentions (India, Yugoslavia), that the item following adoption of the agenda should be "Complaint of aggression upon the Republic of Korea". It rejected by 5 votes to 5 (China, Cuba, Ecuador, France, United States), with 1 abstention (Egypt), the proposal to include the item "Recognition of the representative of the Central People's Government of the People's Republic of China". It also rejected, by 7 votes to 3 (Egypt, India, the USSR), with 1 abstention (Yugoslavia), the proposal to include the item entitled "Peaceful settlement of the Korean question".

Representation of Korea

At the 483rd meeting of the Council on 4 August, the President, speaking as the representative of the USSR, introduced a draft resolution, the first operative paragraph of which would have the Council decide:

(a) To consider it necessary, in the course of the discussion of the Korean question, to invite the representative of the People's Republic of China and also to hear representatives of the Korean people.

In introducing his draft resolution, the USSR representative stated that it was a tradition and practice established in the Security Council to invite both parties involved in the hostilities to participate in the consideration and discussion of such questions regardless of whether or not they were Members of the United Nations or whether or not they had been granted diplomatic recognition by all members of the Security Council. That practice had been followed by the Security Council in the consideration of a number of questions. Besides that, the United States draft resolution contained a paragraph directed against the North Korean authorities. In such circumstances, it would be unfair and inadmissible for the Security Council not to give a due hearing to the accused party.

The representatives of China, the United States, the United Kingdom, Norway and India considered that the Council had already taken a decision on 25 June to invite the representative of the Republic of Korea, under which that representative had participated in the discussions during June and July, and that this decision was binding. After the representative of the Republic of Korea had been seated the question of inviting a representative of the North Korean authorities could be considered; these authorities had, however, by defying the Security Council's decision, put themselves in a state of hostility with the United Nations and, while this continued, they should not be invited to be represented at the Council table.

The President, speaking as the representative of the USSR, considered that to reject the proposal to invite both parties would imply that the Council was unwilling to assist in halting hostilities. To invite both sides in what, he stated, was a civil war would be taking the most objective and the fairest decision possible. He rejected the assertion that the North Korean authorities had refused to comply with the decisions of the United Nations, since these decisions were not legal, having been adopted with the participation of only three permanent members of the Council. He also charged that resolutions had been adopted on the basis of the one-sided version given to the Council by the representative of the Syngman Rhee régime and of the United Nations Commission on Korea, which he termed "an obedient tool of the United States Department of State". United States pressure, he alleged, had been responsible for excluding representatives of the People's Democratic Republic of Korea from the United Nations discussions on this question since 1947, when it had prevented the hearing of these representatives by the Assembly when it was establishing the Commission.

At the 484th meeting of the Council the representative of China, on a point of order, requested that the President immediately rule on the following question: "Does the President consider it obligatory upon him to carry out the decision of the Security Council on 25 June by inviting the representative of the Republic of Korea to take his place at the Council table?"

The President stated that he was not in a position to give a ruling on the subject.

The representatives of China, the United States, Ecuador, Cuba and France held that the President was not acting in accordance with the rules of procedure.

The discussion on the seating of the representative of the Republic of Korea continued at the 484th and 485th meetings of the Council on 8 and 10 August, but no decision was taken. At the meeting on 10 August, the President stated that, as President, he was not in a position to rule on the question of the seating of the representative of the Republic of Korea. The question was also the subject of informal talks among Council members on 10 and 21 August, but no decision was reached during August.

At the 494th meeting of the Council on 1 September, the President, the representative of the United Kingdom, invited the representative of the Republic of Korea to take his seat at the Council table ''in accordance with the previous decision of the Council''. Mr. John M. Chang took his seat as that representative. The President's ruling was challenged by the representative of the USSR, but, on being put to the vote, was upheld by 3 votes to 1 (USSR), with 1 abstention (United Kingdom).

The USSR representative then introduced a draft resolution by which the Council would decide ''that during the discussion of the Korean question it shall be necessary to invite and hear at its meetings the representatives of the Korean people, i.e. the representatives of North and South Korea''. Before taking the vote on this draft resolution, the President ruled that if the USSR motion was put to the vote and rejected, nothing in that rejection should prejudice the right of the representative of the Republic of Korea to be present at meetings of the Council when the Korean question was discussed. This ruling was challenged by the representative of the USSR, but was upheld by 8 votes to 1 (USSR), Yugoslavia abstaining. The representative of Egypt did not participate in the vote, stating that such a matter could not be subject to a ruling by the President.

. . .

Special report of the UN Command in Korea: consideration by the Security Council

At the 518th meeting of the Security Council on 6 November 1950 the representative of the United States brought to the attention of the Council the text of a special report, dated 5 November, from the United Nations Command in Korea. The report stated that in certain areas of Korea United Nations forces had been in contact with Chinese communist military units deployed for action against the forces of the United Nations Command. At the next meeting of the Council on 8 November, the representative of the Soviet Union objected to the Council considering this special report on the ground

that the Council's decision establishing that command had been in violation of the Charter. Furthermore, he contended, General MacArthur's reports could not be relied upon. The history of war, it was claimed, showed that army commanders always gave a biased interpretation of events, which they considered exclusively from the points of view of their own military interests. The representative of the Soviet Union recalled, further, that as far back as 27 September, the Government of the People's Republic of China had submitted a complaint of violation of China's frontier by American troops in Korea. The Council had been prevented by the United States from taking a just and legal decision in connexion with that complaint. Since the United States delegation had then argued against discussing that communication, he said, there were no grounds for discussing now the tendentious and highly unreliable reports from an American general in Korea.

After the Council had decided to place the matter on its agenda, the representative of the USSR presented a draft resolution which would have the Council decide that during the discussion of the Korean question it would be necessary to invite the representative of the People's Republic of China.

While agreeing that as a matter of equity the representative of the People's Republic of China should be present during the discussion of this item, the representative of the United Kingdom nevertheless felt that the USSR draft was not appropriate.

He therefore submitted the following amendment to the USSR draft:

The Security Council,
Decides to invite, in accordance with rule 39 of the Rules of Procedure, a representative of the Central People's Government of the People's Republic of China to be present during discussion by the Council of the Special Report of the United Nations Command in Korea.

The representative of the United Kingdom felt that if this counter-draft was adopted, the Council would not be debarred in the interval, pending the arrival of a representative from Peking, from considering the item on the agenda and from taking any decision in that respect which it deemed essential.

The representative of the United States said that since the Chinese communist military units deployed against the United Nations were not merely volunteers interspersed in the North Korean army but were regular military units, the question arose as to whether the Council should invite representatives of aggressors. By their intervention the Chinese communists had, it was claimed, imposed upon the world the danger of an extension of the Korean conflict. This had been done despite assurances to them by both the United Nations and, individually, the United States. He was in favour of the Council making the objectives of United Nations action in Korea clear to the Chinese communists, but such an assurance should not imply that the Council was prepared to condone the intervention of Peking authorities in Korea. The invitation to the Central People's Government of China should not be in the form used by the Council in its efforts to adjust controversies by peaceful means. It should rather be a summons to the Peking régime to appear before the Council and to offer to the world community an explanation of the state of affairs which the Council was "forced to consider".

The representative of China stated that he opposed the proposal to extend an invitation to representatives of the Chinese communists on the grounds that the Peking régime was not Chinese in origin or character but the fruit of Soviet intervention and aggression in China, and that the matter under discussion was not a dispute.

The representative of the USSR, while emphasizing the necessity of inviting a representative of the People's Republic of China before considering the charges brought against that Government by the United States, considered that the United Kingdom amendment was not an amendment but a separate draft resolution. He therefore asked that the two proposals be voted on separately. He further took exception to the use, by the representative of the United States, of the word "summons" in connexion with the invitation to the representative of a sovereign State.

The representative of Yugoslavia stated that, having always considered the People's Republic of China as an interested party in the Korean question as a whole, he would vote in favour of the USSR draft resolution. If it was not adopted, he would vote in favour of the proposal submitted by the United Kingdom.

At the 520th meeting of the Council, on 8 November, the USSR draft resolution was rejected by the Council by a vote of 2 in favour (USSR, Yugoslavia) and 3 against (China, Cuba, United States), with 6 abstentions.

Before a vote was taken on the United Kingdom proposal, the representative of the USSR proposed an amendment to it which would replace the words "special report of the United Nations Command in Korea" by the words "the question submitted by the delegation of the United States of America." This amendment was rejected by 1 vote in favour (USSR) and 2 against (China, Cuba), with 8 abstentions.

The representatives of the United States, France and Ecuador explained that while they would vote in favour of the United Kingdom draft resolution, their vote should not be construed as implying recognition by their Governments of the Central People's Government of the People's Republic of China, named in that draft resolution.

The representative of the USSR stated that he would also vote in favour of the United Kingdom draft resolution, even though his delegation did not recognize the United Nations Command and its so-called special report.

The representative of Egypt, after having stated that he would not vote against the United Kingdom proposal, also stressed that his Government's position with regard to the question of the recognition of the Government of China remained unchanged.

At the same meeting (520th), the United Kingdom draft resolution was adopted by 8 votes to 2 (China, Cuba), with one abstention (Egypt).

At the 521st meeting of the Council on 10 November, the representatives of Cuba, Ecuador, France, Norway, the United Kingdom and the United States submitted the following joint draft resolution:

The Security Council,
Recalling its resolution of 25 June 1950, determining that the North Korean forces had committed a breach of the peace and calling upon all Members of the United Nations to refrain from giving assistance to the North Korean authorities,
Recalling the resolution adopted by the General Assembly on 7 October 1950, which sets forth the policies of the United Nations in respect to Korea,
Having noted from the special report of the United Nations Command in Korea dated 5 November 1950 that Chinese Communist military units are deployed for action against the forces of the United Nations in Korea,
Affirming that United Nations forces should not remain in any part of Korea otherwise than so far as necessary for achieving the objectives of stability throughout Korea and the establishment of a unified independent and democratic government in the sovereign State of Korea, as set forth in the resolution of the General Assembly dated 7 October 1950,
Insistent that no action be taken which might lead to the spread of the Korean conflict to other areas and thereby further endanger international peace and security,
Calls upon all States and authorities, and in particular those responsible for the action noted above, to refrain from assisting or encouraging the North Korean authorities, to prevent their nationals or individuals or units of their armed forces from giving assistance to North Korean forces and to cause the immediate withdrawal of any such nationals, individuals, or units which may presently be in Korea;
Affirms that it is the policy of the United Nations to hold the Chinese frontier with Korea inviolate and fully to protect legitimate Chinese and Korean interests in the frontier zone;
Calls attention to the grave danger which continued intervention by Chinese forces in Korea would entail for the maintenance of such a policy;
Requests the Interim Committee on Korea and the United Nations Commission for the Unification and Rehabilitation of Korea to consider urgently and to assist in the settlement of any problems relating to conditions on the Korean frontier in which States or authorities on the other side of the frontier have an interest, and suggests that the United Nations Commission for the

Unification and Rehabilitation of Korea proceed to the area as soon as possible, and, pending its arrival, that it utilize the assistance of such States members of the Commission as now have representatives in the area for this purpose.

. . .

At the 525th meeting of the Council on 27 November, the President proposed that the Council should consider together the items entitled "Complaint of armed invasion of Taiwan (Formosa)", and "Complaint of aggression upon the Republic of Korea". He explained that the two problems were closely inter-related and further that the Security Council had invited the representatives of the People's Republic of China, then present in New York, to take part in the Council's discussion of both the questions.

. . .

At the 526th meeting on 28 November, the representative of the People's Republic of China took his seat at the Council table. . . .

The representative of the United States, speaking first in the debate, stressed the fact that, while the complaint of aggression on the Republic of Korea and the complaint of armed invasion of Taiwan were two distinct matters, they were closely related aspects of the gravest question then confronting the world. That question, he stated, was whether there would be peace or war in the Far East. The facts of the situation in Korea, he said, were that Chinese communist forces totalling more than 200,000 were engaged in North Korea, in what the United States Government believed to be aggression.

The United States representative then reviewed past Chinese-American relations, stressing the aid and assistance given by the United States to China in the economic, political and cultural fields. Referring to the Korean problem, the representative of the United States put the following questions to the representative of the People's Republic of China:

What was the number of Chinese communist troops who had entered Korea, their organization and composition. How had supplies been organized, dispatched across the frontier and distributed? What motives had led the Peking Government to ignore the reiterated statements of the United Nations and of the United States Government that there were no designs on Chinese territory or legitimate interests. What were the interests of the Peking Government in Korea. Was the Peking Government ready to respond to the central paragraph of the six-Power draft resolution, calling upon all States and authorities to refrain from assisting or encouraging the North Korean authorities? That proposal, the representative of the United States commented, represented the conscience of the world. Would the Peking authorities heed the judgment of the United Nations, or would they defy the Organization, thus further endangering peace and security?

With regard to the complaint of violation of the Chinese territorial air, he recalled the United States proposal for a commission of investigation, which had been vetoed by the USSR. He stated that despite the subsequent intervention of Chinese communists, the Unified Command had maintained its instructions strictly prohibiting United Nations aircraft crossing the Korean frontier.

Referring to the question of Formosa, he emphasized that the Government of China, which was recognized by the United States Government and by a majority of the Members of the United Nations, was in effective control of the island. The representative of that Government had clearly repudiated the charge of United States aggression against Formosa. Recalling the statements of the President of the United States on 27 August and the letter dated 21 September from the United States Secretary of State to the Secretary-General, he reaffirmed that the sole mission of the United States Fleet was to prevent any attack from the mainland on Formosa or vice versa.

The representative of the Central People's Government of the People's Republic of China stated, *inter alia*, that because of the fact that the item "Complaint of aggression upon the Republic of Korea" was not in conformity with the wording proposed by his Government, he would not participate in the discussion of that item. His statement was therefore largely concerned with the question of Taiwan.

The representative of the People's Republic of China, however, charged that from 27 August to 10 November 1950, military aircraft of the United States in Korea had violated the air space of China ninety times, bombing its peaceful cities, towns and villages. Now, he said, the United States forces of aggression were approaching China's northeastern frontier. Only a river separated the two countries geographically, and the security of the People's Republic of China was gravely endangered. The Chinese people, he said, could not afford to stand idly by in the face of this serious situation. They were volunteering in great numbers to go to the aid of the Korean people. Resistance to the United States aggression, it was maintained, was based on self-evident principles of justice and reason. In making Japan its main war base in the Far East, launching armed aggression against Korea and Taiwan, carrying out active intervention against Vietnam and tightening its control over other countries in Asia, the United States Government, he stated, was systematically building up a military encirclement of the People's Republic of China for a further attack upon that country and to stir up a third world war. The American imperialists, he said, claimed that the United States "defence line" must be pushed to the Yalu River, to the Strait of Taiwan, and to the border regions between China and Vietnam, or the United States would have no security. But, he said, in no sense could it be maintained that the Korean people's struggle for liberation, or the exercise of sovereignty by the People's Republic of China over its own territory of Taiwan, or the volunteering of the Chinese people to resist the United States and aid Korea, or the struggle for national independence of the Vietnam Democratic Republic, affected the security of the United States in North America, 5,000 miles away.

The fact was that the civil war in Korea was created by the United States, and was designed solely to furnish a pretext for launching armed aggression against Korea and against China's territory, Taiwan, and for tightening its control in Vietnam and in the Philippines. Clearly, in carrying out aggression simultaneously against Korea and Taiwan under the pretext of the Korean civil war, which was of its own making, the United States Government had vastly extended the scale of the Korean war. It was the United States armed aggression, launched under the pretext of "maintaining security in the Pacific", that had shattered the security of that area.

The representative of the People's Republic of China therefore submitted a draft resolution which, *inter alia*, would have the Council demand the withdrawal from Korea of the armed forces of the United States and all the other countries and leave the people of North and South Korea to settle the domestic affairs of Korea themselves, so that a peaceful solution of the Korean question might be achieved.

. . .

The representative of the USSR considered that the representative of the United States had falsified the whole history of the Korean question in order to conceal and justify its aggression against North Korea. In violation of the agreements made during the war and of Article 107 of the Charter, the United States Government, counting on the support of the Anglo-American bloc in the United Nations had, in 1947, dragged the Korean question into the United Nations, and had "forced" the Organization to adopt a number of illegal resolutions favourable to the United States and its South Korean puppets.

In ordering the United States armed forces to invade Korea on 27 June, several hours before the Security Council was convened, the United States, it was asserted, had brought the whole world face to face with the *fait accompli* of its aggression in Korea. It had afterwards forced the Council to adopt an illegal resolution for the purpose of concealing the aggression already committed. Moreover, the representative of the USSR argued, the decisions taken by the Council on 25 and 27 June had been adopted by an illegally constituted Council, i.e. without the participation of two permanent members, the USSR and China. The United States Government's attempt to convince public opinion that the war against the Korean people was being waged by "United Nations Troops under United Nations Command" was a falsification of facts.

. . .

The six-Power draft resolution was put to the vote and received 9 votes in favour and 1 against (USSR), with 1 member (India) not participating. Since the negative vote was cast by a permanent member, the draft resolution was not adopted.

Intervention of the Central People's Government of the People's Republic of China in Korea

In a telegram dated 4 December 1950, the representatives of Cuba, Ecuador, France, Norway, the United Kingdom and the United States requested the inclusion of the item "Intervention of the Central People's Government of the People's Republic of China in Korea" in the agenda of the fifth session of the General Assembly. In an explanatory memorandum submitted on 5 December, they stated that armed forces of the Central People's Government of the People's Republic of China were conducting military operations against the United Nations forces in Korea, and recalled that the draft resolution submitted jointly by their delegations in the Security Council with a view to dealing with this question had failed of adoption because of the negative vote of one of the permanent members, the USSR. Under those circumstances, they believed that the Assembly should consider the problem urgently, with a view to making appropriate recommendations.

The General Assembly, at its 319th plenary meeting on 6 December 1950, decided, on the recommendation of the General Committee made at its 74th meeting on 5 December, to include this item in its agenda and to refer it to the First Committee for consideration and report.

Representatives of Czechoslovakia and the USSR in the General Committee, and representatives of Czechoslovakia, Poland and the USSR in the General Assembly, had expressed opposition to the inclusion of the item, on the grounds that there was no Chinese armed intervention in Korea (there were only Chinese volunteer forces in Korea who were hastening "to succour their brethren"), and that the real intervention in Korea was being carried out by the armed forces of the United States and its allies.

Discussion in the First Committee

The First Committee, during 1950, considered the question at its 409th to 417th meetings, 7-9 and 11-13 December.

At its 409th meeting on 7 December, the First Committee, by 42 votes to 5, with 4 abstentions, adopted a French motion that priority should be given to the consideration of the item. Representatives of the Byelorussian SSR, Czechoslovakia, Poland, the Ukrainian SSR and the USSR opposed the French motion. At the same meeting, the Committee, by 48 votes to 5, with 4 abstentions, adopted a motion, presented by the United States, that the representative of the Republic of Korea should be invited to participate in the discussions. Representatives of Poland and the USSR spoke in opposition to the United States motion. They maintained that there was no such thing as intervention on the part of the Central People's Government of the People's Republic of China, and, accordingly, it would be wrong to invite South Korean representatives to participate in the discussion, particularly because they would be unable to give an objective picture.

The following draft resolutions were submitted during 1950:

(a)　Joint draft resolution, submitted at the 409th meeting on 7 December, by *Cuba, Ecuador, France, Norway, the United Kingdom and the United States*, which, after recalling the Security Council resolution of 25 June 1950 and the General Assembly resolution of 7 October 1950, and noting that armed forces of the Central People's Government of the People's Republic of China were conducting military operations against the United Nations forces in Korea, called upon all States and authorities, *inter alia*, to prevent their nationals or individuals or units of their armed forces from giving assistance to the North Korean forces and to cause immediate withdrawal of such nationals or units; affirmed that it was the policy of the United Nations to hold the Chinese frontier with Korea inviolate and fully to protect legitimate Chinese and Korean interests in the frontier zone; and requested the United Nations Commission for the Unification and Rehabilitation of Korea to assist in the settlement of any problems relating to conditions on the Korean frontier.

(b)　Draft resolution, submitted by *the USSR* at the 412th meeting on 9 December, which recommended that all foreign troops should be withdrawn immediately from Korea and that the decision on the Korean question should be entrusted to the Korean people themselves.

(c)　Joint draft resolution, submitted at the 415th meeting on 12 December, by *Afghanistan, Burma, Egypt, India, Indonesia, Iran, Iraq, Lebanon, Pakistan, Philippines, Saudi Arabia, Syria and Yemen*, requesting the President of the General Assembly to constitute a group of three persons, including himself, to determine the basis on which a satisfactory cease-fire in Korea could be arranged and to make recommendations to the General Assembly as soon as possible.

(d)　Joint draft resolution, submitted at the 415th meeting on 12 December by *the same countries with the exception of the Philippines*, which, considering that the situation in the Far East was likely to endanger the maintenance of world peace and security, recommended the establishment of a committee to meet as soon as possible and make recommendations for the peaceful settlement of existing issues.

On 5 December 1950, Afghanistan, Burma, Egypt, India, Indonesia, Iran, Iraq, Lebanon, Pakistan, the Philippines, Saudi Arabia, Syria and Yemen appealed to the North Korean authorities and the Central People's Government of the People's Republic of China immediately to declare that it was not their intention that any forces under their control should cross to the south of the 38th parallel of latitude. Such a declaration, the appeal stated, would give time for considering what further steps were necessary to resolve the conflict in the Far East and thus help to avert the danger of another world war. No action was taken on this appeal.

At the 410th meeting of the First Committee on 8 December, the first report of the United Nations Commission for the Unification and Rehabilitation of Korea, dated 7 December 1950, was read. In connexion with Chinese communist intervention in Korea, it stated that, on the basis of existing evidence, the Commission had concluded that Chinese forces in great strength were attacking the United Nations forces in North Korea and that they formed part of the armed forces of the People's Republic of China. Definitely identified forces totalled 231,000 men, drawn from eight armies and comprising 26 divisions. One responsible estimate placed the total number as high as 400,000. Interrogation of prisoners showed that they were not volunteers in any possible meaning of the term. The Commission also called attention to a large-scale exodus of refugees fleeing southwards from North Korea, with one estimate placing the number in the west coast areas alone as high as 500,000. This number would increase, the Commission believed, as additional territory became threatened by invading forces from the north.

Representatives of Belgium, Cuba, the Dominican Republic, Ecuador, France, Greece, the Netherlands, Peru, the Philippines, the United Kingdom, the United States, Uruguay and Venezuela, among others, spoke in support of the joint six-Power draft resolution. They considered that since the veto of the USSR had prevented the Security Council from undertaking effective action to restore peace, it was now the General Assembly's duty to exercise its powers under Article 11 of the Charter and under the resolutions adopted under the title "Uniting for Peace". Only after this question had been settled could other matters relating to the peace and security of Asia be dealt with.

It was argued that just when the armed forces of the United Nations had almost completed the task entrusted to them as a result of the aggression committed by the North Koreans, whose vanquished armies had disappeared into the frozen wastes of

North Korea, in their stead there had appeared a vast contingent of the communist armies of China, which nobody had attacked and with which everyone wished to have peaceful relations. By crossing the border into North Korea, those armies had not only invaded Korea but they had attacked the forces of the United Nations and had brought about a state of undeclared war against the Organization, against each Member State and particularly those which had supported General Assembly resolution 376(V) of 7 October 1950. Such action, they said, constituted a breach of international security; it also imperilled world peace. It was not only the prestige of the democratic nations of the world which was involved, but also the prestige and the moral authority of the United Nations itself that represented all peace-loving nations. Not only were the solemn declarations of principle and the plans for moral and material progress—so carefully worked out to bring peace to all human beings—in danger, but the world was at present on the edge of a catastrophe of immeasurable consequences.

. . .

Representatives of the Byelorussian SSR, Czechoslovakia, Poland, the Ukrainian SSR and the USSR spoke against the six-Power draft resolution and in support of the USSR draft. They rejected the views put forth by the supporters of the six-Power draft, considering them to be based on a complete distortion of the facts. Those views, the five representatives stated, had already been refuted by them during the debates in the Security Council and in the General Assembly on the Korean question.

. . .

The six-Power draft, offered as a justification of the intervention of American troops in Korea, was completely contrary to the purposes and principles of the United Nations, they declared. In point of fact, it was at the instigation of General MacArthur and the United States Government that the Government of South Korea had launched its aggression. That Government had remained in office only because of the support of the American armed forces controlling the country. Fascism, illegality, terrorism and violence had marked a régime which had endeavoured to stifle the aspirations of the Korean people. It was ridiculous to represent the aid given to that régime as a defence of democracy and freedom.

. . .

The American representative, they said, had spoken as if the Chinese were at the frontier of the United States, instead of American troops having advanced toward the Chinese frontier with hostile designs. Long before the outbreak of hostilities, American bombs supplied to Chiang Kai-shek had helped to massacre Chinese citizens; now American aircraft were bombing Manchuria. When the American forces, after crossing the 38th parallel, had continued to advance northward in large numbers, the Chinese people had become indignant and alarmed in the face of the dangerous situation created by the American intervention.

. . .

The real intervention, the representatives of the five Powers reiterated, had been from the side of the United States, and the purpose of the six-Power draft resolution was to divert the attention of the world from United States aggression against Korea and China. The aim of the USSR draft resolution, on the other hand, they added, was to make an effective contribution to the strengthening of peace, and to end the intervention of the United States and of certain other countries which were taking advantage of the United Nations.

The representative of China declared that the communist forces fighting in Korea were regular units of the Fourth Field Army of the Peking régime. The volunteers comprised only those engaged in clerical work, propaganda, first-aid and, to a minor degree, transportation in the rear areas. Such volunteers numbered less than 2,000. The Chinese people, he affirmed, firmly believed that the surest guarantee of the inviolability of their frontier between Korea and Manchuria lay in the existence of a free and united Korea, since an independent Korea could not possibly conduct an imperialistic invasion of China. There was also no suspicion or fear of United States imperialism among the Chinese people, he added. After more than a century of Sino-American relations, the United States had not acquired a single inch of Chinese territory. On the contrary, it had always provided relief for the Chinese people whenever they had been struck by any natural disaster. Therefore, all those contentions and fears were un-Chinese and concocted, and the intervention in Korea was being carried out by a totally un-Chinese régime. It was only when China once again became Chinese that peace and security would reign in the Far East.

The representative of the Republic of Korea asserted that the opponent to the unification of Korea had been the USSR, although it had signed the Potsdam Declaration providing for the establishment of a united and independent Korea. The USSR, he said, had refused to permit general elections in North at the same time as in South Korea, and in this way had succeeded in establishing and maintaining in North Korea a puppet régime which it contended was a government elected by the people, although the elections in North Korea had been carried out under police pressure, and United Nations observers had not been able to see that they were properly held.

. . .

The Korean conflict was not a limited war, he asserted; on the contrary, the United Nations was confronted by an aggressor set on a policy of extermination. The United Nations had already condemned the aggression committed by the North Koreans against the Republic of Korea. Now the Chinese communists had committed a similar act of aggression. He declared that the free world was well aware that the new aggression was a product of the USSR in origin, direction and execution.

Now that the Republic of Korea was once again in grave danger, it again appealed to the Members of the United Nations to adopt a policy of resistance to aggression, in order to prevent further aggression in other parts of the world.

After introducing the joint thirteen-Power draft resolution at the 415th meeting, the representative of India informed the First Committee of the substance of the conversations he had held with the representatives of the Peking Government. His main object throughout those conversations, he explained, had been to understand the point of view of the Peking Government in respect to the Korean conflict and other connected issues and then to make certain proposals for the consideration of the Peking Government. Towards the end of those talks, he had asked General Wu Hsiu-chuan, representative of the Central People's Government of the People's Republic of China, whether it was correct to suppose that the Peking Government did not want a war with the United Nations or with the United States. General Wu Hsiu-chuan replied that most certainly his Government did not want a war but that the forces of the United States and the United Nations were carrying on military operations near the Chinese border and thus a war had been forced upon the Chinese people.

The representative of India felt that, since China had been ravaged by wars of one kind or another for almost a generation, it was understandable that the people of China should not want another war and would welcome a spell of peace. At the same time, the ordeals through which they had passed had made them unduly suspicious and apprehensive. In fact, China seemed to be moving towards a Monroe Doctrine of its own. Nevertheless the United Nations had, for the moment, an assurance that the Peking Government desired a peaceful settlement. Since that was also the wish of the members of the First Committee, India, together with other countries, had introduced the joint thirteen-Power draft resolution.

He then pointed out that the joint draft did not impose an immediate cease-fire order. He had felt that in order to obtain an effective cease-fire order, it would be better to have first an exploratory proposal as embodied in the joint draft. According to that proposal, the President of the General Assembly, together with two other persons of his choice, would consult both High Commands or their representatives and report back to the General Assembly on the most suitable basis for a cease-fire. On the basis of that report, the General Assembly could recommend the actual cease-fire.

At the same meeting, the representative of India introduced the joint twelve-Power draft resolution, but moved, however, that priority of discussion should be given to the joint thirteen-Power draft because of its urgency and importance.

In the discussion that followed, representatives of Australia, Syria and Yugoslavia supported the Indian motion with respect to priority. Representatives of Poland and the USSR opposed the Indian motion. They argued that the First Committee was engaged in a general debate and several draft resolutions had been presented. It was unusual, they stated, to select one for special attention, and there had already been too many changes in the order of their discussions.

The Indian motion was adopted by 48 votes to 5, with 4 abstentions.

The representatives of Brazil, Canada, Egypt, France, India, Iran, Israel, Mexico, the Netherlands, Norway, Pakistan, the Philippines, Syria, Turkey, the United Kingdom, the United States and Yemen, among others, spoke in support of the thirteen-Power draft resolution.

. . .

Viewing the thirteen-Power draft with misgivings, the representative of China declared that in ordinary circumstances, it would be natural for the United Nations to begin with a cease-fire order. That had already been done by the Security Council on 25 June 1950, but the aggressor had paid no attention and the Security Council had then taken police action. Now it was proposed that the General Assembly should seek a cease-fire, but that was equivalent to asking the police to stop at the same time as the gangster. It was doubtful, he observed, whether such a procedure was right, or would enhance the prestige or usefulness of the United Nations.

The representative of the USSR . . . considered that the objective sought by the United Kingdom and United States representatives boiled down to the narrow aim of obtaining a cease-fire but not peace and security in the Far East. Thus, the proposal for a cease-fire constituted merely a hypocritical and camouflaged attempt to obtain a breathing spell before embarking upon further military action and would redound solely to the benefit of the United States and the United Kingdom.

The representative of the USSR added that a correct solution of the Korean question could be found only through the evacuation of all foreign troops from Korea, which would enable the Korean people to settle all issues and problems relating to the future of their country. The USSR draft resolution, he said, laid down the basic conditions for a peaceful settlement of the Korean question and for the restoration of peace and security in the Far East.

These views were shared by the representatives of Czechoslovakia and Poland, who also spoke in favour of the USSR draft and in opposition to the thirteen-Power draft.

The thirteen-Power draft resolution was put to the vote at the 417th meeting of the First Committee on 13 December and was adopted by 51 votes to 5, with 1 abstention.

Resolution adopted by the General Assembly

The interim report of the First Committee, containing the text of the draft resolution adopted, was considered by the General Assembly at its 324th plenary meeting on 14 December.

. . .

The Committee draft resolution was adopted by a roll-call vote of 52 to 5, with 1 abstention. . . . The text of the resolution adopted (384(V)) read as follows:

The General Assembly,

Viewing with grave concern the situation in the Far East,

Anxious that immediate steps should be taken to prevent the conflict in Korea spreading to other areas and to put an end to the fighting in Korea itself, and that further steps should then be taken for a peaceful settlement of existing issues in accordance with the Purposes and Principles of the United Nations,

Requests the President of the General Assembly to constitute a group of three persons, including himself, to determine the basis on which a satisfactory cease-fire in Korea can be arranged and to make recommendations to the General Assembly as soon as possible.

The President of the General Assembly, at the 325th plenary meeting on 14 December, announced the constitution of a Group on Cease Fire in Korea consisting of the following persons: L. B. Pearson (Canada), Sir Benegal Rau (India) and N. Entezam (Iran).

Report of Group on Cease Fire in Korea

The Group on Cease Fire in Korea met almost immediately after it was constituted by the President of the Assembly. It decided to associate the Secretary-General of the United Nations with its work. A report on its work, dated 2 January 1951, was submitted to the General Assembly. The report stated that, as a first step, it had consulted the representatives of the Unified Command as to what they considered to be a satisfactory basis for a cease-fire. The suggestions which had emerged from this consultation could be summarized as follows:

(1) All Governments and authorities concerned, including the Central People's Government of the People's Republic of China and the North Korean authorities, should order and enforce a cessation of all acts of armed force in Korea. The cease-fire should apply to all of Korea.

(2) There should be established across Korea a demilitarized area of approximately twenty miles in depth, with the southern limit following generally the line of the 38th parallel.

(3) The cease-fire should be supervised by a United Nations commission, whose members and designated observers should have free and unlimited access to the whole of Korea.

(4) All Governments and authorities should cease promptly the introduction into Korea of any reinforcement or replacement units or personnel, including volunteers, and additional war equipment and material.

(5) Appropriate provision should be made in the cease-fire arrangements in regard to steps to ensure the security of the forces, the movement of refugees, and the handling of other specific problems arising out of the cease-fire.

(6) The General Assembly should be asked to confirm the cease-fire arrangements, which should continue in effect until superseded by further steps approved by the United Nations.

The Group then had attempted to consult the Central People's Government of the People's Republic of China and, for that purpose, had sent a message to that Government's representative in New York and repeated it by cable to the Minister for Foreign Affairs in Peking. The message stressed that, in the interests of stopping the fighting in Korea and of facilitating a just settlement of the issues there in accordance with the principles of the Charter, the Group was prepared to discuss cease-fire arrangements with the Government of the People's Republic of China or its representatives either in New York or elsewhere, as would be mutually convenient.

On 16 December, the Group requested the Central People's Government to instruct its representative in New York to stay there and to discuss with the Group the possibility of arranging a cease-fire. In its reply, on 21 December, the Government of the People's Republic of China had recalled that its representative had neither participated in or agreed to the adoption of the General Assembly resolution establishing the Group. The Central People's Government had repeatedly declared that it would regard as illegal and null and void all resolutions on major problems, especially regarding Asia, which might be adopted by the United Nations without the participation and approval of duly appointed representatives of the People's Republic of China. After the Security Council had unreasonably voted against the question "Complaint of armed invasion of Taiwan (Formosa)" raised by the Government of the People's Republic of China, that Government had instructed its representatives to remain in New York for participation in the discussion of the question "Complaint by the Union of Soviet Socialist Republics regarding aggression against China by the United States of America''. However, he had still not been given the opportunity to speak. Under those circumstances, the Central People's Government deemed that there was no further necessity for its representatives to remain in New York.

On 19 December, acting on a recommendation from the sponsors of the twelve-Power draft resolution, the Group had sent another message to the Minister for Foreign Affairs of the People's Republic of China, which was intended to remove any possible misunderstandings which might have arisen out of the separation of the twelve-Power draft resolution from the thirteen-Power resolution adopted by the Assembly on 14 December. The message stressed that the Group's clear understanding and also that of the twelve Asian sponsors was that, once a cease-fire arrangement had been achieved, the negotiations envisaged in the twelve-Power draft resolution should be proceeded with at once, and that the Government of the People's Republic of China should be included in the Negotiating Committee referred to in that draft resolution.

On 23 December, the President of the General Assembly, in his capacity as such, had received from the Minister for Foreign Affairs of the People's Republic of China the text of a statement issued by the Government in Peking on 22 December, in which it was noted that that Government, from the very beginning of hostilities in Korea, had stood for the peaceful settlement and localization of the Korean problem. However, the United States Government had not only rejected the proposals made by his Government and by the USSR for the peaceful settlement of the problem, but had rejected negotiations on the question. The statement then reiterated the basic views on the problems involved, as set forth in the Security Council by the representative of the People's Republic of China and in that organ, as well as in the General Assembly, by the representative of the USSR. In conclusion, the statement held that if the Asian and Arab nations wished to achieve genuine peace, they must free themselves from United States pressure, no longer make use of the Group on Cease Fire and give up the idea of achieving a cease-fire first and negotiations afterwards. The Central People's Government of the People's Republic of China insisted that, as a basis for negotiating a peaceful settlement of the Korean problem, all foreign troops must be withdrawn from the peninsula, Korea's domestic affairs must be settled by the Korean people themselves, the American aggression forces must be withdrawn from Taiwan and the representative of the People's Republic of China must obtain a legitimate status in the United Nations.

The Group concluded its report by stating that, in those circumstances, it regretted that it had been unable to pursue the discussion of a satisfactory cease-fire arrangement and, therefore, felt that it could not usefully make any recommendation in regard to a cease-fire for the time being.

Report of the UN Commission on Korea

Pursuant to General Assembly resolution 293(IV) of 21 October 1949, the United Nations Commission on Korea transmitted to the fifth regular session of the Assembly a report of its activities covering the period from 15 December 1949 to 4 September 1950.

Facts of Aggression

The Commission, in Part One of its report, declared that on Sunday, 25 June 1950, at 1:30 P.M. (Korean time), it was officially informed by the Foreign Minister of the Republic of Korea that the territory of the Republic had been invaded early that morning by the armed forces of the North Korean authorities, and was still under attack all along the 38th parallel of latitude. At 5 P.M. the same day, the Commission's field observers reported that Northern armed forces had that morning taken the Southern defences completely by surprise in a well-mounted attack all along the 38th parallel. The strategic plan of the Northern forces appeared to be to draw off Southern defensive reserves by launching heavy attacks on the east and west, and then to make the main attack through the centre along the shortest route to Seoul.

The Commission immediately drew the attention of the Secretary-General to the situation, suggesting that he might consider the possibility of bringing the matter to the notice of the Security Council.

It then approved the text of a broadcast to be made by the Chairman to North Korea, in which the Commission deplored the tragic outbreak of military conflict on a large scale in Korea. The Commission appealed for an immediate cessation of hostilities.

. . .

Korea prior to act of aggression

In its survey of the situation in Korea prior to the act of aggression, the Commission, in Part Two of its report, explained its own task and the attitudes toward it. The Republic of Korea, it said, continued to regard the Commission as an important symbol of the United Nations interest in Korea and looked upon it for assistance in solving many of Korea's problems. The North Korean authorities, on the other hand, were hostile toward the Commission.

With respect to the question of unification, the Commission called attention to the fact that this question remained the fundamental objective towards which it should work. Consequently, on 7 February 1950 it established a Sub-Committee which decided to approach its task: (1) by hearing the views of leading personalities in Korea in regard to the removal of existing barriers to economic, social and other friendly intercourse and in regard to the question of unification of Korea, and (2) by informing the people of both South and North Korea by means of broadcasts of the objects and aims of the Commission, with particular emphasis on the question of unification.

. . .

In early June, while the Commission was collating the reports of its election observation teams, Radio Pyongyang gave wide publicity to an article in the North Korean Press calling for an intensification of measures aimed at unifying the country. On 5 June 1950, the Central Committee of the Democratic Front for the Attainment of Unification of the Fatherland announced that agreement had been reached on a fundamental policy for expediting the peaceful unification of Korea on the basis of proposals arising out of the above article. This was followed on 7 June by the broadcasting of an appeal outlining a detailed programme for unification. Broadcasts on the following days invited the representatives of almost all political parties and social organizations in the South to appear on 10 June at Yohyon station, just north of the parallel, to receive copies of the appeal. Included in the list of those invited was the United Nations Commission on Korea.

The Commission appointed its Acting Deputy Principal Secretary as its representative to meet the three representatives from the Democratic Front for the Attainment of Unification of the Fatherland, who would be waiting above the parallel to deliver the appeal. The Commission's representative was authorized to receive a copy of the appeal and to attempt, at the same time, to transmit to the Northern representatives copies of its previous broadcasts to North Korea. These, however, were not accepted by the Northern representatives on the grounds that they were mere agents and were without authority to enter into any discussions or accept any documents.

On 11 June, Radio Pyongyang announced that the three emissaries had been directed to cross the 38th parallel and proceed to Seoul in order to deliver copies to the designated organizations. As soon as the three emissaries crossed the parallel they were placed under detention, and efforts were made to induce them to accept the point of view of the Republic of Korea. This step of detaining "envoys of peace" touched off a violent chain of denunciation by Radio Pyongyang.

The Commission reported that arrangements for the unification drive from Radio Pyongyang were still continuing on the eve of the invasion.

The Commission went on to report that the Republic of Korea's programme for developing its shaky economy was directly dependent upon the assistance of the United States Economic Co-operation Administration. The Republic, it said, was faced with excessive defence expenditures, deficiencies in plants, shortages of raw materials and consumer goods, serious inflation and general nervousness about the future. It had begun, though belatedly, to grapple with these difficulties through the medium of a careful economic stabilization programme, and the future appeared rather brighter on the eve of the invasion.

The building of security forces, the Commission pointed out, absorbed energies and resources which were urgently needed to develop politically the new form of democratic representative government and carry out the economic and social programme necessary to nourish and keep healthy the infant State.

Up to the end of May 1950, the Executive and the Legislature were continually engaged in a bitter struggle for the recognition by the other of what each deemed its proper power and authority. The Executive, the Commission said, possessed an advantage in that it already controlled the administration, and the Legislature felt that the Executive tended to ignore it in the transaction of day-to-day business. The Legislature, not willing to be thus ignored, and resentful of the treatment meted out to it by the Executive, tried again and again to assert its right of control. It had become clear, long before the act of aggression occurred, that the Legislature would not rest content until its relationship with the Executive was satisfactorily adjusted.

New general elections, the first to be conducted by the Government of the Republic of Korea, were due to take place before 31 May 1950, the date when the mandate of the first National Assembly would expire. Early in 1950, the Commission disclosed, considerable prominence was given to the question of the date on which these elections would be held, and it soon became evident that the Executive and the National Assembly were at odds on this issue.

. . . The President finally fixed 30 May as the date for the election.

The Commission was invited by the Republic of Korea to observe the general elections. Teams were organized by the Commission to cover the whole of South Korea. They were charged with studying the election law and regulations and their application, the organization and arrangements for the elections, the balloting and the subsequent counting of ballots and the declaration of the results. The teams were also to examine the attitude of the authorities, the platforms and activities of political parties and organizations and the reaction of the people to the elections. They were further to study the nature and extent of freedom of expression and of assembly, freedom from intimidation, violence and threats of violence, and undue interference with or by voters, candidates and political parties and groups.

The Commission arrived at the following general conclusions regarding the elections of 30 May 1950:

(a) Very considerable enthusiasm was everywhere shown by the electorate. A high percentage, almost 90 per cent, cast their votes.

(b) The electoral law and regulations were adequate and generally enforced. The organization of the elections and the work of the various election committees were commendable, and the electoral machinery functioned well.

(c) The secrecy of the ballot was respected.

(d) The lack of a developed party system and discipline led to an excessive number of candidates and made the choice of the voters needlessly difficult.

(e) As no clearly defined party programmes were placed before the electorate, votes were cast for individual candidates on their personal rather than on their party merits. In fact, a party label was regarded as a disadvantage.

(f) No undue pressure was exerted to influence the vote in favour of a particular candidate.

(g) There was certain concrete evidence of interference by the authorities with candidates and their election campaigns. This interference, in the main, was carried out by local police. Some candidates who were under arrest were actually elected, and the voters seemed to react against police interference by supporting those candidates with whom the police had interfered.

The safeguarding of its national security, the Commission reported, was a constant anxiety for the Republic of Korea.

. . .

Analysis and conclusions

After dealing with its functions since the aggression, in the third part of its report, the Commission went on to analyse the issues involved and to give its conclusions. The analysis and conclusions, reproduced as given in Part Four of the Commission's report, were as follows:

The invasion of the territory of the Republic of Korea by the armed forces of the North Korean authorities, which began on 25 June 1950, was an act of aggression initiated without warning and without provocation, in execution of a carefully prepared plan.

This plan of aggression, it is now clear, was an essential part of the policy of the North Korean authorities, the object of which was to secure control over the whole of Korea. If control could not be gained by peaceful means, it would be achieved by overthrowing the Republic of Korea, either by undermining it from within or, should that prove ineffective, by resorting to direct aggression. As the methods used for undermining the Republic from within proved unsuccessful, the North Korean authorities launched an invasion of the territory of the Republic of Korea.

The origin of the conflict is to be found in the artificial division of Korea and in the failure, in 1945, of the occupying Powers to reach agreement on the method to be used for giving independence to Korea. This failure was not due to anything inherent in the attitude of the people of Korea themselves, but was a reflection of those wider and more fundamental differences of outlook and policy which have become so marked a feature of the international scene.

This artificial division was consolidated by the exclusion from North Korea of the United Nations Temporary Commission, which had been charged by the General Assembly to observe the holding of elections on a democratic basis in the whole of Korea. In the circumstances, it was decided to hold such elections in South Korea alone.

Had internationally-supervised elections been allowed to take place in the whole of Korea, and had a unified and independent Korea thereby come into existence, the present conflict could never have arisen.

The Korean people, one in race, language and culture, fervently desire to live in a unified and independent Korea. Unification can be the only aim regarding Korea. It did, however, appear to the Commission, before the aggression took place, that unification through negotiation was unlikely to be achieved if such negotiation involved the holding of internationally-supervised elections on a democratic basis in the whole of Korea. Experience suggested that the North Korean authorities would never agree to such elections.

It was hoped that, at some stage, it might be possible to break down the economic and social barriers between the two political entities as a step toward unification. That too proved illusory, as the North Korean authorities persisted in their policy of aiming at the overthrow of the Republic of Korea.

After the consolidation of the division of Korea, propaganda and hostile activities on the part of the North Korean authorities accentuated tension which, in turn, stiffened the attitude of the Government and people of the Republic of Korea, and even further prejudiced such possibility of unification by negotiation as might have remained. Notwithstanding the continued efforts of the Commission, it appeared on the eve of the aggression that the Korean peninsula would remain divided indefinitely, or at least until international tension had slackened.

The necessity to safeguard the stability and security of the Republic of Korea from the threat from the North gradually became a controlling factor in all the major activities of the administration of the Republic, and absorbed energies and resources which were needed to develop the new form of representative government and to carry out the economic and social reconstruction programme.

The first two years of the new National Assembly reflected clearly the difficulties which it would be normal to expect in a body dealing with a new and unfamiliar political structure. It had become clear, long before the act of aggression occurred, that the Legislature was making good progress in its efforts to exert parliamentary control over all departments of government, and would not rest content until its relations with the Executive had been satisfactorily adjusted. The growing civic responsibility shown by the Legislature augured well for the future of representative government in Korea.

At the elections of 30 May 1950, the people showed very considerable enthusiasm, and the electoral machinery functioned well. Among the cases of interference with candidates which occurred, some were explainable in the light of the stringent precautions which the Government found it necessary to take in order to safeguard the stability and security of the State against the threat from the North. Although there appeared to be little justification for interference in some other cases, the results of the elections, in which many candidates critical of the Administration were returned, showed that the voters were in fact able to exercise their democratic freedom of choice among candidates, and had cast their votes accordingly. The results also showed popular support of the Republic, and a determination to improve the Administration by constitutional means.

The division of Korea added to the economic difficulties that had arisen at the end of the Japanese domination, and made it most difficult for the Republic of Korea to become self-supporting. Funds which might have been expended for the execution of the social and economic programme of the Republic were consumed by heavy defence expenditures. Nevertheless, when the aggression occurred, substantial progress was being made with that programme.

Serious problems of reconstruction and rehabilitation, particularly the grave refugee problem, already confront the country. To these problems will be added problems of greater magnitude when the military conflict comes to an end. It will be quite beyond the capacity of the country to provide from its own resources means for rehabilitation. A healthy and viable democracy in Korea cannot come into being unless very considerable aid and assistance are provided from outside Korea.

Finally, as the division of the country and the resulting antagonisms were artificial, the Commission believes that, when the conditions under which they arose disappear, it will be possible for the Korean people of both North and South to come again together, to live in peace and to build the strong foundations of a free, democratic Korea.

(YUN 1950, pp. 232-57)

Armistice and reconstruction

Armistice negotiations between the military commanders of the opposing sides in Korea began in July 1951, but were recessed over the question of exchange and repatriation of prisoners. In April 1953, agreement was reached on the exchange of sick and wounded prisoners, followed by an agreement in June on the question of all prisoners of war. Fighting continued until 27 June 1953, when an Armistice Agreement was signed between the United Nations Command and the Chinese-North Korean Command. A Military Armistice Commission was established to supervise implementation of the Agreement and to settle any violations through negotiations.

The United Nations Commission for the Unification and Rehabilitation of Korea (UNCURK) replaced the United Nations Commission on Korea in 1950. It remained in the country until its dissolution in 1973 when the General Assembly, by unanimous decision, considered UNCURK's mandate to have been fulfilled in view of a joint communiqué issued by North and South Korea in July 1972, stating that their common aim was to promote national unity and achieve reunification by peaceful means, without reliance on, or interference by, outside forces. In 1974, the Assembly urged North and South Korea to continue their dialogue to expedite reunification, and the question of Korea was taken off the Assembly's agenda.

United Nations Command reports

Reports of the United Nations Command operations in Korea were submitted by the representative of the United States to the Security Council, in accordance with the Security Council resolution of 7 July 1950. The following information on the progress of truce negotiations and of operations is taken from reports Nos. 61 to 76 and from a special report of the Unified Command to the Security Council dated 7 August 1953.

Truce negotiations

By the end of 1952, agreement had been reached on all major questions relating to the conclusion of an armistice and a tentative draft armistice agreement had been worked out covering all agreed points. The differences between the United Nations Command and the Chinese-North Korean side which had prevented the conclusion of an armistice had been narrowed by the end of April 1952, to the question of the disposal of prisoners of war. The United Nations Command had insisted that force should not be used to repatriate any prisoner of war. The Chinese-North Korean side had insisted on the unconditional repatriation of all prisoners of war. Armistice negotiations were recessed on 8 October 1952, following the rejection by the Chinese-North Korean side of United Nations Command proposals on the question of repatriation of prisoners of war. They were resumed on 26 April 1953.

Following a resolution adopted by the Executive Committee of the League of Red Cross Societies on 13 December 1952, which appealed to the parties, as a gesture of good will, to implement the humanitarian principles of the Geneva Convention by repatriating sick and wounded prisoners of war, the Commander-in-Chief of the United Nations Command, on 22 February, addressed a letter to the Chinese-North Korean Commanders, stating that the United Nations Command still remained ready to implement, immediately, the repatriation of sick and wounded prisoners of war and asking if the other side was prepared to proceed with such repatriation.

On 28 March, the Chinese-North Korean Command agreed to the principle of the exchange of the sick and wounded, which, they stated, "should be made to lead to the smooth settlement of the entire question of prisoners of war". Arrangements for the exchange were initiated through the respective liaison officers on 6 April.

The agreement was followed on 30 March by a statement by Chou En-lai, Foreign Minister of the People's Republic of China, subsequently endorsed by the Prime Minister of the North Korean regime, indicating a desire to resume negotiations on the entire prisoner-of-war question.

On 11 April 1953, agreement was formally reached on the repatriation of sick and wounded prisoners of war. The initial Chinese-North Korean figure for prisoners of war to be repatriated was 600, including 450 Koreans and 150 non-Koreans. The United Nations Command initially agreed to repatriate 5,800 prisoners, including 5,100 Koreans and 700 Chinese. Pursuant to the agreement, sick and wounded prisoners of war were exchanged between 20 April and 3 May.

Total deliveries of both sides including those recently wounded, are summarized in the following table:

Delivery of United Nations Command Personnel

United States	149
United Kingdom	32
Canada	2
Colombia	6
Greece	11
Australia	5
Turkey	15
South Africa	1
Philippines	1
Netherlands	1
Republic of Korea	471
Total	684

Delivery of Chinese-North Korean Personnel

North Korea	5,194
China	1,030
Civilian Internees	446
Total	6,670

On 17 April, in response to the Chinese-North Korean suggestion for a resumption of the armistice negotiations for settling the entire prisoner-of-war question, the Commander-in-Chief of the United Nations Forces proposed that prisoners of war not directly repatriated should be released in Korea to the custody of a neutral State, such as Switzerland, and that after allowing a reasonable time, such as 60 days, for determining the attitudes of individuals in its custody with respect to their status, the neutral State should make arrangements for the peaceable disposition of those remaining in its custody.

The armistice negotiations, which had been in recess since 8 October 1952, were resumed on 26 April 1953 when the Senior Delegate of the Chinese-North Korean Command presented a six-point proposal under which all prisoners desiring repatriation would be returned within two months after an armistice. Within one month after completion of direct repatriation, the remainder would be sent to a neutral State, where, for six months, representatives of their home countries would be enabled to explain to them matters regarding their repatriation. Prisoners requesting repatriation would be afforded a speedy return. If at the end of six months any prisoners were unrepatriated, the question of their disposition would be submitted to the political conference which, in accordance with the draft armistice agreement, was to take place after the armistice.

In reply, the United Nations Command stated that the period of detention proposed by the Chinese-North Korean Command would result in the indefinite detention of those prisoners who were opposed to repatriation. On 29 April, the Chinese-North Korean Command indicated that the neutral State proposed should be an unnamed Asian country.

On 2 May, the Chinese-North Korean side asked whether it could be said that India, Burma, Indonesia and Pakistan were not suitable as neutral nations. It also asked if the United Nations Command would agree to sending to Switzerland, Sweden, Poland and Czechoslovakia all the prisoners not directly repatriated.

The United Nations Command pointed out that it had suggested that the neutral State agreed upon should keep custody of the prisoners in Korea and that it could not agree to the prisoners being transported to another country.

On 4 May, the United Nations Command nominated Pakistan as the neutral nation to assume custody of the prisoners.

On 7 May, the Chinese-North Korean side put forward a new proposal, providing for the establishment of a Neutral Nations Repatriation Commission to be composed of the four States already nominated for membership of the Neutral Nations Supervisory Commission (namely, Czechoslovakia, Poland, Sweden and Switzerland) and India, as agreed upon by both sides. This Commission, it was proposed, was to take custody of the prisoners in Korea.

On 13 May the United Nations Command presented a counter-proposal shortening the period of time in which the non-repatriates would remain in neutral custody, providing for the release of Korean non-repatriates immediately after the armistice, and proposing that only Indian forces take actual custody of the non-repatriates. The Chinese-North Korean side rejected these proposals.

On 25 May, the United Nations Command made a new proposal, providing for the transfer of both Korean and Chinese non-repatriates to neutral custody and for consideration of the disposition of any remaining non-repatriates by the political conference for a limited period, after which they might either be released to civilian status or the question of their disposition referred to the General Assembly.

On 4 June, the United Nations Command stated, the Chinese-North Korean Command offered a counter-proposal in effect based on "the mechanics of General Assembly resolution 610(VII)", also closely paralleling the United Nations Command proposals of 25 May (see above), but vague on the basic principle of "non-forcible repatriation". The United Nations Command reported that it succeeded in reaching agreement with the other side on the elaboration of the Neutral Nations Repatriation Commission's terms of reference to ensure that the principle approved by the General Assembly that force should not be used to compel or to prevent repatriation of any prisoners of war would be fully observed.

On 8 June, it was stated, the Senior Delegates for the United Nations Command and for the Communists signed the Prisoner of War Agreement, which was incorporated by reference in the Armistice Agreement. The delegations then proceeded to the final arrangements toward an early conclusion of the armistice.

The United Nations Command further reported that on 18 June "officials of the Republic of Korea brought about a break-out from prisoner-of-war camps of some 27,000 Korean prisoners of war who had previously indicated that they would resist repatriation to North Korea". This action by the Republic of Korea, it was stated, was inconsistent with the Agreement of 8 June on prisoners of war and the United Nations Command at once protested to the Republic of Korea Government. It also informed the Chinese-North Korean Command of the event and told them that, while efforts would be made to recover as many of the escapees as possible, there was not much hope that many of these could be recaptured since they had melted into the South Korean population. This incident, it was reported, led to immediate conversations with the Republic of Korea by the representatives of the Unified Command. After prolonged discussions, it was stated, the Republic of Korea gave assurances that it would not obstruct the implementation of the terms of the Armistice Agreement.

The conclusion of an armistice was, however, further delayed, the United Nations Command stated, since the Chinese-North Korean side demanded assurances that the United Nations Command would "live up" to the terms of the Armistice Agreement. While giving these assurances, the United Nations Command made it clear that it would not use force against the Republic of Korea forces to ensure compliance with the armistice by the Republic of Korea.

The Armistice Agreement was finally signed on 27 July 1953, at 10 a.m. Korean time.

In its special report to the Security Council, the Unified Command stated that it had agreed to waive certain safeguards, e.g., in regard to the construction and rehabilitation of military airfields in North Korea, but had asked that governments with forces under the Command should make it clear in a declaration to be issued after the signing of an armistice that "if there was an unprovoked renewal of the armed attack by the Communists the sixteen governments would again be united and prompt to resist". The Declaration, which was signed by representatives of the sixteen participating nations in Washington on 27 July 1953, was as follows:

We the United Nations Members whose military forces are participating in the Korean action support the decision of the Commander-in-Chief of the United Nations Command to conclude an armistice agreement. We hereby affirm our determination fully and faithfully to carry out the terms of that armistice. We expect that the other parties to the agreement will likewise scrupulously observe its terms.

The task ahead is not an easy one. We will support the efforts of the United Nations to bring about an equitable settlement in Korea based on the principles which have long been established by the United Nations, and which call for a united, independent and democratic Korea. We will support the United Nations in its efforts to assist the people of Korea in repairing the ravages of war.

We declare again our faith in the principles and purposes of the United Nations, our consciousness of our continuing responsibilities in Korea, and our determination in good faith to seek a settlement of the Korean problem. We affirm, in the interests of world peace, that if there is a renewal of the armed attack, challenging again the principles of the United Nations, we should again be united and prompt to resist. The consequences of such a breach of the armistice would be so grave that, in all probability, it would not be possible to confine hostilities within the frontiers of Korea.

Finally, we are of the opinion that the armistice must not result in jeopardizing the restoration or the safeguarding of peace in any other part of Asia.

The report of the United Nations Command covering the period 1 to 15 August stated that the period had marked the beginning of the implementation of the Armistice Agreement. During this period, it was stated, agreement was reached on the method of operation of joint observer teams, which were dispatched to their assigned areas. Marking of boundaries, clearing of hazards and construction of the various installations were begun within the demilitarized zone. Agreement was also reached on the civil police and the type of arms they might carry within the demilitarized zone. Neutral nations inspection teams were dispatched to the ports of entry of both sides.

The report stated that, during the first week of August, an advance party representing the Indian contingent of the Neutral Nations Repatriation Commission and the Custodial Forces of India arrived in Tokyo. A "Memorandum of Understanding" between the Indian group and the group representing the Senior Member of the United Nations Command Military Armistice Commission and his staff was drafted. It related to facilities and support to be furnished by the United Nations Command to the Neutral Nations Repatriation Commission installation within the demilitarized zone on the United Nations Command side of the demarcation line.

Dealing with the repatriation of Chinese-North Korean prisoners, the report of the United Nations Command for 1 to 15 August stated that the United Nations Command had provided adequate food, clothes and medical care for all the prisoners of war in its custody but that, for propaganda purposes, Communist prisoners had torn newly issued clothing and cast aside comfort items. At the same time, the report mentioned that United Nations Command repatriates bore evidence of brutal treatment. In their individual stories, these prisoners stated that the Communists had taken every possible measure for their indoctrination. The idea had been instilled into their minds that the United Nations and, in particular, the United States had started the war.

The United Nations Command report for the period 15 to 31 August stated that by the end of that period a total of 61,415 prisoners had been returned by the United Nations Command to Communist control. By the same date, the following numbers of United Nations Command personnel had been released from Communist captivity:

United States	2,827
Other United Nations	1,208
Republic of Korea	6,979
Total	11,014

The United Nations Command reported that Communist members of the joint Red Cross teams had not acted in conformity with the Armistice Agreement since they had not been interested in providing humanitarian service to the prisoners, but in propaganda.

On 19 August, it was reported, the Communist side delivered a roster of deceased United Nations Command military personnel. The total number reported was 1,078. Agreement was reached later on the recovery of bodies of deceased personnel from the demilitarized zone under the control of both sides, the reports said.

. . .

Economic and relief assistance

The United Nations Command report for the period 1 to 15 February stated that although the United Nations Command was able to assist the Government of the Republic of Korea in meeting the basic minimum needs of the Korean people for food from United States appropriated funds and contributions made by Member States, such aid was necessarily adapted to meet the general needs and usually involved bulk foods, such as grain.

However, there was an ever present need for specialized and supplementary foods not adaptable to normal programming in large quantities. These special needs, it was reported, related to hospitals, welfare institutions, convalescent centres and, particularly, to feeding stations. Forty-five feeding stations, the report stated, were providing 44,000 meals a day to persons with certificates from medical authorities, all requiring special or supplementary foods, the principal recipients being the sick, pregnant mothers and children. The United Nations Command asked for voluntary contributions of powdered eggs, fats, yeast, sugar, cereals, cod liver oils, dry foods and canned meats which, it said, it could transport to Korea at no expense to the donors.

On 25 February, the United States agreed to pay $85,800,000 to the Republic of Korea for full and final settlement of all unpaid Korean currency provided to the United States forces prior to 7 February 1953. This payment brought to $163,490,444.99 the total which the United States Government had paid for Korean currency provided by the Republic of Korea.

The United Nations Command stressed the shortage of trained medical personnel in Korea and acknowledged the valuable work of the Italian Red Cross and of a Swedish group in this field. It also acknowledged the aid provided by the American-Korean Foundation to help disabled persons. This group, the United Nations Command said, in conjunction with the Republic of Korea, the United Nations Korean Reconstruction Agency (UNKRA) and the United Nations Command, had initiated a programme of voluntary assistance from the people of the United States in the rehabilitation of Korean disabled civilian and military personnel—including medical, prostheses and training aspects.

In June the United Nations Command reported that the United Nations Civil Assistance Command (UNCACK) was reorganized and redesignated as the Korea Civil Assistance Command (KCAC), so as to operate under the direct supervision of the Commander-in-Chief, United Nations Command. The purpose of the change was to assure a more efficient administration of the economic assistance being extended to the Republic of Korea by Member States through the Unified Command. Under the new arrangement, the Korean Civil Assistance Command would administer all phases of civil assistance rendered by the United Nations Command to the Republic of Korea, including the formulation of programmes for the relief and support of the civilian population, the distribution of relief supplies and the carrying out of projects of reconstruction and rehabilitation other than those undertaken by the United Nations Korean Reconstruction Agency.

(YUN 1953, pp. 109-15)

Both the Democratic People's Republic of Korea and the Republic of Korea maintained observer status in the General Assembly until September 1991, when they were simultaneously admitted to the United Nations as Member States. In December of that year, the two countries signed an Agreement on Reconciliation, Non-Aggression, Cooperation and Exchange between the North and the South. In February 1992, they exchanged ratification documents and agreed to implement the Agreement as well as a Joint Declaration on Denuclearization of the Korean Peninsula, initialled in December 1991. In September 1992, the two sides established four joint commissions—a reconciliation commission, a military commission, an economic exchanges commission and a socio-cultural commission—to supervise implementation of the Agreement. The commissions never functioned, however, as the Democratic People's Republic of Korea, protesting the "Team Spirit" joint military exercises of the Republic of Korea and the United States, refused to attend any of the initial commission meetings scheduled in November 1992. Later meetings in 1993, intended to arrange for summit talks and resolve South-North issues, including joint nuclear inspections, resulted in no substantive progress.

In March 1993, the Democratic People's Republic of Korea announced its intention to withdraw from the Treaty on the Non-Proliferation of Nuclear Weapons, effective June 1993, blaming "Team Spirit" and United States influence over the International Atomic Energy Agency (IAEA). When the Republic of Korea proposed resuming talks to discuss the Joint Declaration on Denuclearization of the Korean Peninsula and the Non-Proliferation Treaty, the Democratic People's Republic rejected the proposal, insisting that it must settle the nuclear issue with the United States. Following bilateral negotiations, the two sides reached agreement that the Democratic People's Republic of Korea was prepared to remain a party to the Non-Proliferation Treaty and to allow implementation of its safeguards measures. Accordingly, IAEA resumed its activities in the Democratic People's Republic in November 1994.

Central America and the Caribbean

During the late 1970s and throughout the 1980s, Central America experienced deepening civil conflicts, military *coups d'état* and guerrilla activities.

The United Nations played a crucial role in accelerating the efforts towards peaceful settlement of the civil conflicts in Costa Rica, El Salvador, Guatemala, Honduras, Nicaragua and Panama. In the late 1980s, the Security Council authorized the undertaking of peace-keeping missions to Central America, including the United Nations Observer Group in Central America (ONUCA) which, during the period from November 1989 to January 1992, was charged with verifying compliance with the security undertakings agreed upon by five Central American countries in 1987. Following the February 1990 presidential elections, supervised by the United Nations Observer Mission to Verify the Electoral Process in Nicaragua (ONUVEN), ONUCA's mandate was enlarged to allow it to play a part in the voluntary demobilization of the members of the Nicaraguan resistance. With the support of the United Nations Observer Mission in El Salvador (ONUSAL), beginning in 1991, the peace process in that country advanced steadily, despite obstacles and slow progress in certain areas. Peace negotiations continued in Guatemala. To strengthen the peace process, a United Nations Mission for the Verification of Human Rights and of Compliance with the Commitments of the Comprehensive Agreement on Human Rights in Guatemala (MINUGUA) was established in September 1994.

El Salvador

The United Nations undertaking in El Salvador was innovative in many respects. The Organization played a central role in negotiating the 1992 peace accords and remained engaged in the transition from peace-keeping to post-conflict peace-building. This involved security-related aspects, including the abolition of the old military-controlled national police and the creation of a national civil police following the redefining of the role of the armed forces as limited to defence against external threat, as well as key institutional reforms designed to entrench the rule of law and to guarantee respect for human rights. The United Nations also supported a complex set of programmes for reintegration into society of former combatants of both sides and of the rural populations who occupied land in conflict zones during the years of armed confrontation. In endorsing the Secretary-General's negotiating efforts and subsequently the peace accords themselves, the Security Council accepted the request of the parties that the United Nations verify compliance with all the agreements reached.

Following the effective verification of a prolonged cease-fire and separation of forces, the demobilization of the Frente Farabundo Martí para la Liberación Nacional (FMLN), the reduction of the armed forces and formation of a new civilian police, the United Nations Observer Mission in El Salvador (ONUSAL), established in May 1991, focused on the democratization of the Salvadorian system and the promotion of national reconciliation. With the support of ONUSAL's Electoral Division, the first post-conflict elections, in which FMLN participated as a political party, were successfully completed in April 1994. In May, the parties agreed on a further revised timetable for the solution of outstanding issues. The Council, in November 1994, extended ONUSAL's mandate for one final period until 30 April 1995.

Guatemala

The Secretary-General, in the exercise of his good offices, continued the efforts to settle the civil conflict in Guatemala, initiated in 1990 by that country's Government and the Unidad Revolucionaria Nacional Guatemalteca (URNG). In January 1994, an agreement was signed for the resumption of negotiations between the parties, establishing a framework for reaching firm and lasting peace at an early date.

The new agreement retained some of the features of the previous process, especially the negotiation agenda adopted in April 1991, but introduced some important changes, such as the creation of an Assembly of the Civil Society in order to promote consensus among the various sectors of society on a number of key issues. In addition, the parties requested the Secretary-General to appoint a representative to serve as Moderator of the negotiations and asked the United Nations to verify implementation of all agreements reached between them. In February, the Secretary-General appointed Jean Arnault as Moderator.

In March 1994, a Comprehensive Agreement on Human Rights was signed, as well as an agreement on a timetable for the negotiation of a firm and lasting peace. Talks relating to the resettlement of the population groups uprooted by the armed conflict were concluded successfully with the signing of an agreement in June. Under another June agreement, the parties decided to establish a Commission to clarify past human rights violations and acts of violence against the Guatemalan people.

In September, the General Assembly established MINUGUA for an initial period of six months to support the early establishment of peace and help strengthen democracy in the country.

Haiti

The crisis in Haiti in the early 1990s preoccupied the United Nations. The Secretary-General and his Special Envoy actively supported the intensive efforts of the Organization of American States (OAS) to find a solution to that crisis, prompted by the *coup d'état* of September 1991 which overthrew the democratically elected President of Haiti, Jean-Bertrand Aristide, forcing him into exile. Through those efforts, the Governors Island Agreement and the New York Pact were concluded in 1993, the first by President Aristide and the Commander-in-Chief of the Armed Forces of Haiti, General Raoul Cédras, and the second by the political parties represented in the Haitian Parliament. According to both documents, President Aristide was to return to Haiti on 30 October.

As part of the Agreement, the Security Council authorized the dispatch of the United Nations Mission in Haiti (UNMIH), which was prevented by the Haitian military authorities, together with the police, from entering the country. Consequently, the sanctions imposed against Haiti by the Council in mid-June, shortly before signing of the Agreement, and suspended in August when certain measures in the Agreement were implemented, were promptly reinstated in October and thereafter strengthened.

The joint United Nations/OAS International Civilian Mission in Haiti (MICIVIH), in operation in the country since February 1993 and whose United Nations component had been authorized by the General Assembly in April to verify compliance with Haiti's human rights obligations, was withdrawn immediately following the prevention of UNMIH's emplacement amidst mounting demonstrations and threats of violence against the two missions and President Aristide's return.

In July 1994, the Security Council authorized Member States to form a multinational force and to use all necessary means to facilitate the departure from Haiti of the military leadership, consistent with the Governors Island Agreement, the prompt return of President Aristide and the restoration of the legitimate Government. At the same time, the Council revised and extended UNMIH's mandate for six months, to assist the democratic Government of Haiti in maintaining the secure and stable environment established by the multinational force, protecting international personnel and key installations, professionalizing the Haitian armed forces and creating a separate police force, and establishing an environment conducive to the organization of free and fair legislative elections. UNMIH's strength was increased to 6,000 troops.

In September, the lead elements of the 28-nation force, spearheaded by the United States, landed in Haiti without opposition. Following their deployment, the top military and political leaders left the country and President Aristide returned to Haiti on 15 October. That same day, the Security Council lifted the sanctions. At the end of October, MICIVIH resumed its activities, its mandate having been renewed by the General Assembly in July for another year. By the time the new Government took office in November, the UNMIH advance team was fully operational and preparations for the Mission's deployment had begun. In December, the President, with the approval of the Parliament, established a Provisional Electoral Council in preparation for elections to take place during the first half of 1995.

Nicaragua

Following a bitter armed conflict in Nicaragua, major steps were taken towards national reconciliation with the establishment of a cease-fire and demobilization arrangements in March 1990 after the elections held in February of that year under the supervision of the United Nations Mission to Verify the Electoral Process in Nicaragua (ONUVEN). For the first time in Nicaraguan history, the presidency was peacefully transferred to an opposition party. The process of pacification and democratization then advanced significantly. More than 20,000 members of the Nicaraguan resistance were demobilized and the army was reduced from 92,000 combatants to slightly over 15,000, the smallest in Central America. About 350,000 displaced persons and refugees returned.

Recognizing that the consolidation of peace in the country was a key factor in the Central American peace process, the General Assembly, in December 1993, expressed support for the Government's efforts in that regard. To help rehabilitate the country's post-conflict economy and assist in its social reconstruction, thus strengthening its democratic institutional structures, a Support Group for Nicaragua, composed of Canada, Mexico, the Netherlands, Spain and Sweden, was established in May 1994, with the office of the United Nations Development Programme (UNDP) in Nicaragua serving as its technical secretariat. The Group worked under the coordination of the Secretary-General.

Europe, CIS and other States

Peace-keeping and peacemaking efforts in newly independent States

The 15 constituent republics of the USSR broke away in 1991 from the 1922 Union Treaty on the Formation of the Union of Soviet Socialist Republics and declared their independence. On 21 December, 11 of these—Armenia, Azerbaijan, Belarus (formerly Byelorussian SSR), Kazakhstan, Kyrgyzstan, the Republic of Moldova (formerly Moldavian SSR), the Russian Federation, Tajikistan, Turkmenistan, Ukraine and Uzbekistan—constituted the Commonwealth of Independent States (CIS) and supported continuance by the Russian Federation of the membership held by the dissolved USSR in the United Nations, including its permanent membership in the Security Council and in other international organizations.

The United Nations focused its efforts in those newly independent States on facilitating the withdrawal of foreign armed forces from the Baltic States and assisting the countries riven by civil unrest and ethnic strife. By 1994, United Nations interim offices had been established in Armenia, Azerbaijan, Belarus, Georgia, Kazakhstan, Ukraine and Uzbekistan to coordinate operational development activities. In Armenia and Azerbaijan, the Security Council provided unanimous support to the Conference on Security and Cooperation in Europe (CSCE) (now Organization on Security and Cooperation in Europe (OSCE)) in its peacemaking efforts for Nagorny Karabakh—an enclave in Azerbaijan marked by years of fighting between its Armenian and Azerbaijani inhabitants—where, since May 1994, a cease-fire agreement between Armenia and Azerbaijan was holding. In July, both countries and the military representative of Nagorny Karabakh signed a declaration committing themselves to continue to abide by the cease-fire until the signing of a comprehensive political agreement.

In 1994, negotiations on the withdrawal of foreign forces from the Baltic States were successfully completed. To facilitate their withdrawal, the Secretary-General sent a Special Envoy to the Baltic States and the Russian Federation in August/September 1993 and held consultations with all the parties concerned. Armed forces of the Russian Federation left Lithuania in August 1993 and Latvia a year later. In Estonia, agreements were signed in July 1994 on the troop withdrawal and on the dismantling of nuclear reactors at the Russian Federation's naval training centre at Paldiski by September 1995.

In Georgia, Government and Abkhaz forces were fighting for the control of Abkhazia, strategically located on the Black Sea in the north-western part of the Republic of Georgia. In September 1993, while the United Nations Observer Mission in Georgia (UNOMIG) was being established, the cease-fire between the parties to the conflict broke down and UNOMIG's deployment was suspended. In November, the Security Council decided that UNOMIG, with five military observers, would be given an interim mandate to maintain contacts with both sides to the conflict and with military contingents of the Russian Federation in order to monitor and report on the situation on the ground. Subsequently, the Council authorized the deployment of 50 additional observers and instructed UNOMIG to concentrate particularly on developments relevant to United Nations efforts to promote a comprehensive political settlement. In May, the United Nations peace-keeping force and the parties agreed on the deployment of a CIS peace-keeping force to monitor compliance with a cease-fire and separation of forces. They also appealed to the Security Council to expand UNOMIG's mandate in order to participate in the operation. Following consultations by the Secretary-General with the Government of Georgia, the Abkhaz authorities, the Russian Federation and the CIS peace-keeping force, the Council in July expanded UNOMIG's mandate, increased its strength up to 136 military observers and extended its mandate period until 13 January 1995.

The explosive situation in Tajikistan, especially on its borders with Afghanistan, led the Secretary-General, through his Special Envoy, to undertake mediation efforts in order to start a political dialogue between the Tajik parties and to reach agreement on a cessation of hostilities. In September 1994, the Tajik parties signed at Tehran, Iran, an agreement on a temporary cease-fire and the cessation of other hostile acts on the Tajik-Afghan border and within the country. A United Nations Secretariat team visited Tajikistan in October to examine the possibility of a United Nations observer mission there to assist in implementing the cease-fire agreement, which was extended until February 1995. Responding to a request by the Tajik parties, the Security Council, in December, established a United Nations Mission of Observers in Tajikistan (UNMOT) for up to six months, with 44 military observers and 44 civilians.

Situation in the former Yugoslavia

In 1991, the former Yugoslavia disintegrated. Of its six republics (Bosnia and Herzegovina, Croatia, Macedonia, Montenegro, Serbia and Slovenia), four unilaterally declared independence between June and October—the Republics of Croatia, Slovenia, Macedonia, and Bosnia and Herzegovina. The Republic of Serbia strongly disapproved of those declarations and expressed grave concern over the fate of some 600,000 Serbs resident in Croatia and of Serbs resident in Bosnia and Herzegovina. This raised questions of border delineations of those two Republics with Serbia, and resulted in the eruption of violence in a country where political boundaries rarely coincided precisely with demographic distribution.

In the face of escalating violence, the European Community and later the United Nations attempted to bring about a cessation of hostilities and promote a peaceful dialogue.

The increasingly complex situation in the former Yugoslavia compelled the United Nations to carry out a multiplicity of mandates in an environment characterized by vicious cycles of death and destruction, by the intermittent flare-up of conflicts, and by the vicissitudes in the search for a peaceful solution. The efforts of the Organization included preventive diplomacy and deployment of troops in the former Yugoslav Republic of Macedonia; peace-making in support of the search for negotiated solutions; efforts to bring to trial those guilty of war crimes; a major humanitarian operation; and the first steps towards reconstruction and rehabilitation.

Since the establishment of the United Nations Protection Force (UNPROFOR) in February 1992, the challenges to peace-keeping both in Croatia and in Bosnia and Herzegovina increased in complexity. With a total of over 38,000 military personnel, UNPROFOR is the largest operation in the history of the United Nations, but still nearly 7,000 short of its authorized strength.

In the absence of an overall peace agreement in both Croatia and Bosnia and Herzegovina, UNPROFOR acquired responsibilities and became involved in undertakings not originally foreseen, while at the same time being prevented from carrying out other crucial parts of its mandate. Despite the limitations of its mandate and military resources, UNPROFOR played a major stabilizing role and contributed to normalizing the situation, particularly in and around Sarajevo and along the confrontation lines in both Croatia and Bosnia and Herzegovina. In 1994, UNPROFOR's activities in Croatia focused on monitoring and verification of the cease-fire agreement of March, which brought to an end several months of active hostilities and allowed for a certain normalization of life, but was repeatedly violated starting in October. An economic agreement between the two sides was signed in December.

As a political solution to the crisis in the former Yugoslavia continued to elude diplomatic efforts, the international community was called upon to sustain an unparalleled humanitarian operation to address the basic needs for survival of an ever-growing number of persons affected by the conflict. Over 4 million persons were in need of assistance, 2.7 million in Bosnia and Herzegovina alone. There, humanitarian operations continued to be obstructed, however, and UNPROFOR and the United Nations High Commissioner for Refugees were repeatedly denied access to populations in need and the security of their personnel was threatened. Efforts to obtain a cease-fire in the Republic failed, despite the Secretary-General's personal initiative.

On the initiative of a special session of the United Nations Commission on Human Rights in August 1992, a Special Rapporteur was appointed to investigate the human rights situation in the former Yugoslavia and in particular within Bosnia and Herzegovina. A Commission of Experts, established to investigate violations of humanitarian law, including grave breaches of the 1949 Geneva Conventions, concluded in its May 1994 report to the Security Council that grave violations had been committed in the territory of the former Yugoslavia on a large scale. With the appointment in August 1994 of Justice Richard J. Goldstone of South Africa as Prosecutor of the International Tribunal for the Prosecution of Persons Responsible for Serious Violations of International Humanitarian Law Committed in the Territory of the Former Yugoslavia, some major investigations were completed and the first indictment submitted.

The Middle East

The Middle East problem arose out of the conflicting claims of the Arab and Jewish communities over the future status of the territory of Palestine which was, under a Mandate from the League of Nations, administered by the United Kingdom. Palestine had a population of about 2 million, two thirds of whom were Arabs and one third Jews. Unable to find a solution acceptable to both communities, the United Kingdom brought the matter before the General Assembly which, in November 1947, endorsed a plan for the partition of the territory into an Arab State and a Jewish State, with an international regime for Jerusalem. The plan was not accepted by the Palestinian Arabs and Arab States.

As a result of the impasse, violent fighting broke out and the Security Council on 23 April 1948 established a Truce Commission for Palestine, composed of the consular representatives of Belgium, France and the United States, to supervise a ceasefire. The Assembly appointed a United Nations Mediator who was to promote a peaceful adjustment of the situation of Palestine. On the same day, the United Kingdom relinquished its Mandate and the Jewish Agency for Palestine proclaimed the State of Israel (which became a United Nations Member a year later) on the territory allotted to it in the partition plan. On the following day, full-fledged war broke out between Israelis and the Palestinian Arabs, assisted by Arab States.

Partition of Palestine

Organization of the *ad hoc* Committee on the Palestinian Question

Establishment and terms of reference of the ad hoc *Committee*

During its second session, the General Assembly, at its 90th meeting on September 23, 1947, established an *ad hoc* Committee on the Palestinian Question, composed of all Members, and referred to it the following agenda items for consideration and report:

"Question of Palestine": item proposed by the United Kingdom.

Report of the United Nations Special Committee on Palestine ("UNSCOP").

"Termination of the Mandate over Palestine and the Recognition of its Independence as One State": item proposed by Saudi Arabia and Iraq.

Organization of the ad hoc *Committee*

At its first meeting on September 25, 1947, the Committee elected H. V. Evatt (Australia) Chairman, Prince Subha Svasti Svastivat (Siam) Vice-Chairman and Thor Thors (Iceland) Rapporteur. It also decided to invite the Arab Higher Committee and the Jewish Agency for Palestine to be represented at its deliberations in order to supply such information or render such assistance as the Committee might require. The invitation was accepted, and representatives of both organizations attended all meetings of the *ad hoc* Committee.

Summary of agenda of the *ad hoc* Committee

Question of Palestine

The representative of the United Kingdom, in a letter to the Secretary-General dated April 2, 1947, had requested, on behalf of his Government, that the "Question of Palestine" be placed on the agenda of the General Assembly at its next regular annual session. In the same communication, the representative of the United Kingdom had requested the convening of a special session of the Assembly "for the purpose of constituting and instructing a special committee" to prepare for the consideration of the question of Palestine at the subsequent (second) regular session.

*Report of the UN
Special Committee on Palestine (UNSCOP)*

The report of the Special Committee related the events leading up to the establishment of UNSCOP and gave a summary of its activities. It surveyed the elements of the conflict with relation to geographic and demographic factors, relevant economic factors, Palestine under the Mandate and the conflicting claims, and dealt with the question of the religious interests and Holy Places in Palestine. The report also reviewed the main proposals previously propounded for the solution of the Palestine question.

The Committee made twelve recommendations, eleven of which were adopted unanimously and the twelfth by a substantial majority.

The report contained a majority proposal for a Plan of Partition with Economic Union and a minority proposal for a Plan for a Federal State of Palestine. Reservations and observations of certain members of the Committee were included in the report.

Summary of UNSCOP's activities

Pursuant to the request of the United Kingdom, the General Assembly had convened at Flushing Meadow, New York, on April 28, 1947, and, on May 15, 1947, had established and instructed a Special Committee on Palestine (UNSCOP).

UNSCOP was composed of representatives of Australia, Canada, Czechoslovakia, Guatemala, India, Iran, Netherlands, Peru, Sweden, Uruguay and Yugoslavia, and was given the "widest powers to ascertain and record facts, and to investigate all questions and issues relevant to the problem of Palestine"; it was under instructions to report its recommendations to the Secretary-General not later than September 1, 1947. It actually completed its work on August 31.

The Special Committee held its first meeting at Lake Success on May 26. From that date until August 31, 1947, when the report was signed, the Committee held 16 public and 36 private meetings.

After an exploratory discussion, UNSCOP agreed to create a Preparatory Working Group which would produce some suggestions on various organizational matters for the Committee's consideration.

Justice Emil Sandstrom (Sweden) was elected Chairman of the Special Committee and Alberto Ulloa (Peru) Vice-Chairman.

UNSCOP members arrived in Palestine on June 14 and 15, meeting in Jerusalem for the first time on June 16, 1947 (its fifth meeting in all). The Special Committee subsequently visited various parts of Palestine to gain a first-hand impression of conditions.

In response to a request from the Special Committee, the Government of Palestine and the Jewish Agency for Palestine appointed liaison officers. The Palestine Government's liaison officer was D. C. MacGillivray, while Aubrey S. Eban and David Horowitz served as liaison officers of the Jewish Agency.

At the same meeting, the Special Committee was informed by the Secretary-General of the decision of the Arab Higher Committee to abstain from collaboration with UNSCOP.

. . .

In addition to hearing representatives of the Palestine Government and of the Jewish Agency, the Special Committee also heard representatives of a number of other Jewish organizations and religious bodies, as well as Chaim Weizmann, to whom the Special Committee granted a hearing in his personal capacity.

Upon the suggestion of some members of UNSCOP, the Committee resolved to invite the Arab States to express their views on the question of Palestine. It was decided that a letter to this effect should be addressed by the personal representative of the Secretary-General to the consular representatives in Jerusalem of Egypt, Iraq, Lebanon, Saudi Arabia, Syria and Transjordan, and to the Government of Yemen through the Consul-General of Lebanon. To the Arab States in conference among themselves was left the choice of a time and place mutually convenient to them and to the Special Committee.

Letters of acceptance were received from Egypt, Iraq, Lebanon, Saudi Arabia and Syria with the information that Beirut, Lebanon, had been designated as the place of meeting.

The Consul-General of Transjordan replied for his Government that, since Transjordan was not a Member of the United Nations, it was not prepared to send a representative outside the country to give evidence, but that it would welcome the Special Committee or any of its members who might wish to pay a visit for that purpose to Transjordan.

On July 20, UNSCOP proceeded to Lebanon, and on the following day paid an informal visit to Damascus, the capital of Syria. On July 22, the Special Committee met in Beirut to hear the views of the Arab States expressed by the Lebanese Minister of Foreign Affairs, Hamid Frangie.

On July 25, several members of the Special Committee—the Chairman and the representatives of Canada, Czechoslovakia, Iran, Netherlands, Peru and Yugoslavia—paid a visit to Amman, capital of Transjordan, where they had an exchange of views with King Abdullah and members of his staff.

In addition to oral testimony, UNSCOP received many written statements from various persons and organizations.

A number of petitions addressed to the Special Committee asked its intervention in securing the release of prisoners and detainees. The Committee decided that these and similar appeals to investigate the methods of the British police in Palestine, the conditions of Jews in Yemen and the plight of refugees in Aden fell outside UNSCOP's terms of reference. The Committee also rejected petitions that it visit camps for Jewish detainees on Cyprus or permit these detainees to appear before it in Jerusalem to give evidence.

UNSCOP also recorded its concern over acts of violence which had occurred in Palestine since its arrival, declaring that such acts constituted a flagrant violation of the General Assembly's resolution of May 14, 1947.

On July 28, 1947, the Special Committee began work on the drafting of its report in Geneva, Switzerland. Between August 8 and 14, the Committee had decided, by vote of 6 to 4, with 1 abstention, to set up a sub-committee to visit displaced persons' camps. During its tour, the Sub-Committee visited camps at or near Munich, Salzburg, Vienna, Berlin, Hamburg and Hanover, and met the Austrian Chancellor, the Military Governor of the United States zones of Germany and Austria and several United States and United Kingdom officials in charge of displaced persons' affairs, as well as officials of the Preparatory Commission of the International Refugee Organization. The Sub-Committee was under the chairmanship of J. D. L. Hood (Australia).

The Special Committee also established a sub-committee to study the question of religious interests and Holy Places in Palestine. The status of Jerusalem was also referred to that Sub-Committee, which was under the chairmanship of A. I. Spits (Netherlands). Its suggestions, with various amendments, were incorporated into both the majority and the minority plans eventually submitted by UNSCOP.

. . .

General recommendations of the Committee

The eleven unanimously-adopted resolutions of the Committee were:

That the Mandate should be terminated and Palestine granted independence at the earliest practicable date (recommendations I and II);

That there should be a short transitional period preceding the granting of independence to Palestine during which the authority responsible for administering Palestine should be responsible to the United Nations (recommendations III and IV);

That the sacred character of the Holy Places and the rights of religious communities in Palestine should be preserved and stipulations concerning them inserted in the constitution of any state or states to be created and that a system should be found for settling impartially any disputes involving religious rights (recommendation V);

That the General Assembly should take steps to see that the problem of distressed European Jews should be dealt with as a matter of urgency so as to alleviate their plight and the Palestine problem (recommendation VI);

That the constitution of the new state or states should be fundamentally democratic and should contain guarantees for the respect of human rights and fundamental freedoms and for the protection of minorities (recommendation VII);

That the undertakings contained in the Charter whereby states are to settle their disputes by peaceful means and to refrain from the threat or use of force in international relations in any way inconsistent with the purposes of the United Nations should be incorporated in the constitutional provisions applying to Palestine (recommendation VIII);

That the economic unity of Palestine should be preserved (recommendation IX);

That states whose nationals had enjoyed in Palestine privileges and immunities of foreigners, including those formerly enjoyed by capitulation or usage in the Ottoman Empire, should be invited to renounce any rights pertaining to them (recommendation X);

That the General Assembly should appeal to the peoples of Palestine to co-operate with the United Nations in its efforts to settle the situation there and exert every effort to put an end to acts of violence (recommendation XI).

In addition to these eleven unanimously approved recommendations, the Special Committee, with two members (Uruguay and Guatemala) dissenting, and one member recording no opinion, also approved the following twelfth recommendation:

> "RECOMMENDATION XII. THE JEWISH
> PROBLEM IN GENERAL
> *"It is recommended that*
> "In the appraisal of the Palestine question, it be accepted as incontrovertible that any solution for Palestine cannot be considered as a solution of the Jewish problem in general."

Majority Proposal: Plan of Partition with Economic Union

According to the plan of the majority (the representatives of Canada, Czechoslovakia, Guatemala, Netherlands, Peru, Sweden and Uruguay), Palestine was to be constituted into an Arab State, a Jewish State and the City of Jerusalem. The Arab and the Jewish States would become independent after a transitional period of two years beginning on September 1, 1947. Before their independence could be recognized, however, they must adopt a constitution in line with the pertinent recommendations of the Committee and make to the United Nations a declaration containing certain guarantees, and sign a treaty by which a system of economic collaboration would be established and the economic union of Palestine created.

The plan provided, *inter alia*, that during the transitional period, the United Kingdom would carry on the administration of Palestine under the auspices of the United Nations and on such conditions and under such supervision as the United Kingdom and the United Nations might agree upon. During this period a stated number of Jewish immigrants was to be admitted. Constituent Assemblies were to be elected by the populations of the areas which were to comprise the Arab and Jewish States, respectively, and were to draw up the constitutions of the States.

These constitutions were to provide for the establishment in each State of a legislative body elected by universal suffrage and by secret ballot on the basis of proportional representation and an executive body responsible to the legislature. They would also contain various guarantees, e.g., for the protection of the Holy Places and religious buildings and sites, and of religious and minority rights.

The Constituent Assembly in each State would appoint a provisional government empowered to make the declaration and sign the Treaty of Economic Union, after which the independence of the State would be recognized. The Declaration would contain provisions for the protection of the Holy Places and religious buildings and sites and for religious and minority rights. It would also contain provisions regarding citizenship.

A treaty would be entered into between the two States, which would contain provisions to establish the economic union of Palestine and to provide for other matters of common interest. A Joint Economic Board would be established consisting of representatives of the two States and members appointed by the Economic and Social Council of the United Nations to organize and administer the objectives of the Economic Union.

The City of Jerusalem would be placed, after the transitional period, under the International Trusteeship System by means of a Trusteeship Agreement, which would designate the United Nations as the Administering Authority. The plan contained recommended boundaries for the city and provisions concerning the governor and the police force.

The plan also proposed boundaries for both the Arab and Jewish States.

Minority Proposal: Plan of a Federal State

Three UNSCOP members (the representatives of India, Iran and Yugoslavia) proposed an independent federal state. This plan provided, *inter alia*, that an independent federal state of Palestine would be created following a transitional period not exceeding three years, during which responsibility for administering Palestine and preparing it for independence would be entrusted to an authority to be decided by the General Assembly.

The independent federal state would comprise an Arab State and a Jewish State. Jerusalem would be its capital.

During the transitional period a Constituent Assembly would be elected by popular vote and convened by the administering authority on the basis of electoral provisions which would ensure the fullest representation of the population.

The Constituent Assembly would draw up the constitution of the federal state, which was to contain, *inter alia*, the following provisions:

The federal state would comprise a federal government and governments of the Arab and Jewish States, respectively.

Full authority would be vested in the federal government with regard to national defence, foreign relations, immigration, currency, taxation for federal purposes, foreign and inter-state waterways, transport and communications, copyrights and patents.

The Arab and Jewish States would enjoy full powers of local self-government and would have authority over education, taxation for local purposes, the right of residence, commercial licenses, land permits, grazing rights, inter-state migration, settlement, police, punishment of crime, social institutions and services, public housing, public health, local roads, agriculture and local industries.

The organs of government would include a head of state, an executive body, a representative federal legislative body composed of two chambers, and a federal court. The executive would be responsible to the legislative body.

Election to one chamber of the federal legislative body would be on the basis of proportional representation of the population as a whole, and to the other on the basis of equal representation of the Arab and Jewish citizens of Palestine. Legislation would be enacted when approved by majority votes in both chambers; in the event of disagreement between the two chambers, the issue would be submitted to an arbitral body of five members including not less than two Arabs and two Jews.

The federal court would be the final court of appeal regarding constitutional matters. Its members, who would include not less than four Arabs and three Jews, would be elected by both chambers of the federal legislative body.

The constitution was to guarantee equal rights for all minorities and fundamental human rights and freedoms. It would guarantee, *inter alia*, free access to the Holy Places and protect religious interests.

The constitution would provide for an undertaking to settle international disputes by peaceful means.

There would be a single Palestinian nationality and citizenship.

The constitution would provide for equitable participation of representatives of both communities in delegations to international conferences.

A permanent international body was to be set up for the supervision and protection of the Holy Places, to be composed of three representatives designated by the United Nations and one representative of each of the recognized faiths having an interest in the matter, as might be determined by the United Nations.

For a period of three years from the beginning of the transitional period Jewish immigration would be permitted into the Jewish State in such numbers as not to exceed its absorptive capacity, and having due regard for the rights of the existing population within that State and their anticipated natural rate of increase. An international commission, composed of three Arab, three Jewish and three United Nations representatives, would be appointed to estimate the absorptive capacity of the Jewish State. The commission would cease to exist at the end of the three-year period mentioned above.

The minority plan also laid down the boundaries of the proposed Arab and Jewish areas of the federal state.

Termination of the Mandate over Palestine and the recognition of its independence as one State

The representative of Saudi Arabia, in a letter dated July 7, 1947, and addressed to the Secretary-General, requested, on behalf of his Government, that the following item be placed on the agenda of the next (second) regular annual session of the General Assembly:

"The termination of the mandate over Palestine and the recognition of its independence as one State."

The same request was addressed to the Secretary-General by the representative of Iraq in a letter dated July 14, 1947.

Initial statements of parties immediately concerned

During its second meeting on September 26, 1947, the *ad hoc* Committee agreed to hear the views of the representatives of the three parties immediately concerned in the Palestine question— i.e., the United Kingdom (as Mandatory Power), the Arab Higher Committee and the Jewish Agency for Palestine—before embarking upon a general debate. The report of the Special Committee on Palestine was introduced by its Chairman, Justice Sandstrom, during the second meeting of the *ad hoc* Committee.

United Kingdom viewpoint

The representative of the United Kingdom placed the views of his Government before the *ad hoc* Committee at the second meeting on September 26, 1947. Congratulating UNSCOP on the way in which it had carried out its task, he declared that the United Kingdom Government was in substantial agreement with the twelve general recommendations. In particular, the United Kingdom Government endorsed and wished to emphasize three of these recommendations: Recommendations I (Termination of the Mandate) and II (Independence), both of which were an exact expression of the guiding principle of British policy, and Recommendation VI (Jewish Displaced Persons). Concerning the latter, the United Kingdom Government believed that the entire problem of displaced persons in Europe, Jewish and non-Jewish alike, was an international responsibility demanding urgent attention. His Government would make proposals in this connection subsequently.

The United Kingdom Government endorsed without reservation the view that the Mandate for Palestine should now be terminated.

He recalled that the representative of the United Kingdom had informed the General Assembly during its first special session that His Majesty's Government would be in the highest degree reluctant to oppose the Assembly's wishes in regard to the future of Palestine. At the same time, he further recalled, the United Kingdom representative had drawn a distinction between accepting a recommendation, in the sense of not impeding its implementation by others, and accepting responsibility for carrying it out by means of a British administration and British forces in Palestine.

The attitude of the United Kingdom Government remained as then stated, the representative of the United Kingdom said. His Government was ready to co-operate with the Assembly to the fullest extent possible. He could not easily imagine circumstances in which the United Kingdom would wish to prevent the application of a settlement recommended by the Assembly. The crucial question for His Majesty's Government was, however, the matter of enforcement of such a settlement.

His Government was ready to assume responsibility for implementing any plan on which agreement was reached by the Arabs and the Jews. If, on the other hand, the Assembly were to recommend a policy which was not acceptable to both parties, the United Kingdom Government would not feel able to implement it, and the Assembly should therefore provide, in such a case, for some alternative authority to implement it. Specifically, the United Kingdom Government was not prepared by itself to undertake the task of imposing a policy in Palestine by force of arms; as to the possibility of his Government's participation with other Governments in the enforcement of a settlement, his Government would have to take into account both the inherent justice of the settlement and the extent to which force would be required for its implementation.

In the absence of a settlement, the United Kingdom Government must plan for an early withdrawal of British forces and of the British Administration from Palestine.

In conclusion, the representative of the United Kingdom declared that if no basis of consent for a settlement could be found, it seemed to him of the highest importance that any recommendations made by the General Assembly should be accompanied by a clear definition of the means by which they were to be carried out.

Viewpoint of the Arab Higher Committee

Addressing the *ad hoc* Committee at the third meeting on September 30, 1947, the representative of the Arab Higher Committee stated that it was obviously the sacred duty of the Arabs of Palestine to defend their country against all aggression, including the aggressive campaign being waged by the Zionists with the object of securing by force a country—Palestine—which was not theirs by right. The *raison d'être* of the United Nations was, he said, to assist self-defence against aggression.

The rights and patrimony of the Arabs in Palestine had been the subject of no fewer than eighteen investigations within 25 years, and all to no purpose. Commissions of inquiry had either reduced the national and legal rights of the Palestine Arabs or had glossed them over. The few recommendations favorable to the Arabs had been ignored by the Mandatory Power. For these and for other reasons already communicated to the United Nations, it was not surprising that the Arab Higher Committee should have abstained from the nineteenth investigation (i.e., UNSCOP's) and refused to appear before the Special Committee.

The representative of the Arab Higher Committee concluded from a survey of Palestine history that Zionist claims to that country had no legal or moral basis. In particular, he denied the legal or moral justification of the Balfour Declaration and the Mandate for Palestine, both of which, he declared, had been laid down by the Zionist Executive and the United Kingdom Government. As a result of Anglo-Zionist co-operation, Palestine's Jewish minority was placed in a privileged position *vis-à-vis* the Arab majority, while Arabs were being made the victims of discrimination.

The representative of the Arab Higher Committee emphasized the importance of the problem of immigration into Palestine. He accused the Mandatory Power of having overstepped the provisions of Article 6 of the Mandate by permitting Jewish immigration into Palestine to the detriment of the political, social and economic rights of the Palestine Arabs. If any room existed in Palestine for an increase in population, that room should be left for its natural increase. He emphasized the increasing determination of the Arabs to oppose all immigration.

The representative of the Arab Higher Committee stated that, yielding to Zionist pressure, the United Kingdom Government had failed to implement its own decision, made in 1939, that Jewish immigration into Palestine must cease and that Palestine must become an independent unitary state within a fixed time.

No people would be more pleased than the Arabs to see the distressed Jews of Europe given permanent relief. But Palestine already had absorbed far more than its just share, and the Jews could not impose their will on other nations by choosing the place and manner of their relief, particularly if that choice was inconsistent with the principles of international law and justice and prejudicial to the interests of the nation directly concerned. He recalled the relevant resolutions concerning refugees and displaced persons passed by the General Assembly on February 12 (8(I)) and December 15 (62(I)), 1946, in that connection and mentioned the offer of the United Kingdom, made more than 40 years ago, to place Uganda at the disposal of the Jews as a national home, and, more recently, the efforts of the U.S.S.R. to create a Jewish national home in Biro-Bidjan.

Both places had more to offer the Jews than the tiny country of Palestine, but the Zionists had turned them down. The Zionists did not want Palestine for the permanent solution of the Jewish problem nor for the relief of the distressed Jews; they wanted power; they had political ambitions and designs on strategically important Palestine and the Near East.

Then, too, it would be illogical for the United Nations to associate itself with the introduction of an alien body into the established homogeneity of the Arab world, a process which could only produce a ''new Balkans''.

The solution of the Palestine problem was simple. It lay in the Charter of the United Nations in accordance with which the Arabs of Palestine, constituting the majority of the population, were entitled to a free and independent state. He welcomed the statement by the representative of the United Kingdom that the Mandate should be terminated and its termination followed by independence, and expressed the hope that the United Kingdom Government would not, as in the past, reverse its decision under Zionist pressure.

Declaring that, once Palestine was found to be entitled to independence, the United Nations was not legally competent to decide or impose Palestine's constitutional organization, the representative of the Arab Higher Committee outlined the following principles as the basis for the future constitutional organization of the Holy Land:

1. That an Arab State in the whole of Palestine be established on democratic lines.

2. That the Arab State of Palestine would respect human rights, fundamental freedoms and equality of all persons before the law.

3. That the Arab State of Palestine would protect the legitimate rights and interests of all minorities.

4. That freedom of worship and access to the Holy Places would be guaranteed to all.

He added that the following steps would have to be taken to give effect to the abovementioned four principles:

(a) A Constituent Assembly should be elected at the earliest possible time. All genuine and law-abiding nationals of Palestine would be entitled to participate in the elections of the Constituent Assembly.

(b) The Constituent Assembly should, within a fixed time, formulate and enact a Constitution for the Arab State of Palestine, which should be of a democratic nature and should embody the abovementioned four principles.

(c) A government should be formed within a fixed time, in accordance with the terms of the Constitution, to take over the administration of Palestine from the Mandatory Power.

Such a program was the only one which the Arabs of Palestine were prepared to adopt, and the only item on the Committee's agenda with which the Arab Higher Committee would associate itself was Item 3, i.e., the item proposed by Saudi Arabia and Iraq.

The representative of the Arab Higher Committee said he had not commented upon the UNSCOP Report because the Arab Higher Committee considered that it could not be used as a basis for discussion. Both the majority and the minority plans contained in the Report were inconsistent with the United Nations Charter and the Covenant of the League of Nations. The Arabs of Palestine were solidly determined to oppose with all the means at their disposal any scheme which provided for the dissection, segregation or partition of their country or which gave to a minority special and preferential rights and status.

Viewpoint of the Jewish Agency for Palestine

The representative of the Jewish Agency for Palestine, addressing the *ad hoc* Committee at the fourth meeting on October 2, 1947, praised the Special Committee for its conscientious labors and good faith. The Jewish Agency had regarded it as an inescapable obligation to co-operate fully with the United Nations and had placed all the required information and data at the disposal of UNSCOP, while the Arab Higher Committee had refused to heed repeated UNSCOP invitations for co-operation. It was strange that, after having flouted its authority, the Arab Higher Committee asked the United Nations to support the Arab stand.

The representative of the Jewish Agency said that it would appear from the statement made by the representative of the United Kingdom that the latter did not intend to accept the General Assembly's impending recommendation on Palestine. If this be so, he wondered why the United Kingdom had asked the Assembly to place the Palestine problem on its agenda. Given the present realities of the Palestine situation, the undertaking of the United Kingdom Government to implement any settlement agreeable to both Jews and Arabs meant very little and did not advance the solution of the Palestine problem at all.

He welcomed the announcement that British troops were to be withdrawn at an early date, adding that this made a decision even more urgent than it had been at the time of the (first) special session.

On behalf of the Jewish Agency, he supported ten of the eleven recommendations unanimously adopted by UNSCOP. The exception was Recommendation VI (Jewish Displaced Persons). The Jewish Agency, he said, did not disapprove of this recommendation but did wish to call attention to the "intense urge" of the overwhelming majority of Jewish displaced persons to proceed to Palestine, a fact noted both by the Anglo-American Committee and by UNSCOP. While hoping that nations would welcome displaced persons wishing to emigrate to countries other than Palestine, the Jewish Agency considered that it would be unjust to deny the right to go to Palestine to those who wished to do so.

The representative of the Jewish Agency regarded the twelfth recommendation (The Jewish Problem in General) as unintelligible. He called it a mere postulate which, moreover, had not been accepted unanimously by the Special Committee. The "Jewish Problem in General" was, he said, none other than the age-old question of Jewish homelessness, for which there was but one solution, that given by the Balfour Declaration and the Mandate: the reconstitution of the Jewish National Home in Palestine.

The solution proposed by the minority of the Special Committee was unacceptable to the Jewish Agency; although it referred to "States", it actually made provision only for semi-autonomous cantons or provinces. Palestine would become an Arab state with two Jewish enclaves. The Jews would be frozen in the position of a permanent minority in the proposed federal state, and would not even have control over their own fiscal policies or immigration. It entailed all the disadvantages of partition without the compensating advantages of a real partition: statehood, independence and free immigration.

The majority proposal was not really satisfactory to the Jewish people, either. According to David Lloyd George, then British Prime Minister, the Balfour Declaration implied that the whole of Palestine, including Transjordan, should ultimately become a Jewish state. Transjordan had, nevertheless, been severed from Palestine in 1922 and had subsequently been set up as an Arab kingdom. Now a second Arab state was to be carved out of the remainder of Palestine, with the result that the Jewish National Home would represent less than one eighth of the territory originally set aside for it. Such a sacrifice should not be asked of the Jewish people.

Referring to the Arab States established as independent countries since the First World War, he said that 17,000,000 Arabs now occupied an area of 1,290,000 square miles, including all the principal Arab and Moslem centres, while Palestine, after the loss of Transjordan, was only 10,000 square miles; yet the majority plan proposed to reduce it by one half. UNSCOP proposed to eliminate Western Galilee from the Jewish State; that was an injustice and a grievous handicap to the development of the Jewish State.

The representative of the Jewish Agency also criticized the UNSCOP majority proposal concerning Jerusalem, saying that the Jewish section of modern Jerusalem (outside the Walled City) should be included in the Jewish State. He reserved the right to deal at a later stage with other territorial modifications.

If this heavy sacrifice was the inexorable condition of a final solution, if it would make possible the immediate re-establishment of the Jewish State with sovereign control of its own immigration, then the Jewish Agency was prepared to recommend the acceptance of the partition solution, subject to further discussion of constitutional and territorial provisions. This sacrifice would be the Jewish contribution to the solution of a painful problem and would bear witness to the Jewish people's international spirit and its desire for peace.

In spite of the heavy sacrifices which the Jewish State would have to make in this matter also, the Jewish Agency accepted the proposal for an economic union, terming it a promising and statesmanlike conception. The limit to the sacrifices to which the Jewish Agency could consent was clear: a Jewish State must have in its own hands those instruments of financing and economic control necessary to carry out large-scale Jewish immigration and the related economic development, and it must have independent access to those world sources of capital and raw materials indispensable for the accomplishment of these purposes.

The Jews of Palestine wanted to be good neighbors of all the Arab States. If their offer of peace and friendship were rejected, they would defend their rights. In Palestine there had been built a nation which demanded its independence, and would not allow itself to be dislodged or deprived of its national status. It could not, and would not, go beyond the enormous sacrifice which had been asked of it. It would not be cowed by idle threats.

The representative of the Jewish Agency urged that the transitional period leading to the establishment of the Arab and Jewish States in Palestine be made as short as possible; at any rate, shorter than the two-year limit proposed by UNSCOP. He favored an international authority to be entrusted, under United Nations auspices, with the task of administering Palestine during the transitional period.

General debate

In the general debate, which began during the *ad hoc* Committee's fifth meeting on October 4,

1947, and ended during the sixteenth meeting on October 16, 1947, opinion was sharply divided. Proponents of the UNSCOP majority plan in general held that the claims of Jews and Arabs both had merit and that no perfect solution of the Palestine problem could be devised. Under the circumstances, a compromise solution was indicated. The partition plan would demand sacrifices from both sides; but, in its emphasis on economic union, it laid the foundation for the eventual development of friendly relations among the two contending parties. Without committing themselves to all the details of the UNSCOP majority plan for partition with economic union, they would support the plan in principle, as the best and most equitable that could be achieved at present. Participants in the general debate who expressed themselves in these or similar terms were the representatives of Canada, Czechoslovakia, Guatemala, Haiti, New Zealand, Norway, Panama, Peru, Poland, South Africa, Sweden, United States, Uruguay and U.S.S.R. The representatives of Colombia and El Salvador dealt with particular aspects of the Palestine problem— displaced persons, appeals for an end to violence— without taking a stand on UNSCOP's majority and minority plans as such. The representative of China, declaring that he could not support the UNSCOP majority or minority plan, urged that new efforts be made to secure Arab-Jewish agreement on a solution of the Palestine problem. Other Committee members held that the Assembly had no right under the Charter to decide to partition Palestine or to enforce such a decision. Representatives of several Arab States formally proposed that the advisory opinion of the International Court of Justice be obtained on this legal aspect of the question before the Assembly proceeded to act on the UNSCOP majority recommendation. Holding that partition violated both the Charter and a people's democratic right to self-determination, the representatives of the Arab States—Egypt, Iraq, Lebanon, Saudi Arabia, Syria and Yemen—declared themselves in favor of an independent unitary state embracing all of Palestine, in which the rights of the minority would be scrupulously safeguarded. These Arab States were supported in their opposition to the partition plan by the representatives of Afghanistan, Argentina, Cuba, India, Iran, Pakistan and Yugoslavia, although not all of the latter explicitly expressed themselves in favor of the Arab States' objective of a unitary Palestine. Yugoslavia, in particular, strongly supported UNSCOP's minority recommendation for a federated state, and India indicated a preference for a large measure of autonomy for areas of the future state of Palestine having Jewish majorities.

Following the conclusion of the initial general debate, the *ad hoc* Committee, during its seventeenth and eighteenth meetings on October 17 and 18, 1947, once again heard representatives of the Jewish

Agency and of the Arab Higher Committee reaffirm their positions.

Proposals submitted during the general debate

In the course of the general debate, seventeen proposals were submitted to the *ad hoc* Committee.

El Salvador proposed that the General Assembly call on the Jewish Agency and the Arab Higher Committee to appoint three representatives each to confer, under United Nations auspices, with a view to reaching agreement on a settlement of the Palestine question.

Uruguay suggested that 30,000 Jewish children be admitted to Palestine at once on humanitarian grounds.

Colombia submitted two proposals, the first being in the nature of an appeal to all interested parties to abstain from violence, the second calling for the creation of a special committee to study the observations and suggestions contained in the report of UNSCOP in so far as these deal with the problem of Jewish displaced persons, i.e., General Recommendations VI and XII and Sections VI and VII of the minority proposal.

Guatemala proposed acceptance, with certain modifications, of the UNSCOP majority plan, to be implemented by an international military police force composed of contingents contributed, on a proportional basis, by States Members other than permanent members of the Security Council, the cost of maintaining such a force to be borne by the five permanent members of the Security Council.

The United Kingdom proposed that each Member of the United Nations "adopt urgent measures for settling a fair share of displaced persons and refugees in its country" and co-operate with other nations through the International Refugee Organization, or its Preparatory Commission, in the development of overall plans to accomplish this end.

Sweden and the United States jointly proposed that the Committee accept the basic principles of the unanimous UNSCOP recommendations, as well as the UNSCOP majority plan, as the basis for its own recommendations to the General Assembly concerning the future government of Palestine.

The United States proposed the formation of a sub-committee to draw up a detailed plan for the future government of Palestine in accordance with the majority plan and the unanimous recommendations of UNSCOP, and to incorporate this plan in the form of recommendations to be transmitted to the *ad hoc* Committee not later than October 27, 1947.

Canada submitted an amendment to this proposal of the United States. Under the Canadian amendment, the sub-committee was to be given the following additional terms of reference:

"To consider the exercise of administrative responsibility in Palestine during the transitional period, including the possibility of the application of Chapter XII of the Charter; [and]

"To consider methods by which recommendations of the *ad hoc* Committee on the Palestinian Question . . . [based on the UNSCOP majority plan] would be put into effect."

The Netherlands called on the Committee to draft "(a) proposals for a fair and practicable solution of the Palestine question, as far as possible acceptable to both parties involved; (b) recommendations for the adequate and effective implementation of this solution, and (c) recommendations for an early solution of the problem of Jewish refugees and displaced persons".

Yugoslavia recommended the immediate admission to Palestine of all Jewish refugees detained in Cyprus.

Uruguay proposed acceptance of the UNSCOP majority plan as a basis for discussion in the *ad hoc* Committee with these modifications: that the territory of Galilee remain under the jurisdiction of the Jewish State, that the Arab city of Jaffa be transferred to the Arab State, that the Arab town of Beersheba be transferred to the Arab State, that the Jewish district of the new City of Jerusalem be included in the territory of the Jewish State, and that the Arab district of the new City of Jerusalem be included in the Arab State. Uruguay further proposed the establishment of a special *ad hoc* committee to study the plan for an economic union of Palestine, if the UNSCOP majority plan were adopted. Uruguay further proposed that the United Nations should take over the government and administration of Palestine during the transitional period (i.e., until September 1, 1949, at the latest) referred to in Section B of the UNSCOP majority report, these functions to be exercised by a Provisional Council composed of five members appointed by the General Assembly, three to be chosen from citizens of Member States, and two to be appointed on the proposal, respectively, of the Jewish Agency and the Arab Higher Committee. Decisions of this Provisional Council should be by a simple majority, except that all proposals voted for by both the Arab and Jewish representative on the Council, or introduced by them jointly, should be considered as adopted. Uruguay further proposed the following substantive proposal "in view of the letter and the spirit of Recommendation No. XII adopted by a majority vote of the Special Committee on Palestine . . .":

"The creation of a Jewish State will be the territorial solution for the European Jewish problem and will permit to reparate in part the terrible damage suffered under the Nazi persecution by the Jewish people, which is still exposed to new wrongs and racial discrimination."

Finally Uruguay reiterated its earlier proposal to admit at once into Palestine some 30,000 Jewish children from displaced persons camps in Europe and other places of detention or assembly.

Iraq proposed that the General Assembly submit the following "legal point" to the International Court of Justice for an advisory opinion under Article 96 of the Charter:

"Did not the pledges given by Great Britain to the Shereef Hussein of Mecca and her subsequent declarations, promises and assurances to the Arabs that in the event of Allied victory the Arab countries would obtain their independence include Palestine and its inhabitants?"

Syria submitted two proposals. The first of these proposed that the General Assembly recommend

"that the United Kingdom prepare as soon as possible an agreement under Article 79 of the Charter and submit it for approval to the General Assembly authorizing Great Britain, as administering authority, to complete her task in Palestine during the transitionary period in accordance with the said agreement, which shall contain the following provisions:

"1. That a Sovereign State for the whole of Palestine be established on a democratic basis,

"2. That a Constituent Assembly shall be elected at the earliest possible date, all genuine and law-abiding nationals of Palestine being entitled to vote,

"3. This Constituent Assembly shall within a fixed period formulate and enact a Constitution for the State of Palestine which shall be of a democratic character and contain provisions

"(a) guaranteeing human rights, fundamental freedoms and the equality of all persons before the Law,

"(b) guaranteeing the legitimate rights and interests of all minorities,

"(c) safeguarding the Holy Places and guaranteeing freedom of worship and access to the Holy Places to all.

"4. That a government shall be formed within a fixed period in accordance with the terms of the Constitution to take over the administration of Palestine from the administering authority."

The second Syrian proposal called for the addressing of a request for an advisory opinion to the International Court of Justice concerning the following questions:

"1. Are the terms of the Act of Mandate [i.e., United Kingdom Mandate for Palestine] . . . consistent or not consistent with the Covenant of the League of Nations . . . and with the fundamental rights of peoples and their right to self-determination and International Law?

"2. Is a forcible plan of partition . . . consistent with the objectives of the mandate and with the principles of the Charter and with the ultimate fate of mandated territories referred to in Chapter XII of the Charter?

"3. Does the plan of partition in its adoption and forcible execution fall within the jurisdiction of the General Assembly?"

Egypt also proposed that a request for an advisory opinion be addressed to the International Court of Justice. The Egyptian proposal would have submitted the following two questions to the Court: Does it lie "within the competence of the General Assembly to recommend any of the two solutions proposed by the majority or by the minority of the United Nations Special Committee on Palestine"? and, Does it lie "within the rights of any Member State or group of Member States to implement any of the proposed solutions without the consent of the people of Palestine"?

Lebanon suggested that the General Assembly,

"*Recognizing* the danger that assistance in transport, arms and money, to immigrants destined for Palestine is calculated to accentuate the existing tension in that country and to endanger peace in the Middle East,

"*Recommends* that the Governments of Members of the United Nations refrain, and prohibit their nationals, from giving assistance in any form whatsoever to the said immigrants."

Finally, Syria verbally suggested, at the nineteenth meeting of the *ad hoc* Committee on October 21, 1947, the establishment of a sub-committee to study the agenda items jointly proposed by Iraq and Saudi Arabia for the creation of a unitary, independent state embracing all of Palestine. At the same meeting, Syria further proposed the establishment of a sub-committee composed of jurists to consider the Assembly's competence to take and enforce a decision (as distinct from making a recommendation) and to deal with the legal aspects of the Palestine Mandate. The question of referring the whole issue to the International Court of Justice could be discussed after the *ad hoc* Committee had received the report of the committee of jurists, the representative of Syria declared.

Establishment of sub-committees

Following the conclusion of the general debate and the hearing of statements by the representatives of the Arab Higher Committee and the Jewish Agency, the *ad hoc* Committee, at its nineteenth meeting on October 21, 1947, discussed its future procedure. The Chairman proposed that no vote should be taken at that stage on matters of principle, but that the Committee should establish:

1. a Conciliation Group, which would try to bring the parties together, as suggested by El Salvador and the Netherlands;

2. a sub-committee (Sub-Committee 1), entrusted with drawing up a detailed plan based on the majority proposals of the Special Committee on Palestine (UN-

SCOP), as provided by the draft resolution of the United States, amended by Canada;

3. a sub-committee (Sub-Committee 2), to draw up a detailed plan in accordance with the proposal of Saudi Arabia and Iraq for the recognition of Palestine as an independent unitary state, and the proposal to the same effect submitted by the delegation of Syria.

. . .

With regard to the various draft resolutions which the Committee had not yet considered, it was decided at the twentieth meeting that (1) the discussion of the draft resolution by Sweden and the United States approving the principles of UNSCOP's majority plan should be deferred until the report of Sub-Committee 1 had been received; (2) the various resolutions proposing to amend the UNSCOP majority plan should be referred to Sub-Committee 1; (3) the Colombian draft resolution on acts of violence should be considered when the *ad hoc* Committee discussed its recommendations to the General Assembly; (4) either Sub-Committee was empowered to take up and consider any or all written proposals before the *ad hoc* Committee which it deemed relevant to the performance of its functions, such as the draft resolutions relating to the problem of Jewish refugees and displaced persons. (A proposal by the representative of Colombia to set up a special sub-committee to study this latter problem was rejected by a vote of 19 to 4.)

. . .

Reports of Sub-Committees

Report of Sub-Committee 1

. . .

In its report Sub-Committee 1 recommended the adoption of a draft resolution embodying a Plan of Partition with Economic Union, along the general lines of the UNSCOP majority plan (two independent states, an international regime for the City of Jerusalem and economic union of these three units).

As regards the Holy Places and the question of citizenship, the recommendations of Sub-Committee 1 virtually coincided with those of the UNSCOP majority plan.

As regards international convention, Sub-Committee 1—unlike UNSCOP—recommended that disputes about their applicability and continued validity be referred to the International Court of Justice.

The Sub-Committee's recommendations on financial obligations—unlike UNSCOP's proposal—provided for the creation in Palestine of a Court of Claims to settle any disputes between the United Kingdom and either state respecting claims not recognized by the latter.

The Sub-Committee, while accepting the recommendations of UNSCOP regarding economic union, adopted certain technical modifications designed to strengthen the powers of the proposed Joint Economic Board while ensuring the widest measure of autonomy to the future states.

As for boundaries, the Sub-Committee, accepting the recommendations of UNSCOP in principle, proposed certain changes with a view to reducing, as far as reasonably possible, the size of the Arab minority in the Jewish State, and to taking into account considerations of security, communications, irrigation and possibilities of future development.

Among the most important suggested changes was that the Arab sections of Jaffa—placed in the Jewish State in the UNSCOP majority plan—should be excluded from the Jewish State and created as an Arab enclave, thus reducing the Arab minority in the Jewish State by between 78,000 and 81,000, depending on whether the Karton quarter of Jaffa, which is inhabited by both Jews and Arabs, was included in the proposed Arab enclave. The final decision on this question, as well as on details on boundary questions, would be left, according to the Sub-Committee's recommendations, to a demarcation commission which would fix the exact boundary lines on the spot.

In its report to the *ad hoc* Committee, Sub-Committee 1 reported that the most difficult problem which it had faced was that of the implementation of the Plan of Partition with Economic Union.

The Working Group on Implementation, taking into account the statement made by the representative of the United Kingdom prior to the general debate in the *ad hoc* Committee (that the United Kingdom Government planned an early withdrawal of its troops and administration from Palestine) agreed on November 10, 1947, to the outlines of a plan for implementation. This plan provided for the termination of the Mandate and the withdrawal of the armed forces of the Mandatory Power by May 1, 1948, and the creation of independent Arab and Jewish States by July 1, 1948. The implementation of the proposed General Assembly resolution was to be entrusted to a commission of from three to five members appointed by the Assembly, but acting under the guidance of the Security Council.

This plan was reconsidered by the Working Group in the light of an additional statement, and replies to questions of Sub-Committee members, made by the representative of the United Kingdom on November 13, 1947, before the Sub-Committee. From the replies and the statement, the Sub-Committee learned that the United Kingdom Government planned to withdraw its troops from Palestine by August 1, 1948. Neither British troops nor the Mandatory Civil Administration in Palestine would be prepared to enforce a settlement against either Arabs or Jews. The United Kingdom Government reserved the right to lay down the Mandate at any time after it became evident that the Assembly's decision was not acceptable to both Arabs and Jews. On the other hand, the United Kingdom Government would not take any action contrary to any resolution adopted by a two-thirds vote of the General Assembly. Subject to the general reservation that the Mandatory Power must retain sufficient control in areas still under military occupation to ensure the safety of British troops and their orderly withdrawal, the Mandatory Power would not obstruct the task of the Commission appointed to implement partition, nor, subject to that same reservation, would it obstruct the establishment of Provisional Councils of Government for the Jewish and Arab States, the work of the Boundary Demarcation Commission, and the recommendations in regard to immigration and land regulations for the territory of the future Jewish State.

In the light of these additional observations of the representative of the United Kingdom, the Working Group unanimously proposed, and the Sub-Committee, with minor modifications, approved, a new plan of implementation, which may be summarized as follows:

The Mandate was to be terminated and British troops were to be withdrawn at a date to be agreed on by the Commission, consisting of five members (Guatemala, Iceland, Norway, Poland and Uruguay), and the Mandatory Power, with the approval of the Security Council, but in any case not later than August 1, 1948.

The proposed Jewish and Arab States, and the Special International Regime for the City of Jerusalem, would come into existence two months after the evacuation of the armed forces of the Mandatory Power, but in any case not later than October 1, 1948. During the transitional period, the Commission would administer Palestine under the guidance of the Security Council, and would take the necessary measures to implement the Plan of Partition with Economic Union. Until the termination of the Mandate, the Mandatory Power was to maintain order and direct the main public services to the extent that these had not yet been placed under the direction of the Commission, Provisional Councils of Government and the Joint Economic Board, respectively. The Commission and the Mandatory Power were to co-operate, and there was to be a progressive transfer from the Mandatory Power to the Provisional Councils of Government and the Joint Economic Board, respectively, of responsibility for all the functions of government. During the transitional period, the Provisional Councils of Government, acting under the Commission, would have full authority in the areas under their control, including authority over

matters of immigration and land regulation. Following the termination of the Mandate, the whole administration would be in charge of the Provisional Councils of Government and the Joint Economic Board, acting under the Commission. The Provisional Council of Government of each State was to recruit an armed militia from the residents of that State to maintain internal order. If by April 1, 1948, a Provisional Council of Government could not be selected, or could not carry out its functions in either of the States, the Security Council would take such action with respect to that State as it deemed proper.

Concerning the City of Jerusalem, the Sub-Committee adopted, with minor extensions, the boundaries proposed by UNSCOP. The Sub-Committee decided to recommend that the City of Jerusalem be placed under a Special International Regime in relation with the Trusteeship Council, rather than under an International Trusteeship, as recommended by UNSCOP.

The Sub-Committee also adopted a number of other amendments to various portions of the text of the recommendations of UNSCOP with a view to giving greater clarity and precision to details.

The Plan of Partition with Economic Union, as adopted by the Sub-Committee, was incorporated into a draft resolution and submitted to the *ad hoc* Committee for approval. All the recommendations and the draft resolution were adopted unanimously by the Sub-Committee, with the exception of a single paragraph relating to the composition of the special police force for the City of Jerusalem, the text of which was adopted by a vote of 6 to 1, with 2 abstentions.

Report of Sub-Committee 2

. . .

The conclusions of the Sub-Committee were embodied in three resolutions which were recommended to the *ad hoc* Committee for its recommendation, in turn, to the General Assembly.

. . .

The three resolutions submitted by Sub-Committee 2 to the *ad hoc* Committee for recommendation to the General Assembly read as follows:

Resolution No. I

DRAFT RESOLUTION REFERRING CERTAIN LEGAL QUESTIONS TO THE INTERNATIONAL COURT OF JUSTICE

"*Considering* that the Palestine Question raises certain legal issues connected, *inter alia*, with the inherent right of the indigenous population of Palestine to their country and to determine its future, the pledges and assurances given to the Arabs in the first World War regarding the independence of Arab countries, including Palestine, the validity and scope of the Balfour Declaration and the Mandate, the effect on the Mandate of the dissolution of the League of Nations and of the declaration by the Mandatory Power of its intentions to withdraw from Palestine;

"*Considering* that the Palestine question also raises other legal issues connected with the competence of the United Nations to recommend any solution contrary to the Covenant of the League of Nations or the Charter of the United Nations, or to the wishes of the majority of the people of Palestine;

"*Considering* that doubts have been expressed by several Member States concerning the legality under the Charter of any action by the United Nations, or by any Member State or group of Member States, to enforce any proposal which is contrary to the wishes, or is made without the consent, of the majority of the inhabitants of Palestine;

"*Considering* that these questions involve legal issues which so far have not been pronounced upon by any impartial or competent tribunal, and it is essential that such questions be authoritatively determined before the United Nations can recommend a solution of the Palestine question in conformity with the principles of justice and international law,

"*The General Assembly of the United Nations Resolves* to request the International Court of Justice to give an advisory opinion under Article 96 of the Charter and Chapter IV of the Statute of the Court on the following questions:

"(i) Whether the indigenous population of Palestine has not an inherent right to Palestine and to determine its future constitution and government;

"(ii) Whether the pledges and assurances given by Great Britain to the Arabs during the first World War (including the Anglo-French Declaration of 1918) concerning the independence and future of Arab countries at the end of the war did not include Palestine;

"(iii) Whether the Balfour Declaration, which was made without the knowledge or consent of the indigenous population of Palestine, was valid and binding on the people of Palestine, or consistent with the earlier and subsequent pledges and assurances given to the Arabs;

"(iv) Whether the provisions of the Mandate for Palestine regarding the establishment of a Jewish National Home in Palestine are in conformity or consistent with the objectives and provisions of the Covenant of the League of Nations (in particular Article 22), or are compatible with the provisions of the Mandate relating to the development of self-government and the preservation of the rights and position of the Arabs of Palestine;

"(v) Whether the legal basis for the Mandate for Palestine has not disappeared with the dissolution of the League of Nations, and whether it is not the duty of the Mandatory Power to hand over power and administration to a Government of Palestine representing the rightful people of Palestine;

"(vi) Whether a plan to partition Palestine without the consent of the majority of its people is consistent with the objectives of the Covenant of the League of Nations, and with the provisions of the Mandate for Palestine;

"(vii) Whether the United Nations is competent to recommend either of the two plans and recommendations of the majority or minority of the United Nations Special Committee on Palestine, or any other solution involving partition of the territory of Palestine, or a permanent trusteeship over any city or part of Palestine, without the consent of the majority of the people of Palestine;

"(viii) Whether the United Nations, or any of its Member States, is competent to enforce or recommend the enforcement of any proposal concerning the constitution and future Government of Palestine, in particular, any plan of partition which is contrary to the wishes, or adopted without the consent of, the inhabitants of Palestine.

"*The General Assembly* instructs the Secretary-General to transmit this resolution to the International Court of Justice, accompanied by all documents likely to throw light upon the questions under reference."

Resolution No. II

DRAFT RESOLUTION ON JEWISH REFUGEES AND DISPLACED PERSONS

"*The General Assembly*, having regard to the unanimous recommendations of the United Nations Special Committee on Palestine, that the General Assembly undertake immediately the initiation and execution of an international arrangement whereby the problem of the distressed European Jews will be dealt with as a matter of extreme urgency for the alleviation of their plight and of the Palestine problem;

"*Bearing* in mind that genuine refugees and displaced persons constitute a problem which is international in scope and character;

"*Considering* that the question of refugees and displaced persons is indivisible in character as regards its possible solution;

"*Considering* that it is the duty of the Governments concerned to make provision for the return of refugees and displaced persons to the countries of which they are nationals;

"*Being* further of the opinion that where repatriation proves impossible, solution should be sought by way of resettlement in the territories of the Members of the United Nations which are willing and in a position to absorb these refugees and displaced persons;

"*Considering* that Palestine, despite its very small area and limited resources, has absorbed a disproportionately large number of Jewish immigrants and cannot take any more without serious injury to the economy of the country and the rights and position of the indigenous population;

"*Considering* that many other countries with much greater area and larger resources have not taken their due share of Jewish refugees and displaced persons;

"*Having* adopted a resolution (No. 62(I)) on 15 December 1946 calling for the creation of an international refugee organization with a view to the solution of the refugee problem through the combined efforts of the United Nations; and

"*Taking* note of the assumption on 1 July 1947 by the Preparatory Commission of the International Refugee Organization of operational responsibility for displaced persons and refugees;

"Recommends:
"(i)   That countries of origin should be requested to take back the Jewish refugees and displaced persons belonging to them, and to render them all possible assistance to resettle in life;
"(ii)   That those Jewish refugees and displaced persons who cannot be repatriated should be absorbed in the territories of Members of the United Nations in proportion to their area, economic resources, per capita income, population and other relevant factors;
"(iii) That a Special Committee of the General Assembly should be set up to recommend for acceptance of the Members of the United Nations a scheme of quotas of Jewish refugees and displaced persons to be resettled in their respective territories, and that the Special Committee should, as far as possible, work in consultation with the International Refugee Organization or its Preparatory Commission."

Resolution No. III

DRAFT RESOLUTION ON THE CONSTITUTION AND FUTURE GOVERNMENT OF PALESTINE

"*The General Assembly,* taking note of the declaration by the Mandatory Power of its intention to withdraw from Palestine;
"*Considering* that Palestine is a mandated territory whose independence was provisionally recognized by virtue of paragraph 4 of Article 22 of the Covenant of the League of Nations;
"*Recognizing* that the only solution in consonance with the objectives of the Covenant of the League of Nations and the principles of the Charter of the United Nations is one that is acceptable to the majority of the people of Palestine;
"*Being* satisfied that the partition of Palestine is unjust, illegal and impracticable and that the only just and workable solution is the immediate establishment of a unitary, democratic, and independent state, with adequate safeguards for minorities;
"*Believing* that peaceful and orderly transfer of power from the Mandatory to the Government of the people of Palestine is necessary in the interest of all concerned;
"*Recommends:*
"1.   That a Provisional Government, representative of all important sections of the citizenry in proportion to their numerical strength, should be set up as early as possible in Palestine;
"2.   That the powers and functions of the present Administration of Palestine should be vested in the Provisional Government as soon as the latter is constituted;
"3.   That the Mandatory Power should begin the withdrawal of its forces and services from Palestine as soon as the Provisional Government is installed, and should complete the withdrawal within one year;
"4.   That the Provisional Government should, as soon as practicable, enact an electoral law for the setting up of a Constituent Assembly, prepare an electoral register, and hold elections for the Constituent Assembly;
"5.   That the Constituent Assembly should also function as a Legislature and that the Provisional Government should be responsible to it until elections for a Legislature are held under the new constitution;

"6.   That while the task of framing a constitution for Palestine must be left to the Constituent Assembly, the following basic principles shall be strictly adhered to:
"(i)   Palestine shall be a unitary and sovereign State;
"(ii)   It shall have a democratic constitution, with an elected Legislature and an Executive responsible to the Legislature;
"(iii) The constitution shall provide guarantees for the sanctity of the Holy Places covering inviolability, maintenance, freedom of access and freedom of worship in accordance with the *status quo;*
"(iv)   The constitution shall guarantee respect for human rights and fundamental freedoms without distinction as to race, sex, language or religion, and freedom of religious belief and practice in accordance with the *status quo* (including the maintenance of separate religious courts to deal with matters of personal status);
"(v)   The constitution shall guarantee the rights of religious bodies or other societies and individuals to maintain, in addition to educational establishments administered by public authority, educational institutions of their own, subject to normal government supervision and inspection;
"(vi)   The constitution shall recognize the right of Jews to employ Hebrew as a second official language in areas in which they are in a majority;
"(vii) The Law of Naturalization and Citizenship shall provide, amongst other conditions, that the applicant should be a legal resident of Palestine for a continuous period to be determined by the Constituent Assembly;
"(viii) The constitution shall ensure adequate representation in the Legislature for all important sections of the citizenry in proportion to their numerical strength;
"(ix)   The constitution shall also provide for adequate reflection in the Executive and the Administration of the distribution of representation in the Legislature;
"(x)   The constitution shall authorize the Legislature to invest local authorities with wide discretion in matters connected with education, health and other social services;
"(xi)   The constitution shall provide for the setting up of a Supreme Court, the jurisdiction of which shall include, *inter alia,* the power to pronounce upon the constitutional validity of all legislation, and it shall be open to any aggrieved party to have recourse to that tribunal;
"(xii) The guarantees contained in the constitution concerning the rights and safeguards of the minorities shall not be subject to amendment or modification without the consent of the minority concerned expressed through a majority of its representatives in the Legislature."

Report of Conciliation Group

At the twenty-third meeting of the *ad hoc* Committee on November 19, 1947, the Chairman, speaking on behalf of the conciliation group, reported that the efforts of the group had not been fruitful. Both parties seemed too confident as to the success of their case before the General Assembly and there appeared to be little hope of conciliation, at least at the present time.

Ad hoc Committee considers Sub-Committee reports

The reports of the two Sub-Committees and of the Conciliation Group were placed before the *ad hoc* Committee at the 23rd meeting on November 19, 1947, and their consideration began at the next meeting on November 20.

. . .

Among the more important amendments adopted by the *ad hoc* Committee (in addition to the United States proposal to transfer to the proposed Arab State a part of the Beersheba area and a portion of the Negeb) was one, proposed by Denmark, calling upon the Security Council to consider whether the situation in Palestine constituted a threat to the peace (if circumstances warranted this) and, if the answer was in the affirmative, to supplement the authorization of the Assembly by taking measures to empower the Commission to exercise its functions under the Partition Plan; and to determine as a threat to the peace, breach of the peace or act of aggression, any attempt to alter by force the settlement envisaged in the Partition Plan. Then, too, the Committee endorsed the joint proposal by Norway and Pakistan to leave the composition of the five-member Commission to the General Assembly rather than recommend specifically that it be composed of Guatemala, Iceland, Norway, Poland and Uruguay, as suggested by Sub-Committee 1.

During the general debate on the recommendations of Sub-Committees 1 and 2, opinion in the *ad hoc* Committee once again was sharply divided.

. . .

Recommendations of the *ad hoc* Committee

Voting on the recommendations occupied the *ad hoc* Committee during its 32nd meeting on November 24, its 33rd on November 25 and its 34th and final meeting on November 25, 1947.

First to be put to the vote were the three draft resolutions submitted by Sub-Committee 2.

Draft Resolution I, providing for the reference to the International Court of Justice for an advisory opinion concerning eight legal questions connected with or arising out of the Palestine problem, was voted on in two parts. The first, comprising questions 1 to 7 inclusive, was rejected by a vote of 25 to 18, with 11 abstentions. The second, comprising the last question, was rejected by a vote of 21 to 20, with 13 abstentions.

Draft Resolution II dealing with Jewish refugees and displaced persons was put to the vote paragraph by paragraph. Paragraphs 1, 2, 5 and 9 of the preamble, as well as the first two paragraphs of the operative part were adopted, the others rejected. The modified draft resolution as a whole received 16 votes in favor, 16 against, with 26 abstentions, and the Committee decided, in view of this result, to include the text of the modified draft resolution verbatim in its report to the General Assembly.

Draft Resolution III of Sub-Committee 2 (dealing with the establishment of an independent, unitary State of Palestine) was rejected by a vote of 29 to 12, with 14 abstentions.

The Committee then turned to the recommendations of Sub-Committee 1. After voting on the amendments, the Committee, during its 34th meeting, on November 25, 1947, voted on the amended draft resolution embodying the Plan of Partition with Economic Union. The draft resolution was adopted by a vote of 25 to 13, with 17 abstentions.

Before this vote, the representative of New Zealand announced that he would abstain, without prejudice to the vote he might cast in the General Assembly, because he regarded the implementation provisions as inadequate. He urged, as a duty which the United Nations owed to itself as well as to Arabs and Jews, that all Members, particularly the big Powers, pledge at the current Assembly that, if bloodshed and upheaval broke out in Palestine, a united effort to suppress it would be made by means of an international force to which all would contribute in proportionate strength.

The delegations of Syria, Iraq and Egypt protested against the partition resolution as being unjust, impractical, against the Charter and a threat to peace. The representative of Egypt reserved the right of his Government to consider the resolution null and void.

The report of the *ad hoc* Committee on the Palestinian Question was then forwarded to the General Assembly for its consideration.

General Assembly adopts recommendations of *ad hoc* Committee

The recommendations of the *ad hoc* Committee on the Palestinian Question were considered by the General Assembly at the 124th to 128th plenary meetings, from November 26 to 29, 1947.

The Plan of Partition with Economic Union, in the form recommended by the *ad hoc* Committee, was supported, often with certain misgivings concerning particular aspects (e.g., the provisions for the Plan's implementation), by the representatives of Sweden, Canada, Brazil, United States, Poland, Uruguay, Netherlands, New Zealand, U.S.S.R., Belgium and Guatemala. The Plan was opposed, on the grounds that it violated the Charter and the principle of the right of self-determination of the Palestine population, by the representatives of the Philippines, Yemen, Greece, Iran, Egypt, Saudi Arabia, Syria, Lebanon, Haiti, Pakistan, Cuba and Iraq.

Representatives of several other Members declared themselves equally dissatisfied with the Partition Plan and with the rival plan for a unitary Palestine. Those who under these circumstances announced that they would abstain from voting were the representatives of China and Ethiopia.

During the 127th meeting on November 28, the representative of Colombia submitted a draft resolution which provided that a decision on the Palestine question be deferred and that the matter be referred back to the *ad hoc* Committee for further efforts at producing a solution acceptable to both Arabs and Jews. At the same meeting, the representative of France proposed a 24-hour adjournment to permit a last-minute effort at conciliating Arabs and Jews and at arriving at an agreed solution of the Palestine problem. The French motion was supported by the representatives of Denmark and Luxembourg, and opposed by those of Colombia and Poland. It was approved by the Assembly by a vote of 25 to 15, with 10 abstentions, and, consequently, the Assembly thereupon adjourned for 24 hours.

Following this 24-hour adjournment, the representative of Lebanon, at the 128th plenary meeting on November 29, 1947, deploring that since the beginning of the discussions "no *démarche* was attempted with the Arab delegations and no attempt was made to find any conciliation formula . . ." until the representatives of France and Colombia had intervened during the preceding plenary meeting, assured the Assembly that the Arab States had been and were always ready to listen to and study "any conciliatory formula susceptible of providing a reasonable and just solution of the Palestine question". They would have been happy to present a detailed plan embodying such a formula, but time had been lacking to do so between the present and the preceding plenary meeting. Nevertheless, the Arab States were in position to submit the "general principles which ought to serve as a basis for a compromise formula", namely:

"*Principle number one:* A federal independent state shall be set up in Palestine not later than 1 August 1948.

"*Principle number two:* The government of the independent state of Palestine shall be constituted on a federal basis and shall comprise a federal government and cantonal governments of Jewish and Arab cantons.

"*Principle number three:* The delimitation of the cantons shall be effected with a view to leaving as few Arab or Jewish minorities as possible in each canton.

"*Principle number four:* The population of Palestine shall elect by direct universal suffrage a Constituent Assembly which shall draft the future constitution of the federal state of Palestine. The Constituent Assembly shall comprise all the elements of the population in proportion to the number of their respective citizens.

"*Principle number five:* The Constituent Assembly, in defining the powers of the federal state of Palestine, as well as the powers of the judicial and legislative organs, in defining the functions of the cantonal governments, and in defining the relationships between the cantonal governments and the federal state, will be guided by the provisions of the Constitution of the United States of America, as well as the constitutions of the individual states of the United States of America.

"*Principle number six:* Among other necessary and essential provisions, the constitution shall provide for the protection of the Holy Places, freedom of access, visit and worship, in accordance with the *status quo*, as well as the safeguarding of the rights of religious establishments of all nationalities which are now found in Palestine."

In formulating these suggestions, the Arab States, the representative of Lebanon said, did not wish to exclude any suggestion or proposal which might be submitted by other delegations and which might be calculated to conciliate the points of view of Jews and Arabs.

The statement that no attempt at conciliation had been made was challenged by the representative of Iceland, who had been the Rapporteur of the *ad hoc* Committee. He recalled the efforts by the *ad hoc* Committee's Conciliation Group, adding that, as previously reported, these efforts had been doomed to failure in view of the vast gap between the contending parties.

The representative of the United States declared that the suggestions outlined by the representative of Lebanon coincided very largely with the plan recommended in the UNSCOP minority report, a plan which the *ad hoc* Committee had rejected. He moved that the recommendations of the *ad hoc* Committee be put to the vote immediately.

The representative of Iran submitted a draft resolution calling for a delay until January 15, 1948, in the deliberations of the Assembly on the Palestine question to enable the *ad hoc* Committee to reconvene and to study the matter further. The representative of Syria declared that the Chairman of the *ad hoc* Committee, in his capacity as Chairman of the Conciliation Group, had requested the chief of the Saudi Arabian delegation to make arrangements for consultations with the chief of the United States delegation to see if conciliation were possible. The representative of Syria further declared that the chief of the Saudi Arabian delegation had immediately notified the Chairman of the Conciliation Group of its readiness to accept this suggestion, but had never received an answer. Nor had another approach been made for such consultations to any of the delegations most directly concerned. Therefore, he maintained, the *ad hoc* Committee had not fulfilled its duties.

The representative of the U.S.S.R. opposed the proposal of the representative of Lebanon, and suggested that a vote be taken promptly on the recommendations of the *ad hoc* Committee.

The President ruled that the recommendations of the *ad hoc* Committee must be voted on before the Iranian proposal could be put to the vote.

The representative of Lebanon said he wished to call the Assembly's attention to the fact that the twelve general recommendations of UNSCOP had not been voted on in the *ad hoc* Committee. He therefore suggested that this be done now, before a vote was taken on the Plan of Partition with Economic Union. The President ruled that these twelve recommendations had been a matter for the *ad hoc* Committee, and not for the General Assembly. He then submitted the report of the *ad hoc* Committee to a roll-call vote.

. . .

The report, including the Plan of Partition with Economic Union, was therefore adopted by a vote of 33 to 13, with 10 abstentions.

Following the vote, the representative of the United Kingdom pointed out that a number of details connected with the application of the resolution just adopted would closely affect his Government. He expressed the hope that the United Nations Commission (envisaged in the resolution) would communicate with his Government in order that arrangements might be agreed upon for the arrival of the Commission in Palestine and for the co-ordination of its plans with those of the Mandatory Power for the withdrawal of British administration and British military forces. Earlier, the representative of the United Kingdom had reaffirmed the policy of his Government as outlined before the beginning of the general debate in the *ad hoc* Committee, and had reaffirmed that, subject to the limitations of that policy, the Government of the United Kingdom would not obstruct the implementation of the Partition Plan.

Also, following the adoption of the resolution on Partition, the representatives of Saudi Arabia, Pakistan, Iraq, Syria and Yemen denounced the Partition Plan as being anti-Charter, illegal and immoral, and declared that their respective Governments, regarding the resolution embodying the plan as a recommendation (rather than a binding decision), would not feel bound by it.

The President then proposed, and the Assembly endorsed, the following Members for membership on the United Nations Palestine Commission: Bolivia, Czechoslovakia, Denmark, Panama and the Philippines.

[YUN 1947-48, pp. 227-47]

On 29 November 1947, the General Assembly adopted resolution 181(II) A on the future Government of Palestine — Plan of Partition with Economic Union. The Plan detailed proposals for the future Constitution and Government of Palestine; termination of the Mandate; partition and independence; boundaries of the Arab State, the Jewish State and the City of Jerusalem; statute of the City of Jerusalem; and capitulations.

UN Palestine Commission

One of the consequences of the General Assembly's resolution 181(II) of November 29, 1947, concerning the Plan of Partition with Economic Union of Palestine, was the establishment of a five-member United Nations Palestine Commission, composed of the representatives of Bolivia, Czechoslovakia, Denmark, Panama and the Philippines, whose terms of reference were laid down in the resolution.

. . .

Under the partition resolution, the Commission had been assigned a major part in the implementation of the Plan of Partition with Economic Union, a task in which it was to avail itself of the guidance and assistance of the Security Council whenever necessary.

At the outset of its work, the Commission invited the United Kingdom as the Mandatory Power, the Arab Higher Committee and the Jewish Agency for Palestine to designate representatives who might furnish the Commission such authoritative information and other assistance as it might require in the discharge of its duties. The United Kingdom and the Jewish Agency complied with this request, while the Arab Higher Committee declared itself unable to accept the invitation, stating that it was "determined to persist in rejection partition and in refusal recognize UNO resolution this respect and anything deriving therefrom". Early in March, the Commission dispatched to Palestine an advance party of six Secretariat members for purposes of observation and exploratory discussions.

The Commission rendered to the Security Council two monthly progress reports as required by the Assembly's resolution, and, in addition, a Special Report on the Problem of Security in Palestine on February 16, 1948. In the last-mentioned report, the Commission reported to the Security Council *inter alia:*

"It is the considered view of the Commission that the security forces of the Mandatory Power, which at the present time prevent the situation from deteriorating completely into open warfare on an organized basis, must be replaced by an adequate non-Palestinian force which will assist law-abiding elements in both the Arab and Jewish communities, organized under the general direction of the Commission, in maintaining order and security in Palestine, and thereby enabling the Commission to carry out the recommendations of the General Assembly. Otherwise, the period immediately following the termination of the Mandate will be a period of uncontrolled, widespread strife and bloodshed in Palestine, including the City of Jerusalem. This would be a catastrophic conclusion to an era of international concern for that territory.

"The Commission submits this report with a profound appreciation of its duty to the United Nations. The sole motivation of the Commission is to obtain from the Security Council that effective assistance without which, it is firmly convinced, it cannot discharge the great responsibilities entrusted to it by the General Assembly."

. . .

The Palestine Commission, in a resolution adopted on April 2, 1948, recalled the mandate entrusted to it by the General Assembly on November 29, 1947, stated that it had "received no guidance or instructions from the Security Council concerning the implementation of the General Assembly's resolution", and noted the Council's decisions of April 1 calling for steps to be taken to arrange a truce in Palestine, and requesting the convocation of a special session of the General Assembly to consider further the question of the future government of Palestine. In the same resolution, the Commission decided:

"I. To continue its work, bearing in mind the resolutions adopted by the Security Council, in the understanding that all of its decisions will be subject to such final action on the future government of Palestine as may be taken by the special session of the General Assembly convening on 16 April;

"II. To undertake the preparation of a report to be presented to the special session of the General Assembly which will include an exposition of the reasons which have prevented the Commission from discharging all of the responsibilities assigned to it by the resolution of 29 November 1947."

The reasons which, in the Commission's opinion, prevented it from discharging all of the responsibilities assigned to it by the Assembly's resolution, were summed up by the Commission in its report to the General Assembly in the following terms:

"The Commission . . . has the duty to report to the General Assembly that the armed hostility of both Palestinian and non-Palestinian Arab elements, the lack of co-operation from the Mandatory Power, the disintegrating security situation in Palestine, and the fact that the Security Council did not furnish the Commission with the necessary armed assistance, are the factors which have made it impossible for the Commission to implement the Assembly's resolution."

In the same report, the Commission also outlined a number of "problems which require an urgent solution", regardless of the ultimate decision of the Assembly on the future government of Palestine, including questions concerned with security, administration, economics and finance. The report also registered the concern of the Commission concerning the food situation in the Holy Land, adding that "in view of the urgency of this matter, the Commission is presenting a special report on the subject to the Security Council with a request for its guidance . . .".

In the concluding paragraph of its report to the General Assembly, the Commission warned once again ". . . [that] in the absence of forces adequate to restore and maintain law and order in Palestine following the termination of the Mandate, there will be administrative chaos, starvation, widespread strife, violence and bloodshed in Palestine, including Jerusalem. These calamitous results for the people of Palestine will be intensified unless specific arrangements are made regarding the urgent matters outlined above well in advance of 15 May 1948."

The report to the General Assembly was adopted by the Palestine Commission on April 10, 1948.

Following the decision of the General Assembly to relieve the Commission of its duties, the Commission held its 75th and last meeting on May 17, 1948, took cognizance of the Assembly's action and adjourned *sine die*.

[YUN 1947-48, pp. 256-57]

Palestine refugees

United Nations aid to Palestine refugees began in November 1948, when the General Assembly authorized the advance of $5 million for relief. United Nations Relief for Palestine Refugees, established on 1 December 1948, received voluntary contributions of $35 million. On 8 December 1949, the Assembly established the United Nations Relief and Works Agency for Palestine Refugees in the Near East (UNRWA).

In October 1993, UNRWA launched its Peace Implementation Programme, which was developed in consultation with the Palestine Liberation Organization (PLO) and major donors. The Programme's main objectives in the West Bank and the Gaza Strip were to improve basic physical and social services infrastructure and to create new employment opportunities for Palestinians. UNRWA prepared over $120 million in project proposals and by mid-1994 had raised about $85 million of the target of $137 million, or over 60 per cent.

Assistance to Palestine refugees

The urgency of the problem of providing assistance to Arab refugees was emphasized by the United Nations Mediator on Palestine in his progress report of 16 September 1948 to the General Assembly. His recommendations included a proposal that the United Nations adopt a plan of assistance which would integrate the activities of the specialized agencies, the United Nations International Children's Emergency Fund, and appropriate voluntary bodies. As one of the minimum conditions for the success of any effort to bring peace to Palestine, he held that it was incumbent upon the international community to accept its share of responsibility for the refugees of that land. The Mediator asked the United Nations to affirm the right of the Arab refugees to return to their homes in Jewish-controlled territory at the earliest possible date, and he recommended the establishment by the United Nations of a conciliation commission for Palestine, which would supervise their repatriation, resettlement and economic and social rehabilitation and also assure the payment of adequate compensation for the property of those choosing not to return to their former homes. In a covering letter attached to the progress report, the Mediator drew special attention to the necessity for humanitarian measures to relieve the desperate condition of Arab refugees, and he asked that the matter be included in the agenda of the third session of the General Assembly.

Consideration by the
General Assembly at its third session

. . .

At the 186th plenary meeting of the General Assembly on 11 December 1948, the United Nations Conciliation Commission for Palestine was established to assist the Governments and authorities concerned to achieve a final settlement of all outstanding questions. Specific reference was made to the Palestine refugees and paragraph 11 of the Assembly resolution 194(III) which reads:

> "*Resolves* that the refugees wishing to return to their homes and live at peace with their neighbours should be permitted to do so at the earliest practicable date, and that compensation should be paid for the property of those choosing not to return and for loss of or damage to property which, under principles of international law or in equity, should be made good by the Governments or authorities responsible;
>
> "*Instructs* the Conciliation Commission to facilitate the repatriation, resettlement and economic and social rehabilitation of the refugees and the payment of compensation, and to maintain close relations with the Director of the United Nations Relief for Palestine Refugees and, through him, with the appropriate organs and agencies of the United Nations."

. . .

Consideration by the
General Assembly at its fourth session

At the fourth regular session of the General Assembly, the United Nations Conciliation Commission for Palestine presented four progress reports covering its activities during the period January-September 1949. Considered by the *Ad Hoc* Political Committee, these reports dealt extensively with the work of assisting the Palestine refugees.

Progress reports of the Conciliation Commission

The first progress report reviewed the preliminary arrangements for the establishment of close relations with the United Nations Relief for Palestine Refugees and with the Governments concerned. The Commission stated that, as a result of preliminary talks, held with the authorities in Egypt, Saudi Arabia, Transjordan, Iraq, Syria, Lebanon and Israel, it found the Governments of the Arab States and the Government of Israel to be in an attitude of mind definitely favourable to peace. The continuation of negotiations by repeated visits to the various capitals was considered a practical impossibility, and the Commission had decided to invite the Arab States to hold meetings for the purpose of exchanging views on the refugee problem.

The second progress report reviewed the substance of preliminary talks held in Beirut with the Arab delegations and in Tel Aviv with the Prime Minister of Israel. The principal subject of those conversations had been the refugee question. Separate meetings between the Commission and each of the Arab delegations were held in Beirut from 21 March to 5 April 1949, and the Arab representatives were unanimous in recognizing: *(a)* the necessity of giving absolute priority to the refugee question; *(b)* the requirement that any solution of the problem must be contingent upon the acceptance by the Government of Israel of the principle established in General Assembly resolution 194(III) of 11 December 1948.

. . .

The Commission's third progress report covered the discussions which took place in Lausanne, Switzerland, during the period 27 April to 8 June 1949. In support of its contention that the refugee question and the territorial question were closely interlinked, the Commission drafted a protocol which accepted the use of a specific map of Palestine as a basis for discussions. The map showed the territory attributed to the Arab and Jewish States respectively, by the General Assembly resolution of 29 November 1947. The protocol was signed by the Commission and the Arab delegations (Egypt, Jordan, Lebanon, Syria) on the one hand, and by the Commission and the Israeli delegation on the other.

. . .

In reaching its conclusions, the Commission stated that its immediate problem consisted in linking together negotiations on the refugee problem and those concerned with territorial questions. It held that a solution of the refugee problem must relate not only to the general aspect of the question, that of the repatriation, resettlement and economic and social rehabilitation of the refugees, but also to its more immediate aspect concerning preliminary measures to be taken for the safeguarding of their rights and property.

The fourth progress report of the Commission, covering the period 9 June to 15 September 1949, noted a willingness of the Israeli Government to give immediate consideration to the problem of refugees, with the proviso that its contribution to the solution of the question would be limited by considerations affecting the security and the economy of the State. Subject to certain conditions which provided that the refugees would be settled in areas where they would not come in contact with possible enemies of Israel, and that it reserved the right to resettle repatriated refugees in specific locations in order to ensure that their reinstallation would fit into the general plan of Israel's economic development, the Israeli Government would be prepared to accept the return to Israel, in its present limits, of 100,000 refugees. This figure was in addition to the total Arab population existing at the end of hostilities and would increase the total number of that population to a maximum of 250,000. It was further stated that this repatriation would form part of a general plan for resettlement of refugees which would be established by a special organ to be created for the purpose by the United Nations.

. . .

On 15 August, the Commission submitted to all delegations present in Lausanne a memorandum asking whether the various delegations were prepared to sign a declaration according to which (a) the solution of the refugee problem should be sought in the repatriation of refugees in Israeli-controlled territory, and in the re-settlement of those not repatriated in Arab countries or in the zone of Palestine not under Israeli control; (b) in the event that an Economic Mission was charged by the United Nations with the establishment of major work projects in the Middle East, all parties would undertake to facilitate the task of the Mission and aid in the implementation of such solutions as it might propose; (c) agreement to the above-mentioned conditions should not prejudice the rights reserved in connexion with the final settlement of the territorial question; (d) renewal of funds for emergency aid to refugees until technical and financial aid should be allotted by the international community.

The delegations were also asked to present a provisional estimate of the approximate number of refugees which their Governments would be ready to accept.

The reply from the Arab delegations, received on 29 August, indicated that they were prepared to study the implementation of the Commission's proposal with respect to repatriation and resettle-

ment, subject to observations contained in their earlier memorandum, which asked for international guarantees against discrimination on grounds of race or faith. With regard to work which might be undertaken by the Economic Mission, the Arab delegations undertook to recommend that their Governments facilitate its operations and assist in the implementation of such solutions as it might propose.

The delegations of Jordan and Syria stated that their Governments were prepared to receive such refugees as might not return to their homes, but the representatives of Egypt and Lebanon declared that it would be difficult to contemplate the resettlement of a number of refugees on their existing territory. They would, however, study the question in the light of the prevailing situation and within the framework of international technical and financial aid. Collectively, the Arab delegations urged that the United Nations continue to supply the funds necessary for emergency aid to refugees.

The Government of Israel, in its reply of 31 August, announced its willingness to sign a declaration subject to precision on the following points: (a) that solution of the problem be sought primarily in resettlement in Arab territories; (b) that Israel would facilitate the task of the Economic Mission without binding itself in advance to implement the solutions proposed; (c) that non-discrimination against refugees also apply to Arab States; (d) that international financial assistance also be extended to the resettlement of Jewish refugees from Arab-controlled areas of Palestine.

. . .

In its report, the Commission announced the establishment of an Economic Survey Mission pursuant to the authorization granted under paragraph 12 of the General Assembly resolution 194(III) of 11 December 1948. The Mission stopped in Lausanne on 8 September 1949 for discussions with the Commission, the Arab and Israeli delegations and various specialized agencies of the United Nations, and departed on 11 September for Beirut where headquarters were established. The terms of reference of the Economic Survey Mission were contained in Annex I to the Commission's fourth progress report.

A fifth progress report of the United Nations Conciliation Commission for Palestine covered the period 16 September to 9 December 1949 and was submitted later during the session. The Commission reconvened in New York on 19 October and reported that conversations with regard to blocked Arab accounts were proceeding favourably in an effort to arrive at a mutually acceptable method of unfreezing the accounts in question.

In connexion with the reunion of separated refugee families, it was reported that Lebanon, Egypt and Jordan had appointed representatives to discuss and carry out, in collaboration with the competent Israeli authorities, the actual plan for the return of these refugees. Syria had also indicated its readiness to appoint a representative.

Further discussions relative to arrangements for Arabs living in territory under Arab control close to the Armistice demarcation line, to cultivate their lands which lie within territory under Israeli control, resulted in an agreement to discuss the matter in the Special Committee set up by the Armistice Agreement.

The question of compensation to be paid to refugees not wishing to return to their homes was included in the terms of reference given to the Economic Survey Mission, and the Commission reported that it proposed taking the matter up again in January 1950 after having heard from the Mission.

. . .

United Nations Relief for Palestine Refugees (UNRPR)

The *Ad Hoc* Political Committee also had before it the Secretary-General's report covering the activities of the United Nations Relief for Palestine Refugees (UNRPR) for the period 1 December 1948 to 30 September 1949.

UNRPR came into existence on 1 December 1948 at which time the Secretary-General appointed its Director in accordance with the terms of the General Assembly resolution 212(III) of 19 November 1948. The problem of refugees became acute in July 1948 and was dealt with principally by the Governments of Lebanon, Syria, Transjordan and Egypt, with some outside assistance received from voluntary organizations in response to appeals by the late United Nations Mediator for Palestine. During the month of September, a Disaster Relief Project was initiated by the Mediator and continued until it was replaced by UNRPR. A UNICEF Middle East feeding programme also contributed substantially to the relief work.

Agreements were signed by UNRPR on 19 December 1948 with the International Committee of the Red Cross, the League of Red Cross Societies and the American Friends Service Committee, whereby the three agencies, as independent and autonomous organizations, assumed full responsibility for the distribution of supplies to be obtained and allocated by UNRPR. Arrangements were also made for UNICEF to continue its work of caring for Palestine refugee mothers and children as an integral phase of the UNRPR relief programme.

The geographical assignment of responsibilities for relief operations was as follows: International Committee of the Red Cross—Israel, Israeli-occupied areas and Transjordanian-occupied areas of Palestine; League of Red Cross Societies— Lebanon, Syria and Jordan; American Friends Service Committee—Gaza area, under Egyptian occupation, and a degree of participation in Israel by arrangement between the agencies.

The operation of the relief programme was examined by the *ad hoc* Advisory Committee on Palestine Refugees on 20 April 1949, at which time the Secretary-General and the Director of UNRPR reviewed measures which had already been taken and made recommendations with respect to future activities. It was felt that operations could be maintained until November 1949 provided the full amount of $25,000,000, pledged by twenty-one Governments, was received. . . .

In June 1949, the agreements with the three operating agencies were extended. Certain reservations were made regarding the maintenance of the level of rations and other supplies, notification as to the availability of funds, and other operational phases of the work. The agencies also stated that they could not continue a purely relief programme indefinitely.

The financial status of UNRPR was again considered by the *ad hoc* Advisory Committee on 4 October 1949 and, as a result of the discussions, the Secretary-General appealed to the three operating agencies to continue their collaboration through March 1950. His request was also communicated to UNICEF, WHO, IRO, UNESCO and FAO. In every instance the Secretary-General received assurance of continued collaboration.

The first shipload of UNRPR supplies reached Beirut on New Year's Day 1949 and total daily rations were initially established at 600,000. The number increased steadily, and from June through September 1949 it reached 940,000. It was possible to provide slightly less than 1,600 calories per daily ration in the three areas of operation, in addition to which shelter, clothing and fuel were made available as circumstances permitted. UNICEF beneficiaries represented over half of the refugee population cared for and substantial supplies were donated by IRO. No serious or widespread malnutrition had been observed among the refugee population during the period UNRPR was in operation, but it was stressed that the food programme, measured by any normal acceptable standard for meeting human needs, had been dangerously low.

Health and medical services were given high priority in the UNRPR programme, and a relatively adequate health programme was instituted in collaboration with WHO. There was provision for emergency surgery and a number of polyclinics, public health clinics and mobile clinics were established.

Shelter for refugees was totally inadequate during the winter of 1948-49, and many people were obliged to live in caves, huts or even out in the open air. In spite of the acquisition of approximately 36,000 tents and over 1,000,000 blankets, it was estimated that requirements for the winter 1949-50 would still be short.

The need for clothing was stressed and, it was stated that, in spite of numerous donations of used clothing and cotton piece goods, supplies were totally insufficient for the needs of the refugees.

. . .

In the field of educational services, it was stated that the programme of educational relief for Arab refugee children in the Middle East was making good progress under the sponsorship of UNESCO. As a result of contributions from the UNESCO Emergency Fund, Norwegian UNAC Committee, Lord Mayor of London's Fund, Arab League, Australian Government, Belgian UNAC Committee, and from the Council for Education in World Citizenship (Great Britain), it was possible to sponsor the establishment of thirty-nine schools, which were attended by over 21,000 children and placed under the supervision of the three operating agencies.

. . .

Economic Survey Mission

The *Ad Hoc* Political Committee was also asked to consider an interim report prepared by the Economic Survey Mission, which had been created by the United Nations Conciliation Commission for Palestine on 29 August 1949. The Mission examined the possibility of introducing measures which might alleviate economic dislocations resulting from hostilities in Palestine, and sought to stabilize the economic life of the area. It also undertook a study of problems relating to repatriation, resettlement and social and economic rehabilitation of the refugees. The Mission, frequently referred to as the Clapp Mission, consisted of a chairman nominated by the United States and three deputy chairmen nominated respectively by the United Kingdom, France and Turkey.

The Mission estimated that a total of 652,000 persons were eligible for relief from the United Nations. After describing their location, their effect on local resources and their dilemma, the report asserted that the repatriation of Arab refugees required political decisions outside the competence of the Economic Survey Mission, and indicated that the only immediate constructive step in sight was to give the refugees an opportunity to work in their current location.

In presenting its interim findings on 16 November 1949, the Mission stated that the refugees themselves were the most serious manifestation of economic dislocation created by the Arab-Israeli hostilities and that they represented about 7 per cent of the population in the countries in which

they had sought refuge. It contended that to resolve the refugee problem with its demoralizing, unproductive and costly aspects was the most immediate requirement conducive to the maintenance of peace and stability in the area, and added that the continuing political stalemate in the relations between the Arab countries and Israel precluded any early solution of the problem by means of repatriation or large-scale resettlement.

. . . the Economic Survey Mission recommended that the present UNRPR system of relief be continued through the winter months until 1 April 1950 without reducing the existing minimum ration but with the number of rations reduced from 940,000 to 652,000. It advocated the adoption of a programme of public works calculated to improve the productivity of the area, and such continuing relief as it would be necessary to organize in co-operation with the Governments of the countries where the refugees were located.

It was suggested that the United Nations should be prepared to continue the works programme until 30 June 1951 and that the programme be planned and arrangements negotiated with the appropriate Near Eastern Governments to begin 1 April 1950. These Governments should assume responsibility for the maintenance of such refugees as might remain within their territories after 31 December 1950, and no further rations should be supplied by the United Nations after that date unless otherwise ordered by the General Assembly at its fifth session. The cost of relief and works projects for the eighteen-month period of 1 January to 30 June 1951 was estimated at $53,700,000.

The Economic Survey Mission recommended that an agency be established to organize and, on or after 1 April 1950, direct the programmes of relief and public works, and it asked that the personnel and assets of the UNRPR be turned over to the new agency in order that the functions of direct relief be directed by the new agency in appropriate relation to the works programme.

. . .

Resolution adopted by the General Assembly

. . . The resolution adopted by the Assembly (302(IV)) read as follows:

"*The General Assembly,*

. . .

"7. *Establishes* the United Nations Relief and Works Agency for Palestine Refugees in the Near East:

"*(a)* To carry out in collaboration with local governments the direct relief and works programmes as recommended by the Economic Survey Mission;

"*(b)* To consult with the interested Near Eastern Governments concerning measures to be taken by them preparatory to the time when international assistance for relief and works projects is no longer available;

"8. *Establishes* an Advisory Commission consisting of representatives of France, Turkey, the United Kingdom of Great Britain and Northern Ireland and the United States of America, with power to add not more than three additional members from contributing Governments, to advise and assist the Director of the United Nations Relief and Works Agency for Palestine Refugees in the Near East in the execution of the programme; the Director and the Advisory Commission shall consult with each Near Eastern Government concerned in the selection, planning and execution of projects;

"9. *Requests* the Secretary-General to appoint the Director of the United Nations Relief and Works Agency for Palestine Refugees in the Near East in consultation with the Governments represented on the Advisory Commission;

"*(a)* The Director shall be the chief executive officer of the United Nations Relief and Works Agency for Palestine Refugees in the Near East responsible to the General Assembly for the operation of the programme;

"*(b)* The Director shall select and appoint his staff in accordance with general arrangements made in agreement with the Secretary-General, including such of the staff rules and regulations of the United Nations as the Director and the Secretary-General shall agree are applicable, and to the extent possible utilize the facilities and assistance of the Secretary-General;

"*(c)* The Director shall, in consultation with the Secretary-General and the Advisory Committee on Administrative and Budgetary Questions, establish financial regulations for the United Nations Relief and Works Agency for Palestine Refugees in the Near East;

"*(d)* Subject to the financial regulations established pursuant to clause *(c)* of the present paragraph, the Director, in consultation with the Advisory Commission, shall apportion available funds between direct relief and works projects in their discretion, in the event that the estimates in paragraph 6 require revision;

"10. *Requests* the Director to convene the Advisory Commission at the earliest practicable date for the purpose of developing plans for the organization and administration of the programme, and of adopting rules of procedure;

"11. *Continues* the United Nations Relief for Palestine Refugees as established under General Assembly resolution 212(III) until 1 April 1950, or until such date thereafter as the transfer referred to in paragraph 12 is effected, and requests the Secretary-General in consultation with the operating agencies to continue the endeavour to reduce the numbers of rations by progressive stages in the light of the findings and recommendations of the Economic Survey Mission;

"12. *Instructs* the Secretary-General to transfer to the United Nations Relief and Works Agency for Palestine Refugees in the Near East the assets and liabilities of the United Nations Relief for Palestine Refugees by 1 April 1950, or at such date as may be agreed by him and the Director of the United Nations Relief and Works Agency for Palestine Refugees in the Near East;

"13. *Urges* all Members of the United Nations and non-members to make voluntary contributions in funds or in kind to ensure that the amount of supplies and funds required is obtained for each period of the programme as set out in paragraph 6; contributions in funds may be made in currencies other than the United States dollar in so far as the programme can be carried out in such currencies;

"14. *Authorizes* the Secretary-General, in consultation with the Advisory Committee on Administrative and Budgetary Questions, to advance funds deemed to be available for this purpose and not exceeding $5,000,000 from the Working Capital Fund to finance operations pursuant to the present resolution, such sum to be repaid not later than 31 December 1950 from the voluntary governmental contributions requested under paragraph 13 above;

"15. *Authorizes* the Secretary-General, in consultation with the Advisory Committee on Administrative and Budgetary Questions, to negotiate with the International Refugee Organization for an interest-free loan in an amount not to exceed the equivalent of $2,800,000 to finance the programme subject to mutually satisfactory conditions for repayment;

"16. *Authorizes* the Secretary-General to continue the Special Fund established under General Assembly resolution 212(III) and to make withdrawals therefrom for the operation of the United Nations Relief for Palestine Refugees and, upon the request of the Director, for the operations of the United Nations Relief and Works Agency for Palestine Refugees in the Near East;
. . ."

[YUN 1948-49, pp. 199-212]

Suez Canal crisis

On 26 July 1956, Egypt proclaimed the nationalization of the Suez Canal Company and placed in the hands of an Egyptian operating authority management of the Canal traffic which, in 1955, amounted to some 14,000 ships with a net tonnage of some 107 million tons. The decree provided for compensation on the basis of the market value of the shares on 25 July upon receipt of all the assets and property of the Canal Company.

Nationalization of the Canal Company was followed by a series of events which included lengthy negotiations over how to settle the Suez question, the further deterioration of the situation, especially along the Egyptian-Israel and Jordan-Israel Armistice Demarcation Lines in September and October, and military action in Egypt by Israel and Anglo-French forces. After eventually successful efforts by the United Nations to obtain the withdrawal of those forces, involving the creation of the United Nations Emergency Force and clearance of the blocked Suez Canal under United Nations auspices, there came renewed negotiations concerning the Canal and renewed efforts to promote peaceful conditions in the area by re-establishing full compliance with the Armistice Agreement.

After the nationalization of the Canal in July 1956, France, the United States and the United Kingdom agreed, in talks at London between 29 July and 2 August 1956, that the Egyptian action threatened "the freedom and security of the Canal as guaranteed by the Convention of 1888", and the United Kingdom issued invitations to a conference in London of parties to the 1888 Convention and of other nations largely concerned with the use of the Canal. The announced purpose was to consider steps to establish operating arrangements, consistent with legitimate Egyptian interests, under an international system designed to assure operation of the Canal as guaranteed by the Convention.

Meanwhile, Egypt had seized the Canal, its installations and all property of the Canal Company in Egypt. France and the United Kingdom countered by refusing to pay tolls to the new Egyptian authority. Together with the United States, they blocked all Egyptian accounts, including those of the Canal Company.

Egypt refused to attend the London Conference, stating that it had been convened without consulting Egypt to discuss the future of an integral part of that nation's territory. Egypt proposed instead a conference of the 45 users of the Canal to reconsider the Constantinople Convention of 1888 and to confirm and guarantee freedom of navigation through the Canal.

At the London Suez Conference held between 16 and 24 August 1956, 18 of the 22 Powers who attended agreed on proposals to be presented to Egypt. The 18 Powers proposed a definite system to guarantee at all times and for all Powers free use of the Canal, with due regard to the sovereign rights of Egypt. The system was to assure: (1) efficient operation and development of the Canal and a free, open and secure international waterway; (2) insulation of that operation from the politics of any nation; (3) an equitable financial return to Egypt, increasing as the Canal was enlarged and used by more shipping; and (4) Canal dues as low as was consistent with the above provisions. To achieve those results, a Suez Canal Board was to operate, maintain and develop the Canal, the Board to include Egypt and to make periodic reports to the United Nations. There would be an arbitral commission to settle disputes and effective sanctions which would treat any use or threat of force to interfere with the operating of the Canal as a threat to peace and violation of the Charter.

. . .

The 18-Power plan was presented to the Egyptian Government in Cairo on 3 September 1956, by a five-nation Committee headed by the Prime Minister of Australia. On 9 September, the Committee reported rejection of the plan by the Government of Egypt which, it stated, resisted any control or management of the operation and development of the Canal by anybody other than itself. In a memorandum of 10 September, Egypt stated that the essence of the proposals was the establishment of international, in place of Egyptian, control over the Canal and stipulations for sanctions. Egypt proposed instead the establishment of a negotiating body representative of the different user views to seek solutions for questions relating to freedom of navigation of the Canal, its development and equitable tolls. This proposal, which Egypt announced had been accepted by 21 States, was considered by the second London Suez Conference, held between 19 and 21 September by the supporters of the 18-Power plan, as too imprecise to afford a useful basis for discussion.

On 12 September, the representatives of France and the United Kingdom informed the Security Council that the situation created by the action of Egypt in attempting unilaterally to bring to an end the system of international operation of the Suez Canal which was confirmed and completed by the Convention of 1888 might endanger the free and open passage of shipping through the Canal. The refusal of Egypt to negotiate on the 18-Power proposals which, in their opinion, offered means for a just and equitable solution, was regarded by them as an aggravation of the situation which, if allowed to continue, would constitute a manifest danger to peace and security.

On the same day, the Prime Minister of the United Kingdom announced that, in agreement with France and the United States, an association would be set up to enable the users of the Canal to exercise their rights. The second London Suez Conference provided for a voluntary Suez Canal Users Association, a body originally suggested by the United States. The Association, of which 15 of the 18 conferring nations became members, was an interim formula, pending a more permanent solution, designed to assist its members in the exercise of their rights as users of the Canal in consonance with the 1888 Convention, with due regard for the rights of Egypt.

Meanwhile, on 15 September, a statement by the USSR, transmitted to the Security Council, declared that military preparations of the United Kingdom and France, conducted with the support of the United States, for the purpose of exerting pressure on Egypt over the Suez question, were grossly at variance with the principles of the Charter and could not be regarded otherwise than an act of aggression against Egypt, which had exercised its legitimate rights as a sovereign State in nationalizing the private Suez Canal Company. The whole plan of the 18-Power proposals and the Users Association was aimed at removing administration of the Canal from the hands of Egypt and transferring it to a foreign administration, although plainly such a plan could only be implemented by force. To impose a solution of the Suez Canal issue by force of arms risked immense destruction in the Suez Canal and in the oil fields and pipelines "in the countries of the Arab East". A foreign invasion of Egypt would rouse the peoples of Asia and Africa, who were aware that no forces were capable of stopping the historical development leading toward liquidation of colonialism. In an age of destructive atomic and hydrogen weapons, it was useless to threaten in a manner characteristic of past colonial conquests. The USSR was convinced that the important questions of freedom of navigation and normal functioning of the Canal could and must be solved by peaceful means and expressed support for the Egyptian proposals of 10 September. The USSR could not stand aside from the Suez problem because any violation of peace in the area could not but affect its security.

On 17 September, Egypt informed the Council by letter that the claim in the Anglo-French letter of 12 September that the Company was part of the system established by the Convention of 1888 was considered devoid of any legal, historical or moral foundation. The act of nationalization had been taken by Egypt in the full exercise of its sovereign rights and Egypt had simultaneously reaffirmed its determination to continue to guarantee the freedom of passage through the Canal in conformity with the 1888 Convention, which did not in any way deprive Egypt of its right to administer the Canal. Reviewing threats of force and hostile economic measures taken by France and the United Kingdom, the letter contrasted Egypt's proposals for a negotiating body with the proposed Suez Canal Users Association, which was declared incompatible with the sovereign rights of Egypt and a violation of the 1888 Convention. Such acts, it concluded, were aimed, particularly by France and the United Kingdom, at taking virtual possession of the Canal and destroying the very independence of Egypt. The proposed Association was especially unjustifiable in view of the fact that for nearly 60 days, and in spite of the difficulties created by France, the United Kingdom and the former Suez Canal Company, the traffic had been going on with regularity and efficiency, with more ships passing than during the corresponding period of 1955.

. . .

On 26 September, the Council included both items in its agenda and decided to give priority to the discussion of the item submitted jointly by the United Kingdom and France. The question was discussed at seven open meetings and three closed meetings held between then and 13 October, in which the representative of Egypt took part.

. . .

The Council, at its next meeting, on 5 October, had before it a draft resolution submitted by France and the United Kingdom. By this the Council, recognizing that, in subjecting the operation of an international public service to exclusive Egyptian control, the Egyptian Government had created a situation likely to endanger the maintenance of international peace and security, would: (1) reaffirm the principle of freedom of navigation of the Suez Canal in accordance with the Suez Canal Convention of 1888; (2) endorse the proposals advanced by 18 of the 22 States which had attended the August conference in London, as suitably designed to bring about a solution of the question by peaceful means and in conformity with justice; (3) recommend that the Government of Egypt should co-operate by negotiation in working out, on the basis of those proposals, a system of operation to be applied to the Canal and should co-operate with the Suez Canal Users Association established at the second London Conference in September to assist its members in the exercise of their rights.

Discussion in the Council ranged over the history of the Canal and the legal status of the Suez Canal Company, the economic importance of the Canal, particularly its role in the transport of Middle Eastern oil, and the political background and implications of nationalization of the Canal. It was said that the crux of the problem was to bring Egypt's sovereign rights with regard to the Suez Canal into harmony with the legitimate interests of the world community in obtaining adequate assurances regarding the freedom and security of navigation established by the Convention of 1888 through a waterway of exceptional international importance.

While no supporter of the Anglo-French draft resolution questioned Egyptian sovereignty over the Canal or the principle of the right of nationalization, it was urged that Egyptian sovereignty did not mean absence of international rights, and some maintained that nationalization of the Suez Canal Company was illegal. The character of the Canal as an international waterway dedicated to the free passage of the vessels of all nations had been guaranteed for all time by the 1888 Convention. The act of nationalization had upset the balance of the system of concessions, the Turkish declaration of 1873 regarding tolls and the Constantinople Convention of 1888, which had safeguarded the rights of Egypt and the users.

. . .

Not only were the economic future and vital interests of many countries east and west of the Canal at stake, but so was the system of operation which was likely to bring the greatest material benefits to the people of Egypt. If the Canal could be used as an instrument of national policy by any Government which physically controlled it, no nation depending on the Canal could feel secure. An instance of discrimination was the refusal of Egypt to allow passage of Israel vessels in accordance with the Security Council resolution of 1 September 1951.

. . .

Opponents of the Anglo-French draft resolution, on the other hand, maintained that nationalization of the Suez Canal Company, an Egyptian company which had amortized its capital many times over, was a legitimate act of Egyptian sovereignty. The claim that the Canal Company was part of the system established by the Convention of 1888 was wholly unwarranted. The question of ownership and operation of the Canal, which was under Egyptian jurisdiction, had nothing to do with Egypt's international obligations under the 1888 Convention to ensure free passage, it was said. Egypt had been faithfully discharging those obligations. Despite many obstructions put in the way, navigation through the Canal had been proceeding with perfect efficiency, and nationalization of the Canal Company could not conceivably endanger international peace and security.

The different plans of the Western Powers for settling the Suez problem, including the Anglo-French draft resolution, were violating Egypt's sovereignty by interfering in its internal affairs and imposing an international authority as the master of the Canal.

The problem, it was recognized, was of vital interest to a large number of user countries, but of at least equal interest to Egypt, as the sovereign Government concerned. Emphasis was laid on Egypt's offers to negotiate on equal terms a peaceful and just solution. What Egypt refused, it was said, was not negotiation but dictation.

On 8 October, the representative of Egypt restated his Government's willingness to negotiate a peaceful settlement on the basis of the 1888 Convention principle of guaranteeing for all and for all time the freedom of navigation in the Suez Canal with a view to: (1) establishing a system of co-operation between the Egyptian operating authority and the users, taking into account the sovereignty and rights of Egypt and the interests of the users; (2) establishing an equitable system of tolls; and (3) allotting a reasonable percentage of the Canal revenues for improvements.

. . . At the next open meeting of the Council, on 13 October, the United Kingdom and France submitted another draft resolution. By this, as amended on the suggestion of Iran, the Council, noting the account of the Secretary-General on these exploratory conversations, would: (1) agree that any settlement of the Suez question should meet the following six requirements: (i) there should be free and open transit through the Canal without discrimination, overt or covert—this covered both political and technical aspects; (ii) the sovereignty of Egypt should be respected; (iii) the operation of the Canal should be insulated from the politics of any country; (iv) the manner of fixing tolls and charges should be decided by agreement between Egypt and the users; (v) a fair proportion of the dues should be allotted to development; and (vi) in case of disputes, unresolved

affairs between the Suez Canal Company and the Egyptian Government should be settled by arbitration with suitable terms of reference and suitable provisions for the payment of sums found to be due; (2) consider that the 18-Power proposals corresponded to those requirements, while recognizing that other proposals, corresponding to the same requirements, might be submitted by the Egyptian Government; (3) note that that Government, while declaring its readiness to accept the principle of organized collaboration between an Egyptian Authority and the users, had not yet formulated sufficiently precise proposals to meet those requirements; (4) invite the Governments of Egypt, France and the United Kingdom to continue their interchanges and, in this connexion, invite the Egyptian Government to make known promptly its proposals for a system meeting those requirements; and (5) consider that, meanwhile, the Suez Canal Users Association, which had been qualified to receive the dues payable by ships belonging to its members, and the competent Egyptian authorities, should co-operate to ensure the satisfactory operation of the Canal and free and open transit through the Canal in accordance with the 1888 Convention.

The representative of Egypt hoped that the Council would adopt the first part of the new draft resolution which outlined the six basic principles which had been presented to the Council by the Secretary-General. . . .He said that the practical approach to a peaceful settlement was by negotiation on the concrete proposals made by Egypt on 8 October and at the six recent meetings of the Ministers for Foreign Affairs of France, the United Kingdom and Egypt in the presence of the Secretary-General. The approach outlined in the second part of the draft resolution would make the Canal the prey of the politics of many nations.

. . .

On 13 October, the Council voted on the amended Anglo-French draft resolution in two parts. The first part outlining the six requirements was adopted unanimously. The second, which received 9 votes in favour to 2 against (USSR, Yugoslavia), was not adopted since one of the negative votes was that of a permanent member.

. . .

Between 13 and 19 October, the Secretary-General held private talks with the Minister of Foreign Affairs of Egypt and, on 24 October, set out in a confidential letter to him his conclusions on possible arrangements for meeting the six ''requirements'' which would have to be studied if exploratory talks between the three Governments directly concerned were to be resumed. The Secretary-General stated that he understood that there should be no difficulty as regards (1) legal reaffirmation of all the obligations under the 1888

Convention and widening those obligations to cover the question of maximum of tolls, maintenance and development, and reporting to the United Nations; (2) the Canal Code and regulations, with revisions to be subject to consultation; (3) the question of tolls and charges and the reservation of a proportion for development, both of which would be subject to agreement; (4) the question of disputes between the Suez Canal Company and the Egyptian Government, which seemed fairly well covered by the sixth principle; and (5) the *principle* of organized co-operation between an Egyptian authority and the users. "Organized co-operation" required provision for necessary joint meetings between an organ on the Egyptian side and a representation of the users entitled to raise all matters affecting the users' rights or interests, for discussion and consultation or by way of complaint, but exercising its functions so as not to interfere with the administrative functions of the operating organ. Such organized co-operation would not give satisfaction to the first three "requirements" unless completed with arrangements for fact-finding, reconciliation, recourse to appropriate juridical settlement of possible disputes, and guarantees for execution of the results thereof. Suggested methods of juridical settlement included a standing local organ for arbitration, the International Court of Justice, the jurisdiction of which should in this case be mandatory, and the Security Council. Normal rules should apply concerning implementation of findings of a United Nations organ. The parties should undertake to carry out in good faith awards of organs of arbitration. "In case of a complaint because of alleged non-compliance with an award, the same arbitration organ which gave the award should register the fact of non-compliance. Such a 'constatation' would give the complaining party access to all normal forms of redress, but also the right to certain steps in self-protection, the possible scope of which would be subject to an agreement in principle."

If there were no objection in principle to that set of arrangements, the Secretary-General would, from a legal and technical point of view, consider the framework sufficiently wide to make a further exploration of a possible basis for negotiations along the lines indicated worth trying.

On 2 November, the Secretary-General received a reply to his letter of 24 October. In his reply the Egyptian Foreign Minister declared that, with the exception of the part referring to entitlement to certain action in self-protection quoted above, he shared the view of the Secretary-General that the framework was sufficiently wide for the purpose expressed.

On 3 November the Secretary-General circulated these letters, which represented in his opinion a significant further development in the consideration of the matter as initiated by the Security Council.

(YUN 1956, pp. 19-24)

Search for a peaceful settlement

In October 1973, war erupted again between Egypt and Israel in the Suez Canal area and the Sinai and between Israel and the Syrian Arab Republic on the Golan Heights. As fighting reached a critical stage, the Security Council on 24 October set up a second United Nations Emergency Force (UNEF II). Within 24 hours, UNEF II was moving into place in the Suez Canal area and its arrival effectively stabilized the situation. Following an agreement on the disengagement of Egyptian and Israeli forces in January 1974, UNEF II supervised their redeployment and manned a buffer zone between them. In September 1975 both countries concluded a second disengagement agreement which led to a further limited Israeli withdrawal from the occupied territories. UNEF II carried out its task successfully until July 1979, when its mandate lapsed.

On the Golan Heights, the United Nations Disengagement Observer Force (UNDOF) continues to supervise the separation between Israeli and Syrian troops and the limitation of armament and forces provided for in the May 1974 disengagement agreement.

In southern Lebanon, the United Nations Interim Force in Lebanon (UNIFIL) has not been able to make tangible progress towards the objectives for which it was established in 1978 following a first Israeli invasion—namely, to confirm the withdrawal of Israeli forces, restore international peace and security, and assist the Lebanese Government in ensuring the return of its effective authority in the southern part of the country. Nevertheless, the presence of UNIFIL contributed to stability in the area and afforded a certain measure of protection to the population.

Middle East peace process

The process of multilateral negotiations among Israel, Arab countries and other States, in which the United Nations acted as a full participant and which were sponsored by the Russian Federation and the United States and assisted by Norway, began in 1991 with a peace conference on the Middle East (Madrid, Spain, 30 October–1 November). In 1993, those negotiations as well as bilateral talks between Israel and the Palestine Liberation Organization (PLO) resulted in the signing, on 13 September in Washington, D.C., of the Declaration of Principles on Interim Self-Government Arrangements between Israel and PLO. Prior to that, on 9 September, the two parties had exchanged letters of mutual recognition, whereby PLO recognized the right of Israel to exist in peace and security, accepted Security Council resolutions 242(1967) and 338(1973) and renounced terrorism and violence, while Israel recognized PLO as the representative of the Palestinian people.

By the Declaration, Israel and PLO agreed that it was time to recognize their mutual legitimate and political rights, to strive to live in peaceful coexistence and mutual dignity and security and to achieve a just, lasting and comprehensive peace settlement and reconciliation through the agreed political process. According to the text, the aim of the Israeli-Palestinian negotiations within the current Middle East peace process was to establish a Palestinian Interim Self-Government Authority, as proposed by PLO in 1992, as the elected Council for Palestinians in the West Bank and Gaza, for a transitional period of not more than five years, leading to a permanent settlement based on Security Council resolutions 242(1967) and 338(1973).

The Declaration, which was to enter into force one month after its signing, also pertained, *inter alia*, to the framework for the interim period, elections, jurisdiction, the transitional period and permanent status negotiations, the preparatory transfer of powers and responsibilities, an interim agreement on the structure of Palestinian authorities, public order and security, laws and military orders, a joint Israeli-Palestinian Liaison Committee to deal with issues requiring coordination, liaison and cooperation with Egypt and Jordan, the redeployment of Israeli forces and the resolution of disputes. Attached to the Declaration were protocols on the mode and conditions of elections, on withdrawal of Israeli forces from the Gaza Strip and Jericho area, on Israeli-Palestinian cooperation in economic and development programmes, and on Israeli-Palestinian cooperation concerning regional development programmes.

The agreement provided that upon the entry into force of the Declaration and Israeli withdrawal, authority would be transferred from the Israeli military government and its Civil Administration to the Palestinians authorized for that task until the inauguration of the Palestinian Council; authority would also be transferred to the Palestinians in the spheres of education and culture, health, social welfare, direct taxation and tourism. After the Council's inauguration, the Israeli Civil Administration would be dissolved and its military government withdrawn. Public order and internal security for Palestinians in the West Bank and Gaza were to be provided by a Palestinian police force, while Israel was to continue to be responsible for defence against external threats and for the overall security of Israelis. An Israeli-Palestinian Continuing Committee for Economic Cooperation was to be set up to focus on water, electricity, energy, finance, transport and communications, trade, industry, labour relations and social welfare issues, human resource devel-

opment and cooperation, environmental protection, and communications and the media. The agreement also outlined a two-part development programme for the region, including an economic development programme for the West Bank and Gaza and a regional economic development programme, to be initiated by the seven most powerful industrialized nations (Group of Seven).

Permanent status negotiations between Israel and Palestinian representatives were to commence as soon as possible, but not later than the third year of the interim period, and were to cover remaining issues, including Jerusalem, refugees, settlements, security arrangements, borders, and relations and cooperation with other neighbours.

Subsequent to the signing of the Declaration, Israel and Jordan agreed on 14 September in Washington, D.C., to a Common Agenda, which sought steps to arrive at a state of peace based on Security Council resolutions 242(1967) and 338(1973) in all their aspects, regulated matters in the fields of security, water, refugees and displaced persons and borders, and explored potentials of future bilateral cooperation in natural and human resources, infrastructure and economic areas, including tourism.

Also in September, the Secretary-General established a high-level task force to identify new projects and activities that could be rapidly implemented by UNRWA, UNDP and UNICEF in the occupied territories. The task force assessed immediate additional needs of Palestinians at $138 million. On 1 October, at the Conference to Support Middle East Peace held in Washington, D.C., 46 countries and organizations pledged some $2.4 billion over five years to finance social and economic development in the West Bank and Gaza Strip. On 4 November, the PLO Executive Committee, meeting at Tunis, Tunisia, established the Palestinian Economic Council for Development and Construction to define priorities of development projects as well as their implementation, control and management.

In December, Israel, speaking before the General Assembly, said it was making progress with the Palestinians and 13 other Arab delegations in the multilateral negotiations, thus creating opportunities for regional cooperation. Forty-seven countries and international organizations, including the United Nations, were participating in those multilateral talks, and five working groups were discussing refugees, arms control, regional economic cooperation, water and environment. States participating in the talks on regional economic development agreed on a plan of action, which included 35 projects, workshops and studies in diverse areas. Israel noted that for the first time in the multilateral negotiations, talks about the Middle East were being held in the Middle East.

On 14 December 1993, the General Assembly, by a recorded vote of 155 to 3, with 1 abstention, adopted resolution 48/58, in which it welcomed the peace process started at Madrid, expressed its full support for the Declaration and the Common Agenda, and urged Member States to provide economic, financial and technical assistance to the Palestinian people during the interim period.

On 25 February 1994, the peace process suffered a set-back when an armed Israeli settler killed more than 50 Palestinian worshippers and injured several hundred others in the Mosque of Ibrahim in the West Bank town of Hebron. On 18 March, the Security Council, in resolution 904(1994), strongly condemned the massacre and called for measures to guarantee the safety and protection of Palestinian civilians throughout the occupied territory, including the establishment of a temporary international or foreign presence. A contingent of observers known as the Temporary International Presence in Hebron (TIPH) was deployed in the area from May to August 1994.

In April, the peace talks were frustrated once again when Palestinian attacks were launched against passenger buses in the Israeli towns of Afula and Hadera, resulting in casualties among Israeli civilians. Nevertheless, on 4 May 1994 at Cairo, Egypt, Israel and PLO signed the Agreement on the Gaza Strip and the Jericho Area, effective immediately, and exchanged letters in which they committed themselves to implementing the Agreement. The Agreement provided for an accelerated and scheduled withdrawal of Israeli forces from the Gaza Strip and the Jericho Area; establishment of the Palestinian Authority with territorial jurisdiction covering the Gaza Strip and the Jericho Area, except Israeli settlements and the Military Installation Area; the Authority's structure and composition, as well as its legislative, executive and judicial powers and responsibilities; transfer of power from the Israeli military government and its Civil Administration to the Palestinian Authority; arrangements for security and public order and establishment of a Palestinian police force; arrangements regarding the Gaza-Egypt and Jericho-Jordan passages and other agreed international crossings, as well as arrangements for safe passage between the Gaza Strip and the Jericho Area; economic relations between Israel and the Palestinian Authority; establishment of a joint Israeli-Palestinian Liaison Committee to ensure the smooth implementation of the Agreement; liaison and cooperation with Jordan and Egypt; settlement of differences and disputes; and rights, liabilities and obligations.

In other clauses of the Agreement, Israel and PLO undertook to: foster mutual understanding and tolerance and to abstain from and take measures to prevent incitement, including hostile propaganda, against each other, as well as acts of terrorism, crime and hostilities directed at each other; cooperate in combating criminal activity and in searching for missing persons; carry out a number of confidence-building measures concerning the release of Palestinian prisoners and detainees and non-prosecution of Palestinians arriving from abroad for offences committed prior to 13 September 1993 and of those Palestinians who were in contact with Israeli authorities; and exercise their powers and responsibilities under the Agreement with due regard to internationally accepted norms and principles of human rights and the rule of law. The two sides also undertook to view the West Bank and the Gaza Strip as a single territorial unit and the Jericho Area as an integral part of that territory, and agreed to a temporary international or foreign presence in the Gaza Strip and the Jericho Area.

Those arrangements were to remain in force until and to the extent superseded by the Interim Agreement, with the five-year interim period commencing on 4 May 1994. Attached to the Agreement were protocols concerning withdrawal of Israeli military forces and security arrangements, civil affairs, legal matters and economic relations.

Under the protocols, a number of bodies were established to coordinate the implementation of the Agreement. The Joint Security Coordination and Cooperation Committee was to monitor Israeli withdrawal, to be completed within 21 days from the date of the signing of the Agreement, as well as security arrangements. The Joint Civil Affairs Coordination and Cooperation Committee and two Joint Regional Civil Affairs Subcommittees were to supervise the transfer of powers and responsibilities in the spheres of interior affairs, fisheries, surveying, statistics, comptrol, employment of Civil Administration employees, legal administration, labour, education, social welfare, assessments, housing, tourism, parks, religious affairs, employee pensions, commerce and industry, health, transportation, agriculture, employment, land registration, natural reserves, electricity, public works, postal services, population registry and documentation, government and absentee lands and other immovables, telecommunications, archaeology, water and sewage, planning and zoning, direct and indirect taxation, environmental protection, gas and petroleum, insurance and treasury. The Joint Economic Committee was to serve as the continuing committee for economic cooperation in the areas of import taxes and import policy, monetary and financial issues, direct taxation, indirect taxes on local production, labour, agriculture, industry, tourism and insurance issues. In addition, the Protocol concerning Legal Matters determined criminal and civil jurisdiction of Israel and of the Palestinian Authority and included provisions for legal assistance in criminal and in civil matters.

Parallel to the success of the Israel-PLO negotiations, progress was made in negotiations between

Israel and Jordan on borders, territorial matters, security, water, energy, environment and the Jordan Rift Valley. As a result, agreement was reached to recognize mutually the rightful allocations of the two sides in Jordan River and Yarmouk River waters and to respect and comply with those allocations. On 25 July 1994 in Washington, D.C., Israel and Jordan signed a Declaration which reaffirmed the underlying principles of the Common Agenda agreed on in 1993 and announced that the state of belligerency between the two countries had been terminated. Both countries undertook to refrain from actions or activities by either side that could adversely affect the security of the other or prejudice the final outcome of negotiations, not to threaten the other by use of force and to thwart threats to security resulting from all kinds of terrorism. Within the framework of regional infrastructural development plans, Israel and Jordan decided to open direct telephone links, link their electricity grids as part of a regional concept, give, in principle, free access to third-country tourists travelling between the two countries, accelerate negotiations on opening an international air corridor between them, ensure cooperation of their police forces in combating crime, and continue negotiations on economic matters so as to prepare for future bilateral cooperation, including the abolition of all economic boycotts.

Subsequent to the signing of the Washington Declaration, a peace treaty was signed between Israel and Jordan on 26 October 1994. In November, the Secretary-General, reporting to the General Assembly on the situation in the Middle East, expressed his hope that that historic achievement would generate further momentum in the Israeli-Palestinian negotiations and encourage progress in the Israeli-Lebanese and Israeli-Syrian tracks of the peace process.

" . . . to save succeeding generations from the scourge of war . . . and to ensure, by the acceptance of principles and the institution of methods, that armed force shall not be used . . . "

Chapter II

The disarmament quest

Before the General Assembly opened its first session in January 1946, nuclear and other weapons of mass destruction were critical issues for the newly established United Nations. The elimination of these weapons from national arsenals and the control of atomic energy for peaceful purposes were objectives that in the heady days following the end of the Second World War many believed were achievable. However, the difficulty of reaching agreement soon became clear during the early chill of the cold war.

In 1959, the United Nations proclaimed the goal of general and complete disarmament under effective international control. The USSR and the United States agreed in 1961 to a set of disarmament principles and the following year offered proposals aimed at achieving the goal set by the United Nations. Nevertheless, years of discussion failed to bring agreement on key issues, particularly on a comprehensive test-ban treaty. In 1969, therefore, the General Assembly declared the 1970s as a Disarmament Decade, calling on Governments to intensify efforts for effective measures relating to the cessation of the arms race, nuclear disarmament and the elimination of weapons of mass destruction and for a treaty on general and complete disarmament. With the nuclear and conventional arms race growing even more intense, the Assembly in 1978 held its first special session devoted to disarmament. By consensus, it re-embraced general and complete disarmament under effective international control.

The Final Document of the session emphasized the role of the United Nations in working for disarmament and elaborated a world-wide programme of action with specific measures. However, despite the encouraging outcome of the session, the situation continued to deteriorate. Military expenditures by major military Powers reached ever-higher levels during the 1980s, resulting in turn in the 1980s being declared the Second United Nations Disarmament Decade setting out the priorities and main areas on which attention should be focused, and in the launching of the World Disarmament Campaign.

Since the beginnings of the United Nations, efforts at disarmament did result in measured successes in some areas. Notable among these were the Treaty Banning Nuclear Weapon Tests in the Atmosphere, in Outer Space and under Water (partial test-ban Treaty) signed in 1963; the 1967 Treaty for the Prohibition of Nuclear Weapons in Latin America; the 1968 Treaty on the Non-Proliferation of Nuclear Weapons; the 1972 Convention on the Prohibition of the Development, Production and Stockpiling of Bacteriological (Biological) and Toxin Weapons and on Their Destruction; the 1981 Convention on Prohibitions or Restrictions on the Use of Certain Conventional Weapons Which May Be Deemed to Be Excessively Injurious or to Have Indiscriminate Effects; and the 1985 South Pacific Nuclear-Free Zone Treaty. (Figure 2 shows dates of entry into force of various international and regional disarmament agreements.) However, it was only with the end of the cold war that slowing the escalation of deadly weaponry came within reach.

Nuclear weapons

First proposals

Establishment of the Atomic Energy Commission

Mr. Harry S. Truman, President of the United States; Mr. C. R. Attlee, Prime Minister of the United Kingdom; and Mr. W. L. Mackenzie King, Prime Minister of Canada, met in Washington, D.C., in November 1945 "to consider the possibility of international action: (a) To prevent the use of atomic energy for destructive purposes, and

FIGURE 2

**Number of States parties and signatories
to major global and regional arms control and disarmament treaties
showing date of opening for signature and status as at 31 March 1995 ***

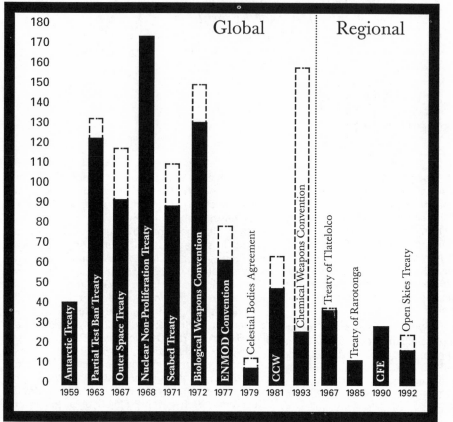

1959 Antarctic Treaty: 42 parties (entered into force: 1961)

1963 Treaty Banning Nuclear Weapon Tests in the Atmosphere, in Outer Space and under Water: 124 parties (entered into force: 1963)

1967 Treaty on Principles Governing the Activities of States in the Exploration and Use of Outer Space, including the Moon and Other Celestial Bodies: 93 parties (entered into force: 1967)

1968 Treaty on the Non-Proliferation of Nuclear Weapons: 175 parties (entered into force: 1970)

1971 Treaty on the Prohibition of the Emplacement of Nuclear Weapons and Other Weapons of Mass Destruction on the Seabed and the Ocean Floor and in the Subsoil Thereof: 90 parties (entered into force: 1972)

1972 Convention on the Prohibition of the Development, Production and Stockpiling of Bacteriological (Biological) and Toxin Weapons and on Their Destruction: 132 parties (entered into force: 1975)

1977 Convention on the Prohibition of Military or Any Other Hostile Use of Environmental Modification Techniques: 63 parties (entered into force: 1978)

1979 Agreement Governing the Activities of States on the Moon and Other Celestial Bodies: 9 parties (entered into force: 1984)

1981 Convention on Prohibitions or Restrictions on the Use of Certain Conventional Weapons Which May Be Deemed to Be Excessively Injurious or to Have Indiscriminate Effects: 49 parties (entered into force: 1983)

1993 Convention on the Prohibition of the Development, Production, Stockpiling and Use of Chemical Weapons and on Their Destruction: 27 parties and 132 additional signatories (not yet in force)

1967 Treaty on the Prohibition of Nuclear Weapons in Latin America and the Caribbean: 38 parties (including Protocols) (Once the additional signatory has ratified, the Treaty will be in force for all States of the region)

1985 South Pacific Nuclear Free Zone Treaty: 13 parties (including Protocols) (entered into force: 1986)

1990 Treaty on Conventional Armed Forces in Europe: 30 parties (entered into force: 1992)

1992 Treaty on Open Skies: 18 parties and 9 additional signatories (not yet in force)

Source: Centre for Disarmament Affairs
*Data provided by one or more depositaries

(b) to promote the use of recent and future advances in scientific knowledge, particularly in the utilization of atomic energy, for peaceful and humanitarian ends.''

On November 15, 1945, the three heads of Government issued a declaration which stated, among other things, that ''in order to attain the most effective means of entirely eliminating the use of atomic energy for destructive purposes and promoting its widest use for industrial and humanitarian purposes, we are of the opinion that at the earliest practicable date a Commission should be set up under the United Nations Organization to prepare recommendations for submission to the Organization.''

. . .

The General Assembly referred the establishment of the proposed commission to its First Committee (Political and Security), which considered the proposed resolution at its second and third meetings on January 21 and 22, 1946. . . .

On January 24 the report and resolution authorizing the Commission on Atomic Energy were approved in the General Assembly with no dissenting votes. According to the resolution, the Commission was to be composed of one representative from each of the States represented on the Security Council, and Canada when that State was not a member of the Security Council.

The Commission was required to inquire with the utmost despatch into all phases of the problems, and to submit its reports and recommendations to the Security Council. . . .

The resolution set forth the terms of reference of the Commission as being to make specific proposals:

(a) for extending between all nations the exchange of basic scientific information for peaceful ends;

(b) for control of atomic energy to the extent necessary to ensure its use only for peaceful purposes;

(c) for the elimination from national armaments of atomic weapons and of all other major weapons adaptable to mass destruction;

(d) for effective safeguards by way of inspection and other means to protect complying States against the hazards of violations and evasions.

. . .

At the first meeting of the Atomic Energy Commission, the representative of the United States presented a plan for the creation of an International Atomic Development Authority entrusted with all phases of the development and use of atomic energy. Under this plan the Authority would conduct continuous surveys of world supplies of uranium and thorium, and would bring the raw materials under its control. It would possess the exclusive right to conduct research in the field of atomic explosives, and all other research would be open only to nations under license of the Authority, which would provide them with denatured materials. Dangerous activities of the Authority and its stockpiles would be decentralized and strategically distributed. All nations would grant the freedom of inspection deemed necessary by the Authority. The representative of the United States stressed the importance of immediate punishment for infringements of the rights of the Authority. He urged that ''there must be no veto to protect those who violate their solemn agreements not to develop or use atomic energy for destructive purposes.''

At the second meeting of the Commission on June 19, 1946, the representative of the U.S.S.R. suggested that the first measure to be adopted should be the conclusion of an international agreement to prohibit the production and use of atomic energy weapons. Within three months from the entry into force of the agreement, he urged, all atomic weapons should be destroyed. Violation of the agreement should be severely punished under the domestic legislation of the contracting parties. The agreement should be of indefinite duration, coming in force after approval by the Security Council and ratification by the Council's permanent members. All States, whether or not Members of the United Nations, should be obliged to fulfil all provisions of the agreement.

. . .

At its sixth meeting on November 13, 1946, the Atomic Energy Commission decided by 10 affirmative votes, with 2 abstentions, to submit to the Security Council before December 31, 1946, a report on its work, its findings and recommendations. . . .

While this report was being prepared, the second part of the first session of the General Assembly was considering various proposals concerning the regulation and reduction of armaments, including atomic weapons.

. . .

Meanwhile, the General Assembly on December 14, 1946, approved unanimously a resolution on the principles governing the general regulation and reduction of armaments, which, among other things, urged the expeditious fulfilment by the Atomic Energy Commission of its terms of reference. It also recommended that the Security Council expedite consideration of the reports made to it by the Atomic Energy Commission, that it facilitate the work of the Commission and that the Security Council expedite consideration of a draft convention or conventions for the creation of an international system of control and inspection, these conventions to include the prohibition of atomic and all other major weapons adaptable now and in the future to mass destruction and the control of atomic energy to the extent necessary to ensure its use only for peaceful purposes.

. . .

On December 30 the Commission, with 10 votes in favor and abstentions on the part of the U.S.S.R. and Poland, adopted the draft report of its Working Committee as the report of the Commission and submitted it to the Security Council on December 31, 1946.

. . .

On the basis of its findings, the Commission recommended the creation of a strong and comprehensive international system of control and inspection by a treaty or convention in which all Members of the United Nations would participate on fair and equitable terms.

. . .

At a meeting of the Security Council on February 18 the representative of the U.S.S.R. proposed twelve specific amendments and additions to the general findings and recommendations contained in the first report of the Atomic Energy Commission. The U.S.S.R. proposals included a provision that inspection, supervision and management by an international agency should apply to all existing atomic plants immediately after the entry into force of an appropriate convention or conventions. Another proposal suggested that an effective system of control of atomic energy must be international in scope and established by an enforceable multilateral convention administered within the framework of the Security Council. Further amendments would provide for the destruction of stocks of manufactured and unfinished atomic weapons, and for elimination of the recommendation in the Commission's report that in case of violation there should be no legal right, by veto or otherwise, whereby a wilful violator of the terms of the treaty or convention should be protected from the consequences of violation of its terms.

On March 10 the Security Council adopted unanimously a resolution which, among other things, stated that the Council would transmit the record of its consideration of the first report of the Atomic Energy Commission to the Commission; urged the Commission to continue its enquiry into all phases of the problem of the international control of atomic energy; and requested the Commission to submit a second report to the Security Council before the next session of the General Assembly.

(YUN 1946-47, pp. 444-48)

Shaping the issue

Consultations among the six Powers—Canada, China, France, the USSR, the United Kingdom and the United States—took place on the Atomic Energy Commission's plan for the international control of atomic energy, which would make effective the prohibition of atomic weapons. However, agreement could not be reached on the elimination of atomic weapons under a system of effective inter-national control. In July 1949, the Commission stated that no useful purpose could be served by discussion in the Commission until the six Powers reported that a basis for agreement existed. In December 1950, the Assembly, recognizing the failure to reach agreement on both the elimination of nuclear weapons and the regulation and reduction of other armaments and armed forces, established a Committee of Twelve (resolution 496(V)) to examine the establishment of a new consolidated disarmament commission by merging the functions of the Atomic Energy Commission with those of the Commission for Conventional Armaments.

Regulation, limitation and balanced reduction of all armed forces and all armaments

The item "Regulation, limitation and balanced reduction of all armed forces and all armaments" was placed on the agenda of the sixth session of the General Assembly at the joint request of France, the United Kingdom and the United States. The explanatory memorandum accompanying the request referred briefly to the manner in which the problems of the regulation of armaments and the international control of atomic energy had been dealt with in the United Nations in previous years. It also referred to a joint statement issued by the Governments of France, the United Kingdom and the United States on 7 November 1951.

This statement, a copy of which was attached to the memorandum, declared the intention of the three Governments to submit proposals to the current Assembly session for proceeding with the regulation, limitation and balanced reduction of all armed forces and all armaments including atomic weapons. . . .

It outlined the main elements of the tripartite proposal, stating, among other things, that the first and indispensable step was disclosure and verification. This, it stated, must be on a continuing basis and reveal in successive stages all armed forces—including para-military, security and police forces—and all armaments, including atomic. It must also provide for effective international inspection to verify the adequacy and accuracy of the information.

The three Governments also believed that a workable programme should include criteria according to which the size of all armed forces would be limited, the portion of national production which could be used for military purposes would be restricted, and mutually agreed national military programmes would be arrived at within the prescribed limits and restrictions. The United Nations plan for the international control of atomic energy and the prohibition of atomic weapons should continue to serve as the basis for the atomic energy aspects of any general programme, unless and until a better and more effective plan could be devised.

. . .

At the following plenary meeting of the General Assembly, the representative of the USSR submitted alternative proposals under the title "Measures to combat the threat of a new world war and to strengthen peace and friendship among nations" which would, among other things: (1) condemn participation in the "Atlantic bloc" and the establishment by certain States, and primarily by the United States, of bases in foreign territories; (2) deem essential the withdrawal of troops from Korea and a cease-fire there; (3) call for a five-Power peace pact to which other States might adhere; and (4) provide for the calling of a world disarmament conference before 1 June 1952.

Report of the Committee of Twelve

On 23 October the Committee of Twelve, established by resolution 496(V) of 13 December 1950, submitted its report.

The Committee, consisting of the members of the Security Council as of 1 January 1951, together with Canada, had been established to consider and report to the sixth session of the Assembly on ways and means whereby the work of the Atomic Energy Commission and the Commission for Conventional Armaments might be co-ordinated and on the advisability of their functions being merged and placed under a new and consolidated disarmament commission.

The report recommended that the General Assembly should establish a new commission, to be known as the Commission for the Control of Armaments and Armed Forces, which should be under and report to the Security Council. This Commission should carry forward the tasks currently assigned to the Atomic Energy Commission and the Commission for Conventional Armaments which, it proposed, should be dissolved.

Consideration by the First Committee

The General Assembly referred the tripartite proposal, the report of the Committee of Twelve and the USSR proposals to the First Committee.

The Committee considered the tripartite proposal and the report of the Committee of Twelve concurrently at 24 meetings between 19 November and 19 December 1951. The general debate on the items took place from the 447th to 460th meetings from 19-30 November.

The discussion in the Committee was based on a joint draft resolution submitted by France, the United Kingdom and the United States, and on USSR amendments to the joint draft.

[YUN 1951, pp. 161-62]

Appointment and report of
Sub-Committee of the four Powers

A draft resolution was submitted jointly by Iraq, Pakistan and Syria calling for the establishment of a sub-committee consisting of the President of the General Assembly as Chairman and the representatives of France, the USSR, the United Kingdom and the United States, with a view to formulating agreed proposals concerning the control and reduction of armed forces and armaments and the abolition of atomic and other weapons of mass destruction.

. . .

Areas of agreement and possible agreement

The four Powers had agreed to the establishment of a new commission to replace the Atomic Energy Commission and the Commission for Conventional Armaments. They had agreed that it should be called the "Atomic Energy and Conventional Armaments Commission" and that it should be under the Security Council. There was also agreement on its membership and rules of procedure.

There was some agreement on the functions of the new commission—to prepare proposals or measures to be embodied in a draft treaty or treaties (conventions) and intended to achieve "the universal desire for peace, for the regulation, limitation and balanced reduction of all armed forces and all armaments, and for the abolition of atomic and other weapons of mass destruction." The USSR, the memorandum stated, preferred to define those objectives as the prohibition of atomic weapons, the effective (strict) international control of atomic energy and its use for peaceful (civilian) purposes only, and the limitation and reduction of armaments and armed forces. Grave differences existed as to the principles and methods according to which those tasks should be executed. During the discussions, nevertheless, opinions had been expressed on the possibility of embarking on a common course to solve the problems posed by those questions.

All the four Powers agreed that all armed forces, including para-military, security and police-forces, and all armaments, including atomic, should be included in the commission's terms of reference.

There was agreement also that there should be full disclosure of information regarding all armaments and all armed forces. While there were some differences regarding the publication of the information disclosed, it was stated that it did not appear that those differences could not be solved, and that they might well be left to the commission. However, the USSR, which favoured the simultaneous disclosure of information on both atomic and non-atomic weapons within one month, was absolutely opposed to the whole concept of "progressive" disclosure or disclosure by stages. France, the United Kingdom and the United States maintained that disclosure should be both progressive and on a continuing basis.

While all four Powers agreed on the necessity of verification and inspection, the USSR objected to inspection on a continuing basis on the ground that the permanent presence at establishments of inspectors or controllers would hinder efficient operation and was incompatible with sovereignty. It held that effective international inspections should be carried out in accordance with decisions of the international control organ, provision being made for control to include also verification of the information submitted. The commission should, further, be entrusted with the task of working out all details and procedures in the draft convention, the USSR representative stated.

. . .

All four Powers appeared to agree that the control organ should decide the times and places of inspection and that a majority decision by the control organ in that regard would be binding on all, with no right of veto.

. . .

Areas of disagreement

Serious and fundamental divergence of views was expressed on the specific means for attaining the general objectives of the two proposals and the principles to be established for the guidance of the commission, the memorandum stated. The USSR, for example, was opposed to the three-Power formulation of balanced reduction to levels adequate for defence but not for aggression, on the ground that the levels envisaged might mean an increase of armaments rather than a reduction, and that that was not a concrete proposal for the reduction of armaments.

The three-Power proposal to achieve effective international control to ensure the prohibition of atomic weapons was opposed by the USSR on the ground that it did not provide for immediate and unconditional prohibition of atomic weapons, that it put control before prohibition, and that unless there was prior prohibition there would be nothing to control.

Other USSR objections concerned: the proposal to use as a basis the United Nations plan for the international control of atomic energy; the system of stages of disclosure proposed by the three Powers; and the directives to be given to the commission.

The United Nations plan for the international control of atomic energy which the three Powers wished to retain as a basis for the commission to work on was, it was stated, unacceptable to the USSR for the many reasons which it had repeatedly advanced, but chiefly because it would infringe on the sovereignty of nations, would set up a monopolistic trust under the United States, and would indefinitely postpone the prohibition of the atomic weapon.

The USSR proposed that the system of control should be implemented by an international control organ responsible for control of the enforcement of the prohibition of atomic weapons, provision also being made for effective international inspection to be carried out in accordance with the decisions of the control organ.

The USSR was also absolutely opposed to the concept of disclosure of information by stages, as contained in the three-Power proposal, on the ground that this would only result in the indefinite postponement of disclosure of information on the most destructive and dangerous arms, such as the atomic weapon.

The USSR was also opposed to the directives to be given to the commission, as set out in the tripartite proposal, concerning: (1) the formulation of criteria; (2) proposals for the over-all limits on armed forces and armaments; and (3) the allocation of armaments and armed forces within national military establishments. The three Powers maintained that it was necessary to give the commission directives for working out its plans. The USSR stated that it had no objection to the commission's being given directives, but proposed that it should be instructed to prepare and submit to the Security Council within three months practical proposals for implementing the Assembly resolution.

Similarly, the three Powers could not accept the USSR proposals, contained in its amendments to the joint draft resolution, that the General Assembly should immediately and simultaneously declare the unconditional prohibition of the production of atomic weapons and the establishment of strict international control over the enforcement of that prohibition, and should recommend to the Great Powers that they reduce their existing armaments and armed forces by one third within one year.

That was opposed on the ground that, until a system of control was in operation, the prohibition would be unenforceable and illusory, and that the mere declaration of control would have little value unless there were prior agreement on the precise nature of the control and unless the control system was actually put into operation. As regards the one-third reduction of arms, the three Powers stated that the reduction by a fraction arbitrarily fixed, would preserve or possibly even intensify, the present imbalance between them and the USSR. Moreover, they held, the measure of the necessary balanced reduction could be determined only on the basis of verified information as to the existing state of armaments.

The memorandum concluded by stating that, despite the disagreements which existed on a number of matters of major importance in the two proposals, it seemed clear that there was some agreement on a number of aspects. The discussions in the Sub-Committee, it was stated, appeared to have helped to widen the areas of agreement on some points.

. . .

Establishment of the Disarmament Commission

Consideration by the
General Assembly in plenary session

The report of the First Committee containing the draft resolution adopted by it was placed before the General Assembly at its 358th meeting on 11 January 1952.

. . .

The resolution (502(VI)) adopted by the General Assembly at its 358th plenary meeting on 11 January 1952 read:

"*The General Assembly,*

"*Moved* by anxiety at the general lack of confidence plaguing the world and leading to the burden of increasing armaments and the fear of war,

"*Desiring* to lift from the peoples of the world this burden and this fear, and thus to liberate new energies and resources for positive programmes of reconstruction and development,

"*Reaffirming* its desire that the United Nations develop an effective collective security system to maintain the peace and that the armed forces and armaments of the world be progressively reduced in accordance with the Purposes and Principles of the Charter,

"*Believing* that a necessary means to this end is the development by the United Nations of comprehensive and co-ordinated plans, under international control, for the regulation, limitation and balanced reduction of all armed forces and all armaments, for the elimination of all major weapons adaptable to mass destruction, and for the effective international control of atomic energy to ensure the prohibition of atomic weapons and the use of atomic energy for peaceful purposes only,

"*Recognizing* that a genuine system for disarmament must include all kinds of armed forces and armaments, must be accepted by all nations whose military resources are such that their failure to accept would endanger the system, and must include safeguards that will ensure the compliance of all such nations,

"*Noting* the recommendation of the Committee of Twelve established by resolution 496(V) that the General Assembly should establish a new commission to carry forward the tasks originally assigned to the Atomic Energy Commission and the Commission for Conventional Armaments,

"1. *Establishes* under the Security Council a Disarmament Commission. This Commission shall have the same membership as the Atomic Energy Commission and the Commission for Conventional Armaments, and shall function under the rules of procedure of the Atomic Energy Commission with such modifications as the Commission shall deem necessary;

"2. *Dissolves* the Atomic Energy Commission and recommends to the Security Council that it dissolve the Commission for Conventional Armaments;

"3. *Directs* the Disarmament Commission to prepare proposals to be embodied in a draft treaty (or treaties) for the regulation, limitation and balanced reduction of all armed forces and all armaments, for the elimination of all major weapons adaptable to mass destruction, and for effective international control of atomic energy to ensure the prohibition of atomic weapons and the use of atomic energy for peaceful purposes only. The Commission shall be guided by the following principles:

"*(a)* In a system of guaranteed disarmament there must be progressive disclosure and verification on a continuing basis of all armed forces—including paramilitary, security and police forces—and all armaments including atomic;

"*(b)* Such verification must be based on effective international inspection to ensure the adequacy and accuracy of the information disclosed; this inspection to be carried out in accordance with the decisions of the international control organ (or organs) to be established;

"*(c)* The Commission shall be ready to consider any proposals or plans for control that may be put forward involving either conventional armaments or atomic energy. Unless a better or no less effective system is devised, the United Nations plan for the international control of atomic energy and the prohibition of atomic weapons should continue to serve as the basis for the international control of atomic energy to ensure the prohibition of atomic weapons and the use of atomic energy for peaceful purposes only;

"*(d)* There must be an adequate system of safeguards to ensure observance of the disarmament programme, so as to provide for the prompt detection of violations while at the same time causing the minimum degree of interference in the internal life of each country;

"*(e)* The treaty (or treaties) shall specifically be open to all States for signature and ratification or adherence. The treaty (or treaties) shall provide what States must become parties thereto before the treaty (or treaties) shall enter into force;

"4. *Directs* the Commission, when preparing the proposals referred to in the preceding paragraph, to formulate plans for the establishment, within the framework of the Security Council, of an international control organ (or organs) to ensure the implementation of the treaty (or treaties). The functions and powers of the control organ (or organs) shall be defined in the treaty which establishes it;

"5. *Directs* the Commission, in preparing the proposals referred to in paragraph 3 above, to consider from the outset plans for progressive and continuing disclosure and verification, the implementation of which is recognized as a first and indispensable step in carrying out the disarmament programme envisaged in the present resolution;

"6. *Directs* the Commission, in working out plans for the regulation, limitation and balanced reduction of all armed forces and all armaments:

"*(a)* To determine how over-all limits and restrictions on all armed forces and all armaments can be calculated and fixed;

"*(b)* To consider methods according to which States can agree by negotiation among themselves, under the auspices of the Commission, concerning the determination of the over-all limits and restrictions referred to in sub-paragraph *(a)* above and the allocation within their respective national military establishments of the permitted national armed forces and armaments;

"7. *Directs* the Commission to commence its work not later than thirty days from the adoption of the present resolution and to report periodically, for information, to the Security Council and to the General Assembly, or to the Members of the United Nations when the General Assembly is not in session. The Commission shall submit its first report not later than 1 June 1952;

"8. *Declares* that a conference of all States should be convened to consider the proposals for a draft treaty (or treaties) prepared by the Commission as soon as the work of the Commission shall have progressed to a point where in the judgment of the Commission any part of its programme is ready for submission to governments;

"9. *Requests* the Secretary-General to convene such a conference when so advised by the Commission;

"10. *Requests* the Secretary-General to furnish such experts, staff and facilities as the Commission may consider necessary for the effective accomplishment of the purposes of the present resolution."

(YUN 1951, pp. 168-77)

Non-proliferation

One of the principal objectives of the international community in the field of disarmament was reaching agreement to prevent the further spread of nuclear weapons. In November 1961, the General Assembly, following a request by Ireland that it discuss the prevention of a wider dissemination of nuclear weapons, called on nuclear-weapon States to conclude an international agreement under which they would refrain from relinquishing control of nuclear weapons and from transmitting the information necessary for their manufacture to States not possessing such weapons, and those States would undertake not to manufacture or otherwise acquire control of such weapons (resolution 1665(XVI)). In making the request, Ireland said that its proposal was aimed at preventing the danger of a nuclear war from becoming greater during the period of time it must take to evolve and strengthen a generally accepted system of world security based on international law and law enforcement. In 1965 and 1966, the Assembly called for the early conclusion of a treaty to prevent the proliferation of nuclear weapons and requested the Eighteen-Nation Committee on Disarmament to work towards the achievement of that objective and to report to it in 1968.

Treaty on Non-Proliferation of Nuclear Weapons

*Report of the Conference of the
Eighteen-Nation Committee on Disarmament
on the non-proliferation of nuclear weapons*

The Conference of the Eighteen-Nation Committee on Disarmament reconvened in Geneva, Switzerland, from 18 January to 14 March 1968. In view of the urgency of concluding a treaty on the non-proliferation of nuclear weapons, and pursuant to a General Assembly resolution of 19 December 1967, the Conference devoted this period exclusively to the negotiation of the treaty. By the same resolution the General Assembly had also asked the Committee to report on or before 15 March 1968 and had decided it would resume its session at an early date after 15 March to consider the report.

. . .

Consideration by General Assembly of Treaty on Non-Proliferation of Nuclear Weapons

As decided by the General Assembly on 19 December 1967, an agenda item entitled "Non-proliferation of nuclear weapons: report of the Conference of the Eighteen-Nation Committee on Disarmament" was maintained on the agenda of the General Assembly's twenty-second session. This session was resumed on 24 April 1968.

The General Assembly had before it the report of the Conference of the Eighteen-Nation Committee on Disarmament, to which were annexed the text of a draft treaty on the non-proliferation of nuclear weapons, submitted on 11 March 1968 by the USSR and the United States—Co-chairmen of the Conference—and other related Conference documents.

The Assembly referred the agenda item to its First Committee which discussed it at meetings held between 26 April and 10 June 1968.

. . .

On 31 May, the representatives of the USSR and the United States . . . agreed to certain revisions of the text of the draft treaty on the non-proliferation of nuclear weapons, which were accepted by the sponsors of the revised draft resolution.

. . .

On 10 June 1968, the First Committee approved the 48-power draft resolution . . .

On 12 June, the text was adopted at a plenary meeting of the General Assembly.

. . .

The General Assembly,

Recalling its resolutions 2346 A (XXII) of 19 December 1967, 2153 A (XXI) of 17 November 1966, 2149(XXI) of 4 November 1966, 2028(XX) of 19 November 1965 and 1665(XVI) of 4 December 1961,

Convinced of the urgency and great importance of preventing the spread of nuclear weapons and of intensifying international co-operation in the development of peaceful applications of atomic energy,

Having considered the report of the Conference of the Eighteen-Nation Committee on Disarmament, dated 14 March 1968, and appreciative of the work of the Committee on the elaboration of the draft non-proliferation treaty, which is attached to that report,

Convinced that, pursuant to the provisions of the treaty, all signatories have the right to engage in research, production and use of nuclear energy for peaceful purposes and will be able to acquire source and special fissionable materials, as well as equipment for the processing, use and production of nuclear material for peaceful purposes,

Convinced further that an agreement to prevent the further proliferation of nuclear weapons must be followed as soon as possible by effective measures on the cessation of the nuclear arms race and on nuclear disarmament, and that the non-proliferation treaty will contribute to this aim,

Affirming that in the interest of international peace and security both nuclear-weapon and non-nuclear-weapon States carry the responsibility of acting in accordance with the principles of the Charter of the United Nations that the sovereign equality of all States shall be respected, that the threat or use of force in international relations shall be refrained from and that international disputes shall be settled by peaceful means,

1. *Commends* the Treaty on the Non-Proliferation of Nuclear Weapons, the text of which is annexed to the present resolution;

2. *Requests* the Depositary Governments to open the Treaty for signature and ratification at the earliest possible date;

3. *Expresses the hope* for the widest possible adherence to the Treaty by both nuclear-weapon and non-nuclear-weapon States;

4. *Requests* the Conference of the Eighteen-Nation Committee on Disarmament and the nuclear-weapon States urgently to pursue negotiations on effective measures relating to the cessation of the nuclear arms race at an early date and to nuclear disarmament, and on a treaty on general and complete disarmament under strict and effective international control;

5. *Requests* the Conference of the Eighteen-Nation Committee on Disarmament to report on the progress of its work to the General Assembly at its twenty-third session.

ANNEX
TREATY ON THE NON-PROLIFERATION OF NUCLEAR WEAPONS

The States concluding this Treaty, thereinafter referred to as the ''Parties to the Treaty'',

Considering the devastation that would be visited upon all mankind by a nuclear war and the consequent need to make every effort to avert the danger of such a war and to take measures to safeguard the security of peoples,

Believing that the proliferation of nuclear weapons would seriously enhance the danger of nuclear war,

In conformity with resolutions of the United Nations General Assembly calling for the conclusion of an agreement on the prevention of wider dissemination of nuclear weapons,

Undertaking to co-operate in facilitating the application of International Atomic Energy Agency safeguards on peaceful nuclear activities,

Expressing their support for research, development and other efforts to further the application, within the framework of the International Atomic Energy Agency safeguards system, of the principle of safeguarding effectively the flow of source and special fissionable materials by use of instruments and other techniques at certain strategic points,

Affirming the principle that the benefits of peaceful applications of nuclear technology, including any techno-

logical by-products which may be derived by nuclear-weapon States from the development of nuclear explosive devices, should be available for peaceful purposes to all Parties to the Treaty, whether nuclear-weapon or non-nuclear-weapon States,

Convinced that, in furtherance of this principle, all Parties to the Treaty are entitled to participate in the fullest possible exchange of scientific information for, and to contribute alone or in co-operation with other States to, the further development of the applications of atomic energy for peaceful purposes,

Declaring their intention to achieve at the earliest possible date the cessation of the nuclear arms race and to undertake effective measures in the direction of nuclear disarmament,

Urging the co-operation of all States in the attainment of this objective,

Recalling the determination expressed by the Parties to the 1963 Treaty banning nuclear weapon tests in the atmosphere, in outer space and under water in its Preamble to seek to achieve the discontinuance of all test explosions of nuclear weapons for all time and to continue negotiations to this end,

Desiring to further the easing of international tension and the strengthening of trust between States in order to facilitate the cessation of the manufacture of nuclear weapons, the liquidation of all their existing stockpiles, and the elimination from national arsenals of nuclear weapons and the means of their delivery pursuant to a treaty on general and complete disarmament under strict and effective international control,

Recalling that, in accordance with the Charter of the United Nations, States must refrain in their international relations from the threat or use of force against the territorial integrity or political independence of any State, or in any other manner inconsistent with the Purposes of the United Nations, and that the establishment and maintenance of international peace and security are to be promoted with the least diversion for armaments of the world's human and economic resources,

Have agreed as follows:

Article I

Each nuclear-weapon State Party to the Treaty undertakes not to transfer to any recipient whatsoever nuclear weapons or other nuclear explosive devices or control over such weapons or explosive devices directly, or indirectly; and not in any way to assist, encourage, or induce any non-nuclear-weapon State to manufacture or otherwise acquire nuclear weapons or other nuclear explosive devices, or control over such weapons or explosive devices.

Article II

Each non-nuclear-weapon State Party to the Treaty undertakes not to receive the transfer from any transferor whatsoever of nuclear weapons or other nuclear explosive devices or of control over such weapons or explosive devices directly, or indirectly; not to manufacture or otherwise acquire nuclear weapons or other nuclear explosive devices; and not to seek or receive any assistance in the manufacture of nuclear weapons or other nuclear explosive devices.

Article III

1. Each non-nuclear-weapon State Party to the Treaty undertakes to accept safeguards, as set forth in

an agreement to be negotiated and concluded with the International Atomic Energy Agency in accordance with the Statute of the International Atomic Energy Agency and the Agency's safeguards system, for the exclusive purpose of verification of the fulfilment of its obligations assumed under this Treaty with a view to preventing diversion of nuclear energy from peaceful uses to nuclear weapons or other nuclear explosive devices. Procedures for the safeguards required by this article shall be followed with respect to source or special fissionable material whether it is being produced, processed or used in any principal nuclear facility or is outside any such facility. The safeguards required by this article shall be applied on all source or special fissionable material in all peaceful nuclear activities within the territory of such State, under its jurisdiction, or carried out under its control anywhere.

2.   Each State Party to the Treaty undertakes not to provide: *(a)* source or special fissionable material, or *(b)* equipment or material especially designed or prepared for the processing, use or production of special fissionable material, to any non-nuclear-weapon State for peaceful purposes, unless the source or special fissionable material shall be subject to the safeguards required by this article.

3.   The safeguards required by this article shall be implemented in a manner designed to comply with article IV of this Treaty, and to avoid hampering the economic or technological development of the Parties or international co-operation in the field of peaceful nuclear activities, including the international exchange of nuclear material and equipment for the processing, use or production of nuclear material for peaceful purposes in accordance with the provisions of this article and the principle of safeguarding set forth in the Preamble of the Treaty.

4.   Non-nuclear-weapon States Party to the Treaty shall conclude agreements with the International Atomic Energy Agency to meet the requirements of this article either individually or together with other States in accordance with the Statute of the International Atomic Energy Agency. Negotiation of such agreements shall commence within 180 days from the original entry into force of this Treaty. For States depositing their instruments of ratification or accession after the 180-day period, negotiation of such agreements shall commence not later than the date of such deposit. Such agreements shall enter into force not later than eighteen months after the date of initiation of negotiations.

Article IV

1.   Nothing in this Treaty shall be interpreted as affecting the inalienable right of all the Parties to the Treaty to develop research, production and use of nuclear energy for peaceful purposes without discrimination and in conformity with articles I and II of this Treaty.

2.   All the Parties to the Treaty undertake to facilitate, and have the right to participate in, the fullest possible exchange of equipment, materials and scientific and technological information for the peaceful uses of nuclear energy. Parties to the Treaty in a position to do so shall also co-operate in contributing alone or together with other States or international organizations to the further development of the applications of nuclear energy for peaceful purposes, especially in the territo-

ries of non-nuclear-weapon States Party to the Treaty, with due consideration for the needs of the developing areas of the world.

Article V

Each Party to the Treaty undertakes to take appropriate measures to ensure that, in accordance with this Treaty, under appropriate international observation and through appropriate international procedures, potential benefits from any peaceful applications of nuclear explosions will be made available to non-nuclear-weapon States Party to the Treaty on a non-discriminatory basis and that the charge to such Parties for the explosive devices used will be as low as possible and exclude any charge for research and development. Non-nuclear-weapon States Party to the Treaty shall be able to obtain such benefits, pursuant to a special international agreement or agreements, through an appropriate international body with adequate representation of non-nuclear-weapon States. Negotiations on this subject shall commence as soon as possible after the Treaty enters into force. Non-nuclear-weapon States Party to the Treaty so desiring may also obtain such benefits pursuant to bilateral agreements.

Article VI

Each of the Parties to the Treaty undertakes to pursue negotiations in good faith on effective measures relating to cessation of the nuclear arms race at an early date and to nuclear disarmament and on a treaty on general and complete disarmament under strict and effective international control.

Article VII

Nothing in this Treaty affects the right of any group of States to conclude regional treaties in order to assure the total absence of nuclear weapons in their respective territories.

Article VIII

1.   Any Party to the Treaty may propose amendments to this Treaty. The text of any proposed amendment shall be submitted to the Depositary Governments which shall circulate it to all Parties to the Treaty. Thereupon, if requested to do so by one third or more of the Parties to the Treaty, the Depositary Governments shall convene a conference, to which they shall invite all the Parties to the Treaty, to consider such an amendment.

2.   Any amendment to this Treaty must be approved by a majority of the votes of all the Parties to the Treaty, including the votes of all nuclear-weapon States Party to the Treaty and all other Parties which, on the date the amendment is circulated, are members of the Board of Governors of the International Atomic Energy Agency. The amendment shall enter into force for each Party that deposits its instrument of ratification of the amendment upon the deposit of such instruments of ratification by a majority of all the Parties, including the instruments of ratification of all nuclear-weapon States Party to the Treaty and all other Parties which, on the date the amendment is circulated, are members of the Board of Governors of the International Atomic Energy Agency. Thereafter, it shall enter into force for any other Party upon the deposit of its instrument of ratification of the amendment.

3.   Five years after the entry into force of this Treaty, a conference of Parties to the Treaty shall be held in

Geneva, Switzerland, in order to review the operation of this Treaty with a view to assuring that the purposes of the Preamble and the provisions of the Treaty are being realized. At intervals of five years thereafter, a majority of the Parties to the Treaty may obtain, by submitting a proposal to this effect to the Depositary Governments, the convening of further conferences with the same objective of reviewing the operation of the Treaty.

Article IX

1. This Treaty shall be open to all States for signature. Any State which does not sign the Treaty before its entry into force in accordance with paragraph 3 of this article may accede to it at any time.

2. This Treaty shall be subject to ratification by signatory States. Instruments of ratification and instruments of accession shall be deposited with the Governments of the Union of Soviet Socialist Republics, the United Kingdom of Great Britain and Northern Ireland and the United States of America, which are hereby designated the Depositary Governments.

3. This Treaty shall enter into force after its ratification by the States, the Governments of which are designated Depositaries of the Treaty, and forty other States signatory to this Treaty and the deposit of their instruments of ratification. For the purposes of this Treaty, a nuclear-weapon State is one which has manufactured and exploded a nuclear weapon or other nuclear explosive device prior to 1 January 1967.

4. For States whose instruments of ratification or accession are deposited subsequent to the entry into force of this Treaty, it shall enter into force on the date of the deposit of their instruments of ratification or accession.

5. The Depositary Governments shall promptly inform all signatory and acceding States of the date of each signature, the date of deposit of each instrument of ratification or of accession, the date of the entry into force of this Treaty, and the date of receipt of any requests for convening a conference or other notices.

6. This Treaty shall be registered by the Depositary Governments pursuant to Article 102 of the Charter of the United Nations.

Article X

1. Each Party shall in exercising its national sovereignty have the right to withdraw from the Treaty if it decides that extraordinary events, related to the subject-matter of this Treaty, have jeopardized the supreme interests of its country. It shall give notice of such withdrawal to all other Parties to the Treaty and to the United Nations Security Council three months in advance. Such notice shall include a statement of the extraordinary events it regards as having jeopardized its supreme interests.

2. Twenty-five years after the entry into force of the Treaty, a conference shall be convened to decide whether the Treaty shall continue in force indefinitely, or shall be extended for an additional fixed period or periods. This decision shall be taken by a majority of the Parties to the Treaty.

. . .

[YUN 1968, pp. 4-19]

The nuclear non-proliferation Treaty entered into force on 5 March 1970; as at 31 March 1995, there were 175 parties to it. On the basis of the Treaty, a global nuclear non-proliferation regime has been established, supported by the safeguards system of the International Atomic Energy Agency to prevent the diversion of nuclear material to military activities. Four conferences have been held (1975, 1980, 1985 and 1990) to review the Treaty's operation. The 1995 conference will decide on the Treaty's extension.

Seabed Treaty

Another important achievement in preventing the further spread of nuclear weapons was the successful conclusion in 1970 of a Treaty on the Prohibition of the Emplacement of Nuclear Weapons and Other Weapons of Mass Destruction on the Seabed and the Ocean Floor and in the Subsoil Thereof. Parties to this Treaty, which was jointly proposed by the United States and the USSR, undertook not to emplant nuclear weapons or other weapons of mass destruction, as well as structures, launching installations or other facilities designed for storing, testing or using such weapons, in the seabed zone or on the ocean floor. The General Assembly, in commending the Treaty to Members in December 1970, expressed the conviction that the prevention of a nuclear-arms race on the seabed and the ocean floor served the interests of maintaining world peace and reducing international tensions. It also recognized the common interest of mankind in reserving the seabed and the ocean floor exclusively for peaceful purposes. The Treaty was signed on 11 February 1971 and entered into force on 18 May 1972.

Nuclear test-ban treaty

The first concrete step in the halting and eventual banning of nuclear testing was the adoption in 1963 of the Treaty Banning Nuclear Weapon Tests in the Atmosphere, in Outer Space and under Water (also known as the partial test-ban Treaty). Parties to that Treaty expressed the aspiration to achieve the discontinuance of all test explosions of nuclear weapons for all time. This determination was also recalled in the 1968 Treaty on the Non-Proliferation of Nuclear Weapons. However, the goal of a comprehensive ban on nuclear testing could not be realized as the question of the suspension of nuclear and thermonuclear tests still remained to be resolved. It was first raised by India in August 1959, and in 1969 the basic differences remained among the members of the Disarmament Commission with regard to extending the test ban of the partial test-ban Treaty to underground tests. The USSR favoured the conclusion of an immediate agreement based on national means of verification, while the United States preferred some form of on-site inspection. In April 1969, Sweden submitted proposals for a possible treaty banning underground tests, except for peaceful purposes, and for the international exchange of seismological data.

Suspension of nuclear and thermonuclear tests

The urgent need for suspension of nuclear and thermonuclear tests was discussed at the 1971 session of the General Assembly during the disarmament debate in the Assembly's First Committee.

. . .

On 16 December 1971, the General Assembly adopted three resolutions concerning the suspension of nuclear and thermonuclear testing.

By the first of these—resolution 2828 A (XXVI)—the Assembly reiterated solemnly and most emphatically its condemnation of all nuclear weapon tests and urged the Governments of the nuclear-weapon States to halt all such tests at the earliest possible date and, in any case, not later than 5 August 1973. In taking this decision, the Assembly expressed its conviction that whatever might be the differences on the question of verification, there was no valid reason to delay the conclusion of a comprehensive test ban.

The Assembly also asked the Secretary-General to transmit the resolution to the nuclear-weapon States and to inform the Assembly at its 1972 session of any measures taken in implementation.

. . .

By the second resolution, adopted on 16 December 1971, the General Assembly: (1) appealed to the nuclear powers to desist from carrying out further nuclear tests of any kind; (2) urged all nuclear powers to reach agreement on a cessation of tests without delay; and (3) requested the nuclear powers not to deploy nuclear weapons of mass destruction. By the preamble to this resolution, the Assembly called attention to the health and other hazards arising from nuclear testing.

. . .

In its third decision on this question, the Assembly stressed anew the urgency of bringing to a halt all nuclear weapon testing in all environments by all States. The Assembly urged all States to adhere without delay to the Treaty Banning Nuclear Weapon Tests in the Atmosphere, in Outer Space and under Water and meanwhile to refrain from testing in the environments covered by that Treaty. It called on all Governments conducting nuclear weapon tests, particularly those of parties to the partial test ban Treaty, immediately to undertake unilateral or negotiated measures of restraint to suspend testing or reduce the size and number of tests, pending the early entry into force of a comprehensive ban.

The Assembly also urged Governments to develop and use more effectively existing capabilities for seismological identification of underground tests in order to facilitate the monitoring of a comprehensive test ban.

It asked the Conference of the Committee on Disarmament (CCD) to give highest priority to an underground test ban treaty and asked testing Governments, in particular, to take an active and constructive part in developing in CCD specific proposals for such a ban.

Finally, the Assembly expressed the hope that these efforts would enable all States to sign in the near future a treaty banning underground tests.

(YUN 1971, pp. 22-24)

Comprehensive test-ban treaty

Multilateral discussions relating to a comprehensive test ban continued in the Conference on Disarmament. The General Assembly in the latter half of the 1980s called on the parties to the partial test-ban Treaty to hold a conference to convert that Treaty into a total ban. An Amendment Conference was held in New York in January 1991 but could not arrive at a substantive decision on conversion or agree on its suitability as the forum for achieving a comprehensive test ban. However, the President of the Conference, at its request, continued to conduct consultations on the matter. The Assembly (resolution 46/29) requested the Conference on Disarmament to intensify its work on specific and interrelated test-ban issues.

The USSR, on 6 August 1985, unilaterally declared a moratorium on all its nuclear explosive testing for a limited time—eventually 18 months. Between 1988 and 1992, there was a progressive and considerable reduction in the total number of nuclear tests conducted by all the nuclear-weapon States. In October 1991, the USSR again unilaterally declared an immediate moratorium. This led, in 1992, to declarations of unilateral moratoriums by France and by the United States; the United Kingdom maintained a de facto moratorium. As of March 1995, no further tests have been conducted by France, the Russian Federation, the United Kingdom or the United States.

. . . the Conference gave the Ad Hoc Committee a mandate to negotiate a comprehensive nuclear-test-ban treaty and requested the Chairman to conduct consultations in the inter-sessional period—between 3 September 1993 and 17 January 1994—on the specific mandate for, and the organization of, the negotiation. On the basis of that action, the Ad Hoc Committee's Chairman initiated consultations on adopting specific wording for a negotiating mandate and on organizing the negotiations to begin in January 1994.

The Ad Hoc Committee also discussed a draft comprehensive test-ban treaty proposed by Sweden in June, for which verification protocols were yet to be prepared. It devoted considerable attention to questions related to verification, a crucial element of the future treaty. . . . Some of the issues discussed during the session were: the substantial role that a global seismic monitoring network would have, especially in underground testing; the possible use of additional non-seismic verification technologies to detect nuclear tests in various environments, including in relation to evasion, and the possible use of such techniques to detect pre-testing preparations; the costs of a future verification system *vis-à-vis* its capabilities; the implementing agency, its powers, functions and costs; the close interrelationship between applicable verification techniques and the scope of obligations under the treaty; and a possible mix of national and international means of verification, taking into account cost effectiveness.

. . .

Moratoriums on testing

[In 1993], there were developments on moratoriums on testing, pending the achievement of a comprehensive test-ban treaty, which were closely connected with the unilateral moratoriums that had been declared or extended by three nuclear-weapon States—France, the Russian Federation and the United States—in 1992.

On 2 July 1993, President William Clinton of the United States announced his decision to extend the 1992 United States moratorium on nuclear testing, at least until the end of September 1994, as long as no other nation tested, and called on the other nuclear Powers to do the same. If those nations were to join the United States in observing the moratorium, the President said, the five nuclear Powers would be in the strongest possible position to negotiate a comprehensive nuclear-test ban and to discourage other nations from developing their own nuclear arsenals. If, however, the moratorium was broken by another nation, approval would be sought from the United States Congress for additional tests.

In a 5 October statement, China informed the Secretary-General that it had conducted an underground nuclear test. It stated that it possessed a small number of nuclear weapons entirely for the purpose of self-defence and that it stood for the complete prohibition and thorough destruction of nuclear weapons and for a comprehensive nuclear-test ban. China believed that a comprehensive test-ban treaty would have positive significance and it would take an active part in the negotiating process. After the treaty had been concluded and had come into effect, China would abide by it and carry out no more nuclear tests. Several States, either at the time the text was announced or later in the First Committee, voiced disappointment that China had resumed nuclear testing. On 21 October, the Russian Federation, expressing deep regret over China's

action, declared its intention to continue to adhere to the nuclear-testing moratorium, of which it had been the initiator, while retaining the right to reconsider its decision in the event of further unfavourable developments in the nuclear-testing area.

[YUN 1993, pp. 114-15]

In December 1993, the General Assembly (resolution 48/70) supported the commencement of multilateral negotiations on a comprehensive nuclear-test-ban treaty. Parallel to this effort was that of the parties to the 1963 Treaty Banning Nuclear Weapon Tests in the Atmosphere, in Outer Space and under Water which held an Amendment Conference on 10 August 1993. They agreed to pursue the work on a comprehensive test ban in the Amendment Conference and the Conference on Disarmament.

Chemical and biological weapons

In 1925, concerned with the possible use of chemical and bacteriological weapons in war, 42 States signed the Geneva Protocol for the Prohibition of the Use in War of Asphyxiating, Poisonous or Other Gases, and of Bacteriological Methods of Warfare. Its general objectives were reinforced by the General Assembly in 1947, when it recommended that the Security Council consider proposals for the adoption of measures, *inter alia*, for the early general regulation of all other major weapons adaptable to mass destruction. One issue that impeded progress with respect to chemical and biological weapons was the question of whether these two categories of weapons should be dealt with jointly or separately.

The use of chemical and bacteriological weapons was brought to the attention of the United Nations in March 1952 during consideration of the work programme of the Disarmament Commission, when the USSR asked the Commission to consider, with reference to charges of the use of bacterial weapons in Korea and China, the violation of the prohibition of bacterial warfare so as to prevent its further use and to bring the violators to account. The request was not accepted by the Commission but the issue was later considered by the Security Council.

Bacterial warfare

The following item was included in the provisional agenda of the 577th meeting of the Security Council on 18 June 1952 by the President (representative of the USSR): "Appeal to States to accede to and ratify the Geneva Protocol of 1925 for the prohibition of the use of bacterial warfare". Following a proposal by the representative of the United States, the item was changed to read: "Question of an appeal to States to accede to and ratify the

Geneva Protocol of 1925 for the prohibition of the use of bacterial warfare''. . . .

The Security Council considered the question at its 577th to 579th and 581st to 583rd meetings between 18 and 26 June 1952. Before it was a draft resolution by the USSR, under which the Council, having regard to the existence of differences of opinion concerning the admissibility of the use of bacterial weapons, noting that the use of such weapons had been justly condemned by world public opinion, as expressed in the signature by 42 States of the Geneva Protocol of 17 June 1925, would decide to appeal to all States, both Members and non-members, which had not yet acceded to or ratified the Protocol, to accede to and ratify it.

Introducing his draft resolution, the President, speaking as the representative of the USSR, stressed the importance of the Geneva Protocol as a factor in restraining the use of bacterial and chemical weapons by the aggressive States which had precipitated the Second World War. He said that 48 States, including all of the Great Powers, had signed or acceded to the Protocol, and only six States, Brazil, El Salvador, Japan, Nicaragua, the United States and Uruguay, had not ratified it. The development of the production of bacterial and chemical weapons, the preparations being made in certain countries for bacterial warfare and the differences of opinion among statesmen and leaders on the use of bacterial weapons created a threat to the peace.

. . .

During the debate in the Council, the following points of view emerged. The representatives of Chile, China, Greece, Turkey, the United Kingdom and the United States concurred in the view that the USSR proposals had been timed to coincide with an organized propaganda campaign on the part of the USSR and its supporters that the United Nations Forces in Korea had used germ warfare. The proposals therefore could not be accepted as a genuine effort to secure the prohibition of bacterial weapons. Moreover, these representatives maintained, however praiseworthy and humane the provisions of the Geneva Protocol might have been, they were now obsolete since they contained no safeguards or guarantees and were not accompanied by any system of international control. Mere declarations, they argued, could not secure any real or effective control. What was really needed, they said, was a comprehensive plan of disarmament which would guard against aggression. They therefore supported a United States motion that the question be referred to the Disarmament Commission.

. . .

At the 583rd meeting of the Security Council on 26 June 1952, the USSR draft resolution was rejected. There was one vote in favour (USSR) and 10 abstentions.

[YUN 1952, pp. 323-26]

The issue of bacterial warfare was further considered during June and July 1952 at four meetings of the Security Council. At that time, there were contentious debates and serious charges and countercharges between the United States and USSR representatives concerning the use of bacterial weapons in Korea. Various draft resolutions put to the vote were not adopted because of the negative vote of a permanent member of the Council.

At the request of the United States, the General Assembly considered the matter during its March/April 1953 session. The Assembly decided (resolution 706(VII)) that after its President had received acceptance of the proposal to investigate the issue, a commission, comprising Brazil, Egypt, Pakistan, Sweden and Uruguay, should be established to investigate the charges. Replies were received only from Japan, the Republic of Korea and the United States. The Assembly further considered the matter at its October session and decided (resolution 714(VIII)) to refer to the Disarmament Commission for consideration a draft resolution proposed by the USSR which would have the Assembly call on all States that had not done so to accede to the 1925 Geneva Protocol prohibiting the use of bacterial weapons.

At the August meeting of the Disarmament Commission, the United States had made a statement on bacterial warfare, emphasizing that its elimination must be an essential part of a comprehensive disarmament programme. Such a programme should include safeguards for disclosure and verification and provide for the progressive curtailment, dismantling and destruction of stockpiles of bacterial weapons and related appliances. In September, the United States subsequently submitted a working paper setting out its proposals for the elimination of bacterial weapons in connection with the elimination of all major weapons adaptable to mass destruction.

Convention on bacteriological weapons

The General Assembly and the negotiating body, the Conference of the Committee on Disarmament, continued to work on all aspects of the problem of the elimination of chemical and bacteriological (biological) weapons. In 1969, two proposals for a draft convention on the prohibition of the development, production and stockpiling and the destruction of such weapons were submitted to the General Assembly for consideration, one by Bulgaria, the Byelorussian SSR, Czechoslovakia, Hungary, Mongolia, Poland, Romania, the Ukrainian SSR and the USSR, and the other by the United Kingdom. The two drafts reflected the differences between the major blocs on the approach to such a convention. The USSR and many other States supported a joint treatment of chemical and bacteriological (biological) weapons in a comprehensive convention, while the United States and the United Kingdom and others preferred a separate convention banning biological weapons as a first step. In 1971, agreement was reached on separating these two categories of weapons. Subsequently, on the basis of draft texts submitted by the USSR and the United States, the Conference of the Committee on Disarmament agreed on a draft convention.

In dealing with the question of chemical and bacteriological (biological) weapons at its 1971 session, the General Assembly's First Committee had before it the report of the Conference of the Committee on Disarmament to which was annexed the text of the draft convention on the prohibition of the development, production and stockpiling of bacteriological (biological) and toxin weapons and on their destruction. In the course of the debate in the First Committee, a majority of States gave general support to the draft convention and welcomed it as the first measure of genuine disarmament, providing for the elimination of one type of weapons of mass destruction. Satisfaction was also widely expressed over the fact that the draft convention was the result of compromise, reflecting the views and suggestions of many States.

At the same time, however, a number of Members expressed disappointment that it had not proved possible to achieve a joint prohibition of chemical and bacteriological (biological) weapons.

. . .

On 16 December 1971, the Assembly adopted a resolution by which it commended the Convention on the Prohibition of the Development, Production and Stockpiling of Bacteriological (Biological) and Toxin Weapons and on Their Destruction, and requested the depositary Governments to open it for signature and ratification at the earliest possible date. At the same time, it expressed hope for the widest possible adherence to the Convention.

By the preamble of this resolution, the Assembly, among other things, made the following points. It expressed its conviction of the importance and urgency of eliminating from the arsenals of States such dangerous weapons of mass destruction as those using chemical or bacteriological (biological) agents. The Assembly recognized the important significance of the Protocol for the Prohibition of the Use in War of Asphyxiating, Poisonous or Other Gases, and of Bacteriological Methods of Warfare, signed at Geneva, Switzerland, on 17 June 1925, and expressed its awareness also of the contribution the Geneva Protocol had already made and continued to make to mitigating the horrors of war.

. . .

These Assembly decisions were set forth in resolution 2826(XXVI), which was adopted by a recorded vote of 110 to 0, with 1 abstention. The text of the resolution was approved by the First Committee by acclamation on 8 December.

[YUN 1971, p. 15]

The Convention was further strengthened through review conferences held in 1980, 1986 and 1991. At the 1991 Review Conference, the parties to the Convention agreed to expand the confidence-building measures they had agreed to at the Second Review Conference. They also decided on the requirement that parties declare what legislation and other regulations they had enacted to implement the Convention's provisions and to control trade of pathogenic micro-organisms. In addition, the Ad Hoc Group of Governmental Experts to Identify and Examine Potential Verification Measures from a Scientific and Technical Standpoint, established by the Third Review Conference, in its report submitted in 1993, concluded that potential verification measures could be useful in enhancing confidence, through transparency, and that States parties were fulfilling their obligation, thereby strengthening the Convention. At the end of 1973 there were 130 parties to the Convention.

In September 1994, a special conference of the States parties was held to consider the experts' report. It decided to establish a further Ad Hoc Group to consider appropriate measures, including possible verification, and to draft proposals to strengthen the Convention, to be included, as appropriate, in a legally binding instrument.

Convention on chemical weapons

The parties to the 1971 Convention on bacteriological (biological) weapons had undertaken, by the terms of article IX of that Convention, to continue negotiations with a view to reaching early agreement on a comprehensive ban on chemical weapons. This intention was reinforced by the General Assembly in November 1972 (resolution 2933(XXVII)). Multilateral negotiations on the elaboration of a global convention banning chemical weapons were conducted within the framework of the Conference on Disarmament through its Ad Hoc Committee on Chemical Weapons.

After more than a decade of negotiations, the Conference on Disarmament adopted the Convention on the Prohibition of the Development, Production, Stockpiling and Use of Chemical Weapons and on Their Destruction in 1992. It was the first disarmament agreement negotiated within a multilateral framework that provided for eliminating an entire category of weapons of mass destruction.

. . .

On 3 September [1992], the Conference on Disarmament adopted the report of the Ad Hoc Committee and its appendix containing the draft convention and a text on establishing a preparatory commission for the Organization for the Prohibition of Chemical Weapons. The report also incorporated statements of members on their positions regarding the Convention as a whole and on specific provisions. The Conference agreed by consensus to transmit the draft Convention to the General Assembly.

. . .

The Convention on the Prohibition of the Development, Production, Stockpiling and Use of Chemical Weapons and on Their Destruction consisted of a preamble, 24 articles and three annexes. The Convention was to enter into force 180 days after the date of the deposit of the sixty-fifth instrument of ratification, but in no case earlier than two years after its opening for signature in January 1993.

. . .

Three annexes—Annex on Chemicals, Annex on Implementation and Verification and Annex on the Protection of Confidential Information—formed an integral part of the Convention.

[YUN 1992, pp. 64-66]

On 30 November 1992, the General Assembly welcomed the draft convention and requested the Secretary-General to open it for signature in Paris on 13 January 1993. It called on States to sign the convention and to ensure its effective implementation. By the end of 1993, 154 States had signed and 4 States had ratified the Convention.

Conventional weapons

Reduction of armaments

The question of the reduction of armaments arose in 1946 within the context of the General Assembly's consideration of a USSR proposal that the presence of troops of the United Nations in non-enemy territories be discussed by the Assembly. The USSR suggested that all Member States submit information on their armed forces and air and naval bases located in the territory of non-enemy States. It had also accepted a United States proposal to include information on Allied troops in former enemy States as well. The USSR therefore proposed that the Assembly recommend that the Security Council ask Member States to furnish information on the number of their armed forces present in both categories of territory as well as information on air and naval bases and the size of their garrisons. The United Kingdom amended the proposal to the effect that the submission of information of armed forces was only one aspect of the larger problem of the regulation and reduction of armaments, and that the scope of the information be widened to include all enlisted forces wherever stationed; that it be submitted by 1 January 1947; and that it be subject to a United Nations verification system. On 28 November 1946, the First Committee, after considering further amendments, accepted the United Kingdom proposal as an amendment to the USSR proposal with the exception of the verification provision.

The General Assembly took up the issue on 10 December 1946 and was unable to arrive at a compromise on the various amendments submitted.

. . . the General Assembly decided to refer the matter to the Sub-Committee of the First Committee on Disarmament.

After long discussion the Sub-Committee concluded that there was no practical possibility of arriving at a balanced text incorporating the amendments submitted by the U.S.S.R. and the United Kingdom. Moreover, the Sub-Committee found that in dealing with the problem of disarmament it had at the same time dealt with the presence of troops on foreign territory. In the circumstances the Sub-Committee considered it logical to propose that the resolution adopted by the First Committee be dropped and that instead the following resolution be adopted:

THE GENERAL ASSEMBLY

DESIROUS of implementing, as soon as possible, the resolution of 14 December 1946 on the Principles governing the Regulation and Reduction of Armaments;

CALLS UPON the Security Council to determine, as soon as possible, the information which the States Members should be called upon to furnish, in order to give effect to this resolution.

. . .

The General Assembly at its 63rd plenary meeting on December 14, 1946, adopted the substitute resolution as quoted by 36 votes to 6, with 4 abstentions.

Principles governing the general regulation and reduction of armaments

By a letter of October 29, 1946, the delegation of the U.S.S.R. submitted a "Proposal Concerning the General Reduction of Armaments" for inclusion in the agenda of the General Assembly. At its 46th plenary meeting on October 31, 1946, the Assembly referred the matter to the First Committee.

On November 26, 1946, the U.S.S.R. delegation submitted a supplementary proposal concerning the establishment of a system of international control and inspection. The U.S.S.R. delegation subsequently submitted the following resolution combining the abovementioned proposals:

1. With a view to strengthening peace and international security in conformity with the aims and principles of the United Nations, the General Assembly recognizes the necessity of a general reduction of armaments.

2. The implementing of the decision concerning the reduction of armaments should include as the primary object the prohibition to produce and use atomic energy for military purposes.

3. To ensure the adoption of measures for the reduction of armaments and prohibition of the use of atomic energy for military purposes, there shall be established within the framework of the Security Council, which has the primary responsibility for international peace and security, international control operating on the basis of a special provision which should provide for the establishment of special organs of inspection for which purpose there shall be formed:

(a) A Commission for the control of the execution of the decision regarding the reduction of armaments;

(b) A Commission for the control of the execution of the decision regarding the prohibition of the use of atomic energy for military purposes.

. . .

The First Committee discussed the question of a general regulation and reduction of armaments at its 30th, 31st, 32nd, 34th, 38th and 44th meetings held on November 28, 29, 30 and December 2, 4 and 13 respectively. Commenting on the U.S.S.R. delegation's proposal, the Soviet representative stressed the necessity for taking serious measures to put an end to the armament race. Not only armed personnel, but military technique and technical means of war must be considered in the problem of disarmament. The Soviet delegation attached particular importance in this connection to the problem of atomic energy. The conclusion of a convention prohibiting both the production and use of atomic weapons was the first step the United Nations must take if a program of general disarmament was to be successful. The U.S.S.R. resolution therefore included a specific recommendation to this effect.

Many representatives commended the U.S.S.R. delegation for taking the initiative in submitting a proposal for the general reduction of armaments, and expressed agreement with the aims of the U.S.S.R. resolution. A number of representatives, however, felt that the wording of the U.S.S.R. resolution was too vague and that it was desirable to formulate more precisely the principles which would have to guide a general program of disarmament.

. . .

At the 34th meeting of the First Committee the representative of the United States submitted the following draft resolution:

1. With a view to strengthening international peace and security in conformity with the purposes and principles of the United Nations, the General Assembly recognizes the necessity of an early general regulation and reduction of armaments. Accordingly, the General Assembly recommends that the Security Council give prompt consideration to working out the practical measures, according to their priority, which are essential to provide for the general regulation and reduction of armaments pursuant to international treaties and agreements and to assure that such regulation and reduction will be generally observed by all participants and not unilaterally by only some of the participants.

2. The General Assembly recognizes that essential to the general regulation and reduction of armaments is the early establishment of international control of atomic energy and other modern technological discoveries to ensure their use only for peaceful purposes. Accordingly, in order to ensure that the general regulation and reduction of armaments are directed towards the major weapons of modern warfare and not merely towards the minor weapons, the General Assembly recommends that the Security Council give first consideration to the report which the Atomic Energy Commission will make to the Security Council before 31 December 1946, and facilitate the progress of the work of that Commission.

3. The General Assembly further recognizes that essential to the general regulation and reduction of armaments is the provision of practical and effective safeguards by way of inspection and other means to protect complying States against the hazards of violations and evasions. Accordingly, the General Assembly recommends to the Security Council that it give prompt consideration to the working out of proposals to provide such practical and effective safeguards in connection with the control of atomic energy and other limitations or regulation of armaments.

4. The General Assembly calls upon the Governments of all States to render every possible assistance to the Security Council and the Atomic Energy Commission in order to promote the establishment of international peace and collective security with the least diversion for armaments of the world's human and economic resources.

At the 38th meeting of the First Committee the representative of the U.S.S.R. announced his willingness to accept the United States resolution as a basis of discussion and submitted a number of amendments to that resolution which would render it acceptable to the U.S.S.R. delegation.

. . .

At its 44th meeting on December 13, 1946, the First Committee, after making some further drafting changes, unanimously and by acclamation adopted the resolution recommended by the Sub-Committee. Likewise by unanimous vote, the General Assembly at its 63rd plenary meeting on December 14, 1946, adopted the resolution, which read as follows:

1. In pursuance of Article 11 of the Charter and with a view to strengthening international peace and security in conformity with the Purposes and Principles of the United Nations,

THE GENERAL ASSEMBLY,

RECOGNIZES the necessity of an early general regulation and reduction of armaments and armed forces.

2. ACCORDINGLY,
THE GENERAL ASSEMBLY,

RECOMMENDS that the Security Council give prompt consideration to formulating the practical measures, according to their priority, which are essential to provide for the general regulation and reduction of armaments and armed forces and to assure that such regulation and reduction of armaments and armed forces will be generally observed by all participants and not unilaterally by only some of the participants. The plans formulated by the Security Council shall be submitted by the Secretary-General to the Members of the United Nations for consideration at a special session of the General Assembly. The treaties or conventions approved by the General Assembly shall be submitted to the signatory States for ratification in accordance with Article 26 of the Charter.

3. As an essential step towards the urgent objective of prohibiting and eliminating from national armaments atomic and all other major weapons adaptable now and in the future to mass destruction, and the early establishment of international control of atomic energy and other modern scientific discoveries and technical developments to ensure their use only for peaceful purposes,
THE GENERAL ASSEMBLY,

URGES the expeditious fulfilment by the Atomic Energy Commission of its terms of reference as set forth in Section 5 of the General Assembly Resolution of 24 January 1946.

4. In order to ensure that the general prohibition, regulation and reduction of armaments are directed towards the major weapons of modern warfare and not merely towards the minor weapons,
THE GENERAL ASSEMBLY,

RECOMMENDS that the Security Council expedite consideration of the reports which the Atomic Energy Commission will make to the Security Council and that it facilitate the work of that Commission, and also that the Security Council expedite consideration of a draft convention or conventions for the creation of an international system of control and inspection, these conventions to include the prohibition of atomic and all other major weapons adaptable now and in the future to mass destruction and the control of atomic energy to the extent necessary to ensure its use only for peaceful purposes.

5. THE GENERAL ASSEMBLY,

FURTHER RECOGNIZES that essential to the general regulation and reduction of armaments and armed forces is the provision of practical and effective safeguards by way of inspection and other means to protect complying States against the hazards of violations and evasions.

Accordingly,
THE GENERAL ASSEMBLY,

RECOMMENDS to the Security Council that it give prompt consideration to the working out of proposals to provide such practical and effective safeguards in connection with the control of atomic energy and the general regulation and reduction of armaments.

6. To ensure the adoption of measures for the early general regulation and reduction of armaments and armed forces, for the prohibition of the use of atomic energy for military purposes and the elimination from national armaments of atomic and all other major weapons adaptable now or in the future to mass destruc-

tion, and for the control of atomic energy to the extent necessary to ensure its use only for peaceful purposes,
THERE SHALL BE ESTABLISHED,

within the framework of the Security Council, which bears the primary responsibility for the maintenance of international peace and security, an international system, as mentioned in paragraph 4, operating through special organs, which organs shall derive their powers and status from the convention or conventions under which they are established.

7. THE GENERAL ASSEMBLY,

regarding the problem of security as closely connected with that of disarmament,

RECOMMENDS the Security Council to accelerate as much as possible the placing at its disposal of the armed forces mentioned in Article 43 of the Charter;

RECOMMENDS the Members to undertake the progressive and balanced withdrawal, taking account of the needs of occupation, of their armed forces stationed in ex-enemy territories, and the withdrawal without delay of their armed forces stationed in the territories of Members without their consent freely and publicly expressed in treaties or agreements consistent with the Charter and not contradicting international agreements.

FURTHER RECOMMENDS a corresponding reduction of national armed forces, and a general progressive and balanced reduction of national armed forces.

8. Nothing herein contained shall alter or limit the resolution of the General Assembly passed on 24 January 1946, creating the Atomic Energy Commission.

9. THE GENERAL ASSEMBLY,

CALLS upon all Members of the United Nations to render every possible assistance to the Security Council and the Atomic Energy Commission in order to promote the establishment and maintenance of international peace and collective security with the least diversion for armaments of the world's human and economic resources.

(YUN 1946-47, pp. 138-43)

The general regulation and reduction of armaments and information on armed forces of the United Nations

By a letter dated December 27, 1947, addressed to the Secretary-General, the representative of the U.S.S.R. submitted a proposal regarding the implementation of the resolution adopted by the General Assembly on December 14, 1946, on the ''Principles Governing the General Regulation and Reduction of Armaments''. The letter advocated the establishment of a commission, to be composed of the representatives of countries members of the Security Council, which should be charged with preparing and submitting to the Council, within a period of not later than three months, proposals for the general regulation and reduction of armaments and armed forces.

At its 88th meeting on December 31, 1946, the Security Council placed the U.S.S.R. proposal on its agenda, but discussion of the substance of the question was postponed to a later date. The United States representative, however, submitted a draft resolution at the meeting which proposed that the

Security Council give first priority to the establishment of international control over atomic energy by considering and acting on the report of the Atomic Energy Commission to the Council.

(YUN 1946-47, p. 375)

The issue was further discussed at meetings of the Security Council held on 9 January and 11 February 1947, during which the views of the United States and USSR were reconciled.

The final text of the resolution of the Security Council concerning the implementation of the resolutions of the General Assembly regarding the principles governing the general regulation and reduction of armaments and information on armed forces of the United Nations was as follows:

The Security Council, having accepted the resolution of the General Assembly of 14 December 1946 and recognizing that the general regulation and reduction of armaments and armed forces constitute a most important measure for strengthening international peace and security, and that the implementation of the resolution of the General Assembly on this subject is one of the most urgent and important tasks before the Security Council,

RESOLVES:

1. to work out the practical measures for giving effect to the resolutions of the General Assembly on 14 December 1946 concerning, on the one hand, the general regulation and reduction of armaments and armed forces, and the establishment of international control to bring about the reduction of armaments and armed forces, and, on the other hand, information concerning the armed forces of the United Nations;

2. to consider as soon as possible the report submitted by the Atomic Energy Commission and to take suitable decisions in order to facilitate its work;

3. to set up a Commission consisting of representatives of the Members of the Security Council with instructions to prepare and to submit to the Security Council within the space of not more than three months, the proposals:

(a) for the general regulation and reduction of armaments and armed forces, and

(b) for practical and effective safeguards in connection with the general regulation and reduction of armaments which the Commission may be in a position to formulate in order to ensure the implementation of the above-mentioned resolutions of the General Assembly of 14 December 1946, in so far as these resolutions relate to armaments within the new Commission's jurisdiction.

The Commission shall submit a plan of work to the Council for approval.

Those matters which fall within the competence of the Atomic Energy Commission as determined by the General Assembly Resolution of 24 January 1946 and 14 December 1946 shall be excluded from the jurisdiction of the Commission hereby established.

The title of the Commission shall be the Commission for Conventional Armaments. The Commission shall

make such proposals as it may deem advisable concerning the studies which the Military Staff Committee and possibly other organs of the United Nations might be asked to undertake.

. . .

The Commission for Conventional Armaments held its first meeting at Lake Success on March 24, 1947.

(YUN 1946-47, pp. 380-81)

The Commission for Conventional Armaments was subsequently dissolved by the Assembly in 1951 and the Disarmament Commission, established in its place, was requested to consider proposals for the control of conventional weapons within the context of the process of general disarmament.

Convention on certain conventional weapons

The objective of an early general regulation and reduction of armaments and armed forces, enunciated by the General Assembly in 1946, remained elusive. The growth in nuclear arsenals was also accompanied by increased stockpiles of conventional weapons as the arms race continued unabated. In 1978, the General Assembly, in the Final Document of its tenth special session, the first session devoted to disarmament, again called for negotiations on the balanced reduction of armed forces and of conventional weapons as well as on the limitation of international transfer of conventional weapons. It further called for international action to prohibit or restrict for humanitarian reasons the use of specific conventional weapons, including those which might be excessively injurious, cause unnecessary suffering or have indiscriminate effects. The General Assembly took up the question of incendiary and other conventional weapons which might be subject to prohibition or restriction of use for humanitarian purposes and decided (resolution 32/152) to convene in 1979 a United Nations conference with a view of reaching agreement on banning such weapons. The United Nations Conference on Prohibitions or Restrictions of Use of Certain Conventional Weapons Which May Be Deemed to Be Excessively Injurious or to Have Indiscriminate Effects met at Geneva from 10 to 28 September 1979 to work towards concluding a general treaty. The Conference produced partially agreed texts and adopted a resolution on small-calibre weapons, but was unable to resolve other issues. It decided to reconvene in 1980.

UN Conference on prohibiting or restricting use of certain conventional weapons

The United Nations Conference on prohibiting or restricting use of certain excessively injurious or indiscriminate conventional weapons . . . resumed its work on 15 September 1980 at Geneva.

. . .

The Conference itself held four plenary meetings at its resumed session. On 10 October, it approved the reports of the Working Group, of the Committee of the Whole and of a Drafting Committee. On the same date, it unanimously adopted its final report to the Assembly to which was annexed the Final Act of the Conference together with the texts of the Convention and its three Protocols. The Conference recommended that the Assembly commend the instruments to States with a view to achieving the widest possible adherence.

(YUN 1980, p. 76)

The report of the Conference was considered by the First Committee on 20 November 1980, when it approved a draft resolution for consideration by the General Assembly. On 12 December 1980, the Assembly adopted, without vote, resolution 35/153 commending the Convention and the three Protocols:

The General Assembly,

. . .

Recalling that, by its resolutions 32/152 and 33/70, it decided to convene in 1979 the United Nations Conference on Prohibitions or Restrictions of Use of Certain Conventional Weapons Which May Be Deemed to Be Excessively Injurious or to Have Indiscriminate Effects and established the mandate of the Conference,

. . .

1. *Takes note with appreciation* of the Final Report of the United Nations Conference on Prohibitions and Restrictions of Use of Certain Conventional Weapons Which May Be Deemed to Be Excessively Injurious or to Have Indiscriminate Effects, held at Geneva from 10 to 28 September 1979 and from 15 September to 10 October 1980;

2. *Welcomes* the successful conclusion of the Conference, which resulted in the adoption, on 10 October 1980, of the following instruments:

(*a*) Convention on Prohibitions or Restrictions on the Use of Certain Conventional Weapons Which May Be Deemed to Be Excessively Injurious or to Have Indiscriminate Effects;

(*b*) Protocol on Non-Detectable Fragments (Protocol I);

(*c*) Protocol on Prohibitions or Restrictions on the Use of Mines, Booby Traps and Other Devices (Protocol II);

(*d*) Protocol on Prohibitions or Restrictions on the Use of Incendiary Weapons (Protocol III);

3. *Takes note* of article 3 of the Convention, which stipulates that the Convention shall be open for signature on 10 April 1981;

4. *Commends* the Convention and the three annexed Protocols to all States, with a view to achieving the widest possible adherence to these instruments;

5. *Notes* that, under article 8 of the Convention, conferences may be convened to consider amendments to the Convention or any of the annexed Protocols, to con-

sider additional protocols relating to other categories of conventional weapons not covered by the existing Protocols, or to review the scope and operation of the Convention and the Protocols annexed thereto and to consider any proposal for amendments to the Convention or to the existing Protocols and any proposals for additional protocols relating to other categories of conventional weapons not covered by the existing Protocols;

6. *Requests* the Secretary-General, as the Depositary of the Convention and its annexed Protocols, to inform the General Assembly from time to time of the state of adherence to the Convention and its three annexed Protocols;

. . .

(YUN 1980, p. 88)

Convention

The Convention on Prohibitions or Restrictions on the Use of Certain Conventional Weapons Which May Be Deemed to Be Excessively Injurious or to Have Indiscriminate Effects consisted of a preamble and 11 articles.

It was to serve as the legal framework for the application of the three Protocols annexed to it, and it was based on such stated principles as the general principle of the protection of civilian populations against the effects of hostilities, the principle of international law that the right to choose methods or means of warfare was not unlimited, and the principle that prohibited the employment of weapons and methods of warfare of a nature to cause superfluous injury, unnecessary suffering, or long-term and severe damage to the natural environment.

. . .

Article 1 included in the scope of the Convention the situations referred to in the 1949 Geneva Conventions for the protection of war victims, as well as their Additional Protocol I providing protection in conflicts involving national liberation movements. The relationship between the 1949 Conventions and their Protocol and this Convention and its Protocols, and the circumstances in which the various instruments applied to States parties to a conflict in which both parties and nonparties to the relevant instruments were involved, were set forth in article 7.

The review mechanism contained in the Convention (article 8) included arrangements for convening a conference of States parties to consider amendments to the Convention and its Protocols, or for the development of new rules for prohibition or restriction. The convening of such a conference would take place if requested by a majority that was not less than 18 States parties, or by any State party if no conference had been convened for 10 years.

Other provisions prevented the Convention and its Protocols from detracting from obligations under international humanitarian law applicable in armed conflicts (article 2), provided for ratification, acceptance, approval or accession, as well as optional expressions of consent to be bound by any of the Protocols (article 4), contained an undertaking by States parties to disseminate the texts of the instruments to their armed forces (article 6), set forth the terms and means of denunciation of the instruments (article 9), and designated the United Nations Secretary-General as Depositary and indicated his functions (article 10), one of which was to receive the six authentic texts—Arabic, Chinese, English, French, Russian and Spanish (article 11). The Convention was to be opened for signature at New York on 10 April 1981 (article 3), and the instruments were to enter into force separately six months after deposit of the twentieth instrument of ratification, acceptance, approval, accession or, in the case of each of the Protocols, notification of consent to be bound by it (article 5).

Protocols

The 26-word Protocol on Non-Detectable Fragments (Protocol I) prohibited the use of non-detectable fragmentation weapons against both civilians and combatants. The weapons in question were those composed of substances such as wood, glass or plastics which in the human body escaped detection by X-rays, making extraction difficult and prolonging suffering and risk of infection.

The Protocol on Prohibitions or Restrictions on the Use of Mines, Booby Traps and Other Devices (Protocol II), consisting of nine articles and a technical annex, applied to the devices mentioned in its title, but not to the use of anti-ship mines at sea or in inland waterways (article 1).

Article 2 defined mines and booby traps, as well as the term "other devices," which meant manually emplaced munitions and devices, actuated by remote control or automatically after a lapse of time, and designed to kill, injure or damage.

Article 3 set general restrictions on the use of mines, booby traps and other devices. It prohibited in all circumstances the directing of weapons, either in offence, defence or by way of reprisals, against civilians, or the indiscriminate use of such weapons. Indiscriminate use meant placement which was not on or directed against a military objective, whose means of delivery could not be directed at a specific military objective, or which might be expected to cause incidental loss of civilian life, injuries or damage to non-military objectives which would be excessive in relation to the anticipated military advantage.

Other provisions restricted the use of mines (other than remotely delivered mines), booby traps and other devices in populated areas (article 4), and of remotely delivered mines (article 5). The locations of the latter type were to be recorded or

they were to contain a mechanism for rendering them harmless. Article 6 prohibited the use of booby traps in the form of apparently harmless portable objects or attached to or associated with internationally recognized protective emblems, the wounded or dead, grave sites, medical facilities or supplies, products for children, animals, food or drink, civilian kitchen equipment, religious objects, historic monuments, works of art or places which constituted a cultural or spiritual heritage, or any booby trap designed to cause superfluous injury or unnecessary suffering.

The text contained guidelines for the recording and publication of the location of minefields, mines and booby traps (article 7) and for international co-operation in providing information on and assistance for the removal of such devices (article 9). Guidelines were also laid down for the protection of United Nations forces and missions from the effects of these devices (article 8).

A technical annex attached to Protocol II provided guidelines for recording the location of pre-planned minefields and of large-scale, pre-planned use of booby traps, by maps, diagrams or other records to indicate the extent of the affected area.

The Protocol on Prohibitions or Restrictions on the Use of Incendiary Weapons (Protocol III) was agreed after an attempt to develop rules for the protection of combatants was abandoned in the interest of a consensus. This was on the understanding that consideration of that question would be resumed during the follow-up to the Conference.

The two-article Protocol thus provided for the protection of civilians and civilian objects against incendiary weapons, as defined in the first article. Military objectives located within a concentration of civilians could not be the object of an air-delivered incendiary-weapons attack; such objectives which were clearly separated from civilian concentrations were excluded from these restrictions, provided that all feasible precautions were taken to limit the incendiary effects to the military objective and to avoid or minimize incidental civilian deaths, injury or damage. It prohibited making forests or other plant-cover the object of incendiary-weapons attack except when they concealed combatants or other military objectives or were themselves military objectives.

(YUN 1980, pp. 76-78)

The Convention and Protocols entered into force in 1983.

Anti-personnel mines

In 1993, the question had arisen of broadening the scope of the 1980 Convention to include matters related to the prohibition of certain conventional weapons considered to be excessively injurious, especially anti-personnel mines. An enormous quantity of mines had been sown on the territory of many countries causing suffering of civilians, not only in time of war but also after the cessation of hostilities. As a result, three related subjects were discussed: the Convention and its Protocol II (on mines); a moratorium on the export of anti-personnel mines; and assistance in mine clearance. In June, the Secretary-General reported that he had instituted a coordinated programme for demining. In December, the General Assembly (resolution 48/79) welcomed the request by France to convene a conference to review the 1980 Convention and welcomed (resolution 48/7) the establishment of the Secretariat's mine-clearing programme. It also noted (resolution 48/75 K) the 85 million uncleared mines throughout the world which killed hundreds of persons each week and prohibited the return of refugees and internally displaced persons. The Assembly called on States to agree to a moratorium on the export of anti-personnel land-mines that posed grave dangers to civilian populations.

In 1994, in preparation for the autumn 1995 conference to review the Convention and its Protocols, a group of governmental experts of States parties met three times, focusing on Protocol II.

International arms transfers

Recent crises in various parts of the world have brought into sharper focus the necessity to curb illicit arms trade. The Register of Conventional Arms has become an important instrument in that endeavour.

[A study by] the group of experts encouraged States to make all their military activities as open as practicable and to ensure that they had the legal and administrative machinery to regulate and monitor effectively their arms transfers. It recommended establishing, as soon as possible, a universal and non-discriminatory arms transfer register under United Nations auspices and outlined the broad characteristics of such a register. The group further encouraged States to make efforts to achieve regional and subregional measures of transparency in relation to arms transfers by means of consultations, arrangements and agreements. The wider sharing of information on defence might be reflected in the provision of information to the United Nations or in the context of possible regional arrangements or both.

. . .

On 9 December 1991, on the recommendation of the First Committee, the General Assembly adopted resolution 46/36 L by recorded vote.

Transparency in armaments
The General Assembly,

. . .

7. *Requests* the Secretary-General to establish and maintain at United Nations Headquarters in New York a universal and non-discriminatory Register of Conventional Arms, to include data on international arms transfers as well as information provided by Member States on military holdings, procurement through national production and relevant policies, as set out in paragraph 10 below and in accordance with procedures and input requirements initially comprising those set out in the annex to the present resolution and subsequently incorporating any adjustments to the annex decided upon by the General Assembly at its forty-seventh session in the light of the recommendations of the panel referred to in paragraph 8 below;

8. *Also requests* the Secretary-General, with the assistance of a panel of governmental technical experts to be nominated by him on the basis of equitable geographical representation, to elaborate the technical procedures and to make any adjustments to the annex to the present resolution necessary for the effective operation of the Register, and to prepare a report on the modalities for early expansion of the scope of the Register by the addition of further categories of equipment and inclusion of data on military holdings and procurement through national production, and to report to the General Assembly at its forty-seventh session;

9. *Calls upon* all Member States to provide annually for the Register data on imports and exports of arms in accordance with the procedures established by paragraphs 7 and 8 above;

10. *Invites* Member States, pending the expansion of the Register, also to provide to the Secretary-General, with their annual report on imports and exports of arms, available background information regarding their military holdings, procurement through national production and relevant policies, and requests the Secretary-General to record this material and to make it available for consultation by Member States at their request;

. . .

ANNEX
Register of conventional arms

1. The Register of Conventional Arms ("the Register") shall be established, with effect from 1 January 1992, and maintained at the Headquarters of the United Nations in New York.

2. Concerning international arms transfers:

(a) Member States are requested to provide data for the Register, addressed to the Secretary-General, on the number of items in the following categories of equipment imported into or exported from their territory:

I. *Battle tanks*

A tracked or wheeled self-propelled armoured fighting vehicle with high cross-country mobility and a high level of self-protection, weighing at least 16.5 metric tonnes unladen weight, with a high muzzle velocity direct fire main gun of at least 75 millimetres calibre.

II. *Armoured combat vehicles*

A tracked or wheeled self-propelled vehicle, with armoured protection and cross-country capability, either: (a) designed and equipped to transport a squad of four or more infantrymen, or (b) armed with an integral or organic weapon of at least 20 millimetres calibre or an anti-tank missile launcher.

III. *Large calibre artillery systems*

A gun, howitzer, artillery piece combining the characteristics of a gun and a howitzer, mortar or multiple-launch rocket system, capable of engaging surface targets by delivering primarily indirect fire, with a calibre of 100 millimetres and above.

IV. *Combat aircraft*

A fixed-wing or variable-geometry wing aircraft armed and equipped to engage targets by employing guided missiles, unguided rockets, bombs, guns, cannons, or other weapons of destruction.

V. *Attack helicopters*

A rotary-wing aircraft equipped to employ anti-armour, air-to-ground, or air-to-air guided weapons and equipped with an integrated fire control and aiming system for these weapons.

VI. *Warships*

A vessel or submarine with a standard displacement of 850 metric tonnes or above, armed or equipped for military use.

VII. *Missiles or missile systems*

A guided rocket, ballistic or cruise missile capable of delivering a payload to a range of at least 25 kilometres, or a vehicle, apparatus or device designed or modified for launching such munitions.

(b) Data on imports provided under the present paragraph shall also specify the supplying State; data on exports shall also specify the recipient State and the State of origin if not the exporting State;

(c) Each Member State is requested to provide data on an annual basis by 30 April each year in respect of imports into and exports from their territory in the previous calendar year;

(d) The first such registration shall take place by 30 April 1993 in respect of the calendar year 1992;

(e) The data so provided shall be recorded in respect of each Member State;

(f) Arms "exports and imports" represent in the present resolution, including its annex, all forms of arms transfers under terms of grant, credit, barter or cash.

3. Concerning other interrelated information:

(a) Member States are invited also to provide to the Secretary-General available background information regarding their military holdings, procurement through national production, and relevant policies;

(b) The information so provided shall be recorded in respect of each Member State.

4. The Register shall be open for consultation by representatives of Member States at any time.

5. In addition, the Secretary-General shall provide annually a consolidated report to the General Assembly of the data registered, together with an index of the other interrelated information.

[YUN 1991, pp. 55-59]

Other issues

Disarmament decades

The General Assembly had in 1959 (resolution 1378(XIV)) proclaimed the goal of general and complete disarmament and in 1961 (resolution 1722(XVI)) welcomed the agreed principles for disarmament negotiations by the United States and the USSR. Ten years later, in 1969, the goal was far from being achieved. Therefore, in the light of the increased militarization of States and the ever-present threat of nuclear war, the United Nations declared the 1970s, the 1980s and the 1990s as disarmament decades.

First Disarmament Decade

On 16 December 1969, the General Assembly adopted a resolution (2602 E (XXIV)) by which, among other things, it declared the 1970s as a Disarmament Decade and took decisions concerning the work of the Conference of the Committee on Disarmament (CCD). . . .

By the operative paragraphs of this resolution, the Assembly: (1) declared the 1970s as a Disarmament Decade; (2) called upon Governments to intensify without delay their concerned and concentrated efforts for effective measures relating to the cessation of the nuclear arms race at an early date and to nuclear disarmament and the elimination of other weapons of mass destruction, and for a treaty on general and complete disarmament under strict and effective international control; (3) requested the Conference of the Committee on Disarmament to resume its work as early as possible, bearing in mind that the ultimate goal was general and complete disarmament; (4) further requested CCD, while continuing intensive negotiations with a view to reaching the widest possible agreement on collateral measures, to work out at the same time a comprehensive programme, dealing with all aspects of the problem of the cessation of the arms race and general and complete disarmament under effective international control, which would provide the Conference with a guideline to chart the course of its further work and to report thereon to the General Assembly at its twenty-fifth (1970) session; (5) decided to draw the attention of CCD to all pertinent proposals made during the First Committee's debates on disarmament; (6) recommended that consideration be given to channelling a substantial part of the resources freed by measures in the field of disarmament to promote the economic development of developing countries and, in particular, their scientific and technological progress; (7) requested the Secretary-General and Governments to publicize the Disarmament Decade; and (8) requested the Secretary-General to provide all appropriate facilities to further the implementation of this resolution.

[YUN 1969, p. 17]

Second Disarmament Decade

. . . The General Assembly on 3 December 1980 adopted, without vote, the Declaration of the 1980s as the Second Disarmament Decade. The Declaration, whose elements had been prepared by the Disarmament Commission in May/June, was annexed to Assembly resolution 35/46. . . .

The Declaration consisted of three main sections. A "General" section (section I) enumerated the objectives of the first Disarmament Decade (the 1970s) and briefly outlined the situation at the end of those 10 years, which had ended without the accomplishment of those objectives, although some limited agreements had been reached. . . .

Section II, on "Goals and principles," listed the aims and expectations of the Decade. Consistent with the overall objective of general and complete disarmament under effective international control, the goals of the Decade should include: halting and reversing the arms race, particularly the nuclear arms race; concluding and implementing agreements on disarmament, particularly nuclear disarmament; strengthening international peace and security; and making available a substantial part of the resources released by disarmament measures to attain the objectives of the Third United Nations Development Decade (the 1980s). . . .

Section III of the Declaration set out in eight subsections the priorities and main areas on which attention should be focused. The Decade should witness renewed intensification of efforts to reach agreement and implement disarmament measures leading to discernible progress towards the ultimate goal. Special attention should be focused on certain identifiable elements in the Assembly's 1978 Programme of Action. The comprehensive programme of disarmament should be elaborated with a view to its adoption at the 1982 special session.

[YUN 1980, p. 93]

Third Disarmament Decade

On 4 December 1990, the General Assembly declared the 1990s as the Third Disarmament Decade (resolution 45/62 A) and adopted the text of the following Declaration:

Declaration of the 1990s as the Third Disarmament Decade

1. The present Declaration of the 1990s as the Third Disarmament Decade is addressed to the global community and deals with the hopes and aspirations of people for lasting peace and security.

2. After a period of heightened tensions, the latter part of the decade of the 1980s saw a noticeable improvement in the way many States conducted their relations with one another. Despite this favourable trend, the specific goals of the Second Disarmament Decade were not fully realized.

3. In a world of growing interdependence, it is essential for the international community to stimulate and deepen awareness of the common interests of the global society and of the universal interest in achieving disarmament and strengthening international peace and security. The challenges facing the international community today are enormous. Accordingly, the solution of these difficult and complex issues will require the political will of States in conducting dialogue and negotiations and in promoting international co-operation, including confidence-building measures aimed at reducing tensions and the risk of military confrontation among States, bearing in mind specific conditions prevailing in the region concerned. It will also require acknowledgement of the profound interrelationship of questions relating to disarmament, social and economic development and environmental protection.

4. The international community stands on common ground in determining to make progress in the 1990s by resolutely pursuing disarmament along with other efforts necessary for attaining genuine peace and security. As members of the international community, we have identified the following common goals. In the nuclear field, we must continue urgently to seek early reductions in, and the eventual elimination of, nuclear weapons and work towards a comprehensive nuclear-test ban. To achieve the objective of non-proliferation in all its aspects, all States are encouraged to make every effort further to strengthen the non-proliferation régime and other measures to halt and prevent the proliferation of nuclear weapons. The aim of the international community should be to promote co-operation in the peaceful use of nuclear energy on a non-discriminatory basis and under agreed and appropriate international safeguards. The prevention of an arms race in outer space remains an important area to be further addressed. Many States also see the need to address naval confidence-building measures and disarmament issues. In the conventional field, we must seek reductions in arms and armed forces in all areas of the world and, in particular, where levels of concentrations of armaments are highest. In this regard, we urgently seek the successful conclusion of the negotiations on conventional forces in Europe. We aim for continued consideration of arms transfers in all their aspects. In the chemical field, we must work for the earliest conclusion of a convention on the prohibition of the development, production, stockpiling and use of all chemical weapons and on their destruction. The international community also calls for strict compliance with the Protocol for the Prohibition of the Use in War of Asphyxiating, Poisonous or Other Gases, and of Bacteriological Methods of Warfare, signed at Geneva on 17 June 1925. As further steps forward, openness and transparency on all appropriate military matters should be developed, the scope and techniques of verification advanced, the use of science and technology for peaceful purposes promoted and non-military threats to security addressed. All other initiatives to halt and reverse the arms race, in particular the nuclear-arms race, in both its qualitative and quantitative aspects deserve careful consideration. Such initiatives include the establishment of nuclear-weapon-free zones on the basis of arrangements freely arrived at among States of the region concerned and the creation of zones of peace under appropriate conditions defined and determined freely by the States concerned in the zone. In the pursuit of the foregoing goals, the international community acknowledges the particular responsibility of countries with the largest military arsenals. Resources freed through disarmament could be used for the benefit of a balanced world development. These goals should be included in a comprehensive programme of disarmament, which should be concluded at an appropriate time.

5.   The United Nations will continue to foster multi-lateral co-operation for disarmament, wherein bilateral and regional efforts can be complementary and mutually supportive in attaining the purposes and principles of the United Nations. The international community can further promote disarmament through the United Nations by building upon its achievements in this field, including the Final Document of the Tenth Special Session of the General Assembly, which was adopted by consensus.

6.   The international community affirms the positive role that an informed public can play in the process of disarmament by promoting a constructive and realistic dialogue on issues related to disarmament. In this regard, the pursuit of the World Disarmament Campaign and the observance of Disarmament Week will continue to play a useful role. Reflecting a growing understanding and commitment in dealing with the global problems of peace and security, it recognizes that non-governmental organizations play an invaluable role. It also supports an enhanced role for women in developing the conditions for enduring peace.

7.   As the world moves towards the twenty-first century, it is evident that future generations will need increasing knowledge and understanding of the interdependent nature of life on the planet. Education on international peace and security issues will play a fundamental part in allowing every individual to realize his or her role as a responsible member of the world community.

By a 1994 resolution (49/75 B), the General Assembly called for a review and appraisal of the implementation of the Declaration.

World disarmament conference

The Ad Hoc Committee on the World Disarmament Conference held two sessions in 1980. At the final meeting, on 20 June, it unanimously adopted its report to the General Assembly.

In its report, the Ad Hoc Committee stated that it had maintained close contact, through its Chairman, with the representatives of the nuclear-weapon States, and set out the information gained from those contacts. The USSR continued to stress the need to convene a world disarmament conference, to make it possible to concentrate government attention and world public opinion on the solution of the question of how to halt the arms race and move forward to real disarmament. The four other nuclear Powers maintained their reservations on the practicability or value of such a conference.

The Committee reiterated that the idea of a world disarmament conference had received wide support from United Nations Member States with varying degrees of emphasis and differences. It was also evident that no consensus with respect to the convening of such a conference under current conditions had been reached among the nuclear-weapon States, whose participation was generally deemed essential. It suggested the Assembly might wish to decide that, after its 1982 special session, such a conference would take place, as soon as the necessary consensus was reached.

On 12 December, the General Assembly adopted, without vote, resolution 35/151 by which it renewed the mandate of the Ad Hoc Committee and requested it to maintain close contact with nuclear-weapon and other States.

General Assembly special sessions on disarmament

From 23 May to 1 July 1978, towards the close of the first Disarmament Decade, the General Assembly held its tenth special session, the first to be devoted to disarmament. The holding of a special session devoted to disarmament was originally proposed by the first Conference of Heads of State or Government of Non-Aligned Countries in 1961. It laid the foundation of an international disarmament strategy aimed at general and complete disarmament under effective international control.

On 30 June 1978, at the end of the special session, the General Assembly adopted resolution S-10/2 by which it adopted also the Final Document which set out a broad framework for further efforts by the United Nations in the field of disarmament. The Final Document was composed of four sections: an introduction, a Declaration, a Programme of Action, and recommendations concerning new international machinery for disarmament negotiations.

Other special sessions of the Assembly devoted to disarmament were held in 1982 and 1988, but did not result in substantive final documents. In 1994 (resolution 49/75 I), the Assembly decided, in principle, to convene, in 1997 if possible, the fourth special session on disarmament, the date to be determined in 1995.

World Disarmament Campaign

In the Final Document of the tenth special session of the General Assembly, Governments and governmental and non-governmental organizations were urged to develop programmes of education for disarmament to create a greater understanding and awareness of the need for disarmament. In 1982, the Secretary-General, in a report to the General Assembly, outlined a programme for a world disarmament campaign which was launched at the twelfth special session of the Assembly, the second devoted to disarmament, held in 1982.

The World Disarmament Campaign, aimed at informing, educating and generating public understanding and support for the disarmament objectives of the United Nations, was launched by the General Assembly on 7 June 1982, at the start of its second special session devoted to disarmament. In December, the Assembly approved the general framework for the Campaign and a 1983 programme of activities. It also invited Member States to co-operate with the United Nations to ensure a better flow of information on disarmament and called on them to encourage their citizens to express their views on disarmament questions.

. . .

The Secretary-General proposed a series of activities for 1983, selected on the basis of their immediate impact, their multiplier effect and their ability to be carried out without extensive preparation. This programme called for the production of United Nations publications and audio-visual materials, interpersonal communication through such means as seminars and training, special events including Disarmament Week activities, publicity for the Campaign, and activities by United Nations information centres and other field offices.

. . .

On 13 December 1982, the General Assembly adopted three resolutions dealing with the World Disarmament Campaign (resolutions 37/100 H, 37/100 I and 37/100 J).

By one of these, the Assembly approved the general framework of the Campaign as specified by the Secretary-General, including the submission of an annual report to the Assembly, as well as his proposals for a programme of activities for 1983. The Assembly again invited Member States to make voluntary contributions and decided to hold a pledging conference in 1983.

. . .

By another resolution, Member States were invited, in implementing activities for the Campaign, to take into account views expressed at the special session, including the proposal on a worldwide collection of signatures in support of disarmament. They were also invited to co-operate with the United Nations to ensure a better flow of disarmament information and to avoid disseminating false and tendentious information.

. . .

By the third resolution, adopted without vote, the Assembly called on Member States to facilitate the flow of a broad range of accurate information on disarmament matters, both governmental and non-governmental, to and among their citizens, so as to advance the objectives of the Campaign and of general and complete disarmament under effective international control. Member States were also called upon to encourage their citizens freely and publicly to express their views on disarmament questions and to organize and meet publicly for that purpose. The Secretary-General was requested to report to the Assembly annually on implementation of the resolution.

. . .

In a 10 December resolution (resolution 37/94 B) on United Nations public information activities, based on the recommendations of the Committee on Information, the Assembly requested the Secretary-General to ensure that the Campaign gave full consideration to the role of mass media as the most effective way to promote in world public opinion a climate of understanding, confidence and co-operation conducive to peace and disarmament.

(YUN 1982, pp. 31 and 33-34)

In 1992 (resolution 47/53 D), the General Assembly decided that the World Disarmament Campaign would henceforth be known as the United Nations Disarmament Information Programme with the following constituencies: elected representatives, research institutes, educational communities, non-governmental organizations and the media.

Disarmament and development

In 1977, the General Assembly (resolution 32/88 A) expressed concern over the vast human and material resources being spent on armaments and agreed to initiate a study on the relationship between disarmament and development.

The subject was further considered at the tenth and twelfth special sessions of the Assembly devoted to disarmament which noted the vast increase worldwide in military budgets. In 1984, the Assembly decided to hold an International Conference on the Relationship between Disarmament and Development (resolution 39/160).

Conference on the relationship between disarmament and development

The International Conference on the Relationship between Disarmament and Development, convened in August/September 1987, considered the relationship in all its aspects, the implications of the level and magnitude of continuing military expenditures, and ways and means of releasing additional resources through disarmament measures. It adopted by consensus a Final Document, aimed at fostering an interrelated perspective on disarmament, development and security, and promoting multilateralism and strengthening the central role of the United Nations in that regard.

In November, the General Assembly welcomed the adoption of the Final Document, requested the Secretary-General to implement the Document's action programme, and requested the Preparatory Committee for the Assembly's third (1988) special session on disarmament to include a relevant item on that session's agenda (resolution 42/45).

(YUN 1987, pp. 82-83)

At the third special session devoted to disarmament, in May/June 1988, a proposal was made regarding the relationship between disarmament and development. The Assembly, however, did not take action on any of the proposals submitted and was unable to reach agreement on a concluding document.

Follow-up

In accordance with the recommendation contained in the Final Document of the International Conference, a High-Level Task Force in May 1988 identified areas of specific activities in the area of development and disarmament which included: monitoring trends in military spending; facilitating exchange of experiences in conversion from military to civilian production; and promoting collective knowledge of non-military threats to international security. In 1990, the Task Force felt that the international situation called for a closer look at the economic aspects of disarmament, including its implications for national and global economy. It decided to continue work on the earlier activities as well as on new projects on the impact of arms reductions on the world economy and a publicity and information strategy. A conference was held in Moscow in August 1990 on "Conversion: economic adjustments in an era of arms reduction". The United Nations has established a theoretical framework of indicators for measuring military expenditures as well as to examine the post-cold-war developments for maximizing the benefits from arms reduction.

As a result of the end of the cold war, there have been some peace dividends: global military spending has declined by almost a quarter since 1987, reflecting approximately 4 per cent per annum reduction by the United States and former USSR and about 2 per cent a year by the developing countries, giving a saving of some $935 billion.

The 1995 Review and Extension Conference of the Parties to the Treaty on the Non-Proliferation of Nuclear Weapons was held in New York from 17 April to 12 May. The Conference reviewed the implementation of the Treaty, which entered into force in 1970, and decided to extend it indefinitely.

This landmark international treaty has the objective of preventing the spread of nuclear weapons and weapons technology and furthering the goal of general and complete disarmament. It has been ratified by 178 countries at the time of the Conference—more than any other arms limitation and disarmament agreement. Along with other measures in the nuclear non-proliferation regime, it has succeeded in stemming the proliferation of nuclear weapons and in reducing existing arsenals. The outcome of the Conference has significant impact on the non-proliferation regime, military expenditures and thus on international peace and security.

The future of the peace dividend will, however, depend on a more aggressive strategy of disarmament in the developing countries and investing resources released from armaments into human development. Peace and development are intertwined and mutually reinforcing. One will not flourish without the other.

PART TWO

International law

"All Members shall settle their international disputes by peaceful means . . . parties to any dispute, the continuance of which is likely to endanger the maintenance of international peace and security, shall, first of all, seek a solution by negotiation, enquiry, mediation, conciliation, arbitration, judicial settlement . . . "

Chapter I

Judicial settlement of international disputes

The United Nations was charged under the Charter to promote the settlement of international disputes by peaceful means, in conformity with the principles of justice and international law. Among the methods of peaceful settlement of disputes, the Charter specifies arbitration and judicial settlement.

International Court of Justice

The International Court of Justice is the principal judicial organ of the United Nations. Its Statute, which is based on the Statute of the Permanent Court of International Justice that functioned under the League of Nations, forms an integral part of the United Nations Charter.

The Court has a dual role: to settle in accordance with international law the legal disputes submitted to it by States, and to give advisory opinions on legal questions referred to it by duly authorized international organs and agencies.

Only States may apply to and appear before the Court. The States Members of the United Nations (at present numbering 185), and two States not Members (Nauru and Switzerland) which have become parties to the Court's Statute, are so entitled.

Both the General Assembly and the Security Council may request from the Court an advisory opinion on any legal question; other United Nations organs and the specialized agencies, when authorized by the Assembly, may also request an advisory opinion on legal matters within the scope of their activities.

In accordance with Article 25 of its Statute, the Court generally sits in its full composition. However, the Statute also provides for the possibility of Chambers of the Court dealing with a case. With a view to the speedy dispatch of business, the Court annually forms a Chamber of Summary Procedure. In 1993, in view of the developments in the field of environmental law and protection that took place in the preceding few years, and considering that it should be prepared to the fullest possible extent to deal with any environmental case falling within its jurisdiction, the Court created a seven-member Chamber for Environmental Matters. The Court has further in four cases, upon the request of the Parties, formed a so-called ad hoc Chamber.

Establishment of the Court

In 1942, during the Second World War, the United States Secretary of State, the Foreign Secretary of the United Kingdom and the Inter-American Juridical Committee declared themselves in favour of the continuation of an international court after the war.

In 1943, the United Kingdom took the initiative to establish an Informal Inter-Allied Committee of 12 international legal experts, which presented a report in early 1944. In that report, the Committee concluded that the Permanent Court of International Justice had on the whole functioned well and that its Statute should be used as a basis for any new international court. It further recommended retaining the advisory jurisdiction, but did not consider that the new court should have compulsory jurisdiction or deal with essentially political matters.

In the Moscow Declaration on General Security of 30 October 1943, the four Allied Powers—China, the USSR, the United Kingdom and the United States—recognized the necessity "of establishing at the earliest practicable date a general international organization, based on the principle of the sovereign equality of all peace-loving States, and open to membership by all such States, large and small, for the maintenance of international peace and security". Following that Declaration, the four Powers exchanged views at Dumbarton Oaks, resulting in proposals (bearing the name of that place) which provided for the establishment of a general international organization, the principal judicial organ of which was to be an International Court of Justice.

The United States, acting on behalf of itself and the other Governments sponsoring the San Francisco Conference, invited a Committee of Jurists to meet in Washington, D.C., to prepare a draft statute of the Court and to submit it to the Conference. Jurists from 44 countries met in April 1945 and used the Statute of the Permanent Court as a basis to draft the Court's statute. The Committee did not reach agreement on the nomination of the judges to the Court or on the question of obligatory jurisdiction. It called to the attention of the Conference the importance of formulating rules for execution of the Court's decisions and the necessity of adjusting the situation with regard to States parties to the Statute of the Permanent Court but not Members of the United Nations.

Chapter VII of the Dumbarton Oaks Proposals and the report of the Committee of Jurists constituted the agenda of Conference Committee IV/1. The basic question that that Committee had to resolve was whether the Court should have *ipso facto* compulsory jurisdiction over the Member States of the United Nations and, in view of a decision on that question, whether the Permanent Court of International Justice should be continued or an entirely new court created as a principal organ of the United Nations, on the same footing as the General Assembly, the Security Council, the Economic and Social Council, the Trusteeship Council and the Secretariat. The Committee recommended the establishment of a new court, with provisions to be incorporated in the Charter under which all United Nations Members were *ipso facto* parties to the Statute of the International Court of Justice and a non-member could become a party on conditions to be determined by the Assembly on the recommendation of the Security Council.

The Committee recommended that each Member State undertake to comply with the decision of the Court in any case to which it was a party. It added another provision to the effect that, should any party fail to comply with the Court's decision, the other party could have recourse to the Security Council, which might make recommendations or decide on measures to give effect to the decision.

With regard to the nomination of judges, the Committee decided to recommend nomination by national groups. It recommended that both the General Assembly and the Security Council take part in the elections, with an absolute majority required by each body.

The Committee proposed that the procedure in amending the Statute be the same as that in amending the Charter, but it added that the Court itself should have the power to propose amendments to its Statute.

The Court thus differed from its predecessor, the Permanent Court of International Justice, in that it was created on a basis of equality with the other principal organs as the principal judicial organ of the United Nations. And, as recently observed by the President of the Court in an address to the General Assembly, "As such, the Court is clearly an essential part not just of the machinery for the peaceful settlement of disputes set up by the Charter, but also of the general system for the maintenance of international peace and security that it introduced . . . the Court has always considered the referral of a dispute to more than one principal organ as not, in itself, constituting any impediment to its performance of its duty". It has consequently, in a number of cases, been able to contribute to the maintenance or restoration of peace between the parties in a dispute. The Court's Judgment of February 1994 in the case concerning the territorial dispute between the Libyan Arab Jamahiriya and Chad is only the most recent example.

The first election for the membership of the Court took place in February 1946. The Court held its inaugural sitting in the Peace Palace in The Hague on 18 April of that year.

In May 1946, Rules of Court were adopted, which were based on the Rules of the Permanent Court, with certain formal and substantive changes. From 1946 to 1972, the Rules remained unchanged, although from time to time the Court, which keeps its procedure under constant review, considered their modification. In 1967, a revision was undertaken which led to the adoption in 1972 of some partial amendments of immediate interest. The revision was subsequently resumed and culminated in 1978 in the adoption of a new set of Rules.

By a 1946 decision of the Court, its internal judicial practice was governed until 1968 by the resolution of the Permanent Court, dating from 1931 and amended in 1936. In 1968, the Court adopted a new resolution which it revised in 1976.

Since its inauguration in 1946, the Court has had before it 73 contentious cases, 11 of which are still pending. It has handed down 21 advisory opinions, with two more requests still before it.

Cases before the Court have covered a broad spectrum, ranging from disputes concerning land frontiers and maritime boundaries, territorial sovereignty, the non-use of force, non-interference in the internal affairs of States, diplomatic relations, hostage-taking, the right of asylum, nationality and guardianship to those over rights of passage and economic rights.

Territorial disputes

A number of cases in this field, including ones involving situations of high tension and eventually armed confrontation, were brought before the Court.

In a 1953 case between France and the United Kingdom involving territorial rights, the Court found that certain Channel islets were under British sovereignty. In 1959, it upheld Belgium's claims to an enclave near its frontier with the Netherlands. In 1960, the Court found that India had not acted contrary to the obligations imposed on it by the existence of Portugal's right of passage between enclaves. And in 1962, it decided that the Temple of Preah Vihear was situated on Cambodian territory and that Thailand had to withdraw its military or police force.

Fighting took place while the delimitation of the frontier between Burkina Faso and Mali was pending before a Chamber of the Court. Its decision of 1986 was, however, accepted by the two countries, the Presidents of which sent appreciative letters to the President of the Court. Another case before a Chamber, also involving territorial claims, was between El Salvador and Honduras. Having originated at the beginning of the century and having led to a war between the two countries in 1969, the dispute was solved to their satisfaction by the Court's delimitation of the frontier.

In February 1994, the Court delivered its Judgment on the territorial dispute between the Libyan Arab Jamahiriya and Chad; it found that the boundary between the two States was defined and determined by a treaty concluded in 1955 between France and the Jamahiriya. In May 1994, the Security Council established the United Nations Aouzou Strip Observer Group to observe implementation of an April agreement whereby the parties pledged to abide by the Court's Judgment. By the end of May, all Libyan troops had been withdrawn from the Strip.

Court deliberations on maritime delimitation and territorial questions between Qatar and Bahrain are ongoing; in a Judgment of February 1995, the Court found that it had jurisdiction to adjudicate on the dispute and that the application of Qatar was admissible. In 1994, Cameroon instituted proceedings against Nigeria in a case in which the Court was requested to determine the land frontier between the two countries from Lake Chad to the sea, as well as part of the maritime boundary.

Law of the sea issues

Other cases involved the law of the sea. In 1949, the Court found Albania responsible for damage caused by mines in its territorial waters to British warships exercising the right of innocent passage. In a fisheries dispute between the United Kingdom and Norway, the Court defined a number of basic criteria governing the delimitation of territorial waters and held, in its 1951 Judgment, that the method employed by Norway in delimiting its territorial waters was not contrary to international law. In 1974, the Court found that Iceland was not entitled unilaterally to exclude fishing vessels of the United Kingdom and the Federal Republic of Germany from areas between fishery limits agreed in 1961 and the 50-mile limit proclaimed by Iceland in 1972.

The Court has further played an active role in the determination of the criteria for the delimitation of the continental shelf. In 1969, at the request of Denmark, the Federal Republic of Germany and the Netherlands, the Court indicated the principles and rules of international law applicable to the delimitation of the areas of the North Sea continental shelf appertaining to each of them. In 1982, at the request of Tunisia and the Libyan Arab Jamahiriya, and in 1985, in a case referred to it by the Libyan Arab Jamahiriya and Malta, the Court indicated the principles and rules of international law applicable to the delimitation of the areas of the Mediterranean continental shelf appertaining to each of them, respectively. In 1984, a Chamber of the Court determined the course of the maritime boundary dividing the continental shelf and fisheries zones of Canada and the United States in the Gulf of Maine area. In 1993, the Court delivered a Judgment determining the delimitation line that divided the continental shelf and fisheries zones of Denmark and Norway. A case on the subject of maritime boundaries between Guinea-Bissau and Senegal is still pending. The Court's rulings on the delimitation of fishing rights and of the continental shelf established precedents which contributed to the work of the Third United Nations Conference on the Law of the Sea in formulating the Convention on the Law of the Sea.

Jurisdictional, diplomatic and consular issues

In the beginning of the 1950s, the Court dealt with several cases between Colombia and Peru concerning the granting of asylum in the Colombian Embassy at Lima to a Peruvian national named Víctor Raúl Haya de la Torre. Other cases involved the rights of United States nationals in Morocco (France v. United States, 1951) and a question of nationality (Liechtenstein v. Guatemala, 1955).

In 1980, in a case concerning the seizure of the United States Embassy at Tehran, Iran, and the detention of its diplomatic and consular staff, the Court ruled that Iran must release the hostages, hand back the Embassy and make reparation. Before the Court had occasion to set the amount of reparation, the case was withdrawn following agreement reached between the two States. Another case concerns the downing of an Iranian aircraft in July 1988 by the guided-missile cruiser USS *Vincennes*; Iran asked the Court in 1989 to condemn the incident and find the United States responsible to pay compensation. The hearings in that case, to be held in September 1994, were postponed *sine die* at the request of the two Parties.

Commercial disputes

The Court has also dealt with several cases involving commercial disputes. In a 1952 Judgment, in a case between Greece and the United Kingdom, the Court held that it had jurisdiction to decide whether the United Kingdom was under a duty to submit the dispute to arbitration, but that it was not competent to deal with the merits of the claims made by Nicolas Ambatielos, a Greek national. In a further Judgment, of 1953, the Court decided that the United Kingdom should submit to arbitration. In two subsequent cases (France v. Norway, 1957; Switzerland v. United States, 1957) the Court found that it had no jurisdiction. In a case brought by Belgium against Spain, first in 1958 and again in 1962, the Court rejected the claim by Belgium that it could exercise diplomatic protection of shareholders in a Canadian company in respect of measures taken against that company in Spain. And in a case of the United States against Italy, the Court found, in a 1989 Judgment, that Italy had not violated the Treaty of Friendship, Commerce and Navigation by its actions with regard to the bankruptcy as an Italian company which was wholly owned by two United States corporations.

The law of international organizations

Certain advisory opinions requested by the General Assembly concerned relations between the United Nations and its Members. The first two opinions treated the procedure for the admission of new Members. In 1949, by an opinion on a question put after the assassination of the United Nations Mediator in Palestine, the Court found that the United Nations had international legal personality and the capacity to maintain a claim for reparation from a Member for injuries to an agent of the Organization. In an advisory opinion of 1962, again requested by the Assembly, regarding the expenses incurred for peace-keeping operations in the Congo and the Middle East—expenditures which were opposed by several States—the Court found that the expenditures were legitimate expenses of the Organization and that they should be borne by the Member States as apportioned by the Assembly. In 1988, the Court expressed the opinion that by virtue of the 1947 Agreement between the United Nations and the United States of America regarding the Headquarters of the United Nations, the United States was under the obligation to submit to arbitration a dispute with the United Nations concerning an order to close the office maintained by the Palestine Liberation Organization observer mission in New York. An opinion rendered by the Court in 1989 concerned a request submitted by the Economic and Social Council on the applicability to a former human rights rapporteur of certain provisions of the 1946 Convention on the Privileges and Immunities of the United Nations.

In a 1960 opinion, the Court replied in the negative to a question of whether the Maritime Safety Committee had been constituted in accordance with the Convention for the establishment of the Inter-Governmental Maritime Consultative Organization (now the International Maritime Organization). And in a 1980 opinion, the Court indicated which obligations derived for the World Health Organization (WHO) and Egypt from the Agreement of 1951 concerning the WHO Regional Office for the Eastern Mediterranean Region.

In a contentious case of 1972 between India and Pakistan, the Court found that the Council of the International Civil Aviation Organization had jurisdiction to deal with a case of suspension by India of overflights of its territory by Pakistani civil aircraft.

Decolonization questions

In the area of decolonization, the Court's decisions were crucial in creating or reinforcing a legal framework for the General Assembly in 1966 to terminate South Africa's Mandate over Namibia, formerly South West Africa, which finally resulted in the independence of that country in 1990. The Court further made a considerable contribution to the development of the law of self-determination and had occasion to confirm that the protection of basic human rights is an obligation deriving from the United Nations Charter and the rules of international law. In a 1950 advisory opinion, requested by the Assembly, the Court found that South Africa was under the obligation to give an account to the United Nations of its administration of the League of Nations–mandated Territory and that it had no competence to modify unilaterally the international status of the Territory. However, the effort by Ethiopia and Liberia, in 1960, to bring a case against South Africa failed when a divided Court, seven to seven, ultimately rejected the claims of the two African States through a tie-breaking vote of the President. In 1971, the Court issued a further advisory opinion, requested of it by the Security Council, on the question of Namibia and found that South Africa's continued presence in Namibia was illegal and that South Africa was under an obligation to withdraw its administration immediately. It also found that Member States of the United Nations were under an obligation to recognize the illegality of South Africa's presence in Namibia and the invalidity of its acts concerning Namibia, and to refrain from any acts implying recognition of the legality of, or lending support or assistance to, such presence and administration.

Another advisory opinion, requested by the Assembly, concerned Western Sahara, a Non-Self-Governing Territory to which both Morocco and Mauritania laid claim. The Court found in 1975 that neither country had established any ties of territorial sovereignty and that there were no impediments to decolonization, in particular to the application of the principle of self-determination through the free and genuine expression of the will of the peoples of Western Sahara.

Questions of international peace and security

A dispute affecting international peace and security was brought by Nicaragua in the 1984 complaint of military and paramilitary activities against it by the United States. The United States, however, refused to recognize the 1986 Judgment by which the Court determined that it had acted in breach of its obligations towards Nicaragua by laying mines outside that country's ports and by supporting the contras there and that it should make reparation. Nicaragua's request that the Court determine the amount of reparation was withdrawn in 1991. In 1986, Nicaragua also brought proceedings against both Costa Rica and Honduras, alleging their responsibility in connection with armed activities in border areas. The two cases were later withdrawn.

In 1992, the Libyan Arab Jamahiriya brought cases against the United Kingdom and the United States concerning the crash of a Pan Am flight over Lockerbie, Scotland, on 21 December 1988. In 1993, Bosnia and Herzegovina instituted a case against Yugoslavia (Serbia and Montenegro) for violating the 1948 Convention on the Prevention and Punishment of the Crime of Genocide. These two cases are still pending.

"The General Assembly shall initiate studies and make recommendations for the purpose of . . . encouraging the progressive development of international law and its codification"

Chapter II

Development and codification of international law

The General Assembly, at the first part of its first session from 10 January to 14 February 1946, considered the issue of the development and codification of international law. By a resolution of 10 February 1946, it instructed the Secretary-General to submit detailed proposals relating to the implementation of Article 102 of the Charter of the United Nations dealing with the registration and publication of treaties and international agreements entered into by any Member State of the United Nations.

Acting on the recommendation of the Sixth (Legal) Committee, the Assembly, on 14 December 1946, adopted the proposals of the Secretary-General to regulate the registration, filing, recording and publication of treaties and international agreements. The Assembly also established a Committee on the Progressive Development of International Law and Its Codification, which first met in New York from 12 May to 17 June 1947. The Committee recommended the creation of an International Law Commission to promote the progressive development of international law and its codification. On 21 November 1947, the General Assembly, by resolution 174(II), established the International Law Commission and approved its Statute. The Commission's sessions began in 1949.

Work of the International Law Commission

The Commission's work consists in the preparation of drafts on topics of international law. Some topics are chosen by the Commission itself, and others are referred to it by the General Assembly.

When the Commission completes draft articles on a particular topic, the General Assembly has usually, in the past, convened an international conference of plenipotentiaries to finalize and incorporate the draft articles into a convention, which is then open to States to become parties. In some cases, the finalization of the draft articles for incorporation into a convention has been carried out in the framework of the Sixth (Legal) Committee of the General Assembly. Occasionally, rather than becoming a convention, the draft articles have been drawn to the attention of States.

Among the important conventions which have originated in drafts prepared by the International Law Commission, the following may be mentioned: the 1958 Geneva Convention on the Territorial Sea and the Contiguous Zone; the 1958 Geneva Convention on the High Seas; the 1958 Geneva Convention on Fishing and Conservation of the Living Resources of the High Seas; the 1958 Geneva Convention on the Continental Shelf; the 1961 New York Convention on the Reduction of Statelessness; the 1961 Vienna Convention on Diplomatic Relations; the 1963 Vienna Convention on Consular Relations; the 1969 Convention on Special Missions; the 1969 Vienna Convention on the Law of Treaties; the 1973 New York Convention on the Prevention and Punishment of Crimes against Internationally Protected Persons, including Diplomatic Agents; the 1975 Vienna Convention on the Representation of States in Their Relations with International Organizations of a Universal Character; the 1978 Vienna Convention on Succession of States in Respect of Treaties; the 1983 Vienna Convention on Succession of States in respect of State Property, Archives and Debts; and the 1986 Vienna Convention on the Law of Treaties between States and International Organizations or between International Organizations.

Other important drafts prepared by the Commission, which have not become the subject of an international convention, are the 1949 draft declaration on rights and duties of States; the principles of international law recognized in the Charter of the Nürnberg Tribunal, formulated in 1950; the 1954 draft code of offences against the peace and security of mankind; the 1958 model rules on arbitral procedure; and the 1978 draft articles on most-favoured-nation clauses.

Recent drafts prepared by the Commission which are still being considered by the General Assembly include the following: the 1989 draft articles on the status of the diplomatic courier and the diplomatic bag not accompanied by diplomatic courier; the 1991 draft articles on jurisdictional immunities of States and their property; the 1994 draft articles on the law of non-navigational uses of international watercourses; and the 1994 draft statute for an international criminal court. The proposed establishment of a permanent international criminal court would be a major contribution to the rule of law and would complete the work begun by the United Nations almost half a century ago. As envisioned in the draft adopted by the Commission, the court would be established by treaty and would be a permanent institution which would act when called upon to consider a case. The court's jurisdiction would encompass serious crimes of international concern, including genocide, aggression, war crimes, crimes against humanity, terrorism and illicit drug trafficking.

Topics on which the Commission is currently working include State responsibility; international liability for injurious consequences arising out of acts not prohibited by international law; a draft code of crimes against the peace and security of mankind; reservations to treaties; and State succession and its impact on the nationality of national and legal persons.

Other multilateral agreements and international legal texts

In addition to the agreements, texts and topics referred to in the preceding sections, which relate to fundamental fields of general international law, the United Nations has secured the conclusion of many other international agreements, or has elaborated international legal texts intended to regulate areas of great interest in international relations. By December 1994, more than 465 such agreements and other texts had been adopted. They cover areas such as human rights, disarmament, outer space, economic development, crime prevention and criminal justice, environment, international trade and the law of the sea. In this overview, reference will be made to a representative cross-section of them, with emphasis on the most recent.

With regard to human rights, the United Nations has articulated values and negotiated agreements without precedent. In new areas of global concern, such as international terrorism, the environment, the sea, outer space, drug trafficking and others, its work has been pioneering.

The atrocities committed during the Second World War compelled the Organization to take strong measures in the protection of human rights. It adopted in 1948 the Convention on the Prevention and Punishment of the Crime of Genocide, which entered into force in 1951. It also adopted in 1948 the Universal Declaration of Human Rights. As an important step towards racial equality, the International Convention on the Elimination of All Forms of Racial Discrimination was adopted in 1965 and it entered into force four years later. The promotion of human rights was further reinforced by the adoption in 1966 of the International Covenant on Economic, Social and Cultural Rights and the International Covenant on Civil and Political Rights, which had been submitted to the General Assembly in 1954 for its consideration. Both Covenants entered into force in 1976. To ensure implementation of certain principles of the latter Covenant and of the Universal Declaration of Human Rights, the 1984 Convention against Torture and Other Cruel, Inhuman or Degrading Treatment or Punishment was adopted and entered into force in 1987. The International Convention on the Suppression and Punishment of the Crime of Apartheid, adopted in 1973 and in force since 1976, as well as the International Convention against Apartheid in Sports, adopted in 1985 and in force since 1988, were important contributions to the dismantling of the system of racial segregation in South Africa.

The United Nations has made significant progress to advance equal rights for women and to promote the rights of children in society. The Convention on the Elimination of All Forms of Discrimination against Women, adopted in 1979, entered into force in 1981. Special protection for children was advocated in the Convention on the Rights of the Child, which was adopted in 1989 — ten years after the International Year of the Child — and entered into force in 1990. Migrant workers were another group whose rights were to be safeguarded, under the International Convention on the Protection of the Rights of All Migrant Workers and Their Families, adopted in 1990.

Among recent activities, the Commission on Human Rights is elaborating a draft optional protocol to the Convention against Torture and Other Cruel, Inhuman or Degrading Treatment or Punishment in order to establish a preventive system of visits to places of detention. It is further working on an optional protocol to the Convention on the Rights of the Child, on the involvement of children in armed conflicts, and on a possible optional protocol to the same Convention on the sale of children, child prostitution and child pornography as well as the basic measures needed for their prevention and eradication. Among the questions being studied by the Commission's Subcommission on Prevention of Discrimination and Protection of Minorities is the right to a fair trial, including the possibility of a third optional protocol to the International Covenant on Civil and Political Rights.

To counter the rising trend in drug production, distribution and trade and the threat of trafficking organizations operating on a global scale, the United Nations Convention against Illicit Traffic in Narcotic Drugs and Psychotropic Substances was adopted in 1988; it entered into force in 1990. Recognizing that drug traffickers and mercenaries were increasingly linked in the perpetration of violent actions against the constitutional order and sovereignty of States, the General Assembly in 1989 adopted the International Convention against the Recruitment, Use, Financing and Training of Mercenaries.

In the area of disarmament, some of the most intensive multilateral negotiations took place in order to protect mankind from the scourge of modern warfare. The 1963 Treaty Banning Nuclear Weapon Tests in the Atmosphere, in Outer Space and under Water was the first instrument to control the disastrous effects of constant exposure to nuclear explosions.

Another notable achievement was the Treaty on the Non-Proliferation of Nuclear Weapons, adopted in 1968. This landmark international treaty, which entered into force in 1970, has the objective of preventing the spread of nuclear weapons and weapons technology and furthering the goal of general and complete disarmament. As at 31 March 1995, it had been ratified by 175 countries—more than any other arms limitation and disarmament agreement (see Figure 2, p. 140). Along with other measures in the nuclear non-proliferation regime, it has succeeded in stemming the proliferation of nuclear weapons and in reducing existing arsenals.

The 1995 Review and Extension Conference of the Parties to the Treaty on the Non-Proliferation of Nuclear Weapons was held in New York from 17 April to 12 May. The Conference reviewed the implementation of the Treaty and its possible extension. By the terms of three decisions and a resolution adopted without a vote on 11 May, the Conference indefinitely extended the Treaty, adopted principles and objectives for nuclear nonproliferation and disarmament, adopted a text on strengthening the Treaty review process and called for the establishment of a Middle East zone free of weapons of mass destruction—nuclear, chemical and biological.

Other valuable achievements in the area of disarmament include the 1971 Convention on the Prohibition of the Development, Production and Stockpiling of Bacteriological (Biological) and Toxin Weapons and on Their Destruction; and the 1980 Convention on Prohibitions or Restrictions on the Use of Certain Conventional Weapons Which May Be Deemed to Be Excessively Injurious or to Have Indiscriminate Effects.

The Conference on Disarmament continues to conduct multilateral negotiations on a universal and effectively verifiable comprehensive test-ban treaty. It is also exploring ways to undertake negotiations on a non-discriminatory, multilateral and effectively verifiable treaty banning the production of fissile material for nuclear weapons or other nuclear explosive devices. The Conference continues to deal with issues relevant to the prevention of an arms race in outer space. Following the establishment by the Secretary-General of the Register of Transfers of Conventional Arms with effect from 1 January 1992, the Conference continues to address the issue of transparency in armaments, with a view to elaborating universal and non-discriminatory practical means to increase openness with regard to the excessive and destabilizing accumulation of arms, military holdings, procurement through national production and transfer of high technology with military application and weapons of mass destruction.

In the area of economic development, the United Nations Conference on Trade and Development adopted in January 1994 the International Tropical Timber Agreement. The Uruguay Round of multilateral trade negotiations, held under the auspices of the General Agreement on Tariffs and Trade, was concluded with the signing of the Final Act in April 1994, resulting in, among other things, the adoption of an agreement establishing a World Trade Organization.

Since the creation of the United Nations Commission on International Trade Law (UNCITRAL) by the General Assembly in 1966, the following conventions originating in UNCITRAL's work have been adopted by the Assembly and opened to States to become parties: the 1974 Convention on the Limitation Period in the International Sale of Goods (New York); the 1980 United Nations Convention on Contracts for the International Sale of Goods (Vienna); the 1980 Vienna Protocol amending the Convention on the Limitation Period in the International Sale of Goods; the 1978 United Nations Convention on the Carriage of Goods by Sea (Hamburg); and the 1988 United Nations Convention on International Bills of Exchange and International Promissory Notes (New York).

The General Assembly has also either recommended to States the adoption of or requested them to give due consideration to a number of drafts emanating from UNCITRAL, which took the form of "Rules", "Provisions", "Model Rules",

"Model Law" or "Uniform Rules". Among them are the 1976 UNCITRAL Arbitration Rules; the 1980 UNCITRAL Conciliation Rules; the 1982 UNCITRAL Provisions for a unit of account and adjustment of limitations of liability; the 1983 Uniform Rules on Contract Clauses for an Agreed Sum Due Upon Failure of Performance; the 1985 UNCITRAL Model Law on International Commercial Arbitration; and the 1993 UNCITRAL Model Law on Procurement of Goods and Construction.

In April 1994, the Code of Ethics on the International Trade in Chemicals was concluded at Geneva as a result of a two-year consultative process organized by the United Nations Environment Programme (UNEP). Work is also continuing on developing a legally binding instrument for the application of the prior informed consent procedure concerning banned or severely restricted chemicals.

UNEP has undertaken work on the development of protocols to existing environmental treaties. The Convention on Biological Diversity was opened for signature at the United Nations Conference on Environment and Development in 1992 and entered into force in 1993. However, the Intergovernmental Committee on that Convention considered the need for a protocol on biosafety. Protocols are also being developed to other treaties, including the 1989 Basel Convention on the Control of Transboundary Movements of Hazardous Wastes and Their Disposal and the 1979 Convention on the Conservation of Migratory Species of Wild Animals. An Intergovernmental Negotiating Committee adopted, in June 1994, the International Convention to Combat Desertification in Those Countries Experiencing Serious Drought and/or Desertification, particularly in Africa.

Law of the sea

One of the major achievements of the United Nations in international law was the Convention on the Law of the Sea, which entered into force in November 1994, more than 12 years after its adoption.

The first United Nations Conference on the Law of the Sea, convened at Geneva in 1958 to consider the drafts prepared by the International Law Commission (see above), resulted in the adoption of four conventions — on the high seas, on the territorial sea and the contiguous zone, on the continental shelf, and on fishing and conservation of the living resources of the high seas. The Second United Nations Conference on the Law of the Sea, which took place in 1960, made an unsuccessful attempt at reaching agreement on the breadth of the territorial sea and on the question of fishing zones.

In 1967, the General Assembly established a committee to study all aspects of the peaceful uses of the seabed and its resources beyond the limits of national jurisdiction. On the basis of the work of the Seabed Committee, the Assembly unanimously adopted the Declaration of Principles stating that the seabed and ocean floor, and the subsoil thereof, beyond the limits of national jurisdiction, as well as the resources of the area, were the common heritage of mankind, to be reserved for peaceful purposes, not subject to national appropriation and not to be explored or exploited except under an international regime to be established.

The Assembly decided in 1970 to convene a new conference to prepare a single comprehensive treaty. The Third Conference on the Law of the Sea at its second session, in 1974, endorsed the Seabed Committee's recommendation that it work on a new treaty as a "package deal". The new Convention on the Law of the Sea was approved in April 1982 and opened for signature at Montego Bay, Jamaica, on 10 December 1982. The Convention was signed by 117 States and two other entities — the largest number of signatures ever affixed to a treaty on its first day.

The Convention constitutes a comprehensive codification of the law of the sea. It has 17 parts and 320 articles, which cover the following: Use of Terms and Scope; Territorial Sea and Contiguous Zone; Straits Used for International Navigation; Archipelagic States; Exclusive Economic Zone; Continental Shelf; High Seas; Regime of Islands; Enclosed or Semi-Enclosed Seas; Right of Access of Land-locked States To and From the Sea and Freedom of Transit; The Area (the seabed and ocean floor and subsoil thereof, beyond the limits of national jurisdiction); Protection and Preservation of the Marine Environment; Marine Scientific Research; Development and Transfer of Marine Technology; Settlement of Disputes; General Provisions; and Final Provisions.

The Convention also contains nine annexes: Highly Migratory Species; Commission on the Limits of the Continental Shelf; Basic Conditions of Prospecting, Exploration and Exploitation; Statute of the Enterprise; Conciliation; Statute of the International Tribunal for the Law of the Sea; Arbitration; Special Arbitration; and Participation by International Organizations.

Through national and international legislation and related decision-making, States have consistently asserted the authority of the Convention on the Law of the Sea as the pre-eminent international legal instrument in the area. The Convention's provisions relating to the passage of ships in the territorial sea or through straits used for international navigation have been incorporated into the legislation of many coastal States. Its major impact so far has been on the establishment of maritime jurisdictional zones. The Convention also influenced the law of naval warfare. The establishment of a territorial sea and precise rules for innocent passage in it, for transit passage in straits, and for archipelagic sea-lanes passage contributed to the clarification of the rights and duties of neutral States and those of belligerent forces. These rules assumed some importance in the context of the Persian Gulf War.

On the other hand, by July 1990, it was widely recognized that problems related to certain aspects of the deep seabed mining provisions in Part XI of the Convention prevented some States from ratification or accession. Informal consultations were convened with the aim of achieving wider participation in the Convention by the major industrialized States. Those consultations culminated in the adoption by the General Assembly in July 1994 (resolution 48/263 of 28 July 1994) of the "Agreement relating to the Implementation of Part XI of the United Nations Convention on the Law of the Sea of 10 December 1982", whose operative Annex refers to the following areas: costs to States parties and institutional arrangements; the Enterprise; decision-making; Review Conference; transfer of technology; production policy; economic assistance; financial terms of contracts; and the Finance Committee.

Under the terms of the Agreement, States parties undertake to implement Part XI of the Convention in accordance with the Agreement. Both the provisions of the Agreement and of Part XI shall be interpreted and applied together as a single instrument, although, in the event of inconsistency between the Agreement and Part XI, the provisions of the Agreement shall prevail. After the adoption of the Agreement, any instrument of ratification or formal confirmation of or accession to the 1982 Convention shall also represent consent to be bound by the Agreement.

As at 31 December 1994, there were 158 signatories and 70 parties to the Convention. There were also 71 signatories of the Agreement but 113 parties thereto, by virtue of the simplified procedure and provisional application provided for in articles 5 and 7 of the Agreement.

Congress on public international law

The General Assembly decided, by resolution 48/30 of 9 December 1993, that a Congress on public international law should be held within the framework of the United Nations Decade of International Law (1990-1999). The Congress, which took place at United Nations Headquarters in New York from 13 to 17 March 1995, was organized around the general theme: "Towards the twenty-first century: international law as a language for international relations". Participants exchanged views on the codification, progressive development and implementation of public international law, both in theory and in practice, as well as on its teaching and dissemination. The purpose of the Congress was thus to assist the international community, in particular the legal profession, to meet the challenges and expectations of the present-day world.

Participants focused on the main goals of the United Nations Decade of International Law: the principles of international law; means of peaceful settlement of disputes between States; conceptual and practical aspects of the codification and progressive development of international law; new approaches to research, education and training in the field of international law and its wider appreciation; and towards the twenty-first century — new challenges and expectations.

PART THREE

Emerging nations

"Members of the United Nations which have or assume responsibilities for the administration of territories whose peoples have not yet attained a full measure of self-government . . . accept as a sacred trust the obligation to promote to the utmost, within the system of international peace and security . . ., the well-being of the inhabitants of these territories"

Chapter I

International trusteeship and decolonization

When future historians look back on our times it may well be that they see the prime characteristic of the era to be one when political liberation swept the world, beginning with the process of decolonization. In 1945, more than 750 million people lived in colonies; a half century later the number was only about 1.3 million. The 11 Trust Territories which came under the International Trusteeship System are now all self-governing as independent States or voluntarily associating with another.

An anti-colonial stand was built into the Charter (whose original signatories included the Powers administering Non-Self-Governing Territories) with the principle of "equal rights and self-determination of peoples" incorporated into Article I, and three specific chapters, XI, XII and XIII, setting out the Organization's role and responsibilities in relation to colonial Territories.

The Charter went beyond any previous international agreements regarding decolonization, emphasizing the paramountcy of the interests of the inhabitants, and making the promotion of their well-being "a sacred trust". Chapter XI contained no measure for international supervision of the decolonization process (other than the minority of Trust Territories); administering Powers were merely required to list dependent Territories and to periodically supply the United Nations with reports on specific conditions. Other than for Trust Territories, information on "political" conditions was voluntary under these provisions.

The innovative, but somewhat passive, assertions of accountability with which the Organization began its involvement in decolonization were complemented by the 1960 landmark Declaration on the Granting of Independence to Colonial Countries and Peoples (resolution 1514(XV)), and the 1961 creation of a watchdog committee to implement it. There was also active involvement of the international community in overseeing and accelerating the movement to self-government, including support of national liberation movements. Decolonization became, in the General Assembly's later view, a legal requirement, since the 1960 Declaration stated that subjection of peoples to alien domination and exploitation was a denial of fundamental human rights and contrary to the Charter.

Non-Self-Governing Territories

The Charter of the United Nations contains three chapters concerned with the destiny of peoples who have not yet attained their independence or self-government. Chapter XI of the Charter deals with Non-Self-Governing Territories in general, and Chapters XII and XIII deal in particular with the International Trusteeship System, which is applicable to only some of the Non-Self-Governing Territories.

. . .

Chapter XI

The history of Chapter XI goes back to the last century, to a gradually developing sense of responsibility on the part of the international community toward those peoples who were not yet independent. The struggle against slavery and the slave trade, growing out of this same sense of responsibility, led to international cooperation in colonial affairs. The Congo Basin Treaties signed at the Berlin Conference of 1885 and the Mandates System established under the League of Nations at the end of the First World War marked new steps in this direction. However, international responsibility remained confined to a mere fourteen territories in Africa, Asia and in the Pacific of which Germany and Turkey had been deprived at the end of the war.

During the Second World War the concept of international responsibility took on more definite shape. The Atlantic Charter, in 1941, expressed concern for the well-being of "all men of all lands." At the Yalta Conference, in 1945, it was agreed to undertake discussions on the principles and machinery of trusteeship. The United Nations Conference on International Organization held at San Francisco in the spring of 1945 considered articles on dependent territories. Their discussion resulted in the Declaration Regarding Non-Self-Governing Territories which is now an integral part of the Charter of the United Nations.

The implementation of Chapter XI

The General Assembly of the United Nations, during the first part of its first session in London, in February 1946, with a view to implementing the Declaration Regarding Non-Self-Governing Territories, passed unanimously Resolution 9(I) entitled "Non-Self-Governing Peoples." This drew attention to the fact that the obligations assumed under Chapter XI were already in full force and not contingent upon the conclusion of Trusteeship Agreements or the creation of the Trusteeship Council (Chapters XII and XIII of the Charter). The resolution read:

NON-SELF-GOVERNING PEOPLES

The United Nations, meeting in its first General Assembly, is keenly aware of the problems and political aspirations of the peoples who have not yet attained a full measure of self-government and who are not directly represented here.

Chapters XI, XII and XIII of the Charter recognize the problems of the non-self-governing peoples as of vital concern to the peace and general welfare of the world community.

By Chapter XI, all the Members of the United Nations which have or assume responsibilities for the administration of territories whose peoples have not yet attained a full measure of self-government recognize the principle that the interests of the inhabitants of these territories are paramount. They accept, as a sacred trust, the obligation to promote to the utmost the well-being of the inhabitants of these territories. To that end they accept certain specific obligations, including the obligation to develop self-government and to assist the inhabitants in the progressive development of their free political institutions.

By Chapters XII and XIII, the Charter provides for the establishment of an international trusteeship system, the basic objectives of which are, among others, to promote the political, economic, social and educational advancement of the inhabitants of trust territories, and to promote their progressive development towards self-government or independence.

The General Assembly regrets that the Trusteeship Council cannot be brought into being at this first part of the first session, not because of any lack of desire to do so but because, before the Trusteeship Council can be established, trusteeship agreements must be concluded.

The General Assembly holds the view that any delay in putting into effect the system of international trustee-

ship prevents the implementation of the principles of the trusteeship system, as declared in the Charter, and deprives the populations of such territories as may be brought under the trusteeship system of the opportunity of enjoying the advantages arising from the implementation of these principles.

With a view to expediting the conclusion of these agreements and the establishment of the Trusteeship Council, the Preparatory Commission recommended that the General Assembly should call on those Members of the United Nations which are now administering territories held under mandate to undertake practical steps, in concert with the other States directly concerned, for the implementation of Article 79 of the Charter.

Without waiting for the recommendation of the Preparatory Commission to be considered by the General Assembly, the Members of the United Nations administering territories held under mandate took the initiative in making declarations in regard to these territories.

THEREFORE

WITH RESPECT TO CHAPTER XI OF THE CHARTER, THE GENERAL ASSEMBLY:

1. DRAWS ATTENTION TO the fact that the obligations accepted under Chapter XI of the Charter by all Members of the United Nations are in no way contingent upon the conclusion of trusteeship agreements or upon the bringing into being of the Trusteeship Council and are, therefore, already in full force.

2. REQUESTS the Secretary-General to include in his annual report on the work of the Organization, as provided for in Article 98 of the Charter, a statement summarizing such information as may have been transmitted to him by Members of the United Nations under Article 73 (e) of the Charter relating to economic, social and educational conditions in the territories for which they are responsible other than those to which Chapters XII and XIII apply.

WITH RESPECT TO CHAPTERS XII AND XIII OF THE CHARTER, THE GENERAL ASSEMBLY:

3. WELCOMES the declarations, made by certain States administering territories now held under mandate, of an intention to negotiate trusteeship agreements in respect of some of those territories and, in respect of Transjordan, to establish its independence.

4. INVITES the States administering territories now held under mandate to undertake practical steps, in concert with the other States directly concerned, for the implementation of Article 79 of the Charter (which provides for the conclusion of agreements on the terms of trusteeship for each territory to be placed under the trusteeship system), in order to submit these agreements for approval, preferably not later than during the second part of the first session of the General Assembly.

IN CONCLUSION, THE GENERAL ASSEMBLY:

5. EXPECTS that the realization of the objectives of Chapters XI, XII and XIII will make possible the attainment of the political, economic, social and educational aspirations of non-self-governing peoples.

The General Assembly thus requested the Secretary-General to include in his annual report on the organization a statement summarizing such information as might have been transmitted to him by Members of the United Nations under Article 73 (e) of the Charter relating to economic, social and educational conditions in Non-Self-Governing Territories other than those which might fall under the Trusteeship System as stated in Chapters XII and XIII.

In reply to a letter by the Secretary-General, written in compliance with this directive, a number of Member Governments[1] stated their views regarding certain problems raised in the letter which arose out of the General Assembly's action. . . .

These problems of transmission of information under Article 73 (e) were discussed by a Sub-Committee of the Fourth (Trusteeship) Committee of the General Assembly, as well as by the full Committee and by the Assembly itself in plenary session.

It was agreed to refrain, for the time being, from attempting a definition of the term ''Non-Self-Governing Territories'', but to note the territories which the governments themselves had enumerated as coming within the scope of Chapter XI.

The territories enumerated by the governments were the following:

AUSTRALIA
1. Papua

BELGIUM
2. Belgian Congo

DENMARK
3. Greenland

FRANCE
4. French Equatorial Africa
5. French Establishments in India
6. French Establishments in Oceania
7. French Guiana
8. French Somaliland
9. French West Africa
10. Guadeloupe and Dependencies
11. Indochina
12. Madagascar and Dependencies
13. Martinique
14. Morocco
15. New Caledonia and Dependencies
16. New Hebrides (under Anglo-French Condominium)
17. Reunion
18. St. Pierre and Miquelon
19. Tunisia

NETHERLANDS
20. Curacao
21. Netherlands Indies
22. Surinam

NEW ZEALAND
23. Cook Islands
24. Tokelau Islands

UNITED KINGDOM
25. Aden (Colony and Protectorate)
26. Bahamas
27. Barbados
28. Basutoland

29. Bechuanaland Protectorate
30. Bermuda
31. British Guiana
32. British Honduras
33. Brunei
34. Cyprus
35. Dominica
36. Falkland Islands
37. Fiji
38. Gambia
39. Gibraltar
40. Gilbert and Ellice Islands Colony
41. Gold Coast (Colony and Protectorate)
42. Grenada
43. Hong Kong
44. Jamaica
45. Kenya (Colony and Protectorate)
46. Leeward Islands
47. Malayan Union
48. Malta
49. Mauritius
50. Nigeria
51. North Borneo
52. Northern Rhodesia
53. Nyasaland
54. Pitcairn Islands
55. St. Helena and Dependencies
56. St. Lucia
57. St. Vincent
58. Sarawak
59. Seychelles
60. Sierra Leone
61. Singapore
62. Solomon Islands Protectorate
63. Somaliland Protectorate
64. Swaziland
66. Trinidad and Tobago
66. Uganda Protectorate
67. Zanzibar Protectorate

UNITED STATES OF AMERICA
68. Alaska
69. American Samoa
70. Guam
71. Hawaii
72. Panama Canal Zone
73. Puerto Rico
74. Virgin Islands

It was further agreed that the information transmitted should reach the Secretary-General by June 30 of each year, and should be of such a nature as to cover economic, social and cultural conditions as requested in Article 73 (e), while information on political progress, although not mandatory, would be desirable and of great importance. Such information was to be summarized, classified and analysed by the Secretary-General, and to be examined by an *ad hoc* committee of representatives of

[1]Australia, Belgium, Brazil, Canada, Costa Rica, Czechoslovakia, the Dominican Republic, Egypt, France, Guatemala, Honduras, India, Mexico, the Netherlands, New Zealand, Norway, Syria, Turkey, the United Kingdom, the U.S.S.R., the United States and Venezuela.

Members transmitting information and of representatives of Members elected by the General Assembly. The *ad hoc* committee, elected for one year, was to be convened by the Secretary-General before the next opening session of the General Assembly.

. . .

The General Assembly then elected Brazil, China, Cuba, Egypt, India, the Philippines, the U.S.S.R. and Uruguay to serve on the *ad hoc* committee together with Australia, Belgium, Denmark, France, the Netherlands, New Zealand, the United Kingdom and the United States, the latter group of States having transmitted or having expressed their intention of transmitting information in respect of Non-Self-Governing Territories under their jurisdiction.

. . .

The task of the *ad hoc* Committee was to be to examine the information transmitted by Member Governments, as summarized and analyzed by the Secretary-General. The Committee was to examine the summaries and analyses with a view to aiding the General Assembly in its own consideration of such information; to recommend procedures to be followed in the future; and to attempt to find the best means of ensuring to Non-Self-Governing Territories the full use of the advice, experience and expert knowledge which the specialized agencies could put at their disposal.

The Trusteeship System

The principles of Chapter XI are applicable to all Territories "whose peoples have not yet attained a full measure of self-government." For some of these Territories, however, wider obligations are provided by the International Trusteeship System as outlined in Chapters XII and XIII of the Charter.

. . .

The League of Nations and the mandates

In accordance with Article 22 of the Covenant of the League of Nations, a number of territories had been placed under mandate in the early years following the First World War. By 1945 some of the territories had achieved independence; the following twelve, however, were still under mandate:

Under mandate to	*Name of territory*
United Kingdom, New Zealand and Australia (administered by Australia)	Nauru[2]
Australia	New Guinea
Belgium	Ruanda-Urundi
France	Cameroons Togoland
Japan	Caroline, Marshall and Marianas Islands[3]

Under mandate to	*Name of territory*
New Zealand	Western Samoa
Union of South Africa	South-West Africa[2]
United Kingdom	Cameroons, Togoland, Tanganyika, Palestine[2]

At its final session in Geneva in 1946 the Assembly of the League of Nations discussed the question of the fulfilment by the League of its responsibilities to the peoples of the mandated territories. On April 18, 1946, the Assembly adopted unanimously, with Egypt abstaining, the following resolution:

THE ASSEMBLY,
RECALLING that Article 22 of the Covenant applies to certain territories placed under mandate the principle that the well-being and development of peoples not yet able to stand alone in the strenuous conditions of the modern world form a sacred trust of civilization:

1. EXPRESSES its satisfaction with the manner in which the organs of the League have performed the functions entrusted to them with respect to the Mandates System and in particular pays tribute to the work accomplished by the Mandates Commission;

2. RECALLS the role of the League in assisting Iraq to progress from its status under an "A" Mandate to a condition of complete independence, welcomes the termination of the mandated status of Syria, Lebanon and Transjordan, which have, since the last session of the Assembly, become independent members of the world community;

3. RECOGNIZES that, on the termination of the League's existence, its functions with respect to the mandated territories will come to an end, but notes that Chapters XI, XII and XIII of the Charter of the United Nations embody principles corresponding to those declared in Article 22 of the Covenant of the League;

4. TAKES NOTE of the expressed intentions of the Members of the League now administering territories under mandate to continue to administer them for the well-being and development of the peoples concerned in accordance with the obligations contained in the respective mandates, until other arrangements have been agreed between the United Nations and the respective mandatory Powers.

The interim period

The meetings of the Executive Committee, the Preparatory Commission and the first part of the first session of the General Assembly of the United Nations all reflected the desire of the Members of the United Nations to set up the Trusteeship Council at the earliest possible date. It was generally recognized that the mandated territories would probably be among the first to be transferred to

---

[2]No Trusteeship Agreements exist[ed] as yet for these territories [in 1946].

[3]By 1945, these islands were under United States Naval Administration.

the International Trusteeship System by means of individual Trusteeship Agreements.

In the resolution on Non-Self-Governing Peoples of February 9, 1946, cited above, the General Assembly expressed regret that the Trusteeship Council could not be brought into being at that time; recognized that any delay in putting into effect the International Trusteeship System would prevent the implementation of the principles of the system and would deprive the populations of the Trust Territories of its advantages; and noted that the Preparatory Commission had recommended that the General Assembly should call upon those Members of the United Nations now administering territories held under mandate to undertake practical steps in concert with the other States directly concerned to place them under the International Trusteeship System. Before the recommendation of the Preparatory Commission had been considered by the General Assembly, several of the mandatory States had in fact declared their intention to negotiate Trusteeship Agreements for the purpose of placing mandated territories under the International Trusteeship System.

The resolution of the General Assembly welcomed these declarations, and invited all the States administering mandated territories to undertake the necessary steps to negotiate the Trusteeship Agreements by means of which the mandated territories would be placed under the International Trusteeship System, with a view to the submission of these agreements for approval, preferably not later than during the second part of the first session of the General Assembly.

In view of the unequivocal expression, in the resolution on Non-Self-Governing Peoples, of the General Assembly's desire that the establishment of the Trusteeship Council should be expedited, letters, dated June 29, 1946, were addressed by the Secretary-General to the States administering territories then held under mandate, i.e., Australia, Belgium, France, New Zealand, the Union of South Africa and the United Kingdom, calling their attention to the resolution

In reply, the Governments of Australia, Belgium, France, New Zealand and the United Kingdom stated that they had either already prepared draft Trusteeship Agreements, or were in process of preparing the terms of such Agreements, with respect to the mandated territories under their control, and expressed the hope that they would be able to submit such Trusteeship Agreements to the General Assembly before or during the second part of its first session. The Government of the Union of South Africa requested that a statement on the outcome of its consultations with the peoples of South-West Africa as to the future status of the mandated territory, and as to the implementation to be given to the wishes thus expressed be included in the agenda for the second part of the first session of the General Assembly.

Establishment of the Trusteeship Council

The essential conditions for the establishment of the Trusteeship Council and for bringing the International Trusteeship System into operation, as envisaged in Chapters XII and XIII of the Charter, were fulfilled in the course of the second part of the first session of the General Assembly.

The first Trust Territories

As a result of the approval by the General Assembly on December 13, 1946, of the eight Trusteeship Agreements which had been submitted by five of the mandatory Powers with regard to territories administered by them under mandate, the International Trusteeship System came into effect. The responsibility for supervising the administration of the first eight Trust Territories was thereby vested in the General Assembly and, under its authority, in the Trusteeship Council.

The Territories thus far placed under Trusteeship by means of individual Trusteeship Agreements are:[4]

a) New Guinea, administered by Australia;

b) Ruanda-Urundi, administered by Belgium;

c) Togoland and Cameroons, administered by France;

d) Western Samoa, administered by New Zealand; and

e) Tanganyika, Togoland and Cameroons, administered by the United Kingdom.

In each of these first eight Trusteeship Agreements a single State was designated as the Administering Authority. It is to be noted, in this connection, that the Charter, in Article 81, also makes provision whereby a Trusteeship Agreement may designate more than one State, or the United Nations itself, as the Administering Authority.

With respect to the first Trust Territories, the former mandatory powers, which had administered them under League of Nations mandates, had proposed Trusteeship Agreements for consideration and approval by the General Assembly, during the second part of its first session. The General Assembly, through its Fourth Committee (Trusteeship) and Sub-Committee 1 of that Committee, examined the proposed Agreements with great care. Numerous proposals for modification of the terms of the Trusteeship Agreements were presented by Members of the United Na-

---

[4] On April 2, 1947 the Security Council approved after some modification, a draft strategic area Trusteeship Agreement in respect of the Pacific Islands, formerly mandated to Japan, which named the United States of America as the Administering Authority. Due, however, to constitutional requirements, the Agreement could not take effect until it had been approved by the United States Government.

tions. Some of the suggested modifications were acceptable to the mandatory powers and were incorporated in the Agreements. In some instances the mandatory powers themselves proposed modifications in the light of the discussions in Sub-Committee 1. In other instances, proposed modifications were not acceptable to the mandatory powers and were not included in the Agreements.

A controlling factor in the General Assembly's consideration and approval of the Trusteeship Agreements was the provision in Article 79 of the Charter making it essential that the mandatory power, as a State directly concerned, approve the terms of Trusteeship. Certain of the mandatory powers had submitted proposed Trusteeship Agreements, but they were not obliged to accept any specific modifications thereto. The General Assembly, on the other hand, could propose modifications of the draft Agreements, and could, in its final decision, determine the conditions on which it would approve them. There was no limitation whatsoever on the authority of the General Assembly to approve or reject the proposed Agreements.

With regard to the terms of the eight Agreements already in effect, a number of issues were raised in the course of the General Assembly's discussions. These issues were thoroughly discussed prior to the final approval of the Agreements by the General Assembly. The Trusteeship Agreements as finally approved constitute the basic instruments by means of which the International Trusteeship System is applied to the Trust Territories. The administration of the eight Trust Territories thus created is henceforth to be subject to the international supervision provided for in Chapter XII of the Charter.

. . .

Trusteeship Agreements

In pursuance of Resolution 64(I) adopted by the General Assembly on December 14, 1946, the Trusteeship Council was established as a principal organ of the United Nations. It was the last such organ to be established. The Council met at Lake Success for its first session on March 26, 1947.

On the basis of the eight Trusteeship Agreements approved by the General Assembly, the Trusteeship Council came into being with ten members. As at present constituted, five of its members are Administering Authorities, namely, Australia, Belgium, France, New Zealand and the United Kingdom. Three of its members, namely, China, the United States and the U.S.S.R., hold membership in accordance with Article 86 of the Charter, by virtue of being permanent members of the Security Council but did not, at the time of the first meeting, administer Trust Territories. The other two members, Iraq and Mexico, were elected for three-year terms by the General Assembly at the second part of its first session, in accordance with Article 86, paragraph 1 (c), of the Charter.

. . .

All of the Territories which remained under mandate status have now been placed under the Trusteeship System, or are in process of being transferred to it, with the exception of Nauru, Palestine and South-West Africa.

In its resolution on the future status of South-West Africa, adopted on December 14, 1946, the General Assembly recommended that the mandated territory of South-West Africa be placed under the International Trusteeship System and invited the Government of the Union of South Africa to submit for the consideration of the General Assembly a Trusteeship Agreement for that territory.

In respect to Nauru, the representative of Australia, at the 15th plenary meeting of the first part of the General Assembly's first session, announced the intention of his Government to submit a Trusteeship Agreement for this mandated territory. This decision had been concurred in by the Governments of the United Kingdom and of New Zealand, with whom Australia shared the mandate. The Australian representative before the Fourth Committee during the second part of the first session of the General Assembly, reaffirmed the intention of his Government to submit a draft Agreement for Nauru.

A United Nations Special Committee on Palestine was created by a resolution of the General Assembly at its first special session on May 15, 1947. In accordance with its terms of reference, the Committee went to Palestine in June 1947 to "investigate all questions and issues relevant to the problem of Palestine." The report of the Special Committee was to be considered at the second regular session of the General Assembly in September 1947.

. . .

During its first session, the Trusteeship Council had before it 26 petitions, two of a general nature and the others referring to specific Trust Territories.

(YUN 1946-47, pp. 569-79)

The 1960 Declaration on Granting Independence to Colonial Countries and Peoples

The year 1960 marked a watershed in United Nations involvement in decolonization. In that year 16 newly independent African States and Cyprus became Members of the Organization, bringing to 30 the number of Trust and Non-Self-Governing Territories that had attained self-government or independence.

More than 80 million people, however, remained under colonial status. The international community now decided that the Charter principles were being too slowly applied. Under a new agenda item proposed by the Soviet Union, 43 African and Asian States presented a draft resolution intended to expand the scope and intensity of the Organization's involvement in the decolonization process. On 14 December 1960, a "Declaration on the Granting of Independence to Colonial Countries and Peoples" was adopted by the General Assembly.

By this, among other things, the Assembly solemnly proclaimed "the necessity of bringing to a speedy and unconditional end colonialism in all its forms and manifestations".

The 43 sponsors of the draft were: Afghanistan, Burma, Cambodia, Cameroun, Central African Republic, Ceylon, Chad, Congo (Brazzaville), Congo (Leopoldville),[5] Cyprus, Dahomey,[6] Ethiopia, Federation of Malaya, Gabon, Ghana, Guinea, India, Indonesia, Iran, Iraq, Ivory Coast, Jordan, Laos, Lebanon, Liberia, Libya, Madagascar, Mali, Morocco, Nepal, Niger, Nigeria, Pakistan, Philippines, Saudi Arabia, Senegal, Somalia, Sudan, Togo, Tunisia, Turkey, United Arab Republic and Upper Volta.

Many representatives of Asian-African Members referred to the Bandung Conference in 1955, where countries of Asia and Africa had initiated a number of fundamental principles which had become the cornerstone of their policy towards the colonial countries and peoples and which had been re-emphasized at the conferences of African States at Accra in 1958, at Monrovia in 1959 and at Addis Ababa in 1960. The draft declaration they were now submitting was the culmination of those principles, they stressed.

The draft resolution sponsored by 43 Asian and African countries was then adopted, on 14 December 1960, as resolution 1514(XV), by a roll-call vote of 89 to 0, with 9 abstentions. Honduras did not press its draft resolution to the vote.

. . .

Abstaining: Australia, Belgium, Dominican Republic, France, Portugal, Spain, Union of South Africa, United Kingdom, United States.

"*The General Assembly*,

"*Mindful* of the determination proclaimed by the peoples of the world in the Charter of the United Nations to reaffirm faith in fundamental human rights, in the dignity and worth of the human person, in the equal rights of men and women and of nations large and small and to promote social progress and better standards of life in larger freedom,

"*Conscious* of the need for the creation of conditions of stability and well-being and peaceful and friendly relations based on respect for the principles of equal rights and self-determination of all peoples, and of universal respect for, and observance of, human rights and fundamental freedoms for all without distinction as to race, sex, language or religion,

"*Recognizing* the passionate yearning for freedom in all dependent peoples and the decisive role of such peoples in the attainment of their independence,

"*Aware* of the increasing conflict resulting from the denial of or impediments in the way of the freedom of such peoples, which constitute a serious threat to world peace,

"*Considering* the important role of the United Nations in assisting the movement for independence in Trust and Non-Self-Governing Territories,

"*Recognizing* that the peoples of the world ardently desire the end of colonialism in all its manifestations,

"*Convinced* that the continued existence of colonialism prevents the development of international economic co-operation, impedes the social, cultural and economic development of dependent peoples and militates against the United Nations ideal of universal peace,

"*Affirming* that peoples may, for their own ends, freely dispose of their natural wealth and resources without prejudice to any obligations arising out of international economic co-operation, based upon the principle of mutual benefit, and international law,

"*Believing* that the process of liberation is irresistible and irreversible and that, in order to avoid serious crises, an end must be put to colonialism and all practices of segregation and discrimination associated therewith,

"*Welcoming* the emergence in recent years of a large number of dependent territories into freedom and independence, and recognizing the increasingly powerful trends towards freedom in such territories which have not yet attained independence,

"*Convinced* that all peoples have an inalienable right to complete freedom, the exercise of their sovereignty and the integrity of their national territory,

"*Solemnly proclaims* the necessity of bringing to a speedy and unconditional end colonialism in all its forms and manifestations;

"And to this end

"*Declares* that:

"1. The subjection of peoples to alien subjugation, domination and exploitation constitutes a denial of fundamental human rights, is contrary to the Charter of the United Nations and is an impediment to the promotion of world peace and co-operation.

"2. All peoples have the right to self-determination; by virtue of that right they freely determine their political status and freely pursue their economic, social and cultural development.

"3. Inadequacy of political, economic, social or educational preparedness should never serve as a pretext for delaying independence.

"4. All armed action or repressive measures of all kinds directed against dependent peoples shall cease in order to enable them to exercise peacefully and freely

---

[5]Later Zaire.

[6]Later Benin.

their right to complete independence, and the integrity of their national territory shall be respected.

"5.   Immediate steps shall be taken, in Trust and Non-Self-Governing Territories or all other territories which have not yet attained independence, to transfer all powers to the peoples of those territories, without any conditions or reservations, in accordance with their freely expressed will and desire, without any distinction as to race, creed or colour, in order to enable them to enjoy complete independence and freedom.

"6.   Any attempt aimed at the partial or total disruption of the national unity and the territorial integrity of a country is incompatible with the purposes and principles of the Charter of the United Nations.

"7.   All States shall observe faithfully and strictly the provisions of the Charter of the United Nations, the Universal Declaration of Human Rights and the present Declaration on the basis of equality, non-interference in the internal affairs of all States, and respect for the sovereign rights of all peoples and their territorial integrity."

(YUN 1960, pp. 48-50)

Creation of decolonization Committee

The Declaration did not specify how the United Nations was to implement it and so in the following year, 1961, the Assembly provided a mechanism by establishing a Special Committee with wide-ranging powers to study, investigate and recommend action. The Special Committee of 24 (as it came to be called after expansion of its original membership of 17) became the international community's watchdog on the progress of decolonization. Many of its functions were similar to those of the Trusteeship Council but the Special Committee was mandated to look at all colonial situations. It was directed to examine the application of the 1960 Declaration and make recommendations on the progress and extent of its application. In its early years, administering Powers generally declined to participate in the work of the Committee.

Programme to implement the Declaration

In 1970, ten years after adoption of the Declaration on decolonization, the General Assembly noted that 44 Territories with a population of 28 million still remained under colonial rule. While acknowledging that the 1960 Declaration had contributed to an acceleration of the pace of decolonization, it regretted that certain countries still clung to their colonial possessions. It therefore adopted a programme of action for its full implementation. It declared that further continuation of colonization was a crime and people under such rule had an inherent right to struggle by all necessary means at their disposal against colonial Powers which were suppressing their aspirations for freedom and independence. Member States were urged to render the necessary moral and material assistance to peoples fighting for their freedom. Those imprisoned for that activity should be treated as prisoners of war under the Geneva Convention of 1949. To emphasize the legitimacy of armed struggle, the Assembly invited the representatives of liberation movements to participate in United Nations organs whenever necessary.

In succeeding years the Assembly went further and identified specific liberation movements as "authentic representatives of their people" in the Portuguese territories, in Namibia and in Southern Rhodesia. (See following chapter.)

Future Programme of Action for implementation of Declaration

. . .

RESOLUTION 2621(XXV), as recommended by Special Committee, A/8086, adopted by Assembly on 12 October 1970, meeting 1862, by recorded vote of 86 to 5, with 15 abstentions.

. . .

The General Assembly,

Having decided to hold a special commemorative session on the occasion of the tenth anniversary of the Declaration on the Granting of Independence to Colonial Countries and Peoples,

Considering that, by arousing world public opinion and promoting practical action for the speedy liquidation of colonialism in all its forms and manifestations, the Declaration has played and will continue to play an important role in assisting the peoples under colonial domination in their struggle for freedom and independence,

Conscious of the fact that, although many colonial countries and peoples have achieved freedom and independence in the last ten years, the system of colonialism continues to exist in many areas of the world,

Reaffirming that all peoples have the right to self-determination and independence and that the subjection of the peoples to alien domination constitutes a serious impediment to the maintenance of international peace and security and the development of peaceful relations among nations,

1.   *Declares* the further continuation of colonialism in all its forms and manifestations a crime which constitutes a violation of the Charter of the United Nations, the Declaration on the Granting of Independence to Colonial Countries and Peoples and the principles of international law;

2.   *Reaffirms* the inherent right of colonial peoples to struggle by all necessary means at their disposal against colonial Powers which suppress their aspiration for freedom and independence;

3.   *Adopts* the following programme of action to assist in the full implementation of the Declaration on the Granting of Independence to Colonial Countries and Peoples:

(1)   Member States shall do their utmost to promote, in the United Nations and the international institutions and organizations within the United Nations system, effective measures for the full implementation of the Declaration on the Granting of Independence to Colonial Countries and Peoples in all Trust Territories, Non-Self-Governing Territories and other colonial Territories, large and small, including the adoption by the Security Council of effective measures

against Governments and régimes which engage in any form of repression of colonial peoples, which would seriously impede the maintenance of international peace and security.

(2) Member States shall render all necessary moral and material assistance to the peoples of colonial Territories in their struggle to attain freedom and independence.

(3) *(a)* Member States shall intensify their efforts to promote the implementation of the resolutions of the General Assembly and the Security Council relating to Territories under colonial domination.

(b) In this connexion, the General Assembly draws the attention of the Security Council to the need to continue to give special attention to the problems of southern Africa by adopting measures to ensure the full implementation of General Assembly resolution 1514(XV) of 14 December 1960 and its own resolutions, and in particular:

(i) To widen the scope of the sanctions against the illegal régime of Southern Rhodesia by declaring mandatory all the measures laid down in Article 41 of the Charter of the United Nations;

(ii) To give careful consideration to the question of imposing sanctions upon South Africa and Portugal, in view of their refusal to carry out the relevant decisions of the Security Council;

(iii) To give urgent consideration, with a view to promoting the speedy elimination of colonialism, to the question of imposing fully and unconditionally, under international supervision, an embargo on arms of all kinds to the Government of South Africa and the illegal régime of Southern Rhodesia;

(iv) To consider urgently the adoption of measures to prevent the supply of arms of all kinds to Portugal, as such arms enable that country to deny the right of self-determination and independence to the peoples of the Territories under its domination.

(c) Member States shall also intensify their efforts to oppose collaboration between the régimes of South Africa and Portugal and the illegal racist régime of Southern Rhodesia for the preservation of colonialism in southern Africa and to end the political, military, economic and other forms of aid received by the above-mentioned régimes, which enables them to persist in their policy of colonial domination.

(4) Member States shall wage a vigorous and sustained campaign against activities and practices of foreign economic, financial and other interests operating in colonial Territories for the benefit and on behalf of colonial Powers and their allies, as these constitute a major obstacle to the achievement of the goals embodied in resolution 1514(XV). Member States shall consider the adoption of necessary steps to have their nationals and companies under their jurisdiction discontinue such activities and practices: these steps should also aim at preventing the systematic influx of foreign immigrants into colonial Territories, which disrupts the integrity and social, political and cultural unity of the peoples under colonial domination.

(5) Member States shall carry out a sustained and vigorous campaign against all military activities and arrangements by colonial Powers in Territories under their administration, as such activities and arrangements constitute an obstacle to the full implementation of resolution 1514(XV).

(6) *(a)* All freedom fighters under detention shall be treated in accordance with the relevant provisions of the Geneva Convention relative to the Treatment of Prisoners of War, of 12 August 1949.

(b) The specialized agencies and international institutions associated with the United Nations shall intensify their activities related to the implementation of resolution 1514(XV).

(c) Representatives of liberation movements shall be invited, whenever necessary, by the United Nations and other international organizations within the United Nations system to participate in an appropriate capacity in the proceedings of those organs relating to their countries.

(d) Efforts shall be intensified to provide increased educational opportunities for the inhabitants of Non-Self-Governing Territories. All States shall render greater assistance in this field, both individually through programmes in the countries concerned and collectively by contributions through the United Nations.

(7) All States shall undertake measures aimed at enhancing public awareness of the need for active assistance in the achievement of complete decolonization and, in particular, creating satisfactory conditions for activities by national and international non-governmental organizations in support of the peoples under colonial domination.

(8) The United Nations as well as all States shall intensify their efforts in the field of public information in the area of decolonization through all media, including publications, radio and television. Of special importance will be programmes relating to United Nations activities on decolonization, the situation in colonial Territories and the struggle being waged by colonial peoples and the national liberation movements.

(9) The Special Committee on the Situation with regard to the Implementation of the Declaration on the Granting of Independence to Colonial Countries and Peoples shall continue to examine the full compliance of all States with the Declaration and with other relevant resolutions on the question of decolonization. The question of territorial size, geographical isolation and limited resources should in no way delay the implementation of the Declaration. Where resolution 1514(XV) has not been fully implemented with regard to a given Territory, the General Assembly shall continue to bear responsibility for that Territory until such time as the people concerned has had an opportunity to exercise freely its right to self-determination and independence in accordance with the Declaration. The Special Committee is hereby directed:

(a) To continue to assist the General Assembly in finding the best ways and means for the final liquidation of colonialism;

(b) To continue to give special consideration to the views expressed orally or in written communications by representatives of the peoples in the colonial Territories;

(c) To continue to send visiting missions to the colonial Territories and to hold meetings at places where

it can best obtain first-hand information on the situation in colonial Territories, as well as to continue to hold meetings away from Headquarters as appropriate;

(d) To assist the General Assembly in making arrangements, in co-operation with the administering Powers, for securing a United Nations presence in the colonial Territories to participate in the elaboration of the procedural measures for the implementation of the Declaration and to observe the final stages of the process of decolonization in the Territories;

(e) To prepare draft rules and regulations for visiting missions for approval by the General Assembly.

(YUN 1970, pp. 706-708)

Plan of Action for implementation of the Declaration—20th anniversary

The General Assembly, on 12 December 1980, held a special meeting to mark the twentieth anniversary of the 1960 Declaration on the Granting of Independence to Colonial Countries and Peoples. In reviewing the status of implementation of the Declaration, the Secretary-General said that, in the 20 years that had elapsed, 136 million people in 59 Trust Territories and Non-Self-Governing Territories had emerged from dependent status and the vast majority were represented in the Assembly. The admission of Zimbabwe was a fitting climax to a period which would no doubt be remembered as the era of decolonization. The Chairman of the Special Committee on decolonization said that the current composition of the United Nations was an eloquent testimony to an outstanding achievement—more than one third of the 154 Members were former colonial Territories which had joined the community of nations as sovereign States since 1960. The work of the United Nations, however, could hardly be considered complete: colonialism in any form, in any territory, must be eliminated. On the previous day, the Assembly had adopted the Plan of Action for the Full Implementation of the Declaration.

The Plan of Action for the Full Implementation of the Declaration on the Granting of Independence to Colonial Countries and Peoples, as proposed by the Special Committee, was contained in an annex to resolution 35/118, adopted by the General Assembly on 11 December by a recorded vote of 120 to 6, with 20 abstentions.

The Plan of Action set forth the following measures.

Member States were to: promote the full implementation of the Declaration in the Trust Territory and all non-self-governing and other colonial territories, including the adoption by the Security Council of measures against régimes engaging in repression of colonial peoples thus impeding the maintenance of international peace and security; render all necessary moral and material assistance in the struggle to exercise the right to self-determination and independence; intensify efforts to promote the implementation of Assembly and Security Council resolutions relating to territories and to end any form of collaboration with South Africa, particularly in the nuclear field, taking measures to prevent such collaboration and uranium purchases by bodies or individuals within their jurisdiction; endeavour to achieve the cessation of new foreign investments in and financial loans to South Africa; ensure that the permanent sovereignty of countries and territories under colonial, racist and alien domination over their natural resources was fully respected and safeguarded; discourage immigration to colonial territories; oppose all military activities by colonial and occupying powers in the territories and intensify efforts to secure the immediate and unconditional withdrawal of those powers' military bases and installations; and intensify aid to the national liberation movements recognized by OAU. All States were to enhance public awareness of the need for assistance in eradicating colonialism and were to co-operate with the United Nations Council for Namibia and the Special Committee.

The Assembly drew the Security Council's attention to the need to continue giving special attention to situations where the denial of the right of peoples to self-determination posed a threat to international peace and security and, in particular, the need to consider imposing mandatory economic sanctions against South Africa and to reinforce the arms embargo against that country.

The Committee was to continue to examine States' compliance with the Declaration and was directed: to continue seeking the most suitable ways for the speedy and total application of the Declaration to all territories that had not attained independence and propose to the Assembly specific measures for its complete implementation; to review thoroughly the list of territories to which the Declaration applied and to report thereon to the Assembly in 1981; to continue sending periodic missions to the territories; to continue examining the views expressed by their peoples and by representatives of non-governmental organizations and individuals with knowledge of conditions there; and to assist the Assembly in making arrangements, in co-operation with the administering powers, for a United Nations presence in the territories to help elaborate procedural arrangements for implementing the Declaration and observe or supervise the final stages of the process of decolonization.

The United Nations was to intensify efforts to disseminate information on decolonization, the struggle for self-determination and equal rights, and the role of national liberation movements. United Nations organizations were to render all possible moral and material assistance to colonial peoples and their liberation movements.

Non-governmental organizations opposed to colonialism were asked to intensify their activities in co-operation with the Secretary-General and relevant United Nations organs.

(YUN 1980, p. 1052)

International Decade for the Eradication of Colonialism—30th anniversary of the 1960 Declaration

In 1988, the Conference of Foreign Ministers of Non-Aligned Countries (Nicosia, Cyprus, 7-10 September) adopted a political statement containing a proposal that the General Assembly declare the 1990-2000 period as the International Decade for the Eradication of Colonialism. Acting on this recommendation, the Assembly (resolution 43/47), recognizing that 1990 would mark the thirtieth anniversary of the 1960 Declaration on the Granting of Independence to Colonial Countries and Peoples, declared the period 1990-2000 as the International Decade for the Eradication of Colonialism. It asked the Secretary-General to submit a plan of action aimed at inaugurating the twenty-first century with a world free from colonialism.

The Secretary-General's proposals for a plan of action for the International Decade were considered by the General Assembly in 1991. It called for the international community to assist the people of Non-Self-Governing Territories (NSGTs) to exercise their right to self-determination through such measures as improving educational systems in the Territories, protecting human rights and ensuring that political exercises relating to self-determination were carried out free from intimidation and outside interference. The United Nations would arrange self-determination referendums in each of the Territo-

ries no later than 1999 and the administering Powers would take certain measures, including facilitating United Nations visiting missions, conserving natural resources and preserving the environment. At the national level, the plan called on States to protect NSGTs against environmental damage and to refrain from using them for military purposes.

The Special Committee on the Situation with regard to the Implementation of the Declaration on the Granting of Independence to Colonial Countries and Peoples would prepare analyses of progress on the implementation of the 1960 Declaration, review the impact of the economic and social situation on the constitutional and political advancement of NSGTs, and organize seminars to review the implementation of the plan of action, as well as report annually to the Assembly appraising the activities of the Decade.

The Assembly (resolution 46/181), declaring that the ultimate goal of the Decade was the free exercise of the right of self-determination without outside pressure in a form reflecting the authentic interests and aspirations of the peoples of NSGTs, adopted the Secretary-General's proposals.

" ". . . to develop self-government, to take due account
of the political aspirations of the peoples, and to assist them
in the progressive development of their free political institutions,
according to the particular circumstances of each territory and its peoples "

Chapter II

Dismantling the colonial system

The United Nations Charter formally ushered in the era of decolonization, but it was not until 1960, the great year of African independence, that the winds of change were felt on the continent most widely affected by the colonial system. During that year, 16 African colonial Territories achieved independence and became Members of the United Nations: Cameroun, Central African Republic, Chad, Congo (Brazzaville), Congo (Leopoldville), Dahomey, Gabon, Ivory Coast, Madagascar, Mali, Niger, Nigeria, Senegal, Somalia, Togo and Upper Volta. The United Nations Declaration on the Granting of Independence to Colonial Countries and Peoples, adopted that same year, created the framework for speeding up the independence process in the remaining African Territories under colonial rule. Although this process of constitutional change and accession to independence was a relatively peaceful one in most of the Territories, it was overshadowed by conflict situations which had developed in others. Notable among those were Algeria, Angola, Mozambique, Namibia and Southern Rhodesia, where the struggle for independence became protracted, escalating into armed conflict and requiring the greater involvement of the United Nations. From 1955, when it first became actively involved in the Algerian situation, until 1990, when the last of them, Namibia, achieved independence, the United Nations worked relentlessly to ensure that the rights and wishes of the majority populations were respected. The independence process in southern Africa was particularly painful as the conflicts spread beyond individual borders, creating a precarious humanitarian situation and having serious implications for international peace. The independence of Namibia marked the end of the most difficult period of the decolonization process in Africa and was a vindication of the role played by the United Nations. In 1995, the only Territory on the African continent with which the Organization continued to be concerned was Western Sahara.

The United Nations also supervised the successful conclusion of the trusteeship system as the last Territory under that arrangement—Palau—became a Member of the United Nations in December 1994.

Algerian struggle for independence

The Algerian struggle for independence was first brought to the attention of the United Nations in April 1955 by a group of 17 Asian and African countries which felt that the situation had deteriorated to such an extent that the United Nations could not remain indifferent to the threat to peace and the flagrant violation of human rights. When the General Assembly began consideration of the item "Question of Algeria", France, while challenging the competence of the United Nations to deal with what it considered a domestic problem, stated that it had legitimately occupied Algeria for more than 120 years and was entitled to decide, within its own constitution, what political system it desired for the country. France maintained that the rebellion in Algeria resulted from activities of terrorist groups, with the help of foreign Powers. It was ready to offer a liberal political solution in three stages: an unconditional cease-fire; free supervised elections; and discussion with elected representatives on the future regime of Algeria. Several representatives maintained that the Algerian liberation movement was a mass movement of the Algerian people whose only legitimate objective was to ensure the exercise of their right to self-determination and independence. The United Nations could play a valuable part in a solution by recommending negotiations to those concerned and indicating on what basis they could be held. The General Assembly, on 15 February 1956, by resolution 1012(XI), expressed the hope that, in a spirit of cooperation, a peaceful, democratic and just solution would be found in conformity with the Charter.

The matter was considered by the Assembly in successive years without the attendance of France, which continued to question the competence of the United Nations to deal with the matter. During the Assembly's debate in 1960, Tunisia said that for six years a real war had been going on in Algeria, troubling the international conscience and constituting a grave threat to peace and security. It recalled that both France and the Algerian Provisional Government had accepted the principle of self-determination, and the only dispute still outstanding related to the creation of conditions for the full and genuine expression of the will of the Algerian people in a referendum; the presence of the United Nations would allay fears on both sides. The Assembly, in resolution 1573(XV), recognized the need for adequate and effective guarantees to ensure the successful implementation of the right to self-determination and that the United Nations had a responsibility to contribute to the implementation of that right.

On 25 September 1961, the General Assembly, acting on the recommendation of its General Committee, decided to place the question of Algeria on the agenda of its sixteenth session.

. . .

On 21 September 1961, the Assembly's General Committee decided without vote to recommend that the item be placed on the Assembly's agenda. The representative of France said that, as he had pointed out at previous Assembly sessions, discussion of the question would be incompatible with the provisions of the United Nations Charter. Moreover, he said, all impartial Members would recognize that France had spared no effort to find a peaceful, democratic and just solution to the Algerian problem, and a debate in the General Assembly on the item would only further inflame passions. He indicated that his delegation would be unable to participate in any such debate and would consider any resolutions adopted on the subject to be invalid.

The Assembly decided to place the item on its agenda, and referred it to the First Committee which, on 30 November 1961, deferred discussion to 14 December in order not to disturb the cease-fire talks which were then being held in regard to Algeria. The item was subsequently considered by the First Committee between 14 and 19 December 1961.

. . .

A draft resolution on the subject was submitted by the following 34 Members: Afghanistan, Burma, Cambodia, Ceylon, Congo (Leopoldville), Cyprus, Ethiopia, the Federation of Malaya, Ghana, Guinea, India, Indonesia, Iraq, Jordan, Lebanon, Liberia, Libya, Mali, Mauritania, Morocco, Nepal, Nigeria, Pakistan, Saudi Arabia, Senegal, Sierra Leone, Somalia, the Sudan, Syria, Tanganyika, Tunisia, the United Arab Republic, Upper Volta and Yemen.

By [that resolution], the General Assembly would call upon the two parties to resume negotiations with a view to implementing the right of the Algerian people to self-determination and independence respecting the unity and territorial integrity of Algeria.

In the debate co-sponsors of the draft resolution described the evolution of the question of Algeria since it first came before the United Nations in 1955. They believed that the chances for a settlement had improved. Some of them declared that the crucial question was whether France was prepared to crush the "fascist" Secret Army Organization, which was standing in the way of peace and, to that end, they appealed to President de Gaulle to continue along the path he appeared to have chosen and called for the resumption of negotiations which had been broken off recently. They stressed that the draft resolution contained nothing controversial and hoped that it would be unanimously adopted.

The representative of the USSR, supported by spokesmen from various Eastern European countries and Cuba, condemned the Algerian war. In continuing that war, waged in support of the interests of French monopolies, it was pointed out, the French Government was flouting the will of the peoples of the world, as expressed in General Assembly resolution 1514(XV) of 14 December 1960 containing the Declaration on the granting of independence to colonial countries and peoples, and in Assembly resolution 1573(XV) of 19 December 1960 which had recognized the right of the Algerian people to self-determination and independence. The purpose of the war, they said, was to break the resistance of the Algerians so that the French could impose a settlement under which domination and exploitation would continue along the classic colonial lines as well as in the more specific field of oil and gas exploitation and nuclear testing. They also asserted that such a war would not be feasible without the strong support of the NATO members and especially the United States, which had a direct financial interest in Saharan oil.

They also condemned partition as a solution to the problem. Such a measure, they said, would give France supremacy over the regions of greatest natural wealth, undermine the bases of the country's political independence and ensure the total economic subjection of Algeria to the imperialist powers. It would also allow them to retain their military bases on Algerian soil.

Some representatives—including those of Iraq and Saudi Arabia—described the situation in Algeria as a colonialist war. While stressing their adherence to the principle of self-determination, the representatives of some African States expressed also their strong desire to see Africa rid of outside domination. They added that their attitude in the issue involved not only a matter of principle but also a question of self-protection against such abuses as the practice of nuclear testing on African soil.

Representatives of various French-speaking African States, Latin American Members and some Western European Members were among those who pointed out the special character of the Algerian problem and welcomed the efforts made by President de Gaulle for a just and lasting solution. They regretted that the draft resolution had not indicated the need for appropriate guarantees for the European minority in Algeria. The representative of the Ivory Coast declared that the Algerian question could not be regarded as a simple colonialist issue; moreover, those acting in good faith should be encouraged to decolonize not by vilification or demagogic outbursts but by constructive proposals which could accelerate the decolonization process. The representative of Peru, while commending the sponsors of the 34-power proposal for their effort, suggested deleting specific references in the text to the Assembly's resolution of 14 December 1960 on the granting of independence to colonial countries and peoples and to the Provisional Government of the Algerian Republic. The United States representative also objected to the reference to an "Algerian Government" which, he said, was not recognized by the majority of Member States; such a reference, he felt, might infringe on the prerogatives and responsibilities of the negotiators on both sides.

Some of the co-sponsors of the 34-power proposal, among them Morocco and Tunisia, emphasized that the reservations of some Members about the reference in the text to the Assembly's resolution on the granting of independence to colonial countries and peoples were unnecessary, as the French Government itself had abandoned the "myth" of a French Algeria. As to the matter of guarantees for the European minority, they considered that since the Algerian Provisional Government was offering full Algerian citizenship to those concerned, it would be incompatible with the status of a sovereign State to lay down any further conditions. Finally, the explicit mention of the Provisional Government of the Algerian Republic should not be prejudicial as, on many other occasions, régimes which had not been recognized by the majority of Member States had, nevertheless, been called by the name they had given to themselves.

The 34-power draft resolution was put to the vote on 19 December 1961 and was adopted by the First Committee by a roll-call vote of 61 to 0, with 34 abstentions.

On 20 December 1961, it was approved at a plenary meeting of the Assembly by a roll-call vote of 62 to 0, with 38 abstentions as resolution 1724(XVI).

(YUN 1961, pp. 97-98)

Algeria attained independence in 1962 and, on 4 October, the Democratic and Popular Republic of Algeria was admitted to membership in the United Nations.

Angolan situation

Portugal, on becoming a Member of the United Nations in 1955, took the position that it had no Territories under its administration as referred to in Chapter XI of the Charter regarding Non-Self-Governing Territories. Its overseas territories, including Angola and Mozambique, were "overseas provinces" and an integral part of Portugal's national territory.

The question of Portugal's compliance with its obligations under Chapter XI, including the recognition of the right of the inhabitants of the Territories under its administration to self-determination and to self-government or independence, was first raised in 1956. In 1960, the General Assembly decided that the Territories under Portuguese administration were non-self-governing. However, Portugal rejected the Assembly's decision that it had responsibilities under Chapter XI for those Territories.

In February 1961, Liberia requested an urgent meeting of the Security Council "to deal with the crisis in Angola". Despite Portugal's objection that the situation in Angola was a matter within its exclusive jurisdiction, the Council discussed a draft resolution calling on Portugal to implement the 1960 Declaration on the Granting of Independence to Colonial Countries and Peoples. The resolution was not adopted. In March, the matter was brought before the General Assembly, which in April appointed a subcommittee to examine information on Angola and conduct inquiries as it deemed necessary.

Consideration by Security Council

On 26 May 1961, a request was made by 42 United Nations Members—later joined by two other Members—for a Security Council meeting to be called, as a matter of urgency, to consider the situation in Angola. They charged that the massacres in Angola were continuing and human rights were being continually suppressed, and that this, together with the armed suppression of the Angolan people and the denial of the right of self-determination in contravention of the United Nations Charter and of the General Assembly's resolution on Angola, constituted a serious threat to international peace and security.

. . .

In a statement issued on 27 May and transmitted to the Security Council, the USSR drew attention to the situation in Angola and stated that it was the duty of all States and peoples to compel Portugal to end the predatory colonial war in Angola. The USSR also declared that an authoritative inquiry into the situation in Angola must be held immediately with the participation of the African countries.

. . .

The question was taken up by the Security Council on 6 June, when it was included in the agenda. . . .

The representative of Portugal, after protesting against the Council's failure to hear him on the request to place the item on the agenda, stated that his Government objected to the inscription of an item relating to a situation pertaining exclusively to Portugal's internal jurisdiction and security. In placing the item on its agenda, he said, the Council had contravened all relevant Articles of the United Nations Charter and had undermined its authority. The events in Angola were the result of terrorist action instigated and directed from the outside by agents of international subversion with such violence that military means were forced on Portugal as the only immediate way to deal with the situation. Moreover, the terrorism in Angola and the legitimate action taken by Portugal were entirely matters of internal law and order. The Council, instead of interfering in matters of essentially domestic jurisdiction, should condemn as indirect aggression the encouragement of subversion and the fomenting of civil war by one Member State against another.

Spokesmen in the Council for the 44 Member States which requested the meeting said that the fact that such a large number of Member States had asked the Council again to discuss the situation in Angola reflected an almost unanimous expression of grief and anxiety about Angola. The situation there had deteriorated further since its consideration by the Security Council and the General Assembly in March and April 1961. On 20 April 1961, they recalled, the Assembly had adopted a resolution (1603(XV)) calling on Portugal to consider urgently the introduction of measures and reforms in Angola. Instead of implementing that resolution, Portugal had stepped up its military repression of the Angolan people. In spite of strict censorship, news of mass killings, arrests and bombardment of villages had reached the outside world. The urgent nature of the situation required prompt action by the Security Council in order to halt the carnage and colonial war that was spreading in the whole of Angola.

There was no doubt, they added, that the continuation of the present situation in Angola would further embitter relations among States and increase the threat to international peace and security. Under Article 34 of the United Nations Charter, the Council was expressly empowered to deal with situations likely to endanger the maintenance of international peace and security. Moreover, the General Assembly, with the adoption of its resolution 1514(XV) of 14 December 1960 containing a declaration on the granting of independence to colonial countries and peoples, had stipulated its interest in territories like Angola. In fact, the consideration by the Council and the General Assembly, and also by other organs of the United Nations, of the Angolan situation had well established the competence of the United Nations to deal with such matters.

On 6 June, Ceylon, Liberia and the United Arab Republic submitted a draft resolution whereby the Security Council, deeply deploring the large-scale killings and the severely repressive measures in Angola and being convinced that the continuance of that situation was an actual and potential cause of international friction and threat to international peace and security, would, among other things: (1) reaffirm the Assembly's resolution of 20 April 1961 and call on Portugal to act in accordance with that resolution; (2) ask the Sub-Committee on the Situation in Angola (set up by that resolution) to carry out its mandate without delay; (3) call upon the Portuguese authorities to desist forthwith from repressive measures and further to extend every facility to the Sub-Committee to enable it to perform its task expeditiously; and (4) request the Sub-Committee to report to the Security Council and the Assembly as soon as possible.

On 9 June, Chile submitted two amendments to the three-power draft resolution. One was intended to have the preamble express the Council's conviction that the continuation of the situation in Angola was "likely to endanger the maintenance of international peace and security," rather than that it was "a threat to" international peace and security. Chile also proposed an additional operative paragraph whereby the Council would express the hope that a peaceful solution would be found to the problem of Angola in accordance with the United Nations Charter.

. . .

The three-power draft resolution as amended was then adopted by 9 votes to 0, with 2 abstentions.

Report of Sub-Committee

On 20 November 1961, the United Nations Sub-Committee on the Situation in Angola submitted its report to the General Assembly's sixteenth session in accordance with an Assembly decision of 20 April 1961.

The Sub-Committee reported that it had given special attention to the causes of the disturbances and conflicts in Angola. In this connexion, it expressed the view that the policy of assimilation proclaimed by the Portuguese administration had not been accompanied by any active preparation of the indigenous population for the status of citizenship. Further, there had been many complaints about the denial of human rights, abuse of authority, and "high-handedness," especially by local administrative officials. There were also some indications of the existence of forced labour and excessive taxation. Other grievances by the inhabitants of the territory against the Portuguese Government concerned the inadequacy of economic and social development and inadequate educational and medical facilities. Movements for self-government, self-determination or independence were regarded as subversive and were suppressed. With no avenue left for negotiations or discussion with the Portuguese authorities, the report continued, nationalist movements were forced into clandestine activity or into exile and some of them subsequently into "direct action." The Sub-Committee also maintained that instructions from outside or even the arrival of "agitators" would alone be insufficient to explain the scale of the incidents, or their rapid spread, unless there had been genuine dissatisfaction and deeply-felt grievances.

The Sub-Committee regretted that the Government of Portugal had maintained a negative attitude toward the recommendations of the United Nations.

The Sub-Committee noted, however, that there was a limited response, though hardly satisfactory, to its approach for Portugal's co-operation with the United Nations—taking the form, for instance, of an invitation to the Sub-Committee's chairman to visit Lisbon and the transmission to the Sub-Committee of some information (including legislation promulgated on 8 September 1961 which introduced some reforms in Portugal's overseas policy).

The report concluded that the reforms introduced, although limited in scope, did reflect some awareness by Portugal of the need to adjust its policies to the opinion of the international community.

Consideration by General Assembly

The General Assembly discussed the item at its resumed session in 15 plenary meetings held from 15 to 30 January 1962.

In introducing the report, the Chairman of the Sub-Committee regretted that Portugal had refused to allow the Sub-Committee to visit Angola. Nevertheless, the Sub-Committee had paid full attention to the material submitted by the Portuguese Government and the information gathered directly by three members of the Sub-Committee on the frontiers of Angola and in Leopoldville, and to information from persons within the territory, as well as from other available sources.

The representative of Portugal spoke immediately after the statement by the Chairman of the Sub-Committee and then withdrew from further participation in the debate. He criticized the report of the Sub-Committee, and Assembly resolution 1603(XV) of 20 April 1961 establishing this body as being illegal and in violation of the principles and purposes of the United Nations Charter. The Assembly's discussion had not only clearly contravened Article 2(7) of the Charter (which precludes United Nations intervention in matters essentially within the domestic jurisdiction of any State); it also represented sinister moves by some Member States with a view to bringing about the disintegration of Portugal. The situation in Angola was not a threat to international peace and security. The disturbances of 1960 were limited to only 8 per cent of the territory, and no disturbances had occurred since then. While Portugal had denied the Sub-Committee entry into Angola, it had, nevertheless, given it all possible co-operation. The Sub-Committee, he added, had reached conclusions which could not be borne out by facts. The Portuguese delegation would therefore have the strongest possible reservations about any resolutions which the Assembly might adopt on the basis of the Sub-Committee's report.

Most representatives of the African-Asian Members who spoke in the debate regarded the situation in Angola as a threat to international peace. Portugal's assertion that the United Nations did not have the competence under Article 2(7) of the Charter to deal with the question of Angola was, in their view, invalidated by several resolutions adopted at the General Assembly's fifteenth session and the Security Council's resolution of 9 June 1961. . . .

They also disagreed with Portugal's view that Angola was an integral part of metropolitan Portugal and regretted that Portugal had refused to allow the Sub-Committee to enter Angola.

Nearly all delegations urged Portugal to adjust its policies to the realities of modern times and to co-operate with the United Nations in the implementation of the Assembly's resolution 1514(XV) of 14 December 1960 on the granting of independence to colonial countries and peoples. Bulgaria, Poland and the USSR, among others, urged sanctions against Portugal for its consistent violations of the Charter.

(YUN 1961, pp. 89-92)

In December 1962, the Assembly condemned what it described as "colonial war" carried on by Portugal against the Angolan people and requested the Security Council to take appropriate measures, including sanctions, to secure Portugal's compliance with the resolutions of the Assembly and the Council.

A long and bitter war between the two sides continued for well over a decade and by 1974 had reached a military stalemate. During that period the United Nations continued to make repeated calls on the Portuguese authorities to apply the principle of self-determination and independence to the peoples under its domination and on all States to refrain from both military and economic collaboration with Portugal.

Towards a settlement

Following the events of 25 April 1974, during which the Portuguese armed forces overturned the Government and established a new one, Portugal increased its efforts to establish contact and negotiations with the Angolan liberation movements, which resulted in a de facto cease-fire honoured by all parties concerned. A new statute for Angola was discussed between the Portuguese Government and the liberation movements, which envisaged the creation of the office of a High Commissioner who would also be the head of the Government. The Government would prepare the elections for a National Constituent Assembly, which would draw up the Constitution of Angola as an independent State.

On 20 January 1975, the representative of Portugal transmitted to the United Nations Secretary-General the text of an agreement negotiated at Alvor, Portugal, from 10 to 15 January 1975, between Portugal and the three liberation movements of Angola—the *Frente Nacional para a Libertação de Angola* (FNLA), the *Movimento Popular de Libertação de Angola* (MPLA) and the *União Nacional para a Independência Total de Angola* (UNITA)—by which Portugal recognized these liberation movements as the sole and legitimate representatives of the people of Angola.

According to the agreement, Angola constituted a single indivisible entity within its current geographical and political boundaries, including Cabinda. Until the independence of Angola, to be proclaimed on 11 November 1975, all power was to be exercised by a High Commissioner, appointed by the President of Portugal, and by a Transitional Government to be inaugurated on 31 January 1975 and to be presided over by a Presidential Council of three members—one from each liberation movement. The members of the transitional cabinet were to be appointed, in equal proportion, by the three liberation movements and the President of Portugal.

By the terms of the agreement, Portugal and the three liberation movements formalized the general cease-fire which was being observed throughout the territory. Also provided for was a National Defence Commission responsible for national defence, for peace, safety and public order, and for promoting the progressive integration of the armed forces of the three liberation movements. The Portuguese armed forces were to be withdrawn from the territory by 29 February 1976.

On 21 August, the Chargé d'affaires a.i. of the Permanent Mission of Portugal to the United Nations brought to the attention of the Secretary-General a letter from the Portuguese Minister for Foreign Affairs informing him that the current situation in Angola was causing serious apprehension to the Portuguese Government. The Alvor agreement—which established the political framework for the transition to independence—had been subjected to repeated violations by the liberation movements, which were incapable of overcoming their differences. Those differences, which had led to an intense political confrontation and an armed conflict that was spreading throughout the territory, had necessitated the temporary suspension of the agreement. The Portuguese Government had sought to maintain a policy of strict active neutrality, defending the territorial integrity of Angola against separatism and outside interference. The situation had led to a breakdown of government machinery and administrative structures and to economic and financial deterioration, bringing the territory almost to the brink of collapse. The Portuguese Government, concerned with the protection of the Angolan people, had been compelled to adopt emergency measures, declaring a state of siege with total or partial suspension of constitutional guarantees. A plan of assistance was also under way for the evacuation of all those who wished to leave the territory. Under these conditions, the Portuguese Government hoped to receive from the United Nations continued and reinforced support.

[YUN 1975, p. 863]

As stipulated under the agreement, Angola became independent on 11 November 1975, in the wake of three other Territories that achieved independence from Portugal earlier that year: Mozambique (25 June), Cape Verde (5 July) and Sao Tome and Principe (12 July).

Mozambican issue

In 1962, the Special Committee on the Implementation of the Declaration on the Granting of Independence of Colonial Countries and Peoples heard petitions on the situation in Mozambique from the Mozambique African National Union, the União Nacional Africana de Moçambique Independente and the Mozambique National Democratic Union. The General Assembly did not adopt a resolution on Mozambique as proposed by the Special Committee, in view of its adoption of resolution 1807(XVII) in December covering all the Territories under Portuguese administration. By that resolution, the Assembly called on Portugal to recognize the right of the peoples in the Territories under its administration to self-determination and independence, to cease all acts of repression and withdraw its military and other forces, establish conditions for the free functioning of political parties and negotiate with those parties with a view to transferring power to freely elected representatives and grant independence immediately thereafter.

By 1973, the liberation struggle against Portugal, led by the Frente de Libertação de Moçambique, succeeded through armed action in liberating areas of the territory of Mozambique. On 11 July 1973, the Special Committee adopted a consensus noting with abhorrence reports of atrocities committed by Portugal against the populations of the African Territories under its domination, in particular the massacre of villagers in Mozambique. It felt that such crimes should be investigated by the United Nations. In December, the General Assembly, by resolution 3114(XXVIII), established a Commission of Inquiry on the Reported Massacres in Mozambique.

In 1974, the Commission reported that the new Government of Portugal had conceded that violations of human rights had taken place under the previous regime. The Commission had no doubt that the Portuguese colonial Government was responsible for a number of atrocities in Mozambique.

Resolving the crisis

Following the events of 25 April 1974 in Portugal, the Special Committee on the Situation with regard to the Implementation of the Declaration on the Granting of Independence to Colonial Countries and Peoples, on 27 April, received a communication from the *Frente de Libertação de Moçambique* (FRELIMO) explaining its position on the future of Mozambique. . . .

The statement by FRELIMO said that the new Government in Portugal brought about by the armed forces on 25 April 1974 had announced its intention of finding a solution to the current crisis resulting from 13 years of colonial war.

The objectives of FRELIMO were the total and complete independence of the Mozambican people and the liquidation of Portuguese colonialism; FRELIMO emphasized that it was up to the Portuguese Government to learn from past experience and understand that only through recognition of

the right to independence of the Mozambican people, led by FRELIMO, their authentic and legitimate representative, would the war end.

The FRELIMO statement further said that at that moment it was important that all the forces in solidarity with the peoples of Mozambique, Angola, Guinea-Bissau, Cape Verde and São Tomé e Príncipe continue their action for the recognition of their right to complete independence and their support of and assistance to the liberation movements.

On 9 May 1974, the Chairman of the Special Committee, the Chairman of the Special Committee on *Apartheid* and the President of the United Nations Council for Namibia issued a joint statement, saying that the developments in Portugal since 25 April were a clear demonstration of the bankruptcy of Portuguese colonialism and a recognition of the futility of the murderous colonial wars waged by the Portuguese military forces in Angola, Mozambique and the illegally occupied parts of Guinea-Bissau. They emphasized that although developments in Portugal proper were a matter for the Portuguese people, these developments had serious implications for the general situation in southern Africa. They believed that the evolving situation in Portugal provided the opportunity for the new régime to abandon completely the misguided policy of its predecessors. Portugal must not only recognize the legitimate right of the peoples of Angola, Mozambique and Cape Verde to self-determination and independence, but must also take decisive and concrete measures towards the realization of that right.

The statement reiterated previous calls on the Portuguese authorities to enter immediately into negotiations with the national liberation movements recognized by the Organization of African Unity for the purpose of ending Portuguese colonialism in those territories.

The Chairmen and the President expressed the hope that the authorities in Portugal would recognize the needs of the hour and seize the opportunity which it presented. They also said that they firmly believed that the time had come for the military allies of Portugal, as well as her trading partners, to demonstrate their goodwill towards Africa and their commitments to the United Nations by taking measures calculated to end once and for all Portuguese colonialism in Africa. Such a course of action would, in their opinion, also be in the best interests of the people of Portugal.

On 24 July, the Chairman of the Special Committee received a communication from the representative of Portugal, informing him that the Government of Portugal intended to co-operate with the Committee.

In response to an invitation by the Government of Portugal, the Secretary-General visited Lisbon in August. During his visit, he received a memorandum setting out Portugal's position on the question of the African territories under its administration within the context of a new law (Constitutional Law No. 7/74 of 17 July 1974) and a statement made by President António de Spínola on 27 July. Portugal reaffirmed its obligations with regard to Chapter XI of the Charter of the United Nations and the Declaration on the granting of independence. It pledged full co-operation to the United Nations in the implementation of the provisions of the Charter, the Declaration, and the relevant United Nations resolutions with respect to the territories under Portuguese administration.

It also reaffirmed its recognition of the right of self-determination and independence for all the overseas territories under its administration, pledged full support for the territorial unity and integrity of each territory and opposed any secessionist attempts or attempts at dismemberment from any quarter.

. . .

The Government of Portugal expressed the hope that since it had taken concrete steps to comply fully with the provisions of the Declaration, the General Assembly would reconsider its previous decisions and enable Portugal to participate fully in the social, economic, financial and technical programmes of the United Nations and the specialized agencies as well as in the activities of those bodies.

By a letter of 6 August to the Secretary-General, the Government of Portugal transmitted the text of a Constitutional Law approved on 24 July 1974 which abrogated article 1 of the existing Constitution wherein the overseas territories were defined as an integral part of the Portuguese national territory. By this constitutional change, the Portuguese Government formally recognized the right to self-determination, with all its consequences, including the acceptance of independence for the overseas territories.

On 29 August 1974, the Special Committee considered developments relating to the question of territories under Portuguese domination subsequent to the change of Government in Portugal on 25 April 1974. It recorded its position on this question on 5 September in a statement by the Chairman which said that the overthrow of the fascist régime in Lisbon on 25 April had been made possible only through the determined efforts of the peoples of the territories led by their national liberation movements.

The Special Committee noted that the Government of Portugal had since indicated its intention to renounce categorically the colonialist policy of the previous régime and had accepted fully the relevant provisions of the United Nations Charter and the right of the peoples concerned to self-

determination and independence in accordance with the Declaration on the granting of independence, as well as with the provisions of all relevant resolutions of the United Nations.

. . .

By a letter dated 20 September 1974, the representative of Portugal transmitted to the Secretary-General the text of an agreement between Portugal and FRELIMO signed at Lusaka, Zambia, on 7 September, aiming at the establishment of self-determination and independence for Mozambique.

Under the terms of the agreement, Portugal accepted the progressive transfer of the powers it held over the territory and set the date for the complete independence of Mozambique as 25 June 1975, the anniversary of the founding of FRELIMO.

The agreement provided for the appointment of a High Commissioner designated by the President of Portugal and the establishment of a transitional Government and a Joint Military Commission, both appointed by agreement between FRELIMO and Portugal. In addition, the two parties agreed to a cease-fire, and to act jointly in the defence of the territorial integrity of Mozambique against aggression.

The two parties agreed to establish and develop links of friendship and constructive co-operation between their respective peoples in the cultural, technical, economic and financial fields, on a basis of independence, equality, community of interests and respect for the personality of each people.

(YUN 1974, pp. 812-14)

Mozambique became independent on 25 June 1975. In September of that year, it was admitted to United Nations membership.

Namibian question

Namibia, under the name South West Africa, was declared a German protectorate in 1890. South Africa seized the Territory from Germany in 1915 during the First World War; in 1920, the League of Nations gave South Africa a Mandate over the Territory.

Namibia was the only one of the seven African Territories once held under the League of Nations Mandate System that was not placed under the United Nations Trusteeship System. The General Assembly, in 1946, recommended that South Africa do so, having refused its request that the Assembly approve the proposed incorporation of South West Africa into South Africa. South Africa took the position that the Mandate in respect of the Territory had lapsed and, while it continued to administer the Territory in the spirit of the trust originally accepted, as a result of the demise of the League of Nations, it had no other international commitments. In 1950, the International Court of Justice (ICJ) held that South Africa continued to have international obligations towards the Territory. In 1966, the Assembly declared that South Africa had failed to fulfil its obligations under the Mandate and placed the Territory under direct responsibility of the United Nations. In 1967, the United Nations Council for South West Africa was established to administer the Territory until independence; in 1968, it was renamed the United Nations Council for Namibia when the Assembly proclaimed that the Territory would be known as Namibia.

Consideration at special session of General Assembly

Report of Ad Hoc Committee

The *Ad Hoc* Committee for South West Africa, established by the General Assembly on 27 October 1966, to recommend practical means by which the territory should be administered until independence, met between January and March 1967 and reported to the General Assembly's fifth special session, held between 21 April and 13 June 1967. In this report, the Committee stated that it had been unable to arrive at an agreed conclusion, and submitted three separate proposals: one sponsored by Ethiopia, Nigeria, Pakistan, Senegal and the United Arab Republic; one sponsored by Canada, Italy and the United States; and one sponsored by Chile and Mexico and supported by Japan. Also included in the report were suggestions by Czechoslovakia and the USSR, reflecting a fourth position not formulated as a formal proposal.

The proposal put forward by Ethiopia, Nigeria, Pakistan, Senegal and the United Arab Republic called for the direct temporary administration of South West Africa through a United Nations Council for South West Africa assisted by a Commissioner. The Council would be given legislative authority and would proceed immediately to South West Africa with a view to taking over the administration and ensuring the withdrawal of South African police, military and other personnel and their replacement by United Nations personnel. The Council would also, in consultation with the people, establish a constituent assembly to draft a constitution. New elections by universal adult suffrage would be held to establish a legislative assembly and, upon the formation of a government, South West Africa would be declared independent no later than June 1968. Any action by South Africa to impede the Council's work would be considered to constitute a flagrant defiance of United Nations authority and call for action by the Security Council under Chapter VII of the United Nations Charter.

. . .

Action by General Assembly

During its fifth special session, the General Assembly considered the report of the *Ad Hoc* Committee for South West Africa at plenary meetings, beginning on 24 April 1967.

. . .

During the ensuing debate, the majority of African and Asian Member States strongly endorsed the five-power proposals made in the *Ad Hoc* Committee (*i.e.*, by Ethiopia, Nigeria, Pakistan, Senegal and the United Arab Republic), particularly those calling for direct administration of the territory by the United Nations and envisaging enforcement action by the Security Council in the event of non-compliance by South Africa. . . .

The representative of Ethiopia, voicing the opinion of the majority of African States, said that the establishment of a United Nations administration within South West Africa was the only logical course of action to discharge the responsibility which the United Nations had assumed under the Assembly's resolution of 27 October 1966. Since the territory no longer had a lawful administration, the United Nations was obliged to fill the vacuum while the necessary preparations were made to enable the people to exercise their right of self-determination and attain independence. He also maintained that, in view of South Africa's past disregard for United Nations resolutions on the territory, it would be unrealistic not to provide for eventual enforcement action by the Security Council in the event that South Africa should persist in its defiance of the will of the Assembly.

. . .

The representative of Canada believed that it was essential to explore all possibilities for a negotiated settlement with South Africa for the orderly transfer of the administration in accordance with the Assembly's resolution of 27 October 1966, before recommending coercive measures which might not have the support of the major powers. He considered that the most practical way of implementing that resolution was to envisage from the start that the territory would be administered by its own inhabitants and to seek, in co-operation with the *de facto* administration, to establish a nucleus of self-government in the territory. The proposal, of which his delegation was a co-sponsor, envisaged that the United Nations representative would have broad powers to investigate the situation and to make recommendations which would include the nature and amount of international assistance required to establish a viable self-administration.

. . .

The United Kingdom spokesman regretted that the terms of reference of the *Ad Hoc* Committee had not required it to consider all aspects of the future course open to the United Nations in order to attain the agreed objectives of self-determination and independence for all the people of South West Africa. To arrive at conclusions which could not be put into effect would raise false hopes and damage the reputation and effectiveness of the United Nations. He favoured the proposal put forward by Canada, Italy and the United States which called for further study of the situation because he considered that it represented the most practical course, offering the best hope of achieving the desired objectives.

In the view of the representative of the USSR, no transition period of United Nations administration was necessary and South West Africa should be declared independent immediately. He maintained that in other former colonial territories it had been demonstrated that problems such as the establishment of a government apparatus could be solved more successfully under conditions of independence without outside interference. He feared that if special United Nations machinery were set up to administer the territory, it would be used by the opponents of independence for purposes other than those envisaged in the Charter. The immediate task was to eliminate the South African racist régime from the territory and the proposals of Canada, Italy and the United States showed the desire of the Western powers to prevent this.

The United States assured the Assembly that the proposals it had co-sponsored were in no way intended to delay the independence of South West Africa, but were designed to seek practical ways of putting into effect the Assembly's resolution of 27 October 1966. The United States considered that the Assembly would be remiss if it did not seek a peaceful solution to the problem through diplomatic dialogue and instead adopted a policy which seemed to lead to confrontation with South Africa.

Sweden recommended that the useful elements of all the proposals should be combined to give practical expression to the direct responsibility undertaken by the United Nations and observed that direct administration of the territory by the United Nations was only one possibility. No matter which course was taken, Sweden stressed, it was of major importance that there be broad consultations with the people of the territory prior to convening a constituent assembly, a comprehensive programme of assistance to the territory continuing beyond independence, and contact with South Africa in order to try to explore further the chances for a peaceful solution.

The representative of Jamaica favoured a United Nations body which would administer the territory and at the same time carry out economic and other surveys and help in the establishment of a viable economy and representative organs of government. In view of the continued intransigence of the Republic of South Africa, he declared, recourse to action by the Security Council was a necessary component of any resolution to be adopted.

. . .

The representatives of Burma, the Ivory Coast and Lesotho also believed that the differences between the five-power proposals and the Latin American proposals were differences of degree and that there was no reason not to reach agreement on a compromise formula acceptable to both groups.

Botswana maintained that so long as the major powers were not prepared to use force, the only realistic approach to giving effect to the Assembly's resolution of 27 October 1966 was by seeking the co-operation of South Africa.

. . .

On 26 April 1967, a five-part draft resolution was introduced, sponsored by 58 Members.

. . .

On 27 April, the representative of Saudi Arabia introduced a draft resolution, which was not put to the vote, whereby the Assembly would appoint two Member States to co-administer the territory with South Africa until the Council for South West Africa began its task.

On 5 May 1967, the Assembly adjourned its consideration of the item to enable further consultations to take place. A revised draft resolution, sponsored by 79 Members, was put before the Assembly on 18 May and was adopted on 19 May by a roll-call vote of 85 to 2, with 30 abstentions as resolution 2248(S-V).

. . .

Thus, by the preamble to the resolution adopted, the General Assembly: reaffirmed its resolution of 14 December 1960 containing the Declaration on the granting of independence to colonial countries and peoples, and its resolution of 27 October 1966 terminating the Mandate of South Africa and assuming direct responsibility for South West Africa; and recognized that it was incumbent upon the United Nations to take practical steps to transfer power to the people of South West Africa.

By the operative parts of the resolution, the Assembly reaffirmed the territorial integrity of South West Africa and the inalienable right of its people to freedom and independence. It established an 11-Member United Nations Council for South West Africa with powers to: (*a*) administer South West Africa until independence, with the maximum possible participation of the people of the territory; (*b*) promulgate laws and regulations necessary to administer the territory until a legislative assembly was established following elections conducted on the basis of universal adult suffrage;

(c) take immediately measures to establish a constituent assembly to draw up a constitution on the basis of which elections would be held; *(d)* take all necessary measures for the maintenance of law and order in the territory; and *(e)* transfer all powers to the people of the territory upon the declaration of independence. The Assembly also decided that the Council would be responsible to the General Assembly and would be assisted by a United Nations Commissioner for South West Africa.

In addition, it decided that the administration of South West Africa was to be financed from revenues collected in the territory and that expenses of the Council and Commissioner were to be met from the regular budget of the United Nations. The Assembly asked the specialized agencies and appropriate organs of the United Nations to give technical and financial assistance to South West Africa through a co-ordinated emergency programme.

The Assembly further decided that the Council was to be based in South West Africa and it requested the Council to enter immediately into contact with the authorities of South Africa in order to lay down procedures, in accordance with the Assembly's resolution of 27 October 1966 and the present resolution, for the transfer of the administration of the territory with the least possible upheaval. It requested the Council to proceed to South West Africa with a view to: *(a)* taking over the administration of the territory; *(b)* ensuring the withdrawal of the South African police and military forces; *(c)* ensuring the withdrawal of South African personnel and their replacement by personnel operating under the Council; *(d)* ensuring that in the utilization and recruitment of personnel preference was given to the indigenous people. The Assembly also called upon the Government of South Africa to comply without delay with the terms of the resolution of 27 October 1966 and the present resolution and to facilitate the transfer of the administration of South West Africa to the Council. It also requested the Security Council to take all appropriate measures to enable the Council for South West Africa to discharge its functions and responsibilities and requested all States to co-operate and to assist the Council for South West Africa in its task. The South West Africa Council was asked to report to the Assembly at intervals not exceeding three months and to make a special report to the twenty-second session of the Assembly (later in 1967) on the implementation of the present resolution.

By the final part of its resolution, the Assembly decided that South West Africa was to become independent on a date to be fixed in accordance with the wishes of the people and that the Council should do all in its power to enable independence to be attained by June 1968.

. . .

On 13 June, the General Assembly, by secret ballot, elected Chile, Colombia, Guyana, India, Indonesia, Nigeria, Pakistan, Turkey, the United Arab Republic, Yugoslavia and Zambia to the United Nations Council for South West Africa.

At the same time, the Assembly considered a note by the Secretary-General in which he informed the Assembly that he had been unable to undertake all the consultations necessary for nominating the United Nations Commissioner for South West Africa. He proposed, as an interim arrangement, the appointment of the United Nations Legal Counsel as Acting Commissioner until the Assembly's twenty-second regular session. The Assembly agreed to this proposal without objection.

. . .

Consideration by Special Committee of Twenty-four (June 1967)

The General Assembly's 24-member Special Committee on the Situation with regard to the Implementation of the Declaration on the Granting of Independence to Colonial Countries and Peoples considered the question of South West Africa at meetings held in Africa between 7 and 19 June 1967. The Special Committee examined numerous written petitions and heard four petitioners representing political organizations: Solomon Mifimo, Moses M. Garoeb and Jacob Kuhangua, of the South West Africa People's Organization (SWAPO), and T. T. Letlaka of the Pan Africanist Congress (PAC).

The petitioners told the Special Committee that the people of South West Africa were disappointed by the delay in the establishment of the United Nations Council for South West Africa and with the functions finally entrusted to it. They had hoped that the General Assembly would decide upon the use of force to terminate South Africa's control over South West Africa, but the great powers, because of their financial interests in South Africa, seemed to have sabotaged proposals for such action by the General Assembly. The petitioners said that the people of South West Africa consequently felt that they could not rely entirely on the United Nations to liberate the territory and were determined to fight on their own behalf. The representatives of SWAPO said that their organization had launched an armed struggle for liberation in August 1966 and had since fought engagements against the South African police in Ovamboland leaving many killed on both sides. The South African authorities had reacted by launching a campaign of oppression, arresting many SWAPO members, some of whom were detained in South West Africa, while about 70, including all the leaders, had been taken to South Africa and imprisoned under the 180-day detention law. In May 1967, a so-called "Terrorism Bill" had been introduced under which persons charged with participating in "terrorist" activities would be tried by a judge without a jury and, if convicted, would be liable to the same penalties as for treason. South Africa had also set up military bases throughout South West Africa and was patrolling the borders, particularly the border with Zambia, in an effort to capture freedom fighters. The petitioners said that, if the United Nations wished to prevent bloodshed, it should act before it was too late; withdrawal of economic support by the major Western powers would be sufficient to bring about the collapse of the South African régime without armed intervention, but the participation of the great powers should not be made a condition for any United Nations action.

The petitioners told the Special Committee that it was the South African Government's intention to grant a form of so-called self-government to Ovamboland, in line with its policy of dividing the African people so as better to exploit them. They vigorously denounced this plan which, they said, would result in the creation of another *Bantustan* like the Transkei. Finally, the petitioners said that the people of South West Africa would not falter in their struggle until their country was freed from foreign domination and a Republic of Namibia had been created. In a free Namibia, the real needs of the people would be served, citizens would have equal opportunity to share in the progress towards prosperity, there would be compulsory education, and private property would be respected.

. . .

Consideration by UN Council for South West Africa

The 11-member United Nations Council for South West Africa, elected on 13 June 1967, held its first meeting on 16 August 1967. On 28 August, the Council approved the text of a letter from its President to be addressed to South Africa's Minister for Foreign Affairs on behalf of the Council. The letter informed the Minister that by terms of the General Assembly's resolution of 19 May 1967, the Council had been requested to enter immediately into contact with the authorities of South Africa in order to lay down procedures for the transfer of the administration of the territory to the Council, and it requested an early reply indicating the measures which the Government of South Africa proposed to facilitate such transfer.

On 27 September 1967, the Council received from the Secretary-General a copy of a letter dated 26 September which he had received from the South African Minister for Foreign Affairs. In this letter the Minister informed the Secretary-General that he had received the President's letter and that since the South African Government considered the Assembly's resolutions terminating the Mandate and authorizing the Council to administer the territory to be illegal, it would not comply with those resolutions and would continue to administer the territory notwithstanding them.

In its report to the General Assembly, dated 30 October 1967, the Council stated that because of the refusal of the Government of South Africa to co-operate, it had found it impossible to discharge effectively all of the functions and responsibilities entrusted to it by the Assembly. The Council stated that the Government of South Africa was not only defying the United Nations but was continuing to act in a manner which was designed to consolidate its control over South West Africa. The Council considered that the continued presence of South African authorities in South West Africa constituted an illegal act, a usurpation of power and a foreign occupation of the territory which seriously threatened international peace and security. In these circumstances, it recommended that the General Assembly should take the necessary measures, including addressing a request for appropriate action to the Security Council, to enable the Council for South West Africa to discharge all its functions and responsibilities effectively. The Council also commented that the South African Government's defiance of the General Assembly was rendered even more blatant by the application in South West Africa of the so-called "Terrorism Act" and the illegal arrest and trial in South Africa of 37 South West Africans, which had shocked international opinion.

The Council informed the Assembly that although it had been unable to undertake its administrative responsibilities in South West Africa, it had given consideration to certain administrative matters regarding the territory, among them the question of issuing passports to South West Africans and the question of the participation of representatives of South West Africa in the work of the Economic Commission for Africa (ECA).

. . .

Consideration by General Assembly (twenty-second session)

At its twenty-second regular session which opened in September 1967, the General Assembly considered the question of South West Africa at plenary meetings held between 5 and 16 December. The discussion centred mainly on two issues: *(a)* the situation arising from South Africa's non-compliance with the Assembly's resolutions of 27 October 1966 and 19 May 1967 by which the Assembly had terminated the Mandate and established the Council for South West Africa; and *(b)* the arrest and trial by South African authorities of 37 South West Africans on charges under the South African Terrorism Act of 1967—which had been applied to the territory after the termination of the Mandate—and the Suppression of Communism Act.

. . .

The report of the Special Committee of Twenty-four included information concerning the arrest and trial of the 37 South West Africans, as well as the provisions of the Terrorism Act. It also set out further measures taken by the South African Government, subsequent to the termination of the Mandate, with respect to the implementation of the recommendations of the Odendaal Commission to partition the territory into 10 self-governing "homelands." The most important of these measures were reported to be the offer of self-government to Ovamboland in March 1967 and the announcement that major constitutional changes affecting the status of South West Africa would soon be introduced in the South African Parliament.

. . .

Resolution on general aspects
of South West African question

Concerning the issue of Assembly action in relation to South Africa's refusal to comply with General Assembly resolutions of 27 October 1966 (2145(XXI)) and 19 May 1967 (2248(S-V)), the debate revealed a divergence of views.

. . .

On 16 December 1967, the General Assembly, by a roll-call vote of 93 to 2 (Portugal and South Africa), with 18 abstentions, adopted a text sponsored by 49 Member States as resolution 2325(XXII).

. . .

By the operative paragraphs of the resolution, the Assembly: (1) noted with appreciation the report of the United Nations Council for South West Africa and the Council's efforts to discharge the responsibilities and functions entrusted to it; (2) requested the Council to fulfil by every available means the mandate entrusted to it by the General Assembly; (3) condemned the refusal of the Government of South Africa to comply with General Assembly resolutions of 27 October 1966 and 19 May 1967; (4) declared that the continued presence of South African authorities in South West Africa was a flagrant violation of South West Africa's territorial integrity and international status; (5) called upon the South African Government to withdraw from the territory of South West Africa, unconditionally and without delay, all its military and police forces as well as its administration, to release all political prisoners and to allow all political refugees who were natives of the territory to return to it; (6) urgently appealed to all United Nations Member States, particularly the main trading partners of South Africa and those which had economic and other interests in South Africa and South West Africa, to take effective economic and other measures designed to ensure the immediate withdrawal of the South African administration from the territory, thereby clearing the way for implementation of the Assembly's resolutions; (7) requested the Security Council to take effective steps to enable the United Nations to fulfil the responsibilities it had assumed with respect to South West Africa; (8) further requested the Security Council to take all appropriate measures to enable the United Nations Council for South West Africa to discharge fully the functions and responsibilities entrusted to it by the General Assembly; . . .

[YUN 1967, pp. 690-706]

Towards a negotiated settlement

South Africa, in defiance of the United Nations, continued to occupy Namibia. The Security Council, in 1969, described the continued presence of South Africa in Namibia as illegal and called on it to withdraw its administration from there immediately. In 1970, the Council declared for the first time that all acts taken by South Africa concerning Namibia after the termination of the Mandate were "illegal and invalid", a view upheld by ICJ in 1971. In 1976, the Council for the first time demanded that South Africa accept elections for the Territory under United Nations supervision and control.

To end the stalemate, the five Western Powers — Canada, France, the Federal Republic of Germany, the United Kingdom and the United States — submitted to the Security Council in 1978 a proposal for settling the question of Namibia, according to which elections for a Constituent Assembly would be held under United Nations auspices. Every stage of the electoral process would be conducted to the satisfaction of a Special Representative appointed by the Secretary-General. A United Nations Transition Assistance Group (UNTAG) would be at the disposal of the Special Representative to help him supervise the political process and ensure that the parties observed all provisions of an agreed solution.

The Security Council requested the Secretary-General to appoint a Special Representative for Namibia and submit recommendations for implementing the settlement proposal. By resolution 435(1978), the Council endorsed the United Nations plan for Namibia and decided to establish UNTAG. Later that year, the General Assembly, at a special session, adopted the Declaration on Namibia setting out a course of action for implementing its decisions ending South Africa's illegal occupation of the Territory and achieving Namibia's independence.

In 1980, South Africa accepted the plan proposed by the five Powers and in 1981 participated in a pre-implementation meeting. However, it did not agree to proceed towards a cease-fire, one of the conditions set by the United Nations for implementing resolution 435(1978). Negotiations were again stalled when South Africa attached new conditions which the United Nations did not accept, in particular linking the independence of Namibia to the withdrawal of Cuban troops from Angola. The situation was complicated further by South Africa's decision in 1985 to establish an interim government in Namibia.

In December 1988, after many years of guerrilla warfare and diplomatic efforts, Angola, Cuba and South Africa signed an agreement which opened the way to implementation of the United Nations independence plan endorsed by resolution 435(1978). To supervise implementation of that plan, including the holding of free and fair elections for a Constituent Assembly, was the mandate of UNTAG.

In 1990, on the occasion of the thirtieth anniversary of its 1960 Declaration on the Granting of Independence to Colonial Countries and Peoples, the General Assembly (resolution 45/33) noted with satisfaction the attainment of independence by Namibia following the holding of free and fair elections under United Nations supervision, which led to its independence on 21 March 1990 and its subsequent admission to membership of the United Nations on 23 April.

Southern Rhodesia

Southern Rhodesia (which later, upon achieving independence, came to be known as Zimbabwe) was administered by the British South African Company under a Royal Charter from 1899 until 1923, when the United Kingdom annexed it to the Crown and granted the settlers internal self-government. In 1953, Southern Rhodesia, with Northern Rhodesia and Nyasaland, became part of the Central African Federation, which was dissolved in 1963.

In a July 1961 referendum, the Southern Rhodesian electorate, consisting almost entirely of Europeans, approved proposals for a new Constitution which provided for a franchise system, excluding the African population almost completely. In the meantime, the new activism signified by the adoption of the 1960 Declaration on the Granting of Independence to Colonial Countries and Peoples led the United Nations to take up the question of Southern Rhodesia.

On 23 February 1962, . . . the General Assembly adopted a resolution (1745(XVI)) asking its Special Committee on the Situation with regard to the Implementation of the Declaration on the Granting of Independence to Colonial Countries and Peoples to advise whether Southern Rhodesia had attained a full measure of self-government. In May 1962, the Special Committee recommended that the question of Southern Rhodesia should be considered as a matter of urgency and in June 1962 it was taken up by the Assembly at its resumed sixteenth session. On 28 June 1962, the Assembly adopted a resolution (1747(XVI)) by which it affirmed that Southern Rhodesia was a non-self-governing territory. Among other things, it also requested the United Kingdom urgently to convene a conference of all political parties to formulate a new constitution on the basis of "one man, one vote"; to restore all rights of the non-European population; to repeal all discriminatory legislation; and to release all political prisoners.

. . . By its resolution 1760(XVII) of 31 October 1962, the Assembly also requested the United Kingdom to take necessary measures to secure the immediate suspension of the enforcement of the Southern Rhodesian Constitution of December 1961 and the cancellation of the general elections scheduled to take place under the Constitution. It asked the Secretary-General to lend his good offices to promote conciliation by initiating discussions between the United Kingdom and other parties concerned to achieve the objectives set out in the Assembly's resolutions on Southern Rhodesia.

During the course of consideration of this item by the Special Committee and by the Assembly (at its sixteenth and seventeenth sessions) the United Kingdom took the position that Southern Rhodesia was not a non-self-governing territory in the context of Article 73 of the United Nations Charter. The United Kingdom declared that Southern Rhodesia was a self-governing colony with a responsible government. Since 1923 the United Kingdom Government had had no effective power to legislate for Southern Rhodesian internal affairs. The United Kingdom maintained that the United Nations had no right to intervene in the affairs of Southern Rhodesia and that the existence of a United Nations resolution which asserted that the United Nations had that right did not establish it.

On 1 November 1962, the whole of the Constitution of December 1961 came into force and elections for the Legislative Assembly under the new Constitution were held on 14 December 1962. These elections, which were boycotted by the African nationalist parties, resulted in the formation of a new government by Winston Field, leader of the Rhodesian Front.

In accordance with the request addressed to him by the Assembly under resolution 1760(XVII) of 31 October 1962, the Secretary-General submitted reports to the Assembly on 19 December 1962 and on 5 June 1963. Transmitted with the second report was the text of a letter from the United Kingdom Government stating that there were difficulties in the way of compliance by it with the Assembly resolutions, owing to the United Kingdom's constitutional relationship with Southern Rhodesia.

. . .

Consideration by Special Committee

The question of Southern Rhodesia was considered by the Special Committee at meetings held between 15 March and 20 June 1963. On 25 and 26 March a petitioner, Joshua Nkomo, National President of the Zimbabwe African People's Union (ZAPU), made a statement describing events which had taken place in the territory since October 1962. He asked the Special Committee to send a sub-committee to London to impress upon the United Kingdom Government the seriousness of the situation in Southern Rhodesia and the necessity for taking immediate action. On 28 March, at the conclusion of the general debate, the Chairman expressed the consensus of the Special Committee, to the effect that if immediate measures were not taken, the situation in Southern Rhodesia might in the near future constitute a real threat to international peace and security. The Special Committee decided to send a sub-committee immediately to London to draw the attention of the United Kingdom Government to the explosive situation in the territory, and to undertake conversations with that Government aimed at ensuring the implementation of the various General Assembly resolutions concerning Southern Rhodesia.

. . .

Report of Sub-Committee

The Sub-Committee, which was composed of the representatives of Mali (Chairman), Uruguay (Vice-Chairman), Syria (Rapporteur), Sierra Leone, Tanganyika and Tunisia, visited London from 20 to 26 April, and unanimously adopted its report on 8 May 1963.

In this report, the Sub-Committee stated that it had gained the impression that the United Kingdom Government intended to seek, through persuasion, a compromise solution aimed at widening the franchise but not, the Sub-Committee felt, in a manner desired by the Africans or according to the terms of the General Assembly's resolutions. The Sub-Committee was of the opinion, among other things, that the present situation in Southern Rhodesia demanded that the United Kingdom should take a more direct and positive position concerning future action, consistent with its obligations to protect the interests of the majority of the territory's inhabitants. It considered that a fully representative constitutional conference should be held; it did not believe that the pre-

independence conference—which the United Kingdom had stated would include discussion of constitutional matters but which, the Sub-Committee noted, would not provide for participation by the African people—would succeed in producing a solution securing the objectives of the General Assembly's resolutions. The Sub-Committee felt that there would be serious repercussions should the present stalemate be permitted to continue and accordingly recommended that, in the absence of any favourable developments in the immediate future, the Special Committee should consider ways and means of dealing with the question on an urgent basis.

. . .

Decisions by Special Committee

The Special Committee considered its Sub-Committee's report from 12 to 20 June, when it adopted, by a roll-call vote of 19 to 0, with 4 abstentions, a 13-power draft resolution on matters arising out of its consideration of the report. The United Kingdom did not participate in the vote. The four members abstaining were Australia, Denmark, Italy and the United States.

By this resolution, the Special Committee called upon the United Kingdom Government: to abrogate Southern Rhodesia's 1961 Constitution; to hold without delay a constitutional conference in which representatives of all political parties of Southern Rhodesia would take part with a view to making constitutional arrangements for independence on the basis of universal suffrage, including the fixing of the earliest date for independence; and to declare unequivocally that it would not transfer the powers and attributes of sovereignty to any government constituted under the 1961 Constitution. It recommended that, if developments necessitated and circumstances warranted, a special General Assembly session should be convened to consider the situation in the territory; and that in any event the question of Southern Rhodesia should be placed as a matter of high priority and urgency on the agenda of the Assembly's eighteenth regular session (scheduled to open in September 1963). It also drew the attention of the Security Council to the deterioration of the explosive situation which prevailed in Southern Rhodesia.

. . .

Consideration by Security Council

. . .

The Security Council considered the question at six meetings between 9 and 13 September 1963, inviting Mali, Tanganyika, Uganda and the United Arab Republic, at their request, to participate in the discussion.

Prior to adoption of the agenda, the United Kingdom representative stressed his Government's view that the Council was not competent to deal with the question as the United Kingdom did not accept that Southern Rhodesia was a non-self-governing territory and therefore Article 2(7) of the United Nations Charter applied. He contended that the onus was on the countries which had brought the item to the Council to establish that a situation existed in Southern Rhodesia calling for action under Chapter VII of the Charter (which deals with action with respect to threats to the peace, breaches of the peace and acts of aggression) and thereby justifying the derogation from Article 2(7) provided for therein. He did not believe this could be done. Moreover, he declared, it was not the function of the Security Council to pronounce on whether a territory was or was not self-governing.

During the debate on the question, Ghana, Mali, the United Arab Republic, Uganda, Tanganyika, and Morocco emphasized that the Council was called upon to consider any issue which in the opinion of a United Nations Member State was likely to endanger peace or was a threat to peace and security. . . .

These speakers expressed the view that the United Kingdom Government had ultimate authority and power in Southern Rhodesia, and it must exercise those powers, however residual, in the name of African advancement and peace, and not for settler entrenchment in Southern Rhodesia. If the contention of the United Kingdom Government that it did not have such power was valid, they declared, it would follow that, contrary to its expressed assurances, the United Kingdom would have no control over the very powerful air and land units that were to be handed over to the Southern Rhodesian régime, and which would be a dangerous element affecting the whole area. No one could say for certain how the white minority were going to utilize those forces, but it could easily be guessed that it would not be in the interest of the African minority, nor in the interest of the neighbouring countries. That was where the threat to peace and security lay. They further asserted that it was the duty of the United Kingdom Government to state in no uncertain terms that it would not grant the right of independence to Southern Rhodesia until such time as political power was taken away from the white minority and transferred to the indigenous people who formed the vast majority of the population.

The representative of the United Kingdom said it would be evident that little further progress could be made towards a solution of the problem of Central Africa until the Federation of Rhodesia and Nyasaland was dismantled. Upon dissolution, powers conferred upon the Federation by Territorial Governments reverted to the latter. But such reversion did not change the status of Southern Rhodesia. In reference to the assertion that the armed forces reverting to Southern Rhodesia might be used for external adventures, he said these armed forces would be no more available for such action than they were at present, and the United Kingdom Government would retain control of their use outside the frontiers of Southern Rhodesia as long as its responsibility in relation to Southern Rhodesia was unchanged. The United Kingdom representative disputed the statement that the United Kingdom had the authority to effect the reforms requested by the United Nations and that the United Kingdom could deny even powers of taxation to the Southern Rhodesian régime. He said that the freedom of the Southern Rhodesian Government to conduct its own internal affairs was an inescapable constitutional and political fact. As for the status of Southern Rhodesia, the present position was that its Government had been informed that prior to consideration of the question of independence, it must make proposals to the United Kingdom Government for amendments to its Constitution, which would result in broadening the basis of representation in the legislature to take effect as soon as practicable.

On 12 September, Ghana, Morocco and the Philippines submitted a draft resolution by which the Council would: (1) invite the United Kingdom Government not to transfer to its colony of Southern Rhodesia as at present governed any powers or attributes of sovereignty until the establishment of a government fully representative of all the inhabitants of the colony; (2) further invite the United Kingdom Government not to transfer to its colony of Southern Rhodesia the armed forces and aircraft as envisaged by the Central African Conference, 1963; (3) invite that Government to implement the General Assembly resolutions on the question, in particular resolutions 1747(XVI) of 28 June 1962 and 1760(XVII) of 31 October 1962; and (4) request the General Assembly to continue its examination of the question with a view to securing a just and lasting settlement.

. . .

On 13 September the Council voted upon the draft resolution. There were 8 votes in favour, 1 against (United Kingdom), and 2 abstentions (France, United States). Owing to the negative vote of a permanent member (United Kingdom), the draft resolution was not adopted.

Explaining his negative vote, the representative of the United Kingdom stated that he had voted against the draft resolution because his Government was convinced that orderly dissolution of the Federation and further progress in Central Africa would be irretrievably damaged if it acceded to the demands not to permit the reversion of powers to the Government of Southern Rhodesia.

. . .

Consideration by General Assembly

On 18 July 1963, 23 United Nations Members asked that an item entitled "The Question of Southern Rhodesia" be placed on the agenda of the eighteenth regular session of the General Assembly (due to open in September 1963). . . .

On the recommendation of its General Committee, the Assembly agreed to place this item on its agenda.

. . .

The United Kingdom representative . . . reviewed events leading to the Central African Conference held at Victoria Falls in July 1963 where an agreement was reached on procedures for the dissolution of the Federation of Rhodesia and Nyasaland. Part of the agreement, he pointed out, had been that control of the armed forces contributed by the territories should revert to them. Dissolution of the Federation, he added, was an essential preliminary to the achievement of independence by Northern Rhodesia and Nyasaland. In regard to the desire of the Southern Rhodesian Government for independence, he noted that the United Kingdom had indicated that amendments to Southern Rhodesia's Constitution would have to precede the granting of independence. Southern Rhodesia, however, had been a self-governing colony when it had joined the Federation and would have the same status when the Federation was dissolved. No resolution by any United Nations body could make its status what it was not.

Other Members—such as Ghana, Libya, Somalia, Syria, Tanganyika, Togo and the USSR—considered, however, that the United Kingdom was in a position to take action in Southern Rhodesia as requested by the Assembly. They criticised the United Kingdom's vote against the draft resolution in the Security Council and felt that the situation in Southern Rhodesia—already a threat to peace and security in Africa—was deteriorating rapidly. One of the points made was that the situation would be aggravated by the proposed transfer of armed forces recruited along racial lines and of a powerful air force to the Southern Rhodesian Government, which was now an extremist European settler régime. The world, however, was living in an era in which all vestiges of colonialism should disappear. The United Kingdom had handed a defenceless African majority over to the mercy of a Government which had already shown its capacity for racial discrimination and oppression. The United Kingdom should show more realism before blood began to flow and the settler minority which it supported should take advantage of the opportunity offered it to live in equal and legal terms with the African majority, which was being denied justice.

. . .

Discussed by the Fourth Committee was a draft resolution proposed by . . . 44 Members . . .

By this resolution, the terms of which were similar to those of the draft resolution which failed of adoption in the Security Council, the Assembly would invite the United Kingdom not to transfer to Southern Rhodesia, as presently governed, any of the powers or attributes of sovereignty, but to await the establishment of a fully representative government, and not to transfer armed forces and aircraft to Southern Rhodesia as envisaged by the Central African Conference. The Assembly would, further, invite the United Kingdom to put into effect previous Assembly resolutions on the question of Southern Rhodesia.

. . .

Continuing its consideration of the question of Southern Rhodesia, the Fourth Committee heard two petitioners: Robert Mugabe (Secretary-General of the Zimbabwe African National Union) and T. George Silundika (Secretary for Publicity, Zimbabwe African Peoples Union), who made statements and responded to Members' questions.

. . .

The Fourth Committee also debated a second draft resolution introduced on 17 October by Somalia. . . .

By this 46-power text, the General Assembly, mindful of the aggravation of the situation in Southern Rhodesia, "which constitutes a threat to international peace and security," would, among other things: (1) approve the Special Committee's report, especially its conclusions and recommendations; (2) reaffirm the inalienable right of the people of Southern Rhodesia to self-determination and independence; (3) express appreciation to the Secretary-General for his efforts in connexion with the Southern Rhodesian question; (4) express deep regret that the United Kingdom Government had not implemented the Assembly's various resolutions on Southern Rhodesia; (5) call upon the United Kingdom not to grant independence to the present Government of Southern Rhodesia until majority rule based on universal adult suffrage was established; (6) invite once more the United Kingdom to hold, without delay, a constitutional conference, in which all political parties of Southern Rhodesia would take part; and (7) urge all Member States, and in particular those having the closest relations with the United Kingdom Government, to use their influence to the utmost with a view to ensuring the realization of the legitimate aspirations of the peoples of Southern Rhodesia. In addition, the Assembly would ask the Secretary-General to continue to lend his good offices to promote conciliation in the territory as stated in the Assembly's resolution 1760(XVII) of 31 October 1962.

On 18 October 1963, the Fourth Committee adopted the 46-power proposal by a roll-call vote of 79 in favour to 2 against, with 19 abstentions.

The United Kingdom did not participate in the voting.

. . .

On 6 November 1963, the Fourth Committee's text was approved at a plenary meeting of the Assembly as resolution 1889(XVIII) by a roll-call vote of 73 to 2, with 19 abstentions. The United Kingdom did not participate in the vote.

On 11 December 1963, the Secretary-General reported to the Assembly on the implementation of that paragraph of the resolution asking him to continue to lend his good offices to promote conciliation in Southern Rhodesia and to report both to the General Assembly and to the Special Committee on the results of his efforts. The Secretary-General stated that he had transmitted the text of resolution 1889(XVIII) of 6 November 1963 to the Permanent Representative of the United Kingdom on 8 November 1963, and subsequently had discussed the question with him.

On 10 December 1963, the Secretary-General had received in reply a letter from the Permanent Representative of the United Kingdom recalling that difficulties lay in the way of his Government's compliance with the United Nations resolutions on Southern Rhodesia. By its participation in United Nations discussions the United Kingdom acknowledged the honest concern shown by many Members of the United Nations about the future of Southern Rhodesia, this letter continued; despite the United Kingdom's attitude on the question of United Nations competence to deal with Southern Rhodesia, his Government thought it right to inform the United Nations of its policy regarding Southern Rhodesia's constitutional status. His Government's intention was to work towards a solution to the problems which faced the territory in a manner best calculated to achieve such a solution.

The Secretary-General further reported that, bearing in mind the mandate given by the General Assembly, he had also undertaken conversations with representatives of African countries in the hope that the Organization of African Unity might assist in preparing the ground for initiating discussions with the other parties concerned.

(YUN 1963, pp. 469-78)

Unilateral declaration of independence

In 1965, the Southern Rhodesian Government announced the holding of general elections on 7 May under the 1961 Constitution. The Sub-Committee on Southern Rhodesia expressed concern that the election results might be used by the minority regime as a pretext for a unilateral declaration of independence. After the regime unilaterally declared independence on 11 November, both the General Assembly and the United Kingdom called for the Security Council to meet. The Council, with the United Kingdom voting in favour, called on the United Kingdom to quell what it termed rebellion of the racist minority and asked all States to stop supplies of arms, equipment and other material to the territory.

On 16 December 1965, the United Kingdom Prime Minister, Harold Wilson, in addressing the General Assembly, reiterated the United Kingdom Government's position on the question of Southern Rhodesia and called for the support of all Member States for the United Kingdom's sanctions against Southern Rhodesia.

On 17 December 1965, the Permanent Representative of the United Kingdom, in a letter to the President of the Security Council, said that the United Kingdom Government, in exercise of powers conferred upon it by the Southern Rhodesia Act of 1965, had prohibited the import of oil and petroleum products into the territory. In a letter dated 12 December 1965, Kenya proposed the convening of the Security Council to resume its consideration of the question of Southern Rhodesia. On 20 December 1965 a subsequent letter was received from the representative of Kenya requesting the postponement of the proposed Security Council meeting on the question of Southern Rhodesia.

By the end of 1965, 29 Member States had informed the Secretary-General of action they had taken against the illegal régime in Southern Rhodesia. In general terms, all the 29 Member States stated that they did not recognize the illegal régime and would have no dealings with it. The replies also informed the Secretary-General of sanctions which the Member States had imposed on Southern Rhodesia.

(YUN 1965, pp. 127-28)

Sanctions

In December 1966, the Security Council, for the first time in United Nations history, imposed selective mandatory economic sanctions on Southern Rhodesia, which were widened in 1968.

. . . On 29 May 1968, the Security Council, noting that the measures so far taken had failed to bring the rebellion in Southern Rhodesia to an end, adopted a resolution (253(1968)), condemning all measures of political repression in Southern Rhodesia and deciding on more comprehensive sanctions.

. . .

On 12 March, a letter requesting an urgent meeting of the Security Council to examine the situation in Southern Rhodesia (Zimbabwe) was sent to the President of the Council by . . . 36 African States. . . .

The letter recalled that more than a year previously the Council had adopted selective mandatory sanctions (by its resolution of 16 December 1966) and that obviously these had failed, as the African States had anticipated, and as had been dramatically demonstrated by the recent tragic assassination of political prisoners by the racist régime in Southern Rhodesia. Meanwhile, the United Kingdom had made no effort to enter into negotiations with the leaders of the African political parties with a view to establishing a government which met the legitimate aspirations of the people of Zimbabwe.

. . .

At a meeting held on 19 March 1968, the Security Council decided without objection to include the question in its agenda and further agreed to invite the representatives of Jamaica and Zambia, at their request, to participate in the discussion without the right to vote. Discussion was continued at five additional meetings which were held on 20 and 26 March, 18 and 23 April and 29 May 1968, interspersed with periods of private consultations among Council members on the text of a resolution on the question.

The representatives of Algeria, Ethiopia and Senegal, who had been appointed by the Organization of African Unity (OAU) to present the views of the African Member States signatories to the request for the meeting, stressed the continuing responsibility of the United Kingdom, as the administering power, to advance the people of Southern Rhodesia to self-determination and independence. Having so far utterly failed to carry out that responsibility, they said, the United Kingdom should recognize the ineffectiveness of selective sanctions, apply more energetic economic sanctions and, if necessary, resort to the use of force.

. . .

Unfortunately, the selective economic sanctions imposed by the Security Council in December 1966 had proved ineffective, and had not been fully complied with by all States. The attitude of the Governments of Portugal and South Africa had been one of complete disregard of the Council's decision. Trade to and from Southern Rhodesia had been "denationalized," and most transactions were being carried out through South African and Portuguese intermediaries. . . .

In view of the complicity and duplicity displayed by Portugal and South Africa, the African representatives considered that no sanction measures, no matter how comprehensive, could work unless they included the Portuguese territories and South Africa as well. . . . Accordingly, they called upon the Council to adopt total and binding economic sanctions against Southern Rhodesia, and also to decide on specific and appropriate measures to enable it to follow up the implementation of its de-

cisions, a process in which they hoped that the United Kingdom would play a major role.

The representative of the United Kingdom urged Council members to avoid controversy that would distract from their overriding duty to make clear, in unmistakable and unanimous terms, their condemnation of the illegal executions carried out in Southern Rhodesia and to demand that no more illegal hangings should occur. . . . Accordingly, he urged that the Council proceed initially, and in full agreement, to adopt a resolution which would express the force of international condemnation and call for a stop to the illegal and inhuman actions. Immediately thereafter, the Council should proceed to consider, on the basis of hard facts and practical possibilities, the whole question of what further action could be taken to restore the situation in Southern Rhodesia, end the rebellion and prepare for the advance to free, democratic government. In reply to those who said that there was no way but force, he stated his conviction that there were effective measures still to be taken. In spite of the difficulties and limitations, Council members had a duty not to decide that sanctions had failed, not to pronounce that one of the main weapons of international enforcement had proved useless, but to explore and examine every effective and practicable method to supplement and sustain the measures already taken.

(YUN 1968, pp. 126-30)

The Council, on 29 May, unanimously adopted resolution 253(1968).

The Security Council,

. . .

Reaffirming its determination that the present situation in Southern Rhodesia constitutes a threat to international peace and security,

Acting under Chapter VII of the Charter of the United Nations,

1. *Condemns* all measures of political repression, including arrests, detentions, trials and executions which violate fundamental freedoms and rights of the people of Southern Rhodesia, and calls upon the Government of the United Kingdom to take all possible measures to put an end to such actions;

2. *Calls upon* the United Kingdom as the administering Power in the discharge of its responsibility to take urgently all effective measures to bring to an end the rebellion in Southern Rhodesia, and enable the people to secure the enjoyment of their rights as set forth in the Charter of the United Nations and in conformity with the objectives of General Assembly resolution 1514(XV);

3. *Decides* that, in furtherance of the objective of ending the rebellion, all States Members of the United Nations shall prevent:

(a) The import into their territories of all commodities and products originating in Southern Rhodesia and exported therefrom after the date of this resolution (whether or not the commodities or products are for consumption or processing in their territories, whether or not they are imported in bond and whether or not any special legal status with respect to the import of goods is enjoyed by the port or other place where they are imported or stored);

(b) Any activities by their nationals or in their territories which would promote or are calculated to promote the export of any commodities or products from Southern Rhodesia; and any dealings by their nationals or in their territories in any commodities or products originating in Southern Rhodesia and exported therefrom after the date of this resolution, including in particular any transfer of funds to Southern Rhodesia for the purposes of such activities or dealings;

(c) The shipment in vessels or aircraft of their registration or under charter to their nationals, or the carriage (whether or not in bond) by land transport facilities across their territories of any commodities or products originating in Southern Rhodesia and exported therefrom after the date of this resolution;

(d) The sale or supply by their nationals or from their territories of any commodities or products (whether or not originating in their territories, but not including supplies intended strictly for medical purposes, educational equipment and material for use in schools and other educational institutions, publications, news material and, in special humanitarian circumstances, food-stuffs) to any person or body in Southern Rhodesia or to any other person or body for the purposes of any business carried on in or operated from Southern Rhodesia, and any activities by their nationals or in their territories which promote or are calculated to promote such sale or supply;

(e) The shipment in vessels or aircraft of their registration, or under charter to their nationals, or the carriage (whether or not in bond) by land transport facilities across their territories of any such commodities or products which are consigned to any person or body in Southern Rhodesia, or to any other person or body for the purposes of any business carried on in or operated from Southern Rhodesia;

4. *Decides* that all States Members of the United Nations shall not make available to the illegal régime in Southern Rhodesia or to any commercial, industrial or public utility undertaking, including tourist enterprises, in Southern Rhodesia any funds for investment or any other financial or economic resources and shall prevent their nationals and any persons within their territories from making available to the régime or to any such undertaking any such funds or resources and from remitting any other funds to persons or bodies within Southern Rhodesia, except payments exclusively for pensions or for strictly medical, humanitarian or educational purposes or for the provision of news material and in special humanitarian circumstances, food-stuffs;

5. *Decides* that all States Members of the United Nations shall:

(a) Prevent the entry into their territories, save on exceptional humanitarian grounds, of any person travelling on a Southern Rhodesian passport, regardless of its date of issue, or on a purported passport issued by or on behalf of the illegal régime in Southern Rhodesia;

(b) Take all possible measures to prevent the entry into their territories of persons whom they have reason to believe to be ordinarily resident in Southern Rhodesia and whom they have reason to believe to have fur-

thered or encouraged, or to be likely to further or encourage, the unlawful actions of the illegal régime in Southern Rhodesia or any activities which are calculated to evade any measure decided upon in this resolution or resolution 232(1966) of 16 December 1966;

6. *Decides* that all States Members of the United Nations shall prevent airline companies constituted in their territories and aircraft of their registration or under charter to their nationals from operating to or from Southern Rhodesia and from linking up with any airline company constituted or aircraft registered in Southern Rhodesia;

. . .

20. *Decides* to establish, in accordance with rule 28 of the provisional rules of procedure of the Security Council, a committee of the Security Council to undertake the following tasks and to report to it with its observations;

(a) To examine such reports on the implementation of the present resolution as are submitted by the Secretary-General;

(b) To seek from any States Members of the United Nations or of the specialized agencies such further information regarding the trade of that State (including information regarding the commodities and products exempted from the prohibition contained in operative paragraph 3 *(d)* above) or regarding any activities by any nationals of that State or in its territories that may constitute an evasion of the measures decided upon in this resolution as it may consider necessary for the proper discharge of its duty to report to the Security Council;

. . .

[YUN 1968, pp. 152-54]

Towards independence

Despite the sanctions imposed by the Security Council, almost a decade later a settlement of the Southern Rhodesia independence issue had still not been reached. The armed struggle continued under the leadership of the Patriotic Front of Zimbabwe, and efforts to negotiate a settlement had so far failed. On 1 September 1977, the United Kingdom and the United States put forward proposals for the transfer of power and transition to independence. They included the surrender of power by the illegal régime; independence in 1978; elections based on universal adult suffrage; establishment of a transitional administration; and a United Nations presence, including a United Nations force during the transition period. However, the situation continued to deteriorate with the conclusion of a so-called internal settlement to the conflict. On 3 March 1978, the "Salisbury agreement", called the Rhodesia Constitutional Agreement, was announced by Ian Smith and representatives of the United Africa National Council (Bishop Abel Muzorewa), the African National Council (Sithole) (the Reverend Ndabaningi Sithole) and the Zimbabwe United People's Organization (Chief Jeremiah Chirau). The General Assembly, in December, rejected the so-called internal settlement and deemed it imperative that the scope of sanctions be widened to include all the measures envisaged under Article 41 of the Charter.

Beginning in 1979, a number of events took place leading towards a settlement of the conflict. In April, the General Assembly's Special Committee on the Situation with regard to the Implementation of the Declaration on the Granting of Independence to Colonial Countries and Peoples adopted a Final Document on the Decolonization of Zimbabwe and Namibia. The foundation for a solution to the conflict was laid at the meeting of heads of Commonwealth countries held at Lusaka, Zambia, in August. This was followed by a Constitutional Conference at Lancaster House, London. The Lancaster House agreement was reached in December, providing for a constitutional settlement and the transition of the territory to independence under majority rule.

Accordingly, the Security Council, in December, terminated the sanctions previously imposed and dissolved the Committee that had supervised their implementation. In February 1980, it called on all parties to comply with the Lancaster House agreement and on the United Kingdom to create conditions for free and fair elections. The machinery for transition to majority rule was put into operation and the first general election under the principle of universal adult suffrage took place from 27 to 29 February. The former Territory of Southern Rhodesia became the sovereign independent State of Zimbabwe at midnight on 17/18 April 1980 and was admitted to the United Nations in August.

The end of the Trusteeship System

In November 1994, the Security Council determined, in the light of the entry into force on 1 October of the new status agreement for Palau—a group of islands located in the Western Caroline Islands which had remained the last Trust Territory—that the objectives of the 1947 Trusteeship Agreement had been fully attained and that the applicability of that Agreement had terminated with respect to Palau. The adoption of the resolution marked the completion of the work entrusted to the Trusteeship Council under the United Nations Charter.

Negotiations between the United States, the Administering Authority under the Trusteeship Agreement, and Palau began in 1969 and resulted in the conclusion of a Compact of Free Association, which was approved by a plebiscite in November 1993 and came fully into force on 1 October 1994. Palau's succession to independence brought to a successful conclusion a very important phase in United Nations history and was testimony to the ideals set out in the Charter.

PART FOUR

Economic and social development

"To achieve international co-operation in solving international problems of an economic, social, cultural, or humanitarian character . . .''

Chapter I

Humanitarian challenges

Before the end of the Second World War and the establishment of the United Nations, a number of international conferences were held to discuss special humanitarian problems that would have to be dealt with following the cessation of hostilities. Organizations would be needed to address major emergencies in war-ravaged areas, particularly to assist and repatriate displaced persons and refugees and to provide massive relief to destitute young victims of the war.

Humanitarian assistance

UNRRA

The first United Nations agency formally to come into being was the United Nations Relief and Rehabilitation Administration (UNRRA). The Agreement creating UNRRA was signed in Washington on 9 November 1943 by representatives of 44 nations; on the following day, the first meeting of the UNRRA Council began in Atlantic City, New Jersey. UNRRA's mandate was to provide the populations of devastated countries with relief—in the form of food, clothing, shelter and medical supplies—and rehabilitation—in the form of materials and services required to resume urgently needed agricultural and industrial production and to restore essential services—and to arrange for the return of prisoners and exiles to their homes.

UNRRA carried out these tasks in Asia and Europe with varying degrees of success until 1946, when its member nations decided that it would be terminated and the General Assembly began to discuss how UNRRA's work could be continued.

On 1 February 1946, the General Assembly established a Committee on UNRRA and requested it to submit a report on its activities to the second part of the Assembly's first session. On 11 December 1946, on the recommendation of the Second (Economic and Financial) Committee, the Assembly adopted a resolution in which it noted with

satisfaction Member Governments' support of UNRRA activities as described in the report of the Committee on UNRRA. It urged Member Governments to make available the balance of their expected contributions in order that UNRRA could have at its disposal for completing its task the full amount recommended by its Council.

Relief needs after the termination of UNRRA

In its resolution of February 1, 1946, establishing a Committee on UNRRA, the General Assembly instructed the Secretary-General to make arrangements with the Director-General of UNRRA whereby the General Assembly might be furnished with full reports on the work of UNRRA. In accordance with this resolution the Director-General of UNRRA submitted an extensive report to the second part of the first session of the General Assembly on the progress made towards economic rehabilitation in the countries being assisted by UNRRA.

The General Assembly also received a recommendation from the Economic and Social Council on the question of relief needs in 1947 after the termination of UNRRA's activities. At its fifth session the Council of UNRRA had adopted a resolution recommending to the General Assembly of the United Nations the establishment or designation of an agency to review the needs in 1947 for urgent imports of basic essentials of life for the various receiving countries of UNRRA and to make recommendations regarding financial assistance that might be required to meet such needs. By a resolution of October 3, 1946, the Economic and Social Council endorsed the recommendation of the Council of UNRRA and recommended that the General Assembly take appropriate action as soon as possible.

At its 46th plenary meeting on October 31, 1946, the General Assembly referred the question of post-UNRRA relief to the Second Committee (Economic and Financial) for consideration. . . .

The Director-General of UNRRA, who was invited to participate in the Committee's discussions, told the Committee that the countries receiving UNRRA aid would be faced with a considerable deficit of foodstuffs after the termination of UNRRA's work in 1947. He urged that the United Nations adopt definite plans to remedy these deficits and continue to provide assistance on an international basis. To this end he proposed the establishment of a United Nations Emergency Food Fund of at least $400,000,000 to which the Members of the United Nations would be called upon to contribute in money or in goods. This fund would operate until after the 1947 harvest, at which time the General Assembly could determine whether further action would be necessary.

The delegation of Denmark submitted a draft resolution embodying the proposal of the Director-General of UNRRA for the establishment of a United Nations Emergency Food Board.

. . . most representatives favored continued relief, after the termination of UNRRA, through an international agency such as that recommended by the Director-General of UNRRA and the Danish delegation.

The representatives of the United States and the United Kingdom, however, the two largest potential contributors to any international relief agency which the General Assembly might set up, opposed the establishment of such an agency. The representative of the United States considered that the world economic situation had improved considerably and that certain nations which had received UNRRA aid were now able to export their own products. His Government was aware, the United States representative stated, that some countries still needed relief, but it was opposed to the establishment of an international organization to handle the residual problem. Moreover, UNRRA resources would in the main be exhausted by the end of February. The most critical period would be the late winter and early spring. It was imperative, therefore, to move quickly and the United States Government favored simpler and more direct methods of relief than the establishment of an international agency. Hence, the United States representative submitted a draft resolution to the Second Committee providing for relief to be furnished by Members of the United Nations on a bilateral and voluntary basis. Specifically, the resolution:

(1)   directed the Secretary-General to transmit to all Members of the United Nations and international organizations concerned information on the needs for urgent imports of basic commodities in 1947 and on the financial assistance which might be required to meet such needs;

(2)   called upon Members of the United Nations to assist in the furnishing of relief during the ensuing year and to develop their relief programs with the greatest possible speed;

(3)   invited contributing governments to co-ordinate their respective programs by informal consultation so as to achieve the maximum results from their efforts.

The representative of the United Kingdom supported the resolution of the United States representative. He suggested that Members of the United Nations which were receiving or contributing relief should use the Secretariat of the United Nations as a clearing house for information and the co-ordination of relief.

As a compromise, certain delegations suggested that contributions of money or in kind should be made by Members of the United Nations on a voluntary basis, with a United Nations committee, however, handling the task of collection and distribution. The representative of Brazil submitted a draft resolution which recommended the establishment of such an international pool of voluntary contributions. This pool was to be created and administered by a special committee consisting of representatives of the Secretary-General of the United Nations, of UNRRA, of the Sub-Commission on Devastated Areas of the Economic and Social Council, of FAO, of the International Emergency Food Council and of the International Bank for Reconstruction. This special committee, moreover, was (a) to survey essential food requirements of the devastated areas in 1947, their need for imports, and the prospective food supply position in the exporting areas; (b) to determine what proportion of those needs could be met with available exchange resources or expected foreign exchange receipts; (c) to consult with the governments of the countries requiring assistance and of potential supplying countries concerning the extension of credit facilities to the needy countries, either on a long or a short-term basis; and (d) to study the possibility of employing the sum in arrears due to UNRRA by Member countries, for the coverage of part of the needs of the devastated areas in 1947.

(YUN 1946-47, pp. 155-57)

The Second Committee appointed a 19-member Sub-Committee to prepare a single draft resolution; the Sub-Committee was unable to reach any agreement on the basic issue as to whether relief was to be provided on a bilateral and voluntary basis or through an international agency.

In his report to the Second Committee the Chairman of the Sub-Committee stated that the overwhelming majority of the Sub-Committee had preferred the principle of action by an international agency. According to ordinary parliamentary practice, the Sub-Committee would have proceeded to vote on a draft proposal to implement the principle of international action. The representative of the United States and the United

Kingdom, however, had explicitly stated before the Sub-Committee that they could not bow to the majority in this case and that they would not adhere to any decision of the Committee which did not meet their point of view. Even if contributions were to be on a voluntary basis, the representatives of the United States and the United Kingdom had informed the Sub-Committee that they would not give their contributions in conformity with principles established by an international agency. They wished to be free to judge on their own when and where relief was needed, and were convinced that the needs which would exist in 1947 could best be met through bilateral action, which would be more direct and immediate than action through an international agency. The representative of the U.S.S.R., on the other hand, informed the Sub-Committee that his Government was not prepared to make a contribution except to an international organization.

Although favoring international action, the majority of the Sub-Committee felt that it would not serve any useful purpose to vote for the establishment of an international agency which would not receive the support of the two largest contributing countries. The Sub-Committee therefore did not take a vote on the proposals before it, and decided by majority vote to refer the matter back to the Second Committee with the request that the Chairman of the Sub-Committee give a factual report.

At the 26th meeting of the Second Committee on December 5, 1946, the United States resolution was resubmitted in revised form as a resolution sponsored jointly by the representatives of the United States, the United Kingdom and Brazil. In addition to the recommendations contained in the original United States resolution, the revised resolution (1) recommended that all Members of the United Nations keep the Secretary-General informed concerning their plans for assisting in meeting relief needs in 1947 and the progress of their relief activities; (2) directed the Secretary-General to make available to all Members of the United Nations the information thus received, together with information concerning existing relief needs, in order that this information might be used by the Members of the United Nations to facilitate the co-ordination of their respective relief programs; (3) directed the Secretary-General to facilitate informal consultation among governments concerning their relief plans and to furnish such technical assistance as governments might request.

The Director-General of UNRRA submitted a revised proposal to the Second Committee, which he hoped might be accepted by all members of the Committee. The resolution proposed that the General Assembly establish a United Nations Emergency Food Board whose functions would include:

(a) A review of the needs in 1947 for financing urgent imports of the basic essentials of life, particularly food, after the termination of UNRRA programs to the extent that they cannot be otherwise met;

(b) The making of recommendations as to the financial assistance that might be required to meet such needs as are found to exist as a result of foreign exchange difficulties which cannot be dealt with by existing agencies;

(c) The making of recommendations to governments as to allocations of resources which they make available for relief purposes on the basis of need and free from political considerations; and

(d) The making of periodic reports at such time and in such form as the Economic and Social Council may provide.

If the Committee should fail to accept this revised proposal, the Director-General of UNRRA urged that at least the following amendments to the resolution sponsored jointly by the representatives of the United States, the United Kingdom and Brazil should be adopted: (1) The resolution should state that relief should be furnished "when and where needed," and that it should be free from political considerations; (2) provision should be made for formal, rather than informal consultation from time to time among governments concerning their relief plans.

The representatives of the United States and the United Kingdom opposed the revised resolution of the Director-General of UNRRA. They were, however, willing to accept the above amendments and submitted a draft of the joint resolution revised accordingly.

In view of the opposition of the United States and the United Kingdom to the establishment of an international agency, the representative of Denmark withdrew his resolution.

After further discussion . . ., the representative of Canada submitted a compromise proposal as an amendment to the United States-United Kingdom-Brazil resolution. He proposed that a special technical committee be appointed, composed of eight experts in the fields of finance and foreign trade to be designated in their personal capacities by the Governments of Brazil, Canada, China, France, Poland, the U.S.S.R, the United Kingdom, and the United States. This committee would study minimum import requirements of countries which were suffering from considerable deficits in foodstuffs and other basic commodities, it would survey the available means of each country to finance such imports, and would report concerning the financial assistance which might be required. The report of the special technical committee was to be submitted to the Secretary-General for submission to Member Governments not later than January 15, 1947.

The representatives of the United States and the United Kingdom were willing to accept the

Canadian proposal. The representative of Denmark and several other representatives who had supported the principle of international action urged support of the Canadian compromise for the sake of unanimity, although this compromise fell short of their aims.

At its 29th meeting on December 9, 1946, the Second Committee decided to increase the membership of the proposed special technical committee to ten, adding Argentina and Denmark to the list of members. The Committee then unanimously adopted the joint resolution of the United States, the United Kingdom and Brazil as amended by the representative of Canada.

As a means of helping to meet relief needs during 1947, the representative of Norway proposed that the General Assembly direct the Secretary-General of the United Nations to consider ways and means of collecting and utilizing contributions by individuals and organizations all over the world equivalent to the value of one day's work. This proposal, submitted in the form of an amendment to the joint resolution of the United States, the United Kingdom and Brazil, was adopted by the Second Committee at its 29th meeting on December 9, 1946, by 33 votes with 4 abstentions.

(YUN 1946-47, pp. 157-58)

Special Technical Committee on relief needs

On 11 December 1946, the General Assembly established a Special Technical Committee of 10 experts serving in their individual capacities, designated by the Governments of Argentina, Brazil, Canada, China, Denmark, France, Poland, the USSR, the United Kingdom and the United States. The Committee was charged with studying the minimum import relief requirements of the basic essentials of life, particularly food and supplies of agricultural production, as well as determining the level of financial requirements of countries in need of assistance to prevent suffering or economic retrogression. The Committee submitted its report to the Secretary-General on 23 January 1947, listing the import needs and outlining the financing requirements.

The Committee reviewed the data supplied by the Secretary-General in accordance with the General Assembly's resolution on the needs and resources for international payment of the following countries: Austria, Czechoslovakia, Finland, Greece, Hungary, Italy, Korea, Philippine Commonwealth, Poland and Yugoslavia. The Committee also heard additional evidence submitted by representatives of Austria, Czechoslovakia, Finland, Greece, Hungary, Poland and Yugoslavia, the Secretary-General of the International Emergency Food Council and the Chief of the Bureau of Supply of UNRRA. Replies were not received

from the Byelorussian S.S.R. and the Ukrainian S.S.R.

The Committee drew up a minimum list of import requirements consisting of the basic essentials of life and of such other imports as were necessary to prevent suffering on the one hand or economic retrogression on the other, under the headings of food, agricultural supplies, textiles and footwear, medical supplies, fuel and industrial supplies; it calculated the foreign currency resources available to the countries under consideration for meeting the minimum import programs.

In calculating import requirements the Commitee considered that capital items and imports required for reconstruction and rehabilitation of agriculture and industry damaged or destroyed by the war, or imports intended to increase agricultural and industrial activity, were outside its terms of reference. It also made allowance for the carry-over of assistance from UNRRA during 1947.

In calculating the means of the countries concerned to finance the minimum import requirements out of their own resources, the Committee considered that such requirements should be regarded as a first charge upon the proceeds of exports and other free resources in foreign currency of these countries. At the same time the Committee recognized that certain exports, e.g. those governed by barter arrangements, could not be freely used to finance minimum import requirements and that certain loans were earmarked for other purposes.

The report of the Special Technical Committee was communicated by the Secretary-General to Members, and was noted by the Economic and Social Council at its fourth session. The Secretary-General also reported to the Council on activities under the General Assembly resolution on relief needs.

The U.S.S.R. representative on the Committee had made a statement criticizing the Committee's report on the ground that, owing to an inequitable approach to the assessment of relief requirements for various countries, the estimates computed were too high for certain countries and too low for others. Referring to this statement, the U.S.S.R. representative on the Council said that in numerous cases the present economic conditions of a country and the degree of devastation caused by the war were ignored, and that the requirements for fuel, capital equipment, clothing and other articles had been calculated on a purely mechanical basis, and were therefore frequently erroneous.

The Czechoslovak representative pointed out certain deficiencies in that part of the Committee's report which concerned Czechoslovakia, e.g. the statement that no grain deficiency was to be expected from Czechoslovakia, whereas that country had imported grain before the war and still needed to do so.

The resolution adopted by the General Assembly had also called on Members to assist in furnishing relief and had recommended that they should keep the Secretary-General informed concerning their plans for assisting in meeting relief needs in 1947, and concerning the progress of their relief activities.

In his letter of February 7, 1947, transmitting the report of the Special Technical Committee, the Secretary-General called the attention of Members to the provisions of the resolution inviting information. The Secretary-General reported to the Council that he had not received official statements from Members concerning their plans, although in response to informal inquiries he had been assured that the matter would be seriously considered by appropriate government departments and that he would be informed as soon as possible concerning plans for assisting in meeting relief needs in 1947. He would make this information available to Members when he had received it and was arranging for informal consultations among interested governments, in accordance with the General Assembly's resolution.

On February 19, 1947, the Secretary-General received a communication from the Director-General of UNRRA, requesting that the United Nations consider taking over the functions of UNRRA with regard to proceeds in the form of local currency derived from the sale of UNRRA supplies by receiving countries.

The matter was considered by the Economic and Social Council at its fourth session, and the Secretary-General was authorized to receive reports on the manner in which the proceeds were used and to transmit a report to the Council. The Cuban and U.S.S.R. representatives abstained from voting on this decision. The Cuban representative felt that the Economic and Social Council was not competent to make such a decision without previous authorization by the General Assembly. The U.S.S.R. representative objected to items being placed on the agenda at the last moment, pointing out that such a procedure made it impossible for representatives to consult competent organizations. He believed that there was no need for the Council to take any decision in the matter.

The General Assembly in its resolution of December 11, 1946, on relief needs after the termination of UNRRA directed the Secretary-General "to consider the ways and means of collecting and utilizing contributions from persons, organizations, and peoples all over the world, equivalent to the earnings of one day's work for the purpose of helping to meet relief needs during 1947" and to report to Member Governments and to the Economic and Social Council. The Economic and Social Council was to take what action it thought appropriate.

The Secretary-General's report estimated that such a collection would materially help in furnishing funds for urgent relief needs, and would have a powerful moral and psychological effect. Countries which had themselves suffered should also participate, it was recommended, and the collection should be linked with an equitable system for the allocation of funds.

The report recommended that the collection be made available for the alleviation of distress among the world's children, adolescents, expectant and nursing mothers, without discrimination because of race, creed, nationality status, or political belief. For this purpose it was suggested that the International Children's Emergency Fund should be the main recipient of the proceeds of the collection.

(YUN 1946-47, pp. 489-91)

In August 1946, the UNRRA Council adopted resolutions regarding the transfer of its social welfare functions (the training of social welfare personnel; rehabilitation of the physically handicapped; restoration of social welfare activities and institutions; co-ordination of the activities of voluntary agencies; and child welfare) to the United Nations and the creation of an international children's fund to rehabilitate children and adolescents of countries that were victims of aggression (see below). In December, the General Assembly approved the Constitution of the International Refugee Organization (IRO), which would assume UNRRA's work on behalf of refugees (see below) and, in December of 1946 and during the early part of 1947, UNRRA's health activities were transferred to the newly established World Health Organization. Also in 1947, a number of UNRRA's technical advisory services to increase food production in war-devastated areas were taken over by the Food and Agriculture Organization of the United Nations, the Constitution of which was signed in October 1945.

Establishment of an International Children's Emergency Fund

In 1945, with the declaration of peace in Europe in May and in the Pacific in August, the most destructive war the world had witnessed was over. Millions of children were orphaned or separated from their families and millions were refugees in foreign lands, displaced within their own countries, or without homes.

From 1943 until the end of 1946, and for months afterwards, UNRRA helped to feed and treat those youngest victims and to fend off famine and epidemic.

At its last meeting in August 1946 at Geneva, the UNRRA Council voted unanimously to propose to the United Nations that it create an international children's emergency fund to feed and care for the over 5 million youngsters in Asia and Europe who were receiving UNRRA assistance.

On the basis of the conclusions of the Special Technical Committee and the Secretary-General's recommendations, a collection of "One Day's Pay" was to be made available for the alleviation of distress among the world's children, adolescents, expectant and nursing mothers. For that purpose, an International Children's Emergency Fund was to be the main recipient of the proceeds of the collections. The Economic and Social Council approved the "One Day's Pay" collection in the following resolution:

THE ECONOMIC AND SOCIAL COUNCIL
HAVING CONSIDERED the report of the Secretary-General in virtue of paragraph 8 of the General Assembly resolution No. 48(1) of 11 December 1946 and
TAKING NOTE of the General Assembly resolution No. 57(1) of the same date and the need of the International Children's Emergency Fund for contributions:
1.   APPROVES in principle the proposal for a special world-wide appeal for non-governmental voluntary contributions to meet emergency relief needs of children, adolescents, expectant and nursing mothers, without discrimination because of race, creed, nationality status, or political belief, by way of a "One Day's Pay" collection or some alternative form of collection better adapted to each particular country;
2.   REQUESTS the Secretary-General to continue his exploration of the most appropriate procedures for carrying forward this work and to make such arrangements as may be necessary for this purpose, taking into account the circumstances, including the foreign exchange position, of each country;
3.   REQUESTS the Secretary-General to report to the next session of the Economic and Social Council on the progress of this project;
4.   URGES Governments to facilitate this voluntary effort, on the understanding that agreement will be reached between the Secretary-General and each country
    (a)   as to the disposal of the national collections,
    (b)   as to the purchase of supplies within the country for use elsewhere; and
5.   AUTHORIZES the Secretary General, after due consultations, to fix a date most suitable for the collection.
                                                            (YUN 1946-47, p. 491)

At its third session, on September 30, 1946, the Economic and Social Council had adopted a resolution, drafted by the Standing Committee of UNRRA in consultation with representatives of the Secretary-General of the United Nations and with the Acting President of the Economic and Social Council, recommending that the General Assembly arrange for the creation of an International Children's Emergency Fund subject to the Economic and Social Council; and that the Secretary-General of the United Nations, in consultation with the Director-General of UNRRA, the President of the Economic and Social Council and the Standing Committee of UNRRA prepare a draft

resolution to establish the necessary international machinery for this purpose.

In compliance with this recommendation the Secretary-General, on October 30, 1946, transmitted a draft resolution to the second part of the first session of the General Assembly. The General Assembly referred the question to its Third Committee (Social, Humanitarian and Cultural), which in turn, on November 20, 1946, instructed a Sub-Committee to examine the Secretary-General's recommendations and to present a report.

The Sub-Committee took note of the situation facing Europe and parts of Asia during the next few years insofar as it affected the rehabilitation of children. Although the Sub-Committee stressed that in its view the prime responsibility for the rehabilitation of children rested with national governments, it concluded that many governments would not be able to meet all the existing needs as regards adequate food supplies for children, the rehabilitation and manning of children's institutions and the training of personnel. Although voluntary relief efforts were generous and widespread, the Sub-Committee considered that such efforts touched only the fringe of the problem. Hence the necessity for an International Children's Emergency Fund. The Sub-Committee worked out detailed recommendations for the operation of the Fund and drew up a resolution based in the main on the Secretary-General's draft resolution.

. . .

The Third Committee then unanimously adopted the report and the resolution of the Sub-Committee. Likewise by unanimous vote, the General Assembly, at its 56th plenary meeting on December 11, 1946, adopted the resolution recommended by the Third Committee, which read as follows:

I.   THE GENERAL ASSEMBLY,
HAVING considered the resolution adopted by the Economic and Social Council at its third session recommending the creation of an International Children's Emergency Fund to be utilized for the benefit of children and adolescents of countries which were the victims of aggression, and recognizing the desirability of establishing such a Fund in accordance with Article 55 of the Charter of the United Nations;
DECIDES THEREFORE:
1.   There is hereby created an International Children's Emergency Fund to be utilized and administered, to the extent of its available resources:
    (a)   For the benefit of children and adolescents of countries which were victims of aggression and in order to assist in their rehabilitation;
    (b)   For the benefit of children and adolescents of countries at present receiving assistance from the United Nations Relief and Rehabilitation Administration;
    (c)   For child health purposes generally, giving high priority to the children of countries victims of aggression.

2. (a) The Fund shall consist of any assets made available by UNRRA or any voluntary contributions made available by Governments, voluntary agencies, individual or other sources. It shall be authorized to receive funds, contributions or other assistance from any of the foregoing sources; to make expenditures and to finance or arrange for the provision of supplies, material, services and technical assistance for the furtherance of the foregoing purposes; to facilitate and co-ordinate activities relating thereto; and generally to acquire, hold or transfer property, and to take any other legal action necessary or useful in the performance of its objects and purposes;

. . .

[YUN 1946-47, pp. 162-63]

Continuation of UNICEF

In the postwar years, UNICEF provided food, clothing, blankets and shoes, milk and dietary supplements, medicine and medical assistance to millions of needy children. From its establishment to the end of 1950, contributions and pledges to the Fund totalled $152,900,000. Of that amount, 71 per cent was from voluntary contributions from 47 Governments and two territories, 21 per cent from UNRRA assets, and 8 per cent from the United Nations Appeal for Children, which had conducted campaigns in 45 countries and more than 30 territories. The 8 per cent included donations from other private sources, some $100,000 of which was in the form of personal contributions from staff members of the United Nations and the specialized agencies.

Since its inception, UNICEF had spent $119 million for the benefit of children in 60 countries and territories. During 1950, the Fund devoted increasing attention to countries outside Europe.

In October 1950, the Assembly's Third Committee considered UNICEF's future. The United States, which continued to provide the lion's share of UNICEF funding, felt that the Fund, while not ignoring emergency needs, should develop long-range programmes of technical assistance and advice in order to help nations to help themselves. A number of developing countries and Poland wished to see the Fund's work continued, with particular attention being paid to the needs of underdeveloped areas.

In resolution 417(V) of 1 December, the Assembly reaffirmed its approval of the policy of UNICEF's Executive Board to devote a greater share of the Fund's resources to developing programmes outside Europe. It decided to reconsider the Fund's future in another three years, with the object of continuing it on a permanent basis.

The Social Commission, at its ninth session from 4 to 20 May 1953, proposed a draft resolution for adoption by the Economic and Social Council, by which the Council would express its opinion that the regulations which governed

UNICEF had enabled it to achieve satisfactory techniques, to acquire valuable experience, and to accomplish its tasks successfully, and would recommend that the Assembly reaffirm the pertinent provisions of its resolutions 57(I) and 417(V) with the exception of any reference to time limits contained in these resolutions.

. . .

In the general discussion on the future of UNICEF, the Council unanimously paid tribute, as had the Social Commission, to the work of UNICEF and to the principles of its administration. UNICEF, by its far-reaching effects, had brought help to millions of children throughout the world, particularly in under-developed areas. Among others, the representatives of Australia, Belgium, France and India expressed satisfaction with the excellent co-operation between UNICEF and the specialized agencies and hoped that such co-operation would continue.

The majority expressed the hope that contributions would be forthcoming in amounts sufficient to enable UNICEF to continue to work effectively. In this connexion, the representatives of Belgium, Egypt and Yugoslavia announced their Governments' contributions to either the 1953 or 1954 budgets, and the representative of Uruguay stated that his Government was studying the possibility of making an additional grant. The representative of Turkey also indicated the amounts his Government was intending to pay towards the aid being given Turkey by UNICEF. The Australian representative, while supporting the continuation of UNICEF, emphasized that it was essential that the Fund should have the guarantee of continued financial support. If that support were not forthcoming, his Government, he stated, would have to review its attitude.

The majority noted with approval that, during the last two years, the emphasis of UNICEF's activities had shifted from Europe to under-developed countries and from emergency to long-range programmes for economic and social development, but agreed that it was important to continue to render emergency aid when necessary. The representative of China stressed that countries outside Europe were three years behind so far as assistance from UNICEF was concerned; therefore, they should certainly not be regarded as no longer in need of any but long-term assistance. It would be regrettable, he thought, if the change of emphasis should debar those countries from benefiting from the emergency programmes in which they stood of such need.

In view of the change of emphasis and the fact that UNICEF was not only concerned with international emergency situations, the representatives of Argentina, France, India, the Philippines and the United States presented a joint amendment to the draft resolution recommended by the Social Commission to:

(1) change the name of the organization to the United Nations Children's Fund, retaining the symbol UNICEF;

(2) provide for a periodic review of UNICEF's work;

(3) request the Secretary-General to ensure effective co-ordination with other United Nations agencies and to report thereon; and

(4) commend UNICEF, the United Nations Secretariat and the specialized agencies for their close working relations and request that they strengthen them.

The joint amendment was adopted unanimously and the draft resolution, as thus amended, was also adopted unanimously by the Council at its 733rd meeting on 20 July.

By this resolution, the Council recommended that the General Assembly:

(1) reaffirm the pertinent provisions of its resolutions 57(I) and 417(V) with the exception of any reference to time limits contained in those resolutions;

(2) change the name of the organization to the United Nations Children's Fund, retaining the symbol UNICEF;

(3) request the Council to continue to review periodically the work of UNICEF and to make recommendations to the Assembly as appropriate;

(4) request the Secretary-General to ensure that the programme carried out by UNICEF should continue to be co-ordinated effectively with the regular and technical assistance programmes of the United Nations and the specialized agencies and to report thereon to the Council in 1954 and subsequently as appropriate; and

(5) that the Assembly commend UNICEF, the United Nations Secretariat and the specialized agencies concerned for the close working relations which have developed progressively, and request them to strengthen those relations in giving full effect to the desires of the General Assembly as expressed in General Assembly resolution 417(V) and in this resolution.

At its eighth session, the General Assembly considered the question of continuing UNICEF . . .

Opening the debate, the representative of Iraq said that UNICEF was currently assisting more than 200 child-care projects in 75 countries. The major categories of these projects were: maternal and child welfare; control of malaria; BCG vaccination and other tuberculosis control; child nutrition; and control of communicable diseases and emergency aid projects. He recalled that the United States had thus far contributed over $97,250,000 to the Fund and other governments approximately a total of $45 million. He stressed that, moreover, these amounts did not take into account the extensive "internal matching" of governments. Out of every dollar spent on child-care projects the local government concerned was

spending 61 cents, as compared to 39 cents contributed by UNICEF.

. . .

On 6 October 1953, the Assembly unanimously adopted resolution 802(VIII).

"*The General Assembly,*

"*Considering* the world-wide disproportion between the magnitude of social service tasks to be undertaken and the available means of implementation,

"*Considering* the role that the United Nations International Children's Emergency Fund plays in the whole international programme for the protection of the child,

"*Considering* that the Fund's activities are useful, not only because they realize some of the high objectives which have been adopted by the United Nations, but also because they create favourable conditions for the development of the long-range economic and social programmes of the United Nations and the specialized agencies, particularly the World Health Organization and the Food and Agriculture Organization of the United Nations.

"*Considering* the urgent need for continuing the work of UNICEF, particularly in the under-developed regions of the world,

"*Considering* that the number of governments making contributions to UNICEF has increased constantly since 1950,

"1. *Affirms* that the regulations which govern the activity of the United Nations International Children's Emergency Fund have enabled it to achieve satisfactory techniques, to acquire valuable experience and to accomplish its task successfully;

"2. *Reaffirms* the pertinent provisions of General Assembly resolutions 57(I) and 417(V), with the exception of any reference to time-limits contained in these resolutions;

"3. *Decides* to change the name of the organization to the *United Nations Children's Fund*, retaining the symbol UNICEF;

"4. *Requests* the Economic and Social Council to continue to review periodically the work of UNICEF and to make recommendations to the General Assembly as appropriate;

"5. *Requests* the Secretary-General:

"(a) To ensure that the programmes carried on by UNICEF continue to be co-ordinated effectively with the regular and technical assistance programmes of the United Nations and the specialized agencies;

"(b) To report thereon to the Economic and Social Council in 1954 and subsequently as appropriate;

"6. *Commends* UNICEF, the United Nations Secretariat and the specialized agencies concerned for the close working relations which have developed progressively and requests them to strengthen those relations in giving full effect to the desires of the Assembly as expressed in resolution 417(V) and the present resolution."

[YUN 1953, pp. 466-68]

Refugee emergencies

Organized international assistance to refugees first came into being in 1921 when an Office of

High Commissioner was established to safeguard the interests of the thousands of people who left their countries of origin as a result of the great political changes following the First World War. In 1930, the duties of legal and political protection passed to the League of Nations. In the 1930s, the office of High Commissioner was again created to deal with the exodus of refugees from Germany and, in 1939, the Office of the High Commissioner for All Refugees was established under League of Nations protection. From 1939, the High Commissioner also headed the Intergovernmental Committee on Refugees, which had been established in the inter-war period to facilitate the movement of refugees.

As the Second World War drew to a close, UNRRA was constituted with the onerous responsibility, among many others, of repatriating millions of displaced persons (see above). By 1946, some 7 million people had been repatriated but over 1.6 million remained, many of whom refused to return to their home countries. Today, 50 years later, the refugee crisis has reached unprecedented proportions. The escalation of ethnic and regional conflicts in many parts of the world has forced more than 20 million people to flee their homes into refugee life, and another 30 million have been displaced within their own countries (see figure 3).

International Refugee Organization

Origin

The General Assembly of the United Nations, recognizing the immediate urgency of the international problem of refugees and displaced persons, recommended, on February 12, 1946, that the Economic and Social Council establish a special committee for the purpose of examining this problem. . . .

On June 21, 1946, the Economic and Social Council in turn recommended to the General Assembly the establishment of an International Refugee Organization and requested the Secretary-General to forward the draft Constitution to governments for their comments. The Council also recommended that the Secretary-General take such steps as might be appropriate to plan, in consultation with UNRRA and the Intergovernmental Committee on Refugees (IGC), the initiation of the work of the IRO. It further established a Committee on the Finances of the IRO to prepare provisional administrative and operational budgets for the first financial year of IRO and scales according to which contributions to these budgets might be allocated equitably among the Members of the United Nations. This Committee met in London from July 6 to 20, 1946.

At its third session the Economic and Social Council had before it the comments of governments on the draft Constitution and on the report of the Committee on the Finances of the IRO, and a report from the Secretary-General relating to the initiation of the work of the projected Organization. It established an *ad hoc* Committee on Finances to review the report of the Committee on the Finances of the IRO. The Council finally approved and submitted to the General Assembly a draft Constitution of IRO together with a resolution regarding Interim Arrangements which provided for the establishment of a Preparatory Commission. It also transmitted to the General Assembly the report of the Committee on the Finances of the IRO together with the report of the *ad hoc* Committee on Finances.

The General Assembly on December 15, 1946, approved, with certain modifications, the Constitution of the International Refugee Organization, including a budget for its first year of operation and the arrangements for a Preparatory Commission, and urged Members of the United Nations to sign both of these instruments.

The Constitution of IRO will come into force when at least fifteen States, whose required contributions to the operational budget ($151,060,500) amount to not less than 75 per cent of the total, have become parties to it. States may become parties to the Constitution by signature without reservation as to approval, signature subject to approval followed by acceptance, or acceptance. As of July 1, 1947, representatives of nineteen governments had signed the Constitution and the Agreement on Interim Measures; of this number, however, only seven, with contributions amounting to 65.26 per cent of the operational budget, had accepted the Constitution unconditionally.

Functions

According to its Constitution the functions of IRO will be the repatriation; identification, registration and classification; care and assistance; legal and political protection; transport; and resettlement and re-establishment, in countries able and willing to receive them, of refugees and displaced persons.

These functions are to be exercised with a view to:

(1) encouraging and assisting the repatriation of persons the concern of the Organization, having regard to the principle that no person shall be compulsorily repatriated;

(2) promoting repatriation by all possible means, especially by providing repatriated persons with adequate food for a period of three months, provided that they are returning to a country suffering as a result of enemy occupation during the war, and provided such food is distributed under the auspices of the IRO.

The term "refugee" is intended to apply to a person who has left, or who is outside of, his country of nationality or of former habitual residence, and who is a victim of the nazi, fascist or falan-

FIGURE 3
Global number of refugees 1960–1995

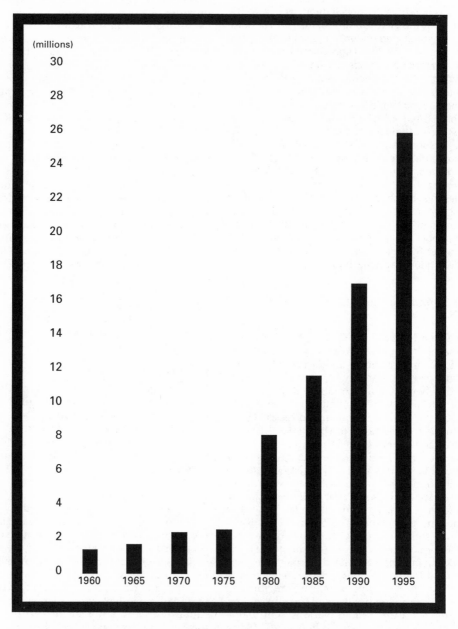

Sources: United Nations High Commissioner for Refugees
Reports of the Secretary-General (A/49/1; A/50/60-S/1995/1)

gist regimes or who was considered a refugee before the outbreak of the Second World War for reasons of race, religion, nationality or political opinion.

The term "displaced person" is intended to apply to an individual who has been deported from his country of nationality or of former habitual residence to undertake forced labor, or has been deported for racial, religious or political reasons.

(YUN 1946-47, pp. 805-806)

IRO continued the work of UNRRA in providing for repatriation, care and maintenance and medical attention, to which it added resettlement, vocational training and language courses for emigrants. Although IRO was due to cease operations in 1950, it was decided that it should continue its activities until October 1951. The High Commissioner for Refugees was due to begin his duties on 1 January 1951 (see below).

Report of the International Refugee Organization

The [Economic and Social] Council considered the Third Annual Report of IRO and heard an oral statement from the Director-General at its 526th plenary meeting on 29 August 1951. . . .

Certain major factors were emphasized in the report and in the statement made by the Director-General. From 1 July 1947 to 31 December 1950, IRO had given assistance of one kind or another to 1,525,643 refugees. It had repatriated 71,695 to their countries of origin, resettled 879,403 to new homes in many parts of the world, and had made rapid progress toward the satisfactory local settlement of a large number of others in countries of asylum.

During 1950, a total of 191,119 persons had been resettled, and the Director-General estimated that another 142,000 refugees would be resettled during 1951. The relaxation of immigration restrictions affecting refugees and the liberalization of selection criteria in Western countries were the major factors in the attainment of the latter two figures.

The year 1950 had been marked by the first major success in resolving the most difficult problem facing IRO—that of finding resettlement opportunities and making suitable permanent arrangements for handicapped, sick and aged refugees in need of institutional care. By the end of 1950, arrangements had been made for more than two thirds of the entire institutional group of some 35,000 persons, and it was anticipated that the remainder of the problem would be solved by the end of the operations of IRO. Some of these refugees had been established in countries of resettlement, while for others suitable permanent arrangements had been made in the countries of their residence.

Only 2,917 refugees had chosen to return home in 1950, and 607 of these were overseas Chinese.

Repatriation was reported to be a decreasing factor in the organization's work, since most persons desiring to do so had returned to their own countries before IRO had come into existence.

As the work of IRO developed, it had become apparent that, for a certain number of refugees who had valid objections against repatriation and for whom no resettlement opportunities could be found within the lifetime of IRO, the only solution would be local settlement in countries of asylum, under the best possible conditions obtainable. On 1 July 1950, responsibility for the care and maintenance of more than 111,000 refugees in countries of Western Europe, in the Federal Republic of Germany and in Austria had been transferred to local authorities. Most of those who were in the countries of Western Europe had desired to remain where they were, whereas those in the Federal Republic of Germany and Austria had desired resettlement. Efforts toward that end had been continued concurrently with attempts to achieve the most satisfactory conditions of local settlement.

During 1950, IRO had continued to render various other services to the refugees within its mandate. Legal and political protection had been continued both on the general plane and in respect of individual refugees. Care and maintenance had been provided to all refugees in process of resettlement, to those in the institutional "hard core" group, and to unaccompanied children. Health services had been extended to those in IRO camps and on board ships carrying them to countries of resettlement. Throughout the year, the International Tracing Service had continued its endeavours to establish the fate of millions of persons, mostly non-German nationals, who had disappeared during the Second World War.

. . .

The majority of members of the Council expressed appreciation of the work done by IRO in accomplishing the substantial completion of the task. It was suggested by the representatives of Belgium and Mexico that the experience of the specialized staff and the transportation facilities of IRO might profitably be put at the disposal of whatever body would deal with migration of workers from Europe. Some representatives, among them those of Chile and France, paid special tribute to the success of the organization in making suitable arrangements for the permanent care of refugees in the institutional "hard core" group.

On the other hand, the representatives of Czechoslovakia, Poland and the USSR felt that IRO had not carried out its assigned task of repatriating displaced persons to their countries of origin. They complained that IRO itself and the Occupation Authorities of the Western Zones of Germany and Austria had prevented repatriation and had conducted a campaign of recruitment of refugees and displaced persons for cheap labour and armed services in Western capitalist countries. They criticized conditions in camps as well as the treatment accorded by IRO to refugees in the so-called "hard core" category and to unaccompanied children.

The representative of the USSR introduced a draft resolution to recommend that Members of the United Nations, and in particular the Governments of the United States, the United Kingdom and France, should remove all obstacles to the repatriation of refugees and displaced persons, and should complete such repatriation in 1952. It would further recommend that governments having refugees and displaced persons on their territories, or under their control, should provide the Secretary-General of the United Nations by 1 January 1952 with full information concerning such persons. Finally, it would instruct the Secretary-General to report to the Council at its fourteenth session on the implementation of the resolution by Members of the United Nations.

The Council rejected this draft resolution by 15 votes to 3 and adopted a draft resolution, proposed by the United States.

Resolution 411(XIII), adopted by 15 votes to 3, at the Council's 526th plenary meeting on 29 August, recognized the great contribution made by IRO to the alleviation of human suffering, commended IRO upon the substantial completion of its task, and expressed appreciation of the manner in which it had carried out its assigned duties.

(YUN 1951, pp. 524-25)

High Commissioner for Refugees

In response to a 1948 Economic and Social Council request, the Secretary-General prepared a study on improving the status of stateless persons and eliminating statelessness. At its ninth (1949) session, the Council considered the study in conjunction with a communication from IRO containing a memorandum from its General Council on the problem, with particular reference to international protection after the termination of IRO activities.

On 6 August 1949, the Council adopted resolution 248(IX) A, in which it requested Members of the United Nations and all other States to provide, after the termination of IRO, the necessary legal protection for refugees. The Secretary-General was asked, in consultation with the Advisory Committee on Administrative and Budgetary Questions, to prepare for the General Assembly a plan for such an organization, taking into account two alternatives: the establishment of a High Commissioner's Office under the control of the United Nations; and the establishment of a service within the United Nations Secretariat.

On 3 December 1949, following discussion of the question in the Third and Fifth Committees, the

General Assembly adopted resolution 319(IV) A by 35 votes to 7, with 13 abstentions.

"*The General Assembly,*

"*Considering* that the problem of refugees is international in scope and nature and that its final solution can only be provided by the voluntary repatriation of the refugees or their assimilation within new national communities,

"*Recognizing* the responsibility of the United Nations for the international protection of refugees,

"*Having examined* resolution 248(IX)A of the Economic and Social Council of 6 August 1949, the report of the Secretary-General of 26 October 1946, and the communications from the General Council of the International Refugee Organization of 11 July 1949 and of 20 October 1949,

"*Considering* that in its aforementioned resolution the Economic and Social Council requested the Governments of States Members of the United Nations, and of other States, to provide the necessary legal protection for refugees who have been the concern of the International Refugee Organization and recommended that the General Assembly at its fourth session should decide the functions and organizational arrangements, within the framework of the United Nations, necessary for the international protection of refugees after the International Refugee Organization terminates its activities,

"1. *Decides* to establish, as of 1 January 1951, a High Commissioner's Office for Refugees in accordance with the provisions of the annex to the present resolution to discharge the functions enumerated therein and such other functions as the General Assembly may from time to time confer upon it;

"2. *Decides* that, unless the General Assembly subsequently decides otherwise, no expenditure other than administrative expenditures relating to the functioning of the High Commissioner's Office should be borne on the budget of the United Nations, and that all other expenditures relating to the activities of the High Commissioner should be financed by voluntary contributions;

"3. *Requests* the Secretary-General:

"*(a)* To prepare detailed draft provisions for the implementation of the present resolution and the annex attached thereto, to circulate these draft provisions to Governments for comments, and to submit them to the Economic and Social Council at its eleventh session, together with such comments thereon as may have been received from Governments;

"*(b)* To prepare, in consultation with the Advisory Committee on Administrative and Budgetary Questions, a draft budget for the operation in 1951 of the High Commissioner's Office for Refugees;

"4. *Requests* the Economic and Social Council:

"*(a)* To prepare, at its eleventh session, a draft resolution embodying provisions for the functioning of the High Commissioner's Office for Refugees and to submit the draft resolution to the General Assembly for consideration at its fifth regular session;

"*(b)* To transmit to the General Assembly at its fifth regular session such recommendations as the Council may deem appropriate regarding the definitions of the term "refugee" to be applied by the High Commissioner;

"5. *Decides* to review, not later than at its eighth regular session, the arrangements for the High Commissioner's Office for Refugees with a view to determining whether the Office should be continued beyond 31 December 1953.''

ANNEX

1. The High Commissioner's Office for Refugees should:

(*a*) Be so organized within the framework of the United Nations as to possess the degree of independence and the prestige required for the effective performance of the High Commissioner's duties;

(*b*) Be financed under the budget of the United Nations; and

(*c*) Receive policy directives from the United Nations according to methods to be determined by the General Assembly.

2. Means should be provided whereby interested Governments, non-members of the United Nations, may be associated with the work of the High Commissioner's Office.

3. .Persons falling under the competence of the High Commissioner's Office for Refugees should be, for the time being, refugees and displaced persons defined in annex I of the Constitution of the International Refugee Organization and, thereafter, such persons as the General Assembly may from time to time determine, including any persons brought under the jurisdiction of the High Commissioner's Office under the terms of international conventions or agreements approved by the General Assembly.

4. The High Commissioner, in order to promote, stimulate and facilitate the execution of the most suitable solution to the problem with which he is entrusted, should provide for the protection of refugees and displaced persons falling under the competence of the Office by:

(*a*) Promoting the conclusion and ratification of international conventions providing for the protection of refugees, supervising the application of the provisions of such conventions, and proposing any necessary amendments thereto;

(*b*) Promoting through special agreements with Governments, the execution of any measures calculated to improve the situation of refugees and to reduce the number of refugees requiring protection;

(*c*) Assisting Governments and private organizations in their efforts to promote voluntary repatriation of refugees or their assimilation within new national communities;

(*d*) Facilitating the co-ordination of the efforts of voluntary agencies concerned with the welfare of refugees.

5. The High Commissioner should distribute among private and, as appropriate, official agencies which he deems best qualified to administer such assistance any funds, public or private, which he may receive for this purpose. He should not, however, appeal to Governments or make a general appeal to non-governmental sources except with the prior approval of the General Assembly. The accounts relating to these funds should be periodically verified by the auditors of the United Nations. For the information of the General Assembly, the High Commissioner should include in his annual report a statement of his activities in this field.

6. The High Commissioner should engage in such additional activities, including repatriation and resettlement activities, as the General Assembly may determine.

7. The High Commissioner should report annually on his work to the General Assembly through the Economic and Social Council.

8. The High Commissioner's work should be of an entirely non-political character and relate as a rule to groups and categories of refugees. In this performance of his duties he should:

(*a*) Keep in close touch with the Governments and inter-governmental organizations concerned and invite the assistance of the various specialized agencies;

(*b*) Establish contact in such manner as he may think best with private organizations dealing with refugee questions.

9. The High Commissioner should be elected by the General Assembly, on the nomination of the Secretary-General, for a term of three years from 1 January 1951.

10. The High Commissioner should appoint for a period of three years a deputy High Commissioner, who should not have the same nationality as the High Commissioner. He should also appoint, under the regulations of the United Nations, a small staff of persons devoted to the purposes of the Office to assist him.

11. The High Commissioner should consult the Governments of the countries of residence of refugees as to the need for appointing representatives therein. In any country recognizing such need, he may appoint a representative approved by the Government of that country. Subject to the foregoing, the same representative may serve in more than one country.

12. The High Commissioner's Office for Refugees should be located in Geneva.

(YUN 1948-49, pp. 598-99)

Report of the United Nations High Commissioner for Refugees

In September 1951, the Economic and Social Council considered the first report by the High Commissioner.

. . .

The report by the High Commissioner contained an account of the activities undertaken by the High Commissioner's Office during the first five months, an appraisal of the task to be done, and a note on the Convention relating to the Status of Refugees. It drew attention to the fact that although IRO had settled over a million persons, the problem was by no means solved.

For example, in Western Germany, apart from the nine million expelled persons who were outside the mandate of the High Commissioner, there was a residual group of at least 100,000 displaced persons and refugees together with a further one and a half million refugees from the Eastern Zone of Germany. In Austria, in addition to the 25,000 displaced persons and refugees, there were within the mandate of the High Commissioner another 300,000 expelled persons, about 50,000 of whom were living in camps. In France, asylum had been given to 300,000 refugees and in other European countries there were residual groups amounting to between 20,000 and 80,000 persons. Further-more, the assimilation of tens of thousands of refu-gees who had been transported to other countries had not yet reached its final stage.

The situation was further complicated, it was stated, by the fact that new refugees were constantly appearing in the countries of first asylum and that the residual groups from IRO, for the most part, fell into the category of difficult cases and failed to meet the criteria of immigration countries. They therefore needed more care and had to be treated on a more-or-less individual basis.

The High Commissioner stated in his report that, although he had no direct mandate to en-gage in repatriation and resettlement without the Assembly's approval, he considered it his duty to look for any possibilities of voluntary repatriation or resettlement which would provide a solution for refugees within this mandate. Should this fail, his chief task then must be to assist, where feasible, the local settlement of those refugees within the competence of his Office for whom there were no chances for resettlement, and to promote the com-plete assimilation of all the refugees who had been resettled.

He estimated that the essential machinery for carrying out the task entrusted to him would con-sist of a headquarters office at Geneva and eleven field offices situated in the countries where impor-tant numbers of refugees were resident. During the period under review, he reported that no funds, public or private, had been given or offered to the High Commissioner's Office. He noted, however, the grant of $100,000 given by the Rockefeller Foundation to carry out an independent analyti-cal survey of the problems and conditions of refu-gees under his mandate.

The High Commissioner also referred to the Convention relating to the Status of Refugees adopted by the Conference of Plenipotentiaries held in Geneva in July 1951. Under the Statute of his Office, the High Commissioner was en-trusted with the duty of supervising the applica-tion of international conventions for the protec-tion of refugees within his mandate. He noted that article 35 of the Convention confirmed this func-tion in respect of the Convention.

In the course of the Council's debate, as well as in his report, the High Commissioner drew at-tention to the connexion between the problem of the residual groups of IRO refugees and, in par-ticular, the German refugee problem.

Large numbers of refugees outside the mandate of his Office still existed in countries in Central Europe, he pointed out. As a result, in these coun-tries the prospects of final assimilation of the refu-gees transferred by IRO were unfavourable.

He referred specifically to the situation in Ger-many and Austria and to the complications aris-ing out of the problem of the *Volksdeutsche* refugees. In Austria these refugees were within his mandate and within the scope of the Convention. In Ger-many, on the other hand, they were not, because they were regarded by the competent authorities as having the rights and obligations attaching to the possession of nationality.

Western Germany, which, before the Second World War, had had a population of 39 million, had now, due to the influx of expelled persons and of refugees from the Eastern Zone of Germany, a population of 47.5 million.

In this connexion, the High Commissioner re-ferred to the report of the United States–German Technical Assistance Commission on the Integra-tion of Refugees in the Federal Republic of Ger-many, which, he stated, showed that economic as-similation of non-German refugees was not feasible unless the problem of assimilating German refu-gees was tackled at the same time. The problem, he felt, was so serious that the United Nations could not afford to ignore it. It was not merely a refugee problem; it was the problem of the social and economic stability of Central Europe, and, if not settled soon, could develop into a threat to in-ternational peace and security.

Most members of the Council expressed appreci-ation for the report and the oral supplementary state-ment. They felt that the points raised by the High Commissioner were of great interest and impor-tance but required further study. Therefore, full discussion of them at this time would not serve any purpose. Some representatives, among them those of Poland and the USSR, stated their intention of voting against the report, as they considered the refugee problem had been artificially created.

On the basis of a proposal by the United States, the Social Committee, at its 209th meeting on 3 September, by 12 votes to 3, with 1 abstention, and the Council, at its 544th plenary meeting on 10 September 1951, by the same vote, adopted a reso-lution (393 A (XIII)) taking note of the report and commending the High Commissioner on the pro-gress made in organizing his Office.

. . .

Consideration by the General Assembly at its sixth session

The General Assembly considered the question of refugees and assistance to them at the 373rd to 386th meetings of its Third Committee from 2-14 January, and at its 371st plenary meeting on 2 February 1952.

The Assembly had before it the report of the High Commissioner for Refugees which, in addi-tion, included further observations on problems of assistance; a report from the International Refugee Organization (IRO); and a note by the Secretary-General concerning a resolution adopted on 6 December 1951 by the United Nations High Commissioner's Advisory Committee on Refugees. This resolution, in general, expressed the Committee's agreement with the High Commissioner's proposals for action.

Report of the United Nations High Commissioner for Refugees

The High Commissioner, in his observations on problems of assistance emphasized that unless countries of immigration approached the problems of refugees in a new manner, there was very little chance that a continuation of international machinery for resettlement or migration could solve the difficulties of the residual groups of IRO refugees. Two distinct problems existed: an emergency relief problem affecting refugees in areas where political or economic conditions made it impossible for them to rely on public relief funds or to engage in any economic activity which would permit them to support themselves; and a long-term problem connected with the assimilation of refugees in certain areas.

The emergency relief problem, he stated, was most serious in the Far East where the situation of refugees in Shanghai and in Samar (Philippines) appeared to be hopeless, unless some government was willing to accept full responsibility for them or unless a fund was made available to help them until a permanent solution could be found.

With regard to the long-term assimilation problem, which was particularly difficult in the main areas in Central Europe, a definite programme would have to be initiated if the refugees within the mandate of IRO were to be absorbed into the local economies. The transfer in Central Europe in July 1950 of care and maintenance from IRO to the governments concerned was in the nature of an administrative transfer and provided no firm basis for the integration of refugees into the economic life of the countries.

In conclusion, the High Commissioner, in his report, recommended three lines of action with respect to assisting the refugees:

(*a*) A limited relief fund should be established which would provide for the basic needs of certain refugee groups, such as those in the Far and Middle East, whose conditions would be desperate after the cessation of IRO emergency relief. The High Commissioner's Office should be able to administer the fund which should also provide for assistance in temporary emergency situations which might arise from the influx of refugees in countries of first asylum.

(*b*) Long-term plans should be made and methods evolved for financing and implementing economic reconstruction measures calculated to afford to residual groups in some areas possibilities of a normal livelihood. Accordingly, governments and appropriate specialized agencies should be urged to work out in close collaboration with his Office all suitable plans toward that end.

(*c*) Those States willing to make a further international effort to promote migration should consider the possibility of taking the necessary measures to ensure that refugees within the mandate of his Office would receive a fair share in any opportunities for migration provided.

Report of the International Refugee Organization

In its report to the Assembly, IRO stated that at the eighth session of its General Council (October 1951) it had determined that it had sufficient funds available to continue operations until 1 January 1952 and that, if additional assets were realized out of its operations, it might prove possible to assist and to re-establish several thousand more refugees in January and February 1952. The communication stated that the organization had already repatriated and resettled more than a million refugees, and, by the end of 1951, would have made reasonably satisfactory provision for approximately 47,000 refugees and their dependents who, because of age or infirmity, required permanent institutional or other forms of care. However, there would remain a limited number in various areas for whom the problem would not have been satisfactorily resolved: Germany—80,000; Austria—24,000; Italy—24,000; Trieste—7,000, of whom 900 were seriously ill; Greece—4,500; Turkey—300; Spain—500; Portugal—100; Middle East—250; China—5,000 of European Origin; and the Philippines—150.

IRO pointed out that the prospects for these refugees were doubtful either because of the level of economic activity in the countries of their asylum, or because local measures for their relief or care were unavailable or inadequate, or because the refugees were unwelcome on political grounds but were unable to depart.

IRO further estimated that between 1,000 and 1,500 refugees were each month entering Germany, Austria, Turkey, Greece, Trieste and Italy from Eastern European countries, and that the impact of this influx was felt also in nearly every country in Western Europe, where political asylum was an established tradition. This continuous influx, in the opinion of IRO, emphasized the permanent character of the refugee problem. Moreover, the report concluded, the situation of refugees coming within the mandate of IRO was rendered precarious by the large numbers of refugees or other persons entering these areas, who, while outside the scope of the competence of IRO, at the same time reduced considerably the opportunities of housing and employment available to refugees under the protection of the organization.

(YUN 1951, pp. 525-29)

Following discussion of the two reports in the Third Committee, the General Assembly, on 2 February, adopted resolutions 538(VI) A and B as proposed by the Committee, by 28 votes to 5, with 21 abstentions, and by 38 votes to 5, with 2 abstentions, respectively:

A

"The General Assembly

"1. *Takes note* of part I and part II of the annual report of the United Nations High Commissioner for Refugees submitted through the Economic and Social Council to the General Assembly in accordance with paragraph 11 of the Statute of his office;

"2. *Expresses its satisfaction* at the conclusion of the Convention relating to the Status of Refugees;

"3. *Invites* Member States and non-member States which have demonstrated their interest in the solution of the refugee problem to become parties to that Convention as soon as possible;

"4. *Reiterates* its call upon governments to co-operate with the High Commissioner as recommended in its resolution 428(V) of 14 December 1950.

B

"The General Assembly,

"*Taking note* of the communication of the General Council of the International Refugee Organization on residual refugee problems and the observations of the United Nations High Commissioner for Refugees contained in his report on the problem of assistance submitted in accordance with resolution 430(V) of 14 December 1950,

"*Having noted* the serious unsolved problems which in certain areas will face refugees who will not have been repatriated or resettled by the end of the operations of the International Refugee Organization,

"*Bearing in mind* the urgency of finding solutions for the refugee problem, including the repatriation to their countries of origin of refugees who express the desire to return there,

"1. *Authorizes* the High Commissioner, under paragraph 10 of the Statute of his Office, to issue an appeal for funds for the purpose of enabling emergency aid to be given to the most needy groups among refugees within his mandate;

"2. *Recommends* all States directly affected by the refugee problem, as well as the appropriate specialized agencies and other inter-governmental agencies concerned, to pay special attention to this problem when drawing up and executing programmes of economic reconstruction and development; and requests the High Commissioner to contribute to the promotion of activities in this field, paying due regard to the desirability of repatriating to their countries of origin refugees who express the desire to return there;

"3. *Appeals* to States interested in migration to give to refugees within the mandate of the High Commissioner every possible opportunity to participate in and benefit from projects to promote migration."

[YUN 1951, p. 531]

Assistance

The Office of the United Nations High Commissioner for Refugees came into existence in January 1951 for a three-year period, following which its mandate was extended for five-year periods, most recently in 1992 until 31 December 1998.

In 1992—over 40 years after UNHCR's establishment—the refugee situation was more severe than ever and affected all regions of the world. Africa, which hosted almost a third of the 19 million global refugee population, also saw its internally displaced persons rise to 15 million. Refugee and asylum issues again became a major concern for European States due to the events in the former Yugoslavia and in the Central Asian republics of the former USSR.

During 1992, UNHCR continued to implement the High Commissioner's three-pronged strategy of prevention, preparedness and solutions, as the global refugee situation again deteriorated. While responding to refugee situations in countries of asylum, it also sought to prevent and contain refugee movements. UNHCR began to provide assistance not only to refugees, returnees and displaced persons, but also, in the case of the former Yugoslavia, to people directly threatened by expulsion or ethnic cleansing.

UNHCR was confronted with emergency situations in many parts of the world. It actively pursued durable solutions for refugees, especially through voluntary repatriation, while seeking to interest Governments, development agencies and financial institutions in improving infrastructure in areas of return devastated by war.

The UNHCR Emergency Fund was used frequently in response to emerging refugee situations. It was used in 1992 to assist Somali refugees in Yemen ($3.8 million) and Kenya ($2.5 million), Bhutanese refugees in Nepal ($3.4 million), Sierra Leonean refugees in Liberia ($2.5 million), Mozambican refugees in Zimbabwe ($1.5 million), as well as refugees and displaced persons from Armenia and Azerbaijan ($1.5 million). Total expenditure from the Emergency Fund in 1992 amounted to $19.2 million. In December, the Executive Committee approved an increase, effective 1 January 1993, raising the ceiling of the Fund from $20 million to $25 million, and increasing the amount available for a single emergency in a given year from $6 million to $8 million. Emergency assistance programmes that were funded from special appeals included: the former Yugoslavia, to assist those uprooted by the ongoing conflict ($294.4 million); Bangladesh, to assist a new influx of Rohingya refugees from Myanmar ($18.4 million); and Iraq, for assistance to the Kurdish population in the north of the country ($17.7 million).

Following the emergency phase of a refugee operation, the basic needs of the refugees were met through care and maintenance assistance. During 1992, such assistance amounted to $214.7 million under General Programmes and $91.3 million under Special Programmes. In Africa, care and maintenance programmes continued in Kenya

($59 million), Ethiopia ($29 million), Malawi ($27.4 million) and Guinea ($16.3 million). The situation in the Horn of Africa required large-scale care and maintenance assistance, which was mostly provided in Kenya for Somali refugees. A significant cross-border operation inside Somalia aimed to avert further influxes of refugees into Kenya. Substantial care and maintenance programmes were also implemented in Côte d'Ivoire, the Sudan and Zimbabwe. Elsewhere, care and maintenance assistance continued for Vietnamese in South-East Asian camps and Hong Kong. The largest programmes were in Hong Kong ($17.1 million) and Thailand ($16.4 million). During 1992, however, new arrivals of Vietnamese asylum-seekers virtually ceased. In addition, major programmes were carried out in South-West Asia, particularly in Pakistan where a sizeable Afghan refugee population remained ($24.1 million). In Latin America, the only significant care and maintenance programme was in Mexico for Guatemalan refugees ($3.1 million), pending their voluntary repatriation.

UNHCR also continued its efforts to provide durable solutions to refugees through local integration and resettlement in addition to voluntary repatriation. In 1992, expenditures to promote durable solutions under both General and Special Programmes amounted to some $319 million.

An estimated 2.4 million refugees returned to their homes during the year. Among the most significant repatriation movements were 360,000 persons to Cambodia, principally from Thailand, and 1,274,016 from Pakistan to Afghanistan. Another 250,000 Afghans returned from Iran. About 1.5 million Mozambican refugees were also being prepared for repatriation. Expenditures on voluntary repatriation under both General and Special Programmes totalled $229 million.

UNHCR supported the local settlement of refugees within host countries, obligating some $76 million under General and Special Programmes. Assistance included the promotion of agricultural and non-agricultural activities, improvements in infrastructure, and skills training in Côte d'Ivoire, Guinea and Senegal. Organized rural settlements were supported in China, Ethiopia, Mexico, Uganda, Zaire and Zambia.

Resettlement was sought for some 42,300 persons in 1992 and, of that number, UNHCR registered 34,510 departures. The main focus for resettlement activity was the Middle East, where UNHCR sought to resettle some 30,000 Iraqi refugees from Saudi Arabia. About 7,200 of them were accepted for resettlement, including almost 3,000 in Iran. More than 5,600 Iraqis and Iranians were resettled from Turkey. In addition to these two operations, some 2,300 refugees from the Middle East and South-West Asia were also resettled. An emergency operation started on 1 October 1992 for Bosnian former detainees whose release was secured by ICRC and who were transferred to Croatia. By the end of the year, about 5,100 had been registered by UNHCR.

In Africa, resettlement efforts remained focused on countries in the Horn of Africa. A total of 6,010 African refugees departed for resettlement during the year.

In South-East Asia, a total of 19,516 refugees from seven countries were resettled during 1992. Global expenditures on resettlement were estimated at $15 million.

In 1992, expenditures on UNHCR assistance activities in Africa totalled $284 million; in the Americas, $50 million; in Asia and Oceania, $175 million; in Europe, $337 million; and in South-West Asia, North Africa and the Middle East, $159 million.

[YUN 1992, pp. 896-97]

Disaster and emergency relief

Following an extensive review of the Organization's humanitarian emergency relief and assistance efforts, the General Assembly, in resolution 46/182 of 19 December 1991, set down basic principles for humanitarian assistance and recommended specific measures to ensure a prompt and coordinated response to complex emergencies and natural disasters. The resolution provided the United Nations with four instruments for coordination: the Office of the Emergency Relief Coordinator, the Central Emergency Revolving Fund, the Inter-Agency Standing Committee and the Consolidated Appeals Process. Those instruments enhanced the Organization's capacity to respond promptly in emergency situations with an effective division of labour between the executing agencies.

In April 1992, the Secretary-General established a new Department of Humanitarian Affairs (DHA) and appointed an Under-Secretary-General for Humanitarian Affairs to head the Department and occupy the role of Emergency Relief Coordinator. DHA subsumed the former Office of the United Nations Disaster Relief Coordinator—which was established in 1972 to mobilize assistance in the aftermath of natural disasters and to make recommendations with regard to prevention and preparedness—as well as former emergency units for Africa, Iraq and South-East Asia.

In order to ensure that all aspects of humanitarian assistance were addressed in a comprehensive and coordinated fashion, DHA's mandate was to work closely with all concerned organizations of the United Nations (such as UNICEF, UNHCR, the World Food Programme and the World Health

Organization), other intergovernmental organizations (the International Federation of Red Cross and Red Crescent Societies, the International Organization for Migration) and non-governmental organizations (Médecins sans frontières, Save the Children Fund). Also, emergency relief was no longer to be seen as an isolated issue; it would be provided in ways to support recovery and long-term development.

In the early 1990s, the work of the United Nations was increasingly dominated by peace-keeping operations and the Security Council took action to establish security for the distribution of emergency relief and assistance, invoking Chapter VII of the Charter for the first time for that purpose in the former Yugoslavia and in Somalia.

Rwanda

Rwanda has a long history of ethnic conflict between the majority Hutu and minority Tutsi populations. Following a full-scale armed conflict which broke out in October 1990 between the Rwanda Government Forces and the Rwanda Patriotic Front, the two parties signed a Peace Agreement in August 1993 at Arusha, United Republic of Tanzania. The two parties also requested the United Nations to deploy a neutral international force in Rwanda to oversee the implementation of that Agreement. After the adoption of Security Council resolution 872(1993) of 5 October 1993, the United Nations Assistance Mission for Rwanda (UNAMIR) was established and subsequently deployed.

On 6 April 1994, Rwanda was plunged into chaos and massive ethnic violence following a plane crash in which the Presidents of both Rwanda and Burundi were killed near Kigali. In the ensuing weeks, over 500,000 people were killed, 2 million were internally displaced and more than 2 million sought refuge in neighbouring Burundi, Uganda and United Republic of Tanzania.

In view of the unfolding humanitarian disaster in Rwanda, the Security Council adopted resolution 918(1994) on 17 May 1994, authorizing the expansion of the UNAMIR force level up to 5,500 troops in order to enable it to carry out an expanded mandate, which included the protection of displaced persons, refugees and civilians at risk, and the provision of security to humanitarian relief operations.

In mid-July 1994, the refugee crisis escalated in the western part of Rwanda, as more than 1 million refugees crossed the border into the Kivu region of Zaire. The challenge presented by this sudden and massive influx of refugees was enormous. It required the urgent organization of logistic arrangements to supply and distribute daily 30 million litres of clean water and emergency relief in food, nutrition, health, shelter and sanitation. Massive international efforts were marshalled to respond to the disaster.

In the early stage of the crisis, intense fighting prevented substantial delivery of humanitarian assistance. As relatively safe areas were identified, humanitarian agencies brought in relief supplies, often through Burundi and Uganda to reach the needy population in the adjoining areas in Rwanda. UNAMIR played a key role in providing protection to the displaced persons and civilians at risk; it saved countless lives, treated injured persons, protected targeted civilians and provided relief supplies.

On 25 April 1994, a United Nations Inter-Agency "Flash Appeal" calling for $16 million was launched covering projected emergency needs up to 31 May. In addition, UNHCR made a request for $56 million to cover the needs of refugees for its Burundi and Rwanda emergency operations from January to 15 July 1994.

The Secretary-General launched the United Nations Consolidated Inter-Agency Appeal for Persons Affected by the Crisis in Rwanda on 22 July 1994. He had drawn the attention of the international community in May to the genocide occurring in Rwanda; in July he stated that it was the "genocide" of hunger, thirst and disease which had to be addressed. The appeal called for $434,861,649 to cover humanitarian requirements for the period between July and December 1994.

On 2 August 1994, the Rwanda pledging conference was held at Geneva. It resulted in contributions amounting to $137 million against the $434.8 million July appeal. As at 1 September 1994, the overall requirements had increased to $552,055,246 with contributions against the appeal amounting to $384,061,506 covering 70 per cent of the revised United Nations humanitarian requirements.

Humanitarian emergency relief was provided by Governments, organizations of the United Nations system, and intergovernmental and non-governmental organizations (NGOs). Witnessing the massive refugee emergency in late July 1994 and heeding the call of the Secretary-General when he launched the United Nations Consolidated Appeal, the international community reacted quickly and in solidarity to contribute cash and relief supplies and to make available teams of doctors, nurses and emergency and logistics experts. Some countries made available military assets to carry out humanitarian activities.

During the periods of intense fighting, massive violence and throughout the refugee crisis, NGOs, in addition to their own programmes, were in many instances the implementing partners of the various United Nations programmes. By September 1994, there were 93 NGOs operating in Rwanda to assist the victims of the crisis. The international community responded generously to the humanitarian situation in Rwanda. However, the major task of rehabilitation of over 4 million Rwandese will require the continuing assistance of the international community.

Somalia

From the ouster of its President in January 1991, Somalia became embroiled in a clan-based civil war that resulted in extensive death and destruction, forced hundreds of thousands of civilians to flee Mogadishu, the capital, engendered dire need for emergency humanitarian assistance and threatened widespread famine. On 23 January 1992 (resolution 733(1992)), the Security Council urged all parties to the conflict to cease hostilities and decided that all States should immediately implement a complete embargo on deliveries of weapons and military equipment to Somalia. On 17 March, it supported the Secretary-General's decision to dispatch a technical team to Somalia to prepare a plan for a cease-fire monitoring mechanism and requested the team to develop a high-priority plan to deliver humanitarian assistance.

In accordance with a 1991 General Assembly request, the Secretary-General submitted an October report on emergency assistance for humanitarian relief and the economic and social rehabilitation of Somalia. The report contained information on the impact of the crisis, initiatives taken by the United Nations for emergency relief and rehabilitation, progress achieved and assistance by 12 Member States and the United Nations system.

In the 22 months since the overthrow of the Government, the situation in Somalia had continued to deteriorate. Almost 4.5 million people were threatened by severe malnutrition and related diseases. Of those, at least 1.5 million were at immediate mortal risk, with 300,000 people having already died since November 1991. No functioning government existed in most parts of the country and inter- and intra-clan violence abounded. The power struggle hampered the delivery of vitally needed humanitarian assistance and increasingly threatened relief workers.

Despite a situation which for most of the year bordered on anarchy, ICRC and a determined band of NGOs had maintained a continuous presence, principally at Mogadishu and Hargeisa. UNICEF re-established its presence in Mogadishu on 24 December 1991, while WFP re-established its operations in March 1992. Deliveries of humanitarian assistance were subject to extensive theft and looting, with relief workers labouring under extremely hazardous conditions. The breakdown in law and order had resulted in the deaths of many local and expatriate relief staff.

United Nations initiative for emergency relief and rehabilitation

In March, following a series of meetings in Mogadishu and New York, the United Nations successfully negotiated a cease-fire between the two factions contesting Mogadishu, making it possible for humanitarian assistance to reach both sides of the divided city. In May, it negotiated and established a vital route along the beach for convoys to pick up food from the port. On 18 March, the Secretary-General appointed a United Nations Coordinator for Humanitarian Assistance for Somalia. The Security Council, in April, approved deployment of a 50-member observer force to monitor the cease-fire; agreed to the deployment of a 500-member security force to protect relief goods and personnel; and endorsed a 90-Day Plan of Action for Emergency Humanitarian Assistance to Somalia, as proposed by a technical mission that had visited the country. Those elements were brought under the aegis of the United Nations Operation in Somalia (UNOSOM), and the Secretary-General appointed a Special Representative for Somalia to provide overall direction of United Nations activities and assist in promoting peace and national reconciliation. The 50 military observers were deployed in July and August, while the 500-member security force arrived at Mogadishu in September.

A United Nations technical team visited Somalia from 6 to 15 August to examine ways to expand UNOSOM's scope and effectiveness. On the basis of the team's findings, the Secretary-General recommended to the Security Council a substantial increase in airlift operations; the establishment of a preventive zone on the Kenya-Somalia border for special deliveries of food and seed to reduce famine-induced population movements; deployment of four additional security units of up to 750 persons each in different parts of the country; and the establishment of four UNOSOM zone headquarters headed by civilian officials as the operational basis for a comprehensive approach to the Somali problem. . . .

100-day Action Programme for Somalia

The Under-Secretary-General for Humanitarian Affairs led a high-level inter-agency mission, including high-level officials of FAO, UNDP, UNHCR, UNICEF, WFP and WHO, to Somalia from 10 to 12 September, meeting with political leaders, clan elders, ICRC, NGOs and United Nations relief workers. A major outcome of the mission was the decision to develop the 100-day Action Programme for Accelerated Humanitarian Assistance for Somalia, covering the period until the end of 1992. The Programme was drafted and refined through a collaborative process involving United Nations agencies, NGOs and other entities and reviewed at a coordination meeting on humanitarian assistance for Somalia (Geneva, 12 and 13 October). The Programme's priority actions included: massive infusion of food aid; expansion of supplementary feeding; provision of basic health services and a mass immunization campaign; urgent provision of clean water, sanitation and hygiene and of shelter material, including blankets and clothes; simultaneous delivery of seeds, tools and animal vaccines with food rations; prevention of further refugee outflows and displacements and initiation of returnee programmes; and promotion of rebuilding of civil society and local institutions, economic and social recovery and rehabilitation.

Resources of up to $83 million were required to implement the Programme, which called for some 50,000 metric tons of food per month to be delivered and distributed in Somalia.

In a December review of the 100-day Action Programme, DHA noted that deaths from starvation had been substantially reduced in most of the worst-affected famine areas, but remained, overall, at unacceptably high levels. The response from the donor community had been prompt and generous: of the $83 million requested under the Programme, $53 million was either received or pledged by early December. While food requirements were fully resourced, in some sectors underfunding or slow honouring of pledges prevented the start of activities.

[YUN 1992, pp. 593-94]

In November 1992, the Secretary-General reported that the situation in Somalia was deteriorating by the day. Difficulties faced by UNOSOM in implementing its mandate included the absence of a governing authority; the failure of factions to cooperate; the extortion of large sums of cash from donor agencies and organizations to allow them to operate; the hijacking of vehicles, looting of relief convoys and warehouses; and the detention of expatriate personnel. On 3 December (resolution 794(1992)), the Security Council endorsed the Secretary-General's recommendation that action under Chapter VII of the Charter should be taken to establish a secure environment for humanitarian relief operations and welcomed the offer of the United States to establish an operation to create such an environment. The first elements of the Unified Task Force, led by United States marines, arrived at Mogadishu on 9 December and, by 18 December, airfields, port facilities and major relief centres had been secured.

By the beginning of 1993, the worst of the emergency in Somalia appeared to be under control and the United Nations began to consider the possibility of moving from relief to rehabilitation.

The 100-Day Action Programme, initiated in October 1992, was extended to the end of March 1993 and received $74 million of the $83 million required. The Unified Task Force (UNITAF) helped to open access to remote areas and enabled the delivery of relief supplies. It opened the port of Mogadishu and repaired major supply routes. The combined efforts of humanitarian organizations and security forces dramatically reduced levels of malnutrition and mortality; however, theft, looting and extortion plagued relief efforts, and the resettlement of internally displaced persons and refugees was affected by ongoing security problems.

. . . The 1993 relief and rehabilitation programme, with requirements of $166.5 million, was launched at the Third Coordination Meeting for Humanitarian Assistance for Somalia (Addis Ababa, Ethiopia, 11-13 March). The Conference on National Reconciliation (15 March) endorsed the outcome of the Meeting and condemned attacks on relief personnel and supplies.

The mandate of the United Nations Operation in Somalia (UNOSOM) was expanded by the Security Council in March (resolution 814(1993)), following reports by the Secretary-General. The Council requested him to provide assistance covering: economic relief and rehabilitation; the repatriation of refugees and resettlement of displaced persons; the re-establishment of national and regional institutions, civil administration and the Somali police force; and mine clearance. UNOSOM II took over from UNITAF the task of facilitating the delivery of humanitarian assistance and expanding efforts to establish security throughout Somalia.

In July, the Secretary-General reported to the Council on attacks on UNOSOM II forces on 5 June. The attack and insecurity in Mogadishu South resulted in the temporary curtailment of many humanitarian programmes, but relief operations in the country were not disrupted. Pockets of acute malnutrition and medical problems persisted and about 1 million Somalis required shelter and life-sustaining assistance. Of the 1.7 million Somalis forced to leave their homes, over 1 million had crossed into Kenya and Ethiopia, while others moved to Mogadishu, Kismayo and Baidoa.

The rehabilitation of social services also continued with NGOs reporting that some 23,000 primary grade students had enrolled in 22 schools in the Bay, Bakool, Mogadishu and Lower Shabelle regions. In the Juba Valley, schools were rehabilitated and provided with textbooks and other equipment. An education development centre was established at Mogadishu, together with a scholarship programme to allow Somali university students to complete their studies abroad. Some 32 hospitals and 81 child health centres were operating throughout the country, and mobile vaccination teams were providing immunization. The water supply systems at Mogadishu, Afgoi, Hargeisa and Berbera were rehabilitated and sanitation projects were maintained. Some success was reported with the reactivation of food-crop and livestock production. Commercial and trading activities showed encouraging signs of recovery, limited telecommunication services were available and local companies provided fuel throughout the country. UNOSOM II, the World Bank and UNDP developed a draft planning framework for the reconstruction and recovery of Somalia, which was reviewed by the third informal meeting of donors, United Nations agencies and NGOs, sponsored by the World Bank (Paris, 22 October).

On 16 November, the Under-Secretary-General for Humanitarian Affairs told the Assembly's Second Committee that Somalia required short-term assistance and rehabilitation measures and long-term development and reconstruction work. The Fourth Coordination Meeting for Humanitarian Assistance for Somalia (Addis Ababa, 29 November–1 December) considered implementation of those measures.

(YUN 1993, pp. 728-29)

Despite sustained efforts by the Secretary-General to bring Somali factions together in national reconciliation, the Security Council, following a visit by a mission to the country, recognized that the lack of progress in the peace process had undermined United Nations objectives there and decided in November 1994 that the mandate of UNOSOM II should terminate on 31 March 1995 (resolution 954(1994)). The Secretary-General was asked to keep the Council informed about the situation, particularly developments affecting the humanitarian situation, the security situation for humanitarian personnel, repatriation of refugees and impacts on neighbouring countries.

Citing the political stalemate in Somalia and the insecurity persisting in certain areas, DHA, on 22 December 1994, issued the United Nations Consolidated Inter-Agency Appeal for Somalia to cover the first six months of 1995 as UNOSOM completed its withdrawal. In stable areas, extended relief and short-term rehabilitation activities would continue. United Nations agencies and the International Organization for Migration requested a total of $70,310,235, $24.8 million of which was sought by WFP, which planned to use its food resources to fund a variety of institutional rehabilitation programmes. The second largest amount was the $14.6 million sought by UNICEF to carry out programmes in primary health care, nutrition, drinking-water and sanitation and education. Other agencies requesting funding for projects under the appeal were: UNHCR, UNDP, WHO, IOM, FAO, the United Nations Volunteers, UNESCO and DHA itself, which required $403,511 to fund the Relief and Rehabilitation Coordination Unit to serve as the secretariat of the United Nations Coordination Team

in Somalia and monitor and report on emergency relief and rehabilitation needs and support in-country coordination efforts.

Although it could hardly be said that the planned continuum from emergency relief to rehabilitation and development in Somalia had been successful, DHA learned much from the operation.

Strengthening coordination

In a November 1994 report, the Secretary-General outlined United Nations efforts, in cooperation with NGOs and other humanitarian partners, to respond to humanitarian emergencies. He noted that an effective humanitarian response based on strengthened and closer cooperation among all humanitarian organizations was needed to tackle the manifold problems attendant upon complex emergencies, which often involved ethnic and civil strife. With the rapid increase in the magnitude and scope of such crises, the capacities of United Nations organizations and other humanitarian bodies were stretched to the limit. In order to improve the organization and management of response mechanisms, the humanitarian, political and security dimensions of those crises needed to be faced in tandem.

The Secretary-General described mechanisms that had been established to carry out that coordinating function and outlined improvements that could be made to strengthen field coordination of humanitarian assistance in complex emergencies, especially in the pre-emergency and initial response phases. They included the establishment, in all situations of potential emergency, of disaster management teams, chaired by the United Nations Resident Coordinator and including all United Nations organizations concerned with humanitarian assistance. As to early warning measures, the Resident Coordinator and disaster management team member agencies in-country had primary responsibility for alerting the Emergency Relief Coordinator and the headquarters of member agencies to signs of an impending complex emergency and for recommending preventive and preparedness action.

The Secretary-General went on to describe measures to be taken when complex emergencies arose and the functioning of the Central Emergency Revolving Fund—a cash-flow mechanism to ensure the rapid and coordinated response of the United Nations system to humanitarian emergencies. He noted that an arrangement had been established by which rapid response coordination was financed from interest earned by the Fund. That arrangement had been used successfully in the emergency operation in Rwanda in 1994 and the Inter-Agency Standing Committee recommended its continuation.

"... the United Nations shall promote higher standards
of living, full employment, and conditions
of economic and social progress and development "

Chapter II

International economic development and cooperation

The emergence of newly independent nations and the wide disparities in economic development among its Member States compelled the United Nations beginning in the 1960s to place greater emphasis on the promotion of economic and social development. As a first step it designated the period from 1961 to 1970 as the United Nations Development Decade, aimed at accelerating progress towards self-sustaining economic growth and social advancement. The objectives of the Decade were further advanced by the adoption in 1970 of the International Development Strategy for the 1970s, and thereafter successive strategies for the 1980s and 1990s, in response to changing world economic situations and the persistence of the problems of developing countries. At the initiative of the developing countries, the United Nations in 1974 adopted the Declaration on the Establishment of a New International Economic Order designed to restructure international economic relationships so as to redress the disadvantaged economic position of developing countries. The General Assembly in the same year adopted the Charter of Economic Rights and Duties of States. As the gap between developed and developing countries continued to widen, the 1980s marked the beginning of fundamental rethinking towards the achievement of economic development. This was followed in 1990 by the Declaration on International Economic Cooperation, in particular the Revitalization of Economic Growth and Development of the Developing Countries and in 1992 by the adoption at the eighth session of the United Nations Conference on Trade and Development (Cartagena, Colombia) of "A New Partnership for Development: The Cartagena Commitment" which outlined action to strengthen multilateral cooperation for sustained economic growth and development and to revitalize international trade and development. In 1993, the Uruguay Round of multilateral trade negotiations was concluded, leading to the establishment of the World Trade Organization.

During these efforts, the United Nations paid particular attention to special problems affecting individual regions and groups of countries. In Africa, where development was affected by a host of other problems caused by environmental disasters, adverse climatic conditions and civil unrest, the United Nations adopted the United Nations Programme of Action for African Economic Recovery and Development 1986-1990. This was succeeded in 1991 by the United Nations New Agenda for the Development of Africa in the 1990s, with a system-wide plan to facilitate its implementation. In 1988 a Special Plan of Economic Cooperation for Central America was established to deal with the situation in those countries affected by natural disasters and political instability. At the global level, the United Nations developed particular strategies for the assistance of the least developed countries, land-locked developing countries and small island developing countries.

Central to all the development initiatives of the United Nations was the concern for people and the human environment. In 1974, it adopted the World Population Plan of Action to support economic development, quality of life, human rights and fundamental freedoms. Those goals were further promoted by the 1984 Mexico City Declaration on Population and Development and the Programme of Action of the 1994 International Conference on Population and Development. In accordance with the 1976 Vancouver Declaration on Human Settlements and the 1988 Global Strategy for Shelter to the Year 2000, the United Nations continued its efforts to provide shelter and improve living conditions throughout the world.

The first global statement on improving the environment together with peace and economic development was articulated at Stockholm in 1972, followed in 1992 by the United Nations Conference on Environment and Development at Rio de Janeiro, Brazil. The Rio Declaration on Environment and Development sought new international agreements. The Conference also adopted "Agenda 21", which reflected the global consensus on development and environmental issues leading into the twenty-first century.

UN development decades

The United Nations sought to fulfil the objective of the Charter for the promotion of economic and social progress and development through the creation in 1958 of the United Nations Special Fund to assist Governments in accelerating the economic development of their countries, and to provide technical assistance from its regular budget and through its Expanded Programme of Technical Assistance, established in 1950 and financed by voluntary contributions. The question of formulating a declaration or general statement of the economic objectives of the United Nations as a means of furthering international economic cooperation was considered by several United Nations bodies. The General Assembly, by resolution 1515(XV) of December 1960, recognized the need for diversification and development of economic activity, for trade "free from artificial restrictions", increasing the provision of public and private capital and the expansion of technical, scientific and cultural cooperation, and adopted recommendations with regard to commodity trade problems, technical training, education, pre-investment assistance and an increase in the supply of technical assistance and development capital. The Assembly, by resolution 1521(XV) of 15 December 1960, also decided in principle to establish a United Nations Capital Development Fund. The following year, as it was recognized that concerted action was required to assist the developing countries, the Assembly took up again the question of the declaration of the economic objectives of the United Nations.

First UN Development Decade

On 25 September 1961, speaking in the general debate at the sixteenth session of the General Assembly, the President of the United States proposed that the 1960's should be officially designated as the "United Nations Development Decade." He considered that the present efforts of the United Nations in promoting economic growth could in this way be expanded and coordinated. He spoke of regional surveys, training programmes, technical assistance and pilot projects as the means of achieving this goal and emphasized that development could become a cooperative rather than a competitive enterprise, which would enable all nations, however diverse their systems and beliefs, to become free and equal in fact as well as in law.

The Assembly's Second (Economic and Financial) Committee considered the proposal for a Development Decade on the basis of a draft resolution submitted by Brazil, Colombia, Denmark, Ethiopia, the Federation of Malaya, Greece, Iran,

Madagascar, Pakistan, the Philippines, Senegal, Thailand, Turkey, the United States and Uruguay, later joined by Afghanistan.

By this text, the General Assembly would designate the 1960's as the United Nations Development Decade for the purpose of mobilizing and sustaining support for the measures required on the part of both developed and developing countries to accelerate economic and social progress. . . .

RESOLUTION 1710(XVI), as proposed by Second Committee, A/5056, adopted unanimously by Assembly on 19 December 1961, meeting 1084.

"The General Assembly,

. . .

"1.　*Designates* the current decade as the United Nations Development Decade, in which Member States and their peoples will intensify their efforts to mobilize and to sustain support for the measures required on the part of both developed and developing countries to accelerate progress towards self-sustaining growth of the economy of the individual nations and their social advancement so as to attain in each under-developed country a substantial increase in the rate of growth, with each country setting its own target, taking as the objective a minimum annual rate of growth of aggregate national income of 5 per cent at the end of the Decade;

"2.　*Calls upon* States Members of the United Nations and members of the specialized agencies:

"*(a)* To pursue policies designed to enable the less developed countries and those dependent on the export of a small range of primary commodities to sell more of their products at stable and remunerative prices in expanding markets, and thus to finance increasingly their own economic development from their earnings of foreign exchange and domestic savings;

"*(b)* To pursue policies designed to ensure to the developing countries an equitable share of earnings from the extraction and marketing of their natural resources by foreign capital, in accordance with the generally accepted reasonable earnings on invested capital;

"*(c)* To pursue policies that will lead to an increase in the flow of development resources, public and private, to developing countries on mutually acceptable terms;

"*(d)* To adopt measures which will stimulate the flow of private investment capital for the economic development of the developing countries, on terms that are satisfactory both to the capital-exporting countries and the capital-importing countries;

"3.　*Requests* the Secretary-General to communicate to the Government of Member States any documentation useful for the study and application of the present resolution and to invite them to make proposals, if possible, concerning the contents of a United Nations programme for the Decade and the application of such measures in their respective plans;

"4.　*Requests* the Secretary-General, taking account of the views of Governments and in consultation, as appropriate, with the heads of international agencies with responsibilities in the financial, economic and social fields, the Managing Director of the Special Fund, the Executive Chairman of the Technical Assistance Board and the regional economic commissions, to develop proposals for the intensification of action in the fields of economic and social development by the United Nations system of organizations, with particular reference, *inter alia*, to the following approaches and measures designed to further the objectives of paragraph 1 above:

"*(a)* The achievement and acceleration of sound self-sustaining economic development in the less developed countries through industrialization, diversification and the development of a highly productive agricultural sector;

"*(b)* Measures for assisting the developing countries, at their request, to establish well-conceived and integrated country plans—including, where appropriate, land reform—which will serve to mobilize internal resources and to utilize resources offered by foreign sources on both a bilateral and a multilateral basis for progress towards self-sustained growth;

"*(c)* Measures to improve the use of international institutions and instrumentalities for furthering economic and social development;

"*(d)* Measures to accelerate the elimination of illiteracy, hunger and disease, which seriously affect the productivity of the people of the less developed countries;

"*(e)* The need to adopt new measures, and to improve existing measures, for further promoting education in general and vocational and technical training in the developing countries with the co-operation, where appropriate, of the specialized agencies and States which can provide assistance in these fields, and for training competent national personnel in the fields of public administration, education, engineering, health and agronomy;

"*(f)* The intensification of research and demonstration as well as other efforts to exploit scientific and technological potentialities of high promise for accelerating economic and social development;

"*(g)* Ways and means of finding and furthering effective solutions in the field of trade in manufactures as well as in primary commodities, bearing in mind, in particular, the need to increase the foreign exchange earnings of the under-developed countries;

"*(h)* The need to review facilities for the collection, collation, analysis and dissemination of statistical and other information required for charting economic and social development and for providing a constant measurement of progress towards the objectives of the Decade;

"*(i)* The utilization of resources released by disarmament for the purpose of economic and social development, in particular of the under-developed countries:

"*(j)* The ways in which the United Nations can stimulate and support realization of the objectives of the Decade through the combined efforts of national and international institutions, both public and private;

"5. *Further requests* the Secretary-General to consult Member States, at their request, on the application of such measures in their respective development plans;

"6. Invites the Economic and Social Council to accelerate its examination of, and decision on, principles of international economic co-operation directed towards the improvement of world economic relations and the stimulation of international co-operation;

"7. *Requests* the Secretary-General to present his proposals for such a programme to the Economic and Social Council at its thirty-fourth session for its consideration and appropriate action;

"8. *Invites* the Economic and Social Council to transmit the Secretary-General's recommendations, together with its views and its report on actions undertaken thereon, to States Members of the United Nations and members of the specialized agencies and to the General Assembly at its seventeenth session."

[YUN 1961, pp. 228-32]

Second UN Development Decade

In 1966, the Secretary-General reported to the Economic and Social Council that progress achieved in the first half of the United Nations Development Decade had been disappointing. Prospects for attaining the Decade's objectives of an economic growth rate of 5 per cent in the developing countries and an annual transfer of development capital from developed to developing countries equivalent to 1 per cent of gross national product had dimmed. He said that the slow progress made was a consequence of the absence of an effective international development strategy and indicated the need for thorough and systematic advance preparation for future United Nations activities in the field of development. To correct this lack of a structured programme, the General Assembly in 1968, by resolution 2411(XXIII), asked the Secretary-General to prepare a preliminary framework of an international development strategy for the 1970s with specific goals and targets for individual sectors and components.

The International Development Strategy

. . .

Reports Before Council and Assembly

Committee for Development Planning

Early in 1970, the Economic and Social Council's Committee for Development Planning met to prepare guidelines and proposals for the Second United Nations Development Decade. The Committee examined the performances of the developing countries, the developed market economies and the centrally planned economies during the First United Nations Development Decade, the 1960s.

The Committee noted in its report that, despite the gains recorded in investment and savings of the developing countries, there had been marked differences in the rates of growth and that the average increase in gross domestic product was below that of the developed market economies and of the net material product of the centrally planned economies.

Developed countries had made further progress in science and technology and in trade and co-operation, but their contribution towards achieving the objectives of the First United Nations Development Decade had fallen short of expectations, according to the report. Despite the growth of international development finance institutions, the net flow of financial resources to developing countries as a percentage of gross national product had declined.

In its report, the Committee proposed that a general declaration of intent and commitments be adopted by the General Assembly at its twenty-fifth session, which was to open on 15 September 1970. This declaration would enunciate broad commitments to be made by both developed and developing countries with the object of furthering the development process. Each country might then supplement the general declaration with a more specific unilateral declaration of its own intentions.

The Committee went on to define what it considered to be the basic objectives of the Second United Nations Development Decade and the national and international measures necessary to achieve those objectives.

. . .

Preparatory Committee for Second United Nations Development Decade

In 1970, a draft of the international development strategy for the Second United Nations Development Decade was prepared by the General Assembly's Preparatory Committee for the Second United Nations Development Decade, which met between 24 February and 13 March and between 11 and 28 May. . . .

The draft consisted of a preamble and sections on goals and objectives for the Decade, policy measures to be implemented, the need for review and appraisal of performance as well as objectives and policies, and the mobilization of public opinion.

. . .

The objectives of the draft strategy included an average annual rate of growth in the gross product of the developing countries of at least 6 per cent during the Decade, implying a corresponding rate of per capita growth of 3.5 per cent on the basis of an annual increase in population of 2.5 per cent. According to the draft, the over-all expansion in agricultural production would need to be 4 per cent a year, and in industry, 8 per cent.

Among the other recommended goals were an average increase of 0.3 per cent a year in the ratio of gross domestic savings to gross product, a rise of slightly less than 7 per cent in imports and of slightly more than 7 per cent in exports. Qualitative and structural improvements in the economy were also envisaged.

Proposed policy measures were set out under several headings: (1) international trade; (2) economic co-operation and regional integration among developing countries; (3) financial resources for development; (4) invisible earnings including shipping; (5) special measures in favour of the least developed among the developing countries; (6) special measures in favour of the land-locked developing countries; (7) science and technology; (8) human development; (9) expansion and diversification of production; and (10) plan formulation and implementation.

As concerned international trade, the draft urged international action with respect to commodity agreements and the establishment of general principles on pricing policy. Developed countries would aim to eliminate or reduce obstacles to imports of primary products from developing countries. They would also give increased attention to aiding developing countries in accelerating the diversification of their economies and in solving problems arising from the competition to natural products of synthetics and substitutes and surplus disposal.

The developing countries' exports of manufactures and semi-manufactures would be expanded and diversified by, *inter alia*, the establishment of generalized, non-discriminatory, non-reciprocal preferential access to developed countries. Efforts would be made to reduce restrictive business practices that were unfavourable to the exports of developing countries.

With regard to financial resources for development, the draft stipulated that developing countries bore the main responsibility for financing their development and outlined the measures to be taken to mobilize their domestic financial resources. Developed countries would endeavour to devote annually to external aid 1 per cent of their gross national product. It was proposed but not agreed that each developed country would try its best to provide annually 0.75 per cent of its gross national product in the form of official development assistance. Softening and harmonization of the conditions of assistance were called for, as well as untying of aid. Multilateral assistance would be increased, and arrangements to forecast and forestall debt crises would be improved.

Policies to promote foreign private investment were recommended for both developing and developed countries.

The International Bank for Reconstruction and Development was called upon to pursue its efforts to set up a scheme of supplementary financing, and a proposal was made, although not agreed upon, to give serious consideration to establishing a link between the allocation of new reserve assets under the scheme of Special Drawing Rights and the provision of additional development finance for the benefit of all developing countries.

No agreement was reached by the Preparatory Committee on a text on shipping, but certain recommendations were made with regard to insurance and tourism. Special measures were urged in favour of the least developed among the developing countries to be implemented at the national, sub-regional, regional and international levels, with the assistance of developed countries.

Special measures were also called for in favour of land-locked developing countries, attention being paid to the need for financial and technical assistance to develop the transport and communications structures of these countries.

With regard to science and technology, the proposed objective was to reduce the disparity in these fields between developed and developing countries. The latter would endeavour to attain, by the end of the Second Development Decade, a minimum annual expenditure on research and development of 0.5 per cent of their gross product, concentrating especially on appropriate technologies and applied research.

Developed countries would commit themselves to increase substantially their aid in direct support of science and technology in developing countries during the Decade. Quantitative targets were proposed but not agreed upon. Developed and developing countries and competent international organizations would draw up and implement a programme for promoting the transfer of technology to developing countries.

Policy measures for human development were prescribed in the field of population growth, employment strategy, education, health and nutrition, housing and related community facilities, the environment, and the participation of women, children and youth in the development process.

With respect to the expansion and diversification of production in developing countries, the draft strategy envisaged policies that would be carried out in a global context, with a view to achieving an optimal international division of labour. Appropriate strategies for agriculture and industry were outlined, including the roles to be played by developed countries, by regional groupings and by international organizations. Expansion of the basic infrastructure of developing countries was also the subject of recommendations.

Developing countries would establish and strengthen planning mechanisms and improve public administration, having recourse to international assistance where necessary.

The draft international development strategy also referred to subsequent review and appraisal of both objectives and policies and to mobilization of public opinion in the interest of the Second Development Decade effort.

. . .

Decisions of General Assembly

. . .

On 24 October 1970, the General Assembly, on the recommendation of the Second Committee,

adopted, without vote, resolution 2626(XXV) on an International Development Strategy for the Second United Nations Development Decade.

Text of Strategy

The text of the International Development Strategy was similar to the draft text approved by the Preparatory Committee for the Second United Nations Development Decade, but it contained specific provisions relating to the various issues on which the Preparatory Committee had been unable to reach agreement.

The target dates in the final draft were somewhat more flexible than those originally suggested. With regard to the reduction of duties and other barriers to imports of primary products by developed countries and of non-tariff barriers affecting trade in manufactures and semi-manufactures of interest to developing countries, the final version of the document stipulated that efforts would be made with a view to achieving results by 31 December 1972.

With respect to the transfer of financial resources to developing countries, developed countries should endeavour to attain the target of 1 per cent of their gross national product by 1972, where possible, otherwise not later than 1975. The proposed target for official resource transfers was reduced from 0.75 to 0.7 per cent of gross national product, and countries would try to reach it by the middle of the Decade.

Agreement was also reached on the softening and harmonizing of the terms and conditions of assistance.

Whereas, with regard to science and technology, the draft of the Preparatory Committee proposed a target for aid by the developed countries to the developing countries of 0.05 per cent of the gross national product of the former and another target (5 per cent of total research and development expenditure) for outlays on work specifically relating to the developing countries, the final document left consideration of target setting until the first biennial review.

With respect to Special Drawing Rights, whereas the original draft stated that the establishment of a link with development finance would be considered by 1972 at the latest, the final text provided only for an examination of the question before the allocation of Special Drawing Rights in 1972.

On the subject of the establishment of generalized, non-discriminatory, non-reciprocal preferential treatment of manufactured exports of developing countries in the markets of developed countries, for which arrangements had been drawn up in UNCTAD, the final text of the Strategy stated that preference-giving countries were determined to seek the necessary legislative or other sanction with the aim of implementing the preferential arrangements as early as possible in 1971.

A paragraph was agreed upon concerning the need for developed countries to adapt industries adversely affected by imports of manufactures from developing countries: adjustment measures would be considered early in the 1970s. Efforts would be made to identify restrictive business practices affecting the trade and development of developing countries, with a view to achieving remedial measures before 31 December 1972. Action would be taken in favour of the least developed among the developing countries early in the Decade.

It was agreed that the implementation of policies relating to trade in primary products should take into account the resolutions, decisions and agreements of the relevant international and intergovernmental organizations. In the section on special measures in favour of the land-locked developing countries, it was stipulated in the final text that their implementation should take into account the relevant decisions and resolutions of UNCTAD.

Clauses were included on the need to protect the national sovereignty of developing countries, both in connexion with the use of external aid and in connexion with efforts to expand and diversify production.

A section on shipping was inserted in the final document, including a detailed listing of items and policies on which action should be taken.

The final document also contained texts relating to the role to be played by the socialist countries of Eastern Europe in the International Development Strategy.

A paragraph was also added to the preamble outlining the political issues on which the success of international development activities depended.

This paragraph also called for a close link between the Second United Nations Development Decade and the Disarmament Decade and pointed out that disarmament would release resources that could be used for economic and social development.

(YUN 1970, pp. 305-12)

Third UN Development Decade

In 1977, the General Assembly recognized that negotiations conducted so far on the establishment of a new international economic order had produced only limited results, while the gap between developed and developing countries continued to grow. It decided to convene a special session in 1980 to assess progress towards the establishment of the new international economic order and established an intersessional Committee of the Whole to monitor progress and to act as the preparatory committee for global negotiations relating to international economic cooperation for development. At the special session, the Assembly adopted the International Development Strategy for the Third United Nations Development Decade.

The Strategy, recognizing that the objectives of the Second Decade remained largely unfulfilled, saw the continuing negative trends in the world economy as impairing the growth prospects of the developing countries. The Strategy called for special attention to the accelerated development of developing countries, requiring more equitable distribution of economic opportunities and changes in the framework of international relations, and their equitable, full and effective participation in all decisions affecting international economic cooperation for development. It proposed an average annual growth rate of gross domestic product (GDP) for the developing countries of 7 per cent and annual growth rates of 7.5 and 8 per cent for exports and imports respectively of developing countries, as well as improved terms of trade. The level of gross investment was to reach an average of 28 per cent of GDP by 1990 and gross domestic savings 24 per cent of GDP.

The Strategy called for an increase in real terms in the concessional and non-concessional flows of finance to developing countries to reach an official development assistance target of 0.7 per cent of the gross national product of developed countries. It also covered such topics as commodities, strengthening the scientific and technological capacity of developing countries, the elimination of poverty, industrialization, environmental management, and an intensified search for a long-term solution of the energy problem.

Other UN initiatives in the economic field

The New International Economic Order

In 1973, the heads of State or Government of the Movement of Non-Aligned Countries said that the International Development Strategy for the Second United Nations Development Decade had failed and developing countries needed to ensure their growth by having recourse in the first instance to the mobilization of their natural resources. They noted that the recent joint action of the oil-producing countries had enabled them to mobilize their domestic resources for the development and advancement of their nations. In 1974, the Movement's Chairman called for the convening of a special session of the General Assembly to consider the problems of raw materials and development. Consideration of this item led to the adoption by the Assembly in May, by resolutions 3201(S-VI) and 3202(S-VI), of the Declaration and Programme of Action on the Establishment of a New International Economic Order.

The Declaration stated that the current international economic order was in direct conflict with current developments in international political and economic relations. The developing world had emerged as a powerful influence in international activity. Hence an active, full and equal participation of the developing countries was necessary in the formulation and application of all decisions that concerned the international community. It said that the interrelationship between the interests of the developed and the developing countries had been brought into sharp focus, but cooperation must be based on sovereign equality and the removal of the disequilibrium between developed and developing countries. The Declaration listed 20 principles on which the new international economic order was to be based.

The Programme of Action set out measures to deal with raw materials, commodities and trade; the international monetary system and finance; industrialization; transfer of technology; transnational corporations; cooperation among developing countries; sovereignty over natural resources; strengthening the role of the United Nations; and a special programme for the countries most seriously affected by the economic crisis.

In December 1974, on the basis of a 1972 suggestion of the developing countries, the Assembly adopted the Charter of Economic Rights and Duties of States.

Charter of Economic Rights and Duties of States

On 18 May 1972, the third session of the United Nations Conference on Trade and Development (UNCTAD) decided to establish a 31-State Working Group to draw up the text of a draft charter of economic rights and duties of States. The proposal was put forward by the developing countries and took note of the suggestion made at the session by the President of Mexico for such a charter. Later in the year, the General Assembly decided that the Working Group should be enlarged by the addition of nine States, also to be appointed by the Secretary-General of UNCTAD in consultation with member Governments.

. . .

By the preamble to resolution 3281(XXIX) proclaiming the Charter, the Assembly among other things . . . referred to the Declaration and the Programme of Action on the Establishment of a New International Economic Order it had adopted on 1 May 1974, which had stressed that the Charter would constitute an effective instrument towards the establishment of a new system of international economic relations based on equity, sovereign equality and interdependence of the interests of developed and developing countries.

. . .

The Assembly declared that the fundamental purpose of the Charter of Economic Rights and Duties of States was to promote the establishment of the new international economic order based on equity, sovereign equality, interdependence, common interest and co-operation among all States, irrespective of their economic and social systems, with the aim of creating conditions for: wider prosperity among countries; the economic and social progress of all countries, especially the developing ones; the encouragement of co-operation in the economic, trade, scientific and technical fields, regardless of political, economic or social systems; the overcoming of obstacles to development; the acceleration of the economic growth of developing countries; and the protection of the environment.

The Assembly expressed awareness of the need to establish and maintain a just and equitable economic and social order through the achievement of more rational and equitable international economic relations and the encouragement of structural changes in the world economy, the creation of conditions conducive to expansion of trade and intensification of economic co-operation, the strengthening of the economic independence of developing countries and the establishment and promotion of international economic relations.

The Assembly also expressed its determination to promote collective economic security for development, in particular of the developing countries, with strict respect for the sovereign equality of each State, and it observed that genuine co-operation among States was essential for the achievement of a rational development of all parts of the world.

Further, the Assembly stressed the importance of ensuring appropriate conditions for the conduct of normal economic relations between States irrespective of differences in economic and social systems.

It reiterated the responsibility of each country for its own development and pointed out that concomitant and effective international co-operation was an essential factor for the achievement of the development goals of each.

(YUN 1974, pp. 381-83)

Declaration on international cooperation

The 1980 special session failed to reach agreement on launching global negotiations on international economic cooperation for development. In 1989, by decision 43/460, the General Assembly decided to convene a special session in April 1990 devoted to international economic cooperation, in particular the revitalization of economic growth and development of the developing countries. In an annex to that decision, it said that in a rapidly changing and interdependent world, it was in the interest of all States to take stock of the significance of the transformation of the world economy, to consider how to meet the challenges and opportunities ahead and to provide more effective means of multilateral cooperation in the economic field. The special session would focus on enhanced international and regional economic cooperation and provide policy guidelines and recommendations for the international community and the United Nations and for an international development strategy for the 1990s. The resulting document would reflect a new spirit in international cooperation.

The special session was held from 25 April to 1 May 1990. The Assembly adopted, by resolution S-18/3, the Declaration on International Economic Cooperation, in particular the Revitalization of Economic Growth and Development of the Developing Countries. The Declaration noted that for many developing countries the 1980s had been viewed as a decade lost for development. The most important challenge for the 1990s was the revitalization of economic growth and social development of those countries within the context of sustained growth of the world economy. The Declaration outlined commitments and policies for international development cooperation.

African economic recovery and development

New agenda for African development in the 1990s

In 1984, several United Nations reports revealed that the economic and social situation in Africa continued to deteriorate, reflecting the cumulative impact of the effects of natural disasters, inadequate resources, slow economic growth, structural weaknesses, global economic recession, strife and adverse climatic conditions. The Economic and Social Council and the General Assembly for the first time included in their agendas an item on the critical situation in Africa. The Assembly, by resolution 39/29, adopted the Declaration on the Critical Economic Situation in Africa, calling for emergency relief on a massive scale, but emphasizing support for the recovery and rehabilitation of African economies. By 1986, the Secretary-General reported that the situation was considered sufficiently critical to summon a special session of the Assembly, despite the steps taken by African Governments to implement much needed structural institutional changes. The Assembly, at its thirteenth special session (27 May– 1 June 1986), considered the question of the critical economic situation in Africa and adopted the United Nations Programme of Action for African Economic Recovery and Development 1986-1990 (UN-PAAERD). The Programme had two central elements: the determination and commitment of the African countries to launch both national and regional programmes of economic development as contained in the July 1985 priority programme for economic

recovery adopted by African heads of State and Government; and the response of the international community and its commitment to support and complement African development efforts.

The final review and appraisal of UNPAAERD conducted in 1991 noted that it had failed to achieve many of its goals in the face of the general downward trend in the global economy. In response to the worsening situation, the General Assembly, on 18 December by resolution 46/151, adopted the United Nations New Agenda for the Development of Africa in the 1990s with a system-wide plan of action to facilitate its implementation.

Final review and appraisal of the implementation of UNPAAERD

. . .

GENERAL ASSEMBLY ACTION

On 18 December 1991, the General Assembly adopted resolution 46/151 without vote.

Final review and appraisal of the implementation of the United Nations Programme of Action for African Economic Recovery and Development 1986-1990

The General Assembly,

. . .

ANNEX

I.   Assessment of the implementation of the United Nations Programme of Action for African Economic Recovery and Development 1986-1990

A.   Preamble

1.   The United Nations Programme of Action for African Economic Recovery and Development 1986-1990 did not quite become a focal point for economic policy or for resource mobilization on behalf of Africa.

2.   Furthermore, the Programme of Action proved to be too optimistic in two basic senses. First, the concept of a global compact at the continental level was difficult to achieve. Specific arrangements, such as World Bank consultative groups and United Nations Development Programme round-table discussions for individual nations, were not always directly related to the goals and targets of the Programme of Action. Second, hopes for a favourable external economic environment for Africa during the period 1986-1990 were not fulfilled. Sharp export price falls, real interest rate increases, and declines in private sector investment and loans all severely limited the positive effects of efforts made by Africa and its development partners. The Programme of Action itself was silent regarding who was to act if unforeseen exogenous contingencies threw the Programme of Action off course; also, its review machinery did not clearly address this issue.

3.   In most African States, it is recognized that revised economic reforms and good governance are a key to economic development. It is also accepted that recovery and renewed development will take longer to achieve than was hoped and projected in 1986 by Africa, as well as by donor States and international financial institutions.

4.   Bilateral cooperating partners have recognized that speedy, low-cost turn-arounds are the exception, not the rule, or as several have explicitly noted, the time-frame for economic transformation and for agreed agendas for

action should be seen in terms of decades, not years. In addition, perception has come much closer to African warnings of the damage done by the debt overhang and worsening terms of trade. Substantial action to overcome these obstacles to African recovery is now agreed to be urgent.

. . .

9. Many of the African States have made progress in meeting their policy restructuring and resource real-location commitments. However, none of the goals of the Programme of Action were fully realized. Targets for growth, food security, human investment and debt reduction were missed, so declines rather than hoped-for increases have been recorded by many States and for Africa as a whole.

10. One of the principal causes of this decline was that only two thirds of the countries pursued sustained economic reform. Those that did received increased donor assistance and achieved modest gains in per capita gross domestic product, agricultural production and exports. Other countries continued to decline in these indices, causing negative performance for Africa as a whole.

11. The reasons for this record of non-success are clear. The bilateral and multilateral achievements with respect to net real resource transfers and debt burden reduction were below expectations. A number of African States did not, in fact, fully achieve policy and resource allocation adjustment and transformation. Africa suffered from a serious fall in commodity earnings. War and certain exogenous events, such as drought and collapse in the terms of trade, imposed devastating costs. Another reason for this record of non-success may have been inadequate United Nations and Government debate or dialogue on the experience gained in the implementation of the Programme of Action.

12. However, the Programme of Action was far from being a failure. It assisted in focusing the attention of African and other Governments on the basic economic, human and governance problems of Africa. By doing so, it did achieve policy and efficiency gains and averted a more severe decline in net resource inflows. As a result, the economic decline afflicting Africa from 1981 to 1985 was slowed and, in many countries, halted. Furthermore, the process of African policy restructuring and its interaction with the analyses of external partners have led to substantial lessons of experience for all concerned.

. . .

II. United Nations New Agenda for the Development of Africa in the 1990s

A. Preamble

1. The final review and appraisal of the implementation of the United Nations Programme of Action for African Economic Recovery and Development 1986-1990 offers yet another opportunity for renewing the commitment of the international community to support Africa's own efforts to achieve self-sustaining socio-economic growth and development. It is also an occasion to refocus world attention on the socio-economic difficulties which continue to face the African countries. Africa's development is primarily the responsibility of Africans. The international community accepts the principle of shared responsibility and full partnership with Africa and therefore commits itself to giving full and tangible support to the African efforts.

2. The circumstances which led to the adoption of the Programme of Action are as valid today as they were in 1986. Assessments made by African countries themselves or by the Secretary-General and many other organizations and independent observers point to the fact that Africa's socio-economic conditions actually worsened overall over the past five years of the Programme of Action period.

3. The current critical economic situation in Africa calls for solidarity among States Members to act in concert to address the problem. The international community renews its efforts to assist Africa, as enunciated under the Programme of Action and in General Assembly resolution 43/27 of 18 November 1988, in which the Assembly stated, *inter alia*, that ''the African economic crisis is one that concerns the international community as a whole'' and that ''the Programme of Action provides an important framework for cooperation between Africa and the international community'', which needs to be renewed in the 1990s.

4. That is why the international community and the countries of Africa should renew their commitment to an agenda of cooperation for sustainable social and economic development of Africa in the 1990s. The agenda is specific and clearly focused on goals and targets to be achieved within that time-frame.

5. A desirable objective should be an average real growth rate of at least 6 per cent per annum of gross national product throughout the period of the New Agenda in order for the continent to achieve sustained and sustainable economic growth and equitable development, increase income and eradicate poverty.

6. The New Agenda has as its priority objectives the accelerated transformation, integration, diversification and growth of the African economies, in order to strengthen them within the world economy, reduce their vulnerability to external shocks and increase their dynamism, internalize the process of development and enhance self-reliance.

7. The New Agenda also accords special attention to human development and increased productive employment, and promotes rapid progress towards the achievement of human-oriented goals by the year 2000 in the areas of life expectancy, integration of women in development, child and maternal mortality, nutrition, health, water and sanitation, basic education and shelter.

8. Peace is an indispensable prerequisite for development. The end of the cold war has opened up opportunities for the peaceful resolution of conflicts and for the intensification of international cooperation for development, particularly with Africa. Peace initiatives by African countries should be encouraged and pursued in order to bring an end to war, destabilization and internal conflicts so as to facilitate the creation of optimal conditions for development. The international community as a whole should endeavour to cooperate with and support the efforts of African countries for a rapid restoration of peace, normalization of life for uprooted populations and national socio-economic reconstruction. Resources freed from military expenditures in all countries can be redirected to socio-economic growth and development.

9. In order to achieve these broad objectives, it is necessary for the international community to enter into a new and stronger accord with Africa, which would spell out clearly the firm commitment of the international community to support and assist Africa in its efforts to implement successfully its development agenda and to reduce, if not entirely eliminate, external impediments

and obstacles to Africa's accelerated socio-economic transformation. This New Agenda reflects a mutuality of commitments and accountability and is in two parts: what Africa commits itself to do and what the international community commits itself to do.

[YUN 1991, pp. 397-403]

Special economic and humanitarian aid to Africa

The economic and social development of some countries in Africa was further hampered by the effects of drought and desertification and the growing number of civil conflicts in various parts of the region. A major part of United Nations assistance was provided in the form of special economic assistance for recovery and rehabilitation of economic and social infrastructure and for the growing number of refugees, returnees and displaced persons. In the Horn of Africa, the continuing civil conflict in the Sudan and the deteriorating situation in Somalia, which spilled over into the neighbouring countries of Djibouti, Ethiopia and Kenya, created an unprecedented humanitarian need. In 1992, the Secretary-General issued a Consolidated Inter-Agency Appeal for the Horn of Africa. Contributions of $788 million, out of requirements of $1.15 billion, were received for the six countries (Djibouti, Eritrea, Ethiopia, Kenya, Somalia and the Sudan) included in the Special Emergency Programme for the Horn of Africa.

In Angola, where over a decade of civil war had resulted in a significant number of refugees, the United Nations provided assistance for their repatriation and reintegration, the regional drought emergency, plans for progress from emergency to rehabilitation, the peace process in the form of electoral assistance, and assistance to soldiers and families awaiting demobilization. The Special Relief Programme for Angola, launched in 1991, emphasized long-range rehabilitation of infrastructure and basic services. In Liberia, for the period December 1990 to September 1992, contributions totalling $102 million were recorded, mainly for the provision of food aid for the refugees resulting from the civil conflict in that country.

In Mozambique, the years of war had stripped the country of much of its infrastructure, and the country was also affected by drought. Immediately following the signing of the peace agreement in October 1992, an appeal was launched to meet the priority requirements of the internally displaced and the drought-affected population, which was estimated at 3.1 million. Emergency assistance was estimated at $400 million for 1992-1993. However, the greatest challenge facing the United Nations in 1992 was the grave humanitarian situation resulting from the crisis in Somalia, where some 4.5 million people were threatened by starvation and where no functioning government existed. The United Nations responded with the 100-day Action Programme for Somalia to provide a massive infusion of food aid, provision of basic health services and a mass immunization campaign and other basic services. By December, $53 million of the $83 million needed to implement the Programme had been pledged. Assistance was also provided to the Sudan through Operation Lifeline Sudan for those affected by drought, civil conflict and displacement.

Assistance to those countries continued in 1993 and 1994, but the United Nations had to respond to new conflicts in Burundi and Rwanda in 1993. In Burundi, an appeal for $9.5 million was launched to meet basic survival needs of the displaced and $17 million for Burundi refugees in Rwanda, the United Republic of Tanzania and Zaire. In Rwanda, the international community contributed $100 million to meet that country's humanitarian needs. The Government later appealed for international assistance to revive the economy and rebuild and rehabilitate national infrastructure. In 1993, the General Assembly also appealed to the international community to provide adequate assistance for the rehabilitation of the economy of Sierra Leone and the reconstruction of devastated areas as a result of the spill-over effect of the conflict in Liberia. An appeal for $84.2 million was also launched to provide assistance for transportation, health, sanitation, agriculture and shelter, as a result of a combination of political and economic problems in Zaire.

Special economic assistance for Central America

In February 1987, the Secretary-General, reporting to the General Assembly on the situation in Central America following the peace mission to the region's five countries (Costa Rica, El Salvador, Guatemala, Honduras and Nicaragua) in January by the Contadora and Support Groups, drew attention to the natural disasters that had befallen the region and pointed to the growing number of refugees in the neighbouring countries as a result of the crisis, estimated at around 125,000. He underscored the need for an emergency reconstruction and economic development plan to help solve the political crisis. Following the signing on 7 August at Guatemala City of the agreement on ''Procedure for the establishment of a firm and lasting peace in Central America'', the Assembly, by resolution 42/1 of 7 October, urged the international community to increase technical, economic and financial assistance to the Central American countries and asked the Secretary-General to promote a special plan of cooperation for the region.

Special plan of economic co-operation for Central America

A proposed special plan of economic cooperation for Central America was submitted by the Secretary-General to the General Assembly in April 1988, pursuant to a 1987 resolution. The Secretary-General requested funding of $4,370,690 for the special programme.

The proposal gave a brief history of the economies of Central America and the main characteristics of the current crisis. The countries involved had witnessed a deterioration in their levels of economic activity, and the international recession had gradually helped to exacerbate the most conspicuous areas of strangulation in both everyday life and the financial sphere. Significant manifestations of the crisis had emerged in the form of contraction of the subregional common market; capital flight and brain drain from the region; shrinking investment; political and military conflicts; displaced persons and refugees; and increased dependence on and vulnerability to the influence of foreign countries.

The plan was designed to concentrate on those economic and social aspects that were directly linked to the preservation and consolidation of peace, and to coincide with the priorities of the Governments of the region and supplement their national development efforts. Specifically, the Secretary-General pointed to problems requiring immediate action under the plan, caused by the damaging effects of war on the population and infrastructure and by the 1987 drought.

Strategies for emergency assistance were outlined in several areas under the plan, including assistance to refugees and repatriated persons; food aid; and urgent needs for fuel and thermal, hydro-electric and electrical energy.

In order to help reactivate the economy, financial constraints on the region needed to be eased. Several measures were proposed to help reduce the heavy burden of foreign debt carried by the Central American countries, including debt outstanding to private agents, bilateral public debt and multilateral debt. The Secretary-General proposed a method of financing to reactivate the Central American Common Market and reduce temporary imbalances in countries' balance of payments. That suggestion included a proposal for facilitating liquidity in the region's payments system and for strengthening the Central American Monetary Stabilization Fund.

In the area of economic revitalization, programmes were proposed for industrial rehabilitation; agricultural development; trade concessions; reconstruction of the infrastructure; and investments in the energy sector. Social development programmes included investments in the social, health, education and housing sectors; strengthening the productive capacity of marginal groups; food security; reinforcement of co-operatives; and strengthening the Central American Bank for Economic Integration. The report also outlined the

role of the United Nations system in the special plan, internal and international responsibilities, and institutional mechanisms for implementing the plan.

In his October report on the situation in Central America, the Secretary-General stressed that the root of the Central American crisis was to be found in the unjust economic and social structures that had traditionally characterized the region, and which were exacerbated by the current economic recession.

UNDP action. On 1 July, the UNDP Governing Council allocated $20 million for the Special Plan of Economic Co-operation for Central America.

                                                        (YUN 1988, pp. 306-307)

Operational activities

Development assistance

Following the designation of the 1960s as the United Nations Development Decade and the establishment in 1964 of the United Nations Conference on Trade and Development to deal with matters of trade as they related to development, the General Assembly decided to consolidate and streamline its development assistance activities into one agency so as to make it more effective. Consequently it created in 1965 the United Nations Development Programme (UNDP). In 1966, it created the United Nations Capital Development Fund for funnelling developmental capital to developing countries. The Fund became operational in 1974.

Establishment of the UN Development Programme

Until the end of 1965, the United Nations and its related agencies supported the economic development activities of their member nations through three main channels of assistance: (1) the United Nations Special Fund, financed by voluntary contributions from Governments and equipped to carry out large-scale projects of a pre-investment nature; (2) the Expanded Programme of Technical Assistance, also financed from voluntary Government contributions and equipped to carry out medium and smaller-scale projects; and (3) the individual programmes of technical assistance carried out separately by the United Nations and several of the agencies, financed from their own regular budgets and hence referred to as "regular" technical assistance programmes.

In 1962, within the context of studies relating to the co-ordination of the above programmes, a proposal was first made to merge some or all of these activities. In 1963 and 1964, merger possibilities were considered by an *Ad Hoc* Committee on the Co-ordination of Technical Assistance Activities established by the Economic and Social Council, by the Administrative Committee on Coordination (ACC), and by the Secretary-General of the United Nations.

On 31 July 1964, on the basis of recommendations received from the Secretary-General, the *Ad Hoc* Committee and the ACC, the Economic and Social Council adopted a resolution endorsing and forwarding for General Assembly approval a plan to consolidate the Expanded Programme and the Special Fund in a new United Nations Development Programme (UNDP). . . .

Consideration by General Assembly

. . .

In considering the basic proposal and framework for a Development Programme, most Assembly Members expressed their belief that a merged Programme would help to streamline activities, simplify organizational procedures, increase the effectiveness of existing machinery and thus strengthen the impact of United Nations development aid. Some Members expressed reservations about aspects of the proposed arrangements for the merger. They felt either that concrete provisions for administrative procedures were lacking; that a tighter consolidation would have been preferable; or that direct investment work and direct aid in industrial development should be included in the activities to be conducted through UNDP.

. . .

On 16 November 1965, the Second Committee, by 89 votes to 0, with 11 abstentions, approved the Economic and Social Council's draft resolution as a whole, as amended by the Second Committee. On 22 November 1965, this text was adopted at a plenary meeting of the Assembly by 98 votes to 0, with 9 abstentions, as resolution 2029(XX).

By this resolution, the Expanded Programme of Technical Assistance and the United Nations Special Fund were to be combined in a new United Nations Development Programme (UNDP) on 1 January 1966. Within UNDP, the special characteristics and operations of the Expanded Programme and of the Special Fund were to be maintained; the separate funds of the two component programmes were to be maintained, too, so that contributions might be pledged to the two programmes separately as hitherto. The Assembly also reaffirmed the principles, procedures and provisions governing the Expanded Programme of Technical Assistance and the Special Fund not inconsistent with the present resolution and declared that they should continue to apply to relevant activities within the United Nations Development Programme.

The Assembly decided that an intergovernmental committee of 37 members, to be known as the Governing Council of the United Nations Development Programme, was to be established to perform the functions previously exercised by the Governing Council of the Special Fund and by the Technical Assistance Committee, including the consideration and approval of projects and programmes and the allocation of funds; in addition, it was to provide general policy guidance and direction for the United Nations Development Programme as a whole, as well as for the United Nations regular programmes of technical assistance.

The Assembly urged the new Governing Council to consider conditions for an effective implementation of the provisions of section III of its resolution 1219(XII) of 14 December 1957 and part C of its resolution 1240(XIII) of 14 October 1958 concerning the scope and future activities of the Special Fund.

(YUN 1965, pp. 270-72)

UNDP activities

UNDP became operational on 1 January 1966. In that year 137 projects, estimated to cost the equivalent of $417 million, were approved by the Governing Council. UNDP assistance for those projects amounted to $168 million, while recipient Governments undertook to provide $249 million as their share in the partnership. By the end of 1966, 130 countries and territories had received assistance for various sectors of their economies. Africa received the largest share of Programme resources, amounting to 44 per cent of the total funds, the Americas, 27 per cent, Asia and the Far East, 20 per cent, the Middle East, 2 per cent, and Europe, 7 per cent. Contributions for 1966 to UNDP amounted to $154,869,163. Of that amount, $98,584,923 represented pledges to the Special Fund. In June, UNDP established a revolving fund of $7.5 million for financing urgently needed activities.

In 1970, the UNDP Governing Council reviewed an extensive study of the United Nations development system and adopted principles and guidelines for its strengthening and reform. They were subsequently endorsed by the Economic and Social Council and the General Assembly. Known as the Consensus, the guidelines introduced the concept of the programming cycle. However, the key provision of the reform was the introduction of "country programming" by which programming would be carried out for each country within the framework of "indicative planning figures" (IPFs). Governments would then decide on their priority projects within their own national plans. The system of "full funding" covering the total costs of projects was changed to a system of annual funding; the distinction between the Special Fund and technical assistance components was eliminated; and authority delegated to the Administrator to approve projects within country programmes.

In 1975, a set of "new guidelines in technical cooperation" was approved by the Governing Council which expanded the UNDP mandate. The main thrust of the guidelines was the change from past emphasis on inputs for technical cooperation to one of output or results. It introduced more flexibility in both programming and in providing inputs, encouraged Governments to assume responsibility for implementing projects, and provided technical support to all stages of the development process, including assistance in project planning. In 1977, the Governing Council invited the Administrator to improve and expand the country programming framework and asked the Organization to consolidate its planning, appraisal and evaluation functions into a comprehensive feedback system.

The year 1991 marked the twenty-fifth anniversary of the establishment of UNDP as the central funding mechanism for the United Nations system of technical cooperation. UNDP total income had by then risen to $1.2 billion and expenditure to $1.5 billion. Income was primarily from voluntary pledges, but also from cost-sharing contributions by recipient Governments, trust funds established by the Administrator, contributions to local office costs and government cash-counterpart contributions. Regionally, Africa and Asia and the Pacific continued to receive the largest share of field programme expenditures, followed by Latin America and the Caribbean, the Arab States and Europe. The rest was used for interregional and global projects. In 1991, there were 1,129 new projects that were approved at a cost of some $690 million.

In response to the new imperatives of development and the principles outlined by the General Assembly in resolution 44/211 of 1989, following the triennial review of United Nations development activities, the Organization was in the process of reorienting its operational activities. The new orientation was directed towards promoting the programme approach and emphasized impact and results rather than output, the concept of comparative advantage among donors, and the placing of prime responsibility for the effectiveness of technical cooperation with national authorities. New projects would be more supportive of national objectives than previous ones, and the country programmes would coincide more or less with the programming cycle. The new programmes would also set out arrangements for execution and monitoring. Programmes would focus strongly on the environment and sustainable use of natural resources, poverty eradication, management development, the role of women in development, the transfer and adaptation of technology, and technical cooperation among developing countries. An important element of the new orientation was the emphasis on national execution, a practice that had increased with each programming cycle. The Governing Council agreed that recipient Governments should be assisted in building and strengthening sustainable national capacities for executing and implementing UNDP activities. The Council therefore encouraged simplifying rules and procedures governing programmes and projects and shifting support away from project operation and administrative support to providing analytical and technical advice and support. It also emphasized the importance of evaluation as a means of improving the quality of UNDP operations.

Trade and development

In 1961, the General Assembly took up the question of the development of world markets and improvement of terms of trade between industrial and less developed countries. The Secretary-General in his report on the subject noted that while discussions on the reduction of trade barriers within the General Agreement on Tariffs and Trade had proved useful, there was need for a broader approach to trade policy on the part of developed countries given the range of barriers, especially non-tariff barriers limiting the export of primary commodities from the developing countries. The Assembly, by resolution 1707(XVI), asked the Secretary-General to consult Governments on the holding of an international conference on international trade problems relating especially to primary commodity markets. At its 1962 session, the Economic and Social Council drew attention to the problems confronting developing countries in expanding their trade and the difficulty they would face in implementing economic and social development plans if their terms of trade continued to be unfavourable. The Council decided to convene a United Nations conference on trade and development. The General Assembly, in endorsing the Council's decision, recommended that the agenda of the conference should include: the need for increasing the trade of developing countries in primary commodities and semi-manufactured and manufactured goods to ensure rapid expansion of their export earnings; measures to ensure stable, equitable and remunerative prices and rising demand for their exports; measures for the removal of tariff and other trade barriers that adversely affected the expansion of international trade; and methods and machinery to implement measures for the expansion of international trade.

UN Conference on Trade and Development

. . .

The Conference in Geneva

The United Nations Conference on Trade and Development was held in Geneva, Switzerland, from 23 March to 16 June 1964.

. . .

The deliberations of the Conference ranged over a wide area of international trade and development problems, resulting in the adoption of 59 individual recommendations.

. . .

Final Act of the Conference

The Final Act of the Conference, which was formally adopted on 16 June 1964, consisted of three parts. The first of these was a preamble which described the background, constitution and proceedings of the Conference, followed by a statement of the findings by which the Conference had been guided and of the essential reasons and considerations on which its recommendations had been based. The second part consolidated the recommendations of the Conference, and the third part contained the text of these recommendations, together with observations and reservations by groups of countries or individual delegations, and messages from Heads of State.

The preamble to the Final Act drew attention to the need for the international community to combine its efforts to ensure that all countries—regardless of size, wealth, or economic and social system—should enjoy the benefits of international trade for their economic development and social progress. The issues before the Conference were set out in some detail in the part of the preamble which contained the findings of the Conference, where the gravity of the deterioration in the international trade situation of the developing countries was stressed. The developing countries had failed to participate to any substantial degree in the rapid expansion of world trade that had occurred since 1950. Their terms of trade had deteriorated, and their share in world exports had declined from nearly one third in 1950 to only slightly more than one fifth in 1962. These adverse trends had limited the capacity of the developing countries to import the capital goods required for development if even the modest target rate of growth for the Development Decade of 5 per cent per annum was to be reached. Indeed, on the basis of that target and assuming no change in the trends of the 1950's, the gap between the import requirements of the developing countries and their export earnings, covered in the past by the provision of aid and other capital flows, was expected to widen, according to Secretariat estimates, to some $20,000 million by 1970.

The findings drew attention to the fact that the slower growth in the quantity of exports of the developing countries and the adverse movement of their terms of trade were largely the reflection of the present commodity composition of their trade, consisting, as it did, predominantly of the exchange of primary product exports for manufactured imports whose relative positions in world markets had undergone significant changes. The findings also identified some of the specific factors at work principally in the economies of the industrially advanced countries, which tended to reinforce the more general factors inhibiting the expansion of exports of developing countries. In the developed market economies, with which the developing countries conducted over two thirds of their trade, such factors included price support programmes, customs duties and taxes, and fiscal charges imposed on consumption of tropical products, export subsidies on commodities of interest to developing countries, and high levels of tariffs imposed on processed products as compared with those applied to such products when exported in their natural form.

Accordingly, there was need for the elimination of those obstacles by national and international action designed to improve access and expand market opportunities for the exports of primary products, semi-manufactures and manufactures of developing countries in order to increase their export earnings. In the countries with centrally planned economies, with which the developing countries conducted a relatively small but rapidly growing trade, there was still considerable scope for expansion, which could be secured through the removal of certain obstacles that prevented a faster rate of growth and by further positive measures taken by the interested countries. Those measures included, among other things, the establishment of normal trade relations between countries with centrally planned economies and a larger number of developing countries; and increased utilization by countries with centrally planned economies, in addition to bilateral arrangements, of multilateral trade and payment methods when these were considered to be of mutual advantage to all partners in trade. It was also recognized that increased trade between the centrally planned economies and the developed market economies would be in the interest of world trade as a whole; and that the establishment of closer and broader trade ties between developing countries was necessary.

The essential reasons and considerations underlying the recommendations of the Conference were inspired by the belief that the development of equitable and mutually advantageous trade could promote higher standards of living, full employment and rapid economic progress in all countries of the world; some lines of advance in respect of trade in primary products and manufactures and of trade between developing countries were indicated. More specifically, in respect of trade in primary commodities, there was a need for a deliberate effort on the part of all industrialized countries to remedy the adverse tendencies resulting from the dependence of developing countries on primary commodity trade. The comprehensive action needed should include international commodity arrangements as well as an accelerated removal of existing obstacles and the forestalling of the creation of new obstacles to commodity trade.

In the field of manufactures and semi-manufactures, the promotion of industries with an export potential in developing countries was deemed essential, and the diversification and expansion of those exports were seen as important means of assisting the developing countries to achieve in time a balance in their external accounts. Accordingly, it was necessary to secure freer access for industrial exports from developing countries, particularly to the markets of the developed countries, not only for existing and traditional exports of manufactures and semi-manufactures but also for a wider range of more technically advanced manufactures.

In respect of the trade of developing countries with one another, it was recognized that an expansion of such trade would contribute towards the solution of the dilemma posed by the economic and technological requirements of modern industry on the one hand and the limited domestic markets of individual industries on the other. The importance and gravity of problems arising in the financing of development were described.

With regard to international financial co-operation, it was recognized that a need existed for greater and more systematic efforts on the part of all concerned. There had been agreement in some key areas, which included: measures for accelerated growth in developing countries and increases in their foreign exchange availabilities; guidelines for international financial and technical co-operation; supplementary financial measures and measures for dealing with external debt problems; and some aspects of shipping in relation to the trade of developing countries.

Finally, the Conference recognized that a need existed for adequate and effective organizational arrangements if the full potential contribution of international trade to the accelerated growth of developing countries was to be successfully achieved. The functioning of existing international institutions was reviewed and both their contributions and their limitations recognized. It was believed that participating Governments should make the most effective use of institutions and arrangements to which they were or might become parties. The

widespread desire among developing countries for a comprehensive trade organization was also noted, and it was recognized that further institutional arrangements were necessary in order to continue the work initiated by the Conference and implement its recommendations and conclusions.

Recognizing that the problems of trade and development required sustained efforts on the part of the international community, the Conference recommended the establishment of the Conference on Trade and Development as an organ of the General Assembly to be convened at intervals of not more than three years.

The machinery to keep world trade problems under constant review would also include the establishment of a 55-member Trade and Development Board with a permanent secretariat.

. . .

Among the individual recommendations adopted by the Conference were:

> Fifteen "General Principles" and 13 "Special Principles" to govern "international trade relations and trade policies conducive to development"; and eight principles relating to transit trade of land-locked States.
>
> Recommendations relating to commodities; manufactured goods; financing for an expansion of trade; improvement of "invisible trade" (factors such as interest and dividend payments, insurance, shipping costs and receipts from tourism); special problems; and a programme of work in the field of trade and development.
>
> Recommendations on institutional arrangements.

. . .

Joint declaration of 77 developing countries

At the conclusion of the Conference, 77 developing nations issued a "joint declaration" in which they declared that the United Nations Conference on Trade and Development "marks the beginning of a new era in the evolution of international co-operation in the field of trade and development."

The Declaration added that such co-operation "must serve as a decisive instrument for ending the division of the world into areas of affluence and intolerable poverty." The developing countries were united in their resolve to continue the quest for a redress of the "injustice and neglect of centuries," and they looked to "the entire international community for understanding and support in this endeavour."

The developing countries made it clear that they considered the final recommendations of the Conference as only an "initial step" towards the endorsement of a new trade policy for development. They did not consider the progress made in each of the major fields of economic development adequate or commensurate with their essential requirements. For example, they believed that there had not been an adequate appreciation of the problem of the "trade gap," and that only the "most limited approaches" had been made regarding trade in primary commodities and preferences for exports of manufactures. Similarly, they felt that only preliminary steps had been possible relating to schemes for compensatory financing to meet long-term deterioration in the terms of trade.

Nevertheless, the declaration stated, the developing countries "accepted the results of this Conference in the hope that these results would lay the foundation for more substantial progress in the period ahead . . . [and] in recognition of the need for a co-operative effort in the international field."

. . .

Action by General Assembly

In view of the circumstances prevailing during the nineteenth session of the General Assembly, the Final Act and Report of the Trade Conference were not considered in detail by the Assembly. However, on 30 December 1964, the Assembly did adopt, without objection, a resolution (1995(XIX)) embodying the recommendations of the Conference for the establishment, within the United Nations framework, of machinery to promote concrete action, national and international, in the field of trade and of trade as related to development. Details of the conciliation procedures recommended by the Trade Conference were worked out by a Special Committee appointed by the Secretary-General of the United Nations which met at United Nations Headquarters from 28 September to 23 October 1964.

By the Assembly's resolution, it was thus decided to establish the United Nations Conference on Trade and Development as a permanent organ of the General Assembly, to be convened at intervals of not more than three years. Members of the Conference would be those States which were members of the United Nations, the specialized agencies or the International Atomic Energy Agency.

A permanent organ of the Conference, the Trade and Development Board, consisting of 55 members elected by the Conference from among its membership, was to perform the functions of the Conference in the intersessional periods, and would normally meet twice a year. It would keep under review and take appropriate action for the implementation of the recommendations, declarations, resolutions and other decisions of the Conference and to ensure the continuity of its work.

The General Assembly also provided for the immediate establishment of an adequate, permanent and full-time secretariat within the United Nations Secretariat to service the Conference and its subsidiary bodies. . . .

The further evolution of institutional arrangements in the field of trade was to be kept under review. To this end, the Conference was to study all relevant subjects, including matters related to the establishment of a comprehensive organ based on the entire membership of the United Nations system of organizations to deal with trade in relation to development.

(YUN 1964, pp. 195-209)

UNCTAD sessions

Following the General Assembly's decision that the United Nations Conference on Trade and Development should meet at intervals of not more than three years, successive sessions of UNCTAD were held to further the liberalization of international trade.

The second session of the Conference (New Delhi, India, 1 February–29 March 1968) continued consideration of matters raised at the first Conference, but failed to draw up a programme of action due to differences between the developed and developing countries. It was at that session that the membership of South Africa was suspended. The third session (Santiago, Chile, 13 April–21 May 1972) continued to formulate new development-oriented trade policies, particularly within the context of the Second United Nations Development Decade.

At the fourth session of UNCTAD (Nairobi, Kenya, 5-31 May 1976), the agenda was more selective and the position of countries was clarified during preliminary negotiations held at a pre-conference meeting of its Trade and Development Board. A major task of this session was to translate objectives, principles and policy approaches embodied in the decisions taken at the 1974 and 1975 special sessions of the General Assembly. The most prominent result was the acceptance of an integrated programme for commodities, together with a time-frame for its implementation. However, it failed to make any headway in the area of money and finance, particularly with respect to the external debt problem of developing countries. The fifth session of UNCTAD (Manila, Philippines, 7 May–3 June 1979) examined the need for structural change in the world economy, including change in the institutional framework governing economic relations between developed and developing countries. Several of UNCTAD's major ongoing activities received new impetus from the Manila Conference and new initiatives were launched, including a programme to deal with protectionism and the establishment of an intergovernmental group to discuss monetary reform.

The central theme of the sixth session of UNCTAD (Belgrade, Yugoslavia, 6 June–2 July 1983), held against the background of the world economic crisis, was development and recovery in the world economy. Revitalization of development, growth and trade was the theme of the seventh session

(Geneva, 9 July–3 August 1987). The Conference adopted a Final Act recommending approaches to deal with debt problems, resources for development and related monetary issues, commodities, international trade and the problems of the least developed countries.

Eighth session of UNCTAD

International trade and development issues for world economic revitalization and growth received greater focus in 1992, by the convening, in accordance with a General Assembly resolution of 1991, of a high-level eighth session of the United Nations Conference on Trade and Development (UNCTAD-VIII), at Cartagena de Indias, Colombia, from 8 to 25 February 1992.

. . .

The Conference's main substantive agenda item was the strengthening of national and international action and multilateral cooperation for a healthy, secure and equitable world economy.

Proceedings of UNCTAD VIII

. . .

UNCTAD VIII Declaration and final document. On 25 February, the Conference adopted a Declaration entitled "The Spirit of Cartagena" and a five-part final document entitled "A New Partnership for Development: the Cartagena Commitment": Part I outlined the challenges and potentials for international trade and development in the 1990s in the context of the evolving international political and economic situation and the growing convergence on development issues and priorities and a new partnership for development; Part II dealt with the broad policy orientations on the issues of good management at the national and internatioanl levels and with sustainable development; Part III discussed the role of UNCTAD in a changing political and economic environment, focusing on a wide range of issues, including institutional adaptation, UNCTAD's functions, adapting, reorienting and consolidating its substantive work, strengthening its intergovernmental machinery and improving its methods of work; Part IV reviewed policies and measures, particularly in the areas of finance, trade, commodities, technology and services and their interlinkages; and Part V focused on economic cooperation among developing countries (ECDC), noting that such cooperation could enable developing countries to exploit more effectively the latest complementarities in their economies, promote a fuller and more effective mobilization of their resources, gain access to additional resources and knowledge, and enhance the negotiating weight necessary to advance their common interests.

. . .

UNCTAD VIII follow-up

In the Cartagena Commitment, UNCTAD VIII proposed a number of institutional reforms for UNCTAD, particularly its intergovernmental machinery. It called on TDB, at its first session following the Conference, to take the necessary follow-up measures to ensure speedy implementation of the agreed institutional reforms. On 7 May, TDB adopted guidelines for its executive sessions and established the terms of reference for four Standing Committees: the Standing Committee on Commodities; the Standing Committee on Poverty Alleviation; the Standing Committee on ECDC; and the Standing Committee on Developing Services Sectors: Fostering Competitive Services Sectors in Developing Countries. It also established the terms of reference for the following Ad Hoc Working Groups: the Ad Hoc Working Group on Investment and Financial Flows—non-debt-creating finance for development; new mechanism for increasing investment and financial flows; the Ad Hoc Working Group on Trade Efficiency; the Ad Hoc Working Group on Comparative Experiences with Privatization; the Ad Hoc Working Group on Expansion of Trading Opportunities for Developing Countries; and the Ad Hoc Working Group on the Interrelationship between Investment and Technology Transfer. TDB agreed that the Standing Committees and the Ad Hoc Working Groups, in their work, would take into account the results of the review and follow-up by TDB of progress in implementing the Programme of Action for LDCs for the 1990s. TDB would also consider establishing a working group to explore questions related to structural adjustment for the transition to disarmament and the implications for economic growth and development of reductions of military expenditures.

On 9 October, TDB established an Ad Hoc Working Group to explore the issue of structural adjustment for the transition to disarmament. It requested the UNCTAD Secretary-General to prepare a report on the activities of other United Nations organizations in this area, indicate where UNCTAD could best play a role, provide an estimate of the resource implications of establishing the Working Group and prepare draft terms of reference. It would also, at its first session in 1993, establish the timetable for the Group, taking into account the timetable of existing working groups and the availability of resources.

(YUN 1992, pp. 611-13)

GENERAL ASSEMBLY ACTION

On 22 December 1992, the General Assembly adopted resolution 47/183 to endorse the conclusions and recommendations of UNCTAD VIII.

Multilateral trade negotiations

The United Nations Conference on Trade and Employment (Havana, Cuba, November 1947–March

1948) drew up a charter for an International Trade Organization and established an Interim Commission for the International Trade Organization. The charter was never accepted, but the Conference's Preparatory Committee members decided to proceed with tariff negotiations among themselves and drew up the General Agreement on Tariffs and Trade (GATT), which entered into force on 1 January 1948 with 23 contracting parties. By December 1993, the number of contracting parties had risen to 114. By 1964, the contracting parties had held five major negotiating conferences for the reduction of tariffs—in 1947, 1949, 1950-1951, 1956 and 1960-1961. In May 1963, Ministers of the contracting parties decided to hold a sixth negotiating conference on a more comprehensive basis than in any previous tariff negotiation held under GATT. A Trade Negotiations Committee was established to supervise the conduct of the negotiations. Known as the "Kennedy Round", the negotiations opened at Geneva in May 1964. The contracting parties also established the International Trade Centre to provide trade information and trade promotion advisory services to developing countries. In 1967, the General Assembly, to avoid duplication between the activities of UNCTAD and GATT in this area, decided to establish, effective 1 January 1968, a joint UNCTAD/GATT Trade Centre. The "Kennedy Round" of trade negotiations concluded in June 1967 with agreements on tariff concessions and separate agreements on grains, chemical products and anti-dumping policies.

The seventh round of trade negotiations, known as the "Tokyo Round" was conducted between 1973 and 1979. In addition to negotiating the further liberalization of world trade, this Round paid special attention to securing additional benefits for the developing countries. Agreements were reached on tariffs and non-tariff measures, agriculture, tropical products, trade in civil aircraft, a framework for the conduct of world trade and safeguards. In particular, the agreements assured preferential treatment in favour of and between developing countries as a permanent feature of the world trading system.

The eighth round of multilateral trade negotiations, the "Uruguay Round", was launched in September 1986 at Punta del Este. The Ministerial Declaration of 20 September setting out the aims and objectives of the negotiations stressed the interrelationship between trade, money, finance and development. It emphasized the need for new understandings on safeguards and sought to bring trade in agriculture and textiles into the GATT framework. It also provided for negotiations on new issues, such as the relationship between trade flows and the protection of intellectual property rights and trade in services.

Uruguay Round

In response to a 1992 General Assembly request, the Secretary-General submitted a September 1993 report on strengthening international organizations in the area of multilateral trade, in which he reviewed developments in the Uruguay Round—the eighth round of multilateral trade negotiations, launched in 1986 under the aegis of GATT.

The Secretary-General noted that the prospects for a successful conclusion of the Round had brightened with the Tokyo Summit (7-9 July 1993), where leaders of the seven major industrialized countries and the European Community (EC) renewed their determination to achieve a global and balanced agreement before the end of the year. In addition, an agreement on market access issues was reached by Canada, Japan, the United States and EC on 7 July, which led to the resumption of negotiations in the middle of that month. The Secretary-General said it was expected that the negotiations would accelerate with the aim of concluding them by 15 December.

In resolution 48/55, the Assembly deplored the repeated delays in concluding the negotiations and urged all participants to complete the Round by 15 December.

The negotiations, which were concluded on that date, proved to be a landmark in the international trade endeavour to strengthen the multilateral trading system. However, some countries expressed concern over the balance between the likely benefits and shortcomings of the outcome.

(YUN 1993, p. 753)

. . . The Uruguay Round, which would expand world trade by $755 billion annually by the year 2002, produced the most comprehensive trade agreement ever, with new multilateral rules for liberalizing trade in goods and services, intellectual property rights and investment measures.

The Uruguay Round package consisted of a Final Act comprising some 28 new agreements and national schedules on tariff concessions and initial commitments for liberalizing trade in services. The Trade Negotiations Committee—the most senior body of the Uruguay Round—approved a work programme for the post-Round period, including recommendations on the subject of trade and environment for adoption at a Ministerial meeting to sign the Final Act in April 1994 in Marrakesh, Morocco.

The Uruguay Round package, intended to improve market-access, was estimated to produce world income gains of $235 billion and trade gains of $755 billion annually by the year 2002. Developed countries' tariffs on industrial products were reduced by 38 per cent, lowering average duties from 6.3 to 3.9 per cent. Tariff bindings (maximum duties) would cover 99 per cent of industrial products entering developed countries and 72 per cent for developing countries. The General Agreement on Trade in Services had three major elements: the Framework Agreement containing basic obligations (such as most-favoured-nation and national treatment); the annexes addressing the special situations of individual services sectors (financial services, telecommunications, air transport, movement of labour); and market-opening commitments submitted by participants that would be the subject of further liberalization in future rounds of negotiations.

The Uruguay Round produced the most extensive agreement on intellectual property ever negotiated, covering patents, copyrights, the rights of performers and producers of sound recordings, trademarks, geographical indications including appelations of origin, industrial design, layout designs of integrated circuits and trade secrets. Other agreements provided for the progressive integration of textiles and clothing products into the GATT rules over a ten-year period; greater liberalization of trade in agriculture; and bringing all measures affecting import and export competition under more effective GATT rules and disciplines. They also strengthened disciplines and clarified current rules on anti-dumping, subsidies and countervailing measures, safeguards, customs valuation, import licensing and technical barriers to trade. New rules would cover trade-related investments, rules of origin and preshipment inspection. The rules and procedures relating to settlement of disputes would also improve.

GATT, which existed on a provisional basis, would become a permanent world trade body through the establishment of the World Trade Organization (WTO) on 1 January 1995 to implement the results of the Round.

(YUN 1993, pp. 1326-27)

Sustainable development

Demographics and development

The relationship between population problems and development was first considered at the second World Population Conference (Belgrade, 30 August–10 September 1965) convened at the invitation of the Government of Yugoslavia and under the auspices of the United Nations. Held amidst growing concern over the consequences of rapid population growth, especially in the developing countries, the Conference, attended by scientific experts, led to a greater understanding of population problems as they related to development, and stimulated interest in new research and the collection of data on population questions.

In 1970, the Economic and Social Council decided to convene another World Population Con-

ference to consider basic demographic problems, their relationship with economic and social development, and population policies and action programmes needed to promote human welfare and development. The Conference (Bucharest, Romania, 19-30 August 1974) was the first global meeting of Governments convened by the United Nations on population issues. It considered population trends and future prospects; population change and social development; population resources and the environment; and population and family. The Conference adopted the World Population Plan of Action as a policy instrument to support other internationally adopted strategies, such as the International Development Strategy for the Second United Nations Development Decade, and to promote economic development, quality of life, human rights and fundamental freedoms. The Plan was based on the affirmation that of all things in the world, people were the most precious. It stressed that the principal aim of social, economic and cultural development, of which population goals and policies were integral parts, was to improve levels of living and the quality of human life. Recommendations for action contained in the Plan dealt with population goals and policies; socio-economic policies; and the promotion of knowledge and policies.

1984 Conference on Population

The International Conference on Population was held at Mexico City from 6 to 14 August 1984 to appraise the implementation of the World Population Plan of Action, adopted in 1974 at Bucharest, Romania, by the World Population Conference.

. . .

On 14 August, the Conference adopted the Mexico City Declaration on Population and Development in which it reaffirmed the full validity of the principles and objectives of the 1974 Plan of Action and adopted by consensus a set of recommendations for its further implementation. Those recommendations comprised a preamble, a short section on peace, security and population, 76 recommendations for action by Governments, and 12 recommendations for implementation.

In its Declaration, the Conference stated that, although the world had undergone far-reaching changes since 1974, population growth, high mortality and morbidity, and migration problems continued to be causes of great concern requiring immediate action. The Conference confirmed that the principal aim of social, economic and human development, of which population goals and policies were integral parts, was to improve people's living standards and quality of life. The Declaration constituted a solemn undertaking by the nations and international organizations gathered in Mexico City to respect national sovereignty, combat all forms of racial discrimination, including *apartheid*, and promote social and economic development, human rights and individual freedom.

Regarding the global population growth rate, the Declaration noted that it had declined from 2.03 to 1.67 per cent per year in the previous decade, but would decline more slowly in the next. Moreover, the annual increase in numbers was expected to continue and could reach 90 million by the year 2000. Ninety per cent of the increase would occur in developing countries and 6.1 billion people were expected to inhabit the Earth. Demographic differences between developed and developing countries remained striking with an average life expectancy of 73 years in developed countries and only 57 years in developing countries. In addition, families in the latter tended to be much larger. This caused concern since social and population pressures could contribute to continuing the wide disparity in welfare and the quality of life between developing and developed countries.

Although progress had been made since 1974, millions still lacked access to safe, effective family planning methods. Major efforts were needed to ensure that all could exercise their basic human right to decide freely the number and spacing of their children and to have the information and means to do so.

Also emphasized in the Declaration were: the importance of recognizing the link between population and development; the positive influence of improving the status of women on family life and size; the need to increase funding to develop new contraceptive methods; the need for special attention to be given to maternal and child health services; and rapid urbanization and migratory movements.

. . . Major challenges and problems of primary concern to the international community included: reducing poverty, expanding employment and encouraging economic growth; promoting the status of women; reducing population growth rates; changes in population structures; infant and maternal mortality; unmet family planning needs; internal and international migration and high urbanization rates; and the increasing number of persons lacking sufficient food, pure water, shelter, health care, education and other facilities.

The 88 recommendations for action to implement further the 1974 World Population Plan of Action dealt with socio-economic development, the environment and population; the role and the status of women; the development of population policies; population goals and policies; morbidity and mortality; reproduction and the family; population distribution and internal migration; international migration; population structure; promotion of knowledge and policy; the role of national

Governments and international co-operation in implementing the Plan; and the monitoring, review and appraisal of the Plan's implementation.

. . .

The Conference's recommendations for implementation of the Plan of Action by national Governments dealt with management of population programmes, and utilization of technical cooperation among developing countries. With regard to international co-operation in the Plan's implementation, the Conference recommended the provision of substantial international support by developed countries, other donor countries and intergovernmental organizations and NGOs. Areas identified as requiring particular emphasis by the international community included: research and action programmes; integration of population planning in the development process; improving the status of women; biomedical and social science research; collection and analysis of data; identification of successful programmes and dissemination of information on them; implementation of monitoring and evaluation systems; promotion of exchanges between countries with common experiences; and education and training. The Conference also urged Governments to increase assistance for population activities, urged further strengthening of UNFPA and invited national NGOs and other groups and individuals to assist in developing and implementing population policies and programmes.

Finally, the Conference stated that the monitoring of population trends and policies would continue to be undertaken by the Secretary-General and the next review and appraisal of progress made towards achieving the goals and recommendations of the Plan of Action would be in 1989.

(YUN 1984, pp. 714-17)

1994 Conference on Population and Development

In 1989, following review of the implementation of the 1984 Mexico City Declaration on Population and Development which was to have advanced the 1974 World Population Plan of Action, the Economic and Social Council (resolution 1989/91 of 26 July) saw the need for continued attention to be given to population issues at a high policy level to ensure that population concerns were integrated into policies, priorities and programmes for social and economic development. It decided to convene an international meeting to assess progress made in implementing the World Population Plan of Action and provide guidance on the treatment of priority population issues for the next decade.

The International Conference on Population and Development (Cairo, Egypt, 5-13 September 1994) adopted the Programme of Action of the International Conference on Population and Development, in the preamble to which it stated that, with the growing recognition of global population, development and environmental interdependence, the opportunity to adopt suitable macro- and socio-economic policies to promote sustained economic growth in the context of sustainable development and to mobilize human and financial resources for global problem-solving had never been greater. Despite significant progress made in many fields important for social welfare, the developing countries still faced serious economic difficulties, an unfavourable economic environment and an increasing number of people living in absolute poverty. Around the world many of the basic resources on which future generations would depend were being depleted and environmental degradation was intensifying, driven by unsustainable production and consumption patterns, unprecedented growth in population, widespread and persistent poverty, and social and economic inequality. However, there was an emerging global consensus for increased international cooperation in regard to population in the context of sustainable development, for which Agenda 21 of the 1992 United Nations Conference on Environment and Development provided a framework.

Regarding global population growth, the Conference noted that the world population was currently estimated at 5.6 billion and, while the rate of growth had declined, absolute increments had been increasing. By the year 2050, the United Nations projections ranged from 7.9 billion to a medium variant of 9.8 billion and a high of 11.9 billion. Implementation of the goals and objectives contained in the 20-year Programme of Action would result in world population growth during that period and beyond at levels below the United Nations medium projection. Those goals and objectives addressed the critical challenges and interrelationships between population and sustained economic growth in the context of sustainable development. They would require mobilization of resources at the national and international levels and additional resources to the developing countries, as well as resources to strengthen the institutional capacity to implement the Programme of Action. The two decades ahead were likely to produce a further shift of rural populations to urban areas and a continued high level of migration between countries, presenting serious new challenges. The most rapid rate of urbanization would occur in developing countries and would place enormous strain on existing social services and infrastructure, much of which would not be able to expand at the same rate as that of urbanization.

The Programme recommended important population and development objectives, as well as mutually supportive qualitative and quantitative goals, among which were: sustained economic growth in the context of sustainable development; education, especially for girls; gender equity and equality; infant, child and maternal mortality reduction; and universal access to reproductive health services, including family planning and sexual health.

The environment

Recognizing in 1968 that the relationship between man and his environment was undergoing profound changes in the wake of modern scientific and technological developments and that increased attention to the human environment was essential for sound economic and social development, the General Assembly, on the recommendation of the Economic and Social Council, decided to convene a United Nations Conference on the Human Environment in 1972 (resolution 2398(XXIII). The Conference was held at Stockholm, Sweden, from 5 to 16 June 1972 and was attended by 113 Member States.

UN Conference on the Human Environment

Actions taken by the Conference

Declaration of the UN
Conference on the Human Environment

On 16 June 1972, the United Nations Conference on the Human Environment adopted a Declaration on the human environment consisting of a preamble and 26 principles.

By the preamble, the Conference proclaimed that the defence and improvement of the human environment—both natural and man-made—had become an imperative goal for mankind, to be pursued together with the fundamental goals of peace and of world-wide economic and social development. The achievement of this goal was the responsibility of citizens, communities, enterprises and institutions at every level. Although local and national governments would bear the greatest burden for large-scale environmental policy and action within their jurisdictions, international cooperation was also needed, both to raise resources to support the developing countries in carrying out their responsibilities in this field, and because a growing class of environmental problems were regional or global in extent.

By the preamble, the conference also, among other things, affirmed that in the developing countries most environmental problems were caused by under-development, whereas in the industrialized countries they were generally related to industrialization and technological development. The Conference also declared that the natural growth of population continuously presented problems on the preservation of the environment and required the adoption, as appropriate, of adequate policies and measures.

The Conference then laid down . . . 26 principles. [Included among those principles were:]

Man had the fundamental right to freedom, equality and adequate conditions of life, in an environment of a quality that permitted a life of dignity and well-being, and he bore a solemn responsibility to protect and improve the environment for present and future generations; . . .

The natural resources of the earth, including the air, water, land, flora and fauna and, especially, representative samples of natural ecosystems, were to be safeguarded for the benefit of present and future generations through careful planning or management, as appropriate;

. . .

Man had a special responsibility to safeguard and wisely manage the heritage of wildlife and its habitat which were now gravely imperilled by a combination of adverse factors. Nature conservation, including wildlife, was therefore to receive importance in planning for economic development;

. . .

The discharge of toxic substances or of other substances and the release of heat, in such quantities or concentrations as to exceed the capacity of the environment to render them harmless, had to be halted in order to ensure that serious or irreversible damage was not inflicted upon ecosystems. The just struggle of the peoples of all countries against pollution should be supported;

. . .

The environmental policies of all States should enhance and not adversely affect the present or future development potential of developing countries, nor should they hamper the attainment of better living conditions for all, and appropriate steps should be taken by States and international organizations with a view to reaching agreement on meeting the possible national and international economic consequences resulting from the application of environmental measures; [and]

. . .

In order to achieve a more rational management of resources and thus to improve the environment, States should adopt an integrated and co-ordinated approach to their development planning so as to ensure that development was compatible with the need to protect and improve the human environment for the benefit of their population.

. . .

Action Plan for the Human Environment

After considering the reports of its three main committees, the Conference adopted 109 recommendations for environmental action at the international level.

. . .

After their adoption, the 109 recommendations were arranged in a functional framework, which constituted the Action Plan for the Human Environment. The Action Plan consisted of three parts: (i) a global assessment programme, known as Earthwatch, to identify and measure environmental problems of international importance and to warn against impending crises; (ii) environmental management activities; and (iii) supporting measures, such as education and training, public information, and organizational and financing arrangements.

[YUN 1972, pp. 319-22]

The General Assembly in the same year accepted the recommendations of the Conference and decided to establish the Governing Council of the United Nations Environment Programme (UNEP) to promote international cooperation and provide policy guidance in the field of environment; an environment secretariat to serve as a focal point for environmental action and coordination within the United Nations system to be located at Nairobi, Kenya; the Environment Fund to provide additional financing for environmental programmes; and an Environment Coordination Board.

In 1982, on the occasion of the commemoration of the tenth anniversary of the Stockholm Conference, the UNEP Governing Council held a special session (Nairobi, 10-18 May) at which it adopted the Nairobi Declaration, expressing concern about the state of the environment and requesting Governments and people to intensify efforts to improve it.

Out of that special session grew an awareness of the need for far-reaching blueprints and long-term environmental strategies for achieving sustainable development to the year 2000 and beyond in the face of rapid socio-economic, political and technological change. On the basis of reports submitted by an independent special commission made up of government officials, economists and scientists—which later adopted the name World Commission on Environment and Development—and the Intergovernmental Preparatory Committee of the UNEP Governing Council, the General Assembly in December 1987 (resolution 42/186) adopted the Environmental Perspective to the Year 2000 and Beyond. The Perspective stated that, to meet the challenge of continued environmental degradation, the overall aspirational goal must be sustainable development on the basis of prudent management of global resources and environmental capacities, and the rehabilitation of environment previously subjected to degradation and misuse.

In 1989, several United Nations bodies devoted attention to the question of environment and development. The General Assembly, recognizing the global character of environmental problems, stressed that poverty and environmental degradation were closely interrelated. It decided to convene in 1992 a high-level United Nations Conference on Environment and Development to elaborate strategies and measures to halt and reverse the effects of environmental degradation and to promote sustainable and environmentally sound development (resolution 44/228).

UN Conference on Environment and Development—"Earth Summit"

The United Nations Conference on Environment and Development, or "Earth Summit", took place at Rio de Janeiro, Brazil, from 3 to 14 June 1992. On 14 June, it adopted the Rio Declaration on Environment and Development; Agenda 21, a comprehensive plan of action for the sustainable development of the Earth into the twenty-first century; and a statement of principles for a global consensus on the management, conservation and sustainable development of forests. The United Nations Framework Convention on Climate Change and the Convention on Biological Diversity were opened for signature at UNCED and signed by 154 States and 156 States, respectively; each Convention was also signed by one regional economic integration organization.

UNCED coincided with World Environment Day (5 June), which was also the twentieth anniversary of the opening of the 1972 United Nations Conference on the Human Environment.

. . .

Action taken by the Conference

Rio Declaration on Environment and Development

The Rio Declaration aimed to establish a new and equitable global partnership on environment and development through cooperation among States, key sectors of society and individuals. It was hoped that the Declaration would serve as a basis for future negotiation of an Earth Charter that could be approved on the fiftieth anniversary of the United Nations in 1995. The Declaration consisted of the following 27 principles:

1.   Human beings are at the centre of concerns for sustainable development. They are entitled to a healthy and productive life in harmony with nature.
2.   States have, in accordance with the Charter of the United Nations and the principles of international law, the sovereign right to exploit their own resources pursuant to their own environmental and developmental policies, and the responsibility to ensure that activities within their jurisdiction or control do not cause damage to the environment of other States or of areas beyond the limits of national jurisdiction.
3.   The right to development must be fulfilled so as to equitably meet developmental and environmental needs of present and future generations.
4.   In order to achieve sustainable development, environmental protection shall constitute an integral part of the development process and cannot be considered in isolation from it.

5.   All States and all people shall cooperate in the essential task of eradicating poverty as an indispensable requirement for sustainable development, in order to decrease the disparities in standards of living and better meet the needs of the majority of the people of the world.
6.   The special situation and needs of developing countries, particularly the least developed and those most environmentally vulnerable, shall be given special priority. International actions in the field of environment and development should also address the interests and needs of all countries.
7.   States shall cooperate in a spirit of global partnership to conserve, protect and restore the health and integrity of the Earth's ecosystem. In view of the different contributions to global environmental degradation, States have common but differentiated responsibilities. The developed countries acknowledge the responsibility that they bear in the international pursuit of sustainable development in view of the pressures their societies place on the global environment and of the technologies and financial resources they command.
8.   To achieve sustainable development and a higher quality of life for all people, States should reduce and eliminate unsustainable patterns of production and consumption and promote appropriate demographic policies.
9.   States should cooperate to strengthen endogenous capacity-building for sustainable development by improving scientific understanding through exchanges of scientific and technological knowledge, and by enhancing the development, adaptation, diffusion and transfer of technologies, including new and innovative technologies.
10.   Environmental issues are best handled with the participation of all concerned citizens, at the relevant level. At the national level, each individual shall have appropriate access to information concerning the environment that is held by public authorities, including information on hazardous materials and activities in their communities, and the opportunity to participate in decision-making processes. States shall facilitate and encourage public awareness and participation by making information widely available. Effective access to judicial and administrative proceedings, including redress and remedy, shall be provided.
11.   States shall enact effective environmental legislation. Environmental standards, management objectives and priorities should reflect the environmental and developmental context to which they apply. Standards applied by some countries may be inappropriate and of unwarranted economic and social cost to other countries, in particular developing countries.
12.   States should cooperate to promote a supportive and open international economic system that would lead to economic growth and sustainable development in all countries, to better address the problems of environmental degradation. Trade policy measures for environmental purposes should not constitute a means of arbitrary or unjustifiable discrimination or a disguised restriction on international trade. Unilateral actions to deal with environmental challenges outside the jurisdiction of the importing country should be avoided. Environmental measures addressing transboundary or global environmental

problems should, as far as possible, be based on an international consensus.

13. States shall develop national law regarding liability and compensation for the victims of pollution and other environmental damage. States shall also cooperate in an expeditious and more determined manner to develop further international law regarding liability and compensation for adverse effects of environmental damage caused by activities within their jurisdiction or control to areas beyond their jurisdiction.

14. States should effectively cooperate to discourage or prevent the relocation and transfer to other States of any activities and substances that cause severe environmental degradation or are found to be harmful to human health.

15. In order to protect the environment, the precautionary approach shall be widely applied by States according to their capabilities. Where there are threats of serious or irreversible damage, lack of full scientific certainty shall not be used as a reason for postponing cost-effective measures to prevent environmental degradation.

16. National authorities should endeavour to promote the internalization of environmental costs and the use of economic instruments, taking into account the approach that the polluter should, in principle, bear the cost of pollution, with due regard to the public interest and without distorting international trade and investment.

17. Environmental impact assessment, as a national instrument, shall be undertaken for proposed activities that are likely to have a significant adverse impact on the environment and are subject to a decision of a competent national authority.

18. States shall immediately notify other States of any natural disasters or other emergencies that are likely to produce sudden harmful effects on the environment of those States. Every effort shall be made by the international community to help States so afflicted.

19. States shall provide prior and timely notification and relevant information to potentially affected States on activities that may have a significant adverse transboundary environmental effect and shall consult with those States at an early stage and in good faith.

20. Women have a vital role in environmental management and development. Their full participation is therefore essential to achieve sustainable development.

21. The creativity, ideals and courage of the youth of the world should be mobilized to forge a global partnership in order to achieve sustainable development and ensure a better future for all.

22. Indigenous people and their communities and other local communities have a vital role in environmental management and development because of their knowledge and traditional practices. States should recognize and duly support their identity, culture and interests and enable their effective participation in the achievement of sustainable development.

23. The environment and natural resources of people under oppression, domination and occupation shall be protected.

24. Warfare is inherently destructive of sustainable development. States shall therefore respect international law providing protection for the environment in times of armed conflict and cooperate in its further development, as necessary.

25. Peace, development and environmental protection are interdependent and indivisible.

26. States shall resolve all their environmental disputes peacefully and by appropriate means in accordance with the Charter of the United Nations.

27. States and people shall cooperate in good faith and in a spirit of partnership in the fulfilment of the principles embodied in this Declaration and in the further development of international law in the field of sustainable development.

Agenda 21

The preamble of Agenda 21 stated that humanity was confronted with a worsening of poverty, hunger, ill-health and illiteracy and the continuing deterioration of the ecosystems. Integration of environment and development concerns would lead to the fulfilment of basic needs, improved living standards for all, better protected and managed ecosystems and a safer, more prosperous future. Agenda 21 reflected a global consensus and political commitment at the highest level on development and environment cooperation. International cooperation should support and supplement national strategies and plans. In that context, the United Nations system had a key role to play. The objectives of Agenda 21 would require a substantial flow of financial resources to developing countries. The 115 programme areas defining areas of action under Agenda 21 were described in terms of the basis for action, objectives, activities and means of implementation.

Social and economic dimensions

Section I of Agenda 21 covered its social and economic dimensions. The Conference called for an international climate that would promote sustainable development through trade liberalization, make trade and environment mutually supportive, provide adequate financial resources to developing countries and deal with international debt, and encourage macroeconomic policies conducive to environment and development. It recommended halting and reversing protectionism, improving the competitiveness of the commodity sector, and diversifying to reduce dependence on commodity exports.

The Conference declared that an environmental policy focusing on the conservation and protection of resources would have to take into account those who depended on the resources for their livelihoods. A development policy focusing on increasing the production of goods without addressing the sustainability of the resources on which production was based would run into declining productivity. The United Nations system should make poverty alleviation a major priority and assist Governments in formulating action programmes on poverty alleviation and sustainable development.

Changing consumption patterns in regard to natural resources would require a multipronged strategy focusing on demand, meeting the basic needs of the poor, and reducing wastage and the use of finite resources in the production process. Governments should assist individuals and households in making environmentally informed choices.

The Conference agreed that the growth in world population and production combined with unsustainable consumption practices was placing increasingly severe stress on the life-supporting capacities of the planet. Demographic trends should be incorporated in the global analysis of environment and development issues, with full recognition of women's rights.

The Conference said that Agenda 21 should address the primary health needs of the world's population. Countries were urged to develop priority action plans based on the cooperative efforts of various levels of government, NGOs and local communities. Programme areas relating to health dealt with meeting rural health-care needs, controlling communicable diseases, protecting vulnerable groups, meeting the urban health challenge and reducing health risks from environmental pollution and hazards.

On the subject of promoting sustainable human settlements, the Conference called for providing shelter for all, improved management of settlements, sustainable land-use planning and management, the integrated provision of environmental infrastructure (water, sanitation, drainage and solid-waste management), sustainable energy and transport systems, planning and management of settlements in disaster-prone areas, sustainable construction industry activities and human resource development and capacity-building for human settlement development.

Conservation and management of resources for development

Section II of Agenda 21 covered the conservation and management of resources for development. It included four programme areas: improving the scientific basis for decision-making; promoting sustainable development; preventing stratospheric ozone depletion; and transboundary atmospheric pollution.

The Conference called for an integrated approach to the planning and management of soils, minerals, water and biota. Noting major weaknesses in the policies, methods and mechanisms adopted to support and develop the ecological, economic, social and cultural roles of trees, forests and forest lands, it recommended the following: en-

hancing the protection, management and conservation of all forests, as well as the greening of degraded areas, through rehabilitation, afforestation, reforestation and other means; promoting efficient utilization and assessment to recover the full valuation of the goods and services provided by forests, forest lands and woodlands; and establishing or strengthening capacities for the planning, assessment and systematic observations of forests.

Three chapters dealt with managing fragile ecosystems: combating desertification and drought, mountain development, and sustaining small islands and coastal areas. Agenda 21 called for strengthening the desertification knowledge base, developing information and monitoring systems for regions prone to desertification and drought, combating land degradation and promoting alternative livelihood systems in areas prone to desertification. In addition, the Conference proposed integrating comprehensive anti-desertification programmes into national development and environmental plans, developing comprehensive drought preparedness and drought-relief schemes for drought-prone areas, designing programmes to cope with environmental refugees and promoting education on desertification control and management of the effects of drought. The Conference called for the General Assembly to establish an intergovernmental negotiating committee to elaborate an international convention to combat desertification in countries experiencing serious drought and/or desertification.

Mountains were susceptible to accelerated erosion, landslides and rapid loss of habitat and genetic diversity. Programme areas covered strengthening knowledge about the ecology and sustainable development of mountain ecosystems and promoting integrated watershed development and alternative livelihood opportunities.

The protection and development of the marine environment, including the oceans, seas and adjacent coastal areas, was to be carried out in accordance with the 1982 United Nations Convention on the Law of the Sea. Agenda 21 called for the integrated management and sustainable development of coastal areas, including exclusive economic zones; marine environmental protection; the sustainable use and conservation of marine living resources; addressing critical uncertainties for the management of the marine environment and climate change; strengthening international cooperation and coordination; and the sustainable development of small islands. It identified small island developing States as a special case for both environment and development, given their vulnerability to global warming and sealevel rise, as well as their degree of biodiversity. The Conference called for a global conference on the sustainable development of island States and for an intergovernmental conference on straddling and highly migratory fish stocks.

To protect the quality and supply of freshwater resources, the Conference proposed the following programme areas: integrated water resources development and management; water resources assessment; protection of water resources, water quality and aquatic ecosystems; drinking-water supply and sanitation; water and sustainable urban development; water for sustainable food production and rural development; and impacts of climate change on water resources.

In relation to promoting sustainable agriculture and rural development, the Conference stated that by the year 2025, 83 per cent of the expected global population of 8.5 billion would be living in developing countries. Major adjustments were needed in agricultural, environmental and macroeconomic policy to create sustainable agriculture and rural development. Agenda 21 included the following programme areas, among others: agricultural policy review, planning and integrated programming; human resource development for sustainable agriculture; improving of farm production and farming systems through diversification of farm and non-farm employment and infrastructure development; land-resource planning information and education for agriculture; land conservation and rehabilitation; and water for food production and rural development.

Regarding the conservation of biological diversity, the Conference observed that the planet's essential goods and services depended on the variety and variability of genes, species, populations and ecosystems. In its view, the current decline in biodiversity was largely the result of human activity and represented a serious threat to human development. Agenda 21 sought to improve the conservation of biological diversity and the sustainable use of biological resources, and to support the Convention on Biological Diversity.

The Conference considered the environmentally sound management of toxic chemicals. It proposed six programme areas: expanding international assessment of chemical risks; harmonization of classification and labelling of chemicals; information exchange on toxic chemicals and chemical risks; establishment of risk-reduction programmes; strengthening of national capacities for management of chemicals; and prevention of illegal international traffic in toxic and dangerous products.

With respect to hazardous wastes, countries were urged to ratify the 1989 Basel Convention on the Control of Transboundary Movements of Hazardous Wastes and Their Disposal and the 1991 Bamako Convention on the Ban of the Import of All Forms of Hazardous Wastes into Africa and the Control of Transboundary Movements of Such Wastes Generated in Africa.

For safe and environmentally sound management of radioactive wastes, the Conference said that States, in cooperation with international organizations, should limit the generation of such wastes; support efforts within the International Atomic Energy Agency to develop radioactive-waste safety standards or guidelines and codes of practice; and promote safe storage, transportation and disposal of radioactive wastes, and proper planning of their management, including emergency procedures.

Strengthening the role of major groups

The third section of Agenda 21 dealt with strengthening the role of various groups in implementing its objectives and policies. The commitment and involvement of all social groups was seen as critical to the success of the programmes. Among the groups addressed were women, children and youth, indigenous people, NGOs, local authorities, workers and trade unions, business and industry, the scientific and technological community, and farmers.

Means of implementation

The fourth and final section of Agenda 21 discussed means of financing its programmes. The Conference secretariat estimated that the average cost of implementing Agenda 21 in developing countries between 1993 and 2000 would exceed $600 billion per year, including $125 billion on grant or concessional terms from the international community.

The Conference stated that for developing countries, official development assistance (ODA) was a main source of external funding; substantial new funding would be required. Developed countries reaffirmed their commitment to reach the target of 0.7 per cent of gross national product for ODA. All available funding sources would be used, including multilateral development banks, the Global Environment Facility, specialized agencies and other United Nations bodies, multilateral institutions, bilateral assistance programmes, debt relief and private funding.

. . . The Conference recommended the creation of a high-level Commission on Sustainable Development to ensure effective follow-up. The Commission, which would report to the Council, would enhance international cooperation, examine progress in implementing Agenda 21 at the national, regional and international levels, provide for the active involvement of organs, programmes and organizations of the United Nations system, international financial institutions and other intergovernmental organizations, and encourage the participation of NGOs.

Statement of Principles on forests

The Non-legally Binding Authoritative Statement of Principles for a Global Consensus on the Management, Conservation and Sustainable Development of All Types of Forests declared that States had the sovereign right to utilize, manage and develop their forests, including the right to convert them to other uses, in accordance with their own development needs and level of socio-economic development. Governments were urged to manage their forest resources and lands so as to meet the social, economic, ecological, cultural and spiritual needs of current and future generations for wood, water, food, fodder, medicine, fuel, shelter, employment, recreation, wildlife habitats, landscape diversity, carbon reservoirs and other forest products.

The Statement called on Governments to recognize that forests played a vital role in protecting fragile ecosystems and water resources, were sources of genetic material for biotechnology products and met energy requirements. In addition, all countries, notably developed countries, were urged to take action towards reforestation, afforestation and forest conservation.

Representative or unique examples of forests that were ecologically viable should be protected, while access to biological resources, including genetic material, should be provided with due regard for the sovereign rights of the countries where the forests were located.

GENERAL ASSEMBLY ACTION

. . .

The Assembly, by resolution 47/189, decided to convene a global conference on the sustainable development of small island developing States, as called for in Agenda 21.

(YUN 1992, pp. 670-75)

The Global Conference on the Sustainable Development of Small Island Developing States was held at Bridgetown, Barbados, from 25 April to 6 May 1994.

Human settlements

Issues relating to human settlements first received global attention at the 1972 United Nations Conference on the Human Environment (Stockholm, 5-16 June). In its Declaration, the Conference stated that rational planning, as a means of reconciling any conflict between the needs of development and the need to protect the environment, should be applied to human settlements and urbanization to avoid the adverse effects on the environment. The Action Plan also adopted by the Conference contained recommendations concerning the planning and management of human settlements. Later that year, the General Assembly, accepting the recommendations of the Stockholm Conference (resolution 2998 (XXVII)), suggested that development assistance agencies should give priority to requests from Governments for assistance in housing and human settlements, and the World Bank should provide funds in

this sector. It endorsed the creation of an international fund or financial institution to provide seed capital and technical assistance for housing and the environmental improvement of human settlements. This led to the establishment in 1974 by the General Assembly (resolution 3327(XXIX)) of the United Nations Habitat and Human Settlements Foundation, designed to strengthen national environment programmes relating to human settlements. The Assembly in 1972 had also decided to hold a Conference-Exposition on Human Settlements.

Habitat: UN Conference on Human Settlements

Convened by the United Nations General Assembly, Habitat: United Nations Conference on Human Settlements met in Vancouver, Canada, from 31 May to 11 June 1976. The purpose of the Conference was to set out guidelines for national and international action to improve the living places of people throughout the world.

. . .

On 11 June 1976, the Conference adopted a Declaration of Principles known as the Vancouver Declaration on Human Settlements, 1976, a set of 64 recommendations for action by Governments intended to assure the basic requirements of human habitation—shelter, clean water, sanitation and a decent physical environment, and the opportunity for cultural growth and the development of the individual—and five resolutions.

. . .

Declaration of principles

The 55-paragraph Vancouver Declaration was composed of a preamble, and three sections setting forth opportunities and solutions, general principles and guidelines for action.

By the preamble, the Conference, among other things, recognized that the circumstances of life for vast numbers of people in human settlements were unacceptable, particularly in the developing countries, and that, unless positive and concrete action was taken, those conditions were likely to be further aggravated.

As factors aggravating the problem, the preamble cited: inequitable economic growth; social, economic, ecological and environmental deterioration; a world population growth, expected to double the population within 25 years; uncontrolled urbanization; rural backwardness and dispersion; and involuntary migration, politically, racially and economically motivated, relocation and expulsion of people from their national homelands.

By the section on opportunities and solutions, the Conference pointed out the need for increased activity by Governments and the international community aimed at mobilization of economic resources, institutional changes and international solidarity. Such a mobilization would include the adoption of bold, meaningful and effective human settlement policies and spatial planning strategies realistically adapted to local conditions, and the creation of more livable, attractive and efficient settlements which would recognize the heritage and culture of people and the special needs of disadvantaged groups, especially children, women and the infirm, in order to ensure the provision of health services, education, food and employment within a framework of social justice. Human settlements, it was noted, had to be seen as an instrument and object of development; the goals of settlement policies were inseparable from the goals of every sector of social and economic life, and the solutions to these problems of human settlements had therefore to be conceived as an integral part of the development process of individual nations and the world community.

The Conference then proclaimed a series of general principles, among which were the following.

The improvement of the quality of life of human beings was the first and most important objective of every human settlement policy; these policies must facilitate the rapid and continuous improvement in the quality of life of all people, beginning with the satisfaction of the basic needs of food, shelter, clean water, employment, health, education, training and social security, without any form of discrimination. Priority was to be given to the needs of the most disadvantaged people.

Human dignity and the exercise of free choice consistent with over-all public welfare were basic rights which must be assured in every society, and it was therefore the duty of all people and Governments to join the struggle against colonialism, foreign aggression and occupation, domination, *apartheid* and all forms of racism and racial discrimination referred to in the resolutions as adopted by the General Assembly.

The establishment of settlements in territories occupied by force was illegal and condemned by the international community; action remained to be taken against the establishment of such settlements.

The right of free movement and the right of each individual to choose the place of settlement within the domain of his own country should be recognized and safeguarded.

Every State had the sovereign right to choose its economic, political, social and cultural system, without interference, coercion or external threat, and the right to exercise full and permanent sovereignty over its wealth, natural resources and economic activities.

Land was one of the fundamental elements in human settlements and every State had the right to maintain under public control the use, possession, disposal and reservation of land; every State had the right to plan and regulate use of land in such a way that the growth of population centres, both urban and rural, was based on a comprehensive land-use plan.

Nations must avoid the pollution of the biosphere and the oceans and should join in the effort to end irrational exploitation of environmental resources. The waste and misuse of resources in war should be prevented.

. . .

The highest priority should be given to homeless persons displaced by natural or man-made catastrophes, and especially by the act of foreign aggression. In the latter case, all countries had the duty to cooperate to guarantee that the parties involved allowed the return of displaced persons to their homes to give them the right to possess their properties without interference.

Historical settlements, monuments and other national heritage items were to be safeguarded against aggression or abuse by an occupying power.

Also, every State had the right to rule and exercise effective control over foreign investments, including the transnational corporations, which affected the human settlements programmes.

All countries were to create conditions making possible the full integration of women and youth in political, economic and social activities, particularly in relation to human settlement proposals, on the basis of equal rights.

. . .

In the section setting out guidelines for action, the Conference among other things stressed that national and international efforts should give priority to improving the rural habitat and to reducing the disparities between rural and urban areas. Human settlements policies and programmes, it stated, should strive for progressive minimum standards for an acceptable quality of life and it drew attention to the detrimental effects of transposing standards and criteria that could only be attained by a minority of the population. Governments should promote programmes that would assist local authorities to participate to a greater degree in national development.

Another guideline enunciated by the Conference stated that land was an essential element in the development of both urban and rural settlements; hence, because of its limited supply the use and tenure of land should be subject to public control through appropriate legislative measures, including agrarian reform, that would facilitate the transfer of economic resources to the agricultural sector and the promotion of the agro-industrial effort.

Also, access should be granted, on more favourable terms, to modern technology, which should be adapted, as necessary, to the specific economic, social and ecological conditions and to the different stages of development of the developing countries. International, technical and financial cooperation by the developed countries with the developing countries must be conducted on the basis of respect for national sovereignty and national development plans and programmes and designed to solve problems relating to projects, under human settlement programmes, aimed at enhancing the quality of life.

Finally, since the resources of Governments were inadequate to meet all needs, the international community should provide the necessary financial and technical assistance, evolve appropriate institutional arrangements and seek new, effective ways to promote them. In the meantime, aid to developing countries must reach the percentage target set in the International Development Strategy for the Second United Nations Development Decade.

Recommendations for national action

The recommendations which the Habitat Conference addressed to Governments concerned action to be taken at the national level to improve human settlements. They were divided into six categories: settlement policies and strategies; settlement planning; shelter, infrastructure and services; land; public participation; and institutions and management.

(YUN 1976, pp. 441-44)

Following up on other recommendations of the Vancouver Conference, the Economic and Social Council established in 1977 the Commission on Human Settlements and the Assembly set up the United Nations Centre for Human Settlements (Habitat) at Nairobi to deal with settlement policies, strategies and planning; shelter infrastructure and services; and land-use policy. The pursuit of the objectives of the Vancouver Declaration was further advanced in 1987 with the observance by the international community of International Year of Shelter for the Homeless, proclaimed by the Assembly in 1982, to improve the shelter and neighbourhoods of the poor and disadvantaged. The Year had stimulated improvements in shelter and services in many countries, and created a strong awareness of the problem of homelessness and inadequate shelter and the need for remedial action.

The Assembly, on the recommendation of the Commission on Human Settlements as a follow-up to the Year, decided that a Global Strategy for Shelter to the Year 2000 should be formulated to stimulate measures that would facilitate adequate shelter for all by the year 2000, including a plan of action for its implementation, monitoring and evaluation.

Global Strategy for Shelter to the Year 2000

In response to a 1987 General Assembly resolution, the UNCHS Executive Director submitted in February 1988 to the Commission on Human Settlements a report on a Global Strategy for Shelter to the Year 2000. The report had four parts: the first discussed the objectives, rationale and general principles of the Strategy; the second, the reorganization of the shelter sector, mobilization and allocation of financial resources, and shelter production and improvement; the third, guidelines for international action; and the fourth, a plan of

action and a timetable for the first phase. The report concluded that the global shelter situation was worsening and that anxiety about it was being expressed not only with regard to its current effects on people but in relation to the future implications for society of the unfavourable supply trend.

To achieve the Strategy's objectives, emphasis would have to be placed on action in the areas of macro-economic policy, institutional coordination, legislation and regulation, data collection and analysis, financial resources and mechanisms for shelter and infrastructure, land, infrastructural development, and building materials and technology.

Implementing the Strategy, Member States would review their shelter policies in the light of the Strategy; formulate national strategies for shelter for all; decide on specific targets; develop plans of action to implement their strategies; and report to the Commission on progress. The plan of action also set forth activities to be carried out by the Commission, the General Assembly, UNCHS, and international and intergovernmental agencies and NGOs.

On 12 April, the Commission adopted the report of the UNCHS Executive Director as an addendum to the report on its eleventh session, and recommended to the General Assembly the adoption of a draft resolution.

(YUN 1988, p. 478)

Conference on human settlements

In September 1992, in response to a General Assembly request, the Secretary-General submitted a report on a proposed United Nations conference on human settlements (Habitat II). The report evaluated the state of human settlements around the world and progress since the 1976 human settlements conference (Vancouver, Canada). It reviewed the objectives, scope and content of the proposed Habitat II and discussed its preparation and financial requirements.

By way of background to the call for Habitat II, the Secretary-General noted that the enormous strides made since 1976 towards solving the shelter problem had not been enough to arrest the deterioration of living conditions in many countries, where rapid urbanization, increasing landlessness and declining income yields from agriculture had led to increasing poverty in both urban and rural areas. The world's population was expanding by about one billion people per decade, with 94.1 per cent of this growth in the current decade in developing countries. Cities in the developing world were expected to absorb some 90 per cent of that population growth but already faced enormous backlogs in the availability of housing, infrastructure and services, and were confronted with overcrowded transportation systems, insufficient water supply, deteriorating sanitation and environmental pollution. One third of the urban population in those countries were living in slums or squatter settlements. The lack of access to modern amenities, the growing scarcity of affordable building materials, and the inadequacy of domestic energy sources were creating equally dramatic conditions for the rural poor. The Secretary-General said the health consequences of the situation were both tragic and appalling, with some 2.5 billion people suffering from ailments related to contaminated water and the lack of sanitation. He further noted that the external debt of developing countries and structural adjustment programmes aimed at strengthening their economies had in fact undermined prospects for improved living conditions in many countries. He also noted that conventional econometric models had failed to measure correctly the economic returns on investments in human settlements which had been given low priority in the mistaken belief that they were "social welfare".

Since Habitat I, Governments had made substantial advances in improving living conditions, and within the United Nations, the human settlements programme had shown considerable gains, he said. Such progress was accompanied by an evolution in thinking with respect to the problems of human settlements development and their solutions. He noted that the 1992 United Nations Conference on Environment and Development (UNCED) had decided to address human settlements as a substantive framework for sustainable development and that programme areas, such as atmosphere, land, coastal areas, freshwater and waste management should include the human settlements dimension.

Referring to the objectives of Habitat II, the Secretary-General recommended that the conference formulate a global plan of action to arrest the deterioration of living conditions and facilitate their improvement, recognizing that the emphasis in solutions to the shelter problem had shifted in the past two decades from direct governmental involvement to government support for private-sector initiatives and the participation of communities and NGOs. He made recommendations on a variety of issues, including the role of Government and NGOs; the mobilization of financial resources; capacity-building and human resources development; sustainable development; new technologies; communications; transportation; water resources; waste management; energy; and information.

GENERAL ASSEMBLY ACTION

On 22 December 1992, the Assembly, on the recommendation of the Second Committee, adopted without vote resolution 47/180.

United Nations Conference on Human Settlements (Habitat II)

The General Assembly,

. . .

Having considered the report of the Secretary-General on a United Nations conference on human settlements (Habitat II),

1. *Decides* to convene the United Nations Conference on Human Settlements (Habitat II) from 3 to 14 June 1996, at the highest possible level of participation;

2. *Also decides* that the Conference, in addressing human settlements issues in the context of sustainable development, shall have the following objectives:

(a) In the long term, to arrest the deterioration of global human settlements conditions and ultimately create conditions for achieving improvements in the living environment of all people on a sustainable basis, with special attention to the needs and contributions of women and vulnerable social groups whose quality of life and participation in development have been hampered by exclusion and inequality, which affect the poor in general;

(b) To adopt a general statement of principles and commitments and formulate a related global plan of action suitable for guiding national and international efforts through the first two decades of the next century;

. . .

(YUN 1992, pp. 702-703)

*" . . . to promote social progress
and better standards of life in larger freedom "*

Chapter III

The expanding social agenda

The promotion of social progress and better standards of life has been one of the least publicized though no less important purposes of the United Nations over the past half century. To achieve lasting global peace and security and prosperity, economic and social development have been an integral part of United Nations activities at both regional and national levels. Over the years, the United Nations has expanded to include social agenda issues relating to women, children, youth, the aged, health, food and nutrition, human resources, social and cultural development, refugees and displaced persons, international drug control and poverty.

The United Nations has recognized the imperative to correct the inequalities affecting women in social advancement and to enhance their participation in economic and social development. Towards this end, it adopted the 1979 Convention on the Elimination of All Forms of Discrimination against Women and the 1993 Declaration on the Elimination of Violence against Women. A 1985 World Conference adopted the Nairobi Forward-looking Strategies for the Advancement of Women to the year 2000, and preparations have continued for the Fourth World Conference on Women, to be held in Beijing in September 1995 to review and appraise progress in implementing the Strategies.

In 1946, the United Nations Children's Fund (UNICEF) was established to provide a framework for advocacy on behalf of children and to increase decision-making and public awareness of their special needs. The protection of children's rights has remained a major concern of the United Nations and led to the adoption of the 1989 Convention on the Rights of the Child. The United Nations in 1990 held a World Summit for Children, which adopted the World Declaration on the Survival, Protection and Development of Children and a Plan of Action for its implementation.

The end of the cold war resulted in renewed focus on the social agenda. In March 1995, heads of State and Government assembled at Copenhagen, Denmark, for the World Summit for Social Development and endorsed a Declaration and a Programme of Action that addressed for the first time, collectively and at the highest level, core issues that would determine the quality of human life into the twenty-first century.

Advancement of women

The Charter of the United Nations in its Preamble reaffirmed faith "in the equal rights of men and women". In 1946, the General Assembly recognized that Member States had not granted to women political rights equal to those granted to men and recommended that they adopt measures to fulfil the purposes and aims of the Charter by granting to women the same political rights as men. Further consideration of women's issues was undertaken by the Commission on the Status of Women, established in 1946 as a functional commission of the Economic and Social Council. From its inception, the Commission was concerned with issues such as the abolition of political inequality, participation of women in government, discrimination against women in respect to nationality, domicile, marriage and divorce, educational opportunities for women, property rights and the right to act as guardians. As time progressed this agenda was expanded to include, among others, equal pay for equal work for men and women, economic opportunities for women, and protection of women's rights in emergency and armed conflict.

The General Assembly in 1952 adopted the Convention on the Political Rights of Women, recognizing their rights to vote, to contest elections, to hold political office and to exercise political functions. United Nations efforts at further advancing the status of women were enhanced by the adoption in 1967 of the Declaration on the Elimination of Discrimination against Women, which envisaged eliminating discrimination in such areas as protection under law, marriage, nationality and political rights.

International Women's Year

Further international focus on women's issues was enhanced in 1972 when the General Assembly proclaimed 1975 the International Women's Year to be devoted to intensifying action to promote equality between men and women, to increase women's contribution to national and international development, and to ensure the full realization of the rights of women and their advancement on the basis of the 1967 Declaration. The main event of the Year was the holding of the World Conference of the International Women's Year (Mexico City, 19 June to 2 July 1975). The Conference adopted the Declaration of Mexico on the Equality of Women and Their Contribution to Development and Peace and a World Plan of Action for the Implementation of the Objectives of the International Women's Year, as well as 35 resolutions on the Year's objectives. By the Declaration, the Conference expressed its awareness that the problems of women, who constituted half of the world's population, were the problems of society as a whole, and that changes in the economic, political and social situation of women had to become part of efforts to transform structures and attitudes that hindered satisfaction of their needs. The Declaration included 30 principles stating the need for measures to advance women's rights and linking that advancement with economic and political objectives. The World Plan consisted of recommendations for national and international action, including economic, legal, social, administrative and educational measures.

In December 1975, the General Assembly endorsed the results of the Conference and proclaimed a United Nations Decade for Women (1976-1985). It also decided to convene a second world conference in 1980.

UN Decade for Women

In 1976, the Commission on the Status of Women adopted a Programme for the United Nations Decade for Women: Equality, Development and Peace (1976-1985). The main objectives of the Programme were the formulation and implementation of international and national standards to eliminate discrimination against women, the integration of women in development, and the increased involvement of women in political life and in international cooperation and the maintenance of peace.

Specific action was identified to achieve those objectives, including elaboration of a convention on the elimination of discrimination against women, public information to advise women of their rights, and regional and global programmes for the integration of women in development. The Programme also outlined measures to increase women's participation in political life and decision-making at all levels. To appraise progress, the Programme called for a review of the World Plan of Action adopted at the 1975 International Women's Year Conference as part of the review process of the International Development Strategy for the Second United Nations Development Decade (the 1970s). The General Assembly approved the Programme in December (resolution 31/136).

At mid-Decade, the World Conference of the United Nations Decade for Women was held (Copenhagen, Denmark, 14-30 July 1980). This Conference evaluated progress made in implementing the 1975 Plan of Action and adopted a Programme of Action for the second half of the Decade aimed at promoting the attainment of equality, development and peace, with special emphasis on employment, health and education. It called for the prohibition of child marriage and included measures to combat the traffic of women and exploitation of prostitution, equal rights in education, equal remuneration with men, and the right to paid maternity leave and guarantee of returning to former employment.

Convention on the elimination of discrimination against women

A major development of the United Nations Decade for Women was the adoption in 1979 of the Convention on the Elimination of All Forms of Discrimination against Women, which concretized and expanded into an international instrument the principles elaborated in the 1967 Declaration on the Elimination of Discrimination against Women.

The Convention consisted of a preamble and 30 articles, divided into six untitled parts. By the preamble, the States parties to the Convention would note various international instruments reaffirming the principle of equal rights of men and women, despite which extensive discrimination against women continued to exist. Convinced that the establishment of the new international economic order based on equity and justice would contribute significantly towards promotion of equality between the sexes, they would emphasize that the eradication of *apartheid*, racism, racial discrimination, colonialism, neo-colonialism, aggression, foreign occupation and domination, and interference in the internal affairs of States was essential to the full enjoyment of men's and women's rights.

States parties would affirm that the strengthening of international peace and security, the relaxation of international tension, mutual co-operation among all States, general and complete disarmament, in particular nuclear disarmament under strict and effective international control, the affirmation of the principles of justice, equality and mutual benefit in inter-State relations and the realization of the right of peoples under alien and colonial domination and foreign occupation to self-determination and independence, as well as respect for national sovereignty and territorial integrity, would promote social progress and development and contribute to the attainment of full equality between men and women. Bearing in mind the great contribution of women to the welfare of the family and to the development of society, and aware that women's role in procreation should not be a basis for discrimination and that a change in the traditional role of men as well as the role of women in society and in the family was needed to achieve full equality, the States parties would express their determination to implement the principles set forth in the 1967 Declaration on the Elimination of Discrimination against Women and adopt measures needed to eliminate such discrimination in all its forms and manifestations.

Discrimination against women was defined in article 1 and condemned under article 2; States parties would agree to pursue policies to eliminate it without delay, undertaking to ensure realization of the principle of equality of men and women through laws and other means, to adopt legislation to prohibit such discrimination, to establish legal protection of women's rights on an equal basis with men and ensure them against discriminatory acts, to take appropriate measures, including legislation, to modify or abolish existing laws, regulations, customs and practices that constituted discrimination against women and to repeal all national penal provisions which discriminated against women.

By article 3, States parties would take all appropriate measures, including legislation, to ensure women full development and advancement to guarantee them human rights and freedoms on a basis of equality with men. Temporary special measures adopted by States parties aimed at accelerating equality between men and women and protecting maternity were not to be considered discriminatory, according to article 4. By article 5, appropriate measures would be taken to modify social and cultural patterns of conduct in order to eliminate prejudices and practices based on the idea of inferiority or superiority of either of the sexes or on stereotyped roles, and to ensure that family education included a proper understanding of maternity as a social function and a recognition of the common responsibility of men and women in the upbringing and development of their children, it being understood that the interest of the children was the primordial consideration. Article 6 called for legislation and other measures to suppress all forms of traffic in women and exploitation of prostitution of women.

Article 7, the first of three articles of part II, provided for women's right to full political and public life on equal terms with men; by article 8, their right to represent their Governments at the international level and to participate in the work of international organizations would be ensured. By article 9, women were to be granted equal rights with men in matters relating to nationality and to the nationality of their children.

Article 10, the first of part III, provided for the elimination of discrimination against women to ensure them equal rights with men in the field of education. Article 11 was to ensure the same rights in employment, including benefits, social security and safe working conditions; measures were to be taken to prevent discrimination against women on the grounds of marriage or maternity, and relevant protective legislation was to be updated periodically in the light of technological knowledge.

Women were to be protected from discrimination in the field of health care under article 12, ensuring access to such services as those relating to family planning, pregnancy, confinement and postnatal care, free where necessary, and nutrition, and from discrimination in other areas of economic and social life by article 13, ensuring equal rights to family benefits, bank loans, mortgages and other forms of financial credit, and participation in recreational activities, sports and cultural life. Article 14 applied the provisions of the Convention to rural women.

Part IV contained two articles: article 15 was to ensure women equality with men before the law, and article 16 was to ensure the absence of discrimination in matters relating to marriage and family relations. Also by article 16, the betrothal and marriage of a child would have no legal effect, and action was to be taken to specify a minimum age for marriage and make marriage registration compulsory.

Article 17, of part V, provided for the establishment by States parties of a Committee on the Elimination of Discrimination against Women to consider progress made in the implementation of the Convention, with staff, facilities and emoluments for its members to be provided by the United Nations. By article 18, States parties would report to the Secretary-General on legislative, judicial, administrative and other measures adopted by them to give effect to the provisions of the Convention. Articles 19 to 22 dealt with the Committee's rules of procedure, officers, meetings, reports (which were to be transmitted to the Commission on the Status of Women for its information), and representation of specialized agencies at meetings.

The first article of part VI, article 23, indicated that the Convention's provisions should not supersede any State-party legislation or other convention or agreement in force whose terms were more conducive to the achievement of equality between men and women. Parties undertook by article 24 to adopt all necessary national measures aimed at achieving the full realization of the rights recognized in the Convention.

Articles 25 to 30 contained technical provisions for the operation of the Convention, including its signatories, the depositary (the Secretary-General), ratification, accession, revision, entry into force (30 days after deposit of the twentieth instrument of ratification or accession), reservations, settlement of disputes concerning interpretation or application, and official languages.

(YUN 1979, pp. 889-90)

At the end of 1993, 130 States were parties to the Convention.

Nairobi Conference on the Decade for Women

The World Conference to Review and Appraise the Achievements of the United Nations Decade for Women: Equality, Development and Peace, was held at Nairobi, Kenya, in July 1985. The Conference assessed progress made towards improving the situation of women during the Decade (1976-1985) which was proclaimed by the General Assembly in 1975—International Women's Year.

On 26 July, the Conference adopted the Nairobi Forward-looking Strategies for the Advancement of Women. It analysed economic, social and political factors and trends expected to have a bearing on the advancement of women over the next 15 years. It stated that the measures proposed were designed for immediate action, with monitoring and evaluation every five years. Each country would have the option to set its own priorities, based on its own development policies and resource capacities. The mode of implementation would vary according to each country's political process and administrative capabilities.

The Conference recommended measures for implementing the basic strategies for equality at the national level in the following areas: constitutional and legal steps; equality in social participation; and equality in political participation and decision-making. Specific measures with regard to development were recommended in the fields of employment; health; education; food, water and agriculture; industry; trade and commercial services; science and technology; communications; housing, settlement, community development and transport; energy; environment; and social services. The chapter on strategies for peace made particular reference to women and children under apartheid, Palestinian women and children, and women in areas affected by armed conflicts, foreign intervention and threats to peace. National measures with regard to peace were recommended under the headings of women's participation in efforts for peace and education for peace.

The Conference dealt with areas of special concern and addressed the situation of women in areas affected by drought; urban poor women; elderly women; young women; abused women; destitute women; women victims of trafficking and involuntary prostitution; women deprived of traditional means of livelihood; women as sole supporters of families; physically and mentally disabled women; women in detention and subject to penal law; refugee and displaced women and children; migrant women; and minority and indigenous women.

Finally, the Conference recommended measures of international and regional co-operation to advance the status of women in such areas as monitoring the implementation of the Forward-looking Strategies; technical cooperation, training and advisory services; institutional coordination; research and policy analysis; participation of women in activities at the international and regional levels and in decision-making; and information dissemination.

In December 1985, the General Assembly (resolution 40/108) endorsed the Nairobi Forward-looking Strategies.

In 1990, the United Nations conducted its first review and appraisal of the implementation of the Strategies, and the Economic and Social Council (resolution 1990/15) called for an improved pace in implementation in the crucial last decade of the twentieth century.

Fourth World Conference

The Fourth World Conference on Women was scheduled to be held in Beijing in September 1995. The Conference would review and appraise progress achieved in implementing the Nairobi Strategies and identify measures to ensure achievement of their objectives during the last five years of the twentieth century.

In 1993, the Secretary-General submitted to the Commission on the Status of Women a draft Platform for Action for consideration by the Conference. The draft comprised sections dealing with a diagnosis of the current situation of the world's women; an analytical statement of the most important obstacles to the advancement of women; key issues and basic needs, linking the status of women to global changes; specific action for reaching goals in key areas; and a statement on an implementation mechanism.

In July 1993, the Economic and Social Council (resolution 1993/16) endorsed a system-wide medium-term plan for the advancement of women for the period 1996-2001. The plan covered action in the areas of discrimination, human resource development, peace and conflict resolution and decision-making; improving international action through the development of statistics and technical cooperation; and action relating to women in development and strengthening national machineries for the advancement of women.

Declaration on the Elimination of Violence against Women

One of the major concerns of the United Nations in the area of women's issues was that of violence against women. The Nairobi Forward-looking Strategies for the Advancement of Women had set out measures to combat such violence. Notwithstanding the principles enshrined in several international instruments to protect women against violence, the Economic and Social Council in 1990 (resolution 1990/15) recognized that such violence was pervasive and had to be matched by urgent and effective steps to eliminate its incidence. In 1991 (resolution 1991/18), the Council recommended the development of an international instrument to address explicitly the issue of violence against women.

An expert group meeting in 1991 prepared the draft Declaration on the Elimination of Violence against Women, which was adopted by the Commission on the Status of Women in 1993. The General Assembly adopted the Declaration in December (resolution 48/104).

The Declaration, in its six articles, defined violence against women to include physical, sexual and psychological violence in all forms, as well as sexual harassment and intimidation, trafficking in women and forced prostitution. It called on States to: condemn such violence and not invoke any custom, tradition or religious consideration to avoid their obligations with respect to its elimination; ratify the 1979 Convention on the Elimination of All Forms of Discrimination against Women; refrain from engaging in violence against women; exercise diligence to prevent, investigate and punish such acts; develop penal, civil, labour and administrative sanctions in domestic legislation to punish and redress wrongs caused to women; develop national plans to promote the protection of women against any form of violence; and adopt measures, especially in the field of education, to modify the social and cultural patterns of conduct of men and women and to eliminate prejudices. It also called on United Nations organs and specialized agencies to contribute to the recognition and realization of the rights and principles contained in the Declaration.

At its January-March 1994 session, the Commission on Human Rights appointed a Special Rapporteur on the Elimination of Violence against Women.

Children

UNICEF

The United Nations International Children's Emergency Fund was created in 1946 for the benefit of children and adolescents of countries which were victims of aggression, those receiving assistance from the United Nations Relief and Rehabilitation Administration, and for child health purposes generally. By 1953, UNICEF's work had shifted from Europe to developing countries, particularly in Africa, the eastern Mediterranean and Latin America and from emergency to long-range programmes for economic and social development. Its activities included assistance in maternal and child welfare, mass health and child nutrition.

In 1976, UNICEF adopted a community-based strategy to meet the basic needs of the millions of children in the developing world. This strategy was given further impetus by the 1978 International Conference on Primary Health Care (Alma-Ata, USSR (now Kazakhstan)), which endorsed the goal of "health for all" by the year 2000. In 1979, the United Nations celebrated the International Year of the Child and the General Assembly designated UNICEF as its lead agency for the concerns of children worldwide.

UNICEF provides a framework for advocacy on behalf of children and works to increase both decision-making and public awareness of their special needs. It helps to plan and design services, delivers supplies and equipment, and provides funds for training purposes.

Rights of the child

Further United Nations initiatives in support of children's issues resulted in the 1959 Declaration on the Rights of the Child and the 1989 Convention on the Rights of the Child.

Declaration on the Rights of the Child

In 1950, a draft preamble and principles of a declaration on the rights of the child were prepared by the Social Commission of the Economic and Social Council. The Commission expressed the view that although there was a close relationship between the draft and the 1948 Universal Declaration of Human Rights, the special needs of the child justified a separate instrument. In 1959, the Commission on Human Rights submitted to the Council a revised draft Declaration on the Rights of the Child, which was adopted by the General Assembly on 20 November (resolution 1386(XIV)) and contained 10 principles which were summarized as follows:

The child without any exception whatsoever and without discrimination shall enjoy all the rights set forth in the Declaration (Principle 1); he shall enjoy special protection and be given opportunities and facilities to enable him to develop in a healthy and normal manner and in conditions of freedom and dignity (Principle 2); he shall be entitled to have a name and a nationality from birth (Principle 3); he shall enjoy the benefits of social security, including adequate nutrition, housing, recreation and medical services (Principle 4); he shall be given special treatment, education and care, if handicapped (Principle 5); he shall grow up in an atmosphere of affection and security and, wherever possible, in the care of and under the responsibility of his parents (Principle 6); he shall be entitled to receive education and to have full opportunity for play and recreation (Principle 7); he shall be among the first to receive protection and relief in time of disaster (Principle 8); he shall be protected against all forms of neglect, cruelty and exploitation (Principle 9); he shall be protected from practices which may foster discrimination, and be brought up in a spirit of understanding, tolerance, friendship among peoples, peace and universal brotherhood (Principle 10).

[YUN 1959, p. 194]

Convention on the Rights of the Child

In 1978, Poland submitted to the Commission on Human Rights a draft convention on the rights of the child, based on the principles of the 1959 Declaration. The Commission requested the Secretary-General to transmit the draft to Member States, specialized agencies and regional organizations for their views and suggestions. In December 1978, the General Assembly requested the Commission to organize its work on the draft convention so that it might be ready for adoption during the 1979 International Year of the Child. The Commission in March 1989 recommended the draft convention for adoption by the Assembly. The draft was endorsed by the Economic and Social Council (resolution 1989/79) and, in November 1989, the General Assembly (resolution 44/25) adopted the Convention on the Rights of the Child.

The Convention entered into force on 2 September 1990. In 1991, the first Meeting of the States Parties to the Convention (New York, 27 February–1 March) established the Committee on the Rights of the Child, provided for under the Convention, to examine progress made by States parties in realizing the obligations undertaken.

By September 1994, there were 159 parties to the Convention.

1990 World Summit for Children

The World Summit for Children was convened in New York on 30 September 1990, with the participation of 71 heads of State and Government. The Summit adopted the World Declaration on the Survival, Protection and Development of Children and the Plan of Action for Implementing the World Declaration in the 1990s.

By that Declaration, the world leaders committed themselves to a 10-point programme to protect the rights of children and improve their lives through promoting the earliest possible ratification and implementation of the Convention on the Rights of the Child; enhancing children's health, lowering infant and child mortality and promoting pre-natal care, provision of clean water for children and universal access to sanitation; eradicating hunger, malnutrition and famine; strengthening the role and status of women and promoting responsible family planning, child spacing, breast-feeding and safe motherhood; promoting the role of the family in providing for children; reducing illiteracy and providing educational opportunities for children; ameliorating the plight of children in especially difficult circumstances; protecting children during armed conflicts; protecting the environment for the benefit of children; and alleviating poverty to improve children's welfare.

The Plan of Action outlined specific activities to be undertaken under the 10-point programme as well as follow-up actions and monitoring mechanisms at the national and international levels, and set major goals for child survival, development and protection in the 1990s. The goals, to be achieved by the year 2000, included reduction of infant and under-five child mortality rates by one third, or to 50 and 70 per 1,000 live births; reduction of maternal mortality rates and of severe and moderate malnutrition among children under five by one half; universal access to safe drinking water and to sanitary means of excreta disposal; universal access to basic education and completion of primary education by at least 80 per cent of primary school age children; reduction of the adult illiteracy rate by at least one half, with emphasis on female literacy; and protection of children in especially difficult circumstances, particularly in situations of armed conflicts.

On 1 October 1990, the World Declaration and the Plan of Action were presented to the President of the General Assembly at a special ceremony during an Assembly plenary meeting.

World Summit for Social Development

The General Assembly, in 1992, decided to convene a World Summit for Social Development to address poverty, social integration and employment, a world-wide commitment to put the needs of people at the centre of development and international cooperation, and the interaction between the social function of the State, market responses to social demands and the imperatives of sustainable development.

The Summit, which was held in March 1995 at Copenhagen, Denmark, adopted the Copenhagen Declaration and Plan of Action. Some 117 heads of State or Government pledged commitments and recommended measures at the national and international levels to eliminate inequalities within and among countries which threaten the security of nations and hamper economic development. The Declaration contained 10 commitments, to be the basis for launching a global drive for social progress and development. The world leaders pledged, among others, to accelerate the socio-economic development of Africa and the least developed countries; to ensure that structural adjustment programmes should include social-development goals; and to strive for a significant increase and/or more efficient utilization of the resources allocated to social development in order to achieve the goals of the Summit. The Declaration also called for reforms in structural adjustment programmes and stressed the importance of productive employment as central elements of development.

The Programme of Action identified measures to promote ''an enabling environment for social development'' including effective, development-oriented and durable solutions to the external debt problems of developing countries, particularly in Africa; an increase in official development assistance (ODA) with an agreed target of 0.7 per cent of gross national product; placing of Governments' emphasis on the expansion of productive employment at the centre of sustainable development strategies and economic and social policies; and safeguarding and promoting respect for basic workers' rights. Recognizing that the implementation of the recommendations and commitments of the Summit would require substantial new and additional resources, world leaders were urged to increase the availability of resources and to agree on a ''mutual commitment between developed and developing partners to allocate, on average, 20 per cent of ODA and 20 per cent of the national budget, respectively, to basic social programmes''.

''the United Nations shall promote: (a) higher standards of living, full employment, and conditions of economic and social progress and development; (b) solutions of international economic, social, health, and related problems; and international cultural and educational cooperation; . . . The various specialized agencies, established by intergovernmental agreement and having wide international responsibilities . . . in economic, social, cultural, educational, health, and related fields, shall be brought into relationship with the United Nations ''

Chapter IV

Intergovernmental organizations related to the United Nations

Over the past 50 years, much of the United Nations work aimed at improving the social and economic conditions of people around the world has been carried out by the specialized agencies and other intergovernmental organizations within the United Nations system.

Some of these organizations existed prior to the creation of the United Nations in 1945. These were the International Telecommunication Union (ITU), established in 1865, the Universal Postal Union (UPU), established in 1874, and the International Labour Organisation (ILO), established in 1919 as an autonomous institution associated with the League of Nations. Before the formal establishment of the United Nations, a number of United Nations conferences were held to discuss certain special problems. As a result of these conferences, a number of specialized agencies were established, namely, the Food and Agriculture Organization of the United Nations (FAO), the United Nations Educational, Scientific and Cultural Organization (UNESCO), the United Nations Relief and Rehabilitation Administration, the International Monetary Fund (IMF), the International Bank for Reconstruction and Development (World Bank) and the International Civil Aviation Organization (ICAO). In 1946, the Economic and Social Council established a Committee on Negotiations with Specialized Agencies to enter into negotiations with those agencies already in existence and to submit preliminary agreements.

The agreements negotiated by the Council were subsequently approved by the General Assembly, thereby bringing into relationship with the United Nations by September 1948 ILO, FAO, UNESCO, ICAO, UPU, ITU, the World Bank and IMF. Similar agreements were subsequently reached with other agencies as they came into existence. The latest agency is the World Trade Organization, established in 1995 to take over the functions of the General Agreement on Tariffs and Trade (GATT).

The agencies were created as separate, autonomous organizations with their own membership, legislative and executive bodies, secretariats and budgets. They work with the United Nations and with each other through the coordinating machinery of the Economic and Social Council, to which they report annually in accordance with Article 64 of the Charter. Each specialized agency has agreed to consider any recommendation made to it by the United Nations and to report to the Organization on the action taken to give effect to any such recommendation. With regard to the World Bank and IMF, the United Nations has agreed to consult with them prior to making any recommendation. The activities of the organizations of the United Nations family are interlinked by the Administrative Committee on Coordination, a body chaired by the Secretary-

General of the United Nations and in which the heads of the special programmes and organs of the United Nations also participate.

As the programmes of the United Nations have expanded in recent years, the activities of these agencies have also proliferated in response to the new challenges in the social, economic and humanitarian spheres. The agencies publish annual reports containing detailed accounts of their operational and budgetary activities. Some agencies also maintain field offices worldwide to implement their activities.

International Atomic Energy Agency

The International Atomic Energy Agency (IAEA), which came into existence on 29 July 1957, serves as the world's central intergovernmental forum for scientific and technical cooperation in the field of the peaceful uses of nuclear energy. Its origin was contained in a proposal made to the General Assembly on 8 December 1953 by Harry S. Truman, President of the United States, suggesting the establishment of a world organization devoted exclusively to the peaceful uses of atomic energy. The general lines of that proposal were unanimously endorsed by the Assembly on 4 December 1954.

The main purposes of IAEA are to ''seek to accelerate and enlarge the contribution of atomic energy to peace, health and prosperity throughout the world'' and to ''ensure, so far as it is able, that assistance provided by it or at its request or under its supervision or control is not used in such a way as to further any military purposes''.

The IAEA policy-making organs are the Board of Governors and the General Conference. The Conference is composed of representatives of IAEA's 121 member States. The Board currently has 35 members, of which 13 are designated by the Board as being the most advanced in atomic energy technology in their regions, and 22 are elected by the General Conference.

The Agency provides technical assistance to member States in the development of self-sufficient nuclear science programmes. Almost half of its work focuses on programmes that can easily be applied in areas such as food and agriculture, health, industry, hydrology and environmental pollution, especially marine.

The Agency helps States to verify their compliance with international treaties meant to ensure that nuclear materials are not diverted for military purposes. Some 200 inspectors are deployed worldwide to more than 900 installations and other locations covered under the IAEA safeguards programme. At the end of 1993, there were 194 safeguards agreements in force with 116 States.

Although IAEA is not an international regulatory body, its nuclear safety work is mainly directed towards assisting national regulatory bodies. IAEA safety recommendations are used by countries as a basis for standards and rules. IAEA has established an International Nuclear Event Scale to rate nuclear events, incidents and accidents. It is the centre point for the Convention on Early Notification of a Nuclear Accident as well as for the Convention on Assistance in the Case of a Nuclear Accident or Radiological Emergency.

IAEA's two scientific laboratories support technical cooperation and assistance activities. With FAO, IAEA operates a joint division promoting application of isotopes and radiation in food and agriculture, and, with WHO, it runs 67 Secondary Standard Dosimetry Laboratories where doses of radiation can be checked.

IAEA has its headquarters at Vienna. Voluntary contributions for technical assistance were set at a target of $58.5 million for 1994.

International Labour Organisation

The International Labour Organisation (ILO) was established in 1919 as an autonomous institution associated with the League of Nations. Its original Constitution formed part of the Treaty of Versailles. In 1946, it became the first specialized agency associated with the United Nations.

The main purposes of the ILO are to contribute to the establishment of lasting peace by promoting social justice; to improve, through international action, labour conditions and living standards; and to promote economic and social stability. Its motto is: ''Poverty anywhere constitutes a danger to prosperity everywhere.'' ILO has 171 members.

ILO is composed of three bodies: (1) The International Labour Conference, which brings together governmental, employer and worker delegates from its member countries every year in June. It elects the Governing Body, adopts the budget, sets international labour standards and provides a world forum for the discussion of social and labour questions. (2) The Governing Body is formed of 28 members representing Governments and 28 members distributed evenly between representatives of employers and workers. Ten countries of major industrial importance have permanent seats. It meets twice a year to direct ILO operations, prepare the programme and budget and examine cases of nonobservance of ILO standards. (3) The International Labour Office, at Geneva, is the permanent secretariat of ILO, providing technical cooperation programmes around the world. It also operates the International Institute for Labour Studies and the International Training Centre in Turin, Italy.

ILO has laid down international labour standards which form a comprehensive code of law and practice. The standards, which are elaborated through the joint efforts of Governments, management and labour, cover a wide range of social issues, including basic human rights, employment promotion, social security, working conditions, occupational safety and health and labour relations.

Directly linked to this standard-setting function are extensive programmes of research and technical cooperation, which are budgeted at about $160 million a year. Current operational priorities are the elimination of child labour, the promotion of democracy, the fight against poverty and protection of working people.

The budget, which is financed by the contributions of all member States, amounted to $466.5 million for 1994-1995.

Food and Agriculture Organization of the United Nations

The Food and Agriculture Organization of the United Nations (FAO) was founded in 1945. The largest of the United Nations specialized agencies, it works to eliminate the hunger and poverty that afflict millions of people in developing countries. The priorities and direction of FAO's efforts to eliminate hunger and poverty are the product of 50 years of thought and experience within and outside the organization. The FAO member countries have pledged: to raise the levels of nutrition and standards of living of their peoples; to improve the production and distribution of all food and agricultural products, including forestry and fisheries; and to improve the condition of rural people. The goal of FAO is world food security — that is, all people, at all times, would have access to the food they need.

As the leading international body in the area of food and agriculture, FAO has four main tasks: to carry out a major programme of technical advice and assistance for the agricultural community on behalf of Governments and development funding agencies; to collect, analyse and disseminate information; to advise Governments on policy and planning; and to provide a neutral forum where Governments and experts can meet and discuss food and agricultural problems.

The supreme governing body of the organization is the Conference, composed of all member nations, which meets every two years to review the state of food and agriculture and FAO's work and to approve the regular programme of work and budget. The Conference elects, as an interim governing body, a Council of 49 member nations, which serve three-year rotating terms. As at 31 December 1993, 169 countries belonged to FAO.

A series of committees and commissions report to the Council on specific issues. FAO cooperates with WHO through the FAO/WHO Codex Alimentarius Commission, which has adopted some 200 international food standards.

The Committee on World Food Security, which monitors developments in food security, adopted in 1983 a new, broader concept of food security which was subsequently endorsed by the FAO Council and Conference. In April 1984, the FAO Director-General proposed the establishment of a World Food Security Compact, a long-term plan to establish a fully effective system for world food security.

FAO's activities include assisting developing countries to increase agricultural production through such means as improved seeds and fertilizer use, soil conservation and better water-resource management; international crop protection, including the reduction of post-harvest crop losses; reducing reliance on pesticides; the conservation and sustainable use of plant and animal genetic resources; fisheries development, especially aquaculture; the promotion of sustainable use of forest resources; and projects aimed at improving household food security and nutrition, especially for women, children and the elderly. It also acts as a neutral forum for discussion of food and agricultural issues; advises Governments on policy and planning; and disseminates information through publications, computer databases, videos and filmstrips.

FAO, which is based in Rome, Italy, had a regular programme budget, funded by its members, of $673.1 million for 1994 and 1995.

United Nations Educational, Scientific and Cultural Organization

The United Nations Educational, Scientific and Cultural Organization (UNESCO) was created on 4 November 1946 to contribute to lasting peace and security in the world by promoting collaboration among nations through education, science, culture and communication in order to further universal respect for justice, for the rule of law, and for human rights without distinction as to race, sex, language or religion.

UNESCO works through a General Conference, an Executive Board and a secretariat. The General Conference, composed of representatives of member countries, meets biennially to decide the policy, programme and budget of the organization. The Executive Board, consisting of 50 members elected by the General Conference, meets at least twice a year and is responsible for supervising the execution of the programme adopted by the General Conference.

UNESCO's secretariat, in Paris, is the executive arm which undertakes both "substantive" and "operational" programmes, consisting of research, studies, information exchange, training, conferences, and projects designed to generate self-reliance in the fields of education, science, culture and communications.

The major focus of UNESCO's educational programmes is education for development, democratization of education, out-of-school and lifelong education, formulation of educational policies, and better financing and administration of educational institutions. In the social and cultural fields, its main emphasis has been the development of research and training in the developing countries and the study, development, preservation and diffusion of cultural heritage. Its programme in communications provides technical assistance for the establishment of schools of journalism, communication research institutes, radio stations, news agencies and television stations, and training in communication professions.

The UNESCO regular budget for 1994-1995 amounted to $455.5 million. UNESCO is supported by National Commissions, UNESCO Associations, Centres and Clubs, and cooperates with more than 600 non-governmental organizations and foundations, as well as international and regional networks.

World Health Organization

The World Health Organization (WHO) came into existence on 7 April 1948 after the twenty-sixth United Nations Member had ratified its Constitution. As a result, 7 April is celebrated each year as World Health Day.

The governing body of WHO is the World Health Assembly, where all 187 member States are represented. It meets annually to review the organization's work and decide on policy, programme and budget. The Executive Board, which has 31 members, acts as the executive arm of the Assembly.

While WHO's headquarters are at Geneva, its activities have been largely decentralized to six regional organizations, each with a regional committee composed of representatives of the Governments in the region and a regional office.

Since 1977, when the World Health Assembly defined "Health for All by the Year 2000" as the organization's overriding priority, a global strategy to assist all people in achieving a level of health that will permit them to lead socially and economically productive lives has been developed. The essential elements of primary health care include: education on prevailing health problems; proper food supply and nutrition; safe water and sanitation; maternal and child health, including family planning; immunization against major infectious diseases; prevention and control of local diseases; appropriate treatment of common diseases and injuries; and provision of essential drugs.

WHO helps countries reinforce their health systems by building up infrastructures; it also helps promote the research required to develop appropriate technologies for all aspects of health. Research programmes administered by WHO, in collaboration with the United Nations Development Programme (UNDP) and the World Bank, include a special programme on research and training in tropical diseases. Working in cooperation with other agencies and several donor countries, WHO is engaged in a programme to combat river blindness in western Africa. It also coordinates the Global Programme on acquired immunodeficiency syndrome (AIDS), which provides the leadership to prevent and control the spread of AIDS through research, technical support to countries and the adoption of effective prevention strategies.

The WHO budget for 1994-1995 was $822.1 million.

International Bank for Reconstruction and Development

The International Bank for Reconstruction and Development (World Bank) was established on 27 December 1945, when representatives of 28 countries signed the Articles of Agreement which had been drawn up at the 1944 United Nations Monetary and Financial Conference at Bretton Woods, New Hampshire, United States. Membership in the Bank is open to all members of IMF.

The Bank assists in the reconstruction and development of member States by facilitating investment for productive purposes; promotes private foreign investment or, when private financing is not readily available on reasonable terms, supplements it with loans from its own capital funds; and promotes a balanced growth of international trade and an equilibrium in the balance of payments of its member States.

Under its charter, the World Bank is permitted to lend only for productive purposes. Each loan must be guaranteed by the Government of the country in which the project is to take place. Except in "special circumstances", loans must be for specific projects.

The World Bank, whose headquarters are in Washington, D.C., is a unique intergovernmental organization in that it relies primarily on private investors for its financial resources. Most of the money lent by it comes from its own borrowing on capital markets around the world. In addition to the money it borrows and paid-in capital subscriptions and charges on its loans, the Bank has two other principal sources of loan finance, the most important of which is the recycling of the payments on previous loans. It also sells portions of its loans to other investors, notably commercial banks, and uses these funds to make additional loans.

In fiscal 1993, the Bank made 122 loans to 45 countries amounting to $16,945 million, bringing its cumulative total of loan commitments to $235,154 million since its inception.

International Development Association

The International Development Association (IDA), an affiliate of the World Bank, was established in September 1960 to provide assistance for the same purposes as the Bank, but on easier terms. Though legally and financially distinct from the Bank, IDA is administered by the same officers and staff. Membership is open to all Bank members.

IDA's assistance is concentrated on countries which are very poor—mainly those with an annual per capita gross national product of less than $635 (1991 dollars). Its objectives are to promote economic development, increase productivity and raise standards of living by providing its members with finances to meet important development needs on terms which are flexible and which bear less heavily on their balance of payments.

Nearly all IDA "credits", as distinct from "Bank loans", have 35- or 40-year maturities, are interest-free, except for a small charge to cover administrative costs, and have a 10-year grace period. Most of IDA resources have come from three sources: transfers from the World Bank's net earnings; capital subscribed in convertible currencies by the members; and general replenishments from the Association's more industrialized and developed members. Total available IDA resources for the 1991-1993 period amounted to 14,425 million special drawing rights (SDR). In December 1992, donor Governments reached agreement on a total replenishment of IDA resources of SDR 13 billion to provide funds to cover credit commitments in fiscal years 1994-1996.

International Finance Corporation

The International Finance Corporation (IFC) was established in 1956 as an affiliate of the World Bank to assist the economic development of the Bank's less developed member countries. IFC promotes private-sector economic growth in these countries through the mobilization of domestic and foreign capital. It is a legal entity separate from the Bank but it does receive a wide range of services from the Bank, and its membership is open to all members of the Bank.

IFC provides risk capital for private enterprise, in association with private investors and management, in order to develop local capital markets and to stimulate the international flow of private capital. Investments are made in the form of share subscriptions and long-term loans. IFC carries out stand-by and underwriting arrangements and provides financial and technical assistance to privately controlled development finance companies; it neither requires nor accepts guarantees from the Governments concerned. Demand for IFC's financial and advisory services increased sharply as many countries accelerated the move to a market economy. IFC expanded its presence worldwide, opening new offices in the former Soviet Union and Latin America. Its headquarters are in Washington, D.C. During fiscal 1993, IFC approved $2.1 billion in financing for 185 projects.

International Monetary Fund

The International Monetary Fund (IMF) was established on 27 December 1945. Like the World Bank, its Articles of Agreement were drawn up by the 1944 International Monetary and Financial Conference, which met at Bretton Woods, and was attended by representatives of 44 nations.

The main purposes of the Fund are: to promote international monetary cooperation and the expansion of international trade; to promote exchange stability, to maintain orderly exchange arrangements among members and to avoid competitive exchange depreciations; to establish a multilateral system of payments for currency transactions between members; and to eliminate foreign exchange restrictions which hamper world trade. It also aims at increasing the confidence of members by making available its financial resources so that balance-of-payments maladjustments can be corrected without resorting to measures that could undermine national or international prosperity.

IMF has a membership of 178 countries and operates through a Board of Governors, the Executive Directors, the Managing Director and the staff. All powers of the Fund are vested in the Board of Governors, which consists of one Governor and one Alternate appointed by each member country. The Board normally holds one meeting each year which takes place in conjunction with the annual meeting of the Board of Governors of the World Bank. The Executive Board is responsible for the Fund's general operations.

The first amendment to the Fund's Articles of Agreement, establishing a new facility based on SDRs, entered into force on 28 July 1969. The SDR allows a country to purchase currency—pounds sterling, United States dollars, French francs, etc.—with which it can transact business. The actual value of an SDR is based on the average of a basket of the currencies of the five countries with the largest share of world exports of goods and services, weighted according to their importance in world trade. With the advent of the SDR, the Fund has been able to supplement the existing reserve assets of participating members.

The second amendment, which entered into force on 1 April 1978, introduced flexible provisions for dealing with international exchange arrangements, reducing the role of gold in the international monetary system and changing the use of the SDR in order to enhance its status as an international reserve asset.

The financial resources of IMF consist primarily of the subscriptions ("quotas") of its member countries, which currently total SDR 144.8 billion, or approximately $205 billion. Quotas, which are the amounts members deposit upon joining IMF, are determined by a formula based on the relative economic size of the members. IMF may also borrow from official lenders to supplement its regular financial resources. It has authority to create and allocate to its members international financial reserves in the form of SDRs. Thus far, IMF has provided additional liquidity totalling SDR 21.4 billion to its members. IMF holds gold reserves of 103.5 million fine ounces.

IMF's main financial role consists of providing temporary credits to members experiencing balance-of-payments difficulties. The amounts that members may borrow are limited in proportion to their quotas. Countries receiving IMF financial support for their economic adjustment programmes over several years may borrow as much as four or five times their quotas.

IMF also offers concessional assistance to low-income member countries through its structural adjustment facility (SAF) and the enhanced structural adjustment facility (ESAF). Members qualifying for ESAF funding may borrow up to 250 per cent of their quotas over a three-year programme period, with provision for up to 350 per cent in special circumstances.

In 1993, IMF created a new temporary facility, the system transformation facility (STF), to provide financial assistance to members facing balance-of-payments difficulties arising from several disruptions of their traditional trade and payments arrangements. Countries that are switching from a centrally planned economic system to a market-oriented system—for instance, countries of the former Soviet Union—may be eligible for STF assistance.

IMF headquarters are in Washington, D.C.

International Civil Aviation Organization

The International Civil Aviation Organization (ICAO) was established on 4 April 1947, 30 days after the Convention on International Civil Aviation had been ratified by 26 States. It became a specialized agency of the United Nations in October 1947. At the end of 1943, membership of ICAO had risen to 182 States.

The Assembly is ICAO's sovereign body, consisting of all Contracting States (ICAO States must be Members of the United Nations). It meets at least once every three years to review in detail the complete work programme of the organization. The governing body of ICAO is the Council, which is elected by the Assembly for a three-year term and consists of 33 States. The Council holds three 12-week sessions a year, providing continuing direction to the work of the organization.

The basic aim of ICAO is to facilitate the safety, regularity and efficiency of civil air transport. As an intergovernmental regulatory organization, its objectives are to prescribe standards, recommended practices and procedures for facilitating civil aviation operations. ICAO studies problems in international civil aviation and establishes international standards and regulations. It fosters the development and planning of international air transport and encourages the use of safety measures, uniform regulations for operation and simpler procedures at international borders. It promotes new technical methods and equipment. With the cooperation of members, it has evolved a pattern for meteorological services, traffic control, communications, radio beacons and ranges, search and rescue organization and other facilities required for safe international flights.

The headquarters of ICAO are in Montreal, Canada.

The budget of ICAO is contributed by its Contracting States. The 1995 budget amounted to nearly $48 million.

Universal Postal Union

The Berne Treaty of 1874, which came into force in 1875, formally established the General Postal Union. In 1878, the General Postal Union became the Universal Postal Union (UPU), with a mandate to improve the postal services of its member countries and to promote international collaboration.

UPU has 188 member countries. Its principal organs are the Universal Postal Congress, the Executive Council, the Consultative Council for Postal Studies and the International Bureau. The Congress meets at five-year intervals and elects the Director-General and the Deputy Director-General. The Executive Council, which holds one session a year, consists of 40 members elected by the Congress on an equitable geographical basis. The Consultative Council for Postal Studies, composed of 35 members elected by the Congress, meets annually; it organizes studies of major technical, economic and operational problems affecting postal administrations in all UPU member countries and examines teaching and training problems in newly independent and developing countries. The International Bureau, at Berne, Switzerland, coordinates, publishes and disseminates information about the international postal service.

UPU is a participating agency in UNDP and manages projects by modernizing existing and introducing new postal and financial services. It assists national postal administrations to accelerate mail deliveries, especially in rural areas; enlarge the number of post offices; expand the use of airmail for international parcel services and maximize air conveyance in all categories; introduce financial services, such as money orders and savings banks where they do not already exist; and improve staff management. It also assists by recruiting and supplying experts, awarding fellowships for vocational training and furnishing equipment or training and demonstration material. It provides technical assistance from other members, usually by means of professional training courses, and through exchanges of information, documents and results of tests or experiments.

UPU's budget for 1994 was $23.5 million.

International Telecommunication Union

The International Telecommunication Union (ITU) was founded in Paris in 1865 as the International Telegraph Union. It changed to International Telecommunication Union in 1934 when the Telegraph and Radiotelegraph Conventions were replaced by the International Telecommunication Convention, adopted at Madrid, Spain, in 1932.

As a result of the international conferences held in the United States in 1947, ITU adjusted its organizational structure, adopted measures designed to take account of advances made in telecommunication techniques and entered into an agreement with the United Nations giving ITU recognition as the specialized agency for telecommunications. A new Convention was adopted in 1947 to give effect to those changes and came into force in January 1949. Since then, ITU has been governed by various Conventions, the latest of which was adopted by the 1965 Montreux Plenipotentiary Conference and entered into force on 1 January 1967.

The supreme organ of ITU is the Plenipotentiary Conference, which meets every four years. It is responsible for laying down ITU's basic policy for fulfilling its purposes. The ITU Council, composed of 43 members of the Union elected by the Plenipotentiary Conference, meets annually and acts as a management body. The Union's secretariat at its Geneva headquarters consists of three bureaux (the Radiocommunication Bureau, the Telecommunication Standardization Bureau and the Telecommunication Development Bureau) and a General Secretariat.

Within ITU, the public and private sectors cooperate for the development of telecommunications and the harmonization of national telecommunication policies. ITU adopts international regulations and treaties governing all space and terrestrial uses of the frequency spectrum as well as the use of the geostationary-satellite orbit, within which countries adopt their national legislation. It also develops standards to facilitate the interconnection of telecommunication systems on a world-wide scale regardless of the type of technology used, and fosters the development of telecommunications in developing countries. It provides specialized technical assistance in the areas of telecommunication policies, choice and transfer of technologies, management, financing of investment projects and mobilization of resources, the installation and maintenance of networks, and the management of human resources as well as research and development.

ITU's ordinary budget for 1995 was $104.6 million.

World Meteorological Organization

The World Meteorological Organization (WMO) was created in 1947 by the World Meteorological Convention, adopted at the Twelfth Conference of Directors of the International Meteorological Organization (IMO), which met in Washington, D.C. WMO commenced operations in 1951 as the successor to IMO.

WMO was established according to the Convention "with a view to coordinating, standardizing and improving world meteorological and related activities and to encouraging an efficient exchange of meteorological and related information between countries in the aid of human activities". Thus, the purposes of WMO are: to facilitate international cooperation in meteorological services and observations; and to promote the rapid exchange of meteorological information, the standardization of meteorological observations and the uniform publication of observations and statistics. It also furthers the application of meteorology to aviation, shipping, water problems, agriculture and other human activities, promotes operational hydrology and encourages research and training in meteorology.

WMO has 173 members, comprising 168 States and 5 territories, all of which maintain their own meteorological and hydrological services. The World Meteorological Congress, the supreme body of WMO, comprises all members, meets every four years and determines general policy, programmes and budget. The Executive Council meets once a year to supervise the implementation of decisions and programmes approved by the Congress.

The 1975 World Meteorological Congress reorganized the organization's activities into the following programmes: world weather; research and development; meteorological applications and environment; hydrology and water resources development; technical cooperation; and education and training. The World Weather Watch provides for surface and upper-air observations from a world-wide network of stations, mobile and fixed ships, commercial aircraft and meteorological satellites.

Together with the Intergovernmental Oceanographic Commission of UNESCO, WMO co-sponsors an international programme called the Integrated Global Ocean Station System, the oceanic counterpart of World Weather Watch, to produce and provide oceanographic analyses and predictions. The Global Atmospheric Research Programme, carried out jointly with the International Council of Scientific Unions, is designed to increase the accuracy of meteorological forecasting and to obtain a better understanding of the physical basis of climate. The Meteorological Application and Environment Programme applies meteorological knowledge to human activities such as agriculture, transport, building climatology, energy, atmospheric and marine pollution and environmental problems in general. WMO has strengthened national agrometeorological services and works closely with FAO in order to increase food production in member countries. The Hydrology and Water Resources Development Programme promotes world-wide cooperation in evaluating water resources and assisting in the development of such resources. The Technical Cooperation Programme assists developing countries to improve national meteorological and hydrological services through the provision of experts, fellowships and equipment. The World Climate Programme seeks to improve knowledge of natural variations in the climate and the effects of climatic changes due to natural causes or human activities.

WMO, with headquarters in Geneva, had a budget for the financial period 1992-1995 of $171 million, with expected extrabudgetary resources in the amount of $120 million.

International Maritime Organization

The International Maritime Organization (IMO), formerly called the Intergovernmental Maritime Consultative Organization, was established by the convention adopted at Geneva in 1948 by the United Nations Maritime Conference. The Convention became operative in March 1958 when it had been accepted by 21 States, including seven with at least 1 million gross tons of shipping each.

The IMO Assembly, consisting of its 149 members, meets every year. It elects the Council, which has 32 members and meets twice a year to oversee the implementation of IMO's work programme.

IMO has developed treaties dealing with safety at sea, prevention of collisions, improvement of radio communications at sea, training and certification of seafarers, creation of an international system for search and rescue and other matters. In the area of marine pollution, IMO has concentrated primarily on combating oil pollution from ships, but has also developed measures to fight pollution by chemicals, sewage and garbage. It has also devel-

oped a number of treaties dealing with liability and compensation issues. In order to facilitate the implementation of these measures, IMO has built up an extensive programme of technical assistance, which concentrates on training in addition to helping maritime training institutes in many parts of the world. It established the World Maritime University in Malmo, Sweden, in 1983 to provide advanced training for administrators, educators and others involved in shipping at a senior level. The offices of IMO itself are located in London. IMO's budget for 1994-1995 was 34,328,800 pounds sterling.

World Intellectual Property Organization

The World Intellectual Property Organization (WIPO) was established by a Convention signed at Stockholm on 14 July 1967, which entered into force on 26 April 1970. Its origins date back to the 1883 Paris Convention and the 1886 Berne Convention, which established the International Union for the Protection of Industrial Property and the International Union for the Protection of Literary and Artistic Works, known as "the Paris Union" and "the Berne Union". These Conventions, each providing for the establishment of an international bureau, were united in 1893 and functioned under various names, including the United International Bureaux for the Protection of Intellectual Property, known by its French acronym "BIRPI".

WIPO became the fourteenth specialized agency in the United Nations system on 17 December 1974. It has 147 member States.

Membership is open to any State member of either Union, and to other States which satisfy any one of the following conditions: is a Member of the United Nations or any of its specialized agencies or IAEA; is a party to the Statute of the International Court of Justice; or is invited by the General Assembly of WIPO to become a party to the Convention.

WIPO has three governing bodies: the General Assembly, the Conference and the Coordination Committee. It also has a secretariat at Geneva called the International Bureau.

WIPO's activities fall into two main categories: the protection of industrial property—inventions, trademarks and industrial designs—and the repression of unfair competition; and copyrights to protect literary, musical, artistic, photographic and cinematographic works.

WIPO's Permanent Programme for Development Cooperation related to Industrial Property encourages inventive and innovative activity in developing countries in an effort to strengthen the technological capacities of those countries. The Programme's Permanent Committee plans and guides the execution of projects, drafts model laws, establishes collections of foreign patent documents, trains people in the use of such documentation and helps establish or modernize government machinery. A Permanent Programme for Development Cooperation has also been established to encourage literary, scientific and artistic creation in developing countries; to facilitate the distribution of such works in those countries; and to strengthen national institutions in those fields.

As a basis for its technical cooperation on patents, WIPO promotes the standardization of documents and patent-office procedures. The International Patent Documentation Centre, established at Vienna in 1972, allows computer access to the principal bibliographic data of almost 1 million patent documents each year and permits the retrieval of the data by patent offices, industry, research and development institutions.

The Organization's programme and budget, which in 1994-1995 amounted to $156.3 million, are established biennially by its governing bodies.

International Fund for Agricultural Development

The International Fund for Agricultural Development (IFAD), one of the newest United Nations specialized agencies, was established in 1976 to provide additional resources for agricultural and rural development in the poorest rural areas, particularly in the least developed countries.

The Fund, one of the major initiatives of the 1974 Rome World Food Conference, resulted from two years of international negotiations. On 13 June 1976 the Agreement was adopted by 91 government representatives at the United Nations Conference on the Establishment of IFAD. That Agreement entered into force on 30 November 1977, following attainment of the target of $1 billion in initial pledges.

IFAD's lending policy provides that its resources be used to support projects which: raise food production, particularly on small farms; provide employment and additional income for poor and landless farmers; and reduce malnutrition by producing, in addition to other crops, foods normally consumed by the poorest populations and by improving food distribution systems. IFAD approved its first projects in April 1978. It initiates, finances and mobilizes co-financing for rural development projects; supports agricultural research programmes; sustains national, regional and international efforts to protect the natural resource base and reverse environmental degradation; promotes the full participation of beneficiaries, grass-roots organizations and non-governmental organizations in its programmes; cooperates with other UN agencies to ensure sound investments in rural poverty alleviation programmes and projects; and cooperates with international and regional financial institutions, as well as bilateral development agencies, in co-financing rural development projects focusing on the poor.

The Governing Council, which is the governing body of the Fund, convenes once a year. Its 157 member States are divided into three categories (each with 600 votes): Category I, consisting of 22 industrialized nations (OECD members), Category II, comprising 12 petroleum-exporting States (OPEC members) and Category III, comprising 123 developing countries. The Council approves the annual budgets, investments and programmes of work and it elects the Executive Board, composed of six executive directors from each of the three categories, with 18 alternates.

The Fund's initial resources were $1.02 billion. Of this, $567.3 million was made available by the developed countries which belong to the Organisation for Economic Cooperation and Development (OECD), $435.5 million by members of the Organization of Petroleum Exporting Countries (OPEC), and $9.3 million by other developing countries.

In line with the Fund's special focus on the rural poor, the bulk of its resources are made available in highly concessional loans, repayable over 50 years with a 10-year grace period and a 1 per cent service charge. There is also provision for loans on ordinary terms, at 8 per cent for 15 to 18 years, and on intermediate terms, at 4 per cent for 20 years. The Fund approved its first projects in April 1978.

IFAD's financial resources are replenished every three years by substantial contributions from Categories I and II and voluntary contributions from countries in Category III. IFAD's average annual investments in loans and grants for projects and research programmes amount to $323 million.

IFAD's main offices are in Rome.

United Nations Industrial Development Organization

The United Nations Industrial Development Organization (UNIDO) was established by the General Assembly in 1967 to promote and accelerate the industrialization of developing countries as well as to coordinate the industrial development activities of the United Nations system.

The principal organ of UNIDO is the General Conference, which consists of all its member States and normally meets every two years. The Industrial Development Board, consisting of 53 member States elected by the General Conference, holds at least one regular session each year to review UNIDO's work and activities. The Programme and Budget Committee, with 27 member States elected by the General Conference, assists the Board in preparing and examining the work programme, budgets and other financial matters. It holds at least one regular session each year.

UNIDO's main activities include: encouraging and extending assistance to developing countries for development, expansion and modernization of their industries; assisting developing countries in the establishment and operation of industries to achieve full utilization of locally available natural and human resources and contribute to self-reliance; providing a forum and acting as an instrument to serve the developing and industrialized countries in their contacts, consultations and negotiations; developing special measures designed to promote cooperation among developing countries and between developed and developing countries; coordinating all activities of the United Nations system relating to industrial development.

UNIDO's regular budget, based on member States' assessed contributions, amounted to $181 million for the biennium 1992-1993. The major sources of funds for its projects have been UNDP and the Industrial Development Fund. Its headquarters are in Vienna.

World Trade Organization

The World Trade Organization (WTO) was established on 1 January 1995, replacing GATT as the major entity overseeing international trade. The origins of WTO date back to the 1947-1948 United Nations Conference on Trade and Employment held at Havana, Cuba, which drew up a charter for an International Trade Organization (ITO) and established an Interim Commission for the International Trade Organization (ICITO). That charter was never adopted and ITO was never established. However,

subsequent negotiations resulted in the creation of GATT, which entered into force on 1 January 1948.

Membership in WTO is automatic for all 128 members of GATT upon acceptance of the agreements reached in December 1994 at the conclusion of the Uruguay Round of multilateral trade negotiations and submission of commitments on trade in goods and services.

WTO administers, through various councils and committees, the 28 agreements on international trading relations contained in the Final Act of the Uruguay Round of trade negotiations, approved at Marrakesh, Morocco, in April 1994. In addition, WTO administers a number of plurilateral agreements, notably on government procurement and civil aircraft. WTO is a watchdog of international trade, regularly examining the trade regimes of individual members. Members are required to notify in detail various trade measures and statistics which are maintained by WTO. Trade disputes between members that cannot be solved through bilateral talks are adjudicated under the WTO dispute-settlement "court".

WTO continues, in a strengthened form, the code of conduct established by GATT for international trade since 1948. This includes the principle of non-discrimination between trading partners—the "most-favoured-nation" clause—and equal treatment for imports and domestic goods in internal markets. Unlike GATT, WTO rules cover trade in services, intellectual property and investment and phase out or reduce protectionist policies in important areas such as agriculture, textiles and clothing.

WTO headquarters are in Geneva.

PART FIVE

Human rights questions

> *"To achieve international co-operation . . . in promoting and encouraging respect for human rights and for fundamental freedoms for all without distinction as to race, sex, language or religion"*

Chapter I

Human rights

With the exception of the pursuit of peace, no cause is more closely identified with the United Nations than human rights.

Concern for human dignity is enshrined in the United Nations Charter although it does not fully define the contents of human rights. The framers of the Charter left to the Organization itself the task of drawing up an International Bill of Human Rights. This finally led to the Universal Declaration of Human Rights in 1948, the International Covenant on Economic, Social and Cultural Rights in 1966, the International Covenant on Civil and Political Rights and the Optional Protocol thereto, providing for the right of individual petition in 1966, and the Second Optional Protocol aiming at the abolition of the death penalty in 1989, which together constitute the International Bill of Human Rights. These texts provide the most authoritative interpretation of the human rights clauses of the Charter.

The coming into force of the Covenants in 1976 launched a new era in the history of human rights. For the first time, States were bound before the international community to promote the rights of their individual citizens, and victims of human rights violations had a means of recourse outside the jurisdiction of the authorities which oppressed them.

The United Nations human rights programme has a three-pronged approach: promotion of human rights—setting standards, legislation, declarations and conventions; protection of human rights—appointing special rapporteurs and applying procedures and mechanisms established by conventions or by resolutions of authorized United Nations bodies; and prevention of human rights violations—providing United Nations advisory services, education and information.

Promotion of human rights

Some 70 human rights treaties and declarations have been negotiated under the aegis of the United Nations to promote human rights. The following are a few examples.

Convention on the Prevention and Punishment of the Crime of Genocide (1948, in force since 1951) was a direct response to the atrocities committed during the Second World War. In recent years, the crime of genocide has been addressed in resolutions adopted by the Commission on Human Rights at its three special sessions, two of them held in 1992 on the human rights situation in the former Yugoslavia and another held in 1994 on the issue of human rights in Rwanda.

International Convention on the Elimination of All Forms of Racial Discrimination (1965, in force since 1969) is one of the most universally accepted international human rights instruments. It obliges States parties to eliminate racial discrimination, prohibit discriminatory practices and, where warranted, ensure the adequate development and protection of certain racial groups.

International Convention on the Suppression and Punishment of the Crime of Apartheid (1973, in force since 1976) reaffirms that systematic, legalized racial discrimination known in South Africa as apartheid is a crime under international law and establishes international criminal responsibility of individuals or groups that "abet, encourage or cooperate in the commission of apartheid". Periodic reports from States parties are reviewed by a "Group of Three", which reports to the Commission on Human Rights.

Convention against Torture and Other Cruel, Inhuman or Degrading Treatment or Punishment (1984, in force since 1987) holds States parties responsible for preventing torture and making it legally punishable. No exceptional circumstances may be invoked to justify torture, nor can a torturer be excused by virtue of having acted under orders.

Convention on the Rights of the Child (1989, in force since 1990) recognizes the particular vulnerability of children and brings together in one comprehensive code benefits and protections for children contained in scores of other agreements. It places special attention on children who are refugees, disabled or members of minorities.

International Convention on the Protection of the Rights of All Migrant Workers and Members of Their Families (1990, not yet in force) defines basic rights and principles and protects migrant workers, whether legal or illegal, throughout the process of migration.

Protection of human rights

The Commission on Human Rights, set up by the Economic and Social Council in 1946, meets annually to review human rights matters. It conducts studies, prepares recommendations and drafts international instruments relating to human rights. It also undertakes special tasks assigned to it by the General Assembly or the Economic and Social Council, including the investigation of allegations concerning human rights violations and the handling of communications relating to such violations.

The Commission has set up various organs to investigate human rights problems in specific countries and territories as well as on thematic situations. Some of the groups include: the Ad Hoc Working Group of Experts on southern Africa; the Group of Three established under the 1973 International Convention on the Suppression and Punishment of the Crime of Apartheid; the Working Group to Elaborate a Draft Optional Protocol to the 1984 Convention against Torture and Other Cruel, Inhuman or Degrading Treatment or Punishment; the Working Group on Enforced or Involuntary Disappearances; the Working Group on the Right to Development; and the Working Group on Arbitrary Detention. In addition, the Commission has been actively employing a variety of methods for dealing with human rights violations. These include fact-finding by experts consisting of special rapporteurs, representatives or other designees appointed by the Commission to study the situation of human rights either in specific countries or on thematic situations such as summary or arbitrary executions; mass exoduses; mercenaries; the sale of children; child pornography and child prostitution; human rights and disability; discrimination against people infected with the human immunodeficiency virus or acquired immunodeficiency syndrome; independence and impartiality of the judiciary; religious intolerance; human rights and states of emergency; human rights and environment; rights of restitution, compensation and rehabilitation for victims of gross violations of human rights and fundamental freedoms; the right to a fair trial; and the matter of traditional practices affecting the health of women and children. Appointed in their individual capacity, not as government representatives, special rapporteurs gather facts, maintain contact with local groups and government authorities, visit prisons and other detention centres, interview victims of human rights violations and make recommendations on strengthening human rights institutions.

The Commission has also established informal open-ended working groups to assist in drafting international declarations and conventions.

At its first session in 1947, the Commission on Human Rights established the Subcommission on Prevention of Discrimination and Protection of Minorities. The Subcommission, like the Commission, operates under the rules of procedure of functional commissions of the Economic and Social Council.

The Subcommission has established three working groups which meet before its annual sessions to assist it with certain tasks: the Working Group on Communications, which examines communications containing allegations of violations of human rights and brings to the attention of the Subcommission those which appear to reveal a consistent pattern of gross and reliably attested violations of human rights; the Working Group on Contemporary Forms of Slavery, which reviews developments in the area of slavery, slave-trade practices, exploitation of child labour and exploitation of prostitutes; and the Working Group on Indigenous Populations, which reviews developments relating to the protection of the human rights of such populations. In addition, the Subcommission may establish sessional working groups, which meet during its annual sessions to consider particular agenda items.

Each of the working groups submits its report to the Subcommission for consideration. On some questions, including those relating to the discharge of its functions, the Subcommission adopts its own resolutions and decisions. On others, it formulates draft resolutions and decisions for consideration by the Commission on Human Rights and the Economic and Social Council. The Subcommission submits a report on the work of each session to the Commission.

States parties to human rights treaties are obliged to report periodically to international bodies on measures they have taken, on progress they have made and on any difficulties they have encountered in living up to the various instruments. These bodies—committees or groups of experts—then examine national reports, question government representatives and point out shortcomings. In some instances, they receive complaints from other States parties or individuals. The committees may call on Governments to respond to allegations and may adopt decisions and publish them along with criticisms or recommendations. Treaty mechanisms usually apply to States that have agreed to be bound by the treaty; many procedures for handling complaints are optional.

Committees created to consider reports, hear complaints and monitor compliance include: Committee on the Elimination of Racial Discrimination (for the 1965 International Convention on the Elimination of All Forms of Racial Discrimination); Committee on Economic, Social and Cultural Rights (for the 1966 International Covenant on Economic, Social and Cultural Rights); Human Rights Committee (for the 1966 International Covenant on Civil and Political Rights); Committee on the Elimination of Discrimination against Women (for the 1979 Convention on the Elimination of All Forms of Discrimination against Women); Committee against Torture (for the 1984 Convention against Torture and Other Cruel, Inhuman or Degrading Treatment or Punishment); Committee on the Rights of the Child (for the 1989 Convention on the Rights of the Child); and the Group of Three (for the 1973 International Convention on the Suppression and Punishment of the Crime of Apartheid).

The Secretary-General of the United Nations has at his disposal a confidential diplomatic mechanism—"good offices"—by which he may raise urgent human rights problems with the Governments of Member States. Cases might include the release of a political prisoner or the commutation of a death sentence. The Secretary-General's efforts to intercede are discreet and rarely, if ever, publicized, but he continues, at the same time, to make public appeals on behalf of respect for human rights in general.

In December 1993, the General Assembly established the post of United Nations High Commissioner for Human Rights. The High Commissioner is charged with promoting the effective enjoyment by all of all human rights, promoting the realization of the right to development, providing advisory services to support human rights programmes, coordinating human rights education and public information activities, and preventing human rights violations. His mandate also includes engaging in dialogue with all Governments to improve respect for human rights, enhancing international cooperation in human rights, coordinating human rights activities within the United Nations system, overseeing United Nations machinery and providing overall supervision of the Centre for Human Rights.

Treading new ground, human rights monitors have formed integral components of a number of peace-keeping operations, among them the United Nations Observer Mission in El Salvador and the United Nations Transitional Authority in Cambodia.

The Centre for Human Rights, located at the United Nations Office at Geneva, is the Secretariat unit of the United Nations mostly concerned with human rights questions. The Centre also serves as a clearinghouse for communications on a multitude of human rights issues received from individuals, nongovernmental organizations (NGOs) and Governments.

The continuous increase in requests for advisory services, the establishment of new mandates, and the constant growth in individual petitions submitted to the United Nations have increased the workload of the Centre. During 1994, the Centre increased substantially its activities in programme advisory services and technical assistance in the field of human rights.

Prevention of human rights violations

Since 1955, the General Assembly has authorized the Secretary-General to make arrangements to provide three forms of assistance, to which were added the regional programmes in 1967 and national information and/or training courses in 1985: advisory services of experts; fellowships and scholarships; international and regional seminars; and regional or national training courses. In 1987, the Voluntary Fund for Advisory Services and Technical Assistance in the Field of Human Rights was set up to receive contributions to provide additional financial support for all the specific activities geared to the implementation of international conventions and instruments on human rights.

The amount of assistance and the conditions under which it is rendered are decided by the Secretary-General. Accordingly, he gives due regard to the greater needs of the developing areas. Assistance is provided only in agreement with the Governments concerned, on the basis of requests received from them. This assistance may be extended to any question in the human rights sphere and it is for the Government concerned to decide on the kind of services to be provided to it. The selection of the persons awarded fellowships and scholarships is made by the Secretary-General based on proposals made by Governments.

Information is a powerful deterrent to human rights abuse. Even Governments that initially sought to suppress discussion of human rights have come to recognize that their international image depends to a certain extent on respecting human rights. Unfortunately, it is often the people whose rights are being violated who are the least informed about their rights and about how to take advantage of human rights mechanisms. In response, a world public information campaign was launched to educate people about their entitlements—and countries about their responsibilities.

The World Public Information Campaign on Human Rights, launched by the Assembly in 1988, seeks to increase understanding and awareness of human rights and fundamental freedoms as well as provide education on international human rights machinery and the efforts of the United Nations to promote and protect human rights. Activities within the Campaign focus on preparing and disseminating printed information and reference materials; workshops, seminars and training courses; fellowships and internships; special human rights observances; and coverage and promotion activities.

In 1994, the General Assembly proclaimed the 10-year period beginning on 1 January 1995 the United Nations Decade for Human Rights Education and called on international, regional and national NGOs, in particular those concerned with women, labour, development and the environment, as well as all other social justice groups, human rights advocates, educators, religious organizations and the media, to increase their involvement in formal and non-formal education in human rights and to cooperate with the Centre for Human Rights in implementing the Decade.

Below are some historical highlights surrounding the development of the United Nations human rights programme since the inception of the Organization.

Genocide

The United Nations has taken a strong position against the crime of genocide. International action to prevent genocide came as a direct response to the atrocities committed during the Second World War. The General Assembly in 1946 took up the question of the prevention and punishment of genocide. By a resolution adopted in December, it affirmed that genocide was a crime under international law and those guilty of it were punishable.

In 1948, the Assembly adopted the Convention on the Prevention and Punishment of the Crime of Genocide, which entered into force in 1951. It defined genocide as the commission of certain acts with the intent to destroy a national, ethnic, racial or religious group and confirmed that genocide, whether committed in peace or in war, was a crime under international law which the States parties undertook to prevent and punish. The Convention enumerated the acts to which the definition applied and ensured that anyone charged with genocide would not be shielded from extradition by a "political" defence. It was ratified or acceded to by 112 States as at 31 December 1993.

The General Assembly at its 47th plenary meeting on November 9, 1946, referred to the Sixth Committee a draft resolution submitted by the representatives of Cuba, India and Panama, drawing the attention of the Economic and Social Council to the crime of genocide and inviting the Council to study the problem and to report on the possibility of declaring genocide an "international crime".

The Sixth Committee discussed the question at its 22nd, 23rd and 24th meetings on November 22, 28 and 29 respectively. The representative of Cuba stated that at the Nürnberg trials it had not been possible to punish certain cases of genocide because they had been committed before the beginning of the war. Fearing that such crimes might remain unpunished in the future owing to the principle of *non crimen sine lege*, the representative of Cuba urged that genocide be declared an international crime.

The representative of the United Kingdom expressed the view that the General Assembly should not merely recommend to the Economic and Social Council that it study the matter, but should clearly state at once that aggressive war and genocide constituted punishable crimes. International law should limit the omnipotence of certain States over their citizens and in certain cases protect the citizens against their own government. The representative of the United Kingdom therefore submitted an amendment to the draft resolution before the Committee to the effect that the General Assembly "declares that genocide is an international crime for which the principal authors, accomplices and States concerned will be held responsible."

The representative of France stated that French law did not recognize criminal responsibility on the part of States. He therefore wished to amend the United Kingdom text to read as follows: "The General Assembly . . . declares that genocide is an international crime for which the principal authors and accomplices, whether statesmen or private individuals, should be punished."

. . .

The representative of the U.S.S.R. proposed that the Economic and Social Council be asked to undertake preparatory studies with a view to drafting an international convention against attacks on particular racial groups.

The representative of Saudi Arabia urged the desirability of agreeing to a protocol on genocide similar to the protocols dealing with narcotics and piracy. He submitted to the Sixth Committee a draft protocol to serve as a basis of consideration. Such a protocol, the Saudi-Arabian representative stated, should contain:

(1) a definition of genocide;
(2) an enumeration of all the acts that fall within the definition;
(3) provisions for assuring the prevention and repression of genocide.

The representative of Poland submitted a proposal for the punishment of those responsible for the propagation and dissemination of hatred against national, racial, or religious groups as a step preparatory to the crime of genocide. The representative of Chile submitted an amendment combining several of the amendments submitted by other representatives.

At its 24th meeting on November 29, 1946, the Sixth Committee decided to entrust a Sub-Committee with the task of drafting a unanimously acceptable resolution on the basis of various proposals submitted. The report and draft resolution submitted accordingly by the Sub-Committee were unanimously adopted by the Sixth Committee at its 32nd meeting on December 9, 1946.

On the recommendation of the Sixth Committee the General Assembly at its 55th plenary meeting on December 11, 1946, unanimously adopted the following resolution:

Genocide is a denial of the right of existence of entire human groups, as homicide is the denial of the right to live of individual human beings; such denial of the right of existence shocks the conscience of mankind, results in great losses to humanity in the form of cultural and other contributions represented by these human groups, and is contrary to moral law and to the spirit and aims of the United Nations.

Many instances of such crimes of genocide have occurred when racial, religious, political and other groups have been destroyed, entirely or in part.

The punishment of the crime of genocide is a matter of international concern.

THE GENERAL ASSEMBLY, THEREFORE,

AFFIRMS that genocide is a crime under international law which the civilized world condemns, and for the commission of which principals and accomplices—whether private individuals, public officials or statesmen, and whether the crime is committed on religious, racial, political or any other grounds—are punishable;

INVITES the Member States to enact the necessary legislation for the prevention and punishment of this crime;

RECOMMENDS that international co-operation be organized between States with a view to facilitating the speedy prevention and punishment of the crime of genocide, and, to this end,

REQUESTS the Economic and Social Council to undertake the necessary studies with a view to drawing up a draft convention on the crime of genocide to be submitted to the next regular session of the General Assembly.

[YUN 1946-47, pp. 254-56]

In accordance with the Council's instruction, the Secretary-General prepared a draft convention which, together with the comments received from the Member Governments, was submitted to the second session of the General Assembly. By resolution 180(II) the Assembly requested the continuation of the work begun by the Council.

Accordingly, the Council, at its sixth session, established an *ad hoc* Committee on Genocide which met at Lake Success (April to May 1948) and prepared a Draft Convention on the Prevention and Punishment of the Crime of Genocide.
. . .

At its seventh session, the Council decided to transmit to the third session of the General Assembly the draft convention prepared by the *ad hoc* Committee on Genocide, together with the proceedings on the subject.

Consideration by the General Assembly at its third session

Discussion in the Sixth Committee

The Sixth Committee of the General Assembly, to which the item was referred, began consideration of the draft convention at its 63rd meeting on 30 September 1948. It was decided to examine the text of the draft, article by article, leaving the preamble to be discussed last of all, and to refer the draft, as formulated by the Sixth Committee, to a drafting committee for the preparation of a final text.

The general discussion of the Sixth Committee continued through four meetings and embraced most of the points which the delegations subsequently put forward as amendments. While some representatives thought that there was no need for a convention, since genocide was already illegal, and that the first duty of penal legislation was to prevent crime instead of inventing new measures for punishing it, others voiced the opinion that it was essential to give a precise definition to genocide and to make provisions for outlawing it.

The individual articles of the draft convention were examined by the Sixth Committee, at its 67th to 110th meetings, between 5 October and 18 November 1948. Then, the text was considered by the drafting committee during four meetings, held from 16 to 22 November. The drafting committee examined, also, the text of the preamble to the convention, as adopted by the Sixth Committee at a later stage (meetings 109, 110, 132 and 133), and drew up the text of a draft resolution recommending the adoption by the General Assembly of the draft convention on genocide. In addition, the drafting committee examined the texts of the draft resolutions adopted by the Sixth Committee dealing *(a)* with the study of the question of an international criminal jurisdiction, and *(b)* with the application of the convention on genocide with respect to dependent territories. The text, as revised by the drafting committee, was examined by the Sixth Committee from its 128th to 134th meetings, held between 29 November and 1 December 1948.

In the debates of the Sixth Committee, several articles of the proposed convention, especially those of a substantive character, gave rise to divergent opinions, and a number of amendments were submitted. The following were some of the most important points raised.

In dealing with article II (2) of the draft convention,[1] which defines the acts of genocide, the Committee had, in particular, to resolve three im-

---

[1]The article numbers in roman figures are those appearing in the final text adopted by the General Assembly. The numbers in parentheses are those of the draft text submitted by the Committee on Genocide.

portant problems. In the first place, the question arose whether the acts of genocide should be explicitly enumerated in the article, as was done in the text prepared by the *ad hoc* committee, or whether a general definition of genocide should be adopted, as proposed in an amendment submitted by the French delegation. The Committee, at its 72nd meeting, decided on the principle of enumeration, the French amendment having been withdrawn.

Secondly, the Committee discussed whether political groups should be included in the groups to be protected by the convention, as proposed by the *ad hoc* committee, or whether these groups should be excluded from the article. At the 75th meeting, the Committee decided to retain this clause, the vote being 29 in favour to 13 against, with 9 abstentions. However, this decision was later reversed when, at its 128th meeting, on the proposal of the representatives of Egypt, Iran and Uruguay, the Committee decided to re-examine the question of excluding the words ''political groups'' from this article. It decided by vote of 22 to 6, with 12 abstentions, to exclude political groups from those groups protected by the article.

Thirdly, it had to be decided whether the Committee should retain the words ''on grounds of the national or racial origin, religious belief, or political opinion of its members'', proposed by the *ad hoc* committee. This was settled when the Committee, at its 77th meeting, by 27 votes to 22, with 2 abstentions, adopted an amendment submitted by the representative of Venezuela, whereby the phrase in question was deleted and the words ''as such'' added after the word ''group'', thus making the first part of article II (2) read as follows:

> ''In this Convention genocide means any of the following acts committed with the intent to destroy, in whole or in part, a national, ethnical, racial, political or religious group as such.''

During the discussion of various categories of acts constituting genocide, the representative of China called the attention of the Committee to the desirability of including acts of genocide committed through the use of narcotics. The Committee, at its 81st meeting, met this point by inserting in subparagraph 2 the words ''or mental'', whereby the text in question came to read: ''Causing serious bodily or mental harm to members of the group''.

At its 82nd meeting, the Committee adopted by 20 votes to 13, with 13 abstentions, an amendment submitted by the representative of Greece to include as point 5 in the acts of genocide the act of forcibly transferring children from one group to another.

Article 3 (subsequently deleted) of the draft convention, which dealt with ''cultural'' genocide, gave rise to a discussion on the question of whether this particular form of genocide should be covered by the convention. At its 83rd meeting, the Committee decided by 25 votes to 16, with 4 abstentions, not to include provisions relating to cultural genocide. It was pointed out, however, by several representatives that, in expressing their views on the retention or suppression of this article, no position was taken on cultural genocide as such, and that they felt that action to safeguard against such form of genocide might more appropriately be taken within the sphere of human rights.

With respect to article III (4), which listed the different punishable acts, prolonged debates took place, particularly on the question of the retention or suppression of sub-paragraph *(c)* providing that ''direct incitement in public or in private to commit genocide shall be punishable whether such incitement be successful or not''. At its 85th meeting, the Committee rejected by 16 votes in favour to 27 against, with 5 abstentions, an amendment of the representative of the United States to omit the whole of this sub-paragraph. On the other hand, the Committee decided, at the same time, to delete the words ''in private'' and the words ''whether such incitement be successful or not'' from the original text.

When the report of the drafting committee was being considered by the Sixth Committee, the United States delegation again proposed that the words ''direct and public incitement to commit genocide'' should be deleted from this article. However, at the 128th meeting, held on 29 November 1948, the representative of the United States withdrew this proposal.

At its 92nd meeting, the Committee took up article IV (5), dealing with the authors of the crime of genocide. It examined, in the first place, the amendment submitted by the USSR delegation which would add to this article a second paragraph as follows: ''Command of the law or superior orders shall not justify genocide''. This amendment was rejected by 15 votes in favour to 28 against, with 6 abstentions. The Committee then discussed the terminology to be used, in order to describe adequately the authors of the crime of genocide. It was pointed out by several representatives that the expression ''Heads of State'' used in the English text would appear to include Heads of State of constitutional monarchies who, according to the constitutions of their countries, enjoyed immunity and could not be brought before a national court. At its 95th meeting, the Committee therefore adopted by 31 votes to 1, with 11 abstentions, a Netherlands amendment, as amended by Thailand, whereby the English text came to read ''constitutionally responsible rulers, public officials or private individuals''. Consequently, the Committee rejected, at its 96th meeting, an amendment submitted by Syria, which would have included in the article as authors of genocide also *de facto* Heads of State and persons having usurped authority. It was felt that such persons already came within the scope of article IV (5).

Article VI (7) provoked a lengthy discussion. As drafted by the *ad hoc* committee, this article provided that persons charged with genocide should be tried by a competent tribunal of the State in the territory of which the act was committed *or* by a competent international tribunal. At the 98th meeting, the Committee decided by 23 votes to 19, with 3 abstentions, to delete the reference to trial before an international tribunal.

In the Sixth Committee's consideration of the drafting committee's report, however, the representative of the United States proposed that the following words should be added to the end of the article: ". . . or by a competent international penal tribunal subject to the acceptance at a later date by the Contracting Party concerned of its jurisdiction". The Sixth Committee discussed the question at its 129th and 130th meetings. It decided to reconsider the draft article VI and, by 29 votes to 9, with 5 abstentions, adopted a revised text of the United States amendment submitted by the representative of France and drawn up in consultation with the representatives of Belgium, France and the United States. By this text, the following words were added at the end of article VI (7): ". . . or by such international penal tribunal as may have jurisdiction with respect to such Contracting Parties as shall have accepted the jurisdiction of such tribunal".

At its 131st meeting, the Sixth Committee had agreed to insert in its report to the General Assembly the substance of an amendment to article VI submitted by the representative of India, according to which nothing in the article should affect the right of any State to bring to trial before its own tribunals any of its nationals for acts committed outside the State. Following this, the representative of Sweden had requested that the report should also indicate that article VI did not deprive the State of jurisdiction in the case of crimes committed against its nationals outside national territory. After some discussion of the questions raised in this connexion, the Committee adopted at its 134th meeting, by 20 votes to 8, with 6 abstentions, the following explanatory text for insertion in its report to the General Assembly:

> "The first part of Article 6 contemplates the obligation of the State in whose territory acts of genocide have been committed. Thus, in particular, it does not affect the right of any State to bring to trial before its own tribunals any of its nationals for acts committed outside the State."

The Sixth Committee, at its 99th meeting, adopted a joint draft proposal of the Netherlands and Iran (resolution B), by which the International Law Commission was invited to study the desirability and possibility of establishing an international judicial organ for the trial of persons charged with genocide or other crimes, over which jurisdiction would be conferred upon that organ by international conventions.

In article IX (10) of the proposed convention, as drafted by the *ad hoc* committee, it was laid down that disputes relating to the interpretation or application of the convention should be submitted to the International Court of Justice, provided that no dispute should be submitted to the Court involving an issue which had been referred to and was pending before, or had been passed upon by a competent international criminal tribunal. At its 104th meeting, however, the Committee adopted by 23 votes to 13, with 8 abstentions, in substitution for this article, a joint amendment submitted by the United Kingdom and Belgium and amended by India, according to which any dispute between the contracting parties relating to the interpretation, application or fulfilment of the convention, including disputes relating to the responsibility of a State for any of the acts enumerated in articles II and IV, should be submitted to the International Court of Justice at the request of any of the contracting parties.

In replying to the objections raised on this point by the USSR and Polish delegations, the United Kingdom representative stated that he had always taken into consideration the enormous practical difficulties of bringing rulers and Heads of State to justice, except perhaps at the end of a war. For that reason, his delegation had thought that provision to refer acts of genocide to the International Court of Justice, and the inclusion of the idea of international responsibility of States or Governments, was necessary for the establishment of an effective convention on genocide.

. . .

Texts of a new article dealing with the application of the convention to dependent territories was proposed by the United Kingdom as well as by the Ukrainian SSR. The United Kingdom amendment provided that the application of the convention might, by a notification to the Secretary-General, be extended to all or any of the territories for the conduct of whose foreign relations the party in question is responsible. The Ukrainian SSR amendment provided that the convention should apply equally to the territory of the contracting parties and to all territories in regard to which they perform the functions of the governing and Administering Authority, including Trust Territories and other Non-Self-Governing Territories. At its 107th meeting, the Committee rejected the Ukrainian amendment by 10 votes in favour to 19 against, with 14 abstentions, but adopted the United Kingdom proposal by 18 votes to 9, with 14 abstentions (article XII of the final text).

The Committee also adopted, at its 108th meeting, a draft resolution presented by Iran (resolution C), recommending Members of the United Nations administering dependent territories to take such measures as are necessary and feasible to enable the provisions of the convention to be extended to those territories as soon as possible.

After having disposed of the final clauses in the draft convention of the *ad hoc* committee (articles XI to XIX), the Sixth Committee took up, at its 100th meeting, the question of the preamble of the convention, and adopted, by 38 votes to 9, with 5 abstentions, a text proposed by Venezuela.

Apart from the amendments already mentioned above, new proposals were submitted when the report of the drafting committee and the texts revised by it were considered by the Sixth Committee. The delegation of India submitted minor amendments concerning articles II, VI, IX and XVII. Only one of these was adopted and became part of the final text of the convention, namely, paragraph *(b)* in article XVII.

Belgium, the United Kingdom and the United States introduced a joint proposal for an alternative text of article IX, to read as follows:

"Disputes between Contracting Parties relating to the interpretation, application or implementation of the Convention, including disputes arising from a charge by a Contracting Party that the crime of genocide or any other of the acts enumerated in Article III has been committed within the jurisdiction of another Contracting Party, shall be submitted to the International Court of Justice at the request of one of the parties to the dispute."

However, before putting this proposal to the vote, the Chairman ruled that the joint amendment concerned the substance of the article. According to him, article IX provided that, among others, disputes relating to the responsibility of a State for genocide or any other acts enumerated in article III should be submitted to the International Court of Justice; whereas according to the amendment in question disputes were not considered to be the responsibility of the State, but the result of a charge that the crime had been committed within the territory of one of the contracting parties. Thereafter, the Chairman put to the vote the Syrian motion for reconsideration of article IX. The result of the vote was 16 in favour, 13 against, and 11 abstentions. Consequently, the motion was not adopted, having failed to obtain the required two-thirds majority.

At its 133rd meeting, the Sixth Committee proceeded to vote on the three draft resolutions. By 30 votes to none, with 8 abstentions, the Committee adopted the draft of the covering resolution A, with the annexed draft convention as amended. Next, by 27 votes to 5, with 6 abstentions, the Committee adopted draft resolution B on the study by the International Law Commission of the question of an international criminal jurisdiction. Finally,

by 29 votes to none, with 7 abstentions, the Committee adopted draft resolution C on application of the convention with respect to dependent territories.

A number of representatives made explanatory statements as to why they voted for or against the adoption of the draft convention, or why they abstained. Some, for instance the representatives of the USSR and India, reserved their right to raise reservations and objections when the matter came before the General Assembly. This happened at the 178th and 179th plenary meetings of the Assembly, on 9 December 1948.

Discussion by the General Assembly in plenary meeting

Altogether, representatives of twenty-one countries made their statements before the Assembly. Several of them admitted that the proposed convention was not perfect; but while some thought that this was natural and could not have been otherwise because the text was the outcome of a compromise between the conflicting views, others put their objections on specific grounds. For instance, a number of delegations considered it a shortcoming that there was no clause in the draft convention which would cover cases of "cultural" genocide (USSR, Venezuela, Pakistan, Egypt, Byelorussian SSR, United Kingdom, Poland and China). The USSR and Venezuela submitted therefore amendments on this point. The Pakistan delegation stated that it recognized that the original text of the proposed article, as discussed by the Sixth Committee at its 83rd meeting, had provided too wide a definition of cultural genocide, and that it would, therefore, have been difficult to bring the offences enumerated in it before the courts. The delegation had, therefore, submitted an amendment which narrowed cultural genocide to two specific crimes—forcible mass conversion of persons and the destruction of religious edifices. The Venezuelan delegation wished to add to the convention the following definition of cultural genocide: "Systematic destruction of religious edifices, schools or libraries of the group". To this the representative of India objected, saying that it could not be asserted that a group, as such, would be annihilated by the destruction of its religious edifices, schools or libraries. Faced with these objections, the delegation of Venezuela withdrew its amendment immediately before a vote was taken on the corresponding Soviet proposal (see below).

However, the main division of opinion took place with respect to three other items. First, there was the question concerning the widening of the definition of genocide in the preamble of the convention. The USSR delegation, supported by the Czechoslovakian, Polish and Byelorussian SSR delegations, argued that it was not sufficient merely to state that genocide had inflicted enormous losses upon humanity. It should also be pointed out that there was a connexion between genocide and racial and national hatreds, the domination of the so-called "higher races" and the extermination of the so-called "lower races". The crime of genocide formed an integral part of the plan for world domination of the supporters of racial ideologies. The United States delegation opposed this on the grounds that, should it be adopted, the Soviet amendment would have a limiting effect on the convention, in that it declared genocide to be organically linked to certain doctrines. The United States representative further said that the Nürnberg tribunal, referred to in that connexion by the USSR, had recognized that there existed such an organic link, but it had been concerned only with crimes committed during the last war or during the period of preparation for the war. The convention on genocide, however, should be applicable to all situations, in time of peace as in time of war.

Another division of opinion occurred with respect to the second part of article VI of the proposed convention, by the terms of which the perpetrators of the crime of genocide could be tried by an international criminal court. The USSR delegation objected to this clause on the grounds that it would limit the action Governments might take for the punishment of genocide. Moreover, the establishment of such an international court would be equivalent to interference in the domestic affairs of States, thus infringing upon their sovereignty. For the same reasons, the Soviet delegation objected to the draft resolution of the Sixth Committee requesting the International Law Commission to consider the question of an international criminal jurisdiction and the establishment of an international criminal court to judge questions connected with genocide.

Several delegations disagreed with this interpretation saying that it was sufficient to point out that the crimes with which the draft convention dealt could be perpetrated by a State, or by individuals who might be representatives or agents of a State. If the punishment of such crimes was left to the State in question, the convention on genocide would be in the nature of a fraud (United States). The delegation of India supported the USSR amendment on this question, stating that the Sixth Committee, itself, had decided, at its 98th meeting, to delete the vague reference to the international penal tribunal and to request the International Law Commission to study the possibility of setting up such a tribunal "which would be the only method of dealing with that complicated and difficult matter". The Netherlands delegation, while realizing that no international court yet existed which was competent to try individuals charged with committing genocide, did not consider this to be a sufficient reason for excluding from the convention the possibility

that cases of genocide might one day be referred to such a court.

. . .

Resolution adopted by the General Assembly

The President then put to the vote draft resolution A, B and C proposed by the Sixth Committee. Resolution A was adopted by 56 votes to none.

. . .

Resolution B was adopted by 43 votes to 6, with 3 abstentions.

Resolution C was adopted by 50 votes, with 1 abstention.

All three resolutions (260(III) A, B, and C) were adopted on 9 December 1948. Their text follows:

A. ADOPTION OF THE CONVENTION ON THE PREVENTION AND PUNISHMENT OF THE CRIME OF GENOCIDE, AND TEXT OF THE CONVENTION

"*The General Assembly*

"*Approves* the annexed Convention on the Prevention and Punishment of the Crime of Genocide and proposes it for signature and ratification or accession in accordance with its article XI."

ANNEX
TEXT OF THE CONVENTION
The Contracting Parties,

Having considered the declaration made by the General Assembly of the United Nations in its resolution 96(I) dated 11 December 1946 that genocide is a crime under international law, contrary to the spirit and aims of the United Nations and condemned by the civilized world;

Recognizing that at all periods of history genocide has inflicted great losses on humanity; and

Being convinced that, in order to liberate mankind from such an odious scourge, international co-operation is required;

Hereby agree as hereinafter provided.

Article I

The Contracting Parties confirm that genocide, whether committed in time of peace or in time of war, is a crime under international law which they undertake to prevent and to punish.

Article II

In the present Convention, genocide means any of the following acts committed with intent to destroy, in whole or in part, a national, ethnical, racial or religious group, as such:

(*a*) Killing members of the group;

(*b*) Causing serious bodily or mental harm to members of the group;

(*c*) Deliberately inflicting on the group conditions of life calculated to bring about its physical destruction in whole or in part;

(*d*) Imposing measures intended to prevent births within the group;

(*e*) Forcibly transferring children of the group to another group.

Article III

The following acts shall be punishable:

(*a*) Genocide;

(b)   Conspiracy to commit genocide;
(c)   Direct and public incitement to commit genocide;
(d)   Attempt to commit genocide;
(e)   Complicity in genocide.

Article IV

Persons committing genocide or any of the other acts enumerated in article III shall be punished, whether they are constitutionally responsible rulers, public officials or private individuals.

Article V

The Contracting Parties undertake to enact, in accordance with their respective Constitutions, the necessary legislation to give effect to the provisions of the present Convention and, in particular, to provide effective penalties for persons guilty of genocide or any of the other acts enumerated in article III.

Article VI

Persons charged with genocide or any of the other acts enumerated in article III shall be tried by a competent tribunal of the State in the territory of which the act was committed, or by such international penal tribunal as may have jurisdiction with respect to those Contracting Parties which shall have accepted its jurisdiction.

Article VII

Genocide and the other acts enumerated in article III shall not be considered as political crimes for the purpose of extradition.

The Contracting Parties pledge themselves in such cases to grant extradition in accordance with their laws and treaties in force.

Article VIII

Any Contracting Party may call upon the competent organs of the United Nations to take such action under the Charter of the United Nations as they consider appropriate for the prevention and suppression of acts of genocide or any of the other acts enumerated in article III.

Article IX

Disputes between the Contracting Parties relating to the interpretation, application or fulfilment of the present Convention, including those relating to the responsibility of a State for genocide or any of the other acts enumerated in article III, shall be submitted to the International Court of Justice at the request of any of the parties to the dispute.

Article X

The present Convention, of which the Chinese, English, French, Russian and Spanish texts are equally authentic, shall bear the date of 9 December 1948.

Article XI

The present Convention shall be open until 31 December 1949 for signature on behalf of any Member of the United Nations and of any non-member State to which an invitation to sign has been addressed by the General Assembly.

The present Convention shall be ratified, and the instruments of ratification shall be deposited with the Secretary-General of the United Nations.

After 1 January 1950, the present Convention may be acceded to on behalf of any Member of the United Nations and of any non-member State which has received an invitation as aforesaid.

Instruments of accession shall be deposited with the Secretary-General of the United Nations.

Article XII

Any Contracting Party may at any time, by notification addressed to the Secretary-General of the United Nations, extend the application of the present Convention to all or any of the territories for the conduct of whose foreign relations that Contracting Party is responsible.

Article XIII

On the day when the first twenty instruments of ratification or accession have been deposited, the Secretary-General shall draw up a *procès-verbal* and transmit a copy of it to each Member of the United Nations and to each of the non-member States contemplated in article XI.

The present Convention shall come into force on the ninetieth day following the date of deposit of the twentieth instrument of ratification or accession.

Any ratification or accession effected subsequent to the latter date shall become effective on the ninetieth day following the deposit of the instrument of ratification or accession.

Article XIV

The present Convention shall remain in effect for a period of ten years as from the date of its coming into force.

It shall thereafter remain in force for successive periods of five years for such Contracting Parties as have not denounced it at least six months before the expiration of the current period.

Denunciation shall be effected by a written notification addressed to the Secretary-General of the United Nations.

Article XV

If, as a result of denunciations, the number of Parties to the present Convention should become less than sixteen, the Convention shall cease to be in force as from the date on which the last of these denunciations shall become effective.

Article XVI

A request for the revision of the present Convention may be made at any time by any Contracting Party by means of a notification in writing addressed to the Secretary-General.

The General Assembly shall decide upon the steps, if any, to be taken in respect of such request.

Article XVII

The Secretary-General of the United Nations shall notify all Members of the United Nations and the non-member States contemplated in article XI of the following:

(a) Signatures, ratifications and accessions received in accordance with article XI;

(b) Notifications received in accordance with article XII;

(c) The date upon which the present Convention comes into force in accordance with article XIII;

(d) Denunciations received in accordance with article XIV;

(e) The abrogation of the Convention in accordance with article XV.

(f) Notifications received in accordance with article XVI.

Article XVIII

The original of the present Convention shall be deposited in the archives of the United Nations.

A certified copy of the Convention shall be transmitted to all Members of the United Nations and to the non-member States contemplated in article XI.

Article XIX

The present Convention shall be registered by the Secretary-General of the United Nations on the date of its coming into force.

B. STUDY BY THE INTERNATIONAL LAW COMMISSION OF THE QUESTION OF AN INTERNATIONAL CRIMINAL JURISDICTION

"*The General Assembly,*

"*Considering* that the discussion of the Convention on the Prevention and Punishment of the Crime of Genocide has raised the question of the desirability and possibility of having persons charged with genocide tried by a competent international tribunal,

"*Considering* that, in the course of development of the international community, there will be an increasing need of an international judicial organ for the trial of certain crimes under international law,

"*Invites* the International Law Commission to study the desirability and possibility of establishing an international judicial organ for the trial of persons charged with genocide or other crimes over which jurisdiction will be conferred upon that organ by international conventions;

"*Requests* the International Law Commission, in carrying out this task, to pay attention to the possibility of establishing a Criminal Chamber of the International Court of Justice."

C. APPLICATION WITH RESPECT TO DEPENDENT TERRITORIES, OF THE CONVENTION ON THE PREVENTION AND PUNISHMENT OF THE CRIME OF GENOCIDE

"*The General Assembly* recommends that Parties to the Convention on the Prevention and Punishment of the Crime of Genocide which administer dependent territories should take such measures as are necessary and feasible to enable the provisions of the Convention to be extended to these territories as soon as possible."

[YUN 1948-49, pp. 953-60]

International Bill of Human Rights

The United Nations has worked for some 50 years to develop standards of human rights in the form of international instruments agreed upon by States and to encourage countries to adopt and implement them.

The International Bill of Human Rights consists of the Universal Declaration of Human Rights, the International Covenant on Economic, Social and Cultural Rights, and the International Covenant on Civil and Political Rights and its Optional Protocol.

Universal Declaration of Human Rights

Among the Organization's first tasks was to draft a Universal Declaration of Human Rights. The Declaration, adopted on 10 December 1948, was intended as a "common standard of achievement for all peoples". Its 30 articles spell out basic civil and political rights and fundamental economic, social and cultural rights that human beings in every country should enjoy. As a statement of goals and principles, the Universal Declaration was a giant step. A declaration does not have the same force as a treaty or a convention by which States legally obligate themselves to adhere to international standards. None the less, the Universal Declaration is generally considered to have the weight of customary international law because it is so widely accepted and used as a yardstick for measuring the conduct of States. Many newly independent countries have cited the Universal Declaration or included its provisions in their basic laws or constitutions and many human rights covenants, conventions and treaties concluded since 1948 have restated its principles.

Articles 1 and 2 of the Declaration state that "all human beings are born free and equal in dignity and rights" and are entitled to all the rights and freedoms set forth in the Declaration "without distinction of any kind, such as race, colour, sex, language, religion, political or other opinion, national or social origin, property, birth or other status".

The next 19 articles deal with the civil and political rights to which all human beings are entitled. Articles 22 to 27 set forth their economic, social and cultural rights.

The concluding articles, 28 to 30, recognize that everyone is entitled to a social and international order in which the human rights set forth in the Declaration may be fully realized; that these rights may only be limited for the sole purpose of securing recognition and respect for the rights and freedoms of others and that each person has duties to the community in which she or he lives.

Each year, the anniversary of the adoption of the Declaration, 10 December, is observed internationally as Human Rights Day.

Introduction

One of the major actions of the General Assembly at its third regular session was the adoption of the Universal Declaration of Human Rights. In view of the importance of this Declaration, a brief survey is given here of its background and of the steps leading towards its adoption which were taken prior to 21 September 1948.

Decision of the UN Conference on International Organization

At the United Nations Conference on International Organization, held at San Francisco in 1945, some representatives suggested that the United Nations Charter should contain a bill of rights. Committee I/1 of the Conference, which was charged with the task of considering the Preamble, Purposes and Principles of the Charter, received the idea with sympathy, but decided that "the present Conference, if only for lack of time, could not proceed to realize such a draft in an international contract. The Organization, once formed, could better proceed to consider the suggestion and to deal effectively with it through a special commission or by some other method. The Committee recommends that the General Assembly consider the proposal and give it effect."

At the final plenary session, on 26 June 1945, the President of the United States stated that

"under this document [the Charter] we have good reason to expect an international bill of rights, acceptable to all the nations involved."

Provisions of the United Nations Charter

One of the principal functions of the United Nations is to promote universal respect for, and observance of, human rights.

Prior to the United Nations, provisions for safeguarding human rights had been written into many national constitutions, and certain rights in limited fields had been guaranteed in treaties. The United Nations Charter, however, goes further in its emphasis on the general obligation of all the Members of the United Nations to provide and encourage respect for human rights, and in providing that machinery should be set up for this purpose.

Article 1 of the Charter declares that one of the principal purposes of the United Nations is:

"To achieve international co-operation . . . in promoting and encouraging respect for human rights and for fundamental freedoms for all without distinction as to race, sex, language or religion . . . '

Moreover, universal respect for human rights and fundamental freedoms is recognized as one of the conditions of stability and friendly relations among nations (Article 55). Its encouragement is one of the basic objectives of the trusteeship system (Article 76 c).

The General Assembly may initiate studies and make recommendations for the purpose of assisting in the realization of human rights and fundamental freedoms for all without distinction as to race, sex, language or religion (Article 13). The Economic and Social Council may make recommendations for the purpose of promoting respect for, and observance of, human rights and fundamental freedoms for all (Article 62).

Establishment of a Commission on Human Rights

The importance with which the question of human rights was regarded at the San Francisco Conference is illustrated by the provision in the Charter, obliging the Economic and Social Council to set up a commission or commissions for the promotion of human rights (Article 68). The Commission on Human Rights is thus the only Commission specifically named in the Charter.

The Economic and Social Council, on 15 February 1946, established a Commission on Human Rights in nuclear form. The Council decided that the work of the Commission should primarily be devoted to submitting proposals, recommendations and reports for an international bill of human rights. This Commission met at Hunter College, New York, from 29 April to 20 May 1946. At this meeting, the Commission studied its final composition and asked the Secretary-General to collect all possible information on the subject. At that stage, the Division of Human Rights was set up in the Secretariat. That Division began a study of various drafts submitted by the delegations of Panama, Chile and Cuba and by the American Federation of Labor, as well as private drafts, especially those of Dr. Lauterpacht of Cambridge University, Dr. Alvarez of the American Institute of International Law, the Rev. Parsons, of the Catholic Association for International Peace, Mr. McNitt of the Faculty of Law of South Western University, and Mr. H. G. Wells.

First session of the Commission on Human Rights

The Economic and Social Council, on 21 June 1946, adopted the terms of reference of the permanent Commission on Human Rights, and determined its membership. The Commission held its first session at Lake Success, New York, from 27 January to 10 February 1947.

The Commission, at its first session, had before it a number of working papers prepared by the Secretariat at the request of the nuclear Commission, and also a number of draft bills submitted by Governments and various organizations. The Commission devoted a great deal of its time to a discussion of the form and content of the proposed bill. It decided that the Chairman, together with the Vice-Chairman and Rapporteur, should undertake, with the assistance of the Secretariat, the task of formulating a preliminary draft international bill of human rights, to be submitted to the Commission at its second session for thorough examination. In view of the difficulties encountered by that small drafting group, it was suggested that it be expanded into a drafting committee, consisting of representatives of the Philippines, the Ukrainian SSR, the USSR, the United Kingdom, the United States, Uruguay and Yugoslavia. The Council later endorsed this suggestion.

First session of the Drafting Committee on the Bill of Human Rights

The Drafting Committee held its first session at Lake Success, from 9 to 25 June 1947. In addition to a Draft Outline of an International Bill of Human Rights prepared by the Secretariat, the Drafting Committee had before it the text of a letter from Lord Dukeston, the United Kingdom representative on the Commission on Human Rights, transmitting a draft International Bill of Human Rights and also a draft resolution which might be passed by the General Assembly when adopting the Bill. These two documents were considered and compared by the Drafting Committee, together with certain United States proposals for the rewording of some items appearing in the Secretariat Draft Outline. The Draft Outline prepared by the Secretariat was a compilation of all the rights proposed either in international drafts, or contained in national constitutions or suggested by members of the Commission on Human Rights.

Two views were put forward by the Drafting Committee regarding the form the preliminary draft Bill should take. Some representatives thought that the preliminary draft, in the first instance, should take the form of a declaration or manifesto; others felt that it should be in the form of a convention. (A declaration or manifesto would be a recommendation by the General Assembly to Member States, and, as such, would have moral weight but no legal compulsion on Members. On the other hand, a convention would be legally binding on Members which accepted it. Its application, however, would be limited to the signatories.)

It was agreed by those who favoured the declaration that it should be accompanied or followed by a convention or conventions on specific groups of rights. It was also agreed by those who favoured the convention that the General Assembly in recommending a convention to Member States might make a declaration wider in content and more general in expression. The Drafting Committee, therefore, while recognizing that the decision as to the form of the Bill was a matter for the full Commission on Human Rights, decided to prepare two documents; one, a working paper in the form of a preliminary draft of a declaration or manifesto setting forth general principles, and the second, a working paper outlining a draft convention on those matters which the Committee felt might lend themselves to formulation as binding obligations.

The report submitted by the Drafting Committee to the Commission on Human Rights included, therefore, drafts for an international declaration and an international convention on human rights.

Second session of the Commission on Human Rights

The Commission on Human Rights met for its second session at Geneva, from 2 to 17 December 1947. It was in the course of that session that the conception of an international bill of human rights comprising three parts began to crystallize: a declaration, a convention, and measures for implementation. It had become evident that many Governments were prepared to accept a draft declaration if it were to precede and not to replace a convention. One result of that session was a report on the measures for implementation which remained a basic document for all subsequent study in that field.

Second session of the Drafting Committee

The Drafting Committee met for its second session at Lake Success, New York, from 3 to 21 May 1948. It considered comments on the draft International Bill of Human Rights which had been received from a number of Member Governments. It also took into account (1) the suggestions of the United Nations Conference on Freedom of Information (held at Geneva in March and April 1948) concerning articles on freedom of information in the draft Declaration and the draft Covenant; (2) suggestions made by the Commission on the Status of Women on two articles in the draft Declaration; and (3) the American Declaration of the Rights and Duties of Man, as adopted by the Ninth International Conference of American States, held in Bogotá, Colombia, in March-May 1948. It redrafted the entire draft Covenant, but had time to redraft only parts of the draft Declaration and did not consider the question of implementation.

Third session of the Commission on Human Rights

The third session of the Commission on Human Rights took place at Lake Success, from 24 May to 18 June 1948. The Commission, at that session, based its work on the report of the second session of its Drafting Committee. The individual articles of the draft Declaration were examined anew. The Commission was able to complete a re-draft of the Declaration, which was adopted without opposition, but had no time to consider the Drafting Committee's re-draft of the Covenant, nor to discuss implementation, as requested by the Economic and Social Council at its sixth session (February and March 1948).

Decision of the Economic and Social Council at its seventh session

Because of pressure of business at its seventh session, the Economic and Social Council decided, on 17 August 1948, that the report of the third session of the Commission on Human Rights, which had been referred to the Council's Human Rights Committee, should be recalled to the plenary session; and that in plenary meeting there would be an opportunity for each member to make one general statement of position.

Statements were made on 25 and 26 August by all members of the Council. The Council then decided, on 26 August, to transmit to the General

Assembly the draft International Declaration of Human Rights submitted to it by the Commission on Human Rights in the report of its third session, together with the remainder of the report of the Commission and the records of the proceedings of the Council on the subject.

Consideration by the General Assembly at its third session

Discussion in the Third Committee

The General Assembly, at its 142nd meeting held on 24 September 1948, referred to the Third Committee the draft International Declaration of Human Rights. The Third Committee considered the item at its 88th to 105th, 107th to 116th, 119th to 134th, 137th to 167th, and 174th to 179th meetings, held on 30 September to 18 October, 19 to 29 October, 30 October to 12 Novembers 15 to 30 November, and 4 to 7 December 1948. Altogether, the Third Committee spent eighty-one meetings in considering and discussing the draft Declaration prepared by the Commission on Human Rights. One hundred and sixty-eight formal draft resolutions containing amendments to the various articles of the draft Declaration were submitted during the course of the Committee's debate.

Before beginning a detailed study of each of the articles in the draft Declaration, the Third Committee engaged in a general debate on the draft as a whole. The representatives of the following countries, among others, supported the draft Declaration: Argentina, Australia, Belgium, Bolivia, Brazil, Canada, Chile, China, Colombia, Cuba, the Dominican Republic, Ecuador, France, Greece, Guatemala, Haiti, Lebanon, Mexico, Norway, Pakistan, Panama, the Philippines, the United Kingdom, the United States, Syria and Uruguay.

. . .

Detailed consideration of the articles of the draft Declaration

After concluding the general debate on the draft Declaration, the Third Committee, at its 94th meeting, held on 5 October, decided by 41 votes to 3, with 7 abstentions, to consider only the draft Declaration, as the other two documents (the covenant and measures of implementation) were not yet in a state suitable for consideration. The Committee did not, however, exclude an exposition of views on the other parts of the International Bill of Rights.

The Committee, at its 95th meeting, held on 6 October, decided by 43 votes to 6, with 7 abstentions, to start by discussing article 1 of the draft Declaration. A detailed examination of each article and the preamble of the draft Declaration was then entered into by the Committee, which devoted eighty-one meetings to its task. One hundred and sixty-eight amendments were presented. The Committee's work lasted from 6 October until 7 December.

Examination of the articles by Sub-Committee

At its 166th meeting on 30 November, the Third Committee adopted a Lebanese proposal to set up a sub-committee "to examine the totality of the declaration of human rights, i.e., the twenty-nine articles and the preamble, adopted by the Third Committee, solely from the standpoint of arrangement, consistency, uniformity and style and to submit proposals thereon to the Third Committee." The Sub-Committee was also asked to "set up a language group of five members, one for each of the official languages, to check and secure the exact correspondence of the text in the five official languages."

The Sub-Committee was composed of the representatives of the following eleven countries: Australia, Belgium, China, Cuba, Ecuador, France, Lebanon, Poland, the USSR, the United Kingdom and the United States. It held ten meetings, from 1 to 4 December, and examined in detail each article of the draft Declaration. Among other things, the Sub-Committee proposed the division into two parts of two of the articles of the draft—those dealing with (1) slavery and torture, and (2) equality before the law and right to an effective remedy by competent national tribunals. The Sub-Committee also proposed that the article of the draft dealing with the right to rest and leisure should be placed after the article dealing with the right to work rather than after the article dealing with the right to education.

Adoption of the draft Declaration by the Third Committee

The report of the Sub-Committee was considered by the Third Committee at its 175th to 178th meetings, held on 4 and 6 December. At the Committee's 175th meeting, on 4 December, an oral proposal of the Chairman (the representative of Lebanon) to have the Committee proceed to an examination, paragraph by paragraph, of the text submitted by the Sub-Committee to make certain, first of all, that the sense had not been altered, was adopted by 31 votes to none, with 3 abstentions.

Only minor drafting changes in the text proposed by the Sub-Committee were made by the Committee. The arrangement of articles was discussed at the Committee's 178th meeting on 6 December, at which time a number of changes were agreed to.

After it had adopted separately the substance and the arrangement of the draft Declaration, it also, at its 178th meeting, voted on the text as a whole. The draft Declaration was adopted by a roll-call vote of 29 to none, with 7 abstentions.

. . .

Dissemination of the Declaration

After the Third Committee had adopted the Declaration of Human Rights, it adopted by 28 votes to none, with 8 abstentions, a French draft resolution, which was slightly amended by Cuba, the Dominican Republic, China, Lebanon and Syria, and which called upon the General Assembly to recommend that Member Governments publicize the text of the Declaration and cause it to be disseminated as widely as possible.

USSR draft resolution

At the 179th meeting of the Third Committee on 7 December, the representative of the USSR explained why his delegation had abstained from voting on the draft Declaration. He observed that most of the USSR amendments to the draft Declaration had been rejected, and the text adopted at the 178th meeting was practically identical with the original draft and was unsatisfactory. He therefore submitted a draft resolution which stated that the text of the Declaration considered by the Third Committee required "serious improvements in a whole series of articles", and which requested the Assembly to postpone the final adoption of the Declaration to its next session. The USSR draft was supported by the representatives of the Byelorussian SSR and the Ukrainian SSR.

The representatives of the United States, the Philippines, France and Ecuador opposed the USSR draft. They maintained that the action contemplated in the USSR draft would be illegal in view of the fact that the Committee had already adopted the draft Declaration.

On being put to the vote, the USSR draft resolution was rejected by 6 votes in favour to 26 against, with 1 abstention.

Discussion by the General Assembly in plenary meeting

The report of the Third Committee was considered at the 180th to 183rd plenary meetings of the General Assembly, on 9 and 10 December. Altogether, thirty-five delegations spoke in the general debate, many of them raising points which they had previously raised in the Third Committee.

Views expressed by representatives

Various representatives underlined the importance of the Declaration. The representative of Lebanon stated that the Declaration was destined to mark an important stage in the history of mankind. The representative of the United States said that the Declaration was inspired by a sincere desire for peace, and that it was based on the conviction that man must have freedom in order to develop his personality to the full and have his dignity respected. The representative of Chile maintained that once the Declaration was approved, no one could infringe upon the rights proclaimed in it without becoming an outcast from the community of nations. The representative of France considered the Declaration to be the most vigorous and the most urgently needed of humanity's protests against oppression. The representative of the Philippines pointed out that, during its third session, the United Nations had been on trial for its life and that it was at that very moment that it had justified its existence before an anxious world by producing the Declaration.

The representative of Cuba proclaimed that the Declaration expressed in particularly clear and precise terms the most noble aspirations of twentieth-century man. The representative of Iceland regarded the Declaration as a preamble to a future world constitution. The representative of the United Kingdom stressed the fact that the preparation of the draft Declaration was a milestone on the road of human progress. Never before, he said, had so many nations joined together to agree on what they considered to be the fundamental rights of the individual.

According to the representative of Mexico, the adoption of the Declaration was one of the most important actions in the history of the United Nations. The representative of Pakistan stated that his delegation fully associated itself with what had been said in praise of the Declaration. In the opinion of the representative of Denmark, the Declaration made the promises of the Charter regarding equality of men and women a living reality. The representative of India expressed the hope that the Declaration would pave the way to a new era of international solidarity, because the basis of rights was neither the State nor the individual, but the social human being, participating in social life, and striving for national and international co-operation. The representative of Canada stated that the Declaration was inspired by the highest ideals and expressed the most noble principles and aspirations. As a result of the Declaration, the representative of Bolivia said, humanity would enter upon a new phase which should lead to the establishment of a true international constitution, founded on the limitation of the sovereignty of States for the benefit of the individual. Though imperfect, the Declaration was the most harmonious, comprehensive and universal that had been so far achieved, and its principles were very advanced, compared with the conditions prevailing in some countries, the representative of Paraguay declared.

The representative of Lebanon drew attention to the fact that eighteen articles of the Declaration had been adopted without any opposition. Of a total of 1,233 individual votes, 88.08 per cent had been affirmative, 3.73 per cent negative, and 8.19 per cent had been abstentions.

A number of representatives drew attention to the Declaration's universality and to the attitude of compromise shown by the delegations working on it. The representative of the United States stated that the Declaration represented a compromise which did not contain everything that each country would have wished it to contain; nevertheless, her country regarded it as a satisfactory document. The representative of Chile recalled that fifty-eight civilized nations had succeeded in overcoming ideological and juridical differences, and had agreed on a joint proclamation of human rights. Stressing that it was impossible to attain complete agreement on doctrine, the representative of France pointed out that an agreement based on the practical as well as the ideal had been achieved. The Declaration, he said, represented a considerable effort on the part of individuals, groups and States. To the French representative, the chief novelty of the Declaration was its universality. Because it was universal, he said, the Declaration could have a broader scope than national declarations.

The document, the representative of the Philippines pointed out, could make no claims to perfection since it had been the result of a compromise, but compromise, he stated, was the essence of democracy and the very basis of the United Nations. Nations which had taken part in the preparation of the Declaration, the representative of Australia observed, differed profoundly in their political, economic, social and religious points of view, and divergencies were bound to become apparent regarding the manner in which the various aspects of the question should be approached and treated. The Declaration, therefore, presented an effort at compromise and mutual understanding. He thought that, having been accepted and approved by the majority of Members of the United Nations, the Declaration would go forth to the world with much greater strength and authority.

The representative of Brazil said that the Declaration did not reflect the particular point of view of any one people or of any one group of peoples. Neither was it the expression of any particular political doctrine or philosophical system. It was, he declared, the result of the intellectual and moral co-operation of a large number of nations. The preparation of the Declaration, explained the representative of New Zealand, had been a difficult task, since its authors had different social, economic and philosophical backgrounds, but it had proved that with good will and a sincere desire to co-operate, it was possible for divergent points of view to be reconciled. Thus, he submitted, the Declaration could justly be described as being "universal".

Another point covered in the general debate was the need to supplement the Declaration with a convention and measures for implementation. The representatives of Haiti, Lebanon, France, the United States, the United Kingdom and New Zealand, among others, spoke of this need.

Some representatives spoke of the effect that the adoption of the Declaration would have on men and nations. The representative of the United States considered it to be first and foremost a declaration of basic principles to serve as a common standard for all nations. Although the Declaration was not legally binding on Governments, it should have great moral force, the representative of the Netherlands submitted, and would serve as a guiding light to all those who endeavoured to raise man's material standard of living and spiritual condition. According to the representative of Mexico, the Declaration would serve as the basis for the realization of one of the highest aims of the United Nations, that of developing and encouraging universal respect for human rights. The representative of New Zealand expressed the opinion that the Declaration, as a statement of principles, had moral force only.

Other representatives attributed even far greater importance to the Declaration. The representative of Lebanon recalled that the Members of the United Nations had already solemnly pledged themselves, under the Charter, to promote respect for human rights and fundamental freedoms, but that it was the first time that human rights and fundamental freedoms had been set forth in detail. Hence, every Government knew, at that time, to what extent exactly it had pledged itself, and every citizen could protest to his Government if the latter did not fulfil its obligations. The Declaration, he claimed, would therefore provide a useful means of criticism, and would help to bring about changes in present legal practice. According to the representative of Chile, men everywhere would henceforth know what their rights and freedoms were. All States which were signatories to the Declaration undertook to respect and extend the basic rights proclaimed.

The representative of France explained that, while the Declaration was less powerful and binding than a convention, it had no less legal value, for it was contained in a resolution of the General Assembly which was empowered to make recommendations; it was a development of the Charter which had brought human rights within the scope of positive international law. The Declaration, said the representative of Uruguay, was a natural complement to the Charter. Its enforcement and respect for its provisions would become one of the obligations of Member States. He argued that human rights would in the future be protected and defended by all the peoples of the States Members of the United Nations. The representative of Bolivia declared that he had been instructed by his Government to state that Bolivia would pledge itself solemnly to adhere to all the provisions of the Declaration.

Although supporting enthusiastically the Declaration, the representatives of, *inter alia*, the Netherlands, Belgium, Canada and Egypt criticized certain of its aspects. The representative of the Netherlands regretted that man's divine origin and immortal destiny had not been mentioned in the Declaration, for the fount of those rights was the Supreme Being. The representative of Belgium considered that it would have been desirable to acknowledge the real basis of the equality of rights, namely, the common origin and destiny of all men. He also viewed the order of the articles as being imperfect.

In the view of the representative of Canada, the Declaration was often worded in vague and unprecise language. The imperfections and ambiguities of the Declaration might have been removed, he remarked, if a body of jurists, such as the International Law Commission, had been asked to review the text before it had been submitted to the General Assembly.

Referring to the article in the Declaration concerning the freedom to contract marriage without any restrictions as to race, nationality or religion, the representative of Egypt explained that in his country, as in almost all Moslem countries, certain restrictions and limitations existed regarding the marriage of Moslem women with persons belonging to another faith. Those limitations, he contended, were of a religious character, sprung from the very spirit of the Moslem religion, and therefore could not be ignored. He also feared that, by proclaiming man's freedom to change his religion or belief, the Declaration would be encouraging, even though it might not be intentional, the machinations of certain missions, well-known in the Orient, which pursued their efforts to convert to their own beliefs the masses of the population of the Orient.

The draft Declaration was criticized by the representatives of the Union of South Africa, the USSR, the Ukrainian SSR, Czechoslovakia, the Byelorussian SSR, Poland and Yugoslavia.

In the opinion of the representative of the Union of South Africa, the Declaration went far beyond the rights and freedoms contemplated in the Charter. He expressed doubt as to the wisdom of a declaration which would be honoured in the breach rather than in the observance of its provisions.

According to the representative of the USSR, the Declaration suffered from serious defects and omissions. Some of the articles dealing with extremely important questions—such as the article on slavery and the article on the right to education—were, in his opinion, in a very abstract form. He considered that the article dealing with the freedom to disseminate ideas did not solve the problem of freedom of expression, as the diffusion of dangerous ideas, such as war-mongering and fascist ideas, should be prevented. That same article, he submitted, made no provision for the free dissemination of just and lofty ideas. If freedom of expression was to be effective, the workers, he argued, must have the means of voicing their opinions, and for that they must have at their disposal printing presses and newspapers. The right to street demonstrations, he said, should be guaranteed. He declared that it was necessary to make certain that scientific research would not be used for war purposes which would obviously hinder progress. He drew the Assembly's attention to a defect in the Declaration which he considered to be fundamental: the absence of provisions guaranteeing the rights of national minorities. He also regretted the failure of the Declaration to mention the sovereign rights of States.

He submitted a draft resolution recommending that the General Assembly postpone adoption of the Declaration until its fourth regular session. The representatives of the Byelorussian SSR, Czechoslovakia, Poland, the Ukrainian SSR and Yugoslavia supported the Soviet draft resolution.

The representative of the Ukrainian SSR stated that the Declaration contained a series of rights which could not be exercised, in view of the existing conditions and the economic structure of a great number of countries. Several elementary democratic rights which could be realized even in a capitalist society had been deliberately omitted. Before the right to work, to rest and to education could be put into effect, he submitted, it was necessary to alter drastically the economic system of private enterprise. He said that there could be true equality among men only under an economic system which guaranteed to everyone equal conditions and opportunities for the development of his own potentialities, and that was not the equality mentioned in the Declaration.

The Declaration, maintained the representative of Czechoslovakia, was not imbued with revolutionary spirit; it was neither bold nor modern. The abolition of the death sentence in peace time was not agreed to; nor were "fascism" and "aggression" denounced publicly and formally. The Declaration, he observed, took no account of the practical aspects of the question of the right to work; it simply expressed lofty ideals, making no provision for their implementation in the difficult daily life of the workers. He stressed the fact that there was no point in proclaiming the right to leisure, for example, if some men had no means of exercising that right.

According to the representative of the Byelorussian SSR, the Declaration was merely a proclamation of human rights, and it contained no guarantee of the rights it proclaimed. The right to national culture and democracy's struggle against fascism and nazism were not mentioned.

The Declaration stated only traditional freedoms and rights of the old liberal school, the representative of Poland asserted. It failed to mention that the counterpart of those rights was the duty of the individual towards his neighbours, his family, his group and his nation. It completely ignored the right of every person to speak his own language and to have the protection of his national culture ensured. He stated that the Declaration, in reality, represented a step backward if compared with the Declaration of the Rights of Man and the Citizen, which had been produced during the French Revolution; if compared with the Communist Manifesto, which had declared human rights as binding and necessary a hundred years ago; and if compared with the principles which had inspired the October Revolution.

The representative of Yugoslavia felt that the principles of human rights set out in the Declaration lagged behind the social progress achieved in modern times; and that they did not grant full juridical and social protection to man. He considered that the radical change in social conditions emphasized the necessity of widening the traditional categories of human rights—which generally included political and civil rights—and of establishing a system of social rights, including the collective ones for certain communities. He regarded the Declaration as an instrument of international codification rather than as an instrument which opened a new and bright future for the individual in the vast field of social rights.

The representatives of the United States, the United Kingdom, India and Bolivia, among others, in opposing the USSR draft resolution proposing that the adoption of the draft Declaration be postponed, also spoke against the USSR amendments to the Declaration (see below).

Both the representatives of the United Kingdom and the United States examined critically the USSR amendments. To adopt these amendments, they argued, would limit the universal scope of the Declaration.

While paying a tribute to the USSR delegation for the tenacity with which it had defended its convictions, the representative of the United States remarked that people sometimes had to co-operate loyally with the majority even when they disagreed with its views. The first Soviet amendment, the United States representative said, dealt with the question of minorities, and the Third Committee had already decided that that question required further study, and had recommended that it be referred, for that purpose, to the Economic and Social Council and the Commission on Human Rights. According to the representative of the United States, it was clear from the second USSR amendment that the aim was to guarantee the rights of certain groups, and not the rights of individuals, with which alone the Declaration was concerned. The effect of the third USSR amendment would be to restrict freedom of opinion and expression, argued the representative of the United States. That amendment, she declared, proposed to set up standards which would allow any State to deny freedom of opinion and expression without violating that article. The fourth USSR amendment, the United States representative explained, proclaimed the obligations of the State, a conception which the USSR delegation had tried to introduce into practically every article of the Declaration. She submitted that if that conception were adopted, the entire character of the Declaration would be changed.

The representative of India maintained that the right to hold different opinions was a sacred right and the prerogative of every truly democratic people. She declared that India, like other countries, would never agree to restricting political rights in order to realize social aims, however noble those aims might be.

According to the representative of Bolivia, two opposing schools of thought had confronted each other in the discussion on the Declaration. There had been, on the one hand, the thesis upheld by the USSR, characterized by the "desire to subordinate the individual to the State", and, on the other hand, the thesis supported by all the democratic countries, which was designed "to make the individual capable of organizing a State which, in turn, would respect the rights of the individual." Referring to the objections formulated by the representative of the Ukrainian SSR, the representative of Bolivia stated that the democratic peoples abhorred the thesis that the happiness of mankind should be subordinated to the interests of the all-powerful communist State.

Proposal of amendments

The representative of the USSR repeated his objections to the Declaration, and again stated that the Declaration was directed against national sovereignty and was therefore entirely inconsistent with the principles of the United Nations. The independence and well-being of a nation, he argued, depended on the principle of national sovereignty, and this principle was the sole protector of the smaller countries against the expansionist dreams of more powerful States. He submitted a number of amendments to the draft Declaration proposed by the Third Committee. These amendments, similar to those presented in the Third Committee—and which provided for, *inter alia*, (1) the extension to the population of Non-Self-Governing Territories of the provisions regarding the human and civic rights and fundamental freedoms set out in the Declaration; (2) a declaration that it was the inalienable right of every person freely to express and disseminate democratic views, and to combat fascism; (3) a declaration that every citizen of any State must have the right, among other rights, of access to any State or public office in his country; and (4) the insertion of a new article declaring that the rights and freedoms enumerated in the draft Declaration should be guaranteed by national laws—were all rejected by individual roll-call votes. The USSR draft resolution, calling upon the Assembly to refer the adoption of the Declaration of Human Rights to the fourth regular session, was also rejected, the vote being 6 in favour, 45 against, and 3 abstentions.

The President then put to vote a United Kingdom amendment to delete the additional article of the draft Declaration (referred to as article 3), which declared that the rights proclaimed in the Declaration would also apply to any person belonging to the population of Trust and Non-Self-Governing Territories, and in its place to substitute the following text as an additional paragraph of the second article, regarding the application of the Declaration:

"Furthermore, no distinction shall be made on the basis of the political, jurisdictional or international status of the country or territory to which a person belongs, whether it be independent, Trust, Non-Self-Governing or under any other limitation of sovereignty."

The representative of the United Kingdom explained that article 2 of the draft Declaration laid down that every individual was entitled to the rights and freedoms proclaimed in the Declaration, without distinction of any kind. He argued that, if article 2 had any meaning and if its terms were sufficiently precise and enumerated sufficiently clearly the distinctions to be outlawed, there was no reason to add an additional article (article 3) stipulating that those rights applied to the inhabitants of the Trust and Non-Self-Governing Territories.

The United Kingdom amendment was adopted by 29 votes to 17, with 10 abstentions.

Adoption of the Declaration

At the request of the representative of Poland, a separate vote was then taken on each recital of the preamble, and on each article.

The first recital of the preamble was adopted, with 2 abstentions.

The second, third, fourth, fifth, sixth and seventh recitals of the preamble were adopted unanimously.

Article 1 was adopted by 45 votes, with 9 abstentions.

The first paragraph of article 2 was adopted unanimously.

The second paragraph of article 2 (United Kingdom amendment) was adopted by 36 votes to 1, with 8 abstentions.

Article 3 was deleted; its content was covered by the second paragraph of article 2 (United Kingdom amendment).

Articles 4 to 13 were adopted unanimously.

Article 14 was adopted by 44 votes to 6, with 2 abstentions.

Articles 15 to 18 were adopted unanimously.

Article 19 was adopted by 45 votes, with 4 abstentions.

Article 20 was adopted by 44 votes to 7, with 2 abstentions.

Articles 21 to 26 were adopted unanimously.

Article 27 was adopted by 53 votes, with 3 abstentions.

Article 28 was adopted unanimously.

Article 29 was adopted by 47 votes, with 8 abstentions.

Articles 30 and 31 were adopted unanimously.

A roll-call vote was then taken on the draft Universal Declaration as a whole, including the United Kingdom amendment previously adopted. The President stated that, as a result of the deletion of article 3, the articles in the final text of the Declaration would have to be renumbered.

The Universal Declaration of Human Rights, as a whole, was adopted by 48 votes, with 8 abstentions.

. . .

The President of the General Assembly said that the adoption of that

"very important Declaration by a big majority without any direct opposition was a remarkable achievement . . . [that] the Declaration only marked a first step since it was not a convention by which States would be bound to carry out and give effect to the fundamental human rights; nor would it provide for enforcement; yet it was a step forward in a great evolutionary process. It was the first occasion on which the organized community of nations had made a declaration of human rights and fundamental freedoms. That document was backed by the authority of the body of opinion of the United Nations as a whole and millions of people, men, women and children all over the world, would turn to it for help, guidance and inspiration."

Text of the Universal Declaration of Human Rights

The text of the Declaration adopted (217(III)A) is as follows:

Preamble

Whereas recognition of the inherent dignity and of the equal and inalienable rights of all members of the human family is the foundation of freedom, justice and peace in the world,

Whereas disregard and contempt for human rights have resulted in barbarous acts which have outraged the conscience of mankind, and the advent of a world in which human beings shall enjoy freedom of speech and belief and freedom from fear and want has been proclaimed as the highest aspiration of the common people,

Whereas it is essential, if man is not to be compelled to have recourse, as a last resort, to rebellion against tyranny and oppression, that human rights should be protected by the rule of law,

Whereas it is essential to promote the development of friendly relations between nations,

Whereas the peoples of the United Nations have in the Charter reaffirmed their faith in fundamental human rights, in the dignity and worth of the human person and in the equal rights of men and women and have determined to promote social progress and better standards of life in larger freedom,

Whereas Member States have pledged themselves to achieve, in co-operation with the United Nations, the promotion of universal respect for and observance of human rights and fundamental freedoms,

Whereas a common understanding of these rights and freedoms is of the greatest importance for the full realization of this pledge,

Now, therefore,

The General Assembly

Proclaims this Universal Declaration of Human Rights as a common standard of achievement for all peoples and all nations, to the end that every individual and every organ of society, keeping this Declaration constantly in mind, shall strive by teaching and education to promote respect for these rights and freedoms and by progressive measures, national and international, to secure their universal and effective recognition and observance, both among the peoples of Member States themselves and among the peoples of territories under their jurisdiction.

Article 1

All human beings are born free and equal in dignity and rights. They are endowed with reason and conscience and should act towards one another in a spirit of brotherhood.

Article 2

Everyone is entitled to all the rights and freedoms set forth in this Declaration, without distinction of any kind, such as race, colour, sex, language, religion, political or other opinion, national or social origin, property, birth or other status.

Furthermore, no distinction shall be made on the basis of the political, jurisdictional or international status of the country or territory to which a person belongs, whether it be independent, trust, non-self-governing or under any other limitation of sovereignty.

Article 3

Everyone has the right to life, liberty and the security of person.

Article 4

No one shall be held in slavery or servitude; slavery and the slave trade shall be prohibited in all their forms.

Article 5

No one shall be subjected to torture or to cruel, inhuman or degrading treatment or punishment.

Article 6

Everyone has the right to recognition everywhere as a person before the law.

Article 7

All are equal before the law and are entitled without any discrimination to equal protection of the law. All are entitled to equal protection against any discrimination in violation of this Declaration and against any incitement to such discrimination.

Article 8

Everyone has the right to an effective remedy by the competent national tribunals for acts violating the fundamental rights granted him by the constitution or by law.

Article 9

No one shall be subjected to arbitrary arrest, detention or exile.

Article 10

Everyone is entitled in full equality to a fair, and public hearing by an independent and impartial tribunal, in the determination of his rights and obligations and of any criminal charge against him.

Article 11

1. Everyone charged with a penal offence has the right to be presumed innocent until proved guilty according to law in a public trial at which he has had all the guarantees necessary for his defence.

2. No one shall be held guilty of any penal offence on account of any act or omission which did not constitute a penal offence, under national or international law, at the time when it was committed. Nor shall a heavier penalty be imposed than the one that was applicable at the time the penal offence was committed.

Article 12

No one shall be subjected to arbitrary interference with his privacy, family, home or correspondence, nor to attacks upon his honour and reputation. Everyone has the right to the protection of the law against such interference or attacks.

Article 13

1. Everyone has the right to freedom of movement and residence within the borders of each State.

2. Everyone has the right to leave any country, including his own, and to return to his country.

Article 14

1. Everyone has the right to seek and to enjoy in other countries asylum from persecution.

2. This right may not be invoked in the case of prosecutions genuinely arising from non-political crimes or from acts contrary to the purposes and principles of the United Nations.

Article 15

1. Everyone has the right to a nationality.

2. No one shall be arbitrarily deprived of his nationality nor denied the right to change his nationality.

Article 16

1. Men and women of full age, without any limitation due to race, nationality or religion, have the right to marry and to found a family. They are entitled to equal rights as to marriage, during marriage and at its dissolution.

2. Marriage shall be entered into only with the free and full consent of the intending spouses.

3. The family is the natural and fundamental group unit of society and is entitled to protection by society and the State.

Article 17

1.   Everyone has the right to own property alone as well as in association with others.

2.   No one shall be arbitrarily deprived of his property.

Article 18

Everyone has the right to freedom of thought, conscience and religion; this right includes freedom to change his religion or belief, and freedom, either alone or in community with others and in public or private, to manifest his religion or belief in teaching, practice, worship and observance.

Article 19

Everyone has the right to freedom of opinion and expression; this right includes freedom to hold opinions without interference and to seek, receive and impart information and ideas through any media and regardless of frontiers.

Article 20

1.   Everyone has the right to freedom of peaceful assembly and association.

2.   No one may be compelled to belong to an association.

Article 21

1.   Everyone has the right to take part in the government of his country, directly or through freely chosen representatives.

2.   Everyone has the right of equal access to public service in his country.

3.   The will of the people shall be the basis of the authority of government; this will shall be expressed in periodic and genuine elections which shall be by universal and equal suffrage and shall be held by secret vote or by equivalent free voting procedures.

Article 22

Everyone, as a member of society, has the right to social security and is entitled to realization, through national effort and international co-operation and in accordance with the organization and resources of each State, of the economic, social and cultural rights indispensable for his dignity and the free development of his personality.

Article 23

1.   Everyone has the right to work, to free choice of employment, to just and favourable conditions of work and to protection against unemployment.

2.   Everyone, without any discrimination, has the right to equal pay for equal work.

3.   Everyone who works has the right to just and favourable remuneration ensuring for himself and his family an existence worthy of human dignity, and supplemented, if necessary, by other means of social protection.

4.   Everyone has the right to form and to join trade unions for the protection of his interests.

Article 24

Everyone has the right to rest and leisure, including reasonable limitation of working hours and periodic holidays with pay.

Article 25

1.   Everyone has the right to a standard of living adequate for the health and well-being of himself and of his family, including food, clothing, housing and medical care and necessary social services, and the right to security in the event of unemployment, sickness, disability, widowhood, old age or other lack of livelihood in circumstances beyond his control.

2.   Motherhood and childhood are entitled to special care and assistance. All children, whether born in or out of wedlock, shall enjoy the same social protection.

Article 26

1.   Everyone has the right to education. Education shall be free, at least in the elementary and fundamental stages. Elementary education shall be compulsory. Technical and professional education shall be made generally available and higher education shall be equally accessible to all on the basis of merit.

2.   Education shall be directed to the full development of the human personality and to the strengthening of respect for human rights and fundamental freedoms. It shall promote understanding, tolerance and friendship among all nations, racial or religious groups, and shall further the activities of the United Nations for the maintenance of peace.

3.   Parents have a prior right to choose the kind of education that shall be given to their children.

Article 27

1.   Everyone has the right freely to participate in the cultural life of the community, to enjoy the arts and to share in scientific advancement and its benefits.

2.   Everyone has the right to the protection of the moral and material interests resulting from any scientific, literary or artistic production of which he is the author.

Article 28

Everyone is entitled to a social and international order in which the rights and freedoms set forth in this Declaration can be fully realized.

Article 29

1.   Everyone has duties to the community in which alone the free and full development of his personality is possible.

2.   In the exercise of his rights and freedoms, everyone shall be subject only to such limitations as are determined by law solely for the purpose of securing due recognition and respect for the rights and freedoms of others and of meeting the just requirements of morality, public order and the general welfare in a democratic society.

3.   These rights and freedoms may in no case be exercised contrary to the purposes and principles of the United Nations.

Article 30

Nothing in this Declaration may be interpreted as implying for any State, group or person any right to engage in any activity or to perform any act aimed at the destruction of any of the rights and freedoms set forth herein.

Dissemination of the Declaration

The draft resolution of the Third Committee relating to the dissemination and publication of the Universal Declaration of Human Rights was adopted by 41 votes, with 9 abstentions, its text (217(III)D) being as follows:

"The General Assembly,

"Considering that the adoption of the Universal Declaration of Human Rights is an historic act, destined to consolidate world peace through the contribution of the United Nations towards the liberation of individuals from the unjustified oppression and constraint to which they are too often subjected,

"Considering that the text of the Declaration should be disseminated among all peoples throughout the world,

"1. Recommends Governments of Member States to show their adherence to Article 56 of the Charter by using every means within their power solemnly to publicize the text of the Declaration and to cause it to be disseminated, displayed, read and expounded principally in schools and other educational institutions, without distinction based on the political status of countries or territories;

"2. Requests the Secretary-General to have this Declaration widely disseminated and, to that end, to publish and distribute texts, not only in the official languages, but also, using every means at his disposal, in all languages possible;

"3. Invites the specialized agencies and non-governmental organizations of the world to do their utmost to bring this Declaration to the attention of their members."

[YUN 1948-49, pp. 524-37]

Covenants on Human Rights

Following adoption of the Universal Declaration of Human Rights, work began on drafting two International Covenants on Human Rights. The International Covenant on Economic, Social and Cultural Rights, the International Covenant on Civil and Political Rights and the Optional Protocol to the latter Covenant were adopted unanimously by the General Assembly on 16 December 1966. These agreements take the provisions of the Universal Declaration a step further by making them legally binding on their States parties.

Although the Covenants are based on the Universal Declaration, the rights covered are not identical. The most important right guaranteed by both Covenants and not contained in the Declaration is the right of peoples to self-determination, including the right to dispose freely of their natural wealth and resources.

International Covenant on Economic, Social and Cultural Rights

The International Covenant on Economic, Social and Cultural Rights entered into force on 3 January 1976.

The human rights which the Covenant seeks to promote and protect are of three kinds. Briefly summarized, they are: the right to work in just and favourable conditions; the right to social protection, to an adequate standard of living and to the highest attainable standards of physical and mental well-being; and the right to education and the enjoyment of benefits of cultural freedom and scientific progress.

The Covenant provides for the progressive full realization of these rights without discrimination of any kind. States parties to the Covenant submit periodic reports to the Secretary-General for consideration by the Economic and Social Council. The Committee on Economic, Social and Cultural Rights, a body of experts set up by the Council to assist it in implementing the Covenant, studies these reports and discusses their contents with representatives of the Governments concerned. Its general comments on the Covenant are intended to help States parties in their task of implementation as well as to bring to their attention deficiencies in reports and reporting procedures. The Committee may also make general recommendations to the Council based on its consideration of individual reports.

International Covenant on Economic, Social and Cultural Rights

PREAMBLE

"The States Parties to the present Covenant,

"Considering that, in accordance with the principles proclaimed in the Charter of the United Nations, recognition of the inherent dignity and of the equal and inalienable rights of all members of the human family is the foundation of freedom, justice and peace in the world,

"Recognizing that these rights derive from the inherent dignity of the human person,

"Recognizing that, in accordance with the Universal Declaration of Human Rights, the ideal of free human beings enjoying freedom from fear and want can only be achieved if conditions are created whereby everyone may enjoy his economic, social and cultural rights, as well as his civil and political rights,

"Considering the obligation of States under the Charter of the United Nations to promote universal respect for, and observance of, human rights and freedoms,

"Realizing that the individual, having duties to other individuals and to the community to which he belongs, is under a responsibility to strive for the promotion and observance of the rights recognized in the present Covenant,

"Agree upon the following articles:

PART I

Article 1

"1. All peoples have the right of self-determination. By virtue of that right they freely determine their political status and freely pursue their economic, social and cultural development.

"2. All peoples may, for their own ends, freely dispose of their natural wealth and resources without prejudice to any obligations arising out of international economic co-operation, based upon the principle of mutual benefit, and international law. In no case may a people be deprived of its own means of subsistence.

"3. The States Parties to the present Covenant, including those having responsibility for the administration of Non-Self-Governing and Trust Territories, shall promote the realization of the right of self-determination, and shall respect that right, in conformity with the provisions of the Charter of the United Nations.

PART II

Article 2

''1. Each State Party to the present Covenant undertakes to take steps, individually and through international assistance and co-operation, especially economic and technical, to the maximum of its available resources, with a view to achieving progressively the full realization of the rights recognized in the present Covenant by all appropriate means, including particularly the adoption of legislative measures.

''2. The States Parties to the present Covenant undertake to guarantee that the rights enunciated in the present Covenant will be exercised without discrimination of any kind as to race, colour, sex, language, religion, political or other opinion, national or social origin, property, birth or other status.

''3. Developing countries, with due regard to human rights and their national economy, may determine to what extent they would guarantee the economic rights recognized in the present Covenant to non-nationals.

Article 3

''The States Parties to the present Covenant undertake to ensure the equal right of men and women to the enjoyment of all economic, social and cultural rights set forth in the present Covenant.

Article 4

''The States Parties to the present Covenant recognize that, in the enjoyment of those rights provided by the State in conformity with the present Covenant, the State may subject such rights only to such limitations as are determined by law only in so far as this may be compatible with the nature of these rights and solely for the purpose of promoting the general welfare in a democratic society.

Article 5

''1. Nothing in the present Covenant may be interpreted as implying for any State, group or person any right to engage in any activity or to perform any act aimed at the destruction of any of the rights or freedoms recognized herein, or at their limitation to a greater extent than is provided for in the present Covenant.

''2. No restriction upon or derogation from any of the fundamental human rights recognized or existing in any country in virtue of law, conventions, regulations or custom shall be admitted on the pretext that the present Covenant does not recognize such rights or that it recognizes them to a lesser extent.

PART III

Article 6

''1. The States Parties to the present Covenant recognize the right to work, which includes the right of everyone to the opportunity to gain his living by work which he freely chooses or accepts, and will take appropriate steps to safeguard this right.

''2. The steps to be taken by a State Party to the present Covenant to achieve the full realization of this right shall include technical and vocational guidance and training programmes, policies and techniques to achieve steady economic, social and cultural development and full and productive employment under conditions safeguarding fundamental political and economic freedoms to the individual.

Article 7

''The States Parties to the present Covenant recognize the right of everyone to the enjoyment of just and favourable conditions of work which ensure, in particular:

''*(a)* Remuneration which provides all workers, as a minimum, with:

''(i) Fair wages and equal remuneration for work of equal value without distinction of any kind, in particular women being guaranteed conditions of work not inferior to those enjoyed by men, with equal pay for equal work;

''(ii) A decent living for themselves and their families in accordance with the provisions of the present Covenant;

''*(b)* Safe and healthy working conditions;

''*(c)* Equal opportunity for everyone to be promoted in his employment to an appropriate higher level, subject to no considerations other than those of seniority and competence;

''*(d)* Rest, leisure and reasonable limitation of working hours and periodic holidays with pay, as well as remuneration for public holidays.

Article 8

''1. The States Parties to the present Covenant undertake to ensure:

''*(a)* The right of everyone to form trade unions and join the trade union of his choice, subject only to the rules of the organization concerned, for the promotion and protection of his economic and social interests. No restrictions may be placed on the exercise of this right other than those prescribed by law and which are necessary in a democratic society in the interests of national security or public order or for the protection of the rights and freedoms of others;

''*(b)* The right of trade unions to establish national federations or confederations and the right of the latter to form or join international trade-union organizations;

''*(c)* The right of trade unions to function freely subject to no limitations other than those prescribed by law and which are necessary in a democratic society in the interests of national security or public order or for the protection of the rights and freedoms of others;

''*(d)* The right to strike, provided that it is exercised in conformity with the laws of the particular country.

''2. This article shall not prevent the imposition of lawful restrictions on the exercise of these rights by members of the armed forces or of the police or of the administration of the State.

''3. Nothing in this article shall authorize States Parties to the International Labour Organisation Convention of 1948 concerning Freedom of Association and Protection of the Right to Organize to take legislative measures which would prejudice, or apply the law in such a manner as would prejudice, the guarantees provided for in that Convention.

Article 9

''The States Parties to the present Convention recognize the right of everyone to social security, including social insurance.

Article 10

"The States Parties to the present Covenant recognize that:

"1. The widest possible protection and assistance should be accorded to the family, which is the natural and fundamental group unit of society, particularly for its establishment and while it is responsible for the care and education of dependent children. Marriage must be entered into with the free consent of the intending spouses.

"2. Special protection should be accorded to mothers during a reasonable period before and after childbirth. During such period working mothers should be accorded paid leave or leave with adequate social security benefits.

"3. Special measures of protection and assistance should be taken on behalf of all children and young persons without any discrimination for reasons of parentage or other conditions. Children and young persons should be protected from economic and social exploitation. Their employment in work harmful to their morals or health or dangerous to life or likely to hamper their normal development should be punishable by law. States should also set age limits below which the paid employment of child labour should be prohibited and punishable by law.

Article 11

"1. The States Parties to the present Covenant recognize the right of everyone to an adequate standard of living for himself and his family, including adequate food, clothing and housing, and to the continuous improvement of living conditions. The States Parties will take appropriate steps to ensure the realization of this right, recognizing to this effect the essential importance of international co-operation based on free consent.

"2. The States Parties to the present Covenant, recognizing the fundamental right of everyone to be free from hunger, shall take, individually and through international co-operation, the measures, including specific programmes, which are needed:

"(a) To improve methods of production, conservation and distribution of food by making full use of technical and scientific knowledge, by disseminating knowledge of the principles of nutrition and by developing or reforming agrarian systems in such a way as to achieve the most efficient development and utilization of natural resources;

"(b) Taking into account the problems of both food-importing and food-exporting countries, to ensure an equitable distribution of world food supplies in relation to need.

Article 12

"1. The States Parties to the present Covenant recognize the right of everyone to the enjoyment of the highest attainable standard of physical and mental health.

"2. The steps to be taken by the States Parties to the present Covenant to achieve the full realization of this right shall include those necessary for:

"(a) The provision for the reduction of the stillbirth-rate and of infant mortality and for the healthy development of the child;

"(b) The improvement of all aspects of environmental and industrial hygiene;

"(c) The prevention, treatment and control of epidemic, endemic, occupational and other diseases;

"(d) The creation of conditions which would assure to all medical service and medical attention in the event of sickness.

Article 13

"1. The States Parties to the present Covenant recognize the right of everyone to education. They agree that education shall be directed to the full development of the human personality and the sense of its dignity, and shall strengthen the respect for human rights and fundamental freedoms. They further agree that education shall enable all persons to participate effectively in a free society, promote understanding, tolerance and friendship among all nations and all racial, ethnic or religious groups, and further the activities of the United Nations for the maintenance of peace.

"2. The States Parties to the present Covenant recognize that, with a view to achieving the full realization of this right:

"(a) Primary education shall be compulsory and available free to all;

"(b) Secondary education in its different forms, including technical and vocational secondary education, shall be made generally available and accessible to all by every appropriate means, and in particular by the progressive introduction of free education;

"(c) Higher education shall be made equally accessible to all, on the basis of capacity, by every appropriate means, and in particular by the progressive introduction of free education;

"(d) Fundamental education shall be encouraged or intensified as far as possible for those persons who have not received or completed the whole period of their primary education;

"(e) The development of a system of schools at all levels shall be actively pursued, an adequate fellowship system shall be established, and the material conditions of teaching staff shall be continuously improved.

"3. The States Parties to the present Covenant undertake to have respect for the liberty of parents and, when applicable, legal guardians to choose for their children schools, other than those established by the public authorities, which conform to such minimum educational standards as may be laid down or approved by the State and to ensure the religious and moral education of their children in conformity with their own convictions.

"4. No part of this article shall be construed so as to interfere with the liberty of individuals and bodies to establish and direct educational institutions, subject always to the observance of the principles set forth in paragraph 1 of this article and to the requirement that the education given in such institutions shall conform to such minimum standards as may be laid down by the State.

Article 14

"Each State Party to the present Covenant which, at the time of becoming a Party, has not been able to secure in its metropolitan territory or other territories under its jurisdiction compulsory primary education, free of charge, undertakes, within two years, to work out and adopt a detailed plan of action for the progressive implementation, within a reasonable number of years, to be fixed in the plan, of the principle of compulsory education free of charge for all.

Article 15

"1. The States Parties to the present Covenant recognize the right of everyone:

"*(a)* To take part in cultural life;

"*(b)* To enjoy the benefits of scientific progress and its applications;

"*(c)* To benefit from the protection of the moral and material interests resulting from any scientific, literary or artistic production of which he is the author.

"2. The steps to be taken by the States Parties to the present Covenant to achieve the full realization of this right shall include those necessary for the conservation, the development and the diffusion of science and culture.

"3. The States Parties to the present Covenant undertake to respect the freedom indispensable for scientific research and creative activity.

"4. The States Parties to the present Covenant recognize the benefits to be derived from the encouragement and development of international contacts and cooperation in the scientific and cultural fields.

PART IV

Article 16

"1. The States Parties to the present Covenant undertake to submit in conformity with this part of the Covenant reports on the measures which they have adopted and the progress made in achieving the observance of the rights recognized herein.

"2. *(a)* All reports shall be submitted to the Secretary-General of the United Nations, who shall transmit copies to the Economic and Social Council for consideration in accordance with the provisions of the present Covenant;

"*(b)* The Secretary-General of the United Nations shall also transmit to the specialized agencies copies of the reports, or any relevant parts therefrom, from States Parties to the present Covenant which are also members of these specialized agencies in so far as these reports, or parts therefrom, relate to any matters which fall within the responsibilities of the said agencies in accordance with their constitutional instruments.

Article 17

"1. The States Parties to the present Covenant shall furnish their reports in stages, in accordance with a programme to be established by the Economic and Social Council within one year of the entry into force of the present Covenant after consultation with the States Parties and the specialized agencies concerned.

"2. Reports may indicate factors and difficulties affecting the degree of fulfilment of obligations under the present Covenant.

"3. Where relevant information has previously been furnished to the United Nations or to any specialized agency by any State Party to the present Covenant, it will not be necessary to reproduce that information, but a precise reference to the information so furnished will suffice.

Article 18

"Pursuant to its responsibilities under the Charter of the United Nations in the field of human rights and fundamental freedoms, the Economic and Social Council may make arrangements with the specialized agencies in respect of their reporting to it on the progress made in achieving the observance of the provisions of the present Covenant falling within the scope of their activities. These reports may include particulars of decisions and recommendations on such implementation adopted by their competent organs.

Article 19

"The Economic and Social Council may transmit to the Commission on Human Rights for study and general recommendation or, as appropriate, for information the reports concerning human rights submitted by States in accordance with articles 16 and 17, and those concerning human rights submitted by the specialized agencies in accordance with article 18.

Article 20

"The States Parties to the present Covenant and the specialized agencies concerned may submit comments to the Economic and Social Council on any general recommendation under article 19 or reference to such general recommendation in any report of the Commission on Human Rights or any documentation referred to therein.

Article 21

"The Economic and Social Council may submit from time to time to the General Assembly reports with recommendations of a general nature and a summary of the information received from the States Parties to the present Covenant and the specialized agencies on the measures taken and the progress made in achieving general observance of the rights recognized in the present Covenant.

Article 22

"The Economic and Social Council may bring to the attention of other organs of the United Nations, their subsidiary organs and specialized agencies concerned with furnishing technical assistance any matters arising out of the reports referred to in this part of the present Covenant which may assist such bodies in deciding, each within its field of competence, on the advisability of international measures likely to contribute to the effective progressive implementation of the present Covenant.

Article 23

"The States Parties to the present Covenant agree that international action for the achievement of the rights recognized in the present Covenant includes such methods as the conclusion of conventions, the adoption of recommendations, the furnishing of technical assistance and the holding of regional meetings and technical meetings for the purpose of consultation and study organized in conjunction with the Governments concerned.

Article 24

"Nothing in the present Covenant shall be interpreted as impairing the provisions of the Charter of the United Nations and of the constitutions of the specialized agencies which define the respective responsibilities of the various organs of the United Nations and of the specialized agencies in regard to the matters dealt with in the present Covenant.

Article 25

"Nothing in the present Covenant shall be interpreted as impairing the inherent right of all peoples to enjoy and utilize fully and freely their natural wealth and resources.

PART V

Article 26

"1. The present Covenant is open for signature by any State Member of the United Nations or member of any of its specialized agencies, by any State Party to the Statute of the International Court of Justice, and by any other State which has been invited by the General Assembly of the United Nations to become a party to the present Covenant.

"2. The present Covenant is subject to ratification. Instruments of ratification shall be deposited with the Secretary-General of the United Nations.

"3. The present Covenant shall be open to accession by any State referred to in paragraph 1 of this article.

"4. Accession shall be effected by the deposit of an instrument of accession with the Secretary-General of the United Nations.

"5. The Secretary-General of the United Nations shall inform all States which have signed the present Covenant or acceded to it of the deposit of each instrument of ratification or instrument of accession.

Article 27

"1. The present Covenant shall enter into force three months after the date of the deposit with the Secretary-General of the United Nations of the thirty-fifth instrument of ratification or instrument of accession.

"2. For each State ratifying the present Covenant or acceding to it after the deposit of the thirty-fifth instrument of ratification or instrument of accession, the present Covenant shall enter into force three months after the date of the deposit of its own instrument of ratification or instrument of accession.

Article 28

"The provisions of the present Covenant shall extend to all parts of federal States without any limitations or exceptions.

Article 29

"1. Any State Party to the present Covenant may propose an amendment and file it with the Secretary-General of the United Nations. The Secretary-General shall thereupon communicate any proposed amendments to the States Parties to the present Covenant with a request that they notify him whether they favour a conference of States Parties for the purpose of considering and voting upon the proposals. In the event that at least one third of the States Parties favours such a conference, the Secretary-General shall convene the conference under the auspices of the United Nations. Any amendment adopted by a majority of the States Parties present and voting at the conference shall be submitted to the General Assembly of the United Nations for approval.

"2. Amendments shall come into force when they have been approved by the General Assembly of the United Nations and accepted by a two-thirds majority of the States Parties to the present Covenant in accordance with their respective constitutional processes.

"3. When amendments come into force they shall be binding on those States Parties which have accepted them, other States Parties still being bound by the provisions of the present Covenant and any earlier amendment which they have accepted.

Article 30

"Irrespective of the notifications made under article 26, paragraph 5, the Secretary-General of the United Nations shall inform all States referred to in paragraph 1 of the same article of the following particulars:

"*(a)* Signatures, ratifications and accessions under article 26;

"*(b)* The date of the entry into force of the present Covenant under article 27 and the date of entry into force of any amendments under article 29.

Article 31

"1. The present Covenant, of which the Chinese, English, French, Russian and Spanish texts are equally authentic, shall be deposited in the archives of the United Nations.

"2. The Secretary-General of the United Nations shall transmit certified copies of the present Covenant to all States referred to in article 26.

[YUN 1966, pp. 419-23]

International Covenant on Civil and Political Rights and Optional Protocol

The International Covenant on Civil and Political Rights and the Optional Protocol to that Covenant both entered into force on 23 March 1976.

The Covenant deals with such rights as freedom of movement, equality before the law, presumption of innocence, freedom of thought, conscience and religion, freedom of opinion and expression, peaceful assembly, freedom of association, participation in public affairs and elections and protection of minority rights. It prohibits arbitrary deprivation of life; torture, cruel or degrading treatment or punishment; slavery and forced labour; arbitrary arrest or detention and arbitrary interference with privacy; war propaganda; and advocacy of racial or religious hatred that constitutes an incitement to discrimination or violence.

The only restrictions on these rights are those permitted by the Covenant itself. Moreover, certain rights may never be suspended or limited, even in emergency situations. No State party may derogate from its obligations to protect the right to life, ensure freedom from torture, freedom from enslavement or servitude, protection from imprisonment for debt, freedom from retroactive penal laws, the right to recognition as a person before the law, and freedom of thought, conscience and religion.

The Covenant established the Human Rights Committee, which considers reports submitted by States parties on measures taken to implement the Covenant's provisions. The Committee makes specific recommendations to the States parties, based on its study of their reports. The Committee also makes general comments on the scope and meaning of certain provisions of the Covenant which are designed to help States parties to give effect to its provisions. If certain requirements are met, the Committee may also receive communications from one State party claiming that another State party is not carrying out its obligations under the Covenant.

The Committee receives and considers communications from individuals who claim that their human rights, being those rights protected by the Covenant, have been violated by a State party. This function was established under the first Optional Protocol adopted by the General Assembly at the same time as the Covenant itself. The Committee considers communications from individuals in private meetings. Their letters and other documentation about individual cases remain totally confidential. The findings of the Committee, however, are always made public immediately after the session at which they were adopted and are reproduced in the Committee's annual report to the Assembly. Several countries have changed their laws as a result of decisions taken by the Committee on individual complaints under the first Optional Protocol. In a number of cases, prisoners have been released and compensation paid to victims of human rights violations. Recently, the Committee has instituted a mechanism whereby it seeks to monitor more closely whether States parties have given effect to its final decisions.

The Second Optional Protocol of the Covenant, aiming at abolition of the death penalty, was adopted by the General Assembly on 15 December 1989.

International Covenant on Civil and Political Rights

PREAMBLE

"*The States Parties to the present Covenant,*

"*Considering* that, in accordance with the principles proclaimed in the Charter of the United Nations, recognition of the inherent dignity and of the equal and inalienable rights of all members of the human family is the foundation of freedom, justice and peace in the world,

"*Recognizing* that these rights derive from the inherent dignity of the human person,

"*Recognizing* that, in accordance with the Universal Declaration of Human Rights, the ideal of free human beings enjoying civil and political freedom and freedom from fear and want can only be achieved if conditions are created whereby everyone may enjoy his civil and political rights, as well as his economic, social and cultural rights,

"*Considering* the obligation of States under the Charter of the United Nations to promote universal respect for, and observance of, human rights and freedoms,

"*Realizing* that the individual, having duties to other individuals and to the community to which he belongs, is under a responsibility to strive for the promotion and observance of the rights recognized in the present Covenant,

"*Agree* upon the following articles:

PART I

Article 1

"1. All peoples have the right of self-determination. By virtue of that right they freely determine their political status and freely pursue their economic, social and cultural development.

"2. All peoples may, for their own ends, freely dispose of their natural wealth and resources without prejudice to any obligations arising out of international economic co-operation, based upon the principle of mutual benefit, and international law. In no case may a people be deprived of its own means of subsistence.

"3. The States Parties to the present Covenant, including those having responsibility for the administration of Non-Self-Governing and Trust Territories, shall promote the realization of the right of self-determination, and shall respect that right, in conformity with the provisions of the Charter of the United Nations.

PART II

Article 2

"1. Each State Party to the present Covenant undertakes to respect and to ensure to all individuals within its territory and subject to its jurisdiction the rights recognized in the present Covenant, without distinction of any kind, such as race, colour, sex, language, religion, political or other opinion, national or social origin, property, birth or other status.

"2. Where not already provided for by existing legislative or other measures, each State Party to the present Covenant undertakes to take the necessary steps, in accordance with its constitutional processes and with the provisions of the present Covenant, to adopt such legislative or other measures as may be necessary to give effect to the rights recognized in the present Covenant.

"3. Each State Party to the present Covenant undertakes:

"*(a)* To ensure that any person whose rights or freedoms as herein recognized are violated shall have an effective remedy, notwithstanding that the violation has been committed by persons acting in an official capacity;

"*(b)* To ensure that any person claiming such a remedy shall have his right thereto determined by competent judicial, administrative or legislative authorities, or by any other competent authority provided for by the legal system of the State, and to develop the possibilities of judicial remedy;

"*(c)* To ensure that the competent authorities shall enforce such remedies when granted.

Article 3

"The States Parties to the present Covenant undertake to ensure the equal right of men and women to the enjoyment of all civil and political rights set forth in the present Covenant.

Article 4

"1. In time of public emergency which threatens the life of the nation and the existence of which is officially proclaimed, the States Parties to the present Covenant may take measures derogating from their obligations under the present Covenant to the extent strictly required by the exigencies of the situation, provided that such measures are not inconsistent with their other obligations under international law and do not involve discrimination solely on the ground of race, colour, sex, language, religion or social origin.

"2.   No derogation from articles 6, 7, 8 (paragraphs 1 and 2), 11, 15, 16 and 18 may be made under this provision.

"3.   Any State Party to the present Covenant availing itself of the right of derogation shall immediately inform the other States Parties to the present Covenant, through the intermediary of the Secretary-General of the United Nations, of the provisions from which it has derogated and of the reasons by which it was actuated. A further communication shall be made, through the same intermediary, on the date on which it terminates such derogation.

Article 5

"1.   Nothing in the present Covenant may be interpreted as implying for any State, group or person any right to engage in any activity or perform any act aimed at the destruction of any of the rights and freedoms recognized herein or at their limitation to a greater extent than is provided for in the present Covenant.

"2.   There shall be no restriction upon or derogation from any of the fundamental human rights recognized or existing in any State Party to the present Covenant pursuant to law, conventions, regulations or custom on the pretext that the present Covenant does not recognize such rights or that it recognizes them to a lesser extent.

PART III

Article 6

"1.   Every human being has the inherent right to life. This right shall be protected by law. No one shall be arbitrarily deprived of his life.

"2.   In countries which have not abolished the death penalty, sentence of death may be imposed only for the most serious crimes in accordance with the law in force at the time of the commission of the crime and not contrary to the provisions of the present Covenant and to the Convention on the Prevention and Punishment of the Crime of Genocide. This penalty can only be carried out pursuant to a final judgement rendered by a competent court.

"3.   When deprivation of life constitutes the crime of genocide, it is understood that nothing in this article shall authorize any State Party to the present Covenant to derogate in any way from any obligation assumed under the provisions of the Convention on the Prevention and Punishment of the Crime of Genocide.

"4.   Anyone sentenced to death shall have the right to seek pardon or commutation of the sentence. Amnesty, pardon or commutation of the sentence of death may be granted in all cases.

"5.   Sentence of death shall not be imposed for crimes committed by persons below eighteen years of age and shall not be carried out on pregnant women.

"6.   Nothing in this article shall be invoked to delay or to prevent the abolition of capital punishment by any State Party to the present Covenant.

Article 7

"No one shall be subjected to torture or to cruel inhuman or degrading treatment or punishment. In particular, no one shall be subjected without his free consent to medical or scientific experimentation.

Article 8

"1.   No one shall be held in slavery; slavery and the slave-trade in all their forms shall be prohibited.

"2.   No one shall be held in servitude.

"3.   (a)   No one shall be required to perform forced or compulsory labour;

"(b)   Paragraph 3 (a) shall not be held to preclude, in countries where imprisonment with hard labour may be imposed as a punishment for a crime, the performance of hard labour in pursuance of a sentence to such punishment by a competent court;

"(c)   For the purpose of this paragraph the term 'forced or compulsory labour' shall not include:

"(i)   Any work or service, not referred to in sub-paragraph (b), normally required of a person who is under detention in consequence of a lawful order of a court, or of a person during conditional release from such detention;

"(ii)   Any service of a military character and, in countries where conscientious objection is recognized, any national service required by law of conscientious objectors;

"(iii)   Any service exacted in cases of emergency or calamity threatening the life or well-being of the community;

"(iv)   Any work or service which forms part of normal civil obligations.

Article 9

"1.   Everyone has the right to liberty and security of person. No one shall be subjected to arbitrary arrest or detention. No one shall be deprived of his liberty except on such grounds and in accordance with such procedure as are established by law.

"2.   Anyone who is arrested shall be informed, at the time of arrest, of the reasons for his arrest and shall be promptly informed of any charges against him.

"3.   Anyone arrested or detained on a criminal charge shall be brought promptly before a judge or other officer authorized by law to exercise judicial power and shall be entitled to trial within a reasonable time or to release. It shall not be the general rule that persons awaiting trial shall be detained in custody, but release may be subject to guarantees to appear for trial, at any other stage of the judicial proceedings, and, should occasion arise, for execution of the judgement.

"4.   Anyone who is deprived of his liberty by arrest or detention shall be entitled to take proceedings before a court, in order that that court may decide without delay on the lawfulness of his detention and order his release if the detention is not lawful.

"5.   Anyone who has been the victim of unlawful arrest or detention shall have an enforceable right to compensation.

Article 10

"1.   All persons deprived of their liberty shall be treated with humanity and with respect for the inherent dignity of the human person.

"2.   (a)   Accused persons shall, save in exceptional circumstances, be segregated from convicted persons and shall be subject to separate treatment appropriate to their status as unconvicted persons;

"(b)   Accused juvenile persons shall be separated from adults and brought as speedily as possible for adjudication.

"3. The penitentiary system shall comprise treatment of prisoners the essential aim of which shall be their reformation and social rehabilitation. Juvenile offenders shall be segregated from adults and be accorded treatment appropriate to their age and legal status.

Article 11

"No one shall be imprisoned merely on the ground of inability to fulfil a contractual obligation.

Article 12

"1. Everyone lawfully within the territory of a State shall, within that territory, have the right to liberty of movement and freedom to choose his residence.

"2. Everyone shall be free to leave any country, including his own.

"3. The above-mentioned rights shall not be subject to any restrictions except those which are provided by law, are necessary to protect national security, public order (*ordre public*), public health or morals or the rights and freedoms of others, and are consistent with the other rights recognized in the present Covenant.

"4. No one shall be arbitrarily deprived of the right to enter his own country.

Article 13

"An alien lawfully in the territory of a State Party to the present Covenant may be expelled therefrom only in pursuance of a decision reached in accordance with law and shall, except where compelling reasons of national security otherwise require, be allowed to submit the reasons against his expulsion and to have his case reviewed by, and be represented for the purpose before, the competent authority or a person or persons especially designated by the competent authority.

Article 14

"1. All persons shall be equal before the courts and tribunals. In the determination of any criminal charge against him, or of his rights and obligations in a suit at law, everyone shall be entitled to a fair and public hearing by a competent, independent and impartial tribunal established by law. The Press and the public may be excluded from all or part of a trial for reasons of morals, public order (*ordre public*) or national security in a democratic society, or when the interest of the private lives of the parties so requires, or to the extent strictly necessary in the opinion of the court in special circumstances where publicity would prejudice the interests of justice; but any judgement rendered in a criminal case or in a suit at law shall be made public except where the interest of juvenile persons otherwise requires or the proceedings concern matrimonial disputes or the guardianship of children.

"2. Everyone charged with a criminal offence shall have the right to be presumed innocent until proved guilty according to law.

"3. In the determination of any criminal charge against him, everyone shall be entitled to the following minimum guarantees, in full equality:

"(*a*) To be informed promptly and in detail in a language which he understands of the nature and cause of the charge against him;

"(*b*) To have adequate time and facilities for the preparation of his defence and to communicate with counsel of his own choosing;

"(*c*) To be tried without undue delay;

"(*d*) To be tried in his presence, and to defend himself in person or through legal assistance of his own choosing; to be informed, if he does not have legal assistance, of this right; and to have legal assistance assigned to him, in any case where the interests of justice so require, and without payment by him in any such case if he does not have sufficient means to pay for it;

"(*e*) To examine, or have examined, the witnesses against him and to obtain the attendance and examination of witnesses on his behalf under the same conditions as the witnesses against him;

"(*f*) To have the free assistance of an interpreter if he cannot understand or speak the language used in court;

"(*g*) Not to be compelled to testify against himself or to confess guilt.

"4. In the case of juvenile persons, the procedure shall be such as will take account of their age and the desirability of promoting their rehabilitation.

"5. Everyone convicted of a crime shall have the right to his conviction and sentence being reviewed by a higher tribunal according to law.

"6. When a person has by a final decision been convicted of a criminal offence and when subsequently his conviction has been reversed or he has been pardoned on the ground that a new or newly discovered fact shows conclusively that there has been a miscarriage of justice, the person who has suffered punishment as a result of such conviction shall be compensated according to law, unless it is proved that the non-disclosure of the unknown fact in time is wholly or partly attributable to him.

"7. No one shall be liable to be tried or punished again for an offence for which he has already been finally convicted or acquitted in accordance with the law and penal procedure of each country.

Article 15

"1. No one shall be held guilty of any criminal offence on account of any act or omission which did not constitute a criminal offence, under national or international law, at the time when it was committed. Nor shall a heavier penalty be imposed than the one that was applicable at the time when the criminal offence was committed. If, subsequent to the commission of the offence, provision is made by law for the imposition of a lighter penalty, the offender shall benefit thereby.

"2. Nothing in this article shall prejudice the trial and punishment of any person for any act or omission which, at the time when it was committed, was criminal according to the general principles of law recognized by the community of nations.

Article 16

"Everyone shall have the right to recognition everywhere as a person before the law.

Article 17

"1. No one shall be subjected to arbitrary or unlawful interference with his privacy, family, home or correspondence, nor to unlawful attacks on his honour and reputation.

"2. Everyone has the right to the protection of the law against such interference or attacks.

Article 18

"1. Everyone shall have the right to freedom of thought, conscience and religion. This right shall include freedom to have or to adopt a religion or belief of his choice, and freedom, either individually or in community with others and in public or private, to manifest his religion or belief in worship, observance, practice and teaching.

"2.   No one shall be subject to coercion which would impair his freedom to have or to adopt a religion or belief of his choice.

"3.   Freedom to manifest one's religion or beliefs may be subject only to such limitations as are prescribed by law and are necessary to protect public safety, order, health, or morals or the fundamental rights and freedoms of others.

"4.   The States Parties to the present Covenant undertake to have respect for the liberty of parents and, when applicable, legal guardians to ensure the religious and moral education of their children in conformity with their own convictions.

Article 19

"1.   Everyone shall have the right to hold opinions without interference.

"2.   Everyone shall have the right to freedom of expression; this right shall include freedom to seek, receive and impart information and ideas of all kinds, regardless of frontiers, either orally, in writing or in print, in the form of art, or through any other media of his choice.

"3.   The exercise of the rights provided for in paragraph 2 of this article carries with it special duties and responsibilities. It may therefore be subject to certain restrictions, but these shall only be such as are provided by law and are necessary:

"*(a)*   For respect of the rights or reputations of others;

"*(b)*   For the protection of national security or of public order (*ordre public*), or of public health or morals.

Article 20

"1.   Any propaganda for war shall be prohibited by law.

"2.   Any advocacy of national, racial or religious hatred that constitutes incitement to discrimination, hostility or violence shall be prohibited by law.

Article 21

"The right of peaceful assembly shall be recognized. No restrictions may be placed on the exercise of this right other than those imposed in conformity with the law and which are necessary in a democratic society in the interests of national security or public safety, public order (*ordre public*), the protection of public health or morals or the protection of the rights and freedoms of others.

Article 22

"1.   Everyone shall have the right to freedom of association with others, including the right to form and join trade unions for the protection of his interests.

"2.   No restrictions may be placed on the exercise of this right other than those which are prescribed by law and which are necessary in a democratic society in the interests of national security or public safety, public order (*ordre public*), the protection of public health or morals or the protection of the rights and freedoms of others. This article shall not prevent the imposition of lawful restrictions on members of the armed forces and of the police in their exercise of this right.

"3.   Nothing in this article shall authorize States Parties to the International Labour Organisation Convention of 1948 concerning Freedom of Association and Protection of the Right to Organize to take legislative

measures which would prejudice, or to apply the law in such a manner as to prejudice, the guarantees provided for in that Convention.

Article 23

"1.   The family is the natural and fundamental group unit of society and is entitled to protection by society and the State.

"2.   The right of men and women of marriageable age to marry and to found a family shall be recognized.

"3.   No marriage shall be entered into without the free and full consent of the intending spouses.

"4.   States Parties to the present Covenant shall take appropriate steps to ensure equality of rights and responsibilities of spouses as to marriage, during marriage and at its dissolution. In the case of dissolution, provision shall be made for the necessary protection of any children.

Article 24

"1.   Every child shall have, without any discrimination as to race, colour, sex, language, religion, national or social origin, property or birth, the right to such measures of protection as are required by his status as a minor, on the part of his family, society and the State.

"2.   Every child shall be registered immediately after birth and shall have a name.

"3.   Every child has the right to acquire a nationality.

Article 25

"Every citizen shall have the right and the opportunity, without any of the distinctions mentioned in article 2 and without unreasonable restrictions:

"*(a)*   To take part in the conduct of public affairs, directly or through freely chosen representatives;

"*(b)*   To vote and to be elected at genuine periodic elections which shall be by universal and equal suffrage and shall be held by secret ballot, guaranteeing the free expression of the will of the electors;

"*(c)*   To have access, on general terms of equality, to public service in his country.

Article 26

"All persons are equal before the law and are entitled without any discrimination to the equal protection of the law. In this respect, the law shall prohibit any discrimination and guarantee to all persons equal and effective protection against discrimination on any ground such as race, colour, sex, language, religion, political or other opinion, national or social origin, property, birth or other status.

Article 27

"In those States in which ethnic, religious or linguistic minorities exist, persons belonging to such minorities shall not be denied the right, in community with the other members of their group, to enjoy their own culture, to profess and practice their own religion, or to use their own language.

PART IV

Article 28

"1.   There shall be established a Human Rights Committee (hereafter referred to in the present Covenant as the Committee). It shall consist of eighteen members and shall carry out the functions hereinafter provided.

"2. The Committee shall be composed of nationals of the States Parties to the present Covenant who shall be persons of high moral character and recognized competence in the field of human rights, consideration being given to the usefulness of the participation of some persons having legal experience.

"3. The members of the Committee shall be elected and shall serve in their personal capacity.

Article 29

"1. The members of the Committee shall be elected by secret ballot from a list of persons possessing the qualifications prescribed in article 28 and nominated for the purpose by the States Parties to the present Covenant.

"2. Each State Party to the present Covenant may nominate not more than two persons. These persons shall be nationals of the nominating State.

"3. A person shall be eligible for renomination.

Article 30

"1. The initial election shall be held no later than six months after the date of entry into force of the present Covenant.

"2. At least four months before the date of each election to the Committee, other than an election to fill a vacancy declared in accordance with article 34, the Secretary-General of the United Nations shall address a written invitation to the States Parties to the present Covenant to submit their nominations for membership of the Committee within three months.

"3. The Secretary-General of the United Nations shall prepare a list in alphabetical order of all the persons thus nominated, with an indication of the States Parties which have nominated them, and shall submit it to the States Parties to the present Covenant no later than one month before the date of each election.

"4. Elections of the members of the Committee shall be held at a meeting of the States Parties to the present Covenant convened by the Secretary-General of the United Nations at the Headquarters of the United Nations. At that meeting, for which two thirds of the States Parties to the present Covenant shall constitute a quorum, the persons elected to the Committee shall be those nominees who obtain the largest number of votes and an absolute majority of the votes of the representatives of States Parties present and voting.

Article 31

"1. The Committee may not include more than one national of the same State.

"2. In the election of the Committee, consideration shall be given to equitable geographical distribution of membership and to the representation of the different forms of civilization and of the principal legal systems.

Article 32

"1. The members of the Committee shall be elected for a term of four years. They shall be eligible for re-election if renominated. However, the terms of nine of the members elected at the first election shall expire at the end of two years; immediately after the first election, the names of these nine members shall be chosen by lot by the Chairman of the meeting referred to in article 30, paragraph 4.

"2. Elections at the expiry of office shall be held in accordance with the preceding articles of this part of the present Covenant.

Article 33

"1. If, in the unanimous opinion of the other members, a member of the Committee has ceased to carry out his functions for any cause other than absence of a temporary character, the Chairman of the Committee shall notify the Secretary-General of the United Nations, who shall then declare the seat of that member to be vacant.

"2. In the event of the death or the resignation of a member of the Committee, the Chairman shall immediately notify the Secretary-General of the United Nations, who shall declare the seat vacant from the date of death or the date on which the resignation takes effect.

Article 34

"1. When a vacancy is declared in accordance with article 33 and if the term of office of the member to be replaced does not expire within six months of the declaration of the vacancy, the Secretary-General of the United Nations shall notify each of the States Parties to the present Covenant, which may within two months submit nominations in accordance with article 29 for the purpose of filling the vacancy.

"2. The Secretary-General of the United Nations shall prepare a list in alphabetical order of the persons thus nominated and shall submit it to the States Parties to the present Covenant. The election to fill the vacancy shall then take place in accordance with the relevant provisions of this part of the present Covenant.

"3. A member of the Committee elected to fill a vacancy declared in accordance with article 33 shall hold office for the remainder of the term of the member who vacated the seat on the Committee under the provisions of that article.

Article 35

"The members of the Committee shall, with the approval of the General Assembly of the United Nations, receive emoluments from United Nations resources on such terms and conditions as the General Assembly may decide, having regard to the importance of the Committee's responsibilities.

Article 36

"The Secretary-General of the United Nations shall provide the necessary staff and facilities for the effective performance of the functions of the Committee under the present Covenant.

Article 37

"1. The Secretary-General of the United Nations shall convene the initial meeting of the Committee at the Headquarters of the United Nations.

"2. After its initial meeting, the Committee shall meet at such times as shall be provided in its rules of procedure.

"3. The Committee shall normally meet at the Headquarters of the United Nations or at the United Nations Office at Geneva.

Article 38

"Every member of the Committee shall, before taking up his duties, make a solemn declaration in open committee that he will perform his functions impartially and conscientiously.

Article 39

"1   The Committee shall elect its officers for a term of two years. They may be re-elected.

"2.   The Committee shall establish its own rules of procedure, but these rules shall provide, *inter alia*, that:

"*(a)*   Twelve members shall constitute a quorum;

"*(b)*   Decisions of the Committee shall be made by a majority vote of the members present.

Article 40

"1.   The States Parties to the present Covenant undertake to submit reports on the measures they have adopted which give effect to the rights recognized herein and on the progress made in the enjoyment of those rights:

"*(a)*   Within one year of the entry into force of the present Covenant for the States Parties concerned;

"*(b)*   Thereafter whenever the Committee so requests.

"2.   All reports shall be submitted to the Secretary-General of the United Nations, who shall transmit them to the Committee for consideration. Reports shall indicate the factors and difficulties, if any, affecting the implementation of the present Covenant.

"3.   The Secretary-General of the United Nations may, after consultation with the Committee, transmit to the specialized agencies concerned copies of such parts of the reports as may fall within their field of competence.

"4.   The Committee shall study the reports submitted by the States Parties to the present Covenant. It shall transmit its reports, and such general comments as it may consider appropriate, to the States Parties. The Committee may also transmit to the Economic and Social Council these comments along with the copies of the reports it has received from States Parties to the present Covenant.

"5.   The States Parties to the present Covenant may submit to the Committee observations on any comments that may be made in accordance with paragraph 4 of this article.

Article 41

"1.   A State Party to the present Covenant may at any time declare under this article that it recognizes the competence of the Committee to receive and consider communications to the effect that a State Party claims that another State Party is not fulfilling its obligations under the present Covenant. Communications under this article may be received and considered only if submitted by a State Party which has made a declaration recognizing in regard to itself the competence of the Committee. No communication shall be received by the Committee if it concerns a State Party which has not made such a declaration. Communications received under this article shall be dealt with in accordance with the following procedure:

"*(a)*   If a State Party to the present Covenant considers that another State Party is not giving effect to the provisions of the present Covenant, it may, by written communication, bring the matter to the attention of that State Party. Within three months after the receipt of the communication, the receiving State shall afford the State which sent the communication an explanation or any other statement in writing clarifying the matter, which should include, to the extent possible and pertinent, preference to domestic procedures and remedies taken, pending, or available in the matter.

"*(b)*   If the matter is not adjusted to the satisfaction of both States Parties concerned within six months after the receipt by the receiving State of the initial communication, either State shall have the right to refer the matter to the Committee, by notice given to the Committee and to the other State.

"*(c)*   The Committee shall deal with a matter referred to it only after it has ascertained that all available domestic remedies have been invoked and exhausted in the matter, in conformity with the generally recognized principles of international law. This shall not be the rule where the application of the remedies is unreasonably prolonged.

"*(d)*   The Committee shall hold closed meetings when examining communications under this article.

"*(e)*   Subject to the provisions of sub-paragraph *(c)*, the Committee shall make available its good offices to the States Parties concerned with a view to a friendly solution of the matter on the basis of respect for human rights and fundamental freedoms as recognized in the present Covenant.

"*(f)*   In any matter referred to it, the Committee may call upon the States Parties concerned, referred to in sub-paragraph *(b)*, to supply any relevant information.

"*(g)*   The States Parties concerned, referred to in sub-paragraph *(b)*, shall have the right to be represented when the matter is being considered in the Committee and to make submissions orally and/or in writing.

"*(h)*   The Committee shall, within twelve months after the date of receipt of notice under sub-paragraph *(b)*, submit a report:

"(i)   If a solution within the terms of sub-paragraph *(e)* is reached, the Committee shall confine its report to a brief statement of the facts and of the solution reached;

"(ii)   If a solution within the terms of sub-paragraph *(e)* is not reached, the Committee shall confine its report to a brief statement of the facts; the written submissions and record of the oral submissions made by the States Parties concerned shall be attached to the report.

In every matter, the report shall be communicated to the States Parties concerned.

"2.   The provisions of this article shall come into force when ten States Parties to the present Covenant have made declarations under paragraph 1 of this article. Such declarations shall be deposited by the States Parties with the Secretary-General of the United Nations, who shall transmit copies thereof to the other States Parties. A declaration may be withdrawn at any time by notification to the Secretary-General. Such a withdrawal shall not prejudice the consideration of any matter which is the subject of a communication already transmitted under this article; no further communication by any State Party shall be received after the notification of withdrawal of the declaration has been received by the Secretary-General, unless the State Party concerned has made a new declaration.

Article 42

"1.   *(a)*   If a matter referred to the Committee in accordance with article 41 is not resolved to the satisfaction of the States Parties concerned, the Committee may, with the prior consent of the States Parties concerned, appoint an *ad hoc* Conciliation Commission (hereinafter referred to as the Commission). The good offices of the Commission shall be made available to the States Parties concerned with a view to an amicable solution of the matter on the basis of respect for the present Covenant;

"*(b)* The Commission shall consist of five persons acceptable to the States Parties concerned. If the States Parties concerned fail to reach agreement within three months on all or part of the composition of the Commission, the members of the Commission concerning whom no agreement has been reached shall be elected by secret ballot by a two-thirds majority vote of the Committee from among its members.

"2. The members of The Commission shall serve in their personal capacity. They shall not be nationals of the States Parties concerned, or of a State not party to the present Covenant, or of a State Party which has not made a declaration under article 41.

"3. The Commission shall elect its own Chairman and adopt its own rules of procedure.

"4. The meetings of the Commission shall normally be held at the Headquarters of the United Nations or at the United Nations Office at Geneva. However, they may be held at such other convenient places as the Commission may determine in consultation with the Secretary-General of the United Nations and the States Parties concerned.

"5. The secretariat provided in accordance with article 36 shall also service the commissions appointed under this article.

"6. The information received and collated by the Committee shall be made available to the Commission and the Commission may call upon the States Parties concerned to supply any other relevant information.

"7. When the Commission has fully considered the matter, but in any event not later than twelve months after having been seized of the matter, it shall submit to the Chairman of the Committee a report for communication to the States Parties concerned:

"*(a)* If the Commission is unable to complete its consideration of the matter within twelve months, it shall confine its report to a brief statement of the status of its consideration of the matter;

"*(b)* If an amicable solution to the matter on the basis of respect for human rights as recognized in the present Covenant is reached, the Commission shall confine its report to a brief statement of the facts and of the solution reached;

"*(c)* If a solution within the terms of sub-paragraph *(b)* is not reached, the Commission's report shall embody its findings on all questions of fact relevant to the issues between the States Parties concerned, and its views on the possibilities of an amicable solution of the matter. This report shall also contain the written submissions and a record of the oral submissions made by the States Parties concerned;

"*(d)* If the Commission's report is submitted under sub-paragraph *(c)*, the States Parties concerned shall, within three months of the receipt of the report, notify the Chairman of the Committee whether or not they accept the contents of the report of the Commission.

"8. The provisions of this article are without prejudice to the responsibilities of the Committee under article 41.

"9. The States Parties concerned shall share equally all the expenses of the members of the Commission in accordance with estimates to be provided by the Secretary-General of the United Nations.

"10. The Secretary-General of the United Nations shall be empowered to pay the expenses of the members of the Commission, if necessary, before reimbursement by the States Parties concerned, in accordance with paragraph 9 of this article.

Article 43

"The members of the Committee, and of the *ad hoc* conciliation commissions which may be appointed under article 42, shall be entitled to the facilities, privileges and immunities of experts on mission for the United Nations as laid down in the relevant sections of the Convention on the Privileges and Immunities of the United Nations.

Article 44

"The provisions for the implementation of the present Covenant shall apply without prejudice to the procedures prescribed in the field of human rights by or under the constituent instruments and the conventions of the United Nations and of the specialized agencies and shall not prevent the States Parties to the present Covenant from having recourse to other procedures for settling a dispute in accordance with general or special international agreements in force between them.

Article 45

"The Committee shall submit to the General Assembly of the United Nations, through the Economic and Social Council, an annual report on its activities.

PART V

Article 46

"Nothing in the present Covenant shall be interpreted as impairing the provisions of the Charter of the United Nations and of the constitutions of the specialized agencies which define the respective responsibilities of the various organs of the United Nations and of the specialized agencies in regard to the matters dealt with in the present Covenant.

Article 47

"Nothing in the present Covenant shall be interpreted as impairing the inherent right of all peoples to enjoy and utilize fully and freely their natural wealth and resources.

PART VI

Article 48

"1. The present Covenant is open for signature by any State Member of the United Nations or member of any of its specialized agencies, by any State Party to the Statute of the International Court of Justice, and by any other State which has been invited by the General Assembly of the United Nations to become a party to the present Covenant.

"2. The present Covenant is subject to ratification. Instruments of ratification shall be deposited with the Secretary-General of the United Nations.

"3. The present Covenant shall be open to accession by any State referred to in paragraph 1 of this article.

"4. Accession shall be effected by the deposit of an instrument of accession with the Secretary-General of the United Nations.

"5.　The Secretary-General of the United Nations shall inform all States which have signed this Covenant or acceded to it of the deposit of each instrument of ratification or accession.

Article 49

"1.　The present Covenant shall enter into force three months after the date of the deposit with the Secretary-General of the United Nations of the thirty-fifth instrument of ratification or instrument of accession.

"2.　For each State ratifying the present Covenant or acceding to it after the deposit of the thirty-fifth instrument of ratification or instrument of accession, the present Covenant shall enter into force three months after the date of the deposit of its own instrument of ratification or instrument of accession.

Article 50

"The provisions of the present Covenant shall extend to all parts of federal States without any limitations or exceptions.

Article 51

"1.　Any State Party to the present Covenant may propose an amendment and file it with the Secretary-General of the United Nations. The Secretary-General of the United Nations shall thereupon communicate any proposed amendments to the States Parties to the present Covenant with a request that they notify him whether they favour a conference of States Parties for the purpose of considering and voting upon the proposals. In the event that at least one third of the States Parties favours such a conference, the Secretary-General shall convene the conference under the auspices of the United Nations. Any amendment adopted by a majority of the States Parties present and voting at the conference shall be submitted to the General Assembly of the United Nations for approval.

"2.　Amendments shall come into force when they have been approved by the General Assembly of the United Nations and accepted by a two-thirds majority of the States Parties to the present Covenant in accordance with their respective constitutional processes.

"3.　When amendments come into force, they shall be binding on those States Parties which have accepted them, other States Parties still being bound by the provisions of the present Covenant and any earlier amendment which they have accepted.

Article 52

"Irrespective of the notifications made under article 48, paragraph 5, the Secretary-General of the United Nations shall inform all States referred to in paragraph 1 of the same article of the following particulars:

"(a)　Signatures, ratifications and accessions under article 48;

"(b)　The date of the entry into force of the present Covenant under article 49 and the date of the entry into force of any amendments under article 51.

Article 53

"1.　The present Covenant, of which the Chinese, English, French, Russian and Spanish texts are equally authentic, shall be deposited in the archives of the United Nations.

"2.　The Secretary-General of the United Nations shall transmit certified copies of the present Covenant to all States referred to in article 48.

Optional Protocol to the International Covenant on Civil and Political Rights

"*The States Parties to the present Protocol,*

"*Considering* that in order further to achieve the purposes of the Covenant on Civil and Political Rights (hereinafter referred to as the Covenant) and the implementation of its provisions it would be appropriate to enable the Human Rights Committee set up in part IV of the Covenant (hereinafter referred to as the Committee) to receive and consider, as provided in the present Protocol, communications from individuals claiming to be victims of violations of any of the rights set forth in the Covenant,

"*Have agreed* as follows:

Article 1

"A State Party to the Covenant that becomes a party to the present Protocol recognizes the competence of the Committee to receive and consider communications from individuals subject to its jurisdiction who claim to be victims of a violation by that State Party of any of the rights set forth in the Covenant. No communication shall be received by the Committee if it concerns a State Party to the Covenant which is not a party to the present Protocol.

Article 2

"Subject to the provisions of article 1, individuals who claim that any of their rights enumerated in the Covenant have been violated and who have exhausted all available domestic remedies may submit a written communication to the Committee for consideration.

Article 3

"The Committee shall consider inadmissible any communication under the present Protocol which is anonymous, or which it considers to be an abuse of the right of submission of such communications or to be incompatible with the provisions of the Covenant.

Article 4

"1.　Subject to the provisions of article 3, the Committee shall bring any communications submitted to it under the present Protocol to the attention of the State Party to the present Protocol alleged to be violating any provision of the Covenant.

"2.　Within six months, the receiving State shall submit to the Committee written explanations or statements clarifying the matter and the remedy, if any, that may have been taken by that State.

Article 5

"1.　The Committee shall consider communications received under the present Protocol in the light of all written information made available to it by the individual or by the State Party concerned.

"2.　The Committee shall not consider any communication from an individual unless it has ascertained that:

"(a)　The same matter is not being examined under another procedure of international investigation or settlement;

"(b)　The individual has exhausted all available domestic remedies.
This shall not be the rule where the application of the remedies is unreasonably prolonged.

"3.　The Committee shall hold closed meetings when examining communications under the present Protocol.

"4. The Committee shall forward its views to the State Party concerned and to the individual.

Article 6

"The Committee shall include in its annual report under article 45 of the Covenant a summary of its activities under the present Protocol.

Article 7

"Pending the achievement of the objectives of resolution 1514(XV) adopted by the General Assembly of the United Nations on 14 December 1960 concerning the Declaration on the Granting of Independence to Colonial Countries and Peoples, the provisions of the present Protocol shall in no way limit the right of petition granted to these peoples by the Charter of the United Nations and other international conventions and instruments under the United Nations and its specialized agencies.

Article 8

"1. The present Protocol is open for signature by any State which has signed the Covenant.

"2. The present Protocol is subject to ratification by any State which has ratified or acceded to the Covenant. Instruments of ratification shall be deposited with the Secretary-General of the United Nations.

"3. The present Protocol shall be open to accession by any State which has ratified or acceded to the Covenant.

"4. Accession shall be effected by the deposit of an instrument of accession with the Secretary-General of the United Nations.

"5. The Secretary-General of the United Nations shall inform all States which have signed the present Protocol or acceded to it of the deposit of each instrument of ratification or accession.

Article 9

"1. Subject to the entry into force of the Covenant, the present Protocol shall enter into force three months after the date of deposit with the Secretary-General of the United Nations of the tenth instrument of ratification or instrument of accession.

"2. For each State ratifying the present Protocol or acceding to it after the deposit of the tenth instrument of ratification or instrument of accession, the present Protocol shall enter into force three months after the date of the deposit of its own instrument of ratification or instrument of accession.

Article 10

"The provisions of the present Protocol shall extend to all parts of federal States without any limitations or exceptions.

Article 11

"1. Any State Party to the present Protocol may propose an amendment and file it with the Secretary-General of the United Nations. The Secretary-General shall thereupon communicate any proposed amendments to the States Parties to the present Protocol with a request that they notify him whether they favour a conference of States Parties for the purpose of considering and voting upon the proposal. In the event that at least one third of the States Parties favours such a conference, the Secretary-General shall convene the conference under the auspices of the United Nations. Any amendment adopted by a majority of the States Parties present and voting at the conference shall be submitted to the General Assembly for approval.

"2. Amendments shall come into force when they have been approved by the General Assembly of the United Nations and accepted by a two-thirds majority of the States Parties to the present Protocol in accordance with their respective constitutional processes.

"3. When amendments come into force, they shall be binding on those States Parties which have accepted them, other States Parties still being bound by the provisions of the present Protocol and any earlier amendment which they have accepted.

Article 12

"1. Any State Party may denounce the present Protocol at any time by written notification addressed to the Secretary-General of the United Nations. Denunciation shall take effect three months after the date of receipt of the notification by the Secretary-General.

"2. Denunciation shall be without prejudice to the continued application of the provisions of the present Protocol to any communication submitted under article 2 before the effective date of denunciation.

Article 13

"Irrespective of the notifications made under article 8, paragraph 5, of the present Protocol, the Secretary-General of the United Nations shall inform all States referred to in article 48, paragraph 1, of the Covenant of the following particulars:

"*(a)* Signatures, ratifications and accessions under article 8;

"*(b)* The date of the entry into force of the present Protocol under article 9 and the date of entry into force of any amendments under article 11;

"*(c)* Denunciations under article 12.

Article 14

"1. The present Protocol, of which the Chinese, English, French, Russian and Spanish texts are equally authentic, shall be deposited in the archives of the United Nations.

"2. The Secretary-General of the United Nations shall transmit certified copies of the present Protocol to all States referred to in article 48 of the Covenant."

[YUN 1966, pp. 423-32]

*"Not a day goes by without scenes of warfare or famine,
arbitrary arrest, torture, rape, murder, expulsion, transfers of population,
and ethnic cleansing. Not a day goes by without reports of
attacks on the most fundamental freedoms . . . without reminders of racism
and the crimes it spawns, intolerance and the excesses it breeds,
underdevelopment and the ravages it causes."*

—Secretary-General Boutros Boutros-Ghali,
statement at the opening of the World Conference
on Human Rights in Vienna, 14 June 1993

Chapter II

Human rights gain prominence

The most fundamental human right of all is the right to life itself. Recent events have witnessed an escalation of massive and systematic violations of human rights, including arbitrary detentions, torture, executions and acts of genocide against innocent populations worldwide. The international community has responded vigorously to promote and protect human rights and prosecute and punish the violators of those rights.

As a result of the increasing human rights horrors in Rwanda and the former Yugoslavia, and in the belief that acts of genocide had been committed, the Commission on Human Rights held three special sessions at Geneva, two in 1992 and one in 1994, to review the extent of all breaches of international humanitarian law and all human rights violations.

The General Assembly adopted resolutions to condemn in the strongest terms all acts of genocide and violations and abuses of human rights in Rwanda and the former Yugoslavia. It called for the establishment of United Nations machinery to investigate the massive violations and breaches of international humanitarian law in those States and punish the alleged violators. The Security Council, by resolutions 955(1994) and 808(1993), established international tribunals for Rwanda and the former Yugoslavia to prosecute the persons responsible for serious crimes against humanity. In addition, Bosnia and Herzegovina instituted proceedings before the International Court of Justice against Yugoslavia (Serbia and Montenegro) for alleged vio-

lations of the 1948 Convention on the Prevention and Punishment of the Crime of Genocide.

The Vienna Declaration and Programme of Action, adopted by the 1993 World Conference on Human Rights, constitutes one of the milestones in United Nations history in the area of human rights. It provides the United Nations with a framework of principles and activities, approved by consensus, to achieve the objectives of the Charter in the field of human rights. The implementation of the Programme of Action requires concerted efforts of Governments and national human rights institutions, international organizations, United Nations human rights bodies and non-governmental organizations (NGOs).

The Declaration and Programme of Action reaffirms the solemn commitment of all States to promote and protect all human rights and fundamental freedoms, charting the course of action of the international community well into the next century. It is the crowning piece of a long process of consultation and joint action, with the participation not only of Governments but also of United Nations organs, human rights treaty bodies and regional intergovernmental organizations, as well as organizations representing all segments of civil society, including national institutions and NGOs.

World Conference on Human Rights

On 25 June 1993, representatives of 171 States adopted by consensus the Vienna Declaration and

Programme of Action of the World Conference on Human Rights, thus successfully closing the two-week Conference and presenting to the international community a common plan for the strengthening of human rights worldwide.

Composed of a preamble, a declaration of principles and a plan of action, the Vienna Declaration reaffirmed the crucial principles of equal rights and self-determination of peoples, peace, democracy, justice, equality, rule of law, pluralism, development, better standards of living and solidarity.

The Declaration also stressed the need to fight all forms of racism, discrimination, xenophobia and intolerance, and placed strong emphasis on the rights of women, children, minorities and indigenous people.

The World Conference took an integrated and systematic approach regarding the protection of human rights, strengthening of democracy and sustainable development. It identified major obstacles to the implementation of human rights and shortcomings, especially in the international protection of those rights, and specified concrete measures to help overcome existing difficulties.

In the words of the Secretary-General, the World Conference reaffirmed the universality of all human rights as the birthright of all human beings. It recognized that their promotion and protection were the first responsibility of Governments and, in the framework of the purposes and principles of the United Nations, constituted a legitimate concern of the international community.

The Conference stressed the close interrelationship between democracy, development and respect for human rights and reaffirmed the right to development as a human right. It underlined that all human rights, civil, cultural, economic, political and social, were universal, indivisible, interdependent and interrelated and must be treated globally in a fair and equal manner, on the same footing, and with the same emphasis. Further, it pointed out that United Nations efforts towards universal respect for and observance of human rights and fundamental freedoms for all contributed to the stability and well-being necessary for peaceful and friendly relations among nations, and to improved conditions for peace and security as well as social and economic development. At Vienna, the international community gave priority to action aimed at the full and equal enjoyment by women of all human rights and stressed the importance of the effective protection of the rights of the child.

The Vienna Declaration and Programme of Action reaffirmed the human rights of persons belonging to national or ethnic, religious and linguistic minorities and recognized the inherent dignity of indigenous people and their unique contribution to the development and plurality of society. It reinforced policies and programmes to eliminate racism and racial discrimination, xenophobia and related intolerance. It called on all Governments to enact appropriate legislation to combat all forms of racism and to establish national institutions to prevent such phenomena.

The role of education was underlined repeatedly as a crucial element in building respect for human rights. The World Conference also recognized the value of technical cooperation programmes aimed at strengthening democratic institutions, the rule of law and national human rights infrastructures, and stressed the enhanced role that regional organizations, national institutions and NGOs had to play in the promotion and protection of human rights.

The World Conference recognized the vital role of international cooperation as well as coordination of efforts undertaken in the human rights field by Governments, specialized agencies and programmes and NGOs. It urged United Nations agencies and programmes to cooperate in order to strengthen, rationalize and streamline their activities. It set universal acceptance of international human rights instruments as an important objective and called for concerted efforts to that end.

The General Assembly, by resolution 48/121 of 20 December 1993, endorsed the Vienna Declaration and Programme of Action and called on all States and requested all United Nations organs and bodies dealing with human rights to take further action with a view to implementing fully all recommendations of the Conference. Governments, the United Nations system, regional organizations, national institutions and NGOs have their own role to play in giving effect to the outcome of the Conference. Implementation of the Vienna Declaration and Programme of Action requires more than a number of isolated activities. International cooperation and an organizational framework are strongly needed. A detailed plan for implementation, enriched by the input of United Nations agencies and programmes, continuously verified in practice, has been developed in order to guide the human rights activities of the United Nations.

Strengthening the international legal framework for the promotion and protection of human rights was a fundamental concern of the World Conference, which recommended that a concerted effort be made to encourage and facilitate the universal acceptance of international human rights instruments and invited States to consider limiting the extent of reservations to those instruments, formulating them as precisely and narrowly as possible and reviewing them regularly with a view to withdrawing them. The United Nations High Commissioner for Human Rights (see below) places primary emphasis on the activities of the Centre for Human Rights aimed at facilitating universal ratification.

The Secretary-General addressed letters to all heads of State urging their Governments to accept those principal human rights treaties to which they were not yet party. The High Commissioner, in his contacts and dialogue with high-level government officials, also encourages universal accession to international human rights treaties. The chairmen of the human rights treaty bodies, during their fifth meeting in September 1994, welcomed these initiatives. They considered it of the utmost importance that the issue of ratification be brought regularly to the attention of non–States parties.

The World Conference recognized the necessity of continuing adaptation of United Nations human rights machinery to current and future needs in the promotion and protection of human rights. On its recommendation, the General Assembly, by resolution 48/141 of 20 December 1993, established the post of High Commissioner.

Elimination of racism and racial discrimination

The World Conference stressed that the elimination of racism and racial discrimination was a primary objective of the international community and should constitute a world-wide promotion programme. It urged all Governments to take immediate measures and develop strong policies to prevent and combat all forms of racism, xenophobia or related intolerance. The General Assembly, by resolution 48/91 of 20 December 1993, proclaimed the Third Decade to Combat Racism and Racial Discrimination and adopted a Programme of Action for the Decade. The Commission on Human Rights, in 1993, decided to appoint for a three-year period a Special Rapporteur on contemporary forms of racism, racial discrimination, xenophobia and related intolerance. Advisory services and information concerning various aspects of racism, racial discrimination and xenophobia are available to Member States on request in the Centre for Human Rights.

Minorities

The World Conference urged States and the international community to promote and protect the rights of persons belonging to national or ethnic, religious and linguistic minorities. It called for facilitation of the full participation of persons belonging to minorities in all aspects of the political, economic, social, religious and cultural life of society and in the economic progress and development in their country. The Conference called on the competent bodies to examine ways effectively to promote and protect the rights of persons belonging to minorities and to provide, at the request of Governments, qualified expertise in that regard, as part of the human rights programme of advisory services and technical assistance.

The Subcommission on Prevention of Discrimination and Protection of Minorities, in 1994, recommended that the Commission on Human Rights establish an inter-sessional working group of the Subcommission to examine peaceful and constructive solutions to situations involving minorities. The Human Rights Committee, also in 1994, adopted a general comment to article 27, on protection of persons belonging to ethnic, religious or linguistic minorities, of the International Covenant on Civil and Political Rights.

The High Commissioner attaches great importance to the protection of minorities and systematically draws Governments' attention to it. The Centre for Human Rights, in close cooperation with other Secretariat departments and United Nations bodies and organs, is developing activities aimed at facilitating the full participation of persons belonging to minorities in all aspects of society and in the economic progress and development of their countries. Technical assistance and advisory services, information and education activities concerning various aspects of minority issues are available to Member States upon request in the Centre for Human Rights.

Indigenous people

The World Conference reaffirmed the commitment of the international community to the economic, social and cultural well-being of indigenous people and their enjoyment of the fruits of sustainable development. It called on States to ensure the full and free participation of indigenous people in all aspects of society and, in accordance with international law, to take positive steps to ensure respect for all human rights and fundamental freedoms of indigenous people, on the basis of equality and non-discrimination, and to recognize the value and diversity of their distinct identities, cultures and social organization.

The General Assembly, by resolution 48/133 of 20 December 1993, requested the Commission on Human Rights to convene a meeting of participants in the programmes and projects of the International Year of the World's Indigenous People, 1993, and to report to the Working Group on Indigenous Populations on the conclusions that could be drawn from the activities of the Year for the elaboration of a detailed plan of action and the establishment of a funding plan for the International Decade of the World's Indigenous People. The Assembly, by resolution 48/163 of 21 December 1993, proclaimed the Decade, commencing on 10 December 1994. By the same resolution, the Assembly also requested the Commission to give priority consideration to the establishment of a permanent forum for indigenous people in the United Nations system.

The Subcommission on Prevention of Discrimination and Protection of Minorities in August 1994 adopted the draft United Nations Declaration on the Rights of Indigenous People and decided to submit it to the Commission on Human Rights at its 1995 session. Once adopted by the General Assembly, the Declaration will become the guideline for national and international activities related to indigenous people.

The Working Group on Indigenous Populations, in July 1994, considered the question of establishing a permanent forum for indigenous peoples. It examined expansion of its mandate, including a new role in the mechanism to be established in the context of the International Decade.

The High Commissioner for Human Rights has put primary emphasis on activities in the Centre for Human Rights aimed at implementation of the Decade. A study on ways of ensuring full and free participation of indigenous people in all aspects of society will be undertaken, and a fact sheet and manual relating to indigenous people will be published.

Technical assistance and advisory services, information and education activities concerning various aspects of the protection of indigenous people are available to Member States on request in the Centre for Human Rights.

Migrant workers

The World Conference urged all States to guarantee the protection of human rights of all migrant workers and their families. It attached particular importance to the harmony and tolerance between migrant workers and the society in which they lived. States have again been invited to sign and ratify the International Convention on the Protection of the Rights of All Migrant Workers and Members of Their Families.

The Commission on Human Rights, in February 1994, called on all States to sign and ratify or accede to the Convention as a matter of priority. It requested the Secretary-General to provide all facilities and assistance necessary for active promotion of the Convention, and invited United Nations organizations and agencies as well as NGOs to intensify their efforts to disseminate information on and promote understanding of the Convention.

The General Assembly, in resolution 48/110 of 20 December 1993, called for action to be taken by all countries, trade unions, treaty bodies and NGOs to protect the human rights of women migrant workers, who are doubly vulnerable because of their gender and their status as foreigners. In this regard, particular responsibility is vested with the sending and receiving States.

Technical assistance and advisory services, information and education activities concerning the Convention are available to Member States upon request in the Centre for Human Rights.

Equal status and human rights of women

The World Conference reaffirmed that the full and equal participation of women in political, civil, economic, social and cultural life, at the national, regional and international levels, and the eradication of all forms of discrimination on grounds of sex were priority objectives of the international community. It stressed that the human rights of women should form an integral part of United Nations human rights activities. The Conference urged Governments, institutions, intergovernmental and non-governmental organizations to intensify their efforts for the protection and promotion of human rights of women and the girl-child.

The Conference reiterated the objectives established on global action for women towards sustainable and equitable development, as set forth in the Rio Declaration on Environment and Development and chapter 24 of Agenda 21. It also emphasized that the equal status and human rights of women should be integrated into the mainstream of United Nations system-wide activity, whereas the coordination and integration of objectives and goals of the relevant organs and bodies should be enhanced. The United Nations should encourage universal ratification by all States, by the year 2000, of the Convention on the Elimination of All Forms of Discrimination against Women, adopted in 1979. The High Commissioner emphasized at the beginning of his term of office that achieving true gender equality in practice would be among his priorities. Strong attention would be paid to the preparation, from the human rights perspective, of the Fourth World Conference on Women in Beijing.

The Commission on Human Rights, in March 1994, condemned all violations of the human rights of women, including acts of gender-based violence, and urged Governments to intensify their efforts to promote and protect the human rights of women. It also called for the elimination of violence against women in public and private life. The Commission stressed the need for cooperation and coordination between relevant United Nations organs and bodies. It noted that the Beijing Conference might consider the question of means to integrate the human rights of women into the mainstream of United Nations system-wide activity.

In accordance with the Commission's March resolution, a Special Rapporteur on violence against women, including its causes and consequences, was appointed for a three-year period. The Special Rapporteur will report annually to the Commission, beginning in 1995. In carrying out her mandate, she is requested by the Commission to seek and receive information on violence against women; recommend national, regional and international measures to eliminate such violence and remedy its consequences; and work closely with other special rapporteurs, special representatives, the Subcommission on Prevention of Discrimination and Protection of Minorities and the treaty bodies, and cooperate closely with the Commission on the Status of Women.

The question of traditional practices affecting the health of women and girl-children has been dealt with by the Subcommission since its 1983 session. In August 1994, the Subcommission adopted a Plan of Action for the Elimination of Harmful Traditional Practices affecting the Health of Women and Children, submitted by the Special Rapporteur. The second regional seminar on traditional practices affecting the health of women and children was held at Colombo, Sri Lanka, in July 1994.

The chairmen of the human rights treaty bodies, at their September 1994 meeting, stressed the need to address in a comprehensive manner the obstacles to the realization by women of human rights established in the international instruments. They also recognized the need to revise appropriately the reporting guidelines and procedures of various treaty bodies and to continue consideration of the subject during the next meeting. The chairmen firmly recommended that the sessions and the secretariat of the Committee on the Elimination of Discrimination against Women be relocated to Geneva so that it was no longer separated from the mainstream of the other human rights activities.

Within the Centre for Human Rights, priority has been given to action aimed at ensuring cooperation and coordination with the Division on Women and other United Nations bodies related to women, especially in view of the Beijing Conference, at developing a strategy for greater information and media activities on women's issues in close cooperation with the Department of Public Information (DPI), and at collecting and exchanging information on the human rights of women to be included in the human rights database. Technical assistance and advisory services, information and education activities concerning various aspects of the protection of human rights of women are available to Member States upon request in the Centre for Human Rights.

The rights of the child

The World Conference stressed the importance of major national and international efforts aimed at promoting respect for the rights of the child to survival, protection, development and participation. It urged universal ratification of the Convention on the Rights of the Child by 1995 and its effective implementation by States parties through the adoption of all the necessary legislative, administrative and other measures and the allocation to the maximum extent of the available resources. National and international mechanisms and programmes should be strengthened for the defence and protection of children, in particular the girl-child, abandoned children, street children, and economically and sexually exploited children. International cooperation and solidarity should be promoted to support the implementation of the Convention, and

the rights of the child should be a priority in the United Nations system-wide action on human rights.

The Commission on Human Rights, in March 1994, called on all States that had not done so to sign, ratify or accede to the Convention as a matter of priority, and requested the Secretary-General to continue to provide all facilities and assistance necessary with a view to promoting its universal ratification by 1995.

The Commission, in March 1994, decided to establish two open-ended working groups to draft two optional protocols to the Convention, one on the prevention and eradication of the sale of children, child prostitution and child pornography and the other on the involvement of children in armed conflicts. The two working groups met in November 1994.

The High Commissioner outlined his basic strategy on the rights of the child in ongoing discussion with the United Nations Children's Fund (UNICEF), with which a joint work programme on cooperative endeavours in order to implement the Convention has been concluded. He has also prepared a seven-point plan of action to improve implementation of the Convention. The Centre for Human Rights will enhance cooperation on issues related to the child within the United Nations system, in particular with UNICEF, and with other relevant agencies and bodies, to pursue the achievement of the objectives set in the Plan of Action for Implementing the World Declaration on the Survival, Protection and Development of Children in the 1990s, adopted by the 1990 World Summit for Children, including the integration of the implementation of the Convention into national plans of action. It maintains contacts with relevant organizations related to the protection of children traumatized by war. A specific programme, embracing cooperation with Governments, the Committee on the Rights of the Child and NGOs, aims at universal ratification of the Convention by 1995.

The Working Group on Contemporary Forms of Slavery of the Subcommission on Prevention of Discrimination and Protection of Minorities continues to deal with issues related to children, such as child labour, the sale of children, child prostitution and child pornography.

In accordance with General Assembly resolution 48/157 of 20 December 1993, the Secretary-General appointed an expert to carry out a study on children affected by armed conflict. In this context, action has been taken to create a mechanism of coordination and cooperation between relevant United Nations agencies, including UNICEF, the United Nations High Commissioner for Refugees and the Centre for Human Rights. The study will be finalized for the 1996 session of the General Assembly.

The Centre for Human Rights assists in the coordination of activities between the Special Rapporteur of the Commission on Human Rights on the sale of children, child prostitution and child pornography and the Committee on the Rights of the Child, the Working Group of the Subcommission on Prevention of Discrimination and Protection of Minorities, UNICEF and other United Nations agencies and NGOs. Technical assistance and advisory services, information and education activities concerning various aspects of the protection of the rights of the child, including the ratification and implementation of the Convention on the Rights of the Child, are available to Member States upon request in the Centre for Human Rights.

Freedom from torture

The World Conference classified torture as one of the most atrocious violations against human dignity, which impaired the capability of victims to continue their lives and activities. It reaffirmed that, under human rights law and international humanitarian law, freedom from torture was a right which must be protected under all circumstances, including in times of internal or international disturbance or armed conflict. The Conference urged all States to end immediately the practice of torture and eradicate it for ever. States should abrogate legislation leading to impunity for those responsible for grave violations of human rights, such as torture, and prosecute such violations. The Conference underscored the primary role of prevention in combating torture and in that context called for the early adoption of an optional protocol to the 1984 Convention against Torture and Other Cruel, Inhuman or Degrading Treatment or Punishment, which is intended to establish a preventive system of regular visits to places of detention. The Conference encouraged speedy ratification of the Convention by all Member States that had not yet ratified it.

The Commission on Human Rights, in March 1994, outlined the specific measures that should be taken to prevent or combat torture, as well as to assist victims of torture. The Commission also urged all States to become parties to the Convention as a matter of priority.

The High Commissioner attaches particular importance to the effective implementation of the Convention. On 28 June 1994, at the Copenhagen Centre for the Rehabilitation of Victims of Torture, he made a world-wide appeal for the immediate cessation of all forms of torture, the universal ratification of the Convention and the full implementation of its provisions. He has also initiated an intensive campaign for universal ratification of the Convention.

Member States should strengthen assistance to victims of torture, including by increased support for the United Nations Voluntary Fund for Victims of Torture. The efficiency of measures and methods applied in assisting victims of torture and ensuring their rehabilitation requires further examination.

The open-ended working group created by the Commission on Human Rights in 1993 to draft an optional protocol to the Convention met in October 1993 and October 1994 and made considerable progress. It will continue its work in 1995.

The Centre for Human Rights has taken steps to facilitate action to combat torture. Advisory services with respect to both ratification and implementation of the Convention and resulting reporting obligations are available to Member States upon request. In this context, in cooperation with the World Health Organization (WHO) and NGOs, the Centre will also take concrete measures to ensure that principles of medical ethics are made familiar to physicians and other relevant professions.

Enforced disappearances

The World Conference called on all States to take effective legislative, administrative, judicial or other measures to prevent, terminate and punish acts of enforced disappearances.

The Commission on Human Rights, in March 1994, focused on States' obligations to prevent, combat and punish involuntary disappearances. In this context, it recalled that all acts of enforced disappearance were offences punishable by appropriate penalties which took into account their extreme seriousness under criminal law. The Commission urged the Governments concerned to intensify their cooperation with the Working Group on Enforced or Involuntary Disappearances on any action taken pursuant to recommendations addressed to them by the Group. It noted with concern that some Governments had never provided substantive replies concerning enforced disappearances alleged to have occurred in their countries, and deplored the fact that some Governments had not acted on the relevant recommendations made in the Working Group's reports.

Also in March 1994, the Commission on Human Rights requested the Working Group on Enforced or Involuntary Disappearances, represented by one of its members, to cooperate with the Special Rapporteur of the Commission in dealing with the problem of enforced disappearances in the territory of the former Yugoslavia.

The High Commissioner, in cooperation with the Working Group and relevant United Nations–based treaty bodies, as well as NGOs, has taken steps to study recommendations for the effective implementation of the 1992 Declaration on the Protection of All Persons from Enforced Disappearances.

Advisory services and information concerning the Declaration with regard to administrative, legislative and judicial procedures are available to Member States upon request in the Centre for Human

Rights. The existing database on missing persons will be revised and integrated into an overall database of the Centre.

The rights of disabled persons

The World Conference stressed that persons with disabilities should enjoy all human rights and fundamental freedoms. It called for legislation to be adopted or adjusted as necessary to ensure access for disabled persons to those rights and freedoms.

The General Assembly, by resolution 48/96 of 20 December 1993, adopted the Standard Rules on the Equalization of Opportunities for Persons with Disabilities. These have been brought to the attention of the relevant committees, working groups and special rapporteurs. Publication of the Rules is expected to sensitize public opinion. A special rapporteur has been appointed within the Commission for Social Development to monitor their implementation.

By resolution 48/99 of 20 December 1993, the General Assembly reaffirmed the continuing validity and value of the 1982 World Programme of Action concerning Disabled Persons; reiterated the responsibility of Governments for removing or facilitating the removal of barriers and obstacles to the full integration of persons with disabilities into society; and requested the Secretary-General to continue to give higher priority and visibility to disability issues within the work programme of the United Nations. Member States and the private sector were invited to contribute to the United Nations Voluntary Fund on Disability. The Assembly also commended the launching of the Asian and Pacific Decade of Disabled Persons, 1993-2002.

Advisory services concerning the adoption or adjustment of legislation for disabled persons are available to Member States upon request. Such services can be provided to promote, in the framework of national programmes, the participation of disabled persons in decision-making.

The right to development

The World Conference set out the vision of supporting democracy, development and human rights through increased international cooperation. It put emphasis on developing and building institutions relating to human rights, strengthening a pluralistic civil society and protecting vulnerable groups.

The Conference emphasized that assistance given, on Governments' request, in the human rights aspects of elections, the strengthening of the rule of law, the promotion of freedom of expression and the administration of justice, and to the effective participation of the people in decision-making processes, was of particular importance.

The Conference recommended establishing a comprehensive programme within the United Na-

tions to help States in building and strengthening national structures which had a direct impact on the overall observance of human rights and the maintenance of the rule of law. Within its framework, technical and financial assistance to national human rights projects and to the implementation of plans of action for the promotion and protection of human rights should be made available to Governments. The Conference recommended that each State consider the desirability of drawing up a related national plan of action.

The reaffirmation by consensus that the universal and inalienable right to development, as established in the 1986 Declaration on the Right to Development, must be implemented and realized was one of the major achievements of the Conference. Further, it was emphasized that the human being was the central subject of development. The Conference urged the Working Group on the Right to Development to formulate promptly, for early consideration by the General Assembly, comprehensive and effective measures to eliminate obstacles to implementing and realizing the Declaration, and to recommend ways towards the realization of the right to development by all States. It also recommended that non-governmental and grass-roots organizations active in development and/or human rights be enabled to play a major role in national and international activities.

The Conference appealed to Governments, agencies and institutions to increase considerably the resources devoted to building legal systems to protect human rights and relevant national institutions. It encouraged the establishment of comprehensive programmes, including resource banks of information and personnel with expertise relating to strengthening the rule of law and democratic institutions, and stipulated that those involved in development cooperation should bear in mind the interrelationship between development, democracy and human rights and cooperation.

The General Assembly, by resolution 48/141 of 20 December 1993, creating the post of High Commissioner for Human Rights, entrusted him with the mandate to enhance international cooperation for the promotion and protection of human rights, and to promote and protect the realization of the right to development. The High Commissioner has initiated dialogue with States and NGOs in order to develop or establish regional arrangements in the field of human rights, including through advisory services and technical assistance. He discussed related problems in the framework of the Third Asia-Pacific Workshop on Human Rights Issues (Seoul, Republic of Korea, July 1994) and encouraged the setting up of a regional or subregional human rights structure in Asia.

With a view to integrating the human rights dimension in development programmes, the High

Commissioner will ensure dialogue with inter-governmental and national development agencies. Comprehensive programmes will be set up to strengthen the legal and institutional infrastructures for the protection of all human rights.

The Centre for Human Rights assists in enhancing cooperation between the Committee on Economic, Social and Cultural Rights and NGOs, as well as relevant United Nations organs and agencies, to ensure the effective implementation of those rights. Support is available to the Commission on Human Rights in pursuing the Committee's recommendation with regard to the elaboration of an optional protocol to the 1966 International Covenant on Economic, Social and Cultural Rights, establishing a procedure of individual communications.

The High Commissioner is taking steps, including the convening of a senior-level meeting of experts, to assess the work undertaken so far in realizing cultural, economic and social rights, and to elaborate a strategy for the next four years, bearing in mind the Secretary-General's *Agenda for Development*. In consultation with relevant United Nations agencies and bodies and other institutions, the High Commissioner assists in the formulation of comprehensive measures to eliminate obstacles to the realization of the 1986 Declaration on the Right to Development. The Centre for Human Rights is preparing plans to enable NGOs and grass-roots organizations active in development and human rights to play an increased role in implementing the Declaration, with a view to facilitating dialogue and exploring possible financial assistance.

The Working Group on the Right to Development, established by the Commission in 1993, met in October 1994 for its third session, focusing on the obstacles to implementing the right to development.

The Commission on Human Rights, in March 1994, recommended that the Centre convene expert seminars for chairmen of the human rights treaty bodies and representatives of specialized agencies and NGOs, as well as representatives of States, focusing on the content of specific cultural, economic and social rights, as a follow-up to the conclusions and recommendations of a January 1993 seminar on indicators to measure achievements in the realization of those rights.

Scheduled for submission to the Commission's 1995 session is a report of the Secretary-General on adequate measures for a durable solution to the debt crisis of developing countries, requested by the Commission in 1993. The report is to be drafted in a process of consultations already launched with heads of State and Government, as well as multilateral financial institutions, specialized agencies, and intergovernmental and non-governmental organizations.

A dialogue is being developed with institutions outside the United Nations system, particularly with regional intergovernmental organizations active in the human rights field, for example, the Commission on Human and People's Rights of the Organization of African Unity (OAU), the Council of Europe, the Conference on Security and Cooperation in Europe (CSCE), and the Inter-American Commission on Human Rights, to enhance coordination for better promotion and protection of human rights and implementation of the Vienna Declaration and Programme of Action. In June 1994, the High Commissioner invited all Member States to inform him annually of national implementation of the Declaration and Programme of Action.

Advisory services and technical assistance

The programme of advisory services and technical assistance, through its multidimensional character, takes an essential place in United Nations human rights activities. The World Conference stressed the need to strengthen the programme and increase the resources for it. Upon Governments' requests, assistance is being made available for implementation of comprehensive plans of action to promote and protect human rights, including the strengthening of institutions of human rights and democracy, the legal protection of human rights, training of officials and others, broad-based education and public information aimed at promoting respect for human rights. The Conference also recommended that more resources be made available for establishing or strengthening regional arrangements for the promotion and protection of human rights.

In keeping with resolution 48/141 of December 1993, the High Commissioner is responsible for providing, through the Centre for Human Rights and other institutions, advisory services and technical assistance at the request of the State concerned and, where appropriate, regional human rights organizations.

Advisory services and technical assistance are provided to requesting States to facilitate the ratification or accession to international human rights instruments. Advisory services of experts are also offered on legislative reforms bringing national law in line with international human rights standards. Within this framework, comprehensive country programmes have recently been launched for Burundi, Cambodia, Malawi, Namibia, the Russian Federation and Rwanda. Programmes for Bhutan and Nepal are under preparation.

The Centre for Human Rights has provided assistance in the elaboration of national plans of action. Needs assessment missions have been requested by Armenia and Azerbaijan (July 1994); Bolivia (October 1994); Georgia and Kazakhstan (under consideration); Kyrgyzstan (envisioned for early 1995); Paraguay (January 1995); and the United Republic of Tanzania (September 1994). In

October 1994, a national plan of action for human rights, elaborated with the support of the Centre, was officially approved by Latvia.

Under the programme, special attention has been given to groups rendered vulnerable, such as minorities, indigenous people, women, children, migrant workers, disabled persons, refugees and displaced persons. Two seminars addressing the rights of minorities and the rights of the child were held at Bucharest, Romania, in October 1994.

The Centre for Human Rights also offers, upon request, assistance for the human rights aspects of elections, strengthening the rule of law and democratic institutions, including training of administrators of justice and police officials. The Centre provided electoral assistance to Malawi. Requests for the training of police were received from Argentina (October 1994, March 1995); Brazil (October 1994); Egypt (June 1994); the former Yugoslav Republic of Macedonia (early 1995); Mexico (early 1995); Mozambique (September 1994); and Palestine (November 1995). The Centre published a manual on human rights and elections, and is developing a manual on human rights for law enforcement officials.

To assist States in meeting their reporting obligations under the various human rights treaties, workshops are organized regularly at the subregional or regional levels. A training course on human rights reporting was organized by the Centre in cooperation with the International Labour Organisation Centre (Geneva and Turin, Italy, 31 October–25 November 1994), to help government officials with the preparation and presentation of national reports to human rights supervisory bodies.

Human rights education and dissemination of information

The World Conference considered human rights education, training and public information to be essential. According to the Vienna Declaration and Programme of Action, human rights, humanitarian law, democracy and rule of law should be included in all curricula. States should develop specific programmes and strategies for human rights education. Advisory services and technical assistance programmes should be able to respond immediately to States' requests in this regard.

The Conference underlined the importance of intensifying the World Public Information Campaign for Human Rights. In accordance with one of its recommendations, the General Assembly in December 1994 proclaimed the 10-year period beginning 1 January 1995 the United Nations Decade for Human Rights Education.

In cooperation with the United Nations Educational, Scientific and Cultural Organization (UNESCO) and other relevant agencies and bodies, the Centre for Human Rights assists Member States in developing specific programmes and strategies for ensuring human rights education for all. It supports the development of curricula, pedagogical techniques and teaching materials, and has published or is preparing manuals for public officials and the general public. The Centre maintains ongoing cooperation with regional, subregional and local human rights institutes and information centres for the purpose of organizing educational and promotional activities in the field of human rights.

At a round-table meeting on human rights education, organized jointly by the Centre and the Council of Europe (Geneva, 7 October 1994), participants discussed ways and forms of cooperation and coordination in the field of human rights education. Within the framework of the World Public Information Campaign for Human Rights, the Centre continues to inform people around the world about United Nations human rights activities. Contacts with the media and United Nations information centres have been intensified.

To enhance human rights training for personnel involved in the increasing number of United Nations field operations, the Centre offers courses and special training materials.

UN High Commissioner for Human Rights

The Vienna Declaration, in addressing the need to strengthen United Nations machinery for human rights, called for the General Assembly to consider, as a matter of priority, the establishment of the post of United Nations High Commissioner for Human Rights. Following those recommendations, the Assembly, in December 1993, established such a post.

The High Commissioner has the principal responsibility for United Nations human rights activities under the direction of the Secretary-General and within the competence and decisions of the General Assembly, the Economic and Social Council and the Commission on Human Rights. His mandate spans the whole range of human rights concerns. In particular, the High Commissioner is charged with promoting the effective enjoyment by all of all human rights, promoting the realization of the right to development, providing advisory services to support human rights programmes, coordinating human rights education and public information activities, and preventing human rights violations. The mandate also includes engaging in dialogue with all Governments to improve respect for human rights, enhancing international cooperation in promoting human rights, coordinating human rights activities within the United Nations system, overseeing United Nations machinery and providing overall supervision of the Centre for Human Rights.

Since the General Assembly approved the appointment of José Ayala-Lasso on 14 February

1994, the High Commissioner, who took up his duties on 5 April of that year, has moved to develop a wide-ranging programme of activities, including visits to countries to discuss and strengthen understanding and respect for human rights, and the maintenance of close contacts with United Nations programmes, the specialized agencies and other international organizations, national institutions and NGOs engaged in the promotion and protection of human rights.

The High Commissioner personally visited Rwanda twice in order to assess the situation, evaluate existing needs and, subsequently, strengthen the human rights presence there. The experience in Rwanda exemplifies the spirit in which he may act in emergency human rights situations, as well as in situations of post-conflict reconstruction of the basic human rights infrastructures of a country. In September 1994, the High Commissioner presented to States at a meeting at Geneva a detailed operational plan for human rights field operations in Rwanda, designed to support the work of the Special Rapporteur and the Commission of Experts to examine and analyse information concerning grave violations of international humanitarian law and genocide in Rwanda, and to provide advisory services.

In May and August 1994, the High Commissioner visited Burundi to provide assistance in preserving respect for human rights, contributing to a stabilization of the situation and preventing large-scale violations. Agreement was reached on a human rights assistance programme aimed at strengthening national institutions for the promotion and protection of human rights that will be part of a comprehensive integrated approach to be carried out in close cooperation with all United Nations agencies and programmes present in the country. In June, an office of the High Commissioner was opened at Bujumbura to help implement the first phase of the programme.

In exercise of his mandate to secure respect for and realization of human rights, the High Commissioner engaged in dialogue with Governments, making official visits to Austria, Bhutan, Cambodia, Denmark, Estonia, Finland, Germany, Japan, Latvia, Lithuania, Malawi, Nepal, Norway, the Republic of Korea, Sweden and Switzerland as the host country. During those visits, he urged ratification of outstanding human rights treaties and discussed strengthening national implementation through action plans, establishment of national institutions such as human rights commissions and ombudsmen, and the promotion of human rights education, as well as strengthening international cooperation and support for the United Nations human rights programme. In particular, during his visits to Cambodia, Estonia, Latvia, Lithuania, Malawi and Nepal, the High Commissioner discussed the development of programmes to assist in the transition to democracy.

Entrusted with the responsibility of enhancing international cooperation in the field of human rights and coordinating human rights activities of the United Nations system, the High Commissioner participated in the April 1994 session of the Administrative Committee on Coordination (ACC), which dealt with follow-up to the Vienna Conference. He met with special rapporteurs, experts and chairmen of working groups of the Commission on Human Rights and with the chairmen of human rights treaty bodies during their fifth meeting in September 1994. In May, he held discussions on priority human rights issues at Vienna with the Secretary-General of CSCE and met with the Director of Human Rights of the Council of Europe. In September, the High Commissioner took part in a meeting between the Council of Europe, CSCE and United Nations programmes based at Geneva, where ways of improving cooperation and coordination were discussed. In July, he participated in the Third Asia-Pacific Workshop on Human Rights Issues (Republic of Korea), offering support to efforts aimed at setting up a regional or subregional arrangement for the promotion and protection of human rights in Asia.

Human rights violations and acts of genocide

The Nürnberg Trials established clearly the principle that any individual, regardless of office or rank, shall be held responsible in international law for war crimes, crimes against peace or crimes against humanity.

At its 55th plenary meeting on 11 December 1946, the General Assembly unanimously adopted a resolution affirming the principles of international law recognized by the Charter of the Nürnberg Tribunal and the judgment of the Tribunal. The resolution read as follows:

THE GENERAL ASSEMBLY,

RECOGNIZES the obligation laid upon it by Article 13, paragraph 1, sub-paragraph a, of the Charter, to initiate studies and make recommendations for the purpose of encouraging the progressive development of international law and its codification;

TAKES NOTE of the Agreement for the establishment of an International Military Tribunal for the prosecution and punishment of the major war criminals of the European Axis signed in London on 8 August 1945, and of the Charter annexed thereto, and of the fact that similar principles have been adopted in the Charter of the International Military Tribunal for the trial of the major war criminals in the Far East, proclaimed at Tokyo on 19 January 1946.

THEREFORE,

AFFIRMS the principles of international law recognized by the Charter of the Nürnberg Tribunal and the judgment of the Tribunal;

DIRECTS the Committee on the codification of international law established by the resolution of the General Assembly of 11 December 1946, to treat as a matter of primary importance plans for the formulation, in the context of a general codification of offences against the peace and security of mankind, or of an International Criminal Code, of the principles recognized in the Charter of the Nürnberg Tribunal and in the judgment of the Tribunal.

(YUN 1946-47, p. 254)

At the same meeting, the General Assembly, again unanimously, adopted another resolution strengthening the concept of punishment of major human rights violations, particularly acts of genocide. The resolution read as follows:

Genocide is a denial of the right of existence of entire human groups, as homicide is the denial of the right to live of individual human beings; such denial of the right of existence shocks the conscience of mankind, results in great losses to humanity in the form of cultural and other contributions represented by these human groups, and is contrary to moral law and to the spirit and aims of the United Nations.

Many instances of such crimes of genocide have occurred when racial, religious, political and other groups have been destroyed, entirely or in part.

The punishment of the crime of genocide is a matter of international concern.

THE GENERAL ASSEMBLY, THEREFORE,

AFFIRMS that genocide is a crime under international law which the civilized world condemns, and for the commission of which principals and accomplices—whether private individuals, public officials or statesmen, and whether the crime is committed on religious, racial, political or any other grounds—are punishable;

. . .

(YUN 1946-47, p. 255)

The principle that the individual shall be held responsible for serious violations of human rights — firmly enforced by the Nürnberg Tribunal and today universally recognized under international law — was the basic principle that led to the establishment and presently guides the operation of the International Tribunal for Rwanda and the International Criminal Tribunal for the former Yugoslavia.

Special session of the Commission on Human Rights on Rwanda

The third special session of the Commission on Human Rights took place on 24 and 25 May 1994 on the issue of the human rights situation in Rwanda. The two previous special sessions had dealt with the human rights situation in the former Yugoslavia. The United Nations High Commissioner for Human Rights undertook a mission to Rwanda on 11 and 12 May and submitted a report on the situation there, together with recommendations, to the third special session.

On 25 May, the Commission, believing that genocidal acts might have occurred in Rwanda, condemned in the strongest terms all breaches of international humanitarian law and all violations and abuses of human rights in that country. It called for an immediate cessation of hostilities and called on the responsible authorities, groups and individuals in Rwanda to facilitate the access of humanitarian relief to all in need. The Commission requested its Chairman to appoint a Special Rapporteur, for an initial period of one year, to investigate the human rights situation in Rwanda. It requested the High Commissioner to make arrangements for the Special Rapporteur to be assisted by a team of human rights field officers and to ensure that future United Nations efforts aimed at conflict resolution and peace-building in Rwanda were accompanied by a strong human rights component.

Appointment of Special Rapporteur on Rwanda

As requested by the special session of the Commission, René Degni-Ségui (Côte d'Ivoire) was appointed Special Rapporteur on the situation of human rights in Rwanda. In accordance with his mandate, he visited Rwanda in June, July and October 1994. He called for very rapid action to avoid further massacres and disaster, and made specific recommendations to the Rwandese Government, countries hosting Rwandese refugees and the United Nations which, he said, should require the Rwandese Government to put an end to the serious human rights violations in its territory. He called, among others, for international assistance in all economic, political, social and cultural sectors, including technical assistance to help reconstruct the infrastructure of the police, gendarmerie and judiciary, provide training for them and establish a Bar with a view to safeguarding the independence of the judiciary. He recommended that the number of human rights experts be increased, with some of them acting as observers, investigators and instructors. A legal framework should be established to ensure the protection of widows and unaccompanied children and guarantee their fundamental rights, and compensation should be provided for damage attributable to the perpetrators of massacres or their accomplices. The security in camps for refugees and displaced persons should be ensured by an international force, and arrangements should be created for their repatriation in security and dignity.

In cooperation with OAU, the United Nations should take steps to create conditions and a framework for dialogue between various Rwandese political groups both inside and outside the country, so that the basis might be laid for a political settlement of the conflict in place of a military settlement. The Special Rapporteur also recommended the convening of an international conference on Rwanda, to induce the parties to the conflict to negotiate the conditions for peace, democratic transition, and national reconciliation and unity, taking due account of the 1993 Arusha agreements.

Based on the findings of the Special Rapporteur and the Commission of Experts that acts of genocide and systematic and widespread violations of human rights had been committed in Rwanda, the General Assembly, on 23 December 1994, adopted resolution 49/206 on the situation of human rights in Rwanda. The resolution read as follows:

The General Assembly,

Guided by the Charter of the United Nations, the Universal Declaration of Human Rights, the International Covenant on Economic, Social and Cultural Rights, the International Covenant on Civil and Political Rights, the Convention on the Prevention and Punishment of the Crime of Genocide, and other applicable human rights and humanitarian law instruments,

Recalling Commission on Human Rights resolution S-3/1 of 25 May 1994, by which the Commission established a Special Rapporteur to investigate the human rights situation in Rwanda,

Recalling the establishment of the Commission of Experts pursuant to Security Council resolution 935(1994) of 1 July 1994 to report on grave violations of international humanitarian law in Rwanda,

Deeply concerned by the reports of the Special Rapporteur and the Commission of Experts that genocide and systematic, widespread and flagrant violations of international humanitarian law and crimes against humanity have been committed in Rwanda, resulting in massive loss of life,

Also deeply concerned by the reports of the Special Rapporteur and the Commission of Experts that the situation of ethnic and political armed conflict in Rwanda resulted in other grave violations and abuses of human rights, including violation of the right to life, the right to physical and moral integrity, the right to be free from torture and other cruel, inhuman and degrading treatment and the right to be free from discrimination on the grounds of ethnic origin and to be protected from incitement to such discrimination,

Reaffirming the deep concern expressed by the World Conference on Human Rights about violations of human rights during armed conflicts affecting the civilian population, especially women, children, the elderly and the disabled,

Noting that, following the cease-fire of 18 July 1994, a new Government of Rwanda has been established and has made efforts to restore the rule of law and reconstruct the civil administration and the social, legal, physical, economic and human rights infrastructure of Rwanda after the extensive damage inflicted by the civil conflict,

Noting with concern that, in spite of efforts by the Government of Rwanda to ensure peace and security and the rule of law, a situation of insecurity still exists, evidenced by reports of disappearances, arbitrary arrest and detention, summary executions and destruction of property, and welcoming the commitments of the Government of Rwanda to protect and promote respect for human rights and fundamental freedoms and to eliminate impunity by investigating and prosecuting those responsible for acts of retribution,

Concerned about the danger posed by continuing incidences of violence and intolerance in Rwanda, which impede the full realization of civil, political, economic, social and cultural rights,

Also concerned about the fact that these occurrences create a climate of insecurity, which prevents refugees and displaced persons from returning to their homes, conscious that the return to their homes is essential for the normalization of the situation in Rwanda and countries of the region, and concerned, in addition, about reports of continuing acts of intimidation and violence within the camps for refugees, particularly by the former Rwandese authorities, which prevent refugees from returning home,

Conscious that technical assistance and advisory services will assist the Government of Rwanda in reconstructing the social, legal, physical, economic and human rights infrastructure of Rwanda,

Further concerned by the ongoing interference, particularly by the former Rwandese authorities, in the provision of humanitarian relief, which has already led to the withdrawal of some non-governmental agencies responsible for the distribution of relief supplies within the camps outside Rwanda,

Noting with appreciation the efforts of the Secretary-General, his Special Representative for Rwanda, the United Nations High Commissioner for Refugees, the Department of Humanitarian Affairs of the Secretariat and non-governmental organizations, as well as of the Commission on Human Rights and its special rapporteurs,

Commending the initiatives taken by the United Nations High Commissioner for Human Rights, including his timely visits to Rwanda, and welcoming his efforts to ensure that the Special Rapporteur is assisted by a team of human rights field officers acting in close cooperation with the United Nations Assistance Mission for Rwanda and other United Nations agencies and programmes operating in Rwanda, and his efforts to facilitate coordination and cooperation between the work of the Commission of Experts and the Special Rapporteur,

Conscious of the important role human rights field officers will have in establishing an environment conducive to full respect for human rights and fundamental freedoms and in preventing further violations, mindful of the need for the speedy deployment of a sufficient number of such officers to fulfil this role and endorsing the Secretary-General's encouragement to Member States to provide contributions to expand human rights activities in the field,

Stressing the need for the implementation by all parties in Rwanda of the principles contained in the Peace Agreement between the Government of the Rwandese Republic and the Rwandese Patriotic Front, signed at Arusha on 4 August 1993, which constitutes the framework for peace, national reconciliation and unity in Rwanda, and noting with appreciation the efforts of the Chairman and Secretary General of the Organization of African Unity, the President of the United Republic of Tanzania, Mr. Ali Hassan Mwinyi, in his capacity as the Facilitator of the Arusha peace process,

Recalling Security Council resolution 965(1994) of 30 November 1994, in which the Council expanded the mandate of the Assistance Mission to contribute to the security and protection of displaced persons, refugees and civilians at risk in Rwanda, to provide security and support for the distribution of relief supplies and humanitarian relief operations, to contribute to the security in Rwanda of personnel of the International Tribunal for Rwanda and human rights officers, and to assist in the training of a new integrated police force, and recalling also the Secretary-General's revised deployment schedule for the Assistance Mission, which is intended to promote security in all areas of the country and create conditions conducive to the return of refugees,

Conscious of the fact that the magnitude of the tragedy in Rwanda requires the kind of coordination and resources that can be effectively sustained by the United Nations, and supporting the Secretary-General's encouragement, under the Rwanda Emergency Normalization Plan, to States Members of the United Nations, United Nations agencies and non-governmental organizations to provide immediate and coordinated technical and financial assistance to Rwanda,

Recognizing that effective action to prevent further violations of human rights and fundamental freedoms must be a central and integral element of the overall United Nations response to the situation in Rwanda,

Recognizing also that a strong human rights component is indispensable to the political peace process and the post-conflict reconstruction of Rwanda,

Considering that the international community and the Government of Rwanda must follow closely and continue to support all efforts to consolidate peace, ensure full respect for human rights and fundamental freedoms and undertake the reconstruction of Rwanda,

1. *Welcomes* the reports of the Special Rapporteur on the situation of human rights in Rwanda;

2. *Condemns in the strongest terms* all acts of genocide and violations of international humanitarian law and all violations and abuses of human rights that occurred during the conflict in Rwanda, especially following the tragic events of 6 April 1994;

3. *Also condemns in the strongest terms* the kidnapping and killing of military peace-keeping personnel attached to the United Nations Assistance Mission for Rwanda, the killing of personnel attached to humanitarian organizations operating in the country, the wanton killing of innocent civilians and the destruction of property during the conflict, which constitute a blatant violation of international humanitarian law;

4. *Reaffirms* that all persons who commit or authorize genocide or other grave violations of international humanitarian law or those who are responsible for grave violations of human rights are individually responsible and accountable for those violations and that the international community will exert every effort to bring those responsible to justice in accordance with international principles of due process;

5. *Welcomes* the establishment, pursuant to Security Council resolution 955(1994) of 8 November 1994, of the International Criminal Tribunal for the Prosecution of Persons Responsible for Genocide and Other Serious Violations of International Humanitarian Law Committed in the Territory of Rwanda and Rwandese Citizens Responsible for Genocide and Other Such Violations Committed in the Territory of Neighbouring States between 1 January 1994 and 31 December 1994, and urges States to cooperate fully with the International Tribunal;

6. *Requests* States that have given refuge to persons involved in serious breaches of international humanitarian law, crimes against humanity or acts of genocide to take the necessary steps, in cooperation with the International Tribunal for Rwanda, to ensure that they do not escape justice;

7. *Notes with deep concern* the findings of the Special Rapporteur that disappearances, arbitrary arrest and detention, summary executions and destruction of property are still taking place in Rwanda, encourages the Government of Rwanda to ensure investigation and prosecution of those responsible for such acts in accordance with international principles of due process, and welcomes the commitments of the Government of Rwanda in this regard;

8. *Encourages* the Government of Rwanda to protect and promote respect for human rights and fundamental freedoms, stresses the need to create an environment conducive to the realization of civil, political, economic, social and cultural rights, and to the return by refugees and displaced persons to their homes, and welcomes in this regard the commitments made by the Government of Rwanda;

9. *Encourages* the efforts of the Government of Rwanda to involve, regardless of ethnicity, all citizens not responsible for acts of genocide or other grave violations of international humanitarian law, within its administrative, judicial, political and security structures;

10. *Invites* Member States, the organizations and agencies of the United Nations system and intergovernmental and non-governmental organizations to intensify their efforts to contribute financial and technical support to the efforts of the Government of Rwanda to reconstruct the civil administration and the social, legal, physical, economic and human rights infrastructure of Rwanda;

11. *Welcomes* the efforts of the Government of Rwanda to restore the rule of law and to reconstruct the Rwandese justice system, and invites Member States, the organizations and agencies of the United Nations system and intergovernmental and non-governmental organizations to intensify their efforts to provide technical and financial assistance for the administration of justice, particularly to ensure the independence and impartiality of the judiciary, and welcomes in this regard the efforts of the Centre for Human Rights of the Secretariat to assist the Ministry of Justice of Rwanda;

12. *Also invites* Member States, the organizations and agencies of the United Nations system and intergovernmental and non-governmental organizations to intensify their efforts to provide technical and financial assistance to the system of law enforcement in Rwanda, including police training, and welcomes in this regard the assistance being provided by the Assistance Mission to the Government of Rwanda in its efforts to establish a new integrated police force;

13. *Condemns* those preventing, in some instances by force, the voluntary repatriation of refugees, and those obstructing the access of humanitarian relief to all in need, including those in the camps for refugees, and calls on the appropriate authorities to ensure security in such camps;

14. *Urges* the responsible authorities in Rwanda and in the region to ensure full respect for human rights and fundamental freedoms in the camps for refugees and displaced persons;

15. *Welcomes* the commitment of the Governments of Zaire, the United Republic of Tanzania and Burundi to help resolve the problems facing the refugees, and calls upon them to do all in their power to ensure the safety both of the refugees and of the personnel providing humanitarian assistance to the refugees;

16. *Urges* Governments of the region to take measures to prevent their territory from being used to pursue a strategy of destabilization within Rwanda;

17. *Urges* the Rwandese authorities and the Rwandese people to work for national reconciliation and unity in Rwanda, for peace in the country and the whole region, and to work together to implement the principles contained in the Peace Agreement between the Government of the Rwandese Republic and the Rwandese Patriotic Front, signed at Arusha, which constitutes the framework for peace, national reconciliation and unity in Rwanda;

18. *Welcomes* the efforts of the United Nations High Commissioner for Human Rights to ensure that efforts of the United Nations aimed at conflict-resolution and peace-building in Rwanda are accompanied by a strong human rights component and effectively supported by a comprehensive programme of human rights assistance, drawing as appropriate on the expertise and capacities of all parts of the United Nations system able to contribute to the promotion and protection of human rights in Rwanda;

19. *Also welcomes* the cooperation the Government of Rwanda has extended to the United Nations High Commissioner for Human Rights and to the Special Rapporteur, and the acceptance by the Government of Rwanda of the deployment of human rights field officers, bearing in mind the important role of those officers, acting in close cooperation with the Assistance Mission and other United Nations agencies and programmes operating in Rwanda, in establishing a climate of confidence and a secure environment conducive to full respect for human rights and fundamental freedoms and in preventing further violations;

20. *Invites* Member States to intensify further their efforts to support human rights activities in the field in Rwanda;

21. *Requests* the Secretary-General to take appropriate steps to ensure adequate financial and human resources and logistical support for the speedy deployment of a sufficient number of human rights field officers and for the delivery of programmes of technical assistance and advisory services;

22. *Also requests* the Secretary-General to provide all resources necessary to enable the Special Rapporteur to fulfil his mandate;

23. *Decides* to continue its consideration of this question at its fiftieth session.

International Tribunal for Rwanda

In 1994, in response to the massive violations of human rights and acts of genocide in Rwanda, the Security Council established the Independent Commission of Experts under resolution 935(1994) to investigate those violations of international humanitarian law. The Independent Commission strongly recommended that the Council take all necessary action to ensure that the individuals responsible for the serious violations of human rights in Rwanda were brought to justice before an independent and impartial international criminal tribunal. The Commission concluded on the basis of ample evidence that individuals from both sides to the armed conflict perpetrated serious breaches of international humanitarian law and crimes against humanity. It concluded that there existed overwhelming evidence to prove that acts of genocide against the Tutsi ethnic group were perpetrated by Hutu elements in a concerted, planned, systematic and methodical way.

The Security Council, on 8 November 1994, adopted resolution 955(1994) on the establishment and statute of an International Tribunal for Rwanda. The resolution read as follows:

The Security Council,

Reaffirming all its previous resolutions on the situation in Rwanda,

Having considered the reports of the Secretary-General pursuant to paragraph 3 of resolution 935(1994) of 1 July 1994, and having taken note of the reports of the Special Rapporteur for Rwanda of the United Nations Commission on Human Rights,

Expressing appreciation for the work of the Commission of Experts established pursuant to resolution 935(1994), in particular its preliminary report on violations of international humanitarian law in Rwanda transmitted by the Secretary-General's letter of 1 October 1994,

Expressing once again its grave concern at the reports indicating that genocide and other systematic, widespread and flagrant violations of international humanitarian law have been committed in Rwanda,

Determining that this situation continues to constitute a threat to international peace and security,

Determined to put an end to such crimes and to take effective measures to bring to justice the persons who are responsible for them,

Convinced that in the particular circumstances of Rwanda, the prosecution of persons responsible for serious violations of international humanitarian law would enable this aim to be achieved and would contribute to the process of national reconciliation and to the restoration and maintenance of peace,

Believing that the establishment of an international tribunal for the prosecution of persons responsible for genocide and the other above-mentioned violations of international humanitarian law will contribute to ensuring that such violations are halted and effectively redressed,

Stressing also the need for international cooperation to strengthen the courts and judicial system of Rwanda, having regard in particular to the necessity for those courts to deal with large numbers of suspects,

Considering that the Commission of Experts established pursuant to resolution 935(1994) should continue on an urgent basis the collection of information relating to evidence of grave violations of international humanitarian law committed in the territory of Rwanda and should submit its final report to the Secretary-General by 30 November 1994,

Acting under Chapter VII of the Charter of the United Nations,

1. *Decides* hereby, having received the request of the Government of Rwanda, to establish an international tribunal for the sole purpose of prosecuting persons responsible for genocide and other serious violations of international humanitarian law committed in the territory of Rwanda and Rwandan citizens responsible for genocide and other such violations committed in the territory of neighbouring States, between 1 January 1994 and 31 December 1994 and to this end to adopt the Statute of the International Criminal Tribunal for Rwanda annexed hereto;

2. *Decides* that all States shall cooperate fully with the International Tribunal and its organs in accordance with the present resolution and the Statute of the International Tribunal and that consequently all States shall take any measures necessary under their domestic law to implement the provisions of the present resolution and the Statute, including the obligation of States to comply with requests for assistance or orders issued by a Trial Chamber under Article 28 of the Statute, and requests States to keep the Secretary-General informed of such measures;

3. *Considers* that the Government of Rwanda should be notified prior to the taking of decisions under articles 26 and 27 of the Statute;

4. *Urges* States and intergovernmental and nongovernmental organizations to contribute funds, equipment and services to the International Tribunal, including the offer of expert personnel;

5. *Requests* the Secretary-General to implement this resolution urgently and in particular to make practical arrangements for the effective functioning of the International Tribunal, including recommendations to the Council as to possible locations for the seat of the International Tribunal at the earliest time and to report periodically to the Council;

6. *Decides* that the seat of the International Tribunal shall be determined by the Council having regard to considerations of justice and fairness as well as administrative efficiency, including access to witnesses, and economy, and subject to the conclusion of appropriate arrangements between the United Nations and the State of the seat, acceptable to the Council, having regard to the fact that the International Tribunal may meet away from its seat when it considers it necessary for the efficient exercise of its functions; and decides that an office will be established and proceedings will be conducted in Rwanda, where feasible and appropriate, subject to the conclusion of similar appropriate arrangements;

7. *Decides* to consider increasing the number of judges and Trial Chambers of the International Tribunal if it becomes necessary;

8. *Decides* to remain actively seized of the matter.

ANNEX
Statute of the International Tribunal for Rwanda

Having been established by the Security Council acting under Chapter VII of the Charter of the United Nations, the International Criminal Tribunal for the Prosecution of Persons Responsible for Genocide and Other Serious Violations of International Humanitarian Law Committed in the Territory of Rwanda and Rwandan citizens responsible for genocide and other such violations committed in the territory of neighbouring States, between 1 January 1994 and 31 December 1994 (hereinafter referred to as "the International Tribunal for Rwanda") shall function in accordance with the provisions of the present Statute.

Article 1
Competence of the International Tribunal for Rwanda

The International Tribunal for Rwanda shall have the power to prosecute persons responsible for serious violations of international humanitarian law committed in the territory of Rwanda and Rwandan citizens responsible for such violations committed in the territory of neighbouring States, between 1 January and 31 December 1994, in accordance with the provisions of the present Statute.

Article 2
Genocide

1. The International Tribunal for Rwanda shall have the power to prosecute persons committing genocide as defined in paragraph 2 of this article or of committing any of the other acts enumerated in paragraph 3 of this article.

2. Genocide means any of the following acts committed with intent to destroy, in whole or in part, a national, ethnic, racial or religious group, as such:

    (*a*) Killing members of the group;

    (*b*) Causing serious bodily or mental harm to members of the group;

    (*c*) Deliberately inflicting on the group conditions of life calculated to bring about its physical destruction in whole or in part;

    (*d*) Imposing measures intended to prevent births within the group;

    (*e*) Forcibly transferring children of the group to another group.

3. The following acts shall be punishable:

    (*a*) Genocide;

    (*b*) Conspiracy to commit genocide;

    (*c*) Direct and public incitement to commit genocide;

    (*d*) Attempt to commit genocide;

    (*e*) Complicity in genocide.

Article 3
Crimes against humanity

The International Tribunal for Rwanda shall have the power to prosecute persons responsible for the following crimes when committed as part of a widespread or systematic attack against any civilian population on national, political, ethnic, racial or religious grounds:

    (*a*) Murder;

    (*b*) Extermination;

    (*c*) Enslavement;

    (*d*) Deportation;

    (*e*) Imprisonment;

    (*f*) Torture;

    (*g*) Rape;

    (*h*) Persecutions on political, racial and religious grounds;

    (*i*) Other inhumane acts.

Article 4
Violations of Article 3 common to the Geneva Conventions and of Additional Protocol II

The International Tribunal for Rwanda shall have the power to prosecute persons committing or ordering to be committed serious violations of Article 3 common to the Geneva Conventions of 12 August 1949 for the Protection of War Victims, and of Additional Protocol

II thereto of 8 June 1977. These violations shall include, but shall not be limited to:

(*a*) Violence to life, health and physical or mental well-being of persons, in particular murder as well as cruel treatment such as torture, mutilation or any form of corporal punishment;

(*b*) Collective punishments;

(*c*) Taking of hostages;

(*d*) Acts of terrorism;

(*e*) Outrages upon personal dignity, in particular humiliating and degrading treatment, rape, enforced prostitution and any form of indecent assault;

(*f*) Pillage;

(*g*) The passing of sentences and the carrying out of executions without previous judgement pronounced by a regularly constituted court, affording all the judicial guarantees which are recognized as indispensable by civilized peoples;

(*h*) Threats to commit any of the foregoing acts.

Article 5
Personal jurisdiction

The International Tribunal for Rwanda shall have jurisdiction over natural persons pursuant to the provisions of the present Statute.

Article 6
Individual criminal responsibility

1. A person who planned, instigated, ordered, committed or otherwise aided and abetted in the planning, preparation or execution of a crime referred to in articles 2 to 4 of the present Statute, shall be individually responsible for the crime.

2. The official position of any accused person, whether as Head of State or Government or as a responsible Government official, shall not relieve such person of criminal responsibility nor mitigate punishment.

3. The fact that any of the acts referred to in articles 2 to 4 of the present Statute was committed by a subordinate does not relieve his or her superior of criminal responsibility if he or she knew or had reason to know that the subordinate was about to commit such acts or had done so and the superior failed to take the necessary and reasonable measures to prevent such acts or to punish the perpetrators thereof.

4. The fact that an accused person acted pursuant to an order of a Government or of a superior shall not relieve him or her of criminal responsibility, but may be considered in mitigation of punishment if the International Tribunal for Rwanda determines that justice so requires.

Article 7
Territorial and temporal jurisdiction

The territorial jurisdiction of the International Tribunal for Rwanda shall extend to the territory of Rwanda including its land surface and airspace as well as to the territory of neighbouring States in respect of serious violations of international humanitarian law committed by Rwandan citizens. The temporal jurisdiction of the International Tribunal for Rwanda shall extend to a period beginning on 1 January 1994 and ending on 31 December 1994.

Article 8
Concurrent jurisdiction

1. The International Tribunal for Rwanda and national courts shall have concurrent jurisdiction to prosecute persons for serious violations of international humanitarian law committed in the territory of Rwanda and Rwandan citizens for such violations committed in the territory of neighbouring States, between 1 January 1994 and 31 December 1994.

2. The International Tribunal for Rwanda shall have primacy over the national courts of all States. At any stage of the procedure, the International Tribunal for Rwanda may formally request national courts to defer to its competence in accordance with the present Statute and the Rules of Procedure and Evidence of the International Tribunal for Rwanda.

Article 9
Non bis in idem

1. No person shall be tried before a national court for acts constituting serious violations of international humanitarian law under the present Statute, for which he or she has already been tried by the International Tribunal for Rwanda.

2. A person who has been tried by a national court for acts constituting serious violations of international humanitarian law may be subsequently tried by the International Tribunal for Rwanda only if:

(*a*) The act for which he or she was tried was characterized as an ordinary crime; or

(*b*) The national court proceedings were not impartial or independent, were designed to shield the accused from international criminal responsibility, or the case was not diligently prosecuted.

3. In considering the penalty to be imposed on a person convicted of a crime under the present Statute, the International Tribunal for Rwanda shall take into account the extent to which any penalty imposed by a national court on the same person for the same act has already been served.

Article 10
Organization of the International Tribunal for Rwanda

The International Tribunal for Rwanda shall consist of the following organs:

(*a*) The Chambers, comprising two Trial Chambers and an Appeals Chamber;

(*b*) The Prosecutor; and

(*c*) A Registry.

Article 11
Composition of the Chambers

The Chambers shall be composed of eleven independent judges, no two of whom may be nationals of the same State, who shall serve as follows:

(*a*) Three judges shall serve in each of the Trial Chambers;

(*b*) Five judges shall serve in the Appeals Chamber.

Article 12
Qualification and election of judges

1. The judges shall be persons of high moral character, impartiality and integrity who possess the qualifications required in their respective countries for appointment to the highest judicial offices. In the overall composition of the Chambers due account shall be taken of the experience of the judges in criminal law, international law, including international humanitarian law and human rights law.

2. The members of the Appeals Chamber of the International Tribunal for the Prosecution of Persons Responsible for Serious Violations of International Law

Committed in the Territory of the Former Yugoslavia since 1991 (hereinafter referred to as "the International Tribunal for the Former Yugoslavia") shall also serve as the members of the Appeals Chamber of the International Tribunal for Rwanda.

3.   The judges of the Trial Chambers of the International Tribunal for Rwanda shall be elected by the General Assembly from a list submitted by the Security Council, in the following manner:

(a)   The Secretary-General shall invite nominations for judges of the Trial Chambers from States Members of the United Nations and non-member States maintaining permanent observer missions at United Nations Headquarters;

(b)   Within thirty days of the date of the invitation of the Secretary-General, each State may nominate up to two candidates meeting the qualifications set out in paragraph 1 above, no two of whom shall be of the same nationality and neither of whom shall be of the same nationality as any judge on the Appeals Chamber;

(c)   The Secretary-General shall forward the nominations received to the Security Council. From the nominations received the Security Council shall establish a list of not less than twelve and not more than eighteen candidates, taking due account of adequate representation on the International Tribunal for Rwanda of the principal legal systems of the world;

(d)   The President of the Security Council shall transmit the list of candidates to the President of the General Assembly. From that list the General Assembly shall elect the six judges of the Trial Chambers. The candidates who receive an absolute majority of the votes of the States Members of the United Nations and of the non-member States maintaining permanent observer missions at United Nations Headquarters, shall be declared elected. Should two candidates of the same nationality obtain the required majority vote, the one who received the higher number of votes shall be considered elected.

4.   In the event of a vacancy in the Trial Chambers, after consultation with the Presidents of the Security Council and of the General Assembly, the Secretary-General shall appoint a person meeting the qualifications of paragraph 1 above, for the remainder of the term of office concerned.

5.   The judges of the Trial Chambers shall be elected for a term of four years. The terms and conditions of service shall be those of the judges of the International Tribunal for the Former Yugoslavia. They shall be eligible for re-election.

Article 13
Officers and members of the Chambers

1.   The judges of the International Tribunal for Rwanda shall elect a President.

2.   After consultation with the judges of the International Tribunal for Rwanda, the President shall assign the judges to the Trial Chambers. A judge shall serve only in the Chamber to which he or she was assigned.

3.   The judges of each Trial Chamber shall elect a Presiding Judge, who shall conduct all of the proceedings of that Trial Chamber as a whole.

Article 14
Rules of procedure and evidence

The judges of the International Tribunal for Rwanda shall adopt, for the purpose of proceedings before the International Tribunal for Rwanda, the rules of procedure and evidence for the conduct of the pre-trial phase of the proceedings, trials and appeals, the admission of evidence, the protection of victims and witnesses and other appropriate matters of the International Tribunal for the Former Yugoslavia with such changes as they deem necessary.

Article 15
The Prosecutor

1.   The Prosecutor shall be responsible for the investigation and prosecution of persons responsible for serious violations of international humanitarian law committed in the territory of Rwanda and Rwandan citizens responsible for such violations committed in the territory of neighbouring States, between 1 January 1994 and 31 December 1994.

2.   The Prosecutor shall act independently as a separate organ of the International Tribunal for Rwanda. He or she shall not seek or receive instructions from any Government or from any other source.

3.   The Prosecutor of the International Tribunal for the Former Yugoslavia shall also serve as the Prosecutor of the International Tribunal for Rwanda. He or she shall have additional staff, including an additional Deputy Prosecutor, to assist with prosecutions before the International Tribunal for Rwanda. Such staff shall be appointed by the Secretary-General on the recommendation of the Prosecutor.

Article 16
The Registry

1.   The Registry shall be responsible for the administration and servicing of the International Tribunal for Rwanda.

2.   The Registry shall consist of a Registrar and such other staff as may be required.

3.   The Registrar shall be appointed by the Secretary-General after consultation with the President of the International Tribunal for Rwanda. He or she shall serve for a four-year term and be eligible for reappointment. The terms and conditions of service of the Registrar shall be those of an Assistant Secretary-General of the United Nations.

4.   The staff of the Registry shall be appointed by the Secretary-General on the recommendation of the Registrar.

Article 17
Investigation and preparation of indictment

1.   The Prosecutor shall initiate investigations ex-officio or on the basis of information obtained from any source, particularly from Governments, United Nations organs, intergovernmental and non-governmental organizations. The Prosecutor shall assess the information received or obtained and decide whether there is sufficient basis to proceed.

2.   The Prosecutor shall have the power to question suspects, victims and witnesses, to collect evidence and to conduct on-site investigations. In carrying out these tasks, the Prosecutor may, as appropriate, seek the assistance of the State authorities concerned.

3.   If questioned, the suspect shall be entitled to be assisted by counsel of his or her own choice, including the right to have legal assistance assigned to the suspect without payment by him or her in any such case if he or she does not have sufficient means to pay for it, as

well as to necessary translation into and from a language he or she speaks and understands.

4. Upon a determination that a prima facie case exists, the Prosecutor shall prepare an indictment containing a concise statement of the facts and the crime or crimes with which the accused is charged under the Statute. The indictment shall be transmitted to a judge of the Trial Chamber.

Article 18
Review of the indictment

1. The judge of the Trial Chamber to whom the indictment has been transmitted shall review it. If satisfied that a prima facie case has been established by the Prosecutor, he or she shall confirm the indictment. If not so satisfied, the indictment shall be dismissed.

2. Upon confirmation of an indictment, the judge may, at the request of the Prosecutor, issue such orders and warrants for the arrest, detention, surrender or transfer of persons, and any other orders as may be required for the conduct of the trial.

Article 19
Commencement and conduct of trial proceedings

1. The Trial Chambers shall ensure that a trial is fair and expeditious and that proceedings are conducted in accordance with the rules of procedure and evidence, with full respect for the rights of the accused and due regard for the protection of victims and witnesses.

2. A person against whom an indictment has been confirmed shall, pursuant to an order or an arrest warrant of the International Tribunal for Rwanda, be taken into custody, immediately informed of the charges against him or her and transferred to the International Tribunal for Rwanda.

3. The Trial Chamber shall read the indictment, satisfy itself that the rights of the accused are respected, confirm that the accused understands the indictment, and instruct the accused to enter a plea. The Trial Chamber shall then set the date for trial.

4. The hearings shall be public unless the Trial Chamber decides to close the proceedings in accordance with its rules of procedure and evidence.

Article 20
Rights of the accused

1. All persons shall be equal before the International Tribunal for Rwanda.

2. In the determination of charges against him or her, the accused shall be entitled to a fair and public hearing, subject to article 21 of the Statute.

3. The accused shall be presumed innocent until proved guilty according to the provisions of the present Statute.

4. In the determination of any charge against the accused pursuant to the present Statute, the accused shall be entitled to the following minimum guarantees, in full equality:

(a) To be informed promptly and in detail in a language which he or she understands of the nature and cause of the charge against him or her;

(b) To have adequate time and facilities for the preparation of his or her defence and to communicate with counsel of his or her own choosing;

(c) To be tried without undue delay;

(d) To be tried in his or her presence, and to defend himself or herself in person or through legal assistance of his or her own choosing; to be informed, if he or she does not have legal assistance, of this right; and to have legal assistance assigned to him or her, in any case where the interests of justice so require, and without payment by him or her in any such case if he or she does not have sufficient means to pay for it;

(e) To examine, or have examined, the witnesses against him or her and to obtain the attendance and examination of witnesses on his or her behalf under the same conditions as witnesses against him or her;

(f) To have the free assistance of an interpreter if he or she cannot understand or speak the language used in the International Tribunal for Rwanda;

(g) Not to be compelled to testify against himself or herself or to confess guilt.

Article 21
Protection of victims and witnesses

The International Tribunal for Rwanda shall provide in its rules of procedure and evidence for the protection of victims and witnesses. Such protection measures shall include, but shall not be limited to, the conduct of in camera proceedings and the protection of the victim's identity.

Article 22
Judgement

1. The Trial Chambers shall pronounce judgements and impose sentences and penalties on persons convicted of serious violations of international humanitarian law.

2. The judgement shall be rendered by a majority of the judges of the Trial Chamber, and shall be delivered by the Trial Chamber in public. It shall be accompanied by a reasoned opinion in writing, to which separate or dissenting opinions may be appended.

Article 23
Penalties

1. The penalty imposed by the Trial Chamber shall be limited to imprisonment. In determining the terms of imprisonment, the Trial Chambers shall have recourse to the general practice regarding prison sentences in the courts of Rwanda.

2. In imposing the sentences, the Trial Chambers should take into account such factors as the gravity of the offence and the individual circumstances of the convicted person.

3. In addition to imprisonment, the Trial Chambers may order the return of any property and proceeds acquired by criminal conduct, including by means of duress, to their rightful owners.

Article 24
Appellate proceedings

1. The Appeals Chamber shall hear appeals from persons convicted by the Trial Chambers or from the Prosecutor on the following grounds:

(a) An error on a question of law invalidating the decision; or

(b) An error of fact which has occasioned a miscarriage of justice.

2. The Appeals Chamber may affirm, reverse or revise the decisions taken by the Trial Chambers.

Article 25
Review proceedings

Where a new fact has been discovered which was not known at the time of the proceedings before the Trial

Chambers or the Appeals Chamber and which could have been a decisive factor in reaching the decision, the convicted person or the Prosecutor may submit to the International Tribunal for Rwanda an application for review of the judgement.

Article 26
Enforcement of sentences

Imprisonment shall be served in Rwanda or any of the States on a list of States which have indicated to the Security Council their willingness to accept convicted persons, as designated by the International Tribunal for Rwanda. Such imprisonment shall be in accordance with the applicable law of the State concerned, subject to the supervision of the International Tribunal for Rwanda.

Article 27
Pardon or commutation of sentences

If, pursuant to the applicable law of the State in which the convicted person is imprisoned, he or she is eligible for pardon or commutation of sentence, the State concerned shall notify the International Tribunal for Rwanda accordingly. There shall only be pardon or commutation of sentence if the President of the International Tribunal for Rwanda, in consultation with the judges, so decides on the basis of the interests of justice and the general principles of law.

Article 28
Cooperation and judicial assistance

1.   States shall cooperate with the International Tribunal for Rwanda in the investigation and prosecution of persons accused of committing serious violations of international humanitarian law.

2.   States shall comply without undue delay with any request for assistance or an order issued by a Trial Chamber, including, but not limited to:

(a)   The identification and location of persons;

(b)   The taking of testimony and the production of evidence;

(c)   The service of documents;

(d)   The arrest or detention of persons;

(e)   The surrender or the transfer of the accused to the International Tribunal for Rwanda.

Article 29
The status, privileges and immunities of the International Tribunal for Rwanda

1.   The Convention on the Privileges and Immunities of the United Nations of 13 February 1946 shall apply to the International Tribunal for Rwanda, the judges, the Prosecutor and his or her staff, and the Registrar and his or her staff.

2.   The judges, the Prosecutor and the Registrar shall enjoy the privileges and immunities, exemptions and facilities accorded to diplomatic envoys, in accordance with international law.

3.   The staff of the Prosecutor and of the Registrar shall enjoy the privileges and immunities accorded to officials of the United Nations under articles V and VII of the Convention referred to in paragraph 1 of this article.

4.   Other persons, including the accused, required at the seat or meeting place of the International Tribunal for Rwanda shall be accorded such treatment as is necessary for the proper functioning of the International Tribunal for Rwanda.

Article 30
Expenses of the International Tribunal for Rwanda

The expenses of the International Tribunal for Rwanda shall be expenses of the Organization in accordance with Article 17 of the Charter of the United Nations.

Article 31
Working languages

The working languages of the International Tribunal shall be English and French.

Article 32
Annual report

The President of the International Tribunal for Rwanda shall submit an annual report of the International Tribunal for Rwanda to the Security Council and to the General Assembly.

The International Tribunal for Rwanda is a subsidiary organ of the Security Council with regard to administrative and financial matters, but as a judicial body is independent of any one particular State or group of States, including its parent body. The statute of the Tribunal is an adaptation of the statute of the International Tribunal for the Former Yugoslavia applied to the circumstances of Rwanda.

The Office of the Prosecutor for the International Tribunal was established at Kigali in January 1995 and the Deputy Prosecutor, Honoré Rakotomanana, took office on 20 March. Since January, Tribunal staff have been gathering information and evidence in Rwanda and other countries. In a statement of 5 April, the Chief Prosecutor, Judge Richard Goldstone, announced that the Tribunal was processing about 400 cases and that the first case for trial was expected in the second half of the year.

Human Rights Field Operation

The United Nations High Commissioner for Human Rights visited Rwanda twice in order to assess the situation, evaluate existing needs and strengthen the human rights presence there. The experience in Rwanda exemplifies the spirit in which the High Commissioner may act in emergency human rights situations and in situations of post-conflict reconstruction of a country's basic human rights infrastructures.

In order to monitor the ongoing human rights situation, help redress existing problems and prevent further possible violations, the High Commissioner, in consultation with the Government, has deployed human rights officers to Rwanda. They work directly with the population, as well as with government officials and civic leaders throughout the country, and seek to promote respect for the rights of individual citizens and a sense of confidence and stability through human rights education in the country generally and in particular sectors of society, such as the police.

In close consultation with the relevant government ministries, the Human Rights Field Operation in Rwanda, through its technical cooperation unit, developed and recently issued a comprehensive programme addressing the needs of the Government in establishing a civil society based on respect for human rights. The programme includes recommendations on measures to facilitate the prosecution of suspects accused of serious human rights violations. It also proposes a strategy for introducing human rights education in Rwandese schools and government institutions. The High Commissioner has also launched an international appeal with a view to assisting the Government of Rwanda in re-establishing the judicial system.

Technical assistance is also to be provided in the administration of justice, which includes improvement in prison administration, establishment of civil dispute resolution mechanisms, and recruitment and training of civilian police.

Special sessions of the Commission on Human Rights on the former Yugoslavia

In 1992, the Commission on Human Rights held two special sessions at Geneva (13 and 14 August; 30 November and 1 December), to consider the situation of human rights in the former Yugoslavia.

The Commission condemned in the strongest terms all human rights violations in the former Yugoslavia, especially in Bosnia and Herzegovina, and called on all parties to end such violations immediately and take steps to ensure full respect for human rights, fundamental freedoms and humanitarian law; cease immediately the human rights violations that had produced refugees and displaced persons and ensure conditions conducive to a safe return to their homes; and fulfil their obligations under the provisions of the various covenants and treaties for the protection of human rights. The Commission condemned ethnic cleansing and called on all parties to ensure the protection of the rights of persons belonging to national or ethnic, religious and linguistic minorities.

The Commission demanded that all parties extend full cooperation and protection to the Office of the United Nations High Commissioner for Refugees (UNHCR) and other international humanitarian organizations and relief workers assisting refugees and displaced persons. Calling for the release of all persons arbitrarily arrested or detained, it demanded that the International Committee of the Red Cross (ICRC) be granted access to all camps, prisons and other places of detention and that all parties ensure safety and freedom of movement for ICRC.

The Commission requested its Chairman to appoint a special rapporteur to investigate first-hand the human rights situation in the former Yugoslavia, particularly in Bosnia and Herzegovina; compile information on possible human rights violations, including war crimes; and provide a preliminary report, including recommendations for ending and preventing such violations. The Commission requested United Nations bodies and specialized agencies, Governments and intergovernmental and non-governmental organizations to assist the special rapporteur, as well as the Special Rapporteurs on the question of torture and on summary or arbitrary executions, the Secretary-General's representative on internally displaced persons and the Working Group on Arbitrary Detention.

Appointment of Special Rapporteur for the former Yugoslavia

In accordance with the Commission's request, Tadeusz Mazowiecki (Poland) was appointed Special Rapporteur. He visited the former Yugoslavia on a number of occasions, accompanied by the Chairman of the Working Group on Arbitrary Detention and the Special Rapporteur on extrajudicial, summary or arbitrary executions.

The Special Rapporteur observed that ethnic cleansing was directed against Muslims and ethnic Croatians in the territories of Bosnia and Herzegovina and Croatia under the control of ethnic Serbs. He also described the situation of ethnic Serbs in Croatia, which had resulted in the flight of a large number of ethnic Serbs to Serbia and to those parts of Croatia and Bosnia and Herzegovina under their control. The Special Rapporteur received information on cases of detention, executions, disappearances and other violations such as physical abuse and torture.

The Special Rapporteur concluded that mass and grave human rights violations were occurring in Bosnia and Herzegovina and were being perpetrated by all parties to the conflicts. Violence was tolerated and often encouraged by responsible authorities. The situation of detainees and refugees was particularly dramatic, and the indoctrination of a large part of the population encouraged national and religious hatred.

The Special Rapporteur recommended neutralizing the heavy weaponry in Bosnia and Herzegovina; the continued call by the United Nations for an end to ethnic cleansing; increasing the size and expanding the mandate of the United Nations Protection Force; granting ICRC full access to detention camps and centres; reinforcing the efficiency of the information system on the fate of persons forcibly separated from their families; establishing a commission to determine the fate of disappeared persons; setting up an information agency, independent of local authorities, to counteract the dissemination of hatred; creating a commission to assess and further investigate cases warranting prosecution; and concerted international action to improve the fate of victims of human rights violations.

In response to the grave human rights situation in the former Yugoslavia, the General Assembly on 18 December 1992 adopted resolution 47/147 on the situation of human rights in the territory of the former Yugoslavia. The resolution read as follows:

The General Assembly,

Guided by the principles embodied in the Charter of the United Nations, the Universal Declaration of Human Rights, the International Covenants on Human Rights, the International Convention on the Elimination of All Forms of Racial Discrimination, the Convention on the Prevention and Punishment of the Crime of Genocide, the Convention against Torture and Other Cruel, Inhuman or Degrading Treatment or Punishment, and international humanitarian law, including the Geneva Conventions of 12 August 1949 and the Additional Protocols thereto, of 1977,

Deeply concerned about the human tragedy in the territory of the former Yugoslavia, and at the continuing massive and systematic violations of human rights occurring in most of that territory, particularly in the areas of Bosnia and Herzegovina under Serbian control,

Bearing in mind Security Council resolutions 771(1992) of 13 August 1992, 780(1992) of 6 October 1992 and 787(1992) of 16 November 1992, in which, *inter alia*, the Council demanded that all parties and others concerned in the former Yugoslavia should immediately cease and desist from all breaches of international humanitarian law, and pursuant to which the Secretary-General has established a Commission of Experts to examine and analyse information relating to violations of humanitarian law being committed in the territory of the former Yugoslavia,

Recalling its resolution 46/242 of 25 August 1992, in which it demanded an end to the fighting, condemned the massive violations of human rights and international humanitarian law occurring in the territory of the former Yugoslavia, in particular the abhorrent practice of "ethnic cleansing", rejected recognition of the acquisition of territory by force and demanded the safe, unconditional and honourable repatriation of refugees and deportees to their homes,

Bearing in mind its resolution 47/80 of 16 December 1992 in which it condemned unreservedly "ethnic cleansing", and reiterated its conviction that those who committed or ordered the commission of acts of "ethnic cleansing" were individually responsible and should be brought to justice,

Noting that the Commission on Human Rights, at its first special session, devoted to the consideration of the situation of human rights in the former Yugoslavia, adopted resolution 1992/S-1/1, of 14 August 1992, in which it condemned in the strongest terms all violations of human rights within the territory of the former Yugoslavia, called upon all parties to cease those violations immediately and to take all necessary steps to ensure full respect for human rights and fundamental freedoms and humanitarian law and requested its Chairman to appoint a special rapporteur to investigate the human rights situation in the territory of the former Yugoslavia,

Noting with appreciation the efforts of the Special Rapporteur, as well as those of the Chairman of the Working Group on Arbitrary Detention, the Special Rapporteur on extrajudicial, summary or arbitrary executions, the Special Rapporteur on the question of torture and the Representative of the Secretary-General on internally displaced persons, who accompanied him on one or both of his missions,

Welcoming the decision by the Commission on Human Rights to meet again in special session to consider the reports of the Special Rapporteur,

Encouraging the continuing efforts made in the framework of the International Conference on the Former Yugoslavia to find a peaceful solution to the situation in the former Yugoslavia, including the proposals made by the Co-Chairmen of the Steering Committee of the Conference for a constitution for the Republic of Bosnia and Herzegovina designed to protect human rights on the basis of fundamental human rights instruments,

Welcoming the consideration by the Human Rights Committee of the special reports from the Governments of the Federal Republic of Yugoslavia (Serbia and Montenegro), Croatia and Bosnia and Herzegovina on the human rights situation in those parts of the territory of the former Yugoslavia, with respect to their obligations under the International Covenant on Civil and Political Rights,

Noting with concern the comments adopted by the Human Rights Committee following consideration of those special reports at its meeting held on 6 November 1992,

Welcoming the effort by the Conference on Security and Cooperation in Europe to prevent further human rights violations and its missions dispatched to the territory of the former Yugoslavia, including missions of long duration to Kosovo, Vojvodina and Sandjak, where the human rights situation remains a cause of great concern,

Gravely concerned about the human rights situation in the territory of the former Yugoslavia, and in particular at the continuing, odious practice of "ethnic cleansing", which is the direct cause of the vast majority of human rights violations there and whose principal victims are the Muslim population threatened with virtual extermination,

Alarmed that, although the conflict in Bosnia and Herzegovina is not a religious conflict, it has been characterized by the systematic destruction and profanation of mosques, churches and other places of worship, as well as other sites of cultural heritage, in particular in areas currently or previously under Serbian control,

1.   *Commends* the Special Rapporteur for his reports on the situation of human rights in the territory of the former Yugoslavia;

2.   *Expresses its grave concern* at the Special Rapporteur's detailed reports of violations of human rights and humanitarian law in Bosnia and Herzegovina, Croatia and the Federal Republic of Yugoslavia (Serbia and Montenegro) and at his conclusion that most of the territory of the former Yugoslavia, in particular Bosnia and Herzegovina, is the scene of massive and systematic violations of human rights and grave violations of humanitarian law;

3.   *Condemns* in the strongest possible terms the abhorrent practice of "ethnic cleansing" and recognizes that the Serbian leadership in territories under its control in Bosnia and Herzegovina, the Yugoslav People's Army and the political leadership of the Republic of Serbia bear primary responsibility for this reprehensible

practice, which flagrantly violates the most fundamental principles of human rights;

4. *Condemns also* the specific violations identified by the Special Rapporteur, most of which are caused by "ethnic cleansing", and which include killings, torture, beatings, rape, disappearances, destruction of houses, and other acts or threats of violence aimed at forcing individuals to leave their homes, as well as reports of violations of human rights in connection with detention;

5. *Condemns further* the indiscriminate shelling of cities and civilian areas, the systematic terrorization and murder of non-combatants, the destruction of vital services, the besieging of cities and the use of military force against civilian populations and relief operations by all sides, recognizing that the main responsibility lies with Serbian forces;

6. *Demands* that all parties involved in the former Yugoslavia, and especially those most responsible, cease these violations immediately, take appropriate steps to apprehend and punish those who are guilty of perpetrating or authorizing the violations, including those violations in connection with detention, and take all necessary measures to ensure the enjoyment of human rights and fundamental freedoms, in accordance with their obligations under the Geneva Conventions of 12 August 1949, and the Additional Protocols thereto, of 1977, the International Covenants on Human Rights, and other international human rights instruments;

7. *Reaffirms* that all persons who perpetrate or authorize crimes against humanity and other grave breaches of international humanitarian law are individually responsible for those breaches and that the international community will exert every effort to bring them to justice, and calls upon all parties to provide all pertinent information to the Commission of Experts in accordance with Security Council resolution 780(1992);

8. *Expresses deep concern* at the number of disappearances and missing persons in the former Yugoslavia, and calls on all parties to make all possible efforts to account for those missing;

9. *Demands* an immediate end to the practice of "ethnic cleansing", and in particular that the Government of the former Federal Republic of Yugoslavia (Serbia and Montenegro) use its influence with the self-proclaimed Serbian authorities in Bosnia and Herzegovina and Croatia to bring the practice of "ethnic cleansing" to an immediate end and to reverse the effects of that practice;

10. *Reaffirms* that States are to be held accountable for violations of human rights which their agents commit on the territory of another State;

11. *Expresses its complete support* for the victims of these violations, reaffirms the right of all persons to return to their homes in safety and dignity, considers invalid all acts made under duress affecting ownership of property and other related questions, and recognizes the right of victims of "ethnic cleansing" to receive reparation for their losses;

12. *Condemns* in particular the violations of human rights and humanitarian law in connection with detention, including killings, torture and the systematic practice of rape, and calls upon all parties in the former Yugoslavia to close immediately all detention centres not in compliance with the Geneva Conventions and to release immediately all persons arbitrarily or illegally detained;

13. *Demands* that the International Committee of the Red Cross, the Special Rapporteur, the missions of the Conference on Security and Cooperation in Europe and other relevant international humanitarian organizations be granted immediate, unimpeded and continued access to all camps, prisons and other places of detention within the territory of the former Yugoslavia;

14. *Expresses its grave concern* at the report of the Special Rapporteur on the dangerous situation in Kosovo, Sandjak and Vojvodina, urges all parties there to engage in a meaningful dialogue under the auspices of the International Conference on the Former Yugoslavia, to act with utmost restraint and to settle disputes in full compliance with human rights and fundamental freedoms, and calls upon the Serbian authorities to refrain from the use of force, to stop immediately the practice of "ethnic cleansing" and to respect fully the rights of persons belonging to ethnic communities or minorities, in order to prevent the extension of the conflict to other parts of the former Yugoslavia;

15. *Calls upon* the parties to implement immediately all commitments made in the framework of the International Conference on the Former Yugoslavia and to work together to ensure the success of the Conference, and welcomes in this regard the acceptance by the Government of Bosnia and Herzegovina of the constitutional proposals of the Co-Chairmen of the Steering Committee of the Conference as a basis for negotiations;

16. *Endorses* the resolution adopted by the Commission on Human Rights at its second special session addressing the reports of the Special Rapporteur, in particular its call for all States to consider the extent to which the acts committed in Bosnia and Herzegovina and in Croatia constitute genocide, in accordance with the Convention on the Prevention and Punishment of the Crime of Genocide;

17. *Calls upon* all United Nations bodies, including the United Nations Protection Force and the specialized agencies, and invites Governments and informed intergovernmental and non-governmental organizations to cooperate fully with the Special Rapporteur and in particular to provide him on a continuing basis with all relevant and accurate information in their possession on the situation of human rights in the former Yugoslavia;

18. *Urges* all States, United Nations bodies, including the specialized agencies, the Special Rapporteur and, as appropriate, international humanitarian organizations to make available to the Commission of Experts, pursuant to Security Council resolution 780(1992), substantiated information in their possession or submitted to them relating to the violations of humanitarian law, including grave breaches of the Geneva Conventions, being committed in the territory of the former Yugoslavia;

19. *Urges* all States and relevant organizations to consider implementation of the recommendations of the Special Rapporteur, and in particular:

(*a*) Welcomes the call of the Special Rapporteur for the opening of humanitarian relief corridors to prevent the imminent death of tens of thousands of persons in besieged cities;

(*b*) Welcomes the invitation of the Security Council, in its resolution 787(1992), to the Secretary-General, in consultation with the Office of the United Nations High Commissioner for Refugees and other relevant agencies, to study the possibility of and the requirements for the promotion of safe areas and the recommendation of the Special Rapporteur for the creation of such security zones for the protection of displaced persons, while keeping in mind that the international community must not acquiesce in demographic changes caused by "ethnic cleansing";

(c) Draws the attention of the Commission of Experts established by Security Council resolution 780(1992) to the need for an immediate and urgent investigation by qualified experts of a mass grave near Vukovar and other mass grave sites and places where mass killings are reported to have taken place, and requests the Secretary-General, within the overall budgetary framework of the United Nations, to make available all necessary resources for this undertaking and for the other work of the Commission;

20. *Requests* the Secretary-General to take all necessary steps to ensure the full and effective coordination of all United Nations bodies to implement the present resolution, and calls upon those bodies concerned with the situation in the territory of the former Yugoslavia to coordinate closely with the Special Rapporteur and the Commission of Experts;

21. *Also requests* the Secretary-General, within the overall budgetary framework of the United Nations, to make all necessary resources available for the Special Rapporteur to carry out his mandate and in particular to provide him with a number of staff based in the territories of the former Yugoslavia adequate to ensure effective continuous monitoring of the human rights situation there and coordination with other United Nations bodies involved, including the United Nations Protection Force;

22. *Further requests* the Secretary-General to give all other necessary assistance to the Special Rapporteur to enable him to fulfil his mandate;

23. *Decides* to continue its examination of the situation of human rights in the former Yugoslavia during its forty-eighth session under the item entitled "Human rights questions".

International Tribunal for the former Yugoslavia

The International Tribunal for the Prosecution of Persons Responsible for Serious Violations of International Humanitarian Law Committed in the Territory of the Former Yugoslavia since 1991 was created in 1993. The first in a series of steps leading to that action was the adoption by the Security Council in 1992 of two resolutions. One held that persons who committed or ordered commission of grave breaches of the 1949 Geneva Conventions for the protection of war victims were individually responsible in respect of such breaches and called on States and international organizations to collate substantiated information relating to such breaches (resolution 771(1992)); the other reiterated the call for substantiated information and requested the Secretary-General to establish an impartial Commission of Experts to examine information submitted and report to the Council on the Commission's conclusions (resolution 780(1992)).

Pursuant to that request, the Secretary-General established a Commission of Experts to examine information containing evidence of grave breaches of the 1949 Geneva Conventions and other violations of international law committed in the former Yugoslavia, particularly in Bosnia and Herzegovina. The Commission concluded that the Genocide Convention established the jurisdictional basis for an international tribunal and that it was well recognized that the principle of universality could also apply to genocide as well as to other crimes against humanity.

The Commission requested Physicians for Human Rights, a United States–based NGO, to investigate a mass grave near Vukovar. A four-member international forensic team, assembled by Physicians for Human Rights, conducted a preliminary site exploration near Vukovar from 17 to 19 December. The forensic team concluded that a mass execution had taken place; the grave contained possibly as many as 200 bodies; the grave site's remote location suggested that the executioners had sought to bury their victims secretly; the grave had not been disturbed since the time of execution or interment; and evidence at the site suggested that the grave most likely contained the remains of Croatians. The conclusions of the forensic team were annexed to the Commission's interim report to the Security Council.

In December, the Commission also adopted its rules of procedure, further discussed its mandate and appointed Rapporteurs on the gathering and analysis of facts and for on-site investigations. It began reviewing numerous reports alleging grave breaches of international humanitarian law received from Governments, United Nations bodies, intergovernmental organizations, NGOs and other sources.

In the Commission's opinion, it would be for the Security Council or another competent United Nations organ to establish a tribunal in relation to the events in the territory of the former Yugoslavia. The total lack of progress towards peace in the region and the need to demonstrate to the international community that the United Nations was not sitting back idly while thousands were being brutally abused or massacred prompted the Council to adopt resolution 808(1993), which established the International Tribunal for the Former Yugoslavia. The resolution read as follows:

The Security Council,

Reaffirming its resolution 713(1991) of 25 September 1991 and all subsequent relevant resolutions,

Recalling paragraph 10 of its resolution 764(1992) of 13 July 1992, in which it reaffirmed that all parties are bound to comply with the obligations under international humanitarian law, in particular the Geneva Conventions of 12 August 1949, and that persons who commit or order the commission of grave breaches of the Conventions are individually responsible in respect of such breaches,

Recalling also its resolution 771(1992) of 13 August 1992, in which, *inter alia*, it demanded that all parties and others concerned in the former Yugoslavia, and all military forces in Bosnia and Herzegovina, immediately cease and desist from all breaches of international humanitarian law,

Recalling further its resolution 780(1992) of 6 October 1992, in which it requested the Secretary-General to establish, as a matter of urgency, an impartial commission of experts to examine and analyse the information submitted pursuant to resolutions 771(1992) and 780(1992), together with such further information as the commission may obtain, with a view to providing the Secretary-General with its conclusions on the evidence of grave breaches of the Geneva Conventions and other violations of international humanitarian law committed in the territory of the former Yugoslavia,

Having considered the interim report of the Commission of Experts established pursuant to resolution 780(1992), in which the Commission observed that a decision to establish an ad hoc international tribunal in relation to events in the territory of the former Yugoslavia would be consistent with the direction of its work,

Expressing once again its grave alarm at continuing reports of widespread violations of international humanitarian law occurring within the territory of the former Yugoslavia, including reports of mass killings and the continuance of the practice of "ethnic cleansing",

Determining that this situation constitutes a threat to international peace and security,

Determined to put an end to such crimes and to take effective measures to bring to justice the persons who are responsible for them,

Convinced that in the particular circumstances of the former Yugoslavia the establishment of an international tribunal would enable this aim to be achieved and would contribute to the restoration and maintenance of peace,

Noting in this regard the recommendation by the Co-Chairmen of the Steering Committee of the International Conference on the Former Yugoslavia for the establishment of such a tribunal,

Taking note with grave concern of the report of the European Community investigative mission into the treatment of Muslim women in the former Yugoslavia,

Taking note of the report of the committee of jurists submitted by France, the report of the commission of jurists submitted by Italy, and the report transmitted by the Permanent Representative of Sweden on behalf of the Chairman-in-Office of the Conference on Security and Cooperation in Europe,

1. *Decides* that an international tribunal shall be established for the prosecution of persons responsible for serious violations of international humanitarian law committed in the territory of the former Yugoslavia since 1991;

2. *Requests* the Secretary-General to submit for consideration by the Council at the earliest possible date, and if possible no later than sixty days after the adoption of the present resolution, a report on all aspects of this matter, including specific proposals and where appropriate options for the effective and expeditious implementation of the decision contained in paragraph 1 above, taking into account suggestions put forward in this regard by Member States;

3. *Decides* to remain actively seized of the matter.

Thus, the traditional approach of establishing such a body by treaty was discarded as being too slow (possibly taking many years to reach full ratification) and insufficiently effective as Member States could not be forced to ratify such a treaty. Instead, the Council proceeded to establish the Tribunal by exercising its special powers under Chapter VII of the Charter.

The 11 judges of the Tribunal were elected by the General Assembly in September 1993 and took office on 17 November 1993. An Acting Registrar was appointed by the Secretary-General in January 1994. A Prosecutor-designate was appointed by the Security Council in October 1993 but he stated that he would be unable to serve until February 1994, when he informed the Secretary-General that he was no longer available for appointment. It was not until July 1994 that the Security Council appointed the Honourable Richard J. Goldstone as Prosecutor.

The Tribunal's inaugural session took place in November/December 1993; the second session in January/February 1994 was devoted mainly to discussion on and adoption of the rules of procedure and evidence; at the third session in April/May 1994, rules of detention were adopted to regulate the conditions under which the accused will be held, together with guidelines concerning the assignment of counsel for indigent detainees; and at the fourth session, in July 1994, additional practical arrangements and other administrative matters were considered.

Since July 1994, the Office of the Prosecutor has been investigating crimes committed in Bosnia and Herzegovina, as well as the criminal responsibility of the leadership of Bosnian Serbs in Pale, particularly their political leader Radovan Karadzic; Ratko Mladic, military commander of their army; and Mico Stanisic, former minister of internal affairs and head of their police forces. The investigations regarding those three suspects cover a wide range of alleged offences, from genocide and other serious offences against civilians to the destruction of cultural and historical monuments. The Prosecutor is also investigating the protracted siege of Sarajevo and the unlawful attacks on civilian members of humanitarian agencies, members of the United Nations peacekeeping forces, aid convoys and aircraft at Sarajevo.

In addition, investigations are being conducted on crimes allegedly committed between September 1992 and June 1993 in the Lasva River Valley in central Bosnia and Herzegovina, which culminated in the mass killing of the Muslim ethnic group in the area and the unlawful destruction of real and personal property.

On 7 November 1994, Dragan Nikolic, former commander of a camp at Susica in north-eastern Bosnia and Herzegovina, was indicted on charges of grave breaches of the Fourth Geneva Convention of 1949 relative to the protection of civilians in time of war, as well as on charges of violations of the laws or customs of war and of crimes against humanity.

In February 1995, 21 Serbs were indicted on charges of atrocities inside and outside the Omarska death camp in north-western Bosnia during the short period of its existence from the end of May to the beginning of August 1992.

Application of the Convention on the Prevention and Punishment of the Crime of Genocide

On 20 March 1993 the Republic of Bosnia and Herzegovina instituted proceedings against Yugoslavia (Serbia and Montenegro) for alleged violations of the 1948 Convention on the Prevention and Punishment of the Crime of Genocide.

Bosnia and Herzegovina requested the International Court of Justice to adjudge and declare that Yugoslavia (Serbia and Montenegro) had violated and was continuing to violate several provisions of the Genocide Convention as well as of the Charter of the United Nations, the 1949 Geneva Conventions for the protection of war victims and their 1977 Additional Protocol I, the 1907 Hague Regulations on Land Warfare and the Universal Declaration of Human Rights; that Yugoslavia (Serbia and Montenegro) was using force and the threat of force against Bosnia and Herzegovina, violating its sovereignty and intervening in its internal affairs, as well as encouraging and supporting military and paramilitary actions in and against Bosnia and Herzegovina; that Bosnia and Herzegovina had the sovereign right under the Charter of the United Nations and customary international law to defend itself and to request assistance of any State in doing so, which was not to be impaired by Security Council resolution 317(1991) and subsequent resolutions imposing and reaffirming an arms embargo upon the former Yugoslavia; that those consequent resolutions should not be construed as imposing an arms embargo upon Bosnia and Herzegovina; that, pursuant to the right to collective self-defence, other States had the right to come to the immediate defence of Bosnia and Herzegovina at its request; that Yugoslavia (Serbia and Montenegro) should cease and desist immediately from its breaches of the foregoing legal obligations; and that Yugoslavia (Serbia and Montenegro) should pay reparations for damages sustained by Bosnia and Herzegovina.

On the same day, Bosnia and Herzegovina requested the Court to indicate provisional measures to the effect that Yugoslavia (Serbia and Montenegro) should cease and desist immediately from all acts of genocide against the people and State of Bosnia and Herzegovina, from military or paramilitary actions and support for such actions in or against Bosnia and Herzegovina and from any other use or threat of force against it; that Bosnia and Herzegovina had the right to seek support and assistance from other States in defending itself; and that other States had the right to come to its immediate defence.

By an Order of 8 April 1993 the Court indicated that Yugoslavia (Serbia and Montenegro) should immediately take all measures within its power to prevent commission of the crime of genocide; that in particular it should ensure that any armed units under its control did not commit any acts of genocide or acts leading up to genocide; and also that neither of the parties should in any way aggravate or extend the dispute. Judge Tarassov appended a declaration to the Order.

Following a request by Bosnia and Herzegovina and after the views of Yugoslavia (Serbia and Montenegro) had been ascertained, the Vice-President of the Court, by an Order of 7 October, extended the time-limits for a Memorial by Bosnia and Herzegovina and a Counter-Memorial by Yugoslavia (Serbia and Montenegro) to 15 April 1994 and 15 April 1995, respectively. The Memorial was filed within the prescribed time-limit.

Into the twenty-first century

"Peace, the economy, the environment, society and democracy are interlinked dimensions of development. . . . We must attend to the immediate problems of conflict, under all circumstances keeping in mind the aspects of development which must be strengthened. The peoples of the world look to the United Nations as the institution indispensable to the success of these efforts."

—Secretary-General Boutros Boutros-Ghali
in his 1994 report on the work
of the Organization

Future perspectives: towards a human agenda

The major issues that have shaped the agenda of the United Nations during the past 50 years persist: international peace and security, disarmament, human and equal rights, democracy, population and human settlements, environmental preservation, social and economic development and the eradication of poverty.

The United Nations has played a crucial role as the defender of peace, as the strengthened voice for the poorest countries, as a deliverer of humanitarian relief, as a guardian of human and minority rights, as a rescuer of States in crisis, as a promoter of economic and social development and as an instrument for repairing a damaged global environment.

The tensions caused by the super-Power rivalry subsided with the end of the cold war, but new anxieties for international peace and security arose due to the escalation of ethnic conflicts, both in number and intensity, in different parts of the world, dashing hopes for a more secure international environment. This experience proved that peace cannot be pursued as an end in itself. Therefore, the emerging vision of the United Nations as it moves into the twenty-first century must be the establishment of a more stable world order, built on the three interlocking and mutually reinforcing tenets of peace, democracy and development. The settlement of some long-standing conflicts, such as those in southern Africa and Central America, and the eruption of new ones in Africa, Europe and elsewhere have made it clear that peace can be maintained only with democracy to support it and development to sustain it.

At the same time, development is no longer a matter of economic policy and resources, but involves education, respect for human rights, the eradication of poverty and other social ills and the protection of the human environment. The world body has now been seized by the urgency and the multifaceted nature of the challenge of this evolving human agenda.

The basic foundations for future United Nations actions will thus be defined by the major policy imperatives which have now become common international property. The Secretary-General espoused the emerging visions in his recent reports entitled "An Agenda for Peace", "An Agenda for Development" and "Building Peace and Development", adopted by the General Assembly in 1992, 1993 and 1994, respectively. These policy statements combined with various mandates derived from major United Nations conferences and meetings, including the 1990 World Summit for Children (New York), the Second (1990) United Nations Conference on the Least Developed Countries (Paris), the 1992 United Nations Conference on Environment and Development (Rio de Janeiro, Brazil), the eighth (1992) session of the United Nations Conference on Trade and Development (Cartagena de Indias, Colombia), the 1993 World Conference on Human Rights (Vienna), the 1994 International Conference on Population and Development (Cairo, Egypt), the 1994 Global Conference on the Sustainable Development of Small Island Developing States (Bridgetown, Barbados), the 1995 World Summit for Social Development (Copenhagen, Denmark), the upcoming 1995 World Conference on Women (Beijing), the 1996 United Nations Conference on Human Settlements (Istanbul, Turkey) and the ninth (1996) session of the United Nations Conference on Trade and Development (South Africa), will constitute an integral part of the international agenda to deal more effectively with the pressing human issues of the next century.

The comprehensive nature of this global challenge makes it indispensable for the United Nations to coordinate and consolidate the various mandates and to forge a common path in the quest for lasting peace and prosperity. The Organization has a unique opportunity to fulfil its role as "a centre for harmonizing the actions of nations" as originally envisaged in the Charter.

Preventive diplomacy and peacemaking

In his 1992 report entitled "An Agenda for Peace", the Secretary-General outlined a framework for preventive diplomacy, peacemaking and peace-keeping, to which he added the concept of post-conflict peace-building.

The Secretary-General observed that the global transition from the cold war period was marked by uniquely contradictory trends. Regional and continental associations of States were evolving ways to deepen cooperation and ease some of the contentious characteristics of sovereign and nationalistic rivalries. At the same time, new assertions of nationalism and sovereignty sprang up, and the cohesion of States was threatened by ethnic, religious, social, cultural or linguistic strife.

While the concept of peace was easy to grasp, that of international security was more complex, with a pattern of contradictions that had arisen. As major nuclear Powers had begun to negotiate arms-reduction agreements, the proliferation of weapons of mass destruction threatened to increase, and conventional arms continued to be amassed in many parts of the world.

Preventive diplomacy

The Secretary-General defined preventive diplomacy as action to prevent disputes from arising between parties, to prevent existing disputes from escalating into conflicts, and to limit the spread of the latter when they occurred. Peacemaking was action to bring hostile parties to agreement, essentially through such peaceful means as those foreseen in Chapter VI of the Charter. Peacekeeping was the deployment of a United Nations presence in the field, with the consent of the parties concerned, normally involving United Nations military and/or police personnel and frequently civilians as well. Post-conflict peace-building was action to identify and support structures which

strengthened and solidified peace to avoid a relapse into conflict. If successful, preventive diplomacy, peacemaking and peace-keeping strengthened the opportunity for post-conflict peace-building, which could prevent the recurrence of violence among nations and peoples.

Preventive diplomacy could be performed by the Secretary-General personally or through senior staff or specialized agencies and programmes, by the Security Council or the General Assembly, and by regional organizations in cooperation with the United Nations. It required measures to create confidence; it needed early warning based on information gathering and fact-finding; it might also involve preventive deployment and, in some situations, demilitarized zones.

Peacemaking

Peacemaking entails taking action to bring hostile parties to agreement, essentially through peaceful means as those foreseen in Chapter VI of the Charter. Under peacemaking, the report discussed greater reliance on the International Court of Justice; amelioration through assistance; sanctions and special economic problems; use of military force; and the utilization of peace-enforcement units.

Greater reliance on the International Court of Justice would be an important contribution to United Nations peacemaking. The report recommended that all Member States should accept the general jurisdiction of the Court under Article 36 of its Statute, wihout any reservation. In instances where domestic structures prevent this, States should agree bilaterally or multilaterally to a comprehensive list of matters they are willing to submit to the Court and should withdraw their reservations to its jurisdiction in the dispute settlement clauses of multilateral treaties.

Peacemaking at times is facilitated by international action to ameliorate circumstances that have contributed to the dispute or conflict. Therefore, a mechanism should be devised through which the Security Council, the General Assembly or the Secretary-General can mobilize the resources and efforts on an inter-agency basis to improve the United Nations contribution to the peaceful resolution of conflicts.

When peacemaking required the imposition of sanctions under Article 41 of the Charter, it was important that States confronted with special economic problems not only had the right to consult the Security Council under Article 50, but also had the realistic possibility of having their difficulties addressed. The Secretary-General recommended that the Council devise a set of measures involving financial institutions and other components of the United Nations system that could be put in place to insulate States from such difficulties, as a matter of equity and a means of encouraging States to cooperate with Council decisions.

As a result of the developments, demands on the United Nations surged. Its security arm emerged as a central instrument for the preservation of peace. The aims of the United Nations must be to identify at the earliest possible stage situations that could produce conflict, and to try through diplomacy to remove the sources of danger before violence resulted. Where conflict erupted, the United Nations should engage in peacemaking aimed at resolving the issues that had led to conflict and preserve peace through peace-keeping. The Organization must stand ready to assist in peace-keeping in its differing contexts and, in the largest sense, to address the deepest causes of conflict: economic despair, social injustice and political oppression.

Peace-keeping

Peace-keeping could rightly be called the invention of the United Nations, having brought stability to numerous areas of conflict around the world. In view of the volume and unpredictability of peace-keeping contributions, the Secretary-General strongly supported proposals in some States that their peace-keeping contributions be financed from defence, rather than foreign affairs, budgets. He recommended such action to others and urged the General Assembly to encourage that approach. He again requested all States to indicate what military personnel they were in principle prepared to make available. He recommended that arrangements be reviewed and improved for training civilian, police or military peace-keeping personnel and that the strength and capability of military staff serving in the Secretariat be augmented to meet new and heavier requirements.

Post-conflict peace-building

In the aftermath of international war, post-conflict peace-building might take the form of concrete cooperative projects linking two or more countries in a mutually beneficial undertaking. That could not only contribute to economic and social development but also enhance the confidence fundamental to peace. The concept of peace-building as the construction of a new environment should be viewed as the counterpart of preventive diplomacy, which sought to avoid the breakdown of peaceful conditions. Preventive diplomacy was to avoid a crisis; post-conflict peace-building was to prevent a recurrence.

Cooperation with regional arrangements and organizations

Regional arrangements or organizations in many cases possessed a potential that should be utilized in preventive diplomacy, peace-keeping, peace-making and post-conflict confidence-building.

Under the Charter, the Security Council had and would continue to have primary responsibility for maintaining international security, but regional action as a matter of decentralization, delegation and cooperation with United Nations efforts could contribute to a deeper sense of participation, consensus and democratization in international affairs.

Agenda for peace

Concluding with "An Agenda for Peace", the Secretary-General stressed that a genuine sense of consensus deriving from shared interests must govern the Security Council's work, not the threat of the veto or the power of any group of nations. The Secretary-General recommended that the heads of State and Government of members of the Council meet in alternate years, just before the start of the general debate in the General Assembly, and that the Council meet at the Foreign Minister level whenever the situation warranted such meetings.

He cautioned against unilateralism and isolationism and stressed that democracy required respect for human rights and fundamental freedoms as set forth in the Charter. He stated that democracy within the family of nations required fullest consultation, participation and engagement of all States in the work of the Organization, and that the principles of the Charter must be applied consistently, not selectively. Swift and impartial reaction of the Organization presupposed an efficient and independent international civil service and an assured financial basis.

In addition, involvement of non-governmental organizations, academic institutions, parliamentarians, business and professional communities, the media and the public at large would help strengthen the Organization's ability to reflect the concerns of its widest constituency.

Collective security, international law, human rights, economic and social development — these principles of international cooperation were enshrined in the United Nations Charter in 1945. For half a century, it has been the mandate and mission of the United Nations to strengthen these achievements and advance common progress in each of these areas.

Thus, this fiftieth anniversary year calls for serious reflection and renewal. The ideals of the Charter must be enforced and capacities to meet new challenges must be assessed. Member States and their peoples must decide the future role of their United Nations instrument.

But today the world situation is vastly different. The international age is giving way to a global age. The threat to international peace and security is changing dramatically. And as globalization transforms economic relations, the link between worldwide development and international peace is growing stronger.

Since the end of the cold war, United Nations activities in peace and security have increased dramatically, straining the Organization. However, the qualitative changes have been even more significant than the quantitative ones. Throughout most of the United Nations history, the primary security concern was inter-State war. But in recent years, conflicts and confrontations within State borders have become more prevalent than wars between States. Many of these conflicts are religious or ethnic in character. They may be fought not only by regular armies but also by militias and irregular groups. Civilians are the main victims and often the main targets. Humanitarian emergencies are commonplace, and the collapse of State institutions may also be involved.

This means that international involvement must extend beyond military and humanitarian tasks. It must include the promotion of national reconciliation and the restoration of effective government. It may involve helping the parties implement a comprehensive settlement. And over the long term, coordinated programmes may be required to ensure that the original causes of war are removed.

Peacemaking instruments

It is thus imperative to understand the different practical measures the United Nations can take to help control and resolve conflicts between and within States. They included preventive diplomacy and peacemaking, peace-keeping, peace-building, disarmament, sanctions and peace enforcement.

The first three can be used only with the consent of the parties to the conflict. Sanctions and enforcement are coercive measures—they do not require consent. Disarmament can take place on an agreed basis or as a coercive measure under Chapter VII of the Charter.

Preventive diplomacy, as already noted, is action to prevent disputes and conflicts from breaking out, or action to prevent their escalation. It requires measures to build confidence and needs early warning based on information gathering and fact-finding.

Peacemaking is action to bring hostile parties to agreement. In essence, it is negotiation. It uses peaceful means under Chapter VI of the Charter. Like preventive diplomacy, it requires information and an analytical capacity and has hinged on the willingness of the parties to accept United Nations assistance.

United Nations peace-keeping, invented as a practical response to real problems, involves in its original sense a neutral and lightly armed force. The peace-keepers are welcomed by all parties to the conflict, and their task is to monitor an agreed cease-fire already in place. The mission is to help keep peace so that the parties can pursue a negotiated settlement. Respect for certain basic principles of peace-keeping are essential, such as

the consent of the parties, impartiality and the non-use of force except in self-defence. Certain tasks, such as protecting humanitarian operations and protecting civilians in designated safe areas, have made respect for these principles very difficult. Giving enforcement tasks to peace-keeping operations must be avoided; peace-keeping and enforcement are not adjacent points on a continuum—they must be understood as alternative techniques.

Also essential to peace-keeping's success is that various distinct levels of authority between the Security Council, the Secretary-General and the command in the field need to be recognized and respected. Troop contingents from different countries must function together as an integrated whole, and Member States must match mandates with the troops and equipment necessary to do the job.

A third instrument to help control and resolve conflicts is peace-building, used in the aftermath of a conflict. It aims to solidify peace and involves support for structures which build trust and cooperation among former enemies. The tasks range from demilitarization to institutional reform, the monitoring of human rights, and social and economic development.

The United Nations may become involved in peace-building when a peace-keeping operation has been asked to implement a comprehensive settlement. In this situation, the smooth transfer of peace-building tasks from peace-keepers to other actors is critical. Peace-building is more difficult in a country where the United Nations does not already have a peacemaking or peace-keeping mandate. Peace-building cannot be undertaken successfully without the consent of the parties concerned.

In either case, peace-building requires the active support of the international community over the long term. The United Nations has an essential role to play in coordinating international assistance across the full range of peace-building tasks.

The fourth instrument is disarmament, mainly "micro-disarmament", which involves mostly light weapons such as small arms and anti-personnel mines that need to be assembled, controlled and disposed of. Practical disarmament can be undertaken with or without consent and can play an important part in the implementation of a comprehensive settlement. It can be equally important to post-conflict peace-building and can follow peace enforcement. The importance of "micro-disarmament" in conflict prevention and resolution needs to be recognized and advanced.

A fifth instrument is sanctions, designed to change the behaviour of a party which is threatening international peace and security. Sanctions are coercive measures but do not involve the use of armed force.

Increased use of sanctions has revealed a number of practical difficulties, some of them relating to the objectives of the sanctions. For example, a lack of clear definition makes it hard to reach agreement on when to lift sanctions. Other difficulties relate to the monitoring of sanctions, and still others have come from the collateral effect of sanctions — such as humanitarian suffering and long-term damage to the target country's productive capacity, as well as the difficulties of neighbouring countries which implement sanctions and are suffering collateral damages. A mechanism needs to be established for more effective and equitable application of sanctions.

Finally, the sixth instrument is peace enforcement. Under Article 42 of the Charter, the Security Council may decide that a threat to international peace and security requires a military response. At present, neither the Security Council nor the Secretary-General has the capacity to deploy and command such operations. Instead, the Council has authorized a coalition of Member States to take enforcement action.

Such "sub-contracting" provides the United Nations with an enforcement capacity it would not otherwise have. But it also may create the image of the United Nations as incapable of taking action directly, and there is a danger that the States concerned may claim international legitimacy for forceful actions not provided for by the Charter or the Security Council. Particularly where a United Nations operation has been mandated for the same area of conflict, these considerations must be carefully weighed.

This list in itself reveals the complexity of the task faced by the United Nations, as each conflict is different and requires a different set of instruments, used in different combinations, often by multiple actors. We must understand which instruments can work together in which situations. Experience has shown that the paramount consideration should be whether consent is required. Consensual and coercive measures must not be combined. It is in peacekeeping where new tasks have made it hard to maintain this conceptual distinction and where the most serious difficulties have arisen and setbacks have occurred.

In development lies the greatest challenge for international cooperation and the greatest hope for moving towards enduring peace and prosperity. Member States must learn to use the United Nations to handle the new forms of conflict. Only when this is done can the agenda of the United Nations be addressed. We must do this so that we can give development our full attention and attend to the longer-term, deeper requirements of building a better world.

Legal discourse

Legal discourse, as a means of communication between States, is also a factor in the growing in-

stitutionalization of international society. It is becoming more or less clear that the emerging international system will be based on a society which is unsure about its own structures, particularly about its main building-block, the State.

Some people are trying, in tragic spurts of history, to make the rationality of the State appear compatible with the impulses of micro-nationalism. It is possible to respect minorities, to embrace those having a different sense of identity, and to accept diversity, without going so far as to back break-up and fragmentation. To suggest that any social or ethnic entity, which decides that it is different from its neighbours, should be recognized as a State would be a very perverse way of interpreting the right of peoples to self-determination. Such a view of the world is at the other end of the spectrum from the democratization of international society.

Elsewhere, the very State itself is collapsing. In some developing countries the structure of the State has eroded to such an extent that it can no longer be said to possess one or another of the defining features of statehood. This can have incalculable consequences, for the institutional decay may well lead people to fall back on primitive loyalties, many of which also bring fanaticism and exclusion in their wake. So the international community now has to consider what to do about failed States.

At a time when public opinion often doubts the ability of the world Organization to perform its function, it is important to focus our attention on the work being done by the United Nations to ensure peace, on both the jurisdictional and the operational levels.

The recent establishment of tribunals mandated to try those presumed responsible for serious violations of international humanitarian law, both within the territory of the former Yugoslavia and, more recently, in relation to the tragedy in Rwanda, represents a significant advance for law.

A new vision of development

Peace, democracy and development are interlocking concepts that are reinforcing. In his 1993 report entitled "An Agenda for Development", the Secretary-General expanded the dimensions of development to include peace as the foundation; the economy as the engine of progress; the environment as a basis for sustainability; justice as a pillar of society; and democracy as good governance.

Peace and development

Traditional approaches to development presuppose that it takes place under conditions of peace. Yet that is rarely the case. The absence of peace is a pervasive reality in many parts of the world. Most peoples must strive to achieve their development against a background of past, present or threatened conflict. Many carry the burden of recent devastation and continuing ethnic strife. None can avoid the realities of a world of ongoing arms proliferation, regional war and the possibility of a return to potentially antagonistic spheres of influence. To the categorization of countries by level of development should be added the categorization of countries in conflict. Because the United Nations is active at the forefront of humanitarian aid, refugee assistance and the range of peace operations, it is deeply and inextricably involved in peace as a fundamental dimension of development.

Development cannot proceed easily in societies where military concerns are at or near the centre of life. Societies whose economic effort is given in substantial part to military production inevitably diminish the prospects of their people for development. The absence of peace often has led societies to devote a higher percentage of their budget to the military than to development. Preparing for war absorbs inordinate resources and impedes the development of social institutions.

Reduction of military expenditure is a vital link in the chain between development and peace. Although world-wide military expenditures continue to consume too large a share of productive resources and capacity, progress has been made in recent years. Worldwide, between 1987 and 1992 a cumulative peace dividend of $500 billion was realized; $425 billion in industrial and transitional countries and $75 billion in developing countries. Little of this peace dividend appears to have been channelled into development.

While figures for exports of weapons show substantial declines in real terms in the early years of the 1990s, major concerns persist. Imported stocks of conventional weapons from countries rapidly reducing their military establishments are finding their way to third countries. Relatively unsophisticated weapons such as mortars, machine-guns and rocket launchers, even in the hands of those with rudimentary military training, have caused immense death and destruction. Paradoxically, those expressing great concern over the rising stocks of arms worldwide are also the source of that phenomenon. The five permanent members of the Security Council account for 86 per cent of the arms supplies now flowing to the countries of the world.

Imports of armaments are often purchased at the expense of capital or consumer goods. Reducing military expenditures makes more funds available to finance development, satisfy consumer demands and meet basic social welfare needs. A decrease in military outlays may support budgetary reform and promote macroeconomic stability. National efforts can be reoriented away from military priori-

ties towards more productive and peaceful objectives. Global tensions and rivalries can be reduced. The overall impact on development is potentially profound.

The armed forces absorb some of the most talented members of society, whose training costs are considerably above the social average and whose energies are directed to the operation of increasingly sophisticated military hardware. Armament production utilizes industrial skills and capacity that could be put to other uses.

Among many of the countries in transition, procurement of new weapons systems has collapsed and most military expenditure is now for personnel costs, including pensions. Whole communities which were dependent on defence industries are now threatened, unless they can adapt themselves to changing requirements. Fears of further increases in unemployment are slowing reductions in the size of armed forces, while military industries are being kept solvent by massive subsidies to the detriment of overall macroeconomic goals.

Arms control and disarmament reduce the threat of destruction, economic decline and tensions that lead to war. A world of lower military expenditures, reduced military establishments, smaller stocks of weapons and less environmental destruction by military-related activities is not only desirable in itself, but propitious for development.

Even remote conflicts can pose security and developmental concerns far beyond a State's borders. This new recognition gives international peace and security a wider meaning, calls for measures that can further development even during conflict, and indicates that development, when successfully pursued, is another way to define peace.

The concept of development and decades of effort to reduce poverty, illiteracy, disease and mortality rates have been great achievements of this century. But development as a common cause is in danger of fading from the forefront of our agenda. The competition for influence during the cold war stimulated interest in development. The motives were not always altruistic, but countries seeking to develop could benefit from that interest. Today, the competition to bring development to the poorest countries has ended. Many donors have grown weary of the task. Many of the poor are dispirited. Development is in crisis.

The poorest nations fall farther behind. Nations in transition from command to open economies face immense hardships. Nations that have achieved prosperity see their success accompanied by a new array of problems—social, environmental, cultural and economic—and many are consequently reluctant even to pursue their assistance policies at former levels.

While national Governments bear the major responsibility for development, the United Nations has been entrusted with important mandates for assisting in that task. The involvement of the United Nations in development has spanned four development decades and encompassed the full range of global problems of an economic, social, cultural and humanitarian character. It has operated in all categories and at every level of development.

In the light of the new vision of development that is emerging, an alternative to the United Nations in development simply does not exist. The United Nations is a forum where the voices of all States, great and small, can be heard with equal clarity, and where non-State actors can make their views known to the widest audience.

The economy as the engine of progress

Economic growth is the engine of development as a whole. Without economic growth, there can be no sustained increase in household or government consumption, in private or public capital formation, in health, welfare and security levels. By whatever social processes distributional choices are made, the capacity to make them is severely limited in poor societies and is enhanced by economic growth. Progress in the other aspects of development, including peace, the environment, society and democracy, will have a positive effect on economic growth.

It is not sufficient, however, to pursue economic growth for its own sake. It is important that growth be sustained and sustainable. Growth should promote full employment and poverty reduction, and should seek improved patterns of income distribution through greater equality of opportunity.

If poverty persists or increases and there is neglect of the human condition, political and social strains will endanger stability over time. The reduction of poverty requires development in which access to the benefits of economic progress are as widely available as possible, and not concentrated excessively in certain localities, sectors or groups of the population.

Improved education, health and shelter, together with an increase in meaningful employment opportunities, will contribute directly to reducing poverty and its consequences. Apart from being desirable goals in themselves, education, health and shelter are all essential to a productive workforce and hence to economic growth. The elimination of hunger and malnutrition should be targets in their own right.

Governments can no longer be assumed to be paramount economic agents. They nevertheless retain the responsibility to provide a regulatory framework for the effective operation of a competitive market system. Governments have to intervene where appropriate: to invest in infrastructure, to facilitate the development of productive sectors, to provide an enabling environment for the promotion of private enterprise, to ensure that proper social safety nets are in place, to invest in human capital and to protect the environment. Governments provide the framework in which individuals can plan their long-term prospects.

Increasing interdependence among nations has accelerated the transmission of both positive growth impulses and negative shocks. As a result, economic problems, even at the national level, now have to be seen in their global context. The distinction between national and international economic policies is fading. No nation, however successful, can insulate itself from the demographic, environmental, economic, social and military problems which exist in the world. The effects of deprivation, disease and strife in one part of the globe are felt everywhere. They will not be successfully managed until global development is under way.

The expansion of international trade is essential to economic growth and is an integral part of the economic dimension of development. The benefits of increased commerce and trade are not in doubt: lower transaction costs, greater economic opportunities and enhanced international confidence, trust and security.

The mechanisms for integrating responsible economic policies at the international level and growth at the national level are not yet fully developed. Leading the list of priorities are adequate measures to reduce the crippling burden of international debt, policies to discourage tendencies towards protectionism, and ensuring that the developing world shares in the benefits of the new World Trade Organization regime.

The lack of financial resources necessary for economic development is exacerbated by the debt crisis, which makes an already difficult situation much worse. In the last decade, indebted developing countries have had to transfer on average between 2 and 3 per cent of their gross domestic product (GDP) abroad; in some instances transfers have amounted to 6 per cent or more of GDP. Perversely, some developing countries have now become net exporters of financial resources.

Large amounts are owed to commercial banks by some countries. Many low-income countries owe large amounts to official bilateral and multilateral creditors. Efforts have been made to restructure commercial debt and, in certain cases, forgive bilateral official debt. But not enough has been done to alleviate the burden of multilateral debt or to assist countries that, despite a large debt-servicing burden, are not in default.

No single formula for generating economic growth exists, but, half a century after the emergence of development as an independent field of inquiry, certain basic conditions are recognized as essential. Foremost among these is the need to take a strategic decision for development.

The experience of countries that have achieved rapid development in the past few years can be seen as the outcome of a conscious choice by the State to give strategic priority to growth. The influence of State policies in encouraging research and development or providing infrastructural and educational support has been crucial. This does not mean, however, that growth takes place through State institutions. The State gives an impetus to the economy to grow.

The basic lesson of recent decades remains valid: as conditions, circumstances and capacities differ, so too must the mechanisms for generating growth. Growth requires political commitment and vision. The United Nations can act as facilitator and communicator, but it cannot substitute for the commitment of individual States and their domestic and international partners.

The environment as a basis for sustainability

The environment, like peace, the economy, society and democracy, permeates all aspects of development, and has an impact on countries at all levels of development. In the developing world, ecological pressure threatens to undermine long-term development. Among many countries in transition, decades of disregard for the environment have left large areas poisoned and unable to sustain economic activity in the long term. Among the wealthiest nations, consumption patterns are depleting world resources in ways that jeopardize the future of world development.

Preserving the availability and rationalizing the use of the earth's natural resources are among the most compelling issues that individuals, societies and States must face. In the context of development, each society must confront the difficult challenges associated with protecting the long-term potential of its natural resources. Competing needs and interests must be balanced. Present social and economic needs must be satisfied in ways that do not undermine long-term resource availability, or the viability of the ecosystems on which the present and future generations depend.

Environmental degradation reduces both the quality and the quantity of many resources used directly by people. Water pollution damages fisheries. Increasing salinity and erosion of topsoil lowers crop yields. Agricultural degradation and deforestation have promoted drought and soil erosion, and made malnutrition and famine increasingly familiar occurrences in certain regions. Overfishing and the exhaustion of marine resources have put ancient communities at risk. Excessive logging and the destruction of rain forests have destroyed important natural habitats and undermined global biodiversity. Environmentally unsound practices in the extraction of natural resources have left large regions barren and contaminated.

The link between the environment and development involves not only the sound exploitation of natural resources but also preserving and protecting the ecological equilibrium of the environment, a vital component of human development and human survival.

Solutions to international environmental problems must be based on common principles and rules of collaboration among States, backed up by persuasion and negotiation. There are also global environmental resources, such as the atmosphere and the oceans, that must be a target of multilateral action. Sustainability must be strengthened as a guiding principle of development. Partnership is required at all levels of development efforts: among different departments and levels of administration within States, as well as between international organizations, Governments and non-State actors.

Justice as a pillar of society

Development does not take place in a vacuum, but occurs within a specific societal context and in response to specific societal conditions. Thus, existing social conditions are the starting-point for development efforts. To a large extent, they determine its priorities and its direction. Throughout much of the developing world, poverty, disease and the need for education and sustainable livelihoods are the most urgent and compelling priorities for development. In many of the countries in transition, sudden economic hardship, decaying industries and infrastructures and profound social disorientation are problems that development must urgently address. Among the richest countries, the growth of a permanent and disaffected underclass, the arrival of increasing numbers of economic migrants and a rise in xenophobia and exclusionary attitudes are realities that must be faced as these societies continue to advance and develop.

People are a country's principal asset. Their well-being defines development. Their energy and initiative drive development. Their characteristics determine the nature and direction of sustainable human development. The benefits of investing in people, however, go beyond increasing the productivity of labour and facilitating access to global opportunities. A healthy, well-educated citizenry contributes to the social cohesion of a country and imparts a dynamism to all aspects of life and culture.

Absolute poverty, hunger, disease and illiteracy are the lot of one fifth of the world's population. There can be no more urgent task for development than to attack both the causes and the symptoms of these ills. It is a task that requires action and commitment. It is an agenda that requires the widest possible distribution of development efforts, the implementation of broad-based strategies and the orientation of development efforts towards projects that enhance people rather than national prestige.

The importance of social integration as a development priority is evident worldwide and among countries across the development spectrum. Manifestations of the lack of social integration include discrimination, fanaticism, intolerance and persecution. The consequences are social disaffection, separatism, micronationalism and conflict.

A vigorous civil society is indispensable to creating lasting and successful social development. Social development must spring from society itself. Government must lead and facilitate, but government cannot, and should not, be the only force for social progress. Non-governmental organizations (NGOs), community organizations, private enterprise, workers' organizations and other groups must all be actively involved. Locally based NGOs, in particular, can serve as intermediaries and give people a voice and an opportunity to articulate their needs, preferences and vision of a better society. In countries where civil society is weak, strengthening civil society should be a major purpose of public policy.

To create the conditions within which social development can take place, popular participation at all levels of society is of vital importance. People must participate actively in formulating their own goals, and in decision-making bodies to pursue appropriate paths to social development.

The significance of the social dimension to development must be recognized and acted upon. The political profile of social development issues must be raised both nationally and internationally. Each country has a duty to address social development within its own society, and each also has a duty to contribute to progress towards a more global solution in this area. The present period provides an historic opportunity to do so in an environment that is relatively free from excessive ideological tensions. It is an opportunity to be seized and turned to advantage.

Democracy as good governance

Democracy and development are linked in fundamental ways. Democracy provides the only long-term basis for managing competing ethnic, religious and cultural interests in a way that minimizes the risk of violent internal conflict. Democracy is inherently attached to the question of governance, which has an impact on all aspects of development efforts. Democracy is also a fundamental human right, the advancement of which is itself an important measure of development. Democracy, as people's participation in the decision-making processes which affect their lives, is a basic tenet of development.

The accumulation of economic despair and the lack of democratic means to effect change have sparked or exacerbated violent and destructive impulses even within relatively homogeneous societies. Civil conflict and strife have increasingly become threats to international peace and profound obstacles to development. Ethnic antagonism, religious intolerance and cultural separatism threaten the cohesion of societies and the integrity of States in all parts of the world. Alienated and insecure minorities, and even majorities, have increasingly turned to armed conflict as a means of addressing social and political grievances.

Democracy is the only long-term means of both arbitrating and regulating the many political, social, economic and ethnic tensions that constantly threaten to tear apart societies and destroy States. In the absence of democracy as a forum for competition and a vehicle for change, development will remain fragile and be perpetually at risk.

Holding elections is only one element in democratization. Member States have sought and received United Nations assistance in facilitating decolonization, thereby implementing the right to self-determination, in designing procedures to smooth and facilitate transitions to democracy and in building democratic alternatives to conflict. United Nations support has also been provided for activities such as drafting constitutions, instituting administrative and financial reforms, strengthening domestic human rights laws, enhancing judicial structures, training human rights officials and helping armed opposition movements transform themselves into democratically competitive political parties.

Improving and enhancing governance is an essential condition for the success of any agenda or strategy for development. Improved governance means the design and pursuit of a comprehensive national strategy for development. It means ensuring the capacity, reliability and integrity of the core institutions of the modern State, and improving the ability of government to carry out governmental policies and functions, including the management of implementation systems. It also means accountability for actions and transparency in decision-making.

The mandate of the people to govern provides legitimacy; it does not carry with it, however, the guarantee of skill or wisdom. Democracy cannot instantly produce good governance, nor will democratic government immediately lead to substantial improvements in growth rates, social conditions or equality. By providing channels for participation of people in decisions which affect their lives, democracy brings government closer to the people.

This is a time of dramatic global change; the State is being challenged as the mechanism for solving national problems. It is challenged as the basic element of the international system. Economic, political and military interconnections are pressing the State from above. From below, citizens are demanding more accountability, more representation and more participation in national and international life. Some States are threatened by fragmentation, as people seek security from change by identifying themselves with ever-smaller ethnic groups.

Democracy is essential to ensure the viability of the State as an institution of governance and a mechanism for human progress. Democracy, within and among States, is key to peace and to development. It is, therefore, essential that the international community pursue democracy within and among States. The United Nations can offer invaluable help in this quest, as the United Nations system has a number of elements that can support efforts to build democracy.

The international community must help the United Nations to strengthen its ability to help States cultivate democracy. The world Organization is a crucial resource in the process of building the democratic system, the system that can best support international peace and development. It is also vital that the international community seek to support democracy among States. The structures that support international relations must be strengthened to include more actors in international decision-making.

Six aspects of this process can be identified. First, there is the need to democratize the United Nations system itself. As it enters its second half-century, there are calls to rethink the relation between the Security Council and the General Assembly. There are also increasing calls for a more representative Security Council and a broadening of its membership.

Second, the United Nations needs to improve its coordination with regional organizations and regional arrangements.

Third, the growth of NGOs can be a powerful factor for democratization throughout the international system. Not only has popular participation dramatically increased, but NGOs have become increasingly involved with the establishment of democratic institutions.

Fourth, guaranteeing an independent communications media is a way to guarantee freedom of thought and the flow of ideas.

Fifth, a series of global conferences convened by the United Nations has reinforced democratic principles in world affairs. These conferences amount to an ongoing democratic process between nations. They can help the world community articulate a new, comprehensive vision of development. The solutions that are found through international debate must be backed by national action for this democratic process to have real meaning.

The sixth aspect of democratization is the growing importance of international law. Increasingly, States are coming to recognize that turning to the International Court of Justice is a democratic alter-

native to conflict. The belief that international relations should be governed by laws is a positive development and one of the most important developments of our time in its implications for human welfare.

The promise of development

A culture of development is emerging in which every major dimension of life is considered as an aspect of social development.

In the past few years near-universal recognition has been achieved of the need for fresh consideration of ways in which the goals of peace, freedom, justice and progress may be pursued in a dramatically transformed global context. A culture of development can encompass these goals in a single, comprehensive vision and framework for action. At the basis of this culture, there is the fundamental commitment of the Charter to ''the dignity and worth of the human person''. In this context, the institution of the United Nations is irreplaceable.

Development has to be oriented towards each person in the world. It must recognize that the human community includes the generations yet to come.

Signs of a global era of development can be observed. The agricultural and industrial revolutions are now being succeeded by an age of information, communication and advanced technology. This presents the potential for freeing humanity from limits of time, place and resources that in the past were regarded as given. At the same time, however, these changes are accompanied by old forces that test the human condition in natural and human disasters, demography, disease, political confrontation, cultural and religious animosity, unemployment and ecological decay.

From an understanding of development as limited to the transfer of funds and other resources from the haves to the have-nots, the perspective has shifted towards a broader concept encompassing the full range of human endeavour. The welfare of future generations must not be compromised by incurring debts that cannot be repaid, whether financial, social, demographic or environmental.

For the human community to continue to advance, it is essential to recognize that current achievements must be accessible to all and to ensure that the United Nations work must stand as a platform for future progress.

Whether this vision is fulfilled or not will be measured by what this living generation of the world's peoples makes or fails to make of the United Nations. Created at a unique moment of unanimity, the United Nations has the mechanisms required to bring practical results and it now stands at the meeting point of past, present and future.

This analysis has described both the nature and scope of development efforts. It has set out both the dimensions of the development process and the actors involved in it, in the hope that a new vision and culture of development will emerge. Such a vision must, however, be firmly anchored in agreed objectives and commitments on development adopted by the international community, and on a record of demonstrated results. The United Nations can offer such a record and bring to bear not only the unparalleled broadness of its scope, but also its unique potential to integrate the many actors and dimensions of development.

In order for this promise to be fulfilled, all organs and entities must perform fully the roles assigned to them by the Charter, roles clearly described but which have yet to be performed entirely as intended.

Human rights

The United Nations has made significant accomplishments in the area of human rights and a consciousness of human rights now pervades the globe. The various international instruments adopted, including the 1948 Universal Declaration of Human Rights and the two 1966 International Covenants, together with institutional arrangements established, have laid the foundations for a universal culture of human rights. Not only has the United Nations protected and defended the traditional civil and political rights over the past 50 years, but it has also defended and promoted the rights of peoples to self-determination and economic, social and cultural rights, and the rights to development, to an adequate standard of living, to own property and to adequate housing. It also defended the rights of the child, women, youth, the disabled, refugees and the internally displaced and the human rights aspects of science and technology.

In spite of these achievements, there is still dismay at the barbaric realities worldwide, arising from the indiscriminate use of power. There is a growing demand that the gulf between the aspirations embodied in international human rights instruments and arrangements and reality be narrowed if they are not to become ineffectual. Crimes of genocide, ethnic cleansing, political repression and denial have returned in new forms to haunt the world community. Effective means of putting an end to such atrocities remain a priority.

In his 1994 report "Building Peace and Development", the Secretary-General stated that the gap between international aspirations for the enjoyment of human rights and the widespread violations of these rights presents the basic challenge to the United Nations human rights programme. To close that gap, the world community must identify and eliminate the root causes of violations. In that respect, United Nations efforts focus on implementing the right to development, defining better and ensuring greater respect for economic, social and cultural rights, and, at the most fundamental level, improving the daily life of the individual.

The protection of human rights has now become one of the keystones in the arch of peace, democracy and development. The 1993 World Conference on Human Rights made a comprehensive review and analysis of the human rights system and of the international machinery for the protection of human rights.

In his statement at the opening of the Conference, the Secretary-General underlined that "the human rights we proclaim and seek to safeguard can be brought about only if we transcend ourselves, only if we make a conscious effort to find our common essence beyond our apparent divisions, our temporary differences, our ideological and cultural barriers". Human rights, he continued, are not the lowest common denominator among all nations, but rather the "irreducible human element", in other words, "the quintessential values through which we affirm together that we are a single human community".

Working towards "a conception of human rights that would make such rights truly universal" is the challenge which involves complex issues. "As an absolute yardstick, human rights constitute the common language of humanity. Adopting this language allows all peoples to understand others and to be the authors of their own history. Human rights, by definition, are the ultimate norm of all politics."

According to the Secretary-General, human rights have a dual nature, expressing timeless injunctions, yet simultaneously reflecting a moment in the development of history. Thus, they are both absolute and historically defined.

It is possible to view political, economic, social and cultural differences as sources of mutual enrichment, yet when they become synonymous with inequalities, they cannot but be perceived as unjust. To move from identifying inequality to rebelling against injustice is only possible in the context of a universal affirmation of the idea of human rights.

The Secretary-General stressed that the consideration of human rights should be guided by three imperatives: universality, guarantees and democratization.

The imperative of democratization is essentially what is at stake as we approach the end of the century. Only democracy, within States and within the community of States, can truly guarantee human rights. It is through democracy that individual rights and collective rights, the rights of peoples and the rights of persons, are reconciled. There is a growing awareness of that imperative within the international community. The process of democratization cannot be separated from the protection of human rights. Democracy is the political framework in which human rights can best be safeguarded.

Universality is inherent in human rights. The Charter is categorical on this score: Article 55 states that the United Nations should promote ''universal respect for, and observance of, human rights and fundamental freedoms for all without distinction as to race, sex, language, or religion''. The title of the 1948 Declaration — universal, not international — reinforces this perspective.

The State should be the best guarantor of human rights. However, the issue of international action must be raised when States prove unworthy of this task, when they violate the fundamental principles laid down in the Charter. In these circumstances, the international community must take over from the States that fail to fulfil their obligations.

The number of procedures for guaranteeing human rights has been increasing for years, but guaranteeing human rights also means setting up jurisdictional controls to punish any violations that occur. In that regard, United Nations efforts to promote both a permanent international criminal court and the establishment of special international tribunals to prosecute the crimes committed in Rwanda and in the former Yugoslavia are to be mentioned.

Within the context of measures taken by the Organization to safeguard human rights, the decisive action by the General Assembly in the area of humanitarian assistance has to be noted. According to the Secretary-General, ''the notion of a right to humanitarian assistance has, to a certain extent, become one of the areas in which human rights can actually be guaranteed''.

The link between democracy, development and human rights is meanwhile being recognized as inescapable. There can be no sustainable development without promoting democracy and, thus, respect for human rights is a matter of concern to the entire international community, for only through individual development can peace for all be ensured.

In its Vienna Declaration and Programme of Action, the Conference recognized that all human rights were universal, indivisible and interdependent and interrelated, and the international community must treat human rights globally in a fair and equal manner, on the same footing, and with the same emphasis. While the significance of national and regional particularities and various historical, cultural and religious backgrounds must be borne in mind, it is the duty of States, regardless of their political, economic and cultural systems, to promote and protect all human rights and fundamental freedoms.

The Conference stated that the efforts of the United Nations system towards the universal respect for, and observance of, human rights and fundamental freedoms for all contribute to the stability and well-being necessary for peaceful and friendly relations among nations, and to improved conditions for peace and security as well as social and economic development, in conformity with the Charter of the United Nations.

The Conference deemed enhancement of international cooperation in the field of human rights as essential for the full achievement of the purposes of the United Nations. The processes of promoting and protecting human rights, it stipulated, should be conducted in conformity with the purposes and principles of the Charter and international law.

As stated in the Declaration and Programme of Action, the promotion and protection of all human rights and fundamental freedoms must be considered as a priority objective of the United Nations in accordance with its purposes and principles, in particular international cooperation. Within that framework, the promotion and protection of all human rights is a legitimate concern of the international community. The organs and specialized agencies related to human rights should therefore further enhance the coordination of their activities based on the consistent and objective application of international human rights instruments.

The Conference reaffirmed the right to development as a universal and inalienable right and an integral part of fundamental human rights, with the human person as the central subject of development.

Recognizing democracy, development and respect for human rights and fundamental freedoms as interdependent and mutually reinforcing, it specified that democracy is based on the freely expressed will of the people to determine their own political, economic, social and cultural systems and their full participation in all aspects of their lives. In that context, the promotion and protection of human rights and fundamental freedoms at the national and international levels should be universal and conducted without conditions attached. The international community should support the strengthening and promoting of democracy, development and respect for human rights and fundamental freedoms in the entire world. The Conference further determined that while development facilitates the enjoyment of all human rights, the lack of development may not be invoked to justify the abridgement of internationally recognized human rights.

In order to foster human rights, priority needs to be given to national and international action to promote democracy, development and human rights, with special emphasis on measures to assist in the strengthening and building of institutions relating to human rights, strengthening of a pluralistic civil society and the protection of vulnerable groups. Assistance provided on the request of Governments for the conduct of free and fair elections, including assistance in the human rights aspects of elections and public information about elections, is of particular importance, as is assistance for strengthening the rule of law, the promotion of freedom of expression and the administration of justice, and for the real and effective participation of the people in the decision-making processes.

Essential for the promotion and achievement of stable and harmonious relations among communities and for fostering mutual understanding, tolerance and peace is human rights education, which should cover peace, democracy, development and social justice, as set forth in international and regional instruments. Governments should promote increased awareness of human rights and mutual tolerance, supporting human rights education and undertaking effective dissemination of information in that field. United Nations programmes should be able to respond immediately to requests from States for educational and training activities in human rights and humanitarian law. The proclamation of a United Nations decade for human rights education in order to encourage related activities should be considered.

The Conference provided substantive guidance for the United Nations in its future work in promoting and defending human rights and called for world-wide action against discrimination and in favour of tolerance.

The Conference addressed a number of contemporary trends and challenges to the realization of human rights of women, including those belonging to other vulnerable groups. It asserted as a priority objective for the international community the speedy and comprehensive elimination of all forms of racism and racial discrimination, xenophobia and related intolerance. It called on United Nations organs and agencies to strengthen their efforts to implement the Programme of Action for the Third Decade to Combat Racism and Racial Discrimination (1993-2003), which was proclaimed by the General Assembly in December 1993.

The Conference urged States to counter intolerance and related violence based on religion or belief, including practices of discrimination against women and the desecration of religious sites. It called on the Commission on Human Rights to examine ways of promoting the rights of persons belonging to ethnic, religious and linguistic minorities. Measures should be taken to facilitate their participation in all aspects of political, economic, social, religious and cultural life, as well as in their countries' development.

States were urged to guarantee the human rights of all migrant workers and their families, and the equal opportunity of disabled persons through the elimination of all restrictive, socially determined barriers, whether they be physical, financial, social or psychological.

The Conference commemorated the International Year of the World's Indigenous People (1993) and, in its Declaration, recognized the inherent dignity and unique contribution of indigenous people to the development and pluralism of society. It strongly reaffirmed the international community's commitment to their economic, social and cultural well-being and their enjoyment of the fruits of sustainable development. The Programme of Action urged States to ensure the full and free participation of indigenous people in all aspects of society, particularly in matters of concern to them. It called on the Working Group on Indigenous Populations of the Subcommission on Prevention of Discrimination and Protection of Minorities to complete the drafting of a declaration on the rights of indigenous people, and on the General Assembly to proclaim an International Decade of the World's Indigenous People, to begin in January 1994, including action-oriented programmes to be decided on in partnership with indigenous people. In the framework of the Decade, the establishment of a permanent forum for indigenous people in the United Nations system should be considered.

The Programme of Action also focused on the rights of women. It urged the eradication of all forms of discrimination against women, both hidden and overt, as well as the full and equal enjoyment by women of all human rights, as a priority for Government and the United Nations. The Programme underlined the importance of integration and full participation of women as agents and beneficiaries in the development process, and called for integration of the equal status and human rights of women into the mainstream of United Nations system-wide activity. It stressed the importance of eliminating violence against women as well as all forms of sexual harassment, exploitation and trafficking in women, the elimination of gender bias in the administration of justice and the eradication of any conflicts which might arise between the rights of women and the harmful effects of certain traditional practices, cultural prejudices and religious extremism. The Conference called on the General Assembly to adopt the draft Declaration on Violence against Women and encouraged universal ratification by the year 2000 of the 1979 Convention on the Elimination of All Forms of Discrimination against Women.

The Programme of Action called for measures to combat exploitation and abuse of children, including such practices as female infanticide, harmful child labour, sale of children and organs, child prostitution, child pornography and other forms of sexual abuse. It supported in particular measures to promote the human rights of the girl child and to protect children in armed conflicts. It urged universal ratification of the 1989 Convention on the Rights of the Child by 1995.

In view of the complexities of the global refugee crisis, the Conference acknowledged that strategies needed to be developed to address the root causes and effects of movements of refugees and displaced persons, that emergency preparedness and response mechanisms needed to be strengthened, and that protection and assistance had to be provided and durable solutions achieved, primarily through safe and voluntary repatriation.

The Conference urged Governments to strengthen national structures and organs which promote and safeguard human rights and the United Nations to strengthen its activities in that regard. It recommended continued work to improve the functioning of treaty bodies, including their monitoring tasks, and called for a more active role in promoting and protecting human rights in situations of armed conflict. It encouraged the International Law Commission to continue its work on an international criminal court and underlined the importance of strengthening the system of special procedures, rapporteurs, representatives, experts and working groups of the Commission on Human Rights and its Subcommission. It called for a concerted effort to ensure recognition of economic, social and cultural rights at the national, regional and international levels.

As a follow-up, the Conference recommended an annual progress review of the implementation of the recommendations contained in its Declaration, including the possibility of proclaiming a United Nations decade for human rights. It requested the Secretary-General to report to the General Assembly at its fifty-third session in 1998 on progress made, with special attention to the assessment of progress towards the goal of universal ratification of international human rights treaties and protocols.

Environmental preservation

Environmental preservation will remain an important preoccupation of the United Nations in the twenty-first century. There is an intricate interdependence of the world's economy with the world's ecology. The development of the Earth to provide a basic level of comfort for all humanity and the protection of the global environment go hand in hand.

Detailed mandates and initiatives to protect the environment were established by the United Nations Conference on Environment and Development (UNCED), commonly called the "Earth Summit", held at Rio de Janeiro, Brazil, in 1992. In its Rio

Declaration, UNCED recognized that peace, development and environmental protection are indivisible. It set out, in its Agenda 21, a programme for achieving the goals of the Declaration.

Agenda 21

Agenda 21 delineates six central themes relating to the protection of the environment: the quality of life on Earth, i.e., the issues of poverty, malnutrition, unemployment, population growth, lack of health care and pollution; efficient use of natural resources; the protection of global commons, i.e., the atmosphere and the oceans; the management of human settlements, i.e, the welfare of villages, towns or cities; the use of chemicals and the management of wastes; and sustainable economic growth. Agenda 21 outlines an implementation regime designed to foster the sustainable use of natural resources for human development while ensuring a basic and healthful standard of living of all humanity.

An essential ingredient for the success of the action programmes that form the core of Agenda 21 is the active and full participation of all groups in society: business and industry, the scientific and technological communities, the educational community, workers and trade unions, farmers, local, state and national administrative and government officials, women, children and indigenous people must all become involved in the process.

Strengthening the roles of each of these major groups in helping to achieve a sustainable global society will involve deep and fundamental changes in education, public awareness and training, and will require far greater public participation in decision-making. Full accountability of government and industry for its action is also a high priority. All actions of Agenda 21 are aimed at placing the issues of environment and sustainable development at the heart of decision-making at all levels, and are directed towards ensuring the maximum possible participation and contribution by all groups of society. Only through a truly universal response to the global environmental and developmental challenges can progress towards the goals of Agenda 21 be achieved.

To promote the most efficient use of land and resources, mechanisms must be created or enhanced which allow for active involvement of all parties concerned in decision-making, particularly at the community and local levels.

In order to implement successfully the broad Agenda 21 programme, modern data and information systems must be made available to every nation, and the capacity of developing countries to assimilate knowledge, apply appropriate technologies and build a workable institutional framework must be enhanced. A monumental and sustained commitment will be imperative to build the human and technological capacity of all countries to implement the necessary changes for the transition to a sustainable world that is crucial to the success of Agenda 21. Behavioural patterns which threaten life on Earth must be changed and environmentally sound technologies must be developed and made available on a world-wide basis.

Meeting the global need for environmentally sound technology will require much greater international scientific integration. The transfer of such technology to the developing countries is crucial, as the desires of their burgeoning populations for an improved life must be met with technology that does not destroy the environment further. The application of modern and safe technology, however, must be carefully made in keeping with the cultural heritage and traditions of developing countries.

The legal and regulatory framework as it relates to environment and development must also be restructured and streamlined in order to promote effectively sustainable development. Current and future laws must be based on the basic principles of democracy, participation, openness of the decision-making process, cost-effectiveness and accountability.

To achieve global environmentally sound and sustainable development, a substantial flow of additional resources to developing countries must be made. Current cost estimates of international financing and aid from industrialized countries for implementing all actions envisioned by Agenda 21 amount to $125 billion annually through the year 2000, equivalent of only 0.7 per cent of their gross national product. In addition, required national expenditures of Governments and industry in developing and industrialized countries is estimated at approximately $400 billion annually through 2000.

International cooperation on all of these aspects is an essential requirement for the success of Agenda 21. Individual initiative and boldness will provide much of the needed stimulus to begin preparing the world for a sustainable society, both through innovative business enterprise and courageous political leadership.

The overall thrust of Agenda 21 is that the global community must be set on a bold new course which strives for a sustainable future and fully implements an understanding of the impact of humanity on the natural world. Agenda 21 is the call for an unprecedented global partnership to confront and overcome the threat of environmental collapse. It is now up to individual citizens to grasp the crucial nature of the twin global problems of environmental destruction and poverty. The prospect of inevitable environmental disaster must not be our legacy. We have the opportunity to create a world in which concern for life is paramount, in which nature is revered and not exploited, a world which is just, secure and prosperous.

Agenda 21 is the blueprint for a future of hope for the human family. Since the Earth Summit, many countries have taken action to follow up on the recommendations and commitments made, in particular by elaborating national sustainable development strategies and action plans, setting up institutional structures to pursue sustainable development goals and objectives, adopting legislative and regulatory frameworks to implement Agenda 21, and involving in that process all sectors of the community. At the international level, two conventions signed at Rio entered into force and the International Convention to Combat Desertification in Those Countries Experiencing Serious Drought and/or Desertification, Particularly in Africa was being finalized. The international community has moved forward in areas of trade, environment and sustainable development; chemical safety; hazardous wastes; and protection of water resources.

Sustainable development of small island developing countries

An area of special concern to the United Nations has been the sustainable development of small island developing countries because of their particular disadvantages. The 1994 Global Conference on the Sustainable Development of Small Island Developing States, in Barbados, addressed the unique development difficulties of these countries and applied the goals and objectives of Agenda 21 to adopt specific policies, actions and measures to enable them to achieve sustainable development.

The Conference's Declaration of Barbados stated that small island developing States should endeavour to achieve the goals of sustainable development by formulating and implementing policies, strategies and programmes that take into account development, health and environmental goals, strengthening national institutions and mobilizing all available resources to improve the quality of life. Those countries should encourage cooperation in the promotion of sustainable development by sharing information and technology, strengthening institutions and building capacity. The international community should cooperate with the States concerned in implementing the Programme of Action by providing financial resources, facilitating the transfer of environmentally sound technology, and promoting fair, equitable and non-discriminatory trading arrangements and a supportive international economic system. The international community had a responsibility to facilitate the efforts of small island developing States to minimize the stress on their fragile ecosystems, including through cooperative action and partnership, and it should build new partnerships for the sustainable development of those States through the implementation of the Programme of Action.

The Programme of Action recommended actions at the national, regional and international levels in four main areas: climate change and sealevel rise, natural and environmental disasters, the management of wastes, and coastal and marine resources.

With regard to climate change and sealevel rise, the Programme stressed the need to ensure early adherence to the United Nations Framework Convention on Climate Change, the Montreal Protocol on Substances that Deplete the Ozone Layer and other related legal instruments. It also called for the formulation of comprehensive adjustment and mitigation policies for sealevel rise in the context of integrated coastal area management. In addition, the Programme outlined a comprehensive list of measures intended to assess the effects and the socio-economic implications of the impact of climate change. They included mapping areas vulnerable to sealevel rise and developing computer-based information systems covering the results of surveys, assessments and observations; improving public and political understanding of the potential impacts of climate change; formulating comprehensive strategies and measures on adaptation to climate change; promoting a more efficient use of energy resources in development planning and using appropriate methods to minimize the adverse effects of climate change on sustainable development; and increasing participation in the bilateral, regional and global research, assessment, monitoring and mapping of climate impacts, including the adoption of oceanographic and atmospheric measures and policies and the development of response strategies.

In the area of natural and environmental disasters, the Programme of Action sought to establish and/or strengthen disaster preparedness and management institutions and policies in order to mitigate, prepare for and respond to the increasing range and frequency of natural and environmental disasters; to strengthen the capacity of local broadcasting to assist remote rural and outer island communities within countries and among neighbouring countries during disaster events; to establish a national disaster emergency fund with joint private and public sector support for areas where insurance is not available in the commercial market; to integrate natural and environmental disaster policies into national development planning processes and encourage the development and implementation of public and private sector pre- and post-disaster recovery plans, drawing on the capacity of the United Nations Department of Humanitarian Affairs and bearing in mind the International Decade for Natural Disaster Reduction; and to strengthen cultural and traditional systems that improve the resilience of local communities to disaster events.

With regard to the issue of management of wastes, the Programme of Action stressed the need to develop fiscal and policy incentives to encourage environmentally sustainable imports and local products; to develop and implement appropriate regula-

tory measures, including emission discharge and pollution standards; to ratify and implement relevant conventions; to formulate and implement public awareness and education campaigns designed to gain local recognition of the need to control wastes at the source; to introduce clean technologies and treatment of waste at the source and appropriate technology for solid waste treatment; to develop information systems and baseline data for waste management and pollution control; to establish port reception facilities for the collection of waste in accordance with the International Convention for the Prevention of Pollution from Ships; and, in conformity with the Basel Convention on the Control of Transboundary Movements of Hazardous Wastes and Their Disposal and relevant decisions taken by the parties to that Convention, to formulate and enforce national laws and/or regulations that ban the importation from States that are members of the Organisation for Economic Cooperation and Development of hazardous wastes and other wastes subject to the Convention.

Finally, concerning the issue of coastal and marine resources, the Programme of Action focused on the need to establish and/or strengthen institutional, administrative and legislative arrangements for developing and implementing integrated coastal zone management plans and strategies for coastal watersheds and exclusive economic zones; to design comprehensive monitoring programmes for coastal and marine resources, including wetlands; to develop and/or strengthen national capabilities for the sustainable harvesting and processing of fishery resources and provide training and awareness programmes for the managers of coastal and marine resources; and to ratify and/or adhere to regional and international conventions concerning the protection of coastal and marine resources and combat unsustainable fishing and related practices.

Issues of demographic dynamics and sustainability and the elimination of poverty as identified in Agenda 21 were dealt with by the 1994 International Conference on Population and Development and the 1995 World Summit for Social Development. Despite these encouraging developments, considerable work remains to be done both nationally and internationally to translate the commitments of Rio into reality. In that regard, the United Nations must play a leading role. The high-level meeting of the Commission on Sustainable Development reported in 1994 that the financing of Agenda 21 fell significantly short of expectations and requirements. It also identified the need for a more focused approach in the areas of the transfer of environmentally sound technologies, cooperation and capacity-building; to address the short-term negative effects on developing countries of the further liberalization of international trade; and to deal with the question of changing production and consumption patterns.

Development and environment

The Vienna Declaration and Programme of Action, adopted by the World Conference on Human Rights in 1993, stated that the right to development should be fulfilled so as to meet equitably the developmental and environmental needs of present and future generations. The Conference recognized that illicit dumping of toxic and dangerous substances and waste potentially constitutes a serious threat to the human rights to life and health of everyone.

In "An Agenda for Development" of May 1994, the Secretary-General said that in the context of development, each society has to confront the difficult challenges associated with protecting the long-term potential of its natural resources, balancing competing needs and interests. Social and economic needs must be satisfied in ways that do not undermine long-term resource availability, or the viability of the ecosystems on which the current and future generations depend.

The link between environment and development involves much more than the sound exploitation of natural resources. Preserving and protecting the ecological equilibrium is vital not only for human development, but also for human survival.

The interconnections between the environment, society, the economy and political participation highlight the importance of addressing the environmental aspect of development in a national context. The link between poverty and environmental sustainability is particularly compelling. Policies that improve the environment, reducing water contamination for example, often bring the greatest benefit to the poorest, and policies that are effective in reducing poverty will help reduce population growth and decrease pressure on the environment.

Policies that promote technological cooperation and the efficient use of resources can also help find solutions to environmental challenges. The relationships between inputs and outputs and the overall effects of economic sustainability is not necessarily to produce less, but rather to produce differently. Rising incomes pay for investments in environmental improvement, and preventing the depletion or degradation of nature is much less expensive than trying to undo the damage.

If sustainable development is to succeed, the Secretary-General stressed, it must become the concern and commitment not just of Governments but of all segments of society. Sustainable development means a commitment to using renewable resources and to avoiding the over-consumption of non-renewable ones. It means choosing products and production processes that have the least adverse impact on the environment.

Consideration must be given to problems at all levels. Some problems, such as damage to the ozone layer, are global, while others, like transborder industrial pollution, may be regional or, like drinking-water contamination, local in effect. Regulations and incentives at different levels can be crucial.

The Secretary-General called for international cooperation in order effectively to address a wide range of common environment and development interests. Solutions to international environmental problems must be based on common principles and rules of collaboration among sovereign States, backed by persuasion and negotiation. Individual States are entitled to international cooperation for the preservation of resources that belong to one country but are of value to the international community, for example ecological habitats and rare species.

Finally, sustainability must be strengthened as a guiding principle of development. Partnership is required at all levels of the development effort, within States, as well as between international organizations, Governments and non-State actors.

The United Nations and the world community must seize the opportunity offered by this particular point in history to make the transition to a sustainable global society. Every effort must be made to ensure that the opportunity is not squandered and that the programmes of Agenda 21 are implemented in the determination of future life on Earth.

Trade and development

UNCTAD VIII

The slow growth in international trade, efforts to liberalize trade in developing countries and in Central and Eastern Europe, the persistence of protectionist threats and managed trade in developed countries, moves towards regional and subregional integration in various parts of the world and tensions among trading partners compelled the United Nations to address trade and development issues for world economic revitalization and growth in the 1990s and beyond. These issues were dealt with by the eighth (1992) session of the United Nations Conference on Trade and Development (UNCTAD VIII) (Cartagena de Indias, Colombia), which concluded with the adoption of the Cartagena Commitment. The Commitment outlined policy measures for the important areas of international trade, protectionism and structural adjustment, trade preferences, trade efficiency, trade and economic cooperation among developing countries (ECDC), restrictive business practices and the Common Fund for Commodities.

International trade

The Cartagena Commitment aimed at more fully reflecting the evolution in the international economy and set out new policy directions, challenges and potentials for international trade. It outlined goals and objectives to halt protectionism; to bring about further liberalization and expansion of world trade; to provide an equitable, secure, non-discriminatory and predictable trading system; to facilitate the integration of all countries into the international trading system; to ensure that environment and trade policies were mutually supportive, with a view to achieving sustainable development; and to strengthen the international trading system through comprehensive and balance agreements in the Uruguay Round of multilateral trade negotiations. It challenged all countries to increase market access, particularly for developing countries. The latter countries should continue their trade policy reforms and structural adjustments and progressively reduce their import barriers.

The Commitment called on the international trading system to support the transition of countries in Central and Eastern Europe, abolish discriminatory measures against them and relax non-tariff measures on a most-favoured-nation basis. It also called on the system to support observance by all countries of their international commitments on the granting of differential and more favourable treatment to developing countries and to provide for their increasing integration into the system.

Protectionism and structural adjustment

The Conference recommended that UNCTAD should promote the establishment by Governments of transparent mechanisms at the national level to evaluate protectionist measures sought by firms/sectors, and the implications of such measures for the domestic economy and their effects on the export interests of developing countries. It also recommended that countries give attention to increasing the transparency of their trade regimes and to replacing non-tariff measures by tariffs where possible.

Trade preferences

UNCTAD VIII noted that many developing countries had benefited from the generalized system of trade preferences (GSP) treatment and encouraged preference-giving countries to continue to improve and renew the schemes and extend their operation periods. It recommended that preference-giving countries comply with the multilaterally agreed principles of GSP, consider appropriate adjustments in country coverage and, if possible, consider comprehensive product coverage. It further recommended minimizing limitations and restrictions on preferential imports, as well as withdrawals of preferential benefits.

The Conference expressed concern over the incidence of non-tariff measures on benefits deriving from GSP schemes, and urged preference-giving countries to reduce or eliminate such barriers. It also called on preference-giving countries to implement fully the provisions of the Paris Declaration, adopted by the Second (1990) United Nations Conference on the Least Developed Countries, in respect of GSP measures in favour of those countries. It urged the United Nations Development Programme and potential donor countries to increase their contributions to the UNCTAD technical assistance programme on GSP in order to allow developing countries to benefit fully. Those preference-giving countries and their exporters that had not yet fully taken advantage of GSP should participate actively in these technical assistance activities. The UNCTAD Special Committee on Preferences was requested to examine the scope and possible modalities for extending preferential treatment to developing countries with respect to goods, in accordance with the principles and objectives underlying GSP. In expectation of most-favoured-nation rates being brought down pending a successful conclusion of the Uruguay Round, preference-giving countries should consider increasing preferential margins and duty-free treatment offered under existing preferential schemes.

Trade efficiency

The Cartagena Commitment noted that new techniques, such as electronic data exchange (EDI) and other procedures in international trade transactions, were capable of producing substantial time and money savings. It recommended that UNCTAD programmes should give special attention to integrating less advanced countries and regions into this process to give them access to new sources of trade competitiveness. It requested the UNCTAD Secretary-General to initiate consultations with member States to establish an expert group on trade efficiency.

Transparency in trade-related information should be fostered by increasing awareness of opportunities to access publicly available market information. Efforts to establish EDI standards should be supported so that the business interests and concerns of all countries, in particular developing countries, should be represented and complemented through international cooperation. The Conference urged countries to increase trade efficiency through the use of information technology, especially in the areas of trade facilitation and customs automation. All countries were encouraged to adopt laws, regulations and policies to reduce barriers to trade facilitation through the use of information technology.

Trade and economic
cooperation among developing countries

The Cartagena Commitment stated that ECDC, in the new context of market-oriented reforms and export-oriented growth strategies being pursued by most developing countries, should be a means to secure the integration of developing countries into the world economy and to increase their capacity to produce, achieve economies of scale and become internationally competitive.

Within subregional groupings, the expansion of trade depended on reducing tariffs, eliminating non-tariff barriers, introducing more transparent and simple customs procedures, macroeconomic policy coordination to ensure convergence of national price trends and exchange-rate stability, and effective clearing and payments arrangements, as well as improving physical infrastructure. The allocation of aid resources should support regional trade liberalization among developing countries, and the international community should support the efforts of regional and subregional groupings of developing countries to promote and encourage enterprise and entrepreneurship.

In the area of monetary and financial impediments to trade, UNCTAD VIII urged the UNCTAD secretariat to assist developing countries to strengthen and develop their national finance mechanisms. All countries and relevant institutions were invited to cooperate fully with the UNCTAD Secretary-General in his consultations on the feasibility of establishing an interregional trade finance mechanism among developing countries.

Restrictive business practices

The Cartagena Commitment urged UNCTAD, through the Intergovernmental Group of Experts on Restrictive Business Practices, to pursue its work with regard to policies and rules for the control of restrictive business practices in order to encourage competition, promote the proper functioning of markets and resource allocation, and bring about further liberalization of international trade. Efforts should be made by national Governments or regional authorities to implement fully the provisions of the Set of Multilaterally Agreed Equitable Principles and Rules for the Control of Restrictive Business Practices and develop cooperation between national competition authorities, including competent authorities of regional groupings.

Commodities

In the area of commodities, the international community's goals should be to improve the functioning of the commodity market by reducing distortions affecting supply and demand; optimize the contribution of the commodities sector to development; achieve a gradual reduction in excessive dependence on the export of primary commodities through horizontal and vertical diversification of production and exports; improve market access for commodity products through a progressive removal of barriers to international trade and improve market transparency; and ensure proper management

of natural resources to achieve sustainable development. UNCTAD VIII agreed to a number of policy measures to achieve those goals. It urged producers and consumers of individual commodities to examine ways and means to reinforce and improve their cooperation towards solving problems in the commodity area. It recommended that an optimal functioning of commodity markets should be sought through, *inter alia*, improved market transparency involving exchanges of views and information on investment plans, prospects and markets for individual commodities. Substantive negotiations between producers and consumers should be pursued to achieve viable and more efficient international agreements, with particular attention being paid to the agreements on cocoa, coffee, sugar and tropical timber.

UNCTAD VIII underlined the importance of full and active participation by consumers and producers in international commodity agreements and arrangements, taking into account occupational health and safety matters, technology transfer and services associated with production, marketing and promotion of commodities, as well as environmental considerations. Cooperation among producers and consumers should be strengthened, especially in situations of large stock overhangs.

Comprehensive commodity-sector strategies should be put in place within a macroeconomic policy framework, taking into consideration a country's economic structure, resource endowments and market opportunities. Such strategies should include the setting up of an enabling national environment to encourage the mobilization of domestic and international finance; the provision of specific incentives to encourage private enterprise and private investment; the development and maintenance of commodity-related power, transport and communications infrastructure; the provision of support services and training for human resources development; and support for commodity research arrangements. Strategies should equally encompass measures to improve the competitiveness of traditional commodity exports and programmes and action to encourage diversification, particularly in countries highly dependent on commodities for export earnings. Particular attention should also be paid to the financial and physical support structures for trading commodities and new market possibilities assessed and exploited.

The Conference called for concerted efforts by developed countries and international organizations to support national commodity policies in developing countries and in countries undergoing transition to a market economy, including providing technical cooperation for commodity development. It was urgent to improve market access conditions, notably the progressive removal of barriers restricting imports, particularly from developing countries, of commodity products in primary and processed forms, as well as the substantial and progressive reduction of types of support that induced uncompetitive production, such as production and export subsidies. Improved market access through a successful conclusion to the Uruguay Round would contribute to a favourable international trading environment, and improved flows of technology to developing countries were important for lowering commodity production costs and encouraging economic development. The free flow of information and science to allow innovation and transfer of technology should be promoted and supported through policies to promote increased collaboration among firms in developing and developed countries.

The Conference affirmed the need for adequate official bilateral, multilateral and private resources, including private investment, to finance diversification projects and programmes, and the promotion and development of resource-based industries, including commodity-related services activities. In that regard it agreed that support should be directed towards institution-building, promotion of entrepreneurship, horizontal diversification and crop substitution, and increased participation in processing, marketing and distribution, including transportation, as well as towards achieving a gradual reduction of excessive commodity dependency. It recognized that increased coordination among donor country Governments and international institutions was essential and should avoid inconsistencies in advice and potential over-investment in particular sectors.

Welcoming compensatory mechanisms introduced by the International Monetary Fund (IMF) and the European Economic Community, UNCTAD VIII invited other countries to consider introducing such mechanisms and called on Governments and institutions to improve those already existing.

It also recognized the importance of commodities for sustainable development and recommended the manner in which prices of natural commodities and their synthetic competitors could reflect environmental costs and resource values; the means by which the competitiveness of natural products with environmental advantages could be improved, the commodity sector developed, and environmental concerns made mutually reinforcing; and additional international financial and technical support to developing countries for the development and dissemination of technologies to cope with environment problems that were specific to commodity production and processing.

Common Fund for Commodities

In the Cartagena Commitment, UNCTAD VIII welcomed the coming into force of the Common Fund for Commodities and its potential contribution to support international commodity cooperation. It urged maximum participation in the Fund and stressed that its resources should be fully exploited; arrears in the payment of subscriptions to the Fund's capital, which could be an impediment to the achievement of its objectives, should be paid up; resources of its Second Account should be increased, particularly through the fulfilment of pledges of voluntary contributions; efforts to elaborate and consider appropriate project proposals, including those for diversification, for financing through the Second Account should be speeded up; and every effort should be made to ensure that the account became fully operational to benefit, in particular, least developed countries (LDCs) and the commodities of interest to developing countries, particularly those of small producers-exporters.

Environment and trade

UNCTAD VIII recognized that improved market access for developing-country exports, in conjunction with sound environmental policies, would have a positive environmental impact. It stressed that environmental policies should deal with the root causes of environmental degradation, thus preventing environmental measures from resulting in unnecessary restrictions to trade. Trade policy measures for environmental purposes should not constitute a means of arbitrary or unjustifiable discrimination or a disguised restriction on international trade. Environmental measures addressing transborder or global environmental problems should, as far as possible, be based on an international consensus. The Conference also identified certain rules and principles which should apply should trade policies be required to enforce environmental policies.

The Conference recommended that UNCTAD, at both the intergovernmental and secretariat levels, should undertake in-depth work on clarifying the linkages between trade and environment and on the need for environmental protection to coexist with liberal trade policies and free market access. It should also contribute to consensus building with regard to appropriate principles and rules. The Conference also requested the UNCTAD secretariat to undertake studies, analyse policy measures, and carry out technical cooperation in the area of trade and sustainable development. In particular, the secretariat should analyse the relationship between environmental policy and trade. The Conference requested donor countries to continue contributing extrabudgetary resources to further strengthen UNCTAD's work on interlinkages between environment, trade and sustainable development, including the adjustment of the Trade Control Measures Information System.

Services

UNCTAD VIII agreed that developing countries should pursue policies to develop the services sectors of their economies, particularly producer services. Such policies should include modernization and expansion of infrastructure, particularly telecommunications and information services; development of human resources and of knowledge-intensive services; measures to encourage investment and cross-border trade in the services sector and to make use of services from competitive domestic suppliers in developing countries; the progressive liberalization of the services sector and the formulation of strategies to improve domestic services capabilities and for internationally competitive services; enhancing cooperation at the interregional, regional and subregional levels, including mutual trade liberalization, and the improvement of skills and infrastructures to promote services exports; and improving the infrastructure to support effective participation in negotiations on services at the regional and multilateral levels.

With regard to international policies, UNCTAD VIII agreed that Governments should support progressive multilateral liberalization, under the draft General Agreement on Trade in Services, in order to promote economic growth and expand world trade in services, and to increase the participation of developing countries. The Conference endorsed the obligation that developed countries, and other national Governments, should maintain contact points, as established under the draft General Agreement, to facilitate the access of developing countries' services providers to information related to their respective markets.

It further agreed that the international community should continue support for concerted policy actions, including providing financial assistance on concessional terms, promoting training and the acquisition and transfer of technology on terms and conditions agreed by the parties concerned, building up technological and human capabilities of developing countries to enhance their ability to absorb relevant technologies, and constructing and/or improving basic services infrastructures, including subregional and regional transportation, particularly in low-income countries and LDCs.

The Conference also recognized that technology had increasingly become a determinant of the ability to participate in world trade in manufactures and services and recommended a series of measures for developing technology in developing countries.

Financial policy

UNCTAD VIII recommended that at the national level all countries should deploy sustained efforts to mobilize domestic savings for investment, growth and development to achieve macroeconomic stability and predictability, increased monetary control and greater financial discipline. However, monetary policy should not be overburdened, and use of a wider gamut of policy instruments was needed. Financial liberalization should be accompanied by appropriate institutional reform and by domestic supervisory and prudential arrangements required for a sound national banking system operating in a liberal and secure international financial system. It should be introduced in a context of macroeconomic stability and be compatible with the competitiveness and institutional development of capital markets. Liberalization in those circumstances could help to maximize the contribution of the financial sector to economic development.

UNCTAD VIII agreed that an economically and institutionally efficient public sector would contribute to fostering growth and development. In many countries, public sector reform was essential for improved mobilization and use of savings. Fiscal reform should be introduced, aimed at rationalizing and simplifying the taxation system, protecting government revenues from erosion by inflation and strengthening tax administration. Structural adjustment programmes and international cooperation programmes should take full account of the priorities of the development of human resources, especially with regard to women, particularly to improve the status of rural women, and the provision of basic public goods, including investment in infrastructure, and social services, such as health and education. It also recommended that the efforts of developing countries to improve their policy and regulatory environment so as to attract foreign direct investment, the return of flight capital and other non-debt-creating financial flows should be further strengthened.

It reiterated the need for developed countries to implement necessary adjustment measures to create a more favourable international economic environment so as to stimulate economic growth, as well as to reduce external and fiscal imbalances and adopt appropriate mixes of fiscal and monetary policies. It encouraged countries to adopt policies conducive to a decline in interest rates and consistent with the stability of prices and exchange rates. UNCTAD VIII called on all countries to consider reducing military expenditure and to channel the resulting savings towards socially productive uses. It urged developing countries in particular to reduce military spending, recognizing the positive effects that such a reduction could have on budgetary policies to accelerate growth and development.

Development financing

UNCTAD VIII declared that structural adjustment in developing countries needed to be supported and funded, and a substantial increase in the aggregate level of resources, particularly concessional resources, would provide a needed boost. The related macroeconomic and structural policies should take account of the specific economic needs and conditions of developing countries. The Conference urged the developed country donors to implement their undertakings to attain the agreed international target of devoting 0.7 per cent of gross national product to official development assistance. Donors reaffirmed the commitment undertaken in the Paris Declaration to bring about a significant and substantial increase in the aggregate level of external support to those countries, taking into account that, since the Paris Conference, six States had been added to the list of LDCs.

The Conference recommended that the resources of the World Bank's Special Programme of Assistance for debt-distressed low-income countries, and those of IMF's Structural Adjustment Facility and Enhanced Structural Adjustment Facility, should continue to play a key role in providing medium-term concessional loans to low-income countries. It recommended that industrialized and developing countries should encourage mutually beneficial flows of foreign direct investment to the developing world, including membership in, and wide utilization of, programmes under the Multilateral Investment Guarantee Agency and the International Finance Corporation, as well as the conclusion of bilateral investment and double taxation treaties. The Conference recognized that the problems of the poor countries of Africa, especially the debt problem, needed special treatment, and urged the international community, particularly the donor developed countries and the multilateral financing institutions, to implement fully the measures agreed in the United Nations New Agenda for the Development of Africa in the 1990s, following the final review of the United Nations Programme of Action for African Economic Recovery and Development 1986-1990, as well as the United Nations System-wide Plan of Action for African Economic Recovery and Development.

Debt problems of developing countries

UNCTAD VIII recommended that the international community continue to provide support, including, on a case-by-case basis, further debt relief for countries implementing sound economic reform programmes. With regard to external debt incurred with commercial banks, it encouraged more rapid implementation of the strengthened debt strategy, noting that some countries had already benefited from a combination of sound adjustment policies and commercial bank debt reduction or equivalent measures. It further encouraged other countries with heavy bank debts to negotiate similiar reductions with their creditors.

With regard to debt owed to official bilateral creditors, the Conference welcomed the substantial bilateral debt reduction undertaken by some creditor countries and encouraged others in a position to do so to take similiar action. It recommended that particular attention be paid to the resource needs of low-income countries and other debt-distressed

developing countries that continued to service their debt, safeguard their creditworthiness and meet their external obligations. As to multilateral debt, the Conference urged that serious attention be given to continuing the work towards growth-oriented solutions to the problems of developing countries with serious debt-servicing difficulties. The international community should explore ways to improve coordination between all creditors, official and private, and donors to help meet, in an integrated manner and based on solid economic considerations, financing requirements of debtor countries in relation to their medium-term development programmes. The Conference urged continued technical cooperation among developing countries in the area of external debt, as well as UNCTAD's cooperation with developing countries in debt negotiation and in providing advice on debt issues.

UNCTAD IX

The ninth session of UNCTAD will be held in South Africa in 1996 for the purpose of addressing contemporary and future development concerns and identifying ways to maximize the impact of globalization and liberalization while minimizing the dangers of instability and marginalization. UNCTAD IX will examine four major topics: development policies and strategies in an increasingly interdependent world economy in the 1990s and beyond; promoting international trade as an instrument for development in the post–Uruguay Round world; promoting enterprise development and competitiveness in developing countries and countries in transition; and the future work of UNCTAD.

The Uruguay Round

A major challenge facing the international community is the need to successfully implement and adhere to the agreements reached at the conclusion of the Uruguay Round of multilateral trade negotiations in December 1993. Those agreements—on safeguards, subsidies and countervailing measures, anti-dumping mechanisms, agriculture, and textiles and clothing—provide a mechanism for countries effectively to defend and pursue their interests. The detailed elaboration and tightening of multilateral disciplines, the introduction of new concepts and detailed criteria for their application and the improvement of the dispute settlement mechanism provide new scope for action against trade-restrictive measures. Many developing countries and countries in transition will be faced with serious challenges with respect to institutional, human resource and information capacities for the effective utilization of the agreements. However, the momentum created by the Uruguay Round to liberalize world trade must be maintained and areas for future negotiations due to begin by 1999 have already been identified by both developed and developing countries.

Agreement on an effective and efficient multilateral safeguard system was of paramount importance in improving security of access to markets and re-establishing the credibility of multilateral disciplines. The Agreement on Safeguards has clarified and reinforced the disciplines for the application of safeguard measures, in particular by re-affirming the most-favoured-nation (MFN) clause, and explicitly prohibits voluntary export restraints and similar measures. The Agreement on Textiles and Clothing provides a framework for the phasing out of the Multifibre Arrangement, thus reversing the trend of the past three decades toward the continuous extension and expansion of the discriminatory and restrictive regime directed against developing countries' major industrial export.

A key feature of the Agreement on Subsidies and Countervailing Measures is the agreement reached on the definition of a "subsidy", reflecting an international consensus on the appropriate role for Governments in supporting production and trade. The Agreement identifies which subsidies are to be prohibited (those contingent upon export performance or upon the use of domestic over imported goods), permitted (i.e., "non-actionable"—in not being exposed to the possibility of remedial action), or applied only if they do not adversely affect the trade interests of other countries.

The Agreement on Agriculture constitutes an important first step towards stability and predictability in trade in agricultural products by establishing a binding "standstill and roll-back" of protectionist measures in this sector, as a basis for further negotiations aimed at more meaningful liberalization and reform. Through "tariffication", all non-tariff measures affecting imports of agricultural products will be converted into bound customs duties, to be reduced by a fixed percentage. The Agreement contains commitments for the reduction of export subsidies in terms of value (budget outlays) and volume.

The Agreement on Implementation of Article VI of the General Agreement on Tariffs and Trade (GATT) 1994, which represents the outcome of the third attempt to clarify the GATT rules on anti-dumping measures, provides more detailed rules on the procedure for initiating investigations, calculating dumping margins, determining the existence of injury and reviewing finds and undertakings.

Further trade liberalization

A major outcome of the Uruguay Round is an MFN tariff reduction in developed countries on industrial products by an average of 38 per cent on a trade-weighted basis, bringing tariffs down to 3.9 per cent on average. This significant reduction of tariff levels derived essentially from the "Quad" package negotiated among Canada, the European Union, Japan and the United States. Duty-free access for developing countries to these markets will significantly increase.

One of the objectives of the Uruguay Round was to correct the situation emerging from the Tokyo Round in 1979, where the nine codes on non-tariff measures and certain product sectors had not been subscribed to by many GATT contracting parties, including most of the developing countries. A major result of the Uruguay Round has been the conversion of modified versions of these codes into multilateral trade agreements which are binding on all World Trade Organization (WTO) members. There has consequently been a dramatic increase in the levels of multilateral discipline for developing countries, particularly when the increases in bindings resulting from the tariff negotiations are taken into account.

The remaining four agreements retain their "plurilateral" character and are contained in a separate annex to the WTO Agreement. Of these, the Government Procurement Code was renegotiated in parallel to the Uruguay Round (but with a smaller number of signatories) and the renegotiation of the Agreement on Civil Aircraft is under way. The WTO Agreement leaves open the possibility of incorporating additional plurilateral agreements on the basis of consensus (one of which could well be the multilateral steel agreement, presently under negotiation).

Dispute settlement understanding

On anti-dumping measures, the codification and alignment of current practices of the major trading countries has, in certain cases, resulted in lower levels of discipline and the legitimization of practices unfavourable to developing countries. Anti-dumping actions will be subject to a less stringent standard of review in dispute settlement procedures than that applied in other agreements, obliging panels to accord relatively greater deference to the decisions of the administering authorities and to the provisions of the implementing legislation. In view of the relatively greater stringency introduced in the other agreements, recourse to anti-dumping action may become even more the preferred "trade remedy" for protectionist interests.

Extension of multilateral disciplines

In the present "globalized" world economy, initiatives to establish multilateral rules for the protection of property rights have been broadened to address the whole spectrum of impediments which restrict the global operations of enterprises. They concern not only traditional objectives, such as the "right of establishment" and "national treatment", but also access to telecommunications networks, the movement of executives and specialists, and the avoidance of conditions on investment that in-hibit the execution of a global production strategy. The Uruguay Round embraced the negotiation of new multilateral disciplines in the areas of intellec-tual property and trade in services, linking them to the GATT rights and obligations through the institu-tional "umbrella" of WTO and its dispute settlement mechanism.

The General Agreement on Trade in Services (GATS) establishes an entirely new contractual framework to govern trade in services, based on its definition of such "trade" and the general obliga-tion to provide unconditional MFN treatment for all measures affecting such "trade" in services.

The most impressive feature of GATS is not so much the degree of liberalization that it has achieved, but rather the extension of the scope of multilateral trade rights and obligations to cover measures affecting such diverse aspects as foreign direct investment, professional qualifications, and the movement of persons and electronic data across national frontiers, thus making them legiti-mate subject-matter for inclusion in the negotiation of future trade commitments under GATS, as well as in other trade agreements.

The Agreement on Trade-Related Investment Measures (TRIMs) does no more than prohibit such measures that contravene the GATT obligations and rules on national treatment and quantitative restric-tions. It does not deal with the rights of investors *per se*. Those rights are addressed in GATS (rather than in the TRIMs Agreement), where it is clearly stipulated that neither "establishment" nor "na-tional treatment" are "rights", but can be the sub-ject of qualified concessions exchanged on a reciprocal basis (including concessions in other modes of supply, such as the temporary movement of persons) with respect to specific sectors or sub-sectors.

Through the Agreement on Trade-Related Aspects of Intellectual Property Rights (TRIPs), the essential provisions of the international conventions governing intellectual property protection have been made universally applicable on an MFN basis, given a binding character and incorporated as inherent rights enshrined in the multilateral trading system. The Agreement establishes disciplines for copy-right, trade marks, geographical indications, indus-trial designs, patents, layout designs of integrated circuits, and protection of undisclosed information, in certain instances going beyond the provisions of the conventions of the World Intellectual Property Organization (WIPO). It provides new rules with re-spect to issues which had not been resolved in WIPO forums, the most important of which was acceptance that all products or processes in all fields of technology will be patentable. Other key aspects in this regard relate to copyright protection for computer software, protection for data banks

and phonogram producers, the term of patent pro-tection, the protection of undisclosed information and civil litigation procedures.

Differential and more favourable treatment

The dramatic increase in the level of discipline ac-cepted by developing countries through their acceptance of all the multilateral trade agreements resulting from the Uruguay Round and the binding of their tariff schedules has significantly reduced the flexibility of Governments in the use of trade and domestic policy instruments. The provisions in various agreements for differential and more favour-able treatment go some way to remedy this situa-tion. Many take the form of "best-endeavour" clauses, time-bound exceptions from obligations and longer periods for implementing obligations, flexibility in procedures and access to technical as-sistance and advice. In certain agreements, differen-tial and more favourable treatment has been given a more precise contractual character.

Development strategies in future will neverthe-less have to be adapted to the post–Uruguay Round trading system. The success of such strategies will depend upon the effectiveness of WTO in ensuring secure access to markets and in preserving the momentum to further multilateral trade liberali-zation.

Least developed countries

The Punta del Este Ministerial Declaration recog-nized the need for "positive measures to facilitate the expansion of trading opportunities" for LDCs. The Marrakesh Ministerial Decision on this subject exhorts members to implement expeditiously the provisions contained in the various agreements in favour of those countries. In those agreements which provide for differential and more favourable treatment for developing countries in general, more generous treatment is extended to LDCs, usually in the form of longer periods for compliance with and implementation of obligations. A Ministerial Deci-sion was adopted as a political message to mobi-lize the support of Governments, through techni-cal and financial assistance for food aid, as well as that of the multilateral financial institutions, to take action to mitigate the impact on LDCs and net food-importing countries of the higher food prices that were expected to result from the new multilateral disciplines on agricultural export subsidies.

None the less, the poorer developing countries, including LDCs and other developing countries in Africa, have emerged confronted by special difficul-ties on account of the erosion of the preferential margins they enjoyed (particularly under the Lomé Convention), the expected increase in the cost of imported technology and in the price of imported foodstuffs, and the much higher level of both legal and procedural obligations that they have assumed.

The revival of multilateralism

The Understanding on Rules and Procedures Governing the Settlement of Disputes substantially strengthens the dispute settlement mechanism and hence also the multilateral trading system. It ensures a complainant the right to the establishment of a panel, which must proceed through predetermined successive stages in accordance with a clearly specified timetable. No member will be able to delay, postpone or block a decision. Panel reports are to be approved by the Dispute Settlement Body unless there is a consensus to reject them. Members are committed not to make a determination to the effect that a violation of obligations or other nullification or impairment of benefits has occurred except through recourse to this multilateral mechanism.

The Uruguay Round has also resulted in the extension of multilateral trade disciplines to cover a much larger number of countries, due to the recent accession to GATT of many developing countries. All WTO members will be subject to roughly the same level of multilateral obligation; any exceptions, including differential and more favourable treatment, are defined in precise terms. The Uruguay Round furthermore attempted to adapt to the new situation arising from the dissolution of the USSR and the transition to a market-oriented economy by the newly independent States; in the later stages of the negotiations additions were made to several agreements which took into account the specific problems faced by these countries in the transition process. Most of the countries concerned which are not contracting parties have initiated procedures for accession to GATT.

WTO and future negotiations

Specific provision is made in some agreements for further negotiations, while in others comprehensive reviews of the operation of the agreements are envisaged, usually within five years. Multilateral negotiations will thus begin on a wide range of issues around 1999-2000.

Meanwhile, countries face the challenging task of implementing the Agreements. Many developing countries, as well as the countries in transition, will be faced with serious challenges with respect to institutional capacity, human resource development and information management. Effective utilization of the agreements requires coordinated governmental machinery on trade matters, in order to monitor compliance with the new rules by their trading partners, as well as to bring national legislation into conformity with the new rules and establish the institutional mechanism for the purpose.

The WTO Agreement has as its primary functions the linking of all the multilateral trade agreements together, subjecting them to a common dispute settlement mechanism, and providing the framework for the implementation of the results of negotiations, on either a multilateral or a plurilateral basis. It commits its members to ensure conformity of their laws, regulations and administrative procedures with the obligations in the agreements and also abolishes the "grandfather rights" (with one exception) which enabled countries to maintain mandatory legislation otherwise inconsistent with their GATT obligations. At the initial stage of its activities, the main objectives of WTO would consist of ensuring full and faithful implementation of the Uruguay Round Agreements.

The Uruguay Round resulted in an extension of the scope of multilateral trade disciplines to cover those aspects of technology, investment, immigration policy and communications where Governments were willing to accept contractual obligations linked to their market access concessions. It did not attempt to address these issues in a comprehensive fashion. The extent to which the scope of WTO will be enlarged to encompass additional "trade-related" areas will be determined by the willingness (or reluctance) of countries to submit their policy measures in additional fields to contractual obligations that could expose them to the threat of possible trade sanctions.

Population and human settlements

Issues relating to population and human settlements will continue to feature prominently on the United Nations agenda for decades. With the world population currently estimated at 5.6 billion and expected to increase by more than 86 million annually into the twenty-first century, there is an emerging global consensus on the need for increased international cooperation to deal with population in the context of sustainable development. The number of people living in absolute poverty has continued to increase and so has the number of those poorly housed and homeless in many countries. The next two decades are also likely to witness a further shift of rural populations to urban areas. In this context, the United Nations Centre for Human Settlements (Habitat) is preparing a Global Plan of Action to guide human settlements development and deal with the problems and potentials of urban life.

Population and development

The 1994 International Conference on Population and Development (Cairo, Egypt) addressed a wide range of population and development issues, including: the interrelationships between population, sustained economic growth and sustainable development; gender equality, equity and empowerment of women; population growth and structure; reproductive rights and reproductive health; health, morbidity and mortality; population distribution, urbanization and internal migration; population, development and education; and technology, research and development.

The Conference adopted a Programme of Action recommending specific actions to be taken at the national, regional and international levels in those areas.

The Conference stressed the interrelationship between population, sustained economic growth and sustainable development, and recommended that Governments integrate population issues into policies and programmes relating to sustainable development and development strategies, which should reflect the implications of and consequences for population dynamics and patterns of production and consumption. It urged Governments to adopt macroeconomic policies designed to provide an appropriate international economic environment, as well as good governance, effective national policies and efficient national institutions. Governments should invest in human resource development, eliminate inequalities and barriers to women in the workforce, and facilitate the creation of jobs in the industrial, agricultural and services sectors by creating a more favourable climate for trade expansion and investments. The Programme of Action also recommended the implementation of population policies and programmes to support the objectives of Agenda 21 of the 1992 United Nations Conference on Environment and Development, including the integration of demographic factors into environment impact assessments, paying special attention to income-generation and employment strategies directed at the rural poor and those living on the edge of fragile ecosystems, utilizing demographic data to promote sustainable resource management, implementing policies to address the ecological implications of inevitable future increases in population numbers and changes in population concentration and distribution. The Programme of Action also suggested measures to enhance the full participation of all groups of society and for research on the linkages among population, consumption and production, the environment and natural resources, and human health.

In relation to the family, its roles, rights, composition and structure, the Programme of Action urged Governments to facilitate compatibility between labour force participation and parental responsibilities, increasing the earning power of economically deprived families, and ensuring that children were educated rather than compelled to work; eliminating all forms of coercion and discrimination; and formulating family-sensitive policies in all fields to create an environment supportive of the family. The Programme also recommended that Governments formulate family-sensitive policies in the areas of housing, health, social security and education and give greater attention to poor families as well as those that have been victimized by war, drought, famine, natural disasters and racial and ethnic discrimination or violence.

On the issue of population growth and structure, the Programme of Action urged countries to give greater attention to the importance of population trends for development and to optimize them within the context of social and economic development. In attempting to address population growth concerns, countries should recognize the interrelationship between fertility and mortality levels and aim to reduce high levels of infant, child and maternal mortality so as to lessen the need for high fertility. The Conference recommended that countries give high priority to the protection, survival and development of children and youth; take action to prevent their exploitation and abuse, especially to alleviate their suffering in armed conflict and other disasters; and meet the aspirations of youth in education, training, employment opportunities, housing and health. The Programme of Action also made recommendations with regard to the elderly and the development of social security systems to enhance their self-reliance and strengthen formal and informal support systems and safety nets for them. Concerning indigenous people, recommendations were made to recognize their distinctive perspective relating to population and development and accordingly address their specific needs. The United Nations should develop an enhanced understanding of indigenous people and to that end compile data on their demographic characteristics.

The Programme of Action addressed the problems of reproductive rights and reproductive health, and recommended that countries make accessible, through the primary health-care system, reproductive health to all individuals by 2015; design programmes to serve the needs of women; promote greater community participation in reproductive health-care services; support the principle of voluntary choice in family planning; take steps to meet the family-planning needs of their population by 2015; and provide universal access to safe and reliable family-planning methods. Other recommendations related to sexually transmitted diseases and the prevention of the human immunodeficiency virus (HIV), human sexuality and gender relations and the reproductive health needs of the adolescent population.

In the area of health, morbidity and mortality, the Conference recommended that countries make access to basic health care and health promotion central strategies for reducing mortality and morbidity, assign sufficient resources for full primary health-care coverage of the population, and strengthen health and nutrition education and communication. Countries should aim to achieve by 2005 a life expectancy at birth greater than 70 years and by 2015 a life expectancy greater than 75 years. Through technology transfer, developing countries should be assisted in building their capacity to produce various drugs and vaccines and ensure the wide availability of and accessibility to such services. All countries should give priority to ensuring a safe and sanitary living environment for all population groups with special attention being given to living conditions of the poor and disadvantaged in urban and rural areas.

Population distribution, urbanization and internal migration will become a major feature in the coming decades. Recommendations were made for Governments to increase the competence of city and municipal authorities to manage urban development, safeguard the environment, improve the plight of the urban poor, finance needed infrastructure services, strengthen the capacity for land management and promote the development and implementation of effective environmental management strategies for urban conglomerations. Special attention should be given to water, waste and air management and environmentally sound energy and transport systems.

Countries were also urged to address the causes of internal displacement and assist those persons. Adequate capacities for disaster preparedness should be developed and the United Nations should continue to review the need for protection and assistance to internally displaced persons. Measures should be taken at the national level with international cooperation to find lasting solutions to questions relating to the internally displaced, including the right to voluntary and safe return to their home of origin.

International migration was also an area of concern. The Conference urged Governments to strengthen efforts to achieve sustainable economic and social development and ensure a better economic balance between developed and developing countries and countries in transition; to diffuse international and internal conflicts before they escalate; to ensure the rights of all minorities and indigenous people; and to respect the rule of law, promote good governance, strengthen democracy and promote human rights. Governments of countries of destination should respect the basic human rights of documented immigrants and those Governments should assert their right to regulate access to their territory and adopt policies that respond to and shape immigrant flows. With regard to the admission of migrants, Governments should avoid discriminating on the basis of race, religion, sex and disability. They were also urged to promote, through family reunion, the normalization of the family life of legal migrants who have the right to long-term residence. With respect to undocumented migrants, Governments of countries of origin and countries of destination should cooperate in reducing the causes of undocumented migration, safeguarding the basic human rights of undocumented migrants and preventing their exploitation.

The Conference recommended increased support and assistance to refugees, asylum-seekers and displaced persons. The Programme of Action urged Governments to relieve the causes of such movements. Factors that contribute to forced displacement should be addressed through the alleviation of poverty, democratization, good governance and the prevention of environmental degradation. Governments were urged to strengthen their support for international protection and assistance activities on behalf of refugees and displaced persons and to enhance regional and international mechanisms for that purpose. All measures should be taken to ensure the physical protection of refugees, especially against exploitation, abuse and all forms of violence. Adequate support should be extended to countries of asylum and to assist in the search for durable solutions. Governments should create conditions that would allow for the voluntary repatriation of refugees in safety and dignity. Rehabilitation assistance to repatriating refugees should be linked to long-term reconstruction and development plans. The international community should provide assistance for repatriation programmes, including the removal of land mines and other devices that threaten the safety of the returnees.

In the critical area of population, development and education, the Programme of Action outlined recommendations to achieve universal access to quality education and to eliminate gender disparities in access to, retention in, and support for, education. It recommended that all countries consolidate progress made in the 1990s towards providing universal access to primary education. Countries that have achieved the goal of universal primary education should extend education and training to education at secondary school and higher levels. Investment in education and job training should be given high priority in development budgets at all levels and should take into account the range and the level of future workforce requirements. Countries should take affirmative steps to keep girls and adolescents in school with a view to closing the gender gap in primary and secondary education by 2005.

Population and development issues should be communicated through print, audiovisual and electronic media, including databases and networks such as the United Nations Population Information Network in order to disseminate technical information and to promote and strengthen understanding of the relationship between population, consumption, production and sustainable development.

Technology, research and development should be brought to bear on improving basic data collection, analysis and dissemination and for undertaking reproductive health research as well as social and economic research.

The Programme of Action called on Governments to strengthen their national capacity to carry out sustained and comprehensive programmes on collection, analysis, dissemination and utilization of population and development data. Particular attention should be paid to monitoring population trends, preparing demographic projections and progress towards the attainment of health, education, gender, ethnic and socio-equity goals. Training programmes in statistics, demography, and population and development should be designed and implemented, particularly in developing countries, with enhanced technical and financial support, through international cooperation and greater national resources. Governments, funding agencies and research organizations should promote socio-cultural and economic research on relevant population and development policies and programmes, including indigenous practices. They should also study the links between population, poverty alleviation, environment, sustained economic growth and sustainable development.

The Action programme recommended measures to improve national capacities and the cost-effectiveness, quality and impact of overall national population and development strategies. It recommended that countries formulate and implement human resource development programmes, policies and plans, and give special attention to the development and implementation of client-centred management information systems for population and development. Governments, NGOs, the private sector and local communities should mobilize and effectively utilize the resources for population and development programmes that expand and improve the quality of health care. They should also mobilize resources to reinforce social development goals including those outlined by the 1990 World Summit for Children, UNCED's Agenda 21 and other relevant international agreements. In this regard, Governments were urged to devote an increased proportion of public sector expenditure and of official development assistance to the social sectors, stressing, in particular, poverty eradication.

At the international level, the Conference urged the international community to foster a supportive economic environment by adopting favourable macroeconomic policies for promoting sustained economic growth and development. The international community should strive to fulfil the agreed target of 0.7 per cent of the gross national product for overall official development assistance and increase the share of funding for population and development programmes. It estimated that the need for complementary resource flows from donor countries would be in the order of $5.7 billion (in 1993 US dollars) in the year 2000, rising to $7.2 billion

by 2015. Therefore, recipient countries should ensure that international assistance for population and development activities is effectively used to meet goals so as to assist donors to secure commitment to further resources for programmes. The United Nations Population Fund, other United Nations organizations, multilateral financial institutions, regional banks and bilateral financing sources should coordinate their financial policies and planning procedures to improve the impact and cost-effectiveness of their contributions to the population programmes of the developing countries and countries with economies in transition.

The Programme of Action also envisaged the active participation of NGOs and the private sector to achieve the population goals outlined. It recommended the promotion of an effective partnership between government, NGOs and local community groups in the discussion, design implementation, coordination, monitoring and evaluation of programmes relating to population, development and the environment.

The Conference outlined follow-up measures in the population area. It urged Governments to commit themselves at the highest political level to achieving the goals and objectives of the Programme of Action and to take the lead roles in coordinating its implementation, monitoring and evaluation of population policies and strategies. In this regard, the international community should assist interested Governments in national capacity-building for project formulation and management.

Regional commissions, United Nations organizations and other relevant regional and subregional organizations should play an active role within their mandates in the implementation of the Programme of Action. The implementation of the Programme of Action on population and development was viewed as part of an integrated follow-up effort to all the major United Nations international conferences during the 1990's, requiring new and additional resource inputs from both Governments and the international community.

Human settlements

Despite significant advances over the past two decades in the approach to addressing human settlement issues, many countries, particularly developing ones, are still faced with the problem of providing adequate shelter for a steadily growing population. It is estimated that by the year 2000 half of humanity will be living in urban areas. Rapid urbanization has outpaced the ability of local authorities and national Governments to provide adequate shelter and basic amenities to the urban poor. For centuries, cities have been the source of prosperity and progress, generating economic growth, social cohesion and opportunity. However, more and more they are faced with overcrowding, unemployment, crime and pollution.

The inability of Governments to supply enough dwellings, infrastructure and services has resulted in an understanding that collaboration and a division of labour between Governments, the private sector and community-based organizations are necessary.

Patterns of consumption among dense city populations, concentration of intensive economic processes, demands placed on natural resources by city-based activities and improper waste disposal all suggest that the major environmental problems of the future will be city problems. Hence, efforts to improve all aspects of the living environment must be focused on urban areas where most of the world's population will live and work, most economic activity will take place, and where the most pollution will be generated and most natural resources consumed. Sustainable urban development will be the most pressing challenge facing humanity in the twenty-first century.

It was for these compelling reasons that the General Assembly in 1992 decided to convene a Second United Nations Conference on Human Settlements, to take place at Istanbul, Turkey, in June 1996. Dubbed the "City Summit" by the United Nations Secretary-General, the Conference will confront the emerging urban situation and initiate world-wide action to improve shelter and living environments. Its two overall themes are adequate shelter for all and sustainable human settlements development in an urbanizing world. The Conference, also known as Habitat II, will deepen understanding of urban challenges and opportunities so that realistic steps can be taken at city, country and international levels to develop new patterns of civic partnerships to overcome the problems and enrich the potentials of city life.

Habitat II will be the last in a series of United Nations conferences which span some of the most serious and pressing challenges of human security and development that will confront the world community in the next century. These conferences have begun to deliver a more holistic and humane message about global problems and about the cooperative solutions they require.

Agenda 21 adopted at the 1992 United Nations Conference on Environment and Development, designed to save the planet endangered by excessive consumption and plagued by poverty and underemployment, can only become a reality if the problems associated with urbanization are approached with equal vigour.

Given the primacy of human settlements in future development efforts due to their growing demographic and economic weight, it is at the city level where policy, as it directly affects people and interests, becomes an eminently political affair. This will mean developing a management style at the local level which is not only efficient, transparent and accountable, but also inter-sectoral and capable of balancing and achieving the prime goals of increased productivity, poverty reduction and environmental protection. In fact, rapid urbanization may be the key to maintaining our ecosystem and environment; when people are concentrated in cities, they are less likely to destroy the countryside by using up its resources.

As the Secretary-General pointed out in his 1994 World Habitat Day message, "The challenge of development has become the challenge of urban settlements." Habitat II is a broad spectrum opportunity, perhaps a last chance, for international collaboration in institution-building — to face squarely the pressing challenges of sustainable urban development in the coming century.

The Conference's objective is to produce a Global Plan of Action to guide human settlements development through the first two decades of the twenty-first century. It will draw from current and past research to enhance understanding of the problems and potentials of urban life. It is expected that these lessons will explore traditional biases against cities in developmental thinking and policy. The draft Global Plan, as it stands, now proposes three basic principles — civic engagement, sustainability and equity — as the basis for a strategy to enable citizens, jointly with their Governments, to identify problems, set goals and objectives, mobilize resources, and achieve and evaluate results. The draft Global Plan calls on Governments and international agencies to make commitments to provide resources and to embark on new partnerships with other urban actors, including local authorities, non-governmental organizations, community groups and the private sector, to deliver short- and long-term improvements in the living conditions of people worldwide.

Women and development

The advancement of women has increasingly become an important issue on the United Nations agenda for development. Since the 1985 World Conference on Women, which adopted the Nairobi Forward-looking Strategies for the Advancement of Women, profound political, economic, social and cultural changes have taken place, with both positive and negative effects on women. The world-wide movement towards democratization has opened up the political process in many nations, but the popular participation of women in decision-making has not yet been achieved. Absolute poverty and the feminization of poverty, unemployment, the increasing fragility of the environment, continued violence against and widespread exclusion of half of humanity from institutions of power and governance underscore the need for a continued search for development, peace, security and solutions to ensure a people-centred sustainable development. The participation and leadership of women is essential to the success of this search and only the radical transformation of the relationship between women and men to one of full and equal partnership will enable the world to meet the challenges of the next century.

The Fourth World Conference on Women: Action for Equality, Development and Peace, to be held in September 1995 in Beijing, will set the stage for national and international action to promote the full and equal integration of women in all aspects of society. It will review and appraise progress achieved in implementing the Nairobi Forward-looking Strategies and identify measures to ensure the achievement of their objectives in the future. The Conference will seek to hasten the removal of all remaining obstacles to women's full and equal participation in all spheres of life, to promote and protect women's human rights and to integrate women's concerns into all aspects of sustainable development.

Its Final Document — the Platform for Action — is expected to serve as an agenda for women's empowerment aimed at establishing the principle of shared power and responsibility between women and men as a prerequisite for equality, development and peace and a condition for people-centred sustainable development. The draft Platform, which contains a mission statement and a global framework, identifies strategic objectives and actions in 12 critical areas, and discusses institutional and financial arrangements to promote the advancement of women. It contains recommendations relating to the impact on women of poverty; education; health; violence; armed conflict; economic structures; power sharing and decision-making; mechanisms to promote the advancement of women; human rights; the media; the environment; and the situation of girls.

According to agreed language in the draft's mission statement, a sustained and long-term commitment is essential so that women and men can work together for themselves, their children and society to meet the challenges of the next century. The draft Platform emphasizes that women and men share common concerns that can be addressed only by working together and in partnership towards the common goal of equality.

Among actions agreed on are recommendations for collection of gender- and age-disaggregated data on poverty and for devising statistical means to make visible the full extent of women's contribution to the national economy, including in the unremunerated and domestic sectors.

Agreed text also includes a recommendation that Governments provide, by the year 2000, universal access to basic education and completion of primary education by at least 80 per cent of primary school-age children; closing the gender gap in primary and secondary school education by 2005; and

universal primary education in all countries before 2015. In order to eradicate illiteracy among women by 2000, the text recommends reducing the female illiteracy rate to at least half the 1990 level, with emphasis on rural, migrant, refugee, internally displaced and disabled women.

To improve their access to science and technology, women and girls should be trained in those areas. Governments, educational authorities and academic institutions should aim to develop non-discriminatory education and training. Action to be taken includes the development of appropriate education and information programmes, with due respect to multilingualism, that make the public aware of the importance of non-discriminatory education for children and the equal sharing of family responsibilities between girls and boys.

Also agreed on was the need for multilateral development organizations, bilateral donors and foundations to maintain or increase funding levels for education in structural adjustment and economic recovery programmes. Governments, educational institutions and communities are called upon to provide support for child care and other services to enable mothers to continue their schooling.

With regard to violence against women, agreed language describes the phenomenon as a manifestation of the historically unequal power relations between men and women. Violence against women derives essentially from cultural patterns, particularly the harmful effects of certain traditional practices and all acts of extremism linked to race, sex, language or religion that perpetuate women's lower status. Images in the media of violence against women, including pornography, are seen as contributing factors.

Governments are called on to adopt measures to modify the social and cultural patterns of men and women, and to eliminate cultural practices based on stereotyped roles for men and women. They should also provide well-funded shelters and relief support for girls and women subjected to violence, as well as counselling services and legal aid. There is also agreement on the need for counselling for the perpetrators of violence. There is a call on Governments and organizations to condemn systematic practice of rape and other forms of inhuman and degrading treatment of women as a deliberate instrument of war and ethnic cleansing.

The draft Platform calls for enactment of legislation to guarantee the rights of women and men to equal pay for equal work or work of equal value; to ensure that policies related to trade agreements do not aggressively affect women's new and traditional economic activities; and to pay special attention to women's needs when disseminating market, trade and resource information.

Other agreed text recommends that Governments commit themselves to establishing the goal of gender balance in governmental bodies and that they ensure that responsibility for the advancement of women is invested at the highest possible level. Political parties should consider examining their structures and procedures to remove all barriers discriminating against the participation of women. Gender balance in the composition of delegations to the United Nations and other international forums is also called for, while the Organization is called on to develop mechanisms to nominate women candidates for appointment to senior posts in the United Nations system.

In order to raise awareness of the human rights of women, Governments should develop a comprehensive human rights education programme. There is a call on United Nations bodies to give full and sustained attention to the human rights of women in the exercise of their respective mandates. Governments are also called upon to promote education concerning the equality of women and men in public and private lives, including their rights within the family and in international human rights instruments. There is a call for measures to ensure that refugee and displaced women, migrant women and women migrant workers are made aware of their human rights and of the recourse mechanisms available to them.

It is recommended that Governments take measures to reduce the risks to women from environmental hazards at home, at work and in other environments, including through appropriate applications of clean technologies. Analysis of the structural links between gender relations, environment and development should be conducted.

As follow-up to the World Conference, the draft Platform states that, by the end of 1996, Governments should have developed comprehensive strategies or plans of action to implement the Platform, with time-bound targets, benchmarks for monitoring and proposals for allocating or reallocating resources for implementation. The integration of a gender perspective in budgetary decisions on policies and programmes is required, as well as the adequate financing of specific programmes for securing equality between women and men.

Recommendations are made for subregional and regional action, including a call on the Economic and Social Council to consider reviewing the institutional capacity of the regional commissions to deal with gender issues in the light of the draft Platform. Regional offices of the specialized agencies should develop and publicize a plan of action for implementing the draft Platform. The need to renew, reform and revitalize the various parts of the United Nations system is stressed. Governing bodies within the United Nations system are encouraged to give special consideration to the implementation of the Platform.

The success of the Platform for Action will require strong commitment on the part of Governments, international organizations and institutions, as well as adequate resources to implement the agreements made.

Eradication of poverty

Absolute poverty, hunger, disease and illiteracy afflict more than one fifth of the world's population. Over 120 million people worldwide are officially unemployed and many more underemployed. More women than men live in absolute poverty and the imbalance continues to grow. Each day, more than 40,000 children die from the scourges of poverty, which include hunger, malnutrition, disease epidemics, the lack of clean water, inadequate sanitation and the effects of drug problems. Despite significant progress in the past four decades, both the gap between rich and poor nations and inequalities within nations have widened. There can be no more urgent task for development than to attack both the causes and manifestations of poverty.

In his "An Agenda for Development", the Secretary-General has warned that if poverty persists or increases and there is neglect of the human condition, political and social strains will endanger stability over time. The reduction of poverty requires development in which access to the benefits of economic progress is as widely available as possible, and not concentrated excessively in certain localities, sectors or groups of the population.

Therefore, improved education, health and shelter, together with an increase in meaningful employment opportunities, are among the programmes which will contribute directly to reducing poverty and its consequences. Apart from being desirable goals in themselves, education, health and shelter are all essential to a productive workforce and hence to economic growth. The elimination of hunger and malnutrition should be targets in their own right.

Conditions of poverty

Poverty manifests itself in many forms, including lack of income and productive resources sufficient to ensure sustainable livelihoods; hunger and malnutrition; ill health; limited or lack of access to education and severe deprivation of other basic services; increased morbidity and mortality from illness; homelessness and inadequate housing; unsafe environments; and social discrimination and exclusion.

Many developing countries and countries with economies in transition face major developmental obstacles and lack the means to improve the quality of life of their people in a sustainable manner. Among the main obstacles are persistent trade imbalances, the slow-down in the world economy, chronic debt-servicing problems and the lack of technological and other resources with which to address pressing national problems. In sub-Saharan Africa, Asia, Latin America and other areas, poverty has been further aggravated by political conflicts and social unrest as well as by natural disasters such as floods, hurricanes, volcanic eruptions, drought and desertification, and locust infestation. In recent years, these situations requiring emergency assistance to meet the serious humanitarian needs of the destitute populations have resulted in widespread hunger, malnutrition, disease and high infant mortality.

UN efforts to eradicate poverty

For decades, the eradication of poverty has been at the forefront of United Nations efforts. In the 1940s, the Universal Declaration on Human Rights also called for the mitigation and eventual eradication of poverty. The International Labour Organization in the 1970s advocated the basic needs approaches to poverty reduction, and later the World Bank and other lending institutions placed greater emphasis on poverty eradication programmes of assistance to developing countries. The General Assembly renewed emphasis on poverty in 1988 and 1989 when it called for effective international cooperation and policy measures for the urgent and permanent eradication of poverty in developing countries. Subsequently, as a result of the General Assembly Declaration on International Economic Cooperation and the International Development Strategy for the Fourth United Nations Development Decade, adopted in 1990, as well as a series of "Human Development Reports" published by the United Nations Development Programme, the issue of poverty eradication featured prominently. In 1992, the Economic and Social Council devoted its segment on coordination to policies and activities related to the eradication of poverty and support to vulnerable groups. The Cartagena Commitment, adopted by the eighth session of the United Nations Conference on Trade and Development, demonstrated a consensus of the international community on the eradication of poverty as a priority. To this end UNCTAD VIII established a Standing Committee on Poverty Alleviation to develop approaches and promote effective programmes in this area. The 1992 United Nations Conference on Environment and Development, in its Agenda 21, also identified poverty as one of its major programme areas.

In 1993, the General Assembly, stressing the importance of international cooperation in combating poverty, proclaimed 1996 International Year for the Eradication of Poverty. It requested the Secretary-General, in consultation with States and other organizations, to set out the objectives, principles and main recommendations for the Year and to give widespread publicity to the activities of the United Nations system related to the eradication of poverty, including those contained in Agenda 21.

The Year will concentrate on establishing effective links with other poverty-related strategies emanating from a wide range of programmes, including the programme of action for sustainable development of UNCED's Agenda 21; the Secretary-General's "An Agenda for Development"; the Programme of Action of the 1994 International Conference on Population and Development; the 1995 World Summit for Social Development; the Platform for Action of the 1995 Fourth World Conference on Women; and other upcoming activities. The Year will thus build on the substantial experiences, policies and programmes already in operation to combat poverty. It will also establish mechanisms to promote greater awareness and understanding of various poverty-related strategies and programmes and promote pratical action at the local, national and international levels.

Further international commitment

The 1995 World Summit for Social Development (Copenhagen, Denmark), commonly referred to as the "Social Summit", offers an unprecedented opportunity to fashion new and effective international cooperation and strategies to advance social development and combat poverty. The Summit reviewed a wide range of issues relating to political, economic and social development, and established principles, goals and commitments for international consensus to promote social progress.

In the Copenhagen Declaration and Programme of Action, adopted at the conclusion of the Summit, world leaders committed themselves to the goal of eradicating poverty through national actions and international cooperation as an ethical, social, political and economic imperative of mankind.

The Programme of Action acknowledges that over 1 billion people in the world live under unacceptable conditions of poverty, mostly in developing countries and particularly in rural areas. Women bear a disproportionate burden of poverty, and children growing up in poverty are often permanently damaged. Older persons, those with disabilities, indigenous people, refugees and displaced persons are particularly vulnerable to poverty.

The Programme of Action outlines a wide range of principles and strategies for combating poverty. Poverty is a complex multidimensional problem and no uniform solution can be found for global application. Rather, country-specific programmes to tackle poverty and international efforts supporting national ones, as well as the creation of a supportive international environment, are crucial to a solution. The eradication of poverty cannot be accomplished through anti-poverty programmes alone, but requires democratic participation and changes in economic structures in order to ensure access for all to resources, opportunities and public services; to undertake policies geared to more equitable distribution of wealth and income; to provide social protection for those who cannot support themselves; and to assist those confronted by unforeseen catastrophe, whether individual or collective, natural, social or technological.

The eradication of poverty requires universal access to economic opportunities which promote sustainable livelihood and to basic social services, as well as special efforts to facilitate access to opportunities and services for the disadvantaged. People living in poverty and vulnerable groups must be empowered through organization and participation in all aspects of political, economic and social life, in particular in the planning and implementation of policies affecting them, thus enabling them to become genuine partners in development.

The Programme of Action states that there is an urgent need for national strategies to reduce poverty and eradicate absolute poverty by a target date, as well as for stronger international cooperation in assisting countries in those efforts. The Programme calls for the development of methods to measure all forms of poverty and to monitor the circumstances of those at risk; for regular national reviews of economic policies and national budgets to orient them towards eradicating poverty and reducing inequalities; as well as for expanded opportunities to enable those living in poverty to enhance their capacities and improve their economic and social conditions. Among further requirements, the Programme enumerated human resources development and improved infrastructural facilities; comprehensive provision for the basic needs of all; policies ensuring adequate economic and social protection during unemployment, ill health, maternity, disability and old age; policies that strengthen the family and contribute to its stability; and mobilization of both the public and private sectors, educational and academic institutions and non-governmental organizations to assist poverty-stricken areas.

Policies to eradicate poverty, reduce disparities and combat social exclusion require the creation of employment opportunities and would be incomplete and ineffective without measures to eliminate discrimination and promote participation and harmonious social relationships among groups and nations. According to the Programme of Action, enhancing positive interaction between environmental, economic and social policies is essential for success in the longer term. Also, the well-being of people requires the exercise of all human rights and fundamental freedoms, access to good education, health care and other basic public services. These policies require the creation of an environment favourable to social development, nationally and internationally, and have to be seen in a framework of sustained economic growth and sustainable development.

To achieve these objectives, the Programme recommends various actions, such as the formulation of integrated strategies, improved access to productive resources and infrastructure, meeting the basic needs of all, enhanced social protection and reduced vulnerability.

Formulation of integrated strategies

Among the Programme of Action's specific recommendations are that Governments give greater focus to public efforts to eradicate absolute poverty and reduce overall poverty substantially by promoting sustained economic growth in the context of sustainable development and social progress, offering equal opportunities to all people. They should formulate or strengthen, preferably by 1996, i.e. the International Year for the Eradication of Poverty, as well as implement national poverty eradication plans to address the structural causes of poverty. In cooperation with self-help organizations, they should develop programmes for combating poverty, ensuring the full participation of the people concerned and responding to their actual needs. Community development projects that foster the skills and self-reliance of those living in poverty should be supported. Each country should develop, preferably by 1996, a precise definition and assessment of absolute poverty and elaborate criteria and indicators for determining its extent and distribution. The effective enjoyment by all people of civil, cultural, economic, political and social rights and access to existing social protection and public services should be promoted, particularly through ratification and full implementation of relevant human rights instruments.

Policies and measurable targets should be established to enhance women's economic opportunities and access to productive resources and land ownership. The participation of women in taking and implementing decisions should be encouraged.

Governments are urged to integrate goals and targets for combating poverty into overall economic and social policies and planning at the local, national and regional levels by analysing policies and programmes with respect to their impact on poverty and inequality, assessing their impact on family well-being and conditions, as well as gender implications, and adjusting them to promote more equitable distribution of productive assets, wealth, opportunities, income and services. Public investment policies relating to infrastructure and human resources development should be redesigned to benefit those living in poverty. It should be ensured that development policies benefit low-income communities and rural and agricultural development and that development schemes do not displace local populations. An appropriate policy and legal framework should be designed to compensate the displaced for their losses, help them re-establish their livelihoods and promote their recovery from social and cultural disruption.

Environmental protection and resource management measures should take into account the needs of vulnerable groups and of those living in poverty. Mechanisms to coordinate efforts to combat poverty in collaboration with civil society, including the private sector, should be established and strengthened, and integrated intersectoral and intra-governmental responses developed.

According to the Programme of Action, people living in poverty and their organizations should be empowered by involving them fully into the setting of targets and into the design, implementation and monitoring of strategies and programmes for poverty eradication, which should reflect their priorities; integrating gender concerns in policies and programmes; ensuring that policies and programmes affecting people living in poverty respect their dignity and culture and make full use of their skills; ensuring access of those living in poverty to education; encouraging them to organize so that their representatives can participate in policy making and work more effectively with institutions to obtain needed services and opportunities; placing special emphasis on capacity building and community-based management; educating people about their rights, the political system and the availability of programmes.

The Programme of Action states that there is a need to monitor and share periodically information on the performance of poverty eradication plans, evaluate policies to combat poverty and promote an understanding and awareness of its causes and consequences. This could be done through developing and disseminating indicators of poverty and vulnerability, as well as indicators of national and international causes underlying poverty; monitoring and assessing the achievement of goals and targets agreed to at international forums; evaluating changes in levels of poverty, its persistence and vulnerability to it; and assessing the effectiveness of poverty eradication strategies. To support countries in monitoring social development goals, international data collection and statistical systems could be strengthened and expanded, and public awareness could be mobilized in order to prioritize the struggle against poverty. Resources of universities and research institutions could be mobilized to improve the understanding of the causes of poverty and their solutions, of the impact of structural adjustment measures on people living in poverty and the effectiveness of anti-poverty programmes. The capacity for social research in developing countries could be strengthened and the results of research integrated into decision-making processes. Lastly,

the exchange of knowledge and experience, especially among developing countries, could be facilitated and promoted through regional and subregional organizations.

Members of the international community should, bilaterally or multilaterally, foster an enabling environment for poverty eradication by supporting measures taken to that end particularly in Africa and the least developed countries; promoting international cooperation to assist developing countries in their efforts towards achieving gender equality and the empowerment of women; strengthening developing countries' capacities to monitor the progress of national poverty eradication plans and to address possible negative impact of national and international programmes on those living in poverty; strengthening the capacity of countries with economies in transition to develop social protection systems and policies for the reduction of poverty; addressing the special needs of small island developing States and the problems faced by land-locked developing countries with respect to eradicating poverty; and supporting societies disrupted by conflict in their efforts to do so and to rebuild their social protection systems.

Improved access to productive resources and infrastructure

The Programme of Action called for enhanced opportunities for income generation, diversification of activities and an increase of productivity in low-income and poor communities. To that end, it recommended improving the accessibility of transportation, communication, power and energy services; ensuring that investments in infrastructure support sustainable development at the local or community levels; supporting commodity diversification as a means to increase the export revenues of developing countries and to improve their competitiveness; promoting rural non-farm production and services and other income-generating activities through supportive laws and administrative measures; strengthening financial and technical assistance for community development and self-help programmes, and increasing the availability of credit and market information to small entrepreneurs, small farmers and other low-income, self-employed workers, especially to women; strengthening cooperatives, especially those run by women, in order to improve market access and increase productivity, and strengthening participation in the planning and implementation of rural development; providing alternatives for farmers involved in the cultivation and processing of crops used for illegal drug trade; improving the competitiveness of natural products with environmental advantages and strengthening assistance for research and development of such products; promoting comprehensive rural development, including by land reform, land improvement and economic diversification; and eliminating legal, social, cultural and practical obstacles to women's participation in economic activities and ensuring their equal access to productive resources.

Rural poverty should be addressed by expanding and improving land ownership, ensuring the equal right of women and men in this respect; improving the conditions of agricultural labour and increasing the access of small farmers to water, credit, extension services and technology, including for women, persons with disabilities and vulnerable groups on the basis of equality; improving living conditions in rural areas to discourage rural exodus; promoting opportunities for small farmers and other agricultural workers on terms that respect sustainable development; improving market information and access for small producers; protecting the traditional rights to land and other resources, strengthening land management and developing improved range management systems and access to water, markets, credit, animal production, veterinary and health services, education and information; promoting research and development of farming systems, smallholder cultivation and animal husbandry, particularly in environmentally fragile areas, building on local and traditional practices of sustainable agriculture and taking particular advantage of women's knowledge; strengthening agricultural training and extension services to promote more effective use of existing technologies and indigenous knowledge and to disseminate new technologies, including through the hiring of more women as extension workers; and promoting infrastructural and institutional investment in small-scale farming in resource-poor regions.

Access to credit by small rural or urban producers, landless farmers and others with low or no income should be substantially improved, with special attention to the needs of women and disadvantaged and vulnerable groups, by reviewing legal, regulatory and institutional frameworks that restrict the access of people living in poverty, especially women, to credit; promoting realistic targets for access to affordable credit; providing incentives for improving access to the organized credit system for people living in poverty and vulnerable groups; and expanding financial networks promoting savings opportunities.

Urban poverty is rapidly increasing in pace with overall urbanization worldwide. Urbanization is a growing phenomenon which poses special problems of overcrowding, contaminated water and inadequate sanitation, environmental pollution, homelessness, crime and other social problems. Urban poverty should be addressed by strengthening small and cooperative enterprises and businesses and expanding market and other employment opportunities; promoting sustainable livelihoods for people living in urban poverty through expansion of access to training, education and employment assistance services, in particular for women, youth and the unemployed; promoting investments to improve the overall human environment and infrastructure for the deprived; ensuring that strategies for shelter give special attention to women and children; promoting social and other essential services, including assistance for people to move to areas with better employment opportunities, housing, education, health and other services; ensuring safety through effective criminal justice administration and protective measures that are responsive to the needs and concerns of the community; strengthening the role of municipal authorities, non-governmental organizations, universities and educational institutions, businesses and community organizations, enabling them to be more actively involved in urban planning, policy development and implementation; and ensuring that special measures are taken for the protection and integration of the displaced, the homeless, street children, children in difficult circumstances, orphans, adolescents and single mothers, persons with disabilities and older persons.

Meeting the basic human needs of all

According to the Programme of Action, Governments, in partnership with all other development actors, in particular with people living in poverty and their organizations, should cooperate to meet the basic human needs of all, including those living in poverty and vulnerable groups, by ensuring universal access to basic social services, particularly for those living in poverty and vulnerable groups; creating public awareness that the satisfaction of basic human needs is an essential element of poverty reduction; ensuring full and equal access to social services, especially education, legal and health-care services for women of all ages and children; ensuring that due priority is given and adequate resources made available to combat the spread of HIV/AIDS and the re-emergenc of major diseases; taking particular actions to enhance the productive capacities of indigenous people, ensuring their full and equal access to social services and their participation in the elaboration and implementation of policies affecting their development, with full respect for their cultures, languages, traditions and social organizations, as well as their own initiatives; providing social services to enable vulnerable people and those living in poverty to improve their lives, exercise their rights and participate fully in all social, economic and political activities; recognizing that improving people's health is linked to a sound environment; ensuring physical access to all basic social services for older, disabled or homebound persons; ensuring full and equal access for people living in poverty to justice, making the legal system more responsive to the special needs of vulnerable and disadvantaged groups; and promoting full restorative services, in particular for those who require institutional care or are homebound, and comprehensive community-based, long-term care services for those facing loss of independence.

The Programme of Action recommends that Governments implement the commitments made to meet the basic needs of all with assistance from the international community, including universal access to basic education and completion of primary education by at least 80 per cent of primary school-age children by the year 2000, closing the gender gap in primary and secondary school education by the year 2005, universal primary education in all countries before the year 2015; a life expectancy of no less than 60 years in any country by the year 2000; reduction of mortality rates of mothers, infants and children, aiming at an infant mortality rate below 30 per 1,000 live births and an under-five mortality rate below 45 per 1,000 by the year 2015; and reducing maternal mortality by one half of the 1990 level by 2000 and, by the year 2015, by a further one half; by the year 2000, reduction of malnutrition among children under five years of age by half of the 1990 level; achieving food security by ensuring safe and nutritionally adequate food supply, as well as access to enough food for all, while reaffirming that food should not be used as a tool for political pressure; by the year 2000, ensuring primary health care for all; making accessible reproductive health to all individuals of appropriate ages no later than the year 2015, taking into account the need for parental guidance and responsibility; increasing commitments with the aim, by the year 2000, of reducing malaria mortality and morbidity by at least 20 per cent compared to 1995 levels in at least 75 per cent of affected countries; by that date, eliminating or controlling major diseases that constitute global health problems; reducing adult illiteracy to at least half of its 1990 level, with an emphasis on female literacy, and achieving universal access to quality education; providing access to safe drinking water and proper sanitation for all; and improving the availability of affordable and adequate shelter for all, in accordance with the Global Strategy for Shelter to the Year 2000.

It urges the improvement of access to social services, including quality health care and education for people living in poverty and vulnerable groups. Opportunities for continuing education and training should be expanded. Formal and non-formal preschool education should also be expanded to overcome some of the disadvantages of young children growing up in poverty. Cooperation among government agencies, health-care workers, non-governmental and women's organizations and other institutions should be promoted, in order to develop a comprehensive national strategy for improving

reproductive and child health care. Lastly, health-care outreach services should be made available to low-income communities and rural areas.

Enhanced social protection and reduced vulnerability

The Programme of Action stipulates that social systems should be based on legislation and should be strengthened and expanded in order to protect from poverty those who cannot work due to sickness, disability, old age, maternity, or their caring for children and sick and older relatives, as well as those who cannot find work. Social protection should also be provided to families who have lost a breadwinner through death or marital breakup and to persons who have lost their livelihood due to disasters, civil violence, war or forced displacement. Due attention should be given to people affected by the HIV/AIDS pandemic.

Action to this end should include strengthening programmes for those in need, programmes providing basic protection and social security insurance programmes; developing a strategy for gradual expansion of programmes to provide social security for all; ensuring social safety nets to protect those living in poverty and enable them to find productive employment; designing programmes to help people become self-sufficient as fully and quickly as possible, to assist and protect families, to reintegrate those excluded from economic activity and prevent the social stigmatization of those who need protection; exploring means for raising revenues to strengthen social protection programmes and promoting efforts by the private sector, voluntary and self-help organizations to provide social protection and support; expanding programmes to protect working people from the risk of falling into poverty by extending coverage, providing benefits and ensuring continued entitlements after job changes; ensuring through appropriate regulation the efficiency and transparency of contributory social protection plans; ensuring an adequate social safety net under structural adjustment programmes; and ensuring that social protection and support programmes meet women's needs, taking in particular into account their reintegration into formal work, support for older women and promotion of acceptance of women's multiple roles and responsibilities.

The Programme recommends particular efforts should be made to protect children and youth by promoting family stability and social support to families, including quality child care and working conditions that allow both partners to reconcile parenthood with working life; supporting and involving family organizations and networks in community activities; protecting and promoting the rights of the child, particularly the girl child, through legislative, administrative, social and educational efforts; protecting children in especially difficult circumstances, including armed conflict, and ensuring their access to food, shelter, education and health care and assisting their reintegration into society; enhancing the economic, educational, social and cultural opportunities of youth living in poverty; addressing the special needs of indigenous children and their families, particularly those living in poor areas; and ensuring social support, including adequate housing and child care, to single-parent families and female-headed households.

It also calls for particular efforts to protect older persons, including those with disabilities, by strengthening family support systems; improving the situation especially of those who lack family support; ensuring that older persons are able to meet their basic human needs through access to social services and social security are protected from abuse and violence, and are treated as a resource and not a burden; assisting grandparents required to assume responsibility for children; creating a financial environment that encourages people to save for their old age; strengthening mechanisms to ensure that retired workers do not fall into poverty; and supporting cross-generational participation in policy and programme development and in decision-making.

People and communities should be protected from impoverishment and long-term displacement and exclusion resulting from disasters through national and international actions, such as designing effective mechanisms to reduce the impact and mitigate the effects of natural disasters; developing long-term strategies and contingency plans for effective mitigation of natural disasters and famine, as well as rapid response strategies; developing complementary mechanisms that integrate governmental, intergovernmental and non-governmental efforts, including the establishment of national volunteer corps to support United Nations activities in humanitarian emergency assistance, as well as mechanisms to promote a smooth transition from relief to rehabilitation, reconstruction and development; developing and strengthening emergency food reserves to prevent acute food shortages and stabilize prices, making full use of traditional and market mechanisms; developing drought and flood mitigation agronomic practices and resource conservation and infrastructure, incorporating traditional disaster-response practices; establishing planning and logistical mechanisms for providing quickly and effectively food, medical supplies and other care and relief services in disaster situations; mobilizing and coordinating regional and international assistance to support actions of Governments and communities confronting disaster situations; and reducing vulnerability to natural disasters through the development of early warning systems.

The Programme of Action also makes specific recommendations for the creation of an enabling environment for social development in the economic as well as political and legal fields. It calls for the expansion of productive employment and reduction of unemployment, including enhanced employment opportunities for groups with specific needs; for social integration, promoting equality and social justice, eliminating discrimination, enabling the full participation of all groups and individuals and responding to special social needs.

Follow-up measures

Among the essential requirements for implementation of and follow-up to the Programme of Action are the promotion and protection of human rights and fundamental freedoms, including support for democratic institutions and the empowerment of women; the integration of goals, programme and review mechanisms; partnership between States, local authorities, non-governmental organizations and other major groups, the media, families and individuals; the recognition of diversity; full participation of people in setting goals, designing, implementing and evaluating programmes; efforts to mobilize additional and predictable financial resources; and extension of the concept of partnership among individuals, communities and nations.

A framework for international cooperation in the context of the agenda for development must be created in order to ensure the integrated and comprehensive implementation, follow-up and assessment of the outcome of the Summit, together with the results of other past and future United Nations conferences related to development. On the international level, as on the national, the financial and organizational implications of the commitments, goals and targets should be assessed, priorities established and budgets and work programme planned.

The Programme of Action recommends that the General Assembly, as the highest intergovernmental mechanism and principal policy-making and appraisal organ on matters relating to the Summit follow-up, should review in 1996 the effectiveness of the steps taken to eradicate poverty, as part of the activities relating to the International Year for the Eradication of Poverty.

The Programme further recommends that following the Year, the General Assembly should declare the first United Nations decade for the eradication of poverty. It should hold a special session in the year 2000 for an overall review and appraisal of the implementation of the outcome of the Summit and consider further action and initiatives. The Assembly, as well as the Economic and Social Council, could convene high-level meetings to promote international dialogue on critical social issues and on policies for addressing them through international cooperation. Further, the Assembly should draw upon the initial work of the agenda for development working group on a common framework for the implementation of the outcome of conferences.

System-wide coordination in implementing the Summit outcome would be overseen by the Economic and Social Council. The Council should look at ways to strengthen its role and authority, bringing specialized agencies into a closer working relationship with it. The Council should also be invited to review the mandate, agenda and composition of the Commission for Social Development, including considerations of strengthening it, and to review the reporting system in the area of social development with a view to establishing a coherent system that would result in clear policy recommendations for Governments and international actors. In order to improve the efficiency and effectiveness of United Nations organizations in providing support for social development efforts, and to enhance their capacity to serve the objectives of the Summit, there is a need to reform and revitalize various parts of the United Nations system, in particular its operational activities. All United Nations agencies and organizations should strengthen and adjust their activities and strategies to take into account the follow-up to the Summit.

Finally, the Programme of Action recommends that support and participation of major social groups, as defined in Agenda 21—that is women, youth, children, indigenous people, private organizations, farmers, workers and unions, business and industry, the scientific and technological community as well as the United Nations—are essential to the success of the implementation of the Programme. To ensure the commitment of these groups, they must be involved in planning, elaboration, implementation and evaluation at both the national and international levels. To this end, mechanisms should be created to support, promote and allow their effective participation in all relevant United Nations bodies, including the mechanisms responsible for reviewing the implementation of the present Programme of Action.

. . . And those who were there

. . . *And those who were there:*

Who's Who in the United Nations
at the time of its founding

The following pages of "Who's Who in the United Nations" have been reproduced exactly as they appeared in the *Yearbook of the United Nations*, Volume 1, 1946-47. This list was prepared in 1947 and therefore any reference to the years "48" through "99" should be read as 1848 through 1899.

❖   ❖   ❖

This section contains brief biographical data concerning the principal representatives who attended the conferences leading to the establishment of the United Nations or who have subsequently been accredited to the organization. Leading officials of the United Nations organs and of most of the specialized agencies are also included.

The following abbreviations are used:

acad.—academy; academic
A.D.C.—Aide de camp
adm.—administration, administrator, Admiral
AEC—Atomic Energy Commission
agric. or agr.—agriculture, agricultural
agt.—agreement
a.i.—ad interim
alt.—alternate
Amb.—Ambassador
Amer.—American
A.P.—Associated Press
app.—appointed
asmb.—assembly
assn.—association
assoc.—associate
asst.—assistant
atty.—attorney

b.—born
bd.—board
Belg.—Belgium, Belgian
Br.—British
Brig. Gen.—Brigadier General
bu.—bureau

Cal.—California
Can.—Canada, Canadian
Capt.—Captain
C.B.—Companion of the (Order of the) Bath
C.B.E.—Commander of (the Order of) the British Empire
CCA—Commission for Conventional Armaments
cen.—central
cert.—certificate
C.H.—Companion of Honour
chem.—chemical, chemistry
chm.—chairman
C.I.E.—Companion of the Order of the Indian Empire
C-in-C—Commander in Chief

C.M.G.—Companion of (the Order of) St. Michael and St. George
CNRRA—Chinese National Relief and Rehabilitation Administration
co.—county
cod.—codification
C. of S.—Chief of Staff
Col.—Colonel
coll.—college
com.—committee
comn.—commission
Comdr.—Commander
compar. or comp.—comparative
comr.—commissioner
conf.—conference
cong.—congress
const.—constitution, constitutional
corp.—corporation
corr.—correspondent
ct.—court
C.V.O.—Commander of (the Royal) Victorian Order
Czech.—Czechoslovakia

d.—died
D.C.L.—Doctor of Civil Law
dec.—declaration
del.—delegate, delegation
dem.—democrat
Den.—Denmark
dept. or dep.—department
devel.—development
D.F.C.—Distinguished Flying Cross
dipl.—diplomatic, diplomacy
dir.—director
dir.-gen.—director-general.
dist.—district
div.—division
Dr.—Doctor
D.Sc.—Doctor of Science
D.S.O.—Distinguished Service Order

e.—east
econ.—economic, economics
Ecua.—Ecuador
ed.—education, editor, editorial
elec.—electrical
emp.—emperor
Ency. Brit.—Encyclopaedia Britannica
eng.—engineering, engineer
ESC—Economic and Social Council
Eth.—Ethiopia, Ethiopian
ex.—executive
ext.—external

fac.—faculty
FAO—Food and Agriculture Organization
fed.—federal
F.F.I.—*Front Français de l'Indépendance;*
French Independence Front (French
Underground Movement)
fin.—finance, financial
fmr.—former
F.R.S.—Fellow of the Royal Society.
F.R.S.C.—Fellow of the Royal Society of
Canada

GA—General Assembly
G.C.B.—Knight Grand Cross of (the Order
of) the Bath
G.C.I.E.—Knight Grand Commander of the
Indian Empire
G.C.M.G.—Knight Grand Cross of St. Michael
and St. George
G.C.S.I.—Knight Grand Commander of the
Star of India
gen.—general
geog.—geography, geographical
geol.—geology
Ger.—Germany
gov.—governor, governmental
grad.—graduate
Gr. Brit.—Great Britain

HC—Headquarters Commission
hdqrs.—headquarters
hist.—history
H.M.—His Majesty
H.M.S.—His Majesty's Ship
Hon.—Honorable
hon.—honorary
hosp.—hospital

ICAO—International Civil Aviation Organization
ICEF—International Children's Emergency
Fund
ICJ—International Court of Justice
ILO—International Labour Organisation
imp.—imperial
ind.—independent, independence
Ind.—Indiana
inf.—information
inst.—institute
int.—international
intergov.—inter-governmental
Ire.—Ireland
ITO—International Trade Organization

J.D.—Doctor of Jurisprudence
jr.—junior
jus.—justice

K.B.E.—Knight Commander of (the Order
of) the British Empire
K.C.—King's Counsel
K.C.B.—Knight Commander of (the Order
of) the Bath
K.C.M.G.—Knight Commander of (the Order
of) St. Michael and St. George

K.C.S.I.—Knight Commander of the Star of
India
K.G.—Knight of the Order of the Garter

L. or Lea.—League
leg. or legis.—legislature, legislative
Lieut.—Lieutenant
Litt.D.—Doctor of Letters
LL.D.—Doctor of Laws
LN—League of Nations
Lieut.-Col.—Lieutenant-Colonel
ltd.—limited

Maj.—Major
Mass.—Massachusetts
math.—mathematics
M.C.—Military Cross, Master of Ceremonies
M.D.—Doctor of Medicine
med.—medicine, medical
mem.—member
met.—metropolitan
Mex.—Mexico, Mexican
mgr.—manager
Mich.—Michigan
mil.—military
min.—minister, ministry
mon.—monetary
M.P.—Member of Parliament
MSC—Military Staff Committee
mun.—municipal

n.—north
nat.—natural
natl.—national
Neth.—Netherlands
Nicar.—Nicaragua, Nicaraguan
no.—number
Nor.—Norway
N.S.—Nova Scotia
N.Y.—New York
N.Y.C.—New York City

O.B.E.—Officer of (the Order of) the British
Empire
Ox.—Oxford

pac.—pacific
Para.—Paraguay
parl.—parliament
P.C.—Privy Councillor
Penn.—Pennsylvania
perm.—permanent
phar.—pharmaceutical
Ph.D.—Doctor of Philosophy
Phila.—Philadelphia
philos.—philosophy
phys.—physical
PICAO—Provisional International Civil Aviation Organization
P.M.—Postmaster
P.O.—Post Office
pol.—political
Prep. Comn.—Preparatory Commission
pres.—president
prin.—principal
prob.—problem

prov.—province, provincial
psych.—psychological
pub.—public
publ.—publisher

Q.M.—Quartermaster

R.A.F.—Royal Air Force
Rapp.—Rapporteur
recon.—reconstruction
rep.—representative, republic
Rt. Hon.—Right Honorable
ry.—railway

s.—South
Sask.—Saskatchewan
SC—Security Council
sci.—scientific
SCOP—Special Committee on Palestine
sec.—secretary; secretariat
sec.-gen.—secretary-general
sect.—section
sen.—senator, senate
sesn.—session
soc.—society
spec.—special
stat.—statistics, statistical, statistician
sub.—substitute
sup.—supreme
supt.—superintendent
Swit.—Switzerland

TC—Trusteeship Council
tech.—technical
tel.—telegraph, telephone
temp.—temporary
Tenn.—Tennessee
theol.—theology
trans.—transportation
treas.—treasury

u.—united
U.K.—United Kingdom
Ukr.—Ukraine, Ukrainian
UN—United Nations
UNCIO—United Nations Conference on International Organization (San Francisco, 1945)
UNESCO—United Nations Educational, Scientific and Cultural Organization
univ.—university
U. of S. Afr.—Union of South Africa
Uru.—Uruguay
U.S.A.—United States of America
U.S.S.R.—Union of Soviet Socialist Republics

Venez.—Venezuela

w.—west
Wash.—Washington
WHO—World Health Organization

Abte-Wold, Aklilou (Eth.); b. 12, Eth.; ed. French Lycée, Alexandria, and Univ. of Paris; chargé d'affaires, Eth. Legation Paris 35-40; Vice Min. of Pen (Imp. Secretariat) 42-43; Vice Min. of For. Affairs 43-; rep. UNCIO 45; Chm. Eth. del. GA London 46.

Acikalin, Cevat (Turkey); b. 90; dipl. service in Moscow, Kabul, Prague, Belgrade and Teheran; Amb. to Moscow 42; Perm. Under-Sec. Min. of For. Affairs; Amb. to U.K.; rep. Prep. Comn. 45, GA London 46.

Acosta, César R. (Paraguay); b. 11, Paraguay; ed. Argentina, Paraguay; LL.D. (Univ. of Asunción, Paraguay) 40; fmr. Sec. in Commercial Branch of Dept. of Justice, in Fiscal Dept. of Commercial Branch; fmr. Judge in Commercial Branch; Embassy Counselor of Paraguay, Wash. 45-; mem. Governing Bd. of Pan Amer. Union; rep. to ILO Conf. in Philadelphia 44; Adviser to del. to UNCIO 45; rep. to FAO Conf. in Copenhagen; Chm. Para. del. GA N.Y. 46, first spec. sesn. GA 47.

Acosta, Julio (Costa Rica); b. 72; fmr. Gov. of Alajuela; Min. to El Salvador 14; Sec. of For. Affairs, Welfare, Cult. and Jus. 15-17; Pres. of Costa Rica 20-24; Rep. Cong. 32-36, during which time elected Vice-Pres. of Republic; Rep. Cong. 38-42; app. Pres. Costa Rican Social Security Adm. 43; Sec. of For. Affairs, Welfare, Cult. and Jus. 44-; Chm. Costa Rican del UNCIO 45.

Adarkar, B. N. (India); b. 10, Vengurla; ed. Bombay Univ. and Cambridge Univ.; branch mgr. of Bank of India, Ltd., 34-38; Research Officer of Commerce Dept. 38-40, Chief Research Officer 40-41; Under-sec. of Commerce Dept. 41-43; Sec. of Postwar Recon. Coms. and Consultative Com. of Economists 43-44; Deputy Econ. Adviser 44-; Vice-chm. of Drafting Com. of Prep. Com. of ITO 47.

Adle, Mostafa (Iran); b. 82, Tabriz; ed. Tabriz, Egypt and Univ. of Paris; frm. prof. Univ. of Teheran; fmr. dir. Dept. of Cod. of Laws in Min. of Jus., and Under-Sec. to Min. of Jus.; app. Min. to Berne and del. LN 35; Under-Sec. and later Acting-Min. of For. Affairs 32-38; Min. to Rome 38-41; subsequently Min. of Ed. and Min. of Jus.; Chm. Iranian del. UNCIO 45; rep. GA London 46.

Afifi Pasha, Hafez (Egypt); M.D.; fmr. mem. Liberal Const. Party and Pol. Front in Egypt; fmr. Amb. to London; negotiated treaty of alliance with England 36; Pres. Bank of Egypt; fmr. Min. of For. Affairs; rep. SC 46, AEC 46.

Aghnides, Thanassis (Greece); b. 89, Nigde, Asia Minor; ed. Superior Natl. Greek Coll. Phanar, Istanbul, Anatolia Coll. Asia Minor, and Univs. of Istanbul and Paris; dir. Press Bu. Greek Legation in London 18-19; mem. Minorities Sect. LN Secretariat 19-20, Disarmament Sect. 21-23, Pol. Sect. 23-30, dir. Disarmament Sect. 30-39, Under Sec.-Gen. LN 39-42; Amb. to U.K. 42-; rep. Prep. Comn. 45, GA 46.

Aguilera, Andrés (Para.); b. 01, Asuncion; ed. mil. school; Second Lieut. (Artillery) 24, First Lieut. 27, Capt. 30, Major 33, Lieut.-Col. 36, Col. 41, Brig.-Gen. 44; Min. to London; rep. Prep. Comn. 45, GA London 46.

al-Antaki, Naim (Syria); b. 03, Aleppo; ed. Amer. Univ. of Beirut and Univ. of Sorbonne; fmr. Pres. of the Bar; Dir.-Gen. of For. Affairs 37-38 (resigned); Min. of For. Affairs, of Pub. Works and of Posts and Tel. 43; elected Deputy of Damascus 43; Min. of Fin.; rep. UNCIO 45, first spec. sesn. GA 47.

al-Armanazi, Najeeb (Syria); ed. in Arabic culture, studied law in Paris; Dr. in Int. Law; Sec.-Gen. of Presidency of Syrian Republic; Min. in London; rep. Prep. Comn. 45, GA London 46.

Alberto da Motta e Silva, Alvaro (Brazil); b. 89, Rio de Janeiro; ed. Brazilian Naval Acad.; app. instructor at Naval Acad. 16, present Head of Dept. of Phys. Sciences; perm. tech. and sci. adviser to Navy Min.; mem. Brazilian Com. of Econ. Planning; fmr. Pres. Brazilian Acad. of Sciences and Brazilian Soc. of Chem.; rep. AEC 46-.

Albornoz, Humberto (Ecua.); b. 96, Ambato; LL.D.; fmr. prof. of econ. Quito Univ.; fmr. Min. of Fin.; fmr. Sen.; Mayor of Quito 44-45; Gen. Mgr. Banco de Préstamos, Ecua.; Pres. Advisory Bd. Min. for For. Affairs; Pres. Sup. Bd. of Liberal-Radical Party; del. to Lima, Buenos Aires and Rio de Janeiro Confs.; Chm. Ecua. del. GA London 46.

Alcalde Cruchaga, Enrique (Chile); b. Santiago; ed. Catholic Univ. and Univ. of Chile; mem. Chamber of Deputies since 32; mem. Housing Com.; prof. Catholic Univ.; adviser *Ministerio de Fomento* (Promotion of Production) and Natl. Agric. Soc. of Chile; rep. UNCIO 45.

Alfaro, Ricardo J. (Panama); b. 82, Panama City; ed. Natl. Faculty of Law of Panama; Sec.-Gen. Amer. Inst. of Int. Law 38-; app. Asst.-Sec. for For. Affairs 05; Premier 18-22; Min. to U.S.A. 22-30, 33-36; Vice-Pres. of Panama 28-30, Pres. 31-32; fmr. mem. Perm. Ct. of Arbitration of The Hague; Min. of For. Affairs 45-; rep. UNCIO 45; rep. GA N.Y. 46.

Ali, M. Asaf (India); b. 88, Delhi; ed. St. Stephen's Coll. in Delhi and England; fmr. mem. of Working Com. of Indian Natl. Cong.; mem. Legis. Asmb. 34-46; fmr. Mem. for Transport in Pandit Nehru's cabinet; first Amb. to U.S.A.; rep. first spec. sesn. GA 47.

al-Koudsi, Nazen (Syria); b. 06, Aleppo; ed. Syrian Univ. and Univ. of Geneva; LL.D. (Univ. of Geneva); M.P. 36 and 43, Rapporteur of For. Relations and Budget

Coms.; first Syrian Min. to U.S.A.; rep. UNCIO 45, GA London 46.

al-Omari, Sayid Arshad (Iraq); b. 88; ed. in Constantinople as civil eng.; fmr. head eng. Islands of Constantinople and Mosul, Iraq; fmr. Dir.-Gen. of Post and Tel. and of Irrigation; fmr. Lord Mayor of Baghdad, and twice Min. of For. Affairs; Chm. Iraqi del. Arab Lea. Cong. Cairo 45, UNCIO 45.

Als, Alphonse (Luxembourg); ed. Antwerp; vice-consul in India 30-40; chief of cabinet to Min. of For. Affairs since 43; rep. GA London 46.

Altmeyer, Arthur J. (U.S.A.); b. 91, Wisconsin; ed. Univ. of Wisconsin; Sec. of Wisconsin Industrial Comn. 22-33; Chm. of Social Security Bd. 37-46; mem. of War Manpower Comn. 42-45; Chm. U.S. del. Pan-Amer. Regional Conf. of ILO in Havana 39, First Inter-Amer. Conf. on Social Security in Santiago de Chile 42; Comr. for Social Security Adm. of U.S. 45-; Ex. Sec. of Prep. Comn. of IRO; Chm. Temp. Social Welfare Com. 47.

Alvarez, Alejandro (Chile); LL.D.; del. to various Int. Confs., LN Assemblies and Pan Amer. Congs.; mem. and fmr. Pres. Inst. of Int. Law; Vice-Pres. Int. Dipl. Acad. and Int. Law Assn.; founder and dir. *Inst. des Hautes Etudes Int.*, Paris Univ.; founder Amer. Inst. of Int. Law; mem. Perm. Ct. of Arbitration The Hague 07-20; mem. Hungarian-Czech. Mixed Arbitral Tribunal; Judge ICJ 46-.

Amado, Gilberto (Brazil); b. 87, Sergipe; ed. Univ. of Recife; LL.D. (Univ. of Recife, Brazil); Legal Adviser of For. Office 34; Amb. to Chile 36; fmr. Deputy; Sen.; rep. GA N.Y. 46.

Ameghino, César (Argentina); b. 71, Buenos Aires; Deputy Legis. of prov. of Buenos Aires 06-12; Vice-Pres. Chamber of Deputies 08; head of Min. of Fin. 13; dir. of Revenues 14-16; Pres. Sup. Ct. of Jus. of Buenos Aires 34, 39-41; Min. of Fin. during three intervals from 35-43; fmr. Min. of For. Affairs and Worship; Chm. Argentine del. UNCIO 45.

Amr Pasha, Fattah Bey (Egypt); b. 09; ed. Khedive Coll., Cairo and London; hon. legal attaché to Royal Egyptian Embassy 39-42; Vice-Pres. Anglo-Egyptian Chamber of Commerce 40-42; Amb. to England; rep. GA London 46, SC 46.

Andrade, Víctor (Bolivia); b. 05; ed. Amer. Inst. in La Paz and Univ. of La Paz; fmr. prof. of math. Amer. Inst.; app. Under-Sec. of Pub. Ed. 30; mgr. Office of Workers' Insurance and Savings 37-43; Min. of Labor 43-44; fmr. Min. of For. Affairs; Amb. to U.S.A.; rep. UNCIO 45.

Andrews, Harry Thomson (U. of S. Afr.); ed. Observatory High School and Pretoria Univ.; rep. on Imp. Shipping Com. 32-35;

del. LN Asmb. 34-39; mem. LN Com. 35-36; rep. LN 35-40; Min. in Wash.; rep. UNCIO 45, GA 46, first spec. sesn. GA 47.

Anthony, Frank (India); b. Jubbulpore (Central Provinces); ed. Nagpor Univ.; called to Bar (Inner Temple) 32; specialist in criminal law practice in Jubbulpore; Pres. of Jubbulpore branch of Anglo-Indian and Domiciled European Assn. 34-42; app. mem. of Legis. Asmb. (Central) 42; rep. GA N.Y. 46.

Aramburu, Gonzalo N. de (Peru); b. 99, Lima; ed. Spain and Lima; second sec. to Legation in Berlin 22, Rome 24; first sec. Madrid 29, Rio de Janeiro 33; counselor London 36; dir. of protocol, Min. of For. Affairs 40; Min. Counselor Rio de Janeiro 43; Min. in Paris 44-; rep. GA London 46.

Aranha, Oswaldo (Brazil); b. 94, Alegrete, State of Rio Grande do Sul; hon. degrees of LL.D. (Columbia and Yale); fmr. Mayor of Alegrete; Min. of Jus. and Interior 30, of Fin. 31, majority leader of Constituent Asmb. 34; mem. of Comn. which prepared draft Const.; Amb. to U.S.A. 34-37; Min. for Ext. Relations 38-44 (resigned); Chm. of Brazilian del. to 3rd meeting of Mins. of For. Affairs of Amer. Reps., Rio de Janeiro 42; rep. SC 47, CCA 47; Pres. first spec. sesn. GA 47.

Arca Parró, Alberto (Peru); b. 01, Ayacucho; ed. Univ. of San Marcos in Lima and Univ. of Indiana in U.S.A.; LL.D.; teacher 25-30; mem. of Chamber of Deputies 31-36; Dir. of Natl. Bu. of Statistics 42; Chm. of Inter-Amer. Statistical Institute's Com. on Demographic Statistics 42; mem. of Sen.; rep. GA 46, ESC 46-; Vice-Pres. ESC 47; Chm. of Population Comn. 47.

Arce, José (Argentina); b. 81, Loberia; M.D. 03; fmr. Dean of Med. Sciences, Rector of Univ. of Buenos Aires; Deputy 03-13; Pres. of Chamber of Deputies 12-13; Deputy Natl. Legis. 24-29; Vice-Pres. Natl. Chamber of Deputies 26-27; mem. Const. Convention of Province of Buenos Aires 34; Amb. to China 45-46; app. perm. rep. UN 46; Chm. Argentina del. GA N.Y. 46, first spec. sesn. GA 47.

Argüello - Vargas, Mariano (Nicar.); b. 90, Granada, Nicar.; ed. *Universidad de Oriente y Mediodía* in Granada; prof. Univs. of Oriente and of Managua 17-34; atty. Natl. Bank and Banco Hipotecario of Nicar. 28-30; mem. Com. which drafted present Const.; fmr. Sen.; Min. of For. Affairs 40-46; Chm. Nicar. del. UNCIO 45, GA N.Y. 46.

Argyropoulos, Alexandre J. (Greece); b. 94, Athens; ed. Swit.; served in various posts abroad for Greek Min. of For. Affairs 19-32; app. head of Econ. and Commercial Div. of Min. of For. Affairs in Athens 32; rep. UNCIO 45, Temp. Social Com. 46, ESC 46.

Arikan, Saffet (Turkey); b. 88, Erzincan; ed. Mil. School, Harbiye and Staff Coll.; served in Yemen as an officer; elected Deputy 24; Sec.-Gen. of Ed. 35-38; Min. of Natl. Defence 40-42; Amb. in Berlin 42-44; Deputy for Kenya and Pres. of For. Affairs Com. of Grand Natl. Asmb.; rep. GA London 46.

Arroyo Lameda, Eduardo (Venez.); b. 97, Caracas, Venez.; ed. Cen. Univ. of Venez.; fmr. dir. of Commercial Policy, Min. of For. Affairs; fmr. counselor of Legation in Lima, Bogota and London; rep. Emergency Advisory Com. for Pol. Defence of the Americas; rep. GA 46.

Arze-Quiroga, Eduardo (Bolivia); b. 08; app. prof. of econ. Univ. of Cochabamba 37; private sec. to Pres. Quintanilla 40; chargé d'affaires to the Vatican 42; app. dir. Pol. and Econ. Dept. in Min. of For. Affairs 43, Sub.-Sec. 43; mem. House of Rep.; rep. UNCIO 45.

Attlee, Clement Richard (U.K.); b. 83; ed. Ox. Univ.; Mayor of Stepney 19-20; Labour M.P. for Limehouse 22-; Under-Sec. of State for War 23-24; leader of Parl. Labour Party 35-; Lord Privy Seal and Deputy-Leader, House of Commons 40-42; Deputy-Prime Min. 42-45; Sec. of State for Dominions 42-43; Prime Min. 45-; Chm. U.K. del. GA London 46.

Auriol, Vincent (France); b. 84; ed. Paris Univ.; LL.D.; Deputy for Haute-Garonne 14-; gen. sec. of Socialist group in Chamber 19-36; Min. of Fin. 36-37, of Jus. 37; Pres. of France; rep. GA London 46, SC 46.

Austin, Warren R. (U.S.A.); b. 77, Vermont; studied law; admitted to Vermont Bar 02 and to practice before Sup. Ct. of U.S.A. 14; elected Sen. from Vermont in 31, re-elected in 34 and 40; adviser to U.S.A. del. to Inter-Amer. Conf. on Probs. of War and Peace, Mexico City 45; Chm. of U.S.A. del. GA N.Y. 46, first spec. sesn. GA 47; rep. SC 47, AEC 47, CCA 47.

Azevedo, José Philadelpho de Barros (Brazil); b. 94; Vice-Rector Univ. of Brazil; Pres. Inst. of Lawyers of Brazil 38; del. Eighth Amer. Sci. Cong. Wash. 40; app. Min. of Sup. Ct. of Brazil 42; Judge ICJ 46-.

Aziz, Abdol Hosayn Khan (Afghan.); b. 96, Teheran, Iran; ed. Habibiya Coll. in Kabul, Afghan.; First Sec. then Counselor in Teheran 19-22; Dir. in Min. of For. Affairs 22; Consul-Gen. in India 23-29; Min. in Rome, 29-32; Chm. Afghan. del. at Disarmament Conf. in Geneva 32; Amb. in Moscow 32-28; Min. of Public Works 38-40; Min. of Posts and Tel. 40-43; Min. to U.S.A. 43-; Int. Civil Aviation Conf. in Chicago 44, PICAO Asemb. in Montreal 46, GA N.Y. 46, first spec. sesn. GA 47.

Badawi Pasha, Abdel Hamid (Egypt); b. 87, Mansourah; LL.D.; legal adviser to Govt. 22-26, Chief Legal Adviser 26-40; attended Montreux Conf. 37; Min. for For. Affairs 45-46; Chm. Egyptian del. UNCIO 45; rep. Prep. Comn. 45, GA London 46, SC 46; Judge ICJ 46-.

Baidakov, Georgy Ipatovich (Byelorussian S.S.R.); b. 06; ed. Kharkov Aviation Inst.; fmr. tech. eng. in airplane factory, and later dir.; dir. Inst. of "Gyproavioprom" (Prin. Governmental Bd. of Aviation Industry); rep. UNCIO 45.

Bailey, Kenneth H. (Australia); b. 99, Canterbury, Victoria; ed. Queen's Coll. of Melbourne Univ. and Corpus Christi Coll. of Ox.; Head of Queen's Coll. 24-27; prof. of jurisprudence at Melbourne Univ. 28-30, prof. of public law 31-46; adviser Australian del. to Imp. Conf. in London and LN 37, UNCIO 45; present Solicitor-Gen. and Sec. of Atty.-Gen's Dept.; rep. GA N.Y. 46, Rapp. Sixth Com. (Legal).

Bajan, Milola (Ukr. S.S.R.); b. 04, Kamenets, Ukr.; ed. Kamenets Gymnasium, Co-operative Inst. and Inst. of Ext. Relationship, Kiev; wrote and adapted scenarios for films; revised front newspapers during World War II; Deputy-Chm., Council of People's Commissars of Ukr.; rep. GA London 46.

Bajpai, Girja Shankar (India); b. 91; ed. Merton Coll., Ox.; K.C.S.I., K.B.E., C.I.E.; Under-Sec. Ed., Health and Lands Dept. 23, Joint Sec. 27-29 and Sec. 32-; adviser Indian del. LN Asmb. and Dominion Legislation Conf. 29; mem. Gov.-Gen.'s Ex. Council 35, 36 and 40-41; Agent-Gen. for India in U.S.A. 41-; alt. rep. ESC 46.

Bakr, Abdullah Ibrahim (Iraq); b. 07, Mosul; ed. Amer. Univ. of Beirut; Private Sec. to Prime Min. 31; app. Consul to Kermanshah, Iran 41; fmr. Dir.-Gen. of Agric. and Industrial Bank; app. Consul-Gen. in Bombay 43; present Consul-Gen. in N.Y.; acting-chm. Iraqui del. GA N.Y. 46; rep. Ex. Bd. of ICEF.

Baranovsky, Anatoli Maksimovich (Ukr. S.S.R.); b. 07, Kiev; ed. Inst. of Econ. Planning, Kharkov; fmr. Vice-Pres. and Pres. Ukr. State Planning Com.; prof. Econ. Insts. of Kharkov and Kiev; Vice-Pres. of Soviet of Ministers of Ukr.; rep. UNRRA, ESC 46, GA N.Y. 46.

Bard, Ralph A. (U.S.A.); b. 84, Cleveland, Ohio; ed. Princeton Univ.; mem. Hitchcock, Bard & Co. 19-25; fmr. Pres. Ralph A. Bard Co., later Bard & Co.; Pres. Chicago Investors' Corp. 28-32, later Vice-Pres. and Dir.; Pres. Ralph A. Bard & Co. of Chicago 34-41; app. Asst.-Sect. of Navy 41; Under-Sec. 41; deputy-rep. CCA 47.

Baruch, Bernard M. (U.S.A.); b. 70, S. Carolina; ed. Coll. of City of N.Y.; mem. Advisory Com. of Council of Natl. Defense 16; fmr. Chm. Com. on Raw Materials, Minerals and Metals; Chm. War Industries Bd. 18-19; fmr. mem. Sup. Econ. Council; econ. adviser for Amer. Peace Com.; rendered Rubber Report 42, and Report on Postwar Conversion 43 to Pres. Roosevelt; rep. AEC 46.

Basdevant, Jules (France); b. 87; ed. Univ. of Paris; LL.D.; prof. of law at Rennes and Grenoble 03-18, later at Univ. of Paris; attended Peace Conf. 19; del. LN Asmb. and Disarmament Conf.; mem. Perm. Ct. of Int. Jus. since 23; rep. UNCIO 45; Vice-Pres. ICJ 46-.

Bassi, Juan Carlos (Argentina); b. 89, Buenos Aires; attended Mil. Coll. 07-09; prof. Mil. Coll. and War School; mem. Armaments Purchasing Comn. in U.S.A. 26-29, in Europe 29-31; chief of Secretariat, Min. of War 35-39; fmr. Comdr. First and Third Divs. of Army and of Sixth Mil. Zone, Q.M.-Gen. of Interior and Dir.-Gen. of Army Instruction; rep. UNCIO 45.

Bautista Ayala, Juan (Para.); b. 91, Pilar; ed. in Pilar and Asuncion; app. Second Lieut. 12; fmr. Chief of Gen. Staff; fmr. instructor Mil. Coll. of Asuncion; app. Min. of War and Marine 38; Min. to Brazil 41-42, and first Amb. to Brazil 42-; rep. UNCIO 45.

Bautista de Lavalle, Juan (Peru); ed. Univ. of San Marcos in Lima; First Sec. and chargé d'affaires to Legation in Bolivia 16-18; fmr. First Sec. to Paris Legation; Sec. of Peruvian del. Peace Conf. in Paris 19; elected to Bd. of Dir. of Inter-Amer. Bar Assoc. 41, 43; elected by Cong. to Supreme Ct. of Jus. 45; rep. GA N.Y. 46, first spec. sesn. GA 47.

Baydur, Huseyin Ragip (Turkey); b. 91, Island of Rhodes; ed. Univ. of Istanbul; prof. 11-16; Inspector of Turkish students in Europe 16-19; fmr. ed. *Ifham*, Istanbul, and ed.-in-chief *Hakimiyetti Milliye* (since 29 called *Ulus*), Ankara; later dir. Anatolian Agency (Govt. news agency), and Dir.-Gen. Turkish Press; Amb. in Bucharest 24-29; Amb. in Moscow 29-35 and 43-45; Amb. in Rome 35-43, to U.S.A. 45-; rep. UNCIO 45; Chm. Turkish del. GA N.Y. 46, first spec. sesn. GA 47.

Bayle, Luis Manuel de (Nicar.); b. 95, Leon; ed. *Universidad de Occidente* in Leon and Univs. of Mich. and Penn.; M.D.; asst. dean School of Med., *Universidad de Occidente* 24-26; app. Dir.-Gen. of Pub. Health 25; Consul-Gen. in Baltimore 30, and later chargé d'affaires in Wash.; app. Min. of For. Affairs in 36 and special Amb. to Mex. and El Salvador; rep. UNCIO 45.

Beasley, John Albert (Australia); b. 95, Werribee; ed. Werribee; Pres. Elec. Trades

Union 23-28; Pres. N. S. Wales Labour Council 22-28; mem. Fed. Parl. for W. Sydney 28-; Asst.-Min. for Industry and Ext. Affairs 29-31; del. ILO 26; app. Min. for Supply and Devel. 41; Resident-Min. in UK.; rep. GA London 46.

Bech, Joseph (Luxembourg); b. 87, Diekirch; ed. Paris; mem. Chamber of Deputies 14-21; Min. of Jus. and Home Affairs 21-25; del. LN Asmb. 26-40; Prime Min. and Min. of For. Affairs 26-37; Min. of For. Affairs 37-; Chm. Luxembourg del. UNCIO 45; rep. Prep. Comn. 45; Chm. Luxembourg del. GA 46.

Begtrup, Bodil (Den.); b. 03, Nyborg; ed. Univ. of Copenhagen; Vice-Pres. Danish Natl. Council of Women 31-41, elected Pres. of Council in 46; rep. Asmb. LN 38; mem. Danish Council for Maternal Health 39; Chief Film Censor 39; Chm. Comn. on Status of Women 47.

Belaunde, Victor Andres (Peru); b. Arequipa; ed. San Marcos Univ.; sec. Bolivian-Peruvian Border Com. 08-10; Min. to Uru. 18; prof. San Marcos Univ. until 23, at Univ. of Miami 24-30; Min. to Colombia 34; del. LN 36; Dean, Fac. of Law, Catholic Univ. of Peru; rep. UNCIO 45.

Belehrádek, Jan (Czech.); b. 96; M.D.; conducted sci. research in London 25-26; prof. of med. and Vice-Chancellor of Charles Univ., Prague; mem. Provisional Natl. Asmb.; rep. GA London 46.

Belt y Ramirez, Guillermo (Cuba); b. 05, Havana; ed. Univ. of Havana; app. Sec. of Public Ed. 33; Sec. of Council of State 34; Mayor of Havana 35; Amb. to U.S.A. 44-; mem. Governing Bd. of Pan Amer. Union; del. Inter-Amer. Conf. on Probs. of War and Peace, Mex. 45; Chm. Cuban del. UNCIO 45; rep. Prep. Comn. 45; Chm. Cuban del. GA 46; rep. ESC 46-, first spec. sesn. GA 47.

Benediktsson, Bjarni (Iceland); b. 08, Reykjavik; ed. Univ. of Iceland and in Den. and Ger.; app. prof. of law at Univ. of Iceland 32; app. mem. of Reykjavik Town Council 34; app. mem. of Cen. Com. of Independence Party 36; Mayor of Reykjavik 40-47; Althing mem. for Reykjavik 42-; Min. for For. Affairs and Min. of Jus. 47-; rep. GA N.Y. 46.

Ben-Gurion, David; b. 86, Poland; ed. Univ. of Constantinople; organized Hechalutz (Pioneer Movement) in U.S.A. 16; helped to organize and served in Amer. Jewish Legion in Palestine, World War I; founded Gen. Federation of Jewish Labor in Palestine 20; rep. of Jewish Agency for Palestine at First Com. meetings of first spec. sesn. GA 47.

Berendsen, Sir Carl August (N. Zealand); b. 90, Sydney, Australia; ed. Victoria Univ. Coll. and Univ. of N. Zealand; Sec. of Ext. Affairs 28-32; perm. head of Prime Min's Dept. 32-43; High Comr. in Australia 43-44; Min. to U.S.A. 44-; fmr. mem. Perm. Mandates Comn.; rep. UNCIO 45, GA N.Y. 46; Vice-Pres. TC 47; rep. first spec. sesn. GA 47; mem. of Council of UNRRA and of Far Eastern Comn.

Bernardino, Minerva (Dominican Rep.); b. 07, Seybo; fmr. Chief of Statistics of Dept. of Ed.; fmr. Supervisor of Vocational Schools of Dist. of San Domingo; del. Seventh Int. Conf. of Amer. States, Montevideo 33 and Eighth Int. Conf., Lima 38; served on Inter-Amer. Comn. of Women since 35, becoming Vice-Pres. 39 and Pres. 44; rep. Inter-Amer. Conf. on Probs. of War and Peace, Mex. 45, UNICO 45, GA 46; Vice-Chm. of Sub-Comn. on Status of Women 46.

Bevin, Ernest (U.K.); b. 81; mem. Gen. Council of Trades Union Cong., Chm. 37; fmr. Deputy-Chm. of *Daily Herald Ltd.* and Chm. *Clarion* Co.; Min. of Labour and Natl. Service 40-45; Sec. of State for For. Affairs 45-; mem. Council of For. Mins.; rep. GA London 46; rep. SC 46; Chm. U.K. del. GA N.Y. 46.

Bezroukov, Nikon Y. (U.S.S.R.); b. 02, Kronstadt; ed. Marine School in Leningrad; app. Dir. of Northern Steamship Co. 38; head of U.S.S.R. marine fleet 39-40; app. head of Baltic Steamship Co. in Leningrad 40; attained rank of Comdr. U.S.S.R. Navy, World War II; Chief of Trans. Dept. of Amtorg Trading Corp. of N.Y. 46; Vice-chm. Trans. and Communications Comn. 47.

Bianchi Gundián, Manuel (Chile); b. 95; ed. Natl. Inst. and Univ. of Chile; sec. of Legation, Ger. 22-25; counselor of Embassy, Brazil 25-27; Gen. Mgr. *La Nación*, Santiago 26-27; Min. to Pan., Venez. and Cuba 27-28, to Bolivia 29-33; Amb. to Mex. 33-39; Acting-Amb. to U.S.A. 39-40; Min. of For. Affairs 40-41; Amb. to Gr. Brit. 41-; rep. Ex. Com. of Prep. Comn. 45, Prep. Comn. 45; Chm. Chilean del. GA London 46.

Bidault, Georges (France); b. 99, Moulins; fmr. prof. of hist. in a Paris *lycée;* fmr. for. ed. Catholic daily *L'Aube;* leader of Popular Dem. Party; elected Pres. of Natl. Resistance Council 43; twice elected Min. of For. Affairs since 44 and once Premier-Pres.; mem. Council of For. Mins.; Chm. French del. UNCIO 45, GA London 46; rep. SC 46.

Biddle, Eric Harbeson (U.S.A.); b. 98, Phila.; ed. Ox. Univ. and Univ. of Penn.; Lieut. R.A.F. World War I; Relief Adm. for State of Penn. 32-35; Ex.-Dir. Community Fund of Phila. 35-40; dir. U. S. A. Com. for Care of European Children 40;

head of spec. mission of Bu. of Budget 42-;
Chm. Advisory Group of Experts.

Billote, Gen. Pierre (France); b. 06, Paris; ed.
St. Cyr. Mil. School and *Ecole Supérieure de
Guerre;* fmr. C.-of-S. of Gen. de Gaulle in
London and in Algiers; fmr. mil. attaché
to Belgian Govt.; fmr. Sec. of Natl. Defence; natl. mil. del. to resistance forces of
interior and Comdr. F. F. I. Div., Paris;
Asst.-C.-of-S. for Natl. Defence; rep. MSC
46-.

Billoux, Francois (France); b. 03, Saint Ro-
main Lamotte; joined Communist Party 20;
mem. Cen. Com. of Communist Party, regional sec. 34; elected Communist Deputy
from Marseilles 36; imprisoned during
World War II and freed by Gen. Giraud;
app. Min. of Pub. Health 44; Min. for Recon.; rep. GA London 46.

Blanco, Juan C. (Uru.); b. 79; ed. Faculty of
Law of Univ. of Montevideo; Deputy 07-12;
fmr. Min. of Pub. Works; app. Min. to
France 15; rep. Versailles Peace Conf. 19,
LN 20; Min of For. Affairs 24-25, reapp.
31; fmr. Acting-Min. of Interior; Amb. to
Argentina 27-31; fmr. Amb. to Brazil; app.
Amb. to U. S. A. 41; rep. GA N. Y. 46.

Blom, Nicolaas S. (Neth.); b. 99 Deventer;
ed. in law; fmr. judge in Neth. E. Indies;
app. head of Neth. E. Indies Dept. of Jus.
37; mem. temp. Neth. E. Indies Gov. in
Australia, World War II; fmr. acting Lieut.
Gov.-Gen. of Neth. E. Indies; alt. rep. GA
N.Y. 46; rep. SCOP 47.

Bloom, Sol (U.S.A.); b. 70, Illinois, Con-
gressman from N. Y. continuously since 23;
fmr. Chm. For. Affairs Com. U. S. House
of Rep.; del. Int. Copyright Conf. Rome 28;
rep. Evian and London Confrs. to discuss
aid to refugees 38; rep. Bermuda meeting
where War Refugee Bd. was organized 43;
rep. UNCIO 45, GA N. Y. 46.

**Boetzelaer Van Oosterhout, Baron Van, Carel
G. W. H.** (Neth.); b. 92, Amersfoort; ed.
Municipal Univ. of Amsterdam; fmr. Sec.
to Legation in Wash., Mex. City, Brussels;
Counselor to Legation in Berlin 35-40; fmr.
mem. Dept. of For. Affairs of Gov.-in-Exile;
app. Min. to U.S.A. 40; fmr. head of Sect.
of Pol. Affairs in Min. of For. Affairs; app.
For. Min. 46; rep. GA N. Y. 46.

Bogdenko, Vice-Adm. Vassili L. (U.S.S.R.);
grad. of Naval Acad.; was on service in
fleet on Baltic Sea, Black Sea and in Far
East; fmr. C.-of-S. of Pac. Fleet and asst.
of head of Allied Control Com. in Rumania;
rep. MSC 46-.

Bonnet, Henri (France); b. 88; ed. *Ecole
Normale Supérieure;* mem. LN Secretariat,
first in Div. of Press and Inf., later as ex.-
sec. of Asst. Sec.-Gen. of LN 20-31; app.

Dir. of Int. Inst. of Intellectual Co-operation,
Paris 31; Amb. to U. S. A. 44-; rep. UNCIO
45, SC 46.

Borberg, William (Denmark); b. 85, Copenhagen; ed. in econ.; Sec. to Merchants'
Guild, Copenhagen 15; Chief of For. Trade
Office 16-19; Sec. of Treaty Com. 19; Chief
of pol. trade policy dept. of For. Office
21-26; Sec of Legation in London 26-28;
perm. del. to LN 28-40; app. Min. 34; alt.
rep. GA N.Y. 46; rep. first spec. sesn. GA 47.

Boza, Hector (Peru); b. 88, Lima; ed. U. S. A.;
Amb. of special mission to Colombia 38;
Min. of Pub. Works 34-39; Pres. Peruvian
Com. for Inter-Amer. Co-operation 44; fmr.
Min. to Paris; Sen. 45-; mem. of For. Re-
lations Com. of Sen.; rep. GA 46.

Bracken, John (Canada); b. 83, Ontario; ed.
Univ. of Illinois; prof. of field husbandry
at Univ. of Saskatchewan 10-20; app. Pres.
of Manitoba Agric. Coll. 20; app. Premier
of Manitoba 22; Leader of Opposition in
House of Commons; rep. GA N. Y. 46.

Brilej, Joza (Yugoslavia); b. 10, Celije; ed.
Univ. of Ljubljana; Col. in Yugoslav Army,
World War II; Dir. of Pol. Dept. of Min. of
For. Affairs 45-; fmr. mem. Slovene Natl.
Liberation Com.; elected to First Parl. of
Slovene Rep. 46; rep. first spec. sesn. GA 47;
mem. SCOP 47.

Brunet, Alberto D. (Argentina); b. 92,
Buenos Aires; ed. naval school; in charge
of Com. of "Isla de los Estados" 33-34;
Comdr. minesweeper "Tucuman" 34; Prof.
School of Naval Warfare; Chief of Gen.
Staff of River Fleet 37, of Navy 38; Comdr.
school-ship cruiser "La Argentina" 39;
naval attaché in U. S. A. 40-; rep. UNCIO
45.

Brunn, Alice (Den.); b. 02, Copenhagen; ed.
Univ. of Copenhagen; Dir. of Maternity
Aid Inst. 28-30; fmr. mem. Child Welfare
Sect. and Care of Handicapped Persons
Sect. (Min. of Social Welfare); Sec. Child
Welfare Conf. of Northern Countries 36;
mem. natl. insurance system 41-45, chief of
system 45; Chief of Public Assistance of
Min. for Social Affairs 45-; rapp. Temp.
Social Welfare Com. 47.

Burger, Jacob W. (Neth.); b. 04, Willemstad,
N. Brabant; ed. Univ. of Utrecht, Univ. of
Amsterdam; fmr. atty. in Dordrecht; mem.
Socialist Dem. Labor Party 29-; fmr. Sec.
"Inst. for Ed. of Labourers," Dir. of Re-
gional Office of Dutch Soc. for Agric.; mem.
Municipal and Police Cts. of Arbitration of
Dordrecht, Min. of Internal Affairs; rep.
GA N. Y. 46.

Byrnes, James F. (U. S. A.); b. 79, Charles-
ton, S. Carolina; Solicitor 09-11; Rep. 10-
25; Sen. 30-41; Assoc.-Jus. U. S. A. Sup. Ct.

41-42; Dir. of Econ. Stabilization 42-43; fmr. Dir. of War Mobilization; Sec. of State 45-47; Chm. U. S. A. del. GA London 46; rep. SC 46.

Cáceres, Julián R. (Honduras); b. 92, Comayagua; ed. Univs. of San Salvador and Tegucigalpa; private sec. to pres. Bertrand 16; app. chief clerk in Min. of For. Relations 17; Gov. Dept. of Cortes 26-27; app. Gov. Dept. of Atlantida 28; sec. of Legation, Wash. 33-36, chargé d'affaires 36-39, Min. 39-43, Amb. 43-; mem. Governing Bd. of Pan Amer. Union; Chm. Honduran del. UNCIO 45.

Caclamanos, Demetrius (Greece); b. 72, Nauplia; ed. Athens Univ.; ed. *Asty* 92-01, *Neon Asty* 01-07; first sec. Paris 10-12; chargé d'affaires Rome 12-14; Min. in Petrograd 15-18, in London 18-35; first Greek del. LN Asmb. 26; rep. GA London 46.

Cadogan, Sir Alexander George Montagu (U. K.); b. 84; ed. Eton and Ox.; G. C. M. G., K. C. B.; attaché Constantinople 09; Min. to China 33, Amb. 35-36; Perm. Under-Sec. of State for For. Affairs 38-46; Chm. U. K. del. first phase Dumbarton Oaks Conf. 44; mem. U. K. del UNCIO 45; rep. GA N.Y. 46, SC 46-, AEC 46-, first spec. sesn. GA 47; rep. CCA 47-.

Camillo De Oliveira, Antonio (Brazil); b. 92, State of Minas Gerais; ed. Law School, Belo Horizonte; attaché to Min. of For. Affairs 16; first sec., Paris 34-38; Min. in La Paz 38, later to Costa Rica; head of Pol. and Dipl. Div. of For. Office 39-41; Acting Sec.-Gen., Min. for Ext. Relations; rep. Com. of Jurists Wash. 45, UNCIO 45, GA N. Y. 46.

Campbell, Richard Mitchelson (N. Zealand); b. 97; ed. Victoria Univ. Coll. and London School of Econ.; Ph. D.; private sec. to Prime Min. 26; sec.-economist to Min. of Fin. 31-35; econ. adviser Embassy, London 35-40, official sec. 40-; rep. Prep. Comn. 45, GA London 46.

Cárcano, Miguel Angel (Argentina); b. 89, Buenos Aires; ed. Univ. of Buenos Aires; Min. Plenipotentiary on mission to London to negotiate Anglo-Argentine Commercial Treaty 33; Min. of Agric., Industry and Commerce under Pres. Gen. Justo; Deputy and Pres. of Com. on Agrarian Legislation, Chamber of Deputies 34; Amb. to U. K.; rep. UNCIO 45.

Carías, Jr., Tiburcio (Honduras); b. 08, Tegucigalpa; ed. Univ. of Mex., Ox. and Liverpool Univs.; fmr. Inspector-Gen. of Honduran Consulate in Liverpool, Consul-Gen. 38-46; Min. to U. K. 46-; Chm. Honduran del. Intergov. Com. on Pol. Refugees in Evian and London 38, Prep. Comn. 45, GA 46, first spec. sesn. GA 47.

Cassell, C. Abayomi (Liberia); b. 06, Monrovia; ed. in liberal arts and law; clerk of Circuit Ct. of First Judicial Circuit of Montserrado Co. 28-30 (resigned); practiced law 30-39; revenue solicitor for Dept. of Jus. and atty. for Montserrado Co. 39-44; app. Atty.-Gen. 44; rep. GA N. Y. 46.

Castro, Héctor David (El Salvador); b. 94, San Salvador; ed. Natl. Univ. of El Salvador; LL. D.; dist.-atty. and later judge, San Salvador 17-19; Under-Sec. of Fin. 19; Sec. of Legation in Wash. 20-23, chargé d'affaires 23-27; Under-Sec. of For. Affairs 27-28; Min. of For. Affairs 31; Min. in Wash. 34-43; Amb. to U. S. A. 43-44 and 45-; mem. Governing Bd. of Pan Amer. Union; rep. Com. of Jurists, Wash. 45; Chm. El Salvador del. UNCIO 45; rep. GA N. Y. 46, first spec. sesn. GA 47.

Castro, Rodolfo Barón (El Salvador); b. San Salvador; ed. Natl. Inst. of El Salvador and studied law at Univ. of Madrid; sec. to Legation, Madrid 43-; rep. GA London 46.

Cattan, Henry; b. 06, Jerusalem, Palestine; ed. Paris and London Univs.; lawyer in Jerusalem 32-; rep. of Arab Higher Com. for Palestine at First Com. meetings of first spec. sesn. GA 47.

Chacón, Gustavo (Bolivia); b. 13; app. chief officer, Min. of Econ. 33; Min. of Econ. 43-44; fmr. Min. of For. Affairs; rep. Tin Com., London 41; del. Inter-Amer. Conf. on Probs. of War and Peace, Mex. 45; Chm. Bolivian del. UNCIO 45.

Chagla, Mohammed Ali Currim (India); b. 00, Bombay; ed. St. Xavier's School and Coll. in Bombay and Lincoln's Coll., Ox.; practiced at High Ct. Bar 22-41; Judge of High Ct. 41-; fmr. organizer and Vice-Pres. of Nationalist Party in Bombay; rep. GA N. Y. 46.

Chamoun, Camille (Lebanon); b. 00, Lebanon; ed. *Coll. des Frères* and law school in Beirut; LL. D.; Min. of Fin. 38-43; Min. of Interior 43-44; Min. in London 44-; rep. Prep. Comn. 45, GA London 46; Chm. Lebanese del. GA N. Y. 46.

Chang, Chun-Mai Carson (China); b. 86, Kiangsu; ed. Waseda Univ. Tokyo, Berlin Univ. and in England; became ed.-in-chief *Peking-Tientsin Shih Pao*, Tientsin 11, fmr. ed. *Young Nation* and assoc. ed. *Justice*; fmr. gen. mgr. *China Times*, Shanghai; mem. Council's Presidium 40-42; mem. People's Pol. Council since 38; rep. UNCIO 45.

Chang, P. C. (China); b. 92, Tientsin; ed. Nankai Middle School, China, and Clark and Columbia Univs., U. S. A.; Ph. D (Columbia), acting-principal of Nankai 16 19; dean of Tsing Hua Coll. 23-26; mem People's Pol. Council of China 38-40; Min to Turkey 40-42, to Chile 42-45; rep GA 46, ESC 46-; Vice-Chm. Comn. on Human Rights 47-; Chm. Working Group for Asia and Far East 47.

Charles, Joseph (Haiti); b. 07, Limbo; ed. *Notre Dame du Perpétuel Secours* and Free Law School; LL. D. (Free Law School); fmr. atty. and teacher of Natl. School; fmr. prof. at *Notre Dame Coll.*; fmr. Ct. Registrar, Judge, State-Sec. for Pub. Ed., M. P. and Chm. of Com. of For. Relations; Amb. to U. S. A.; mem. of Governing Bd. of Pan Amer. Union; Chm. of Haitian del. GA N. Y. 46.

Chernyshev, Pavel M. (U. S. S. R.); b. 09, co. of Tver; ed. For. Trade Inst., Moscow Fin. and Econ. Inst.; Dir. of Export Dept., later head of For. Dept. of Gov. Bank of U.S.S.R. 37-46; Adm. chm. of For. Trade Bank 39-44; Econ. adviser to U. S. S. R. del. to UN 46-; Vice-chm. Fiscal Comn., acting-chm. first sesn. of Fiscal Comn. 47.

Chieh, Liu (China); b. 06; ed. Ox. and Columbia Univs.; began pol. career as sec. in Leg. Yuan; adviser to Chinese del. to LN 32-39; first sec. and counsellor, Embassy in London 33-40; counsellor and Min., Embassy in Washington 40-45; Vice-Min. for For. Affairs 46-; mem. Chinese del. to Sugar Conf. 37, to Dumbarton Oaks Conf. 44, to UNCIO 45; rep. GA N. Y. 46, TC 47.

Chisholm, Brock (Can.); b. 96, Oakville, Ontario; M. D. (Univ. of Toronto) 24; Commandant of Northern Area, Med. Div. 42-44; Chm. of Can. Med. Procurement and Assignment Bd. 42-44; Chm. Health Com. 43-44; fmr. Dir.-Gen. and Maj.-Gen. of Med. Service; fmr. Deputy-Min. of Health in Dept. of Natl. Health and Welfare; Ex.-Sec. WHO Interim Comn. 46-.

Chow, Capt. Ying-Tsung (China); b. 01, Foochow, Fukien, China; ed. Chinese Naval Coll. in Chifoo and Nanking Naval Coll.; service and training with British Navy 29-33; senior officer in charge of naval offices outside China 39-41; naval attaché to U. K. 41-45; dir. of Naval Ordnance 45; rep. MSC 46-.

Churchill, Winston Spencer (U. K.); b. 74; ed. Harrow and Sandhurst; LL. D. (Harvard); C. H., M. P., F. R. S.; served in S. Afr. War and in World War I; Home Sec. 10-11; First Lord of Admiralty 11-15, 39-40; Prime Min. and Min. of Natl. Defence 40-45; Leader of Opposition 45-; co-author of Atlantic Charter 41; signer of Dec. by UN 42; attended Cairo and Teheran Confs. 43, Crimea Conf. 45.

Cisneros, Luis Fernán (Peru); b. 82, Paris; ed. San Marcos Univ.; mem. of staff, *La Nación*, Buenos Aires; dir. *La Prensa*, of Lima; Min. to Uru. 34-39; fmr. Amb. to Mex.; Amb. to Brazil; rep. UNCIO 45.

Claxton, Brooke (Can.); b. 98, Montreal; ed. Lower Canada Coll. and McGill Univ., Montreal; admitted to bar 21; app. a King's Counsel 39; elected to House of Commons, Montreal 40, and served as parl. asst. to Prime Min. W. L. Mackenzie King; Min. of Natl. Health and Welfare 44-; rep. ESC 46.

Clementis, Vladimír (Czech.); b. 02, Tisovec; ed. Charles Univ. in Prague; fmr. M. P.; Chief of Slovak Broadcast B. B. C. in London, World War II; Sec. of State in Min. of For. Affairs 45-; rep. GA N. Y. 46.

Cohen, Benjamín (Chile); b. 96, Concepción, Chile; ed. English School of Lota, Univ. of Chile and Georgetown Univ., Wash.; Ph. D. (Univ. of Chile); sec. Embassy, Wash. 23-27; prof. Georgetown Univ. 27-34; Amb. to Bolivia 39-45, to Venez. 45; chief of Inf. Planning Sect. GA London 46; Asst. Sec.-Gen. in charge of Pub. Inf. 46-.

Colban, Eric (Nor.); b. 76, Oslo; mem. of Min. of For. Affairs 16-18; Dir. of Minority Sect. of LN 19-27, of Disarmament Sect. 28-30; app. Min. to France 30, to Belg. and Luxembourg 31; rep. to Council, Asemb., and Disarmament Conf. of LN 30-32; Min. and later Amb. to U. K. 34-46; rep. to Prep. Comn. of UN, GA London 46; Chm. of Drafting Com. of Prep. Com. of ITO 47.

Colbjornsen, Ole (Nor.); b. 97, Vegaardshei; ed. Univ. of Oslo; fmr. fin. ed. *Arbeiderbladet* in Oslo; M. P. 37-40; app. Fin. Counsellor of Embassy in Wash. 40; rep. Int. Labour Conf. in Geneva 34, Conf. of Int. Monetary Stabilization in Wash. 43, Bretton Woods Conf. 44; present Alt.-Gov. Int. Monetary Fund and Int. Bank; rep. Int. Emergency Food Council; alt.-rep. GA N. Y. 46; rep. ESC 46, alt. 47.

Coldwell, J. (Canada); b. 88, Seaton, England; ed. Exeter Univ. Coll.; fmr. teacher in Canada; alderman of Regina, Saskatchewan 22-32; Chm. of Council of Inquiry into pub. service of Saskatchewan 23-30; elected to House of Commons 35; Parl. Leader of Co-operative Commonwealth Federation Party; rep. GA N. Y. 46.

Connally, Tom (U. S. A.); b. 77, McLennan Co., Texas; ed. Baylor Univ. and Univ. of Texas; LL. D.; elected to Texas State Legis. 01; fmr. prosecuting atty. McLennan Co.; Rep. 17-29; Sen. 29-; fmr. Chm. Sen. Com. on For. Relations; del. Inter-Parl. Union Confs. Geneva 24, Wash. 25, London 30 and Istanbul 34; rep. UNCIO 45, GA 46.

Contreras Labarca, Carlos (Chile); b. 99; ed. Univ. of Chile; Deputy 25; del. Seventh World Cong. of Communist Int. 35; fmr. Sec.-Gen. Communist Party of Chile; Sen.; rep. UNCIO 45.

Cordier, Andrew Wellington (U. S. A.); b. 01, Canton, Ohio; ed. Manchester Coll. in Indiana and Univ. of Chicago; chm. of dept. of hist. and pol. science Manchester Coll. 27-44; lecturer in social sciences Indiana Univ. 29-44; expert on int. security, Dept. of State 44-46; tech. expert U. S. A. del. UNCIO 45; chief of sect. Prep. Comn. 45; adviser to Ex.-Sec. of Prep. Comn. 45; to Pres. of GA London 46; Ex.-Asst. to Sec.-Gen. 46-.

Córdova, Roberto (Mex.); lawyer; fmr. Chm. Mex. group in Mex.-Amer. Claims Com.; fmr. legal counsellor Embassy, Wash.; fmr. head of legal dept. of For. Office; fmr. Amb. to Costa Rica; rep. GA 46, SC 46.

Costa Du Rels, Adolfo (Bolivia); b. 91, Sucre; ed. Corsica and Univ. of Paris; app. Second Sec. to Legation in Chile 18; Counsellor to Legation in Paris 21-32; app. Min. to Swit. 33, rep. LN; rep. Bolivian del. Chaco Peace Conf. 36; elected Chm. LN Council 39; Amb. to Argentina 41-44; mem. LN Liquidation Bd. 46; app. perm. rep. UN 46; rep. GA N. Y. 46.

Cranborne, The Right Honorable Viscount; Gascoyne-Cecil, Robert Arthur James (U. K.); b. 93; ed. Eton and Christ Church, Ox.; P. C.; Conservative M. P. for S. Dorset 29-41; Under-Sec. of State for For. Affairs 35-38 (resigned); Sec. of State for Dominion Affairs 40-42; Sec. of State for Colonies 42; Lord Privy Seal 42-43; Leader of House of Lords since 42; Sec. of State for Dominion Affairs since 43; rep. UNCIO 45.

Cruz-Coke, Eduardo (Chile); b. 99, Valparaíso; ed. in med.; rep. Conf. on Sexology in Europe 26; app. Min. of Health 37; fmr. adviser to Office of Worker's Insurance, Pres. Natl. Food Council; present Sen. of Chilean Cong., mem. of Conservative Party; mem. TC Visiting Mission to W. Samoa 47.

Cuenco, Mariano (Philippines); b. 88, Cebu; Rep. of 5th Dist. of Cebu 31-34; Gov. of Cebu 34-37; app. Sec. of Pub. Works 37; Sen. 41-; rep. GA N. Y. 46.

Darwin, Sir Charles Galton (U. K.); b. 87; ed. Marlborough Coll., Cambridge Univ.; O. B. E., M. C., M. A., Sc.D., F. R. S.; prof. of nat. philos., Edinburgh Univ. 23-36; Master of Christ's Coll., Cambridge 36-38; Dir. of Material Phys. Laboratory 38-; alt. rep. AEC 47-.

David, Wilmot A. (Liberia); formerly in For. Office, Monrovia, Liberia; present consul-gen. in Gr. Brit. and Northern Ire.; rep. GA London 46.

Davidson, George F. (Canada); b. 09, Bass River, Nova Scotia; ed. Univ. of Br. Columbia and Harvard Univ.; Ph.D. (Harvard); app. Supt. of Welfare and Neglected Children of Prov. of Br. Columbia 34; Ex.-Dir. of Vancouver Welfare Fed. and Council of Social Agencies 35; Dir. of Social Welfare for Br. Columbia and later Ex.-Dir. of Can. Welfare Council; Deputy-Min. of Welfare 44-; rep. ESC 47-, Social Comn. 47-.

Dávila, Carlos (Chile); b. 87, Los Angeles, Chile; ed. Univ. of Santiago; founder and dir. *La Nación* and *Los Tiempos*, Santiago newspapers, and magazine *Hoy;* awarded Cabot Prize for distinguished service in inter-Amer. relations in field of journalism; Amb. to U. S. A. 27-31; provisional Pres. of Chile 32; author of "Davila Plan" creating Inter-Amer. Devel. Comn.; rep. ESC 46.

De Diego, Mario (Panama); b. 08, Panama City; ed. Natl. Inst. and at Alabama; mem. of consular service 28-32; fmr. Chief of Protocol in For. Office; mem. First Consultative Meeting of Amer. Mins. of For. Affairs 41; app. Second Asst.-Sec. of For. Affairs 45; adviser of Panamanian del. UNCIO 45; Under-Sec. of For. Affairs 46-; rep. first spec. sesn. GA 47.

Dehousse, F. (Belg.); b. 06, Liege; ed. Univ. of Liege; LL.D. (Univ. of Liege); fmr. prin. asst. to Belg. Min. of Labour; co-author of socialist plan for reorganization of Belg. on fed. basis; ed. *Le Monde du Travail;* prof. Acad. of Int. Law, The Hague; prof. of int. law Univ. of Liege; rep. UNCIO 45, ESC 46, Comn. on Human Rights 46-.

Delgado, Francisco A. (Philippines); b. 86, Bulacan, Bulacan; ed. in Manila and Indiana State Univ., Univ. of Chicago, and Yale; LL.B. (Indiana State Univ.); practiced law in Indianapolis and Manila; fmr. Resident Comr. of Philippines to U. S. A.; dir. Philippine Bar Assn., and Int. Bar Assn.; judge Ct. of Appeals; mem. House of Rep.; rep. UNCIO 45.

Dendramis, Vassili (Greece); b. 83, Athens; ed. Univ. of Athens; LL.D. (Univ. of Athens); sec. of Legation in Bucharest 14-19; per. rep. of Greece to LN 23-27; Min. in Sofia 28-32, in Cairo 33-36, to Argentina, Brazil, Chile and Uru. 36-45; Amb. to U.S.A. 47-; rep. ESC 46, GA N. Y. 46, first spec. sesn. GA 47.

Dennis, Gabriel L. (Liberia); LL.D. (Emporia Coll. Kansas); Belg. Consul in Liberia 22-44; Sec. of Treas. 32-40; del. LN 43; Sec. of State 44-; rep. UNCIO 45; Chm. Liberian del. GA London 46.

Dihigo y López Trigo, Ernesto (Cuba); b. 96, Havana; ed. Univ. of Havana; prof. of Roman Law Havana Univ. since 17; dean of Law School 39-42; mem. Superior Electoral Tribunal 33-38; mem. organizing com. for Inter-Amer. Acad. of Compar. and Int. Law, mem. of its Curatorium and dir. of Acad.; rep. UNCIO 45, GA 46.

Djordjevic, Krista (Yugoslavia); b. 92, Zagreb; organized transfer of children from famine-stricken areas to fertile lands, World War I; Pres. Initiative Com. of Red Cross of occupied and liberated Yugoslavia, World War II; rep. Yugoslav Red Cross with Mil. Mission in London 44; Chief of Dept. of Invalids of Min. of Social Affairs of Serbia 45-; Vice-chm. Temp. Social Welfare Com. 47.

Drakeford, Arthur S. (Australia); b. 87; elected to Parl. of State of Victoria (Labour mem.) 27; app. Pres. of Victorian branch of Labour Party 29; elected rep. to House of Fed. Parl. 34; rep. Int. Civil Aviation Conf. in Chicago 44; Second Vice-Pres. of PICAO, Montreal 46; Min. for Air and for Civil Aviation 41-; Pres. of first Asmb. of ICAO.

Ducháček, Ivo (Czech.); fmr. war corr. Prague daily *Lidove Noving* in Paris; chief of cabinet of Min. of State in Min. of For. Affairs in London during World War II; mem. Provisional Natl. Asmb., Chm. of For. Affairs Com.; rep. GA London 46.

Eaton, Charles A. (U. S. A.); b. 69; ed. Newton Theol. Inst., Mass.; first pastorate was First Baptist Church, Natick Mass.; later served as pastor in Toronto, Canada, in Cleveland and in N . Y.; app. head of natl. service sect. of U. S. A. Shipping Bd. Emergency Fleet Corp. 17; Rep. since 24, Chm. of For. Affairs Com. of House of Rep.; rep. UNCIO 45.

Echandía, Darío (Colombia); b. 97; Chaparral, Tolima; ed. *Colegio Mayor de Nuestra Señora del Rosario*, Bogota; mgr. Agric. Mortgage Bank 27-31; Sen. 31-33; Deputy 34; head of Min. of For. Affairs 34-35; Min. of Natl. Ed. 35-36; fmr. Amb. to Holy See; Amb. to U. K.; rep. GA London 46.

Eden, (Robert) Anthony (U. K.); b. 97; ed. Eton and Christ Church, Ox.; LL.D.; P.C., M. P., M. C.; Under-Sec. of State for For. Affairs 31-33; Sec. of State for For. Affairs 35-38 (resigned); Sec. of State for War 40, for For. Affairs 40-45; M. P. 45-; attended Moscow Conf. 43; Chm. U. K. del. UNCIO 45.

Egeland, Leif (U. of S. Afr.); b. 03; ed. Natal Univ. Coll., and Trinity Coll., Ox.; admitted to bar 31; fmr. M. P. for Zululand and Berea, Durban; mem. S. Afr. Goodwill del. to India 36; Min. in Stockholm 44-; rep. GA London 46.

el-Khouri, Faris (Syria); b. 79, Kfeir; ed. Amer. Univ. of Beirut; Deputy of Damascus to Ottoman Parl. in Constantinople 14-18; Counsellor of State 18; Min. of Fin. 20, of Pub. Instruction 26; Deputy of Damascus and Pres. of Parl. 36-39, 43-44 and 45-; prof.

Syrian Univ. of Damascus and mem. Arab Acad. since 19; Prime Min. 44-45; Chm. Syrian del. Arab L. Cong. Cairo 45, UNCIO 45, GA 46, first spec. sesn. GA 47; Chm. Fifth Com. GA 46; rep. SC 47-, AEC 47-, CCA 47.

el-Pachachi, Nedim (Iraq); b. 14, Baghdad; ed. London Univ.; Ph. D. (London Univ.); app. official of Iraq Govt. 35, head of Oil Sect. 37, head of Dept. of Mines 40, Dir. Gen. of Min. of Econ. 43-; rep. GA London 46.

el-Wadi, Shaker (Iraq); b. 99, Baghdad; ed. Instanbul, Staff Coll. in Camberley, and Senior Officers Course in Sheerness; fmr. cadet in Turkish Army; fmr. instructor to Iraq Army; chargé d'affaires Teheran 39-41; consul.-gen. Palestine 43; chargé d'affaires London 44-; rep. Prep. Comn. 45, GA London 46.

Endlakachou, Makonnen S. (Eth.); b. 93; app. controller of Franco-Eth. Ry. 18; Min. of Commerce 26; Min. to England and Eth. rep. LN 31-33; Gov. Addis Ababa 33-34; Gen. commanding Ogaden front during Italo-Eth. War; Pres. Council of Ministers 43-44; Prime Min. 44-; Chm. Eth. del. UNCIO 45.

Entezam, Nasrollah (Iran); b. 00, Teheran; ed. Univs. of Teheran and Paris; sec. Legation in Paris 26, in Warsaw 28, in London 28-29; rep. World Econ. Conf. London 33; chargé d'affaires Berne 34-38; dir. of pol. dept. Min. of For. Affairs 38-40; fmr. Min. of Pub. Health; fmr. Min. of State for For. Affairs; rep. Ex. Com. of Prep. Comn. 45, Prep. Comn. 45, GA 46, first spec. sesn. GA 47.

Eriksson, Gustaf H. (Sweden); b. 92, Upsala; ed. in law, Univ. of Stockholm; app. Under-Sec. of State in Min. of Fin. 31; app. Dir.-Gen. of Swedish Bd. of Trade 36; Min. without Portfolio 38; app. Min. of Food and Supply 39; Min. of Commerce 41; app. Min. to U. S. A. 45; rep. GA N. Y. 46; Chm. Swedish del. first spec. sesn. GA 47.

Erkin, Feridun Cemal (Turkey); b. 00; ed. Paris Fac. of Law; fmr. first sec. Embassy, London; fmr. consul.-gen. in Berlin and Beirut; fmr. dir.-gen. of Pol. Dept.; app. asst. sec.-gen. to Min. of For. Affairs 42; rep. UNCIO 45.

Escudero Guzmán, Julio (Chile); ed. School of Higher Int. Research in Paris, and Int. Acad. of La Haya; prof. of int. affairs Univ. of Chile; adviser to Min. of For. Affairs; del. Conf. on Study of Int. Relations Prague 38, Inter-Amer. Conf. on Probs. of War and Peace Mex. 45; rep. UNCIO 45.

Espil, Felipe (Argentina); b. 87; ed. Univ. of Buenos Aires; first sec. Embassy Wash. 19, counsellor 21; Min. to Neth. 28, to Den. and Nor. 29; Amb. to U. S. A. 31-43; rep. GA London 46.

Evatt, Herbert Vere (Australia); b. 94, New S. Wales; ed. Sydney Univ.; mem. Legis. Asmb., N. S. W. 25-29; Judge Fed. High Ct. of Australia 30-40 (resigned); Min. of Ext. Affairs and Atty.-Gen. 41-; rep. UN-CIO 45, Ex. Com. of Prep. Comn. 45, Prep. Comn. 45, SC 46-, AEC 46-.

Exintaris, George (Greece); b. 88, Margara, Eastern Thrace; ed. Univ. of Paris; Deputy for Kavalla 26; Min. of Agric. 28; Gov.-Gen. of Salonica 32-33; Deputy for Rhodope 33-36; app. Greek rep. on Advisory Council for Italy 44; rep. GA London 46.

Fabela Alfaro, Isidro (Mex.); b. 82, State of Mex.; ed. Univ. of Mex.; LL. D.; Deputy for Dist. of Ixtlahuac, Mex. 12; fmr. Act-ing-Sec. of State for For. Affairs; Mex. rep. Claims Com. between Mex. and Italy 37-40; fmr. Pres. of Mex. del. to LN; Gov. State of Mex. 42-45; Judge ICJ 46-.

Fabregat, Enrique Rodríguez (Uru.); b. 98, San Jose; ed. Univ. of Montevideo; fmr. Deputy, Vice-Pres. of House of Deputies, Min. of Ed. (resigned 32); fmr. prof. Univ. of Rio de Janeiro, visiting prof. Univ. of Illinois, Mills Coll. in California; Chm. of Uru. del. first spec. sesn. GA 47.

Faisal, H. R. H. Ibn Abdul Aziz Al Saud (Saudi Arabia); b. 05, Riad; ed. Riad; headed pol. missions to Europe in 19, 26 and 32; Viceroy of Hedjaz 26-; Min. of For. Affairs 34-; Chm. of Saudi Arabian del. to Palestine Confs. in London in 39 and 46, UNCIO 45, Prep. Comn. 45, GA 46, first spec. sesn. GA 47.

Fawzi, Mahmoud Bey (Eqypt); b. 00, Cairo; ed. Univ. of Cairo, Royal Univ. of Rome, Liverpool Univ. in England and Columbia Univ.; vice-consul in N. Y. and N. Orleans 26-29; consul in Kobe, Japan 29-36; dir. of nationalities dept. Min. of For. Affairs 39-41; consul.-gen. in Jerusalem 41-44; fmr. counsellor Wash.; rep. SC 46; alt.-rep. GA N. Y. 46; rep. first spec. sesn. GA 47.

Fay, Brig. Gen. Pierre (France); b. 99, Dinan; ed. St. Cyr Mil. Coll., *Ecole Supérieure de Guerre;* mem. *"Chasseurs Alpins"* World War I; mem. French Mil. Mission, Brazil 32-35; fmr. instructor *Ecole Supérieur de Guerre aérienne;* Asst. C.-of-S. French Air Force in Far East 39-40; Comdr. of Group in Tunisia with Allied Air Forces 42-43; Dir. Mil. School in Morocco 43-44; asst. to Chief of French Mission in Far East 45; Comdr. French Air Forces in Indo-China 45; Air rep. MSC 47-.

Federspiel, Per (Den.); b. 05; ed. Harrow School, England, and Copenhagen Univ.; practising barrister in Copenhagen since 37; Min. for Special Affairs 45-; rep. GA 46.

Fenard, Vice-Adm. R. (France); b. 87; ed. French Naval School; Capt. destroyer "Vauban" 30; Dir. of Naval Sci. Research Service-Liaisons with British Admiralty 40; perm. Gen.-sec. in French Afr.; head of Naval Mission in Wash. 43; naval attaché in Wash. 45; rep. MSC 46-.

Feonov, Nikolai I. (U.S.S.R.); b. 05; ed. Acad. of For. Trade, Moscow; deputy trade rep. of U .S. S. R. in U. K. 38-44; Deputy Dir.-Gen. of UNRRA 44-46; head of U. S. S. R. del. to UNRRA's fourth session, Atlantic City 46; rep. ESC 46.

Ferguson, George Victor (Can.); b. 97, Cupar, Scotland; ed. Univ. of Alberta in Edmonton, Ox. Univ.; Can. Expeditionary Force 16-19; app. managing ed. of *Winnipeg Free Press* 34, ex. ed. 44-46; ed. *Montreal Daily Star* 46-; Rapp. Sub-comn. Freedom of Inf. and of Press 47.

Fernández y Fernández, Joaquín (Chile); b. 97, Santiago; ed. Univ. of Santiago; app. second sec. of Legation in Holland 19; Intendente of Valparaiso 30; fmr. Mayor of Santiago; Min. to Uru. 39-42, Amb. 42; Min. of For. Affairs 42-46; Amb. to France 47-; Chm. Chilean del. UNCIO 45.

Fernández y Medina, Benjamín (Uru.); b. 73, Montevideo; sec. Bu. of Health 02-05; Under-Sec., Min. of For. Affairs 11; Min. of Interior a. i. 07-10, of For. Affairs a. i. 16; Min. to Ger. and Holland 16, to Spain and Portugal 17-30, to Cuba 30-35; del. LN Asmb. 20 and 22-26; honorary counsellor of Legation in Spain; rep. GA London 46.

Fletcher, Sir Angus Somerville (U.K.); b. 83; ed. S. Afr. Coll. Cape Town; K. C. M. G., C. B. E.; Royal Field Artillery 15-19; mem. Br. War Mission to U.S.A. 18; Natl. Industrial Conf. Bd. (U.S.A.) 19-22; Dir. Br. Library of Inf. N. Y. 28-41; consul Buffalo, N. Y. 43-; Chm. HC 46.

Foo Ping-Sheung (China); b. 95; ed. Hong Kong Univ.; LL.D.; sec. Chinese del. Peace Conf. Paris 21; Vice-Min. of For. Affairs 41; Amb. to U.S.S.R. 43-; attended Moscow Conf. 43; rep. GA London 46, SC 46.

Forde, Francis Michael (Australia); b. 90, Mitchell, Queensland; ed. Christian Brothers' School in Toowoomba, Queensland; mem. Queensland Parl. 17-22; entered Federal House of Rep. 22; deputy-leader of Australian Labour Party since 32; Min. for Army; Deputy Prime Min.; rep. UNCIO 45.

Forsyth, Douglas David (U. of S. Afr.); b. 96, Pietermartizburg, Natal; ed. Transvaal Univ. Coll. in Pretoria; Magistrate 25-34; Pub. Service Inspector 34-37; Under Sec., Dept. of Social Welfare 37-39; Sec. for S.W. Africa and Chief Native Comr. 39-41; Sec. to Prim. Min. and Sec. for External Affairs 41-; rep. UNCIO 45, GA N.Y. 46.

Franco y Franco, Tulio (Dominican Rep.); b. 93, Santiago, Dominican Republic; ed. *Ecole Libre des Sciences Politiques*, Paris; attended Conf. of Signatories of Perm. Ct. of Int. Jus. 26; del. LN Asmb. 26-28; Judge Ct. of Appeals 29-31, Judge of Sup. Ct. 34-44; fmr. Min. to Haiti; rep. UNCIO 45.

Fraser, Peter (N. Zealand); b. 84, Scotland; migrated to N. Zealand in 10; fmr. Pres. Auckland Gen. Labourer's Union, sec. Social Dem. Party, and Pres. Labour Party; first elected to Parl. in 18; Mem. Ex. Council and assumed portfolios of Min. of Ed., Min. of Health, Min. of Marine, and Min. in charge of Mental Hospitals, Inspection of Machinery, and Police Dept.; Chm. N. Zealand del. UNCIO 45, GA London 46; Chm. Third Com. GA London 46.

Freitas-Valle, Cyro de (Brazil); b. 96, Sao Paulo; ed. Sao Paulo Law School; Litt.D.; app. second sec. in Buenos Aires 19; counsellor in Wash. 34-36; Min. to La Paz, Buenos Aires, Havana and Bucharest 36-38; Acting-Min. of For. Affairs 39; Amb. to Berlin 39-42; Dir. Gen. Fed. For. Trade Council 43-44; Amb. to Canada; rep. UNCIO 45, Ex. Com. of Prep. Comn. 45, Prep. Comn. 45, GA London 46, SC 46.

Frisch, Hartvig (Den.); b. 93; ed. Copenhagen Univ.; magistrate 17; asst. at Aarhuus 18 and Met. School Copenhagen 23; Pres. *Studentersamfundet* 23-25; mem. Rigsdag 26; Chm. Social-Dem. Group 35-40; prof. at Univ. of Copenhagen; M.P.; del. LN; rep. UNCIO 45, GA 46.

Frisch, Ragnar (Nor.); b. 95, Oslo; ed. Oslo Univ.; Ph.D. (Oslo Univ.) 26; visiting prof. at Yale Univ. 30; lecturer at Sorbonne 31; prof. of econ. at Oslo Univ. 31-; founder of Econometric Society in 31; chief publ. of *Econométrica* 33-; Dir. of Research of Econ. Inst. of Oslo Univ.; mem. of Nor. Gov.'s Econ. and Fin. Council; Chm. Econ. and Employment Comn. 47.

Fusco, Antonio Gustavo (Uru.); b. Montevideo, Uru.; ed. Univ. of Montevideo; Deputy 30-33; practised law and worked as journalist 33-42; Deputy 43-; rep. GA London 46.

Gallagher, Manuel C. (Peru); b. 85, Lima; ed. *Colegio de la Recoleta* and San Marcos Univ., Lima; dean of Bar Assn.; fmr. adviser to various N. Amer. firms, and counsel to Peruvian Chamber of Commerce; app. Min. of Jus. and Labor 42, Min. of For. Affairs 44; Chm. Peruvian del. UNCIO 45.

Gallais, Hugues le (Luxembourg); b. 96, Dommeldange, Luxembourg; ed. Univ. of Liege and in Zurich; rep. of Luxembourg Steel Industry in Paris, London, Tokyo and Bombay 19-39; chargé d'affaires, U.S.A. 40, Min. 40-; rep. UNCIO 45, GA N.Y. 46, first spec. sesn. GA 47.

Gallego, Manuel Viola (Philippines); b. 93, San Miguel, Bulacan; ed. Univ. of Philippines; J.D. (Northwestern Univ.) 20; Pres. of Manila Tobacco Assn., Katubusan Cigar and Cigarette Factory, United Holding and Management Co.; Mgr. of El Ahorro Insular; Assemblyman 38-46; Sec. of Pub. Instruction 46-; rep. GA London 46.

Gálvez, Virgilio Roberto (Honduras) b. 11, Santa Barbara; ed. Univ. of Leon, Nicar. and Cen. Univ., Tegucigalpa; fmr. prof. *Colegio Independencia of Santa Barbara*; ed. writer *El Crenista* 31-33; Clerk, Min. of Fin. 33-34, chief, legal sect. 34-35, chief adm. officer 35-42; Sub-Sec. of Fin., Pub. Credit and Commerce; rep. UNCIO 45.

García Godoy, Emilio (Dominican Rep.); b. 94, La Vega; fmr. journalist; chargé d'affaires Paris 29-30; first sec. and later counsellor of Legation, Wash. 34-38; Min. to Haiti 38, to Cuba 39-42; sec. to Pres. 42; Min. of Sanitation and Pub. Assistance 44; fmr. Amb. to U.S.A.; del. LN; rep. UNCIO 45; Chm. of del. to GA N.Y. 46.

García Granados, Jorge (Guatemala); b. 00, Guatemala City; ed. in France and *Univ. Nacional* of Guatemala; app. sec. of Legation in El Salvador 20, Gr. Brit. 21; mem. of Cong. 28-43; prof. at Univ. of Guatemala 29-34, Univ. of Mexico 39-43; Pres. of Const. Asmb. 44, of Cong. 45; app. Amb. to U.S.A. 45; mem. Governing Bd. of Pan Amer. Union; alt. rep. GA N.Y. 46; Chm. of Guatemala del. spec. sesn. GA 47; rep. SCOP 47.

Gardiner, James Garfield (Can.); b. 83; ed. Manitoba Coll., Winnipeg; Prin. Temberg Pub. School 11; Mayor of Lemberg, Sask. 20; Premier 26-29; Min. of Ed. 28-29; Premier and Provincial Treas. 34-35; M.P. for Melville Div., Sask. 40-; Commonwealth Min. of Natl. War Services 40-41; Min. of Agric.; rep. GA London 46.

Garreau, Roger (France); b. 91, Dôle, Jura; ed. *Ecole nationale des langues orientales vivantes*, Paris, and also Sorbonne; dipl. service successively in Bangkok, Peiping, Moscow, Indo-China, Zagreb, Cairo, Hamburg, Lausanne and Zurich 13-40; del. of Provisional Govt. of Free France to Moscow 42-45; Amb. to Poland 45-; participated in confs. concerned with settlement of Franco-Siamese question 27-31, for

Franco-Chinese Treaty 32, for settlement of Franco-Turkish dispute over Alexandretta 38; rep. TC 47.

Garrod, Air Chief Marshall, Sir Guy (U.K.); b. 91, London; ed. Ox.; K.C.B., O.B.E., M.C., D.F.C.; fmr. instructor R.A.F. Staff Coll.; deputy-dir. of organization and dir. of equipment, Air Min. 33-39; air mem. for training on Air Council 40-43; later deputy air officer C-in-C for India, then S.E. Asia; Acting Air C-in-C in S.E. Asia 44-45; rep. MSC 46-.

Gavrilović, Stoyan (Yugoslavia); b. 96, Belgrade; ed. Geneva; head of Yugoslav del. to LN Council and Asmb.; fmr. asst. pol. dir. Belgrade For. Office; first Yugoslav dipl. rep. to S. Afr.; Dir. Yugoslav Inf. Office in N. Y. 43; Under-Sec. of State for For. Affairs; rep. Prep. Comn. 45, GA London 46; Chm. Hdqrs. Planning Inspection Group 46.

Gerbrandy, Pieter Sjoerds (Neth.); b. 85, Goengamieden, Prov. of Friesland; ed. Amsterdam Free Univ.; mem. Friesland Prov. Com. 19-30; prof. Amsterdam Free Univ. 30-39; Min. of Jus. 39; fmr. Prime Min. and Min. for the Co-ordination of Warfare; rep. GA London 46.

Gerig, Benjamin (U.S.A.); b. 94, Smithville, Ohio; ed. Goshen (Ind.) Coll., Univ. of Illinois, Univ. of Geneva; prof. of pol. econ. at Univ. of Illinois 21-23; prof. of econ. at Simmons College, Boston 23-28; mem. LN Sec. Inf. and Mandates Sects. 29-39; assoc.-prof. of govt. at Haverford Coll. 40-42; app. to Dept. of State 42, chief of Div. of Dependent Area Affairs; adviser on trusteeship questions to U.S.A. del. to UNCIO 45, to GA 46; mem. of U.S.A. del. to Dumbarton Oaks Conf. 44, to Prep. Comn. 45; rep. TC 47.

Ghani, Ghassam (Iran); b. 94, Sahzevar, Iran; ed. Amer. Univ. of Beirut and in N.Y.; M.D.; rep. Int. Red Cross Lea. 24; fmr. mem. of House of Reps.; Min. of Pub. Health 43, of Ed. 44; prof. of medicine at Univ. of Teheran; rep. UNCIO 45, GA N.Y. 46.

Ghavam, Ahmad (Iran); b. 72; held various cabinet posts 10-23; Gov.-Gen. of Korasan Prov. 18; app. Premier, Min. of Interior, Min. of For. Affairs 46; Chm. Iranian del. GA N.Y. 46.

Giambruno, Cyro (Uru.); b. 98, Mercedes, Uru.; ed. Univ. of Montevideo; M.D. (Univ. of Montevideo); after graduation, practised med. in Fray Marcos, and was dir. of local newspaper at same time; elected Deputy 34, re-elected 38 and became Pres. of Chamber of Deputies; Min. of Pub. Instruction 41-43; app. Sen. 43; rep. UNCIO 45.

Gibson, Joseph Lemuel (Liberia); b. 98, Greenville, Sinoe Co.; ed. Cuttington High School in Maryland Co.; elected to House of Rep. 33, to Sen. 35; Chm. Ways and Means and Fin. Coms. of Sen. and mem. For. Affairs Com.; app. Chm. True Whig Party in Sinoe Co. 44; rep. UNCIO 45.

Gildersleeve, Virginia C. (U.S.A.); b. 77, N.Y.; ed. Brearley School (N.Y.), Barnard Coll. and Columbia Univ.; Ph.D. (Columbia); mem. of fac. of Barnard Coll. since 00; fmr. Dean of Barnard; mem. Bd. of Trustees of Inst. of Int. Ed.; first Chm. of Com. on Int. Relations of Amer. Assn. of Univ. Women; rep. UNCIO 45.

Gjoeres, Axel (Sweden); b. 89, Smedjebacken; ed. in economics at Commercial Coll. in Stockholm, Co-operative Coll. in Manchester, England; Chief of Div. of Co-operative Federation, Stockholm 26-38; app. Dir.-Gen. of Bd. of Trade 38: Min. of Supply 41-47; Min. of Commerce 47-; rep. GA N.Y. 46.

Glass, David V. (U.K.); b. 11, London; ed. Univ. of London; research sec. of Population Investigation Com. 36-; chief stat. of Br. Petroleum Comn. in Wash., chief of overseas munitions stat. in Br. Min. of Supply World War II; present mem. Med. and Biological Com.; Dir. of family census, Mem. Stat. Com. of Royal Comn. on Population; Rapp. Population Comn. 47.

Goedhart, Gerrit Jan van Heuven (Neth.); b. 01, Bussum; ed. Univ. of Leiden; chief ed. of *De Telegraaf* 30-33; app. ed.-in-chief of *Utrechtsch Neuwsblad* 33; co-ed. of underground newspaper *Het Parool* World War II, now chief ed.; Min. of Jus. 44-45 (resigned); Chm. Sub-comn. Freedom of Inf. and of Press 47.

Golunsky, S. A. (U.S.S.R.); b. 95, Moscow; ed. Univ. of Moscow; LL.D.; corr. mem. U.S.S.R. Acad. of Sci.; fmr. prof. All-Union Acad. of Law and Mil. Acad. of Law; Dean of Inst. of Law, Acad. of Science; expert consultant of People's Commissariat of For. Affairs; rep. Dumbarton Oaks Conf. 44, UNCIO 45.

Gómes, Henrique de Souza (Brazil); b. 07, Rio de Janeiro; ed. in law at Univ. of Rio de Janeiro; fmr. Sec. to Embassies at Montevideo and Rome; Asst.-Chief of Pol. and Dipl. Dept. of Min. of For. Relations 42-44; C.-of-S. to Min. of For. Relations 44-46; Sec.-Gen. of del. to UNCIO 45; alt. rep. GA N.Y. 46; alt. rep. first spec. sesn. GA 47, SC 47; rep. Com. of Experts 47.

González Videla, Gabriel (Chile); b. 98; ed. *Liceo de La Serena* and Univ. of Chile; Deputy 30, 32, 37; Pres. of Radical Party 32, 38; Min. to France, Belg. and Luxembourg 39-41; Amb. to Brazil 43-44; rep. UNCIO 45.

González Fernández, Alberto (Colombia); b. 03, Bogota; ed. Columbia Univ., Nuremberg, Ger., and Dipl. and Consular Acad., Vienna; newspaper ed. 29-30; served in Colombian Legations in Wash., Stockholm and the Vatican 34-39; app. sec.-gen. of Min. of For. Affairs in 30 and again in 39; app. Amb. to Ecua. in 44; rep. UNCIO 45.

Gonzalvo, Francisco Antonio (Dominican Rep.); b. 95, La Romana; ed. in med. at Univ. of Maryland, M.D.; Senator 45-46; rep. GA London 46.

Gousev, Feodor Tarasovich (U.S.S.R.); b. 05, Leningrad Region; ed. Leningrad Univ.; Leningrad State Office 31-36; with Commissariat for For. Affairs 37-42, chief of second European dept. 39-42; Min. to Can. 42-43; Amb. to Gr. Brit. 43-; rep. GA 46.

Grant, Moses N. (Liberia); b. 92; ed. in Sierra Leone and in prep. dept. of Liberia Coll. and grad. of a mil. training school; clerk in P.O. of Monrovia 10-12, in Interior Dept. 12-13; Paymaster 22-25; first Inspector Gen. of Troops, Liberian Frontier Force 22-24; Commanding Officer of Liberian Frontier Force; rep. UNCIO 45.

Gromyko, Andrei A. (U.S.S.R.); b. 09, Gromyki near Gomel; ed. Inst. of Econ., Moscow; counsellor Embassy, Wash. 39-43; Amb. to U.S.A. and Min. to Cuba 43-46; Deputy-Min. of For. Affairs 46-; Chm. U.S.S.R. del. Dumbarton Oaks Conf. 44; Acting-Chm. U.S.S.R. del UNICO 45; rep. Ex. Com. of Prep. Comn 45, Prep. Comn. 45, GA 46, SC 46-, AEC 46-, first spec. sesn. GA 47; rep. CCA 47.

Guerra y Sánchez, Ramiro (Cuba); b. 80, Batabano, Havana Prov.; ed. Univ. of Havana; prof. of Spanish colonial and Cuban hist., Univ. of Havana 27-30; rep. Conf. on Food and Agric., Hot Springs 44, Mon. and Fin. Conf., Bretton Woods, UNCIO 45, ESC 46.

Guerrero, J. Gustavo (El Salvador); b. 76, San Salvador; ed. San Salvador and Guatemala Univs.; LL.D.; Min. to France, Italy and Spain respectively 12-30; fmr. Min. of For. Affairs, Jus. and Pub. Ed.; Pres. 10th LN Asmb. 29; Vice-Pres. Perm. Ct. of Int. Jus. 31-36, Pres. 37-40; Pres. Int. Dipl. Acad. Paris; rep. Prep. Comn. 45, GA London 46; Pres. ICJ 46-.

Guichón, Juan F. (Uru.); b. 94, Durazno, Uru.; founded and directed for 26 years newspaper *El Heraldo*, published in Florida, Uru.; sec.-gen. of Batista Party and mem. of its natl. ex. com.; elected to Chamber of Rep. three times; Pres. Cong. of Free Journalists of Interior 33-42; rep. UNCIO 45.

Gutiérrez, Francisco de Paula (Costa Rica); b. 80, San Jose; ed. in econ. sciences, Columbia Univ.; twice elected to Cong.; V.-Pres. of Chamber of Deputies 32-34; Sec. of Treas. 37-39, 43-44; mem. Governing Bd. of Pan Amer. Union; Chm. of Costa Rican del. to Mon. Conf. at Bretton Woods; Amb. to U.S.A. 44-; Chm. of Costa Rican del. GA N.Y. 46, first spec. sesn. GA 47.

Gutt, Camille (Belg.); b. 84; ed. Brussels; LL.D.; sec.-gen. Belgian del. at Reparations Com. 19; Fin. Min. 34-35; Min. of Natl. Defence and of Communications 40-42; fmr. Min. of Fin. and Min. of Econ. Affairs; Managing-Dir. and Chm. of Ex. Bd. of Int. Mon. Fund 46-.

Hackworth, Green H. (U.S.A.); b. 83, Prestonburg, Kentucky; ed. Valparaiso, Georgetown and George Wash. Univs.; atty. State Dept. 16-18, solicitor 25-31, legal adviser 31-46; del. Conf. on Cod. of Int. Law, The Hague 30, 8th Int. Conf. of Amer. States Lima 38, 8th Amer. Sci. Cong. Wash. 40; adviser 2nd meeting of Min. of For. Affairs of Amer. Republics Havana 40; Judge ICJ 46-.

Hadi, Ibrahim Bey Abdel (Egypt); b. 98, Zarka; ed. Univ. of Cairo; fmr. prominent mem. of Students Nationalist Com.; Vice-Chm. of Saadist Party; Min. of Pub. Health; rep. UNCIO 45.

Haekal Pasha, Mohamed Hussein (Egypt); b. 88, Kafr Ghannam; ed. Univ. of Cairo and in Paris; fmr. prof. of public law at Univ. of Egypt, chief ed. of *Assyassa*, Min. of Ed.; present Pres. of Liberal Const. Party and Egyptian Senate; rep. GA N.Y. 46.

Hakim, George (Lebanon); b. Tripoli; ed. Amer. Univ. of Beirut, *Ecole Française de Droit* in Beirut; instructor in econ. at Amer. Univ. of Beirut 34-43, adjunct prof. in econ. 43-46; Counsellor of Legation in Wash. 46-; rep. GA N.Y. 46; alt. rep. ESC 46-.

Halifax, First Earl of; Irwin, First Baron; Wood, Edward Frederick Lindlay (U.K.); b. 81, near Exeter; ed. Eton and Christ Church, Ox.; K.G., P.C., G.C.S.I., G.C.I.E.; Under-Sec. Min. of Natl. Service 17-19; Viceroy and Gov.-Gen. of India 26-31; leader of House of Lords 35-38; Sec. of State for War 35; Lord Privy Seal 35-37; Sec. of State for For. Affairs 38-40; Amb. to U.S.A. 41-46; Chm. U.K. del. second phase of Dumbarton Oaks Conf. 44; rep. UNCIO 45.

Hambro, Carl Joachim (Nor.); b. 85, Bergen; ed. Univ. of Oslo; ed. Oslo daily *Morgenbladet* 13-41; mem. Storting 19-; Pres. of Odelsting of Nor. Parl. 26-; mem. Nor. del. LN Asmb. 26-46; mem. Supervisory Com.

of LN 26-46, Chm. 37-46; Pres. LN Asmb. 39; rep. GA 46.

Hambro, Edvard (Nor.); b. 11, Oslo; ed. Vestheim School in Oslo, Oslo Univ., Geneva Univ. and Yale; temp. collaborator of LN Sec. 33; Sec.-Gen. World Lea. of Norsemen; first sec. Royal Nor. Min. of For. Affairs, London and Oslo 43-45; assoc.-chief of legal sect. Prep. Comn. 45, chief 45; Registrar ICJ 46-.

Hanc, Josef (Czech.); b. 95, Libstat, Czech.; ed. Prague Univ.; entered dipl. service in 31, and has served in Prague, the Far East, London, N.Y., and Wash.; mem. of fac. Fletcher School of Law and Diplomacy, Boston 39-43; fmr. consul-gen. and dir. of Czech. Econ. Service in N.Y.; rep. UNCIO 45, ESC 46, GA N.Y. 46.

Harris, Sir Sidney (U.K.); b. 76; ed. Queen's Coll., Ox.; Sec. of Royal Comn. on Mines 06-09; rep. on Perm. Advisory Com. of LN for Social Questions 22; Asst. Under-Sec. of State, Home Office 35-47; mem. U.K. del. to ESC 46, GA N.Y. 46; rep. Social Comn. 47.

Harrison, Wallace K. (U.S.A.); b. 95, Worcester, Mass.; ed. *Ecole des Beaux-Arts* in Paris, Amer. Acad. in Rome; assoc.-architect for Bd. of Ed. of N.Y.C. 25-26; assoc. prof. in School of Architecture at Columbia Univ. 27, Yale Univ. 38-41; Dir. of Office of Inter-Amer. Affairs 41-45; app. Dir. of Planning, Perm. Hdqrs. 47.

Hasluck, Paul (Australia); b. 05, Fremantle, W. Australia; ed. Perth Modern School and Univ. of W. Australia; hon. sec. W. Australian Hist. Soc. 30-36; lecturer Univ. of W. Australia 39-41; dir. postwar sect. Dept. of Ext. Affairs 41-44, later dir. post-hostilities div.; rep. SC 46 and 47; acting rep. AEC 46 and 47.

Hassan Pasha, Mahmoud (Egypt); b. 93, Cairo; ed. Fac. of Law; fmr. M.C. to his late Majesty King Fuad I; fmr. first sec. Legation, Paris; fmr. chargé d'affaires, Brussels and Prague; first Egyptian Min. to Scandinavian countries 36-38; Min. to U.S.A. 38-; rep. UNCIO 45, SC 46, GA N.Y. 46, first spec. sesn. GA 47.

Hauck, Henri (France); b. 02, Neuilly sur Seine; ed. *Lycée Lakinal*, Paris and Univ. Coll. of Wales; asst.-dir. Pedagogical Museum in Paris 29-39; prof. at Br. Inst. of Univ. of Paris 36-39; app. labor attaché London Embassy 40; dir. of labor French Natl. Com. London 40-43; dir. of Commissariat of Social Affairs in Algiers 43-44; rep. ILO Confs. N.Y. 41, Paris 45, Montreal 46; Chm. Temp. Social Comn. 46; Rapp. of perm. Social Comn. 47.

Henries, Richard A. (Liberia); b. 08; ed. Coll. of W. Afr. and Liberia Coll.; chief clerk of Commonwealth Dist. of Monrovia 33-34; chief clerk of Treas. Dept. 34-38; Supervisor of Schools 38-43; elected to House of Rep. 43; Chm. For. Affairs Com. of House of Rep.; rep. Com. of Jurists, Wash. 45, UNCIO 45.

Henríquez Ureña, Max (Dominican Rep.); b. 85, Santo Domingo; ed. Univ. of Havana; LL.D. 12, Ph.D. 15 (Univ. of Havana); fmr. journalist, lawyer and prof.; Sec. to Pres. of Rep. 16; Supt. of Pub. Ed. 31; Sec. of State 31; perm. del. to LN 35-40; Chm. of Dominican Rep. del. to Pan-American Conf. at Lima 38; app. Amb. to Brazil 43, to Argentina 45; Chm. of Dominican Rep. del. first spec. sesn. GA 47.

Hernáez, Pedro C. (Philippines); b. 99, Talisay, Negros Occidental; ed. St. Augustine Coll., San Juan de Letran; LL.B. (*Escuela de Derecho*) 21; Pres. of Talisay Silay Sugar Planters Assn.; rep. to Const. Asmb. 34; Assemblyman 38-41; Sen. 41-; rep. GA N.Y. 46.

Herrera, Gustavo (Venez.); b. 80, Caracas; ed. Cent. Univ. of Venez.; Min. of Fin. 36; Min. to Holland 36-37, to Ger. 37-38; mem. Inter-Amer. Neutrality Com. 40; dir. of int. policy in Min. of For. Affairs 39-41; Min. of Natl. Ed. 41-43; app. Min. of Devel. 43; rep. UNCIO 45.

Hewitt, Admiral Henry Kent (U.S.A.); b. 87, Hackensack, N.J.; ed. U.S. Naval Acad.; commissioned Admiral 45; Comdr. Cruisers Atlantic Fleet 41, Amphibious Force Atlantic Fleet 42, U.S. Eighth Fleet (U.S. Naval Forces in N.W. Africa) 43, U.S. Twelfth Fleet (U.S. Naval Forces in Europe) 45-46; naval rep. MSC 47.

Hiss, Alger (U.S.A.); b. 04, Baltimore, Maryland; ed. Baltimore City Coll., Johns Hopkins, and Harvard; special atty., Dept. of Jus. 35-36; app. asst. to Asst.-Sec. of State 36, asst. to adviser on pol. relations 42, special asst. to dir., Office of Far Eastern Affairs 44; Sec.-Gen. UNCIO 45.

Hodgson, Lt.-Col. William Roy (Australia); b. 92, Kingston, Victoria; ed. School of Mines in Ballarat, Royal Mil. Coll. in Duntroon and Melbourne Univ.; O.B.E.; attached to Gen. Staff Hdqrs., Melbourne 21-34; sec. Dept. of Ext. Affairs 35-44; High Comr., Ottawa 45-; app. Min. to France 45; rep. GA London 46, SC 46-, AEC 47, CCA 47, first spec. sesn. GA 47.

Hoo, Victor Chi-tsai (China); b. 94, Wash., D. C.; ed. Paris LL.D.; asst.-sec. Chinese del. Paris Peace Conf. 18-19; del. LN 19-21; chargé d'affaires in Berlin 22-24; Min. to Swit. 33-42; Vice-Min. of For. Affairs 42-45; sec.-gen. Chinese del. UNCIO 45; alt. del. GA London 46; Asst. Sec.-Gen. in charge of Dept. of Trusteeship Affairs 46-.

Hood, John D. L. (Australia); b. 04, Adelaide; ed. Univ. of Tasmania, Ox. Univ.; Asst. Ext. Affairs Officer, London 36-39; later head of Pol. Sect.; Sec. of Dept. of Ext. Affairs in Canberra 44; app. chargé d'affaires at The Hague, and Pol. Officer of Australian Mil. Mission in Berlin 45; present Senior Counsellor with Dept. of Ext. Affairs; rep. first spec. sesn. GA 47, SCOP 47.

Ho Ying-chin (China); b. 90, Hsing-I, Kweichow; ed. Wuchang Mil. Acad., Mil. Acad. in Japan; Min. of War 30-44; C. of S. 38-46; C.-in-C., Chinese Army in China Theater 44-46; Chief of Chinese Mil. Mission to U.S.A. since 46; Army rep. MSC 46-.

Hsia, C. L. (China); b. 96; ed. Anglo-Chinese Coll. Tientsin, and Glasgow and Edinburgh Univs.; Principal Medhurst Coll. 27-31; first sec. London Legation 31-32 and Wash. 33; prof. of int. relations Chiaotung Univ., Shanghai; mem. Legis. Yuan 35-; Dir. Chinese News Service 42; alt. rep. SC and AEC 46-.

Hsu Mo (China); b. 93, Soochow; ed. Peiyang and George Wash. Univs.; LL.D.; prof. of law and dean Coll. of Arts, Nankai Univ., Tientsin; judge Shanghai Provisional Ct. 27; dir. of European and Amer. Affairs in For. Office 28-31 and of Asiatic Affairs 31; Vice-Min. of For. Affairs 32-41; Min. to Australia 41-45; Amb. to Turkey 45; Judge ICJ 46-.

Hu Lin (China); b. 93; ed. Tokyo Imp. Univ.; covered Allied expedition in Siberia for _Ta Kung Pao_ 18; only Chinese corr. at Paris Peace Conf.; managing dir. of China's leading ind. daily, _Ta Kung Pao_; rep. UNCIO 45.

Huang, Air Col. Pun-young (China); ed. Jagdschule, Fliegergruppe, Schleissheim bei München, Ger., Cen. Flying School Hangchow, China, and Chinese Air Force Staff School; served in Kwangtung Air Force 31-35; Commanding Officer, No. 5 Fighter Wing, Chinese Air Force 37-41; air attaché Embassy London 42-46; rep. MSC N.Y. 46-.

Hull, Cordell (U.S.A.); b. 71, Tenn.; ed. Cumberland Univ. Law School; LL.D.; mem. Tenn. House of Rep. 93-97; circuit judge, Tenn. 03-07; mem. of Cong., Tenn. Dist. 07-21 and 23-31; Sen. 31-33; Sec. of State 33-44 (resigned); attended Moscow Conf. 43; senior adviser U.S.A. del. UNCIO 45.

Husfeldt, Eric (Den.); b. 01, Sumatra; M.D.; asst. surgeon at Odense Co. and City Hosp. 35-38, and Mun. Hosp. of Copenhagen 38-39; lecturer in surgery Univ. of Copenhagen 41-43; sec. of Scandinavian Surgical Soc. since 39; rep. UNCIO 45.

Hutson, John B. (U.S.A.); b. 90, Murray, Kentucky; ed. Univs. of Kentucky, Wisconsin and Columbia; Ph.D. (Columbia); served for approximately 25 years in Dept. of Agric., of which he became Under-Sec. 45; Deputy-Dir. of Office of War Mobilization and Reconversion 44-45; Pres. of Commodity Credit Corp. 41-44 and 45-46; Asst. Sec.-Gen. in charge of Adm. and Fin. Services 46-47.

Huxley, Julian (U.K.); b. 87; ed. Eton and Balliol Coll.; fmr. lecturer of Zoology at Rice Inst., Houston, Texas, prof. of Zoology at King's Coll., London; Pres. of Natl. Union of Scientific Workers 26-29; Sec. Zoological Soc. of London and dir. of London Zoo 35-42; fmr. adviser Tennessee Valley Authority; mem. Moscow Conf. of World Scientists 45; app. Dir.-Gen. UNESCO 46.

Hvass, Franz (Den.); b. 96, Copenhagen; ed. Univ. of Copenhagen; sec. to For. Min. 25-27 and 30; chief of pol. econ. dept., For. Office 39, of dept. of adm. 40, of pol. juridical dept. 41; sec.-gen. For. Office 45; rep. Prep. Comn. 45.

Ibarra García, Oscar (Argentina); b. 99, Morón; ed. Univ. of Buenos Aires; attaché Min. of For. Affairs 26; Provisional Dir. of Pol. Affairs 33; Provisional Under-Sec. 34; Counsellor 35; mem. of Adm. Council, Perm. Ct. of Arbitration The Hague 28-30; Min. to Den. 37-43; Under-Sec. of Min. of For. Affairs 43; Amb. to U.S.A. 43-45; rep. UNCIO 45.

Jamali, Mohammad Fadhil (Iraq); b. 03, Kadhimain; ed. Baghdad, Amer. Univ. of Beirut, Univ. of Chicago, and Columbia Univ.; Ph.D.; Supervisor-Gen., Dir.-Gen., Inspector-Gen., and again Dir.-Gen. of Ed. and Pub. Instruction 32-43; app. Dir.-Gen. of For. Affairs 45; Min. of For. Affairs 46-; rep. UNCIO 45; Chm. Iraqi del. first spec. sesn. GA N.Y. 47.

Jawdat, Ali (Iraq); b. 86, Mosul, Iraq; ed. Istanbul Mil. Coll.; one of comdrs. with Emir Faisal of Arab revolt; Min. of Interior 23-24, of Finance 30-33; Prime Min. 34-35; Pres. of Chamber of Deputies 35; Min. to Gr. Brit. 35-37, to France 37-39; Min. of For. Affairs 39-41; Min. to U.S.A. 42-; fmr. dir. of Iraq Petroleum Ltd.; rep. UNCIO 45, GA 46, TC 47, first spec. sesn. GA 47.

Jiménez O'Farrill, Federico (Mex.); lawyer; career dipl.; Amb. to Gr. Brit.; rep. GA London 46.

Jiménez, Roberto (Panama); b. 94, Panama; ed. in Panama and Univs. of Cal. and S. Cal.; LL.D. (Univ. of S. Cal.); sec.-gen. of

Pres. of Panama 24; sec. of Legation in Costa Rica 28; Vice-Pres. Natl. Red Cross 31-36; mem. of Natl. Asmb. 36-44, Pres. 42-44; Pres. Canal Zone Bar Assn. 39; Min. of For. Affairs 44-45; Chm. Panamanian del. UNCIO 45; rep. Prep. Comn. 45, GA 46; Chm. Sixth Com. GA 46.

Johannesson, Olafur (Iceland); b. 13, Storholt i Fljotum, Iceland; ed. Univ. of Iceland and in Stockholm; legal adviser of Federation of Icelandic Co-op. Societies 39-44; mem. Icelandic-Amer. Valuation Bd. 42-46; mem. Icelandic Govt. Import Bd. 43-44; prof. of law, Univ. of Iceland 47-; rep. GA N.Y. 46 .

Johnson, Herschel V. (U.S.A.); b. 94, Atlanta, Georgia; ed. Univ. of N. Carolina and Harvard Law School; entered for. service 20; first sec. of Embassy, Mex. City 29-30; chief, div. of Mex. affairs, Dept. of State 30-34; first sec. of Embassy, London 34-39, counsellor 39-41, Min. 41; Min. to Sweden 41-46; alt. rep. SC 46-, first spec. sesn. GA 47.

Jonsson, Finnur (Iceland); b. 94, Hardbak, Sletta, Iceland; ed. Middle School of Akureyri; Postmaster of Isafjordur 20-32; mem. of Town Council 21-42; Althing mem. (Labour) for Isafjordur Town 33-; Mgr. Isafjordur Co-op. Society 28-44; Chm. Icelandic Herring Bd. 35-41; mem. Bd. of State Herring Factories 36-44; Chm. Fisheries' Com. of Althing 34-44; Min. of Jus. 44-46; mem. Govt. Economic Bd. 47-; rep. GA N.Y. 46.

Jung, Nawab Ali Yawar (India); b. 88; ed. Madras Univ. and Ox. Univ.; joined Govt. of Nizam's Own Lancers 06; called to Bar 15; app. Munsif (Judge of lowest ct. with Civil Jurisdiction) 15, later Dist. and Registrar of High Cts.; app. Chief Justice 43; app. Juridical Mem. in Nizam's Ex. Council 44; rep. GA N.Y. 46.

Jurdak, Angela N. M. (Lebanon); b. 15, Shwayr; ed. Amer. Univ. of Beirut, School of Advanced Int. Studies in Geneva; sec. to Registrar and Dean of Beirut Univ. 38-43; fmr. instructor in sociology and psychology at Amer. Univ. of Beirut; attaché to Legation in Wash. 45-; Sec.-Gen. Lebanon del. UNCIO 45; Rapp. Sub-Comn. on Status of Women 46.

Kaeckenbeeck, Georges (Belg.); b. 92, Brussels; ed. Univ. of Brussels; D.C.L. (Univ. of Ox.); fmr. mem. of Legal Sect. of LN Secretariat 19-; Pres. of German-Polish Arbitration Tribunal for Upper Silesia 22-37; Jurisconsult for Min. for For. Affairs in London, World War II; rep. Reparations Conf. in Paris 45, Asmb. of LN in Geneva 46, Peace Conf. in Paris 46, GA N.Y. 46.

Kaminsky, Leonid (Byelorussian S.S.R.); b. 07, Moghilev; ed. Byelorussian State Univ.; fmr. lecturer on hist.; fmr. adviser on social and cultural questions to Byelorussian Govt.; mem. dipl. service 44-; rep. UNCIO 45, FAO Conf. in Quebec 45, GA N.Y. 46; fmr. rep. UNRRA Council; rep. first spec. sesn. GA 47, ESC 47.

Kardelj, Edward (Yugoslavia); b. 10, Ljubljana; obtained teacher's cert. in Ljubljana; publicist; one of the founders of Natl. Liberation Front in Slovenia; Deputy Prime-Min.; Chm. Yugoslav del. GA London 46.

Kauffman, Henrik de (Den.); b. 88; ed. Univ. of Copenhagen; sec. N.Y. Consulate 13-15, Berlin Legation 16; chief of sect. Min. of For. Affairs 20; Min. to Italy 21-24, to China and Japan 24-32, to Siam 28-32, to Nor. 32-39, to U.S.A. 39-47; Amb. to U.S.A. 47-; Chm. Den. del. UNCIO 45, first spec. sesn. GA 47.

Kazemi, Bagher (Iran); b. 91, Teheran; ed. Univ. of Teheran and Amer. Univ., Wash.; Min. of Communications 31; Min. to Iraq 32-36; Min. of For. Affairs and head of Iranian del. to LN; subsequently Amb. to Afghanistan and Turkey; Min. to Sweden, Nor. and Den.; rep. GA London 46.

Keçici, Sevket Fuad (Turkey); b.93, Istanbul; ed. French Coll., Istanbul, and Lausanne Univ.; ind. vice-consul Rome and Budapest 24-26; consul at Geneva and rep. to LN 29; Min. in Copenhagen and Oslo 39, in Lisbon 41, in Budapest 43; rep. GA London 46.

Kenney, Gen. George C. (U.S.A.); b. 89, Yarmouth, Nova Scotia, Can.; ed. Air Corps Tech. School, Air Corps Tactical School, Command and Gen. Staff School, and Army War Coll.; asst. mil. attaché in France 40; Commanding-Gen. of Allied Air Forces, S.W. Pac. Area 42-45; Commanding Gen. of the Far E. Air Forces; app. Commanding Gen., Pac. Air Command 45; rep. MSC 46-.

Kerno, Ivan (Czech.); b. 91, Myjava; ed. Univs. of Budapest and Paris; fmr. Czech. rep. Perm. Ct. of Jus., The Hague; mem. of pol. sect. of LN 28-39; mem. of cabinet of Sec.-Gen. of LN 30-33; Min. to the Neth. 34-38; chief of pol. dept. of Min. for For. Affairs, Prague 38; rep. UNCIO 45; Asst. Sec.-Gen. in charge of Dept. of Legal Affairs 46-.

Kiernik, Wladyslaw (Poland); b. 79; ed. Jagellonian Univ., Cracow; Min. of Internal Affairs 23; Min. of Agric. 25-26; one of the organizers of underground movement of Peasant Party; app. Min. of Pub. Adm. in Govt. of Natl. Unity 45; rep. GA London 46.

King, William Lyon Mackenzie (Can.); b. 74, Kitchener, Ontario; ed. Univ. of Toronto; Ph.D.; C.M.G., P.C.; Deputy-Min. of Labor 00-08 (resigned); Min. of Labor 09-11;

leader of Liberal Party since 21, Prime Min. of Can. five times since 21; concluded with Pres. Roosevelt Ogdensburg Agt. setting up perm. Joint Bd. of Defence 40, and Hyde Park Agt. for war production 41; attended meeting of Prime Mins. of Nations of Commonwealth, England 44; Chm. Can. del. UNCIO 45.

Kiselev, Kuzma Venedictovich (Byelorussian S.S.R.); b. 03, Magivlev Oblast; ed. Voronezh State Univ.; practiced med. for many years; Deputy of Sup. Soviet of U.S.S.R. and of Byelorussia; People's Commissar for For. Affairs of Byelorussia; Chm. Byelorussian del. UNCIO 45; rep. Prep. Comn. 45; Chm. Byelorussian del. GA 46.

Klaestad, Helge (Nor.); b. 85; LL.D.; Pres. Anglo-Ger. Mixed Arbitral Tribunal 25-31; mem. Perm. Ct. of Arbitration, The Hague; Arbitrator between Gt. Brit., Ger., Austria and Hungary in certain disputes under Peace Treaties 26-31; Pres. Conciliation and Arbitration Com. between U.S.A. and Italy; fmr. Judge of Sup. Ct. of Nor.; Judge ICJ 46-.

Konderski, Waclaw (Poland); leading economist; fmr. Pres. Bank of Natl. Economy and Gen. Mgr. British and Polish Trade Bank in Danzig; dir. in Min. of Fin.; alt. rep. GA London 46; Chm. GA Second Com. 46.

Koo, V. K. Wellington (China); b. 88, Shanghai; ed. St. John's in Shanghai and Columbia Univ.; Ph.D. (Columbia); Min. of For. Affairs 22, 24 and 31; Prime Min. 27; mem. of World Ct. 27 and 33; del. to LN Asmb. and Council 32-39; Amb. to France 36-41, to Gr. Britain 41-46, to U.S.A. 46-; Chm. Chinese del. second phase of Dumbarton Oaks Conf. 44; rep. UNCIO 45, Ex. Com. of Prep. Comn. 45, Prep. Comn. 45, GA 46, SC 46.

Koresty, Vladimir M. (U.S.S.R.); b. 90, Dnepropetrovsk; ed. Moscow and Kharkov Univ.; fmr. sci. research worker and lecturer at Kharkov Univ., app. prof. 20, lectured on int. law and legal hist.; fmr. legal adviser U.S.S.R. del. to GA, Council of For. Min., Peace Conf. in Paris, and SC.; Vicechm. Com. on Codification of Int. Law 47.

Kosanovic, Sava (Yugoslavia); b. 94; publicst; fmr. M.P. for Ind. Dem. Party, and fmr. Sec.-Gen. of Party; Min. of Supplies 41; fmr. Min. of Inf.; Amb. to U.S.A.; rep. GA 46; Chm. Yugoslav del. first spec. sesn. GA 47.

Kraft, Ole Bjorn (Den.); b. 93, Copenhagen; studied econ.; mem. Bd. of Directors of Assn. of Danish Journalists 28-32, Vice-Pres. 38-40; mem. Danish del. to LN 33-37; mem. Const. Com. 37 and 45; fmr. Min. of Defence; M.P.; rep. GA 46.

Kramers, Hendrik Anthony (Neth.); b. 94, Rotterdam; ed. Univ. of Leyden; engaged in research work on structure of atom, under Niels Bohr at Univ. of Copenhagen 19-26; fmr. prof. in theoretical physics Univ. of Utrecht; prof. of theoretical physics and mechanics Univ. of Leyden 34-; alt. rep. AEC 46.

Kraus, Frantisek (Czech.); b. 04, Trest-Moravia; ed. Charles Univ. of Prague; LL.D. (Charles Univ. of Prague); fmr. mem. of Min. of Social Welfare; rep. Council of UNRRA in London 45, Int. Labour Conf. in Paris 45, GA London 46, Nuclear Social Comn. 46; Chm. Social Comn. 47.

Kremer, Jean-Pierre (Luxembourg); b. 03; ed. Brussels and Paris; mem. Luxembourg, del. to LN; counsellor of Legation in Min. of For. Affairs 44-; rep. GA London 46.

Krishnamachari, Sir V. T. (India); b. 81; ed. Presidency and Law Coll. in Madras; app. Deputy-Collector 03; del. LN Asmb. 34 and 36; Diwan (Prime Min.), State of Baroda 27-44; Chm. Minister's Com. of Chamber of Princes since 41; rep. UNCIO 45, GA London 46.

Krylov, Sergei Borisovich (U.S.S.R.); b. 88, Leningrad; ed. Univ. of Leningrad; LL.D.; fmr. prof. of int. law Leningrad Univ.; Dean, Leningrad Inst. 30-39; legal adviser of People's Commissariat for For. Affairs of U.S.S.R. 42-46; rep. UNCIO 45; Judge ICJ 46-.

Kulikov, Aleksey F. (Byelorussian S.S.R.); b. 03, Orsha; ed. Fin. Acad., Leningrad; occupied different fin. posts in Republic; Deputy People's Commissar for Control; rep. GA London 46.

Kuznetsov, Vassili Vasilievich (U.S.S.R.); b. 01; ed. in metallurgical eng.; expert on trade unions in U.S.S.R.; fmr. Chm. of Ex. Com. of Trade Unions of Metallurgical Industries in Cen. U.S.S.R.; Chm. All-Union Council of Trade Unions of U.S.S.R.; Chm. Soviet del. World Trade Union Conf., London 45; rep. GA London 46.

Labarca Hubertson, Amanda Pinto (Chile); b. 86; ed. Univ. of Chile, Columbia Univ., and Sorbonne; school dir. 16-28; prof. of psychiatry at Univ. of Chile 22-23, prof. of philosophy 23-28; Dir. Gen. of Secondary School Ed. 31-32; app. gov. rep. on Council of Univ. of Chile 34; present Pres. of Federation of Women of Chile; rep. GA N.Y. 46.

Laleau, Leon (Haiti); ed. Port-au-Prince, Haiti; fmr. Dir. of consular services Min. for For. Affairs; fmr. consul-gen. at Genoa, chargé d'affaires at Rome; fmr. Min. to Chile; Min. for For. Affairs 33-34 and 38-40; Gen. Comr. for Haiti at Paris Conf. 37; Min. at London; rep. Prep. Comn. 45, GA London 46.

Lange, Halvard M. (Nor.); b. 02, Oslo; ed. Univs. of Oslo, Geneva and London; fmr. lecturer econ. hist., Sec. of Workers' Ed. Assn. and Warden of Cen. Labor Coll. in Oslo; app. Min. of For. Affairs 46; chief Nor. rep. to Paris Peace Conf. 46; rep. GA N.Y. 46.

Lange, Oscar (Poland); b. 04, Tomaszow Mazowiecki, Poland; ed. Univs. of Poznan and Cracow; LL.D.; lecturer Univ. of Cracow 31-36; fmr. lecturer Univs. of Michigan and Cal.; prof. of econ. Univ. of Chicago 38-45; Amb. to U.S.A. 45-47; rep. SC 46-, AEC 46-, GA N.Y. 46, first spec. sesn. GA 47, CCA 47.

Lannung, Hermod (Den.); b. 95, Vestervang, Den.; ed. Univ. of Copenhagen; mem. of Copenhagen City Council since 33 and Chm. of its radical group since 35; mem. of Upper House of Danish Parl. since 39; Barrister-at-Law; rep. GA 46.

Laugier, Henri (France); Dr. of Med. and Sci.; fmr. prof. Univs. of Paris, Sao Paulo, Lima, Mex. and Montreal; co-founder New School of Social Research, N.Y.; fmr. dir.-gen. of cultural relations in Min. of For. Affairs; fmr. Pres. "Ligue des Droits de l'homme"; Chm. French del. UNESCO. Conf. London 45; Asst. Sec.-Gen. in charge of Dept. of Social Affairs 46-.

Lavrentiev, Anatoliy I. (U.S.S.R.); b. 04; ed. Moscow; Min. Plenipotentiary to Bulgaria 39-40, to Rumania 40-41; People's Commissar for For. Affairs of the Russian S.S.R. 44-; UNCIO 45, GA London 46.

Leitão da Cunha, Vasco T. (Brazil); b. 03, Rio de Janeiro; ed. Univ. of Rio de Janeiro; joined Min. of For. Relations 27; asst. to sec.-gen. of Min. of For. Relations 39-41; Acting-Min. of Jus. and Internal Affairs 41-42; chargé d'affaires in Rome 44-45; consul-gen. at Geneva; rep. GA London 46.

Leitão de Carvalho, Estevão (Brazil); b. 81, Penedo. State of Alagoas; ed. Mil. School, Rio de Janeiro, and Gen. Staff School; mil. attaché to Chile 18-21; Dir., Gen. Staff School 32-35; Deputy-Chief of Gen. Staff of Army 37; Amb. to Chile 38; Comdr. Third Mil. Region 39-42; mil. attaché in Wash.; Chief Brazilian del. Joint Brazil-U.S. Defense Com.; rep. UNCIO 45.

Leiva, Carlos (El Salvador); b. 88, San Salvador; ed. Univ. of El Salvador, and in Paris and London; fmr. prof. Univ. of El Salvador and Chief Surgeon Hosp. Rosales, San Salvador; app. Min. to U.S.A. 32, then practised med. in N.Y. and in San Francisco since 35; rep. UNCIO 45, GA N.Y. 46.

Leontic, Ljubo (Yugoslavia); b. 87, Dalmatia; ed. in law, Zagreb and Prague, in painting, Prague and Munich; outstanding leader of Yugoslav Youth during last decade of Austro-Hungarian Empire; during first World War worked among Yugoslav emigrants in N. and S. Amer.; fmr. Vice-Pres. of Natl. Liberation Com. in Split; Amb. to U.K.; rep. Ex. Com. of Prep. Comn. 45, GA 46.

Lescot, Gerard (Haiti); b. 14, Port-de-Paix; fmr. Asst.-Sec. of Haitian-Dominican Boundary Com.; fmr. Attaché, Sec. and Consul-Gen., Haitian Legation at Santo Domingo; fmr. Asst.-Sec. of State; For. Min. 43-46; Chm. Haitian del. UNCIO 45.

Liautaud, André (Haiti); b. 06, Port-au-Prince; ed. Haitian School of Agric. and Columbia Univ.; Dir. of Farm School 25-28; Asst.-Dir. of Rural Ed. in Haiti 28-38, Dir. 41-42; Min. to U.S.A. 42-43, Amb. 43-45; rep. UNCIO 45.

Lie, Trygve Halvdan (Nor.); b. 96, Oslo; ed. Oslo Univ. Law School; Pres. Labor Party's branch in Aker, suburb of Oslo 14-19; app. legal adviser to Labor Party 22, mem. of its Natl. Council 26-40; Min. of Jus. 35-39, of Commerce 39-40, of Shipping and Supply 40, of For. Affairs 41-46; Chm. Nor. del. UNCIO 45, GA London 46; app. first Sec.-Gen. of UN Feb. 1, 46.

Li Hwang (China); b. 95, Szechwan prov.; ed. Univ. of Paris; fmr. prof. of Natl. Wuchang and Ntal. Peking Univs.; fmr. ed. of *Young China* and *Awakened Lion* (magazines); helped organize Nationalist Youth Party in 27; elected mem. of People's Pol. Council in 28 and now mem. of its Presidium; connected with Szechwan-Sikang Econ. Com. since 40; rep. UNCIO 45.

Lisicky, Karel (Czech.); b. 93, Holesov, Moravia; ed. Prague Univ. and Strasbourg Univ.; Sec. to Legation in Paris 20-26; Counsellor in Wash. 27-31; fmr. rep. Conf. of Lausanne, Rapp. Reparations Conf.; mem. LN's pol. sect. 34-37; app. chargé d'affaires in London 36; mem. of Min. of For. Affairs 41-; mem. Czech. del. Ex. Com., Prep. Comn., GA London 46; rep. SCOP 47.

Liu Shih-shun (China); b. 00, Hunan; ed. Tsing Hua, Johns Hopkins Coll., Harvard, Michigan and Columbia Univs.; prof. of int. relations at Tsing Hua Univ. 25-27; senior mem. of Treaty Comn. of Min. of For. Affairs and mem. of Legis. Yuan 27-30; app. acting-dir. of Dept. of Int. Affairs of Min. of For. Affairs 32, dir. of Dept. of European and Amer. Affairs 41; Min. to Canada 41-43, to U.S.A. 43-; rep. GA N.Y. 46.

Liu Ten-fu, Rear-Adm. (China); b 87, Menyang, Hupeh, China; ed. Navigation Coll., Naval Communication Coll., Navy Gunnery Coll., Coll. of Torpedo and Mines, and the Naval War Coll. (all in Japan); Supt. of

Chinese Naval Acad. 25-28; Captain of cruisers, "Cheng-hai" and "Hai-shen" 28-31; naval attaché to Chinese Embassy in Tokyo 34-37, in Wash. 43-46; rep. MSC 46-.

Lleras Camargo, Alberto (Colombia); b. 06, Bogotá; ed. *Instituto Ricaurte* and *Colegio del Rosario* in Bogotá; founded *El Liberal,* a daily in Bogotá; fmr. reporter, ed. writer, and ed. of *El Tiempo,* Bogotá; app. Rep. to Cong. 31; sec.-gen. to Pres. López 34-35; Min. of Interior 35-38; Min. of Natl. Ed. 38; elected Pres. of House in 41; Amb. to U.S.A. 43; Min. of For. Affairs 45; Pres. of Colombia 45-46; App. Dir.-Gen. of Pan Amer. Union 47; Chm. Colombian del. UNCIO 45.

Lleras Restrepo, Carlos (Colombia); b. 08, Bogotá; ed. De la Salle Inst., Bogotá and Natl. Univ. of Colombia; Deputy Cundinamarca Asmb. 31-33; sec. of govt., Municipality of Bogotá 33-34; Rep. Natl. Chamber of Reps. 33-34, Pres. 35; Comptroller-Gen. of Colombia 36-38; Min. of Fin. and Pub. Credit 38-41, 41-42, and 43-44; Sen. 43; rep. GA London 46, ESC 46.

López, Alfonso (Colombia); b. 86, Honda, Colombia; ed. in U.K. and U.S.A.; founder and Vice-Pres. of Amer. Mercantile Bank of Colombia, becoming its Pres. in 18; app. Min. to U.K. 31; Pres. of Colombia 34-38 and 42-45 (resigned); founder of *El Liberal* and fmr. ed. and part owner of *El Diario Nacional;* rep. Econ. Conf. in London 33; Chm. of Colombian del. to Pan Amer. Conf. in Montevideo 33, GA N.Y. 46, first spec. sesn. GA 47; rep. SC 47, AEC 47, CCA 47.

López, Pedro (Philippines); b. 06, Cebu; studied law at night school; ed. *The Freeman,* Visayan Islands; publ. of *The Star, The Clarion,* and *The Nasud;* fmr. Pres. of Cebu Press Assn.; fmr. sec. of Cebu Bar Assn.; Pres. of Cebu Lawyers' League since 40; Maj. Bohol Area Command during World War II; mem. House of Rep.; mem. Philippine Rehabilitation Com., Wash.; rep. Prep. Comn. 45, GA London 46.

López, Rafael Ernesto (Venez.); b. 95, Caracas; ed. Cen. Univ. of Venez., Columbia Univ., Paris and Vienna; M.D. (Univ. of Venez.); fmr. resident-surgeon at Lennox Hill and Mt. Sinai Hospitals, N.Y.; founded and organized Inst. of Experimental Surgery in Caracas 38; founded Hispano-Amer. Med. Soc.; Min. of Natl. Ed. in Venez. 36-38; rep. UNCIO 45.

Loudon, Alexander (Neth.); b. 92, The Hague; ed. The Hague and Univ. of Leyden; LL.D. (Univ. of Leyden); fmr. attaché at Sofia, Constantinople and London, Sec. at Buenos Aires, Wash., and Madrid, chargé d'affaires at Mex. City and Lisbon, Min. at Lisbon, Berne and Wash.; Amb. to U.S.A. 44-; Vice-Chm. Neth. del. UNCIO 45; rep. SC 46.

Lubin, Isador (U.S.A.); b. 96, Worcester, Mass.; ed. in econ. Clark Coll. in Worcester; Ph.D. (Robert Brookings Inst.) 26; adviser to Ed. and Labor Com. of U.S. Senate 28-29; Vice-chm. U.S. Cen. Stat. Bd. 33-38; mem. of Temp. Natl. Econ. Com. 38-41; Comr. of Labor Stat. and Stat. Asst. to White House 41-45; Min. and Assoc. U.S. rep. to Allied Reparations Comn. in Moscow 45; Rapp. of Econ. and Employment Comn. 47.

Luisi, Héctor (Uru.); b. 90, Montevideo; fmr. Dir. of Naval School of Hydrographic Service and Gen. Dir. of Naval Training; adviser, Uru. del. to LN 20; fmr. naval attaché in Gr. Brit. and France; Under-Sec. of State in Dept. of Natl. Defence; rep. UNCIO 45.

Lutz, Bertha (Brazil); b. 94, Sao Paulo; ed. Univs. of Paris and Rio de Janeiro; sec. of Natl. Museum in Rio, chief of dept. of nat. hist. and geol.; Pres. of Brazilian Federation for Advancement of Women; rep. Int. Confs. for Women, Rome 23, Berlin 29; mem. Chamber of Deputies 36-37; rep. ILO Conf. Phila. 44, UNCIO 45.

Lynden, R. A. de (Liberia); b. Holland; LL.D.; Min. in London 38-; rep. GA London 46.

MacEachen, Roberto Eduardo (Uru.); b. 99, Montevideo; ed. Univ. of Montevideo; second sec. Uru. Legation in Wash. 26-28; first sec., counsellor and chargé d'affaires Uru. Legation in London 28-40; Min. to Cuba 40-43; Min. to Gt. Brit. 43-44, Amb. 44-; del. World Mon. and Econ. Conf. London 33; rep. Prep. Comn. 45, Chm. Com. Eight; Chm. Uru. del. GA London 46; Chm. Fourth Com. GA 46; rep. GA N.Y. 46.

Machado Hernández, Alfredo (Venez.); b. 89, Caracas; ed. Cen. Univ. of Venez. and *Ecole Libre des Sciences Politiques* in Paris; fmr. prof. School of Dipl. in Caracas; fmr. dir. Cen. Bank of Venez.; Min. to Peru 38-39; Min. of Fin. 41-43; rep. UNCIO 45.

Mackay, Athol Rezy F. (New Zealand); b. 98, Paeroa; ed. Wellington Coll., Victoria Univ. Coll.; Ph.D. (London Univ.); fmr. Inspector, later Accountant to Treas.; Fin. Officer of New Zealand Treas. in London 32-35; rep. LN. 34; app. Asst.-Sec. to Treas. 42; Rapp. Fiscal Comn. 47.

Mackintosh, W. A. (Can.); b. 95, Madoc, Ontario; ed. Queens Univ. in Kingston, Ontario and Harvard; Ph.D. (Harvard); dir. of school of commerce and adm., Queens Univ. 23-; dir. of research Can. Pioneer Probs. Com. 29-34; mem. Natl. Employment Com. 36-38; special asst. to Deputy-Min. of Fin. 39-44; Acting Deputy-Min. of Fin. 45; Can. Chm. Joint Econ. Com. of Can. and U.S.A. 41-43; Dean of Fac. of Arts and Science,

Queens Univ. 46-; Chm. Nuclear Econ. and Employment Com. 46.

Mahalanobis, Prasanta Chandra (India); b. 93; ed. Presidency Coll. in Calcutta and King's Coll. at Cambridge; prof. of physics at Presidency Coll. 15-, present Pres.; hon. sec. and dir. of Indian Stat. Inst. 31-; hon. ed. of *Sankhya* (Indian Journal of stat.) 33-; stat. adviser to Govt. of Bengal 44-; Gen. Sec. of Indian Science Cong. 45-; Vice-chm. Stat. Comn. 47.

Makin, Norman John Oswald (Australia); b. 89, Petersham, N.S.W.; mem. House of Rep. for Hindmarsh 19-46, Speaker 29-31; Min. for Navy and Munitions 41-46, for Aircraft Production 45-46; Amb. to U.S.A. 46-; rep. GA 46, SC 46 and 47, TC 47.

Malik, Charles (Lebanon); b. 06, Bitirram, Lebanon; ed. Amer. Univ. of Beirut and Harvard Univ.; Ph.D. (Harvard); associated with a Rockefeller Foundation unit in Egypt 30-32; asst.-prof. of philos., Harvard 36-37; prof. of philos. and head of dept., Amer. Univ. of Beirut 37-45; first Min. from Lebanon to U.S.A.; rep. UNCIO 45, ESC 46-, GA N.Y. 46, first spec. sesn. GA 47; Rapp. Comn. on Human Rights, 47.

Mance, Sir Harry Osborne (U.K.); b. 75; ed. Bedford School; K.B.E., C.B., C.M.G., D.S.O.; Dir. Rys., Light Rys. and Roads War Office 16-20; trans. adviser to British del. Paris 19-20; Dir. Ger. Ry. Co. 25-30; ry. econ. expert to Austria 34; transport adviser E. Afr. 36; dir. of canals, Min. of War Transport 41-44; Chm. Temp. Transport and Communications Comn. 46.

Manuilsky, Dmitro Zakharvich (Ukr. S.S.R.); b. 83; ed. Leningrad Univ. and Sorbonne; mem. Revolutionary Com. of Ukr. 20-21; app. mem. Presidium of Comintern 24; Commissar for For. Affairs and Deputy-Chm. of Council of People's Commissars of Ukr. 44-; Chm. Ukr. del. UNCIO 45; Vice-Pres. Prep. Comn. 45; Chm. Ukr. del. GA 46; Chm. First Com. GA 46.

Marchal, Comdr. Victor (France); b. 05, Lunéville; ed. *Ecole Navale;* participated in Indo-China campaign 29-32; Ordinance Officer to Adm. of Fleet in Algeria 38-40; Deputy-Chief of Gen. Staff of Submarine Group in Bizerte 40; Chief of Operations of Gen. Staff of Navy at Casablanca and later Algeria 43-44; escort work in Mediter-Oleron 45; Deputy-Chief of French Naval participated in operations at Royan and Oleron 45; Deputy-Chief of French Naval Mission to U.S. 45; Navy rep. MSC 47.

Mariam, Ambaye Wolde (Eth.); b. 06, Eritrea; ed. Lycée of seminary of Vatican in Rome and Univ. of Paris; Ph.D. (Univ. for Propagation of the Faith in Rome); legal adviser to Special Ct. of Addis Ababa 33-

35; app. legal adviser to Duke of Harrar, second son of Emp. 41; fmr. Vice-Min. of Jus.; acting Vice-Min. of For. Affairs; rep. UNCIO 45.

Marshall, Herbert (Can.); b. 87, Toronto; ed. Univ. of Toronto; fmr. lecturer at Univ. of Toronto; app. Prices Stat. in Dominion Bu. of Stat. 22; Chief of Internal Trade Branch 26-42; Sec. at Br. Commonwealth Stat. Conf. 35; Asst. Dominion Stat. 42-45; Dominion Stat. 45-; Chm. of Stat. Comn. 47.

Martin, Paul (Can.); b. 03, Ottawa; ed. St. Michael's Coll., Harvard, Trinity Coll., Cambridge and Geneva School of Int. Studies; mem. House of Commons 35; Chm. Can. del. World Youth Conf. 36; del. 19th LN Asmb. 38; parl. asst. to Min. of Labour 43; Sec. of State 45-; Chm. Com. on Const. of ILO; rep. GA 46; rep. ESC 46.

Martínez Cabañas, Gustavo (Mex.); Dr. in Econ. Science; fmr. econ. adviser at Fin. Min.; prof. of Natl. School of Econ. in Mex.; Dir. *Review of Economics* of Mex.; rep. GA London 46; Chm. Com. on Contributions.

Martins, Carlos (Brazil); b. 84, Rio Grande do Sul; ed. School of Law, Porto Alegre; Amb. to Japan 34, Denmark 34, Belgium 35, U.S.A. 39-; Chm. of Brazil del. to First Meeting of Min. of For. Affairs of Amer. Reps., Panama 39; rep. Inter-Amer. Conf. on Probs. of War and Peace, Mex. City 45; Vice-Chm. of del. to UNCIO 45; rep. GA N.Y. 46.

Masaryk, Jan (Czech.); b. 86, Prague; ed. Prague; served in Min. of For. Affairs in Prague 20-22 and 23-25; Min. to Gr. Brit. 25-38 (resigned); app. For. Min. of Czech. Govt. in London 40, also Vice-Premier 41-45; Chm. Czech. del. UNRRA Conf. Atlantic City 43, UNCIO 45; rep. Ex. Com. of Prep. Comn. 45, Prep. Comn. 45; Chm. Czech. del. GA 46; rep. ESC 46.

Massey, Vincent (Can.); b. 87; ed. Toronto and Ox. Univs.; lecturer in modern hist. Toronto Univ. 13-15; Pres. Massey-Harris Co. 21-25; Min. to U.S.A. 26-30; High Comr. in London 35-; Gov. Toronto Univ.; rep. GA London 46.

Massigli, René (France); b. 88; ed. *Ecole Normale;* prof. *Ecole Française de Rome* 10-13; sec. Lausanne Conf. 22-23; mem. Council of State 24-28; chief of LN sect., Min. of For. Affairs 28-33; asst.-dir. of pol. sect., Min. of For. Affairs 33-37, dir. 37-38; Amb. to Turkey 38-40, to Gt. Brit. 44-; rep. Ex. Com. of Prep. Comn. 45, Prep. Comn. 45, GA London 46, SC 46.

Mayhew, Major Christopher Paget (U.K.); b. 15; ed. Christ Church Coll., Ox.; M.P. (Labour) for S. Norfolk 45-; Parl. Private Sec.

to Lord Pres. of the Council 45; Parl. Under-Sec. of State for Foreign Affairs 46; rep. ESC 47.

Maza, José (Chile); Deputy, House of Rep. 21 and 24; Sen. 25, 32, 36, 37, 45; Pres. of Sen. 36-37; Min. of Jus. and of Pub. Ed. 23; Min. of Interior 24; rep. UNCIO 45.

McCloy, John J. (U.S.A.); b. 95, Philadelphia; ed. Amherst Coll. and Harvard; Capt. in Field Artillery World War I; head of Paris Office of legal firm of Cravath, De Gersdoff, Swaine & Wood 30, 31; app. expert consultant to Sec. of War, later spec.-asst. to Henry L. Stimson 40; Asst.-Sec. of War 41-45 (resigned); app. Pres. Int. Bank for Recon. and Devel. 47.

McIntosh, Agnes F. R. (New Zealand); b. London; ed. Univ. of Edinburgh, Scotland; fmr. mem. of Teachers' Training Coll., Christ Church, New Zealand; life mem. of Farmers Union, active in Women's Div.; Pres. Natl. Council of Women; active in establishing Home Aid for Women, and in establishing Obstetrical Hosp. for spec. research, Auckland; rep. GA N.Y. 46.

McIntosh, Alister Donald (N. Zealand); b. 06, N. Zealand; ed. Marlborough Coll. and Victoria Univ. Coll., N. Zealand; mem. of staff, Gen. Asmb. Library 27-34; app. to Prime Minister's Dept. in 34; sec. to War Cabinet 43-45; sec. of Dept. of Ext. Affairs 43-; rep. GA London 46.

McKenzie, Jean Robertson (N. Zealand); b. 01, N. Zealand; mem. of Prime Minister's Dept. 26; sec. to del. to Ottawa Conf. 32, to N. Zealand Trade Comr., Canada 32-36; attended Asmb. and Council of LN 36-39; first sec. to High Comr. for N. Zealand, Australia 43-; rep. GA London 46.

McNair, Sir Arnold Duncan (U.K.); b. 85, London; ed. Aldenham School and Gonville and Caius Coll. Cambridge; LL.D.; C.B.E., F.B.A.; fellow and law lecturer Gonville and Caius Coll. 12; sec. Coal Controller's Advisory Bd. 17-19; Tagore Prof. Univ. of Calcutta 31; prof. Acad. of Int. Law, The Hague 28, 33 and 37; Vice-Chancellor Liverpool Univ. 37-45; Judge ICJ 46-.

McNarney, Gen. Joseph T. (U.S.A.); b. 93, Emporia, Penn.; ed. West Point Mil. Acad.; promoted to Gen. (temp.) 45; app. Deputy-Sup. Allied Comd. of Mediterranean Theater of Operations and Commanding Gen. of U.S. Army Forces 44; app. Commanding Gen. of U.S. Forces in European Theater and C.-in-C. of U.S. Forces of Occupation in Germany 45; U. S. air rep. MSC 47.

McNaughton, Gen. Andrew G. L. (Can.); b. 87, Moonsomin, Saskatchewan; ed. McGill Univ.; C.H., C.B., C.M.G., D.S.O.; Deputy C. of S. 23-28, Chief 29-35; Pres. Natl. Research Council 35-39; Comdr. First Can. Army in World War II; Min. of Natl. Defence 44-45; Co-Chm. Can.-Amer. Joint Defence Bd. 45-46; rep. AEC 46-.

McNeil, Hector (U.K.); b. 10, Scotland; fmr. parl. private sec. to P. Noel-Baker; fmr. Under-Sec. for For. Affairs; Min. of State; Chm. Special Com. on Refugees and Displaced Persons 46; rep. ESC 46-, GA N.Y. 46.

Medhen, Blatta Ephram Tewelde (Eth.); b. 94, Eritrea; ed. Amer. Univ. of Beirut; Consul-Gen. to France 29-32; app. First Sec. and chargé d'affaires a.i. in London 32; app. Sec.-Gen. of Min. of For. Affairs 42, later Vice-Min.; Min. to U.S.A. 43-45, to UK 45-; Chm. Eth. del. to Bretton Woods Conf., Int. Civil Aviation Conf. in Chicago 44; rep. UNCIO 45, Prep. Comn. 45, GA London 46; Chm. Eth. del. GA N.Y. 46.

Medved, Levko Ivanovich (Ukr. S.S.R.); b. 05, Tchernaya Greblia in the Vinnitsa Oblast; ed. Chem.-Phar. Inst. Vinnitsa and Med. Inst. Kiev; prof. of industrial hygiene, Med. Inst. Kiev; in charge of Kiev Oblast Sect. of Pub. Health 34-37, Health Sec. of Dnieper Basin 37-40; Dir. Kiev Med. Inst. 40-45; app. Deputy-Min. of Pub. Health of Ukr. 45; rep. ESC 46, GA N.Y. 46.

Mendès-France, Pierre (France); b. 97; ed. in econ.; fmr. deputy, advocate at Ct. of Appeals; Under-Sec. for Treas. 38-39; Fin. Comr. for French Provisional Gov. 43-44; fmr. Min. of Natl. Econ.; rep. ESC 47.

Messina Pimentel, Temístocles (Dominican Rep.); b. 94, Sabana de la Mar; ed. San Domingo Univ.; Judge of Ct. of Appeals 22-24; State Atty. 41-43; Judge of Supreme Ct. 43-44; fmr. mem. Perm. Ct. of Arbitration, The Hague; present Pres. of Perm. Consultative Comn. of Min. of For. Affairs, Natl. Comn. on Amer. Int. Law, mem. of Inst. of Comparative Law; Chm. Dominican del. GA London 46; rep. GA N.Y. 46.

Meyer, Eugene (U.S.A.); b. 75; ed. Cal. and Yale Univs.; LL.D.; head of Eugene Meyer, Jr, & Co., N.Y. 01-17; Dir., later Mgr.-Dir. War Fin. Corp. of U.S.A. 18-20 and 21-29; mem. Fed. Farm Loan Com. 27-29; Gov. Fed. Reserve Bd. 30-33; First Chm. Recon. Fin. Corp. 32; publisher and ed. *Wash. Post*; Pres. Int. Bank for Recon. and Devel. 46 (Resigned).

Michalowski, Jerzy (Poland); b. 09; ed. Univ. of Warsaw; active in Polish Co-operative Movement; fmr. mem. Inst. of Social Science in Warsaw; prisoner of war 39-45; app. counsellor to Polish Embassy, London 45; alt.-rep. SC 46, AEC 46.

Modzelewski, Zygmunt (Poland); b. 00; ed. School of Pol. Science, Paris; fmr. journalist; officer in Polish Army during World War II; Amb. in U.S.S.R. 45; app. Under-Sec. of State, Min. of For. Affairs 45; rep. Prep. Comn. 45, GA London 46, SC 46.

Moe, Finn (Nor.); b. 02, Bergen; ed. *Lycée Corneille* and Univ. of Paris; journalist, for. corr. and later co-for. ed. of Labor Party Newspaper *Arbeiderbladet;* winner of *Conrad Mohrs Press Scholarship* 36; Dir. of Nor. broadcasting from U.S.A. 40-43; Press Consultant at Nor. Min. of For. Affairs in London 43-45; mem. of Nor. del. to GA in London 46; fmr. pol. adviser to Sec.-Gen. of UN; rep. ESC 46-, GA N.Y. 46, first spec. sesn. GA 47.

Molotov, Viacheslav M. (U.S.S.R.); b. 90 as V. M. Skriabin; ed. Petersburg Polytechnic; Sec. Gen. Com. of Communist Party of U.S.S.R. 21-; Premier 21; chm. Council of People's Commissars 30-41, Vice-Chm. 41-; Foreign Commissar of U.S.S.R. 39-; attended Moscow Conf. 43; Yalta Conf. 45; Chm. U.S.S.R. del. UNCIO 45, GA N.Y. 46; rep. Council of For. Ministers, Paris Peace Conf.

Moniz de Aragão, J. J. (Brazil); b. 87; ed. Rio de Janeiro Fac. of Law; sec. in Embassy U. S. A. 12, Uru. 13; chargé d'affaires Spain 15, Italy 16; counsellor, del. to Peace Conf. Versailles 19; del. LN 25, ILO 27-28; Min. to Den. 29, to Venez. 31, to Austria 33; Amb. to Ger. 35, to Gr. Brit. 40-; rep. GA London 46.

Montt, Gonzalo (Chile); entered dipl. service 11; fmr. sec. in Bolivia and London, consul-gen. in Swit., chargé d'affaires in Czech., Min. to Para.; Min. to The Neth.; rep. GA London 46.

Moore, Adm. Sir Henry Ruthven (U. K.); b. 86; ed. Sherbourne and H.M.S. "Britannia"; K.C.B., C.V.O., D.S.O.; asst.-sec. of U. K. del. to Limitation of Armaments Conf. Wash. 21-22, Geneva 27; dir. of Plans Div., Admiralty 32-33; A.D.C. to the King 37-38; Lord-Comr. of the Admiralty and Asst.-Chief of Naval Staff 40-41, Vice-Chief 41-43; Vice-Admiral 2nd in command, Home Fleet 43-44; C.-in-C. Home Fleet 44-45; rep. MSC 46-.

Mora, José A. (Uru.); b. 87, Montevideo; ed. Univ. of Montevideo; LL.D.; fmr. Sec. of Legations in Spain, Portugal, Brazil and U.S.A.; fmr. Dir. of Dept. of Inter. Institutions in Min. of For. Affairs; Min. to Bolivia 42-44; Min. of Uru. Embassy in Wash.; mem. of Governing Bd. of Pan Amer. Union; mem. Uru. del. to Meetings of For. Mins. in Panama, Havana and Rio, Mex. Conf. and UNCIO in 45; rep. GA N. Y. 46.

Mora, Marcial (Chile); b. Chillan; ed. Liceo in Chillan and Univ. of Chile; ed. *El Día* of Chillan; Deputy in Natl. Cong. 26-30; Min. of Interior and Aviation 32; Pres. of Natl. Savings Bank 33-39, of Cen. Bank of Chile 39-40; Min. of For. Affairs 40-41, of Fin. 41; fmr. Amb. to U. S. A.; rep. UNCIO 45.

Morgenstierne, Wilhelm Munthe (Nor.); b. 87, Oslo; ed. Oslo Univ.; served Legation in Wash. 10-12, as commercial counsellor 17-21; app. counsellor 21; subsequently chief of Amer. Div. of For. Office in Oslo until 29; consul-gen., N. Y., 29-34; Min. to U.S.A. 34-42, Amb. 42-; rep. UNCIO 45, GA N.Y. 46.

Morozov, Alexander P. (U. S. S. R.); b. 00, Kostroma Dist.; ed. Leningrad Pol. Inst.; fmr. lecturer at Finance Inst.; Chief of Dept. of For. Currency and mem. of Bd. of Min. for For. Trade of U. S. S. R. 39-46; mem. of U. S. S. R. del. to Monetary and Financial Conf., Bretton Woods 44; rep. ESC 47; Vice-Chm. of Econ. and Employment Comn. 47.

Morris, Gen. Sir Edwin Logie (U. K.); b. 89; ed. Wellington and Royal Mil. Acad. Woolwich; K.C.B., O.B.E., M.C.; Imp. Defence Coll. 33; Comdr. Royal Engineers 34; Deputy-Dir. Operations War Office 36-38; Chief of Gen. Staff India 42-44; Gen. Officer, C.-in-C. Northern Command 44-; rep. MSC 46-.

Moullec, Rear-Adm. R. (France); b. 01, Brest; ed in Brest and Paris and Naval Acad., Brest; naval attaché, Embassy in Madrid 36-39; co-organizer with Admiral Muselier of Free French Naval Forces and C.-of-S. 40-42; French rep. to Allied Com. in Italy 45-46; rep. MSC 46.

Mow, Lt.-Gen. Pong-Tsu (China); b. 04, Fenghwa, Chekiang Prov.; ed. Whangpoa Mil. Acad., Canton Aviation Acad., and Second Mil. Aviation Acad. in U. S. S. R.; chief instructor, Cen. Mil. Acad. Aviation Branch, 28-30, Dir. 31; Deputy-Comdr. Chinese Air Force 37-38, Chief of Operations, 38-39, C-in-C 41-43; Deputy-Dir. Com. on Aeronautical Affairs and chief rep. Chinese Air Mission in U. S. A. 43-; rep. MSC 46-.

Mudaliar, Sir A. Ramaswami (India); b. 87; ed. Christian Coll. and Law Coll. Madras; fmr. ed. *Justice;* fmr. Mayor of Madras; fmr. mem. Madras Legis.; mem. Econ. Com. of LN; del. Nine Power Conf. Brussels 37; rep. of India on Imp. War Cabinet and Pac. War Council 42-43; rep. UNCIO 45, Prep. Comn. 45; Chm. Indian del. GA London 46; Pres. ESC 46-; Chm. Com. on Arrangements for Consultation with Non-Gov. Organizations, Com. on Negotiations with Intergov. Agencies 46.

Muniz, João Carlos (Brazil); b. 93, Matto Grosso; ed. in law at Univ. of Rio de Janeiro, Univ. of N. Y.; Dir. of Fed. Council for For. Trade Council 38-41; Min. to Cuba 41-42; Amb. to Ecua. 42-45; mem. of Governing Bd. of Pan Amer. Union; rep. to Bankers' Conf., Phila. 26, Commercial Aviation Conf., Wash. 27, sesns. of Labor Conf., Geneva 23-34, N. Y. 41; rep. GA N. Y. 46, first spec. sesn. GA 47; alt. rep. CCA 47.

Muñoz, Rodolfo (Argentina); b. 08, Buenos Aires; ed. Buenos Aires Univ. and La Plata Univ.; Dir. Internal Revenue 31; Adviser to Min. of Fin. 33-35; Econ. Attaché to Embassy in London 36-39, Sec. 40-44; Counsellor and chargé d'affaires in Paris 45; Sec. Argentinian del. GA London 46; alt. rep. GA N. Y. 46; rep. first spec. sesn. GA 47; Counsellor to Argentinian perm. del. UN 47.

Myrdal, Karl G. (Sweden); b. 98, Delecarlia; ed. Univ. of Stockholm; asst.-prof. of int.-econ. at Post-Graduate Inst. of Int. Studies in Geneva 30-31; fmr. holder of Lars Hurta Chair of Pol. Economy and Public Fin. at Univ. of Stockholm; app. Chm. of Post-War Econ. Planning Comn. 44; Min. of Commerce and Trade 45-47; Ex.-Sec. Econ. Comn. for Europe 47.

Myrddin-Evans, Sir Guildhaume (U. K.); b. 94; ed. Christ Church of Ox.; mem. Prime Min.'s Secretariat 17; Under-Sec. Min. of Labour and Natl. Service 42; mem. Int. Labour Confs. 39 and 44; rep. UNCIO 45; Chm. of Governing Body of ILO.

Naim, Wadih (Lebanon); b. 85, Chiah; ed. in Beirut; has specialized in civil law cases since graduation; Chief of Bar of Beirut 24, 25, 30 and 31; app. Deputy from Dist. of Mt. Lebanon 43, Min. of Interior and Pub. Ed. 45; Chm. Labanese del. UNCIO 45.

Nájera, Francisco Castillo (Mex.); b. 86, Durango; ed. Coll. of State of Durango and Univ. of Mex., special studies in med. in Paris, Berlin and N. Y., also studied in Paris and Brussels; M. D. (Univ. of Mex.); fmr. prof. Univ. of Mex.; dir. Juarez Hosp. 18-19; app. dir. Army Med. School 20; Min. to China, Belg., Holland and France 22-35; Amb. to U. S. A. 35-45; For. Min. 45-46; rep. UNCIO 45, SC 46; Chm. Mex. del. GA N. Y. 46.

Nash, Walter (New Zealand); b. 82; ed. in England; rep. Int. Labour Conf. in Geneva 20; Sec. New Zealand Labour Party 22-32, Pres. 35-36; rep. Imp. Conf. 37; mem. War Cabinet 40-41; Min. to U. S. A. 42; Pres. Int. Labour Conf. Philadelphia 44; rep. ESC 47.

Navarro, Manuel A. (Ecuador); b. 87, Quito; ed. Univ. of Paris, Massachusetts Inst. of Technology; Dir. of Pub. Works in Quito 11; Rep., later Sen. 28-33; Rector of Cen. Univ. of Quito 37-38; rep. Comns. of Inter-Amer. Develop. in N.Y. 44; Min. Counsellor to U. S. A. 46-; rep. GA N. Y. 46.

Nicholls, George Heaton (U. of S. Afr.); b. 76; M.P. 20; rep. of Sugar Industry at Imp. Conf. London 31; mem. Indian Colonization Com.; mem. Perm. Native Affairs Com.; High Comr. for S. Afr. in London 44-; rep. Prep. Comn. 45; Chm. S. Afr. del. GA London 46; rep. GA N. Y. 46.

Nieto Del Río, Félix (Chile); b. 88; Cauquenes; sec. at Embassies in Wash. and in Belg. 17-26; sec. Chilean del. to LN 20; Spec. Min. to Peru 29; Under-Sec. of For. Affairs 30; Amb. to Chaco Peace Conf. 35-37, to Brazil 36-39; fmr. Chilean rep. Perm. Inter-Amer. Juridical Com.; ed. *El Mercurio*; mem. Governing Bd. of Pan.-Amer. Union; rep. UNCIO 45; Chm. Chile del. GA N. Y. 46.

Nisot, Joseph (Belg.); b. 94, Charleroi; ed. in law at Univ. of Gand, Cambridge, Geneva, Freiburg and Harvard; asst. legal consultant, Min. of For. Affairs 19-22; legal adviser, Secretariat of LN 22-40; mem. of Com. of Jurists and of Conf. for Revision of Statutes of Perm. Ct. of Int. Jus., Geneva 29; mem. of Harvard Research Group in Int. Law 40-42; legal adviser, Embassy in Wash. 42; alt. rep. GA 46, first spec. sesn. GA 47, SC, AEC, CCA; rep. Com. of Experts.

Noel-Baker, Philip (U. K.); b. 89; ed. Bootham School, Cambridge Univ. and Haverford Coll. in U. S. A.; fmr. Vice-Pres. Ruskin Coll., Ox. Univ.; mem. LN Secretariat; prof. Univ. of London 24-29; parl. private sec. to Sec. of State for For. Affairs 29-31; parl. sec. to Min. of War Transport during World War II; Min. of State 45-46; Sec. of State for Air 46-; rep. Ex. Com. of Prep. Comn. 45, Prep. Comn. 45, GA 46, SC 46, ESC 46.

Noriega Morales, Manuel (Guatemala); b. 10; ed. School of Science and Econ. in Guatemala and Harvard; counsellor of econ. affairs at Min. for For. Affairs; rep. Bretton Woods Conf. 44, UNCIO 45.

Novikov, K. V. (U. S. S. R.); b. 05, Moscow; ed. Leningrad Univ.; counsellor at U. S. S. R. Embassy in London 41-42; rep. of U. S. S. R. at Moscow Conf. 43; Yalta Conf. 45; rep. UNCIO 45.

Novikov, Nikolai V. (U. S. S. R.); b. 03, Leningrad; ed. Oriental Inst. of Leningrad, Inst. of Profs. of the World's Econ. and Pol. in Moscow; Deputy-Dir. First Eastern Dept. 38, fmr. Dir. Near Eastern Dept., Balkan Dept., Fourth Eastern Dept. of People's

Commissariat for For. Affiars; Amb. to U. S. A. 46-; rep. GA N. Y. 46.

Oreamuno, José Rafael (Costa Rica); b. 90; attaché Costa Rican Mission Wash. 10-14; sec. Costa Rica Legation Wash. 15-17; consul-gen. N. Y. 20-22; Min. to U.S.A. 22-28; fmr. mem. of Office of Co-ordinator of Inter-Amer. Affairs; rep. UNCIO 45.

Orr, Sir John Boyd (U. K.); b. 80, Ayrshire, Scotland; ed. Glasgow Univ.; D.Sc. (Glasgow Univ.); Dir. of Rowett Research Inst. of Animal Nutrition 19-45; Imperial Bu. of Animal Nutrition 29-45; mem. Reorganization Comn. for Milk 35-36; app. Rector of Glasgow Univ. 45, Chancellor 46; M. P. 45-; Dir.-Gen. of FAO 45-.

Osborn, Frederick H. (U. S. A.); b. 89, N. Y., N. Y.; ed. Princeton Univ., Cambridge Univ.; Treasurer, Vice-Pres. Detroit, Toledo, Ironton Ry. 14-17; acting-chief of Mil. Works of Amer. Red Cross World War I; app. Chm. Civilian Com. on Selective Service 40; fmr. Chm. Joint Army-Navy Com. on Welfare and Recreation; fmr. Chief (with rank of Brig.-Gen.) of Morale Branch of Army; fmr. Maj.-Gen. of Spec. Service; app. deputy-rep. AEC 47.

Owen, A. D. K. (U. K.); b. 05; ed. Leeds Grammar School and Leeds Univ.; Co-Dir. Pilgrim Trust Unemployment Enquiry 36; Dir. of Pol. and Econ. Planning 40; personal asst. to Sir Stafford Cripps 41-43; mem. of Foreign Office Recon. Dept. 43-45; mem. of British del. UNCIO 45; Deputy Ex.-Sec. of Prep. Comm. 45; Asst. Sec.-Gen. in charge of Dept. of Econ. Affairs 46-.

Oyevaar, Jan Johan (Neth.); b. 97, Amsterdam; ed. Univs. of Amsterdam and Utrecht; fmr. rep. Amsterdam Shipping Co.. in Br. India and fmr. consul at Calcutta; Econ. Intelligence Dept. of Min. of Econ. Affairs; app. Dir. of Shipping in Min. of Econ. Affairs 39; later Sec.-Gen. of Min. of Shipping; present Dir.-Gen. of Shipping in Min. of Transport; Chm. Trans. and Communications Comn. 47.

Padilla, Ezequiel (Mex.); b. 92, Coyuca, Guerrero; ed. Univ. of Mex., Sorbonne and Columbia; LL.D.(Columbia); fmr. mem. army of Gen. Zapata; lawyer in Cuba and Mex.; fmr. Deputy to Cong.; fmr. prof. Univ. of Mex.; Atty.-Gen. 28-29; Sec. of Pub. Ed. 29-30; Min. to Italy and Hungary 30-32; Sen. 34-40; For. Min. 40-45; Chm. Mex. del. UNCIO 45.

Padilla Nervo, Luis (Mex.); b. 98, Zamora, Michoacan, Mex.; ed. Univs. of Mex. and Buenos Aires, George Wash. Univ. and London School of Econ.; entered dipl. service 20; Min. to U. S. A. 32-34, subsequently to El Salvador, Costa Rica, Panama, Uru., Para., Neth., Den. and Cuba; del. LN 38 and 46; fmr. Under-Sec. of Ed. and Fine Arts; fmr. Asst.-Sec. of Labor; rep. Ex-Com. of Prep. Comn. 45, Prep. Comn. 45, GA 46, SC 46, AEC 46, TC 47, first spec. sesn. GA 47.

Palladin, Alexander Vladimirovich (Ukr. S. S. R.); b. 85; ed. Petersburg Univ.; fmr. prof. at Kharkov; as Dir., organized Ukr. S. S. R. Research Inst. of Bio-Chem. 25; attended Int. Physiological Confs. Boston 29, later in Stockholm, Rome and Leningrad; Vice-Pres. Ukr. S. S. R. Acad. of Sciences; mem. Acad. of Sciences of U. S. S. R.; rep. UNCIO 45.

Palza, Humberto (Bolivia); b. 01, La Paz; ed. Univ. of La Paz; app. Under-Sec. of Ed. 28, Deputy 29; gen. adviser, then Under-Sec. to Min. of For. Affairs 39-43; lecturer Univ. of Santiago 45; prof. Univ. of La Paz; rep. GA N. Y. 46; Chm. Bol. del. first spec. sesn. GA 47.

Pandit, Vijaya Lakshmi (India); b. 00; ed. private instructors; elected mem. Legis. Asmb. of United Provinces, app. Min. for Local Self-Government and Pub. Health 37 and 46; Pres. All-India Women's Conf. 41-43; founder and present Pres. All-India Save the Children Com; Chm. Indian del. GA N. Y. 46.

Papanek, Jan (Czech.); b. 96, Brezova; ed. *l'Ecole libre des Sciences Politiques* and *l'Institut des Hautes Etudes Internationales* in Paris and *l'Académie de Droit* at The Hague; LL.D. (Univ. of Paris and Charles Univ. of Prague); commercial attaché of Legation in Budapest 25-27; sec. of Legation in Wash. 27-32; mem. UN Inf. Organization 42-46; rep. UNCIO 45, ESC 46-, Vice-Pres. ESC 47-; rep. GA N. Y. 46; first spec. sesn. GA 47.

Paul-Boncour, Joseph (France); b. 73, Dept. of Loire-et-Cher; LL. D; Deputy 19-30; elected Sen. 30; rep. at Geneva 24-28; Premier 32-33; Pres. of Socialist and Republican Union 35-38 (resigned); For. Min. 38; Chm. Com. of Twenty to select 60 M. P.s in Paris to sit in Consultative Asmb.; app. mem. Consultative Asmb. 44; rep. UNCIO 45, GA London 46; rep. ESC 46, SC 46.

Parodi, Alexandre (France); b. 01, Paris; ed. Univ. of Paris; Dir.-Gen. of Min. of Labor 38-40; app. Pres. of Underground Press Com. 43; under name of "Cerat" app. del.-gen. of French Com. of Natl. Liberation 44; Pres. of Int. Labour Conf. 45; Amb. in Italy 45; rep. SC 46-, AEC 46-, ESC 46, GA N. Y. 46, first spec. sesn. GA 47, CCA 47-.

Parra Pérez, Caracciolo (Venez.); b. 88, Merida; ed. Univ. of Merida and Univ. of Paris; Attaché, Sec., Counselor and finally chargé d'affaires, Paris Legation 13-17; chargé d'affaires, Swit. 19-26; Min. to Italy,

England, Swit. and Spain between 27-39; Min. of Pub. Instruction 36; Pres. and Sec. Venez. del. at all meetings of LN; fmr. Min. of For. Affairs; Amb. to France; Chm. Venez. del. UNCIO 45.

Parra Velasco, Antonio (Ecua.); del. Pan Amer. Conf. Montevideo 33; fmr. Min. of Fin. and of Pub. Ed.; fmr. prof. of int. law Univ. of Guayaquil; Deputy to Constituent Asmb. 45; Min. in Paris; rep. Prep. Comn. 45, GA London 46.

Pastoriza, Andrés (Dominican Rep.); ed. Dominican Republic and U. S. A.; Min. of Pub. Works and Communications 30; commercial enterprises 31-35; Min. to U. S. A. 36-41, to England 45-; rep. GA London 46; alt.-rep. GA N. Y. 46.

Payssé Reyes, Héctor (Uru.); b. 03, Montevideo; ed. Fac. of Law at Montevideo; fmr. prosecuting-atty. in Criminal Ct. and fmr. journalist; sec.-gen. Natl. Party of Uru.; Pres. Uru. Olympic Com. and of Sports Federation; mem. House of Rep.; rep. UNCIO 45, GA London 46.

Pearson, Lester Bowles (Can.); b. 97, Toronto; ed. Univ. of Toronto, Ox. Univ.; mem. of Dept. of Ext. Affairs 28-35; First Sec. then Counsellor of High Comr. of Canada in London 35-41; Asst.-Sec. of State for Ext. Affairs 41; Min.-Counsellor at Legation in Wash. 42; rep. on UNRRA; app. Min. to U. S. A. 44, Amb. 45; app. Under-Sec. of State for Ext. Affairs 46; Chm. of Can. del. first spec. sesn. GA 47.

Pelt, Adrian (Neth.); b. Koog on the Zaan; ed. *Ecole libre des sciences politiques*, Paris; ed. successively of *Nieuwblad voor Nederland* and *Niews van de Dag en Telegraaf* 19-20 mem. LN staff, Inf. Sect. 20-34, Dir. of Sect. 34-40; fmr. head of Neth. Govt. Inf. Service in London; rep. GA London 46; Asst. Sec.-Gen. in charge of Conf. and Gen. Services 46-.

Peña Battle, Manuel Arturo (Dominican Rep.); b. 02, Ciudad Trujillo; ed. Univ. of Santo Domingo; Pres. Dominican Sect. of Boundary Delimitation Com. set up in 29; Dominican rep. in negotiations of Treaty of Amity and Arbitration with Haiti; mem. of Dominican Com. for Cod. of Int. Law 40; Pres. Chamber of Deputies 42; Sec. of State for Interior and Police 43; fmr. Sec. of State for For. Affairs; Chm. Dominican del. UNCIO 45.

Pérez Cisneros, Guy (Cuba); b. Paris; ed. Univ. of Havana; Ph. D., Litt. D. (Univ. of Havana); Comr. Provisional Com. of Office of LN in Cuban Min. of State 39; commercial attaché in Can.; Vice Sec.-Gen. Inter-Amer. Union of the Caribbean; sec.-gen. Cuban del. UNCIO 45; rep. GA 46; rep. ESC 47.

Pérez-Guerrero, M. (Venez.); b. 11, Caracas; ed. Univ. of Paris; LL.D. (Univ. of Paris);

mem. Dept. of Economy, Fin. and Transit of Secretariat of LN 37-40; sec. of Com. for Importation Control, Venez. 40-42; mem. Econ. and Statistical Sect. of ILO 42-43; acting-dir. Cen. Bank of Venez. 45; rep. Prep. Comn. 45.

Pertzev, Vladimir Nikolaevich (Byelorussian S. S. R.); b. 77, Byelorussia; ed. Moscow State Univ.; mem. Acad. of Sciences of Byelorussia; prof. Byelorussian Univ. of Minsk; rep. UNCIO 45.

Petrovsky, Mikola I. (Ukr. S. S. R.); b. 94; ed. Inst. of Nejin; app. prof. of hist. 28; conducting research at Ukr. S. S. R. Acad. of Science since 34; app. Dir. Inst. of Hist., Ukr. S. S. R. Acad. of Sciences 42; consultant to People's Commissariat of For. Affairs of Ukr. S. S. R.; rep. UNCIO 45, GA London 46.

Phelan, Edward (U. K.); b. 88, Waterford, Ire.; ed. Liverpool Univ.; fmr. mem. of Bd. of Trade, Natl. Health Insurance Comn., Min. of Labour and For. Office; Asst.-Sec. of Organizing Com. of First ILO Conf. in Wash. 19; fmr. Chief of Dipl. Div. of ILO, app. Asst.-Dir. 33, Deputy-Dir. 38, Dir-Gen. 46.

Picón Lares, Roberto (Venez.); Dr. of pol. science; fmr. Rector Univ. of Los Andes; Dir. Inst. of Immigration and Colonization, and dir. Secretariat of Pres.; dir. of Int. and Pol. Depts., Min. of For. Relations; Chm. Venez. del. GA London 46.

Plaza Lasso, Galo (Ecua.); b. 06; ed. Univs. of Cal. and Maryland; co-founder Amer. School in Quito; Pres. of Quito Municipal Council and Min. of Natl. Defence 38-40; fmr. Amb. to U. S. A.; Sen.; rep. UNCIO 45.

Ponce Enríquez, Camilo (Ecua.); b. 12, Quito; ed. Cen. Univ. of Quito and Univ. of Santiago, Chile; founding mem. Ecua. Dem. Alliance 43, and mem. of its Directive Council 44; fmr. Min. of For. Affairs; Chm. del. Inter-Amer. Conf. on Probs. of War and Peace, Mex. 45, UNCIO 45.

Ponce, Neftalí (Ecuador); b. 08, Quito; ed. Univ. of Quito; LL.D. (Univ. of Quito); Consul in Glasgow 34; First Sec. to Embassy in Wash. 41; Dir. of Protocol in Min. of For. Relations 43; counsellor to Embassy in Caracas 43, Bogota 44; Min-Counsellor, chargé d'affaires at Embassy in Wash.; mem. Governing Bd. of Pan Amer. Union; rep. Inter-Amer. Conf. on Probs. of War and Peace, Mexico City 45, UNCIO 45; rep. GA N. Y. 46; Chm. of Ecuador del. first spec. sesn. GA 47, one of Vice-Presidents.

Ponsot, Henri (France); b. 77; Consul-Gen. to Montreal 18-20; Dir.-Gen. of Interior with Tunisian Gov. 22-24; Dir. of African Levant Sect. of For. Office 25; High Comr. of Syria and Lebanon 26-33; Resident-Gen. in Morocco 33-36; Amb. to Turkey 36-39; mem. French del. GA London 46; Chm. IRO Prep. Comn. 47.

Popovic, Vlado (Yugoslavia); b. 14, Montenegro; ed. Univ. of Belgrade; fmr. mem. Sup. Hdqrs. Staff of People's Liberation Army and Partisan Units, Maj.-Gen. and Comdr. of Third Army Corps; app. Pol. and Mil. Rep. to Bulgaria 45; Amb. to U.S.S.R. 45-; rep. Paris Peace Conf., GA N.Y. 46.

Porras, Demetrio A. (Panama); b. 97; ed. Panama Natl. Inst., Bordeaux Univ., The Hague Int. Acad. of Law and London School of Econ; LL.D.; fmr. consul-gen. at Bordeaux and London; Pres. Panama Law School; fmr. mem. Legis. Chamber; fmr. Min. of State; Min. to Gr. Brit. and France; rep. GA London 46.

Portillo, Eduardo del (Bolivia); ed. Univ. of Barcelona and Madrid Univ.; LL.D. (Madrid Univ.); mem. House of Rep. 40-43; fmr. Min. to Spain; rep. GA London 46.

Price, Byron (U.S.A.); b. 91, Topeka, Indiana; ed. Wabash Coll.; LL.D. (Wabash Coll.); joined A.P. 12; Capt. of Infantry in World War I; app. chief of A.P. Wash. Bu. 27; ex. news ed. of A.P. in N.Y. 37-41; Dir. of U.S. Office of Censorship 41-45; Vice-Pres. of Motion Picture Assn. and head of its Hollywood office 45-47; Asst. Sec.-Gen. in charge of Adm. and Fin. Services 47-.

Price, Frederick A. (Liberia); b. Barbados, Br. W. Indies; ed. in Barbados; served for 40 years as missionary of fmr. Methodist Episcopal Church of U.S.A.; fmr. Field Treas. of Mission Bd.; fmr. Inspector of Schools, Maryland Co., Liberia; app. Consul-Gen., N.Y. 45; rep. FAO Conf. in Quebec 45, UNRRA Council in Atlantic City and Wash., GA N.Y. 46, first spec. sesn. GA 47.

Puig-Arosemena, Alberto (Ecua.); fmr. Supt. of Banks; fmr. chargé d'affaires in Paris, Nor., Belg., Neth., Czech.; chargé d'affaires in London; rep. third session of UNRRA, UNESCO, GA London 46.

Putman, Rodolphe (Belg.); b. 81, Waereghem; Pres. of *Comité spécial d'Imposition des Sociétés Coloniales;* mem. of *Conseil Supérieur des Finances;* fmr. Pres. of Fin. Com. of LN; negotiated treaties on double taxation between Belg., Neth., Luxembourg, France and Italy; Chm. Fiscal Comn. 47.

Quirós José Antonio (El Salvador); b. 88, San Miguel; ed. in law at Natl. Univ. of El Salvador, Univ. of Paris; practiced law for a few years; represented El Salvador at a number of conferences; Chm. Salvadorian del. UNCIO 45; app. Min. of For. Affairs 46; rep. GA N.Y. 46.

Quo Tai-chi (China); b. 88, Kwangtzi, Hupeh Prov., China; ed. Williston Acad. in East-

hampton, Mass. and Univ. of Penn.; sec. to Gen. Li Yuan-hung 12-15; mem. Chinese del. to LN 32-38; Min. to Gr. Brit. 32-35, Amb. 35-41; Min. of For. Affairs 41-42; Chm. Sup. Natl. Defence Council 42-46; rep. SC 46-, AEC 46-, GA N.Y. 46, first spec. sesn. GA 47, CCA 47.

Rabichko, V. A. (Ukr. S.S.R.); b. 04, Stalino; ed. Plekhanov Inst. of Natl. Econ. in Moscow; fmr. lecturer on pol. economy; mem. of coal industry of Middle Asia 33-36; fmr. mem. of Central Stat. Adm. in Moscow; Dir. of Stat. Adm. of Ukr. S.S.R. 37-; mem. of State Planning Comn.; Vice-chm. Population Comn. 47.

Rahman, Sir Abdur (India); b. 88; ed. St. Stephen's Coll. at Delhi, Law Coll. at Lahore; Senior Vice-Chm. of Delhi Municipality 25-28; Dean of Faculty of Law, Delhi Univ. 28-34, Vice-Chancellor 30-34; app. to Bench of Madras High Ct. 37; Judge of Lahore High Ct. 43-; rep. SCOP 47.

Rajchman, Ludwik (Poland); b. 81, Warsaw; ed. Univ. of Cracow; M.D. (Univ. of Cracow) 06; Gen. Dir. of Natl. Inst. of Health in Warsaw 19; Dir. of Health Organization of LN 21-39; rep. of LN's Council to Natl. Econ. Com. of China 33-34; adviser to Natl. Gov. of China 39-43; Chm. of Ex. Bd. of ICEF.

Rand, Ivan C. (Can.); b. 84, Moncton, New Brunswick; ed. Mount Allison Univ., Harvard Law School; app. Atty-Gen. for New Brunswick 24; elected to New Brunswick Legislature 25; Counsel to Can. Natl. Ry. 26-43; app. judge to Sup. Ct. 43; rep. SCOP 47.

Rangel, Orlando (Brazil); b. 07, Niteroi, State of Rio de Janeiro; ed. Mil. Acad.; head of laboratory of mil. plant of Piquete 37-38; mem. Brazilian Mil. Com. in Sweden and Hungary 39-40, in Ger. 40-41, in U.S.A. 46; mem. tech. sect. Ordnance Dept., Min. of War 41-46; mem. mil. staff of Pres. of Brazil 45-46; alt. rep. AEC 46-.

Rasmussen, Gustav (Den.); b. 95, Odense; ed. Univ. of Copenhagen; chargé d'affaires in Berne 27-31; counsellor Danish del. to LN 34-35; chief of sect. in For. Office 35-39; counsellor Danish Legation in London 39-42; mem. of Dan. Council and Mil. Mission in London during World War II; Min. of For. Affairs 45-; Chm. Danish del. GA 46; Chm. Credentials Com. 46.

Read, John E. (Can.); b. 88, Halifax, N.S.; ed. Dalhousie Univ., Columbia Univ., Univ. Coll., Ox. (Rhodes Scholar); gen. law practice 13-20; legal adviser, Dept. of Ext. Affairs 29-46; fmr. counsel for Govt. of Can. in various cases before Int. Joint Com., in litigation before Sup. Ct. of Can., Judicial Com. of Privy Council, and U.S.A. Fed. Cts., including U.S.A. Sup. Ct.; Judge ICJ 46-.

Rendis, Constantin (Greece); head of pol. sect. of Greek del., Peace Conf. Paris 18-20; Min. without portfolio in Papandreou Govt., Cairo 44; Min. of Justice and Interior 45; Min. for For. Affairs 46; Chm. Greek del. GA London 46.

Reyes Carías, Marcos (Honduras); b. 06, Tegucigalpa; ed. Univ. of Honduras; sec. First Ct. of Appeals 29-32; fmr. sec. Honduran Legation in Paris; ed. *El Demócrata* and *Vanguardia;* private sec. to Pres. Carías; rep. Conf. on Food and Agric. Hot Springs 43, UNCIO 45.

Riaz, Mamdouh (Egypt); b. 95, Cairo; ed. Faculty of Law, Univ. of Paris and School of Pol. Science, Paris; elected M.P. City of Alexandria 26, re-elected 30, 36, 39 and 44; Parl. Under-Sec. of State for Min. of For. Affairs 36-37; Chm. Com. of For. Relations in House of Deputies 44-45, Fin. and Budget Com. 46; rep. GA London 46, SC 46.

Ribnikar, Vladislav (Yugoslavia); b. 00, Belgrade; owner and manager newspaper *Politika* 24; Vice-Pres. Natl. Liberation Com. of Yugoslavia and Comr. of Information 43; subsequently Min. of Ed. in Federal Govt. and Pres. of Com. for Culture and Art; deputy at Belgrade 45; rep. UNESCO 46; Mem. Comn. on Human Rights 47.

Rice, Stuart Arthur (U.S.A.); b. 89; ed. Univ. of Wash. and Columbia Univ.; prof. of sociology and stat. Univ. of Penn. 26-40; asst.-dir. U.S. Census 33-36; Vice-Chm. U.S. Cen. Stat. Bd. 32-35, Chm. 36-40; asst.-dir. stat. standards, Bu. of Budget, Ex. Office of Pres. 40-; first Vice-Pres. Inter-Amer. Stat. Inst. 41-; Chm. Nuclear Stat. Comn. 46, Rapp. Stat. Comn. 47.

Ridgway, Lt.-Gen. Matthew Bunker (U.S.A.); b. 95, Fort Monroe, Virginia; ed. U.S. Mil. Acad. and Army War Coll.; mem. Amer. Electoral Com. in Nicar. 27-29 and 30; Asst. C.-of-S., G-3, Second Army, Chicago 36; mem. of War Plans Div. War Dept. Gen. Staff 39-42; Commanding Gen. of 82nd Airborne Div. and of 18th Corps (Airborne) 42-45; senior U.S. del. to Inter-Amer. Defense Bd.; rep. MSC 46-.

Ripka, Hubert (Czech.); b. 95, Koberice, Moravia; ed. Prague Univ.; Ph.D.; Ed. *Narodni Osvobozeni;* ed.-in-chief *Demokraticky stred;* Sec. of State for For. Affairs 40-42; Min. of State in charge of Inf. Service 42-44; Min. of For. Trade; rep. GA London 46.

Robertson, Wishart McLee (Canada); b. 91, Barrington Passage, Nova Scotia; ed. Barrington Passage High School; elected to Nova Scotia Legis. 28, to Sen. 43; app. Pres. of Natl. Liberal Fed. 43; app. Sen. Govt. Leader 45; Pres. and mgr. of Robertson Motors, Ltd.; Pres. of Argyle Motor Services, Ltd.; rep. GA N.Y. 46.

Rodionov, K. K. (U.S.S.R.); b. 01; after completing studies at Univ. joined Navy of U.S.S.R.; rep. Dumbarton Oaks Conf. 44, UNCIO 45.

Rolin, Henri (Belg.); b. 91, Ghent; ed. Univ. of Ghent; sec. to For. Min. at Peace Conf. after World War I; del. LN Asmb.; Socialist mem. of Sen.; prof. of int. law Univ. of Brussels; fmr. mem. Perm. Ct. of Arbitration; rep. GA London 46.

Rómulo, Brig.-Gen. Carlos P. (Philippines); b. 01, Manila; ed. Univ. of the Philippines and Columbia; fmr. prof. and later head of English Dept., Univ. of Philippines, mem. Board of Regents of that Univ.; mem. Philippine Ind. Missions 21, 24, 28, 29, 33, 37; head of D.M.H.M. newspapers, a Philippine chain; A.D.C. to Gen. MacArthur; resident Comr. of the Philippines to U.S.A. 44-46; Chm. Philippine del. UNCIO 45, GA N.Y. 46; rep. first spec. sesn. GA 47.

Roosevelt, Franklin Delano (U.S.A); b. 82, Hyde Park, N.Y.; ed. Harvard and Columbia Univs.; LL.D.; mem. N.Y. Sen. 10-13 (resigned); Asst.-Sec. of Navy 13-20; Gov. of N.Y. 29-33; Pres. of U.S.A. 33-45; co-author of Atlantic Charter 41; signer of Dec. by UN 42; attended Cairo and Teheran Confs. 43, Yalta Conf. 45; d. 45.

Roosevelt, Mrs. Franklin D. (U.S.A.); b. 84; married Franklin D. Roosevelt 05; Fin. Chm. Woman's Div. N.Y. State Dem. Com. 24-28: Vice-Pres. N.Y. State Lea. of Woman Voters; radio broadcaster and journalist, writing daily column since 36; asst.-dir. Office of Civilian Defense 41; rep. GA 46; Chm. Comn. on Human Rights 46-, Drafting Com. on Int. Bill of Rights 47.

Roper, Albert (France); b. 91; ed. Paris Univ.; Capt.-Pilot World War I; French aviation expert and Sec. Aeronautical Comn. Peace Conf. 19; fmr. French aviation expert Conf. of Ambs., Wash. Confs., LN; aviation adviser to Min. of For. Affairs 20-22; Sec.-Gen. Int. Comn. for Air Navigation 22-46; fmr. Sec.-Gen. PICAO; Sec.-Gen. ICAO 47.

Rosenzweig Diaz, Alfonso de (Mex.); lawyer; fmr. Min. to Sweden; fmr. Amb. to France and to U.K.; rep. GA London 46, SC 46.

Roy, Herard (Haiti); b. 10, Port-au-Prince; ed. Paris and Port-au-Prince; Asst.-Chief of Service in Pub. Works Office 33-34; Chief of U.S. Service of For. Office 43-45; Chief of Amer. and European Affairs Div. 45-; rep. GA N.Y. 46; mem. Sub-Comn. on Prevention of Discrimination and Protection of Minorities 47.

Runganadhan, Sir Samuel E. (India); b. 77; ed. Madras Univ.; Vice-Chancellor Annamalai Univ. Chidambaram 29-35, Madras Univ. 37-40; mem. Legis. Council Madras

38-40; adviser to Sec. of State for India 40-43; High Comr. in London 43-; rep. GA London 46.

Ryckmans, Pierre (Belgium); b. 91, Antwerp; ed. Louvain Univ.; LL.D. (Louvain Univ.); served in mandated territory of Ruanda-Urundi from end of World War I to 28; Barrister of law and prof. at Univs. of Antwerp and Louvain 28-34; Gov.-Gen. of Belgian Congo 34-46; rep. GA N.Y. 46, TC 47; mem. TC Visiting Mission to W. Samoa 47.

Rzymowski, Wincenty (Poland); b. 83, Warsaw; ed. Univ. of Geneva and Odessa Univ.; mem. Warsaw Dist. Ct. of Law 07-12; journalist 23-27; mem. Cong. of Culture, Lvov 36; dir. *Slowaeki Museum Krzemieniec;* mem. Polish Com. for Natl. Liberation, subsequently Min. for Culture and Art; Min. of For. Affairs 45-; Chm. Polish del. GA 46.

St. Laurent, Louis Stephen (Can.); b. 82, Compton, Prov. of Quebec; ed. St. Charles Coll., Sherbrooke, Quebec, and Laval Univ. Quebec; LL.D.; K.C.; app. prof. of law Laval Univ. 15; fmr. Batonnier of local Quebec Bar, Batonnier-Gen. Quebec Prov. and Pres. Can. Bar Assn.; Min. of Jus. and Atty.-Gen. 41-; rep. UNCIO 45; Sec. of State for Ext. Affairs 46-; chm. Can. del. GA 46.

Saint-Lot, Emile (Haiti); b. 04, Port-au-Prince; ed. in law, Port-au-Prince; prof. at Univ. of Haiti 37-46; Dean of Faculty of Law (Port-au-Prince) 46; Sen. 46; Sec. of State for Natl. Ed., Pub. Health and Labor 47; rep. GA N.Y. 46.

Saka, Hasan (Turkey); b. 86, Trabzon; ed. School of Pol. Science, Istanbul; Deputy for Trabzon since 19, and Vice-Pres. of Turkish Natl. Asmb. since 26; fmr. prof. Univ. of Istanbul and Law Fac. of Ankara; twice Min. of Fin. and four times Min. of Natl. Econ. and Min. of Commerce; For. Min. 44-; Chm. Turkish del. UNCIO 45, GA London 46.

Salamanca, Carlos (Bolivia); b. 07; sec. Bu. of Students Univ. of Cochabamba 28-30; officer in Chaco War; app. prof. of pub. law Univ. of Cochabamba 37; elected to House of Rep. 40; fmr. Min. to Argentina; rep. UNCIO 45, Prep. Comn. 45; Chm. Bolivian del. GA London 46.

Salem, Joseph (Lebanon); b. 97, Tyre; ed. Patriarchal Coll. at Beirut and Univ. of Paris; commissioned Lieut. in Turkish Army 16; fmr. eng. in Waterworks Co. of Beirut and later Gen.-Chm. of that co.; mem. Chamber of Deputies 25-; first Min. from Lebanon to Egypt; rep. Arab Lea. Cong. Cairo 45, UNCIO 45, GA London 46, ESC 46.

Salinas, Octavio (Nicar.); b. 89, Leon; ed. in law; Deputy 14-15, 21-24, 30-35; Pol. Chief of Dept. of Zelaya 26-27; Judge of Sup. Ct. of Nicar. 35-; rep. GA N.Y. 46.

Sánchez Lustrino, Gilberto (Dominican Rep.); b. 02, Ciudad Trujillo; ed. Univ. of Santo Domingo; Under-Sec. of State for Interior and for Police, War and Marine 34-38; Amb. to Brazil and Uru. 39-43, to Para. 43; Amb.-Counsellor to Dominican For. Office 43-44; dir. *La Nación;* rep. UNICO 45.

Sand, René (Belgium); b. 77, Brussels; ed. Univ. of Brussels; M.D. (Univ. of Brussels); founded Belgian Assn. for Social Med. and became ed. of its Bulletin 12; fmr. Sec.-Gen. of Red Cross Societies; organized Int. Confs. of Social Work and Int. Hosp. Assn.; Sec.-Gen. of Min. of Health 36-40, tech. counsellor 45-; Chm. Tech. Preparatory Com. for Int. Health Conf. 46.

Sandoval-Vallarta, Manuel (Mex.); b. 99, Mex. City; ed. Mass. Inst. of Technology; asst.-prof. of physics Mass. Inst. of Technology 26-30, app. assoc.-prof. 30, app. prof. 39; resident-assoc. of Carnegie Inst. Wash. 39-; fmr. Pres. *Academia Nacional de Ciencias de Méx.;* alt. rep. AEC 46.

Sandström, Alfred Emil (Sweden); b. 86, Nykoping; fmr. reporting judge of Supreme Ct., Chief Jus. 31-33, 35-43; Pres. of a div. of Anglo-German Ct. of Arbitration, London 26-29; Chm. of Tribunal on questions of collective labor agts. 29-31; Chm. of Int. Red Cross and Swedish Red Cross Mission to Greece 43-46, Swedish-Swiss Relief Mission in Greece 43-45; Chm. SCOP 47.

Sanjinés, Ernesto (Bolivia); b. 94; ed. Univ. of La Paz; fmr. prof. of econ. and fin. sciences, criminal law; fmr. Sec.-Gen. Assn. of Mining Industrialists of Bolivia, Ex. Counsellor *"Compañia Recaudadora Nacional," "Caja de Seguros y Ahorro Obrero";* app. Under-Sec. of Fin. 30; Dir.-Gen. of Supplies for Army, later Min. of Natl. Def. 28-33 (Chaco War); rep. GA N.Y. 46, Rapp. Second Com. (Econ. and Fin.)

Santa Cruz, Hernán (Chile); b. 06, Santiago; ed. in mil. law; app. Sec. to Superior Mil. Ct. 29; fmr. prof. of criminal and mil. procedure 30; mil. atty. 34-39; legal adviser to Sec. of Interior 38-47; Judge of Superior Mil. Ct. 39-47; Sec.-Gen. and Pres. of Chilean-Brazilian Inst. of Culture; Chm. of Chilean del. first spec. sesn. GA 47; rep. ESC 47.

Sassen, Emanuel M. J. A. (Neth.); b. 11; mem. of Second Chamber of States-Gen., N. Brabant Provincial Gov.; rep. governing body of ILO at Quebec 45; mem. Neth. del. GA N.Y. 46; chief Dutch rep. IRO Prep. Comn., Rapp. 47-.

Sayre, Francis B. (U.S.A.); b. 85, Penn.; ed. Williams Coll. in Mass. and Harvard Univ.;

held acad. posts at Williams and at Harvard 12-23 and 26-33; app. adviser in For. Affairs to Siam Govt. 23; Asst.-Sec. of State 33-39; High Comr. of Philippines 39-42; during World War II held posts as deputy-dir. of Office of For. Relief and Rehabilitation Operations, spec. asst. to Sec. of State Hull, dipl. adviser to UNRRA, and head of UNRRA missions to 23 countries; Pres. TC 47; mem. TC Visiting Mission to W. Samoa 47.

Schermerhorn, Willem (Neth.); b. 94, Schermer, N. Holland prov.; ed. Delft Univ.; fmr. prof. Delft Univ.; Pres. Int. Soc. for Photogrammetry; travels to Neth. E. Indies, China and Australia to discuss aerial survey probs. 36-39; Chm. *Nederlandsche Volksbewegin* (Dutch People's Movement); Prime Min.; Chm. Neth. del. GA London 46.

Schreiber, Ricardo Rivera (Peru); b. 92, Lima; ed. Univ. of Lima; chargé d'affaires London 21-26, Holland 26-28; mem. Int. Ct. of Arbitration The Hague 26; Min. to Ecua. 28-30, to Colombia 36-38, to Japan and China 38-42; Amb. to Spain 43-45, to Italy 45-; rep. Prep. Comn. 45, GA London 46.

Schrijver, August-Edmond de (Belg.); b. 98, Ghent; lawyer since 21; successively M.P., Mem. Com. of For. Affairs and of Judicial Affairs, Chm. of Flemish Catholic Parl. group, Min. of Agric. and Min. of Interior Affairs; Min. of Jus. 39; Min. of Econ. Affairs 40; app. Min. of Interior Affairs of Belg. Govt-in-Exile 43; Vice-Premier in Pierlot Govt. after liberation of Belg.; rep. UNCIO 45.

Selassie, Ras Imru Haile (Eth.); b. 92, Prov. of Harar; ed. Menelek School in Eth.; Vice-Gov. of Harar Prov. 14-22; fmr. Gov.-Gen. of Wallo Prov.; Gov.-Gen. of Godjam Prov. 33-35; Min. to U.S.A. 46-; rep. first spec. sesn. GA 47.

Senin, Ivan Semanovich (Ukr. S.S.R.); b. 03, Donets Basin; ed. Polytechnical Inst. of Kiev and Columbia; app. Deputy People's Commissar of Light Industry of Ukr. S.S.R. 38; People's Commissar of Ukr. S.S.R. 39; Deputy-Chm. Council of People's Commissars of Ukr. S.S.R. 40-; rep. UNCIO 45.

Serrato, José (Uru.); b. 63, Montevideo; ed. Univ. of Montevideo; app. mem. of Econ. Bd. of Montevideo 97; Min. of Devel. 03-04 (resigned), later Min. of Fin.; elected Sen. 07; Min. of Fin. and Min. of Interior 11; app. Pres. of State Mortgage Bank 17, and Pres. of Bank of Republic 33; Pres. of Uru. 23-27; fmr. For. Min.; Chm. Uru. del. UNCIO 45.

Sevilla-Sacasa, Guillermo (Nicar.); b. 11, Leon, Nicar.; ed. in Leon and at Natl. Univ. of Mex.; M.D.; private practice in medicine in Mex. 37-43; app. First Sec. of Embassy in Wash. 43, later app. Amb.; mem. of Governing Bd. of Pan Amer. Union; rep. first and fourth sesns. of UNRRA Council in 43 and 46, first conf. of FAO in 45, GA N.Y. 46, first spec. sesn. GA 47.

Shang Chen, Gen. (China); grad. of Pei-yang Staff Coll.; Comdr. 32nd Army 31-36; Dir. of Main Office and of For. Affairs Bu. of Natl. Mil. Council 42-44; head of Chinese Mil. Mission to U.S.A. 44-45; app. personal C.-of-S. to Pres. of Natl. Govt. 45; rep. MSC 46-.

Sharapov, Lt.-Gen. Andrei R. (U.S.S.R.); grad. of an aviation school and mil. acad.; participated in first and second World Wars; fmr. Comdr. of Air Force of a district; Chief of the Air-Force Acad.; fmr. Chief of the Mil. Mission in Gr. Brit.; rep. MSC 46-.

Shawcross, Sir Hartley (U.K.); b. 03; ed. Dulwich Coll.; senior law lecturer Liverpool Univ. 24-34; bencher Gray's Inn 39; Ind. Chm. Kew District Bd. since 40; Recorder of Salford 41-; Atty.-Gen.; rep. GA 46.

Shepstone, Denis Gem (U. of S. Afr.); b. 88; ed. Natal Univ. Coll. and in England; Solicitor of the Sup. Ct. of S. Afr., Mem. of City Council for City of Durban 39-43; Sen. of U. of S. Afr. 43-; rep. GA N. Y. 46.

Shertok, Moshe; b. 95, Ukraine; ed. Imp. Ottoman Univ. at Istanbul and London School of Econ.; fmr. ed. mem. *Davar* (organ of Palestine Labor Party); Pol. Sec. to Jewish Agency 31-33; head of Pol. Dept. 33-; helped organize Jewish Brigade in World War II; rep. Jewish Agency for Palestine at First Com. meetings of first spec. sesn. GA 47.

Shmigov, Frol Porfirjevich (Byelorussian S.S.R.); b. 13, Byelorussia; ed. Molotov State Univ.; fmr. lecturer Molotov State Univ.; Chief of Pol. Dept. of Byelorussian People's Commissariat for For. Affairs; rep. UNCIO 45, GA 46.

Silva Pena, Eugenio (Guatemala); b. 97, Guatemala City; ed. St. Joseph's Acad., Cal. and Univs. of Guatemala and Honduras; mem. of Cong. for Guatemala, and mem. of Fed. Cong. Tegucigalpa, Honduras 20; sec. of Legations in France and Spain 23-27; Guatemalan del. on comn. on boundary dispute with Honduras, Wash. 30; Amb. to U.S.A. 44-45; Min. of For. Affairs 45-; rep. UNCIO 45; Chm. of del. GA N.Y. 46.

Silver, Abba Hillel; ed. Hebrew Union Coll.; Amer. rep. Zionist Conf. in London 20; Co-Chm. later Chm. United Palestine Appeal 38-43, later Co-Chm. United Jewish Appeal; Dudlian lecturer Harvard Univ. 39-40; present chm. Amer. Sect. Jewish Agency for Palestine; rep. of Jewish

Agency for Palestine at First Com. meetings of first spec. sesn. GA 47.

Simic, Stanoje (Yugoslavia); b. 93, Belgrade; ed. Belgrade; entered dipl. service 19; fmr. chief sec. of Legation in Tirana and then consul in Korcha and later in Zadar; chief of sect. for Cen. Europe in Pol. Dept., Belgrade 32-35; dipl. agent to Slovakia 39-41; Amb. to U.S.S.R. 42-45; to U.S.A. 45-46; Min. of For. Affairs 46-; rep. UNCIO 45, GA London 46; Chm. Yugoslav del. GA N.Y. 46.

Simpson, Clarence L. (Liberia); b. 96; ed. Coll. of W. Afr. and Liberia Coll.; app. collector of customs in Monrovia 25; co.-atty. for Montserrado Co. 27-28; app. sec. of Gen. P.O. 28, and Acting P.M.-Gen. 31; Rep. 31-34; Sec. of State 34-44; Chm. Liberian del. LN Asmb.; Vice-Pres. of Liberia 44-; Chm. Liberian del. UNCIO 45.

Singh, Kanwar Dalip (India); b. 85, Simla, Punjab; ed. Forman Christian Coll. in Lahore, Pembroke Coll. at Cambridge; Barrister-at-Law in Lahore 12-26; app. Sec. of Punjab Legis. Asmb. 21; fmr. Asst. Legal Remembrancer to Punjab gov. 22-24, Advocate-Gen. 24-25, Judge of High Ct. 25-43; Chm. Com. on Codification of Int. Law 47.

Singh, Rajah Sir Maharaj (India); b. 78; ed. Balliol Coll. and Ox. Univ.; joined United Provinces Civil Service 04; Sec. to United Provinces Govt. 19; fmr. Divisional Comr. in Allahabad and Benares; Chief Min. of Jodhpur State 31; Agent Gen. in S. Afr. 32; app. Mem. of United Provinces Legis. Asmb. 36; app. Vice-Counsellor of Lucknow Univ. 41; app. Prime Min. of Kashmir 43; Pres. of Indian Christian Assn. and of Natl. Liberation Federation 44; rep. GA N.Y. 46.

Sipahi, Emin Ali (Turkey; b. 95; ed. Fac. of Law, Istanbul; pub. prosecutor in Yabanabad and later in Zonguldak; Dir.-Gen. of Balkan Affairs at Min. of For. Affairs; Min. in Brussels 33-38, to China 39, to Saudi Arabia 44-; GA London 46.

Skylstad, R. B. (Nor.); b. 93; Attaché in Madrid 22, in Lisbon 23; app. Sec. in For. Min. 24; Sec. to Legation in London 28-30; Dir. of Minorities Sect. of LN 38-40; Dir.-Gen. of For. Office 41-45; app. Min. to Berne 45; Vice-chm. IRO Prep. Comn. 47.

Slávik, Juraj (Czech.); b. 90, Dobrá Niva; ed. Univ. of Budapest, Berlin, Paris; LL.D. (Univ. of Budapest); Sec. of Natl. Council at Bratislava 18; fmr. mem. of Natl. Asmb.; Min. of Agric. 26; elected to Parl. 29; Min. of Interior 29-32; app. Min. to Poland 35; Min. of Interior and Ed. of Govt.-in-Exile in London 40-45; app. Amb. to U.S.A. 46; rep. GA N.Y. 46.

Smoliar, Vassily P. (Byelorussian S.S.R.); b. 03; ed. Geog. Fac. of State Byelorussian Univ.; lectured on econ. geog. at High School of Agric.; Deputy to Sup. Soviet of Byelorussian S.S.R.; rep. European Com. of UNRRA, GA London 46.

Smuts, Jan Christiaan (U. or S. Afr.); b. 70; ed. Cambridge Univ.; P.C., C.H., K.C., M.P.; state atty. to Pres. Kruger 99; mem. Peace Conf. terminating war 08; Min. of Defence 10; Comdr. of Br. forces, Br. E. Afr. 16-17; mem. Br. War Cabinet 17-18; co-founder with Pres. Wilson of LN; Prime Min. 19-24; Leader of Opposition 24-33; Deputy-Premier and Min. of Jus. 33-39; Prime Min. 39-; Chm. S. Afr. del. UNCIO 45, GA N.Y. 46.

Sobolev, Arkady Alexandrovitch (U.S.S.R.); b. 03, Leningrad; ed. Electrotech. Inst. of Leningrad; research work in connection with devel. of power plant equipment 30-39; Sec.-Gen. of People's Commissariat for For. Affairs 39-42; app. Counsellor to Soviet Embassy in London 42; mem. U.S.S.R. del. Dumbarton Oaks Conf. 44, UNCIO 45; pol. adviser to Marshal Zhukov, Comdr. of U.S.S.R. Occupation Forces in Ger., 45-46; participated in Potsdam Conf. 45; Asst. Sec.-Gen. in charge of Dept. of Security Council Affairs 46-.

Sofianopoulos, John (Greece); b. 87, Sopoto, Prov. of Kalavryta, Peloponn-es-us; ed. Univ. of Athens; LL.D.; dir. of Press Bu., Min. of For. Affairs 12-13; fmr. legal adviser Com. for Settlement of Greco-Serbian boundaries; fmr. gen. sec. of Min. of Natl. Econ.; adviser Greek del. Paris Peace Conf.; Chm. Greek del. ILO Confs., Wash. and Geneva; fmr. Min. of For. Affairs; Chm. Greek del. UNCIO 45.

Soheiny, Ali (Iran); b. 97; ed. Teheran Univ.; Under-Sec. of State for For. Affairs 31-36; Min. to Gr. Brit. 36-38; Min. of For. Affairs 38; Gov.-Gen. Kerman Prov. 38; Amb. to Afghanistan 39; Min. of For. Affairs 41-42; Prime Min. 42-43; rep. GA London 46.

Soltesz, Josef (Czech.); b. 09; ed. in Prague and Bratislava; organized anti-Fascist front of Socialist students; del. World Youth Cong. Geneva 36, U.S.A. 38; active in Slovak underground movement; head of Dept. of Jus. in Slovak Natl. Com. during uprising 44; rep. GA London 46.

Soong, Tse Vung (China); b. 94, Shanghai; ed. Harvard and Columbia Univs.; Pres. Canton Cen. Bank 24; Min. of Fin. 28; founder and Chm. Bank of China 35-44; Min. of For. Affairs 41-44; Premier 44-47; signer of Dec. by UN 42; Chm. Chinese del. UNCIO 45.

Soto Harrison, Fernando (Costa Rica); b. 16; fmr. Min. of Govt.; lawyer by profession; rep. GA London 46.

Souza Dantas, Luis Martins de (Brazil); b. 76, Rio de Janeiro; ed. Law Univ. of Rio de Janeiro; first sec. in Buenos Aires 08-13; Min. to Argentina 13-16; Under-Sec. of State in Min. of For. Affairs 16; Min. to Italy 17-19, to Belg. 19; Amb. to Italy 19-22; fmr. Amb. to France; del. to LN 24 and 26; fmr. Min. for Ext. Affairs; Chm. Brazilian del. GA London 46.

Spaak, Paul-Henri (Belg.); b. 99, Brussels; elected Socialist Deputy for Brussels in Belg. Parl. 32; founded newspaper *L'Action Socialiste* 34; Min. of Trans., Posts and Tel. 34-36; For. Min. almost uninterruptedly since 36; Chm. Nine Power Conf. Brussels 37; Premier 38-39; Chm. Belg. del. UNCIO 45; rep. Prep. Comn. 45; Chm. Belg. del. Yalta Conf. 45.

Stalin, Joseph Vissarionovich (U.S.S.R.); b. 79; ed. seminary for priests; leader of Marxist group in Tiflis 97 and Party Com. 00; mem. "The Five" during October Revolution and afterwards of "The Seven"; Commissar for Nationalization 17-23; gen. sec. of Cen. Com. of Communist Party 22-; mem. Presidium Sup. Soviet of U.S.S.R. 25-; Commissar of Defence and C.-in-C. 41-; Premier 46-; attended Teheran Conf. 43, Crimea Conf. 45.

Stampar, Andrija (Yugoslavia); b. 88, Drenovac, Yugoslavia; ed. Univ. of Vienna; Dir. of Health in Yugoslav Govt. 19-31; health expert attached to Chinese Govt. with LN 33-36; mem. Health Organization of LN 36-37; fmr. prof. Univ. of Cal.; present Rector of Zagreb Univ.; rep. ESC 46, acting-Pres. Third Session; Chm. Interim Comn. of WHO 46.

Stanczyk, Jan (Poland); b. 86, Brzesko, Poland; Sec.-Gen. Cen. Mine Workers Union of Poland 18-39; mem. Polish Parl. and Social Affairs Com. 19-35; del. (Polish Workers) ILO 20-39; mem. Ex. Com. Int. Federation of Mine Workers 21-45, Vice-Pres. since 30; mem. Com. Int. Federation Trade Unions 30-39; Min. of Labour and Social Welfare 39-44 and 45-46; del. GA London 46; top-ranking dir., Dept. of Social Affairs 46-.

Stassen, Harold E. (U.S.A.); b. 07, Minnesota; ed. Univ. of Minnesota; fmr. co. atty.; elected Gov. of Minnesota in 38, re-elected 40, 42; served as Lieut.-Comdr. U.S. Navy during World War II; rep. UNCIO 45.

Steenberghe, Maximilien P. L. (Neth.); b. 99, Leyden; ed. in law at Univ. of Utrecht; fmr. Chm. Gen. Roman Catholic Employers Assn.; mem. Council of Industry, High Council of Labor, Cen. Comn. for State 24-34; Min. of Econ. Affairs 34-35, 37-41 (resigned); elected mem. of Second Chamber of States Gen. 37; Head of Dutch Econ.,

Fin. and Shipping Mission in Wash. World War II; rep. GA N.Y. 46.

Stettinius, Edward R., Jr. (U.S.A.); b. 00, Chicago; ed. Univ. of Virginia; LL.D. (Colgate); Chm. Fin. Com. and Dir. U.S.A. Steel Corp. 36-38; Chm. War Resources Bd. 39; Lend-Lease Adm. 41-43; Sec. of State 44-45; Pres. Univ. of Virginia 46-; Chm. U.S.A. del. Dumbarton Oaks 44, UNCIO 45; rep. Ex. Com. of Prep. Comn. 45, Prep. Comn. 45; rep. GA London 46, SC 46.

Strasburger, Henryk (Poland); b. 87; ed. Heidelberg Univ.; Under-Sec. of State in Min. of Commerce and Industry 18-23; del. to LN; Polish Comr. in Free City of Danzig 24-32; Pres. Cen. Organization of Polish Industries 32-39; Min. of Fin. Industry and Commerce 39-42; Amb. to Gr. Brit.; rep. GA London 46.

Stinebower, Leroy D. (U.S.A.); b. 04, Eureka, Michigan; ed. Univ. of Chicago, Brookings Inst.; Chief of Div. of Econ. Studies and mem. of Comn. on Spec. Studies, Dept. of State 43-44; Deputy-Dir. of Office of Int. Trade Policy 45; Adviser U.S. del. UNCIO 45, GA London 46; Spec. Asst. to Asst.-Sec. of State for Econ. Affairs 46-47; Deputy-rep. U.S. del. ESC 46-47, acting-rep. 47. GA 47.

Stolk, Carlos Eduardo (Venez.); b. 12, Caracas, Venez.; ed. Cen. Univ. of Venez.; Informing Magistrate of Fed. Dist. High Ct. 36-39; Pres. Fed. Dist. Law Assn. 39; del. Inter-Amer. Neutrality Com. 41-42; rep. of Venez. on Inter-Amer. Juridical Com. 42-; rep. GA London 46; Chm. Venez. del. GA N.Y. 46; rep. ESC 47-, first spec. sesn.

Street, Jessie Mary G. (Australia); b. 89, Ranchi, India; ed. Univ. of Sydney; rep. to women's and social workers' confs. in Swit., France, India, U.S., and U.K. 11-; Chm. Australian Women's Charter Conf. 43, 46; Mem. of Labor Party; Pres. of United Assns. of Women of New S. Wales; proprietor of *Women's Digest*; rep. UNCIO 45; Vice-chm. Comn. on Status of Women 47.

Subasic, Ivan (Yugoslavia); b. 92, Bukova Gorica; ed. Fac. of Law in Zagreb; elected M.P. 35 and again 38; became First Ban for autonomous Croatian Banovina 39; Yugoslav Premier in London 45; assisted in formation of United Yugoslav Govt. under Marshal Tito 45; Chm. Yugoslavian del. UNCIO 45.

Suetens, Maximilien R. L. M. (Belg.); b. 91, Lierre; ed. Mil. Coll. in Brussels; rep. to int. econ. confs. at Geneva since 30; rep. at Oslo Conf. 30, Emergency Econ. Com. for Europe 45; Min. First-Class and Dir.-Gen. of For. Trade in Min. of For. Affairs and For. Trade 36-; Chm. of Prep. Com. ITO 47.

Sumulong, Lorenzo (Philippines); b. 06, Antipolo, Rizal; ed. Univ. of Philippines, Harvard; LL.M. (Harvard Univ.) 32; prof. at Arellano Law School 45; Assemblyman 46; Chm. of For. Relations Com. of House of Rep.; rep. GA N.Y. 46.

Sychrava, Lev (Czech.); b. 87, Ledec nad Sázavou; ed. Charles Univ. in Prague; collaborator of Pres. Masaryk and Benes World War I; fmr. Czech. dipl. to France; ed.-in-chief *Národní osvobození* in Prague 24-; Vice-chm. sub-comn. on Freedom of Information and of Press 47-.

Sze, Szeming (China); b. 08, Tientsin; ed. Cambridge Univ., St. Thomas' Hosp. Med. School in London; Sec.-Gen. of Chinese Med. Assn. 37-41; Ed. of *Chinese Med. Journal* 42-45; Consultant to Chinese del. UNCIO 45; Med. Dir. of CNRRA, Wash. Office 45-; Vice-Chm. Interim Comn. of WHO; rep. and rapp. Comn. on Narcotic Drugs 46-.

Taqizadeh, Sayyid Hassan (Iran); b. Tabriz; Deputy Tabriz 06 and 09; Gov.-Gen. Khorassan Prov. 29; Min. to Gr. Brit. 29-30; Min. of Roads and Communications 30, of Fin. 30-33; Min. to France 33-34, to Gr. Brit. 41-44; Amb. to Gr. Brit. 44-; Chm. Iranian del. GA London 46.

Tello, J. Manuel (Mex.); b. 98, Zacatecas; ed. Christian Brothers School, Univ. of Mex. and *Escuela Libre de Derechos*; fmr. vice-consul in Antwerp and consul in Geneva; unofficial rep. from Mex. to LN; fmr. dir. of Pol. Affairs and Dipl. Service in Min. of For. Affairs; fmr. Under-Sec.; rep. UNCIO 45.

Tesemma, Ato Getahoun (Eth.); b. 12, Addis Ababa; ed. Amer. Univ. of Beirut; Sec.-Gen. of Com. of Patriots for Ind. of Ethiopia 36-40; Dir.-Gen. of Adm. Services of Min. of Interior 41-43; alt. rep. to UNRRA, to Int. Civil Aviation Conf.; First Sec. of Legation, Wash.; rep. Int. Health Conf. 46, first spec. sesn. GA 47.

Thomas, Ivor (U.K.); b. 05, Cumbran, Monmouthshire, Wales; ed. Ox.; mem. ed. staff of London *Times* 30-37; chief leader-writer for *News Chronicle* 37-39; M.P. 42-; Under-Sec. of State for Colonies; rep. TC 47.

Thomson, Sir George (U.K.); b. 92; ed. Perse School, Cambridge, and Trinity Coll., Cambridge; mem. Royal Flying Corps and Royal Air Force 15-19; prof. of nat. philos., Univ. of Aberdeen 22-30; mem. Aeronautical Research Com. 37-41; received Nobel Prize for physics 37, Hughes Medal of Royal Soc. 39; sci. adviser to Air Min. 43-44; alt. rep. AEC 46-.

Thors, Thor (Iceland); b. 03, Reykjavik; ed. Univ. of Reykjavik, Cambridge Univ. in England, Sorbonne in Paris; LL.D. (Univ. of Reykjavik); M.P. 33-41; Consul-Gen. of Iceland in N.Y. 40-41; Min. to U.S.A. 41-; Rep. Conf. on Food and Agric., Hot Springs, Va. 43; rep. Int. Aviation Conf. in Chicago 44, Int. Labour Conf. in Montreal 46; Chm. of Icelandic del. GA N.Y. 46, first spec. sesn. GA 47.

Toriello, Guillermo (Guatemala); b. 10, Guatemala City; ed. Univ. of Guatemala; practiced law in Guatemala City; Amb. to Mex. 44; Min. for For. Affairs 44-45; Chm. Guatemala del. UNCIO 45.

Toro, Emilio (Colombia); ed. Queens Univ. Can. and Imp. Coll. of Science and Technology, London; fmr. dir. *Banco de la República*, Bogota, Colombia; rep. ESC 46; alt. rep. SC and AEC 47.

Troncoso, Jesús María (Dominican Rep.); b. 02, Ciudad Trujillo; ed. San Domingo Univ.; fmr. lawyer, prof. of law at Univ. of San Domingo, Under-Sec. of State for Jus., of For. Affairs; Min. to U.S.A. 41-42, Amb. 42-43; Sec. of Treas. 44; Sec. of Natl. Econ. 45; Gov. of Reserve Bank 46-; rep. GA N.Y. 46.

Tsaldaris, Constantine (Greece); b. 84, Alexandria, Egypt; ed. Univ. of Athens; elected M.P. (Populist Party) 32; app. Under-Sec. of Communications 32; elected Chm. of Populist Party's Adm. Com. 45, Chm. Populist Party 46; Prime Min. and Min. of For. Affairs 46-; Chm. Greek del. Paris Peace Conf. 46; rep. GA N.Y. 46.

Tsarapkin, S. K. (U.S.S.R.); b. 06, Nikolayev, U.S.S.R.; ed. Inst. of Oriental Studies and Moscow Univ.; fmr. Chief of Second Far Eastern Dept. of People's Commissariat of For. Affairs; Chief of Amer. Dept. of People's Commissariat of For. Affairs; rep. Dumbarton Oaks Conf. 44, UNCIO 45, first spec. sesn. GA 47.

Tsien Tai (China); b. 87, Chekiang; ed. China, and Paris Univ.; LL.D.; dir. of Treaty Dept., Min. of For. Affairs 21-28; tech. del. to LN Asmb. 32, sub. del. 33-36; Min. to Spain 33-37; del. LN Asmb. 37-38; Amb. to Belg. 37-39, to Nor. 43, to Belg. 43, to France 44-; rep. GA London 46.

Tung Pi-wu (China); b. 85, Hopeh Prov.; participated in Wuchang uprising; connected with Hopeh Prov. Kuomintang Hdqrs. for many years; fmr. mem. of Cen. Ex. Com. of Chinese Communist Party and Pres. of its Sup. Ct.; mem. of People's Pol. Council; mem. Com. for Promotion of Const. Govt.; rep. UNCIO 45.

Turgeon, William Ferdinand Alphonse (Can.); b. 77; ed. N.Y., and Levis Coll., Quebec; P.C., K.C.; Atty.-Gen. Saskatchewan Prov. 07; mem. Prov. Parl. for Prince Albert, Sask. and Humboldt; Chief Justice

Sask. 38-41; Min. to Argentina and Chile 41-44; Amb. to Mex. 44, to Belg. 44-; rep. Ex. Com. of Prep. Comn. 45.

Turner, Adm. Richmond Kelly (U.S.A.); b. 85, Portland, Oregon; ed. U.S. Naval Acad.; Comdr., Aircraft Squadrons, U.S. Asiatic Fleet 28-29; C.-of-S., Aircraft Battle Force 34-35; dir. of war plans Navy Dept. 40-42; Comdr. Third Amphibious Force S. Pac. 42-43, Cen. Pac. 43-44, Pac. Fleet 44-45; commissioned Adm. 45; rep. MSC 46.

Ulloa, Alberto (Peru); b. 92, Lima; ed. Lima and Paris; tech. adviser in juridical matters to Min. of For. Affairs 34-36, 37-39, and 39-40; Min. of For. Affairs 36; del. to LN 37; Min. to Holland 39; mem. Ct. of Int. Arbitration, The Hague; Sen. and Pres. of For. Relations Com. of Peruvian Sen. 45-; Chm. Peruvian del. GA 46; rep. SCOP 47.

Unden, Osten (Sweden); b. 86; ed. in law at Univ. of Lund; app. prof. of civil law at Upsala Univ. 17; fmr. legal expert to gov. 17-20, 32-36; fmr. Min. of Jus.; Min. of For. Affairs 24-26, 45-; elected Pres. of Upsala Univ. 29; app. Chancellor of the Universities 37; fmr. rep. LN; rep. GA N.Y. 46.

Uralova, Evdokia I. (Byelorussian S.S.R.); b. 02, Smolensk; ed. Juridical Inst. in Minsk; occupied various guiding posts in organs of ed. in Byelorussian Republic; Deputy to Sup. Soviet of Byelorussian Republic; People's Commissar for Ed.; rep. GA London 46; Rapp. of Comn. on Status of Women 47-.

Valin, Martial, Air Marshal (France); b. 98; ed. St. Cyr Mil. Acad.; awarded "Croix de Guerre" for action in Campaign of Champaigne; took part in Riff campaign, Morocco 25; fmr. head of intelligence dept. of N.E. Air Force Hdqrs.; commanded Free French Air Force and was head of Air Mission in London during World War II; app. Chief of Air Staff 44; rep. MSC 46-.

Vandenberg, Arthur Hendrick (U.S.A.); b. 84, Michigan; ed. Univ. of Michigan; apprentice-reporter *Grand Rapids Herald* and eventually ed. and publisher; Sen. from Michigan since 28; Chm. of Sen. Com. on For. Relations; rep. UNCIO 45, GA 46.

van Kleffens, Eelco (Neth.); b. 94, Heerenveen, Friesland; ed. Groningen, The Hague and Univ. of Leyden; LL.D. (Univ. of Leyden); mem. LN Secretariat 19-21; app. to Bu. of Judicial Affairs in For. Office 22, head of Bu. 24-27; mem. Bu. of Pol. Affairs of Foreign Office 27-29, app. head of Bu. 29; Min. of For. Affairs 39-46; Amb. to U.S.A. 47-; Chm. Neth. del. UNCIO 45; rep. GA 46, SC 46, AEC 46, ESC 47.

van Langenhove, Fernand (Belg.); b. 89, Mouscron, Belg.; prof. of sociology and social policy Univ. of Brussels since 20; mem. Belg. del. Assemblies of LN 29-38; del. Int. Reparations Confs. London 24, Int. Econ. Confs. in Geneva 26 and Stresa 32; del. Int. Conf. on Commerce London 33; fmr. sec.-gen. of Min. of For. Affairs and For. Trade; rep. GA 46, SC 47-, AEC 47-, CCA 47-, first spec. sesn. GA 47.

van Roijen, J. H. (Neth.); b. 05, Istanbul; ed. Utrecht Univ.; attaché Legation in Wash. 30-32; attached to Min. of For. Affairs 33; sec. in Wash. Legation 33-35; sec. of Legation in Tokyo 36; app. head of Pol. Div. Neth. For. Office 39; Min. of State and later Min. of For. Affairs 45-46; Amb. to Can. 46-; rep. Ex. Com. of Prep. Comn. 45, Prep. Comn. 45, GA N.Y. 46; Chm. Neth. del. first spec. sesn. GA 47.

van Verduynen, E. F. M. J. Michiels (Neth.); b. 85, The Hague; ed. Leyden Univ.; deputy-head of sect. of Econ. Affairs 18; Min. in Prague 20-25; head of Pol. Dept. of Min. of For. Affairs 27-29; Min. in London 39; Min. of State 42; subsequently Amb. in London; rep. GA London 46, SC 46.

Varela, Jacobo D. (Uru.); b. 76, Montevideo; ed. Univ. of Montevideo; app. Min. of For. Affairs 07; Deputy and Sen. between 10-19; mem. Uru. del. Paris Peace Conf. 19; Min. to U.S.A. 19-34; Chm. Uru. Com. on Postwar Probs.; alt. Chm. Uru. del. UNCIO 45.

Varvaressos, Kyriakos (Greece); b. 84, Athens; ed. Univ. of Athens; fmr. prof. Athens Univ.; Min. of Fin. 32; Vice-Pres. of Bank of Greece 33-39, Gov. 39-46; Min. of Fin. in Greek Govt.-in-Exile 41-43 (resigned); rep. GA London 46, ESC 46.

Vasiliev, Lt.-Gen. Alexandre P. (U.S.S.R.); grad. from a mil. school and mil. acad. of the Red Army; fmr. C.-of-S. of an Army; fmr. head of the mil. Mission in London; rep. MSC 46-.

Velázquez, Celso R. (Para.); b. 97, Asuncion; ed. Natl. Univ. of Asuncion; fmr. prof. and later Rector of Univ. of Asuncion; fmr. judge of Civil Ct., Commercial Ct. and mem. of Civil Tribunal; Maj. in Para. Army during Chaco War 33-35; fmr. Amb. to U.S.A.; Amb. to Brazil; Chm. Para. del. UNCIO 45.

Velebit, Vladimir L. (Yugoslavia); b. 07, Zadar; ed. Univ. of Zagreb; Dist. Judge 32-37 (resigned); Gen. in Army of Natl. Liberation; app. first Envoy of Marshal Tito to U.K. 44; Asst. Min. of For. Affairs; rep. first spec. sesn. GA 47.

Velkoborsky, Jiri (Czech.); b. 94, Prague; ed. Charles Univ. in Prague; mem. Czech. State Ry. 21-25; fmr. mem. commercial service in Min. of Ry., present deputy-chief of commercial dept.; fmr. rep. Int. Transport Com. Confs. in Berne; Vice-chm. of Temp. Transport and Communications Comn. of ESC 46.

Velloso, Pedro Leão (Brazil); b. 87, Pindamonhangada, Sao Paulo; ed. fmr. Free School of Juridical and Social Sciences, Rio de Janeiro; rep. in Brazilian Legations at Rome, Paris, Berne, and Copenhagen 10-18; sec. Brazilian del. Peace Conf. Versailles; Min. to China 29-35; Amb. to Japan 35-39; Sec.-Gen. of Min. of For. Affairs 41-44; Min. of For. Affairs 44-46; Chm. Brazilian del. UNCIO 45 and GA N.Y. 46; rep. SC 46-47; d. 47.

Vergara Donoso, Germán (Chile); b. 02, Constitucion; ed. Catholic Univ. in Santiago and School of Pol. Research, Paris; chief of Dipl. Dept. of Min. of For. Affairs 30; Under-Sec. of Internal Affairs 31-38; chargé d'affaires to Spain 39-44; adviser to Min. of For. Affairs 44-; rep. UNCIO 45, GA 46, ESC 46.

Villegas, Silvio (Colombia); b. 02, Manizales; ed. *Invistituto Universitario de Caldas* and Univ. of Columbia LL.D.; fmr. ed. of *La Patria* (Manizales), *El Debate* and *El Nuevo Tiempo* (Bogota); fmr. prof. of Spanish grammar and world hist. in several insts.; mem. of House of Rep.; rep. UNCIO 45.

Visscher, Charles de (Belg.); b. 84, Ghent; prof. of int. law Univs. of Louvain and Ghent; mem. Inst. of Int. Law since 21 and Sec.-Gen. 27-37; mem. Perm. Ct. of Arbitration since 23; mem. Perm. Ct. of Int. Jus. The Hague since 37; rep. Com. of Jurists, Wash. 45, UNCIO 45, GA London 46; Judge ICJ 46-.

Viteri Lafronte, Homero (Ecua.); b. 92, Ambato; ed. *Colegio de San Gabriel*, Quito and Univ. of Quito; LL.D.; dean of Fac. of Jurisprudence and Social Sciences, Univ. of Quito 26-30; fmr. mem. Ct. of Int. Jus., The Hague; Min. of Pub. Instruction 26, of For. Affairs 26-30; Min. to U.S.A. 30-32, in Lima 35-36, to U.K.; rep. GA 46.

Voina, Olexa D. (Ukr. S.S.R.); b. 07, Vinnitzky dist., Ukr.; ed. Moscow Econ. Inst. and Higher Dipl. Inst.; fmr. consul to Sweden; Chief of Pol. Dept. of People's Commissariat for For. Affairs; rep. GA London 46.

Vyshinsky, Andrei Y. (U.S.S.R.); b. 83; LL.D.; mem. Communist Party 20-; mem. Staff Commissariat for Food Supply 20-23; Commissar for Jus., Deputy Pub.-Prosecutor and Pub. Prosecutor 35-39, present Vice For.-Min.; Chm. U.S.S.R. del. GA London 46; rep. GA N.Y. 46, SC 46.

Waerum, Ejnar (Den.); b. 90, Aarhus; ed. Copenhagen Univ.; Sec. to Legation at Brussels 23; chargé d'affaires at Tokio 24; chief of Office 1 of econ.-pol. sect. of For. Office 28, later head of sect.; mem. Council on For. Currency 36-40; rep. Second Conf. on Econ. Co-operation in Geneva 31, Econ. World Conf. in London 33, Emergency Econ. Com. for Europe 45; Chm. Econ. Comn. for Europe 47.

Wahba, Hafiz (Saudi Arabia); b. 92, Cairo; ed. Cairo School of Law; app. attaché at Saudi-Arabian Legation in Cairo 23; Min. of Ed. and asst. to Viceroy 27-28; Min. to Gr. Brit. 30-; rep. GA 46.

Waithayakon, Prince Wan (Siam); b. 91, Bangkok; ed. at Ox. in England, *Ecole des Sciences Politiques* in Paris; Sec. of Legation in Paris 17-19; private sec. of Min. of For. Affairs 19-24; Under-Sec. of State for For. Affairs 24-26; Min. to U.K. 26-30; Adviser to Premier's Office and For. Office 33-46; Chm. of Siamese del. first spec. sesn. GA 47.

Wang Chung-hui (China); b. 84; ed. China, Japan, England, France, Ger. and U.S.A.; D.C.L. (Yale); fmr. Min. of Ed., of Jus., of For. Affairs and Pres. of Judicial Yuan; Judge Perm. Ct. of Int. Jus., The Hague 23-24 and 30-35; translated Ger. Civil Code into English; Sec.-Gen. of China's Sup. Defence Council; rep. UNCIO 45.

Wang, Lt.-Col. Ko-tsan (China); b. 07, Honan Prov., China; ed. Cen. Mil. Coll., Chinese Aeronautical Acad., H.M. Mil. Acad. in Gr. Brit.; C.-of-S. 8th Air Group 33; sect. chief of Intelligence, Chinese Aeronautical Com. 40; Dir. of Ed., Chinese Air Com. 42; asst. air-attaché Embassy Wash. 44, acting air-attaché 46; rep. MSC 46-.

Wang Shih-chieh (China); b. 92, Hupeh; ed. London and Paris; mem. Perm. Ct. of Arbitration, The Hague 28; Chancellor, Natl. Wuhan Univ. 29-34; Min. of Ed. 33-37, of Inf. 39-42 and 44-45; app. Min. of For. Affairs 45; Chm. Chinese del. GA London 46.

Warner, Edward (U.S.A.); b. 94, Pittsburgh, Penn.; ed. Harvard and Mass. Inst. of Technology; prof. of aeronautical eng. Mass. Inst. of Technology 20-26; Asst. Sec. of Navy for Aeronautics 26-29; ed. *Aviation* 29-34; Pres. Interim Council PICAO 46-; Pres. ICAO Council 47.

Wehrer, Albert (Luxembourg); b. 95; ed. Geneva; LL.D.; counsellor for Int. Affairs and del. to LN 26; chargé d'affaires, Berlin 38-40; Sec.-Gen. Grand-Ducal Govt. since 36; rep. GA London 46.

Wei Tao-ming (China); b. 99, Kiangsi prov.; ed. Univ. of Paris; LL.D.; Sec.-Gen. of Min. of Jus., Vice-Min. and later Min. of Jus.; Mayor of Nanking 30-31; Sec.-Gen. of Ex. Yuan 37-41; fmr. Amb. to U.S.A.; rep. UNCIO 45.

Wilgress, L. D. (Can.); b. 92, Vancouver; ed. McGill Univ.; mem. Can. Econ. Mission to Siberia 18-19; Trade Comr. at Hamburg 23-32; Dir. of Commercial Intelligence Service 32-35; first Can. Amb. to U.S.S.R.; alt. rep. UNCIO 45; rep. Prep. Comn. 45.

Wilkinson, Ellen (U.K.); b. 91, Manchester; ed. Univ. of Manchester; organized Natl. Union of Women's Suffrage Societies and Natl. Union of Distributive and Allied Workers; M.P. Middlesborough 24-31; M.P. Jarrow 35-47; mem. Min. of Home Security 40-47; Min. of Ed. 45-47; Pres. Prep. Comn. UNESCO 45-46; rep. GA London 46; d. 47.

Wilson, David (New Zealand); b. 82, Glasgow, Scotland; ed. Board School, Glasgow; mem. of trade union movements, of Socialist and Labour Party; elected campaign organizer, Labour Party 35, 38; High Comr. to Can. 44-; Chm. of del. to FAO in Quebec 46, ILO Conf. in Montreal 46, PICAO Interim Asmb. 46; rep. GA NY 46.

Wilson, Joseph Vivian (N. Zealand); b. 94, N. Zealand; ed. in N. Zealand, and Trinity Coll., Cambridge; mem. N. Zealand Expeditionary Force 15-19; fmr. mem. LN Secretariat as asst. to Sec.-Gen. and later head of Cen. Sect.; Asst.-Dir. of Research Royal Inst. of Int. Affairs London 40; mem. Dept. of Ext. Affairs, Wellington 44-; rep. GA 46.

Wilson, Roland (Australia); b. 04, Tasmania; ed. in econ. Univ. of Tasmania; D. Phil. (Ox. Univ.) 29; Ph.D. (Univ. of Chicago) 30; app. Commonwealth Stat. and Econ. Adviser to Treas. 36-; Perm. Head of Dept. of Labour and Natl. Service 41-46; Pres. of Econ. Soc. of Australia and New Zealand; Vice-chm. Econ. and Employment Comn. 47.

Winant, John G. (U.S.A.); b. 89, N.Y.; ed. St. Paul's School and Princeton and Dartmouth Univs.; N. Hampshire State Sen. 21-23, Gov. 25-26, re-elected 31; fmr. Asst.-Dir. and Dir. of ILO; Chm. Social Security Bd. 35-37; Amb. to Gr. Brit. 41-46; rep. ESC 46.

Winiarsky, Bogdan (Poland); b. 84; ed. Warsaw, Cracow, Paris and Heidelberg Univs.; LL.D.; legal adviser to Polish del. Peace Conf.; fmr. Pres. of LN Com. on Inland Navigation; del. Int. Com. of Oder 22-30; Polish rep. Perm. Ct. of Int. Jus. in Oder case 29; prof. Acad. of Int. Law, The Hague 33; Dean of Fac. of Law, Poznan 36-39; Pres. Bank of Poland 41-46; Judge ICJ 46-.

Winiewicz, Jozef (Poland); b. 05; ed. Univ. of Poznan; ed.-in-chief of *Dziennik Poznanski* 30-39; ed. of *Wiesci Polski* in Budapest 39-41; fmr. mem. Polish Min. of Prep. Work for Peace Conf.; fmr. Counsellor of Legation in London; rep. Peace Conf. in Paris 46; app. Amb. to U.S.A. 47; rep. GA N.Y. 46, first spec. sesn. GA 47.

Wold, Terje (Nor.); b. 99; lawyer 21-; advocate 31; judge Appeal Ct. 36-39; Judge of Sup. Ct.; Chm. Nor. For. Relations Com.; M.P.; rep. GA 46.

Worm-Müller, Jacob Stenersen (Nor.); b. 84; ed. Oslo, Copenhagen, Berlin and Paris Univs.; del. LN Asmb. 26-27; ed. *Samtiden* since 25; prof. of hist. Oslo Univ. since 28; rep. GA London 46.

Wrong, Humphrey Hume (Can.); b. 94; ed. Upper Can. Coll. in Toronto, Ridley Coll. in Ontario, Univ. of Toronto and Balliol Coll., Ox.; asst.-prof. Univ. of Toronto 21-27; first sec. of Legation in Wash. 27, counsellor 30; perm. Can. del. to LN 37-40; Min.-Counsellor of Legation in Wash. 41-42; Asst. Under-Sec. of State for Ext. Affairs 42-; rep. GA London 46.

Wu Yi-fang (China); b. 93, Hupeh; ed. Ginling Coll. in Nanking and Univ. of Michigan; Ph.D. (Univ. of Michigan); fmr. head of English Dept. of Peking Girls' Higher Normal School; Pres. of Ginling Coll. for Women since 28; mem. of People's Pol. Council since 38 and one of its presiding officers since 40; rep. UNCIO 45.

Yafi, Abdallah (Lebanon); b. 01, Beirut; ed. Univ. of Paris; LL.D. (Univ. of Paris); barrister-at-law in Lebanon since 26; mem. Chamber of Deputies from city of Beirut 37-39 and 43-; Prime Min. and Min. of Jus. 38-39; rep. UNCIO 45.

Yepes, Jesús M. (Colombia); b. 92, Granada; ed. Univ. of Antioquia in Colombia, *Ecole Consulaire* in Antwerp and Catholic Univ. in Louvain; LL.D.; Sec.-Gen. in Antwerp 12-16; prof. of law, Univ. of Antioquia 17-23; dir. and ed. *El Colombiano*, Medellin 17-29; judicial adviser to Min. of For. Affairs 26-30; app. Colombian del. to LN 34; Dean of consular corps in Geneva 33-45; del. 19th session of ILO, Geneva; rep. UNCIO 45.

Yllescas, Francisco (Ecua.); b. 01, Bahia de Caraquez; ed. in social sciences and law: rep. and sec. Natl. Asmb. 28-29; app. Min. to Peru on Spec. Mission, Amb. to Argentina 45; app. Amb. to U.S.A. 46; Chm. Ecua. del. GA N.Y. 46.

Zaldumbide, C. Tobar (Ecua.); sec. of Legation in Spain, Brazil and Peru 33-40; Under-Sec. of Min. of For. Affairs 44-45; rep. UNCIO 45.

Zephirin, Mauclair (Haiti); b. 14, Cape Haitien; ed. *Notre-Dame du Perpétuel Secours Coll.* and *Ecole Libre de Droit* at Cape Haitian; prof. of science, literature and history 32-45, of const. law, adm. law and fin. 38-46; Dir. of *Le Messager du Nord* 38-42; Sec. Haitian del. Eighth Int. Conf. of Inter-Amer. Reps. in Lima 38; rep. first spec. sesn. GA 47.

Zhebrak, Anton Romanovich (Byelorussian S.S.R.); b. 01, Byelorussia; ed. Timirazov Moscow Agric. Acad.; prof. Agric. Acad. in Moscow and Minsk; mem. Acad. of Science of Byelorussia; rep. UNCIO 45.

Zlotowski, Ignace (Poland); b. 07, Warsaw; ed. Warsaw Inst. of Technology, Univ. of Paris, Univ. of Warsaw; associated with Mme Curie at Radium Inst. of Paris 33-35; Research Assoc. (Rockefeller Foundation) at Univ. of Minnesota 41-42; acting-Dir. Pol. Dept. for Amer. Affairs at Min. of For. Affairs, Warsaw 46; Min. to U.S.A. 46-47; alt. rep. GA N.Y. 46, AEC 47-.

Zoricic, Milovan (Yugoslavia); b. 84, Zagreb; ed. Univ. of Zagreb; LL.D.; legal agent for Treas. to Atty.-Gen. at Zagreb 10; mem. Governing Com. of Saar in charge of Jus. 32; app. mem. Perm. Ct. of Int. Jus. 35; *ad hoc* Judge of Perm. Ct. of Int. Jus. 36; fmr. Pres. Adm. Ct. of Zagreb; Judge ICJ 46-.

Zuleta Angel, Eduardo (Colombia); b. 99; ed. Paris; LL.D.; prof. and Dean Natl. Fac. of Law; fmr. Pres. Sup. Ct. of Jus.; Amb. to Peru 43-45; Min. of Ed. 47-; rep. UNCIO 45; Pres. of Prep. Comn. 45; rep. GA 46, ESC 46; Chm. Perm. Hdqrs. Com. 46.

Zuloaga, Pedro (Venez.); b. 98, Caracas; ed. Central Univ. of Venez., Harvard, Paris Law School; Comr.-Gen., World Exposition, Paris 37; rep. International Statistical Institute, Prague 38; Commercial Attaché, Paris 38-39; Comr. of Immigration and Colonization in U.S.A. 41-; Mem. Venez. del. UNCIO 45; rep. GA N.Y. 46; alt. rep. ESC 47.

Zurayk, Costi K. (Syria); b. 09, Damascus; ed. Amer. Univ. of Beirut, Univ. of Chicago; Ph.D. (Princeton Univ.) 30; asst.-prof. of hist. at Amer. Univ. of Beirut 30-40, assoc.-prof. 40-43, head of hist. dept. 43-45; First Counsellor of Legation in Wash. 45, chargé d'affaires 45-; rep. GA N.Y. 46, first spec. sesn. GA 47.

(YUN 1946-47, pp. 915-53)

Selected bibliography

Selected bibliography

ORIGINS OF THE UNITED NATIONS

An organization for the postwar world

Basic Facts about the United Nations. New York, 1992. E.93.I.2.

Everyman's United Nations. A Complete Handbook of the Activities and Evolution of the United Nations During its First Twenty Years, 1945-1965. 8th ed. New York, 1968. E.67.I.5

The United Nations at Forty—A Foundation to Build On. New York, 1985. E.85.I.24.

Yearbook of the United Nations, vol. 1, *1946-47.* 1947.I.18.

PART ONE: INTERNATIONAL PEACE AND SECURITY

Chapter I: The evolving UN agenda: making and keeping peace

Basic Facts about the United Nations. New York, 1992. E.93.I.2.

The Blue Helmets. A Review of United Nations Peace-keeping. 2nd ed. New York, 1990. E.90.I.18.

Boutros-Ghali, Boutros, Secretary-General of the United Nations. *Building Peace and Development—1994. Report on the Work of the Organization from the Forty-eighth to the Forty-ninth Session of the General Assembly.* New York, 1994. E.95.I.3.

Everyman's United Nations. A Complete Handbook of the Activities and Evolution of the United Nations During its First Twenty Years, 1945-1965. 8th ed. New York, 1968. E.67.I.5.

The United Nations and Apartheid, 1948-1994. The United Nations Blue Books Series, vol. I. New York, 1994. E.95.I.7.

The United Nations and Cambodia, 1991-1995. The United Nations Blue Books Series, vol. II. New York, 1995. E.95.I.9.

The United Nations at Forty—A Foundation to Build On. New York, 1985. E.85.I.24.

UN Chronicle, vol. XXVII, No. 2, June 1990.

United Nations Peace-keeping. 1995. E.95.VII.1.

Report of the Secretary-General on the work of the Organization (September 1993). New York, 1994. A/48/1.

Report of the United Nations High Commissioner for Refugees. New York, 1994. A/49/12.

Eighth progress report of the Secretary-General on the United Nations Observer Mission in Liberia. 6 January 1995. S/1995/9.

Ninth progress report of the Secretary-General on the United Nations Observer Mission in Liberia. 24 February 1995. S/1995/158.

Report of the Secretary-General on the situation in Burundi. 11 October 1994. S/1994/1152.

Third progress report of the Secretary-General on the United Nations Observer Mission Uganda-Rwanda. 19 September 1994. S/1994/1073.

Letter dated 15 June 1994 from the Permanent Representative of the United States of America to the United Nations addressed to the President of the Security Council transmitting report on the activities of the United Nations Command in Korea, 1993. S/1994/713.

Report of the Secretary-General on the United Nations Iraq-Kuwait Observation Mission (for the period 1 April–29 September 1994). 29 September 1994. S/1994/1111 & Corr.1.

International assistance for the rehabilitation and reconstruction of Nicaragua: aftermath of the war and natural disasters. Report of the Secretary-General. 7 November 1994. A/49/487.

Letter dated 24 October 1994 from the Permanent Representative of the United States of America to the United Nations addressed to the President of the Security Council transmitting the third report of the Multinational Force in Haiti. S/1994/1208.

Letter dated 19 December 1994 from the Permanent Representative of the United States of America to the United Nations addressed to the President of the Security Council transmitting the seventh report of the Multinational Force in Haiti. S/1994/1430.

Letter dated 23 January 1995 from the Permanent Representative of the United States of America to the United Nations addressed to the President of the Security Council transmitting the ninth report of the Multinational Force in Haiti. S/1995/70.

Report of the Secretary-General on the United Nations Observer Mission in El Salvador. 31 October 1994. S/1994/1212 & Add.1.

The situation in Central America: Procedures for the establishment of a firm and lasting peace and progress in fashioning a region of peace, freedom, democracy and development. Report of the Secretary-General. 7 October 1994. A/49/489 & Corr.1.

Report of the Secretary-General, concerning the situation in Abkhazia, Georgia. 6 January 1995. S/1995/10 & Add.1,2.

Report of the Secretary-General on the situation in Tajikistan. 30 November 1994. S/1994/1363.

Report of the Secretary-General pursuant to paragraph 4 of Security Council resolution 947(1994). 14 January 1995. S/1995/38.

The situation in Bosnia and Herzegovina. Report of the Secretary-General. 6 December 1994. A/49/758.

Letter dated 27 May 1994 from the Permanent Representatives of the Russian Federation and the United States of America to the United Nations addressed to the Secretary-General transmitting Agreement on the Gaza Strip and the Jericho Area. A/49/180-S/1994/727.

Letter dated 5 August 1994 from the Permanent Representatives of Israel, Jordan, the Russian Federation and the United States of America to the United Nations addressed to the Secretary-General transmitting Washington Declaration, signed at Washington, D.C., on 25 July 1994 by the Governments of the Hashemite Kingdom of Jordan and of the State of Israel, and witnessed by the United States of America. A/49/300-S/1994/939.

Report of the Secretary-General (on the question of Palestine). 3 November 1994. A/49/636-S/1994/1240.

Yearbook of the United Nations: vol. 1, *1946-47.* 1947.I.18; vol. 6, *1952.* 1953.I.30; vol. 7, *1953.* 1954.I.15; vol. 13, *1959.* 60.I.1; vol. 15, *1961.* 62.I.1; vol. 21, *1967.* E.68.I.1; vol. 23, *1969.* E.71.I.1; vol. 24, *1970.* E.72.I.1; vol. 31, *1977.* E.79.I.1; vol. 32, *1978.* E.80.I.1; vol. 33, *1979.* E.82.I.1; vol. 36, *1982.* E.85.I.1; vol. 45, *1991.* E.92.I.1; vol. 46, *1992.* E.93.I.1; vol. 47, *1993.* E.94.I.1.

Chapter II: The disarmament quest

Boutros-Ghali, Boutros, Secretary-General of the United Nations. *New Dimensions of Arms Regulation and Disarmament in the Post-Cold War Era.* 1992. E.93.IX.8.

The United Nations and Disarmament: 1945-1970. E.70.IX.1.

The United Nations and Disarmament: 1970-1975. February 1978. E.76.IX.1.

The United Nations and Disarmament: A Short History. New York, 1988.

The United Nations Disarmament Yearbook: vol. 1, *1976.* E.77.IX.2; vol. 2, *1977.* E.78.IX.4; vol. 3, *1978.* E.79.IX.3; vol. 4, *1979.* E.80.IX.7; vol. 5, *1980.* E.81.IX.4; vol. 6, *1981.* E.82.IX.7; vol. 7, *1982.* E.83.IX.7; vol. 8, *1983.* E.84.IX.3; vol. 9, *1984.* E.85.IX.4; vol. 10, *1985.* E.86.IX.7; vol. 11, *1986.* E.87.IX.1; vol. 12, *1987.* E.88.IX.2; vol. 13, *1988.* E.89.IX.5; vol. 14, *1989.* E.90.IX.4; vol. 15, *1990.*

E.91.IX.8; vol. 16, *1991.* E.92.IX.1; vol. 17, *1992.* E.93.IX.1; vol. 18, *1993.* E.94.IX.1; vol. 19, *1994.* E.95.IX.1.

New realities: disarmament, peace-building and global security. New York, 1992. E.93.IX.14.

Status of Multilateral Arms Regulation and Disarmament Agreements, vols. 1 and 2, 4th ed. New York, 1992. E.93.IX.11.

The United Nations and Nuclear Non-Proliferation. The United Nations Blue Books Series, vol. III. New York, 1995. E.95.I.17.

Yearbook of the United Nations: vol. 1, *1946-47.* 1947.I.18; vol. 6, *1952.* 1953.I.30; vol. 7, *1953.* 1954.I.15; vol. 13, *1959.* 60.I.1; vol. 15, *1961.* 62.I.1; vol. 21, *1967.* E.68.I.1; vol. 23, *1969.* E.71.I.1; vol. 24, *1970.* E.72.I.1; vol. 31, *1977.* E.79.I.1; vol. 32, *1978.* E.80.I.1; vol. 33, *1979.* E.82.I.1; vol. 36, *1982.* E.85.I.1; vol. 45, *1991.* E.92.I.1; vol. 46, *1992.* E.93.I.1; vol. 47, *1993.* E.94.I.1.

PART TWO: INTERNATIONAL LAW

Chapter I: Judicial settlement of international disputes

Basic Facts about the United Nations. New York, 1992. E.93.I.2.

Boutros-Ghali, Boutros, Secretary-General of the United Nations. *Building Peace and Development—1994. Report on the Work of the Organization from the Forty-eighth to the Forty-ninth Session of the General Assembly.* New York, 1994. E.95.I.3.

Everyman's United Nations. A Complete Handbook of the Activities and Evolution of the United Nations During its First Twenty Years, 1945-1965. 8th ed. New York, 1968. E.67.I.5.

Report of the International Court of Justice (1 August 1993–31 July 1994). New York, 1994. A/49/4.

The United Nations at Forty—A Foundation to Build On. New York, 1985. E.85.I.24.

Yearbook of the United Nations: vol. 1, *1946-47.* 1947.I.18; vol. 38, *1984.* E.87.I.1; vol. 46, *1992.* E.93.I.1; vol. 47, *1993.* E.94.I.1.

Chapter II: Development and codification of international law

Basic Facts about the United Nations. New York, 1992. E.93.I.2.

Everyman's United Nations. A Complete Handbook of the Activities and Evolution of the United Nations During its First Twenty Years, 1945-1965. 8th ed. New York, 1968. E.67.I.5.

The Results of the Uruguay Round of Multilateral Trade Negotiations—The Legal Texts. 15 December 1993. GATT/1994-4.

Multilateral Treaties Deposited with the Secretary-General: Status as at 31 December 1994. E.95.V.5.

Report of the International Law Commission on the work of its fortieth session (2 May–22 July 1994). A/49/10.

Report of the United Nations Commission on International Trade Law on the work of its twenty-seventh session (31 May–17 June 1994). 15 July 1994. A/49/17.

The United Nations at Forty—A Foundation to Build On. New York, 1985. E.85.I.24.

United Nations Convention against Illicit Traffic in Narcotic Drugs and Psychotropic Substances, adopted by the United Nations Conference for the Adoption of a Convention against Illicit Traffic in Narcotic Drugs and Psychotropic Substances (Vienna, 25 November–20 December 1988). Vienna, 19 December 1988. E/CONF.82/15.

United Nations Decade of International Law. Report of the Secretary-General. 19 August 1994. A/49/323 & Add.1,2.

Yearbook of the United Nations: vol. 20, *1966.* E.67.I.1; vol. 23, *1969.* E.71.I.1; vol. 33, *1979.* E.82.I.1; vol. 36, *1982.* E.85.I.1; vol. 45, *1991.* E.92.I.1; vol. 46, *1992.* E.93.I.1; vol. 47, *1993.* E.94.I.1.

PART THREE: EMERGING NATIONS

Chapter I: International trusteeship and decolonization

The United Nations at Forty—A Foundation to Build On. New York, 1985. E.85.I.24.

Basic Facts about the United Nations. New York, 1992. E.93.I.2.

Yearbook of the United Nations: vol. 1, *1946-47.* 1947.I.18; vol. 14, *1960.* 61.I.1; vol. 15, *1961.* 62.I.1; vol. 24, *1970.* E.72.I.1; vol. 34, *1980.* E.83.I.1; vol. 42, *1988.* E.93.I.100; vol. 45, *1991.* E.92.I.1.

Chapter II: Dismantling the colonial system

Yearbook of the United Nations: vol. 14, *1960.* 61.I.1; vol. 15, *1961.* 62.I.1; vol. 17, *1963.* 64.I.1; vol. 19, *1965.* 66.I.1; vol. 21, *1967.* E.68.I.1; vol. 22, *1968.* E.70.I.1; vol. 23, *1969.* E.71.I.1; vol. 27, *1973.* E.75.I.1; vol. 28, *1974.* E.76.I.1; vol. 29, *1975.* E.77.I.1; vol. 31, *1977.* E.79.I.1; vol. 32, *1978.* E.80.I.1; vol. 33, *1979.* E.82.I.1; vol. 34, *1980.* E.83.I.1; vol. 39, *1985.* E.88.I.1; vol. 46, *1992.* E.93.I.1.

PART FOUR: ECONOMIC AND SOCIAL DEVELOPMENT

Chapter I: Humanitarian challenges

Consolidated inter-agency appeal for Somalia, Part I. New York, December 1994.

Protecting the Refugees: The Story of United Nations Effort on Their Behalf. New York, 1953. 1953.I.35.

Yearbook of the United Nations: vol. 1, *1946-47.* 1947.I.18; vol. 2, *1947-48.* 1950.I.11; vol. 4, *1950.* 1951.I.24; vol. 5, *1951.* 1952.I.30; vol. 46, *1992.* E.93.I.1; vol. 47, *1993.* E.94.I.1.

Chapter II: International economic development and cooperation

Report of the International Conference on Population and Development (Cairo, 5-13 September 1994). 18 October 1994. A/CONF.171/13.

Report of the International Conference on Population (Mexico City, 6-14 August 1984). New York, 1984. E/CONF.76/19. E.84.XIII.8 & Corr.1-3.

Yearbook of the United Nations: vol. 2, *1947-48.* 1950.I.11; vol. 15, *1961.* 62.I.1; vol. 17, *1963.* 64.I.1; vol. 18, *1964.* 65.I.1; vol. 19, *1965.* 66.I.1; vol. 20, *1966.* E.67.I.1; vol. 21, *1967.* E.68.I.1; vol. 22, *1968.* E.70.I.1; vol. 24, *1970.* E.72.I.1; vol. 26, *1972.* E.74.I.1; vol. 28, *1974.* E.76.I.1; vol. 30, *1976.* E.78.I.1; vol. 31, *1977.* E.79.I.1; vol. 33, *1979.* E.82.I.1; vol. 36. *1982.* E.85.I.1; vol. 37, *1983.* E.86.I.1; vol. 38, *1984.* E.87.I.1; vol. 40, *1986.* E.90.I.1; vol. 41, *1987.* E.91.I.1; vol. 45, *1991.* E.92.I.1; vol. 46, *1992.* E.93.I.1; vol. 47, *1993.* E.94.I.1.

Chapter III: The expanding social agenda

Boutros-Ghali, Boutros, Secretary-General of the United Nations. *Building Peace and Development—1994. Report on the Work of the Organization from the Forty-eighth to the Forty-ninth Session of the General Assembly.* New York, 1994. E.95.I.3.

Commission on Human Rights: report on the forty-fifth session, 30 January–10 March 1989. New York, 1989. E/1989/20.

Preparations for the Fourth World Conference on Women: Action for Equality, Development and Peace: Draft Platform for Action. 27 February 1995. E/CN.6/1995/2.

Provisional verbatim record of the 14th meeting held at Headquarters, New York, on Monday, 1 October 1990. General Assembly, 45th session. 5 October 1990. A/45/PV.14.

Report of the World Summit for Social Development (Copenhagen, 6-12 March 1995). A/CONF.166/9.

World Summit for Children, "World Declaration on the Survival, Protection and Development of Children and Plan of Action". New York, 30 September 1990. A/45/625.

Yearbook of the United Nations: vol. 1, *1946-47.* 1947.I.18; vol. 2, *1948-49.* 1950.I.11; vol. 6, *1952.* 1953.I.30; vol. 7, *1953.* 1954.I.15; vol. 13, *1959.* 60.I.1; vol. 21, *1967.* E.68.I.1; vol. 26, *1972.* E.74.I.1; vol. 29, *1975.* E.77.I.1; vol. 30, *1976.* E.78.I.1; vol. 32, *1978.* E.80.I.1; vol. 33, *1979.* E.82.I.1; vol. 45, *1991.* E.92.I.1; vol. 47, *1993.* E.94.I.1.

Chapter IV: Intergovernmental organizations related to the United Nations

Everyone's United Nations. A Handbook on the United Nations, its Structure and Activities. 9th ed. New York, December 1979. E.79.I.5.

Basic Facts about the United Nations. New York, 1992. E.93.I.2.

A Guide to Information at the United Nations. New York, February 1995. E.95.I.4.

Yearbook of the United Nations: vol. 1, *1946-47.* 1947.I.18; vol. 2, *1947-48.* 1950.I.11; vol. 47, *1993.* E.94.I.1.

PART FIVE: HUMAN RIGHTS QUESTIONS

Chapter I: Human rights

An agenda for development. Report of the Secretary-General. 6 May 1994. A/48/935.

An agenda for development: recommendations. Report of the Secretary-General. 11 November 1994. A/49/665.

Boutros-Ghali, Boutros, Secretary-General of the United Nations. *Building Peace and Development—1994. Report on the Work of the Organization from the Forty-eighth to the Forty-ninth Session of the General Assembly.* New York, 1994. E.95.I.3.

Commission on Human Rights: report on the fiftieth session, 31 January–11 March 1994. E/1994/24 & Add.1,2.

Human rights. Fact Sheet No. 1. Human rights machinery. Geneva, 1987.

Human rights. Fact Sheet No. 3. Advisory services and technical assistance in the field of human rights. Geneva, 1988.

Human rights, questions and answers. New York, 1987.

Manual on human rights reporting. Geneva, 1991. HR/PUB/91/1.

Chapter II: Human rights gain prominence

An agenda for development. Report of the Secretary-General. 6 May 1994. A/48/935.

Follow-up to the World Conference on Human Rights. Report of the Secretary-General. 15 November 1994. A/49/668.

Letter dated 9 February 1993 from the Secretary-General addressed to the President of the Security Council transmitting interim report of the Commission of Experts established pursuant to Security Council resolution 780(1992). 10 February 1993. S/25274.

Letter dated 24 May 1994 from the Secretary-General to the President of the Security Council transmitting final report of the Commission of Experts established pursuant to Security Council resolution 780(1992). S/1994/674.

Letter dated 1 October 1994 from the Secretary-General addressed to the President of the Security Council transmitting preliminary report of the Independent Commission of Experts established in accordance with Security Council resolution 935(1994). S/1994/1125.

Letter dated 9 December 1994 from the Secretary-General addressed to the President of the Security Council transmitting final report of the Commission of Experts established pursuant to Security Council resolution 935(1994). S/1994/1405.

Note by the Secretary-General transmitting the first annual report of the International Tribunal for the Prosecution of Persons Responsible for Serious Violations of International Humanitarian Law Committed in the Territory of the Former Yugoslavia since 1991, dated 28 July 1994. 29 August 1994. A/49/342-S/1994/1007.

Note by the Secretary-General transmitting sixth periodic report on the situation of human rights in the territory of the former Yugoslavia submitted by Mr. Tadeusz Mazowiecki, Special Rapporteur of the Commission on Human Rights, pursuant to paragraph 32 of Commission resolution 1993/7 of 23 February 1993. 7 March 1994. S/1994/265.

Progress report of the Secretary-General on the United Nations Assistance Mission for Rwanda. 6 February 1995. S/1995/107.

Progress report of the Secretary-General on the United Nations Assistance Mission for Rwanda. 9 April 1995. S/1995/297.

Report of the Commission on Human Rights on its first special session (Geneva, 13 and 14 August 1992). New York, 14 August 1992. E/1992/22/Add.1.

Report of the Commission on Human Rights on its second special session (Geneva, 30 November and 1 December 1992). 3 December 1992. E/1992/22/Add.2.

Report of the Commission on Human Rights on its third special session (Geneva, 24 and 25 May 1994). 1 June 1994. E/1994/24/Add.2.

Report of the Subcommission on Prevention of Discrimination and Protection of Minorities on its forty-sixth session (Geneva, 1-26 August 1994). Geneva, 28 October 1994. E/CN.4/1995/2.

Report of the Secretary-General pursuant to paragraph 5 of Security Council resolution 955(1994). 13 February 1995. S/1995/134.

Report of the United Nations High Commissioner for Human Rights. 11 November 1994. A/49/36.

Report of the World Conference on Human Rights (Vienna, 14-25 June 1993). A/CONF.157/24.

Situation of human rights in Rwanda. Note by the Secretary-General transmitting reports prepared by Mr. Rene Degni-Segui, Special Rapporteur of the Commission on Human Rights on the situation in Rwanda, in accordance with paragraph 20 of Commission on Human Rights resolution S-3/1 of 25 May 1994 and Economic and Social Council decision 1994/223 of 6 June 1994. 13 October and 14 November 1994. A/49/508-S/1994/1157 & Add.1.

Vienna Declaration and Programme of Action. 12 July 1993. A/CONF.157/23.

World Conference on Human Rights: The Vienna Declaration and Programme of Action, June 1993, with the opening statement of United Nations Secretary-General Boutros Boutros-Ghali. New York, 1993. DPI/1394.

Yearbook of the United Nations: vol. 33, *1979.* E.82.I.1; vol. 36, *1982.* E.85.I.1; vol. 40, *1986.* E.90.I.1; vol. 46, *1992.* E.93.I.1; vol. 47, *1993.* E.94.I.1.

INTO THE TWENTY-FIRST CENTURY

Future perspectives: towards a human agenda

Agenda 21. The Earth Summit Strategy To Save Our Planet. Introduction by Senator Paul Simon. Edited by Daniel Sitarz. Boulder, Colorado, 1994.

An agenda for development. Report of the Secretary-General. 6 May 1994. A/48/935.

An agenda for development: recommendations. Report of the Secretary-General. 11 November 1994. A/49/665.

Boutros-Ghali, Boutros. *An Agenda for Peace. Preventive Diplomacy, Peacemaking and Peace-keeping.* Report of the Secretary-General pursuant to the statement adopted by the summit meeting of the Security Council on 31 January 1992. New York, 1992. DPI/1247.

Boutros-Ghali, Boutros, Secretary-General of the United Nations. *Building Peace and Development—1994. Report on the*

Work of the Organization from the Forty-eighth to the Forty-ninth Session of the General Assembly. New York, 1994. E.95.I.3.

The Results of the Uruguay Round of Multilateral Trade Negotiations—The Legal Texts. 15 December 1993. GATT/1994-4.

International Year for the Eradication of Poverty. Report of the Secretary-General. 25 October 1994. A/49/572.

Preparations for the Fourth World Conference on Women: Action for Equality, Development and Peace: Draft Platform for Action. 27 February 1995. E/CN.6/1995/2.

Proceedings of the United Nations Conference on Trade and Development, Eighth Session (Cartagena de Indias, Colombia, 8-25 February 1992). Report and Annexes. New York, 1993. E.93.II.D.5.

Report of the Commission on Sustainable Development on its second session (New York, 16-27 May 1994). 12 July 1994. E/1994/33.

Report of the Global Conference on the Sustainable Development of Small Island Developing States (Bridgetown, Barbados, 26 April–6 May 1994). E.94.I.18.

Report of the International Conference on Population and Development (Cairo, 5-13 September 1994). 18 October 1994. A/CONF.171/13 & Add.1.

Report of the United Nations Conference on Environment and Development (Rio de Janeiro, 3-14 June 1992). Vol. I, 25 June 1993. E.93.I.8.

Report of the World Summit for Social Development (Copenhagen, 6-12 March 1995). A/CONF.166/9.

Trade and Development Report, 1993. New York, 1993. E.93.II.D.10.

UN Chronicle, vol. XXX, No. 3, September 1993.

United Nations Development Programme, *Human Development Report.* New York, 1991.

United Nations Development Programme, *Human Development Report.* New York, 1992.

Vienna Declaration and Programme of Action. 12 July 1993. A/CONF.157/23.

World Conference on Human Rights: The Vienna Declaration and Programme of Action, June 1993, with the opening statement of United Nations Secretary-General Boutros Boutros-Ghali. New York, 1993. DPI/1394.

World Summit for Children, "World Declaration on the Survival, Protection and Development of Children and Plan of Action". New York, 30 September 1990. A/45/625.

Yearbook of the United Nations, vol. 47, *1993.* E.94.I.1.

Index

Index

NOTES

NOTES

NOTES

NOTES

NOTES

NOTES

NOTES

NOTES